WORD ASSOCIATION NORMS

Word Association Norms

GRADE SCHOOL THROUGH COLLEGE

by

DAVID S. PALERMO

and

JAMES J. JENKINS

UNIVERSITY OF MINNESOTA PRESS · MINNEAPOLIS

Lithographed in the United States of America at
the Lund Press, Inc., Minneapolis

Library of Congress Catalog Card Number: 64-13766

PUBLISHED IN GREAT BRITAIN, INDIA, AND PAKISTAN BY THE OXFORD UNIVERSITY PRESS
LONDON, BOMBAY, AND KARACHI, AND IN CANADA BY THOMAS ALLEN, LTD., TORONTO

ACKNOWLEDGMENTS

The data included in this volume were collected as part of a research project supported by grant MH-04286 from the National Institute of Mental Health, U. S. Public Health Service. The book itself was subsidized in part by a supplement to that grant.

The authors wish to acknowledge the help of a number of graduate students who devoted a great deal of effort to collecting, tabulating, and analyzing these data as well as preparing the materials for the book. Among these were Ann M. Banovetz, George B. Flamer, Herman O. Hormel, Nancy L. Nikkel, M. Elizabeth Reinecke, and David A. Wicklund. In addition, the work of undergraduates Sharon Thompson, Elaine Cartier, and Katharine H. A. Johnson made the book possible. Miss Johnson deserves special praise for the devoted effort and care she expended on these data from the time of their collection through the organization, typing, and proofreading involved in preparing them for publication.

Finally, the authors wish to express their appreciation to the teachers, principals, and children of the many schools in Minneapolis who so generously gave their time to this research project. Mr. Locksley D. Berg, acting assistant superintendent in charge of elementary education, Dr. Arthur J. Lewis, former assistant superintendent in charge of elementary education, and Mr. Adner I. Heggerston, assistant superintendent in charge of secondary education, were particularly helpful in arranging for the project to be conducted in the schools.

D. S. P.
J. J. J.

Minneapolis, Minnesota
November 1963

CONTENTS

WORD ASSOCIATION NORMS

INTRODUCTION

In 1959 the senior author of this project participated in a seminar on verbal learning and verbal behavior conducted by Professor James Jenkins at the University of Minnesota. After listening for nearly a year to the discussions analyzing and attempting to account for the myriad of problems in this area, he had two major impressions: (1) the approach to verbal behavior through word associations is extraordinarily fruitful and (2) understanding the complexities of the verbal behavior of the adult subject, with his tremendously intricate verbal skills, appeared almost too difficult to achieve. It seemed that if an attempt were made to study some of the same problems with children, who are of course less experienced in language skills, there might be a greater chance of isolating some of the relevant variables before they become as intertwined as is the case with adults.

After discussion of the problem at some length with Dr. Jenkins, it was decided that one way to open up the area, stimulate research, and provide the raw materials for the investigation of a wide variety of psycholinguistic and verbal learning problems would be to establish a comprehensive set of word association norms over a wide age range. Although some efforts had been made to establish norms (see Palermo, 1963, for a complete review of the literature) no extensive age or grade norms had ever been attempted. We felt that these data would broaden the scope of the norms available at the college level and would be of immediate use in examining questions relating to the development of language habits and the change in associative habits in this country over time. In addition, and perhaps more significant, the norms would provide the necessary data for clinical uses of the association test over a wide age range and would furnish the essential raw data for experimental work on the role of language habits among children and young adults in important behaviors such as recall, learning, perception, and generalization. By happy circumstance, Minneapolis appeared to be the ideal place for such a study since Woodrow and Lowell (1916) had collected their norms for fourth- and fifth-grade children in this city approximately 45 years earlier.

With these objectives in mind, we set out to collect normative word association data, testing subjects from the fourth grade through the college level.* The next several pages provide a description of the methods used in the study followed by the main body of the book which reports the data obtained.

THE LIST OF WORDS

A list of 200 stimulus words was developed for use in the present study. The list included the 100 words of the Kent-Rosanoff list (1910) plus 100 additional stimulus words.

---

*Data have been since collected by the present authors from children in grades one through four using the method of oral presentation and oral response. The data for the 100 stimulus words administered to 50 boys and 50 girls in each grade will be published at a later date.

STIMULUS WORDS, WITH PARTS OF SPEECH

1. Table (noun)
2. Dark (adjective)
3. Music (noun)
4. Sickness (noun)
5. Man (noun)
6. Deep (adjective)
7. Soft (adjective)
8. Eating (verb, participial form)
9. Mountain (noun)
10. House (noun)
11. Black (adjective)
12. Mutton (noun)
13. Comfort (transitive verb)
14. Hand (noun)
15. Short (adjective)
16. Fruit (noun)
17. Butterfly (noun)
18. Smooth (adjective)
19. Command (transitive verb)
20. Chair (noun)
21. Sweet (adjective)
22. Whistle (intransitive verb)
23. Woman (noun)
24. Cold (adjective)
25. Slow (adjective)
26. Wish (transitive verb)
27. River (noun)
28. White (noun)
29. Beautiful (adjective)
30. Window (noun)
31. Rough (adjective)
32. Citizen (noun)
33. Foot (noun)
34. Spider (noun)
35. Needle (noun)
36. Red (noun)
37. Sleep (intransitive verb)
38. Anger (noun)
39. Carpet (noun)
40. Girl (noun)
41. High (adjective)
42. Working (verb, participial form)
43. Sour (adjective)
44. Earth (noun)
45. Trouble (transitive verb)
46. Soldier (noun)
47. Cabbage (noun)
48. Hard (adjective)
49. Eagle (noun)
50. Stomach (noun)
51. Stem (noun)
52. Lamp (noun)
53. Dream (noun)
54. Yellow (noun)
55. Bread (noun)
56. Justice (noun)
57. Boy (noun)
58. Light (noun)
59. Health (noun)
60. Bible (noun)
61. Memory (noun)
62. Sheep (noun)
63. Bath (noun)
64. Cottage (noun)
65. Swift (adjective)
66. Blue (noun)
67. Hungry (adjective)
68. Priest (noun)
69. Ocean (noun)
70. Head (noun)
71. Stove (noun)
72. Long (adjective)
73. Religion (noun)
74. Whiskey (noun)
75. Child (noun)
76. Bitter (adjective)
77. Hammer (noun)
78. Thirsty (adjective)
79. City (noun)
80. Square (noun)
81. Butter (noun)
82. Doctor (noun)
83. Loud (adjective)
84. Thief (noun)
85. Lion (noun)
86. Joy (noun)
87. Bed (noun)
88. Heavy (adjective)
89. Tobacco (noun)
90. Baby (noun)
91. Moon (noun)
92. Scissors (noun)
93. Quiet (adjective)
94. Green (noun)
95. Salt (noun)
96. Street (noun)
97. King (noun)
98. Cheese (noun)
99. Blossom (noun)
100. Afraid (adjective)
101. Dogs (plural noun)
102. At (preposition)
103. Sell (transitive verb)
104. Always (adverb)
105. And (conjunction)
106. That (adjective)
107. Cry (intransitive verb)
108. Only (adjective)
109. Doors (plural noun)
110. Hotter (adverb)
111. On (preposition)
112. Is (intransitive verb)
113. Quickly (adverb)
114. A (adjective, indefinite article)
115. Carry (transitive verb)
116. However (adverb)
117. Very (adverb)
118. Appear (intransitive verb)
119. You (pronoun)
120. Salty (adjective)
121. Cars (plural noun)
122. Because (conjunction)
123. Oh (interjection)
124. Running (verb, participial form)
125. He (pronoun)
126. Find (transitive verb)
127. Of (preposition)
128. Then (adverb)
129. People (plural noun)
130. Although (conjunction)
131. What (pronoun)
132. Live (intransitive verb)
133. Broader (comparative adjective)
134. There (adverb)
135. Get (intransitive verb)
136. Why (adverb)
137. For (preposition)
138. Was (intransitive verb)
139. Or (conjunction)
140. Hardly (adverb)
141. Children (plural noun)
142. It (pronoun)
143. In (preposition)
144. Sit (intransitive verb)
145. Younger (comparative adjective)
146. With (preposition)
147. Take (transitive verb)
148. Easier (comparative adjective)
149. Go (intransitive verb)
150. How (adverb)
151. But (conjunction)
152. Lift (transitive verb)
153. They (pronoun)
154. Guns (plural noun)
155. Who (pronoun)
156. If (conjunction)
157. Come (intransitive verb)
158. Thinner (comparative adjective)
159. From (preposition)
160. Kittens (plural noun)
161. Me (pronoun)
162. Now (adverb)
163. See (transitive verb)
164. Faster (comparative adjective)
165. Playing (verb, participial form)
166. I (pronoun)
167. Farther (adjective)
168. Speak (intransitive verb)
169. Where (adverb)
170. As (adverb)
171. Shoes (plural noun)
172. To (preposition)
173. Am (intransitive verb)
174. Clearer (comparative adjective)
175. Ah (interjection)
176. Become (intransitive verb)
177. The (adjective, definite article)
178. By (preposition)
179. Stand (intransitive verb)
180. His (pronoun)
181. Make (transitive verb)
182. Closer (comparative adjective)
183. So (adverb)
184. Numbers (plural noun)
185. We (pronoun)
186. Over (preposition)
187. Slowly (adverb)
188. Jump (intransitive verb)
189. My (pronoun)
190. This (pronoun)
191. Tell (transitive verb)
192. An (adjective, indefinite article)
193. Buying (verb, participial form)
194. Here (adverb)
195. Fingers (plural noun)
196. Us (pronoun)
197. Therefore (adverb)
198. Have (transitive verb)
199. Quietly (adverb)
200. Him (pronoun)

The entire list of words in the order in which they were administered is shown on the facing page.

The Kent-Rosanoff words were used to allow comparisons with older data where appropriate. Since the Kent-Rosanoff list consists primarily of singular nouns and simple adjectives, it was decided to add words of other form classes to broaden the norm base and allow greater flexibility in future research based upon these norms. The second 100 words systematically sampled verbs, pronouns, adverbs, etc., which occur at relatively high frequency levels in the speech and writing of children and young adults. All the words in their root form were A or AA on the general count in the Thorndike-Lorge list (1944) except kittens which occurs 35 times in a million according to the count. All the words were above 100 on the juvenile count of the Thorndike-Lorge list. Included in the second 100 words were 10 plural nouns, 10 transitive verbs, 10 intransitive verbs, 3 forms of the verb "to be," 3 participles, 6 conjunctions, 2 interjections, 10 prepositions, 14 pronouns, 17 adverbs, and 15 additional adjectives, 9 of which were comparative and 3 of which were articles. The grammatical classifications are based upon the Thorndike-Barnhart Comprehensive Desk Dictionary (Barnhart, 1951). The Thorndike-Barnhart Dictionary lists the meanings of words in order of their frequency of usage. In cases in which words could be classified as more than one part of speech, the first and presumably most frequent classification was arbitrarily used. The part of speech of each word is given in the accompanying list.

PROCEDURE

Since all the tests were to be administered in written form, it was necessary to determine how young a group of children could be used. It was felt that children in the fourth grade were probably as young as could be administered the test. Accordingly, a pilot study was conducted to test the limits by administering the test to two elementary schools which drew from families of low socioeconomic level. It was found that the children in grades four and five of these schools did not have adequate reading and writing skills to provide usable data. Out of a class of 25 or 30 pupils, typically, only about five scorable tests were obtained. Thus, it was necessary to limit the sample in the lower grades to children drawn from schools of middle and upper socioeconomic level. With this limitation, the schools selected were drawn from a wide geographical dispersion within the city limits of Minneapolis.

It was considered desirable to administer the tests in a manner as similar as possible to the one employed in previous studies with adults. Therefore, the instructions were taken from the previous study of Russell and Jenkins (1954) with some additional elaborations to make them clear to children; Goodenough's (1942) instructions used with children were of help here, along with the pilot work mentioned earlier.

The instructions for administration of the test may be found on the next page. Emphasis was placed upon (1) giving the first response produced by the stimulus word, (2) responding with only one word, (3) the experimenter's lack of concern with spelling, and (4) speed of responding. The subjects were told that they would be timed and were requested to record the time it took them to finish the test on the back of their booklets at the end of each session. The experimenter indicated the time on the blackboard as each minute passed during the test. Following the instructions, the subjects read the stimulus words and responded by writing their association in the spaces provided. Each page contained 25 words as may be seen on the sample page reproduced below. Subjects were allowed to work until a show of hands indicated that everyone was finished.

All subjects were given the Kent-Rosanoff list of 100 words plus the list of 100 additional words in that order. In grades four through six, 50 words were presented in each

INSTRUCTIONS FOR WORD ASSOCIATION TEST FOR PUBLIC SCHOOL CHILDREN

Today you are going to have a test to see how quickly you can think of words. I will hand out the test booklets but do not open them until I tell you to. (Hand out the blanks.)

On the front page fill in the blanks. (High school and college students were told to "write your name, age, sex, and birthday and so on" and the rest of this paragraph was omitted.) Put your name on the first line. Fill in your age. Circle whether you are a boy or a girl. Put down your birth date. Write in your grade, which is _____. Then put down the name of the school, which is _____, and the name of the teacher, which is _____. On the last line fill in the date, which is _____.

When I tell you to open your booklets you will find inside a list of words. You are to write next to each word the first word that it makes you think of. It doesn't make any difference what word you write as long as the word on the paper makes you think of it. There are no right or wrong answers. The purpose of the test is just to see how quickly words will come to your mind.

For example (writing on the board), suppose that Coat is the word you see. It will look just like this in the list with a line beside it for you to write the first word that you think of. Your job will be to write down the first word that Coat makes you think of on the line next to Coat. For example, Coat might make you think of Hat or Man or Wear or Brown or Big or Warm or you might think of some other word. Whatever the first word is that you think of write it down on the line next to Coat.

You are to do the same thing for each word in the list. Be sure to write the word clearly but don't worry if you are not sure how to spell the word. Spell it as best you can. We are not interested in spelling; we are just interested in the word you think of each time. (This sentence was omitted from the high school and college instructions.)

This is a test of speed. When I tell you to start I want you to work straight down the list as fast as you can. When you finish a page, go right on to the next one. Write only one word on each line but do not skip any words and be sure to write clearly since words that cannot be read will not count toward your score. I am going to time you and at the end of each minute I will write the number of minutes that it is taking you to finish. When you get through with all the words on the list write the number that I have on the board on the back page of your test. That will tell me how long it took you to finish.

Now we are ready to start. When I say "start" turn the page and begin with the first word.

Be sure to write clearly.

Be sure to write the first word that you think of.

And be sure to write just one word for every word on the list.

All right, "Start."

RETEST INSTRUCTIONS

Today we are going to have another word association (these two words were omitted from instructions given below the high school level) test like the one I gave you the other day (the last six words were replaced by "you took before" for high school and college students). It is a test to see how quickly you can think of words (sentence omitted for high school and college). This time the words will be different ones but it will be the same kind of test. (This sentence read as follows for the high school and college students: The instructions are the same but the words on the list are different this time.)

On the front page fill in the blanks. Put your name on the first line. Fill in your age. Circle whether you are a boy or a girl. Put down your birth date. Write in your grade, which is _____. Then put down the name of the school, which is _____, and the name of your teacher, which is _____. On the last line fill in the date, which is _____. (This paragraph was shortened to the following for the high school and college students: On the front page fill in the blanks. Write your name, age, sex, birthday and so on. Where it says grade put in your year in high school (college).)

Now let's review what I told you last time. (High school and college instructions read: Let me review the instructions briefly.)

When I tell you to open your booklets you will find inside a list of words. You are to write next to each word the first word that it makes you think of. It doesn't make any difference what word you write as long as the word on the paper makes you think of it. There are no right or wrong answers. The purpose of the test is just to see how quickly words come to your mind.

Be sure to write the word clearly but don't worry if you are not sure how to spell the word. Spell it as best you can. We are not interested in spelling. We are just interested in the word you think of each time. (This paragraph was omitted for high school and college students.)

This is a test of speed. (High school and college instructions read: Remember this is a test of speed.) When I tell you to start I want you to work straight down the list as fast as you can. When you finish a page go right on to the next one. (High school and college instructions read: When I tell you to start, I want you to work down the list as fast as you can until you are through with all the pages.) Write only one word on each line but do not skip any words and be sure to write clearly since words that cannot be read will not count toward your score. If you don't know a word, guess so that you don't have to skip any words. (This sentence was omitted from high school and college instructions.) I am going to time you and at the end of each minute I will write on the board the number of minutes that it is taking you. When you get through with all the words on the list, write the number that I have on the board on the back of your test. That will tell me how long it took you to finish. (This sentence was omitted from high school and college instructions.)

Now we are ready to start. When I say "start" turn the page and begin with the first word. (These two sentences were replaced in high school and college instructions by "Remember.")

Be sure to write clearly.

Be sure to write the first word that you think of.

And be sure to write just one word for every word on the list.

(The words "Be sure to" were omitted from the high school and college instructions.)

All right, "Start."

Become	_____
The	_____
By	_____
Stand	_____
His	_____
Make	_____
Closer	_____
So	_____
Numbers	_____
We	_____
Over	_____
Slowly	_____
Jump	_____
My	_____
This	_____
Tell	_____
An	_____
Buying	_____
Here	_____
Fingers	_____
Us	_____
Therefore	_____
Have	_____
Quietly	_____
Him	_____

(SAMPLE PAGE)

session. The sessions were ordinarily on consecutive school days, although for some classes a single day or a weekend intervened between sessions. All other subjects were given the Kent-Rosanoff list in one session and the second 100 words in the second session. All tests were administered in the regular classroom by the experimenters.

SUBJECTS

The test was administered to 250 boys and 250 girls in each of the grades 4-8, 10, and 12 in the Minneapolis public schools and 500 male and 500 female students in introductory psychology classes at the University of Minnesota. Following data collection, each test was examined to determine whether it met criteria for inclusion in the final sample. Test forms were excluded from further analysis if: (1) the subject had not completed the last five words in the first form given him; (2) sentence-like continuations from one response to the next involved four or more consecutive responses; (3) ten or more responses appeared which were also stimulus words on a page of 25 items; (4) the subject was seen to be copying response words from the blackboard or other classroom source during the test; or (5) responses to more than 10 per cent of the total set of words were "response faults." Response faults consisted of illegible or incomplete words, omissions, and the occurrence of the same response ten or more times on a page of 25 items. Although these criteria appear complex and arbitrary, their development was necessitated primarily by the behavior of only the youngest subjects. They resulted in the rejection of a relatively small percentage of the total population tested, as may be seen in the table below where numbers of subjects rejected for the various reasons are indicated. During the initial examination of the test forms, misspelled words were corrected but in no case was a word changed which appeared misspelled but actually spelled another word; i.e., to the stimulus word "take" the response "steel" was not changed to "steal." Numbers which were given in numeral form were counted with numbers written as words. All multiple word responses were included in the final tabulations.

More than the required number of subjects were tested at each grade level. Final

Number of Subjects Rejected in Each Grade-Sex Group

Reason for Rejection	4 M	4 F	5 M	5 F	6 M	6 F	7 M	7 F	8 M	8 F	10 M	10 F	12 M	12 F	College M	College F
Absent one or more days . .	51	49	40	63	59	59	35	30	76	65	43	36	26	33	120	3
Response faults	73	34	43	13	13	5	31	10	34	7	6	1	8	4	2	1
Ten stimulus words	14	10	2	2	5	1	4	0	0	0	1	0	1	0	0	0
Last five omitted. . . .	11	1	0	0	0	1	5	0	2	3	2	0	3	0	1	2
Copied response . . .	4	0	0	0	1	0	0	0	0	0	0	0	0	0	0	0
Word continuations	8	7	10	2	3	0	3	3	1	0	0	0	0	0	0	0
Total . .	161	101	95	80	81	66	78	43	113	75	52	37	38	37	123	6

membership in the sample was based upon random selection of the number specified from the total pool of tests. When a test form was rejected for one of the reasons cited above, a replacement was drawn at random from the appropriate grade-sex group.

RESULTS

All data were transferred to IBM cards. Each response made by each subject to each stimulus word was put on a separate card. The cards were then sorted by stimulus word for each of the 16 grade-sex groups, and the frequency of each response to each of the stimulus words was printed out. The body of this book is divided into three sections which give the raw data obtained.

Response Frequencies. In the first and longest section each stimulus word, appearing in alphabetical order, is followed by an alphabetical listing of each response to it. The original data were tabulated in such a way that the frequency of each response by each grade-sex group was obtained for each stimulus. The response words which were given by only one subject in any particular grade-sex group were identified and omitted from this table if the response was not given by more than one subject in some other grade-sex group. Therefore, the responses listed are those which occurred with a frequency of two or more in at least one of the grade-sex groups. The table may be read by looking up a particular stimulus word, selecting the response of interest, and reading along the row the frequency of that response for each grade-sex group. The groups are ordered from the fourth-grade boys in column one to the college women in column sixteen. It should be remembered in reading the college frequencies and comparing them with the other groups that the sample size of the college students was 500 in each sex group while the sample size was only 250 for all other grade-sex groups.

Idiosyncratic Responses. All the responses which are not in the response frequency table are listed for each stimulus word alphabetically beginning on p. 359. An idiosyncratic response, as indicated above, was any word which appeared with a frequency of one in some grade-sex group but did not occur with a frequency of greater than one in any other grade-sex group. Such responses could have occurred with a frequency of one in more than one grade-sex group but never with a frequency of more than one in any subgroup. No effort has been made to identify which grade or sex group made each of the idiosyncratic responses.

Response Index. The data for the study were sorted to yield an index showing all response words in alphabetical order. This ordering with the accompanying listing of stimulus word numbers for each response constitutes the final section of this book.

For reasons of economy, the index has been abridged by the exclusion of certain classes of responses. First, all multiple-word responses have been omitted. It was felt that this was little loss since most investigators are unlikely to use such material experimentally and in general such responses are themselves rare and even more rare as responses to several stimuli. Second, responses which occurred to only one stimulus word were omitted. While it may possibly be an inconvenient exclusion, this procedure saved a great deal of space and seems to impose little restriction on the use of materials. If one is interested in a particular response found in the frequency table, it may be looked up in the index to determine its other occurrences. If it is not in the index, it did not occur to any other stimulus word in the list. If it is in the index, the list numbers of the other stimuli to which it was a response will be found there. Under the word abbreviation, for example, one notes that it occurred as a response to stimulus words 1, 4, 8, 94, and 172.

One other difference which should be noted between the listings of the frequency table and the index is that idiosyncratic responses which appeared for more than one stimulus are listed in the index. Thus, responses will be found in the index which are not in the frequency table because they did not occur to a particular stimulus with a frequency of two or more in any of the groups but did occur to more than one stimulus word at some frequency. Any particular response listed in the index can be looked for under the appropriate stimulus listings in the table to obtain frequency of occurrence and groups for which the response appeared. If the response is not listed under a particular stimulus word, it means that the response was idiosyncratic for that word.

REFERENCES

Barnhart, C. L. Thorndike-Barnhart Comprehensive Desk Dictionary. Garden City, N.Y.: Doubleday, 1951.

Goodenough, F. L. "The Use of Free Association in the Objective Measurement of Personality," Studies in Personality, edited by Q. McNemar and M. A. Merrill. New York: McGraw-Hill, 1942. Pp. 87-103.

Kent, G. H., and A. J. Rosanoff. "A Study of Association in Insanity," American Journal of Insanity, 1910. Pp. 67, 37-96, 317-390.

Palermo, D. S. "Word Associations and Children's Verbal Behavior," Advances in Child Development and Behavior, edited by L. P. Lipsitt and C. C. Spiker. New York: Academic Press, 1963 (in press).

Russell, W. A., and J. J. Jenkins. "The Complete Minnesota Norms for Responses to 100 Words from the Kent-Rosanoff Word Association Test." Technical Report No. 11. Contract N8-ONR-66216, Office of Naval Research, and University of Minnesota, 1954.

Thorndike, E. L., and I. Lorge. The Teachers' Word Book of 30,000 Words. New York: Teacher's College, Columbia University, 1944.

Woodrow, H., and F. Lowell. "Children's Association Frequency Tables," Psychological Monographs, 1916, 22, No. 5 (Whole No. 97).

RESPONSE FREQUENCIES

Response Word	4th M	4th F	5th M	5th F	6th M	6th F	7th M	7th F	8th M	8th F	10th M	10th F	12th M	12th F	College M	College F

1. A

Response Word	4th M	4th F	5th M	5th F	6th M	6th F	7th M	7th F	8th M	8th F	10th M	10th F	12th M	12th F	College M	College F
A......	0	0	0	0	3	0	0	0	0	0	0	0	0	0	0	0
About ...	1	1	0	2	1	0	0	0	0	0	0	0	0	0	0	0
Adjective .	0	0	0	0	0	0	0	1	1	3	0	1	1	1	2	0
Ah	0	0	0	0	0	0	0	1	0	1	1	2	1	0	5	0
All	0	2	0	0	0	0	2	0	0	0	0	0	1	0	0	0
Alphabet ..	1	5	5	6	1	11	5	2	3	6	3	6	3	1	3	2
Am....	0	1	0	1	2	0	2	1	0	0	1	0	0	0	0	1
An	10	7	9	17	8	14	12	28	17	31	16	30	19	58	62	97
And	11	6	11	6	6	12	7	8	8	8	7	9	9	12	17	28
Animal...	0	0	0	0	0	2	0	1	0	0	0	1	0	0	0	0
Another ..	0	3	0	0	1	0	0	0	0	0	0	0	0	0	0	0
Apple ...	5	6	8	4	3	4	5	7	5	13	9	7	5	4	10	5
Are....	2	1	0	0	1	1	0	0	4	2	0	1	2	0	2	0
Article...	0	0	0	1	0	0	0	0	0	1	0	2	0	2	7	4
As	2	1	1	0	0	1	3	0	0	0	1	0	3	0	0	1
At	11	4	10	12	8	5	6	14	17	4	10	10	7	4	9	5
B	16	11	15	10	16	12	27	18	23	14	18	14	25	11	49	28
Baby	3	3	3	1	1	3	3	0	0	0	0	0	1	2	1	2
Bad	2	0	0	0	0	0	0	0	0	0	0	0	0	0	1	0
Ball	0	2	1	2	1	3	0	4	1	1	1	1	0	0	6	8
Be	3	2	2	1	5	2	3	3	2	1	4	2	6	1	7	6
Bear	0	0	0	2	0	1	0	0	0	0	0	1	0	0	1	0
Bee	3	0	0	1	1	2	4	2	2	1	2	0	2	1	4	0
Bird	3	0	2	1	1	2	0	1	2	3	3	0	3	1	2	7
Boat	1	0	0	2	1	2	0	1	0	0	0	0	1	0	1	1
Book	0	0	2	1	0	0	0	1	0	1	2	0	0	4	1	1
Boy	3	6	6	2	7	5	4	9	2	8	14	10	7	5	25	21
But	0	0	1	0	1	0	1	2	0	0	1	1	0	0	5	5
By	0	0	0	0	0	0	1	2	1	0	0	0	2	1	1	0
Can	1	1	2	1	1	1	0	0	0	0	1	0	0	0	1	0
Car	3	3	4	3	3	3	3	3	1	3	6	6	3	2	11	2
Cat	5	7	7	9	5	4	3	5	6	8	3	7	9	4	11	9
Cow	0	0	1	1	0	0	1	0	1	0	1	1	2	1	1	1
Dog	14	11	10	9	9	12	19	15	7	14	18	14	11	13	29	37
Door	0	0	0	3	1	0	0	1	0	0	0	0	0	0	1	1
English ..	0	0	0	0	0	0	3	0	0	1	0	0	0	0	0	0
F......	0	0	0	0	0	0	0	0	0	0	0	0	0	0	2	0
Fail	0	0	0	0	0	0	0	0	2	1	0	1	0	0	1	0
First ...	2	0	0	1	0	0	0	0	0	0	1	0	1	1	1	0
Girl	2	3	1	0	0	3	1	1	1	3	3	2	9	4	6	5
Good	3	1	0	0	1	3	1	0	1	1	0	1	1	0	0	0
Grade ...	0	0	1	0	0	0	1	0	1	2	1	1	0	1	3	1
Hat.....	1	1	0	0	0	0	1	0	1	0	0	0	0	0	1	2
Horse ...	0	0	1	1	1	0	0	0	0	1	1	2	1	0	1	1
House ...	1	1	1	0	1	0	0	1	3	3	1	3	2	2	3	2
I	8	11	11	8	4	5	14	4	9	5	7	0	2	3	6	1
In	2	3	1	0	2	1	0	1	0	1	0	0	0	2	1	0
Is	6	8	5	10	8	4	6	7	2	3	5	1	2	1	6	0
It	2	6	5	5	11	7	5	4	8	6	3	5	5	0	9	9

Response Word	4th		5th		6th		7th		8th		10th		12th		College	
	M	F	M	F	M	F	M	F	M	F	M	F	M	F	M	F

A

Response Word	M	F	M	F	M	F	M	F	M	F	M	F	M	F	M	F
Letter	6	12	9	13	15	10	4	3	6	6	7	8	8	1	7	6
Little	2	0	0	0	1	1	1	0	0	0	0	0	0	2	1	2
Man	3	4	3	5	5	0	3	1	8	3	5	2	5	6	10	13
Many	0	0	0	0	0	1	0	1	1	2	2	0	0	0	1	2
Mark	0	0	0	0	0	0	2	1	0	0	1	0	0	1	1	1
Me	0	3	2	0	3	3	2	0	1	0	2	2	0	0	2	0
Mouse	1	0	0	1	2	0	0	1	0	1	0	3	0	1	2	1
My	0	1	1	0	0	0	0	0	0	0	1	0	0	0	3	0
None	0	0	0	0	0	0	0	0	0	0	0	1	0	0	0	2
Not	0	1	0	3	0	1	0	0	0	0	0	0	0	1	1	0
Noun	0	0	0	0	0	0	1	0	1	1	0	0	0	0	1	0
Now	1	0	0	0	2	1	0	2	0	0	0	0	0	0	0	1
Nut	0	2	0	0	1	0	1	0	2	1	0	0	1	0	0	0
O	1	0	1	0	0	1	0	0	1	0	0	0	0	0	2	2
Object	0	0	0	0	0	1	1	2	0	1	0	1	0	1	4	0
Of	0	1	0	0	0	1	0	0	1	1	2	0	0	0	0	2
Oh	0	1	0	3	0	1	0	2	1	3	2	3	0	0	3	1
On	0	0	1	0	1	1	2	0	0	0	0	1	0	0	0	3
One	16	22	13	23	16	21	26	38	25	29	21	22	21	30	37	60
Only	0	2	0	0	1	0	0	0	0	0	0	0	1	0	0	0
Person	0	4	3	1	1	5	1	2	3	3	2	2	3	1	0	1
Pig	1	2	1	1	0	1	0	1	0	0	0	0	0	0	1	0
Place	1	3	0	1	0	1	1	0	1	1	0	0	1	0	0	0
Say	0	1	1	0	1	1	0	0	1	0	0	0	2	0	0	0
See	0	2	0	2	0	0	0	0	0	0	0	0	0	0	1	0
Sentence	1	0	0	1	0	2	0	0	0	0	0	0	0	0	0	1
Single	1	1	0	1	1	0	1	0	1	0	0	1	3	0	1	3
Small	0	0	0	0	1	0	1	0	1	0	0	1	0	0	2	0
Some	2	1	0	0	1	0	2	0	0	0	0	0	0	0	1	0
Something	7	6	4	4	8	2	6	1	2	2	1	0	4	3	3	1
That	3	4	4	1	4	5	0	5	2	0	4	1	1	1	1	0
The	3	4	2	2	7	12	3	9	5	10	7	8	11	12	30	46
There	0	1	2	0	0	1	1	0	0	0	0	2	0	1	0	0
Thing	13	8	17	12	13	12	17	8	12	6	16	11	3	10	12	7
To	0	0	0	0	0	0	0	0	0	1	0	1	2	1	6	9
Truck	2	0	0	0	0	0	0	0	0	0	0	0	0	0	0	0
Vowel	2	0	1	1	0	2	0	0	0	0	0	0	0	0	0	1
Way	1	1	0	0	3	0	1	0	0	0	0	0	0	0	2	0
What	1	0	0	0	1	0	1	1	1	0	4	3	4	2	4	1
Word	8	3	15	7	8	6	4	0	1	4	3	7	2	2	2	2

2. AFRAID

Response Word	M	F	M	F	M	F	M	F	M	F	M	F	M	F	M	F
Africa	2	1	0	0	0	0	0	2	1	2	2	0	1	0	0	1
Alone	0	0	0	1	0	0	0	0	0	0	1	1	0	2	2	3
Anger	0	0	0	0	0	0	0	0	1	1	2	1	0	0	2	0
Angry	0	0	1	1	0	2	1	1	1	0	1	0	2	1	2	2
Animal	0	0	0	0	1	0	0	1	0	1	2	0	0	0	0	0
Bad	1	1	4	4	2	1	2	1	0	0	1	0	1	1	1	4
Bear	0	1	1	1	0	0	0	0	0	0	0	0	0	1	0	2

Response Word	4th M	4th F	5th M	5th F	6th M	6th F	7th M	7th F	8th M	8th F	10th M	10th F	12th M	12th F	College M	College F
								AFRAID								
Big	1	0	0	0	0	0	0	0	0	0	2	0	0	0	1	1
Bold ...	0	0	0	0	0	0	1	0	0	0	1	0	1	1	3	0
Boy	3	0	2	1	0	0	0	0	0	0	0	0	0	0	1	0
Brave ...	13	11	7	7	6	5	12	3	14	4	8	6	9	8	15	15
Bugs ...	0	0	0	0	0	0	0	0	0	2	0	0	0	0	0	0
Calm ...	0	0	0	0	0	1	0	0	0	0	0	0	1	0	1	2
Cat	0	0	1	0	0	1	0	0	0	1	1	0	1	0	3	1
Chicken ..	1	0	4	0	4	0	8	1	6	0	5	2	2	0	5	0
Child ...	0	0	0	0	0	0	0	0	0	0	1	1	0	1	0	4
Come ...	0	0	0	0	2	0	0	0	0	0	0	0	0	0	0	0
Comfort ..	0	0	0	0	0	0	0	0	0	0	0	0	0	2	0	0
Cord ...	0	0	2	0	0	0	0	0	0	0	0	0	0	0	0	0
Country ..	0	0	0	2	0	1	0	0	0	0	0	1	0	0	0	1
Courage ..	1	1	0	0	0	0	1	0	0	1	2	2	1	0	3	3
Courageous	0	0	0	0	0	0	0	1	0	1	0	0	0	1	2	0
Coward ..	0	0	2	1	0	1	3	2	4	1	0	0	3	3	5	0
Cry	0	3	0	0	0	1	0	0	1	1	0	1	0	1	2	4
Danger ..	1	1	0	0	0	0	1	1	1	0	4	1	0	3	2	5
Dark ...	1	5	5	5	6	8	3	7	1	16	9	25	14	14	21	63
Darkness .	0	0	0	0	0	0	0	1	0	0	0	1	3	0	0	3
Dog	3	1	0	0	2	2	0	0	0	1	0	0	0	1	0	1
Don't ...	0	2	1	1	0	0	0	0	0	0	0	0	0	1	0	2
Dream ..	0	0	0	0	0	0	0	0	0	0	0	0	0	0	2	0
Fail	0	0	0	0	0	0	0	0	0	0	0	0	1	0	0	2
Fear ...	3	3	10	7	15	13	23	15	34	26	48	53	50	62	146	132
Fearful ..	2	0	1	1	0	0	1	1	1	0	2	0	0	0	1	0
Fearless .	0	0	0	0	0	0	0	0	1	0	0	0	0	1	1	2
Fierce ..	0	0	0	1	0	0	0	0	2	0	0	0	1	0	0	0
Fight ...	0	0	1	0	0	0	0	0	0	1	3	0	0	0	6	1
Friend ..	1	0	0	2	0	0	0	0	1	0	0	0	0	0	0	0
Fright ..	3	0	1	3	4	1	1	1	1	5	3	3	3	0	6	5
Frighten .	3	7	1	0	2	4	0	4	1	7	0	0	0	1	1	3
Frightened	7	8	4	13	9	17	6	16	2	12	3	5	6	8	8	6
Good ...	3	1	1	2	2	0	0	0	3	0	1	0	0	0	0	0
Happy ...	2	4	2	4	6	2	0	2	1	2	3	0	0	1	2	4
Height ...	0	0	0	0	0	0	0	0	0	0	0	1	0	0	0	3
Help	3	3	1	2	2	0	0	0	1	1	0	0	1	0	3	1
Hurt	0	0	0	2	0	0	0	0	0	0	1	0	0	2	1	2
Knife ...	0	0	0	0	0	0	0	0	2	0	0	0	0	0	0	0
Lion	2	2	4	2	5	2	2	1	0	0	2	1	1	0	1	0
Lonesome .	0	1	0	1	0	0	2	0	0	0	0	1	0	0	0	0
Mad	1	1	0	3	0	1	3	1	0	1	1	0	1	1	3	1
Man	0	0	1	0	0	0	0	0	2	0	0	0	0	0	0	1
Me	1	1	0	1	4	0	0	1	1	1	0	1	2	0	0	0
Mean ...	1	0	1	3	0	0	0	1	1	0	0	0	0	1	0	0
Nervous ..	0	0	1	0	0	1	1	0	0	2	1	1	1	0	2	1
Never ...	0	0	0	0	0	0	0	0	1	1	1	0	2	0	0	1
Night ...	0	2	2	3	1	4	0	2	0	3	0	4	1	7	7	9
No	1	0	1	0	0	0	1	0	1	0	1	0	2	1	5	0
Noise ...	0	0	0	0	0	0	0	0	0	0	0	0	0	0	4	2

Response Word	4th M	4th F	5th M	5th F	6th M	6th F	7th M	7th F	8th M	8th F	10th M	10th F	12th M	12th F	College M	College F
AFRAID																
Not	2	4	0	2	6	0	1	0	0	1	2	0	0	1	1	0
Not afraid .	1	0	2	0	0	1	1	1	0	0	0	0	0	1	2	0
Run	6	1	1	2	2	0	3	0	2	1	7	2	6	1	13	4
Sad	1	0	1	1	0	3	1	0	1	0	0	0	1	0	2	1
Safe	4	0	0	1	0	0	0	0	1	0	0	2	0	1	0	2
Scare. . . .	3	12	7	8	6	11	3	6	3	4	2	3	2	3	7	6
Scared . . .	107	121	113	118	117	128	126	144	108	114	77	94	82	77	116	126
Scary. . . .	0	3	1	1	0	0	0	0	0	0	0	1	0	0	0	1
Scream . .	1	0	0	0	0	2	0	0	0	1	0	1	0	1	3	1
Shy	0	1	0	1	0	1	1	0	0	0	1	1	0	0	2	2
Snake . . .	0	0	0	0	0	0	0	1	0	2	0	0	0	1	1	1
Snakes . . .	0	0	0	0	0	0	0	0	0	0	0	0	0	1	0	2
Sorrow. . .	0	0	0	0	0	0	0	0	0	0	0	0	0	0	2	0
Spider . . .	0	0	0	0	0	0	0	0	2	0	0	0	0	0	0	1
Spiders . .	0	0	0	0	0	0	0	1	0	2	0	0	0	1	0	0
Strong . . .	0	0	1	0	0	0	0	0	1	0	1	0	0	0	3	2
Tense . . .	0	0	0	0	0	0	0	0	0	0	0	0	0	0	2	0
Terrified .	0	2	0	0	0	0	1	1	0	0	0	0	1	0	0	0
Terror. . .	0	0	1	1	0	1	0	1	1	0	1	3	0	1	1	4
Tests . . .	0	0	0	0	0	0	0	2	0	0	0	0	0	0	0	0
Tremble . .	0	0	0	0	0	0	0	0	0	0	1	0	0	0	2	1
Trouble . .	0	1	0	1	0	1	1	0	0	1	0	1	2	0	0	0
Unafraid . .	2	1	1	1	1	0	0	1	0	1	1	0	1	0	7	1
Unhappy . .	2	0	0	1	0	0	0	0	0	1	1	1	0	0	0	1
War	0	0	0	0	0	0	1	0	0	0	0	0	0	0	0	2
Worried . .	0	1	0	0	0	1	1	0	0	0	1	0	0	0	2	1
Worry . . .	0	0	0	0	0	0	0	0	0	0	0	1	2	0	1	0
Yellow . . .	2	0	0	1	1	0	0	0	5	1	1	0	0	0	0	1
Yes	1	0	0	0	2	0	0	0	0	1	0	1	0	0	1	0
3. AH																
A	11	11	4	8	9	4	1	0	5	2	2	1	1	0	2	0
Ah	0	0	0	0	2	2	0	0	0	0	0	0	0	0	1	0
Air.	0	0	0	1	0	0	3	0	0	0	0	0	0	0	0	0
Alas	0	0	0	0	0	0	1	1	0	0	0	0	0	0	0	2
Am.	2	3	1	1	3	6	0	0	0	3	0	0	0	0	0	0
An	0	0	2	1	1	0	1	0	0	1	0	1	0	0	0	0
And	3	0	2	1	2	1	0	0	1	0	0	0	1	2	0	0
Apple . . .	0	0	0	0	2	0	0	0	0	0	0	0	0	0	0	0
Are.	2	0	1	0	0	0	1	0	1	0	0	0	1	0	0	0
As	0	0	1	0	0	2	1	1	0	0	0	0	0	0	0	0
Bad	2	0	0	2	0	0	0	0	0	0	0	0	1	0	0	0
Beautiful. .	0	1	0	1	0	3	0	0	0	0	0	0	1	0	0	0
Better . . .	0	1	0	0	0	0	1	0	1	0	0	2	0	0	0	0
Big.	0	0	0	0	0	2	0	0	0	0	0	0	0	0	0	0
Bliss. . . .	0	0	0	0	0	0	0	0	0	0	0	0	0	0	0	2
Boo	0	0	0	0	0	1	2	1	0	0	0	0	0	1	1	0
Boy	0	1	1	1	0	0	0	2	1	1	1	3	1	0	4	0
But	2	1	2	0	0	1	0	1	0	0	0	0	1	1	3	2

6

Response Word	4th M	4th F	5th M	5th F	6th M	6th F	7th M	7th F	8th M	8th F	10th M	10th F	12th M	12th F	College M	College F

AH

Response Word	4th M	4th F	5th M	5th F	6th M	6th F	7th M	7th F	8th M	8th F	10th M	10th F	12th M	12th F	College M	College F
Choo	6	2	7	3	1	0	1	1	11	3	8	2	10	1	6	5
Comfort	1	2	0	0	0	0	2	0	2	3	0	0	0	0	1	1
Cool	2	0	1	0	1	1	1	0	0	0	0	0	0	0	0	0
Cute	0	0	0	0	0	0	0	0	0	0	0	2	0	0	0	0
Dentist	0	1	0	0	1	0	2	0	0	0	0	1	2	0	2	1
Doctor	1	1	4	0	4	6	2	6	6	3	5	2	3	3	8	9
Don't	0	0	0	2	1	0	0	0	0	0	0	0	0	0	0	0
Drink	0	0	0	0	0	0	0	0	0	0	0	0	1	0	2	0
Easy	0	0	1	0	1	0	0	0	1	0	2	0	1	0	1	0
Eek	0	0	0	0	0	0	0	0	0	0	0	2	0	0	0	0
Eh	0	0	1	0	0	2	0	1	0	0	0	0	0	0	0	1
Enjoyment	0	0	0	0	0	0	0	0	0	0	0	0	1	0	2	0
Excited	0	0	0	0	0	0	0	1	0	0	0	0	0	0	2	0
Exclaim	0	0	0	0	0	1	2	1	0	1	0	2	3	2	2	3
Exclamation	0	0	0	0	1	4	2	3	0	2	1	3	2	4	5	7
Express	0	0	0	0	1	0	0	0	0	0	0	0	0	0	0	2
Expression	0	3	1	3	0	4	1	2	0	4	2	2	3	4	3	5
Feel	0	0	0	1	0	0	0	0	0	0	2	0	1	0	1	0
Feeling	0	0	0	0	0	0	0	0	1	0	1	0	0	2	0	0
Fine	2	1	2	1	0	1	0	1	0	1	0	1	1	1	0	0
Food	2	1	1	0	1	2	1	1	1	3	0	0	0	0	0	2
Fun	3	1	0	0	0	1	1	0	0	0	4	1	1	0	0	0
Funny	1	3	2	1	0	1	0	1	1	1	1	0	0	0	0	0
Gee	0	1	1	2	0	0	1	3	1	2	0	0	0	0	0	1
Glad	0	0	0	2	0	0	0	0	0	0	0	2	0	0	0	1
Go	1	0	0	1	2	1	0	0	0	0	0	1	1	0	1	0
Good	9	12	21	18	13	17	13	21	15	17	23	15	13	13	26	32
Great	0	0	0	0	0	0	0	0	0	0	2	0	0	1	0	0
Ha	6	16	17	10	16	14	8	9	11	10	7	10	10	8	21	21
Had	2	0	0	0	0	0	0	0	0	0	0	0	0	0	0	0
Hah	0	0	0	0	0	0	0	0	0	0	0	1	0	1	6	0
Happy	1	3	1	2	0	1	1	2	1	0	0	1	0	1	0	1
Hard	0	0	0	0	0	2	0	0	0	0	0	0	0	0	0	0
Hay	1	1	0	0	1	0	2	0	0	0	0	0	0	0	0	0
He	1	1	2	0	3	2	2	1	1	0	0	0	0	0	0	0
Hem	0	0	0	0	0	0	0	0	0	0	0	0	1	0	0	2
Here	1	0	0	0	0	2	0	0	0	0	0	0	0	0	0	1
Hi	0	1	1	3	2	0	0	0	0	0	0	0	0	0	1	0
Ho	1	3	3	0	3	2	6	2	0	2	0	0	1	0	1	1
Home	0	0	0	0	0	1	0	0	0	0	2	0	1	0	0	0
How	2	0	1	1	0	1	0	0	0	0	1	0	0	1	0	0
Huh	0	0	0	0	0	0	1	0	1	3	0	0	0	0	2	0
Hum	1	1	2	2	0	0	0	3	1	0	0	1	0	0	1	1
I	2	2	4	2	0	0	2	0	0	1	0	1	0	0	2	0
Il	0	0	0	0	0	0	0	0	2	0	0	0	0	0	0	0
Is	0	2	1	3	0	1	1	1	2	2	2	1	1	0	2	1
Ish	0	0	0	0	0	1	0	2	0	0	1	1	0	0	0	0
It	3	2	1	2	5	2	1	1	0	0	0	0	2	0	1	0
Joy	0	0	0	0	1	1	0	0	0	0	1	0	0	0	2	1

Response Word	4th M	4th F	5th M	5th F	6th M	6th F	7th M	7th F	8th M	8th F	10th M	10th F	12th M	12th F	College M	College F
							AH									
Laugh . . .	6	14	8	7	8	3	1	3	2	3	1	0	2	1	2	2
Laughing . .	0	0	3	0	1	1	0	0	1	0	0	0	0	0	0	0
Let	0	0	0	0	0	0	2	0	0	0	0	0	0	0	0	0
Look	1	1	1	1	0	0	0	2	0	0	0	0	0	0	0	0
Love	0	0	0	0	0	0	0	0	0	2	0	1	0	1	0	2
Ma	1	1	0	0	2	1	1	0	0	0	0	0	0	0	0	0
Mad . . .	0	2	2	1	1	1	0	1	1	0	0	1	0	0	0	0
Man	1	0	1	3	1	0	2	1	1	0	0	1	0	0	0	2
Me	7	5	6	3	5	1	13	3	4	5	4	7	4	10	14	14
Men	0	1	0	1	0	1	0	0	0	0	0	0	1	1	3	3
Mouth . . .	1	3	2	2	2	0	1	1	0	3	1	0	0	0	4	2
My	0	1	0	1	0	1	1	0	0	2	3	1	1	1	1	4
Nice	2	3	1	5	3	6	1	2	2	4	2	2	3	4	2	9
No	5	5	7	3	2	3	5	5	4	5	5	10	4	6	9	4
Not	1	1	1	1	1	0	0	0	1	1	2	0	0	1	0	0
Nothing . .	0	1	0	0	1	0	0	0	1	0	0	0	0	0	2	0
Now	0	4	3	1	2	1	2	1	1	2	4	0	0	1	7	1
Nuts	1	0	1	0	1	2	3	0	0	1	1	0	1	0	2	1
Of course .	0	0	0	0	0	0	0	0	0	0	0	0	0	0	0	2
Oh	20	35	21	37	20	45	38	74	39	59	55	81	51	80	136	177
Okay	0	0	0	0	0	1	0	0	0	2	0	0	0	0	0	1
Ooh	0	0	0	0	0	0	0	0	0	0	0	0	0	0	2	0
Open	0	0	1	0	1	0	1	1	0	0	0	1	0	0	2	2
Ouch	1	0	1	0	1	0	2	1	3	1	0	1	2	1	2	0
Pain	0	0	0	0	1	0	0	0	0	0	0	2	0	0	0	0
Phooey . .	0	1	0	0	2	0	0	0	0	0	2	0	0	0	0	0
Pleased . .	0	0	1	0	0	0	0	1	0	0	0	1	0	0	0	2
Pleasure . .	0	0	0	0	0	0	0	1	0	0	0	0	1	0	7	3
Pretty . . .	0	3	0	1	1	1	0	1	0	0	1	4	0	2	0	2
Question . .	1	1	0	0	2	1	0	0	0	1	0	0	0	0	1	0
Refreshing .	0	0	0	0	0	0	2	0	0	0	0	0	0	0	0	0
Relax . . .	0	0	1	1	2	0	2	2	1	0	3	4	3	1	7	0
Relief . . .	1	1	2	0	1	4	3	6	9	10	15	7	5	8	9	5
Said	0	0	2	0	0	0	0	0	0	0	0	0	0	0	0	0
Satisfaction	0	0	0	2	0	1	0	0	0	2	2	0	2	3	7	2
Satisfied . .	0	1	1	0	0	0	0	0	0	1	0	1	2	0	0	1
Saw	0	0	0	0	0	0	0	1	2	0	0	0	1	0	0	0
Say	1	2	0	1	1	0	1	0	0	0	0	2	0	1	1	1
See	3	1	2	2	1	2	2	1	0	0	1	0	1	0	1	0
Shoot	2	0	2	0	1	0	0	0	0	0	0	0	0	0	0	0
Shutup . . .	0	0	0	0	0	0	0	0	2	0	0	0	0	0	0	0
Sigh	1	2	0	5	2	3	2	3	2	4	2	2	2	11	7	12
Sleep . . .	0	0	0	0	0	0	0	0	2	0	1	1	0	1	0	1
Sneeze . . .	1	2	0	0	1	0	0	1	0	1	0	0	0	1	2	1
So	2	1	3	3	3	3	17	8	26	9	18	11	20	8	66	43
Sod	0	0	0	0	0	0	3	0	0	0	0	0	0	0	0	0
Something .	3	0	1	1	0	0	0	0	0	0	0	0	0	0	0	0
Sound . . .	0	2	0	0	1	2	0	1	0	0	2	1	1	1	2	1
Surprise . .	0	2	0	1	1	4	3	0	1	3	2	2	5	5	4	6

Response Word	4th M	4th F	5th M	5th F	6th M	6th F	7th M	7th F	8th M	8th F	10th M	10th F	12th M	12th F	College M	College F
						AH										
Surprised .	0	3	0	1	1	1	0	1	0	0	0	0	0	0	0	1
Talk	0	1	0	0	0	1	0	2	0	0	0	0	0	0	0	0
That	2	2	1	3	1	1	0	0	0	0	2	1	1	0	0	0
The	0	0	1	2	8	1	0	0	0	0	0	0	1	0	1	0
There . . .	3	1	2	2	2	0	1	1	1	1	0	0	1	1	2	0
Throat . . .	0	0	0	0	0	2	0	0	0	0	0	0	1	0	1	4
Tired . . .	0	0	0	0	0	0	0	0	1	0	0	0	0	0	1	2
To	1	0	1	1	1	1	0	0	2	0	0	0	1	0	0	0
Two	2	0	0	0	0	0	0	0	0	0	0	0	0	0	0	0
Ugh	0	0	0	1	0	1	1	2	0	0	0	0	0	1	0	0
Um	0	1	0	1	2	0	0	1	0	1	0	0	0	0	0	0
Us	0	0	0	0	0	2	0	0	0	0	0	0	0	0	0	0
Well	0	0	0	1	0	0	0	0	1	4	0	2	1	5	1	3
What	5	2	5	6	5	3	1	2	3	3	3	2	1	1	3	6
When	0	0	0	0	0	0	0	0	0	0	0	0	0	0	2	0
Who	2	2	0	2	2	1	0	0	1	1	0	0	0	0	0	0
Why	0	0	0	3	0	1	0	1	2	2	0	1	0	1	0	0
Wonderful .	1	0	0	0	0	0	0	2	0	0	0	0	1	1	0	0
Word	4	2	2	4	0	1	1	1	1	0	0	1	0	3	0	0
Wow	0	0	1	1	1	0	0	0	1	0	0	2	0	0	2	0
Ya	1	0	2	1	0	0	1	0	3	0	3	0	1	0	1	1
Yes	3	5	0	3	8	4	10	3	8	10	5	6	14	6	22	29
You	12	11	13	11	8	1	5	7	6	4	3	0	0	4	2	0
					4.	ALTHOUGH										
Again . . .	0	0	0	0	0	0	0	0	2	1	0	0	0	0	1	0
Al	2	1	1	0	0	0	0	0	1	0	0	0	0	0	0	0
All	14	8	6	9	5	4	5	1	2	2	1	2	3	2	3	1
All right . .	0	0	2	0	0	0	1	0	0	0	0	1	0	1	0	0
Almost . .	0	2	1	2	0	0	3	1	2	1	2	2	1	0	1	0
Alright . . .	0	2	0	3	0	3	0	0	0	1	1	0	3	1	1	0
Also	1	2	1	5	1	7	6	2	5	5	5	5	4	6	8	3
Althrough .	0	2	0	0	0	1	5	2	1	3	1	0	1	0	1	1
Altogether .	0	1	0	1	0	2	3	3	4	2	2	1	5	2	1	2
Always . . .	2	4	4	4	1	3	6	1	4	5	6	4	0	5	7	4
Among . . .	1	0	0	0	0	0	0	0	0	0	1	2	0	1	0	0
And	1	1	0	0	0	2	1	3	1	1	1	1	0	1	3	2
Another . . .	0	0	0	0	1	2	0	0	1	0	0	2	1	0	0	0
Anyhow . .	0	2	0	0	2	2	0	0	0	1	0	2	0	0	0	0
Anyway . .	1	3	3	6	3	5	1	7	3	7	7	5	3	4	2	4
As	0	0	0	0	0	0	0	1	0	0	0	1	1	0	1	3
At	2	3	1	0	1	0	0	4	1	0	0	1	0	1	0	3
Ball	1	0	0	0	2	0	0	0	0	0	0	0	0	0	0	0
Be	0	0	0	0	0	0	1	0	0	0	2	0	0	0	0	0
Because . .	1	6	1	8	6	9	10	21	12	10	9	23	21	25	44	63
Before . . .	0	0	0	0	0	0	0	0	0	0	0	0	2	1	1	0
Besides . .	0	0	0	0	0	0	1	2	0	1	2	3	3	3	3	2
Boy	2	0	0	1	0	1	0	0	0	0	0	0	0	0	0	0
But	10	5	4	5	10	9	14	20	13	17	11	12	11	13	39	54

Response Word	4th M	4th F	5th M	5th F	6th M	6th F	7th M	7th F	8th M	8th F	10th M	10th F	12th M	12th F	College M	College F
							ALTHOUGH									
Can't	2	1	0	0	0	1	0	1	1	0	0	0	0	0	0	0
Do	3	0	0	2	0	0	0	0	0	0	0	0	0	0	0	0
Done	5	7	2	6	5	4	3	0	2	1	1	0	0	0	0	0
Don't	0	1	0	1	2	1	0	0	0	0	1	0	1	0	0	0
Doubt	0	0	0	0	0	0	0	2	0	0	0	0	0	0	1	2
English	0	0	0	0	0	0	2	0	0	0	0	1	1	0	0	2
Enough	0	0	0	0	2	0	0	1	1	2	0	0	1	3	2	0
Even	0	6	3	3	3	5	7	7	4	9	5	12	6	8	9	12
Even so	0	1	0	0	0	0	2	1	0	0	0	1	0	0	0	2
Even though	0	0	0	0	0	0	2	4	0	2	2	2	2	1	5	6
Ever	0	1	0	0	0	1	0	1	1	0	0	0	0	0	2	1
Except	0	0	0	0	0	0	2	2	1	1	2	0	1	1	0	2
Exception	0	0	0	0	0	0	1	0	1	2	1	0	3	1	0	0
Excuse	0	1	0	0	0	0	0	1	0	1	2	1	0	0	0	2
For	1	0	2	0	1	0	0	0	0	0	0	0	1	0	5	0
Girl	2	0	1	0	0	1	0	0	0	0	0	0	1	0	0	0
Go	1	2	1	0	0	1	0	0	0	1	1	0	0	0	1	0
Good	1	1	1	0	2	0	2	0	0	0	0	1	0	0	0	0
Happen	0	1	1	2	0	1	0	0	0	0	0	0	0	0	0	1
He	10	8	11	6	10	7	9	3	11	3	6	2	12	6	15	12
Him	1	0	1	0	3	2	0	1	2	0	0	0	0	0	1	0
House	2	1	2	1	0	2	0	0	0	1	2	0	0	0	0	0
However	1	5	3	7	2	6	3	3	1	13	13	7	7	15	33	53
I	4	2	2	2	2	2	0	2	2	2	0	4	2	1	3	5
If	2	0	0	1	0	0	3	1	0	2	0	3	0	4	4	5
In	0	0	1	2	0	0	2	0	0	0	0	1	0	0	0	3
Instead	0	0	0	0	0	0	0	1	0	0	0	3	0	0	4	1
Is	2	1	0	3	1	0	1	0	0	1	1	0	4	0	1	2
It	5	6	4	7	5	1	8	3	4	5	0	6	5	6	10	7
Know	0	0	0	0	2	1	0	1	0	0	0	0	3	0	0	0
Long	3	1	1	0	1	0	0	0	0	0	0	0	0	0	0	0
Man	0	1	0	0	0	0	0	0	2	0	0	0	1	0	1	0
Many	0	0	1	1	1	1	1	0	0	2	1	1	2	3	1	0
Maybe	3	4	10	10	6	11	5	8	11	6	10	9	2	5	7	8
Me	3	2	2	0	2	2	0	0	1	1	0	2	1	0	0	0
Might	0	2	1	3	3	3	0	0	1	0	0	0	1	0	0	0
Much	0	0	0	0	0	0	0	0	0	0	1	0	0	0	0	2
Never	1	1	3	2	0	3	9	6	12	10	12	8	14	15	36	32
Nevertheless	0	0	0	0	0	0	0	1	0	0	0	3	2	3	3	7
Nice	0	2	0	0	0	1	0	0	0	0	1	0	0	0	1	0
Night	0	2	1	0	3	0	0	1	0	2	0	0	0	0	0	0
No	0	3	0	1	1	1	1	1	4	1	3	0	1	1	4	0
Not	0	5	3	4	2	2	0	2	1	0	0	3	4	0	7	7
Nothing	0	0	0	1	1	1	0	0	2	1	1	0	0	2	1	1
Now	2	3	4	3	1	2	1	2	7	4	2	8	2	2	11	8
Of course	0	1	0	0	0	0	0	2	0	0	0	0	0	0	1	0
Okay	0	0	2	0	2	0	0	0	0	0	0	0	0	0	0	1
Only	0	0	1	1	0	0	1	1	2	0	0	2	1	2	2	1
Out	0	0	0	0	1	0	0	2	0	0	0	0	0	0	0	0

Response Word	4th M	4th F	5th M	5th F	6th M	6th F	7th M	7th F	8th M	8th F	10th M	10th F	12th M	12th F	College M	College F
									ALTHOUGH							
People . . .	3	1	3	1	2	0	1	0	2	1	0	0	0	0	1	0
Perhaps . .	0	0	0	0	0	0	1	0	0	0	0	0	0	2	1	0
Person . .	0	0	0	0	2	0	0	0	0	0	0	0	0	0	0	0
Place . . .	0	1	2	1	0	0	0	0	0	1	0	0	0	0	0	0
Plus	0	0	0	0	0	0	0	0	0	0	0	0	2	1	0	0
Preposition	0	0	0	0	0	0	0	0	0	0	0	0	0	1	2	1
Question . .	0	0	0	1	0	0	2	0	0	0	0	0	0	1	0	1
Really . . .	2	1	0	0	1	2	0	0	0	0	0	1	1	1	0	0
Reason . .	0	0	0	0	0	0	1	0	1	3	3	3	2	0	2	1
See	1	0	0	0	1	0	0	0	2	0	0	1	0	0	2	0
Sentence . .	0	0	0	1	0	1	0	0	0	0	0	1	0	3	0	1
She	0	2	0	3	1	6	0	1	0	2	3	2	2	3	3	2
Since	0	0	0	0	0	1	0	0	0	0	1	0	1	3	1	7
Slow	0	0	0	0	0	0	0	0	0	0	0	0	2	0	0	0
So	1	1	2	1	2	9	0	3	0	2	1	2	0	2	7	7
Some . . .	1	2	0	0	0	1	0	0	1	1	1	0	0	0	1	1
Something .	2	0	2	1	2	2	0	1	1	0	3	1	0	0	0	0
Sometime .	0	0	0	0	0	0	1	0	0	0	0	1	0	0	0	2
Sometimes .	1	1	1	0	0	1	4	3	0	3	2	6	2	3	5	5
Still	0	1	0	0	0	0	0	0	0	0	0	1	1	0	1	2
Strong . . .	0	0	0	0	0	0	0	2	0	0	0	0	0	0	0	0
Sure	0	0	0	0	1	2	0	0	0	1	0	0	0	0	0	0
Talk	0	1	0	0	1	2	0	0	0	0	0	0	0	0	0	0
Talking . .	0	0	0	0	0	2	0	0	0	0	0	0	0	0	0	0
That	3	2	4	2	5	0	1	2	2	2	3	1	2	0	5	4
The	4	2	2	1	11	0	2	0	2	1	4	1	0	1	1	2
Then	0	1	1	1	2	2	0	0	1	2	4	1	1	1	3	2
There . . .	1	4	2	1	2	1	3	0	2	2	2	0	0	0	1	0
Therefore .	1	0	0	0	0	0	2	1	1	3	0	0	1	3	9	7
They	0	4	1	1	2	3	1	1	3	3	1	4	7	2	7	3
Thing . . .	1	0	2	0	1	0	0	0	0	0	0	1	0	0	0	0
Think . . .	2	2	8	3	2	1	0	0	1	1	1	0	0	0	0	0
This	1	1	0	0	0	0	0	1	0	0	4	0	1	0	2	4
Though . . .	17	25	32	27	26	29	22	29	21	19	11	10	8	11	12	8
Thought . .	5	8	7	2	5	7	1	3	3	2	1	2	1	1	1	0
Threw . . .	0	0	0	1	1	0	3	4	0	0	0	0	1	0	1	0
Through . .	5	7	9	9	6	5	8	9	11	14	8	14	8	5	13	7
Throughout.	0	0	0	0	0	1	0	0	0	1	0	0	2	0	0	0
Thus	0	0	0	0	0	0	0	0	0	0	0	0	0	0	1	2
Time	2	0	0	0	0	0	0	1	0	0	0	0	0	0	0	0
To	0	0	0	0	0	2	0	0	0	0	0	0	1	1	1	2
Together . .	0	2	0	1	0	2	7	2	5	2	1	1	7	4	6	1
Too.	0	0	1	0	1	0	0	0	0	0	0	2	2	2	1	2
Way	0	2	0	0	1	0	0	0	0	0	0	0	0	0	0	0
We	2	1	2	3	1	3	7	2	4	2	7	7	3	7	16	11
Well	0	2	0	2	1	0	0	0	0	0	1	1	0	0	0	2
What	4	2	4	3	5	1	4	2	7	4	2	3	3	3	5	3
Whatever .	0	1	1	0	1	0	2	1	0	1	0	0	0	0	0	1
When. . . .	0	1	2	1	0	1	3	4	3	2	3	1	2	2	5	4

Response Word	4th M	4th F	5th M	5th F	6th M	6th F	7th M	7th F	8th M	8th F	10th M	10th F	12th M	12th F	College M	College F
ALTHOUGH																
Whenever .	0	0	0	0	1	0	0	0	0	1	0	3	0	1	3	2
Who	0	0	1	0	0	0	0	0	0	0	2	0	0	0	0	0
Why	3	2	1	2	2	0	5	0	2	3	2	0	1	2	10	5
Word....	2	2	1	1	3	1	1	0	0	0	1	1	2	3	0	0
Yes	1	0	3	6	1	3	0	1	0	1	0	2	0	1	4	3
Yet	2	0	0	1	1	0	0	0	1	0	0	1	0	2	3	12
You	11	2	6	5	5	5	3	10	7	9	10	6	14	7	12	11
5. ALWAYS																
All	9	5	13	6	8	6	4	4	4	1	4	1	1	0	3	0
All the time	2	2	3	1	0	0	2	2	1	2	0	0	1	0	1	2
All times .	0	0	2	0	0	1	0	0	1	0	0	0	0	0	0	0
Almost...	0	4	0	2	0	0	0	1	1	2	1	1	0	0	0	0
An	0	0	0	0	0	0	0	2	0	0	0	0	0	0	0	0
Anytime ..	0	0	2	0	0	2	2	0	1	1	2	2	1	0	0	0
Anyway ..	0	0	0	1	0	2	2	2	1	0	0	1	0	1	3	0
Anyways ..	0	0	1	0	0	1	2	1	0	0	1	1	2	0	0	0
After....	0	0	0	0	0	0	0	2	0	0	0	1	0	0	1	0
Again ...	2	0	2	2	2	0	0	1	2	2	0	0	0	0	1	0
At	0	0	0	1	0	0	1	1	0	0	0	0	0	0	2	0
Away....	8	9	3	2	3	5	1	3	2	1	0	2	0	0	0	0
Be	1	2	3	3	0	3	0	0	1	0	1	1	1	1	3	2
Because ..	0	2	1	2	1	0	1	0	0	0	1	2	1	1	2	0
Before ...	0	0	1	1	1	0	1	0	0	1	1	0	0	0	2	0
Buy.....	0	0	0	0	0	0	0	0	0	1	0	0	0	0	3	0
By	0	1	0	0	1	3	1	0	1	0	0	0	0	0	0	0
Can	0	0	1	1	0	0	0	2	1	0	0	0	0	0	0	1
Car	2	0	3	1	0	0	0	0	0	0	0	0	0	0	0	0
Come ...	5	3	2	2	2	0	0	0	1	0	1	2	0	3	2	1
Constant ..	0	0	0	0	1	0	0	0	1	0	0	3	0	0	1	0
Constantly .	1	0	0	1	0	0	1	2	0	0	0	0	0	0	0	0
Continuous .	0	0	0	0	0	0	2	0	0	0	0	0	0	0	0	0
Do	10	2	8	6	3	4	1	0	1	1	0	0	1	0	0	0
Doing ...	0	3	0	0	0	0	0	0	0	0	0	0	0	0	0	0
Done	0	2	0	0	0	0	1	0	0	0	0	0	0	0	0	0
Did.....	2	0	0	0	2	0	0	0	0	0	0	0	0	0	0	0
Eternity ..	0	0	0	0	0	0	0	0	0	0	3	1	1	0	0	1
Even	0	0	0	0	0	0	0	0	0	0	0	0	0	0	2	0
Ever	1	8	8	9	5	14	12	15	7	8	5	9	6	13	26	32
Evermore .	0	0	0	0	0	0	0	3	0	0	0	0	0	0	0	0
Every ...	12	11	8	10	8	5	7	5	1	3	3	1	1	0	0	0
Everyday..	0	2	1	1	1	2	0	0	0	1	1	0	0	1	0	0
Everytime .	4	2	1	5	5	5	6	2	4	2	3	0	1	0	0	0
Faithful ..	0	0	0	0	0	0	0	0	0	0	0	0	0	1	3	0
Far	2	0	2	2	1	0	0	0	1	0	1	0	0	0	0	0
Fast	1	0	3	0	0	1	0	0	0	0	1	0	0	0	0	0
For	0	0	0	0	0	2	0	0	0	0	0	0	0	0	0	0
Forever ..	10	10	7	17	18	36	21	38	21	36	34	48	28	46	54	82
Fun.....	1	0	1	0	0	1	0	0	0	0	0	1	2	0	0	1

Response Word	4th		5th		6th		7th		8th		10th		12th		College	
	M	F	M	F	M	F	M	F	M	F	M	F	M	F	M	F

ALWAYS

Response Word	M	F	M	F	M	F	M	F	M	F	M	F	M	F	M	F
Glad	0	0	0	0	2	0	0	0	0	0	0	0	0	0	0	0
Go	6	6	3	4	3	5	2	1	3	0	1	1	1	0	1	0
God	0	0	0	0	0	0	0	0	0	2	0	0	0	0	0	0
Going	0	0	2	0	1	1	4	0	0	0	0	0	1	0	0	0
Gone	0	3	5	2	9	0	2	2	1	1	1	0	1	2	3	1
Good	4	6	3	2	4	3	1	1	2	3	2	0	2	1	5	3
Have	0	1	0	2	1	1	0	1	0	0	0	0	0	0	1	1
Here	2	1	1	4	6	3	1	2	3	1	2	2	1	2	4	2
Home	1	2	2	0	2	1	0	1	3	1	3	0	1	1	0	0
Him	0	0	0	0	2	0	0	0	0	0	0	0	1	0	1	0
Is	0	0	0	2	0	1	0	0	0	0	0	0	1	0	0	0
Keep	0	3	1	2	0	1	0	0	0	0	1	0	0	0	0	0
Late	0	1	2	0	0	0	0	0	0	0	1	1	2	2	1	2
Letter	0	0	0	0	0	0	0	0	0	0	2	0	0	1	0	0
Long	1	3	0	1	3	1	1	0	0	0	1	0	0	1	0	0
Look	2	0	0	0	0	0	0	0	0	0	0	0	0	1	0	0
Love	0	0	1	0	0	1	1	0	0	1	5	3	1	9	5	5
Mad	0	0	0	2	0	0	0	0	1	0	0	0	0	0	0	0
Many	0	0	1	1	0	0	0	1	0	1	0	3	0	0	2	0
Me	0	0	0	0	0	1	0	2	0	2	0	0	0	0	0	2
Mine	0	0	1	0	0	0	0	0	0	4	1	1	1	0	1	0
Mom	0	0	0	0	2	0	0	0	0	0	0	0	0	0	0	0
Most	0	0	2	2	2	0	0	1	0	0	1	0	0	2	0	0
Mostly	1	0	0	1	4	1	1	2	0	0	0	0	1	0	0	0
Must	0	0	0	1	1	2	0	0	0	0	0	0	0	1	1	0
My	2	2	1	1	0	0	0	0	0	0	0	0	0	0	0	0
Near	0	1	1	0	0	0	0	0	0	0	1	2	0	1	1	2
Never	34	42	34	54	33	52	76	86	84	93	90	105	116	103	239	268
Nice	0	1	0	1	0	0	0	0	0	2	0	1	1	0	1	0
No	2	1	1	2	3	0	0	0	0	1	0	0	1	1	2	0
None	1	0	1	2	2	0	0	0	1	1	0	0	0	0	0	0
Not	5	0	2	0	3	1	5	1	1	0	0	0	1	1	0	2
Now	2	4	3	3	3	1	4	4	8	5	3	6	1	7	22	14
Often	0	0	0	0	1	1	2	2	0	0	0	0	0	1	4	0
Out	0	0	2	0	0	0	0	0	0	0	0	0	0	0	0	0
Play	1	2	1	0	2	1	1	0	0	0	1	0	0	0	0	0
Ready	2	0	0	2	3	1	3	2	1	3	0	2	3	0	2	1
Remember	0	2	0	1	2	0	1	2	0	0	0	0	1	2	1	1
Right	3	2	3	2	3	4	1	1	2	0	1	0	0	1	4	0
Run	1	1	0	1	2	0	0	0	1	0	0	0	0	0	0	0
Same	1	2	3	0	2	0	0	1	0	4	2	0	0	0	0	0
School	0	0	0	0	0	1	1	0	0	2	1	0	0	2	0	0
Seldom	0	0	0	0	1	0	1	0	0	0	1	0	0	0	0	2
Some	2	0	1	0	0	1	1	0	1	0	1	0	0	0	1	2
Sometime	0	1	2	2	0	0	3	0	4	1	1	0	2	0	2	1
Sometimes	6	4	0	1	3	2	13	5	9	4	10	7	11	5	17	9
Song	0	0	0	1	0	0	0	0	0	0	0	3	1	0	1	4
Soon	0	0	0	0	0	0	1	0	0	0	0	1	0	0	2	2
Stay	0	1	1	2	1	2	0	2	0	1	0	0	0	0	0	0

Response Word	4th M	4th F	5th M	5th F	6th M	6th F	7th M	7th F	8th M	8th F	10th M	10th F	12th M	12th F	College M	College F
						ALWAYS										
Sure	2	1	1	0	2	1	0	0	0	1	0	0	1	1	0	3
The	2	0	0	0	0	0	0	0	0	0	0	0	0	0	0	0
Then	0	1	0	0	0	0	1	0	0	1	2	0	1	0	0	0
There . . .	6	4	9	4	5	2	0	2	6	2	3	1	1	3	1	0
Thing . . .	1	0	2	2	0	0	0	0	0	0	1	0	0	0	0	0
Time	10	14	8	8	9	10	8	2	4	6	2	4	4	4	3	4
Together . .	0	0	1	0	1	0	0	2	1	1	2	1	0	0	3	1
True . . .	1	0	0	1	0	0	1	0	1	1	0	3	1	1	2	6
Usually . . .	0	0	0	1	0	1	1	0	0	0	0	0	0	0	2	2
Want	0	4	0	0	0	0	0	0	0	1	0	0	0	0	1	0
Was	0	1	2	3	1	1	0	0	1	0	3	0	0	0	0	0
Way	9	3	10	6	7	1	4	3	3	2	0	0	1	0	0	0
Ways	11	13	13	9	10	6	5	1	1	4	2	0	2	0	0	0
Well	0	0	0	0	0	0	0	0	0	2	0	0	0	0	0	0
Were	0	1	2	0	0	0	0	0	0	0	0	1	0	1	1	0
Word	0	0	2	1	1	2	0	1	2	0	0	0	0	0	0	0
When	1	1	0	1	3	1	5	4	4	0	1	2	3	2	5	5
Why	1	1	1	0	2	0	1	0	0	0	0	0	1	1	1	0
Will	1	1	0	2	0	4	1	0	0	2	0	0	3	2	0	3
With	0	0	0	1	0	0	0	0	0	0	0	0	0	2	0	0
Yes	0	1	2	1	2	0	1	1	3	0	1	2	2	2	4	1
You	0	0	0	1	0	0	0	0	2	0	0	1	1	0	0	0
Young . . .	0	0	0	0	0	0	0	0	0	0	0	0	0	0	0	2
Your . . .	0	0	0	0	0	2	0	0	0	0	0	0	0	0	0	0
Yours . . .	0	0	0	0	0	2	2	1	3	0	2	1	4	1	3	0
						6. AM										
A	8	4	4	6	9	2	4	1	5	2	0	2	0	1	2	5
Ah	1	1	3	1	0	0	0	0	0	0	0	0	0	0	0	0
Aim	1	0	2	1	2	4	5	0	1	1	0	0	2	1	0	0
Alive	0	0	0	0	0	1	0	0	0	0	0	0	0	2	0	4
Also	0	0	0	0	0	0	0	0	1	0	0	3	1	0	0	0
Always . . .	0	0	0	0	0	0	0	0	0	0	0	0	0	1	2	2
America . .	1	0	0	0	0	0	2	0	0	0	2	0	0	1	2	0
American .	0	0	0	0	0	0	0	0	0	0	0	0	0	1	2	0
An	9	10	12	11	4	7	2	8	6	4	0	7	5	1	4	3
And	7	1	3	1	0	2	1	4	0	1	1	1	1	1	2	3
Ann	1	4	0	2	1	0	2	0	0	0	0	1	0	0	0	1
Are	3	4	1	8	2	12	13	22	13	20	17	19	24	22	43	56
Aren't . . .	1	0	0	0	1	0	0	2	2	1	1	1	1	1	2	1
Arm	0	0	1	2	2	1	1	1	0	0	0	0	0	0	1	0
As	2	1	2	2	0	2	1	0	1	1	0	0	0	1	1	1
At	1	0	0	1	1	2	2	1	3	0	2	0	1	0	0	1
Be	0	0	0	0	0	0	0	0	0	1	1	3	1	3	6	12
Being . . .	0	0	0	0	0	0	0	3	1	0	1	0	2	0	4	4
Better . . .	0	0	0	0	0	0	2	0	0	0	0	0	0	0	0	0
Big	0	1	0	0	1	0	0	0	0	1	0	0	0	0	3	0
Boy	1	0	2	0	1	0	1	0	0	0	2	1	0	0	0	0
But	0	1	0	0	0	0	0	1	0	0	0	0	0	0	2	0

Response Word	4th M	4th F	5th M	5th F	6th M	6th F	7th M	7th F	8th M	8th F	10th M	10th F	12th M	12th F	College M	College F
							AM									
Can	2	1	2	1	0	2	0	0	0	1	0	0	1	0	1	1
Clean . . .	0	1	0	0	0	1	0	0	1	0	0	0	0	0	2	0
Clear . . .	0	0	2	0	0	0	0	1	0	2	0	0	0	0	4	0
Closer . . .	0	0	0	0	0	0	1	0	0	0	2	0	0	0	0	0
Cold	0	0	0	0	0	0	0	0	0	0	1	1	0	1	2	0
Doing . . .	0	0	0	0	1	2	0	1	2	0	1	0	1	0	3	1
Dumb . . .	0	0	0	0	0	0	0	0	0	0	0	2	0	1	0	0
Exist . . .	0	0	0	0	0	0	0	0	0	0	0	0	0	1	8	0
Fire	2	0	3	0	0	0	0	0	0	0	0	0	0	0	0	0
Glad	0	2	0	1	0	0	1	0	0	0	1	0	0	0	0	0
Going . . .	5	4	11	4	13	2	7	8	8	11	10	16	16	8	18	24
Good	4	1	2	0	0	0	1	0	3	2	1	1	0	2	7	2
Gun.	1	1	2	1	2	0	1	0	1	0	1	0	0	0	0	0
Ham	2	1	1	0	0	0	0	0	0	0	1	1	1	0	1	2
Happy . . .	1	0	0	0	0	0	0	1	0	2	0	2	0	0	1	4
He	1	0	3	2	0	0	1	0	1	0	0	0	1	0	0	1
Her	0	0	0	0	0	1	0	0	0	0	1	0	3	0	0	1
Here	2	0	0	0	5	4	6	5	4	8	4	5	8	8	20	22
Him	0	1	1	0	1	0	2	0	2	0	0	0	1	0	0	1
Home . . .	0	0	0	0	0	0	2	0	0	1	1	0	0	0	0	0
How	0	1	0	0	0	2	0	0	0	0	0	0	0	0	0	1
I	82	98	78	97	81	89	67	85	68	80	92	90	68	77	133	111
I am	1	1	1	0	1	0	3	0	1	2	1	0	2	1	0	0
I'm	2	10	10	9	7	15	7	8	5	4	4	1	1	2	2	0
In	2	1	0	3	3	1	1	1	3	1	3	0	3	0	4	3
Is	4	2	5	5	7	18	18	18	20	17	21	33	28	29	47	70
Isn't	0	0	2	0	1	0	0	0	2	0	0	0	0	0	0	0
It	2	2	2	3	2	2	0	5	1	1	3	0	1	1	1	0
Man	1	0	0	0	0	0	1	2	0	0	0	0	0	0	0	0
Me	13	22	12	21	22	17	17	13	4	6	6	4	6	11	12	12
More. . . .	1	0	0	0	0	0	0	0	0	0	0	0	0	8	0	1
Myself . . .	3	2	0	4	1	0	0	0	2	0	0	0	2	1	2	1
Near	0	0	0	0	0	0	1	0	0	0	0	0	0	0	5	4
Nice	0	0	0	0	0	0	1	0	1	2	0	0	0	0	0	1
Not.	5	9	6	11	10	10	9	13	21	14	12	12	22	14	44	40
Now	3	0	2	1	1	2	2	2	2	4	3	4	0	3	11	7
Oh	2	0	0	0	1	0	0	1	0	0	1	0	0	0	0	0
Older. . . .	0	0	0	0	0	0	0	0	0	0	0	1	2	0	1	0
On	2	0	1	1	0	0	1	0	0	1	2	0	0	1	3	3
Person . .	0	1	1	2	3	1	0	2	0	0	1	1	0	2	0	3
Question . .	0	1	0	0	1	3	0	0	0	0	0	0	0	0	0	0
Ready . . .	0	0	0	0	0	2	0	0	1	0	1	0	1	0	0	0
Sam	2	1	0	1	1	1	0	0	2	0	0	1	0	0	1	0
See	2	0	0	1	0	1	1	1	0	0	0	0	0	0	0	0
She	0	0	1	0	0	1	0	0	0	2	0	0	0	0	0	0
Shot	0	0	1	3	1	0	0	0	0	0	1	0	0	0	0	0
Sick	0	0	0	0	0	2	1	0	1	3	0	0	0	1	2	2
So	1	0	0	2	0	1	0	0	0	2	0	1	0	0	0	1
Some . . .	0	0	3	0	0	0	0	0	0	0	0	0	0	0	0	0

Response Word	4th M	F	5th M	F	6th M	F	7th M	F	8th M	F	10th M	F	12th M	F	College M	F

AM

Response Word	4th M	4th F	5th M	5th F	6th M	6th F	7th M	7th F	8th M	8th F	10th M	10th F	12th M	12th F	College M	College F
Someone . .	1	2	1	0	0	0	0	0	1	0	0	0	0	0	0	0
Still	0	0	0	0	0	0	0	0	0	0	0	0	0	0	0	2
Than	0	0	0	0	2	0	0	0	0	0	0	1	1	0	0	0
The	2	1	2	0	2	0	1	0	0	1	2	1	0	0	2	0
There . . .	1	3	1	3	3	0	3	1	2	1	0	1	1	1	2	2
They	0	2	0	2	1	1	0	0	0	1	0	0	1	0	0	0
Tired . . .	0	0	0	0	0	0	1	1	0	0	0	2	0	2	1	2
To	6	2	5	4	4	0	1	2	2	0	4	0	0	0	2	1
To be . . .	0	0	0	0	0	0	0	0	0	0	0	1	0	2	0	1
Us	1	0	1	2	0	0	0	0	0	0	0	0	0	0	0	0
Verb	0	0	0	0	0	0	0	0	0	1	1	1	0	2	2	5
Was	0	1	1	2	2	1	6	4	4	8	2	2	3	2	14	21
We	0	0	0	0	2	1	0	1	0	0	1	0	0	0	0	0
Were. . . .	0	0	0	0	0	0	0	0	0	0	0	0	0	3	1	4
What	0	0	1	0	0	0	0	1	9	4	3	5	2	2	6	3
Where . . .	1	0	2	0	0	0	0	0	0	0	0	1	0	0	0	2
Why	0	0	1	0	0	2	0	0	0	0	1	0	0	0	1	0
Will	1	0	1	1	1	1	2	1	0	2	1	3	2	0	2	4
With	0	0	0	1	0	0	2	0	1	0	0	0	0	0	0	0
Word . . .	0	2	2	4	1	1	1	0	1	1	1	0	1	0	1	0
You	7	6	8	7	6	4	3	3	5	3	4	1	4	5	3	4
Yours . . .	0	0	0	0	0	0	0	0	0	0	0	0	0	2	0	0
Yourself . .	0	0	2	1	0	1	0	0	0	0	0	0	0	0	0	0

7. **AN**

Response Word	4th M	4th F	5th M	5th F	6th M	6th F	7th M	7th F	8th M	8th F	10th M	10th F	12th M	12th F	College M	College F
A	28	23	27	26	19	25	21	28	21	27	20	34	29	52	65	120
Adjective .	0	0	0	0	0	0	0	1	2	0	1	0	0	1	2	0
Ah	0	0	0	0	0	0	0	1	0	0	0	0	0	0	2	1
Airplane . .	0	1	2	1	3	0	3	2	1	1	3	1	3	2	6	5
Also	1	3	1	2	3	1	4	3	3	2	1	0	4	4	3	3
Am.	7	10	5	9	8	10	11	7	8	7	2	5	6	3	5	4
An	1	0	0	0	2	1	0	0	0	0	0	0	0	0	0	1
And	26	40	24	26	17	40	36	33	35	18	24	24	17	16	38	39
Angel . . .	0	0	0	0	0	0	0	0	0	1	0	0	1	1	0	2
Animal . .	0	4	4	1	1	3	3	2	1	4	4	6	4	4	6	9
Ann	5	5	9	0	5	4	4	2	5	2	3	0	3	0	6	0
Anne	0	1	0	8	0	0	1	1	0	1	0	0	0	0	0	0
Another . .	0	1	0	6	3	3	2	2	6	5	8	6	3	5	11	4
Answer . .	1	1	0	1	2	1	2	2	0	4	1	2	3	3	4	8
Ant	1	2	5	2	6	2	5	4	3	5	2	1	2	0	5	3
Any	0	0	1	0	0	1	1	0	0	0	2	2	2	0	0	0
Anything . .	1	0	0	0	0	0	1	1	0	1	0	0	2	0	0	1
Apple . . .	21	25	17	39	12	28	27	42	31	56	28	62	19	54	78	97
Are	0	0	3	0	0	1	0	1	1	3	0	1	4	1	4	3
Article. . .	0	0	0	0	0	0	0	0	2	0	0	2	2	1	13	13
At	1	0	0	1	0	5	1	1	2	2	2	2	0	0	0	3
Aunt	0	0	0	0	1	0	0	0	0	0	1	0	0	0	2	1
Auto	0	0	0	0	0	0	0	0	1	1	0	1	1	0	5	2
Awful . . .	0	0	0	0	0	0	0	0	0	0	0	0	2	0	1	0

Response Word	4th M	4th F	5th M	5th F	6th M	6th F	7th M	7th F	8th M	8th F	10th M	10th F	12th M	12th F	College M	College F
							AN									
Ball	3	1	0	0	0	0	0	1	1	1	0	0	0	0	0	0
Ban	0	0	2	2	0	0	1	1	1	0	0	0	1	0	0	1
Band	1	0	2	0	0	0	0	1	0	0	0	0	0	0	0	0
Be	2	0	1	0	0	0	0	0	0	1	1	0	1	2	0	0
Because	1	0	1	0	0	0	0	1	0	0	1	0	2	0	0	1
Bee	0	0	1	0	0	0	0	0	0	2	0	0	1	0	0	0
Book	0	1	2	1	0	0	0	0	0	0	1	0	1	0	3	1
Boy	2	2	0	2	1	0	1	0	2	1	1	0	0	1	0	0
But	1	0	0	0	2	0	0	2	1	1	1	2	2	2	4	2
Buy	1	0	0	0	0	0	2	1	1	1	0	1	0	1	0	0
By	2	1	1	0	0	0	1	1	1	0	1	1	0	0	1	0
Can	3	0	1	4	2	2	2	0	0	0	1	1	1	0	3	0
Car	0	0	1	0	0	0	0	1	3	1	3	0	2	0	1	0
Cat	2	1	0	2	1	3	0	0	1	0	0	1	0	1	1	1
Conjunction	0	0	0	0	0	0	0	0	0	0	1	1	2	0	0	0
Do	2	0	1	0	0	0	0	0	0	0	0	0	1	0	0	0
Dog	0	1	2	2	0	4	0	3	2	2	3	1	1	1	0	1
Eagle	0	1	0	0	0	0	0	0	1	0	0	0	0	0	2	0
Egg	0	1	0	1	2	1	1	0	0	0	1	0	0	2	2	1
Elephant	2	1	1	1	0	1	1	4	0	1	0	1	2	0	3	1
End	0	0	1	2	1	0	0	0	0	0	0	0	0	1	1	1
Evening	0	0	0	0	0	0	1	0	0	0	0	0	1	0	3	2
Example	0	0	0	0	0	0	0	0	0	0	0	0	2	0	1	1
Fruit	0	2	0	0	0	0	0	0	0	0	0	0	0	0	0	0
Girl	2	4	1	3	2	2	3	2	0	0	7	2	4	2	3	0
Go	0	0	1	0	0	0	0	1	2	0	3	0	1	2	1	1
Gun	1	0	1	0	3	0	0	0	0	0	0	0	0	0	0	0
He	0	0	4	1	3	4	2	0	1	0	2	1	1	0	0	0
Hen	0	0	0	0	0	0	2	0	0	0	0	0	0	0	0	0
Her	1	1	0	0	1	3	0	0	1	0	3	0	1	0	0	0
Here	0	2	1	0	0	1	0	1	1	1	1	0	1	0	0	0
Him	2	0	2	1	2	0	1	2	3	0	1	1	2	0	1	0
Horse	0	1	0	1	0	0	0	1	0	0	0	0	0	1	0	2
Hour	0	1	0	1	0	1	0	0	0	1	1	1	2	2	5	5
House	0	0	0	1	3	0	1	0	0	1	0	2	1	1	1	0
How	3	3	0	0	1	2	1	0	3	1	1	0	0	1	0	0
I	7	3	5	5	5	8	6	5	5	5	1	0	3	1	4	0
Idiot	0	0	0	0	0	0	0	0	0	0	0	0	1	0	2	0
If	0	3	2	1	1	0	1	0	0	0	0	0	2	1	5	0
In	2	3	3	4	4	2	3	1	2	0	3	0	3	5	4	8
Inning	0	0	0	0	0	0	0	0	0	0	0	0	0	0	2	0
Iron	0	0	0	0	0	0	0	0	0	0	0	0	0	0	2	0
Is	4	3	3	4	2	2	8	3	7	4	9	3	9	6	10	3
It	2	2	2	8	7	4	7	3	8	3	6	9	6	1	12	6
Man	2	0	1	0	2	0	1	1	1	2	2	0	0	0	0	0
Many	0	0	0	0	0	0	0	0	0	0	0	0	0	1	0	2
Me	2	4	3	2	2	1	1	2	2	0	1	2	0	1	0	1
My	1	0	1	1	3	1	1	2	2	0	0	0	0	0	1	0
Name	1	2	3	0	4	5	0	1	0	0	1	0	0	0	1	0

17

Response Word	4th		5th		6th		7th		8th		10th		12th		College	
	M	F	M	F	M	F	M	F	M	F	M	F	M	F	M	F

AN

Response Word	M	F	M	F	M	F	M	F	M	F	M	F	M	F	M	F
No	1	0	0	0	3	0	0	2	0	0	0	1	0	2	0	0
Noise	0	2	0	0	0	0	0	0	0	0	0	0	0	0	0	0
Now	0	0	1	1	1	0	1	0	2	0	1	1	1	0	3	1
Object	0	0	0	0	0	0	3	2	2	2	6	2	2	3	13	14
Ocean	0	1	0	0	1	0	0	1	0	0	0	0	0	1	1	3
Of	1	0	0	2	0	2	0	0	2	1	2	1	1	1	1	3
Office	0	0	0	0	0	0	0	0	0	0	0	0	0	0	2	0
Oh	1	3	1	1	1	2	0	0	1	1	0	0	0	0	2	0
Old	2	2	2	2	3	0	0	1	1	1	0	0	0	0	3	5
On	0	3	0	0	2	2	0	3	0	2	0	2	1	2	6	2
One	0	3	3	1	5	6	3	13	1	13	2	7	3	6	10	25
Opening	0	0	0	0	0	1	0	0	0	0	1	1	0	1	2	1
Operation	0	0	0	0	0	0	0	0	0	0	0	0	0	0	0	2
Or	0	0	0	0	1	0	1	1	2	1	1	2	1	0	8	4
Orange	0	0	0	0	0	0	1	1	0	1	0	0	0	3	2	6
Other	4	4	9	4	7	3	4	1	4	1	7	7	7	1	15	10
Our	0	0	0	0	0	0	1	0	0	2	0	0	0	0	0	0
Over	0	0	0	0	0	0	0	0	0	2	0	0	0	1	0	1
Pan	0	1	0	0	2	0	1	3	0	0	0	0	0	0	0	0
Person	2	0	1	0	0	0	2	0	0	0	0	0	1	0	0	1
Pig	1	0	0	0	3	0	0	0	0	0	0	0	0	0	0	0
Plus	0	0	0	0	0	0	2	0	0	0	1	0	1	0	0	0
Say	0	0	0	1	0	0	0	2	0	0	0	0	0	0	0	0
Sentence	0	0	0	0	0	0	0	0	0	0	0	2	0	0	0	1
Sister	2	0	0	0	0	0	0	0	0	0	0	0	0	0	0	0
So	3	1	2	3	1	0	0	0	1	0	0	0	1	1	2	2
Something	3	7	2	2	0	3	1	2	1	0	0	3	0	0	0	1
Story	4	7	4	3	5	5	5	0	2	2	4	0	2	0	0	1
Than	0	0	1	2	0	1	0	0	0	0	1	0	1	0	1	0
That	3	0	2	1	0	1	0	0	0	1	1	1	3	0	2	1
The	2	1	1	3	8	3	3	3	4	2	6	2	6	3	18	14
Them	1	0	0	0	0	1	0	0	1	2	0	1	0	0	0	0
Then	0	1	1	1	5	1	1	1	6	3	4	4	4	1	7	4
There	1	1	0	3	0	1	2	0	0	0	1	2	0	1	0	0
They	0	0	0	0	1	1	1	2	1	0	1	0	0	0	0	1
Thing	3	7	8	4	12	7	2	4	1	1	5	0	3	4	4	2
This	1	0	2	3	0	2	0	0	0	0	1	0	0	1	0	0
To	2	1	1	1	1	0	1	1	0	0	0	0	2	1	1	0
Vowel	1	2	1	1	0	1	0	1	1	0	0	1	1	0	2	0
We	1	0	2	1	1	0	2	1	0	0	0	0	1	0	0	0
What	2	1	0	0	0	1	3	2	0	4	2	2	1	2	3	0
Where	3	0	0	0	0	0	0	0	0	0	0	0	0	0	0	0
Why	0	0	1	1	2	0	2	1	0	0	0	0	1	0	1	0
Will	2	0	0	0	1	0	0	0	0	0	0	0	0	0	0	0
With	0	0	0	0	0	0	0	0	0	0	0	0	0	0	2	0
Word	5	5	4	4	3	4	0	2	2	1	2	2	0	4	6	0
You	4	6	12	8	5	3	2	0	3	2	1	0	5	1	1	1
Your	0	0	0	0	2	0	0	0	0	0	0	0	0	0	0	0

Response Word	4th M	4th F	5th M	5th F	6th M	6th F	7th M	7th F	8th M	8th F	10th M	10th F	12th M	12th F	College M	College F

8. **AND**

Response Word	4th M	4th F	5th M	5th F	6th M	6th F	7th M	7th F	8th M	8th F	10th M	10th F	12th M	12th F	College M	College F
A	2	5	4	4	4	1	2	7	1	5	4	4	1	5	1	4
Add	4	1	0	0	4	1	0	1	1	0	2	1	1	0	2	0
Addition . .	0	0	0	0	2	0	0	0	0	1	0	0	0	0	1	0
Again . . .	2	1	4	1	4	4	3	4	2	4	2	0	2	0	3	0
All	0	0	1	0	0	1	2	0	0	0	1	1	0	1	2	0
Also	9	17	12	21	14	30	30	34	21	29	17	33	21	27	38	36
Always . . .	2	1	0	0	2	3	2	1	3	2	0	2	2	2	2	0
An	8	14	14	14	7	12	11	18	6	4	4	5	6	1	1	2
And	1	1	0	0	2	0	0	0	0	0	0	0	0	0	0	0
Andy	3	0	0	1	0	1	0	0	0	1	0	0	0	0	0	1
Ann	3	2	1	2	0	1	0	2	0	1	1	0	0	0	0	0
Another . .	5	8	2	6	4	6	3	1	2	2	1	2	0	0	2	0
Apple	0	1	0	0	1	2	0	1	0	0	0	0	0	0	0	0
At	6	5	3	2	6	2	4	3	1	2	4	0	3	2	3	3
Band	1	1	2	3	0	1	2	1	1	0	1	0	0	0	1	0
Be	1	3	0	0	0	1	1	1	0	1	0	0	0	0	0	0
Because . .	2	2	0	0	2	1	0	3	2	0	3	1	1	1	0	6
Before . . .	0	0	0	0	0	0	0	0	0	1	0	0	1	1	3	1
Begin . . .	1	0	0	2	0	0	0	0	0	0	0	0	0	0	0	0
Besides . .	0	0	1	0	0	0	0	1	0	0	1	1	2	0	2	1
Between . .	0	0	0	0	0	0	0	0	0	1	0	0	0	2	0	1
Book	0	0	0	0	1	1	0	3	0	0	0	0	0	1	0	0
Both	0	0	0	0	0	0	1	0	0	2	0	0	1	0	1	0
But	1	4	4	3	4	4	18	19	34	34	30	31	36	41	96	137
Can	0	1	3	3	1	0	0	0	0	0	1	0	0	0	1	2
Cat	3	0	1	0	0	0	2	0	0	0	1	0	1	0	0	0
Come . . .	2	0	1	0	1	0	0	0	0	0	0	0	0	0	0	0
Comma . .	0	0	0	0	0	0	2	0	0	0	1	0	0	1	0	0
Conjunction	0	0	0	0	0	1	6	3	2	4	3	6	1	7	8	8
Connecting .	0	1	0	0	0	0	0	0	0	0	0	0	0	0	1	2
Do	3	3	1	0	0	0	0	1	1	1	0	0	0	0	0	0
Else	2	1	0	0	0	1	0	0	0	0	0	0	0	0	0	0
End	6	7	8	6	7	9	8	3	2	0	3	0	3	18	2	3
English . .	0	0	0	0	0	0	2	0	2	2	0	0	0	0	0	0
Et	0	0	0	0	0	0	0	0	2	0	0	0	0	0	1	1
Etc	0	0	1	3	0	0	2	1	0	3	0	3	3	2	4	3
Ever	0	0	0	0	0	0	1	0	1	1	0	0	0	0	2	2
For	0	1	0	0	0	0	0	1	0	0	2	2	2	0	6	2
Go	2	1	2	1	6	2	2	0	1	0	1	1	0	0	3	0
Good	1	0	0	2	1	2	0	0	0	0	0	0	0	0	0	0
Hand	2	0	0	0	1	0	3	0	0	0	0	0	0	0	1	0
He	4	3	6	4	3	2	0	0	1	1	3	1	0	0	0	1
Her	0	0	0	0	0	1	0	1	0	0	2	1	1	1	2	0
Here	1	1	0	2	2	0	0	0	0	1	1	0	0	0	0	0
Him	1	0	1	1	2	0	1	0	1	0	1	2	0	0	0	0
House . . .	0	1	0	0	1	0	0	0	0	0	2	0	1	0	0	0
How	3	5	6	2	3	5	1	1	2	4	2	2	1	2	6	1
I	0	1	2	1	0	0	1	0	2	1	0	0	2	0	1	2
If	3	2	0	1	0	3	2	2	0	2	2	3	2	6	5	7

19

Response Word	4th M	4th F	5th M	5th F	6th M	6th F	7th M	7th F	8th M	8th F	10th M	10th F	12th M	12th F	College M	College F
							AND									
In	2	1	0	2	1	4	1	0	3	1	0	0	2	0	4	1
Is	1	2	0	1	2	2	2	0	3	1	4	2	2	3	2	1
It	12	5	9	7	7	8	11	4	3	6	3	1	3	5	6	0
Know	0	0	0	1	2	0	0	0	0	0	0	0	1	0	0	0
Me	5	1	3	1	0	4	1	2	2	2	1	1	1	0	0	0
More	1	3	1	3	2	0	3	1	3	2	2	2	3	2	2	3
My	2	0	1	0	0	0	1	0	1	1	0	0	0	0	0	0
Never	0	0	0	2	0	0	0	1	0	0	0	0	0	0	0	0
No	6	2	2	0	1	3	1	2	5	3	0	0	1	1	1	3
Not	3	1	3	5	4	1	2	0	1	2	1	0	0	2	0	0
Now	1	5	2	3	3	2	3	1	6	11	5	5	5	4	14	9
Of	0	1	0	0	1	1	2	2	3	1	6	3	2	2	3	8
Oh	0	0	0	0	0	0	0	0	1	0	0	1	0	0	1	2
Or	1	2	1	1	1	1	9	10	9	4	10	13	18	17	54	48
Other	1	1	7	0	0	1	0	1	0	0	0	0	0	1	0	0
Plus	12	12	6	8	6	16	18	13	6	11	11	4	7	4	6	11
Said	0	0	2	0	0	0	0	1	0	0	0	0	0	0	0	0
Same	3	0	0	0	0	0	0	1	1	0	0	0	0	0	0	0
Sand	2	1	0	1	0	0	0	3	0	1	2	0	1	1	0	1
See	0	1	2	1	1	0	0	0	0	0	0	1	0	0	0	0
Sentence	1	1	1	2	2	6	0	2	1	1	2	3	2	2	1	0
She	1	0	0	3	0	1	0	2	0	0	0	0	0	1	0	0
So	1	10	10	12	13	10	4	16	9	18	9	15	12	11	27	51
So on	0	0	0	0	0	0	0	1	2	1	0	1	1	2	0	0
So forth	0	0	1	0	0	0	1	1	2	0	2	3	2	3	4	4
Some	2	0	1	0	0	0	0	1	0	0	1	1	0	0	1	4
Something	5	6	3	3	2	1	2	1	0	0	1	1	0	0	0	0
Soon	0	0	0	0	0	0	2	0	0	0	1	0	0	0	0	2
That	11	8	8	15	7	3	8	5	6	4	9	13	15	5	27	15
The	14	15	20	12	33	20	16	12	21	13	16	23	18	10	46	41
Then	5	4	5	3	9	7	2	6	2	3	10	13	5	10	29	15
There	4	2	0	2	0	4	2	1	2	2	2	0	2	0	2	0
Therefore	0	0	0	0	0	0	1	0	0	1	0	0	1	2	2	2
They	2	0	2	1	1	1	1	1	1	1	0	0	0	1	0	1
Thing	0	0	0	1	4	0	1	0	1	0	0	0	0	0	0	1
Think	0	0	0	2	0	0	0	0	0	0	0	0	0	0	0	1
This	1	1	1	2	1	0	1	1	2	0	1	0	1	1	3	2
Though	0	0	1	0	0	1	0	0	0	1	1	0	1	0	5	2
Thus	0	0	0	0	0	0	0	0	0	0	0	0	1	0	3	2
To	4	5	3	5	7	3	1	7	9	4	9	8	12	5	12	4
Together	0	0	0	0	0	4	0	0	0	1	0	1	0	2	0	0
Too	2	3	0	2	3	1	0	3	0	1	0	1	1	4	7	9
Two	0	4	2	1	1	4	0	1	2	0	3	0	0	1	3	1
Typing	0	0	0	0	0	0	0	0	0	0	0	2	0	0	0	0
Us	0	0	0	0	0	0	0	0	1	0	0	0	0	1	0	2
Was	0	0	0	0	0	1	2	0	1	2	0	0	0	0	0	0
We	0	0	0	1	0	0	0	1	2	0	0	0	0	0	0	0
Well	0	0	1	0	0	0	0	2	0	1	0	0	0	0	0	0

Response Word	4th M	4th F	5th M	5th F	6th M	6th F	7th M	7th F	8th M	8th F	10th M	10th F	12th M	12th F	College M	College F

AND

Response Word	4th M	4th F	5th M	5th F	6th M	6th F	7th M	7th F	8th M	8th F	10th M	10th F	12th M	12th F	College M	College F
What	3	1	1	9	2	1	2	1	9	4	5	0	2	4	5	3
When	0	0	1	2	0	0	1	0	1	0	0	0	0	0	1	3
Who	0	0	0	0	0	0	0	0	0	0	0	1	2	0	0	0
Why	1	0	1	0	0	0	0	0	0	1	3	1	0	0	0	0
With	1	0	1	2	2	1	3	4	3	2	1	0	0	1	0	3
Word	4	2	13	5	8	6	1	2	4	3	6	1	0	0	1	1
Words	0	0	0	2	0	0	0	0	0	0	0	0	0	0	0	0
Yes	0	1	2	3	2	1	0	0	1	1	0	1	2	0	2	1
You	7	12	4	5	1	8	2	3	2	5	2	0	7	4	2	2

9. ANGER

Response Word	4th M	4th F	5th M	5th F	6th M	6th F	7th M	7th F	8th M	8th F	10th M	10th F	12th M	12th F	College M	College F
An	2	2	0	0	1	0	0	0	0	0	0	0	0	0	0	0
Angry	9	7	2	3	4	2	2	1	2	1	1	0	1	0	1	0
Aroused	0	0	0	0	0	0	0	0	0	0	0	0	0	0	2	0
Bad	5	6	3	5	2	2	3	0	2	0	3	4	1	3	6	5
Calm	1	1	1	0	0	1	0	0	0	0	0	0	0	0	8	1
Calmness	1	0	0	0	0	0	0	0	0	0	0	0	0	0	0	3
Control	0	0	0	0	0	0	0	0	0	0	0	0	0	0	2	0
Cross	1	2	0	0	0	0	1	0	0	1	0	0	0	0	0	0
Cry	0	1	0	1	0	0	0	2	0	0	0	3	0	1	1	4
Danger	2	2	1	1	1	0	0	0	0	0	2	0	0	0	0	1
Devil	2	1	2	0	1	0	0	1	1	2	1	1	0	0	0	0
Disgust	0	0	0	0	0	0	0	0	0	0	0	0	1	0	0	2
Emotion	0	0	0	0	0	0	0	0	0	0	0	3	0	1	4	4
Excitement	0	0	0	0	0	0	0	0	0	0	0	0	0	0	2	0
Face	0	0	0	0	0	0	0	0	0	0	0	1	0	0	0	3
Father	0	0	1	0	0	0	0	0	0	0	0	1	0	1	0	2
Fear	1	0	0	0	1	2	1	1	2	3	9	10	12	7	29	24
Fierce	0	0	0	0	1	0	0	0	2	1	1	0	1	2	0	0
Fight	3	1	2	5	2	4	4	4	6	4	12	7	11	5	20	18
Fighting	0	0	0	0	0	0	0	0	1	1	0	0	2	0	0	0
Fire	0	0	0	0	0	0	0	0	0	1	0	1	0	0	3	0
Fit	1	0	0	0	0	0	0	0	0	0	1	1	1	0	1	4
Fly	1	0	2	0	0	0	0	0	0	0	0	0	0	0	0	0
Friend	1	0	1	0	0	0	0	0	0	2	0	1	0	0	0	1
Fright	1	1	2	0	2	0	1	1	0	3	3	3	1	1	1	2
Frustration	0	0	0	0	0	0	0	1	0	0	0	2	1	0	2	1
Furious	0	0	0	0	0	1	2	1	0	2	0	1	1	1	0	1
Fury	0	0	0	1	0	0	0	1	0	0	1	0	1	0	0	2
Gentle	1	0	0	0	1	0	1	0	2	1	2	0	0	0	0	0
Glad	1	0	1	0	2	2	0	1	1	2	1	0	0	0	0	0
Good	4	5	3	1	0	4	2	1	2	1	1	0	1	0	0	0
Happiness	0	0	0	0	0	1	0	1	2	3	1	0	1	0	1	2
Happy	9	18	13	14	13	8	20	11	10	10	7	8	3	7	7	8
Hard	0	1	0	0	2	0	1	0	0	0	0	1	1	0	1	0
Harsh	0	0	0	1	0	0	0	2	1	1	0	0	0	0	1	0
Hate	0	2	2	3	4	2	1	7	5	3	8	10	4	12	32	25

Response Word	4th		5th		6th		7th		8th		10th		12th		College	
	M	F	M	F	M	F	M	F	M	F	M	F	M	F	M	F

ANGER

Response Word	4th M	4th F	5th M	5th F	6th M	6th F	7th M	7th F	8th M	8th F	10th M	10th F	12th M	12th F	College M	College F
Hatred ..	0	0	0	0	2	0	2	0	2	2	2	4	5	4	10	10
Heaven	1	1	0	1	2	0	1	1	0	0	1	0	1	0	0	0
Hit	0	0	0	0	1	0	1	0	0	1	2	1	1	0	3	2
Hot	0	0	0	1	1	0	1	2	0	1	0	0	3	1	2	8
Hunger ..	1	1	0	0	0	0	0	1	2	0	0	0	0	0	0	0
Hurt	1	0	0	2	0	0	1	5	0	0	0	2	1	1	3	2
Ire	0	0	0	0	0	0	0	0	0	0	0	0	0	0	7	4
Joy	0	0	0	0	0	0	0	0	0	1	0	1	0	1	1	2
Khrushchev	0	0	0	0	0	0	0	0	0	0	0	0	0	0	2	2
Kind	1	1	1	3	3	1	0	0	2	0	0	0	0	0	0	1
Like	2	0	0	0	0	1	0	0	0	0	0	0	0	0	0	0
Line	0	0	0	0	0	0	1	2	0	0	0	0	0	0	0	0
Loud	0	2	0	0	0	2	0	0	0	1	0	0	0	1	2	8
Love ...	0	0	1	1	1	0	0	1	3	1	1	0	0	6	1	1
Mad	125	119	135	134	126	152	119	123	112	111	107	95	119	122	180	172
Made ...	1	1	2	0	2	1	3	1	0	0	1	0	0	0	0	0
Madness .	0	1	2	0	5	1	3	3	6	2	4	5	1	3	2	5
Man	1	1	0	0	1	0	1	1	2	1	0	1	1	2	8	3
Manager .	2	0	0	0	0	0	0	0	0	0	1	0	0	0	0	0
Me	0	0	0	0	2	1	1	0	1	0	0	0	0	0	1	1
Mean ...	3	14	9	13	7	16	7	13	2	13	9	10	4	4	5	11
Meanness .	0	0	0	1	0	0	0	0	0	2	0	1	0	1	0	0
Mother....	0	0	1	0	0	1	0	0	0	1	0	1	3	2	0	0
Nice	8	15	4	12	7	7	6	6	10	6	2	1	3	2	2	0
No	0	0	0	2	0	0	1	0	0	0	0	0	0	0	0	0
Pain ...	0	0	0	0	0	0	0	0	2	1	0	0	1	1	2	3
Peace ...	0	0	0	0	0	0	0	0	0	0	0	1	0	0	3	0
People ...	0	1	0	0	1	0	2	0	1	0	0	0	0	0	0	1
Person ..	0	1	2	0	1	0	0	0	0	0	0	1	0	0	2	1
Rage ...	0	0	1	0	0	3	2	1	0	0	3	1	2	2	13	18
Red	3	0	0	1	1	0	4	3	6	8	13	13	11	8	31	30
Revenge ..	0	0	0	0	1	1	1	0	2	0	0	3	1	1	0	0
Sad	0	0	1	2	0	1	1	1	1	1	0	1	0	3	1	1
Scream ..	0	1	0	0	0	0	0	0	0	1	0	0	1	2	2	0
Shout ...	0	0	1	0	0	1	2	0	2	1	0	1	0	0	2	10
Shouting ..	0	0	0	0	0	0	0	2	0	0	0	1	0	0	0	0
Sister ...	0	0	0	0	0	0	0	0	0	0	3	1	0	1	0	0
Sky	2	0	0	0	0	0	0	0	0	0	0	0	0	0	0	0
Smile ...	0	0	0	0	1	0	0	0	3	1	0	0	0	0	0	0
Sorrow ..	0	0	0	0	0	0	0	0	2	0	0	1	0	1	2	1
Sweat ...	0	0	2	0	0	0	0	0	0	0	0	0	1	0	0	0
Sweetness .	0	0	0	1	0	0	0	1	1	0	2	1	0	0	1	0
Swing ...	0	0	0	0	0	0	0	0	2	0	0	0	0	0	0	0
Tears ...	0	0	0	0	0	0	0	0	0	2	0	0	0	0	0	0
Temper ..	4	3	1	4	3	4	6	7	4	6	7	13	10	11	17	22
Terrible .	0	0	0	0	0	0	0	0	0	0	2	0	0	0	0	0
Thirst ..	0	0	0	0	0	0	0	0	0	0	0	0	0	1	2	0
Tough ...	0	0	1	0	0	0	0	0	0	0	2	0	0	0	0	0

Response Word	4th M	4th F	5th M	5th F	6th M	6th F	7th M	7th F	8th M	8th F	10th M	10th F	12th M	12th F	College M	College F
ANGER																
Upset . . .	0	1	0	0	0	0	1	0	0	1	0	0	0	1	0	2
Wrath . . .	0	0	0	1	0	0	0	0	2	0	0	0	1	1	1	6
Yell	0	0	1	1	2	1	0	1	0	2	4	1	1	0	1	3
10. APPEAR																
Again . . .	1	0	1	1	2	1	1	0	0	0	0	0	0	0	1	1
Alike . . .	0	0	0	0	0	0	0	0	0	0	0	0	0	0	0	2
Always . . .	0	0	0	0	0	0	0	0	0	0	0	0	0	0	2	1
Angel . . .	0	1	0	1	0	0	0	0	0	3	0	0	0	1	1	0
Angle . . .	0	0	0	0	0	0	0	2	0	0	0	0	0	0	0	0
Appearance	1	1	2	1	1	1	3	2	1	2	0	1	4	3	4	1
Appeared .	1	0	0	1	1	0	3	1	4	0	1	0	0	0	0	1
Apple . . .	5	4	5	1	2	2	3	0	0	0	1	0	2	0	0	0
Approach .	0	0	0	0	0	1	1	0	1	0	0	0	0	2	0	1
Arrive . . .	0	0	0	0	0	1	0	0	0	0	0	0	1	0	2	0
At	4	1	0	0	2	0	1	0	1	3	1	0	1	2	2	2
Away. . . .	0	2	0	1	0	0	0	1	0	0	0	0	0	0	1	0
Bad	0	0	0	0	0	1	2	0	2	0	0	0	0	0	2	0
Be	0	2	1	0	2	1	1	2	2	0	0	0	1	0	5	7
Beautiful . .	0	2	0	1	0	0	0	1	0	2	1	0	0	2	1	2
Become . .	0	0	0	0	0	1	0	0	0	1	1	0	1	0	0	4
Beer. . . .	1	0	0	0	0	0	0	0	0	1	0	0	0	0	2	0
Before . . .	1	1	0	0	1	0	2	4	0	1	1	0	7	3	6	5
Bright . . .	0	0	0	0	0	1	0	0	0	0	0	0	1	2	0	1
Came . . .	0	4	3	1	0	1	0	0	1	0	0	0	1	0	1	1
Car	2	0	0	0	0	0	0	0	0	0	0	0	0	0	0	0
Clean . . .	0	0	0	0	1	0	1	2	1	1	0	1	1	1	1	0
Clear . . .	0	0	0	0	1	0	0	2	0	0	0	0	0	0	1	2
Close . . .	1	0	1	2	0	0	0	0	0	0	1	0	0	0	2	2
Clothes . .	0	0	0	0	0	0	1	0	1	1	0	3	1	2	2	1
Cloths . . .	0	0	0	0	0	0	0	0	0	0	2	0	0	0	0	0
Cold	0	0	0	0	0	0	1	1	0	0	0	0	0	0	3	0
Come . . .	8	22	11	18	8	15	10	15	7	7	5	9	4	8	9	9
Cute	0	0	0	0	0	0	1	0	0	2	0	1	0	0	1	1
Dark	0	0	0	0	0	0	0	0	2	0	0	1	0	0	1	4
Disappear .	46	26	40	38	38	46	63	55	69	58	32	45	37	35	95	86
Disappeared	0	2	0	0	0	0	0	0	0	0	0	0	0	0	0	0
Do	0	1	0	0	0	0	0	0	0	0	0	0	1	0	0	2
Dog	2	0	2	0	0	0	0	0	0	0	0	0	0	0	1	0
Dream . . .	0	0	1	0	1	1	0	0	0	0	0	0	2	2	0	0
Dress . . .	0	0	1	0	0	1	1	0	0	0	1	0	0	0	1	3
Ear	2	2	5	1	1	0	0	0	0	0	0	0	0	0	1	0
Enter . . .	0	0	0	0	0	0	0	0	0	0	0	0	0	0	0	2
Face	0	0	1	1	1	1	0	0	0	0	3	2	1	0	2	2
Fast	2	1	0	1	1	1	0	0	0	0	1	1	0	0	4	0
Find	0	0	1	0	0	2	0	0	0	0	0	0	1	0	0	0
From . . .	0	0	0	0	0	0	0	2	0	0	0	0	0	0	0	0
Genie . . .	1	0	0	2	0	0	0	0	0	0	0	0	0	0	0	0
Ghost . . .	2	3	7	1	3	3	7	4	1	5	1	2	4	4	3	4

Response Word	4th M	4th F	5th M	5th F	6th M	6th F	7th M	7th F	8th M	8th F	10th M	10th F	12th M	12th F	College M	College F
								APPEAR								
Girl	0	1	0	0	1	0	0	0	2	0	3	0	0	0	3	2
Go	2	3	0	2	2	2	1	2	2	2	1	2	4	2	2	4
Gone	5	5	6	3	1	3	1	1	2	0	0	1	0	2	0	0
Good	3	2	2	0	3	1	0	0	4	0	2	0	1	2	7	3
Happen	0	2	0	1	0	0	1	1	0	0	0	0	0	0	0	0
Happy	0	1	0	1	0	0	0	0	0	0	0	1	3	1	1	1
Hear	4	3	0	2	1	1	0	1	0	0	0	0	0	0	2	1
Here	1	10	5	6	3	6	3	3	1	0	5	5	1	7	3	9
Home	0	0	0	0	0	0	0	0	0	0	2	0	0	0	0	2
Image	0	0	0	0	0	0	0	0	1	1	1	1	3	0	2	1
Invisible	1	1	1	0	1	2	0	0	0	0	0	0	0	0	0	0
Is	1	0	0	0	0	0	0	1	1	0	0	0	2	0	5	1
It	0	0	0	0	2	0	0	0	0	0	1	0	0	0	1	0
Light	0	1	1	1	0	0	0	0	3	0	0	1	0	1	4	0
Like	0	0	0	0	1	0	0	0	0	0	0	1	1	1	2	1
Look	5	6	7	13	11	9	13	18	15	26	25	46	29	30	30	31
Looks	1	2	0	0	1	0	2	0	4	3	10	6	2	10	6	3
Magic	2	3	3	4	1	1	5	2	3	2	2	1	0	0	1	0
Magician	0	0	0	0	2	0	1	0	1	1	0	0	1	0	0	0
Me	1	1	1	1	0	0	1	0	1	1	0	0	0	2	1	0
Mirror	0	0	0	0	0	0	0	0	0	2	0	2	0	0	0	0
Near	0	1	1	1	1	1	0	0	0	0	0	2	2	0	1	0
Neat	0	0	0	0	1	1	1	0	0	2	5	6	2	4	6	5
Neatly	0	0	0	0	0	0	0	1	0	0	0	0	2	1	0	0
Never	0	0	2	1	0	0	1	1	0	1	0	0	1	0	3	3
Nice	0	3	1	0	3	3	3	4	2	4	4	2	3	4	3	10
No	0	2	0	2	0	0	0	0	0	0	0	0	0	0	0	1
Normal	0	0	0	0	0	0	0	0	1	0	2	0	0	0	0	0
Not	1	1	2	1	2	0	0	1	1	0	0	0	0	1	0	1
Notice	0	0	0	0	0	1	0	1	0	0	0	0	0	0	1	2
Now	2	1	2	2	1	1	0	1	2	3	3	4	2	3	14	5
On	0	1	0	1	0	0	2	1	0	0	1	1	3	0	0	0
Only	0	0	0	0	0	0	0	0	0	0	0	0	2	0	0	0
Open	2	0	1	0	0	0	0	1	0	0	1	0	0	0	0	0
Pear	2	10	3	4	8	8	5	4	4	2	5	0	0	1	0	0
Person	1	2	3	0	0	2	1	0	0	1	2	1	0	0	3	1
Place	3	0	0	1	0	0	0	0	0	1	1	0	0	0	0	0
Present	0	0	0	0	0	0	0	0	0	0	0	1	2	1	1	2
Pretty	0	0	0	1	1	2	1	2	2	2	3	2	1	1	0	4
Quickly	1	0	0	2	1	0	1	0	1	1	2	1	1	0	0	1
Reappear	2	2	3	3	1	2	1	3	3	3	2	1	0	2	4	2
Said	2	0	0	0	0	0	0	0	0	0	0	0	0	0	0	0
Saw	0	1	1	1	0	2	0	1	2	0	0	0	1	2	1	0
See	39	33	43	41	39	38	35	40	25	43	31	44	33	40	98	120
Seeing	0	0	0	0	0	0	0	0	2	0	0	0	0	0	0	0
Seem	2	1	1	0	1	0	1	2	2	1	0	8	5	6	21	27
Seems	0	0	0	1	0	0	0	1	0	4	1	1	2	3	1	6
Seen	2	6	4	6	3	3	4	5	1	4	0	1	2	4	0	3
Shadow	0	0	0	0	0	0	0	1	0	2	0	0	0	1	0	0

Response Word	4th M	4th F	5th M	5th F	6th M	6th F	7th M	7th F	8th M	8th F	10th M	10th F	12th M	12th F	College M	College F

APPEAR

Response Word	4th M	4th F	5th M	5th F	6th M	6th F	7th M	7th F	8th M	8th F	10th M	10th F	12th M	12th F	College M	College F
Short . . .	0	0	0	0	0	0	0	0	0	0	0	0	0	0	2	1
Show	5	6	9	7	10	14	10	9	9	3	13	4	7	3	15	11
Shown . . .	1	0	0	1	0	3	1	0	0	0	0	0	1	0	0	0
Sight	3	3	1	2	2	3	1	3	2	0	1	1	3	3	2	0
Slow	0	0	0	0	0	0	0	0	0	0	0	0	0	0	0	2
Small . . .	1	0	0	0	1	0	0	0	0	1	0	2	0	1	1	2
So	0	0	0	0	0	0	1	0	0	0	0	2	0	0	0	3
Someone . .	0	0	0	2	0	0	0	0	0	0	0	0	0	0	0	0
Sometimes .	0	0	0	0	0	0	0	1	0	0	0	0	2	0	1	0
Soon	0	0	0	1	0	1	0	0	0	0	0	0	0	1	1	2
Stage	0	0	0	0	1	0	0	0	0	0	1	2	0	0	1	0
Suddenly . .	0	1	0	0	0	2	0	0	0	0	0	0	0	0	0	0
That	0	0	0	0	1	1	1	0	0	0	0	0	0	0	1	2
Their . . .	3	0	1	0	1	2	1	0	0	0	0	0	0	0	0	0
Then	0	1	0	0	0	0	0	0	0	0	0	0	0	0	2	0
There . . .	10	10	9	6	12	8	5	6	1	7	7	1	1	0	8	4
To	3	0	3	4	3	1	2	1	4	1	2	3	7	5	9	8
To be . . .	0	0	0	0	0	0	0	0	1	1	0	0	1	2	2	3
TV	0	0	0	0	0	0	0	1	0	0	2	0	1	0	0	0
Ugly	1	0	1	0	2	1	0	1	1	0	2	0	0	0	1	1
Vanish . . .	4	3	2	4	6	2	5	1	3	0	4	1	2	1	2	2
View	0	0	0	0	2	0	2	1	0	0	0	0	1	0	1	0
Visible . .	2	0	1	1	2	1	3	4	4	2	2	0	2	2	0	2
Vision . . .	0	0	0	1	0	0	1	1	1	0	0	1	0	2	3	4
Well	0	0	0	0	1	1	2	0	0	0	4	2	4	0	4	0
When	0	0	2	1	1	0	0	0	0	1	0	0	0	0	1	2
Where . . .	0	1	0	1	0	0	0	0	0	0	0	0	2	0	0	0
Window . .	0	1	0	0	0	0	0	0	0	1	0	0	0	0	0	2
With	1	0	0	1	0	0	1	0	0	1	0	0	0	0	2	0
You	3	2	4	0	3	2	0	1	1	1	2	1	0	0	1	2

11. AS

Response Word	4th M	4th F	5th M	5th F	6th M	6th F	7th M	7th F	8th M	8th F	10th M	10th F	12th M	12th F	College M	College F
A	11	10	6	13	5	3	6	5	5	3	3	2	1	1	0	2
Also	1	0	1	3	1	0	0	2	2	0	0	1	1	1	3	2
Always . .	0	0	0	0	0	1	0	2	1	1	1	8	5	2	7	7
Am	0	0	0	1	3	1	1	1	1	3	0	1	1	1	1	3
An	1	0	1	1	1	0	0	1	0	1	2	1	0	0	0	0
And	3	1	2	3	1	1	3	1	3	1	0	3	2	2	3	3
Are	0	3	0	0	1	0	1	1	0	0	2	1	1	0	0	1
Ask	1	4	1	0	2	4	2	2	3	1	2	0	0	0	0	0
Ass	0	0	0	0	0	1	0	0	3	1	1	0	2	0	2	0
At	5	5	0	5	2	1	0	1	2	2	3	3	0	3	1	2
Be	0	0	1	1	1	1	0	2	0	1	0	0	0	0	1	0
Because . .	0	0	1	1	0	1	0	2	0	1	3	2	2	6	6	6
Before . . .	0	0	0	0	0	0	0	1	2	1	0	2	3	1	13	9
But	1	1	2	1	2	1	1	2	0	0	2	0	0	1	4	4
By	0	0	0	1	0	0	0	1	1	0	0	2	1	1	1	3
Can	1	2	1	0	0	0	0	1	0	0	0	1	0	0	0	0
Come . . .	1	0	1	0	0	0	0	2	0	0	1	0	0	0	1	0

Response Word	4th		5th		6th		7th		8th		10th		12th		College	
	M	F	M	F	M	F	M	F	M	F	M	F	M	F	M	F

AS

Response Word	4th M	4th F	5th M	5th F	6th M	6th F	7th M	7th F	8th M	8th F	10th M	10th F	12th M	12th F	College M	College F
Could	0	1	0	0	0	0	0	2	0	1	0	1	0	0	0	0
Do	5	4	0	3	0	3	0	1	0	0	0	0	1	2	0	0
Ever	0	0	0	0	0	0	1	0	1	2	0	2	1	4	9	4
Exist	0	0	0	0	0	0	0	0	0	0	0	0	0	2	0	0
Far	1	1	0	1	0	2	1	1	1	1	2	1	1	4	3	3
Fast	4	3	3	1	2	1	1	1	0	1	4	2	3	0	0	2
For	1	3	0	1	1	3	0	0	2	2	4	6	5	0	4	9
Go	5	4	2	0	2	0	2	2	1	0	0	2	1	0	0	2
Going	0	1	2	0	1	0	0	0	0	0	0	0	0	0	0	0
Good	3	1	0	0	1	0	1	0	0	1	0	0	0	0	1	0
Has	2	3	0	1	2	3	5	6	2	1	0	1	0	1	2	2
He	8	7	10	2	6	2	5	7	8	2	5	2	2	1	8	3
Him	2	0	3	1	3	0	0	2	2	0	0	0	0	0	1	0
How	0	0	2	0	1	3	5	2	1	0	1	0	0	2	5	2
I	18	14	15	13	11	12	14	14	8	11	19	12	11	5	15	8
If	8	3	11	23	12	14	22	8	10	19	16	29	40	25	59	76
In	1	0	1	1	1	3	3	3	3	0	3	1	0	2	2	3
Is	9	14	8	16	14	21	18	24	26	26	34	30	43	36	88	81
It	17	22	15	18	20	18	11	15	17	9	9	6	8	9	24	15
Just	1	0	0	0	0	1	1	2	0	0	0	0	1	0	0	0
Know	0	1	0	0	0	0	0	0	2	0	0	0	0	0	0	0
Like	0	2	1	0	1	1	6	3	1	6	6	8	5	13	16	21
Long	0	0	1	2	0	0	0	2	1	2	0	1	1	3	0	2
Many	0	1	2	1	0	1	0	0	0	0	1	1	1	2	0	0
Me	7	5	5	2	4	8	4	3	3	1	0	4	1	0	0	1
Much	0	0	0	0	0	0	0	2	2	3	1	2	4	1	4	1
Mule	0	0	0	0	0	0	0	0	2	0	0	0	0	0	0	0
Never	0	0	0	0	1	0	1	0	0	0	0	1	0	0	2	5
Nice	0	0	2	0	1	0	0	0	0	0	0	0	0	1	0	0
No	2	1	0	0	0	0	1	0	0	0	0	1	0	0	0	0
Not	1	0	0	2	2	1	2	2	0	1	1	0	0	0	0	2
Now	8	16	10	11	8	8	6	8	7	20	2	8	5	9	20	18
Of	3	2	8	6	3	3	8	5	6	8	5	6	8	1	16	22
Of now	0	0	0	0	2	0	0	0	0	0	0	1	0	0	0	0
On	0	0	0	0	1	0	0	2	0	0	0	0	0	0	1	0
One	0	0	0	2	0	1	1	1	0	0	1	1	0	1	0	1
Or	0	1	1	0	1	0	0	0	2	0	0	0	1	1	2	1
People	0	2	1	1	0	0	0	0	1	1	0	0	0	0	0	0
Place	0	0	0	0	0	0	0	0	0	0	2	0	0	0	0	0
Reason	0	0	0	0	0	0	0	0	0	0	0	0	1	1	2	0
Same	2	1	1	0	1	1	1	2	2	1	0	2	1	1	3	4
Saying	0	3	0	0	0	0	0	0	0	0	0	0	0	0	0	0
She	0	1	0	1	1	3	1	3	2	2	4	2	1	2	2	1
Should	0	1	1	0	1	0	0	0	0	1	0	1	1	0	0	2
Since	0	0	0	0	0	0	0	0	0	0	0	0	0	0	2	4
So	2	2	1	3	1	2	0	1	0	3	1	2	1	3	4	5
Some	2	1	1	0	2	2	0	1	0	0	1	1	0	0	2	0
Something	1	2	1	0	1	2	0	0	1	0	0	0	0	0	0	0
Soon	9	4	12	11	7	7	10	6	11	6	11	5	4	13	18	19

Response Word	4th M	4th F	5th M	5th F	6th M	6th F	7th M	7th F	8th M	8th F	10th M	10th F	12th M	12th F	College M	College F
							AS									
Soon as	0	0	0	0	0	0	0	0	0	0	0	0	0	0	0	2
Such	1	0	0	0	0	0	0	0	0	0	0	0	0	2	0	4
Than	0	0	0	0	0	0	0	0	0	2	1	1	0	1	1	0
That	2	1	1	5	1	0	0	2	1	1	1	2	1	3	0	4
The	5	7	6	4	15	5	4	3	1	3	1	3	3	4	3	5
Them	1	0	1	0	0	0	2	1	1	1	1	0	1	0	1	1
Then	0	2	0	0	1	3	4	0	1	4	3	3	1	3	9	5
There	2	1	2	2	1	1	2	1	1	1	2	2	0	0	2	0
They	3	6	5	2	6	4	3	1	2	0	1	0	4	6	5	5
Thing	0	0	2	0	0	0	0	0	0	0	0	0	1	0	0	0
This	1	0	1	0	1	1	0	1	0	0	2	1	1	1	4	3
Those	0	0	0	2	2	0	0	0	1	0	0	1	0	0	0	1
Though	2	1	1	1	2	2	0	1	2	1	4	6	2	6	6	2
Thus	0	0	0	0	0	0	0	0	0	0	1	0	0	0	0	2
To	1	3	3	6	2	4	3	4	8	2	5	6	4	4	7	19
Us	4	2	4	3	4	2	0	4	1	2	1	0	0	0	0	0
Walk	1	2	0	0	0	0	1	0	0	0	0	0	0	0	0	0
Was	3	2	1	3	3	2	13	11	7	14	8	7	10	4	23	23
We	10	9	11	6	8	11	6	5	3	6	6	4	3	0	7	0
Were	1	1	1	0	2	1	0	1	3	1	0	1	1	0	1	1
What	2	3	4	1	0	1	4	4	5	5	5	2	4	5	5	2
When	2	1	1	4	0	6	1	4	2	2	4	1	3	3	4	10
Where	0	1	1	2	2	1	2	2	2	0	1	1	0	0	1	0
While	0	0	0	0	0	0	0	0	0	3	0	1	1	1	1	1
Who	2	0	0	1	3	2	3	1	1	1	1	1	0	0	0	1
Why	2	0	0	0	0	1	0	0	0	0	1	0	0	2	2	1
With	1	0	0	0	0	0	1	0	2	4	0	1	2	1	1	0
Word	2	2	3	3	1	7	0	0	0	2	1	2	0	2	2	2
You	17	17	27	26	29	26	17	18	30	26	18	10	18	17	21	17
You were	0	0	0	0	0	0	0	0	0	0	0	0	1	0	2	0
						12.	**AT**									
A	4	0	1	2	0	1	0	1	1	1	0	0	0	0	0	1
About	0	0	0	0	0	0	0	0	0	2	0	0	1	0	2	2
All	11	8	10	9	6	7	5	6	6	4	6	9	7	8	23	16
And	0	1	1	0	0	1	1	0	0	0	0	0	0	0	0	2
Around	0	0	0	0	1	0	0	0	1	0	0	0	2	0	1	0
At	0	0	0	0	2	0	0	0	0	0	0	0	0	0	0	0
Ate	4	2	2	1	1	0	0	1	3	0	2	0	0	0	1	0
Away	0	1	0	3	2	0	1	0	4	0	0	1	2	0	1	1
Bat	2	3	4	8	1	2	2	5	4	3	4	1	3	2	14	4
Be	1	0	1	0	1	0	0	0	1	0	0	0	2	0	5	3
Before	0	0	0	0	0	0	0	0	1	0	0	1	1	0	0	2
Being	0	0	0	0	0	0	0	0	2	2	0	0	0	0	0	0
But	0	0	0	0	0	0	0	0	0	0	0	1	2	0	2	2
Buy	2	1	0	0	0	0	0	0	0	0	0	0	0	0	0	0
By	1	0	0	0	3	1	8	7	5	8	4	13	5	4	12	22
Can	0	0	0	0	1	0	0	1	0	0	0	0	0	0	0	2
Cat	2	2	2	0	0	0	0	1	3	1	2	2	1	2	4	1

Response Word	4th		5th		6th		7th		8th		10th		12th		College	
	M	F	M	F	M	F	M	F	M	F	M	F	M	F	M	F

AT

Response Word	M	F	M	F	M	F	M	F	M	F	M	F	M	F	M	F
Come ...	2	4	3	3	1	1	4	6	0	0	1	3	2	0	0	2
Cow	0	0	0	0	0	0	0	0	1	2	0	0	0	0	0	0
Door	0	0	0	0	0	0	0	0	1	1	0	2	0	0	1	5
Eat ...	0	0	0	0	0	2	0	1	1	0	0	0	0	0	1	0
Fat	0	0	2	1	2	0	1	1	1	0	3	1	1	0	0	3
For	0	0	0	0	0	1	1	0	0	0	1	1	2	0	5	5
From ...	1	1	0	0	0	2	1	1	4	1	0	4	3	3	3	4
Go	8	6	6	4	9	5	5	2	6	2	5	3	5	4	5	7
Going ...	1	2	1	2	2	0	0	2	0	0	1	1	0	0	0	0
Gone ...	3	2	1	2	1	1	2	1	3	3	2	2	0	0	0	0
Hat	1	1	0	1	1	1	3	0	2	1	1	2	0	0	4	4
Hear	0	1	2	0	0	1	0	0	0	0	0	0	0	0	0	0
Here	13	14	9	13	16	20	19	19	10	20	12	18	6	11	19	31
Him	0	0	2	0	1	0	0	0	1	0	0	0	1	0	2	0
His	2	0	2	0	0	0	1	0	0	0	0	1	0	0	1	0
Home ...	12	28	18	19	26	23	16	26	24	20	26	35	29	31	90	94
House ...	8	17	10	14	10	12	8	12	9	18	13	12	6	5	9	12
In	4	6	7	4	5	9	11	8	10	6	12	10	12	20	19	31
Into	0	0	0	0	0	0	0	0	2	0	0	0	0	0	0	0
Is	6	3	1	9	2	1	2	2	4	3	1	1	1	1	2	2
It	12	7	9	9	12	7	8	2	12	5	13	4	7	17	14	11
Last	1	1	0	0	0	0	0	0	0	0	1	0	2	0	2	0
Mat	2	2	3	0	1	0	0	2	1	2	1	2	0	0	2	2
Me	4	1	3	1	1	2	0	2	1	0	1	0	0	1	1	0
My	0	1	1	2	0	1	0	0	0	0	1	0	0	0	0	0
Near	0	1	0	2	0	0	2	1	1	0	0	2	3	2	7	12
None	0	0	0	0	0	0	0	0	0	0	0	0	0	0	3	1
Not.....	0	0	0	0	0	0	1	0	2	0	0	1	0	0	1	0
Now	1	2	2	3	0	1	2	2	1	1	0	0	0	3	2	2
Of	0	0	0	0	1	1	0	0	0	0	3	0	1	1	1	3
Oh	0	2	1	0	0	0	0	0	0	1	0	0	0	0	0	1
On	1	1	1	2	0	1	4	3	3	0	1	3	2	4	16	11
Once	0	0	0	0	1	1	0	0	0	0	1	0	0	0	2	3
Or	0	0	0	0	0	1	0	0	0	0	1	0	0	0	3	0
Over	0	0	1	0	0	1	0	0	1	0	0	0	0	0	2	0
Party ...	0	1	1	0	1	0	0	2	0	0	1	0	0	0	0	1
Place ...	26	35	34	39	28	47	23	19	9	25	20	12	9	9	10	13
Places ...	2	1	1	0	0	1	0	0	0	0	1	0	0	0	0	0
Preposition	0	0	0	0	0	0	0	0	0	2	0	1	2	1	1	5
Rat	1	1	1	0	1	0	1	2	1	0	0	0	1	2	1	0
Sat	4	4	4	3	0	2	6	5	3	2	3	0	7	6	6	7
School ...	3	5	7	8	3	11	5	7	6	12	6	12	6	4	8	15
Sea.....	1	1	0	0	1	1	0	0	0	0	1	2	0	0	0	0
See	1	1	1	1	1	0	0	0	0	0	1	1	0	0	1	2
Set	0	0	0	0	0	0	0	0	0	0	0	0	0	0	2	1
Show ...	0	0	1	1	1	0	0	0	0	1	1	0	2	1	0	0
Sit	1	0	0	1	0	0	0	0	1	0	1	0	0	0	2	0
Some ...	0	2	1	0	0	0	0	0	0	0	0	2	1	0	0	0

Response	4th		5th		6th		7th		8th		10th		12th		College	
Word	M	F	M	F	M	F	M	F	M	F	M	F	M	F	M	F

AT

Someplace .	3	6	2	2	0	5	2	0	0	0	1	1	1	0	2	0
Somewhere	1	4	1	6	3	4	3	1	1	2	2	0	0	0	0	0
Stare ...	0	0	0	0	0	0	0	0	1	0	0	0	0	0	2	0
Stay	1	3	0	1	0	0	0	0	0	0	0	0	0	0	0	0
Store ...	3	5	3	7	6	6	4	5	3	9	5	7	4	5	2	5
That	0	2	2	2	4	1	3	3	4	4	2	0	7	7	9	5
The	10	4	3	4	16	5	7	8	10	10	3	9	11	14	20	19
Their ...	0	1	2	2	2	0	1	3	0	0	1	2	2	1	0	0
Them ...	0	0	0	0	0	0	1	0	1	0	0	0	2	0	1	0
Then ...	1	0	0	0	0	0	0	0	0	0	0	0	2	1	1	0
There ...	31	21	38	26	42	36	46	42	40	30	44	28	29	29	42	40
This	0	0	0	0	0	0	0	2	0	0	0	1	1	0	0	0
Time ...	2	2	0	0	2	2	1	0	1	0	0	0	2	1	1	0
To	2	3	1	4	0	1	5	2	7	6	8	6	9	9	35	46
Top	0	0	0	0	0	0	0	0	0	0	0	0	0	0	2	0
Toward ..	0	0	0	0	0	0	0	0	0	0	0	1	0	0	5	1
Water ...	0	0	0	0	1	0	0	0	1	0	2	1	4	0	0	1
We	2	0	0	0	0	0	0	0	0	0	0	0	0	0	0	0
Well	0	0	0	0	0	0	0	0	0	0	1	1	3	1	3	1
Were ...	1	0	1	2	2	1	1	1	2	0	0	1	1	1	0	0
What	0	0	0	0	0	0	0	2	2	2	1	1	1	1	0	0
When ...	0	0	1	2	0	0	0	2	0	0	0	0	0	1	0	1
Where ..	7	7	10	8	6	6	10	14	7	16	7	7	5	12	8	5
Will	0	0	0	0	0	0	0	0	0	0	0	0	1	0	5	1
With	0	0	0	0	1	2	2	2	0	0	0	2	2	1	5	2
Word ...	3	1	6	1	2	2	2	0	0	1	3	1	0	1	3	1
Work ...	0	0	0	0	0	0	0	0	0	0	0	0	1	0	2	0
You	1	0	1	0	2	0	0	0	1	0	0	0	2	1	1	0

13. BABY

Adult....	1	0	0	0	0	1	2	0	1	0	1	3	1	1	2	4
Bad	0	1	1	0	0	0	0	0	0	0	2	0	2	0	0	0
Beautiful .	0	0	0	0	0	0	0	0	0	0	0	1	0	0	0	2
Bed	0	1	0	0	3	0	2	2	0	0	1	0	0	0	5	3
Bird	0	0	0	0	0	0	0	0	2	0	0	0	0	0	0	0
Blanket ..	0	0	0	1	1	1	1	0	0	1	0	2	0	0	2	7
Blue	0	0	0	0	0	0	2	1	0	6	2	3	3	4	10	13
Born ...	3	5	1	3	4	2	4	2	1	0	1	1	1	1	2	0
Bottle ...	2	6	2	6	1	1	2	2	2	5	3	4	2	5	8	8
Boy	56	2	58	26	49	23	39	13	32	19	37	20	42	33	56	51
Brat	1	0	1	1	1	1	0	0	4	1	0	0	0	0	0	1
Brother ..	2	2	3	1	4	0	0	2	3	2	3	4	2	1	1	0
Buggy ...	0	1	0	0	0	2	0	1	0	1	1	1	2	0	6	6
Carriage...	1	0	0	0	0	0	0	1	1	0	1	2	4	1	0	1
Child ...	42	43	41	56	48	51	48	48	39	37	33	29	27	28	42	38
Children ..	0	0	0	0	0	2	1	1	0	1	1	0	1	1	1	1
Clothes ..	0	0	0	0	0	0	1	2	0	1	0	1	0	0	1	2
Coo	0	0	0	0	0	0	0	0	0	0	0	0	0	0	1	2
Cousin....	0	0	0	0	0	0	1	0	0	0	0	0	3	0	0	0

Response Word	4th M	4th F	5th M	5th F	6th M	6th F	7th M	7th F	8th M	8th F	10th M	10th F	12th M	12th F	College M	College F
							BABY									
Cradle . . .	0	0	0	3	0	0	1	1	0	1	0	0	2	2	0	0
Crib	2	4	7	3	3	2	2	3	5	5	4	10	6	3	11	11
Cries . . .	1	1	0	1	0	0	0	2	0	0	0	1	0	2	0	3
Cry	12	34	16	30	18	34	18	28	16	24	16	21	22	27	58	61
Crying . . .	1	1	1	2	2	2	1	3	3	5	5	3	1	2	3	5
Cuddle . . .	0	0	0	1	0	0	0	0	0	1	0	0	0	0	0	2
Cuddly . . .	0	0	0	0	0	0	0	0	0	0	0	0	0	4	1	6
Cute	0	1	1	3	0	9	3	8	2	12	3	11	3	10	7	17
Darling . .	0	0	0	0	0	0	0	0	0	3	0	3	0	0	0	2
Diaper . . .	0	1	2	3	2	4	2	1	2	2	1	1	1	0	4	1
Diapers . .	3	1	0	2	2	1	3	2	3	6	2	3	3	5	6	8
Dog	0	1	0	0	0	0	0	1	0	0	0	0	0	0	2	0
Doll	0	1	2	0	3	2	1	1	0	0	1	0	3	0	5	2
Face	0	0	0	0	2	0	0	0	0	0	0	0	0	0	0	1
Family. . .	0	0	0	0	0	0	0	1	0	0	1	1	1	0	1	2
Father . . .	0	2	1	0	0	0	0	1	0	0	1	0	0	0	0	0
Food	0	0	0	0	1	1	0	0	0	0	1	1	0	0	4	0
Fun	0	1	1	0	0	0	1	0	0	0	1	1	2	0	0	0
Gentle . . .	0	0	0	2	0	0	0	0	0	2	0	0	1	0	0	1
Girl	7	11	8	12	8	19	6	15	18	8	14	16	12	10	31	14
Girls . . .	0	0	0	0	0	1	0	0	3	0	1	0	0	0	0	0
Good . . .	0	1	0	0	2	0	0	0	1	0	0	2	0	1	3	1
Happy . . .	0	0	0	0	0	0	1	0	0	0	1	0	1	2	0	1
Helpless . .	0	0	0	0	0	0	0	0	0	0	1	0	1	1	5	2
Hospital . .	0	0	0	1	1	0	0	2	0	1	0	0	0	1	1	0
Human . .	0	1	1	0	1	0	0	0	0	0	2	1	0	0	0	0
Infant . . .	4	4	2	1	5	9	8	10	6	3	1	6	4	3	13	2
Joy.	0	0	0	1	0	0	1	0	0	0	0	0	0	1	2	0
Kid.	1	2	3	1	4	2	1	3	6	2	2	1	3	0	2	0
Kids	0	0	0	0	0	0	0	0	2	0	0	0	0	1	0	0
Lion	0	0	0	0	0	0	1	0	0	2	0	0	0	0	0	0
Little . . .	19	31	22	21	20	19	12	10	11	13	21	13	6	11	11	19
Love . . .	0	0	0	0	0	1	0	1	1	1	1	3	1	5	3	10
Man	4	0	2	0	2	1	3	0	3	0	3	1	1	0	1	0
Marriage .	0	0	0	0	0	0	2	0	0	0	1	0	2	0	2	3
Me	1	0	2	0	1	0	1	0	0	0	0	0	0	0	0	0
Mom	1	3	0	1	0	0	0	0	0	0	0	0	0	0	0	0
Mother . .	8	13	7	12	3	8	7	11	8	20	17	22	14	27	31	47
New	2	0	1	0	2	1	1	0	0	0	0	0	0	0	1	0
Nice	1	2	1	0	2	2	0	1	2	1	0	1	0	1	0	3
Niece . . .	0	0	0	0	1	0	0	0	0	0	2	0	1	0	0	1
Noise . . .	0	0	0	0	1	0	0	1	0	1	0	0	0	0	2	0
Parents . .	0	0	0	0	0	0	0	2	0	0	0	1	0	0	0	0
People . .	3	1	3	1	0	1	0	0	0	1	0	0	0	0	0	0
Person . .	12	9	13	5	5	7	4	4	3	1	3	0	0	0	1	1
Pink	0	0	0	0	1	0	0	0	0	0	0	1	1	3	2	4
Pretty . . .	1	0	0	1	0	1	0	1	1	0	0	0	0	2	2	1
Rattle . . .	0	1	1	3	0	2	1	0	0	3	2	2	1	0	2	3
Sheep . . .	0	0	2	0	0	0	0	0	0	0	0	0	0	0	0	0

Response Word	4th M	4th F	5th M	5th F	6th M	6th F	7th M	7th F	8th M	8th F	10th M	10th F	12th M	12th F	College M	College F
							BABY									
Sister . . .	2	2	2	2	1	3	4	5	3	1	3	1	2	0	2	5
Sitter . . .	0	0	2	0	0	1	2	0	2	1	2	0	9	1	5	1
Sitting . . .	0	0	0	0	0	0	0	0	0	1	2	0	0	0	0	0
Sleep. . . .	2	0	0	3	1	2	0	2	0	3	1	0	1	1	8	5
Small . . .	15	10	7	7	16	10	21	17	19	13	18	18	20	12	51	13
Soft	5	1	2	3	1	1	2	4	2	7	4	5	4	7	13	27
Spoon . . .	0	0	0	0	0	0	0	0	0	0	0	0	0	0	0	3
Sweet . . .	0	0	0	4	0	1	0	9	0	5	0	5	0	7	0	16
Tender . .	1	1	1	0	1	0	2	0	0	0	0	0	0	0	0	1
Tiny	0	1	0	0	0	9	1	7	0	2	0	2	1	0	5	7
Tot . . .	1	0	3	0	0	0	0	1	0	2	0	0	1	1	0	0
Toy	2	1	0	2	1	0	0	0	1	3	0	1	1	2	1	5
Toys . . .	1	0	0	0	0	0	1	0	2	0	2	0	0	2	2	2
Trouble . .	0	0	0	0	1	0	0	0	2	0	0	0	2	0	3	0
Woman . .	0	0	0	0	0	0	2	0	4	0	2	0	1	0	1	2
Women . .	0	1	0	0	0	0	0	0	1	0	1	1	2	0	0	0
Work. . . .	1	0	0	0	0	0	0	0	2	0	0	1	0	0	0	0
Young . . .	6	3	4	4	3	0	5	0	6	4	4	0	1	0	10	3
						14.	BATH									
Bad	0	0	2	0	1	0	1	0	0	0	0	0	0	0	0	0
Bathe . . .	2	0	2	2	2	0	7	3	1	1	0	1	0	0	2	0
Bathroom .	1	2	1	1	4	1	1	0	0	0	2	0	0	1	1	1
Bathtub . .	1	3	1	1	1	1	2	0	1	0	1	2	2	0	1	1
Bed	0	2	0	0	0	0	0	0	0	0	0	0	0	0	1	0
Bubble . . .	2	0	0	1	0	0	0	0	2	1	0	1	1	1	2	7
Bubbles . .	1	3	0	4	0	1	0	1	0	1	0	2	0	3	1	8
Clean . . .	31	43	34	49	51	56	46	78	43	74	72	93	96	106	163	191
Cleanliness	0	0	0	0	0	0	1	7	3	2	2	2	1	6	8	4
Cleanness .	0	0	0	0	0	0	1	0	0	2	0	0	0	0	2	0
Cleanse . .	0	0	0	0	0	0	0	0	1	0	1	3	0	0	0	0
Clothes . .	0	2	0	1	1	0	0	0	0	0	0	0	1	0	0	0
Cold	1	0	3	1	1	2	0	1	0	2	0	1	0	0	0	0
Comfort . .	0	0	0	0	0	0	0	0	0	1	0	0	0	1	2	1
Comfortable	0	0	0	0	0	0	0	1	2	0	0	0	0	0	1	0
Cool	0	0	0	1	0	0	0	1	0	1	1	1	0	1	2	2
Dirt	2	1	2	0	1	1	2	2	7	5	4	5	8	0	4	3
Dirty . . .	1	3	2	1	1	3	4	3	7	5	4	6	2	6	12	2
Fresh . . .	0	0	0	0	0	0	0	0	0	0	0	0	2	0	0	1
Girl	0	1	1	1	1	0	0	0	2	0	0	0	1	0	0	0
Girls . . .	0	0	0	0	0	0	0	0	2	0	0	0	0	0	0	0
Good	1	1	2	0	0	1	0	0	0	0	0	1	0	0	0	0
Health . . .	2	1	0	0	0	0	0	0	0	0	2	0	0	0	0	0
Hot	2	2	7	4	2	1	4	5	3	4	2	3	2	2	7	10
House . . .	0	0	0	1	1	1	0	0	0	0	1	0	3	1	6	2
Naked . . .	0	0	0	0	0	0	1	0	1	0	0	0	0	0	2	0
Nice	2	0	3	0	0	0	0	1	0	0	3	0	1	1	0	2
No	2	0	0	0	0	0	1	0	0	0	0	0	0	0	0	0
Nude	0	0	0	0	0	0	0	0	3	0	0	0	0	0	1	0

Response Word	4th M	4th F	5th M	5th F	6th M	6th F	7th M	7th F	8th M	8th F	10th M	10th F	12th M	12th F	College M	College F

BATH

Response Word	4th M	4th F	5th M	5th F	6th M	6th F	7th M	7th F	8th M	8th F	10th M	10th F	12th M	12th F	College M	College F
Oil	0	0	0	0	1	0	0	1	0	1	1	0	0	0	0	3
Powder . .	0	0	0	0	0	0	0	0	0	0	0	0	0	0	1	2
Refreshing .	0	0	0	0	0	0	0	0	0	3	0	0	0	1	0	0
Relaxing . .	0	0	0	0	0	0	0	0	0	0	1	0	0	2	0	1
Ring	0	0	1	0	0	0	0	0	0	0	1	0	1	0	2	0
Room . . .	2	3	0	1	1	2	0	0	1	0	0	1	1	0	6	2
Saturday . .	0	1	0	1	1	0	3	3	0	1	2	1	2	1	1	0
Scrub . . .	0	2	0	0	1	0	0	1	0	0	0	0	0	0	1	0
Shore . . .	2	0	0	0	0	0	0	0	0	0	0	0	0	0	0	0
Shower . .	3	5	8	6	5	3	13	11	17	11	10	1	14	5	23	13
Sink	1	0	0	1	2	1	0	0	0	0	0	0	0	0	3	0
Soap	11	25	8	13	8	17	9	13	8	15	2	17	14	13	21	41
Sponge . . .	1	1	1	0	0	0	0	0	0	1	0	2	0	1	0	1
Swim . . .	2	0	3	0	0	3	3	0	3	0	0	0	1	1	1	0
Take	0	0	0	1	0	2	1	0	0	0	0	0	2	0	1	0
Towel . . .	1	2	1	2	3	6	1	4	2	3	1	2	2	3	7	3
Tub.	26	27	31	21	17	28	14	15	24	16	15	12	15	10	27	24
Tube . . .	0	1	1	0	2	1	0	0	0	0	0	0	0	0	0	0
Warm . . .	3	3	2	5	2	8	3	2	1	2	5	5	1	7	5	12
Warmth . .	0	0	0	0	0	0	0	0	0	1	0	0	0	0	2	1
Wash . . .	11	12	5	13	12	17	12	17	15	10	11	10	14	9	22	12
Washing . .	0	0	0	0	2	0	0	0	0	1	0	0	1	0	0	0
Water . . .	102	82	96	94	101	92	93	65	80	75	93	72	47	53	135	129
Wet	6	3	3	9	3	1	6	5	6	3	3	3	3	4	6	5

15. BEAUTIFUL

Response Word	4th M	4th F	5th M	5th F	6th M	6th F	7th M	7th F	8th M	8th F	10th M	10th F	12th M	12th F	College M	College F
Adorable . .	0	0	0	2	0	0	0	0	0	0	0	0	0	0	0	0
America . .	0	0	0	2	0	0	0	0	0	0	0	0	0	0	0	0
Art	0	0	1	0	0	0	0	0	1	0	1	0	0	1	1	3
Attractive .	0	0	0	0	0	0	0	0	0	2	0	0	0	0	1	1
Autumn . .	0	0	0	0	0	0	0	0	0	0	0	0	0	0	4	3
Awful . . .	0	2	4	2	2	0	1	0	2	1	0	1	2	0	0	1
Bad	1	2	2	0	0	1	0	1	1	0	0	0	0	0	1	0
Beauty . . .	5	3	1	0	0	3	3	0	0	1	0	0	1	0	1	2
Big	0	0	1	1	0	0	0	0	0	0	1	0	0	0	2	0
Bird	0	0	0	1	0	2	1	0	0	0	0	0	0	1	0	1
Blue	0	1	0	0	1	0	0	2	0	0	0	0	1	0	0	1
Bright . . .	0	0	1	0	2	0	0	1	0	0	2	1	0	1	1	1
Butterfly . .	4	1	7	3	0	2	1	0	0	1	1	0	1	0	2	0
Car	1	0	1	0	1	0	1	0	0	0	3	1	3	0	2	1
Charming .	0	0	0	0	2	2	0	0	1	0	0	0	0	0	0	0
Church . .	0	0	0	0	0	0	0	0	1	2	0	0	0	1	0	1
Clothes . .	0	0	0	0	0	1	0	0	0	2	0	2	0	3	0	4
Coat	0	0	0	0	0	2	0	0	0	0	1	0	0	0	0	1
Color . . .	2	1	3	1	2	0	1	0	0	0	2	2	0	2	4	4
Colorful . .	1	0	0	0	1	1	4	0	0	0	1	0	1	1	0	3
Cute	1	1	0	1	0	0	1	0	3	3	1	3	0	2	1	1
Dark	0	0	0	1	0	0	0	1	0	0	0	0	2	0	1	2
Day	0	0	0	1	0	0	0	0	0	2	0	2	1	0	0	2
Dog	0	0	4	1	1	3	1	0	1	1	0	0	1	0	0	0
Doll	0	0	0	0	0	0	0	0	2	0	0	0	0	1	0	1

Response Word	4th M	4th F	5th M	5th F	6th M	6th F	7th M	7th F	8th M	8th F	10th M	10th F	12th M	12th F	College M	College F
							BEAUTIFUL									
Dream ..	1	0	0	0	0	0	0	0	2	0	0	0	0	0	0	0
Dress ...	0	4	1	0	1	1	0	3	0	5	1	2	0	2	1	1
Dull	0	0	0	1	0	1	0	0	0	0	1	0	1	0	2	1
Eyes	0	0	1	0	0	2	0	0	0	0	0	1	0	1	0	0
Fall	0	0	0	0	0	0	0	0	0	0	0	0	0	0	1	4
Flower ..	4	4	3	6	3	0	8	3	4	7	1	3	1	3	5	6
Flowers ..	1	1	2	1	1	2	1	2	0	3	3	1	2	4	3	3
Full	0	1	1	2	2	0	0	0	0	0	0	0	0	0	0	0
Fun	0	0	0	0	0	0	0	0	0	1	0	0	0	2	0	0
Girl	5	7	7	2	18	3	19	5	28	19	51	39	53	36	95	64
Girls ...	2	0	2	0	2	0	3	0	13	4	5	0	4	1	3	0
Good	1	1	4	0	2	0	1	1	1	0	5	0	1	1	7	2
Goodlooking	0	0	1	0	1	0	2	0	1	0	1	0	0	0	0	0
Gorgeous .	1	3	2	7	3	7	6	11	3	4	4	5	1	2	1	3
Graceful .	0	0	0	0	0	2	0	0	2	0	0	0	0	0	0	0
Hair	1	2	0	0	0	1	1	1	0	5	0	1	1	2	3	8
Handsome .	0	0	0	0	0	1	2	3	2	0	1	0	0	1	0	2
Hard	1	0	0	0	0	0	0	0	0	0	0	0	0	0	2	0
Heavenly .	0	0	0	0	0	0	0	0	0	0	0	0	0	2	0	0
Home ...	0	0	0	0	0	0	0	0	0	0	2	0	0	0	0	0
Homely ..	0	1	0	0	1	1	1	0	0	0	1	1	1	2	2	4
Horrible .	1	2	0	3	1	0	6	0	1	1	0	0	1	0	0	0
Horse ...	0	0	0	0	2	1	0	1	1	0	1	0	1	1	0	3
House ...	1	1	1	0	0	0	0	1	1	1	0	0	1	0	0	6
Lady	0	1	1	4	4	2	0	4	0	4	1	5	0	5	0	7
Lake ...	0	0	0	0	0	0	0	0	1	0	2	3	1	0	4	2
Leaves ..	0	0	0	0	0	0	0	0	0	0	0	0	0	0	2	0
Life	0	0	0	0	0	0	0	0	0	0	0	0	0	0	1	2
Light ...	0	1	0	0	0	0	0	0	0	0	0	0	0	0	2	1
Liz Taylor.	0	0	0	0	0	0	0	0	0	0	1	1	0	2	0	0
Looks ...	0	0	2	0	0	0	0	1	1	0	0	0	0	0	0	0
Love ...	0	0	0	0	1	0	0	0	1	1	0	1	0	0	2	1
Lovely ...	14	16	11	25	19	31	5	19	6	15	12	15	11	13	16	34
Me	0	1	0	0	1	1	0	1	0	0	0	2	1	0	0	0
Mother ..	1	0	0	3	1	0	1	1	1	1	0	0	0	1	0	0
Mountain .	0	1	0	1	1	0	0	0	1	0	1	0	0	0	1	3
Mountains .	0	1	0	0	0	0	0	0	0	0	1	1	2	0	1	1
Music ...	0	0	0	0	0	0	0	1	0	0	0	1	1	1	1	5
Nature ..	0	0	0	1	0	0	0	1	0	0	0	1	0	5	2	4
Neat	0	0	0	0	0	0	2	0	1	0	0	0	0	1	1	0
Nice	21	7	17	8	19	8	14	9	9	6	16	6	15	2	18	10
Not	2	0	1	0	0	1	0	0	0	0	0	0	0	1	0	0
Not pretty .	0	0	0	2	0	0	0	0	0	0	0	0	0	0	0	0
Painting ..	0	0	0	0	1	0	3	0	1	0	0	0	0	0	1	2
Person ..	0	0	0	0	0	2	0	0	0	1	0	0	0	1	0	0
Picture ..	0	0	1	0	2	0	1	1	1	2	0	3	2	1	5	6
Pleasing .	0	0	0	0	0	0	0	0	0	0	0	0	0	0	0	2
Pretty ...	88	115	88	97	52	100	59	67	38	48	28	41	18	45	55	92
Princess..	0	5	0	0	0	0	0	0	0	0	0	0	0	0	0	2

Response Word	4th M	4th F	5th M	5th F	6th M	6th F	7th M	7th F	8th M	8th F	10th M	10th F	12th M	12th F	College M	College F

BEAUTIFUL

Response Word	4th M	4th F	5th M	5th F	6th M	6th F	7th M	7th F	8th M	8th F	10th M	10th F	12th M	12th F	College M	College F
Queen . . .	0	0	0	1	0	0	0	0	0	1	0	0	0	2	0	3
Red	1	1	1	0	3	0	0	0	0	0	0	0	0	0	0	3
River . . .	1	0	0	0	0	0	0	0	0	1	0	0	3	0	1	0
Rose	0	0	0	0	0	0	0	0	1	1	0	0	0	0	0	3
Savior . . .	0	0	0	0	0	0	0	0	0	0	0	0	0	0	2	0
Scene . . .	0	0	0	0	0	0	0	2	0	0	1	1	1	1	3	3
Scenery . .	0	0	0	1	0	1	1	1	0	0	3	2	3	0	8	7
Scenic . . .	0	0	0	0	0	0	0	0	0	0	0	0	1	0	2	0
Sharp . . .	0	0	0	0	0	0	0	0	0	0	0	1	2	0	0	0
Sister . . .	0	0	0	0	0	0	0	2	0	0	0	0	0	0	1	1
Sky	1	1	1	0	1	0	1	2	2	0	0	4	1	3	2	2
Snow	0	1	1	0	2	1	1	2	1	2	0	1	0	0	2	2
Soft	1	1	0	1	1	0	0	1	0	0	0	0	1	0	2	2
Song	0	0	0	0	0	0	0	0	0	0	0	0	0	1	0	2
Summer . .	0	0	1	0	0	0	1	0	0	0	1	2	1	1	0	0
Sunset . . .	0	0	0	0	0	0	1	0	2	0	0	0	0	1	0	1
Sweet . . .	0	2	1	0	2	1	0	2	1	1	1	0	0	0	2	2
Tall	0	0	0	0	0	0	0	0	0	0	0	0	0	0	0	2
Tree	0	0	0	0	0	1	2	2	1	0	1	0	2	0	7	4
Trees . . .	0	0	1	1	0	0	1	1	0	1	0	0	2	0	7	4
Ugly	47	32	38	37	45	32	53	56	72	63	46	51	49	46	93	76
View	0	0	0	0	0	0	0	0	0	0	0	0	0	0	2	0
Water . . .	0	0	0	0	2	0	1	0	0	1	0	0	0	0	1	0
Wedding . .	0	0	0	0	0	0	0	0	0	1	0	0	0	2	0	0
Wife	0	0	0	0	0	0	1	0	0	0	0	0	0	0	2	0
Window . .	1	0	0	0	0	0	0	0	0	0	0	0	0	0	2	0
Winter . . .	0	0	0	0	0	0	0	0	0	0	0	0	0	0	0	2
Woman . .	0	0	3	0	3	1	6	4	7	10	17	10	15	15	52	29
Women . .	2	2	4	1	0	1	2	1	8	0	2	2	10	3	9	2
Wonderful .	1	4	1	3	5	3	3	4	0	2	5	1	1	1	1	3
Woods . . .	0	0	0	0	1	0	0	0	0	0	3	0	1	0	0	0

16. BECAUSE

Response Word	4th M	4th F	5th M	5th F	6th M	6th F	7th M	7th F	8th M	8th F	10th M	10th F	12th M	12th F	College M	College F
Account . .	0	0	0	0	0	0	0	0	0	1	2	0	1	0	1	0
All	0	0	0	0	0	0	0	2	0	0	0	0	0	0	0	0
Also	0	1	0	2	5	1	3	2	2	1	3	2	2	4	4	6
Always . . .	0	1	4	3	0	1	0	5	4	4	1	4	1	4	3	4
And	2	2	1	1	4	4	1	3	4	1	3	3	2	3	9	9
Answer . .	3	10	3	8	4	3	2	2	3	4	4	2	3	1	0	1
Anyway . .	0	1	0	0	0	0	0	0	0	0	1	1	2	0	0	0
As	0	0	0	0	0	1	0	0	0	0	0	0	1	2	0	4
As a result	0	0	0	0	0	0	0	0	0	0	0	0	0	0	0	2
At	0	0	0	0	0	0	0	2	0	0	0	0	0	0	0	0
Be	13	5	10	4	3	6	3	0	2	1	0	0	1	0	1	2
Became . .	5	2	2	2	1	0	4	3	11	8	2	0	1	1	3	0
Because . .	0	0	0	0	1	0	0	0	0	0	0	0	0	0	2	2
Become . .	1	2	0	0	0	0	2	1	1	2	2	0	1	0	1	0
Bee	1	2	2	0	1	1	0	0	0	0	0	0	0	0	0	0
Before . . .	1	0	2	0	0	1	0	1	2	1	1	1	2	1	1	1
Behind . .	0	0	0	0	0	0	0	0	1	0	1	2	0	0	0	0

Response Word	4th M	F	5th M	F	6th M	F	7th M	F	8th M	F	10th M	F	12th M	F	College M	F
							BECAUSE									
Besides ..	0	0	0	0	0	0	0	0	0	0	0	3	0	1	1	0
Boy	0	2	0	0	0	1	0	0	0	0	0	0	0	0	0	0
But	1	2	3	0	0	2	7	6	4	5	3	5	2	4	6	9
Came ...	0	0	2	0	2	0	0	0	0	0	2	0	0	0	0	1
Can	1	1	1	0	0	0	0	2	0	0	0	0	0	1	0	0
Can't ...	2	0	0	0	0	0	1	2	0	0	0	0	0	0	0	0
Cause ...	15	15	19	22	14	14	15	14	8	9	8	4	2	0	10	6
Causes ..	0	0	0	1	0	0	2	0	0	0	0	0	0	0	0	0
Come ...	1	1	0	1	2	2	0	0	0	0	1	0	0	0	1	0
Conjunction	0	0	0	0	0	0	0	0	0	0	2	3	0	2	2	2
Did.....	0	0	1	2	0	0	1	0	0	0	0	1	0	0	0	0
Do	2	0	4	4	3	2	0	0	0	0	1	0	0	0	1	0
Don't ...	0	1	0	1	0	0	2	0	1	0	0	0	0	0	0	0
Due	0	0	0	0	1	0	0	0	0	0	0	0	0	0	1	2
Even	0	0	0	0	1	0	2	0	0	0	0	0	0	0	1	0
Excuse...	1	2	3	4	3	9	4	3	3	4	6	4	6	4	1	8
Explain ..	0	2	0	1	0	1	2	1	0	0	0	0	0	1	0	1
Explanation	0	0	1	1	1	0	0	0	0	0	2	0	0	0	0	0
For.....	1	0	0	2	1	0	2	2	1	2	5	2	2	2	15	17
Good	2	0	1	0	0	0	0	0	1	0	0	0	0	0	0	0
Had	0	0	1	0	1	0	2	0	0	0	0	0	0	0	0	0
Happened .	0	2	0	0	0	0	0	0	0	0	0	0	0	0	0	0
Have	0	0	1	1	0	1	0	2	0	1	0	0	0	0	0	0
He	4	4	7	2	5	2	4	3	3	1	4	0	2	2	3	0
Help	0	0	1	0	0	2	0	0	1	0	0	0	0	0	0	0
House ...	0	0	0	0	0	1	0	2	0	0	0	0	0	0	0	0
How	0	1	0	0	0	2	0	1	1	0	0	1	0	0	0	1
However ..	2	1	1	3	0	2	2	4	1	1	0	2	0	1	1	4
I	9	3	4	3	3	2	4	3	6	5	5	4	4	4	8	5
If	0	1	0	1	0	0	1	1	2	2	1	5	4	3	15	13
I'm	2	0	1	0	1	0	0	0	0	0	0	0	0	0	0	0
Is	2	1	1	2	3	3	1	4	2	3	4	1	3	1	3	2
It	12	5	10	7	11	6	11	4	8	4	1	3	3	2	11	3
Just	1	0	0	1	2	4	0	3	1	2	3	8	2	2	4	1
Know ...	0	0	0	2	1	0	0	0	0	1	0	0	1	0	0	0
Love ...	0	0	1	0	0	0	0	0	0	1	0	1	1	1	0	2
Maybe ...	0	2	1	2	1	1	2	5	3	2	0	4	0	3	4	1
Me	3	1	3	0	5	0	0	1	0	0	0	1	0	0	1	0
Mean....	0	0	0	0	0	0	0	2	0	0	0	0	0	0	0	0
My	1	2	1	1	0	0	1	0	0	0	0	0	0	0	0	1
Never ...	1	2	0	0	1	1	1	2	4	4	6	1	6	3	10	6
Nice	1	2	1	0	0	0	0	0	0	0	0	0	1	0	0	0
No	4	6	5	2	2	4	4	2	4	1	0	0	2	0	1	2
Not	3	3	2	6	2	5	4	2	1	1	1	1	2	1	4	2
Now	3	0	3	3	1	0	1	1	1	2	2	1	0	2	3	5
Of	1	0	2	5	10	4	16	18	27	32	19	27	42	36	84	79
Of you ...	0	0	0	0	0	0	0	0	0	0	2	1	1	5	6	9
Oh	3	4	3	2	3	0	0	0	1	0	0	0	0	0	2	1
Okay	0	2	0	1	0	0	0	0	0	0	0	0	0	0	0	1

Response Word	4th M	4th F	5th M	5th F	6th M	6th F	7th M	7th F	8th M	8th F	10th M	10th F	12th M	12th F	College M	College F
							BECAUSE									
On	3	1	2	1	2	0	1	2	0	1	0	0	2	0	1	0
On account of	0	0	0	0	0	0	0	0	0	0	0	0	0	1	1	2
One	1	0	0	0	1	0	2	0	0	0	0	1	0	0	0	0
Only	5	8	5	6	0	8	3	11	2	5	3	6	2	6	9	6
Or	0	2	1	0	0	0	0	0	0	0	1	0	1	0	4	1
Parece que .	0	0	0	0	0	0	0	0	0	0	0	0	0	0	0	2
Preposition .	0	0	0	0	0	0	0	0	1	0	0	0	0	2	0	1
Question . .	1	2	0	2	2	1	2	0	1	3	0	2	2	1	0	0
Reason . . .	1	7	10	4	4	13	4	12	7	13	14	25	23	25	38	29
Reasons . . .	0	0	0	0	0	0	0	0	0	1	2	0	1	0	1	0
Said	1	2	2	0	1	1	1	0	0	0	0	0	1	0	0	0
See	2	1	1	0	1	0	0	0	1	0	2	0	0	0	0	0
Sentence . . .	0	2	0	2	1	2	1	0	0	0	1	0	0	0	0	1
She	0	3	0	5	0	2	0	0	0	0	0	0	2	1	0	3
Since	0	0	1	0	1	0	0	2	0	0	1	5	2	4	9	8
So	3	3	1	3	2	4	2	5	2	5	5	6	2	7	14	27
Some	1	0	0	2	1	0	3	0	0	0	0	0	0	0	0	2
Something . .	6	7	1	4	2	4	1	1	0	0	0	0	0	0	0	0
Song	0	0	0	0	0	1	1	1	0	1	0	1	2	1	4	9
Story	1	0	0	2	0	1	0	0	1	0	0	0	0	0	0	0
Tell	1	0	1	2	0	0	0	0	1	0	0	0	0	0	0	0
That	8	3	3	2	8	2	2	0	3	1	2	2	5	4	4	3
The	2	0	5	1	7	2	1	0	2	0	2	1	1	1	2	2
Then	0	0	1	2	0	0	1	0	2	2	3	1	1	0	5	2
There	2	1	0	2	1	0	1	1	2	1	1	0	1	0	3	0
Therefore . .	0	0	0	0	0	0	1	0	1	0	2	3	4	3	17	17
They	3	2	1	2	2	1	2	1	1	2	2	2	1	0	5	1
Think	2	1	2	0	0	0	0	0	2	0	1	1	0	0	0	1
This	0	1	0	2	0	2	0	0	2	0	1	0	1	1	4	3
Though . . .	1	0	0	0	0	0	0	1	0	0	0	0	0	0	0	2
Thus	0	0	0	0	0	0	0	0	0	0	0	0	0	0	1	2
To	0	0	3	1	0	0	0	0	1	0	0	0	0	1	1	0
Use	0	0	2	0	0	0	0	0	0	0	0	0	0	0	0	0
Want	1	1	2	1	0	2	0	2	1	1	0	0	0	0	1	0
Wanted . . .	0	1	0	0	0	2	1	0	0	0	0	0	0	0	0	0
Was	0	0	1	0	1	0	2	0	3	0	1	0	0	0	4	1
Way	0	1	0	2	4	0	2	0	2	0	1	0	0	1	0	0
We	2	2	1	2	0	0	0	2	1	0	1	3	0	2	5	0
Wedding . . .	0	0	0	0	0	0	0	0	0	0	0	0	0	0	1	2
Well	1	2	0	2	0	0	0	1	0	2	0	0	0	1	1	0
What	2	1	3	0	0	2	3	0	2	2	2	0	3	1	3	2
When	0	1	1	0	2	2	2	0	2	1	1	2	1	2	2	1
Why	33	41	31	37	32	45	51	53	49	73	47	60	43	48	72	80
Women . . .	2	0	0	0	0	0	0	0	0	0	0	0	0	0	0	0
Word	2	3	10	2	6	2	2	1	0	0	0	0	1	0	0	0
Wrong	0	2	0	1	0	0	0	0	0	0	1	0	0	0	0	0
Yes	1	4	0	3	7	3	2	1	0	1	1	0	0	3	2	2
Yet	0	0	0	0	0	0	0	0	0	0	0	0	0	0	1	2

Response Word	4th		5th		6th		7th		8th		10th		12th		College	
	M	F	M	F	M	F	M	F	M	F	M	F	M	F	M	F

BECAUSE

Response Word	M	F	M	F	M	F	M	F	M	F	M	F	M	F	M	F
You	11	12	14	16	18	22	11	13	21	10	21	12	21	19	34	36
Young ...	0	0	0	0	0	0	0	0	0	0	0	3	0	0	0	2
Your ...	0	0	0	0	1	1	0	0	0	0	1	0	3	0	2	1

17. BECOME

Response Word	M	F	M	F	M	F	M	F	M	F	M	F	M	F	M	F
A	6	0	5	1	10	1	1	0	3	0	0	1	0	0	5	2
Acquainted	0	0	0	1	0	0	0	0	0	2	0	2	2	0	4	1
Afraid ...	1	1	0	1	1	0	1	1	1	2	0	0	1	0	1	0
Am	0	1	1	0	1	0	1	2	1	7	2	3	2	3	4	8
And	0	0	0	0	1	2	0	0	0	0	0	0	0	0	0	0
Appear ..	0	0	0	0	0	2	0	0	1	2	0	1	0	1	2	2
Are	1	1	2	0	1	0	1	5	0	0	1	2	1	1	9	9
Arrive ..	0	0	0	0	0	0	0	0	1	0	1	1	1	0	2	3
As	0	0	0	0	0	0	1	1	0	0	1	0	0	1	2	3
Attached ..	0	0	0	0	0	2	0	0	0	0	0	0	0	0	0	0
Aware ...	0	0	0	0	0	0	0	0	0	0	0	1	0	0	2	3
Bad	0	0	1	1	1	0	1	0	0	2	0	0	1	0	0	0
Be	10	10	9	5	3	15	4	7	2	7	3	9	8	9	24	28
Beautiful .	0	0	0	0	0	1	1	1	0	1	0	1	0	2	1	5
Became ..	24	25	21	26	9	35	51	74	91	97	42	43	53	66	92	100
Because ..	13	8	7	12	10	8	4	7	8	4	7	4	4	2	6	12
Become ..	0	0	0	0	1	2	0	0	0	0	0	0	0	0	0	0
Becoming .	0	0	0	1	0	1	0	1	0	0	1	3	1	0	3	1
Before ...	1	3	0	1	1	2	0	1	0	1	2	0	0	0	1	2
Began ...	0	0	0	0	0	0	0	0	1	0	0	1	1	0	0	2
Begone ..	0	0	0	0	1	0	1	0	2	0	0	0	0	0	0	0
Behind ..	0	0	0	0	0	0	2	1	0	0	0	0	0	0	0	0
Being ...	0	0	0	0	0	0	0	0	0	0	1	1	1	1	2	2
Beside ...	0	0	0	0	0	0	1	0	0	0	0	0	0	0	1	2
Better ...	1	0	3	1	0	1	0	1	0	1	0	1	1	2	1	3
Big	0	0	1	0	0	0	1	0	0	1	1	1	4	1	0	1
Boy	0	0	1	0	0	0	0	1	2	0	1	0	0	1	2	1
Bride ...	0	1	0	0	0	0	0	0	0	0	0	3	0	1	2	1
By	3	0	0	0	0	0	1	1	0	0	0	0	0	1	1	2
Came ...	6	9	15	12	9	7	13	15	7	8	5	5	6	3	8	3
Career ..	0	0	0	0	0	1	0	0	0	0	1	0	0	2	0	0
Change ..	0	1	2	1	1	1	2	3	2	1	2	6	2	1	12	11
Clear ...	0	0	0	0	0	0	1	0	0	1	0	0	0	0	0	2
Closer ...	0	0	0	3	0	0	0	1	1	0	2	0	0	1	1	1
Come ...	43	46	36	35	33	42	22	18	12	6	4	5	11	1	5	5
Coming ..	0	2	0	1	0	1	0	0	0	0	0	1	1	1	0	0
Dead ...	1	0	2	0	0	0	0	0	1	0	0	0	1	0	1	0
Develop ..	0	0	0	0	0	0	0	0	0	0	0	0	0	0	3	0
Did	0	0	0	2	0	0	0	0	0	0	0	1	0	1	0	0
Do	2	1	0	1	2	2	1	1	1	0	0	2	0	1	0	2
Doctor ...	1	0	1	0	0	0	1	0	0	1	0	0	2	0	1	1
Exist ...	0	0	0	0	0	0	0	0	0	0	0	0	0	0	3	2
Famous ..	1	2	0	0	0	0	0	1	0	0	1	1	0	2	0	2
Fast	3	6	4	4	1	2	1	1	0	2	2	1	0	1	3	1

Response Word	4th M	4th F	5th M	5th F	6th M	6th F	7th M	7th F	8th M	8th F	10th M	10th F	12th M	12th F	College M	College F
								BECOME								
Faster . . .	0	0	1	0	0	2	0	1	1	0	2	1	0	1	0	0
Fat	3	0	1	0	4	0	1	2	0	3	4	1	2	2	5	1
Friendly . .	0	0	0	0	0	2	0	0	0	0	0	0	0	1	0	0
Friends . .	0	1	0	0	2	0	0	1	0	0	0	0	0	1	0	0
Frightened	0	1	0	0	0	0	0	0	0	0	0	0	0	2	0	0
From . . .	0	0	0	0	0	1	1	1	3	1	0	0	1	0	0	1
Future . . .	0	0	0	0	1	0	2	1	0	0	0	0	0	3	2	4
Get	0	0	1	0	1	2	1	2	2	2	8	8	2	7	7	8
Girl	1	0	0	1	0	1	0	0	2	2	0	0	0	1	0	0
Go	3	4	5	10	7	5	6	3	6	4	7	3	2	2	12	5
Going . . .	1	0	3	0	0	0	0	1	0	0	1	0	1	0	0	0
Gone . . .	0	0	1	3	1	5	0	0	0	3	1	1	1	1	3	1
Good . . .	4	3	5	1	4	2	6	3	1	1	4	4	3	5	9	6
Great . . .	2	0	2	1	3	1	1	0	0	1	1	0	1	1	0	1
Grow . . .	0	1	2	0	1	1	1	0	0	1	0	1	1	0	4	5
Happen . .	3	2	0	2	1	0	0	0	0	0	0	0	0	0	0	1
Happened .	0	0	1	0	1	1	2	0	0	0	1	0	0	0	1	0
Happy . . .	0	0	0	0	0	2	0	1	1	0	2	0	1	1	1	2
Hard . . .	0	1	0	0	1	1	1	0	0	1	2	0	0	1	0	0
Harder . .	0	0	0	0	1	0	0	0	2	0	1	0	1	0	0	0
Has	0	1	0	0	1	0	1	2	0	0	0	1	0	0	0	1
Have . . .	0	0	0	1	0	0	0	1	0	0	4	0	1	1	1	2
He	0	3	3	0	1	0	1	1	4	0	1	1	1	0	1	0
Hear . . .	1	0	2	0	0	0	0	0	0	1	0	0	0	0	0	0
Help	0	0	0	0	0	0	0	0	2	0	0	0	0	0	1	0
Her	0	2	0	0	0	3	0	1	0	0	0	0	0	0	1	1
Here . . .	5	4	5	1	4	5	4	3	2	4	2	1	1	1	1	1
Him	0	0	3	0	0	1	0	1	0	0	0	3	1	0	0	1
Home . . .	2	0	2	1	1	0	1	1	1	0	1	0	2	0	1	0
Hot	0	0	0	0	0	0	2	0	0	0	0	0	0	0	0	0
I	2	1	1	0	2	0	1	1	1	0	0	0	1	1	3	0
Ill	0	0	1	2	0	2	2	2	2	1	2	0	3	0	0	3
In	0	1	1	1	0	1	0	0	0	0	2	0	0	0	2	0
Into	1	0	2	0	1	2	0	1	0	0	0	0	0	0	0	1
Is	1	6	5	5	4	3	1	2	1	2	5	11	2	15	13	34
It	4	3	1	0	4	3	3	0	2	1	2	2	2	0	5	5
Job	0	1	1	0	0	2	0	0	0	0	0	0	0	0	0	0
King . . .	2	0	0	0	2	0	1	0	0	0	0	0	0	0	0	0
Known . . .	0	0	0	0	0	1	0	0	0	0	1	0	1	3	0	0
Leave . . .	0	1	0	1	0	0	0	0	0	0	2	0	0	0	0	1
Like	1	0	0	0	0	0	0	0	0	0	0	0	2	1	3	1
Little . . .	0	0	0	2	0	2	0	0	0	0	0	0	0	0	0	1
Look	1	0	0	1	1	0	0	1	0	1	0	0	0	0	2	0
Mad	1	0	0	3	0	1	0	0	1	0	1	0	0	0	3	1
Made	0	0	0	1	0	0	0	0	0	0	1	1	0	1	2	2
Make	0	0	1	1	1	1	0	0	0	0	0	1	2	1	5	4
Man	1	0	1	0	0	0	2	0	1	0	1	0	1	2	3	1
Married . .	0	0	0	0	0	0	0	0	0	1	1	0	0	1	0	2

Response Word	4th		5th		6th		7th		8th		10th		12th		College	
	M	F	M	F	M	F	M	F	M	F	M	F	M	F	M	F

BECOME

Response Word	M	F	M	F	M	F	M	F	M	F	M	F	M	F	M	F
Me	2	4	4	1	6	0	1	1	3	2	1	1	2	2	2	0
Mine . . .	0	1	1	0	0	1	0	0	0	1	3	2	1	0	0	1
My	2	0	1	0	1	0	2	0	0	0	3	0	0	0	0	0
Myself . . .	0	0	0	0	1	0	0	0	0	0	0	0	0	2	0	0
New	0	1	1	0	3	0	1	2	1	0	1	0	1	1	0	1
Nice	4	2	3	0	0	3	1	2	2	2	1	1	1	4	1	0
Not	0	0	0	2	1	0	0	0	1	0	0	1	0	0	1	0
Now	3	4	2	4	2	1	1	1	1	2	3	2	2	1	6	4
Nurse . . .	0	0	0	0	0	0	0	1	0	0	0	3	0	2	0	1
Of	3	0	2	4	7	2	4	1	4	3	1	4	4	6	7	4
Old	0	0	1	0	2	2	2	1	1	0	2	2	1	0	7	4
Older . . .	0	0	1	1	0	0	0	2	0	2	1	0	1	2	5	1
One	0	0	1	0	0	0	2	1	2	0	1	2	2	2	6	7
Person . .	1	0	0	0	1	0	0	1	1	0	1	0	1	0	0	2
President .	2	0	1	1	0	0	0	0	1	0	1	0	0	0	0	0
Pretty . . .	0	0	0	2	0	1	1	3	0	2	2	5	0	1	1	7
Queen . . .	0	0	0	0	0	0	0	1	0	0	0	0	0	1	1	2
Ready . . .	0	0	0	0	0	0	0	0	0	0	0	0	1	2	0	0
Receive . .	0	0	0	0	0	0	0	0	0	0	0	2	0	0	0	1
Rich	0	0	0	0	0	0	1	1	0	0	1	0	0	0	3	0
Sad	0	0	1	3	1	1	0	1	0	0	0	1	0	0	0	0
Scared . . .	0	0	0	0	1	1	0	0	0	0	1	2	0	0	0	0
See	1	1	0	1	1	0	0	2	0	0	1	0	0	0	0	0
Seem . . .	0	0	0	0	0	0	0	0	0	0	0	0	0	0	1	4
Sick	0	2	2	0	2	1	4	0	1	1	4	1	1	0	5	2
Slow	1	0	0	0	2	0	0	0	1	0	1	2	1	0	2	1
Small . . .	0	0	0	0	0	0	1	0	0	0	1	0	0	0	2	1
Smart . . .	0	0	1	0	0	0	0	2	0	1	1	0	1	0	1	0
So	1	0	0	1	0	2	0	0	0	0	0	0	0	0	1	1
Some . . .	0	0	0	0	2	0	1	0	0	0	0	0	0	0	0	1
Someone .	2	1	2	1	0	2	0	1	0	2	0	1	0	0	1	2
Something .	4	4	3	4	3	1	2	0	1	1	2	0	0	0	4	6
Soon	0	0	1	1	0	1	0	1	1	0	0	0	0	2	1	2
Start . . .	0	0	0	2	0	2	1	0	0	0	0	0	0	0	2	0
Stay	0	0	0	0	1	0	0	0	0	0	0	1	1	0	3	1
The	7	3	4	2	8	2	1	0	0	0	0	0	2	1	1	1
Them . . .	0	0	1	3	0	0	0	0	0	0	1	0	0	0	1	0
Then	2	0	0	1	0	0	2	0	2	1	0	1	0	0	0	0
There . . .	0	2	2	1	1	1	1	3	0	0	1	3	2	0	0	1
They	1	2	4	2	2	1	2	1	4	1	0	2	1	0	2	0
Thin	0	0	0	0	1	0	0	1	0	0	0	1	1	3	0	1
Time . . .	0	0	0	0	0	0	0	0	0	0	2	0	0	0	0	0
Tired . . .	1	2	0	0	1	0	0	0	0	0	2	5	4	2	4	1
To	2	0	0	3	4	1	2	2	1	0	2	0	0	0	2	3
To be . . .	0	0	0	0	0	0	0	0	1	2	0	1	0	0	0	3
Today . . .	0	0	0	0	0	0	0	0	2	0	0	0	0	0	1	0
Transform .	0	0	0	0	0	1	0	0	0	0	1	0	1	0	1	2
Turn	1	2	0	1	3	1	3	2	0	2	1	1	1	1	2	0
Turn into .	0	0	0	0	0	1	0	0	2	0	0	0	0	0	1	0

Response Word	4th M	F	5th M	F	6th M	F	7th M	F	8th M	F	10th M	F	12th M	F	College M	F

BECOME

Response Word	4th M	F	5th M	F	6th M	F	7th M	F	8th M	F	10th M	F	12th M	F	College M	F
Very	1	0	1	1	2	0	0	0	0	0	0	0	0	0	0	0
Was	2	1	0	0	2	0	6	3	1	2	2	1	1	1	9	14
Welcome	0	1	1	2	1	2	1	0	0	0	0	0	0	0	0	0
Went	1	0	0	0	0	0	1	0	1	2	0	1	0	1	2	0
Were	0	0	0	0	1	0	0	0	0	0	1	1	0	0	0	3
What	3	4	4	1	5	1	4	2	3	2	3	4	5	7	9	10
When	0	0	0	1	0	2	0	0	0	0	0	0	1	0	0	2
Where	0	3	0	5	1	1	0	0	1	1	1	0	2	0	0	0
Why	2	1	0	2	1	1	2	0	0	3	1	1	3	2	4	1
Wild	0	0	0	0	0	0	0	1	0	0	0	0	0	1	2	0
Will	1	1	1	3	2	0	3	2	1	1	2	2	1	1	6	5
Will be	0	0	0	0	0	0	1	0	1	0	1	2	0	2	0	2
Word	0	0	1	0	2	0	0	0	0	1	0	0	0	0	0	0
Work	0	0	0	0	1	0	0	0	1	0	0	0	0	0	2	0
Yes	0	1	0	2	0	0	0	0	0	0	0	0	0	0	0	0
You	3	4	5	3	2	1	0	3	3	1	1	1	3	2	9	2
Your	0	1	0	2	0	0	0	0	0	0	0	1	1	0	0	0

18. BED

Response Word	4th M	F	5th M	F	6th M	F	7th M	F	8th M	F	10th M	F	12th M	F	College M	F
Asleep	1	2	0	0	0	1	0	0	0	0	0	0	0	0	0	0
Awake	0	0	2	0	0	0	1	0	0	0	0	0	0	0	0	0
Bed	0	0	0	0	2	0	0	0	0	0	0	0	0	0	1	0
Bedroom	0	2	1	0	1	0	1	0	1	0	0	0	0	1	1	1
Big	0	1	0	0	1	0	0	0	0	0	0	0	0	0	1	2
Blanket	2	2	2	1	3	6	2	5	2	0	2	6	3	8	7	13
Blankets	2	0	0	1	0	0	0	0	0	4	1	3	1	0	3	3
Board	0	0	0	0	0	0	0	0	0	0	0	0	0	0	2	0
Book	0	0	0	0	0	0	0	0	0	0	2	0	0	0	1	0
Boy	1	0	1	0	0	1	0	0	0	2	0	1	0	0	2	2
Bug	0	1	1	0	0	0	1	0	2	0	0	0	0	0	1	2
Bugs	0	0	0	0	0	0	0	0	2	0	0	0	0	0	0	0
Butter	0	0	0	0	0	0	0	0	0	0	0	0	0	0	3	0
Chair	6	6	3	2	0	4	8	4	6	1	3	2	1	0	4	2
Comfort	0	0	1	0	1	1	3	3	3	5	4	3	3	8	9	11
Comfortable	1	0	1	1	1	2	2	4	0	3	1	2	1	0	1	1
Couch	0	2	1	0	0	0	1	1	0	0	0	0	1	0	2	1
Cover	0	1	1	3	1	2	0	0	2	1	0	0	0	0	0	0
Covers	4	1	5	7	3	1	1	4	2	3	1	4	2	2	4	5
Cushion	0	0	0	0	0	0	1	0	2	0	0	0	0	0	0	0
Dream	1	1	0	2	1	0	1	0	0	0	0	0	3	0	0	0
Dreams	1	0	0	0	0	0	1	0	0	0	1	0	2	0	0	0
Dresser	0	0	0	0	0	0	0	0	0	0	0	0	0	0	1	2
Floor	2	3	0	0	1	1	2	1	2	0	0	0	0	0	1	1
Foot	2	0	0	0	0	0	0	0	0	0	0	0	0	0	0	0
Furniture	0	0	2	0	0	1	0	0	0	1	0	1	0	0	1	0
Girl	1	0	0	0	0	0	0	0	2	0	7	0	5	0	10	0
Good	1	0	3	0	0	1	1	0	0	0	2	0	1	0	0	0
Happy	1	0	0	0	0	0	0	0	0	0	0	1	0	0	2	0
Hard	1	1	3	0	1	0	0	0	1	0	2	0	0	0	1	1

Response Word	4th M	4th F	5th M	5th F	6th M	6th F	7th M	7th F	8th M	8th F	10th M	10th F	12th M	12th F	College M	College F
							BED									
Head . . .	2	1	0	1	0	0	0	0	0	1	0	0	0	0	1	1
Heavy . . .	0	0	0	0	0	0	0	0	0	0	0	0	0	0	2	0
Home . . .	1	1	0	2	0	3	1	0	0	0	0	0	0	1	2	0
House . . .	0	0	1	0	3	3	0	0	3	0	1	1	1	0	3	0
Lay	3	4	3	2	4	4	2	3	5	2	3	2	1	0	2	2
Lie	1	2	0	2	1	0	3	0	0	0	0	1	1	1	0	1
Light . . .	0	0	0	0	0	1	0	1	0	0	0	2	0	0	1	1
Linen . . .	0	0	0	0	0	0	0	0	0	0	0	0	0	0	2	0
Love . . .	0	0	0	0	0	0	0	0	0	0	0	0	2	1	5	1
Man	0	0	1	0	0	0	0	0	2	0	0	1	0	1	0	0
Marriage .	0	0	0	0	0	0	0	0	0	0	0	0	0	0	3	0
Mattress .	0	1	2	0	4	1	2	3	3	2	5	2	2	3	3	6
Morning . .	0	0	2	0	0	0	0	0	0	0	0	0	0	0	0	0
Nice	1	0	2	1	1	0	0	1	2	1	2	1	0	1	2	1
Night . . .	11	8	7	11	8	7	6	1	3	7	5	4	4	3	3	1
People . .	0	0	0	0	0	0	0	0	0	2	0	1	0	0	0	0
Pillow . . .	7	10	8	16	5	13	9	20	9	15	6	13	4	9	9	25
Post	0	0	0	0	1	1	1	0	1	2	1	2	2	0	1	1
Quilt . . .	0	0	0	0	0	0	0	0	0	0	0	0	0	0	0	2
Red	5	2	1	3	1	1	0	0	0	1	1	0	2	0	2	0
Relax . . .	0	0	0	0	0	0	0	0	0	1	0	0	2	1	2	0
Rest . . .	1	2	4	1	2	1	3	3	2	4	5	1	6	14	12	14
Ridden . . .	0	0	0	0	0	0	0	0	0	0	0	0	2	0	0	0
Room . . .	1	0	0	0	2	0	0	2	2	4	1	0	2	3	5	5
Round . . .	1	0	0	0	0	0	0	0	0	0	0	0	0	0	2	0
Sex	0	0	0	0	0	0	0	0	0	0	0	0	3	0	6	2
Sheep . . .	2	0	1	0	0	0	1	0	0	0	0	0	1	0	0	0
Sheet . . .	0	1	1	2	3	3	2	1	4	1	2	3	2	4	7	7
Sheets . . .	0	0	0	0	1	0	1	2	1	2	1	0	0	4	5	5
Sick	1	2	0	1	0	2	0	0	0	1	1	2	0	0	1	0
Sleep . . .	139	135	137	152	144	135	134	141	129	138	142	156	147	142	285	292
Sleeping . .	1	0	1	2	3	2	1	0	1	3	0	1	0	1	0	0
Sleepy . . .	1	3	2	2	0	0	1	3	1	0	1	1	1	1	0	0
Soft	15	15	8	13	23	28	32	26	33	23	19	22	21	23	36	47
Spread . . .	1	1	2	2	1	0	1	1	0	0	0	3	2	0	4	2
Table . . .	1	1	3	1	2	0	0	0	1	0	0	0	0	0	0	0
Time . . .	2	5	5	4	4	3	1	0	0	0	1	0	0	0	3	3
Tired . . .	0	4	3	2	2	5	2	2	1	5	4	3	0	4	4	5
Warm . . .	0	4	2	0	0	3	0	2	1	3	3	0	0	4	2	6
White . . .	1	0	0	0	0	1	0	0	0	0	1	0	0	0	1	2
Woman . .	0	0	0	0	0	0	0	0	0	0	0	0	1	0	4	0
Women . .	0	0	0	0	0	0	0	0	0	0	2	0	0	0	1	0
						19.	BIBLE									
Black . . .	1	0	0	2	0	1	0	1	0	1	0	0	1	2	7	9
Book . . .	48	58	72	56	57	57	54	45	45	43	43	38	55	46	100	73
Christ . . .	2	2	0	3	4	2	2	2	0	4	3	4	4	4	12	6
Church . .	25	19	27	19	30	33	22	29	25	25	31	31	29	25	28	44

Response Word	4th M	4th F	5th M	5th F	6th M	6th F	7th M	7th F	8th M	8th F	10th M	10th F	12th M	12th F	College M	College F

BIBLE

Response Word	4th M	4th F	5th M	5th F	6th M	6th F	7th M	7th F	8th M	8th F	10th M	10th F	12th M	12th F	College M	College F
Confirmation	0	0	0	0	0	0	0	0	2	2	0	0	1	0	0	0
Devil	0	0	1	0	0	0	0	2	0	0	0	0	0	0	0	0
Faith	1	0	0	0	0	0	1	1	0	0	0	1	0	2	2	0
False	0	0	0	0	0	0	0	0	0	0	0	0	0	0	2	0
God	43	44	44	46	55	57	58	74	65	61	83	116	74	92	145	171
God's word .	0	1	0	1	0	0	0	1	0	3	0	0	0	0	0	0
Good	3	1	7	1	5	0	2	6	2	6	12	5	3	8	9	7
History . . .	1	2	1	0	3	1	0	2	2	3	1	0	1	1	6	0
Holy	20	21	20	19	16	12	17	15	20	11	3	6	9	8	9	8
Jesus	15	23	16	16	10	20	19	16	11	17	12	16	14	17	14	23
Jesus Christ	0	1	0	0	0	0	0	0	0	0	0	0	0	0	2	1
Law	0	0	0	0	0	0	2	0	0	0	0	1	1	2	0	1
Learn	0	1	0	2	0	0	0	0	0	0	0	0	0	0	0	0
Learning . . .	0	0	0	0	0	0	0	0	2	0	0	0	0	0	0	0
Life	0	0	0	0	0	0	0	0	0	0	0	0	0	2	2	3
Look	0	2	1	0	0	0	0	0	1	0	0	0	0	0	0	0
Lord	0	3	2	5	6	3	0	0	1	1	2	0	2	1	5	1
Love	0	1	0	3	1	0	0	0	0	0	0	0	0	2	3	4
Man	1	0	2	0	0	0	0	0	0	0	0	0	1	0	0	1
Minister . . .	0	1	0	1	2	0	0	0	0	0	0	0	0	1	1	1
Moses	0	1	0	1	0	0	3	3	4	2	0	2	1	0	6	3
Nice	1	2	1	1	1	0	0	0	0	0	0	0	0	0	1	0
Pray	1	1	2	1	2	1	2	1	2	5	2	0	2	0	0	3
Prayer . . .	1	0	3	1	1	1	2	1	1	2	0	1	0	0	0	3
Priest	1	0	1	2	0	0	0	0	2	0	0	0	0	0	0	0
Psalms . . .	0	2	0	0	0	0	0	0	0	1	0	1	0	0	0	0
Read	16	7	6	15	9	9	3	4	3	5	6	1	8	7	8	8
Religion . . .	1	2	5	2	6	3	13	12	16	19	12	8	10	9	42	35
Religious . .	1	0	0	1	0	3	0	0	3	4	3	2	0	1	3	1
Sacred	0	0	0	0	0	0	1	0	3	1	0	1	0	1	0	0
School	5	1	0	1	0	2	0	0	0	0	0	0	0	0	1	0
Stories . . .	6	5	2	2	4	2	4	8	3	1	2	2	3	2	10	9
Story	17	27	5	21	14	8	9	8	3	7	10	8	9	10	33	39
Study	2	0	0	0	1	0	2	0	0	2	1	0	2	1	1	1
Sunday	2	2	1	3	2	6	1	0	1	1	0	0	0	1	1	0
Sunday school	0	0	0	2	0	1	1	1	0	0	0	0	1	0	0	0
Testament . .	1	0	1	1	0	0	4	0	0	0	3	1	1	1	1	0
True	0	0	0	3	0	1	1	0	0	0	0	0	1	0	1	0
Truth	0	2	0	0	1	0	0	0	0	2	1	0	2	3	6	11
Verse	0	0	1	0	1	1	0	0	2	0	0	0	1	0	1	1
Verses . . .	1	0	0	0	0	0	1	2	0	1	1	0	0	0	0	0
Wonderful . .	0	0	0	1	0	1	0	1	0	2	0	0	0	0	0	0
Word	0	2	0	1	3	0	1	2	2	1	1	0	0	0	1	3
Words	2	0	0	1	1	4	2	1	0	1	2	0	0	0	1	2

20. BITTER

Response Word	4th M	4th F	5th M	5th F	6th M	6th F	7th M	7th F	8th M	8th F	10th M	10th F	12th M	12th F	College M	College F
Acid	0	0	0	0	0	0	1	0	0	0	0	0	0	0	4	1
Acrid	0	0	0	0	0	0	0	0	0	0	0	0	0	0	2	0
Alum	0	0	0	0	0	0	0	0	1	0	0	0	0	0	2	0

Response Word	4th		5th		6th		7th		8th		10th		12th		College	
	M	F	M	F	M	F	M	F	M	F	M	F	M	F	M	F

BITTER

Response Word	4th M	4th F	5th M	5th F	6th M	6th F	7th M	7th F	8th M	8th F	10th M	10th F	12th M	12th F	College M	College F
Anger . . .	0	1	0	1	0	0	0	0	0	0	1	1	0	1	0	3
Angry . . .	0	0	1	4	2	1	0	1	1	4	6	6	6	7	6	5
Apple . . .	1	1	0	0	0	1	0	0	1	0	2	0	1	0	2	0
Apples . .	0	0	0	0	0	0	0	0	0	0	0	2	0	1	0	0
Awful . . .	4	4	4	3	8	12	6	5	3	1	1	1	3	1	1	0
Bad	18	5	22	8	15	4	10	2	4	4	8	4	5	2	2	2
Batter . . .	0	2	0	0	1	1	0	0	0	0	0	0	0	0	1	0
Beer	0	0	0	1	0	0	0	0	2	0	0	0	0	1	0	1
Berries . .	0	0	0	0	0	1	0	0	0	0	0	2	0	0	1	3
Better . . .	1	3	2	2	1	1	0	0	1	0	0	0	0	0	1	0
Bit	3	6	0	1	1	2	0	0	0	0	0	0	0	0	0	0
Bite	2	0	0	0	0	1	0	0	0	1	0	0	0	0	0	1
Bread . . .	0	1	0	0	1	0	0	0	1	0	2	0	0	0	0	0
Butter . . .	8	8	7	6	4	3	0	1	1	2	2	2	1	0	3	0
Candy . . .	2	1	1	1	1	2	0	0	0	1	2	0	1	1	1	0
Cat	0	0	0	2	0	0	0	0	0	0	0	0	0	0	0	0
Chocolate .	1	4	1	2	0	3	4	9	2	7	4	12	4	8	5	6
Coffee . . .	1	0	1	1	0	3	0	0	1	0	0	1	1	0	1	1
Cold	9	8	13	11	7	8	1	3	1	2	0	1	4	1	3	1
Cry	0	3	0	0	0	0	0	0	0	0	0	0	0	0	0	0
Drink . . .	0	0	0	0	1	0	0	0	0	0	0	0	0	0	2	1
Eat	3	1	0	1	3	0	0	1	0	0	0	1	0	0	1	0
Eggs	2	0	0	0	0	0	0	0	0	0	0	0	0	0	0	0
Enemy . . .	0	0	0	0	0	0	0	0	0	0	0	2	1	0	0	1
Food	7	3	5	0	5	1	2	0	2	1	3	0	6	3	5	3
Fruit	0	1	0	0	0	0	0	0	1	1	0	0	2	1	0	1
Good	14	8	11	4	9	3	3	2	4	3	3	1	1	1	1	0
Grapefruit .	0	1	0	1	1	0	2	0	1	1	2	1	1	0	1	0
Happy . . .	0	0	0	0	0	0	2	0	1	0	0	1	2	2	1	0
Hard . . .	1	4	0	0	3	1	5	2	2	4	1	1	2	0	4	4
Harsh . . .	0	0	2	0	1	0	2	1	1	2	0	2	1	1	2	1
Hate	0	3	1	0	1	0	0	0	1	2	2	2	2	2	2	5
Hatred . . .	0	0	0	0	0	0	0	0	0	0	1	0	1	0	1	2
Herb	0	0	0	0	0	0	0	0	1	1	0	0	0	0	2	4
Herbs . . .	0	0	0	0	0	0	0	1	2	2	0	0	0	0	3	4
Hit	2	0	0	0	0	0	0	0	0	0	0	0	0	0	0	0
Honey . . .	1	0	0	0	2	0	1	0	0	0	0	0	0	0	0	1
Horrible . .	1	2	2	1	0	1	3	2	0	0	0	1	0	1	0	0
Hungry . .	0	1	2	0	0	1	0	0	0	0	0	0	0	0	0	0
Hurt	2	1	0	1	2	1	1	0	0	1	0	0	0	0	1	1
Ick	0	0	0	1	2	3	1	0	1	0	1	1	0	0	1	0
Icky	3	3	1	3	2	1	1	0	0	0	0	0	0	0	0	0
Ish	1	5	3	0	2	3	0	2	1	1	0	0	1	2	0	1
Ishy	4	0	4	3	2	0	1	1	2	2	0	1	0	2	0	0
It	0	1	2	1	0	0	0	0	0	0	0	0	0	0	0	0
Lemon . . .	2	2	6	3	6	6	10	5	7	14	14	11	10	4	11	10
Like	0	1	0	2	0	0	0	0	0	0	0	0	0	0	0	0
Mad	4	2	3	2	2	1	2	1	7	6	7	7	8	7	8	6
Man	0	0	0	0	1	0	0	0	0	0	0	0	0	0	2	0

Response Word	4th M	4th F	5th M	5th F	6th M	6th F	7th M	7th F	8th M	8th F	10th M	10th F	12th M	12th F	College M	College F
						BITTER										
Mean . . .	0	2	1	4	1	3	1	3	0	2	2	5	3	1	1	3
Medicine .	0	2	1	1	2	1	0	0	0	2	0	1	0	0	0	1
Nice	2	0	0	1	0	1	0	0	1	0	0	0	1	0	0	0
Not good .	0	2	0	4	1	2	1	1	1	0	1	0	0	0	0	0
Not sweet .	2	0	0	0	0	1	0	1	0	1	0	0	0	0	0	0
Pepper . . .	0	0	1	2	0	0	0	0	0	0	0	0	1	0	0	0
Pickle . . .	0	0	0	1	1	0	1	0	0	0	1	0	0	0	1	2
Pickles . .	0	1	0	0	0	0	0	0	0	0	0	1	1	1	2	0
Pretty . . .	0	0	0	2	0	0	0	0	0	0	0	0	0	0	0	0
Rice	0	0	0	0	0	0	0	0	0	0	0	0	0	0	2	1
Rotten . . .	0	1	0	0	0	2	0	0	0	0	0	0	0	0	0	0
Rough . . .	0	0	0	0	0	0	0	0	0	0	0	2	0	0	1	0
Sad	0	0	0	1	1	0	0	0	1	0	0	0	0	2	0	2
Salt	0	1	0	0	0	0	1	1	2	0	1	1	0	0	3	0
School . . .	1	0	0	0	0	0	0	0	2	0	0	0	0	0	0	0
Sea	2	0	0	0	0	0	0	0	0	0	0	0	0	0	0	0
Shoot . . .	1	2	0	0	0	0	0	0	0	0	0	0	0	0	0	0
Soft	1	0	2	0	0	0	0	0	0	0	0	0	1	0	0	1
Sour	43	63	43	78	55	94	73	91	59	59	40	42	29	57	56	93
Stale	0	0	0	0	1	2	0	0	0	0	0	0	0	0	0	0
Strong . . .	0	2	2	4	1	5	1	1	0	1	0	0	3	0	0	2
Sweat . . .	1	1	2	0	1	1	0	0	1	0	1	2	1	1	0	2
Sweet . . .	33	38	29	43	37	41	76	75	84	85	96	94	107	103	277	267
Tart	0	0	0	0	0	0	0	0	0	0	0	2	1	0	2	0
Taste . . .	16	9	21	13	27	9	12	11	9	8	13	11	12	8	25	18
Tasteless .	0	0	0	1	0	0	0	1	1	0	1	2	0	1	0	0
Tasty . . .	1	2	0	0	0	1	0	1	0	0	0	0	0	0	0	1
Teacher . .	0	0	2	0	0	0	0	0	0	0	0	0	0	0	0	0
Terrible . .	4	3	3	1	1	0	1	0	1	0	3	2	1	1	0	0
Ugly	1	0	0	0	3	1	1	1	1	0	1	0	0	0	0	0
Unsweet . .	2	0	1	0	2	1	0	2	0	0	0	0	0	0	0	0
Vinegar . .	0	0	0	0	2	1	1	1	0	0	1	1	0	1	1	2
Whiskey . .	0	1	0	0	1	0	0	1	0	1	0	0	0	1	0	2
Wine	0	0	0	0	0	0	0	0	0	0	0	0	0	1	2	0
						21. **BLACK**										
Back	0	0	2	0	1	0	0	0	0	0	0	0	0	0	0	0
Bad	0	0	0	0	0	0	2	1	0	0	1	0	1	0	0	2
Big	0	0	0	0	0	0	0	0	0	0	0	2	0	0	0	0
Blue . . .	1	3	6	5	3	1	3	0	6	4	1	4	2	4	6	3
Board . . .	0	0	0	0	0	1	1	0	0	0	0	0	1	0	2	1
Boots . . .	0	0	2	0	0	0	0	0	0	0	0	0	0	0	0	0
Brown . . .	10	4	5	9	6	2	2	3	4	3	1	2	3	8	5	8
Button . . .	0	1	0	0	0	0	0	0	0	1	0	0	2	1	1	4
Car	0	0	1	0	2	0	1	0	2	0	5	1	6	2	5	0
Cat	8	6	11	9	8	4	6	7	3	10	7	6	9	6	6	13
Cloth . . .	0	1	0	0	0	0	0	0	1	0	0	0	1	0	3	0
Coal	0	0	0	0	0	1	0	0	0	3	1	1	0	0	0	0
Coat	0	0	3	4	1	1	1	1	0	3	2	1	0	2	6	7

Response Word	4th M	4th F	5th M	5th F	6th M	6th F	7th M	7th F	8th M	8th F	10th M	10th F	12th M	12th F	College M	College F
							BLACK									
Coffee ...	0	0	0	0	0	0	0	0	0	0	2	0	0	0	0	0
Cold	0	1	0	0	0	0	1	0	0	1	1	1	2	0	1	2
Color ...	30	25	22	27	36	25	11	20	16	12	9	7	11	6	12	5
Colors ...	1	2	0	0	0	1	0	0	0	0	0	0	0	0	0	0
Dark ...	91	87	95	86	89	111	78	67	47	56	51	46	28	32	57	37
Darkness .	2	1	0	0	0	1	0	0	0	0	1	1	2	0	0	1
Death ...	0	0	0	0	1	0	0	0	1	2	0	0	3	1	0	2
Deep ...	0	0	0	0	0	0	0	0	0	1	2	0	1	0	2	2
Dirt	0	0	0	0	0	0	0	2	1	0	0	1	1	1	0	0
Dirty ...	0	0	0	0	0	0	0	1	0	0	0	0	2	0	0	0
Dog	0	1	0	1	3	0	1	2	1	1	3	5	3	5	4	3
Dress ...	0	0	0	0	0	1	0	2	0	2	0	0	0	1	1	4
Funeral ..	0	0	0	0	0	0	0	0	0	0	0	2	0	0	4	0
Gray	0	0	0	1	0	1	1	0	1	0	0	1	1	2	0	0
Green ...	0	1	0	0	3	0	2	0	2	2	0	0	2	1	4	1
Hair	0	0	0	0	0	0	1	1	1	2	0	0	0	1	0	0
Hat	1	2	0	1	0	0	0	2	0	0	0	1	3	1	0	5
Horse ...	3	2	0	2	1	3	0	1	1	2	1	5	1	2	2	6
Light ...	6	6	6	5	9	6	7	9	7	9	8	4	9	3	6	4
Magic ...	0	0	0	0	0	0	0	0	0	0	0	0	0	0	2	0
Man	1	0	0	0	0	0	0	0	0	1	1	2	0	0	2	1
Negro ...	0	0	0	0	0	1	3	0	2	1	1	2	1	1	1	0
Night ...	7	10	9	8	7	9	13	6	15	10	20	24	15	11	19	31
Nothing ..	0	0	0	0	0	0	0	0	0	0	1	0	2	0	1	0
Pink	1	1	0	0	0	0	1	1	1	0	2	0	0	0	0	0
Pretty ...	0	0	0	0	0	2	0	0	0	0	0	0	0	0	0	0
Red	7	11	10	9	6	5	5	2	4	2	4	5	2	4	10	9
Room ...	0	1	0	0	0	0	0	0	0	0	0	0	1	0	2	2
Sad	0	0	0	0	0	0	0	0	0	0	0	0	0	0	2	2
Scarf ...	0	0	0	0	0	0	0	0	0	1	0	2	0	0	0	0
Scary ...	0	2	1	0	0	0	0	0	0	1	0	0	0	1	0	0
See	0	0	0	2	0	0	0	0	0	0	0	0	0	0	0	0
Sheep ...	0	0	0	0	0	0	0	0	0	0	1	0	3	1	7	7
Skirt ...	0	0	0	0	0	0	0	0	0	0	0	1	0	1	0	2
Sweater ..	0	0	0	0	0	0	0	0	0	0	1	1	0	0	0	2
Top	0	0	0	0	0	0	0	0	0	0	0	0	0	0	0	2
White ...	57	67	56	69	53	57	91	104	116	101	107	108	119	132	287	298
Witch ...	0	0	1	0	0	0	0	0	0	0	0	0	0	0	0	2
Yellow ..	5	2	0	0	1	2	0	2	0	1	0	0	0	0	0	2
						22.	**BLOSSOM**									
Apple ...	5	8	5	13	5	11	14	19	7	16	21	28	19	23	30	55
Apples ..	0	0	0	0	0	0	1	0	1	1	0	1	3	1	3	2
Apple tree .	0	1	1	0	0	1	0	1	1	0	0	0	0	2	2	7
Beautiful .	0	0	0	3	1	0	0	1	0	0	2	1	1	0	3	2
Beauty ..	0	0	0	0	0	0	0	0	0	0	2	0	1	0	2	3
Bloom ...	3	7	6	4	5	11	5	6	4	6	3	5	5	3	15	6
Blue	0	0	0	0	0	0	1	0	2	0	1	0	1	0	2	0
Bosom ..	0	0	0	0	0	0	0	0	0	0	0	0	2	0	1	0

Response Word	4th M	4th F	5th M	5th F	6th M	6th F	7th M	7th F	8th M	8th F	10th M	10th F	12th M	12th F	College M	College F

BLOSSOM

Response Word	4th M	4th F	5th M	5th F	6th M	6th F	7th M	7th F	8th M	8th F	10th M	10th F	12th M	12th F	College M	College F
Bright ...	0	0	0	0	0	0	0	0	0	0	1	0	0	1	2	0
Bud	3	5	2	6	2	1	3	6	5	1	4	4	2	3	4	1
Cherry...	0	1	1	1	0	0	3	2	3	2	1	1	2	4	2	4
Color....	0	0	0	0	0	0	0	0	0	0	0	0	0	0	2	0
Floor ...	0	0	0	2	1	2	0	0	0	0	0	0	0	0	0	1
Flour ...	0	0	3	0	3	0	0	0	0	0	0	0	0	0	3	0
Flower ..	1	2	4	2	1	3	3	7	3	8	2	2	5	1	10	1
Flowers ..	159	172	162	176	167	187	174	169	170	177	158	155	155	167	316	313
Food	2	0	0	0	2	0	0	0	0	0	1	0	0	0	0	0
Fragrance .	0	0	0	0	0	0	0	0	0	0	0	0	0	0	2	2
Fruit....	0	0	0	0	0	0	0	1	1	0	0	0	0	0	1	2
Full	0	0	0	0	0	0	0	0	0	0	0	0	2	0	0	0
Girl	1	0	0	0	2	0	2	0	4	2	0	0	1	1	1	0
Good	0	2	0	0	1	0	0	0	0	0	0	0	1	0	0	0
Hurry ...	2	0	0	0	0	0	0	0	0	0	0	0	0	0	0	0
It	2	0	0	0	0	0	0	0	0	0	0	0	0	0	0	0
Lilac ...	0	0	0	0	0	0	0	1	0	0	2	0	0	0	1	0
No	2	0	0	0	0	0	0	0	0	0	0	0	0	0	0	0
Orange ..	0	0	0	0	0	0	0	0	0	0	2	0	2	1	0	1
Petal....	0	0	0	0	0	0	0	2	0	1	0	0	0	0	0	1
Pink	0	0	1	3	2	4	0	1	0	0	2	4	0	5	2	10
Plant ...	2	1	4	1	4	0	0	1	3	1	1	0	3	0	2	0
Pretty ...	5	9	8	9	8	8	6	9	3	3	5	6	3	5	7	11
Red ...	0	1	2	1	2	1	2	0	3	0	3	1	1	1	3	2
Rose ...	3	5	6	3	5	3	3	4	3	1	5	5	6	3	9	6
Seeley ...	0	0	0	0	0	0	0	0	0	0	0	0	0	0	0	2
Smell ...	2	0	2	0	1	1	1	2	0	2	2	0	2	2	6	4
Soft	0	0	0	0	0	0	2	0	0	0	0	0	0	0	1	0
Spring ...	6	4	7	5	1	2	2	2	3	5	8	11	11	9	8	16
Stem	0	0	2	0	1	0	0	0	3	0	0	1	1	0	1	1
Summer ..	0	0	0	0	0	0	0	2	0	0	0	0	0	0	0	0
Sweet ...	0	1	0	1	1	0	1	0	0	0	3	3	1	0	6	5
Time ...	0	0	0	0	0	0	1	0	0	1	0	0	2	2	3	2
Tree	6	6	3	5	4	2	8	2	5	9	7	7	5	6	14	22
Trees ...	0	0	0	0	0	0	1	0	0	0	0	2	1	0	0	2
Tulip ...	2	1	0	0	0	0	0	1	0	0	0	1	0	0	0	0
White ...	0	0	1	0	1	0	0	0	1	1	0	0	0	1	3	1
Wood....	0	0	1	0	2	0	0	0	0	0	0	0	1	0	0	0
Yellow ...	1	1	0	0	1	0	0	0	1	0	0	1	1	0	2	0
Yes	2	0	0	0	0	0	0	0	0	0	0	0	0	0	0	0

23. BLUE

Response Word	4th M	4th F	5th M	5th F	6th M	6th F	7th M	7th F	8th M	8th F	10th M	10th F	12th M	12th F	College M	College F
Angel ...	0	0	1	0	0	1	1	0	0	1	0	0	2	1	6	3
Baby ...	0	0	0	0	0	0	0	2	0	0	0	0	0	2	0	4
Ball	0	0	0	0	0	0	0	0	0	0	0	0	0	0	0	2
Berry ...	0	0	0	0	0	0	0	0	0	1	0	0	1	0	3	1
Bird	0	1	0	3	1	1	2	4	2	4	2	2	3	6	13	9
Black ...	15	7	12	3	10	5	9	5	20	7	16	9	8	9	28	26
Blew	1	0	2	0	0	0	0	0	0	0	0	0	0	0	0	0

Response Word	4th		5th		6th		7th		8th		10th		12th		College	
	M	F	M	F	M	F	M	F	M	F	M	F	M	F	M	F

BLUE

Response Word	M	F	M	F	M	F	M	F	M	F	M	F	M	F	M	F
Bonnet . . .	0	0	0	0	0	0	0	0	0	1	1	0	2	2	1	1
Book	0	0	0	1	0	0	0	0	0	0	1	0	2	0	0	0
Boy	3	1	0	1	0	1	0	2	3	3	1	2	5	5	7	10
Bright . . .	3	3	2	1	4	2	2	0	1	2	1	1	0	1	1	0
Brown . . .	6	0	2	3	0	0	0	1	3	2	0	0	2	1	1	0
Car.	2	0	1	0	0	1	1	1	1	0	5	2	3	1	1	1
Clothes . .	0	0	0	0	0	0	0	0	0	2	0	1	0	0	1	1
Clothing . .	0	0	0	0	0	0	0	0	0	0	0	0	0	0	2	0
Coat	2	0	2	0	1	3	0	2	0	1	2	0	0	1	0	2
Cold	1	1	1	1	0	2	3	0	0	3	3	1	1	0	3	6
Color . . .	72	68	72	74	77	70	52	39	33	38	39	24	19	14	32	27
Colors . . .	1	3	1	0	3	0	0	0	0	0	0	0	0	0	0	0
Cool	0	0	0	0	0	0	1	1	0	4	0	1	1	2	0	11
Danube . . .	0	0	0	0	0	0	1	0	0	0	0	0	0	1	3	0
Dark	1	6	6	4	5	2	4	6	2	1	2	1	0	0	3	0
Dream . . .	0	0	0	0	0	0	0	0	0	0	0	0	0	0	0	2
Dress . . .	1	5	0	3	1	2	0	4	1	5	1	1	0	2	3	9
Earth . . .	0	0	0	0	0	0	0	0	0	0	1	0	3	0	1	0
Eyes	0	2	2	0	1	0	2	3	5	5	1	4	2	9	3	0
Favorite . .	0	0	0	1	0	1	0	0	0	0	0	3	1	1	0	0
Flag	1	0	0	0	1	1	0	0	0	0	4	1	0	2	1	3
Flower . . .	0	0	0	0	1	0	0	2	0	0	0	0	0	0	0	1
Girl	0	0	0	0	1	0	0	0	2	0	0	0	0	0	0	0
Gold	0	0	0	0	0	0	0	3	1	1	5	2	3	0	8	1
Good	0	0	0	0	0	2	0	0	0	0	0	1	0	0	0	0
Gray	8	0	6	1	4	0	0	0	4	1	7	3	8	2	6	6
Green . . .	11	14	11	13	23	15	18	16	23	24	21	26	34	22	49	57
Grey	0	0	0	0	2	0	1	0	2	0	0	0	0	3	4	0
Hat.	0	1	1	0	0	1	1	0	0	2	0	0	0	0	0	1
Heaven . .	0	0	0	0	0	0	0	0	0	0	0	0	0	0	0	2
House . . .	0	1	0	0	0	2	0	1	0	0	1	0	0	0	0	0
Hue	0	0	0	0	0	0	0	0	0	0	0	0	0	0	2	0
Ice	0	0	0	0	0	0	0	0	0	1	0	0	2	1	0	0
Jeans . . .	0	0	0	0	0	0	0	0	0	0	1	1	0	0	0	2
Lake	1	0	3	1	1	0	2	3	1	1	2	3	2	1	1	0
Light. . . .	2	0	3	4	2	1	6	4	1	2	0	2	0	4	0	1
Lonely . . .	0	0	0	0	0	0	0	0	0	0	0	0	0	1	0	2
Monday . .	0	0	0	0	0	0	0	1	0	0	0	0	0	0	2	0
Mood. . . .	0	0	0	0	0	0	0	0	0	1	0	2	1	0	1	2
Moody . . .	0	0	0	0	0	0	0	0	1	0	1	1	0	4	1	1
Moon . . .	0	0	0	0	0	0	0	6	2	0	0	0	4	4	1	2
Navy . . .	1	0	1	0	0	0	0	0	0	0	0	0	2	0	0	1
Nice	0	0	0	0	1	0	2	1	1	0	1	0	0	1	0	0
Ocean . . .	1	0	0	0	0	2	1	2	2	2	2	1	1	0	4	3
Orange . .	0	2	2	1	0	0	2	5	0	5	1	1	2	1	4	3
Paint . . .	0	0	0	0	0	2	1	0	0	0	0	0	1	0	0	0
Pencil . . .	0	2	0	0	0	0	0	0	0	0	0	0	0	0	0	0
Pink	2	2	4	7	1	7	3	6	4	4	2	0	1	6	0	1
Pretty . . .	5	7	4	9	2	11	1	2	1	2	1	6	3	1	4	9

Response Word	4th M	F	5th M	F	6th M	F	7th M	F	8th M	F	10th M	F	12th M	F	College M	F

BLUE

Response Word	4th M	F	5th M	F	6th M	F	7th M	F	8th M	F	10th M	F	12th M	F	College M	F
Purple . . .	0	0	1	2	1	1	1	3	0	0	2	1	0	0	1	0
Red	38	54	35	38	34	28	31	26	34	23	14	21	21	20	58	55
Sad.	2	1	0	1	0	4	2	6	2	4	3	11	5	9	3	10
Sea.	1	1	0	0	1	1	0	0	2	1	0	2	0	1	2	2
Shirt	1	0	0	1	0	0	0	0	2	0	1	3	0	0	3	0
Skirt	0	0	0	1	0	0	0	0	0	2	0	3	0	0	0	1
Sky.	19	25	30	32	32	42	42	42	43	49	60	71	53	59	128	124
Soft . . .	0	0	0	0	0	1	3	2	0	1	1	0	2	1	3	3
Sweater . .	0	1	0	0	0	1	0	0	0	0	0	0	0	0	2	3
Unhappy . .	0	0	0	0	0	0	0	2	0	1	0	2	0	0	1	1
Violet . . .	0	0	0	0	0	0	0	0	0	0	1	0	0	0	2	0
Water . . .	2	4	6	4	10	4	15	5	10	4	4	5	11	6	19	15
White . . .	8	5	11	13	9	5	11	7	5	8	12	5	13	14	17	20
Yellow . . .	18	15	8	11	10	13	7	11	14	7	3	6	5	7	15	16

24. BOY

Response Word	4th M	F	5th M	F	6th M	F	7th M	F	8th M	F	10th M	F	12th M	F	College M	F
Baby	1	0	1	1	0	0	0	0	0	0	0	0	0	0	2	2
Bad	0	2	0	1	0	2	1	0	1	0	0	2	1	2	2	1
Ball	1	0	0	3	2	1	0	0	0	0	1	0	0	0	0	1
Baseball . .	0	1	0	0	2	0	2	1	2	0	2	1	1	0	2	2
Big	2	3	1	0	1	1	0	1	0	1	1	1	1	1	0	0
Bike	0	0	0	1	2	0	0	1	1	0	0	0	0	0	0	1
Blue	0	0	0	0	0	0	0	0	0	1	0	0	1	1	3	1
Boys	2	0	0	0	0	0	2	0	1	0	1	1	0	0	0	0
Brave . . .	0	0	0	1	0	0	0	0	2	0	0	0	0	0	0	0
Brother . .	0	1	0	3	1	2	0	7	2	0	2	3	2	1	3	9
Brothers .	0	0	0	0	0	0	0	0	0	2	0	0	0	0	0	1
Car	1	0	0	0	0	0	0	0	0	2	0	0	4	1	0	2
Cars	0	0	0	0	0	0	0	0	0	0	0	2	0	1	0	0
Child . . .	8	8	9	3	5	5	1	1	2	0	0	1	0	3	4	6
Coat	1	0	0	0	0	0	0	3	0	0	0	0	1	0	0	0
Cute . . .	0	0	0	0	1	4	0	5	0	2	0	11	0	1	0	2
Date . . .	0	0	0	0	0	0	0	1	0	0	0	1	0	1	0	2
Dave . . .	0	0	0	0	0	0	0	0	0	0	0	3	0	0	0	0
Dirty . . .	0	2	0	1	0	0	0	0	0	0	1	0	1	0	0	3
Dog	1	0	0	2	1	0	1	0	0	1	1	1	3	0	3	7
Face . . .	1	0	0	0	0	0	0	0	1	0	0	0	0	0	0	2
Fishing . .	0	0	2	0	0	2	0	0	1	1	0	1	1	2	1	1
Friend . .	0	1	1	2	2	2	5	2	6	6	4	2	4	5	4	2
Fun	0	0	0	0	0	0	2	2	1	0	2	1	1	2	0	1
Girl	132	140	112	136	133	134	129	126	167	149	147	146	173	157	354	350
Girls . . .	0	0	1	1	2	1	2	0	3	2	1	0	2	1	1	0
Good . . .	3	0	3	1	1	0	3	1	0	0	2	1	0	0	1	1
Hair	0	5	0	1	0	1	0	1	0	1	0	1	0	0	0	0
Handsome .	0	1	0	2	2	4	1	5	1	4	0	3	1	3	0	4
Hat	0	0	0	4	1	0	0	0	0	1	1	0	1	0	0	1
Him	0	0	0	0	3	0	0	1	0	1	1	0	1	0	0	0
Human . .	4	3	4	1	5	1	1	0	1	0	2	0	0	0	1	0
Jeans . . .	0	0	0	3	0	0	0	1	0	1	1	0	0	0	1	0

Response Word	4th M	4th F	5th M	5th F	6th M	6th F	7th M	7th F	8th M	8th F	10th M	10th F	12th M	12th F	College M	College F
							BOY									
Kid	0	0	1	0	2	1	0	0	1	0	1	0	3	0	0	0
Lad	0	2	0	0	0	0	1	0	1	0	0	0	0	1	1	2
Like	0	0	0	0	0	0	0	0	0	0	0	2	0	0	0	0
Little	0	2	0	0	0	1	2	1	0	1	5	1	0	1	5	3
Love	0	0	1	1	0	0	1	2	0	5	0	1	0	1	1	2
Male	6	2	2	2	13	4	5	8	4	1	3	1	2	5	5	3
Man	18	21	24	20	19	25	26	26	10	16	20	9	7	8	27	25
Me	2	0	6	0	4	1	5	0	9	0	2	0	1	0	2	0
Mean	0	3	1	4	0	3	1	0	0	2	0	1	0	1	0	1
Men	1	0	2	0	1	0	0	0	1	0	0	0	0	1	0	0
Mischievous	0	0	0	0	0	1	0	0	0	1	0	0	0	0	0	2
Nice	3	2	2	2	3	2	2	3	1	3	0	3	0	1	0	1
Pants	0	5	1	1	0	2	0	1	1	1	1	0	0	0	2	1
People	5	5	3	0	1	0	0	0	0	0	0	0	0	0	0	0
Person	19	17	21	15	18	17	5	6	2	6	2	1	0	1	1	1
Play	0	1	1	0	2	2	0	0	1	0	1	2	2	2	4	3
Rough	0	1	1	2	0	0	3	0	0	2	0	0	0	0	1	0
Run	1	0	1	1	1	1	1	1	0	0	1	0	0	0	2	1
Scout	0	0	1	1	0	1	0	0	2	2	2	1	5	0	9	2
Sex	6	2	7	5	7	5	4	2	0	1	1	1	0	0	1	0
Shirt	0	1	0	1	0	0	1	3	0	2	0	1	1	2	1	1
Shoes	0	0	1	2	0	0	0	1	0	0	0	0	0	0	0	0
Shorts	0	0	0	0	1	0	0	0	0	1	0	2	0	0	1	0
Small	0	1	0	1	1	0	1	1	1	0	7	1	3	5	7	3
Smart	0	0	5	0	0	0	0	0	1	1	0	0	0	0	0	0
Son	1	0	0	4	0	0	1	0	0	0	1	1	0	0	0	1
Sports	0	0	0	0	0	0	0	0	2	1	3	3	3	1	1	0
Strong	1	0	1	2	0	0	4	1	3	0	3	1	0	0	0	2
Tall	0	1	1	1	0	3	1	1	1	0	2	4	1	3	1	0
Toy	0	0	1	0	0	0	0	0	0	0	0	0	0	0	0	2
Trouble	1	1	2	0	0	2	0	0	1	1	2	1	0	0	2	1
Wild	0	0	0	0	0	0	0	0	0	0	0	0	0	0	2	0
Young	0	0	1	2	0	1	6	3	0	1	3	3	3	3	5	8
							25. BREAD									
Bake	1	0	0	0	1	0	0	0	0	0	1	0	0	0	3	2
Baking	0	0	0	0	0	1	0	0	0	0	0	0	0	1	0	2
Banana	0	0	0	0	0	0	0	0	0	0	0	0	0	2	0	0
Box	0	0	3	1	3	0	0	0	2	0	1	0	0	0	2	1
Brown	1	1	0	0	0	2	0	0	0	0	0	0	0	1	2	2
Butter	35	51	26	49	38	54	51	64	62	96	58	112	73	116	197	269
Cake	0	1	0	1	0	0	1	0	0	0	2	0	2	0	2	0
Cheese	1	1	1	0	0	0	0	0	0	0	0	1	2	1	1	2
Crumb	2	1	2	0	0	0	1	1	2	1	2	0	0	0	0	2
Crumbs	1	0	0	0	1	0	0	3	0	1	1	1	1	0	1	0
Crust	0	4	0	0	2	2	1	2	0	1	1	0	1	2	3	3
Cut	2	1	0	0	0	0	0	0	0	0	0	0	0	0	0	0

Response Word	4th M	4th F	5th M	5th F	6th M	6th F	7th M	7th F	8th M	8th F	10th M	10th F	12th M	12th F	College M	College F
							BREAD									
Dark	1	0	0	0	0	0	0	2	0	0	3	1	0	0	0	0
Dough	1	0	1	1	0	3	3	3	2	5	4	1	4	0	4	5
Dry	0	0	0	0	0	0	0	0	0	0	0	1	0	1	0	2
Eat	59	61	57	60	51	45	38	26	27	28	30	16	28	18	71	26
Eating	1	5	1	0	3	2	0	1	0	1	3	0	1	0	1	2
Flour	5	3	5	1	3	3	12	3	11	7	4	4	2	2	6	5
Fluffy	0	0	0	0	0	0	0	0	0	0	0	0	0	0	2	0
Food	63	52	84	53	75	75	64	70	61	41	70	41	62	29	85	51
French	0	0	0	0	0	0	0	0	0	0	0	0	0	0	0	2
Fresh	0	0	0	0	0	1	0	0	1	0	0	1	3	3	2	1
Fruit	0	0	0	0	0	1	0	0	1	0	1	0	0	0	2	0
Good	3	5	7	5	5	8	7	6	0	7	5	5	1	2	5	9
Hair	0	0	0	0	2	0	0	0	1	0	0	0	0	0	0	0
Hard	0	0	3	0	0	1	2	2	0	2	1	1	0	0	0	1
Head	2	0	1	0	0	1	0	0	0	0	1	0	0	0	1	0
Homemade	0	0	0	0	0	0	0	0	0	0	0	0	0	1	0	2
Hunger	0	0	0	0	0	0	1	0	0	2	0	0	0	0	2	2
Hungry	1	1	0	1	1	1	0	1	1	3	0	2	1	0	0	1
Jam	1	6	0	4	2	6	2	3	2	2	1	5	1	7	4	15
Jelly	2	4	0	0	0	2	0	0	1	3	1	3	4	1	7	4
Juice	0	0	0	0	3	0	2	0	0	0	0	1	1	1	0	0
Knife	0	1	1	1	1	0	0	0	2	1	1	3	1	0	1	2
Life	0	0	0	0	1	0	0	0	0	1	0	0	0	1	3	0
Loaf	1	1	4	2	4	4	1	2	2	0	2	0	3	3	4	1
Lunch	1	1	0	0	0	0	2	0	0	0	0	0	2	0	0	0
Meat	1	1	1	2	2	0	5	1	1	0	3	0	2	0	4	1
Milk	4	13	11	16	3	7	6	2	5	10	3	3	7	7	6	6
Mold	0	0	0	0	0	0	0	0	1	0	4	1	1	1	1	2
Oven	0	0	0	0	0	2	0	0	0	0	0	0	0	0	0	0
Pan	0	0	0	0	1	0	1	0	0	0	0	0	0	0	1	2
Pastry	1	0	0	0	0	2	0	0	0	0	0	0	0	0	0	0
Peanut butter	0	0	2	1	2	0	1	1	1	0	0	0	0	0	0	1
Read	2	6	0	1	3	0	0	0	1	0	0	0	0	1	0	0
Red	1	0	3	1	0	0	0	0	1	1	0	0	0	0	0	1
Roll	1	1	0	1	0	0	2	1	1	0	0	0	1	0	0	0
Rolls	0	0	1	0	0	0	2	2	1	1	0	1	0	0	0	1
Rye	1	0	2	0	0	1	0	1	0	0	0	1	2	2	3	2
Sandwich	3	1	1	1	1	1	3	3	2	1	3	4	1	2	5	8
Smell	0	0	0	0	0	0	0	0	0	0	0	0	2	0	0	0
Soft	2	0	0	1	1	2	0	3	1	1	3	0	3	1	1	3
Starch	0	0	0	1	0	0	0	0	1	5	0	2	0	2	0	1
Taste	1	0	2	0	0	0	1	0	0	0	0	2	0	1	1	0
Toast	5	2	2	2	2	1	2	4	1	1	2	4	2	2	2	6
Water	7	4	4	11	3	4	7	11	16	12	5	9	6	10	10	10
Wheat	6	3	2	5	7	2	7	4	8	4	4	0	2	2	3	0
White	2	7	3	6	2	6	4	9	4	9	9	7	7	7	14	9
Wine	0	0	1	0	0	0	0	1	3	0	2	0	1	2	12	8
Winner	0	0	0	0	0	0	0	0	0	0	0	0	2	0	0	0
Yeast	0	0	1	2	1	0	3	6	0	3	1	4	3	3	4	2

Response Word	4th M	4th F	5th M	5th F	6th M	6th F	7th M	7th F	8th M	8th F	10th M	10th F	12th M	12th F	College M	College F
						26.	BROADER									
Across...	2	1	3	0	0	1	0	1	0	3	0	0	0	0	0	0
Around ..	1	0	0	1	0	2	1	1	0	0	2	0	0	1	0	0
Barn....	1	0	1	0	0	0	1	1	0	0	0	0	0	1	0	2
Beam ...	0	0	0	0	0	0	0	0	0	0	0	0	0	0	3	2
Bed	0	0	0	0	1	0	2	0	0	0	0	0	0	0	0	0
Big	1	3	7	9	4	0	4	7	4	5	8	5	5	6	8	3
Bigger...	0	1	2	5	1	2	8	5	6	7	12	4	4	0	3	5
Black ...	0	3	0	1	0	0	0	0	0	0	0	0	0	0	0	0
Board ...	7	7	6	7	6	7	4	4	4	7	3	4	0	5	4	2
Boarder ..	1	0	0	1	1	0	1	1	0	2	0	0	0	1	1	0
Boat	1	2	0	0	0	0	1	1	1	2	1	0	0	0	0	0
Border ..	2	1	0	1	3	0	3	0	0	0	0	0	0	0	2	0
Boundary .	0	3	5	2	3	4	8	3	3	2	0	0	0	0	0	0
Bridge...	6	7	0	5	0	4	0	1	2	0	1	0	1	0	0	0
Brighter ..	0	0	0	0	1	2	0	0	1	0	0	0	0	0	1	0
Broad ...	11	16	11	7	3	8	3	4	4	4	1	3	7	1	7	0
Broadest .	0	0	0	0	0	0	1	0	0	0	1	0	2	0	8	0
Brother ..	0	0	0	2	1	0	0	1	1	0	0	0	0	0	0	0
Built	0	0	0	0	0	0	0	0	0	0	0	0	2	0	0	0
Canada...	3	1	0	0	4	0	1	0	0	0	0	0	1	0	0	1
Chest ...	0	0	0	0	0	0	0	0	1	1	2	0	0	0	0	0
City	2	0	2	1	0	1	0	0	1	0	0	0	1	0	0	0
Come ...	0	0	0	0	2	0	0	0	0	0	0	0	0	0	0	0
Country ..	3	1	1	3	10	2	4	5	0	0	3	2	1	0	0	3
Cross ...	1	1	2	0	1	1	0	0	0	0	0	0	0	0	0	0
Darker ..	0	0	0	0	0	2	0	0	0	0	0	0	0	0	0	0
Day	0	1	0	2	0	1	1	0	0	0	0	0	0	0	0	0
Deeper ..	0	0	0	0	0	0	0	0	1	1	1	0	0	0	3	2
Dock....	1	3	0	0	0	1	0	0	0	0	0	0	0	0	0	0
Edge....	1	3	0	1	1	0	5	2	0	1	0	2	2	0	1	2
Education .	0	0	0	0	0	0	0	0	0	0	0	0	0	0	0	2
End	2	3	2	1	1	2	0	2	1	2	0	0	0	2	0	0
Expanse ..	0	0	0	0	0	0	0	0	0	0	1	0	0	1	2	0
Far	0	0	1	1	0	2	0	0	0	0	0	0	0	0	0	1
Farther ..	0	0	0	0	0	0	0	0	0	0	0	1	0	0	2	1
Fast	1	0	0	0	2	0	1	0	0	0	0	0	0	0	0	0
Fat	7	18	6	7	7	19	13	12	8	12	3	16	4	17	7	16
Fatter ...	3	0	2	7	2	2	5	6	0	6	2	1	1	1	6	5
Fence ...	0	1	0	0	0	0	0	0	0	0	0	0	0	0	0	2
Flat	1	0	0	1	0	1	1	2	0	0	2	2	1	0	1	0
Flatter...	0	0	0	0	0	0	0	0	2	0	3	2	0	0	0	2
Girl	0	0	0	1	1	0	3	0	9	4	16	1	8	0	15	1
Girls....	0	0	0	0	0	0	0	0	3	0	4	0	2	0	2	0
Good....	1	1	2	0	0	0	0	0	1	0	0	0	0	0	0	0
Horizon ..	0	0	0	0	0	0	1	0	0	1	0	0	1	0	2	0
Horizons .	0	0	0	0	0	0	0	2	0	0	0	0	1	0	1	0
House ...	5	3	2	3	2	4	1	2	0	5	1	2	0	2	1	0
Jump ...	0	2	1	0	0	0	0	0	0	0	0	0	0	0	2	1
Jumping ..	0	1	0	0	0	0	0	0	0	2	0	0	0	0	0	0

Response Word	4th M	4th F	5th M	5th F	6th M	6th F	7th M	7th F	8th M	8th F	10th M	10th F	12th M	12th F	College M	College F
								BROADER								
Knowledge .	0	0	0	0	0	0	0	0	0	0	0	0	0	1	2	1
Lake	4	2	0	2	1	0	0	0	0	1	0	2	1	1	1	0
Land	0	1	2	0	0	0	0	0	0	1	0	0	0	0	0	0
Large . . .	0	1	0	1	0	0	1	1	1	0	1	0	0	1	2	1
Larger . .	1	1	0	0	0	0	2	2	0	0	4	0	1	0	0	3
Light . . .	0	1	1	1	0	0	0	0	0	0	0	0	0	0	0	2
Limit . . .	0	0	1	0	0	2	0	0	0	0	0	0	0	0	0	0
Line	32	10	36	29	38	18	23	16	16	13	13	10	10	2	8	4
Live	0	1	1	1	0	0	0	1	0	0	1	1	0	2	0	0
Load . . .	0	0	0	0	0	0	0	2	1	0	0	0	0	0	0	0
Long . . .	1	2	0	4	1	1	2	1	1	0	1	1	0	0	3	2
Longer . .	0	1	1	0	2	3	4	3	0	0	2	1	0	0	1	2
Man	0	0	1	0	1	2	1	0	1	0	2	0	0	0	1	0
Margin . .	0	0	0	0	0	2	0	0	0	0	0	0	0	0	0	0
Me	1	1	2	0	0	1	0	0	0	0	0	0	0	0	0	0
Meaning . .	0	0	0	0	0	0	0	0	0	0	0	0	2	0	0	1
Mexico . .	6	5	2	6	2	3	6	2	1	1	2	3	3	1	1	2
Mind	0	0	0	0	0	0	1	1	0	1	3	2	3	2	1	1
Narrow . .	1	2	2	2	3	8	4	9	2	16	6	10	21	21	46	57
Narrower .	0	0	2	0	0	2	4	5	8	11	8	10	11	8	59	72
Ocean . . .	0	0	0	0	0	1	0	0	0	0	1	0	3	0	1	1
Of	1	0	0	0	0	0	0	0	0	0	0	0	0	0	2	0
Outline . .	0	2	0	0	0	0	0	0	0	0	1	0	0	0	0	1
Patrol . . .	0	0	0	0	1	0	1	0	0	0	0	0	0	0	2	0
People . . .	1	0	0	2	0	0	0	0	0	0	0	2	0	0	1	0
Person . .	0	1	1	2	1	2	0	3	0	0	0	3	0	1	1	0
Place . . .	3	2	3	0	1	0	1	0	0	1	0	0	0	0	0	0
Post	2	0	0	0	0	0	0	0	0	0	0	0	0	0	0	0
Pretty . . .	2	1	0	1	0	0	0	0	0	0	0	0	1	0	0	0
Rent	0	0	1	1	1	1	1	1	0	0	0	0	2	1	0	0
River . . .	1	4	1	2	0	1	3	2	2	3	5	3	2	2	3	2
Road	3	5	4	2	9	2	1	1	3	4	1	2	3	1	2	4
Room . . .	0	0	1	2	0	2	1	1	0	0	2	0	1	3	4	1
Roomer . .	0	0	0	0	0	3	2	0	0	1	0	0	1	0	1	1
Roomier .	0	0	0	0	0	0	0	0	0	0	0	0	0	0	2	0
Roommate .	0	0	0	0	0	0	0	2	0	0	1	1	0	0	0	0
Scope . . .	0	0	0	0	0	0	0	0	0	0	0	0	1	0	2	1
Sea	0	0	1	1	1	0	0	0	1	0	0	1	2	0	0	0
Sense . . .	0	0	0	0	0	0	0	0	0	0	1	1	4	2	4	4
Sew . . .	4	3	1	2	0	2	1	0	1	0	0	0	0	0	0	0
Ship	0	1	0	1	0	2	0	0	0	0	0	0	0	0	0	0
Short . . .	0	1	0	1	1	0	2	0	3	0	0	0	2	0	1	2
Shorter . .	0	1	0	0	0	0	4	3	8	5	0	2	1	2	8	12
Shoulder . .	1	0	0	5	1	3	0	0	2	3	0	3	3	0	5	1
Shoulders .	4	4	1	3	8	6	1	5	7	4	4	3	3	1	3	0
Skinnier . .	0	2	0	1	1	0	1	0	4	3	1	2	1	0	0	0
Skinny . . .	1	2	1	7	2	1	8	3	6	2	2	3	0	2	1	0
Slender . .	1	0	0	1	0	0	0	1	0	0	0	2	0	0	1	1
Slim	3	1	0	1	4	3	0	3	0	1	0	0	2	0	1	1
Slimmer . .	0	0	0	0	0	0	0	2	5	2	3	2	0	3	4	3

Response Word	4th M	F	5th M	F	6th M	F	7th M	F	8th M	F	10th M	F	12th M	F	College M	F
						BROADER										
Small . . .	0	1	0	0	2	1	1	0	1	0	0	0	0	0	0	0
Smaller . .	0	1	0	1	0	0	2	3	0	5	1	3	6	9	3	7
South . . .	0	0	0	2	0	0	0	1	0	1	0	0	0	0	0	0
South of the border. .	2	0	0	0	0	0	0	0	0	0	0	0	0	0	0	0
Square . .	0	2	0	0	1	0	0	0	0	0	0	0	0	0	0	0
Stacked . .	0	0	0	0	0	0	0	0	2	0	0	0	0	0	0	0
State	8	2	11	8	6	2	3	4	8	4	4	5	2	0	0	0
States . . .	1	0	2	0	3	0	0	1	1	1	0	1	0	1	0	0
Still	0	0	1	0	0	0	0	0	0	0	0	0	0	0	2	1
Straight . .	1	3	2	3	1	1	0	1	0	1	0	0	0	0	0	0
Street . . .	2	2	3	2	1	0	2	0	0	3	3	3	4	3	4	4
Stronger . .	0	0	0	0	0	2	0	0	0	0	0	0	0	0	0	0
Texas . . .	0	0	0	0	0	0	0	0	0	0	1	0	1	0	2	0
Than	1	0	0	0	2	0	2	1	3	1	4	4	5	5	9	7
The	0	0	2	0	2	0	0	0	0	0	0	0	0	0	0	0
Then . . .	1	2	1	0	1	0	0	0	1	0	0	0	0	0	1	0
Thicker . .	0	0	0	0	1	3	1	1	1	0	1	0	2	0	0	0
Thin	2	5	1	4	2	6	0	5	1	3	4	0	2	3	3	1
Thinner . .	1	4	2	2	1	4	2	7	13	12	3	6	6	3	6	12
Town. . . .	2	0	0	0	1	0	0	0	0	0	0	0	0	0	0	0
U.S.	0	0	0	0	0	0	0	0	0	0	2	0	0	0	0	0
View	0	0	0	0	0	0	0	0	0	0	0	0	3	2	2	4
Water . . .	0	4	0	2	1	1	0	0	0	0	1	0	1	1	0	0
What	0	0	2	0	0	0	0	0	1	0	0	0	0	0	0	0
Wide	8	10	6	7	18	16	20	26	15	30	24	26	24	37	62	67
Wider . . .	7	5	8	5	9	17	30	31	24	28	27	58	38	62	100	132
Width . . .	0	0	0	0	0	1	0	0	0	0	2	2	2	0	2	0
Woman . .	0	0	0	0	0	0	0	0	0	1	4	1	0	0	3	0
Women . .	0	0	0	1	0	0	0	0	2	0	1	0	2	0	3	0
Wood . . .	3	4	1	0	1	2	0	0	0	0	0	0	0	0	0	0
						27. BUT										
A	3	1	2	0	1	0	0	0	0	0	1	0	0	0	0	0
Again . . .	0	0	0	0	0	0	0	0	3	0	0	0	0	0	0	0
Also	4	1	0	3	5	1	4	4	3	3	3	8	9	8	6	6
Although .	0	0	0	0	1	2	3	2	1	4	2	1	3	1	7	7
Always . . .	0	0	0	0	0	0	0	0	0	0	1	0	0	2	2	1
And	1	1	2	3	2	8	2	4	8	11	8	15	18	26	35	65
Anyway . .	0	2	1	1	0	0	1	2	0	0	1	1	0	0	0	0
Are	0	0	0	0	0	0	0	0	0	0	0	0	1	0	2	0
As	0	0	1	2	0	0	0	0	0	1	1	0	0	0	0	2
Asked . . .	0	0	0	0	0	2	0	0	0	0	0	0	0	0	0	0
At	1	1	0	0	1	0	1	0	0	0	0	0	1	2	0	0
Back . . .	1	1	2	0	1	0	1	0	2	1	0	1	0	0	0	0
Bad	0	1	0	0	0	0	0	0	0	2	0	0	0	0	0	0
Bat	1	0	1	0	1	0	1	0	2	0	1	0	1	0	3	1
Be	1	4	0	2	0	0	0	0	0	1	0	0	1	1	1	3
Because . .	2	2	0	3	0	5	12	16	8	15	10	9	12	14	29	33

Response Word	4th M	4th F	5th M	5th F	6th M	6th F	7th M	7th F	8th M	8th F	10th M	10th F	12th M	12th F	College M	College F
							BUT									
Before . . .	0	0	0	0	0	1	0	0	0	2	0	0	0	1	0	1
Behind . .	0	1	0	0	1	0	1	2	2	0	0	0	0	0	0	0
Besides . .	0	0	0	0	0	0	0	1	0	0	1	0	2	4	1	0
Bet	0	0	0	0	0	0	1	0	1	0	0	1	0	0	2	0
Between . .	0	0	0	0	0	0	0	0	0	0	0	0	0	0	0	2
Big	2	0	0	1	1	0	0	0	0	0	1	0	0	0	0	0
Bit	0	0	1	0	1	2	0	2	2	0	3	0	1	1	2	1
Body . . .	0	2	0	0	0	1	0	0	1	0	0	0	0	0	0	0
Boy	3	1	1	0	0	0	0	0	1	0	0	0	0	0	0	1
Bright . . .	0	2	0	0	0	0	0	0	0	0	0	0	0	0	0	0
Butt	1	0	1	1	1	4	2	0	1	0	1	1	2	0	1	0
Butter . . .	4	3	4	3	1	1	8	3	4	0	2	3	2	1	2	0
Button . . .	1	0	0	0	0	2	0	0	1	1	0	0	0	0	0	1
Buy	0	0	0	0	1	0	0	0	1	2	1	0	0	0	0	0
By	1	0	1	0	3	0	0	4	2	6	4	0	0	1	1	2
Can	2	1	0	3	1	3	0	3	0	0	2	0	0	0	1	2
Can't . . .	0	2	1	1	0	1	0	1	0	1	1	1	1	2	1	2
Cigar. . . .	0	0	0	0	1	0	1	1	0	0	1	0	1	0	3	0
Cigarette .	0	0	0	1	0	2	1	0	2	1	4	1	1	1	2	0
Condition .	0	0	0	0	0	0	0	0	0	0	0	0	0	0	1	2
Conj	0	0	0	0	0	0	0	0	0	0	0	0	4	0	1	0
Conjunction	0	0	0	0	0	1	0	0	2	2	3	2	3	9	3	6
Could . . .	0	0	1	0	0	0	0	0	0	0	0	0	0	2	1	0
Cut	1	1	0	1	0	0	2	2	0	1	0	0	1	0	0	0
Dear . . .	0	0	0	0	0	0	0	0	0	0	2	0	0	0	1	0
Different .	0	0	0	0	0	0	1	0	0	0	3	0	1	0	0	0
Do	3	2	0	0	0	0	0	0	0	0	1	0	0	0	0	0
Don't . . .	2	1	0	1	0	3	0	3	0	0	0	0	1	1	2	2
Doubt . . .	0	0	0	0	0	0	0	0	0	0	0	0	1	1	2	1
Else	1	0	0	0	0	0	0	2	0	1	0	0	0	0	0	0
End	0	0	2	1	2	1	1	3	1	2	3	2	2	1	4	0
Except . .	1	0	1	0	2	1	2	8	5	5	1	10	5	9	4	2
Exception .	0	0	0	0	0	0	0	0	1	3	2	2	4	0	1	0
Excuse. . .	3	3	3	6	2	6	0	2	3	4	4	0	4	3	3	4
For	0	0	0	1	0	0	0	0	0	1	2	1	1	1	8	15
Gee	0	3	0	1	0	0	0	0	0	0	0	0	0	0	0	0
Go	3	1	0	0	1	2	2	1	2	1	0	1	1	0	0	0
Goat	3	2	0	5	0	8	0	0	0	2	0	2	2	0	0	0
Good . . .	3	0	1	0	2	0	1	0	0	0	0	0	0	0	0	0
Gun	0	0	0	0	0	0	1	0	3	0	1	0	2	0	1	0
Hard . . .	0	0	1	0	0	0	0	2	0	0	0	0	0	0	0	0
He	6	6	4	4	8	3	4	1	3	2	1	0	3	0	5	3
Hear . . .	0	0	0	0	2	0	0	0	0	0	0	0	0	0	0	0
Help . . .	0	2	0	1	0	0	1	0	0	0	0	0	0	0	0	0
Him	1	1	2	0	4	1	0	0	0	0	1	0	0	0	0	0
Hit	1	0	0	0	2	1	0	0	1	0	1	0	0	0	0	0
How	0	2	2	2	4	2	4	2	7	4	0	2	0	3	3	4
However .	0	0	1	0	1	0	1	4	3	7	1	7	5	4	19	23
Hut	2	2	2	0	2	1	1	0	1	0	0	0	0	0	0	0

54

Response Word	4th		5th		6th		7th		8th		10th		12th		College	
	M	F	M	F	M	F	M	F	M	F	M	F	M	F	M	F

BUT

Response Word	4th M	4th F	5th M	5th F	6th M	6th F	7th M	7th F	8th M	8th F	10th M	10th F	12th M	12th F	College M	College F
I	6	9	7	3	6	4	0	2	2	2	4	0	0	2	7	1
If	18	18	18	24	19	15	14	15	13	11	9	16	12	9	31	49
In	1	1	0	0	0	2	2	0	0	1	0	0	2	0	0	0
Instead . .	0	0	0	0	0	0	1	0	1	2	0	4	0	1	1	3
Is	0	4	5	2	3	1	2	2	2	0	2	1	1	0	2	4
It	16	12	22	11	15	9	12	3	8	4	2	2	3	4	6	3
Know . . .	1	1	0	0	4	0	0	0	0	0	0	0	0	0	0	0
Left	0	0	0	0	0	0	0	2	0	0	0	0	0	0	0	0
Let	0	0	1	2	1	0	0	2	0	0	0	0	0	1	0	1
Life	0	1	0	0	0	0	1	2	0	0	0	1	2	1	0	0
Lift	0	0	1	0	0	2	0	1	0	0	0	0	0	0	0	0
Little . . .	0	1	1	0	2	0	1	2	1	0	1	0	1	0	0	0
Man	0	1	0	0	2	0	0	0	1	0	0	0	0	0	0	0
Maybe . . .	1	5	1	3	1	2	3	4	5	5	4	8	3	3	4	7
Me	3	2	5	1	3	3	5	1	2	3	0	2	2	1	2	1
Mother . .	0	2	0	0	1	1	0	0	0	0	0	0	0	0	1	1
Mutt	0	1	2	0	0	0	1	1	1	0	0	0	0	0	1	0
My	2	1	0	2	0	0	2	0	0	1	0	0	0	0	0	0
Never . . .	0	0	0	0	0	0	2	4	2	3	5	4	3	7	5	6
No	7	8	11	9	3	8	9	10	4	7	2	12	5	8	8	14
Nor	0	0	0	0	0	0	0	1	0	4	0	1	1	0	2	1
Not	6	9	6	8	6	2	8	1	5	8	15	4	5	4	27	13
Nothing . .	2	0	0	0	0	0	0	0	3	0	1	0	0	0	1	1
Now	2	2	7	3	4	4	0	4	5	6	4	3	1	2	11	5
Nut	5	2	0	2	2	2	1	1	0	1	0	1	0	0	0	2
Object . . .	1	1	0	0	0	0	0	0	0	0	0	0	0	1	0	3
Objection .	0	0	0	0	0	0	0	1	0	0	0	0	0	2	0	1
Of	0	0	0	0	0	0	1	1	2	0	0	3	0	0	4	2
Of course .	0	0	0	0	0	0	0	1	0	0	0	1	1	0	4	1
Oh	3	2	0	1	1	0	2	4	0	0	0	0	0	0	0	0
Okay . . .	0	0	0	0	0	2	0	0	0	0	0	0	0	0	0	0
Only	0	3	0	0	0	4	0	0	0	2	2	2	2	0	1	2
Or	2	1	0	1	0	1	4	0	4	2	11	6	6	3	13	10
People . . .	0	0	0	0	0	0	0	0	0	3	0	0	0	0	0	0
Put	4	3	1	1	5	6	1	2	1	0	0	0	1	0	0	1
Question .	3	2	0	0	1	1	2	2	0	2	1	2	0	3	4	5
Really . . .	0	0	0	0	0	0	0	0	0	0	0	2	0	0	0	0
Rear	1	1	1	1	2	0	2	1	0	1	2	0	0	0	4	0
Reason . .	0	2	1	0	1	1	0	0	0	0	2	1	0	3	3	2
Rifle . . .	0	0	0	0	0	0	0	0	0	0	2	0	0	0	0	0
Seat	4	7	7	10	4	4	4	4	4	2	1	1	3	2	3	0
See	1	0	0	0	1	1	0	0	0	0	0	1	3	0	0	1
Set	1	0	0	0	2	1	0	0	1	0	1	0	1	0	0	0
She	0	0	1	1	0	2	0	0	0	1	2	0	2	0	2	1
Since . . .	0	0	0	0	0	0	0	0	0	0	0	3	0	1	0	2
Sit	0	0	0	3	3	1	1	2	0	0	2	0	1	0	2	0
Smell . . .	0	0	0	0	0	0	0	0	2	0	0	0	0	0	0	0
So	2	3	1	2	0	4	1	3	1	1	0	3	0	4	1	15

Response Word	4th M	4th F	5th M	5th F	6th M	6th F	7th M	7th F	8th M	8th F	10th M	10th F	12th M	12th F	College M	College F
							BUT									
Some . . .	0	0	2	1	1	1	0	0	0	0	0	1	0	0	0	0
Something .	0	4	2	1	0	1	1	1	0	0	0	0	0	0	0	0
Sometimes .	0	0	0	0	0	1	1	0	0	0	2	1	0	0	1	0
Still	0	0	0	0	0	0	1	2	3	0	0	1	0	0	2	2
Stool . . .	0	0	0	0	0	0	0	2	0	0	0	0	0	0	0	0
Stop	1	1	1	0	0	0	0	1	0	1	1	0	2	0	0	1
Stupid . .	0	0	0	0	0	0	0	0	0	2	0	0	0	0	0	0
Stutter . .	0	0	0	3	0	1	0	1	0	0	0	0	0	0	0	0
Take	0	0	0	2	0	0	0	0	0	0	1	0	1	0	0	0
Talk	1	1	0	0	2	0	0	0	0	0	0	0	0	0	0	0
Than	0	0	0	0	0	0	1	2	0	0	0	0	0	0	1	0
That	1	3	4	1	5	0	3	1	1	1	1	2	1	4	5	1
The	4	7	4	6	8	1	1	2	1	2	1	2	0	3	1	2
Them . . .	0	0	0	1	0	0	0	0	4	0	0	0	0	0	0	0
Then . . .	1	3	1	1	3	5	4	2	0	3	7	3	1	2	19	19
There . . .	4	1	0	2	0	2	0	1	1	0	1	0	1	0	0	0
Therefore .	0	0	0	0	0	0	0	0	0	2	0	0	1	0	2	2
They	4	5	4	1	6	1	5	0	3	5	2	2	4	2	4	3
Thing . . .	2	2	1	0	1	0	0	0	0	0	1	0	0	0	0	0
Think . . .	0	0	0	2	1	0	0	0	0	0	0	0	0	0	0	0
This	1	0	0	1	1	0	1	0	1	0	0	2	0	0	2	2
Though . .	0	0	1	0	0	1	0	1	1	1	0	0	2	0	2	0
To	0	1	1	2	1	2	1	0	1	0	0	0	0	0	1	1
Try	0	0	0	0	0	0	0	0	0	0	0	0	0	2	1	0
Until . . .	0	0	0	0	0	2	0	0	0	0	0	1	0	1	0	0
Wait . . .	0	0	0	0	0	3	0	0	0	0	3	0	2	2	1	1
Was	0	0	0	0	0	2	1	0	0	0	0	0	0	0	1	0
We	1	2	0	0	0	0	2	1	4	1	2	1	4	0	1	1
Well	0	0	2	2	0	2	1	2	0	1	0	0	0	1	1	1
What . . .	14	4	11	14	11	8	11	5	9	11	15	6	17	14	26	10
When . . .	1	3	0	5	3	4	2	4	9	4	2	2	1	4	4	6
Where . .	1	0	0	1	2	1	1	0	1	0	0	0	1	0	1	0
Who	0	1	3	1	0	2	0	0	2	1	1	0	0	1	0	1
Why	10	14	12	18	9	16	24	29	13	22	23	30	12	22	43	30
Will	0	0	0	0	0	0	2	1	2	1	0	0	2	0	0	0
With . . .	0	0	0	0	1	0	0	1	1	1	0	1	0	1	3	2
Word . . .	5	5	5	3	2	3	0	0	1	0	0	0	0	2	0	1
Yes	1	0	1	1	1	2	4	1	4	0	1	0	0	2	2	6
Yet	0	0	0	0	1	0	0	1	0	0	0	0	0	1	5	9
You	12	9	16	12	9	11	5	5	6	5	2	7	5	3	4	4
						28.	BUTTER									
Bad	0	0	0	0	0	0	1	0	2	0	1	0	0	0	0	0
Beard . . .	1	1	0	2	0	0	0	0	0	0	0	0	1	0	0	0
Better . . .	1	1	2	1	0	0	0	1	0	0	0	1	0	0	0	0
Bitter . . .	2	7	6	2	4	1	0	0	2	0	1	0	1	0	1	0
Boy	0	0	2	0	0	0	0	0	0	0	0	0	0	0	0	0
Bread . . .	62	92	66	99	82	96	82	96	109	109	103	143	126	133	268	307
Brickle . .	0	0	0	0	0	0	0	0	0	0	0	0	0	0	1	2
But	3	1	1	0	0	1	0	0	0	0	0	0	0	0	0	0

Response Word	4th M	4th F	5th M	5th F	6th M	6th F	7th M	7th F	8th M	8th F	10th M	10th F	12th M	12th F	College M	College F
							BUTTER									
Butterfly....	0	0	0	1	0	2	0	0	0	0	0	0	0	0	0	0
Cheese	0	4	3	4	4	2	5	6	6	3	3	3	2	0	8	0
Churn	0	0	2	1	0	0	1	0	2	0	0	0	1	0	0	1
Cow	1	1	1	2	5	2	9	6	7	5	5	1	3	1	4	2
Cream	12	6	6	7	8	12	8	5	7	14	13	9	11	6	5	6
Creamy	1	1	0	0	0	0	1	1	0	0	1	2	1	1	1	1
Cup	2	1	2	0	0	1	1	0	2	1	3	0	0	0	0	0
Dairy	0	0	2	2	0	0	1	2	0	0	0	0	0	0	1	0
Dish......	2	1	0	1	1	2	0	3	1	1	0	0	0	0	4	1
Eat	14	8	11	17	9	11	4	3	5	2	2	2	4	1	7	1
Eggs	0	0	0	0	0	0	0	0	0	0	0	0	1	2	1	2
Fat	3	3	4	0	2	2	11	8	5	9	9	6	6	8	9	12
Fattening ...	2	1	1	0	0	5	0	1	0	2	1	3	0	3	0	1
Fly	3	1	2	0	2	1	1	1	2	1	2	2	2	0	3	0
Food	24	20	40	19	24	19	15	15	10	7	10	5	14	6	13	6
Good	4	6	5	4	7	8	3	1	0	1	1	2	1	2	3	2
Grease	1	2	3	4	1	0	1	3	5	0	1	4	2	3	5	4
Greasy	0	2	1	2	0	2	2	5	0	2	3	0	3	2	6	6
Hard	1	0	0	0	0	1	0	0	0	0	0	0	0	3	0	1
Jam	1	2	1	0	1	0	0	0	1	0	0	0	0	1	1	4
Knife	9	5	6	3	7	2	6	2	3	6	12	8	17	5	15	11
Lard	0	0	1	0	2	0	2	0	2	1	1	0	0	2	2	1
Margarine ..	0	0	0	1	1	1	4	8	1	3	2	4	2	4	1	1
Melt	0	1	0	3	2	2	3	0	1	2	0	3	1	1	1	3
Mike	0	0	2	0	0	0	0	1	0	0	0	0	0	0	0	0
Milk	26	14	17	20	19	18	24	16	16	11	7	2	6	4	21	9
Oil	0	0	0	1	1	0	1	0	1	0	1	0	0	2	0	2
Oleo	1	0	1	0	0	0	3	2	1	0	0	0	0	4	2	2
Oleomargarine	0	0	0	0	0	0	0	2	0	0	0	0	0	0	0	0
Pad	0	0	0	0	0	0	0	0	0	0	0	0	0	0	0	2
Peanut	0	0	1	0	0	0	0	0	0	0	2	0	1	0	0	0
Rich	0	1	0	0	0	0	2	0	0	0	0	0	1	0	0	0
Rum	0	0	0	0	0	0	0	0	0	0	0	0	0	0	2	1
Salt	4	2	1	0	4	1	1	1	1	1	0	0	0	0	1	0
Slippery	0	0	0	2	0	0	3	0	2	0	0	1	0	1	0	0
Smooth	1	1	0	1	1	0	0	0	0	2	1	0	0	0	2	1
Soft	5	6	12	6	9	3	13	10	17	14	14	14	12	7	28	26
Sour	1	0	0	2	0	0	0	0	0	0	1	0	0	0	1	0
Spread	4	2	2	1	6	4	1	2	3	3	3	2	1	3	4	7
Sugar	0	0	0	0	2	0	0	0	1	0	0	1	0	0	0	1
Sweet	0	1	0	1	0	0	2	1	1	5	1	1	4	2	2	2
Toast	3	5	4	4	1	3	3	3	3	2	2	1	4	1	7	2
Up	0	0	0	0	0	0	0	0	0	0	0	0	2	0	1	0
Yellow	25	29	21	27	21	37	21	32	12	29	30	25	12	33	52	57
						29.	BUTTERFLY									
Air	0	1	2	1	4	0	0	2	1	0	0	1	0	0	1	0
Animal	14	8	9	14	12	12	11	6	9	4	7	6	4	3	5	8
Animals ...	1	4	0	0	1	0	1	0	0	1	1	0	0	0	0	0
Ant	0	0	0	2	1	2	0	1	1	4	1	2	1	1	1	2

Response Word	4th M	4th F	5th M	5th F	6th M	6th F	7th M	7th F	8th M	8th F	10th M	10th F	12th M	12th F	College M	College F
							BUTTERFLY									
Beautiful ...	3	7	1	10	2	10	2	3	4	5	7	9	5	8	11	4
Beauty ...	1	1	0	0	1	1	1	1	0	2	2	3	1	4	5	6
Bee	6	5	2	3	1	2	3	7	4	3	5	2	3	6	5	7
Bees	0	1	0	1	0	0	0	0	0	2	0	1	0	0	1	1
Bird	21	12	29	25	30	27	23	18	32	22	18	15	28	24	37	22
Bread	0	0	0	0	0	1	0	0	0	2	1	0	0	0	0	0
Bug	14	4	6	10	11	3	10	10	13	8	14	2	7	6	28	21
Bugs	2	0	0	0	0	2	0	1	0	0	0	1	0	0	1	0
Butter ...	6	11	8	6	6	4	7	3	3	0	6	1	2	1	1	1
Cat	0	0	0	1	2	0	0	1	1	0	0	0	2	0	1	0
Catch	2	1	1	2	0	0	1	0	1	1	0	1	1	0	1	2
Caterpillar .	0	4	5	2	3	1	4	5	6	3	2	5	7	6	3	10
Cocoon ...	1	2	0	1	1	2	0	1	4	6	5	5	2	3	8	13
Collecting ..	0	0	0	0	0	0	0	0	2	0	0	0	0	0	0	0
Collection ..	1	0	1	0	2	0	0	0	0	0	0	0	1	0	0	1
Color	0	1	1	0	0	1	2	1	2	1	5	0	0	5	10	14
Colorful ...	0	1	0	0	2	0	1	1	1	1	0	0	1	2	0	5
Colors	0	0	1	2	2	1	3	2	0	2	1	1	1	0	2	2
Creature ..	0	0	0	2	0	0	0	0	0	0	0	0	0	0	0	0
Delicate ...	0	0	0	0	0	0	0	0	1	0	0	2	0	0	1	3
Dog	0	0	0	0	1	1	1	1	2	0	2	0	1	0	1	0
Flew	0	0	0	0	0	0	0	0	0	0	1	0	2	0	1	0
Flies	1	2	1	2	1	2	0	1	0	1	0	0	1	1	2	1
Flight	0	0	0	0	0	0	0	0	0	0	1	1	1	0	2	1
Flower ...	3	2	1	4	4	2	2	4	4	8	3	2	4	5	10	15
Flowers ...	0	1	0	0	0	1	0	2	1	0	0	2	3	0	1	1
Fly	39	38	38	29	31	34	17	23	20	19	22	14	16	24	35	34
Flying	8	10	13	2	4	2	3	4	3	1	3	1	2	0	5	1
Garden ...	0	0	0	0	0	0	0	0	0	0	0	2	0	0	0	1
Grasshopper.	0	0	0	1	0	0	2	0	1	1	1	1	0	0	0	0
High	0	1	0	0	1	1	0	0	0	0	0	0	0	2	0	0
Insect	42	38	37	38	43	43	69	50	39	37	40	27	30	25	62	34
Insects ...	0	2	1	2	1	0	1	0	1	2	1	1	0	0	0	0
Lepidoptera .	0	0	0	0	0	0	0	0	0	0	0	0	0	0	2	0
Light.....	0	0	0	0	0	2	0	0	0	0	0	1	1	0	2	3
Madam ...	0	0	0	0	0	0	0	0	0	0	0	4	0	0	0	0
Monarch ...	2	1	5	2	3	2	8	6	7	4	8	5	7	1	8	8
Moth	14	11	10	10	4	4	24	16	24	14	16	20	29	8	71	53
Mouse	1	0	0	0	1	1	0	0	0	0	0	0	1	0	0	2
Mouth	1	1	3	4	1	1	1	0	1	0	2	1	1	0	0	0
Nature ...	0	0	0	0	2	1	1	1	0	0	0	1	1	0	5	3
Net	1	3	5	1	1	2	4	0	8	3	4	1	10	6	20	19
Orange ...	0	2	1	0	1	1	0	1	0	3	1	0	1	0	2	1
Outdoors....	0	0	0	0	1	0	0	0	0	0	1	1	1	0	0	2
Pretty	15	32	21	27	11	35	7	25	4	19	12	20	11	28	14	48
Quick	0	0	0	0	0	0	0	0	0	0	2	0	0	1	0	0
Red	0	0	1	0	0	0	0	0	1	0	0	0	1	0	2	0
Sky	0	0	0	0	0	1	0	0	0	0	0	3	0	1	0	1
Small	1	0	1	1	1	2	1	0	1	1	1	1	2	0	0	1

Response Word	4th M	4th F	5th M	5th F	6th M	6th F	7th M	7th F	8th M	8th F	10th M	10th F	12th M	12th F	College M	College F
BUTTERFLY																
Soft	2	0	0	0	2	0	0	1	0	1	0	0	1	0	1	1
Spider ...	1	1	1	0	1	0	1	0	1	0	0	0	0	0	2	0
Spring ...	0	1	0	3	2	1	1	0	0	2	2	6	3	6	2	4
Stomach ..	0	0	0	0	1	0	0	0	3	3	0	0	0	0	6	6
Summer ..	0	1	2	2	0	1	2	2	0	6	4	5	5	7	6	5
Sun	0	0	0	0	0	0	0	0	0	0	0	0	0	0	1	3
Tree	0	0	0	0	0	0	0	0	0	1	1	0	0	1	0	2
Warm ...	0	0	0	0	0	0	0	0	1	1	0	1	0	0	0	2
Wasp ...	1	0	0	0	0	0	0	0	0	0	0	0	1	0	1	3
White ...	0	0	1	1	0	0	0	0	0	0	0	0	0	2	0	1
Wing	4	2	0	1	6	2	3	2	2	4	4	5	5	2	16	19
Wings ...	7	16	9	12	11	14	8	18	4	14	14	16	12	11	23	23
Worm ...	0	1	2	0	3	1	3	3	5	2	1	2	3	3	5	5
Yellow ...	3	7	2	6	6	14	2	8	6	16	13	25	7	30	32	41
30. BUYING																
A	5	3	2	0	3	2	0	1	2	0	0	0	0	0	0	0
Books ...	0	1	0	0	0	0	1	0	0	0	0	0	1	1	4	2
Bought ..	10	18	20	21	14	36	31	49	35	41	16	17	21	21	29	30
Bread ...	1	2	2	0	0	0	0	0	0	0	2	0	0	1	3	1
Bring ...	0	0	0	0	0	0	0	0	0	1	0	2	0	0	0	0
Brought ..	0	1	0	0	2	1	1	1	0	3	1	0	0	0	0	0
But	3	0	0	0	3	1	1	0	0	1	0	0	0	0	0	0
Buy	33	47	24	31	17	27	17	13	17	3	5	6	4	1	3	4
Buyer ...	0	0	0	0	0	1	0	0	0	0	0	0	2	0	1	0
By	12	16	10	13	5	9	7	5	0	0	3	0	1	1	1	0
Candy ...	1	4	4	4	6	2	4	2	1	1	0	1	0	0	0	0
Car	1	0	0	0	1	1	0	1	2	2	10	2	9	2	7	5
Cars ...	0	0	0	0	0	0	1	1	2	1	6	3	9	1	6	1
Charge ..	0	0	0	0	0	0	0	0	0	0	0	0	1	2	0	0
Cigarettes .	0	0	0	0	0	0	0	0	0	0	2	1	0	0	0	1
Cloth ...	1	0	1	0	1	0	0	1	0	2	0	0	0	0	0	0
Clothes ..	1	3	3	5	3	5	5	15	5	20	11	27	16	24	33	46
Cloths ...	0	0	0	0	0	0	0	0	0	0	2	0	0	0	0	0
Coat	0	0	0	1	0	0	0	0	0	0	0	1	0	1	0	2
Come ...	0	0	0	0	0	2	0	0	0	0	0	0	0	0	0	0
Cost	1	1	0	1	2	0	0	0	0	0	0	0	0	0	1	0
Cow	3	1	0	0	0	0	0	0	0	0	0	0	0	0	0	0
Crying ..	1	0	1	1	2	0	1	0	0	0	0	0	0	0	2	1
Do	2	0	0	0	0	0	0	0	0	0	0	0	0	0	0	0
Dress ...	0	0	0	3	0	0	0	2	0	1	0	1	0	2	0	5
Food ...	5	13	8	9	9	9	6	12	5	9	7	11	10	9	9	9
For	0	0	3	0	1	0	0	0	0	0	0	0	0	0	1	0
From ...	0	0	0	0	2	0	0	0	0	2	0	0	0	0	0	0
Fruit ...	1	1	0	0	0	1	0	2	0	2	0	1	0	1	0	1
Get	0	1	2	1	2	2	0	1	1	1	1	1	0	1	1	2
Getting ..	0	2	1	3	1	0	0	0	1	1	0	2	1	2	5	2
Gift	0	2	1	1	2	1	0	0	0	0	0	1	0	1	0	1
Gifts ...	0	0	0	1	0	1	0	1	0	0	0	0	0	0	0	5

Response Word	4th		5th		6th		7th		8th		10th		12th		College	
	M	F	M	F	M	F	M	F	M	F	M	F	M	F	M	F

BUYING

Response Word	M	F	M	F	M	F	M	F	M	F	M	F	M	F	M	F
Good	2	0	2	0	2	0	0	0	0	0	0	0	0	0	0	0
Goods	0	0	1	0	2	0	2	0	3	1	4	3	3	6	6	5
Groceries . .	1	0	2	1	3	2	0	3	1	4	5	1	3	1	7	2
Guide	0	0	0	0	0	0	0	0	0	0	0	0	2	1	2	1
Hat	0	1	0	0	0	1	0	1	0	0	0	0	0	2	0	0
Hats	0	0	0	0	0	0	0	0	0	1	0	1	0	1	0	2
Here	2	2	0	0	4	0	0	0	2	1	2	1	1	1	5	3
Him	3	1	0	1	0	0	1	0	0	0	0	0	0	0	0	0
Home	0	0	0	0	1	0	0	0	0	1	1	0	0	1	2	0
House	0	0	0	0	0	2	1	1	0	1	2	4	2	3	5	6
I	2	1	0	0	1	0	0	0	0	0	0	0	0	0	0	0
It	7	1	11	5	9	3	7	1	4	0	2	1	3	0	9	0
Look	0	0	2	0	0	0	0	0	0	0	0	0	0	0	0	0
Me	1	3	3	1	3	0	4	2	1	1	0	2	0	1	1	0
Meat	0	0	0	0	0	1	0	1	2	0	0	0	0	0	0	0
Merchandise	1	0	0	0	0	1	1	0	0	1	1	0	0	0	3	0
Money	12	6	10	5	21	11	8	3	8	8	17	23	9	8	20	22
New	0	3	1	0	0	0	0	1	0	0	0	1	0	1	0	0
Now	3	0	0	0	0	0	0	0	1	0	0	0	1	0	2	0
One	1	0	2	0	0	0	1	0	1	0	0	0	0	0	1	0
Paper	0	0	0	0	2	0	0	0	0	0	0	0	0	0	0	0
Pay	0	1	0	1	1	2	2	2	1	0	1	0	2	1	2	0
Paying . . .	0	3	1	0	1	1	0	1	2	0	1	1	2	2	0	2
Price	0	0	0	1	0	0	0	0	0	0	0	0	0	1	0	2
Purchase . .	0	0	0	3	1	6	5	6	0	1	4	3	9	7	12	9
Purchasing .	0	0	0	1	0	1	2	1	2	3	1	1	1	2	4	10
Sale	0	2	0	1	1	0	2	0	2	0	0	1	0	0	1	1
Sell	12	18	21	23	12	18	22	15	19	18	17	16	15	9	29	20
Selling . . .	17	15	27	32	16	25	48	46	58	59	58	70	67	84	187	223
Shoes	1	1	1	2	2	2	1	5	2	2	2	1	1	2	7	7
Shopping . .	5	0	1	2	1	2	0	2	0	2	1	3	1	1	0	3
Sold	3	3	2	2	6	4	4	6	10	6	3	6	8	5	10	7
Some	1	2	1	1	3	0	0	0	2	1	1	0	0	2	0	0
Something . .	4	4	5	4	8	5	1	0	3	3	2	2	0	0	2	0
Spend	0	1	0	0	1	1	0	3	0	0	2	0	0	1	2	1
Spending . .	0	0	0	0	0	0	0	1	0	0	3	1	2	2	2	2
Steal	0	0	1	0	1	0	0	0	3	2	0	0	0	0	0	0
Stealing . . .	0	0	1	0	0	1	2	0	3	1	1	0	0	0	1	2
Store	10	26	9	23	10	22	16	12	5	12	6	5	1	6	7	12
Stores . . .	0	0	0	0	0	0	0	0	0	0	1	0	1	0	0	2
Story	0	0	2	0	0	0	0	1	0	0	0	0	0	0	0	0
Stuff	0	0	0	0	1	0	1	0	3	0	1	0	0	0	0	0
Take	1	1	2	1	0	1	0	2	0	0	0	0	0	0	0	0
Taking . . .	0	0	0	2	0	1	0	1	2	0	0	1	0	0	1	1
That	3	0	1	2	3	0	0	0	3	1	1	0	0	0	1	0
The	5	4	6	2	10	1	3	0	0	0	1	0	0	0	2	1
Them	0	1	0	0	3	1	1	0	0	1	1	2	0	0	1	0
Thing	2	0	3	0	4	0	0	0	0	0	0	0	3	0	0	0

Response Word	4th M	4th F	5th M	5th F	6th M	6th F	7th M	7th F	8th M	8th F	10th M	10th F	12th M	12th F	College M	College F
BUYING																
Things . . .	4	1	3	3	4	4	1	1	2	1	4	4	3	1	7	4
This	3	0	1	1	2	2	0	0	0	1	1	1	2	0	2	2
Toy	3	0	4	3	1	0	0	0	0	0	0	0	0	0	0	0
Toys . . .	5	2	2	0	1	3	1	0	1	2	0	1	1	0	0	0
Trying . .	2	0	0	0	1	1	2	0	1	0	0	0	0	0	0	0
What	1	0	0	0	3	1	1	0	4	0	1	0	0	1	2	0
You	3	3	6	1	1	1	1	1	1	0	0	0	0	1	0	0
31. BY																
A	0	0	0	0	3	0	0	0	0	0	0	0	0	0	1	1
Along . . .	0	0	0	1	0	0	0	2	2	2	0	2	1	0	2	5
Alongside .	0	0	0	0	0	0	1	0	1	0	0	1	1	1	0	2
Also . . .	0	0	0	0	0	0	0	0	0	0	0	0	0	2	0	0
And	5	5	6	4	4	2	2	5	3	3	8	4	2	3	18	10
And by . .	0	2	0	0	1	0	0	1	1	1	1	0	1	0	4	3
And large .	0	0	0	0	0	0	0	0	0	0	0	0	0	0	1	2
Around . .	0	0	0	0	0	0	0	1	0	0	0	0	3	0	0	0
Aside . . .	0	0	0	0	0	0	1	1	0	1	0	0	1	2	2	0
At	1	0	1	0	0	0	2	2	4	0	1	0	2	1	3	3
Author . .	1	1	0	1	3	4	0	3	0	2	0	1	2	2	0	2
Away . . .	1	2	0	1	1	3	0	2	1	4	1	4	1	2	5	2
Baby . . .	0	0	0	4	0	0	0	1	0	1	1	0	0	0	0	0
Be	4	5	4	3	2	3	3	4	3	3	2	2	0	12	3	4
Because . .	0	0	0	0	0	0	1	0	2	0	0	0	1	0	1	3
Beside . .	1	0	1	2	0	0	8	4	3	7	9	5	5	9	9	13
Besides .	0	0	0	0	0	0	0	0	0	1	0	1	0	2	0	1
Bit	0	0	2	0	0	0	1	0	0	0	0	0	0	0	0	0
Bought . .	0	0	0	0	0	0	1	2	6	0	0	0	0	0	1	0
Boy	0	2	0	0	1	0	0	0	0	0	1	1	0	0	1	1
Brook . . .	0	0	0	0	0	1	0	0	0	0	0	0	0	0	2	0
Bus	1	1	0	0	0	1	0	1	0	0	1	0	0	0	0	2
But	1	1	0	1	0	0	1	0	3	6	0	0	1	0	1	0
Buy	19	24	12	29	16	29	23	26	17	13	13	8	9	11	10	6
By	2	0	0	1	4	4	0	0	0	0	0	0	0	0	0	8
By by . .	0	0	2	1	0	0	1	0	0	0	0	0	1	0	0	0
Bye	3	3	1	9	2	7	5	6	2	4	1	9	10	6	8	7
Bye bye . .	0	1	0	4	0	0	0	1	0	0	0	0	0	0	0	0
Car	1	0	2	1	0	0	0	1	0	0	2	1	1	2	0	2
Close . . .	2	3	7	1	3	4	1	4	0	2	2	2	2	0	10	7
Come . . .	3	4	1	1	2	1	0	0	2	3	0	2	0	1	1	0
Corner . .	0	0	0	0	0	0	0	0	0	0	1	0	0	0	1	3
Do	0	0	2	0	0	0	0	0	0	0	0	0	0	0	0	0
Door . . .	0	1	0	0	0	0	0	0	0	0	0	2	0	1	1	3
Far	2	1	3	1	0	7	2	1	4	0	1	2	1	0	0	3
Fast . . .	0	0	1	0	0	0	1	0	2	0	0	1	0	0	0	0
Food . . .	0	0	0	1	1	0	0	0	2	0	0	0	1	0	1	0
For	0	1	0	0	0	0	0	0	0	1	1	1	1	0	8	10

Response Word	4th		5th		6th		7th		8th		10th		12th		College	
	M	F	M	F	M	F	M	F	M	F	M	F	M	F	M	F
							BY									
From ...	0	0	1	1	0	0	1	2	2	2	0	2	0	2	3	7
Get	0	0	1	1	0	1	0	0	0	0	1	0	0	0	2	0
Go	5	13	8	7	9	10	1	5	3	5	7	4	4	9	6	8
Going ...	0	6	4	1	5	4	1	0	1	1	3	1	0	2	1	1
Golly ...	1	0	0	0	1	0	0	0	2	0	0	0	0	0	0	0
Gone ...	1	1	1	3	1	2	1	2	3	2	4	0	6	2	7	3
Good ...	10	9	10	13	9	10	5	5	1	4	6	2	6	4	6	1
Goodby ..	7	0	3	4	0	0	4	2	0	4	0	1	0	0	0	0
Goodbye ..	0	7	0	1	4	7	0	0	4	0	4	0	4	1	2	0
Hand	0	0	0	1	0	0	0	1	0	1	2	0	2	0	0	1
Hear ...	0	0	0	0	2	0	1	0	0	0	0	0	0	0	0	1
Hello ...	3	5	0	5	1	4	1	9	3	1	2	3	1	2	3	1
Her	0	0	0	1	0	0	0	0	0	1	0	0	6	0	2	0
Here ...	3	5	3	1	2	7	2	3	2	3	2	6	0	2	4	3
Hi	5	3	5	7	1	5	5	5	4	5	2	5	1	0	0	0
High	1	1	0	0	0	0	0	0	2	0	0	0	0	0	1	0
Him ...	3	3	8	4	5	1	1	2	3	1	7	3	4	7	6	1
Himself ..	0	0	0	0	0	0	0	0	0	0	0	0	0	0	3	0
His	0	2	1	0	2	0	0	0	1	0	0	0	0	0	1	0
Home ...	1	2	0	1	1	0	1	0	0	4	0	0	0	0	1	1
House ...	1	2	1	0	0	0	1	1	1	0	1	0	1	1	0	3
How	1	0	0	0	0	1	1	2	0	0	0	0	1	1	1	0
In	0	0	0	0	0	3	0	1	0	0	0	0	1	0	0	2
Is	0	1	1	0	0	1	0	0	2	1	0	0	2	0	0	1
It	4	2	8	6	6	2	5	1	5	2	4	4	4	0	8	6
Itself ...	0	0	0	0	0	0	0	0	0	0	1	0	0	0	2	2
Lake ...	0	0	0	0	0	1	0	0	0	1	2	3	0	1	0	2
Large ...	0	0	0	0	0	0	0	0	0	1	0	0	0	1	2	2
Leave ...	0	1	0	2	2	0	0	1	0	0	5	2	1	2	2	0
Love	0	0	0	0	0	0	0	0	0	0	0	0	3	0	0	0
Me	15	11	17	12	16	13	13	8	17	14	8	16	8	11	13	22
Money ...	0	1	3	1	2	0	1	0	0	0	1	1	1	0	0	0
My ...	1	4	8	3	1	4	4	2	2	1	1	0	1	0	2	1
Myself ..	0	1	0	0	2	0	0	1	0	1	0	0	0	2	1	0
Near ...	4	3	3	7	5	2	22	16	6	13	13	21	8	21	55	79
Next	1	0	1	1	1	0	5	2	1	1	4	3	0	1	8	2
Next to ..	0	0	0	0	0	0	1	1	1	0	0	1	1	0	2	1
Night ...	0	4	2	0	0	0	0	0	0	0	0	0	0	0	0	0
Not	0	0	0	0	2	1	0	0	0	0	0	0	0	0	1	1
Now	4	4	4	4	7	9	7	11	8	16	13	16	20	16	46	54
Of	0	0	0	0	0	0	0	0	0	0	0	0	0	0	2	1
On	0	0	0	0	0	0	0	0	0	0	0	2	0	1	0	0
Pass ...	3	3	2	1	4	2	2	1	1	1	3	2	7	3	3	4
Past	4	1	0	0	3	2	1	4	0	3	1	1	2	0	4	1
People ..	1	2	1	0	0	1	1	0	0	1	0	0	0	0	0	0
Place ...	0	1	0	0	1	2	0	0	0	2	2	0	1	0	1	0
Preposition	0	0	0	0	0	0	0	0	0	1	0	1	0	0	4	3
River ...	0	0	0	0	0	2	2	2	0	0	1	4	2	5	2	8
Road ...	0	0	0	1	0	0	0	0	1	0	3	1	3	1	2	1

Response Word	4th M	4th F	5th M	5th F	6th M	6th F	7th M	7th F	8th M	8th F	10th M	10th F	12th M	12th F	College M	College F
							BY									
Sea	0	0	0	0	0	0	0	0	0	2	1	1	1	3	4	5
See	0	2	3	5	0	1	0	3	0	1	2	1	0	1	0	0
Sell	0	0	0	0	1	2	2	0	4	2	5	2	2	1	1	1
Shore	0	0	0	0	0	0	0	1	0	0	0	1	0	1	0	2
Side	3	0	0	0	0	0	2	3	0	0	3	2	2	1	6	2
Sigh	2	0	1	1	0	0	0	1	1	0	1	1	0	0	1	0
Sit	0	0	2	0	1	1	1	1	0	0	0	0	0	0	0	1
So	3	0	1	1	1	0	0	0	0	0	0	0	0	0	0	1
So long	0	0	2	2	0	0	0	3	3	2	0	0	1	2	0	0
Something	0	1	2	1	2	1	0	0	0	0	0	0	0	1	0	0
Stand	11	11	6	8	8	6	9	5	9	7	4	4	12	9	18	11
Standards	0	0	0	0	0	0	0	0	0	0	0	0	0	0	0	2
Stander	0	0	3	1	3	0	7	1	4	2	3	3	1	2	7	5
Stood	0	0	1	0	0	2	0	0	1	0	0	0	0	0	0	0
Store	2	0	1	4	1	4	1	0	1	0	1	1	0	1	1	0
Stream	0	0	0	0	1	2	0	0	0	0	0	0	0	0	0	4
Street	0	0	0	0	0	0	0	0	0	2	0	1	0	2	1	1
That	3	1	2	2	1	0	4	0	1	0	1	4	0	0	2	1
The	21	14	21	11	29	9	15	10	13	9	14	7	16	8	40	26
Them	0	0	1	1	1	1	0	1	3	0	0	1	0	3	1	2
Then	1	2	2	0	2	2	4	1	2	2	2	0	1	2	8	5
There	3	2	2	3	4	2	2	1	3	7	1	1	1	0	1	10
The way	0	0	0	0	0	1	1	0	1	2	2	2	1	0	2	3
They	0	1	2	0	0	1	0	0	0	0	1	0	0	0	0	0
This	1	2	1	2	1	1	0	1	1	0	0	0	1	1	3	1
Through	0	0	0	0	0	0	0	1	0	0	0	1	1	0	2	1
Time	1	4	2	2	0	1	0	4	1	1	1	0	1	1	1	3
To	1	1	0	1	0	3	2	1	0	0	0	2	1	0	2	0
Toys	2	0	0	0	0	0	0	0	0	0	0	0	0	0	0	0
Train	0	0	0	0	0	0	0	0	0	0	0	0	0	0	1	2
Trip	0	0	0	0	0	1	0	1	0	0	0	2	0	0	0	0
Us	0	0	0	0	0	1	2	0	1	0	2	0	1	3	1	2
Walk	0	2	0	0	0	0	0	0	0	0	0	0	0	0	0	0
Wave	0	0	0	1	2	3	0	1	0	0	0	3	0	0	0	1
Way	3	0	0	3	3	1	1	3	2	2	9	5	9	7	14	11
Ways	0	0	0	0	0	0	0	0	0	1	0	0	0	0	2	0
Went	1	1	1	4	1	0	2	3	1	1	1	1	2	1	0	0
What	0	0	1	0	1	0	1	1	3	5	4	1	5	3	7	6
When	1	0	0	0	0	1	0	0	1	0	1	0	0	0	2	0
Where	2	0	0	0	1	1	1	1	2	1	2	2	3	2	4	5
Which	0	0	0	0	0	0	0	0	0	0	0	2	1	3	1	1
Who	1	1	2	1	0	2	0	0	1	1	1	1	2	1	2	1
Whom	0	0	0	0	1	0	0	0	0	1	0	0	0	0	2	5
Why	3	3	1	1	4	2	1	2	3	0	0	1	0	0	1	1
With	2	0	0	0	1	1	2	2	2	1	3	6	1	3	8	6
Word	2	1	1	2	1	1	1	0	0	0	0	0	0	0	1	0
You	8	11	7	2	3	5	6	6	4	13	5	7	7	8	8	16

Response Word	4th M	4th F	5th M	5th F	6th M	6th F	7th M	7th F	8th M	8th F	10th M	10th F	12th M	12th F	College M	College F
						32.	CABBAGE									
Age	1	3	0	3	2	0	0	0	0	0	0	0	0	0	0	0
Apple ...	2	1	1	0	1	0	1	0	1	0	0	0	0	0	0	0
Awful ...	0	0	0	0	1	0	1	1	0	1	0	2	0	1	0	1
Bad	0	0	1	0	0	0	0	1	2	0	2	1	2	0	1	1
Bag	2	1	2	0	1	1	0	1	1	0	1	0	0	0	0	0
Boiled ...	0	0	0	0	0	0	0	0	1	0	1	1	1	0	2	4
Cab	0	4	3	1	0	2	1	0	1	0	0	0	0	0	0	0
Can	0	3	0	3	0	2	1	0	0	0	2	0	2	0	0	0
Carrot ..	7	6	3	3	3	2	1	5	4	2	3	0	3	1	2	0
Carrots ..	2	1	0	0	0	0	1	0	0	2	0	3	0	0	1	5
Celery ..	0	1	0	0	0	0	1	1	2	0	1	0	2	1	0	0
Coleslaw .	0	0	0	0	0	0	0	2	0	1	2	2	2	3	1	10
Collector .	0	0	0	0	0	0	0	0	0	0	2	0	0	0	0	0
Cook	0	0	0	0	1	0	0	0	0	0	0	0	0	0	0	2
Cooked ..	0	0	0	0	0	0	0	0	0	1	0	0	0	0	0	2
Corn	1	0	3	1	4	1	2	0	2	0	0	0	1	0	2	3
Corn beef .	0	0	0	0	0	0	1	0	1	0	1	0	0	0	3	4
Corned beef	0	0	0	0	0	0	0	0	0	0	0	1	0	0	0	3
Dark ...	0	0	0	0	0	0	0	0	0	0	0	0	2	0	0	0
Dislike ..	0	0	0	0	0	0	0	0	0	0	1	0	0	0	2	0
Eat	19	20	25	33	27	17	24	8	10	11	9	8	10	6	35	10
Eating ...	2	2	2	1	3	1	1	0	0	0	0	1	2	2	0	2
Field ...	0	0	0	0	1	0	0	0	0	0	0	1	1	2	0	2
Food ...	55	59	64	44	56	45	35	29	32	31	42	29	37	42	65	50
Fruit ...	7	4	2	5	6	3	10	5	12	2	7	3	6	1	8	1
Garbage ..	0	0	0	0	1	0	1	0	2	3	1	1	3	0	2	0
Garden ..	1	6	3	6	3	2	3	2	3	3	4	6	5	2	15	9
Good ...	3	5	7	9	3	5	1	4	0	1	5	3	1	2	1	3
Green ...	3	9	1	9	8	12	5	22	3	12	11	17	12	24	28	52
Hard ...	1	0	0	0	0	0	0	1	0	0	0	0	2	0	0	0
Head ...	5	3	4	8	6	4	4	2	9	9	10	8	17	8	42	29
Ick	1	0	0	0	1	1	0	1	3	1	2	1	0	0	0	0
Icky	2	0	0	0	0	0	0	0	0	0	0	0	0	0	0	0
Ish	0	0	0	0	0	2	1	1	4	5	4	5	2	5	3	1
King	0	0	0	0	0	0	0	0	0	0	0	0	0	0	2	0
Leaf	0	0	1	1	0	2	0	1	1	0	2	1	2	1	13	8
Leaves ..	0	1	0	0	0	0	0	1	0	2	0	0	1	1	5	1
Letter ...	2	0	0	0	0	0	0	0	0	0	0	0	0	0	0	0
Lettuce ..	38	51	42	50	25	50	54	48	53	56	51	48	42	37	66	74
Man	1	0	0	0	1	0	0	1	0	0	2	1	0	0	1	0
Moth ...	0	0	0	0	0	0	0	0	1	0	0	0	0	0	2	0
Patch ...	0	0	1	0	0	0	1	0	0	2	0	3	1	1	5	2
Plant ...	11	3	5	2	4	1	4	2	1	0	3	0	3	0	4	2
Rabbit ..	6	7	2	5	5	4	2	5	5	4	1	3	8	4	6	9
Rabbits ..	0	1	2	0	0	0	1	1	1	0	0	0	1	0	0	0
Radish ..	0	0	0	0	0	0	0	0	0	0	0	0	1	0	0	2
Round ...	0	0	1	0	2	2	1	2	1	0	2	1	4	2	3	5
Salad ...	0	2	5	2	4	8	6	7	12	13	8	16	12	18	22	50
Sauerkraut.	0	0	0	0	0	1	1	1	2	1	1	4	1	3	11	10

Response Word	4th M	4th F	5th M	5th F	6th M	6th F	7th M	7th F	8th M	8th F	10th M	10th F	12th M	12th F	College M	College F
CABBAGE																
Slaw	0	1	0	0	0	0	0	2	1	0	3	5	1	2	5	9
Slow	0	0	0	0	0	0	0	0	0	0	0	0	0	0	1	3
Smell . . .	0	0	1	0	1	2	4	1	1	4	6	6	3	7	6	14
Soup	1	0	2	0	2	1	1	1	0	1	0	0	0	0	2	2
Sour	0	0	1	0	1	1	2	2	2	1	2	1	0	2	4	1
Stew	0	0	0	0	0	0	0	0	0	1	0	1	0	3	6	4
Stink	0	0	0	0	0	0	1	0	0	0	1	1	0	0	2	0
Taste . . .	0	0	0	0	0	0	0	0	0	0	2	1	1	0	2	0
Tasteless .	0	0	0	0	0	0	0	0	0	0	0	0	1	3	0	0
Terrible .	0	0	0	1	0	0	0	1	0	2	0	0	0	0	0	0
Tomato . .	0	0	1	2	1	0	1	0	1	0	0	0	1	0	1	2
Trash . . .	0	0	1	0	1	1	1	2	1	1	1	0	2	2	1	0
Ugh	0	0	0	0	0	0	0	1	1	1	1	0	0	1	2	1
Vegetable .	34	36	24	39	38	50	53	68	34	59	32	48	34	45	72	65
Vegetables .	5	1	3	2	3	2	1	4	1	3	1	1	0	0	0	1
33. CARPET																
Bag	0	0	1	0	0	0	0	0	3	0	4	0	1	0	4	1
Bagger. . . .	0	0	0	0	0	0	0	0	1	0	1	0	2	0	4	1
Big	0	1	2	0	1	0	0	1	0	0	1	0	0	1	2	1
Blue	0	0	0	2	1	0	1	3	0	1	1	1	0	2	2	2
Brown . . .	1	1	0	2	0	2	0	0	0	0	0	1	1	1	4	5
Car.	3	3	6	2	1	1	1	0	0	0	0	0	0	0	0	0
Cat	2	1	0	0	1	0	0	0	0	0	0	0	0	1	0	0
Chair . . .	1	0	1	1	0	0	1	0	0	0	0	0	0	0	2	2
Clean . . .	0	0	0	2	2	1	0	0	0	0	0	2	0	1	0	1
Cloth . . .	1	0	1	1	2	0	0	0	1	0	0	0	0	0	2	2
Cover . . .	0	0	0	0	0	0	0	1	1	0	0	1	2	0	1	0
Covering .	0	0	0	0	2	0	1	0	1	0	0	0	1	0	1	0
Deep . . .	0	0	0	0	0	0	0	0	1	1	0	2	1	1	5	5
Dirt	0	1	1	0	0	0	2	1	0	0	1	0	1	0	1	0
Dog	0	3	2	2	2	1	2	1	0	0	0	0	0	0	0	0
Drapes . .	0	0	0	0	0	0	0	0	0	0	0	0	0	0	0	2
Feet	1	1	0	1	0	0	0	0	2	0	0	0	0	0	0	1
Flood . . .	0	0	0	0	0	1	0	0	0	2	0	0	0	0	0	0
Floor . . .	27	34	29	24	22	32	33	36	31	36	42	36	34	32	80	73
Fluffy . . .	0	0	0	0	0	0	0	0	0	1	2	0	0	0	0	0
Fly	4	3	2	3	0	0	0	1	1	1	0	0	0	0	0	0
Flying . . .	1	1	2	2	5	3	2	1	3	1	0	0	0	2	0	0
Foot	0	0	0	0	0	0	0	0	0	0	0	0	2	0	3	0
Furniture .	1	0	0	0	0	0	0	0	1	0	0	2	0	1	1	0
Gray . . .	0	1	0	1	1	0	0	1	0	0	1	1	2	4	2	2
Green . .	0	0	0	1	1	0	2	2	0	2	0	2	1	4	1	5
Hair	0	0	0	0	2	0	0	0	0	0	0	0	0	0	0	0
Hall	0	0	0	0	0	0	0	0	0	0	0	0	0	0	2	0
Home . . .	0	0	0	0	1	0	0	0	2	0	0	1	2	0	2	0
House . . .	1	1	1	2	1	2	2	1	5	2	4	2	5	4	4	5
Living room	0	2	0	3	0	0	0	2	1	3	2	5	1	0	1	4
Long	0	0	0	0	2	1	1	0	0	0	0	0	0	0	0	0

Response Word	4th M	4th F	5th M	5th F	6th M	6th F	7th M	7th F	8th M	8th F	10th M	10th F	12th M	12th F	College M	College F
						CARPET										
Luxury	0	0	0	0	0	0	0	0	0	0	0	0	1	0	0	2
Magic	0	2	1	0	2	0	0	0	0	1	0	0	0	0	1	0
Man	0	2	0	2	0	0	1	0	0	0	0	0	0	0	0	0
Mat	1	2	1	0	1	0	0	0	1	2	0	0	0	0	1	0
Money	0	1	1	0	0	0	0	0	0	0	1	0	0	0	2	0
New	0	0	1	1	0	0	0	0	0	0	1	1	0	2	0	0
Nice	1	0	0	1	1	1	0	0	0	0	2	1	0	0	1	0
Old	0	0	0	0	0	0	0	0	0	0	0	0	0	0	2	0
Pet	7	2	5	2	1	1	0	3	0	0	1	0	0	0	0	0
Plush	0	0	0	0	0	0	0	0	0	1	0	2	0	0	1	3
Quiet	0	0	0	0	0	0	0	0	0	0	1	0	0	0	0	2
Rag	3	2	6	3	4	2	1	0	2	0	0	0	0	0	0	0
Red	6	6	3	3	5	1	4	6	10	12	5	13	4	8	24	36
Rich	0	0	0	0	0	0	0	0	0	1	0	1	0	0	2	1
Room	0	0	0	0	4	2	0	2	0	2	3	1	1	2	3	8
Rose	0	0	0	0	0	0	0	0	0	0	0	0	0	0	1	2
Rough	3	2	3	1	3	1	0	0	1	1	0	1	0	0	2	2
Rug	130	137	132	130	128	139	130	115	128	107	94	97	117	99	160	151
Rugs	1	1	2	0	0	0	0	2	1	1	0	0	0	0	0	0
Smooth	1	0	2	2	2	1	2	2	2	3	2	1	1	1	2	2
Soft	10	8	13	22	14	27	32	40	17	38	44	53	33	49	103	103
Stand	0	1	0	0	0	0	0	0	0	0	1	0	0	0	2	0
Sweep	0	1	0	0	1	1	0	1	1	2	1	0	1	0	1	1
Sweeper	2	0	2	1	0	2	1	1	0	2	4	2	7	1	7	5
Tack	0	0	1	0	0	0	1	0	0	0	1	0	1	0	4	1
Thick	0	0	0	0	1	0	1	2	1	3	1	4	4	5	7	10
Vacuum	1	1	0	0	0	0	1	1	1	0	0	1	0	0	0	2
Walk	2	2	4	5	6	6	5	7	2	3	9	7	4	10	17	14
Wall	2	2	0	0	1	0	1	0	0	0	0	0	1	0	0	0
Warm	0	0	0	0	0	1	0	0	1	0	1	0	2	2	1	3
Wool	0	0	0	1	0	0	0	0	0	1	2	4	3	2	6	2
Worn	0	0	0	0	0	0	0	0	0	0	0	0	0	1	0	2
					34.	CARRY										
A	1	1	1	0	2	1	0	0	0	2	1	0	0	0	1	0
Air	0	2	0	0	0	0	0	0	0	0	0	0	0	0	0	0
Along	2	0	0	0	0	0	0	0	0	0	0	0	0	1	0	0
Arm	1	0	0	1	0	0	0	0	0	0	0	0	0	0	2	2
Arms	0	1	0	1	1	3	0	0	2	0	0	2	0	1	1	1
Away	1	1	4	4	1	0	1	2	1	0	1	2	2	0	2	3
Baby	2	7	5	5	2	7	1	5	0	11	7	2	3	7	2	5
Back	2	2	1	2	4	2	1	0	3	0	1	1	1	1	2	0
Bad	2	0	0	0	0	0	0	0	0	0	0	1	0	0	0	0
Bag	2	11	0	5	2	6	2	3	2	5	3	4	5	4	6	12
Baggage	0	0	0	0	0	0	0	0	0	0	0	0	0	0	2	0
Bags	0	0	0	2	1	0	0	0	0	1	1	1	0	0	2	3
Ball	0	0	0	0	2	0	0	0	2	1	0	0	0	0	2	2
Basket	4	2	0	3	1	1	3	3	3	0	0	0	0	0	3	9
Bear	0	0	0	0	0	0	0	0	0	0	0	0	0	4	0	2

Response Word	4th M	4th F	5th M	5th F	6th M	6th F	7th M	7th F	8th M	8th F	10th M	10th F	12th M	12th F	College M	College F
							CARRY									
Berry ...	0	0	0	3	0	0	0	1	0	0	0	1	3	0	0	0
Big	2	1	0	0	0	0	0	0	0	0	0	0	0	0	0	0
Book ...	0	1	1	0	0	2	0	1	0	0	1	1	1	2	2	3
Books ...	0	1	0	3	2	1	1	3	0	4	2	7	2	4	10	15
Box	1	5	2	2	2	0	1	0	2	0	2	3	1	2	3	5
Boxes ...	2	1	0	1	0	0	0	0	0	0	0	1	0	0	0	0
Boy	3	0	0	0	0	0	0	0	2	0	3	3	2	0	1	1
Bring ...	5	5	5	7	5	5	10	7	13	5	18	14	9	10	10	24
Bucket ...	0	0	0	0	0	1	0	1	0	0	1	1	1	0	2	0
Bundle ..	0	0	0	0	0	1	0	0	0	0	0	1	1	4	0	3
Burden ..	0	0	0	0	3	3	2	0	1	1	0	1	2	1	2	4
Bury ...	0	0	0	0	0	0	0	0	0	0	0	0	1	0	2	2
Buy	0	0	0	0	1	0	0	2	0	4	0	0	0	2	2	6
Car	7	3	6	3	2	0	4	2	1	0	0	0	0	0	0	0
Care ...	1	1	2	0	0	1	0	0	0	0	1	0	0	0	0	0
Carried ..	1	2	1	2	1	1	2	2	3	0	2	0	2	0	1	0
Carrying .	3	0	0	1	0	0	0	1	0	1	0	0	0	0	0	0
Cart	0	0	0	0	0	1	0	0	0	2	1	1	1	2	0	5
Cash ...	0	0	0	0	0	0	0	1	0	0	0	1	0	0	2	0
Cover ...	0	0	0	0	0	0	0	1	0	0	0	0	0	2	0	0
Cry	3	3	2	1	4	1	1	4	1	0	0	0	1	1	0	0
Dog	1	0	3	0	0	0	0	1	1	1	1	1	0	1	0	3
Door ...	2	0	0	0	0	0	0	0	0	0	0	0	0	0	0	0
Down ...	1	2	2	1	0	0	0	0	1	1	0	0	0	1	0	1
Drag ...	0	2	2	1	0	2	1	2	1	2	0	1	2	1	1	5
Drop ...	8	5	6	5	8	6	11	9	19	18	5	6	4	8	16	11
Fairy ...	1	0	0	0	0	0	0	1	0	0	0	1	1	1	2	0
Far	0	0	0	0	3	0	1	0	0	0	0	0	1	0	1	1
Fast	0	1	1	1	2	0	1	1	0	0	1	0	0	0	1	1
Flower ..	0	0	0	2	0	0	0	0	0	0	0	0	0	0	0	0
Food ...	0	2	2	2	1	0	1	0	0	1	0	1	1	0	2	1
Girl	0	0	0	0	0	0	2	0	0	0	2	1	2	0	0	1
Go	1	1	3	0	0	1	0	0	0	1	0	0	0	0	1	1
Groceries .	0	1	2	1	2	0	2	3	2	1	5	5	4	5	5	3
Handle ..	0	1	0	1	0	1	2	0	0	0	0	1	1	2	0	3
Happy ...	2	0	1	0	0	0	1	0	0	0	0	0	0	0	0	0
Hard ...	5	3	3	3	3	3	0	0	0	1	0	0	1	0	1	0
Harry ...	2	3	0	0	0	1	0	0	0	1	0	1	3	0	3	1
Haul	1	1	1	0	1	0	5	2	0	0	4	0	2	3	11	5
Have	0	2	1	0	1	1	0	0	2	0	0	0	1	0	0	0
Heave ...	1	0	0	0	1	0	0	0	0	0	1	0	0	0	2	0
Heavy ...	33	37	28	30	21	26	24	24	16	21	16	27	15	19	21	19
Help	0	1	0	0	0	1	3	1	0	1	1	0	1	1	1	0
Her	1	1	0	1	1	0	0	0	0	0	1	0	3	0	1	1
Him	0	0	0	1	2	1	0	0	0	0	0	0	0	0	2	0
Hold	26	39	28	56	28	55	26	46	24	32	25	22	21	22	47	55
Home ...	0	0	4	1	1	4	1	1	3	4	2	2	3	4	10	10
Horse ...	0	0	0	0	0	0	1	0	0	0	0	0	0	0	3	0
How	0	2	0	0	0	0	0	0	0	0	0	0	0	0	0	0

Response Word	4th M	4th F	5th M	5th F	6th M	6th F	7th M	7th F	8th M	8th F	10th M	10th F	12th M	12th F	College M	College F
								CARRY								
Hurry . . .	0	1	2	0	1	0	0	0	0	0	0	1	0	0	0	0
It	0	1	3	4	2	0	1	2	0	2	0	2	0	4	4	1
Lay	0	0	0	0	0	0	0	0	2	0	0	1	2	1	1	0
Leave . . .	0	0	0	1	0	0	0	2	1	0	0	0	0	0	2	0
Left	0	0	2	1	2	3	1	0	1	2	0	1	0	1	0	0
Lift	17	11	21	16	30	19	23	20	24	28	34	34	37	27	39	38
Light . . .	1	0	0	0	0	0	0	0	0	2	0	0	0	0	1	0
Load . . .	15	9	7	15	19	15	14	16	8	9	10	10	11	9	25	19
Lot	0	0	0	2	0	0	0	0	0	0	0	0	0	0	0	0
Lug	0	0	1	0	2	3	2	2	1	1	2	4	2	1	6	3
Mail	0	2	0	0	0	1	0	0	0	0	0	0	0	0	0	1
Man	3	0	0	0	0	0	0	0	0	0	1	0	0	0	0	1
Marry . . .	2	1	2	1	1	0	3	1	1	1	0	0	0	3	2	4
Mary . . .	0	1	3	2	0	0	0	1	1	0	0	0	0	1	0	0
Me	4	9	9	4	14	6	7	4	5	8	4	5	7	5	3	5
Money . . .	1	0	0	0	0	0	0	0	0	1	0	2	0	0	0	0
Move . . .	1	1	1	0	3	1	3	0	1	1	1	1	2	0	5	1
My	0	0	1	0	2	0	0	0	0	0	0	0	0	0	0	0
No	1	0	0	0	2	1	0	0	0	0	0	0	0	0	0	0
Nurse . . .	0	0	0	0	0	0	0	0	0	0	0	1	1	1	4	0
Off	1	0	0	1	0	0	2	0	1	0	0	0	0	0	4	0
On	3	2	5	3	4	3	7	8	7	3	15	11	19	9	52	42
One	0	2	0	0	0	1	0	0	0	0	0	0	0	0	1	0
Out	2	1	0	0	3	1	3	0	12	4	5	0	8	4	16	6
Over . . .	3	3	1	0	1	3	2	1	4	1	2	1	6	1	25	14
Pack . . .	0	0	2	0	0	0	0	0	1	0	0	0	0	0	0	3
Package . .	2	3	2	1	0	1	4	3	1	4	3	5	1	5	3	15
Packages .	0	1	0	0	0	1	0	0	0	2	1	1	0	0	0	1
Pail	0	0	0	0	0	0	0	0	0	3	0	1	0	1	3	2
Paper . . .	0	0	0	0	0	0	0	0	0	0	0	2	0	0	1	3
Pick	0	0	3	1	0	0	1	2	0	1	0	1	0	2	0	1
Pickup . . .	0	0	1	0	0	1	0	0	1	0	1	0	0	0	2	1
Port	0	0	0	0	0	0	0	0	2	0	0	1	0	0	1	2
Portable . .	0	0	0	0	0	0	0	0	0	0	0	1	1	0	3	0
Pull	0	1	2	2	0	1	3	2	3	1	0	0	1	4	2	1
Purse . . .	0	0	0	0	0	1	0	2	0	3	0	0	0	2	0	4
Push . . .	0	0	0	0	0	1	2	0	4	0	1	1	0	2	0	2
Ride	1	2	1	0	0	1	0	1	1	1	1	0	1	1	4	1
Run	1	1	0	1	2	0	1	0	1	2	1	0	1	0	2	3
Shoulder . .	0	0	0	0	0	0	0	0	0	0	1	0	0	1	2	0
Some . . .	1	0	1	0	2	0	0	0	0	0	0	0	0	0	0	0
Something .	2	1	3	2	0	2	1	0	1	3	0	1	0	0	0	1
Suitcase . .	1	0	0	0	0	1	2	0	0	1	0	0	0	0	0	1
Take	1	3	3	3	6	3	3	8	3	4	2	5	5	6	5	11
Tarry . . .	0	0	0	0	0	0	1	0	0	0	0	0	0	0	2	1
That	1	0	0	0	0	0	1	2	1	0	0	1	1	0	3	0
The	1	1	2	0	1	0	0	0	1	1	0	0	1	0	2	1
Them . . .	0	0	0	1	0	1	0	1	0	0	1	0	0	0	2	0
Things . .	2	0	0	0	0	1	2	1	1	0	0	2	0	1	2	0

Response Word	4th		5th		6th		7th		8th		10th		12th		College	
	M	F	M	F	M	F	M	F	M	F	M	F	M	F	M	F

CARRY

Response Word	4th M	4th F	5th M	5th F	6th M	6th F	7th M	7th F	8th M	8th F	10th M	10th F	12th M	12th F	College M	College F
This	0	0	0	0	1	0	2	2	0	0	1	0	1	0	1	0
Throw	0	0	0	0	1	1	0	1	3	0	1	2	1	1	5	6
To	0	0	0	0	1	0	0	0	0	0	0	0	0	2	0	2
Tote	0	1	0	0	1	1	1	1	0	2	1	0	0	1	7	10
Transport	1	0	0	0	0	0	1	0	0	2	1	0	3	2	2	2
Transportation	0	0	2	0	0	0	0	0	0	0	0	0	0	0	0	0
Walk	4	5	2	5	2	5	2	8	4	3	3	5	0	1	5	1
Water	1	1	1	0	2	4	1	2	3	3	10	9	3	8	11	10
Wear	0	0	0	0	0	0	0	0	0	0	1	0	0	2	3	1
Weight	0	0	1	0	1	0	2	1	3	0	4	0	4	0	3	0
What	0	0	0	0	0	0	1	0	3	2	1	0	0	1	1	1
With	0	0	1	1	0	1	1	0	1	0	0	1	1	2	1	0
Work	0	0	2	1	1	0	1	0	1	0	2	0	0	0	5	1
You	0	0	2	1	0	0	0	0	1	0	0	0	0	0	1	1

35. CARS

Response Word	4th M	4th F	5th M	5th F	6th M	6th F	7th M	7th F	8th M	8th F	10th M	10th F	12th M	12th F	College M	College F
Accident	0	0	1	0	0	0	0	0	0	0	0	1	0	0	0	2
Auto	2	4	3	1	11	13	9	7	5	5	4	4	8	2	17	15
Automobile	12	6	9	7	10	12	10	5	3	4	1	2	4	2	4	1
Automobiles	2	2	5	8	6	6	4	4	4	5	2	5	2	0	6	8
Autos	0	0	1	4	5	6	6	6	4	3	6	3	7	3	26	20
Bars	0	0	0	0	0	0	1	1	0	0	0	0	1	1	3	0
Be	2	0	0	0	0	0	0	0	0	0	0	0	0	0	0	0
Bicycle	0	0	2	3	0	1	0	0	1	0	0	0	1	1	0	0
Bicycles	0	0	0	1	0	1	0	0	0	1	0	0	1	1	2	3
Big	2	0	3	4	1	2	0	1	2	1	1	2	2	1	2	3
Bike	0	0	1	2	2	1	3	2	5	2	0	0	0	3	4	2
Bikes	1	2	1	4	1	0	6	4	4	7	3	3	1	9	6	6
Black	0	0	0	0	0	2	0	0	0	0	0	2	1	1	0	1
Blue	1	0	1	1	1	2	2	1	0	5	4	5	1	8	2	6
Boat	0	1	0	0	0	1	0	0	0	1	0	0	1	0	3	0
Boats	0	1	1	0	3	2	3	1	3	2	5	3	7	6	13	7
Boys	0	0	0	0	1	0	0	1	0	18	0	16	2	16	0	9
Bugs	0	0	0	0	2	0	0	0	0	0	0	0	0	0	0	0
Buick	0	0	1	0	0	0	0	0	0	2	0	0	1	0	1	3
Bus	21	18	22	21	12	11	24	15	9	11	9	16	5	1	20	13
Buses	13	12	5	7	3	13	17	20	15	14	11	10	8	8	19	26
Busy	0	2	0	0	0	0	0	0	0	0	0	0	0	0	0	0
Buy	1	0	1	0	0	0	1	0	0	0	0	0	0	0	1	4
Cadillac	0	0	0	0	0	0	0	1	1	2	0	0	0	0	0	0
Car	7	4	9	2	1	2	4	0	0	0	0	0	0	1	1	0
Cat	1	0	0	0	2	0	0	0	1	0	0	0	0	0	0	0
Cats	0	0	1	0	1	0	0	1	1	0	1	0	0	0	2	1
Chev	0	0	0	0	0	0	1	0	1	0	2	1	4	2	2	3
Chevrolet	0	0	0	1	0	0	0	2	1	1	3	0	1	0	3	5
Chevy	0	1	0	0	0	1	1	1	1	1	3	1	0	0	1	3
Color	0	0	1	0	0	1	0	1	0	1	1	0	0	1	2	1
Corvette	0	0	0	0	0	0	1	0	2	0	0	0	3	0	2	0
Crash	1	0	0	0	2	0	1	0	1	1	1	1	0	0	0	1

Response Word	4th		5th		6th		7th		8th		10th		12th		College	
	M	F	M	F	M	F	M	F	M	F	M	F	M	F	M	F

CARS

Response Word	M	F	M	F	M	F	M	F	M	F	M	F	M	F	M	F
Custom	0	0	0	0	0	0	2	0	1	0	1	0	1	0	0	0
Dogs	1	0	1	1	1	0	0	0	0	3	0	0	0	2	2	1
Door	1	3	0	0	0	0	0	1	0	0	0	1	1	2	4	5
Doors	1	1	1	0	0	1	1	1	0	0	0	1	2	2	12	13
Drive	7	11	12	11	6	6	6	13	5	9	10	6	7	8	17	18
Drivers	0	0	1	0	0	0	0	0	0	0	0	3	1	0	0	3
Driving	0	1	0	0	2	0	1	1	0	0	1	0	2	1	0	0
Engine	1	1	0	1	0	1	2	1	4	0	2	0	1	0	2	0
Engines	0	0	1	0	0	0	1	2	0	0	1	0	2	0	0	0
Fast	3	9	6	7	9	5	4	0	5	5	21	12	14	11	11	13
Ford	1	1	3	1	4	4	7	4	8	4	5	3	6	8	13	17
Fords	0	0	0	0	1	1	0	0	0	0	0	1	0	1	3	5
Foreign	0	0	0	0	1	0	0	0	0	0	0	2	0	0	2	0
Fun	0	0	2	1	0	1	0	0	0	0	2	3	2	0	0	0
Garage	0	0	0	0	0	0	0	0	0	0	1	0	2	0	0	0
Gas	1	0	4	2	0	0	4	0	6	3	3	0	1	3	1	3
Girls	0	0	0	0	0	0	1	0	0	0	4	0	4	0	0	0
Go	5	7	6	8	14	1	5	1	5	5	1	2	8	7	11	13
Green	0	0	0	1	0	1	1	2	0	1	0	0	1	0	1	0
Hobby	0	0	1	0	0	0	0	0	0	0	0	0	0	0	2	0
Honk	0	0	1	2	0	1	0	0	0	0	0	1	1	0	1	1
Horn	0	0	0	0	4	4	1	1	0	0	0	0	1	1	0	0
Horse	0	2	0	1	0	2	1	1	2	0	1	0	0	3	1	1
Horses	0	0	0	2	0	1	1	4	1	2	0	3	0	5	11	7
Hotrod	0	0	2	0	2	0	0	0	3	0	4	1	0	0	0	0
Hotrods	0	0	0	0	0	0	2	0	4	2	1	0	0	0	0	1
House	0	0	0	0	0	0	1	1	0	1	0	0	1	1	0	2
Houses	0	0	0	1	0	0	0	0	1	1	0	0	0	1	1	3
Jeep	0	0	0	0	0	0	0	2	0	0	0	0	0	0	0	0
Kill	0	0	0	0	0	0	0	2	0	0	0	0	0	0	0	0
License	0	0	0	0	0	0	0	0	1	1	0	0	0	0	0	2
Lot	0	0	2	0	0	1	0	0	0	1	0	0	0	0	0	1
Lots	0	0	1	0	2	0	0	0	0	0	1	0	0	0	0	0
Machine	0	0	1	0	2	1	0	0	0	0	0	0	0	1	0	0
Many	0	0	0	0	0	0	0	1	0	0	0	2	0	0	1	1
Metal	1	0	2	1	1	1	1	0	0	0	0	0	0	0	1	0
Mine	0	0	0	0	0	0	1	0	1	0	0	0	1	0	2	1
Money	0	0	0	0	1	0	1	0	0	0	1	0	1	0	4	1
Motor	4	1	5	4	4	2	5	2	4	1	2	0	2	2	9	5
Motors	0	1	1	1	0	3	1	0	3	0	4	3	4	1	2	2
Move	1	3	3	2	2	1	1	1	2	0	1	1	3	1	3	5
Moving	0	0	2	0	4	0	2	0	1	1	0	0	0	1	1	1
New	0	0	0	1	0	0	2	0	1	0	1	2	2	2	3	11
Nice	0	2	0	0	0	0	1	0	0	0	0	0	0	2	1	0
Noise	1	0	1	0	0	2	3	1	0	1	1	0	0	2	1	1
Oldsmobile	0	0	0	1	0	0	0	0	1	0	0	1	1	0	2	3
Paint	0	0	0	0	0	0	0	0	0	0	0	0	2	0	1	2
Parked	0	1	0	0	0	0	0	0	0	2	0	0	0	0	0	0
Parking	0	0	0	0	0	0	1	0	0	3	0	0	0	0	1	0
People	2	3	1	2	3	3	0	4	2	4	2	2	1	3	3	4

Response Word	4th		5th		6th		7th		8th		10th		12th		College	
	M	F	M	F	M	F	M	F	M	F	M	F	M	F	M	F

CARS

Response Word	4th M	4th F	5th M	5th F	6th M	6th F	7th M	7th F	8th M	8th F	10th M	10th F	12th M	12th F	College M	College F
Planes	0	0	0	0	0	0	1	0	0	2	0	1	0	1	2	1
Pontiac	0	0	0	0	0	0	0	0	0	0	0	0	0	0	3	0
Race	0	0	0	0	2	1	1	0	0	0	1	1	0	0	3	0
Red	1	1	1	0	0	2	2	3	1	2	2	9	2	5	11	17
Ride	10	13	5	11	7	10	3	11	1	11	2	8	3	6	4	12
Road	1	3	1	4	2	2	2	2	0	1	1	1	0	3	0	3
Roads	0	0	2	1	1	2	0	0	1	1	2	7	0	3	2	5
Rod	0	0	0	0	0	0	1	0	3	0	1	0	1	0	0	0
Rods	0	0	0	0	2	0	0	0	2	0	1	0	0	0	0	1
Run	6	6	9	7	7	3	2	4	2	4	3	1	2	2	4	7
Seats	0	0	0	1	0	1	0	0	0	1	0	0	0	0	0	2
Sell	0	0	0	1	0	0	0	0	0	0	0	0	0	0	2	0
Shine	0	0	0	0	0	0	0	0	0	0	1	0	0	0	0	2
Shiny	0	1	0	0	0	0	0	0	0	0	0	2	0	1	0	5
Small	1	1	1	1	0	0	0	0	0	0	0	0	1	0	2	1
Speed	0	1	1	0	1	0	2	0	3	0	6	4	8	5	7	3
Sports	0	0	0	0	0	0	0	0	0	0	0	0	0	2	2	2
Steel	2	0	3	1	0	3	0	1	1	0	1	0	0	1	0	0
Stop	0	1	0	0	2	1	1	0	1	0	0	0	0	0	0	0
Street	7	10	1	10	2	2	1	3	2	1	2	5	2	7	1	2
Streets	2	2	0	2	1	1	1	3	2	2	2	2	2	5	2	4
Tires	0	0	0	0	1	1	0	1	1	3	3	2	5	1	10	7
Toys	0	0	1	0	0	0	0	1	0	1	0	0	0	2	1	4
Traffic	3	2	0	2	1	2	1	1	0	2	0	2	1	1	3	2
Train	0	1	1	1	0	1	0	1	0	4	4	0	0	0	1	1
Trains	0	3	1	5	1	1	1	0	5	3	3	3	3	5	6	5
Transportation	0	2	1	3	0	3	2	0	0	2	2	3	1	1	2	1
Travel	0	1	0	2	0	1	2	2	1	1	1	1	0	1	5	3
Trouble	0	0	0	0	0	0	0	0	0	1	0	0	3	0	0	0
Truck	16	13	9	13	9	5	9	6	9	4	3	5	4	2	6	3
Trucks	46	53	40	40	49	51	39	42	53	31	30	31	37	21	68	39
Two	0	0	2	0	0	0	0	1	0	0	0	0	0	0	0	0
Vehicles	0	0	0	0	0	3	0	0	1	0	0	0	0	0	0	0
Wagon	1	1	2	0	0	0	1	0	1	0	0	0	0	1	0	1
Wagons	1	0	0	1	0	0	0	0	0	0	0	0	0	0	1	3
Wash	0	0	0	0	0	0	2	0	0	0	0	0	1	0	1	0
Wheel	1	1	0	1	2	1	1	0	1	0	2	0	2	1	3	1
Wheels	11	8	7	3	4	8	2	20	4	9	9	10	6	10	18	19

36. CHAIR

Response Word	4th M	4th F	5th M	5th F	6th M	6th F	7th M	7th F	8th M	8th F	10th M	10th F	12th M	12th F	College M	College F
Air	0	1	1	2	1	0	0	0	0	0	0	0	0	1	0	0
Arm	0	2	3	0	0	0	1	1	1	1	5	1	4	2	2	3
Armchair	0	0	0	0	0	0	0	0	0	0	0	0	0	0	2	0
Back	0	0	0	0	0	0	0	2	0	0	1	1	1	0	4	1
Bed	4	5	2	1	2	3	2	2	8	3	5	2	2	0	3	4
Bench	0	0	1	0	0	2	2	1	1	0	0	0	1	0	1	0
Big	1	0	0	0	3	0	1	3	1	2	3	2	1	0	0	0
Brown	0	0	0	0	0	0	0	0	1	0	0	0	0	2	0	2

Response Word	4th M	4th F	5th M	5th F	6th M	6th F	7th M	7th F	8th M	8th F	10th M	10th F	12th M	12th F	College M	College F
							CHAIR									
Cloth . . .	0	0	0	0	0	0	0	0	1	0	0	0	0	0	2	0
Comfort . .	2	5	4	6	9	8	5	7	6	4	7	4	6	4	12	4
Comfortable	2	1	4	2	1	4	3	5	1	4	2	4	3	2	1	1
Couch . . .	3	4	4	3	0	1	4	4	5	7	2	1	0	2	1	1
Cushion . .	1	0	0	0	1	2	0	2	1	4	1	4	2	1	1	3
Davenport .	2	0	0	0	0	1	0	0	0	1	1	0	0	1	1	1
Desk . . .	1	2	1	3	2	4	4	0	2	5	5	3	7	6	6	7
Easy . . .	0	0	0	0	1	1	1	0	1	1	3	0	2	0	1	2
Floor . . .	4	1	5	0	4	2	3	0	5	0	1	4	3	2	4	6
Furniture .	1	1	6	1	2	4	0	1	2	1	0	1	0	1	0	1
Good . . .	0	0	3	0	0	0	0	0	0	0	1	0	0	0	0	0
Hair	2	2	3	2	1	2	0	0	0	0	0	0	1	0	2	0
Hard . . .	3	1	1	3	0	3	3	5	0	2	3	5	3	1	3	4
High . . .	0	0	3	0	0	1	0	0	0	1	1	1	1	1	4	1
House . . .	1	2	0	1	0	0	0	0	1	0	1	0	3	1	1	1
Kitchen . .	0	0	0	0	0	0	0	0	0	2	0	0	0	1	0	0
Leather . .	0	0	0	0	0	0	1	0	0	0	0	0	0	1	2	1
Leg	1	1	0	1	2	2	3	5	8	4	5	8	4	7	8	7
Legs . . .	2	2	3	2	3	2	4	5	4	2	1	5	3	6	11	9
Man	0	1	1	0	0	0	0	0	2	0	0	0	1	0	0	0
Person . .	0	0	0	1	0	1	1	0	0	2	1	2	0	0	0	0
Pillow . .	0	0	0	0	0	0	1	1	0	0	1	0	1	1	2	4
Red	0	0	0	0	0	1	0	0	1	0	0	1	0	0	1	3
Relax . . .	2	0	0	1	2	1	0	0	0	2	1	1	1	2	1	2
Rest . . .	0	0	1	1	1	1	4	1	2	2	4	1	3	2	4	1
Rocker . .	0	0	0	0	0	0	1	0	0	0	2	1	1	2	1	4
Rocking . .	0	0	0	0	1	2	0	1	0	0	1	2	0	0	1	1
Room . . .	0	0	0	0	0	0	2	0	1	0	2	0	0	0	2	2
Rug	0	0	0	2	1	0	1	0	0	1	0	0	0	0	1	1
Rung . . .	0	0	0	0	0	0	0	0	0	0	0	0	0	0	0	2
Sat	1	2	2	4	1	0	1	1	0	0	0	0	0	0	1	0
Seat	8	7	12	3	10	11	12	16	11	8	11	9	12	7	32	16
Set	9	8	9	8	10	6	4	2	2	0	6	1	1	2	1	0
Set down .	0	0	0	0	2	0	0	0	0	0	0	0	0	0	0	0
Setting . .	0	0	0	0	0	2	0	0	0	0	0	0	0	0	0	0
Sit	69	90	69	91	61	69	64	56	34	58	63	51	51	51	122	102
Sit in . . .	0	0	2	0	0	0	1	0	0	1	0	0	0	0	0	0
Sitting . . .	4	3	2	1	5	3	4	5	1	0	2	1	1	1	3	0
Sofa	1	2	1	3	2	1	1	5	1	4	4	4	1	2	7	7
Soft	4	13	6	7	6	5	7	1	5	6	6	6	6	8	13	20
Something to sit on .	2	0	0	0	0	0	0	0	0	0	0	0	0	0	0	0
Stole . . .	2	0	0	0	0	1	1	0	0	0	0	0	0	1	0	0
Stool . . .	7	2	10	3	6	4	14	7	12	10	4	5	2	2	11	4
Straight . .	0	0	0	0	0	0	0	0	0	0	0	0	0	0	0	3
Study . . .	0	0	0	0	0	0	0	0	0	0	0	0	0	0	0	2
Swivel . .	0	0	0	0	1	0	0	0	0	0	0	0	0	0	2	1
Table . . .	84	90	65	98	81	91	78	99	109	92	68	105	102	116	190	238
TV	0	0	0	0	2	0	0	0	0	0	1	0	1	0	0	0

Response Word	4th M	4th F	5th M	5th F	6th M	6th F	7th M	7th F	8th M	8th F	10th M	10th F	12th M	12th F	College M	College F

CHAIR

Response Word	4th M	4th F	5th M	5th F	6th M	6th F	7th M	7th F	8th M	8th F	10th M	10th F	12th M	12th F	College M	College F
Wheel ...	0	0	0	0	0	0	1	0	0	0	1	2	3	0	4	1
Wheelchair	0	0	0	0	0	0	0	0	0	0	0	0	2	0	0	1
Wicker ..	0	0	0	0	0	0	0	0	0	0	0	0	0	0	0	2
Wood ...	7	1	2	2	1	4	4	2	2	5	3	2	1	4	4	7

37. CHEESE

Response Word	4th M	4th F	5th M	5th F	6th M	6th F	7th M	7th F	8th M	8th F	10th M	10th F	12th M	12th F	College M	College F
American .	0	0	0	0	0	0	0	3	1	0	1	1	1	2	5	4
Apple pie .	0	0	0	0	0	0	0	0	0	0	0	0	0	1	2	0
Apples ..	0	0	0	0	0	0	0	0	0	0	0	0	0	0	0	2
Bacon ...	0	1	0	0	0	0	0	0	0	1	0	0	0	1	2	6
Bitter ...	0	1	1	0	0	0	2	2	0	0	4	2	1	0	1	0
Blue	0	1	0	0	0	2	1	7	4	8	5	4	5	3	11	17
Box	0	0	0	0	0	1	0	0	1	0	0	0	0	0	0	3
Bread ..	9	13	10	18	19	25	6	6	12	16	8	7	16	27	34	52
Burger ..	0	1	1	1	0	1	0	0	1	1	0	2	0	0	3	0
Butter ...	22	19	13	13	21	11	18	18	27	25	16	11	11	11	18	11
Cake ...	0	1	1	0	3	3	5	1	6	2	4	2	8	8	12	13
Cat	1	1	0	0	3	0	1	0	0	0	0	1	0	0	2	0
Cheddar .	1	1	0	1	0	0	1	3	1	4	3	4	3	2	5	12
Cloth ...	0	0	0	0	1	0	0	1	0	0	0	0	0	1	3	0
Colby ...	0	0	0	0	0	0	0	0	0	2	1	0	1	0	0	1
Cottage ..	3	1	2	1	5	4	3	3	13	5	5	7	12	4	11	8
Cow	2	1	1	0	1	6	3	3	2	5	8	4	0	0	4	1
Cows ...	0	0	0	0	0	0	0	0	0	1	0	0	1	0	0	2
Cracker .	0	1	0	2	0	2	0	2	2	6	1	0	2	2	6	6
Crackers .	0	1	3	5	3	4	5	5	5	6	5	24	11	26	30	41
Cream ...	2	3	4	1	1	3	4	4	2	2	3	0	3	1	6	3
Curd ...	0	0	0	0	0	0	0	0	0	0	0	0	0	1	2	0
Dairy ...	0	0	0	3	1	1	1	1	0	1	0	2	0	0	2	2
Eat	25	27	24	31	11	19	6	11	9	15	11	9	14	7	39	12
Eating ..	0	1	0	1	1	0	0	0	0	2	0	0	1	0	0	0
Feet	0	0	0	0	0	0	0	0	2	0	0	0	0	0	0	0
Food ...	41	36	63	23	45	30	36	29	28	16	28	13	24	12	38	23
Friday ..	0	0	0	0	0	0	0	0	0	0	0	0	0	2	1	2
Gold	0	0	0	0	0	0	0	0	0	0	0	2	0	0	0	1
Good ...	12	8	6	16	13	7	5	4	3	3	4	3	2	4	7	5
Green ..	2	1	1	3	4	3	1	6	2	1	1	1	4	7	8	11
Ham	0	1	0	2	2	0	0	0	0	0	1	0	0	1	3	1
Hate ...	0	2	0	0	0	0	0	1	0	2	0	0	0	0	0	0
Hole ...	0	0	0	1	0	0	0	1	0	1	1	0	1	1	3	3
Holes ..	1	2	2	3	0	3	3	5	4	6	5	3	3	5	19	8
Holland ..	2	0	0	0	0	0	0	0	0	0	0	0	0	0	0	1
Hungry ..	2	0	1	0	0	0	1	0	0	0	0	0	0	0	0	0
Ish	1	1	1	0	0	0	1	0	2	2	1	2	0	2	0	0
Knife ...	0	0	1	1	0	0	0	0	0	1	1	0	0	0	1	2
Limburger	1	2	2	2	4	1	4	2	1	2	4	1	3	0	5	2
Longhorn .	0	2	0	0	0	0	0	0	0	0	0	0	0	0	2	0
Macaroni .	0	0	0	0	0	0	0	0	0	2	0	0	0	1	0	0
Me	2	0	0	0	1	0	0	0	0	0	0	0	0	0	0	0
Meat ...	0	2	1	1	1	0	1	2	1	0	0	2	0	0	0	0

Response Word	4th M	4th F	5th M	5th F	6th M	6th F	7th M	7th F	8th M	8th F	10th M	10th F	12th M	12th F	College M	College F

CHEESE

Response Word	M	F	M	F	M	F	M	F	M	F	M	F	M	F	M	F
Mice . . .	12	12	20	15	22	18	26	22	19	15	23	20	20	15	16	18
Mild . . .	0	0	0	0	0	0	1	0	0	0	2	0	0	0	1	1
Milk . . .	10	11	16	18	7	17	18	19	16	14	12	8	12	9	14	31
Mold . . .	0	0	0	0	0	0	0	0	1	0	0	0	1	0	1	2
Moon . . .	2	3	1	0	3	3	4	1	4	5	3	4	3	2	8	6
Mouse . .	34	37	23	41	33	37	40	31	38	30	38	52	36	27	46	60
Nice	0	0	2	0	0	1	0	1	0	0	1	0	0	0	1	1
No	2	0	0	0	1	0	0	0	0	0	0	0	0	0	1	0
Orange . .	1	2	1	5	0	4	1	5	0	2	1	5	0	5	3	0
Pie	0	0	0	0	0	0	0	0	0	0	1	1	1	0	2	3
Pizza . . .	0	0	0	0	0	1	0	0	0	0	0	3	1	3	2	2
Please . .	0	0	0	1	3	0	0	0	0	0	0	0	0	0	0	0
Rat	3	1	1	1	1	1	2	5	3	0	0	0	3	3	8	6
Rats . . .	0	0	1	0	0	0	0	2	1	2	2	1	2	1	1	0
Roquefort .	0	0	0	0	0	0	0	1	0	0	0	1	0	0	0	2
Rye	0	0	0	0	0	0	0	0	0	0	0	0	0	2	0	0
Sandwich .	2	1	1	5	2	2	4	2	2	3	6	7	6	4	6	10
Sandwiches	0	0	0	0	1	0	0	0	1	0	0	0	1	0	2	0
Sharp . . .	0	0	0	0	0	0	0	1	0	0	0	0	0	1	1	3
Smell . . .	2	1	1	3	1	0	1	0	2	2	4	4	2	1	9	7
Soft	0	1	0	0	0	0	2	0	0	0	0	1	0	1	2	0
Sour . . .	1	0	0	1	1	1	0	1	0	1	1	2	0	0	2	4
Spread . .	0	0	0	1	1	0	1	0	0	3	0	0	0	0	2	2
Strong . .	0	1	0	0	0	0	1	1	0	1	1	2	0	0	0	0
Swift	1	2	0	1	2	0	0	0	0	0	0	0	0	0	0	0
Swiss . . .	6	2	5	4	2	2	9	8	5	6	5	2	5	5	13	14
Switzerland	0	0	1	0	0	0	1	0	0	1	1	1	1	2	0	1
Taste . . .	1	0	0	0	3	0	1	2	0	0	0	1	0	0	1	1
Velveeta . .	0	0	0	0	0	0	0	1	0	1	0	0	1	0	0	2
Water . . .	0	2	0	0	0	0	0	0	0	0	0	0	0	0	0	0
We	0	0	2	0	0	0	0	0	0	0	0	0	0	0	0	0
Wisc . . .	0	0	0	0	0	0	0	0	0	0	0	0	0	0	2	0
Wisconsin .	0	0	0	0	0	0	0	0	0	1	1	0	0	0	2	2
Yellow . .	6	12	8	8	5	19	8	6	8	15	13	14	9	22	26	45

38. CHILD

Response Word	M	F	M	F	M	F	M	F	M	F	M	F	M	F	M	F
Adult . . .	4	1	2	3	1	4	4	4	9	4	5	5	6	7	12	18
Babies . .	0	0	0	0	0	0	0	1	1	2	0	1	0	0	0	0
Baby . . .	12	21	16	27	13	39	41	66	27	64	38	66	32	68	75	98
Bad	0	0	1	0	2	0	0	0	1	0	0	0	2	1	1	0
Beautiful .	0	0	0	0	0	0	0	0	0	0	0	0	0	2	0	0
Birth . . .	0	0	0	0	1	0	0	3	1	3	2	0	1	0	5	1
Born . . .	1	1	0	1	0	0	1	1	2	1	0	0	0	0	1	0
Boy	78	17	73	17	70	19	37	13	34	11	21	11	17	9	51	24
Boy or girl	1	0	2	0	0	0	1	0	0	0	0	0	0	0	0	0
Boys	2	0	0	0	0	0	0	0	1	0	0	0	0	0	0	0
Brat . . .	0	0	0	0	2	1	0	2	5	7	3	4	2	0	0	1
Brother . .	0	0	1	0	1	0	1	1	6	0	3	1	2	3	3	4
Care . . .	0	1	0	1	0	1	0	0	1	0	1	1	1	4	5	1

Response Word	4th M	4th F	5th M	5th F	6th M	6th F	7th M	7th F	8th M	8th F	10th M	10th F	12th M	12th F	College M	College F
							CHILD									
Children .	31	39	26	43	23	25	17	17	14	10	10	4	5	4	10	5
Cry	0	0	0	0	1	0	1	0	1	3	4	2	1	1	3	7
Cute	0	1	0	1	0	0	1	4	2	6	2	3	2	3	5	16
Dog	0	0	1	1	0	1	0	0	0	2	1	0	1	1	1	1
Family . .	0	0	0	0	2	0	0	0	0	1	0	1	1	0	2	1
Fun	1	0	0	0	3	1	1	0	1	0	3	0	4	1	4	4
Girl	4	33	4	26	8	26	6	10	6	11	2	6	5	7	9	12
God	0	2	0	0	0	0	0	0	0	0	0	0	0	0	0	0
Good . . .	1	0	1	2	0	2	2	0	0	0	1	0	0	0	3	7
Grown . .	0	2	0	0	0	0	0	0	0	0	0	0	0	0	0	0
Grownup .	2	4	0	3	1	5	1	1	3	3	0	1	0	0	1	0
Happiness .	0	0	0	0	0	0	0	0	0	1	0	0	1	0	2	0
Happy . . .	0	1	0	0	1	0	0	0	0	0	0	2	0	3	2	4
Helpless .	0	0	0	0	0	0	0	1	0	0	0	2	1	0	2	0
Home . . .	0	0	0	0	1	2	0	0	0	0	0	0	0	0	0	0
Human . .	3	2	3	1	2	2	1	0	0	0	1	0	0	0	3	1
Immature .	0	0	0	0	0	0	0	0	0	0	1	0	0	0	0	2
Infant . . .	1	1	0	1	4	1	2	8	5	3	2	3	3	1	8	3
Innocence .	0	0	0	0	0	0	0	0	0	0	0	0	1	0	1	2
Innocent . .	0	0	0	0	0	0	0	0	0	0	0	0	2	0	0	7
Kid	14	12	13	15	23	7	23	13	23	12	16	6	13	3	21	5
Kids . . .	1	1	2	0	3	1	4	1	3	0	5	3	1	2	2	0
Labor . . .	0	0	0	0	0	0	0	0	0	1	0	0	2	0	3	0
Little . . .	9	12	8	11	5	21	10	7	10	17	13	13	12	16	18	16
Love . . .	0	0	0	2	0	1	0	3	1	0	1	3	3	2	6	9
Lovely . .	0	0	0	0	0	0	0	0	0	0	0	0	0	2	0	2
Loving . .	0	0	0	0	0	0	0	0	0	0	0	0	0	2	0	0
Man	9	2	8	3	11	2	9	2	9	1	3	0	9	2	16	1
Many . . .	0	0	0	1	0	1	0	0	0	0	0	0	0	0	2	1
Marriage .	0	0	0	0	0	0	0	0	0	0	2	0	0	0	1	1
Me	7	4	8	6	6	3	5	6	3	0	0	1	1	1	1	0
Mean . . .	0	0	0	0	0	0	0	0	0	2	0	0	0	1	0	0
Men	0	0	1	1	2	0	1	0	0	0	0	0	0	0	0	0
Mild	0	0	0	0	0	0	0	0	0	0	0	0	1	0	2	0
Mine . . .	0	0	0	0	0	0	0	0	0	0	0	0	0	0	2	1
Mother . .	3	12	6	7	5	10	6	7	9	19	15	26	31	30	43	79
Nephew . .	0	0	0	0	0	0	0	0	0	0	0	0	2	0	0	0
Nice	1	3	0	1	1	2	0	1	2	0	1	1	2	1	1	2
Noise . . .	0	0	0	0	0	0	0	0	0	0	0	0	0	0	2	0
Old	1	2	0	2	0	0	0	0	0	0	0	0	0	0	0	0
Parent . .	0	0	1	2	0	2	1	2	2	2	0	1	0	3	5	5
Parents . .	0	1	1	4	0	2	0	0	1	0	0	0	1	1	4	4
People . .	4	6	10	5	3	3	2	0	5	1	1	2	0	2	0	0
Person . .	26	29	29	17	22	23	14	11	4	5	9	3	4	4	4	2
Play	1	6	2	0	2	2	1	4	1	0	4	5	9	4	11	15
School . . .	0	4	1	0	2	1	1	1	1	2	1	1	1	2	2	2
Sex	2	0	0	0	0	0	0	1	0	0	1	0	1	0	1	0
Sister . . .	1	1	0	0	0	0	0	2	1	6	5	3	4	3	2	2
Small . . .	6	4	9	12	6	16	17	21	15	10	27	22	19	12	48	31

Response Word	4th M	4th F	5th M	5th F	6th M	6th F	7th M	7th F	8th M	8th F	10th M	10th F	12th M	12th F	College M	College F

CHILD

Response Word	4th M	4th F	5th M	5th F	6th M	6th F	7th M	7th F	8th M	8th F	10th M	10th F	12th M	12th F	College M	College F
Soft	0	0	0	0	0	1	0	0	1	0	0	0	0	0	1	2
Son	0	0	0	0	1	1	0	0	0	0	0	0	1	0	3	1
Sweet . . .	0	0	0	3	0	1	0	4	0	3	0	4	1	4	1	8
Tender . .	0	0	0	0	0	0	0	0	0	2	0	0	0	2	0	0
Tiny	0	0	0	0	0	0	1	0	0	0	0	0	0	0	1	2
Tot	0	0	0	0	0	0	1	0	0	1	1	0	1	1	1	2
Toy	0	0	1	0	0	0	0	1	0	2	2	3	1	2	1	10
Toys . . .	0	0	0	0	1	0	0	1	0	0	0	4	1	3	2	1
Trouble . .	0	0	0	0	0	0	0	0	1	1	1	0	1	2	2	1
Welfare . .	0	0	1	0	0	0	0	0	0	0	1	0	0	0	6	1
Wife . . .	0	0	0	0	0	0	0	0	0	0	0	0	1	0	2	0
Woman . .	0	1	0	1	2	1	0	1	2	0	4	1	0	1	6	6
Women . .	0	0	0	2	0	1	0	0	0	0	3	1	2	0	0	1
Young . .	2	5	3	7	2	2	8	7	9	6	12	4	12	5	30	11
Youngster .	0	0	0	0	0	1	1	1	0	1	1	1	1	2	0	1
Youth . . .	0	0	0	1	0	0	0	0	0	0	0	0	0	0	4	2

39. CHILDREN

Response Word	4th M	4th F	5th M	5th F	6th M	6th F	7th M	7th F	8th M	8th F	10th M	10th F	12th M	12th F	College M	College F
Adult . . .	1	0	0	1	1	3	4	6	1	3	2	2	0	2	2	4
Adults . . .	2	5	1	2	0	5	5	6	8	10	7	10	6	4	13	21
Are	5	1	2	1	4	2	0	1	4	2	5	3	13	1	11	4
Babies . .	0	2	1	3	1	5	2	14	5	22	7	9	8	17	13	29
Baby	2	3	3	3	7	9	7	13	17	12	5	12	9	10	10	7
Babysit . .	0	0	0	0	0	1	0	0	0	1	0	2	0	0	0	1
Bad	1	0	1	0	0	0	0	0	0	0	0	0	0	0	2	1
Big	1	2	0	0	1	0	0	0	0	0	2	0	1	0	0	0
Boy	13	8	21	5	11	6	6	6	8	1	6	3	5	5	12	2
Boys . . .	11	3	8	3	3	6	8	4	9	7	9	6	7	10	18	16
Brat	0	0	1	0	0	0	1	1	1	4	0	0	0	0	0	2
Brats . . .	0	0	0	0	1	0	1	1	5	4	4	2	4	4	5	3
Brother . .	0	0	1	0	2	0	0	1	1	1	0	0	0	0	0	0
Can	1	0	0	1	2	0	0	0	0	0	1	1	1	1	0	0
Cat	0	1	0	0	0	0	0	0	0	2	0	0	0	0	1	0
Chickens .	0	0	0	0	0	0	0	0	0	0	0	0	0	0	0	2
Child . . .	83	71	69	84	60	57	56	54	43	43	21	18	32	20	50	44
Chill . . .	0	0	0	2	0	0	0	0	0	0	0	0	0	0	0	0
Clothes . .	1	1	0	0	0	0	0	0	2	0	0	0	0	0	0	0
Cry	0	0	0	0	1	0	4	0	1	2	2	2	3	2	6	11
Crying . .	0	0	0	0	0	0	0	0	0	2	0	0	1	0	2	0
Cute	0	0	0	1	0	0	0	1	0	4	0	3	1	2	1	1
Die	0	0	0	0	0	0	0	0	0	0	0	0	2	0	0	0
Dogs . . .	0	1	0	0	0	0	0	0	1	0	0	4	1	1	2	6
Family . .	0	1	1	0	1	1	0	3	0	1	2	2	2	7	3	6
Father . .	0	0	1	0	0	1	1	0	0	0	0	0	0	0	2	1
Fight . . .	0	0	0	0	0	0	0	0	0	0	0	0	0	1	2	0
Fun	1	0	1	1	1	2	0	2	2	2	1	1	1	5	2	8
Girl	1	10	5	5	5	5	5	3	2	2	2	2	3	2	2	3
Girls . . .	3	5	1	5	3	3	4	4	3	2	3	2	2	2	3	5
Good . . .	0	0	0	0	1	1	0	0	0	0	0	0	0	0	3	4

Response Word	4th		5th		6th		7th		8th		10th		12th		College	
	M	F	M	F	M	F	M	F	M	F	M	F	M	F	M	F

CHILDREN

Response Word	M	F	M	F	M	F	M	F	M	F	M	F	M	F	M	F
Group . . .	0	0	1	1	0	1	0	0	0	1	1	0	0	1	0	4
Grownup .	2	1	0	0	0	1	0	0	0	0	0	0	0	0	0	0
Grownups .	3	1	1	4	1	1	3	1	2	2	0	0	1	1	2	2
Happy . . .	0	0	0	2	0	1	0	0	1	0	1	1	0	1	0	2
He	2	0	0	0	0	0	0	0	0	0	0	0	0	0	0	0
Hen	0	2	0	0	0	0	0	0	0	0	0	0	0	0	0	0
Home . . .	1	0	0	0	0	0	0	0	0	0	0	0	0	1	1	2
Human . .	0	2	4	0	1	0	0	2	0	0	0	0	0	0	0	1
Infant . . .	0	0	0	0	0	0	0	1	0	0	1	0	0	1	2	0
Infants . .	0	1	0	0	0	1	4	2	0	0	0	1	0	2	6	3
Kid	5	1	11	4	6	8	6	8	4	2	4	0	2	1	7	1
Kids . . .	14	19	18	18	36	35	43	31	38	30	51	40	39	34	101	87
Laugh . . .	0	0	0	0	0	0	0	1	0	1	1	1	1	0	3	4
Laughing .	0	0	0	0	0	2	0	0	0	0	0	0	0	0	1	0
Like	0	0	2	1	1	0	0	0	0	0	0	0	0	0	1	0
Little . . .	3	5	4	6	5	10	8	5	2	8	16	15	7	11	14	17
Lots	1	0	0	2	0	0	0	0	0	0	0	0	0	0	0	0
Love . . .	0	1	0	0	0	0	0	1	0	0	0	3	0	3	2	3
Man	2	0	2	1	3	0	1	0	0	0	1	0	0	0	0	0
Many . . .	0	1	1	2	0	3	2	0	1	1	3	6	3	8	8	7
Marriage .	0	0	0	0	0	0	0	0	1	0	1	1	1	1	1	2
Me	4	2	6	3	2	2	4	0	2	1	0	0	1	0	0	0
Men	5	0	3	0	2	2	4	0	2	1	2	0	0	1	8	1
Mine . . .	0	0	0	0	1	0	0	0	0	0	1	0	1	0	2	3
Mother . .	0	3	1	1	4	1	3	2	3	6	4	4	4	4	3	6
Noise . . .	1	0	0	2	0	1	1	0	0	1	1	2	1	1	2	2
Noisy . . .	0	1	0	1	0	0	1	0	0	2	0	2	1	0	1	0
Offspring .	0	0	0	0	0	0	0	0	0	0	0	0	0	0	0	2
Parent . .	0	0	0	1	0	0	1	0	0	1	0	1	0	1	2	1
Parents . .	1	4	4	2	0	3	3	5	7	6	5	1	7	3	11	14
People . .	30	43	30	33	25	25	17	15	17	18	11	13	12	10	21	15
Person . .	4	2	5	2	3	1	2	1	2	0	0	0	0	0	0	0
Persons .	2	1	0	0	0	0	0	0	0	1	0	0	0	0	0	0
Pets . . .	0	0	0	0	0	0	0	0	0	0	0	0	0	1	2	4
Play . . .	7	13	6	11	12	5	4	5	4	7	17	15	15	20	25	42
Playing . .	0	0	0	0	1	1	1	0	0	0	2	4	2	1	4	2
Run	2	1	1	0	3	1	1	2	2	0	2	3	1	2	8	4
School . . .	1	3	0	3	3	2	0	2	1	3	2	2	0	0	3	9
Sisters . .	0	0	0	0	0	1	0	0	0	0	0	2	0	0	0	0
Sit	0	0	2	0	0	0	0	0	0	0	0	0	0	0	0	0
Small . . .	2	3	5	2	6	7	6	11	9	8	11	14	22	13	41	11
Tots . . .	1	0	0	0	0	0	0	1	0	0	1	0	1	2	1	1
Toys . . .	0	0	0	0	0	0	0	1	1	1	0	6	0	3	4	4
Trouble . .	0	0	0	0	0	0	0	0	1	0	0	2	1	1	0	0
Us	0	0	2	1	1	0	1	1	0	0	0	0	0	0	0	0
Voices . .	0	0	0	0	0	0	0	0	0	0	0	0	0	0	0	2
Women . .	2	0	0	1	0	0	0	0	1	1	3	0	0	0	0	0
Yes	0	0	0	0	0	0	0	0	0	0	0	0	0	0	1	3	0
You	2	0	0	0	1	0	0	0	0	0	1	0	0	0	0	0

Response Word	4th M	4th F	5th M	5th F	6th M	6th F	7th M	7th F	8th M	8th F	10th M	10th F	12th M	12th F	College M	College F
CHILDREN																
Young . . .	1	1	3	3	0	3	6	1	2	2	3	5	3	4	7	9
Youngster .	0	0	0	0	0	0	0	2	0	0	0	0	0	1	1	0
Youngsters	0	0	0	2	0	1	0	1	0	0	0	0	1	0	1	1
Youth . . .	1	0	0	0	0	0	0	0	0	0	1	0	0	0	1	2
40. CITIZEN																
Alien . . .	0	0	0	0	0	0	3	0	7	1	4	2	9	3	20	12
America .	1	1	3	5	2	3	2	3	3	5	3	14	11	8	8	19
American .	1	4	2	3	2	7	7	13	5	10	18	19	16	21	26	45
A person .	2	0	0	0	0	0	0	0	0	0	0	0	0	0	0	0
Arrest . .	0	0	0	0	0	0	0	0	0	1	0	0	0	0	3	0
Bank . . .	0	0	0	0	0	0	0	0	0	0	0	0	2	1	1	1
Belong . .	1	1	1	1	0	2	0	1	0	0	0	0	0	0	1	0
Boy	0	1	1	1	4	2	0	0	1	0	1	1	1	2	0	1
Burglar . .	0	0	0	2	0	0	0	0	0	0	0	0	0	0	0	0
Car	2	0	0	0	0	1	0	0	0	0	0	0	0	0	0	0
Child . . .	0	1	0	0	0	0	0	0	2	0	1	0	0	0	0	0
Citizenship	0	0	0	0	0	0	0	2	0	1	0	0	0	0	0	1
City	18	13	12	7	12	6	4	5	4	1	2	5	1	2	2	7
Civil . . .	0	0	0	0	0	0	0	0	1	0	3	0	0	0	0	0
Community	0	0	0	1	0	1	1	0	2	2	0	3	1	0	0	1
Country . .	3	3	3	6	1	2	7	7	1	6	8	3	5	8	29	30
Countryman	0	0	1	0	0	0	0	0	3	1	0	0	0	0	0	0
Courthouse	0	0	0	0	0	0	0	0	0	0	0	0	0	0	0	3
Criminal .	0	0	0	2	0	0	0	0	1	0	0	0	0	0	0	0
Democracy	0	0	0	0	0	0	0	0	0	0	1	2	0	0	7	7
DP	0	0	0	0	0	0	0	0	0	0	0	0	0	0	2	0
Enemy . . .	0	0	0	0	0	1	1	0	1	0	0	3	0	0	0	1
Flag . . .	0	0	0	0	0	1	0	0	0	2	0	2	0	3	6	6
Foreign . .	1	0	0	0	3	0	1	1	2	0	0	0	1	4	2	3
Foreigner .	0	0	1	1	1	1	1	1	9	4	1	4	2	4	3	7
Free . . .	0	0	0	0	0	1	0	1	0	0	1	3	1	0	1	0
Friend . .	1	0	5	0	1	4	1	0	1	0	1	2	0	0	0	1
Girl	0	1	0	1	0	0	0	1	0	2	0	0	0	0	0	0
Good . . .	17	34	24	14	13	11	3	7	5	8	3	5	1	7	3	9
Government	0	0	0	0	1	0	0	1	1	1	2	3	2	2	2	3
Happy . . .	0	0	0	0	1	0	0	0	0	0	0	0	0	0	2	0
Human . .	1	0	0	0	2	0	0	1	0	0	0	1	1	0	2	0
I	0	0	0	0	1	0	0	0	2	0	0	0	0	0	1	0
Immigrant .	0	0	0	0	0	0	1	1	4	6	1	4	1	2	2	3
Indian . . .	0	0	0	0	0	0	0	0	2	0	0	0	0	0	0	0
Kennedy . .	0	0	0	1	0	0	0	0	0	1	0	1	2	1	0	0
Kind	2	0	0	0	0	0	0	0	0	0	0	0	0	0	0	0
Leader . .	0	0	0	2	1	0	0	0	1	0	0	0	0	0	0	1
Liberty . .	0	0	0	0	0	0	0	0	0	0	0	0	2	0	0	0
Loyal . . .	0	0	2	0	1	0	0	1	1	0	0	0	1	0	1	2
Man	17	5	22	8	19	8	11	10	26	15	24	26	24	18	86	69
Mayor . . .	1	1	0	0	0	1	1	2	1	2	0	0	1	0	1	3
Me	1	1	1	6	4	1	10	6	4	9	6	7	8	9	9	7

Response Word	4th M	4th F	5th M	5th F	6th M	6th F	7th M	7th F	8th M	8th F	10th M	10th F	12th M	12th F	College M	College F
							CITIZEN									
Member . . .	4	0	5	7	3	8	12	11	4	9	0	4	1	0	3	2
Men	2	1	1	0	1	0	1	0	1	0	1	0	3	1	1	0
Mother . . .	1	0	0	0	0	0	0	0	0	1	2	0	0	1	0	0
Myself . . .	0	0	0	0	0	0	2	0	0	0	2	0	1	2	1	1
Native	0	0	0	1	0	0	1	3	0	1	2	0	2	0	1	0
Natural . . .	0	0	0	0	0	0	0	0	0	0	0	0	0	0	2	0
Neighbor . .	0	0	0	1	1	0	0	1	2	1	0	0	0	0	3	1
Nice	1	1	1	1	3	2	0	2	0	1	0	0	0	0	0	0
Nixon	0	0	0	0	0	0	0	0	0	0	0	0	0	0	0	2
Noncitizen .	0	0	0	0	0	0	1	1	0	0	0	0	0	0	0	2
Outlaw . . .	0	0	0	0	0	0	0	2	2	0	0	0	0	0	0	0
Part	1	0	0	0	2	0	0	0	0	0	0	0	0	1	0	0
Patriot . . .	0	0	0	0	1	1	1	0	0	1	3	2	3	1	5	7
Patriotic . .	0	0	0	0	0	0	0	0	0	0	1	0	2	1	1	4
Pedestrian .	0	0	0	0	2	0	1	0	0	0	0	0	0	0	0	0
People	41	48	52	54	38	48	34	28	32	37	36	33	30	25	28	18
Person . . .	74	70	63	76	78	105	93	91	69	77	70	58	53	62	67	55
Policeman .	0	0	0	0	0	0	0	0	0	0	0	2	0	0	0	0
Polite	0	0	0	2	0	0	0	0	0	0	0	0	0	0	0	0
Politics . . .	0	0	0	1	0	0	1	0	0	0	0	0	1	0	1	3
President . .	0	1	1	1	0	0	0	1	0	1	2	0	0	1	2	3
Prisoner . .	0	0	0	0	0	0	0	1	2	0	1	0	0	0	0	0
Pupil	0	2	0	1	0	0	0	2	1	0	0	0	0	0	0	0
Roman . . .	0	0	0	0	0	0	0	1	0	0	2	0	0	0	0	1
School	1	3	0	0	0	0	1	0	0	0	0	1	0	0	0	0
Ship	1	0	2	1	2	0	1	1	1	1	1	0	1	1	1	0
Sit	0	0	2	1	0	0	0	0	0	0	0	0	0	0	0	0
Soldier . . .	0	1	2	1	3	0	1	1	3	1	4	1	6	1	19	3
State	0	2	1	0	0	2	0	0	1	1	1	3	4	0	6	10
Student . . .	1	2	1	1	2	0	1	0	1	0	0	0	0	1	0	1
Tax	0	0	0	0	2	0	0	0	0	0	0	0	0	0	0	0
Tom Paine .	0	0	0	0	0	0	0	0	0	0	0	0	0	0	0	2
Town.	3	3	3	2	2	1	0	3	0	2	2	0	0	3	3	1
US	0	0	0	0	0	0	0	0	1	1	1	0	4	5	1	0
USA	0	0	0	0	3	4	3	5	1	3	4	9	9	10	39	58
United States	0	0	1	2	0	1	4	3	1	9	3	6	6	10	6	14
Us	1	0	0	0	0	0	0	0	0	2	0	0	0	0	0	0
Vote	0	0	0	1	0	2	0	1	0	3	0	0	2	0	21	25
Voter	0	0	0	0	0	0	1	0	2	0	1	0	2	1	14	1
							41. CITY									
Big	9	9	21	9	6	12	6	3	3	6	13	19	11	16	29	22
Block	1	0	1	0	0	1	1	0	1	0	2	1	1	0	17	6
Brainerd . .	0	0	0	0	0	0	0	0	0	0	0	0	0	0	2	0
Building . . .	3	2	3	4	8	2	2	0	0	2	1	3	2	1	7	7
Buildings . .	3	2	9	4	6	7	7	11	11	3	9	9	12	1	14	21
Busy.	0	3	0	2	1	2	0	2	1	5	1	2	2	4	4	9
Car	2	2	0	1	1	0	1	0	0	0	0	0	1	0	0	0

Response Word	4th M	4th F	5th M	5th F	6th M	6th F	7th M	7th F	8th M	8th F	10th M	10th F	12th M	12th F	College M	College F

CITY

Response Word	M	F	M	F	M	F	M	F	M	F	M	F	M	F	M	F
Cars	2	3	1	1	0	2	2	2	1	2	3	3	1	2	2	2
Chicago . . .	0	0	0	0	1	0	1	2	1	0	0	0	0	1	0	5
Cities	1	0	2	1	0	0	1	0	2	0	0	0	0	0	0	0
Citizen . . .	1	0	0	1	2	0	1	0	0	0	0	0	0	0	0	1
Community .	1	0	0	0	0	0	0	0	2	0	0	0	1	1	1	0
Country . . .	8	18	9	13	4	10	7	20	9	8	6	5	6	9	15	18
County . . .	1	2	0	0	0	1	1	1	0	1	1	0	0	0	1	0
Crowded . .	1	0	0	0	0	0	0	0	0	0	0	1	0	2	0	1
Dirt	0	0	0	0	0	0	0	0	0	0	0	0	0	0	2	5
Dirty	0	0	0	0	0	0	0	0	0	0	0	1	3	2	3	3
Duluth . . .	0	0	0	0	0	0	0	0	0	1	0	0	0	0	3	2
Farm	2	0	0	1	0	0	1	0	1	0	0	0	0	0	1	1
Good	1	0	2	0	0	0	1	0	0	0	0	0	0	1	0	0
Hall	0	2	0	0	1	1	0	0	1	1	0	0	1	1	1	2
Home	1	2	3	2	3	3	1	3	4	0	0	2	1	0	4	3
House	3	3	9	2	5	3	1	0	2	1	1	0	0	1	3	2
Houses . . .	2	1	0	0	2	1	1	3	3	1	3	3	1	1	3	3
It	0	2	1	0	0	0	0	0	0	0	0	0	0	0	0	0
Large	0	0	1	0	0	0	2	4	2	3	5	4	3	4	10	10
Life	0	0	0	0	0	0	0	0	0	0	0	0	0	0	3	3
Lights	0	0	0	0	0	1	0	0	0	2	0	0	1	1	1	5
Live	1	7	1	2	3	3	2	1	1	2	1	1	1	0	0	3
London . . .	0	0	0	0	0	0	0	1	0	0	0	0	0	2	0	0
Metropolis .	1	0	0	0	1	1	1	2	0	1	0	0	0	1	2	1
Mile	0	0	0	0	1	0	0	2	0	0	0	0	0	0	0	0
Mine	0	0	0	0	0	0	0	0	0	0	0	0	0	0	0	2
Minn	2	1	2	1	1	0	0	1	3	0	0	0	0	0	0	0
Minneapolis .	8	7	8	26	14	7	20	25	25	39	32	31	28	21	8	12
Minnesota . .	0	2	1	1	1	1	0	1	0	0	0	0	0	0	0	0
Mpls	2	6	2	2	9	26	9	15	19	28	30	20	41	35	40	64
New York . .	0	0	0	0	0	0	2	1	2	1	2	3	3	2	10	7
Nice	0	2	0	0	1	0	0	0	0	0	0	0	0	0	0	0
Noise	1	1	0	0	1	2	1	2	0	0	0	4	0	0	3	6
Park	1	0	0	0	0	0	0	1	1	0	1	0	0	1	5	2
People . . .	14	14	11	13	15	5	14	13	16	13	12	15	12	11	36	28
Place	11	9	9	13	7	11	3	6	1	5	1	3	1	3	2	2
San Francisco	0	0	0	0	0	0	0	0	0	0	0	0	0	0	0	2
Sewer	0	0	0	0	0	0	0	0	0	0	1	0	0	1	3	0
Skyscrapers .	0	0	0	0	0	0	2	0	0	0	0	0	1	0	0	0
Square . . .	2	0	2	0	2	3	0	0	2	2	2	2	5	5	24	12
State	19	29	29	32	8	25	16	19	23	29	33	34	13	31	15	29
Stores	0	0	0	2	1	0	0	1	0	1	0	1	0	1	0	0
St. Paul . . .	1	0	0	1	2	0	0	0	1	0	1	0	0	0	22	23
Street	1	1	4	6	2	4	2	2	6	5	8	7	9	5	14	9
Streets . . .	1	1	0	2	0	0	1	0	1	1	1	1	3	0	7	7
Suburb . . .	0	0	1	1	0	0	3	0	0	0	0	1	0	2	1	2
Town	118	103	106	99	111	100	126	90	85	70	63	57	73	57	130	102
Traffic . . .	0	0	0	0	1	0	0	1	0	0	1	1	0	1	2	7

Response Word	4th M	4th F	5th M	5th F	6th M	6th F	7th M	7th F	8th M	8th F	10th M	10th F	12th M	12th F	College M	College F
CITY																
Urban	0	0	0	0	0	0	0	0	0	0	0	2	0	0	1	1
Village	1	0	1	1	2	0	0	1	2	1	1	2	1	0	7	2
Water	0	0	0	0	0	0	0	0	0	2	0	1	2	1	1	1
42. CLEARER																
Ah	0	2	0	1	0	0	0	0	0	0	0	0	0	0	0	0
Air	0	1	0	1	1	0	0	0	0	0	0	1	0	1	2	0
Better	5	3	3	5	4	6	3	1	2	3	1	2	3	3	5	3
Black	1	0	2	1	1	2	1	0	1	0	1	0	2	0	0	1
Blacker	0	2	2	0	0	0	0	0	1	0	0	0	0	0	0	0
Blue	0	0	0	0	0	1	1	1	1	1	0	1	0	0	3	0
Blur	0	0	1	0	1	0	2	2	2	2	1	1	2	1	1	1
Blurred	0	0	0	0	1	0	0	2	1	1	1	2	0	0	2	1
Blurry	0	3	1	3	1	7	2	6	2	6	0	4	0	4	1	5
Bright	5	1	7	6	7	6	2	4	4	5	3	8	4	5	7	8
Brighter	4	6	1	9	1	8	4	7	8	6	8	11	4	9	16	17
Broader	0	0	0	0	0	0	0	0	0	0	0	0	0	0	3	0
Clarity	0	0	0	0	0	0	0	0	0	0	0	0	0	0	0	2
Class	0	0	2	1	1	0	0	0	0	0	0	0	0	0	0	0
Clean	16	22	21	12	10	19	10	15	8	10	14	10	8	10	11	10
Cleaner	3	6	2	3	2	4	6	5	2	4	5	5	6	6	16	10
Clear	33	41	29	20	22	29	11	15	18	10	14	8	11	5	20	7
Clearest	0	1	1	0	1	1	2	1	3	1	5	2	3	1	8	3
Clearly	0	0	1	1	0	1	0	0	0	0	0	1	2	4	0	2
Closer	0	0	0	0	0	0	0	0	1	0	2	1	0	1	2	2
Cloudier	0	0	0	0	0	0	2	2	3	0	0	1	1	0	5	6
Cloudy	0	0	3	1	1	1	2	5	6	8	7	3	12	11	20	27
Coat	2	0	0	0	1	0	0	0	0	0	0	0	0	0	0	0
Confused	0	0	0	0	0	0	0	0	1	0	0	0	2	0	2	1
Crystal	0	1	0	0	0	0	0	1	1	0	0	0	1	0	3	2
Dark	5	6	2	6	10	4	7	1	7	1	5	2	2	1	7	5
Darker	6	5	5	4	5	5	17	14	8	10	11	6	6	4	26	12
Day	0	1	0	1	1	0	0	3	1	0	2	2	0	1	4	0
Deeper	0	0	0	0	0	0	0	0	0	0	0	1	0	0	0	3
Dense	0	0	0	0	0	0	0	0	1	0	1	0	0	1	1	2
Denser	0	0	0	0	0	0	0	1	0	1	1	0	1	1	1	3
Dim	1	0	0	0	0	0	0	2	1	1	2	0	0	0	3	0
Dimmer	0	0	0	1	1	1	1	0	1	1	0	1	1	3	4	14
Dirt	5	5	3	5	5	3	3	2	1	1	1	0	2	1	3	1
Dirtier	1	1	2	2	1	2	1	3	3	4	2	2	2	1	1	0
Dirty	7	5	5	3	7	8	6	8	8	3	2	5	5	3	4	2
Distinct	0	0	0	0	1	0	2	0	0	0	0	0	2	2	5	3
Dull	1	0	2	0	0	2	1	1	1	2	2	1	2	5	2	3
Duller	1	0	0	3	1	1	1	2	1	1	4	2	2	1	3	9
Ear	3	0	0	0	0	0	1	0	1	0	0	0	0	0	0	0
Easier	1	0	0	1	0	1	4	1	0	4	3	1	1	2	1	5
Easy	0	0	0	0	0	1	0	1	1	0	0	0	0	3	3	1
Eyes	0	0	0	1	0	0	1	0	0	1	0	0	1	1	2	0
Fade	0	0	0	1	0	0	0	0	0	2	0	0	0	0	0	0

Response Word	4th		5th		6th		7th		8th		10th		12th		College	
	M	F	M	F	M	F	M	F	M	F	M	F	M	F	M	F

CLEARER

Response Word	M	F	M	F	M	F	M	F	M	F	M	F	M	F	M	F
Faint ...	0	0	0	0	0	0	1	0	0	0	1	1	0	1	0	2
Fainter ..	0	0	0	1	1	0	0	0	0	2	1	0	0	0	0	1
Farther ..	0	1	0	1	0	1	1	2	2	1	0	1	0	0	0	1
Fast	2	5	4	1	1	3	0	2	1	1	2	0	1	2	1	1
Faster ..	0	1	2	0	0	0	0	0	1	3	0	1	0	2	0	2
Fear	0	0	0	0	0	0	0	0	1	0	0	0	0	0	2	0
Fine ...	0	0	0	0	2	0	0	0	0	0	0	0	0	0	2	0
Floor ...	0	0	0	1	0	0	2	0	0	0	0	0	0	0	0	0
Focus ...	0	0	0	0	0	0	1	2	0	0	0	0	0	1	0	0
Fog	7	2	3	7	7	3	4	1	2	8	3	3	3	3	10	9
Foggier ..	0	2	1	1	0	0	3	5	3	2	2	3	3	2	11	9
Foggy ...	1	2	1	5	4	6	13	13	9	19	9	20	9	16	21	37
Fuzzy ...	0	0	0	0	1	2	2	3	3	2	1	2	1	0	0	3
Glass ...	5	5	6	4	7	5	4	4	10	4	10	7	10	3	11	9
Glasses ..	0	1	3	1	2	3	1	5	0	1	0	2	1	3	0	2
Good	1	3	4	1	3	0	0	1	1	2	1	1	1	0	0	0
Hands ...	0	0	0	0	0	0	0	0	0	0	0	0	0	0	2	0
Happy ...	3	0	0	0	0	0	0	0	0	0	0	0	0	0	0	0
Hard	0	0	0	1	0	0	1	0	1	1	0	2	0	0	0	0
Harder ..	1	1	1	1	0	1	3	2	1	4	0	0	2	1	6	0
Hazier ..	0	0	0	0	0	0	0	0	2	0	0	0	1	0	0	2
Hazy	0	0	0	0	0	2	0	0	0	5	0	0	4	5	4	3
Hear	3	0	0	1	0	0	1	0	0	0	0	0	0	1	0	0
Her	2	0	0	0	0	0	0	0	0	0	0	0	0	0	0	0
Is	0	0	2	0	1	0	0	0	1	0	2	0	0	0	0	0
Lake ...	1	0	0	0	3	2	0	0	0	0	2	0	1	0	1	0
Land ...	1	1	2	0	0	0	0	0	0	0	0	0	0	0	0	0
Light ...	0	1	1	0	0	0	0	1	1	0	1	3	0	1	1	4
Lighter ..	0	1	0	1	0	0	0	1	0	0	1	1	0	1	2	3
Look ...	0	0	1	2	0	2	1	1	1	0	1	0	0	1	1	0
Louder ..	1	0	1	2	0	0	1	1	1	2	0	0	0	3	1	3
Lucid ...	0	0	0	0	0	0	0	0	0	0	0	1	0	0	1	2
Meaning ..	0	0	0	0	0	0	0	0	0	0	0	0	2	0	0	0
Messy ...	1	1	0	1	0	2	0	0	0	1	0	0	0	0	0	0
Misty ...	0	0	1	0	0	0	1	1	0	1	3	2	0	0	0	0
Mud	0	0	0	0	0	0	0	3	5	1	2	4	4	3	4	4
Muddier ..	0	0	0	0	0	0	0	0	0	0	0	0	0	0	1	2
Muddy ...	0	0	0	0	0	0	0	0	1	0	0	2	1	0	3	2
Near	0	1	1	2	0	0	0	0	1	0	0	0	0	0	0	3
Nearer ..	2	0	0	1	0	0	0	2	1	2	0	1	1	2	6	5
Neat	0	1	0	2	0	1	1	1	0	0	0	0	0	2	0	1
Neater ..	0	0	0	1	1	3	0	0	1	1	0	1	2	0	0	1
Nice	2	8	1	0	2	1	1	0	0	1	1	0	1	0	0	0
Nicer ...	0	1	0	1	1	2	0	4	0	0	0	1	0	0	2	0
No	0	0	1	0	2	2	0	0	0	0	2	2	0	0	0	0
Noisy ...	0	0	0	0	0	0	0	0	0	0	0	0	2	0	0	0
Not	2	1	1	0	0	0	2	0	0	0	0	1	1	1	1	1
Now	0	1	0	0	1	0	3	0	0	0	1	1	3	0	2	0
Opaque ..	0	0	0	0	0	0	0	0	0	0	0	0	0	1	2	0

Response Word	4th		5th		6th		7th		8th		10th		12th		College	
	M	F	M	F	M	F	M	F	M	F	M	F	M	F	M	F

CLEARER

Response Word	M	F	M	F	M	F	M	F	M	F	M	F	M	F	M	F
Picture	0	2	0	1	0	1	1	2	0	0	0	3	0	3	3	7
Plain	0	1	0	3	1	4	0	1	0	2	0	3	2	3	4	7
Plainer	1	1	0	2	1	1	2	4	0	2	0	2	0	2	4	9
Plane	0	2	0	0	0	0	0	0	1	0	0	0	0	1	0	0
Rain	0	0	1	0	0	0	0	0	0	0	1	0	0	1	3	0
Read	1	0	3	0	1	2	0	0	0	1	0	0	0	0	0	1
Right	3	0	0	0	0	1	0	0	0	0	0	0	0	0	0	0
Rough	0	0	0	0	0	0	0	0	2	1	0	0	0	0	0	0
See	9	26	9	18	14	10	8	9	2	7	9	13	7	7	15	31
Seeing	0	0	0	0	1	0	0	0	1	1	2	0	0	0	0	0
Seen	0	1	0	1	0	0	0	0	1	2	0	0	1	1	0	1
Sharp	0	0	0	0	0	0	0	2	1	0	0	1	0	0	3	2
Sharper	0	0	0	0	0	2	0	3	0	0	1	4	0	2	2	12
Shiny	1	0	2	0	2	0	1	1	1	1	0	1	0	0	1	1
Shorter	0	0	0	0	0	0	0	0	0	0	0	0	0	0	0	2
Sight	1	0	2	0	0	1	0	1	0	0	1	0	0	0	1	0
Skin	0	0	0	0	0	0	0	0	1	0	1	1	0	0	2	1
Sky	3	7	7	4	4	3	7	5	3	5	9	11	6	9	10	9
Sloppy	0	0	1	0	0	2	0	0	0	0	0	0	0	0	0	0
Slower	0	0	1	0	0	0	0	0	0	1	0	0	0	2	1	0
Smoke	1	0	2	0	0	0	0	0	1	0	0	1	0	0	0	0
Smooth	1	0	0	1	0	1	2	0	1	1	1	0	0	0	1	2
Soft	0	0	0	2	0	0	0	0	0	0	0	1	0	2	0	1
Softer	0	0	0	0	0	2	2	0	2	1	1	1	2	0	4	2
Speak	0	1	0	2	0	0	0	1	0	1	0	3	0	0	0	0
Steer	0	0	2	0	0	0	0	0	0	0	0	0	0	0	0	0
Stronger	0	0	0	0	0	0	0	0	0	0	0	0	0	0	0	2
Sunny	0	0	0	2	0	0	0	1	0	1	0	1	1	1	0	0
Than	8	2	5	6	13	2	14	4	12	5	13	7	22	11	37	21
The	1	0	0	0	2	0	0	0	0	0	1	0	0	0	0	0
Then	3	1	3	4	7	1	4	1	3	1	0	0	2	0	2	0
Thick	0	0	0	1	0	0	0	0	1	0	1	0	0	0	2	3
Thicker	3	0	2	0	0	1	0	1	0	0	4	1	1	1	3	2
Thin	0	0	0	0	1	1	1	0	2	0	0	0	1	0	1	0
Think	0	0	0	0	1	0	0	1	0	0	0	0	0	1	2	0
Thinking	0	0	0	0	0	0	0	0	1	1	0	1	3	2	0	2
To	0	0	0	0	2	0	0	0	0	0	0	0	0	0	0	0
Transparent	0	0	0	0	0	0	3	0	1	0	1	2	4	3	2	3
Unclear	0	1	0	0	0	1	1	0	2	1	1	0	1	0	1	3
Understand	0	0	0	1	0	0	0	0	0	1	0	1	2	1	4	2
Understandable	0	0	0	0	0	0	0	0	0	0	1	0	0	2	1	1
Vague	0	0	1	1	0	2	0	0	0	0	1	1	0	1	2	4
Visible	0	0	0	0	0	0	2	2	0	0	0	2	1	0	1	1
Vision	0	0	0	0	0	3	1	0	1	0	0	3	3	4	2	5
Wash	0	0	3	0	0	0	1	0	0	0	0	1	0	0	0	0
Water	1	1	3	1	8	3	8	4	8	5	10	10	12	4	22	14
Weather	0	1	0	0	0	0	0	0	0	0	2	0	4	0	2	0
White	2	2	1	1	1	0	5	6	0	3	4	2	0	0	2	2
Who	2	0	0	0	1	0	0	0	0	0	0	0	0	0	0	0

Response Word	4th M	4th F	5th M	5th F	6th M	6th F	7th M	7th F	8th M	8th F	10th M	10th F	12th M	12th F	College M	College F
							CLEARER									
Window	1	2	1	5	4	4	4	4	6	1	6	0	3	4	7	12
Write	0	2	3	4	1	5	0	0	0	0	0	0	0	0	0	1
Writing	0	0	0	0	0	0	0	0	0	1	0	2	0	0	1	0
You	2	2	1	1	0	2	0	0	1	1	0	0	0	0	0	0
							43. CLOSER									
Away	0	0	1	3	0	2	0	2	2	0	1	4	1	2	3	5
Back	2	0	0	2	1	0	0	1	0	0	1	0	0	0	0	0
Beside	0	0	0	0	0	0	1	1	0	0	2	0	0	0	1	0
Better	0	0	2	1	0	1	0	1	0	0	1	0	1	0	0	0
Boy	1	0	0	0	0	0	0	1	0	2	0	0	0	1	0	2
By	2	3	3	1	1	3	1	1	0	1	3	2	1	0	2	4
Came	1	2	2	2	1	0	0	0	0	0	0	0	0	0	0	0
Car	0	0	0	0	0	0	0	0	0	2	1	0	0	0	1	1
Clearer	0	0	0	3	0	0	1	3	0	0	0	0	0	0	0	1
Close	36	43	36	24	26	31	22	19	14	13	13	4	8	6	16	5
Closed	0	1	1	1	0	1	0	0	1	2	0	0	1	0	0	0
Closely	0	0	0	0	0	0	0	0	0	0	0	2	0	0	0	0
Closest	1	0	2	0	1	0	3	1	3	4	7	1	3	1	5	2
Closet	1	2	2	4	1	2	1	2	1	0	0	1	1	0	0	2
Clothes	0	1	1	1	0	1	2	0	2	0	0	1	0	0	0	0
Come	10	10	12	7	11	10	7	3	2	2	8	4	5	2	9	11
Coming	0	1	3	1	2	2	0	0	0	0	0	0	0	0	0	0
Companionship	0	0	0	0	0	0	0	0	0	0	0	0	0	0	2	0
Contact	0	0	0	0	0	0	0	0	0	0	0	0	0	0	'2	0
Crowd	0	0	0	0	0	0	0	0	0	0	2	0	0	0	0	0
Dear	0	0	0	0	0	0	0	0	0	1	0	0	0	0	0	2
Distance	0	0	0	0	0	0	0	1	0	0	3	0	1	0	3	0
Door	2	6	2	2	4	5	3	3	3	0	4	0	0	2	3	2
Family	0	0	0	0	0	0	0	0	0	0	0	0	1	0	0	2
Far	14	15	14	12	13	23	10	14	18	10	9	13	9	5	14	18
Fare	0	0	0	0	0	0	0	0	0	0	2	0	0	0	0	0
Farther	42	46	46	65	38	59	73	82	72	92	55	75	67	63	101	134
Fast	1	2	3	1	2	2	1	1	0	0	1	1	0	0	2	1
Faster	2	1	3	0	2	3	1	1	3	2	0	0	3	2	3	0
Father	5	3	1	0	3	1	6	4	8	3	0	0	0	1	1	1
For	0	0	0	0	2	0	0	1	0	1	2	1	1	1	0	0
Friend	0	0	0	0	0	1	0	0	0	0	2	0	0	0	0	0
Further	0	1	0	0	1	3	1	5	2	2	3	1	2	4	7	4
Girl	0	0	0	0	0	0	3	0	3	0	7	0	1	0	4	0
Go	2	1	2	2	1	0	0	0	0	0	0	0	0	1	0	0
Her	1	0	1	0	1	1	0	0	0	2	1	0	1	0	1	0
Here	1	0	1	2	4	0	2	0	1	2	0	3	0	2	1	3
Hold	0	0	0	0	0	0	1	0	0	0	0	2	0	0	0	1
Hot	0	0	0	1	0	1	1	1	0	0	0	2	0	1	0	0
House	0	1	0	0	0	0	0	0	2	0	0	1	0	0	0	0
In	0	1	1	1	2	0	0	1	1	0	1	0	1	1	0	1
Intimate	0	0	0	0	0	0	0	0	0	0	0	0	0	0	0	2
It	2	0	0	1	0	1	0	0	0	0	0	0	0	0	0	1

Response Word	4th M	4th F	5th M	5th F	6th M	6th F	7th M	7th F	8th M	8th F	10th M	10th F	12th M	12th F	College M	College F
CLOSER																
Kiss	0	1	0	0	0	1	0	1	0	2	1	0	1	0	0	2
Longer . .	1	0	0	1	1	0	0	0	3	0	0	0	0	0	1	0
Look . . .	0	1	1	1	1	1	0	0	0	0	0	1	2	0	3	2
Lose . . .	2	0	0	2	1	0	1	0	0	1	0	0	0	0	0	0
Love . . .	0	1	0	0	1	1	0	1	0	1	0	0	2	4	3	1
Make . . .	2	1	0	0	0	0	1	0	0	0	0	0	0	0	0	0
Me	2	1	2	0	2	2	0	3	1	0	2	1	1	2	1	1
Move . . .	0	0	2	0	1	0	0	1	0	0	2	2	1	4	2	0
Near . . .	9	27	17	21	12	17	18	14	16	13	12	23	13	39	55	71
Nearer . .	13	16	8	17	12	15	29	29	15	28	23	34	33	44	115	132
Necking . .	0	0	0	0	0	0	0	0	2	0	0	0	0	0	0	0
Next . . .	0	0	1	1	1	0	0	2	1	0	0	0	0	0	3	0
Nice . . .	0	0	0	0	0	0	0	0	0	0	2	0	0	0	0	0
No	0	0	1	0	1	1	0	0	2	0	0	1	0	0	0	1
Now	1	4	0	0	1	1	2	0	0	1	1	2	1	0	2	2
Open . . .	1	3	3	1	4	2	1	0	3	1	4	0	2	1	0	0
Opener . .	0	0	0	1	0	0	0	0	2	0	0	0	0	0	0	0
People . .	0	1	0	0	0	0	1	0	0	1	0	0	0	0	2	1
Please . .	0	0	2	0	0	0	0	1	2	0	1	1	0	0	0	0
See	1	4	1	0	1	0	0	0	0	0	1	1	0	2	0	0
Shut . . .	1	1	1	3	1	1	1	1	0	0	1	2	0	2	1	1
Sit	0	0	0	0	0	0	0	0	1	1	1	1	2	0	1	1
Sitting . . .	0	0	0	0	0	0	0	0	0	0	0	0	0	0	2	0
Slower . .	0	0	0	2	0	0	0	0	4	0	0	0	0	0	1	0
Smaller . .	0	0	0	0	0	1	2	0	1	0	0	0	0	0	0	0
So	2	2	0	1	2	1	0	0	1	0	0	0	0	0	0	0
Stand . . .	0	0	0	0	0	0	0	1	0	1	2	2	1	1	1	0
Still	0	0	0	0	0	0	0	0	0	0	1	1	1	0	0	2
Stop	0	0	0	0	0	1	2	1	0	0	0	0	0	0	0	0
Than . . .	3	0	6	3	11	4	9	2	4	2	8	3	13	3	24	7
The	3	0	0	1	2	1	0	0	0	0	1	0	0	0	0	0
Then . . .	3	5	1	2	6	3	1	0	1	1	0	0	3	0	3	0
Tight . . .	0	0	1	0	0	2	1	2	1	1	1	2	4	5	2	1
Tighter . .	0	0	0	0	1	0	0	1	0	1	1	1	0	1	2	2
To	20	8	16	10	18	4	7	11	17	12	17	14	18	13	32	22
Together .	1	1	0	4	7	3	2	6	2	8	4	7	5	6	11	13
Too	0	0	0	0	2	0	0	0	2	0	0	0	0	0	0	0
Touch . . .	1	0	0	0	0	0	0	1	0	1	1	1	0	2	2	1
Up	2	0	1	1	1	1	1	0	1	0	1	1	0	2	1	0
Walk . . .	0	0	0	1	0	1	1	0	0	0	1	1	1	1	3	4
Warm . . .	0	0	0	0	0	0	0	0	0	0	1	0	0	0	4	1
Yet	0	0	1	1	1	0	1	0	0	1	2	0	0	1	0	1
You	1	0	2	3	1	0	0	1	0	2	1	2	0	0	2	3
44. COLD																
Air	1	0	1	3	0	1	0	0	0	0	0	0	0	1	1	0
Bad	0	0	3	0	1	0	1	0	0	0	2	1	0	0	0	2
Bed	1	0	0	0	0	0	0	0	0	0	2	0	0	0	0	0
Bitter . . .	1	0	2	2	0	5	1	1	0	1	0	0	0	0	0	1

Response Word	4th		5th		6th		7th		8th		10th		12th		College	
	M	F	M	F	M	F	M	F	M	F	M	F	M	F	M	F

COLD

Response Word	4th M	4th F	5th M	5th F	6th M	6th F	7th M	7th F	8th M	8th F	10th M	10th F	12th M	12th F	College M	College F
Blue	0	0	0	0	0	0	0	0	0	0	0	1	1	0	2	1
Brrr	1	1	1	3	1	3	3	2	2	0	0	2	0	0	0	0
Chill	0	1	0	0	1	1	2	0	0	1	1	0	2	1	2	0
Chilled	0	0	0	0	0	2	1	0	0	0	0	1	0	0	0	0
Chilly	3	6	4	1	9	2	3	8	2	2	4	0	0	0	1	0
Coat	5	1	3	1	5	6	1	6	2	2	3	5	4	2	5	3
Cool	3	3	5	4	2	2	2	7	1	3	2	1	0	2	0	2
Cough	0	0	1	0	1	0	2	4	1	1	1	2	0	2	1	1
Damp	0	1	0	0	0	0	0	1	0	0	0	1	3	0	0	0
Dank	0	0	0	0	0	0	0	0	0	0	0	0	0	0	2	0
Dark	0	0	1	1	0	0	2	0	1	1	3	3	2	2	1	3
Day	0	0	0	1	0	0	0	0	0	0	1	0	0	0	0	4
Drink	0	0	0	0	0	0	0	1	0	0	2	0	0	0	0	0
Feet	0	0	0	0	0	0	0	0	0	0	0	0	0	0	0	3
Freeze	9	21	9	15	15	16	7	11	12	8	11	5	5	4	3	4
Freezer	0	0	0	0	1	0	2	0	0	0	0	0	0	0	0	0
Freezing	6	17	17	11	16	23	6	9	6	6	5	4	1	3	2	0
Frigid	0	0	0	0	1	2	0	0	0	0	1	1	0	1	0	1
Frost	0	2	1	1	1	0	0	0	1	0	0	0	0	0	0	1
Froze	0	1	1	1	3	2	3	1	0	1	0	1	0	2	0	0
Frozen	3	3	2	4	1	3	1	1	1	0	1	0	1	0	0	0
Hard	0	0	0	0	0	0	1	1	2	1	1	3	2	0	3	3
Harsh	0	0	0	0	0	1	2	0	0	0	0	0	0	0	0	0
Heat	2	0	0	0	0	0	0	0	1	2	0	1	0	0	3	2
Hot	59	45	56	53	42	40	69	69	87	72	55	59	68	72	163	166
House	0	0	0	0	0	0	2	0	0	0	1	0	0	0	0	0
Ice	15	10	8	4	9	10	13	13	7	17	14	12	7	8	23	16
Ill	1	0	0	0	1	0	0	0	0	0	0	0	0	1	3	0
Jacket	0	1	0	1	1	0	1	1	2	0	1	0	0	0	0	0
Nice	0	2	0	0	0	0	0	0	0	0	0	0	1	0	0	0
Nose	0	0	1	0	0	0	0	0	1	1	0	0	1	1	1	3
Not warm	1	2	0	0	2	0	0	1	0	0	0	0	0	0	0	0
Old	1	2	3	1	1	1	0	0	0	0	0	0	0	0	0	0
Outside	1	1	1	0	0	2	1	0	0	0	0	0	0	0	0	0
Shiver	8	2	5	4	1	3	2	3	1	1	1	1	2	2	0	4
Shivering	2	0	0	2	0	0	1	1	0	0	1	0	0	0	0	0
Shower	0	0	0	0	0	0	0	0	0	1	0	0	0	0	5	1
Sick	7	4	3	2	3	2	4	5	4	1	4	6	3	4	2	6
Sickness	0	0	2	0	0	0	1	0	1	4	2	2	4	0	1	1
Sneeze	0	0	0	0	1	1	0	1	0	1	1	2	0	1	0	2
Snow	23	34	23	24	27	22	29	34	22	24	37	53	46	47	100	109
Soft	0	0	0	0	1	0	0	0	0	0	0	0	1	0	1	2
Today	0	1	0	0	0	1	0	0	0	0	0	0	0	0	3	2
Uncomfortable	1	0	1	0	1	3	1	1	0	0	1	1	1	2	2	3
Warm	48	46	43	64	59	56	49	38	57	50	52	33	52	47	89	76
Warmer	1	2	0	0	0	0	0	0	0	0	0	0	0	0	0	0
Water	2	0	0	0	0	0	1	0	2	1	1	0	0	1	2	3
Weather	1	1	3	4	4	1	0	0	0	3	4	3	5	3	7	3
Wet	0	0	0	0	0	1	1	1	3	2	2	5	1	2	4	5

Response Word	4th M	4th F	5th M	5th F	6th M	6th F	7th M	7th F	8th M	8th F	10th M	10th F	12th M	12th F	College M	College F
							COLD									
White ...	0	0	1	0	0	0	1	0	1	1	0	0	0	0	2	2
Wind ...	5	5	3	2	2	4	1	1	0	1	0	4	0	2	2	1
Windy ...	1	3	1	0	4	0	1	0	0	0	0	0	0	1	0	0
Winter ..	14	15	20	19	9	17	17	10	15	24	21	25	17	29	35	47
Worm ...	2	1	0	0	0	1	0	0	0	0	0	0	0	0	1	0
Zero ...	0	0	0	2	0	0	0	0	0	0	0	0	0	0	0	0
						45.	COME									
All	2	0	3	0	1	1	0	1	0	0	0	0	0	0	0	0
Along ...	1	1	3	6	1	3	3	2	6	0	4	0	1	0	4	1
Arrive ..	0	0	0	0	0	1	0	0	0	0	0	2	1	0	3	1
Back ...	1	2	4	1	1	0	3	0	0	2	2	3	2	1	1	0
Bring ...	0	0	0	1	0	1	1	0	0	0	3	2	1	1	0	1
Came ...	31	33	22	36	19	33	43	47	43	38	23	19	38	34	59	33
Can	0	0	1	0	0	1	0	0	0	0	0	2	0	0	0	0
Close ...	0	1	0	0	0	0	1	0	2	1	1	1	0	2	1	2
Closer ..	1	0	2	3	1	1	2	1	1	3	4	0	2	3	6	2
Coming ..	2	2	1	0	1	2	0	0	1	1	1	0	0	1	1	0
Command .	0	0	0	0	0	1	0	0	0	0	0	0	0	1	2	2
Dinner ..	0	1	0	2	0	0	0	0	0	1	0	0	0	0	0	1
Don't ...	0	0	3	0	0	0	0	0	0	0	0	0	0	0	0	0
Down ...	0	1	2	0	1	1	0	0	0	1	0	0	1	0	2	2
Enter ...	0	0	1	0	0	0	0	0	1	1	0	0	1	0	5	0
Fast	2	0	1	0	0	0	0	0	0	0	0	0	0	0	3	1
Follow ..	2	0	0	0	1	1	0	0	0	0	1	0	0	0	0	0
Forward .	0	0	0	1	1	2	0	0	0	0	0	0	0	0	0	0
From ...	0	0	0	0	1	0	0	0	0	0	0	0	2	2	1	0
Game ...	0	0	0	0	0	0	0	0	0	0	0	0	2	0	0	0
Get	0	0	0	0	0	1	0	2	0	0	1	1	3	0	1	3
Go	50	52	35	57	39	61	59	88	62	81	72	106	53	84	143	212
Going ...	3	0	1	0	1	2	0	0	0	0	1	1	0	0	0	0
Gone ...	0	0	0	1	1	0	3	4	4	0	4	0	5	6	1	1
Hear ...	4	3	2	1	2	4	0	0	0	0	0	0	0	0	1	0
Heard ..	2	0	0	0	0	0	0	1	0	0	0	0	0	0	0	0
Her	1	0	0	1	2	0	1	0	0	0	2	1	0	0	0	0
Here ...	38	41	45	43	60	43	27	28	34	47	37	44	34	37	62	88
Hither ..	0	0	0	0	0	0	0	0	1	0	0	2	1	1	4	5
Home ...	11	6	11	8	10	10	13	10	9	12	13	10	19	18	26	21
House ...	1	3	0	0	1	3	2	2	0	0	0	0	0	0	1	0
Hurry ...	1	0	3	1	1	0	2	4	1	0	0	2	0	0	0	0
In	10	15	16	17	16	17	15	6	11	6	11	6	12	5	17	13
Into	0	0	0	2	0	1	1	0	0	0	0	0	2	1	1	0
Invitation .	0	0	0	0	0	0	0	0	0	0	0	0	0	0	0	2
Leave ...	0	0	0	0	0	0	1	0	0	1	1	0	1	1	1	3
Look ...	0	2	0	1	0	0	0	0	0	0	0	0	0	0	0	0
Me	5	3	1	0	3	0	0	0	3	1	0	1	1	0	1	0
Move ...	1	0	0	0	1	0	1	1	0	0	0	0	0	0	1	2
Near ...	3	1	1	1	1	0	2	0	0	0	1	0	1	0	1	4
No	1	0	0	0	0	1	0	0	1	0	0	0	0	2	0	2

Response Word	4th M	4th F	5th M	5th F	6th M	6th F	7th M	7th F	8th M	8th F	10th M	10th F	12th M	12th F	College M	College F
							COME									
Now	1	0	5	1	3	0	6	9	6	3	7	10	7	3	17	15
On	12	19	21	12	15	6	6	3	10	3	4	1	5	1	11	7
One	0	0	2	0	1	0	0	0	0	0	0	1	0	0	0	0
Out	2	2	1	0	1	0	3	2	1	1	3	1	2	4	5	1
Over	5	9	0	10	1	2	2	7	2	5	7	3	6	4	12	4
People	1	0	0	0	0	0	0	0	0	0	1	1	0	1	2	0
Place	1	0	2	0	0	2	1	0	0	0	0	0	0	0	1	0
Please	0	1	0	0	1	1	0	0	0	0	0	0	0	0	2	1
Proceed	0	0	0	0	0	0	0	0	0	0	0	0	0	0	2	0
Quick	0	1	0	0	0	0	1	0	1	0	1	0	0	0	2	2
Quickly	0	1	0	1	0	0	0	0	2	1	1	1	1	0	0	1
Return	0	0	0	0	0	0	0	0	1	1	0	0	0	0	0	2
Run	3	0	3	0	0	3	2	2	0	4	0	0	2	0	5	3
Running	0	0	0	0	0	0	0	0	0	0	0	0	0	0	2	0
See	0	2	1	1	1	2	1	0	0	0	0	2	0	2	3	2
Some	1	1	1	1	2	1	0	1	0	0	0	0	0	0	0	1
Soon	0	2	0	0	0	2	0	1	0	0	1	0	0	0	0	2
Stay	1	3	0	2	0	1	1	1	2	5	0	1	1	0	1	4
Stop	0	0	0	0	0	1	0	0	0	2	0	0	1	0	0	0
Then	0	2	0	0	0	1	0	0	0	0	0	0	0	0	2	0
There	2	1	1	1	2	3	3	1	0	0	0	0	0	1	0	0
Think	0	0	0	0	1	0	0	0	0	0	0	0	0	0	0	2
Through	0	0	0	0	0	0	1	0	0	0	0	0	1	0	3	0
To	9	6	9	10	14	4	9	4	7	4	6	1	13	5	15	7
Together	1	0	0	0	0	0	0	0	1	0	2	1	1	1	5	0
Toward	1	0	3	0	0	2	0	1	0	1	1	1	0	2	1	2
Up	0	0	0	0	0	0	0	0	0	0	0	0	0	0	2	1
Walk	1	5	8	0	4	4	1	2	2	3	3	3	0	1	1	2
Went	0	1	0	1	0	0	2	0	2	1	1	1	1	2	2	2
Where	1	3	2	0	2	0	0	0	3	2	2	1	2	3	5	2
With	5	3	4	9	7	4	5	7	8	5	9	8	8	8	14	9
						46.	COMFORT									
Ah	0	0	0	0	0	0	2	0	0	0	0	0	0	0	0	0
At ease	0	0	0	0	0	0	2	0	3	0	0	0	1	1	0	0
Bed	9	12	5	11	12	12	19	28	30	32	28	29	30	35	34	63
Blanket	0	1	0	0	0	0	0	2	1	2	0	2	1	1	1	7
Car	0	0	2	0	0	0	0	0	1	0	5	1	1	1	1	0
Chair	17	18	9	16	26	15	20	18	25	22	29	20	37	25	53	38
Cold	0	0	1	0	1	0	0	0	0	0	0	1	1	1	5	3
Come	3	1	4	1	2	1	0	0	0	1	0	0	0	0	0	0
Comfort	0	0	0	0	0	2	0	0	0	0	0	0	0	0	0	0
Comfortable	17	8	7	10	10	10	7	5	5	3	2	1	1	0	0	1
Console	0	0	0	0	0	0	0	1	0	0	0	0	0	1	2	0
Cool	2	1	0	0	0	1	0	0	1	0	0	0	0	0	1	1
Couch	2	3	1	2	2	0	1	4	7	1	9	3	3	1	6	1
Cozy	1	3	2	5	5	3	1	1	2	3	0	2	2	1	4	2
Davenport	1	2	2	0	1	1	0	0	0	2	0	1	0	0	2	0
Discomfort	1	0	1	1	1	1	4	5	6	6	6	2	6	5	15	8

Response Word	4th		5th		6th		7th		8th		10th		12th		College	
	M	F	M	F	M	F	M	F	M	F	M	F	M	F	M	F

COMFORT

Response Word	M	F	M	F	M	F	M	F	M	F	M	F	M	F	M	F
Ease ...	1	2	0	5	4	5	6	9	11	10	5	11	10	12	42	23
Easily ..	0	1	3	0	1	0	0	0	0	1	0	0	0	0	0	0
Easy ...	12	3	10	13	9	17	11	12	5	5	8	12	9	8	4	3
Easy chair.	1	0	0	0	0	0	0	1	1	0	1	0	1	0	2	1
Enjoying .	0	0	0	2	0	0	0	1	0	0	0	0	0	0	0	0
Enjoyment .	0	0	0	0	0	0	0	0	1	2	1	0	1	0	0	0
Feel	1	2	1	3	2	2	0	0	0	0	0	0	0	1	0	1
Feel good .	1	2	0	0	2	0	0	0	0	0	0	0	0	0	0	0
Feeling ..	0	0	2	1	1	1	0	2	0	0	0	0	0	1	0	0
Fine	1	1	1	1	0	0	1	3	0	1	0	0	0	0	0	1
For	0	0	0	2	0	0	0	0	0	0	0	0	0	0	0	0
Fort	3	4	3	2	2	1	0	0	0	0	0	0	0	0	0	0
Fun	0	0	1	1	0	0	1	0	2	0	1	1	0	0	2	0
Good ...	8	5	6	5	9	3	8	0	5	1	4	1	2	0	6	6
Hand ...	2	0	0	0	0	1	1	0	0	0	0	0	1	0	0	2
Happiness .	0	0	0	0	0	0	0	1	0	0	2	0	0	0	3	2
Happy ...	5	9	2	1	3	8	0	2	2	2	1	3	1	1	1	7
Hard ...	6	4	14	11	12	5	5	9	12	10	5	5	3	4	10	7
Hardness .	0	0	0	0	1	0	0	0	2	2	0	0	1	0	0	0
Hardship .	0	0	0	0	0	0	1	1	0	0	1	1	1	1	1	3
Health ...	0	0	0	0	0	0	0	0	0	0	0	0	2	1	6	10
Heat	0	0	0	0	0	1	0	0	0	0	0	0	0	1	2	0
Help	0	2	0	2	0	1	1	2	1	1	1	3	0	1	0	1
Home ...	2	3	3	4	1	4	2	3	2	13	6	13	17	21	26	35
House ...	0	0	0	1	0	0	2	1	3	0	6	1	2	4	7	4
Hug	0	0	0	0	0	0	0	0	0	2	0	0	0	0	0	0
Lay	0	1	2	0	0	0	1	0	0	0	0	0	0	0	0	0
Laziness .	0	0	0	0	0	0	0	0	0	1	1	1	0	0	2	0
Lazy ...	1	2	3	0	4	4	3	5	2	3	3	5	1	7	3	5
Leisure ..	0	0	0	0	0	0	0	1	1	0	1	0	2	4	5	2
Like	0	2	1	1	1	0	0	0	1	0	0	2	0	0	0	0
Love ...	0	4	0	0	0	1	0	2	0	2	1	0	0	0	1	2
Luxury ..	1	0	1	2	2	3	0	1	0	5	7	3	3	3	2	0
Man	0	3	0	1	0	1	0	0	0	1	0	0	0	0	1	0
Miserable .	0	0	0	0	0	0	0	2	1	0	0	0	0	0	0	0
Misery...	0	0	0	0	0	0	0	0	0	0	0	0	1	0	1	2
Money ...	0	0	0	0	0	0	0	0	1	0	0	1	0	0	0	4
Mother ..	0	3	0	2	0	2	1	2	0	5	1	1	1	0	0	3
Nice	18	23	24	22	9	14	5	13	4	6	6	7	3	5	15	9
Pain	0	0	0	0	0	0	1	1	1	0	2	0	0	0	4	4
Peace ...	0	0	0	0	0	0	0	1	0	4	0	0	0	1	0	1
Pillow ...	1	2	2	2	0	1	0	3	3	4	1	2	2	3	6	10
Place ...	0	2	0	0	0	0	0	0	0	0	0	0	0	0	0	0
Pleasant .	0	0	0	1	0	0	0	0	0	0	0	0	0	0	0	2
Pleasure .	2	1	2	0	1	3	5	0	3	1	0	2	5	2	2	3
Quiet ...	0	0	0	0	0	0	0	0	0	0	0	0	1	1	2	1
Quilt ...	0	0	0	0	0	0	0	0	0	0	0	0	0	1	0	2
Relax ...	14	6	10	14	7	16	11	5	10	9	9	6	8	6	7	8
Relaxation .	0	1	0	1	2	0	0	3	1	1	4	1	3	1	2	3

Response Word	4th M	4th F	5th M	5th F	6th M	6th F	7th M	7th F	8th M	8th F	10th M	10th F	12th M	12th F	College M	College F
COMFORT																
Relaxed	4	2	4	2	3	6	3	5	3	4	1	4	1	0	4	1
Relaxes	2	0	0	0	0	0	0	0	0	0	0	0	1	0	0	0
Relaxing	1	0	2	0	1	1	2	1	2	2	0	1	2	1	0	0
Relief	0	0	2	0	0	0	0	0	1	0	0	0	0	0	0	0
Rest	7	2	7	6	3	3	9	8	4	5	6	4	4	2	13	6
Resting	0	1	1	0	0	0	2	0	3	0	0	0	0	0	0	0
Rich	0	0	0	0	0	0	1	0	0	0	0	0	0	0	3	0
Rock	0	0	0	0	0	0	0	0	0	0	2	0	0	0	0	0
Safety	0	0	0	0	0	0	2	0	0	0	0	2	0	0	0	1
Satisfy	0	0	0	0	0	0	1	0	0	0	0	0	0	0	0	2
Security	0	0	0	0	0	0	0	0	0	1	0	1	1	0	5	6
Setting	0	2	0	0	0	0	0	0	0	0	0	0	0	0	0	0
Sex	0	0	0	0	0	0	0	0	0	0	0	0	0	0	2	0
Sick	0	0	0	0	1	0	1	0	1	0	1	2	2	2	2	3
Sit	1	2	0	4	1	0	1	0	0	1	1	2	0	1	0	0
Sitting	1	2	1	1	0	2	1	0	0	0	0	0	0	0	0	0
Sleep	4	7	4	4	8	2	7	4	6	4	15	9	8	11	28	36
Sleeping	1	1	0	2	1	0	2	1	0	1	1	1	2	1	0	0
Sofa	2	3	0	1	1	0	1	1	2	2	4	1	5	1	3	3
Soft	27	23	36	39	36	46	46	26	18	17	23	29	22	17	43	58
Softness	0	0	0	2	0	0	0	0	0	2	1	1	1	2	2	1
Sooth	0	0	0	0	2	0	0	0	0	0	0	0	0	0	0	0
Soothe	1	0	0	2	0	0	0	0	1	0	0	2	0	0	0	1
Sorrow	0	0	0	0	0	0	0	0	0	1	1	1	0	1	4	1
Table	3	0	0	0	1	0	0	0	0	1	0	0	0	0	0	0
Terrible	0	0	0	2	0	1	0	0	0	0	0	0	0	0	0	0
Uncomfort	9	12	4	7	2	5	5	3	5	1	2	1	0	3	4	1
Uncomfortable	4	4	2	3	2	2	9	11	9	7	4	5	2	4	5	3
Uneasy	0	0	4	0	1	1	0	3	2	2	1	2	0	1	0	0
Warm	1	6	4	4	10	2	3	4	4	3	8	9	3	11	21	24
Warmth	1	1	1	0	0	2	0	0	1	1	2	2	2	5	19	19
Well	0	1	1	0	2	1	0	0	0	0	1	0	1	1	0	1
Woman	0	0	0	0	0	0	0	0	0	0	0	0	2	0	1	0
47. COMMAND																
Action	0	0	0	0	0	0	2	0	3	0	0	1	0	0	1	2
Admiral	0	0	0	0	0	0	1	0	0	0	2	0	0	0	1	0
Ahoy	0	0	0	0	2	0	1	0	0	0	0	0	0	Ahoy	0	0
Air	0	0	0	0	0	0	1	0	0	0	0	1	1	0	3	1
Air Force	0	0	0	0	0	0	0	0	0	1	0	0	1	1	5	2
And	0	4	2	0	1	1	0	0	0	0	0	0	0	0	0	0
Answer	0	0	1	0	1	3	0	2	2	1	2	0	1	0	1	5
Army	3	2	9	3	3	2	10	5	15	7	10	7	15	6	42	28
Ask	1	0	0	1	0	1	2	4	2	4	2	3	1	2	4	2
Attention	1	0	0	1	2	1	0	1	1	0	2	1	2	2	6	0
Authority	0	0	0	0	0	0	0	0	0	1	0	0	1	0	3	3
Bad	0	0	0	1	0	0	3	0	0	0	0	0	0	0	1	0
Bark	0	0	0	0	0	0	0	0	0	0	0	0	0	0	4	0
Boat	3	0	0	0	0	0	0	1	0	0	0	0	3	0	0	0

Response Word	4th		5th		6th		7th		8th		10th		12th		College	
	M	F	M	F	M	F	M	F	M	F	M	F	M	F	M	F

COMMAND

Response Word	M	F	M	F	M	F	M	F	M	F	M	F	M	F	M	F
Boss	3	0	1	1	2	4	1	0	0	1	3	2	1	4	4	1
Bossy . . .	0	0	0	0	0	1	0	0	0	2	0	0	0	0	0	0
Captain . .	1	3	3	1	0	1	1	1	4	2	3	6	6	2	5	0
Charge . .	2	0	1	1	1	0	0	0	2	1	3	1	0	0	1	2
Chief . . .	0	0	1	3	1	0	0	0	2	0	2	2	1	1	4	0
Come . . .	1	3	4	1	1	2	0	0	0	0	1	2	0	2	1	2
Commander	1	0	3	2	0	1	0	1	0	0	0	1	1	0	1	0
Control . .	1	0	0	0	0	0	0	0	0	1	0	0	1	0	1	2
Decision .	0	0	0	0	0	0	0	0	0	0	0	0	1	0	2	1
Demand . .	0	2	0	6	3	3	3	3	1	12	3	3	3	5	4	12
Direct . . .	0	0	0	0	2	1	1	2	0	0	0	2	2	2	4	3
Direction .	0	0	0	1	1	0	1	0	1	1	0	0	0	1	1	0
Disobey . .	1	1	1	1	1	1	1	2	6	2	4	0	3	0	0	1
Do	24	39	20	30	20	32	13	16	7	7	6	8	4	8	16	19
Dog	0	0	1	0	1	3	1	1	0	0	0	1	3	0	1	0
Do it . . .	1	0	0	2	1	3	4	0	1	1	1	2	0	0	0	0
Duty . . .	0	1	0	0	0	0	0	0	0	2	0	0	0	2	0	2
Father . .	0	0	0	0	1	0	0	0	0	1	1	2	1	4	1	1
Follow . .	0	0	0	0	0	0	0	1	0	0	0	1	1	0	1	2
Force . . .	1	0	0	0	0	0	1	1	1	1	3	0	1	0	1	0
General . .	3	1	2	1	1	2	6	3	3	5	18	3	7	5	14	13
Give	0	0	2	1	2	0	1	2	0	0	2	1	1	1	2	1
Go	6	1	2	1	1	7	4	4	4	6	7	5	6	8	12	16
God	0	0	0	1	0	0	0	1	0	0	0	0	0	1	0	3
Good . . .	1	0	2	0	0	1	0	0	0	1	0	0	0	0	0	0
Hair	0	1	0	0	0	0	0	0	0	1	2	0	0	0	0	0
Hair tonic .	0	0	0	0	0	0	1	0	1	0	0	0	2	0	0	0
Halt	0	1	0	1	1	0	2	0	0	0	3	2	2	0	6	3
Hand . . .	3	0	0	1	0	0	0	1	0	1	0	1	0	0	0	0
Hard . . .	3	0	1	0	3	1	0	0	0	0	1	0	1	2	2	1
Harsh . . .	0	0	0	0	1	1	2	0	0	1	1	1	3	2	3	5
Hear . . .	2	1	0	0	0	0	0	0	0	1	2	1	0	1	0	1
High . . .	2	0	0	0	0	0	0	0	0	0	0	0	0	0	0	0
Holler . . .	0	0	0	0	1	0	1	0	0	0	0	0	0	0	1	2
Hurry . . .	0	0	0	1	1	1	0	2	0	0	0	0	0	0	0	0
In charge .	1	0	0	0	1	0	1	0	2	0	0	1	0	1	1	0
Instruct . .	0	0	0	0	0	0	2	0	1	1	0	0	0	1	0	0
Jump . . .	0	0	0	0	0	0	0	0	0	0	0	0	2	0	0	0
King	0	3	2	0	0	0	1	2	0	0	0	0	0	0	0	1
Know . . .	0	1	0	0	0	2	0	0	0	0	0	0	0	0	0	0
Law	1	1	0	0	0	3	1	0	0	1	0	2	0	7	0	0
Lead . . .	1	0	1	0	2	0	0	1	3	0	0	0	1	0	3	2
Leader . .	5	1	5	1	4	0	1	0	5	3	3	1	6	3	7	3
Leadership	0	0	0	0	0	0	0	0	2	0	0	0	1	0	0	0
Lieutenant	0	0	0	0	0	0	0	0	1	0	1	0	1	0	0	2
Listen . . .	0	0	0	0	0	0	0	0	2	0	0	3	0	0	1	2
Loud	1	0	0	0	1	1	1	4	2	1	3	1	1	2	6	8
Mad	0	0	0	2	1	0	0	2	0	0	0	0	0	1	0	1
Make . . .	0	2	2	1	1	0	0	0	0	0	0	0	0	0	0	1

Response Word	4th M	4th F	5th M	5th F	6th M	6th F	7th M	7th F	8th M	8th F	10th M	10th F	12th M	12th F	College M	College F
							COMMAND									
Man	1	0	4	1	1	3	4	0	1	3	3	3	1	5	4	4
March . .	1	0	2	0	0	1	0	1	0	0	0	0	1	0	1	0
Master . .	0	0	1	3	0	0	0	0	0	0	1	0	0	0	0	0
Mean . . .	0	1	0	1	0	2	0	3	0	2	2	1	0	0	2	4
Men	2	0	0	0	0	0	0	0	0	0	0	0	0	0	0	0
Military . .	0	0	0	0	0	0	0	0	0	0	0	0	0	1	5	3
Mind . . .	2	1	1	1	1	1	0	0	0	0	0	0	0	0	0	0
Mother . .	3	1	0	1	0	0	1	1	0	2	0	4	0	2	0	0
Navy	2	0	2	0	1	0	0	0	0	1	0	0	6	2	7	2
Nice . . .	0	2	1	0	0	0	0	0	0	0	0	0	0	0	0	0
No	1	1	0	1	0	0	1	0	0	0	0	2	0	0	1	2
Now	0	1	2	0	2	0	1	0	0	1	0	0	2	0	0	0
Obey . . .	2	13	8	13	5	7	6	20	20	20	8	18	19	13	12	33
Officer . .	2	3	3	4	3	1	3	6	6	6	9	2	4	7	23	17
Order . . .	68	53	80	75	92	94	80	78	72	60	57	73	62	65	129	125
Ordered . .	3	0	1	0	0	0	0	1	0	0	0	0	0	0	0	0
Orders . .	5	2	3	1	3	0	0	4	2	1	1	2	2	5	0	2
Performance	0	0	0	0	1	1	1	0	1	1	0	0	1	0	6	3
Power . . .	0	0	0	0	0	0	1	0	0	0	1	0	1	1	2	0
Principal .	0	0	0	0	0	0	0	0	0	2	0	0	0	0	0	0
Private . .	0	0	0	0	0	0	0	0	3	0	0	0	0	0	0	0
Reply . . .	0	0	0	0	0	0	0	0	0	0	0	0	0	0	1	3
Request . .	0	0	0	0	4	4	1	4	2	3	1	0	0	2	1	1
Respect . .	0	0	0	0	0	0	0	0	0	0	0	0	0	0	3	1
Right . . .	1	2	0	0	0	0	0	0	0	0	0	0	0	0	0	0
ROTC . .	0	0	0	0	0	0	0	0	0	0	0	0	0	0	2	0
Rule	1	8	0	6	0	3	1	0	3	1	0	0	0	3	1	1
Ruler . . .	0	1	0	0	0	0	2	0	0	0	0	0	0	0	0	0
Salute . .	0	0	0	0	0	1	0	0	0	2	0	0	2	0	0	1
Say	2	8	2	2	2	1	1	4	1	0	1	1	0	2	0	2
Sergeant .	0	0	2	0	1	0	3	2	4	1	4	3	3	5	7	10
Sharp . . .	0	0	0	0	1	2	0	0	0	1	0	1	1	3	2	5
Ship	0	0	2	1	1	0	0	1	3	1	2	0	4	1	1	1
Shout . . .	0	1	2	1	1	1	3	4	4	4	3	5	2	4	7	12
Signal . . .	0	0	0	0	0	0	1	0	1	2	0	0	1	0	2	2
Sir	0	0	1	1	0	0	0	0	0	0	0	1	0	1	2	0
Soldier . .	1	1	1	0	0	1	3	1	2	1	1	7	1	3	6	13
Something .	0	0	0	1	3	0	0	0	0	1	0	0	0	0	0	0
Speak . . .	1	1	0	0	0	0	0	2	0	0	3	1	1	0	2	2
Statement .	0	0	0	0	0	0	1	0	0	2	0	0	1	0	0	1
Stay	0	0	0	0	2	0	0	0	0	0	0	0	0	0	0	0
Stern . . .	1	0	0	0	0	0	3	0	0	1	0	1	1	0	1	0
Stop	0	1	1	0	1	0	1	1	2	2	5	5	2	0	7	7
Strict . . .	0	0	0	1	0	2	0	1	1	0	0	2	0	1	2	3
Strong . .	0	0	0	1	1	0	1	0	0	0	0	0	0	0	1	1
Take	0	0	1	0	0	0	1	0	1	0	0	0	0	0	2	1
Talk . . .	1	0	2	2	0	0	2	4	1	2	2	0	0	2	2	2
Teacher .	0	1	0	3	0	2	3	1	0	10	4	8	6	3	2	4

92

Response Word	4th M	4th F	5th M	5th F	6th M	6th F	7th M	7th F	8th M	8th F	10th M	10th F	12th M	12th F	College M	College F
						COMMAND										
Teachers .	0	0	0	0	0	0	0	0	0	3	1	0	0	0	0	0
Tell	14	16	8	19	12	13	11	13	7	4	8	5	7	11	15	14
Telling . .	0	0	1	0	2	0	1	0	1	1	0	0	0	0	0	0
Ten	0	0	0	0	0	0	0	0	0	0	1	1	0	0	0	2
Told . . .	1	0	3	1	0	0	0	1	1	3	0	0	0	0	0	0
Uncommand	1	2	0	2	0	0	0	0	2	0	1	0	0	0	0	0
Voice . . .	0	1	0	0	0	0	0	2	1	2	0	1	1	1	10	1
Word . . .	0	0	0	1	0	1	1	0	1	1	0	0	1	0	0	2
Work . . .	3	2	2	2	0	2	1	1	0	1	2	3	0	1	0	0
Yell	1	1	1	0	2	1	4	2	0	5	6	4	1	6	6	9
You	2	1	1	0	0	0	0	0	0	0	0	0	0	0	0	1
					48.	COTTAGE										
Age	0	3	1	1	0	0	0	0	0	0	0	0	0	0	0	0
Alone . . .	0	0	0	0	0	0	0	0	2	0	0	0	0	0	0	0
Beach . . .	0	0	0	0	0	0	0	0	0	0	0	0	0	0	1	2
Big	0	0	0	0	2	1	0	0	0	0	0	0	0	0	0	0
Blue . . .	2	0	0	0	0	0	0	0	0	0	0	0	0	0	0	0
Boat . . .	0	0	1	0	1	0	0	0	1	2	0	1	1	1	1	0
Brook . . .	0	0	0	0	0	0	0	0	0	0	0	0	0	0	2	0
Cabin . . .	17	10	17	20	17	16	21	23	13	17	18	15	14	11	26	17
Camp . . .	1	0	0	2	1	0	1	0	0	0	0	0	0	0	0	0
Cheese . .	23	15	16	16	28	19	18	18	34	32	24	21	25	22	49	45
Cot	2	0	0	0	0	0	0	0	0	0	0	0	0	0	0	0
Cotton . . .	2	3	3	4	0	1	0	0	1	0	0	0	0	0	0	0
Country . .	0	0	0	1	0	0	1	0	1	2	1	4	2	6	2	2
Cozy	1	0	0	0	0	1	0	0	0	0	0	1	0	3	4	3
Cute	0	0	0	0	0	0	0	0	0	0	0	5	0	2	0	3
Do	2	0	0	0	0	0	0	0	0	0	0	0	0	0	0	0
Door	0	0	0	0	0	0	0	0	0	1	0	1	0	1	5	4
Eat	0	1	2	0	2	0	0	0	1	0	0	0	0	0	0	0
Farm . . .	0	1	0	1	0	0	0	0	0	0	0	1	0	0	2	2
Fence . . .	0	0	0	0	0	0	0	0	0	1	0	2	2	0	2	10
Fish	0	0	0	0	1	0	0	0	0	1	0	0	0	0	2	1
Fishing . .	0	0	0	0	0	0	2	1	4	0	1	0	1	0	0	0
Flowers . .	0	0	1	0	0	1	0	0	0	0	0	2	0	1	1	5
Food . . .	7	4	7	2	0	0	2	2	2	1	1	0	0	0	2	0
Forest . .	0	0	0	0	1	0	1	0	0	0	0	0	1	0	1	4
Fun	0	0	2	2	2	0	7	5	4	7	8	3	9	10	5	5
Girls . . .	0	0	0	0	0	0	0	0	2	0	0	0	0	0	0	0
Grass . . .	1	0	0	0	1	0	0	2	0	0	0	1	1	0	0	2
Green . . .	0	0	0	0	0	0	0	0	0	1	0	0	1	0	1	2
Grove . . .	0	0	0	0	0	0	0	0	0	0	0	0	1	0	3	1
Happy . . .	0	0	0	0	0	0	0	0	0	0	0	0	0	0	2	0
Home . . .	21	17	23	15	16	11	13	14	14	6	11	15	10	12	39	36
Honeymoon	0	0	0	0	0	0	0	0	0	1	0	3	1	1	1	1
House . . .	85	108	106	104	92	115	87	99	85	104	51	50	60	74	141	123
Hut	0	7	3	3	0	3	3	7	2	0	0	1	1	3	6	1
Ivy	0	0	0	0	0	0	0	0	0	0	0	0	0	0	2	3

Response Word	4th M	4th F	5th M	5th F	6th M	6th F	7th M	7th F	8th M	8th F	10th M	10th F	12th M	12th F	College M	College F

COTTAGE

Response Word	4th M	4th F	5th M	5th F	6th M	6th F	7th M	7th F	8th M	8th F	10th M	10th F	12th M	12th F	College M	College F
Lake	25	25	16	19	35	38	45	32	45	24	74	63	56	42	87	74
Lettuce . .	0	0	1	0	0	0	0	0	2	0	0	0	0	0	0	0
Little . . .	2	2	1	2	1	3	0	1	0	2	1	0	0	1	1	1
Live	1	3	0	5	0	1	2	2	0	0	1	1	3	1	10	4
Log	0	0	1	0	1	1	0	0	0	0	1	2	1	0	1	0
Logs . . .	2	0	0	0	1	2	0	0	0	1	0	0	1	0	2	2
Love . . .	0	0	0	0	0	0	0	0	0	1	0	1	0	2	0	1
Marriage .	0	0	0	0	0	0	0	0	0	0	0	0	2	0	1	1
Me	1	2	0	0	1	0	0	0	0	0	0	0	0	0	0	0
Mountains .	0	0	0	0	1	0	0	0	0	1	0	2	0	0	0	1
Nice	3	1	2	0	1	0	0	0	2	1	1	1	1	1	3	3
Peace . . .	0	0	0	0	0	0	0	0	0	0	0	0	0	1	1	2
Place . . .	1	0	3	2	1	1	0	1	2	1	1	0	0	0	0	0
Pleasant .	0	0	0	0	0	0	0	0	0	0	0	0	1	0	0	2
Pretty . . .	0	1	2	0	0	0	0	0	0	0	0	0	1	0	1	1
Quaint . . .	0	0	0	0	0	0	0	0	0	1	0	0	0	0	0	2
Resort . .	0	0	0	0	0	1	1	0	2	0	4	0	0	0	0	0
Rest	0	0	0	0	1	0	0	0	2	0	2	0	3	1	3	1
Room . . .	1	1	0	0	0	0	0	0	0	1	0	0	0	0	2	1
Roses . . .	0	0	0	0	0	0	0	0	0	1	0	0	0	1	0	5
Round . . .	0	0	2	1	0	0	0	0	0	0	0	0	0	0	0	0
Rustic . . .	0	0	0	0	0	0	0	0	0	0	0	0	1	0	0	2
School . . .	8	8	5	4	7	4	4	3	1	0	1	0	0	0	0	0
Shack . . .	0	1	1	0	0	0	1	0	1	1	2	2	0	0	1	0
Shutters . .	0	0	0	0	0	0	0	0	0	0	0	0	0	0	0	2
Sleep . . .	1	0	1	1	0	0	0	1	1	2	0	0	2	0	3	0
Small . . .	1	2	0	2	0	1	1	6	1	3	4	8	2	10	13	21
Summer . .	0	0	0	5	2	5	4	4	2	3	2	7	6	3	2	5
Swim . . .	0	1	0	2	1	0	4	0	3	0	1	1	1	0	0	1
Swimming .	0	1	0	0	0	0	0	1	1	3	0	1	0	0	0	1
Thatch . . .	0	0	0	0	0	0	0	0	0	0	0	2	0	0	0	0
Trees . . .	0	0	0	0	0	0	0	0	0	0	0	0	0	2	1	2
Vacation .	1	3	1	3	1	0	2	2	1	3	6	2	6	3	6	5
Village . .	2	1	1	1	0	0	1	1	0	1	0	0	1	0	1	0
Vine	0	0	0	0	0	0	0	0	0	0	0	0	0	0	2	1
Vines . . .	0	0	0	0	0	0	0	0	0	1	0	0	1	1	1	4
Water . . .	1	0	1	1	1	0	0	0	0	0	2	2	0	0	4	1
White . . .	0	1	0	1	0	2	0	2	0	1	2	3	4	10	11	24
Wood . . .	0	2	0	3	1	1	0	1	1	1	1	0	1	0	4	5
Woods . . .	1	2	2	4	4	1	4	4	1	2	2	6	5	4	7	10

49. CRY

Response Word	4th M	4th F	5th M	5th F	6th M	6th F	7th M	7th F	8th M	8th F	10th M	10th F	12th M	12th F	College M	College F
Aloud . . .	0	0	0	0	0	0	0	0	1	0	1	0	7	0	2	2
Anger . . .	0	0	0	0	0	0	0	1	0	0	2	0	0	0	0	1
Babies . .	1	2	0	0	0	0	0	0	0	2	0	0	0	0	0	0
Baby . . .	38	48	33	55	50	64	56	53	55	68	72	64	48	57	138	146
Bad	3	5	3	1	1	1	0	1	0	0	2	0	2	0	0	1
Ball	4	3	4	2	7	3	1	1	0	0	4	0	0	0	3	0
Bawl . . .	5	6	9	5	8	5	16	8	15	5	7	8	6	12	23	17

Response Word	4th M	F	5th M	F	6th M	F	7th M	F	8th M	F	10th M	F	12th M	F	College M	F
							CRY									
Boohoo ...	0	0	0	0	0	0	1	2	3	2	0	0	0	0	0	0
Boy	1	0	0	0	1	0	0	0	0	0	1	1	0	0	2	0
Buy	1	0	0	1	0	1	0	1	0	0	1	0	2	0	1	1
By	3	2	2	1	0	2	1	3	1	1	1	0	1	0	4	0
Carry ...	0	2	1	0	1	0	1	0	0	0	0	0	1	0	0	0
Child ...	0	0	0	0	1	2	1	0	1	1	0	1	2	3	2	1
City	0	0	2	2	0	0	0	0	0	0	0	0	0	0	1	0
Cried ...	4	1	1	2	0	0	1	3	1	1	0	0	0	0	1	1
Crying ..	5	2	4	4	2	0	3	0	1	0	1	0	4	0	0	1
Die	0	0	2	1	0	0	2	0	0	0	0	0	3	0	0	0
Dog	1	0	0	0	0	0	1	0	0	0	0	0	0	0	2	3
Doll	0	0	1	0	0	0	1	0	0	0	1	0	0	0	2	3
Don't ...	3	1	0	0	0	2	0	0	0	0	0	1	0	0	0	0
Dry	0	5	4	0	2	2	3	3	1	0	0	0	3	3	2	0
Face ...	2	0	0	0	0	0	0	0	0	0	1	0	0	0	0	0
For	0	0	0	0	0	0	0	0	2	1	1	0	1	1	1	0
Girl	2	0	1	0	2	0	2	1	0	0	1	1	2	1	3	0
Happy ...	8	7	12	11	3	3	15	18	16	12	5	6	4	10	5	2
Hard ...	1	1	2	0	3	0	0	0	0	1	1	4	1	1	3	2
Heard ...	0	0	0	0	2	0	0	0	0	0	0	0	0	0	0	0
Help	1	0	0	0	1	0	0	0	1	1	0	0	2	2	0	1
Hi	2	1	0	0	0	0	0	0	0	0	0	0	0	0	0	0
Hit	1	0	0	0	1	1	2	0	0	0	0	0	0	0	1	0
Holler ..	0	0	1	1	0	2	2	1	0	1	0	1	0	1	3	2
Howl	0	0	0	1	0	0	0	2	0	0	0	0	1	1	2	3
Hurt ...	3	7	8	6	5	6	4	0	2	2	2	2	3	3	6	4
Joy	1	0	0	0	0	0	1	2	0	0	0	0	0	0	0	0
Laugh ...	9	12	6	12	7	12	12	30	16	26	14	27	9	20	34	37
Loud ...	6	4	6	3	8	9	9	8	6	2	10	9	12	7	16	22
Mad	3	4	1	3	4	3	2	0	1	0	2	0	4	1	0	0
Me	0	0	0	0	2	0	0	0	0	2	0	0	1	1	1	1
My	1	4	2	1	1	1	2	2	0	1	0	0	1	0	1	0
No	1	1	0	0	0	0	0	0	0	0	0	0	0	0	2	1
Noise ...	2	5	6	6	5	3	5	2	2	2	3	4	4	2	3	3
Not	1	1	0	1	0	0	0	0	0	0	0	0	0	0	0	2
Now	1	1	0	0	0	0	0	0	1	1	0	0	0	0	1	2
Only	1	0	1	1	2	0	0	0	0	0	0	2	0	0	1	0
Out	5	2	4	2	6	2	2	0	3	1	6	3	6	6	11	10
Out loud ..	0	0	0	0	0	0	0	0	1	0	0	0	0	0	2	0
Pain	0	0	1	0	0	0	0	0	2	0	0	0	3	1	3	2
Person ..	2	1	1	0	0	0	0	0	0	0	0	0	0	0	0	0
Pout	1	2	0	1	1	0	0	1	1	0	0	0	0	1	1	0
Sad	17	18	11	16	12	18	13	16	10	18	5	18	13	23	10	18
Say	0	0	0	0	0	2	0	0	1	0	0	0	0	0	0	0
Scream ..	2	1	4	2	6	5	5	6	3	4	2	10	2	3	7	16
Shout ...	0	2	1	0	0	0	1	0	2	0	6	2	4	3	1	5
Shy	0	2	0	0	0	0	0	0	0	0	0	0	0	0	0	0
Sigh	0	1	0	1	0	0	0	1	1	3	0	1	2	1	5	4
Sing	0	1	0	0	1	0	1	0	0	3	0	1	1	2	5	2

Response Word	4th M	4th F	5th M	5th F	6th M	6th F	7th M	7th F	8th M	8th F	10th M	10th F	12th M	12th F	College M	College F

CRY

Response Word	4th M	4th F	5th M	5th F	6th M	6th F	7th M	7th F	8th M	8th F	10th M	10th F	12th M	12th F	College M	College F
Sleep ...	1	2	1	0	0	0	0	0	0	0	0	1	0	1	1	4
Smile ...	2	3	0	1	5	2	3	2	5	2	1	1	3	3	7	6
Sob	2	5	1	8	5	5	5	6	11	10	7	8	7	10	13	32
Sorrow ..	0	0	0	0	0	1	0	1	3	0	4	2	1	1	4	6
Sorry ...	0	1	1	1	0	3	0	0	0	2	1	0	0	0	2	0
Sound ...	0	0	1	0	1	0	0	1	0	0	0	0	1	1	0	3
Talk	0	2	0	1	0	1	0	1	1	1	0	1	2	0	0	0
Tear ...	5	5	4	5	1	3	4	2	2	4	5	9	4	6	17	16
Tears ...	29	38	39	39	30	42	26	31	28	29	31	40	19	24	48	45
Terror ..	0	0	0	0	0	0	0	0	1	0	0	0	0	1	4	0
That	2	0	0	0	0	0	0	1	1	0	0	0	0	0	0	0
Tough ...	0	0	0	0	0	0	0	0	0	0	0	0	0	0	3	0
Try	3	1	1	2	0	2	1	1	2	1	1	0	0	0	1	1
Unhappy ..	5	3	1	3	0	1	3	2	1	4	0	2	0	0	1	4
Wail	1	1	0	1	0	1	0	2	0	2	0	0	3	0	3	3
Water ...	6	2	11	4	8	2	1	4	5	1	6	0	4	3	2	2
Weep ...	6	8	8	12	4	6	3	5	6	14	11	3	10	12	20	26
Wet	3	1	2	0	4	1	2	1	2	0	1	1	1	1	0	0
Whimper .	0	0	1	2	1	1	0	0	1	0	0	0	1	0	3	2
Whine ...	1	1	2	3	1	5	4	3	2	1	1	3	3	2	2	2
Why	0	0	0	1	1	0	0	0	2	1	2	0	4	1	3	0
Wind ...	0	0	2	0	0	0	0	0	0	0	0	0	0	0	0	0
Wine ...	1	1	2	0	2	1	0	0	0	0	0	0	0	0	1	0
Wolf	0	0	0	0	0	0	0	0	0	0	1	0	1	0	2	0
Word ...	2	0	0	0	0	0	0	0	0	0	0	0	0	0	0	0
Yell	1	0	2	2	7	1	7	4	11	5	8	4	7	3	10	5

50. DARK

Response Word	4th M	4th F	5th M	5th F	6th M	6th F	7th M	7th F	8th M	8th F	10th M	10th F	12th M	12th F	College M	College F
Afraid ..	1	2	1	0	0	2	0	0	0	0	0	2	0	0	0	0
Alley ...	0	0	0	0	0	0	0	0	0	0	0	1	2	0	1	0
Bark ...	2	0	0	0	3	0	0	0	0	0	0	0	0	0	0	0
Bed	1	1	0	2	0	0	1	2	3	0	1	1	0	0	1	0
Black ...	47	37	43	26	51	44	39	40	20	20	28	12	21	16	28	22
Blue	1	0	0	0	0	1	0	1	0	0	2	1	1	1	0	4
Bright ...	3	3	2	1	2	0	0	0	1	2	4	0	1	0	2	0
Brown ...	1	1	1	0	1	2	0	0	0	1	1	0	0	2	0	1
Clear ...	0	1	2	0	0	0	0	1	0	0	0	0	0	0	0	0
Closet ..	0	2	0	2	2	1	0	1	2	4	2	3	3	0	1	2
Cold	3	0	1	4	1	2	2	1	0	2	4	3	3	0	3	4
Color ...	0	1	0	0	1	2	0	1	2	0	0	3	1	0	0	2
Darkness .	2	0	0	0	0	0	0	0	0	0	0	0	0	0	0	0
Day	1	4	0	0	0	0	0	1	1	0	1	0	0	1	1	0
Fear ...	0	0	0	0	1	0	0	0	1	0	0	0	0	0	0	2
Ghost ...	1	0	0	0	0	0	2	1	0	1	0	0	0	0	0	0
Girls ...	0	0	0	0	0	0	0	0	2	0	0	0	0	0	0	0
Gloomy ..	3	0	1	1	0	0	0	2	0	1	0	0	0	0	0	1
Hair	0	0	1	1	0	1	2	0	0	1	1	0	0	0	0	2
Handsome .	0	0	0	0	0	0	1	1	0	0	0	1	0	2	0	0
House ...	0	0	0	0	0	0	0	0	0	1	0	0	0	1	3	1

Response Word	4th M	4th F	5th M	5th F	6th M	6th F	7th M	7th F	8th M	8th F	10th M	10th F	12th M	12th F	College M	College F

DARK

Response Word	4th M	4th F	5th M	5th F	6th M	6th F	7th M	7th F	8th M	8th F	10th M	10th F	12th M	12th F	College M	College F
Light . . .	98	103	90	112	88	99	123	122	126	140	114	135	138	136	305	313
Lonely . .	0	0	0	0	2	1	0	1	0	0	0	0	0	1	0	0
Love	0	0	0	0	2	0	0	0	0	0	0	0	1	1	1	0
Milk . . .	2	0	0	0	0	0	0	0	0	0	0	0	1	0	0	0
Monster . .	0	0	0	0	0	0	2	0	0	0	0	0	0	0	0	0
Moon . . .	0	1	1	1	1	0	1	1	0	1	2	1	1	2	2	3
Music . . .	1	0	0	0	0	0	0	0	0	0	0	2	1	1	0	2
Night . . .	52	52	60	54	43	61	36	42	52	38	46	59	52	61	86	95
Party . . .	0	0	0	0	0	0	0	2	0	0	0	0	0	0	0	0
Quiet . . .	0	2	0	1	0	0	0	0	0	0	0	0	0	0	0	0
Red	0	0	0	0	0	0	1	0	0	0	0	0	0	0	2	0
Room . . .	3	2	4	5	9	1	6	7	7	13	15	11	12	11	20	14
Scare . . .	1	0	2	1	1	1	1	1	0	0	0	0	1	0	0	1
Scared . .	1	1	1	7	3	3	4	2	1	0	0	4	0	1	0	2
Scary . .	5	4	3	11	4	6	2	2	0	3	0	1	0	1	0	0
See	3	3	6	4	6	1	0	0	2	0	0	0	0	0	0	0
Sky	0	1	0	0	0	0	0	0	2	0	0	0	0	1	0	0
Sleep . . .	3	6	0	0	1	0	0	1	4	3	1	0	0	0	3	2
Spooky . .	0	3	3	2	2	3	1	2	0	1	1	0	0	0	0	0
Stairs . . .	0	0	0	0	0	0	0	0	1	1	0	0	0	0	2	1
Warm . . .	1	0	0	0	0	0	0	0	0	1	0	0	0	0	2	1
Water . . .	0	1	0	0	3	2	0	0	0	0	1	0	0	0	0	0
White . . .	0	0	1	0	2	0	0	1	2	1	1	1	1	0	4	5

51. DEEP

Response Word	4th M	4th F	5th M	5th F	6th M	6th F	7th M	7th F	8th M	8th F	10th M	10th F	12th M	12th F	College M	College F
Below . . .	0	0	0	0	0	1	0	1	1	0	0	0	1	0	2	0
Big	5	10	3	6	7	7	4	4	1	0	3	3	3	0	2	2
Black . . .	0	0	1	0	1	0	2	1	2	2	0	4	2	0	1	2
Blue	0	0	0	0	1	1	1	1	0	3	3	3	3	5	9	9
Can	0	2	0	0	0	0	0	0	0	0	0	0	0	0	0	0
Canyon . .	0	0	0	0	1	1	0	0	0	1	2	0	0	0	0	1
Cave . . .	0	0	0	0	0	0	0	0	0	1	0	2	0	0	1	2
Clear . . .	0	1	0	0	1	0	0	0	0	0	0	0	0	2	1	0
Cold	1	0	0	0	1	1	1	0	1	0	0	2	2	0	4	1
Dangerous .	0	0	0	1	1	0	2	0	0	0	0	1	0	1	0	0
Dark . . .	7	15	14	19	15	21	22	30	16	25	33	32	34	43	73	96
Depth . . .	1	0	1	0	1	2	4	4	1	3	1	0	2	1	1	3
Ditch . . .	1	0	0	0	0	0	0	1	1	1	1	0	0	0	0	2
Down . . .	32	29	32	26	28	22	19	16	15	9	10	6	5	6	9	5
Empty . . .	0	0	0	1	0	0	0	2	0	0	0	0	0	0	1	0
Fall . . .	2	0	1	3	3	3	2	2	1	0	0	2	0	0	3	0
Far	12	9	21	10	18	12	12	4	8	3	4	4	6	2	9	6
Grave . . .	0	0	0	0	0	0	0	0	1	0	0	0	0	0	1	2
Ground . .	0	2	1	2	1	0	0	3	1	0	0	0	0	0	0	0
Gully . . .	0	1	2	0	0	0	1	0	0	0	0	0	0	0	0	2
Hard . . .	0	0	2	0	1	0	0	2	0	1	0	0	1	0	3	0
Heavy . . .	0	0	1	1	0	0	0	0	2	0	0	0	0	0	1	1
Help	0	0	0	2	2	1	0	0	0	0	0	0	0	0	0	0
Hi	0	0	2	0	0	0	0	0	0	0	0	0	0	0	0	0

Response Word	4th M	4th F	5th M	5th F	6th M	6th F	7th M	7th F	8th M	8th F	10th M	10th F	12th M	12th F	College M	College F
							DEEP									
High	24	20	15	13	17	13	12	14	11	12	7	13	11	18	13	24
Hole ...	41	39	29	39	27	36	23	22	12	13	18	9	7	9	29	18
Hollow ..	0	2	2	3	0	6	0	3	4	3	0	9	1	3	2	1
In	2	0	1	1	0	0	0	0	0	0	0	0	0	0	0	0
Lake ...	1	0	1	2	1	0	2	2	5	1	4	2	3	3	6	8
Large ...	1	1	0	3	1	3	0	2	0	3	0	0	0	3	4	0
Light ...	2	1	1	0	1	2	1	2	4	1	2	4	0	1	1	3
Little ...	0	0	0	1	1	1	0	2	0	0	0	0	1	0	1	1
Long ...	5	10	6	8	7	4	8	14	3	6	3	4	2	1	3	3
Loud ...	0	0	0	0	0	0	1	2	0	0	0	0	0	2	0	0
Low	16	30	12	22	16	24	14	17	17	19	15	8	6	3	6	12
Magic ...	0	0	0	0	0	0	0	0	0	0	2	0	0	1	0	0
Mountain .	0	1	0	0	0	0	0	0	2	1	0	0	0	0	0	0
Mud	1	0	2	1	0	0	0	0	0	1	0	1	0	0	0	0
Narrow ..	0	0	0	0	0	0	1	1	1	3	0	0	1	3	4	1
O	0	0	0	0	0	2	0	0	0	0	0	0	0	0	0	0
Ocean ...	2	2	1	0	1	4	7	4	4	9	16	8	15	12	26	24
Peep ...	2	1	2	0	0	0	0	0	0	0	0	0	0	0	0	0
Pit	2	2	3	2	2	2	3	3	0	0	3	2	1	2	2	4
Purple ..	0	0	0	0	0	0	0	0	1	0	0	0	0	0	1	2
River ...	0	1	1	1	0	0	0	0	2	3	3	6	2	6	5	7
Scary ...	2	0	1	0	1	1	0	1	0	0	0	2	0	0	0	0
Sea	1	0	2	5	1	6	6	4	6	3	7	16	15	15	22	25
Shallow ..	19	8	18	16	29	10	51	32	68	47	50	39	51	37	98	73
Short ...	3	1	2	0	1	0	0	1	2	1	1	0	0	1	1	0
Six	0	0	0	0	0	0	0	0	0	0	0	0	0	0	2	0
Skin	0	0	0	0	0	0	0	0	0	0	0	0	0	1	0	2
Sleep ...	1	3	3	4	8	8	3	1	4	2	4	5	8	3	34	25
Slow	0	0	0	1	0	1	0	0	0	0	0	2	0	1	1	0
Small ...	2	3	0	0	1	3	0	0	0	0	2	0	0	0	1	1
Snow ...	2	4	3	7	1	2	1	2	0	1	1	3	2	1	1	2
Soft	3	4	1	1	1	4	4	6	3	7	6	4	5	3	16	23
Steep ...	2	6	3	6	2	6	0	3	3	4	1	2	0	1	1	2
Thick ...	1	0	0	0	0	1	3	1	0	1	0	1	1	0	0	0
Tunnel ..	1	0	0	0	0	1	0	2	0	0	0	0	0	0	0	0
Under ...	2	0	2	0	0	0	1	0	0	3	0	0	0	1	0	0
Up	1	2	0	2	2	0	2	0	0	0	0	0	0	0	0	0
Valley ...	1	2	1	0	3	2	1	1	1	2	2	3	0	0	1	0
Voice ...	0	0	2	0	0	0	0	1	0	2	0	2	0	0	2	1
Warm ...	0	0	0	0	0	1	0	0	0	0	0	0	0	0	0	4
Water ...	15	10	16	9	21	9	8	11	22	20	27	20	35	30	53	49
Weep ...	0	0	0	2	0	0	0	0	0	0	0	0	0	0	0	0
Well ...	0	0	1	4	1	1	5	6	2	5	4	5	8	11	17	18
Wide ...	1	4	3	6	2	6	0	3	1	4	2	8	4	8	4	14
							52. DOCTOR									
Aid	0	0	1	0	0	0	0	0	0	1	0	0	0	0	2	1
Anderson .	0	0	0	0	0	0	0	2	1	0	1	0	0	0	0	0
Apple ...	0	1	0	0	0	0	1	0	1	1	0	0	0	0	0	2

DOCTOR

Response Word	4th M	4th F	5th M	5th F	6th M	6th F	7th M	7th F	8th M	8th F	10th M	10th F	12th M	12th F	College M	College F
Baby	0	0	0	0	0	1	1	0	0	1	0	1	0	2	0	0
Bad	1	0	2	1	3	0	3	0	0	0	0	0	1	0	2	0
Bag	0	0	0	0	0	0	0	0	1	0	0	1	1	1	3	2
Bed	1	1	2	0	0	0	0	0	0	1	0	0	0	0	1	0
Bill	0	0	1	0	0	0	0	1	0	0	1	0	2	0	1	1
Bills	0	0	0	0	0	0	1	1	0	0	0	0	0	0	2	0
Black bag	0	0	0	0	0	0	0	0	0	0	0	0	0	0	1	2
Blood	0	0	0	0	0	0	0	0	0	1	2	0	0	0	0	1
Boy	1	1	2	0	1	0	0	0	0	0	0	0	0	0	0	1
Care	0	1	0	0	1	2	1	2	0	0	0	0	0	1	2	1
Checkup	0	1	0	0	1	0	0	1	0	0	2	0	0	0	0	0
Child	0	0	0	2	0	0	0	0	0	0	0	0	0	0	0	0
Clinic	0	0	0	1	0	0	0	0	0	0	1	0	0	0	2	1
Cure	0	0	0	0	1	1	0	2	0	0	1	0	1	1	0	1
Degree	0	0	0	0	0	0	0	0	0	0	0	0	0	0	2	0
Dentist	5	2	5	4	5	6	3	1	2	3	6	4	7	6	11	6
Disease	0	0	0	0	0	0	0	0	0	0	1	0	0	0	2	0
Do	0	0	0	0	2	0	0	0	0	0	0	0	0	0	0	0
Doc	2	2	4	2	0	1	2	1	4	0	1	0	0	0	0	0
Father	0	0	0	0	0	0	0	0	0	1	0	0	0	0	2	2
Fix	1	1	1	1	2	0	0	0	1	0	1	0	1	0	1	0
Friend	0	1	0	0	4	3	1	0	2	0	5	1	1	5	3	2
Good	2	2	7	4	1	1	2	4	0	0	3	0	2	2	6	3
Heal	0	0	0	0	1	0	3	0	2	0	0	0	2	2	5	0
Healer	0	0	0	0	0	0	1	0	3	0	2	1	1	1	0	1
Health	21	17	18	17	24	15	10	12	12	14	16	12	22	16	36	39
Healthy	0	1	2	1	0	0	0	2	0	0	0	0	0	0	1	0
Heart	2	0	1	1	0	1	1	0	0	1	0	0	0	0	0	1
Help	22	17	17	14	9	22	13	7	8	4	6	7	8	6	20	13
Helper	2	3	2	5	1	3	2	4	0	2	3	1	0	0	0	2
Helpful	0	0	0	0	2	1	0	0	0	1	2	3	1	0	1	0
Helps	1	3	1	2	0	0	0	0	0	0	0	0	1	0	0	0
Hospital	4	3	4	2	8	5	12	5	4	6	9	11	7	5	8	25
House	0	0	0	0	1	0	0	1	0	0	0	1	0	0	4	1
Hurt	0	3	3	1	1	2	1	3	1	1	0	2	1	1	1	4
Husband	0	0	0	0	0	0	0	0	0	0	0	0	0	1	0	2
Ill	1	5	0	3	2	4	1	2	6	2	1	6	4	3	4	4
Illness	0	1	1	0	0	0	0	1	1	3	1	4	0	5	6	11
Ish	0	0	0	0	0	0	0	0	0	0	0	2	0	0	0	0
Jones	0	0	0	0	0	0	0	0	0	0	1	0	1	0	1	2
Kind	0	0	0	0	1	0	0	0	0	0	0	1	0	1	0	3
Lawyer	4	1	2	1	1	3	4	1	7	3	6	3	15	8	24	24
Life	0	0	0	0	0	0	1	0	0	0	0	0	0	0	3	0
Man	18	14	15	11	15	12	9	15	13	14	10	12	11	15	24	25
MD	1	1	2	2	4	1	4	1	7	1	1	0	1	1	8	2
Me	0	0	1	1	1	0	0	2	0	1	0	0	0	1	0	0
Mean	0	1	1	0	0	0	2	3	0	1	1	2	1	0	0	0
Medic	0	0	1	0	0	0	0	0	0	0	1	0	0	0	2	0
Medical	0	0	0	0	1	0	2	3	0	0	0	1	0	1	0	0

Response Word	4th M	4th F	5th M	5th F	6th M	6th F	7th M	7th F	8th M	8th F	10th M	10th F	12th M	12th F	College M	College F
							DOCTOR									
Medicine	4	5	15	4	12	13	17	12	12	15	14	9	16	14	27	33
Money	0	0	0	0	0	0	1	0	0	0	1	1	4	0	4	1
Needle	2	0	4	0	4	1	1	1	3	5	7	4	2	4	3	4
Needles	0	0	0	0	0	0	0	0	2	0	1	0	0	0	0	0
Nice	4	3	3	2	1	1	1	3	1	2	1	0	0	2	1	1
Nurse	60	95	65	93	53	72	59	80	59	68	59	67	43	58	70	103
Nurses	0	0	0	0	2	1	0	0	1	0	0	0	0	0	0	0
Office	1	1	1	4	2	1	2	2	1	3	1	3	1	4	3	3
Operation	0	0	1	0	1	0	0	0	1	1	0	0	2	0	0	0
Or	3	1	0	0	0	0	0	0	0	0	0	0	0	0	0	0
Ouch	1	1	0	0	0	0	4	0	0	0	0	1	1	0	0	0
Pain	1	0	0	0	0	0	2	1	3	2	4	1	0	0	3	2
Patient	6	2	4	1	4	1	2	4	3	3	1	1	1	2	9	8
People	0	1	2	1	2	0	0	0	0	0	1	0	0	0	0	0
Person	3	0	6	5	7	3	6	0	3	3	1	2	0	0	1	0
Ph. D	0	0	0	0	0	0	0	0	0	0	0	0	2	0	0	0
Physician	0	1	0	0	1	0	4	3	4	4	4	2	8	3	5	2
Pill	0	0	0	0	0	1	2	0	1	0	0	0	0	0	0	0
Pills	0	1	0	1	0	0	1	1	4	0	2	1	4	1	1	5
Prescription	0	0	0	0	0	0	0	0	0	0	0	0	0	0	2	0
Quack	0	0	0	0	0	0	0	0	2	0	0	0	0	0	1	0
School	0	0	0	0	0	0	0	0	0	0	0	0	2	0	4	1
Sergeant	0	0	2	0	0	0	1	0	1	0	0	0	0	0	0	0
Shot	6	5	5	9	6	14	2	10	2	12	3	3	3	2	2	3
Shots	2	4	6	5	9	9	2	2	4	11	6	8	1	1	1	1
Shout	0	0	2	0	0	2	0	1	0	0	0	0	0	0	0	0
Sick	24	29	9	32	19	20	27	30	33	25	20	33	25	26	56	54
Sickness	1	1	0	1	0	3	4	5	5	8	13	13	8	10	30	24
Stethoscope	0	0	0	0	0	1	0	0	1	0	0	1	1	0	3	4
Surgeon	0	0	0	0	1	1	1	0	4	0	1	0	1	1	1	1
Surgery	1	0	0	1	0	1	0	0	0	0	0	0	0	0	0	2
Well	3	0	2	0	2	0	1	2	0	1	0	0	1	2	0	3
White	0	0	0	1	0	0	1	1	0	1	1	0	5	2	12	12
Witch	0	0	0	0	0	0	0	2	0	0	0	0	0	0	0	0
Zhivago	0	0	0	0	0	0	0	0	0	0	0	0	0	0	0	2
						53.	DOGS									
Animal	31	27	21	25	20	27	20	22	7	13	10	3	1	3	7	2
Animals	19	25	17	20	19	19	9	12	7	7	6	4	2	4	6	3
Bark	6	11	12	21	13	16	12	15	3	11	6	8	2	5	9	19
Barking	1	0	1	0	1	1	0	3	0	0	1	0	0	0	0	1
Big	0	1	1	0	1	1	0	1	1	0	3	1	0	0	1	0
Bit	0	0	0	0	2	2	1	0	0	0	0	0	0	0	0	0
Bite	0	3	2	1	3	0	5	2	1	1	2	1	1	1	1	4
Black	0	0	1	1	0	0	3	1	0	3	0	2	1	2	1	1
Bone	0	1	0	0	3	0	0	2	4	1	1	1	1	0	0	3
Bones	0	2	1	1	2	1	2	1	2	3	2	2	1	1	1	4
Boy	0	0	2	0	2	1	1	0	0	0	0	0	1	0	0	0
Boys	0	1	0	0	1	0	0	2	0	1	1	2	0	2	0	0

Response Word	4th		5th		6th		7th		8th		10th		12th		College	
	M	F	M	F	M	F	M	F	M	F	M	F	M	F	M	F

DOGS

Response Word	4th		5th		6th		7th		8th		10th		12th		College	
Brown	1	0	2	0	1	3	0	1	0	1	2	33	0	1	3	2
Butch	0	0	0	0	0	0	0	0	0	2	0	0	0	0	0	0
Call	0	0	0	0	0	0	0	0	0	0	0	0	0	0	1	2
Cat	48	26	48	32	35	26	72	43	56	32	47	0	42	31	84	63
Cats	95	113	87	109	100	94	85	98	108	133	115	157	170	165	333	346
Collie	0	0	1	0	0	1	0	1	2	0	2	1	0	0	0	1
Creature	0	0	0	0	0	2	0	0	0	0	0	0	0	0	0	0
Cute	0	0	0	0	0	0	0	1	0	0	1	2	0	0	0	0
Dog	2	0	0	0	2	1	0	0	1	0	0	0	0	0	1	0
Fight	0	0	0	0	2	0	2	0	1	0	0	0	0	2	0	0
Food	2	0	0	1	0	0	0	1	1	1	1	0	1	0	2	0
Friend	1	0	1	0	2	1	0	0	0	0	1	0	0	0	0	0
Fun	0	0	1	0	2	1	0	0	0	0	0	1	0	0	1	0
Fur	0	1	1	1	1	0	0	0	2	1	2	2	0	2	1	3
Hair	1	0	1	1	0	0	0	3	6	0	2	0	3	1	3	0
Hairy	0	1	0	0	0	0	0	0	2	2	0	0	1	0	0	0
Hot	1	0	0	0	0	0	0	0	1	0	0	0	1	0	2	1
House	1	0	0	0	2	1	1	1	1	0	1	1	2	0	0	0
Hunting	0	0	0	0	0	0	0	0	0	1	0	0	0	1	3	1
It	2	0	0	0	0	0	0	1	0	0	0	0	0	0	0	0
Kennel	0	0	0	0	0	0	0	0	0	0	0	0	0	0	3	0
Large	0	0	0	0	0	0	0	0	0	0	2	0	0	0	0	1
Leash	0	2	1	0	0	2	0	0	1	0	0	0	0	1	1	0
Linda	0	0	0	0	0	0	0	0	2	0	0	0	0	0	0	0
Mutt	0	0	0	0	1	0	0	0	2	1	0	0	1	0	1	0
Nice	4	0	1	0	0	1	0	0	0	0	0	0	0	0	0	0
Pet	5	6	8	3	4	9	3	3	4	2	1	1	3	0	1	1
Pets	3	4	5	4	7	9	3	3	2	3	4	1	0	2	3	3
Play	1	0	1	0	2	0	0	0	0	0	0	0	0	1	0	0
Poodle	0	0	0	0	0	3	0	1	0	0	0	1	0	0	0	1
Puppies	0	3	0	3	1	1	1	1	3	2	1	1	2	3	1	2
Puppy	1	5	0	3	0	0	1	6	0	3	0	2	0	0	0	1
Pups	0	1	0	2	0	0	0	0	0	0	0	0	0	0	0	0
Rover	0	0	0	0	0	0	1	0	0	0	2	0	0	0	0	0
Run	1	0	1	0	2	0	0	0	0	0	0	0	0	0	1	0
Sheep	0	0	0	0	1	0	0	0	0	0	0	0	0	0	2	0
Smell	0	0	0	0	0	0	0	0	0	1	0	1	0	0	2	0
Tail	0	0	0	0	1	0	1	3	1	1	1	1	0	0	1	1
Tails	0	0	0	3	1	0	0	0	0	1	1	1	1	0	0	0
Trees	0	0	0	0	0	0	1	1	4	0	0	0	0	0	0	2
Trouble	0	0	2	0	0	0	0	0	0	0	0	0	0	0	0	0

54. DOORS

Response Word	4th		5th		6th		7th		8th		10th		12th		College	
Back	0	2	0	0	0	0	2	0	0	0	0	0	0	0	0	0
Bell	1	1	1	2	0	0	0	1	1	0	0	0	0	0	2	0
Bells	1	1	0	0	1	0	0	1	0	0	0	0	3	1	1	0
Big	1	2	3	1	0	0	1	0	0	1	1	0	1	0	2	0
Boars	0	0	0	0	0	0	0	0	0	1	0	0	2	0	0	0
Brown	0	0	0	2	0	0	1	0	0	0	0	2	0	2	1	1

Response Word	4th M	4th F	5th M	5th F	6th M	6th F	7th M	7th F	8th M	8th F	10th M	10th F	12th M	12th F	College M	College F
								DOORS								
Building . .	1	0	1	0	1	0	0	0	0	0	2	1	0	0	1	0
Buildings .	0	0	0	0	0	0	0	0	0	0	0	0	0	0	0	3
Car	2	0	1	1	1	0	1	0	1	0	3	4	10	2	0	1
Cars . . .	0	2	0	0	0	0	1	1	2	2	0	3	1	0	3	4
Cat	0	0	1	0	0	2	0	0	0	1	0	0	0	0	0	0
Cats . . .	0	0	0	1	0	0	0	0	0	0	1	0	0	0	1	4
Car	0	0	0	0	0	0	0	0	0	0	0	0	0	0	4	0
Chair . . .	1	1	0	0	0	0	0	0	2	2	1	0	0	0	0	1
Chairs . .	0	1	0	0	0	1	1	1	1	1	0	0	0	1	4	2
Close . . .	5	5	7	7	5	10	5	3	4	6	3	5	4	6	12	9
Closed . .	1	1	2	1	2	1	1	1	2	2	1	6	1	2	3	1
Closet . . .	1	1	0	1	1	2	0	0	1	0	2	2	0	0	0	2
Closets . .	0	0	0	1	0	0	0	0	1	2	0	0	0	1	3	0
Do	3	0	1	0	0	0	0	0	0	0	0	0	0	0	0	0
Dogs . . .	0	0	0	1	1	0	0	0	0	0	1	0	0	0	2	0
Door . . .	8	9	8	5	4	3	8	0	4	1	3	1	1	0	3	0
Doorknob .	0	1	0	0	0	3	0	0	0	1	1	0	0	0	1	2
Doorknobs	0	0	0	0	1	0	0	0	1	0	1	1	2	0	0	0
Enter . . .	0	0	0	0	0	0	0	0	0	0	0	2	0	0	1	1
Entrance .	0	0	0	0	0	0	0	0	1	0	1	0	0	1	4	0
Entrances .	0	0	0	0	0	0	0	0	0	0	0	0	0	0	0	2
Exit	0	0	1	1	0	0	3	1	0	1	2	0	0	0	0	1
Exits . . .	0	0	0	0	0	1	0	0	0	0	0	0	0	0	2	0
Floor . . .	3	1	1	0	3	0	2	1	0	0	0	0	1	0	0	0
Floors . .	2	2	2	0	0	2	3	0	0	3	0	0	2	1	3	3
Frames . .	0	0	0	0	0	0	0	0	0	0	0	0	1	0	3	0
Garage . .	0	0	0	0	0	0	0	0	1	0	3	0	2	1	0	0
Gate	0	0	0	1	0	0	0	0	2	0	0	0	0	0	1	2
Gates . . .	2	0	1	0	0	0	0	0	0	0	0	0	0	0	0	0
Glass . . .	0	0	0	2	1	1	3	0	0	2	2	0	4	0	2	0
Go	0	0	2	0	1	0	0	0	0	0	0	1	0	0	1	0
Green . . .	0	0	0	0	0	1	1	1	0	0	2	1	0	4	1	2
Hall	1	0	0	0	1	1	0	0	5	0	0	0	0	0	1	0
Handle . . .	3	0	2	4	1	0	2	5	1	0	2	1	1	0	8	3
Handles . .	0	0	1	0	0	0	0	2	2	1	3	3	3	3	7	7
Hinge . . .	0	0	1	0	0	0	2	1	0	0	0	1	2	1	3	1
Hinges . .	2	0	2	1	3	1	1	1	2	1	0	2	1	1	6	1
Home . . .	3	3	2	0	3	3	2	0	1	0	0	0	0	0	1	1
Hot	1	0	0	0	0	0	0	0	0	0	0	0	0	0	3	0
House . . .	25	30	31	31	41	27	23	26	22	22	25	31	20	32	33	38
Houses . .	2	2	1	3	3	4	0	2	1	2	2	4	2	2	7	14
In	0	5	2	4	3	5	2	0	1	2	1	0	1	2	3	1
Indoors . .	0	3	0	1	0	1	0	0	0	0	0	0	0	0	0	0
Jams . . .	0	0	0	0	0	0	0	0	0	0	0	0	0	0	2	0
Keys . . .	0	0	0	0	0	0	0	0	0	1	0	2	0	0	1	0
Knob . . .	4	3	1	3	6	2	5	6	5	1	4	5	1	5	14	5
Knobs . . .	2	1	1	2	1	4	1	1	4	6	4	8	5	8	16	17
Knock . . .	2	1	0	1	1	1	0	0	1	1	0	0	0	0	1	0
Large . . .	0	0	0	0	0	0	0	0	0	0	2	0	0	1	1	0

Response Word	4th M	4th F	5th M	5th F	6th M	6th F	7th M	7th F	8th M	8th F	10th M	10th F	12th M	12th F	College M	College F

DOORS

Response Word	4th M	4th F	5th M	5th F	6th M	6th F	7th M	7th F	8th M	8th F	10th M	10th F	12th M	12th F	College M	College F
Lock . . .	3	0	2	2	1	2	2	2	1	3	2	1	3	0	2	2
Locked . .	0	0	1	0	1	0	1	0	0	1	1	2	0	2	0	0
Locks . . .	1	0	0	0	0	0	0	0	0	1	3	1	2	2	1	3
Mats . . .	0	0	0	0	0	0	0	0	0	0	0	0	0	0	2	0
Open . . .	40	44	42	44	49	52	42	44	31	37	32	31	42	38	61	55
Opened . .	0	1	0	0	0	2	1	0	1	0	1	0	0	0	1	0
Opening . .	0	0	0	0	1	0	2	1	4	2	1	1	1	1	0	1
Openings .	0	0	1	0	0	2	3	1	0	1	1	0	1	1	4	1
Out	6	8	9	9	7	6	0	3	3	2	3	1	2	4	4	2
Outdoors .	1	2	0	1	0	0	1	0	0	1	0	0	0	0	1	0
Outside . .	4	7	2	7	2	6	0	2	0	1	0	1	0	2	1	0
Red	0	0	0	0	0	0	0	1	0	0	0	0	0	0	2	0
Revolving .	0	0	0	0	0	0	1	0	1	1	2	0	0	1	1	1
Roof . . .	0	0	0	0	1	0	2	0	0	0	1	1	0	0	0	0
Room . . .	0	2	2	0	2	0	2	4	1	0	0	0	0	3	1	4
Rooms . .	1	0	0	0	0	1	0	0	1	1	3	1	1	1	3	1
School . .	0	1	0	0	1	1	4	1	1	4	4	4	3	1	2	0
Screen . .	3	1	1	2	1	0	4	1	0	1	0	0	0	1	2	3
Screens . .	1	0	1	1	1	0	1	0	3	2	0	1	1	1	4	2
Shot	0	2	0	0	0	0	0	0	0	0	0	0	0	0	0	0
Shut	11	8	11	10	4	9	3	10	2	3	6	7	2	2	7	8
Shutters . .	0	0	1	0	0	0	1	0	0	1	0	0	1	0	1	3
Side	0	0	0	2	0	0	0	0	0	0	0	0	0	0	0	0
Slam . . .	0	6	0	3	0	2	1	1	4	2	1	0	1	2	3	1
Square . .	2	0	1	0	0	0	0	0	0	1	1	0	0	0	0	0
Stairs . . .	1	0	0	0	0	0	1	3	2	1	0	0	1	0	1	0
Steps . . .	0	0	0	1	0	1	1	0	0	1	2	0	0	0	0	1
Swing . . .	0	4	1	1	3	1	3	2	2	0	2	1	2	1	2	1
Swinging .	0	0	0	1	1	1	0	0	0	2	0	3	2	0	2	2
Tables . .	0	0	0	0	0	0	0	1	0	0	2	0	0	1	0	1
Two	2	2	3	1	2	0	4	1	1	0	0	3	2	1	0	0
Walk . . .	3	0	0	1	2	0	1	0	1	0	2	0	0	1	0	0
Walls . . .	0	1	0	0	1	0	3	3	1	1	0	0	0	1	5	2
Way	0	0	0	2	1	0	1	0	0	0	0	0	0	0	0	0
Wide . . .	0	2	0	0	0	0	0	0	0	0	1	0	0	0	0	0
Window . .	12	10	8	15	10	14	16	16	23	21	15	17	11	3	21	18
Windows . .	33	39	33	39	23	42	49	65	69	79	53	69	67	79	144	214
Wood . . .	13	4	19	4	15	15	10	14	6	3	11	8	5	8	14	18
Wooden . .	0	0	0	0	0	1	0	0	0	0	2	0	0	1	0	0

55. DREAM

Response Word	4th M	4th F	5th M	5th F	6th M	6th F	7th M	7th F	8th M	8th F	10th M	10th F	12th M	12th F	College M	College F
About . . .	2	0	0	0	0	1	0	0	0	0	0	1	0	0	0	0
Asleep . .	0	2	0	0	1	0	1	0	2	0	0	0	0	0	0	0
Awake . .	4	1	2	1	0	2	1	2	1	0	0	0	0	0	3	0
Bad	1	1	1	1	1	0	2	0	3	1	1	2	1	2	3	2
Beautiful .	0	0	2	2	3	2	3	0	2	2	2	3	0	1	0	0
Bed	14	14	11	8	11	4	4	1	5	8	6	6	3	3	12	3
Blue	0	0	0	0	1	0	0	0	0	0	1	0	0	1	1	4
Boat	2	2	7	1	9	8	5	1	3	2	1	0	2	0	1	1

Response Word	4th		5th		6th		7th		8th		10th		12th		College	
	M	F	M	F	M	F	M	F	M	F	M	F	M	F	M	F

DREAM

Response Word	M	F	M	F	M	F	M	F	M	F	M	F	M	F	M	F
Boy	0	1	0	2	1	3	0	4	0	3	0	5	1	4	1	3
Boys ...	0	0	0	0	0	2	0	11	0	4	0	5	0	0	0	0
Car	0	0	0	0	0	1	1	0	0	0	3	0	0	0	0	0
Cloud ...	0	2	0	4	3	3	1	1	1	2	1	2	3	2	5	3
Clouds ...	0	1	1	3	1	1	0	2	0	0	2	0	1	1	2	2
Color ...	0	0	0	0	1	0	0	0	0	0	0	2	0	0	1	2
Cream ..	4	3	0	0	1	1	1	0	0	1	0	0	0	0	0	0
Dark ...	0	1	3	1	0	1	0	0	1	0	0	0	2	0	0	0
Dave ...	0	0	0	0	0	0	0	0	0	0	0	3	0	0	0	0
Day	2	0	1	0	1	0	1	0	1	0	1	0	3	1	8	3
Dick ...	0	0	0	0	0	0	0	0	0	0	0	1	0	2	0	0
Fairies ..	0	2	1	0	0	1	0	0	0	0	0	0	0	0	0	0
Fairy ...	2	3	0	1	0	0	0	0	0	0	0	0	0	0	0	0
Fairyland .	0	0	0	0	0	0	0	2	0	0	0	0	0	0	0	0
Fairy tale .	0	0	0	1	0	2	0	0	0	0	1	0	0	0	0	0
Fantasy ..	0	0	0	2	0	1	0	0	2	1	4	3	0	4	3	2
Float ...	0	0	0	0	2	1	0	0	0	0	0	0	0	0	1	0
Freud ...	0	0	0	0	0	0	0	0	0	0	0	0	0	0	4	3
Fun	3	1	1	2	2	0	1	2	0	2	2	3	3	2	2	0
Funny ...	0	2	3	0	0	0	2	0	0	1	1	0	1	0	1	0
Girl	1	0	5	0	2	1	3	1	11	0	12	0	9	1	15	4
Girls ...	0	0	0	0	2	0	8	0	10	0	6	0	2	0	4	0
Go	0	0	0	0	2	0	0	0	0	0	0	0	0	0	0	0
Good ...	5	6	2	3	5	2	2	4	3	3	2	3	4	3	3	4
Happy ...	1	3	0	0	0	2	2	1	2	1	1	1	0	1	3	5
Head ...	3	3	2	1	1	0	0	0	0	0	0	0	0	0	0	0
Hope ...	0	0	0	0	2	2	1	0	2	2	0	3	0	2	2	3
Horse ...	0	2	0	0	0	1	0	0	0	0	0	1	0	0	0	0
Idea	0	0	0	0	1	0	0	0	0	0	0	0	2	0	0	1
Illusion ..	1	0	0	0	0	0	0	0	2	0	0	1	0	2	0	0
Imagine ..	1	0	3	1	2	2	3	2	0	1	0	1	1	0	0	1
It	2	0	0	0	0	0	0	0	0	0	0	0	0	0	0	0
Lady ...	0	1	0	0	0	2	0	0	0	0	0	0	0	0	0	0
Lamb ...	0	2	0	0	0	0	0	0	0	0	0	0	0	0	0	1
Land ...	0	0	0	0	2	0	0	0	2	2	0	0	1	0	1	1
Lazy ...	0	0	1	0	0	0	0	0	0	0	0	0	0	0	2	0
Long ...	0	0	0	1	0	0	0	0	0	0	0	0	2	0	1	0
Love ...	1	0	2	0	2	1	0	2	3	2	0	1	0	2	5	3
Lovely ..	0	1	1	3	0	2	1	0	0	1	0	1	0	1	1	3
Man ...	2	2	0	0	2	1	0	0	1	0	0	1	0	0	0	1
Me	1	2	0	2	0	0	0	0	0	1	1	0	0	0	1	0
Money ..	0	0	0	1	0	0	0	0	1	0	0	0	0	2	1	1
Movie ...	0	0	0	0	0	0	1	2	0	0	1	0	0	0	0	2
Nice	6	5	6	6	2	4	5	9	1	10	7	6	4	6	7	5
Night ...	24	31	33	34	25	26	18	18	11	14	18	14	6	13	24	28
Nightmare .	13	12	9	11	9	12	17	14	17	13	14	10	12	9	11	20
No	0	0	0	0	1	0	0	0	0	0	0	0	0	0	2	0
People ..	0	2	0	0	0	0	0	0	1	1	0	3	1	0	0	0
Picture ..	2	0	1	0	1	1	0	1	0	3	0	1	2	0	2	2

Response Word	4th M	4th F	5th M	5th F	6th M	6th F	7th M	7th F	8th M	8th F	10th M	10th F	12th M	12th F	College M	College F

DREAM

Response Word	4th M	4th F	5th M	5th F	6th M	6th F	7th M	7th F	8th M	8th F	10th M	10th F	12th M	12th F	College M	College F
Pillow ..	0	2	1	2	1	1	1	3	2	3	2	2	3	1	4	5
Play	0	0	0	0	2	0	0	0	0	0	0	0	1	0	0	0
Pleasant .	1	2	1	1	1	0	2	2	1	1	1	4	2	4	6	10
Pleasure .	0	0	0	0	0	0	0	0	0	1	0	0	0	0	2	1
Pretty ..	0	1	3	2	0	1	0	1	0	0	0	0	0	0	1	1
Real	2	0	0	0	0	0	0	0	0	0	0	0	0	0	1	2
Reality ..	0	0	0	0	0	0	1	0	2	0	0	1	0	0	1	0
Rest ...	0	0	0	0	0	0	1	0	0	2	1	0	0	0	1	4
Scare ...	2	1	0	0	0	1	0	0	0	0	0	0	0	0	0	0
Scared ..	2	0	0	0	1	0	0	0	0	0	1	0	0	1	0	0
Scary ...	0	0	1	0	0	2	0	0	0	0	0	0	0	0	0	0
See	4	0	1	1	1	1	0	0	0	0	0	0	0	0	3	1
Sheep ...	0	0	4	1	1	0	1	0	1	0	0	0	0	0	0	0
Sleep ...	65	73	64	80	68	87	78	85	72	87	102	88	112	98	247	238
Sleeping ..	1	1	3	1	2	4	1	1	2	3	1	2	1	1	0	1
Slumber ..	0	0	0	0	1	0	0	0	1	0	0	0	1	2	1	1
Soft	0	0	1	3	1	1	3	1	0	4	2	4	1	2	3	4
Something .	2	1	2	0	1	1	1	0	0	0	0	0	0	0	0	0
Story ...	4	1	1	1	2	0	0	1	1	0	0	0	1	1	1	0
Stream ..	1	0	3	1	0	0	0	0	1	0	0	0	0	0	0	0
Sweet ...	0	0	1	0	0	1	0	0	1	4	3	1	1	3	2	8
Sweetly ..	0	0	0	0	0	0	0	0	0	0	0	0	0	2	0	0
Thing ...	1	0	3	1	1	1	1	2	0	1	2	0	0	0	0	0
Think ...	7	12	6	9	13	9	11	5	13	6	8	7	3	1	3	6
Thinking .	3	1	0	1	0	1	0	1	2	1	0	2	0	0	0	0
Thought ..	1	0	5	4	1	3	13	1	8	1	4	3	1	3	8	2
Thoughts .	0	0	0	0	0	0	0	1	0	1	1	0	0	0	2	3
True ...	2	1	1	1	2	6	0	2	1	0	0	0	1	4	1	2
Truth ...	0	0	0	0	0	0	0	0	0	0	0	0	0	0	0	2
Unreal ...	0	0	0	0	0	0	1	0	0	0	0	0	1	2	0	0
Vision ...	0	0	0	1	1	0	2	1	1	4	0	0	2	5	5	5
Wake ...	1	1	0	3	0	0	1	0	1	0	1	0	2	0	2	2
Wet	0	0	0	0	0	0	0	0	0	0	0	0	0	0	2	0
Wish ...	8	14	4	11	7	14	20	29	14	16	7	21	17	28	18	29
Women ..	0	0	0	0	0	0	0	0	2	0	0	0	1	0	1	0
Wonder ..	0	0	2	0	2	1	0	1	1	0	2	4	2	0	2	1
Wonderful .	1	2	2	2	2	2	1	5	0	0	2	4	4	3	1	3
World ...	0	0	1	0	0	0	0	0	0	0	0	0	2	1	4	1
You	1	0	0	0	2	0	0	0	0	0	0	0	0	0	0	0

56. EAGLE

Response Word	4th M	4th F	5th M	5th F	6th M	6th F	7th M	7th F	8th M	8th F	10th M	10th F	12th M	12th F	College M	College F
America ..	1	1	1	1	1	1	2	1	3	2	3	2	2	1	1	2
American .	2	1	0	0	0	0	0	0	0	0	0	0	0	0	0	1
Animal ..	2	0	1	4	0	0	4	0	3	2	1	0	0	1	0	1
Awful ...	0	0	0	0	0	2	0	0	0	0	0	0	0	0	0	0
Bald ...	4	0	3	2	1	0	3	2	12	7	6	8	9	3	7	4
Beagle ...	0	0	0	0	2	0	1	0	1	1	0	1	0	1	0	0
Beak ...	0	0	0	0	2	0	0	1	0	0	3	1	1	0	6	5
Big	3	1	4	3	4	2	1	1	1	0	5	2	2	4	0	3

EAGLE

Response Word	4th M	4th F	5th M	5th F	6th M	6th F	7th M	7th F	8th M	8th F	10th M	10th F	12th M	12th F	College M	College F
Bird	178	199	174	175	167	205	181	189	155	184	148	164	158	171	285	291
Birds	2	2	1	4	1	0	1	2	3	1	0	1	0	2	0	3
Boy scout	0	0	0	0	0	0	0	0	0	0	0	1	1	2	0	1
Brave	0	0	0	0	0	0	0	0	1	0	0	0	2	0	1	0
Bride	0	0	0	0	2	0	0	0	0	0	0	0	0	0	0	0
Claw	0	0	1	0	0	0	1	0	0	0	1	0	3	1	1	1
Claws	0	0	1	0	0	0	0	1	1	1	0	0	1	0	1	2
Cliff	1	0	1	0	0	0	0	1	0	0	0	0	2	0	0	0
Coin	0	0	0	0	0	0	0	0	0	0	0	0	0	0	2	2
Country	0	0	0	0	0	0	0	0	1	0	0	2	0	0	2	0
Dollar	0	0	0	0	1	0	0	0	0	0	1	0	0	0	2	0
Eat	1	0	0	0	2	0	0	0	0	0	0	0	0	1	0	0
Egg	0	1	0	1	0	1	1	0	0	0	0	1	0	0	2	2
Emblem	0	0	0	0	0	0	1	0	0	0	0	1	0	1	1	3
Eye	1	0	1	0	4	1	2	1	0	0	1	0	1	0	5	1
Eyes	0	0	0	0	2	1	1	0	0	0	0	0	0	0	0	1
Fast	1	0	0	1	1	1	2	1	1	0	0	0	0	0	2	1
Feather	3	2	0	2	1	0	1	1	2	1	2	0	2	0	6	3
Feathers	1	0	1	1	1	1	0	2	2	0	1	3	1	0	4	2
Flag	1	0	0	1	0	2	0	0	0	1	2	2	1	2	4	3
Flight	0	0	0	0	0	0	0	0	0	0	0	1	0	0	1	4
Fly	7	3	14	10	8	3	10	8	9	13	18	12	10	11	49	46
Flying	0	1	2	0	1	2	0	0	2	1	3	3	2	1	4	3
Grace	0	0	0	0	0	1	0	0	0	0	0	0	0	0	0	2
Hawk	3	0	2	2	6	1	8	2	9	1	1	1	1	1	5	1
High	0	1	1	1	1	0	2	0	1	2	5	2	0	2	9	6
Huge	0	0	1	0	0	0	0	0	0	0	0	2	0	0	0	0
Indian	1	2	0	0	0	0	0	0	0	0	0	0	0	0	0	0
Majestic	0	0	0	0	0	0	0	0	0	0	1	1	3	0	0	1
Mean	0	0	1	0	1	2	0	0	0	1	0	3	0	1	0	1
Money	0	0	0	0	0	0	2	0	1	2	2	3	2	0	3	1
Mountain	0	1	1	2	2	1	0	0	2	1	1	2	2	1	3	3
Nest	2	0	1	1	1	0	1	2	2	1	2	3	5	5	12	9
Nice	1	1	2	1	0	0	0	0	0	0	0	0	0	0	0	0
People	0	0	0	0	0	1	0	0	0	0	0	0	0	2	0	0
Power	0	0	0	0	0	0	0	0	0	0	0	0	0	0	2	0
Robin	0	1	0	0	0	0	2	1	1	1	1	1	0	1	0	1
Scout	0	0	0	0	0	0	0	0	1	1	6	2	9	5	2	7
Sky	0	1	1	0	0	0	0	1	0	1	1	0	3	2	5	5
Soar	0	0	1	0	0	0	0	0	1	0	1	0	1	2	7	4
Soaring	0	0	0	0	0	0	0	0	0	0	0	1	1	0	1	3
Strong	0	0	0	1	0	0	2	0	2	0	1	1	1	0	2	0
Swift	0	0	0	2	1	1	1	2	0	0	2	1	1	0	2	2
Symbol	0	0	1	2	1	0	0	1	1	0	3	0	0	1	2	1
US	0	0	0	0	0	0	0	1	1	1	2	0	0	0	3	6
USA	0	0	0	0	1	0	1	0	0	0	0	1	0	0	5	1
Ugly	0	0	1	2	0	0	0	0	0	0	0	0	0	2	0	1
United States	0	0	0	0	0	0	0	1	1	0	3	4	1	0	3	1
Vulture	1	0	0	0	0	0	1	0	0	0	2	0	0	0	0	1

Response Word	4th M	F	5th M	F	6th M	F	7th M	F	8th M	F	10th M	F	12th M	F	College M	F

EAGLE

Response Word	4th M	F	5th M	F	6th M	F	7th M	F	8th M	F	10th M	F	12th M	F	College M	F
White ...	0	0	0	1	1	0	0	0	0	0	2	0	0	0	1	0
Wing ...	1	1	0	0	0	1	0	2	2	2	2	1	0	0	2	3
Wings ...	0	1	0	1	1	0	0	1	0	8	3	3	0	1	1	20

57. EARTH

Response Word	4th M	F	5th M	F	6th M	F	7th M	F	8th M	F	10th M	F	12th M	F	College M	F
Air	0	2	0	2	0	0	0	0	0	1	0	0	0	0	3	2
Around ...	0	1	2	0	2	0	0	0	0	0	0	0	0	0	0	0
Atmosphere	0	1	0	1	0	0	0	0	3	1	0	0	0	0	0	1
Ball	3	1	4	4	7	2	1	2	1	0	1	1	3	0	5	2
Big	2	1	3	1	3	4	5	2	1	1	5	4	5	4	5	5
Black ...	0	0	0	0	0	1	1	1	3	1	1	0	3	8	10	7
Blue ...	0	0	0	0	0	0	0	0	0	0	0	0	0	0	1	3
Brown ...	0	0	1	1	1	2	1	0	1	2	2	3	1	4	1	13
Circle ...	2	0	1	0	1	0	0	0	0	0	0	0	1	2	0	1
Corn ...	0	0	0	0	0	0	0	0	2	0	0	0	0	0	0	0
Dark ...	0	0	0	0	0	0	0	0	1	0	0	0	0	1	1	5
Dirt	7	8	14	14	13	15	24	15	24	22	28	33	31	27	78	65
Dirty ...	1	0	0	0	0	0	0	0	1	0	1	0	1	0	1	2
Ear	0	2	0	1	0	0	0	0	0	0	0	0	0	0	0	0
Farm ...	0	0	0	0	0	0	0	2	0	1	0	0	0	1	2	3
Garden ..	0	0	1	0	0	0	1	0	0	0	0	3	0	1	0	3
Globe ...	5	1	2	1	2	5	3	2	2	3	4	5	3	1	13	9
God	0	0	0	2	1	0	0	2	0	0	1	2	1	4	1	4
Good ...	0	0	2	0	1	0	0	0	0	0	3	4	1	0	1	6
Grass ...	0	1	0	1	0	1	1	2	0	1	0	2	0	2	2	3
Gravel ...	0	0	0	0	2	1	0	0	0	0	0	1	0	0	0	0
Green ...	0	0	0	0	0	0	0	1	0	0	1	1	0	3	0	3
Ground ..	40	41	49	50	41	42	45	56	34	38	41	39	39	57	65	62
Hard ...	0	2	2	3	3	2	1	3	3	1	3	1	1	4	3	3
Heaven ..	0	5	0	2	0	0	1	3	0	3	0	7	4	5	4	4
High	0	1	1	2	0	0	0	0	0	0	0	0	0	0	0	0
Hill	0	0	0	0	0	0	0	0	0	0	0	0	0	0	2	1
Hole	0	0	0	0	0	0	0	0	0	1	1	0	0	0	2	0
Home ...	1	0	1	1	1	2	1	0	2	0	3	0	0	1	2	1
Huge ...	0	0	0	0	0	0	0	1	0	0	0	2	0	0	0	5
Lake ...	0	0	2	0	0	0	0	0	0	0	0	0	0	0	0	0
Lakes ..	0	0	2	0	0	0	0	0	0	0	0	0	0	0	0	0
Land ...	13	14	9	13	18	14	7	19	10	11	4	7	3	10	11	18
Large ...	0	0	0	1	0	1	0	0	0	0	3	0	1	2	5	0
Life	0	1	0	0	2	0	0	0	0	2	0	1	1	1	0	1
Live	1	2	0	2	0	2	1	2	1	2	0	0	0	0	1	0
Lovely ...	0	0	0	0	0	0	0	0	0	0	0	0	0	2	0	0
Man	0	2	0	0	1	0	1	1	1	1	1	0	2	0	6	3
Mars ...	5	6	9	2	7	1	10	5	13	9	6	3	3	5	6	3
Moon ...	38	18	26	12	21	12	18	9	29	12	11	7	27	11	41	17
Mother ..	1	0	0	0	0	0	0	0	0	0	0	0	1	0	4	2
Mountain .	0	0	0	0	0	0	0	0	0	1	2	0	0	0	1	0
Mover ...	0	0	0	0	0	0	0	0	0	0	0	0	3	0	3	0
Mud	0	1	0	0	0	2	0	2	0	4	0	1	0	2	3	5

Response Word	4th		5th		6th		7th		8th		10th		12th		College	
	M	F	M	F	M	F	M	F	M	F	M	F	M	F	M	F

EARTH

Response Word	M	F	M	F	M	F	M	F	M	F	M	F	M	F	M	F
Nature	0	0	0	1	0	0	0	1	0	0	0	0	0	0	0	2
Ours	0	0	0	0	0	2	0	0	0	0	0	0	0	0	0	0
People	4	4	2	2	2	5	3	2	1	2	2	7	1	4	0	1
Place	3	2	2	2	2	2	1	1	0	1	1	0	0	0	0	0
Planet	26	26	20	22	18	28	32	12	35	31	21	8	14	8	25	18
Planets	2	2	0	1	1	0	0	1	1	1	2	0	0	0	0	1
Plant	9	0	1	1	6	1	4	3	0	0	2	0	0	0	1	1
Plow	0	0	0	0	0	0	0	0	0	0	0	0	0	0	2	0
Quake	1	2	1	2	2	1	1	0	2	0	1	1	5	1	2	2
River	0	0	0	0	0	2	0	1	1	0	0	0	0	0	0	0
Rocks	0	0	1	0	0	0	0	0	0	1	0	0	0	0	0	3
Round	21	28	22	29	19	33	17	20	9	17	29	33	28	16	49	60
Sand	4	0	0	1	0	0	0	0	1	2	0	2	0	1	3	0
Satellite	0	0	0	0	0	0	2	0	0	0	1	0	0	0	1	0
Science	0	0	0	0	0	1	0	0	1	2	0	0	0	0	0	1
Sea	0	0	0	1	0	0	0	2	2	0	0	0	0	1	1	1
Sky	2	15	2	8	3	4	2	4	3	5	6	8	13	5	20	31
Snow	0	0	0	0	0	0	0	0	0	0	0	0	0	0	0	2
Soil	1	1	7	2	2	9	12	10	9	7	13	8	5	11	16	18
Solid	0	0	0	0	0	0	0	0	1	1	0	0	1	2	0	0
Space	1	2	3	6	4	4	4	3	4	2	3	0	1	0	0	1
Sphere	0	0	0	0	0	0	2	1	0	2	1	1	1	2	2	3
Star	0	0	0	0	0	0	0	0	0	0	2	0	0	0	0	1
Stars	0	0	0	1	0	0	0	0	0	0	0	0	2	0	2	1
Sun	5	7	3	6	2	1	2	6	3	8	4	3	3	5	13	4
Surface	0	1	0	0	1	2	1	2	0	1	0	0	0	0	1	0
Terra	0	0	0	0	0	0	0	0	0	0	0	0	0	0	3	0
Trouble	0	1	0	0	1	0	0	0	0	0	1	0	0	0	2	0
Universe	1	1	0	1	1	0	1	3	2	2	4	2	1	2	9	7
Us	0	0	1	0	0	2	0	1	1	1	0	0	0	0	0	0
Venus	2	1	1	0	0	0	1	1	3	0	0	0	0	0	0	1
Ware	0	0	0	0	0	0	0	0	0	0	0	0	0	0	1	2
Warm	0	0	0	0	0	1	1	0	0	0	0	1	1	0	1	3
Water	1	2	1	1	1	1	1	1	1	1	1	2	1	0	2	3
World	19	21	21	23	24	23	17	28	12	28	10	21	14	12	20	24
Worm	0	0	0	1	1	0	0	0	4	1	3	5	8	1	5	1
Worms	0	0	0	0	0	0	1	0	0	1	3	1	0	1	2	0

58. EASIER

Response Word	M	F	M	F	M	F	M	F	M	F	M	F	M	F	M	F
Arithmetic	0	0	2	2	1	0	0	0	0	0	0	0	0	0	0	0
Better	3	2	2	4	6	0	2	2	1	0	3	4	2	1	4	4
Bunny	1	4	2	0	2	1	0	0	0	0	1	0	0	0	0	0
Candy	0	1	2	0	0	0	0	0	0	0	0	0	0	0	0	0
Cheat	0	0	0	0	0	0	0	2	1	0	0	0	1	0	1	0
Class	0	0	0	0	0	0	0	0	0	0	0	0	0	0	0	2
Coming	0	0	2	0	0	0	0	0	0	0	0	0	0	0	0	0
Day	0	0	2	0	0	0	0	0	1	0	0	0	0	0	0	0
Difficult	0	0	0	0	0	0	0	0	0	1	0	1	1	2	4	3
Do	2	1	1	0	2	1	0	0	0	1	1	0	0	1	1	2

	4th		5th		6th		7th		8th		10th		12th		College	
	M	F	M	F	M	F	M	F	M	F	M	F	M	F	M	F

EASIER

Response Word	M	F	M	F	M	F	M	F	M	F	M	F	M	F	M	F
Done . . .	0	0	0	1	1	0	1	0	0	1	1	0	1	1	2	3
Ease . . .	0	0	2	0	3	0	2	0	0	1	2	0	0	0	1	0
Easiest . .	0	0	0	0	0	1	1	0	4	4	8	1	7	1	6	4
Easily . . .	0	1	0	0	2	0	3	0	0	1	0	0	0	1	0	2
East . . .	3	2	0	0	0	0	0	1	0	0	0	0	0	0	0	0
Easter . .	2	1	3	2	2	1	1	0	0	1	0	1	0	1	0	0
Easy . . .	44	36	31	39	28	39	18	17	19	15	21	15	15	17	22	9
Eat	0	0	0	2	1	0	0	0	0	0	0	0	0	0	0	0
Egg	6	0	2	2	0	2	1	0	0	0	0	0	0	0	0	0
Eggs	2	2	2	1	0	1	0	0	0	0	0	1	0	0	0	0
Eraser . .	0	0	0	0	2	0	0	0	2	0	0	0	0	0	0	0
Facility . .	0	0	0	0	0	0	0	0	0	0	2	0	0	0	1	0
Fast	8	5	12	10	6	12	8	5	6	7	7	7	3	14	11	8
Faster . . .	6	12	10	11	10	12	12	18	4	13	8	14	18	15	15	22
Find	0	0	0	0	0	0	0	0	0	0	0	0	0	1	0	2
Fun	3	6	5	4	2	5	2	4	2	0	4	1	4	3	3	3
Get	0	1	0	1	0	0	0	0	0	0	0	0	1	0	2	2
Go	4	5	3	2	6	3	1	3	2	0	2	0	2	1	5	0
Goes . . .	0	0	2	1	0	0	0	0	0	0	0	0	0	0	1	0
Going . . .	2	2	0	1	0	0	1	0	1	0	3	2	1	1	7	1
Good . . .	6	4	4	1	3	1	1	0	0	0	1	0	2	0	3	5
Happy . . .	1	1	1	0	2	0	0	0	0	0	0	0	0	0	0	0
Hard . . .	29	38	41	34	35	38	39	43	46	46	28	31	30	28	48	52
Harder . .	34	55	41	57	49	60	68	90	84	98	74	93	72	84	176	243
Holiday . .	2	0	3	1	0	0	0	0	0	1	0	0	0	0	1	0
How	0	0	0	1	2	1	0	0	1	0	0	1	0	0	3	0
In	2	0	1	1	0	0	0	0	0	0	1	0	0	0	1	0
It	1	0	0	1	0	1	1	2	0	0	0	0	0	0	1	0
Job	1	0	0	0	0	0	1	0	0	0	0	1	3	0	2	0
Lazy	0	0	2	1	0	0	5	2	2	2	3	2	1	1	4	3
Less	0	0	0	1	1	0	1	1	1	0	0	0	4	1	0	1
Lesser . .	0	0	0	0	0	0	0	0	0	0	1	0	0	0	2	0
Life	0	0	0	0	0	0	0	1	1	0	2	0	0	0	0	1
Light . . .	0	1	1	1	1	0	1	1	1	0	2	0	0	1	1	1
Lighter . .	0	1	1	0	0	1	1	0	0	0	1	2	3	3	2	3
Like	0	2	0	0	0	0	0	0	0	0	0	0	0	0	0	0
Make . . .	0	0	0	0	0	0	0	1	0	0	0	0	0	1	2	0
Man	0	0	4	0	2	0	0	0	0	0	0	0	0	0	0	0
Math . . .	0	0	0	0	0	2	1	0	0	1	0	0	0	0	0	0
Me	3	0	1	1	1	0	1	0	0	0	0	0	0	0	0	0
Never . . .	0	0	0	0	1	1	0	0	0	0	1	0	0	0	2	3
Nice	1	0	1	0	1	2	1	1	0	0	0	0	1	1	3	2
No	2	1	0	1	0	0	0	0	0	0	0	0	0	1	1	0
Not	1	1	2	1	2	1	0	0	0	0	0	0	0	0	0	0
Not hard . .	3	2	2	1	1	1	2	0	1	1	0	1	0	1	0	0
Now	3	1	1	1	0	1	1	1	0	0	0	1	1	0	11	2
Paper . . .	4	1	0	0	0	1	1	0	1	0	0	1	0	0	0	0
Pencil . . .	0	0	1	1	1	2	3	0	2	1	0	0	0	0	0	0
Quick . . .	0	0	1	0	0	2	0	0	0	2	0	3	1	2	2	3

Response Word	4th M	4th F	5th M	5th F	6th M	6th F	7th M	7th F	8th M	8th F	10th M	10th F	12th M	12th F	College M	College F
							EASIER									
Quicker ..	0	0	1	2	1	1	2	2	1	3	0	5	1	1	5	2
Quickly ..	0	0	0	0	0	0	0	0	0	0	0	2	0	0	0	0
Rabbit ...	3	0	1	1	0	0	0	0	0	0	1	0	0	0	0	0
Run	0	0	0	0	1	0	0	0	0	0	2	0	0	0	0	0
Running ..	2	0	0	0	0	0	0	0	0	0	0	0	0	0	0	0
School ...	0	0	1	0	0	0	0	0	0	0	1	2	0	0	0	0
See	0	1	0	1	2	1	0	0	0	0	0	0	0	0	0	0
Simple ..	4	7	2	6	7	12	4	14	7	14	8	12	6	17	13	20
Simpler ..	1	0	1	2	1	2	3	0	1	0	0	0	0	0	4	8
Simplier ..	0	0	0	0	0	0	0	0	0	0	0	0	0	0	2	0
Slow	2	0	0	1	1	0	1	1	0	0	0	0	0	1	2	4
Slower ...	0	0	0	0	0	0	4	0	0	2	0	1	0	0	3	5
Smooth ..	0	0	0	0	0	0	0	0	0	0	0	1	1	0	1	2
Smoother .	0	2	0	0	1	0	0	0	0	0	0	1	2	0	1	4
Snap	0	0	0	0	0	0	0	0	0	0	0	0	0	0	2	1
Soft	1	1	0	1	1	0	4	1	1	0	1	0	3	1	8	2
Softer ...	0	0	0	0	0	1	1	0	4	0	1	2	4	2	4	3
Spelling ..	0	0	0	0	0	2	0	0	0	0	0	0	0	1	0	0
Take ...	0	1	0	0	2	0	2	0	0	0	0	0	0	0	0	0
Task ...	0	0	0	0	0	0	0	0	0	0	0	0	0	0	0	2
Test ...	1	1	0	0	0	4	2	1	0	1	3	2	0	1	4	3
Than ...	4	3	2	4	6	3	9	3	14	8	10	10	17	10	34	23
The	0	0	0	0	2	0	0	0	0	0	0	0	0	0	0	0
Then ...	4	1	2	2	2	1	1	2	0	2	1	1	2	1	1	0
Thing ...	1	2	0	0	0	0	0	0	0	0	0	0	0	0	0	0
Time ...	2	0	0	1	0	0	0	0	0	0	0	1	1	0	0	0
To	4	2	3	3	5	1	5	3	3	1	4	2	4	3	6	6
Unhard ..	0	0	0	0	3	2	0	0	0	0	0	0	0	0	0	0
Was	0	1	0	1	1	0	1	0	0	0	2	0	0	0	0	0
Way	0	4	0	0	1	0	0	0	0	1	1	0	1	1	0	1
With	1	0	0	1	1	0	0	0	1	0	0	0	1	1	2	0
Work ...	4	5	2	6	3	1	1	1	5	3	7	3	3	3	10	3
							59. EATING									
Apple ...	0	1	0	1	0	3	1	5	0	0	1	2	0	1	1	2
Ate	13	16	14	12	12	11	8	4	5	3	3	1	8	3	1	1
Bread ...	1	1	1	4	1	0	0	2	3	1	0	1	0	0	1	2
Breakfast .	2	0	1	3	0	1	0	1	0	0	2	0	0	1	3	0
Cake	0	2	1	0	0	1	0	0	0	0	2	0	2	2	2	1
Calories ..	0	0	0	0	0	0	0	0	0	1	0	2	1	1	0	1
Candy ...	2	1	2	0	0	1	0	0	0	0	0	1	0	1	0	2
Cat	0	0	0	2	0	0	0	0	0	0	0	0	0	0	0	2
Chew ...	2	0	0	1	1	1	1	0	0	0	0	1	0	0	0	0
Chewing ..	2	0	4	1	4	3	4	5	4	5	1	3	0	4	2	2
Dessert ..	0	0	0	0	0	2	0	0	0	0	0	0	0	0	0	0
Diet	0	0	0	0	0	0	0	0	1	0	0	1	2	0	0	2
Dieting ..	0	0	0	0	0	0	0	0	0	0	0	2	1	0	1	0
Digesting .	0	0	0	0	1	0	0	1	0	0	2	0	0	0	1	0
Dinner ...	3	1	0	4	1	1	4	2	3	2	1	1	3	1	3	6

Response Word	4th M	4th F	5th M	5th F	6th M	6th F	7th M	7th F	8th M	8th F	10th M	10th F	12th M	12th F	College M	College F
							EATING									
Dish	0	1	0	1	1	2	0	0	0	0	0	0	0	0	0	0
Done . . .	2	0	1	1	0	2	0	1	0	0	0	0	0	0	0	0
Drink . . .	6	1	2	4	4	3	2	4	2	1	0	1	0	0	2	4
Drinking . .	13	11	7	9	8	14	15	16	21	13	11	17	16	11	62	54
Eat	7	11	6	10	6	9	7	4	2	1	4	0	2	0	1	0
Enjoyment .	0	0	0	0	0	0	0	0	0	0	2	0	1	0	0	1
Fast	0	1	3	0	4	2	2	0	0	2	1	2	1	1	5	1
Fat	4	3	3	5	7	4	8	14	5	19	9	10	12	16	15	28
Feeding . .	0	0	0	2	0	1	1	1	0	0	0	0	0	0	0	0
Fish	0	1	0	0	0	2	1	0	0	0	0	0	0	0	1	0
Food . . .	78	76	89	92	83	93	108	95	104	102	108	132	104	104	207	216
Fork . . .	1	1	2	1	2	2	2	4	2	2	3	3	1	1	3	1
Full	2	3	6	3	9	5	4	7	6	4	9	6	4	8	25	13
Fun	0	0	0	1	1	3	1	1	0	0	0	0	2	0	1	5
Good . . .	12	16	16	18	23	17	4	10	5	5	5	6	3	4	6	9
Habit . . .	0	0	0	0	0	0	0	0	0	0	0	2	0	0	2	0
Habits . . .	0	0	0	0	0	0	0	0	0	0	1	0	0	0	2	0
Hamburger	0	0	0	0	0	0	0	1	0	0	0	1	0	1	0	2
Hunger . .	2	1	0	0	5	1	1	0	4	1	5	0	3	2	7	9
Hungry . .	22	24	15	20	19	22	16	21	13	14	11	19	16	22	24	23
Ice cream .	0	0	0	0	0	0	0	0	0	2	0	0	0	0	0	2
Lunch . . .	2	3	3	1	2	1	1	3	0	3	2	0	1	1	1	4
Man	2	0	0	0	1	0	1	0	0	0	1	1	0	1	3	1
Manners .	1	0	0	0	0	0	0	0	0	0	1	0	0	2	0	0
Meal . . .	2	0	0	0	0	3	1	2	0	0	0	0	2	1	2	4
Meals . . .	0	0	0	0	0	1	0	0	0	0	0	0	0	0	2	0
Meat . . .	3	1	2	3	2	2	2	1	0	1	0	2	3	2	2	1
Milk . . .	0	3	1	3	0	0	0	0	0	0	0	0	0	0	0	0
Mouth . . .	0	1	0	1	1	2	0	1	1	4	2	1	2	0	4	6
Munching .	0	0	0	0	0	1	1	0	1	3	0	1	0	0	0	1
Not eating .	0	2	2	0	0	0	0	1	2	0	0	0	0	0	0	0
Obesity . .	0	0	0	0	0	0	0	0	0	0	0	0	0	0	0	2
Out	0	0	0	0	0	0	0	0	0	0	0	0	0	1	2	1
Pie	0	1	3	0	0	1	1	1	0	1	2	0	0	0	2	1
Pig	0	0	0	1	0	0	0	2	0	0	0	0	0	0	1	0
Pizza . . .	0	0	0	0	0	0	1	1	0	0	0	2	1	0	0	0
Plate . . .	2	2	2	1	0	1	1	0	1	1	0	0	2	0	0	1
Sandwich .	0	0	0	0	0	0	1	0	0	0	0	0	0	1	1	5
Satisfying .	0	0	0	0	0	0	1	0	0	0	0	0	0	0	2	0
Sleep . . .	2	0	1	0	0	0	0	1	1	2	2	1	3	1	1	3
Sleeping . .	2	3	3	5	6	2	5	4	15	16	17	13	16	21	43	30
Soup	0	0	0	3	0	0	0	0	0	0	0	0	1	0	0	0
Spoon . . .	3	7	2	1	2	4	1	3	2	3	3	0	2	2	1	3
Starve . .	1	1	0	1	2	1	1	0	1	0	0	0	0	0	0	0
Starving . .	0	1	1	0	0	3	3	3	8	4	1	1	1	2	4	6
Steak . . .	1	0	0	0	1	0	3	1	1	2	4	2	3	2	4	1
Stomach . .	0	0	1	0	0	0	1	2	0	1	0	0	0	0	2	0
Stop	3	1	1	0	0	0	1	0	1	0	0	1	0	0	0	0

111

Response Word	4th M	4th F	5th M	5th F	6th M	6th F	7th M	7th F	8th M	8th F	10th M	10th F	12th M	12th F	College M	College F

EATING

Response Word	4th M	4th F	5th M	5th F	6th M	6th F	7th M	7th F	8th M	8th F	10th M	10th F	12th M	12th F	College M	College F
Stuffed ..	0	0	0	0	0	1	0	0	2	1	0	0	1	0	0	1
Supper ..	4	5	2	1	3	3	1	0	0	1	2	0	0	0	3	0
Table ...	9	12	5	8	2	2	5	2	2	1	3	4	3	1	7	7
Talking ..	0	1	0	3	0	0	0	0	0	0	0	0	0	0	0	0
Taste ...	0	0	2	1	2	1	0	1	0	0	0	0	0	0	2	0
Tasting ..	0	0	0	1	2	0	0	0	0	0	0	0	0	0	0	0
Weight ..	0	0	1	0	0	0	0	0	0	1	0	0	0	1	0	2
Yum	0	0	0	0	0	0	1	0	0	2	0	0	1	0	0	0

60. FARTHER

Response Word	4th M	4th F	5th M	5th F	6th M	6th F	7th M	7th F	8th M	8th F	10th M	10th F	12th M	12th F	College M	College F
Ahead ..	0	1	1	0	1	0	0	0	1	1	0	2	0	0	1	1
Apart ...	1	0	0	1	1	0	0	0	0	0	2	0	3	4	7	3
Away ...	13	24	9	16	20	23	21	28	17	30	25	36	23	32	83	107
Back ...	1	2	1	1	1	2	0	1	0	1	1	1	2	0	5	4
Beyond ..	0	1	0	1	0	3	2	0	0	0	0	0	0	0	0	1
Bird ...	0	2	0	0	0	0	2	1	0	0	0	0	0	0	0	0
Can	0	0	0	0	2	0	0	0	0	0	0	0	0	0	1	0
Close ...	4	1	5	1	6	5	8	4	14	2	0	5	5	3	9	11
Closer ..	7	16	11	32	6	15	23	47	43	52	26	36	17	31	61	63
Country ..	0	1	1	1	0	1	0	0	1	0	2	0	0	0	1	0
Dad	7	2	19	6	11	8	7	4	3	5	8	2	5	3	7	2
Daddy ...	0	2	3	3	0	1	0	0	0	0	0	0	0	0	0	0
Distance .	1	3	3	4	5	7	5	6	4	3	14	12	18	11	31	23
Distant ..	0	0	0	1	0	0	2	0	0	2	1	0	6	1	8	3
Down ...	0	3	1	0	1	0	2	0	0	2	3	4	7	4	7	3
Eyes	0	0	0	0	0	0	2	0	0	0	0	0	0	0	0	0
Far	27	35	16	22	16	32	12	13	8	20	8	10	4	8	7	12
Far away .	0	0	0	0	2	0	0	0	0	0	0	1	0	0	0	1
Farthest ..	0	1	0	1	1	0	1	1	3	3	4	1	4	1	6	1
Fast	4	6	0	5	3	9	5	4	4	2	3	4	2	1	5	1
Faster ...	0	7	5	6	4	5	5	8	7	7	11	11	8	2	14	13
Father ...	10	8	4	1	6	3	1	6	2	3	3	0	4	2	8	1
Feather ..	0	0	0	0	0	2	0	1	0	0	0	0	0	0	0	0
Forth ...	0	0	0	0	0	0	2	0	0	0	0	0	0	0	0	0
From ...	1	0	1	2	0	1	0	1	0	2	0	1	1	0	4	2
Further ..	1	1	2	3	2	4	7	6	5	4	6	14	16	24	25	27
Furthest .	0	0	0	0	0	0	0	0	0	0	1	0	2	0	1	0
Go	6	1	3	4	2	5	1	1	2	3	2	2	2	3	4	9
Going ...	0	0	1	0	0	0	1	1	0	0	1	2	1	0	0	1
Gone ...	1	0	0	1	2	2	1	1	3	1	1	1	1	1	2	6
Good ...	1	0	3	1	1	0	0	0	0	0	0	0	0	0	0	0
Here ...	2	3	0	2	0	0	1	0	0	0	0	0	0	1	1	3
Home ...	0	0	0	0	1	1	0	0	0	2	0	1	0	1	3	1
Horizon ..	0	0	0	0	1	0	0	0	1	0	0	0	0	0	1	3
I	1	1	0	1	0	2	0	0	0	0	0	0	0	0	0	0
In	0	0	0	0	0	0	1	1	1	0	2	1	0	0	0	1
Is	1	0	2	1	1	0	0	0	1	0	0	0	2	0	0	0
It	0	0	1	0	2	0	0	0	0	1	0	0	0	0	0	0
Light ...	0	0	0	0	2	0	0	0	0	2	0	0	0	0	0	0

Response Word	4th M	4th F	5th M	5th F	6th M	6th F	7th M	7th F	8th M	8th F	10th M	10th F	12th M	12th F	College M	College F
						FARTHER										
Long . . .	6	6	11	16	5	9	10	7	6	3	5	4	6	13	14	4
Longer . .	5	4	4	12	7	8	9	7	3	11	12	9	7	7	7	8
Lower . .	0	2	0	0	0	0	0	0	0	0	0	0	0	0	0	0
Man	4	0	2	3	5	1	2	4	3	0	2	0	4	0	0	0
Mile . . .	0	3	1	2	2	1	0	1	2	2	0	0	0	0	0	0
Miles . . .	1	1	1	1	0	3	0	3	0	1	1	5	0	4	0	3
Mom . . .	4	3	3	2	3	0	0	0	1	0	0	0	0	0	0	0
More . . .	2	0	1	1	1	2	1	3	1	0	1	0	0	1	0	0
Mother . .	65	39	60	42	53	26	37	26	24	13	23	9	22	17	27	11
Near	5	4	4	2	0	7	2	7	4	10	2	1	5	7	12	18
Nearer . .	4	14	4	4	2	12	11	18	17	19	13	25	8	16	58	90
Neither . .	0	0	0	0	0	0	0	2	1	0	0	0	0	0	0	0
Nice . . .	0	1	2	0	0	0	1	0	0	0	1	0	0	0	0	0
No	1	1	2	0	0	0	0	0	0	0	1	1	0	1	0	0
On	1	2	1	1	2	1	0	0	0	1	1	1	0	2	4	2
Out	0	1	1	0	2	0	0	0	0	1	3	0	1	1	5	3
Over . . .	0	0	0	0	0	1	0	0	1	0	0	2	0	0	1	1
Parent . .	1	3	2	0	1	1	1	1	1	0	0	0	1	0	0	0
Parents . .	1	0	0	2	1	0	0	0	1	0	0	0	0	0	0	0
People . . .	0	0	2	0	0	0	0	1	0	0	0	0	0	0	0	0
Person . .	1	3	1	0	3	0	1	0	0	0	0	0	0	0	0	0
Plane . . .	0	0	0	0	0	0	0	0	0	0	0	1	0	0	0	2
Road . . .	0	0	1	0	0	2	0	1	0	0	0	3	1	1	0	1
Run	1	1	0	3	0	1	1	1	1	0	1	2	1	1	0	3
See	2	1	0	0	3	1	2	0	0	2	1	1	0	0	1	1
Short . . .	2	1	2	2	2	2	3	0	5	1	0	0	1	0	1	0
Shorter . .	7	3	4	3	1	4	8	3	10	6	5	4	5	12	5	5
Slow	0	2	1	0	3	1	1	1	0	2	0	0	0	0	0	1
Slower . .	1	2	0	2	0	1	0	3	3	4	1	4	0	2	1	3
Son	1	0	0	0	0	0	2	0	0	0	1	0	0	1	1	1
Speak . . .	0	0	0	0	3	0	0	0	0	0	1	0	0	0	0	0
Than . . .	1	3	5	3	10	3	7	2	8	3	8	4	12	3	23	10
Then . . .	2	4	2	3	3	1	3	1	2	1	1	0	2	0	1	0
Throw . . .	0	0	0	0	3	1	1	1	2	1	5	0	1	0	2	1
To	1	0	1	1	4	0	0	0	0	0	0	0	2	0	0	1
Town . . .	0	0	0	2	0	0	0	0	0	0	0	0	0	0	0	0
Travel . . .	1	0	0	0	0	0	0	0	0	0	0	2	1	2	1	0
Up	0	0	1	0	0	2	0	1	1	0	0	0	4	1	0	0
Walk . . .	0	4	3	1	1	2	2	0	0	0	0	2	1	4	2	2
Way out . .	0	0	0	0	0	0	0	0	2	0	0	0	0	0	0	0
We	2	0	0	0	0	0	0	0	0	0	0	0	0	0	0	0
Who . . .	0	0	0	0	2	0	0	0	0	0	0	0	0	0	0	0
Yet	1	0	0	1	0	0	0	0	0	0	2	0	0	0	1	1
You	0	2	0	0	0	2	0	0	0	1	1	0	0	0	0	0
					61.	FASTER										
Airplane .	0	0	0	0	0	1	0	1	1	1	2	2	2	0	0	2
And	2	1	0	0	0	0	0	0	0	0	0	0	0	0	0	0
At	2	0	0	0	0	0	0	0	0	0	0	0	0	0	0	0

Response Word	4th M	4th F	5th M	5th F	6th M	6th F	7th M	7th F	8th M	8th F	10th M	10th F	12th M	12th F	College M	College F
							FASTER									
Bike	0	0	0	0	0	3	0	0	1	0	0	0	0	1	0	0
Boy	0	1	2	1	0	0	1	1	0	0	0	0	0	0	0	1
Car ...	1	0	2	2	4	0	3	0	3	2	10	8	3	8	11	6
Cars ...	0	0	0	0	0	0	0	1	0	1	0	1	0	1	3	2
Cat	0	0	0	2	0	0	0	0	1	0	0	0	0	0	0	0
Christmas .	0	0	2	0	0	0	0	0	0	0	0	0	0	0	0	0
Decoration	0	0	0	2	0	0	0	0	0	0	0	0	0	0	0	0
Easier ...	2	1	0	1	1	0	0	2	1	2	1	1	0	3	1	0
Easter ...	0	3	1	1	2	2	1	2	0	0	0	0	3	0	0	0
Farther ..	2	0	0	2	0	0	0	0	2	0	1	1	0	1	3	1
Fast	39	33	33	18	15	25	16	8	9	13	10	8	3	8	15	5
Fastest ..	0	1	2	3	1	4	6	1	3	6	3	3	2	2	14	4
Father ..	3	0	0	0	1	0	0	0	0	0	0	0	0	0	0	0
Fatter ...	0	0	0	0	0	0	0	0	0	0	1	2	0	0	0	0
Fly	0	0	0	0	0	0	0	1	0	0	1	0	1	0	4	7
Flying ...	0	0	0	0	0	0	0	0	0	0	1	0	0	2	3	0
Fun	0	0	0	0	0	1	0	2	0	0	0	0	0	1	0	0
Girl	2	0	0	0	0	1	0	0	0	0	0	0	0	0	0	0
Go	3	6	9	14	13	8	5	3	5	5	11	6	6	3	7	4
Going ...	0	0	0	1	2	0	0	0	0	0	1	0	0	1	2	0
Good ...	0	0	2	0	0	0	0	0	1	0	0	0	0	0	0	0
Hard ...	1	0	2	0	0	0	1	0	1	0	0	0	0	0	1	0
Harder ..	0	0	1	1	1	0	1	1	0	0	1	1	1	1	2	4
Higher ..	0	1	0	0	1	0	0	1	0	0	0	0	0	0	4	0
Hurry ...	2	4	3	4	3	4	2	0	0	4	0	1	0	4	1	6
In	0	0	2	0	0	0	0	0	0	0	1	0	0	0	0	0
Jet	0	0	0	0	0	0	2	0	2	0	1	0	1	0	2	0
Light ...	0	0	0	0	0	0	0	0	0	0	0	0	2	0	1	0
Long ...	2	0	1	0	1	0	0	0	0	0	0	0	0	0	0	0
Longer ..	1	2	0	1	0	1	0	0	0	0	0	0	0	0	0	0
Lower ..	0	0	0	0	0	0	0	2	0	0	0	0	0	0	0	0
Me	1	0	1	0	1	0	2	0	0	0	0	0	0	0	0	0
Move ...	0	0	1	0	0	0	0	0	0	1	0	0	0	0	2	3
Now ...	2	1	2	1	2	0	0	1	0	0	1	1	0	0	1	0
Pace ...	0	0	0	0	0	0	0	0	0	0	0	0	0	0	2	0
Plane ...	0	1	0	0	0	0	1	0	0	0	6	4	1	1	11	4
Play	0	0	2	0	1	0	0	0	0	2	0	0	0	2	0	3
Quick ...	3	3	3	8	1	2	3	9	5	4	2	5	2	6	7	13
Quicker ..	1	0	2	1	2	5	4	5	4	2	3	4	4	5	8	25
Quickly ..	1	4	1	1	0	1	0	3	2	4	2	3	1	2	3	7
Race	1	1	1	0	0	2	3	1	0	1	0	0	0	1	0	0
Ran	2	1	1	1	0	0	1	1	0	0	0	0	2	0	1	0
Run	16	31	24	35	28	26	17	27	8	10	26	26	22	23	42	36
Runner ..	1	1	2	1	2	0	2	0	0	0	0	0	2	1	4	0
Running ..	3	4	6	4	2	6	1	3	0	3	2	5	5	1	4	5
Show ...	2	1	0	1	0	0	1	0	0	0	0	0	0	0	0	0
Slow ...	41	39	46	38	40	38	37	25	42	36	21	20	25	20	38	35
Slower ..	50	69	43	68	51	74	97	111	114	127	88	110	101	116	226	268
Slowly ..	2	1	0	0	1	2	0	0	2	2	1	0	0	0	0	3

Response Word	4th M	4th F	5th M	5th F	6th M	6th F	7th M	7th F	8th M	8th F	10th M	10th F	12th M	12th F	College M	College F
FASTER																
Sooner ..	0	0	0	0	1	0	0	1	0	0	0	0	0	0	0	2
Speed ...	7	4	16	4	10	10	7	6	7	1	21	12	17	7	18	14
Speedier ..	0	0	0	0	3	1	1	0	2	0	1	1	1	0	2	0
Speeding .	0	1	0	0	0	0	0	0	0	0	0	1	0	0	0	2
Speedy ..	0	1	1	1	2	0	0	2	2	0	0	1	0	1	1	0
Swift ...	0	2	0	2	3	3	1	3	0	0	3	2	2	1	4	2
Swifter ..	0	0	1	1	3	1	1	1	0	0	0	0	0	0	0	1
The	1	0	0	0	2	0	0	0	0	0	0	0	0	0	1	0
Than ...	4	0	3	4	15	1	11	3	9	4	13	3	15	9	22	12
Then ...	8	3	2	2	2	4	0	0	1	1	1	0	0	0	0	0
Train ...	1	0	0	0	0	0	0	1	1	1	0	2	0	0	2	0
Why	3	0	0	0	0	0	0	0	0	0	0	0	0	0	0	0
Win	3	0	0	0	0	0	0	0	0	0	0	0	0	0	0	0
Write ...	0	0	0	1	0	0	0	0	0	0	0	0	2	0	1	1
62. FIND																
A	2	0	2	0	1	0	0	0	0	0	0	0	0	0	1	0
Ball ...	1	1	1	1	3	2	0	1	0	0	0	0	1	2	2	1
Book ...	0	1	2	0	1	0	0	0	1	1	2	2	0	2	2	2
Bring ...	0	0	1	0	0	0	0	0	1	0	1	1	0	0	3	0
Buy	0	0	0	0	0	0	1	0	0	1	0	0	0	0	2	0
Can	0	0	0	0	0	0	0	2	0	0	0	0	0	0	0	0
Cat	2	0	1	1	1	0	0	1	0	0	0	0	0	1	0	1
Catch ...	0	0	1	0	0	0	0	0	0	1	1	0	1	0	2	0
Come ...	0	0	0	0	1	0	0	0	0	0	0	0	0	0	2	0
Discover..	3	3	3	3	7	5	9	3	5	2	7	4	8	5	20	17
Dog	3	3	0	0	1	1	2	1	1	0	0	0	0	1	1	1
Fond	0	0	2	0	0	0	0	1	0	0	0	0	0	0	0	0
Found ...	46	47	32	35	32	41	41	34	33	20	20	17	17	18	25	30
Fun	0	1	0	0	0	1	0	0	0	0	2	0	0	0	0	0
Get	5	4	1	4	6	3	2	9	4	2	2	2	1	2	2	6
Give	2	3	0	0	0	0	0	0	2	1	0	1	0	0	1	4
Go	0	2	1	0	1	0	0	0	2	0	0	0	1	0	0	0
Gold	0	0	0	0	0	1	2	0	1	1	6	5	1	1	3	3
Good ...	3	2	4	2	1	2	1	0	1	1	1	2	1	0	0	0
Got	0	2	2	1	4	0	2	1	0	0	1	0	0	0	0	0
Help	1	1	2	1	1	1	0	0	0	0	0	0	0	0	0	0
Her	2	1	0	0	0	1	1	0	1	2	0	1	0	1	1	1
Here ...	0	2	0	0	0	0	0	1	0	0	0	0	1	0	0	1
Hid	1	1	1	3	2	1	0	0	0	0	0	0	0	1	0	0
Hide	3	3	4	3	2	3	3	1	1	5	2	2	0	1	2	7
Him	3	2	3	2	7	1	1	1	4	1	2	0	3	3	3	0
Hope ...	0	2	0	0	0	0	0	0	0	0	0	0	0	0	0	0
Hunt	0	1	0	2	0	1	0	3	1	0	0	2	0	2	1	4
In	1	2	0	1	0	0	0	0	0	0	0	0	0	0	0	0
It	11	6	11	9	11	5	3	3	8	5	5	3	4	9	17	11
Keep ...	1	3	4	7	4	10	11	6	5	4	3	9	5	8	12	13
Kind ...	1	0	1	1	2	0	1	1	0	0	0	0	0	0	1	0
Locate	0	1	0	0	2	1	5	3	1	3	1	0	6	4	8	8

Response Word	4th M	4th F	5th M	5th F	6th M	6th F	7th M	7th F	8th M	8th F	10th M	10th F	12th M	12th F	College M	College F
							FIND									
Look . . .	16	15	24	17	19	31	17	26	23	22	27	36	13	29	30	53
Looked . .	0	0	0	1	2	1	0	0	0	0	0	0	0	0	0	0
Loose . . .	1	0	1	3	2	1	0	1	0	0	8	13	0	0	0	0
Lose . . .	5	9	12	23	13	14	27	27	32	33	20	26	44	42	90	100
Loss . . .	0	0	1	0	1	0	0	0	1	3	3	0	1	0	1	1
Lost . . .	38	37	45	42	27	45	49	52	42	68	48	50	49	48	92	88
Me	3	2	4	2	5	1	1	1	1	2	0	1	2	3	4	3
Mind . . .	0	1	1	0	0	1	0	0	0	0	0	1	1	2	2	0
Money . . .	2	0	2	2	3	1	7	3	12	6	12	9	9	6	13	8
Never . . .	0	0	0	0	0	0	0	0	0	0	0	0	0	0	2	0
No	3	1	0	1	0	0	0	0	1	0	0	0	0	0	0	0
Not	1	3	0	0	0	0	1	0	0	0	0	0	0	0	0	0
Object . .	0	0	0	0	0	0	1	0	0	0	1	0	0	0	3	1
Of	2	0	0	1	1	0	0	0	0	0	0	0	0	0	1	1
OK	1	0	0	0	2	0	0	0	0	0	0	0	0	0	0	0
Out	32	36	29	25	29	26	13	15	33	18	26	15	24	16	51	28
People . . .	0	0	2	0	1	0	0	0	0	0	0	0	1	0	0	0
Recover . .	0	0	0	0	2	0	0	1	0	0	0	0	1	0	0	1
Return . .	0	0	0	0	1	2	0	0	1	1	0	0	0	0	0	0
Ring	0	0	0	1	0	0	0	0	0	1	0	0	1	0	0	2
Saw	0	2	1	2	0	1	1	1	0	1	0	0	0	0	1	1
Search . . .	0	0	0	2	0	0	0	1	0	3	2	0	1	4	6	8
See	6	5	2	6	1	12	2	8	2	2	3	5	0	6	6	12
Seek	1	2	0	1	1	2	1	2	1	2	0	2	1	4	10	15
Sell	0	0	0	0	0	0	0	0	0	0	0	0	1	0	2	0
Some . . .	2	2	0	0	0	0	0	0	1	0	0	0	1	0	1	1
Something .	6	2	4	8	5	3	1	4	2	4	3	3	2	1	2	4
Steal	0	0	0	0	0	0	0	0	1	0	2	0	0	0	0	1
Take	0	0	0	1	0	0	0	1	0	3	3	0	1	0	0	1
That	3	4	1	1	1	0	2	1	0	0	0	1	2	0	1	1
The	2	1	4	2	5	3	2	0	2	0	2	0	2	1	3	0
Them . . .	1	2	0	0	1	0	2	0	1	0	2	4	7	2	0	3
There . . .	0	0	1	2	0	0	0	1	0	0	1	1	0	0	1	0
Thing . . .	0	0	4	0	1	0	1	0	0	0	1	0	0	0	2	2
Things . . .	1	1	0	2	0	0	0	0	0	2	0	0	0	1	0	1
This	0	0	0	0	0	0	0	1	0	0	2	0	0	0	1	0
Toy	1	0	0	1	2	2	1	1	0	0	0	0	0	0	0	0
Treasure .	1	2	0	2	1	1	5	7	3	5	7	8	9	2	10	7
Watch . . .	0	0	0	0	0	0	0	0	1	0	0	0	1	0	2	0
What	0	0	2	1	2	1	3	1	2	1	2	0	0	1	4	1
Where . . .	0	2	0	1	1	0	1	1	0	0	0	1	0	2	2	1
You	2	1	2	1	2	1	1	0	2	2	1	1	0	0	2	0
Your	0	0	0	0	2	1	0	0	0	0	0	0	0	0	0	0
							63. FINGERS									
Are	3	2	3	3	6	4	1	2	2	0	5	0	10	3	6	0
Arm	0	0	0	2	2	2	3	3	1	0	0	0	0	1	0	0
Arms . . .	0	1	0	0	0	0	1	0	0	2	0	0	0	0	1	1
Big	2	0	0	0	0	0	0	0	0	0	0	0	0	0	1	0

116

Response Word	4th M	4th F	5th M	5th F	6th M	6th F	7th M	7th F	8th M	8th F	10th M	10th F	12th M	12th F	College M	College F
							FINGERS									
Body . . .	3	2	5	2	2	1	0	1	0	2	0	1	0	0	0	0
Bones . . .	2	0	2	1	0	1	1	0	0	0	0	0	0	0	3	0
Bowl . . .	0	0	0	0	0	0	0	0	0	0	0	0	1	0	3	0
Broke . . .	0	0	2	0	0	0	0	0	0	0	0	0	1	0	0	0
Can	0	0	0	0	0	0	0	0	0	0	2	0	1	0	0	0
Count . . .	1	3	1	1	2	0	1	0	0	0	1	0	2	2	2	2
Cross . . .	0	0	0	0	0	0	0	0	0	0	0	0	1	0	3	1
Crossed . .	1	0	0	0	1	0	0	0	0	1	1	1	3	1	2	2
Cut	0	1	1	0	0	0	1	0	3	0	2	0	1	0	1	0
Digits . . .	0	0	0	0	1	0	0	0	2	0	0	0	0	0	7	2
Dirty . . .	0	0	0	0	0	0	1	0	1	0	1	0	1	0	1	2
Discount . .	0	0	0	0	0	0	0	0	2	0	0	0	0	0	0	0
Doug . . .	0	0	0	0	0	0	0	0	2	0	0	0	0	0	0	0
Eat	2	1	0	1	1	0	0	0	0	0	0	2	0	0	1	0
Fast . . .	0	2	1	0	0	0	0	0	0	0	0	0	0	0	2	2
Fat	1	1	0	0	0	1	0	3	1	0	1	1	0	0	1	0
Feel . . .	0	0	0	2	0	0	1	2	3	0	2	3	2	0	0	1
Feet . . .	3	7	3	2	2	6	1	1	9	1	3	4	4	5	9	5
Fin	1	1	2	0	1	0	0	0	0	0	0	0	0	0	0	0
Find . . .	0	2	2	3	0	1	1	1	1	0	0	1	0	0	0	0
Finger . .	10	9	8	6	7	7	4	1	4	3	3	1	1	1	1	0
Fingernails	0	0	0	0	0	3	0	2	0	1	0	2	1	0	0	1
Five	8	11	6	15	16	12	12	16	8	11	13	6	10	11	21	21
Flesh . . .	0	0	1	1	1	2	1	0	0	1	1	0	0	0	0	0
Food . . .	0	0	0	0	0	0	1	0	0	0	2	0	0	0	0	0
Foot . . .	3	3	7	2	3	1	1	2	1	1	2	0	3	1	1	1
Funny . . .	2	0	0	0	0	0	0	0	0	0	0	0	0	0	0	0
Glove . . .	0	0	0	0	0	0	1	0	0	0	1	0	2	0	0	1
Gloves . .	0	0	0	0	1	1	0	1	0	0	1	1	0	0	4	0
Go	1	0	1	2	1	1	0	0	0	0	0	1	0	0	0	0
Good . . .	2	2	1	0	1	0	0	0	0	0	0	0	0	0	0	0
Hand . . .	63	79	74	87	80	81	92	92	93	79	86	84	88	69	187	154
Hands . . .	11	9	7	15	10	14	16	15	18	23	10	22	16	29	46	70
Hard . . .	2	0	1	0	0	0	1	0	0	0	0	1	0	0	0	0
Head . . .	0	1	0	0	1	2	0	0	0	0	0	0	0	0	0	0
Here . . .	0	0	2	0	0	0	0	0	0	0	0	0	0	0	0	0
Hurt . . .	0	0	2	1	0	0	2	0	0	0	0	1	3	1	1	3
In	1	0	0	1	1	0	0	0	0	0	3	0	1	0	1	0
It	1	0	1	0	1	2	0	0	0	0	0	0	0	0	0	0
Legs . . .	0	2	0	0	0	0	0	0	1	0	0	1	0	0	0	0
Long	1	3	2	2	4	1	0	1	1	1	5	3	4	3	3	7
Many . . .	1	0	2	0	0	0	1	0	0	0	0	0	1	1	1	2
Me	1	0	3	0	2	0	1	0	0	1	0	1	0	0	0	0
Middle . .	0	0	0	0	0	0	0	0	2	0	0	0	0	0	0	0
Mouth . . .	0	0	0	0	0	0	0	1	0	0	0	0	0	0	2	0
Move . . .	3	6	1	0	2	1	1	1	0	1	0	0	0	1	1	5
My	0	1	1	0	0	0	0	2	0	0	0	0	1	0	0	1
Nail . . .	5	2	1	4	2	1	0	2	2	1	1	1	0	1	4	2

117

Response Word	4th M	F	5th M	F	6th M	F	7th M	F	8th M	F	10th M	F	12th M	F	College M	F
							FINGERS									
Nails	2	6	4	5	5	7	8	10	10	27	13	14	10	18	13	28
No	4	1	0	0	0	0	0	0	1	0	0	0	0	0	0	0
Now	1	1	1	2	0	1	0	0	0	0	0	0	0	0	0	0
Numb . . .	0	0	0	0	2	0	0	0	0	0	0	0	0	0	2	0
Numbers .	1	1	2	0	0	0	2	2	0	0	0	0	0	2	0	0
Part	0	1	2	0	0	0	0	0	0	0	0	0	0	0	0	0
Phalanges .	0	0	0	0	0	0	0	0	0	0	0	1	0	1	3	0
Piano . . .	0	0	0	0	0	1	0	2	1	0	1	4	1	5	5	11
Play	1	0	1	0	0	1	0	0	0	2	2	1	1	0	4	10
Point . . .	0	2	0	1	0	1	0	0	0	0	0	0	2	0	1	1
Prints . . .	0	0	0	0	1	0	0	0	0	0	0	0	0	0	2	0
Right	0	0	0	0	0	2	0	0	0	0	1	0	0	0	0	0
Ring	0	0	0	1	0	0	1	1	0	3	2	8	3	9	7	14
Rings . . .	0	0	0	0	0	0	0	0	0	1	0	2	2	4	2	12
Short . . .	0	1	0	0	0	0	0	0	1	0	0	2	0	1	0	0
Skin	1	0	2	0	2	0	1	0	1	0	2	1	0	1	1	0
Small . . .	1	0	1	0	0	0	0	0	2	0	1	1	1	1	0	1
So	1	0	0	2	0	0	0	0	0	0	0	0	0	0	0	0
Teeth . . .	0	0	0	0	0	0	0	0	2	0	0	0	1	0	0	0
Ten	1	4	3	6	1	3	2	1	0	4	5	2	0	1	7	1
The	2	1	1	0	0	0	0	0	0	0	1	0	0	0	0	0
There . . .	0	1	2	0	0	0	0	1	0	0	0	0	0	0	0	0
Things . .	0	0	2	0	1	0	1	0	0	0	0	0	0	0	0	0
Three . . .	0	0	1	1	1	1	0	0	0	0	1	1	0	0	0	0
Thumb . .	18	17	22	17	19	23	14	23	16	16	13	5	14	9	16	11
Thumbs . .	5	2	0	2	2	6	4	5	8	5	5	5	3	4	6	11
Tip	2	0	0	0	0	0	1	1	1	0	0	0	2	0	1	1
Tips	1	0	2	0	2	2	1	3	2	4	1	1	0	1	5	2
Toe	1	2	2	1	0	0	0	3	1	1	2	0	1	0	1	1
Toes	8	15	9	17	6	15	26	26	17	31	19	38	23	44	53	82
Touch . . .	3	0	1	3	4	4	4	1	1	0	5	2	4	1	6	1
Up	2	1	1	1	2	2	2	0	2	1	1	0	0	0	4	0
Us	4	0	0	1	1	1	0	0	0	0	0	0	0	0	0	0
Use	1	3	2	2	1	1	1	0	0	0	0	0	0	0	0	1
Words . . .	0	0	0	0	0	0	0	0	0	0	0	0	0	0	2	0
Work . . .	0	1	1	1	0	2	0	1	0	0	1	0	0	1	0	2
Write . . .	0	1	0	2	0	3	1	2	1	1	1	6	1	1	0	1
Writing . .	0	0	0	0	0	0	0	0	0	0	1	1	0	2	0	0
You	2	1	1	3	2	0	2	1	0	0	0	0	0	0	0	0
						64.	FOOT									
Ankle . . .	2	1	3	2	2	4	3	4	5	5	8	4	3	2	8	6
Appendage .	0	0	0	0	0	0	0	0	0	0	0	0	2	0	0	0
Arm	2	8	1	3	3	3	4	4	3	6	2	2	2	3	6	6
Ball	4	4	2	0	4	0	0	0	1	0	4	0	2	3	12	5
Bed	1	0	0	0	0	0	0	0	0	0	0	0	1	0	2	0
Big	1	2	4	2	5	1	2	2	1	6	7	3	1	5	1	2
Body . . .	7	10	8	5	13	12	9	6	1	8	2	0	1	0	4	0
Bottom . .	0	1	1	0	1	2	1	1	0	0	2	0	0	0	1	0

Response Word	4th M	4th F	5th M	5th F	6th M	6th F	7th M	7th F	8th M	8th F	10th M	10th F	12th M	12th F	College M	College F
FOOT																
Cold	0	2	0	0	0	1	0	0	0	0	0	0	0	0	0	2
Corn	0	0	2	0	0	0	1	0	3	0	0	1	0	0	0	0
Disease . .	0	0	0	0	0	0	0	0	0	2	0	0	0	0	0	0
Doctor . .	0	0	0	0	0	0	0	0	0	1	0	0	2	1	0	1
Down . . .	0	0	0	2	0	0	0	1	0	0	0	0	0	0	0	0
Feet	30	33	34	29	39	29	26	18	30	18	14	7	16	7	12	9
Flat	0	0	0	0	3	1	1	0	0	0	0	0	0	0	1	0
Football . .	0	0	0	0	2	0	0	0	1	0	2	0	0	0	0	1
Ground . .	0	0	1	0	1	0	2	0	0	0	0	0	0	0	0	0
Hand	37	32	34	38	17	21	27	25	49	26	30	28	43	27	59	73
Head	4	4	2	3	1	1	1	2	0	0	3	1	2	0	6	3
Heel	1	0	1	1	0	1	3	3	0	2	1	2	1	2	0	3
Hurt	1	0	0	0	1	1	0	0	0	0	1	2	0	1	1	0
Inch	2	0	0	0	0	1	2	2	0	0	1	2	0	0	6	2
Kick	1	0	0	0	2	0	0	0	0	0	1	1	1	0	2	1
Knee	1	0	0	1	0	0	0	0	0	1	0	1	0	0	2	0
Large . . .	0	0	1	0	1	1	0	0	0	0	0	1	1	0	1	2
Leg	36	33	25	36	35	33	35	45	29	37	32	34	25	30	60	54
Legs	2	0	0	1	0	0	0	1	2	1	0	0	0	1	0	0
Limb	0	0	0	0	2	0	1	2	0	0	1	0	1	1	0	1
Long	2	0	7	3	1	3	0	1	2	2	1	2	0	3	1	2
Man	0	0	1	1	0	0	3	0	0	0	2	0	1	1	1	3
Measure . .	0	0	0	0	0	0	0	1	0	0	0	1	0	0	3	2
Mouth . . .	0	0	0	1	1	1	0	0	4	1	1	0	1	1	0	1
Nail	0	0	0	0	0	0	0	1	0	1	1	0	0	0	2	0
Part	3	0	2	1	2	0	0	0	0	0	0	1	0	0	0	0
Person . . .	0	1	1	1	1	0	0	0	0	0	0	0	0	0	2	0
Pound . . .	0	0	0	0	0	0	0	0	0	0	0	0	0	0	0	2
Powder . .	0	0	0	0	0	0	0	0	0	0	0	0	0	2	1	1
Root	0	0	2	0	0	0	0	0	0	0	0	0	0	0	0	0
Ruler . . .	0	0	1	0	0	0	3	1	0	0	3	1	1	0	3	0
Run	1	1	4	0	0	0	1	1	0	0	0	0	3	0	1	0
Shoe	7	14	17	27	16	21	19	26	26	32	38	64	45	43	117	138
Shoes . . .	2	0	3	2	2	4	0	6	0	5	2	8	4	11	1	6
Show	1	1	0	1	1	0	2	0	0	0	0	0	0	0	1	1
Skin	3	3	1	0	0	0	0	1	0	1	0	0	0	0	0	0
Slipper . .	0	0	0	2	0	1	0	0	0	0	0	1	0	1	0	1
Small . . .	1	2	2	2	1	1	0	0	0	0	0	1	1	1	0	0
Smell . . .	1	0	2	0	1	1	1	1	1	1	0	0	1	0	2	1
Sock	0	0	0	1	0	1	0	1	0	1	1	0	1	0	2	2
Soldier . .	1	0	0	0	0	0	0	0	1	1	2	0	6	2	12	1
Sore	0	0	2	0	1	1	2	2	1	1	5	0	5	0	4	5
Spider . . .	0	0	0	0	0	0	0	0	0	0	0	0	0	0	3	1
Step	5	3	2	2	2	4	1	2	2	1	1	0	0	0	2	1
Stink . . .	0	0	0	2	0	1	1	0	2	0	0	0	0	0	0	0
Support . .	0	0	0	0	0	0	1	0	0	0	0	0	0	0	2	0
Thing . . .	1	0	3	1	2	0	0	0	0	0	0	0	0	0	0	0
Tired . . .	0	0	0	0	0	0	0	0	0	0	0	0	0	0	0	2
Toe	39	22	23	21	26	20	43	31	31	34	32	24	25	36	80	70

Response Word	4th M	4th F	5th M	5th F	6th M	6th F	7th M	7th F	8th M	8th F	10th M	10th F	12th M	12th F	College M	College F
							FOOT									
Toes	21	33	17	21	19	30	19	28	29	27	23	26	18	30	25	46
Twelve inches	0	0	0	0	0	1	2	0	1	0	2	0	2	0	1	0
Two	0	0	1	1	0	1	0	0	0	1	0	2	0	1	0	0
Ugly	0	0	0	0	0	0	0	0	0	0	0	2	0	0	0	0
Walk	8	11	14	21	12	25	9	11	5	6	6	11	13	16	20	13
Walking . . .	0	5	0	1	2	2	0	0	1	0	2	4	2	1	1	0
Yard	1	0	1	0	1	0	4	0	0	1	1	0	0	0	0	3
						65.	FOR									
A	1	0	2	1	0	0	1	0	0	0	0	0	0	0	2	1
Against . . .	0	0	0	0	1	0	2	0	1	1	1	4	3	3	12	8
All	1	1	0	1	1	0	0	0	0	0	0	0	0	1	3	1
Always . . .	0	0	0	3	1	1	0	0	1	2	1	2	2	3	3	6
And	0	0	1	0	0	0	0	0	1	0	0	0	0	0	2	1
As	2	1	0	1	3	1	2	0	2	1	1	1	1	2	2	6
At	0	0	0	0	0	0	0	0	0	0	0	0	0	0	2	2
Awhile . . .	0	0	0	0	0	0	0	0	2	0	5	1	0	1	1	1
Be	0	0	0	0	0	0	0	0	0	1	0	0	1	0	2	0
Because . . .	1	0	1	3	1	2	1	3	4	2	4	2	7	7	22	32
Before	0	0	1	0	1	1	0	0	0	0	0	0	1	0	2	0
Bore	0	0	2	0	1	1	2	0	0	0	0	0	0	0	0	0
But	0	0	0	0	0	0	0	0	0	0	0	0	0	0	1	2
By	0	0	0	0	0	0	0	0	0	0	0	0	0	0	2	2
Did	0	0	0	0	0	2	1	0	0	0	0	0	0	0	0	0
Do	0	1	0	0	0	1	0	1	0	0	0	1	0	0	1	2
Door	5	0	1	0	1	2	0	3	0	0	0	0	0	0	0	1
Ever	3	3	2	4	6	2	8	4	8	13	11	0	12	3	26	25
Example . . .	0	0	0	0	0	0	0	0	0	0	0	0	0	0	0	2
Far	0	1	1	0	0	1	0	1	2	0	1	0	0	1	1	0
Five	0	3	2	4	1	0	2	2	2	5	4	2	1	0	4	0
Fore	3	2	2	3	2	2	3	2	2	2	2	0	2	0	1	0
Forever . . .	0	1	0	0	0	0	0	1	2	0	0	0	0	1	2	2
Four	15	15	16	35	8	13	17	16	6	9	6	11	17	9	7	9
From	3	2	0	4	1	4	7	15	7	9	3	4	3	1	4	12
Fun	0	0	1	0	1	0	0	2	0	0	1	0	1	0	1	0
Fur	0	0	0	0	0	0	0	1	1	0	0	1	0	0	0	2
Get	2	9	5	5	1	4	3	2	0	4	2	2	1	3	3	1
Gift	0	1	0	2	0	2	0	2	1	0	1	2	1	1	0	3
Give	6	6	2	8	3	9	6	2	7	7	3	4	3	1	2	8
Go	1	0	0	0	1	0	2	0	0	0	0	0	0	0	0	0
Golf	0	0	1	0	0	1	1	0	0	1	7	3	5	1	7	0
Good	2	1	1	2	0	1	0	0	0	0	1	0	0	0	0	0
Goodness . .	1	0	0	1	0	0	1	0	0	1	0	0	1	0	2	0
Got	2	2	0	3	1	1	0	0	0	0	1	0	0	0	0	1
He	4	1	3	2	3	1	4	0	2	1	1	1	3	1	2	1
Her	1	7	1	5	2	6	0	4	1	1	4	2	5	3	2	3
Here	0	0	1	0	1	1	0	1	1	0	1	0	0	0	0	2
Him	5	8	4	6	10	6	10	6	13	2	3	5	9	9	9	9
His	0	0	0	0	0	0	0	0	1	0	1	0	0	2	1	1
How	0	2	1	1	1	1	0	2	1	0	2	0	0	0	0	2

Response Word	4th M	4th F	5th M	5th F	6th M	6th F	7th M	7th F	8th M	8th F	10th M	10th F	12th M	12th F	College M	College F
							FOR									
If	0	2	0	0	0	0	2	0	0	0	1	2	3	1	3	5
In place of	0	0	0	0	0	0	0	0	0	2	0	0	0	0	0	0
Is	1	1	2	3	1	1	3	1	1	1	0	0	1	0	3	3
It	9	5	7	7	4	7	5	4	9	7	5	2	5	1	13	11
Let	0	0	0	0	2	0	0	0	0	0	0	0	0	0	0	0
Like	0	0	0	0	0	0	1	2	0	0	0	0	0	0	0	0
Man	0	0	0	0	2	0	0	0	0	0	0	0	0	0	0	0
Me	22	18	25	18	16	22	18	21	18	17	21	33	17	19	25	48
More	1	1	1	2	2	2	0	0	3	1	1	0	0	0	1	1
Nor	0	0	0	0	0	0	0	1	0	1	1	0	0	0	4	1
Not	3	1	0	1	2	0	0	0	0	0	1	1	0	2	1	0
Nothing	1	1	0	0	1	0	0	0	0	1	0	0	2	0	1	2
Now	1	3	3	0	2	4	0	2	4	2	4	5	0	1	12	8
Number	3	1	3	2	2	9	1	1	2	2	2	2	1	0	1	0
Of	3	1	0	0	2	2	0	2	2	1	1	0	0	1	1	6
One	0	0	0	1	3	0	0	0	1	0	1	0	0	0	1	0
Or	3	7	4	3	1	1	3	1	1	2	2	3	4	1	6	3
People	1	0	0	0	0	1	0	2	2	0	1	1	0	1	0	0
Person	0	1	0	2	0	2	0	0	1	0	1	0	0	3	4	1
Preposition	0	0	0	0	0	0	0	0	0	2	2	4	5	5	7	5
Present	3	3	0	0	0	2	1	3	2	2	2	2	0	1	0	1
Purpose	0	0	1	0	0	0	0	2	0	2	0	1	0	0	3	2
Reason	0	1	4	2	0	1	1	3	1	0	2	4	2	7	11	9
Receive	0	0	0	0	0	0	0	2	0	0	0	0	0	0	0	0
Sake	2	0	1	1	0	2	0	0	0	0	0	0	1	0	3	0
Sale	0	0	0	0	1	1	2	1	0	0	6	1	2	5	1	0
See	1	0	1	2	1	1	1	1	1	1	0	0	0	0	0	0
She	0	0	0	2	0	3	0	0	0	0	0	0	0	0	0	1
Since	0	0	1	0	0	0	0	0	0	0	0	1	0	1	1	2
So	0	0	0	0	0	0	1	0	0	1	0	1	0	1	1	2
Some	0	0	2	0	0	0	0	1	1	0	0	0	0	0	0	0
Somebody	0	0	0	1	0	4	0	0	0	0	1	0	0	0	1	0
Someone	2	8	5	4	2	4	0	1	0	3	1	4	0	1	1	2
Something	1	4	2	2	5	3	0	0	2	4	1	1	0	0	1	0
That	8	6	3	2	4	7	1	0	6	4	2	1	1	4	4	4
The	2	7	7	2	7	2	6	1	3	1	2	1	2	4	6	6
Them	1	0	2	0	0	2	3	1	3	0	0	3	2	1	3	5
Then	0	0	1	1	1	0	0	2	0	0	0	0	0	0	1	1
There	1	1	0	2	3	0	0	3	3	1	0	0	2	1	1	1
Things	0	0	0	0	2	0	0	0	0	0	0	0	0	0	0	0
This	1	2	3	0	0	0	1	1	1	2	2	3	1	2	14	9
Three	0	0	1	2	2	1	1	1	0	0	3	1	2	3	2	1
Time	0	0	1	0	0	0	2	0	0	0	0	0	0	0	0	0
To	1	5	4	5	3	9	11	9	11	10	4	10	4	8	20	12
Two	1	0	1	2	1	3	1	1	0	1	0	0	0	0	0	0
Us	14	8	13	5	13	6	9	17	11	6	7	11	8	13	14	14
Want	1	0	1	0	0	2	0	0	0	0	0	0	1	0	1	0
Ward	0	0	0	0	0	0	1	0	0	0	1	0	0	0	2	0
Was	2	1	2	2	3	3	1	0	0	0	0	0	1	1	1	1

Response Word	4th		5th		6th		7th		8th		10th		12th		College	
	M	F	M	F	M	F	M	F	M	F	M	F	M	F	M	F

FOR

Word	M	F	M	F	M	F	M	F	M	F	M	F	M	F	M	F
What	20	19	23	20	30	18	27	24	25	32	46	37	42	41	84	64
When	1	0	0	0	0	0	1	3	3	1	0	0	0	0	2	4
Which . . .	0	0	0	0	0	0	0	0	0	0	0	0	0	1	4	0
Who	4	2	1	1	1	2	5	5	10	9	10	6	8	13	9	16
Whom . . .	0	0	0	0	0	1	0	2	4	4	0	5	4	4	12	16
Why	4	2	4	1	8	3	6	1	4	4	5	8	2	4	8	7
With	1	0	2	0	0	0	1	1	0	0	0	1	0	0	0	2
Word	2	0	1	0	2	0	0	1	1	2	1	0	1	1	0	2
Yes	0	2	0	0	0	0	0	0	0	0	1	0	1	0	0	1
You	29	31	31	30	31	20	25	29	26	27	21	27	26	22	29	42
Your . . .	1	0	0	0	1	0	0	0	1	2	0	0	0	0	1	1

66. FROM

Word	M	F	M	F	M	F	M	F	M	F	M	F	M	F	M	F
A	2	0	2	0	0	0	1	0	0	0	0	1	0	0	1	0
Afar	0	0	0	0	0	0	0	0	0	0	0	0	0	0	2	0
At	1	0	1	0	1	1	1	0	0	0	1	0	0	0	3	2
Away . . .	2	0	2	0	2	2	2	0	2	2	4	10	5	7	19	19
Bill	0	0	0	0	0	0	0	0	0	0	0	0	0	2	0	0
Bring . . .	0	0	0	1	1	0	0	0	0	0	0	2	0	1	0	0
By	0	1	1	3	0	0	0	0	0	2	0	0	0	0	0	5
Came . . .	3	5	2	4	5	6	12	2	3	5	6	1	2	3	5	5
City	2	1	0	0	0	0	0	0	1	0	0	0	0	0	0	0
Come . . .	9	7	5	9	6	6	9	13	4	5	7	2	10	11	7	9
Coming . .	0	1	0	0	0	2	0	1	0	0	1	0	0	0	1	0
Country . .	0	0	1	3	0	0	1	0	0	0	0	0	0	0	0	0
Dear	0	0	0	0	0	2	0	0	0	0	0	1	0	0	0	0
Exit	0	0	0	0	0	0	0	0	0	0	0	0	0	0	2	0
Far	1	3	3	2	0	1	0	2	0	0	2	2	0	0	0	5
Farm . . .	7	2	2	0	1	2	0	1	1	1	0	0	0	1	2	0
For	5	2	5	5	0	5	7	16	9	14	5	7	3	3	4	13
Form . . .	3	7	6	7	3	0	6	3	6	4	3	1	0	1	1	0
Frame . .	0	2	0	0	0	0	0	2	1	0	1	0	0	0	2	0
Get	1	2	1	0	0	0	1	0	1	2	0	0	0	2	0	1
Gift	0	0	0	1	0	1	1	1	2	0	0	1	0	1	0	0
Girl	0	2	0	0	0	0	0	0	0	0	0	0	0	0	0	0
Give	2	0	0	2	1	1	0	2	0	1	0	1	0	0	1	1
Go	9	4	4	7	7	3	4	5	6	7	6	9	10	12	6	9
Going . . .	2	3	1	0	0	1	1	1	0	1	2	2	2	0	2	1
Gone	1	0	0	0	2	0	2	0	3	0	1	0	0	1	0	0
Hear	0	0	2	0	1	1	1	0	0	0	0	0	0	0	2	0
Her	1	2	2	1	4	2	0	0	1	1	3	1	1	1	4	4
Here	16	9	4	5	7	16	14	9	18	9	14	17	11	15	37	34
Him	1	2	4	1	3	1	2	3	7	1	1	1	4	4	6	4
His	0	0	0	0	0	0	0	0	1	0	0	0	2	0	2	0
Home . . .	3	7	2	1	2	4	4	7	3	3	7	3	5	6	9	13
House . . .	2	3	4	3	3	3	1	2	3	2	5	3	2	1	1	4
How	0	0	0	1	3	0	0	0	0	0	0	0	0	0	1	0
In	1	1	0	0	0	0	2	2	2	1	1	1	0	6	1	3
Into	0	0	0	0	1	0	1	0	0	0	0	0	2	1	0	1

Response Word	4th M	4th F	5th M	5th F	6th M	6th F	7th M	7th F	8th M	8th F	10th M	10th F	12th M	12th F	College M	College F
							FROM									
Is	0	2	1	1	1	0	0	0	0	0	0	0	0	0	0	1
It	5	3	8	2	10	5	6	1	6	2	2	2	4	0	5	6
Kitchen . .	1	0	0	1	0	0	2	5	0	2	3	4	0	1	1	5
Letter . . .	1	7	2	8	1	6	0	1	1	5	2	3	0	4	3	2
Love	0	0	1	2	0	1	0	0	0	1	0	0	0	2	0	1
Many . . .	0	0	0	0	0	0	0	0	0	0	2	0	0	0	0	0
Mars . . .	1	0	1	0	1	0	1	0	1	0	0	0	1	0	0	2
Me	9	10	17	12	16	13	5	10	12	11	4	11	5	11	8	7
Minnesota .	2	1	0	0	0	0	0	0	0	0	0	1	0	0	0	1
Move . . .	0	0	0	0	0	0	0	0	0	0	0	0	0	0	2	0
Near	0	1	2	0	0	0	0	0	0	0	1	1	1	0	0	2
Not	2	0	0	0	0	0	0	0	0	0	0	0	0	0	0	0
Now	1	1	1	3	2	2	2	1	2	5	2	2	3	2	14	7
Nowhere . .	1	0	0	0	0	0	0	2	0	0	0	0	0	0	1	1
Now on . .	0	0	0	0	0	0	0	0	0	1	0	1	0	3	0	0
Of	0	1	0	0	1	0	0	1	1	0	1	1	0	0	5	9
On	1	0	1	0	1	0	0	0	0	0	0	0	0	0	2	1
Origin . . .	0	0	0	0	0	0	2	0	0	0	0	0	0	0	2	1
Out	1	0	0	0	2	0	1	2	0	0	1	0	1	0	10	5
Out of . . .	0	0	0	0	0	0	0	0	0	1	0	0	0	1	0	2
Over	3	1	0	0	0	0	1	0	0	0	2	0	0	0	0	1
People . . .	0	2	1	0	1	0	0	0	0	0	0	0	0	0	0	0
Person . . .	0	3	0	0	0	1	0	1	0	0	0	1	1	0	0	1
Place . . .	8	2	9	2	13	4	4	0	2	2	5	4	3	3	4	4
Preposition	0	0	0	0	0	0	0	0	0	1	0	0	2	1	2	1
Present . .	1	0	0	1	0	2	0	3	0	2	0	0	0	0	0	1
Receive . .	1	1	0	2	2	1	2	0	0	1	0	1	0	1	1	1
Received .	0	0	0	1	0	1	0	3	0	0	0	0	0	0	0	1
Room . . .	1	2	1	1	1	0	3	0	0	0	0	0	0	0	0	0
School . . .	1	2	1	1	1	1	3	1	1	3	0	1	2	1	0	2
Sent	0	2	1	0	0	1	1	0	1	0	1	1	0	0	0	0
Sign	0	0	0	0	0	2	0	0	0	0	0	0	0	0	0	0
Sincerely .	0	3	0	2	0	2	0	1	0	0	0	1	0	0	0	1
Somebody .	1	0	1	0	0	2	0	0	0	0	0	0	0	0	1	1
Someone . .	1	3	1	1	1	3	0	0	0	0	0	1	0	0	0	0
Space . . .	0	0	0	0	0	0	0	0	2	0	0	0	0	0	1	0
Store . . .	0	1	0	1	0	0	1	2	0	0	0	2	0	1	0	0
Sun	0	0	0	0	0	0	0	2	0	0	0	0	0	0	0	0
Take	0	0	0	3	1	0	0	1	2	4	2	5	1	4	3	2
Taken . . .	0	0	0	0	0	0	2	0	0	1	0	1	0	1	1	0
Texas . . .	0	0	0	0	3	0	0	1	2	0	2	0	1	0	0	0
That	2	3	3	2	4	2	0	1	1	2	2	0	1	0	1	2
The	17	11	9	7	16	6	8	1	6	1	3	2	3	3	6	8
Their . . .	4	1	1	2	3	1	1	0	0	1	2	1	1	0	1	0
Them . . .	0	2	6	4	1	1	3	1	2	3	0	1	7	8	9	8
Then	2	0	1	2	1	2	0	0	2	0	2	0	1	0	4	3
There . . .	10	14	16	12	24	18	26	21	24	22	24	23	22	22	46	40
These . . .	0	0	2	0	0	1	2	0	1	1	3	1	0	0	2	0
This	2	2	0	0	3	3	0	0	1	1	3	0	6	1	6	3

Response Word	4th M	4th F	5th M	5th F	6th M	6th F	7th M	7th F	8th M	8th F	10th M	10th F	12th M	12th F	College M	College F
							FROM									
To	21	36	29	57	21	48	32	65	35	50	47	62	39	38	89	109
Too	1	1	0	2	0	0	1	0	1	1	0	1	0	0	0	0
Toward	0	0	0	0	0	0	0	0	2	0	0	0	0	0	4	1
Town	0	1	1	1	0	0	1	0	1	0	2	1	1	0	2	2
Us	4	1	0	0	0	0	2	2	3	1	1	2	0	3	5	3
Way	0	2	0	0	0	0	0	0	0	0	0	0	0	0	0	0
Went	0	0	1	0	0	0	0	1	2	1	0	0	0	2	0	0
Were	0	0	3	0	3	1	1	0	1	0	1	0	1	0	0	1
What	1	0	1	0	0	0	1	0	2	2	1	0	4	2	6	4
When	0	1	0	1	0	0	2	1	0	1	0	0	1	0	1	2
Whence	0	0	0	0	0	0	0	0	0	0	0	0	0	1	3	4
Where	10	7	11	10	16	17	18	15	17	19	25	16	22	19	58	56
Who	4	6	4	6	3	6	0	2	0	3	3	6	5	1	3	2
Whom	0	0	0	0	0	2	1	1	1	3	1	1	2	3	9	5
With	0	0	0	0	1	0	1	0	0	1	0	0	3	0	0	3
Within	0	0	0	0	0	0	0	1	0	0	1	0	2	1	4	2
Word	0	1	3	0	2	0	0	0	0	0	1	0	0	0	0	0
You	9	16	15	10	4	9	3	6	10	5	2	3	6	9	10	9
							67. FRUIT									
Apple	63	64	69	62	72	76	87	90	96	96	116	98	91	111	205	245
Apples	1	2	4	4	1	3	0	3	4	4	0	2	4	3	0	4
Banana	7	4	5	6	7	11	12	13	3	12	9	19	16	20	13	20
Bananas	0	0	1	1	3	0	0	1	0	3	0	0	2	0	0	1
Basket	0	1	1	2	0	1	0	0	0	1	1	3	0	0	2	3
Berry	1	1	0	0	0	0	2	0	1	0	1	2	1	1	3	2
Bowl	0	1	0	1	1	0	0	0	2	0	0	1	2	4	5	4
Cake	1	0	2	1	1	1	3	0	3	0	5	0	1	0	5	1
Candy	0	1	0	1	1	1	2	1	1	0	4	2	0	0	0	0
Celery	0	0	0	0	0	2	0	0	0	0	0	0	0	1	0	0
Cereal	0	0	1	0	0	0	0	2	0	0	0	0	0	0	1	0
Cherry	0	0	2	0	2	0	2	2	1	0	3	0	2	0	1	1
Citrus	2	1	0	0	0	2	0	2	0	0	1	0	0	0	0	0
Cocktail	0	0	1	0	1	0	0	0	1	0	0	0	2	1	1	0
Colors	0	2	0	1	0	0	0	0	0	0	0	0	0	0	0	0
Delicious	0	1	0	2	2	0	0	1	1	0	0	2	0	1	1	0
Dish	0	2	0	0	0	1	0	1	1	1	0	0	1	0	1	0
Drink	0	0	0	0	2	1	0	0	0	0	0	0	0	0	0	1
Eat	33	37	28	46	29	24	23	18	11	13	11	16	13	10	32	22
Eating	1	2	4	3	2	3	2	0	2	0	2	1	2	0	1	0
Eats	0	1	0	0	0	2	1	0	1	0	0	0	0	0	0	0
Flies	0	0	0	0	0	0	0	0	0	0	0	0	0	2	0	1
Flower	0	0	0	0	0	1	0	0	0	0	0	0	1	0	0	3
Fly	0	0	0	0	0	1	2	1	1	0	1	0	4	2	51	40
Food	20	30	28	18	24	29	17	22	20	11	12	9	8	10	13	13
Fresh	0	0	0	0	1	0	0	0	0	0	1	0	0	0	1	2
Good	13	19	31	18	18	18	9	10	2	9	8	12	6	6	7	11
Goodies	0	0	0	0	2	0	0	0	0	0	0	0	0	0	0	0
Grape	4	1	1	1	1	0	2	2	0	1	0	1	0	1	5	0

Response Word	4th M	4th F	5th M	5th F	6th M	6th F	7th M	7th F	8th M	8th F	10th M	10th F	12th M	12th F	College M	College F
							FRUIT									
Grapefruit . . .	0	0	0	0	0	0	0	2	1	0	1	0	0	0	0	0
Grapes	1	0	0	0	1	0	1	0	2	1	1	0	1	0	1	1
Juice	3	1	4	3	2	2	4	2	1	1	2	2	3	3	0	5
Juicy	0	5	0	0	3	0	2	1	0	1	2	4	1	3	2	1
Lemon	0	0	1	1	1	0	0	0	1	1	0	0	0	0	0	2
Man	0	0	1	0	0	0	0	0	0	0	0	0	2	0	0	0
Meat	0	1	0	0	0	1	1	1	3	0	2	0	0	1	0	0
Nut	0	0	0	0	1	0	0	0	2	1	0	0	2	0	1	1
Orange	15	12	8	13	12	18	24	13	15	20	20	21	26	27	35	27
Oranges	0	0	1	1	1	0	0	1	1	0	0	2	0	0	2	0
Peach	0	0	0	1	2	0	2	5	1	6	2	4	2	2	5	4
Pear	3	6	1	5	2	4	5	8	7	7	3	8	7	6	15	17
Pears	0	0	0	1	0	0	0	0	0	2	0	1	0	1	0	0
Person	0	0	0	0	0	0	0	0	0	0	2	0	0	0	0	0
Pie	2	0	0	1	0	0	0	0	0	0	0	0	0	0	2	0
Pineapple . . .	0	0	2	0	1	0	0	0	2	1	2	0	0	1	2	0
Queer	0	0	0	0	0	0	0	0	0	0	0	0	2	0	0	0
Red	1	1	0	1	0	1	0	1	0	1	1	0	0	1	0	3
Salad	0	0	0	1	0	1	2	1	2	4	0	1	8	1	5	3
Soft	0	0	2	0	0	0	0	0	0	0	0	0	0	0	0	0
Something to eat	2	0	0	1	0	0	0	0	0	0	0	0	0	0	0	0
Sour	0	0	0	1	0	2	0	1	0	1	0	1	1	0	1	0
Suit	0	0	3	0	0	1	0	0	0	0	0	0	0	0	0	1
Sweet	1	2	2	4	1	2	3	2	2	0	2	5	2	4	9	5
Table	1	1	1	0	0	0	0	1	0	1	1	1	0	1	2	2
Taste	1	1	2	0	1	1	0	0	2	1	0	0	0	0	1	1
Tree	0	0	1	1	0	1	4	2	3	1	0	2	4	1	17	8
Trees	0	1	2	0	0	1	0	0	1	0	1	0	0	1	0	0
Veg	0	0	2	0	0	0	0	1	0	0	0	0	0	0	0	0
Vegetable . . .	24	23	17	21	24	10	23	22	33	29	19	17	16	16	23	26
Vegetables . .	14	9	4	7	7	5	4	2	1	7	2	6	0	1	2	1
Vine	0	0	0	0	0	0	0	0	1	0	0	0	0	0	2	0
Yellow	1	0	0	1	1	0	0	3	0	0	0	1	0	0	0	0
							68. GET									
A	0	1	0	0	2	0	0	0	1	0	0	0	0	0	2	1
Acquire	0	0	0	0	0	0	0	0	0	1	0	0	0	0	7	2
Anger	0	0	0	0	0	0	0	0	0	0	0	0	0	0	2	0
At	1	0	0	0	0	0	1	0	0	1	0	1	0	0	0	2
Away	22	15	19	22	21	16	19	17	14	13	25	22	11	16	45	34
Back	2	1	1	1	0	0	0	0	0	0	0	0	0	0	2	0
Ball	0	1	0	0	0	0	0	2	0	1	0	1	0	1	1	1
Book	0	0	0	1	0	0	0	0	2	0	1	3	0	0	0	0
Bring	3	2	2	3	3	5	3	3	2	2	8	7	7	4	5	9
Buy	0	3	2	10	2	8	5	8	3	5	7	12	4	7	12	22
By	0	0	2	0	0	0	0	0	1	0	1	1	0	0	2	2
Car	0	2	1	0	0	0	0	1	1	0	0	0	0	0	0	1
Carry	0	0	0	0	0	1	0	0	0	0	0	0	0	1	0	3
Cat	1	0	3	0	0	0	2	1	0	0	0	0	0	0	0	0

Response Word	4th M	4th F	5th M	5th F	6th M	6th F	7th M	7th F	8th M	8th F	10th M	10th F	12th M	12th F	College M	College F
								GET								
Catch . . .	0	0	0	2	0	1	1	1	1	0	1	0	1	0	0	1
Come . . .	3	1	2	5	1	0	3	1	1	2	3	3	1	1	1	3
Command .	0	0	0	0	0	0	0	0	0	0	2	0	0	0	0	0
Do	0	0	0	0	0	0	0	0	0	0	0	0	0	0	2	0
Don't . . .	1	1	0	2	0	2	2	1	0	0	0	0	0	1	0	0
Down . . .	2	0	0	0	0	0	0	0	0	0	2	0	0	0	0	0
Fast	2	1	1	0	0	0	2	0	1	0	2	0	0	0	0	1
Fetch . . .	1	3	5	4	4	4	4	4	6	2	4	2	6	8	5	9
Find . . .	2	4	4	4	3	3	3	6	6	3	4	3	4	6	7	5
Food . . .	0	1	1	1	0	0	0	1	0	1	2	1	0	0	1	1
For	0	0	1	2	0	0	0	0	0	0	0	0	0	0	1	0
Forget . . .	0	2	0	0	0	0	1	0	2	0	0	1	0	0	0	1
Found . . .	2	0	1	2	0	0	0	0	0	0	0	0	0	0	0	0
Four	0	2	0	0	0	0	0	0	0	0	0	0	0	0	0	0
Get it . . .	0	0	0	0	0	2	0	0	0	0	0	0	1	0	0	0
Getting . .	2	5	2	1	1	2	2	2	1	1	0	1	1	0	0	0
Give	2	5	2	3	1	4	3	2	6	6	1	6	5	6	7	18
Go	24	24	22	24	31	34	28	31	28	30	31	37	19	29	46	52
Going . . .	2	3	8	5	8	5	4	7	10	6	9	8	10	8	19	25
Gone . . .	0	1	2	2	0	0	2	3	4	1	1	2	0	2	3	3
Good	1	3	0	0	0	0	0	0	0	0	0	0	0	0	0	0
Got	21	27	29	25	18	26	54	47	43	47	24	21	39	32	65	67
Grab	1	0	0	0	1	1	2	0	0	2	1	1	3	0	5	1
Have . . .	2	2	3	4	2	6	3	7	2	2	8	7	3	5	7	10
Her	0	0	1	2	0	1	0	0	2	1	1	0	0	0	2	0
Here . . .	1	3	1	0	1	3	1	0	1	0	0	1	0	1	1	0
Him	4	4	4	0	6	0	0	0	1	0	1	1	0	1	1	0
Hit	1	0	0	0	3	0	0	0	0	0	0	0	0	0	0	0
Hold	0	1	0	0	0	0	1	1	2	0	0	0	0	0	1	0
Home . . .	1	2	1	1	1	3	0	0	1	0	1	3	3	1	4	1
In	2	2	2	1	1	2	1	1	0	1	2	4	2	2	2	1
Into	0	0	0	1	1	0	0	0	0	0	0	1	0	1	2	1
It	15	13	14	13	16	8	5	4	6	5	5	4	5	4	13	11
Jet	0	0	0	1	0	0	2	0	0	0	0	0	0	0	1	0
Keep	1	0	0	0	1	1	1	1	0	0	0	1	0	0	1	3
Leave . . .	0	0	0	0	1	0	1	0	0	3	1	2	1	3	4	2
Let	1	0	0	0	1	0	0	0	1	0	0	0	2	2	1	0
Loose . . .	0	0	0	0	0	0	0	0	0	1	1	0	0	1	0	2
Lose	0	0	0	0	0	1	2	1	2	3	0	1	1	4	4	5
Lost	1	1	2	4	4	3	1	3	7	5	7	3	10	12	13	8
Mad	0	1	2	0	0	0	0	0	0	2	0	0	0	0	1	0
Man	0	2	0	0	0	0	0	0	0	0	0	0	0	0	0	0
Me	7	1	6	0	1	1	1	2	2	0	1	1	3	1	2	4
Met	2	1	2	1	2	0	1	1	1	1	0	0	0	0	0	1
Money . . .	0	0	0	1	0	0	0	0	4	1	0	0	1	0	4	3
More . . .	0	1	0	0	2	0	1	0	0	0	0	0	0	0	0	0
Move . . .	0	0	1	0	2	1	0	0	0	1	2	0	0	1	1	3
My	1	1	1	3	1	1	0	1	0	1	0	0	0	1	0	0
Not	3	3	1	2	0	0	0	0	0	0	0	0	0	0	0	0

Response Word	4th M	4th F	5th M	5th F	6th M	6th F	7th M	7th F	8th M	8th F	10th M	10th F	12th M	12th F	College M	College F
								GET								
Now	0	4	2	1	0	1	2	0	0	1	1	0	0	0	1	1
Obtain . . .	0	0	0	0	0	0	0	1	2	2	2	4	1	6	19	16
Of	0	2	0	0	0	0	0	0	0	0	0	0	0	0	1	0
Off	0	1	2	0	1	1	5	2	2	3	1	1	2	0	4	3
On	1	1	1	2	0	1	0	0	1	1	1	0	1	0	0	3
One	0	0	2	1	1	1	0	0	0	1	0	0	1	0	1	0
Out	12	13	15	14	23	17	16	10	15	10	20	21	22	24	53	39
Over . . .	1	0	0	0	0	0	1	1	0	0	0	0	0	0	1	2
Pet	1	0	2	0	0	0	0	0	0	0	0	0	0	0	0	0
Pick . . .	0	0	0	1	1	2	3	0	0	1	0	0	0	0	1	2
Please . .	0	2	0	0	0	1	0	1	0	0	0	0	0	0	0	0
Present . .	0	0	0	0	0	1	0	0	0	0	0	1	0	0	0	2
Procure . .	0	0	0	0	0	0	0	0	0	0	0	0	0	0	2	0
Purchase .	0	0	0	0	0	0	1	0	0	0	0	1	0	0	0	2
Ready . . .	5	4	4	2	2	3	1	3	1	3	2	1	1	1	1	1
Receive . .	6	0	6	10	4	7	7	11	3	8	2	4	10	8	12	15
Rich	0	0	0	0	0	0	0	0	0	0	0	0	0	0	2	0
Run	1	0	0	0	3	1	3	1	0	0	1	0	0	2	0	0
Scat	2	1	0	0	0	2	1	0	0	0	0	0	0	0	0	0
Scram . . .	0	3	0	1	1	1	1	1	1	0	0	0	1	0	0	0
Secure . .	0	0	0	0	0	0	0	0	0	0	0	0	0	0	2	1
Set	0	0	2	2	0	1	1	4	3	0	2	0	0	0	2	2
Sit	0	0	1	0	2	0	0	1	0	0	0	0	0	0	0	0
Some . . .	5	2	3	4	2	2	1	1	2	3	2	2	4	2	4	7
Something .	5	8	5	9	4	3	2	2	2	3	0	2	0	1	0	4
Steal . . .	0	0	0	0	0	0	2	0	0	0	0	1	0	0	0	0
Stop	0	0	0	0	0	1	2	0	0	0	0	0	0	0	0	0
Store . . .	0	3	0	0	0	1	0	0	0	0	0	1	0	0	0	0
Take	1	6	2	11	7	7	6	11	9	17	13	15	8	13	20	25
That	3	3	1	1	5	5	4	3	4	3	7	3	0	2	2	4
The	1	0	3	2	2	0	2	0	0	1	2	1	4	2	2	0
Them . . .	1	0	1	0	0	1	1	0	0	0	2	0	0	0	0	2
There . . .	9	7	6	4	7	4	1	1	4	4	3	4	4	1	4	1
This	2	0	2	0	0	0	0	0	2	0	1	0	0	1	1	1
To	1	1	1	1	1	1	2	1	0	0	0	0	1	0	4	6
Up	0	2	0	0	3	2	0	1	1	2	0	2	1	1	1	3
Want . . .	1	1	2	0	1	3	1	2	0	3	1	4	3	2	4	1
Way	1	1	1	0	2	0	1	0	0	1	0	1	0	0	0	0
Well	2	5	1	1	3	3	1	3	1	1	4	2	4	2	3	3
Wet	4	3	2	4	4	2	1	1	5	2	2	1	4	2	7	3
What . . .	3	1	2	0	1	0	3	5	2	4	2	3	3	4	3	6
Where . .	1	0	0	0	0	1	1	0	1	2	0	0	2	0	2	0
Why	1	0	2	1	1	0	0	3	0	0	0	0	0	0	0	1
						69.	GIRL									
Baby . . .	1	0	1	0	0	2	0	1	0	0	0	0	0	0	0	0
Bad	1	0	0	0	1	0	0	0	0	0	0	0	0	0	2	0
Beautiful .	1	0	3	2	5	1	5	0	5	2	18	1	4	1	3	2
Beauty . . .	0	0	0	0	0	1	0	0	0	0	1	0	0	1	3	0

Response Word	4th		5th		6th		7th		8th		10th		12th		College	
	M	F	M	F	M	F	M	F	M	F	M	F	M	F	M	F

GIRL

Response Word	M	F	M	F	M	F	M	F	M	F	M	F	M	F	M	F
Blonde . . .	0	0	0	0	0	0	1	1	0	0	0	0	0	0	3	0
Boy	144	145	119	135	102	119	120	142	121	159	117	154	123	156	259	339
Boys . . .	0	0	0	1	0	0	2	0	1	1	0	0	0	1	0	0
Braids . . .	0	0	0	0	0	0	0	0	0	0	0	0	0	1	0	2
Car	0	0	0	0	0	0	0	1	0	0	0	0	3	0	0	0
Carol . . .	0	0	0	0	0	0	0	0	0	0	0	0	0	0	2	1
Child . . .	3	3	3	4	1	2	0	0	0	1	0	3	0	2	2	6
Clothes . .	0	0	0	0	0	0	0	2	1	1	1	5	2	4	2	4
Cute	0	0	0	1	1	1	1	3	2	4	7	4	4	1	3	4
Date . . .	0	0	0	0	0	0	0	1	0	0	6	0	4	0	6	0
Doll	0	0	0	0	0	0	0	0	0	0	0	0	0	0	0	2
Dress . . .	7	7	4	9	9	6	4	6	6	6	4	6	1	3	13	7
Fat	0	0	0	0	0	1	2	0	0	0	0	0	1	0	0	0
Female . .	2	3	5	3	10	2	5	9	4	3	2	1	3	2	2	2
Feminine .	0	0	0	0	0	1	0	0	0	0	0	1	1	1	0	2
Figure . .	0	0	0	0	0	0	0	0	0	0	0	0	0	1	2	0
Friend . .	2	0	1	4	0	4	2	3	5	2	7	5	4	7	5	6
Friends . .	0	1	0	0	0	0	0	1	0	2	0	0	0	0	0	0
Fun	0	0	1	1	1	1	1	0	3	0	2	0	8	0	6	0
Girls . . .	0	0	0	0	1	1	0	0	1	0	3	1	1	0	1	0
Good . . .	0	0	1	0	0	2	1	0	2	0	0	0	1	0	1	0
Gym	0	0	0	0	0	0	2	0	0	0	0	0	0	0	0	0
Hair	5	4	5	3	2	6	6	6	3	2	1	2	2	3	6	5
Hat . . .	0	0	0	0	1	1	0	1	1	0	1	2	1	0	2	0
Her	0	0	0	0	3	0	0	0	0	0	0	0	0	0	0	0
House . . .	0	0	0	0	0	0	0	0	1	0	0	0	0	0	2	0
Human . .	3	1	3	1	4	0	0	0	1	0	1	0	0	0	1	0
Judy	0	0	0	0	0	0	0	0	0	0	0	0	2	0	1	0
Kid	0	0	0	0	2	0	0	0	0	0	0	0	0	0	1	0
Lady . . .	12	15	8	3	8	8	4	1	3	3	1	1	0	4	2	5
Laugh . . .	0	0	0	1	0	0	0	1	0	1	0	2	0	0	0	0
Little . . .	0	2	2	1	0	1	1	1	0	0	3	1	0	4	2	5
Long hair .	0	2	1	0	0	1	1	0	1	0	1	1	1	0	0	0
Love	0	0	1	1	2	0	2	0	5	0	4	1	7	0	7	0
Man	3	0	5	2	2	0	1	0	2	0	2	1	2	1	6	0
Mary . . .	0	0	0	0	0	0	0	0	0	0	2	0	1	0	0	0
Me	0	3	0	5	0	8	0	7	0	9	0	4	0	1	0	2
Neat	0	0	0	0	0	0	1	0	2	1	0	0	0	0	1	0
Nice	2	5	6	5	3	7	11	3	4	3	16	3	11	1	16	4
People . .	1	1	0	1	2	1	0	0	0	1	0	0	0	0	0	0
Person . .	11	14	18	11	15	16	7	6	1	4	0	1	0	1	0	1
Pretty . . .	2	6	4	5	9	14	9	12	7	9	7	11	7	6	18	16
School . . .	0	1	1	0	0	0	0	1	0	1	1	0	1	2	1	2
Scout	0	0	1	0	1	0	0	0	0	0	0	1	2	2	2	2
Sex	4	1	1	4	6	2	2	1	0	1	3	1	4	0	9	0
Sharp . . .	0	0	0	0	0	0	1	0	0	0	0	0	2	0	0	0
Sissy . . .	0	0	2	0	0	0	0	0	0	0	0	0	0	0	0	0
Sister . . .	0	0	3	1	2	2	0	1	2	1	2	0	0	2	5	6
Sisters . .	0	0	0	0	0	0	0	0	0	0	2	0	0	0	0	0
Sitter	0	0	0	0	2	0	0	0	0	0	0	0	0	0	0	0

Response Word	4th M	F	5th M	F	6th M	F	7th M	F	8th M	F	10th M	F	12th M	F	College M	F

GIRL

Response Word	4th M	F	5th M	F	6th M	F	7th M	F	8th M	F	10th M	F	12th M	F	College M	F
Skirt	0	0	0	1	0	0	0	0	0	0	0	1	1	0	0	2
Small . . .	2	0	1	0	2	1	2	3	0	0	1	2	1	0	1	1
Soft	0	0	1	0	0	0	0	0	0	0	0	0	2	0	0	0
Stupid . . .	2	0	1	0	1	0	0	0	1	0	0	0	0	0	0	0
Sweater . .	0	0	0	1	0	0	0	0	0	0	0	0	0	0	2	2
Sweet . . .	0	1	0	3	1	1	0	1	1	4	0	5	0	2	3	6
Tall	0	1	1	0	0	0	0	0	2	0	1	0	0	1	2	0
Thin . . .	0	0	0	0	0	2	0	1	0	0	0	0	0	1	0	0
Warm . .	0	0	0	0	0	0	0	0	0	0	0	0	1	0	3	0
Woman . .	12	5	8	12	10	9	18	9	17	6	9	5	7	5	24	18
Women . .	3	6	9	3	4	5	6	3	1	3	2	3	6	3	6	0
Wow	0	0	0	0	3	0	3	0	4	0	0	0	2	0	2	0
Young . . .	1	2	3	5	2	2	4	6	1	3	0	5	2	12	17	19

70. GO

Response Word	4th M	F	5th M	F	6th M	F	7th M	F	8th M	F	10th M	F	12th M	F	College M	F
Ahead . . .	0	1	0	2	1	0	2	2	0	1	2	2	1	3	0	1
Away . . .	5	12	6	4	4	9	1	8	7	8	11	14	7	9	30	28
Back . . .	0	0	0	0	0	0	0	1	0	0	1	0	1	0	0	2
Boy	0	0	0	0	0	0	2	0	0	0	0	0	0	0	0	0
Buy	1	0	2	0	0	0	0	0	0	0	0	0	0	0	0	0
By	0	2	1	0	1	3	1	0	1	3	1	0	1	0	0	1
Bye	0	0	0	0	0	0	0	3	0	0	0	0	0	0	0	0
Came . . .	1	0	1	0	0	0	0	0	0	0	0	0	1	2	1	1
Car	1	0	1	3	1	2	1	0	0	1	1	1	2	1	2	1
Cart . . .	0	0	0	0	0	0	2	0	1	0	0	0	0	0	0	0
Come . . .	13	14	13	19	18	24	15	29	22	35	33	47	23	38	70	95
Command .	0	0	0	0	0	1	0	0	0	0	0	0	0	0	0	2
Down . . .	1	1	3	5	0	1	1	1	2	1	0	0	2	1	4	3
Easier . .	0	0	1	0	0	0	0	0	0	0	0	0	0	0	2	0
Easy	0	0	0	0	0	0	0	0	0	0	0	0	0	0	0	2
Far	2	0	0	4	1	0	1	0	1	1	0	1	2	1	2	5
Fast	35	40	57	46	55	30	22	21	22	24	35	32	26	20	49	38
Faster . . .	3	0	1	1	0	1	1	1	3	2	2	0	1	1	1	3
Find	0	0	1	0	0	1	0	0	2	1	1	0	0	0	1	1
For	2	0	0	0	0	0	0	0	2	0	0	0	0	0	2	1
From . . .	0	0	0	0	0	0	0	0	0	0	1	2	1	0	0	4
Fun	0	0	2	0	0	0	0	0	0	0	0	0	0	0	0	0
Get	5	6	7	6	5	14	5	8	6	4	4	4	7	6	17	14
Going . . .	2	1	2	2	2	1	3	0	2	0	2	1	1	3	2	0
Gone	3	2	3	3	5	8	11	9	22	15	8	9	18	24	13	14
Good	2	1	0	0	1	0	0	0	0	0	0	0	0	0	0	0
Goodbye . .	0	0	0	0	0	1	0	2	0	0	0	0	0	0	0	0
Got	0	0	0	0	0	0	1	1	0	0	2	0	2	1	0	1
Green . . .	2	0	0	1	1	0	1	3	0	1	5	7	3	2	3	6
Here	5	3	0	0	0	1	0	1	0	0	0	0	0	1	0	1
Home . . .	10	6	7	7	12	7	9	7	6	9	8	12	11	8	25	15
How	1	3	1	1	1	0	0	0	1	0	0	0	0	1	1	1
In	0	4	0	1	2	1	1	1	0	1	0	3	0	0	4	3
Know . . .	2	0	0	0	0	0	0	0	0	0	0	0	0	0	0	0

Response Word	4th M	4th F	5th M	5th F	6th M	6th F	7th M	7th F	8th M	8th F	10th M	10th F	12th M	12th F	College M	College F
							GO									
Leave . . .	1	1	1	3	0	2	3	1	1	5	5	14	8	11	11	11
Light . . .	0	0	0	0	1	0	0	0	1	0	2	0	0	1	0	4
Low	4	0	0	0	0	0	0	0	0	0	0	0	0	0	0	0
Move . . .	2	0	1	0	3	1	3	3	1	3	6	1	0	1	4	6
No	5	0	1	0	0	2	0	1	0	0	0	0	0	0	0	0
Now	6	17	11	6	9	7	7	3	8	3	10	9	13	11	33	18
On	5	6	10	5	8	4	3	3	3	1	1	2	1	3	8	6
Order . . .	0	0	0	0	0	0	2	0	0	0	0	0	0	0	0	0
Out . . .	4	4	3	3	3	3	0	2	6	3	3	2	3	7	8	7
Place . . .	1	4	1	2	0	0	0	1	0	1	0	1	0	0	0	0
Places . .	0	1	0	1	0	1	0	0	0	0	0	0	2	2	0	0
Quick . . .	0	0	0	0	0	0	0	1	2	1	0	0	0	0	1	0
Quickly . .	0	0	0	0	0	0	1	2	1	0	1	1	0	0	2	3
Race . . .	1	0	1	1	0	0	1	0	0	0	0	0	2	0	1	0
Red	0	0	0	0	0	0	0	0	1	1	0	0	1	1	0	2
Run	5	3	6	10	5	12	9	21	6	12	9	10	6	6	17	18
Scram . . .	0	1	0	1	2	0	0	0	0	0	0	0	0	0	0	1
Sign . . .	0	1	0	1	0	4	0	1	0	1	0	0	1	1	0	0
Slow	9	3	9	5	6	2	8	2	7	4	4	3	3	9	15	10
Slowly . . .	0	0	0	0	0	0	0	0	1	0	0	0	0	0	0	2
So	1	1	3	0	1	0	0	0	0	0	0	0	0	0	0	0
Someplace .	1	2	0	4	0	3	0	0	0	0	0	0	1	0	1	1
Speed . . .	0	0	1	0	0	0	0	1	1	0	2	0	0	0	0	0
Start	4	2	2	2	6	4	3	5	0	4	2	1	1	0	3	0
Stay	0	7	3	5	5	10	4	9	7	8	3	5	2	4	7	10
Stop	49	59	50	55	45	57	75	57	66	59	38	36	32	24	50	81
Store . . .	0	0	0	1	0	0	1	2	0	0	0	1	0	1	0	0
Take	0	0	0	2	1	0	0	0	1	0	1	0	0	3	0	0
Their . . .	2	0	0	0	0	0	0	2	0	0	0	0	0	0	0	0
There . . .	5	2	5	0	1	1	2	1	1	4	5	6	1	4	5	5
To	7	3	7	6	11	1	7	2	6	5	5	2	8	3	19	15
Too	0	0	0	1	2	0	0	1	0	0	0	0	0	0	0	0
Town . . .	0	0	0	0	0	0	0	0	0	0	0	0	0	0	2	0
Travel . .	0	0	0	0	1	0	1	0	0	0	0	1	0	0	2	3
Walk	0	0	1	0	2	0	3	3	0	4	0	1	3	2	1	1
Went	0	5	1	3	2	3	8	14	9	6	10	5	15	15	27	18
What	0	0	0	0	0	0	0	0	0	0	0	0	2	0	0	0
Where . . .	0	1	1	1	1	1	0	0	2	3	3	4	8	4	6	4
With	5	0	2	0	2	6	1	2	6	1	3	0	1	4	5	6
						71.	GREEN									
Apple . . .	0	1	0	1	0	0	0	0	0	0	1	1	0	1	2	2
Bay	0	0	0	0	0	0	0	0	0	0	0	0	0	0	2	0
Bean . . .	0	0	0	0	0	1	0	0	1	0	0	0	0	0	2	0
Beans . . .	0	0	0	1	0	1	0	0	0	0	0	0	0	0	1	2
Beautiful .	0	0	0	0	0	0	0	2	0	0	0	0	0	0	0	0
Black . . .	8	5	7	5	10	7	5	2	11	4	3	2	3	3	9	3
Blouse . .	0	0	0	0	0	0	0	0	0	2	0	0	0	1	0	0
Blue	25	22	24	24	17	21	20	18	37	27	25	14	23	17	37	58

Response Word	4th M	F	5th M	F	6th M	F	7th M	F	8th M	F	10th M	F	12th M	F	College M	F
							GREEN									
Bright . . .	2	1	1	1	1	2	1	1	0	0	1	0	1	0	0	0
Brown . . .	0	1	0	0	1	2	6	2	1	1	0	2	3	2	2	2
Car	0	0	0	0	0	0	1	0	0	0	2	0	3	0	1	0
Cat	0	0	1	0	1	2	0	0	0	0	0	0	0	0	0	0
Cheese . .	0	0	0	2	1	0	1	1	0	1	1	0	1	0	3	0
Coat	1	0	0	0	0	0	0	1	0	0	0	1	0	0	3	0
Color . . .	73	68	72	57	79	57	47	37	37	31	36	15	14	13	33	15
Colors . .	1	2	1	0	2	0	0	0	0	0	0	0	0	0	0	0
Cool	0	0	0	0	0	0	3	2	0	1	1	2	0	1	0	2
Dark	0	1	2	6	1	1	2	2	0	2	4	1	0	0	3	1
Dress . . .	0	1	0	0	0	0	0	1	0	1	0	1	0	2	1	6
Envy	0	0	0	0	0	0	0	1	0	1	0	0	1	1	2	1
Field . . .	0	0	0	0	0	0	0	0	0	0	1	1	1	0	2	2
Fields . .	0	0	0	0	0	0	0	1	0	0	1	2	1	1	5	2
Go	0	0	1	0	0	1	0	2	3	0	7	2	4	4	3	3
Golf	0	0	0	0	0	0	0	0	0	0	1	2	0	1	3	0
Grass . . .	38	49	52	61	50	72	66	73	52	86	77	116	87	127	182	230
Hat.	0	1	0	0	0	0	0	0	0	1	0	0	0	0	2	0
House . . .	1	0	0	0	1	0	4	0	1	0	0	0	0	1	0	0
Ireland . .	0	0	0	0	0	0	1	0	0	1	0	0	0	1	3	0
Irish	0	0	0	0	0	0	0	0	0	1	2	0	2	2	2	0
Lake	0	0	0	0	0	0	0	0	0	0	0	2	1	0	0	0
Lawn . . .	0	0	1	0	0	0	1	3	2	2	0	2	1	2	3	2
Leaf	2	1	1	1	1	0	1	1	2	3	0	0	1	1	2	1
Leave . . .	0	1	0	0	0	2	0	0	0	0	0	0	0	0	0	0
Leaves . .	1	1	0	3	0	1	1	3	1	1	0	2	4	1	4	4
Lettuce . .	0	0	0	0	0	0	0	1	1	3	0	0	0	0	1	1
Light. . . .	0	0	1	0	0	0	5	1	3	1	2	1	1	3	9	3
Man	0	0	0	0	1	0	0	0	2	0	0	0	0	0	0	0
Money . . .	0	0	0	1	2	4	0	0	1	0	0	0	1	0	2	0
Moon . . .	2	1	0	0	3	0	0	0	1	1	0	0	0	0	0	0
Ocean . . .	0	0	1	0	1	0	0	0	1	0	0	1	2	1	1	0
Orange . .	3	3	0	1	0	2	1	3	4	4	0	1	0	1	2	1
Outdoors .	0	0	0	0	0	0	0	1	0	0	0	0	0	0	0	2
Pasture . .	0	0	1	0	0	1	1	0	0	0	0	0	2	1	0	0
Pastures .	0	0	0	1	1	0	1	0	0	0	0	0	2	1	2	1
Peas	1	0	0	0	1	0	0	0	1	1	0	1	0	0	2	2
Pepper . .	0	0	0	0	0	0	0	0	0	0	1	1	0	0	1	2
Pink	1	4	1	5	2	0	5	1	2	2	2	0	0	2	1	1
Plant . . .	2	0	1	2	2	1	3	4	2	0	0	0	0	2	3	1
Plants . .	0	0	0	1	0	0	1	0	0	1	0	0	0	0	2	1
Pretty . .	1	4	3	1	0	2	1	5	0	0	1	1	0	1	1	0
Purple . .	4	5	1	2	1	0	2	2	4	2	3	0	0	1	2	2
Queen . . .	0	2	0	0	0	1	0	0	0	0	0	1	0	0	0	0
Red	33	30	28	17	26	16	29	18	30	24	18	16	35	15	54	46
Robin Hood	0	0	0	0	0	0	0	0	0	0	0	0	2	0	0	0
Salt	1	0	0	0	2	0	0	0	1	0	1	0	0	0	1	0
Sea	0	0	1	0	1	0	0	0	0	0	0	1	2	0	1	6
Sick	0	1	0	0	0	0	0	1	3	0	1	0	0	1	1	0

Response Word	4th M	4th F	5th M	5th F	6th M	6th F	7th M	7th F	8th M	8th F	10th M	10th F	12th M	12th F	College M	College F

GREEN

Response Word	4th M	4th F	5th M	5th F	6th M	6th F	7th M	7th F	8th M	8th F	10th M	10th F	12th M	12th F	College M	College F
Skirt	0	0	0	0	0	1	0	1	0	0	0	1	0	1	1	2
Sleeves	0	0	0	0	0	0	1	0	0	0	0	0	2	0	1	1
Soft	0	0	0	0	0	0	1	0	0	0	1	3	1	0	0	4
Stem	0	2	0	2	0	0	1	0	0	1	0	0	0	0	0	0
Suit	0	0	0	0	0	0	0	0	0	0	0	0	1	1	2	0
Summer	0	1	0	1	0	1	0	1	0	0	1	2	0	0	1	0
Thumb	0	0	0	0	1	0	0	0	1	1	1	0	0	0	0	0
Tree	4	2	2	3	1	5	3	3	4	3	4	2	0	2	6	7
Trees	1	0	1	1	1	0	1	4	4	3	4	3	4	2	7	6
Ugly	0	0	2	0	0	0	0	0	0	0	0	0	0	0	0	0
Warm	0	0	0	0	0	0	0	0	0	0	0	0	0	0	0	3
Water	0	0	0	0	0	1	0	1	1	2	2	0	0	0	2	1
White	3	2	7	8	4	5	2	0	1	1	7	7	5	6	14	7
Yellow	21	22	19	21	11	18	14	24	23	14	18	19	15	10	25	26

72. GUNS

Response Word	4th M	4th F	5th M	5th F	6th M	6th F	7th M	7th F	8th M	8th F	10th M	10th F	12th M	12th F	College M	College F
Ammo	0	0	0	0	0	0	5	0	4	0	2	0	1	0	1	0
Ammunition	2	0	6	4	2	2	6	9	8	19	8	7	12	6	17	19
Are	1	0	0	1	1	1	1	0	0	0	1	0	4	0	1	1
Arms	0	0	1	0	2	2	1	0	0	0	2	0	0	0	0	3
Army	2	0	1	1	0	0	2	1	2	2	1	0	2	0	2	3
Arrows	1	0	0	0	0	0	0	0	2	2	1	1	2	1	1	2
Artillery	0	0	0	1	0	0	0	0	0	1	0	0	0	1	0	2
Bad	0	3	2	1	0	0	0	1	1	0	0	1	0	1	0	0
Bam	2	0	0	0	0	0	0	0	0	0	0	0	0	0	0	0
Bang	11	12	14	22	19	17	20	19	11	18	11	12	11	11	11	23
Barrel	0	0	0	1	0	0	0	0	0	0	0	0	0	0	2	0
Barrels	0	0	0	0	0	0	1	0	1	2	0	0	0	0	1	0
Birds	0	0	0	0	0	0	0	0	1	0	0	0	3	0	1	0
Black	0	0	0	0	0	0	0	0	0	0	1	0	0	1	3	1
Blast	0	0	0	0	0	0	0	0	2	1	0	0	0	0	0	0
Blood	0	0	0	0	0	0	1	0	0	2	0	1	0	0	0	0
Boat	0	0	0	0	0	0	0	0	0	0	1	0	0	2	0	0
Boom	3	0	1	0	1	1	0	1	1	0	0	0	0	0	2	4
Boys	0	2	0	0	0	1	1	1	0	1	0	0	0	2	0	3
Bullet	4	2	5	4	8	4	6	1	5	1	2	5	2	4	11	4
Bullets	15	8	8	9	19	15	20	14	20	17	23	18	22	18	38	53
Buns	0	2	1	0	1	0	1	2	0	0	0	0	0	0	0	1
Cannon	0	0	1	1	0	0	0	1	2	2	0	0	2	0	2	2
Cars	0	0	0	0	0	0	2	0	1	0	0	1	0	1	1	1
Case	0	0	0	0	0	0	0	0	0	0	0	0	0	0	2	0
Cops	0	0	0	1	0	0	0	0	2	0	1	1	0	0	0	0
Cowboy	3	4	1	2	2	2	1	4	2	0	2	2	0	1	2	8
Cowboys	1	3	2	5	2	3	5	6	1	7	5	9	5	14	2	14
Danger	0	0	1	0	0	3	0	0	0	0	0	2	0	0	0	0
Dangerous	0	0	1	0	0	2	2	1	0	0	0	1	1	2	0	0
Dead	1	0	0	0	1	1	0	0	1	2	2	0	0	1	2	0
Death	0	0	0	0	1	0	2	0	1	0	0	0	1	1	5	1
Dogs	0	0	0	0	2	0	0	0	0	1	0	0	0	0	1	0

Response Word	4th M	4th F	5th M	5th F	6th M	6th F	7th M	7th F	8th M	8th F	10th M	10th F	12th M	12th F	College M	College F
							GUNS									
Fight	0	1	0	0	0	1	1	0	1	0	1	1	0	1	3	5
Fire	4	6	14	5	6	7	6	10	5	12	8	18	7	14	29	34
Firearms .	1	0	1	0	2	1	2	2	0	1	0	0	0	0	1	0
Fun	0	0	2	0	0	0	3	0	3	0	1	0	0	0	0	0
Game . . .	2	1	0	0	0	1	0	0	0	0	1	0	1	0	1	1
Go	2	0	1	1	3	1	0	0	0	0	2	0	1	1	0	2
Good . . .	2	0	0	0	1	0	0	0	0	0	0	0	0	0	0	0
Gum	2	1	2	5	0	1	1	1	1	1	0	0	0	0	0	0
Gun	8	10	7	3	4	6	6	1	3	0	3	0	0	0	1	0
Gym	2	0	0	0	0	0	0	2	0	0	0	0	0	1	0	0
Holster . .	1	1	2	3	2	3	1	8	4	3	1	8	1	8	2	9
Holsters .	0	1	0	1	1	1	1	1	0	4	1	2	1	1	4	9
Horses . . .	0	0	0	0	0	1	0	1	1	0	0	0	0	2	1	0
Hunt	1	0	0	0	0	0	2	0	0	0	12	1	1	0	15	5
Hunters . .	0	0	0	0	0	0	0	0	0	0	0	2	0	0	0	0
Hunting . .	1	0	0	0	3	0	0	0	1	0	5	1	6	1	4	4
Hurt	1	1	1	0	0	1	1	0	2	3	1	3	0	4	2	0
Is	2	1	0	0	1	0	0	0	0	0	0	0	0	0	0	0
Kill	2	1	4	3	4	5	6	3	3	3	3	2	7	2	7	6
Killing . . .	1	0	0	0	0	0	0	0	0	0	0	0	0	1	3	0
Knives . . .	0	0	0	1	0	1	1	1	0	2	3	1	1	3	3	3
Loud	1	1	0	0	5	1	0	1	0	1	3	2	0	1	0	2
Machine . .	0	0	0	0	0	0	0	0	0	0	1	0	1	1	0	2
Machine gun	0	0	0	0	0	0	0	0	2	0	0	0	0	0	0	0
Machinery .	0	0	0	0	0	0	0	0	0	0	0	0	0	0	0	2
Man	1	0	3	0	0	1	2	0	0	0	0	1	0	0	0	0
Men	3	1	2	0	2	0	0	1	1	3	0	0	1	2	2	1
Muskets . .	0	0	0	3	0	0	0	0	0	1	0	0	0	0	0	0
Noise . . .	1	1	3	3	4	5	0	2	4	2	2	5	7	3	8	9
People . .	0	0	2	0	0	0	0	1	1	0	0	1	2	1	0	1
Pistol . . .	6	2	6	3	6	3	11	4	7	3	5	2	2	1	8	2
Pistols . .	1	1	2	1	0	4	10	4	3	0	5	0	2	2	4	5
Play	1	6	0	0	1	0	0	1	0	1	0	0	0	0	0	0
Police . . .	0	0	0	0	0	0	0	0	1	0	1	2	0	0	0	1
Pow	0	0	0	3	0	0	0	1	1	0	0	0	0	0	0	0
Powder . .	1	3	4	3	4	3	3	1	4	3	4	2	2	2	3	4
Power . . .	1	0	0	1	0	1	1	1	0	2	2	1	0	0	3	0
Rifle . . .	20	8	11	12	14	15	13	9	13	8	6	6	10	5	21	5
Rifles . . .	3	3	5	10	5	9	13	11	9	9	5	6	11	7	18	11
See	1	0	0	0	2	0	0	0	0	0	0	0	0	0	0	0
Shell	0	0	0	0	1	0	1	0	0	0	1	0	0	1	2	0
Shells . . .	2	1	2	0	0	0	3	0	6	1	3	2	7	3	21	5
Shoot . . .	31	62	34	40	31	48	29	51	35	53	31	54	39	54	102	99
Shooting . .	0	1	1	3	1	0	1	1	0	1	0	4	0	1	1	2
Shoots . . .	2	1	1	0	0	0	0	0	0	0	0	0	0	0	0	0
Short	2	0	1	0	0	0	0	0	0	0	0	0	0	0	0	0
Shot	21	35	22	32	22	28	13	14	10	17	13	19	14	17	11	27
Shots . . .	4	2	1	0	3	3	0	5	1	3	2	2	2	2	3	4
Shout . . .	2	8	2	2	2	4	0	3	1	0	2	1	1	0	0	0

133

Response Word	4th M	F	5th M	F	6th M	F	7th M	F	8th M	F	10th M	F	12th M	F	College M	F

GUNS

Response Word	4th M	F	5th M	F	6th M	F	7th M	F	8th M	F	10th M	F	12th M	F	College M	F
Shouts . . .	0	0	2	0	0	0	0	0	0	0	0	0	0	0	0	0
Smoke . . .	11	3	6	9	6	2	3	5	2	3	7	5	4	2	12	11
Soldier . .	0	0	0	0	0	0	0	0	0	0	0	1	0	0	2	0
Soldiers . .	0	0	0	0	0	0	0	0	1	1	0	2	1	0	3	3
Sound . . .	0	0	0	0	0	1	0	0	0	0	0	0	0	0	2	0
Steel	1	0	2	0	0	0	0	0	0	0	0	0	0	1	0	0
Sun	0	0	1	0	0	2	0	0	0	0	0	0	0	0	0	0
Teeth . . .	3	1	0	0	0	0	0	0	2	0	0	0	0	0	0	0
The	0	0	0	0	2	0	0	0	0	0	0	0	0	0	0	0
Toy	1	3	1	3	0	0	0	0	0	0	0	0	0	0	1	0
Toys . . .	1	1	0	3	1	1	2	2	1	2	1	1	1	0	2	4
Trigger . .	0	0	0	0	0	0	0	0	0	1	0	1	0	0	3	2
TV	0	0	0	0	1	1	0	1	0	0	0	0	0	0	2	0
Twenty two	0	0	2	0	1	0	2	0	1	0	2	0	0	0	0	0
Two	2	0	1	0	1	2	1	2	0	0	1	0	0	1	0	1
War	2	0	1	5	4	1	3	3	5	4	2	1	5	9	12	31
Wars . . .	0	0	1	0	0	0	0	0	0	0	0	0	0	0	0	2
Weapon . .	1	3	2	2	2	1	1	4	0	0	1	1	1	1	2	0
Weapons .	3	0	5	1	7	2	6	4	2	2	3	4	5	2	4	0
Were . . .	0	0	0	0	0	0	0	0	0	0	0	0	1	0	2	0
West . . .	0	1	2	1	3	0	0	1	0	0	1	3	0	0	4	0
Western . .	0	0	0	0	0	1	0	0	0	1	2	0	0	1	1	1
Westerns .	1	0	0	0	0	0	0	0	0	0	1	0	2	0	2	5
Who	0	0	0	0	2	0	1	0	0	0	0	0	0	0	0	0
Will	0	0	0	0	0	0	0	0	1	0	1	0	1	0	0	2

73. HAMMER

Response Word	4th M	F	5th M	F	6th M	F	7th M	F	8th M	F	10th M	F	12th M	F	College M	F
Anvil	0	0	0	0	0	0	0	0	1	0	1	0	2	1	5	5
Arm	0	0	0	0	0	0	0	0	0	1	0	0	1	0	2	0
Axe	0	0	0	1	1	0	2	0	0	0	0	0	0	0	0	1
Bang . . .	2	0	1	3	1	1	2	2	0	2	1	0	0	1	2	1
Bench . . .	0	0	0	0	0	0	0	0	0	0	0	0	0	0	0	2
Blow	0	0	0	0	0	1	0	0	1	0	1	0	3	0	1	1
Board . . .	1	2	0	1	1	0	0	0	0	1	0	0	0	0	0	1
Bond	2	0	0	0	0	1	0	0	0	0	0	0	0	0	0	0
Bound . . .	0	0	1	3	0	1	0	0	0	0	0	0	0	0	0	0
Build . . .	0	1	0	0	0	1	0	1	0	0	0	1	0	1	2	0
Carpenter .	0	0	0	0	0	0	1	0	0	0	0	0	1	2	1	1
Chisel . . .	1	0	1	0	0	0	0	0	0	1	0	0	3	0	2	1
Drum . . .	0	0	0	0	0	0	0	0	0	2	0	0	0	0	0	0
Finger . .	0	0	1	0	2	0	1	1	0	1	0	0	0	0	2	2
Fist	0	0	0	0	0	0	0	0	0	0	0	2	0	0	1	0
Fix	0	0	0	0	0	0	0	1	0	0	1	0	0	1	1	2
Good . . .	2	0	3	0	0	0	0	0	0	0	0	0	0	0	0	0
Gun	0	1	0	0	2	0	0	0	1	0	0	0	0	0	0	0
Ham	6	6	2	4	2	2	0	1	1	0	0	0	0	0	0	0
Hand . . .	0	1	0	1	2	0	0	1	0	0	0	0	0	1	0	0
Handle . .	1	0	1	0	1	0	0	0	1	1	2	0	0	1	0	0
Hard	15	19	36	17	23	29	32	23	23	15	29	14	18	16	20	22

Response Word	4th M	4th F	5th M	5th F	6th M	6th F	7th M	7th F	8th M	8th F	10th M	10th F	12th M	12th F	College M	College F
						HAMMER										
Head	7	4	9	5	11	3	17	4	19	4	10	2	6	3	26	4
Heart	0	0	0	0	0	0	0	0	0	0	0	2	0	0	0	0
Heavy	2	1	1	2	0	0	0	2	1	0	6	0	0	2	1	2
Hit	16	4	8	5	13	6	21	16	21	10	20	7	11	11	46	31
Hurt	1	4	2	2	2	3	1	4	2	4	2	5	0	7	1	4
Iron	1	0	2	0	0	1	2	0	1	0	0	0	1	0	1	1
Knock	0	1	2	1	0	0	0	1	0	0	0	0	0	0	1	2
Loud	0	0	0	4	0	5	0	1	0	2	0	1	0	0	0	0
Mallet	0	0	0	0	0	0	2	0	1	1	0	0	0	0	0	0
Nail	69	98	84	93	91	93	92	97	100	120	105	133	128	111	214	235
Nails	6	13	11	16	4	14	7	10	14	18	5	14	5	15	13	33
Noise . . .	1	4	0	1	0	4	1	1	2	0	0	2	0	3	4	7
Ouch	0	1	3	1	1	2	3	2	3	1	1	1	0	1	3	0
Pound	36	34	28	35	22	36	16	36	10	22	7	29	10	24	25	45
Pounding . .	0	1	1	1	1	0	0	0	1	1	2	1	3	2	0	0
Russia	0	0	0	0	0	0	0	0	0	0	1	0	0	0	2	1
Saw	16	14	10	9	8	8	3	11	7	5	9	16	8	17	27	39
Screw	0	0	2	0	0	0	0	0	0	0	0	0	0	0	0	0
Screw driver	0	0	0	1	2	1	2	0	3	0	1	1	1	1	1	1
Sickle	1	0	0	0	0	0	0	0	0	0	1	1	5	0	21	6
Slam	0	1	0	2	0	0	1	1	0	0	0	1	0	1	0	0
Sledge	0	0	0	0	3	1	0	0	0	1	0	0	1	0	2	0
Sound	0	0	2	1	2	0	0	1	0	1	0	0	0	0	0	1
Steel	4	1	4	0	6	1	0	1	2	1	3	0	1	0	6	1
Strike	0	0	0	0	0	0	0	0	0	1	0	0	2	0	1	0
Strong . . .	0	0	1	0	0	0	0	0	0	0	0	1	1	0	0	2
Thor	0	0	0	0	0	0	5	1	0	0	0	0	4	0	0	0
Throw	0	0	0	0	1	0	0	0	1	0	3	1	3	0	15	2
Thumb	0	0	0	1	1	0	1	1	1	2	4	1	1	0	2	3
Tong	0	0	0	0	0	0	0	0	0	0	0	0	0	0	4	1
Tongs	0	0	0	0	0	0	0	0	0	0	0	0	2	0	2	1
Tool	17	23	13	14	25	22	26	17	12	18	12	6	6	11	11	13
Tools	2	3	1	0	1	3	0	2	0	0	1	0	0	1	0	0
Wood	3	2	0	2	3	2	4	4	3	0	6	2	3	0	4	2
Work	3	1	2	3	1	1	0	3	1	1	2	0	6	6	2	2
					74.	HAND										
And	1	3	2	2	0	0	0	0	0	0	0	0	0	0	0	0
Arm	40	22	30	34	41	39	55	57	47	51	52	47	48	44	71	77
Ball	0	0	0	0	0	0	0	0	0	0	2	1	0	0	2	0
Band	1	0	2	1	2	0	0	0	1	0	0	0	0	1	0	0
Big	0	0	4	2	3	5	2	1	0	1	7	1	1	0	2	3
Body	9	7	8	11	13	16	7	4	3	4	1	8	1	2	6	2
Chair	0	1	0	0	0	0	0	0	0	0	0	0	0	0	2	0
Clasp	0	0	0	0	0	0	0	0	0	0	0	0	0	1	2	0
Ear	0	0	1	0	0	1	0	1	0	2	0	0	0	0	0	0
Eat	0	0	2	0	0	0	0	0	0	0	0	0	0	0	0	0
Eye	2	0	0	0	0	0	0	0	0	0	0	0	0	0	1	1
Face	1	4	5	2	0	1	1	1	2	1	1	2	2	0	7	2

Response Word	4th M	4th F	5th M	5th F	6th M	6th F	7th M	7th F	8th M	8th F	10th M	10th F	12th M	12th F	College M	College F
							HAND									
Feel	0	2	2	0	1	3	0	0	1	2	0	1	0	0	1	1
Feet	11	10	4	5	5	1	0	0	15	3	3	2	2	2	4	3
Finger . .	25	22	21	32	17	24	47	25	31	38	26	36	29	28	67	67
Fingernail	1	1	0	0	1	1	1	1	1	1	1	1	1	2	2	4
Fingernails	0	0	0	1	0	1	0	0	0	3	1	2	1	2	0	1
Fingers . .	18	37	19	35	30	27	13	33	26	34	25	30	21	31	36	32
Fist	3	1	3	0	6	3	3	0	3	0	1	0	1	0	0	0
Five	0	1	1	1	0	0	3	0	0	2	0	0	0	0	1	0
Flesh . . .	0	1	1	1	3	2	2	0	1	0	0	0	0	2	0	0
Food	0	0	1	0	0	1	0	0	1	0	0	0	1	0	0	2
Foot	20	27	34	17	17	22	37	31	50	42	36	33	58	52	112	116
Girl	0	2	0	0	0	0	1	0	0	0	1	0	1	0	0	0
Give	1	2	2	1	0	1	1	1	1	0	0	0	0	0	2	1
Glove . . .	3	0	4	0	2	2	1	3	3	2	4	3	10	4	28	25
Grab	0	0	0	1	0	0	2	0	0	0	0	0	0	0	0	0
Grasp . . .	0	0	0	0	0	0	0	0	0	0	0	0	0	0	2	1
Grip	0	0	0	0	2	1	2	0	0	0	0	0	0	0	0	0
Hard	2	1	1	1	0	0	1	2	0	0	3	0	2	2	0	1
Harm . . .	0	0	1	0	0	0	1	2	0	0	0	0	0	0	0	0
Hat	2	0	0	0	0	1	0	0	0	0	0	0	0	0	0	0
Head . . .	10	3	4	6	3	4	0	1	2	2	3	0	4	0	2	3
Heart . . .	0	0	1	0	0	0	0	1	0	0	0	2	0	0	1	2
Help	2	1	3	2	0	3	3	1	1	1	1	0	0	0	2	2
Hold	4	3	2	7	6	2	2	1	0	0	1	2	3	3	7	3
Large . . .	0	0	1	0	1	1	1	0	1	0	1	0	0	1	3	0
Left	2	0	1	2	0	0	0	0	0	0	0	0	0	0	0	1
Leg	11	15	2	8	8	5	8	9	12	4	6	2	2	2	9	6
Limb . . .	0	0	0	0	2	0	4	1	0	0	3	0	0	0	0	0
Little . . .	0	3	0	2	0	0	0	0	0	0	0	0	0	0	0	0
Man	4	0	1	1	1	2	1	0	1	1	1	1	1	1	3	1
Me	2	1	0	0	2	0	0	0	0	0	0	0	1	0	1	0
Mine	1	0	1	0	1	1	1	0	0	0	0	0	0	1	2	1
Mitten . . .	0	0	0	2	0	0	0	0	0	0	0	0	0	0	0	0
Mouth . . .	1	0	0	0	1	0	0	0	0	0	1	0	1	1	5	5
Nail	0	1	1	1	0	2	0	2	1	0	1	1	0	3	1	3
Nails . . .	0	1	0	0	0	0	1	1	0	3	1	0	0	2	1	5
Nice . . .	1	0	0	0	1	2	0	0	0	0	0	1	0	0	1	0
Palm . . .	5	8	5	7	11	4	3	3	3	2	4	0	0	0	2	4
Part . . .	3	0	1	0	1	1	0	0	1	0	0	0	1	0	0	0
Pencil . . .	0	1	2	0	0	0	1	0	1	1	1	0	0	0	0	1
People . . .	1	1	1	0	0	2	0	1	0	0	0	1	1	0	0	0
Person . .	2	0	0	2	2	0	0	3	1	1	1	1	0	0	1	1
Rest	0	0	2	0	0	0	0	0	0	0	0	0	0	0	0	0
Right . . .	2	1	1	2	2	2	1	3	0	0	3	0	0	0	1	1
Ring	0	1	0	2	0	2	1	2	2	10	3	16	8	17	16	33
Shake . . .	5	3	2	1	2	2	1	1	2	4	8	7	4	1	16	11
Short . . .	0	2	0	0	0	1	0	0	0	0	1	0	0	0	2	0
Skin	3	6	5	3	0	3	4	3	0	1	3	2	2	3	1	1
Small . . .	1	2	1	3	0	0	0	4	0	0	1	2	1	0	0	1

Response Word	4th M	4th F	5th M	5th F	6th M	6th F	7th M	7th F	8th M	8th F	10th M	10th F	12th M	12th F	College M	College F
HAND																
Soft	1	7	5	7	5	12	3	10	1	10	6	16	7	14	14	29
Some ...	0	0	0	0	0	0	0	0	0	0	0	0	2	0	2	0
Something .	0	1	0	0	0	2	0	0	0	0	0	0	0	0	0	0
Strong ...	0	0	2	0	0	1	1	2	1	0	3	0	0	0	2	2
Thing ...	2	0	3	2	3	0	0	1	0	0	0	0	0	0	0	0
Thumb ..	1	0	1	1	1	1	3	1	0	0	2	0	0	0	4	1
Toe	0	0	0	1	0	0	0	0	1	1	0	1	2	1	2	1
Tool	0	0	1	0	1	0	0	0	0	0	0	0	4	0	0	0
Touch ...	1	1	0	0	1	1	1	1	0	1	1	1	1	0	6	3
Use	0	1	2	3	1	3	0	0	0	0	1	0	0	0	0	0
Useful ...	0	0	0	0	0	1	0	0	0	2	1	0	0	0	0	0
Warm ...	0	0	1	1	0	1	0	2	0	0	1	1	0	0	3	3
Warmth ..	0	0	0	0	0	0	0	0	0	0	0	2	0	0	0	0
Wash ...	0	1	0	0	0	0	0	0	0	0	0	0	0	0	1	2
White ...	1	1	0	0	0	0	0	1	0	1	1	1	0	0	1	3
Work ...	5	4	7	4	4	1	0	0	2	0	3	0	3	2	1	1
Wrist ...	3	0	0	0	3	1	3	1	3	2	4	3	3	2	3	0
Write ...	2	4	0	5	0	7	0	5	1	1	3	1	2	3	2	6
Writing ..	0	1	1	1	1	0	0	0	0	1	0	1	0	1	0	2
75. HARD																
Bad	2	0	2	2	2	0	0	1	0	1	1	0	1	0	2	0
Ball	1	1	1	1	0	1	1	1	2	0	3	0	1	1	2	1
Baseball .	0	0	0	0	0	0	0	0	2	0	2	0	0	0	1	0
Bed	0	1	0	0	0	2	0	0	1	1	1	2	0	2	0	1
Big	1	0	2	1	0	0	0	0	0	0	0	0	0	0	0	0
Board ...	1	0	0	2	1	1	2	0	0	1	1	1	1	1	0	5
Boiled ...	1	0	0	0	0	0	1	0	1	1	1	0	2	1	3	1
Book	0	0	0	0	0	1	0	1	0	0	0	2	0	0	0	1
Bread ...	0	1	0	0	0	0	0	0	0	0	0	0	0	0	0	0
Brick ...	1	0	1	2	0	1	0	0	0	0	0	0	2	0	0	1
Brittle ..	0	0	0	0	0	0	0	1	1	0	1	0	1	1	2	1
Candy ...	0	0	1	0	0	2	0	1	0	2	2	0	2	3	0	0
Cement ..	3	0	1	0	0	2	1	0	2	0	0	2	0	0	6	1
Chair ...	0	1	0	2	0	1	0	2	0	0	0	3	0	0	3	3
Cold	0	0	0	1	0	0	0	0	0	0	3	1	1	1	3	3
Core	0	0	0	0	0	0	0	0	0	0	0	0	1	0	0	2
Desk ...	0	0	0	1	0	0	0	0	0	1	1	2	2	2	0	0
Diamond .	0	0	0	0	0	1	1	0	1	0	0	1	3	0	7	1
Difficult ..	1	0	1	3	1	2	0	1	3	2	3	1	0	0	2	6
Earth ...	0	0	0	2	0	0	0	0	0	0	0	0	0	1	1	2
Ease	0	1	1	0	0	0	2	0	0	0	0	0	0	0	0	0
Easy ...	21	14	23	17	19	12	9	11	14	9	9	13	7	14	9	16
Edge	0	0	0	0	0	0	0	0	1	0	0	0	1	0	2	0
Egg	0	1	1	0	1	1	2	3	4	11	5	12	9	10	28	18
Eggs	0	0	0	0	0	0	0	0	2	1	0	3	1	1	0	4
Fast	1	0	0	0	0	1	0	0	0	0	1	0	0	0	1	3
Firm....	1	0	0	0	0	0	0	1	0	0	0	0	0	0	0	3
Floor ...	0	2	3	3	0	3	1	0	2	4	3	4	2	5	2	6

Response Word	4th		5th		6th		7th		8th		10th		12th		College	
	M	F	M	F	M	F	M	F	M	F	M	F	M	F	M	F

HARD

Response Word	M	F	M	F	M	F	M	F	M	F	M	F	M	F	M	F
For	2	0	0	0	0	0	0	0	0	0	0	0	0	0	0	0
Glass	0	0	0	0	0	0	1	0	0	0	2	0	0	0	0	0
Ground . . .	1	1	2	2	0	2	1	1	0	1	0	1	2	4	3	3
Hammer . .	0	0	0	0	1	0	2	0	0	1	3	0	0	0	0	0
Hand	2	2	1	0	1	1	0	1	0	0	0	0	0	0	1	0
Harder . . .	0	0	0	0	0	1	2	0	0	0	0	0	0	0	1	0
Head	5	2	3	1	4	2	1	2	5	2	3	1	3	0	8	4
Heavy . . .	0	1	0	3	0	3	0	0	0	1	0	2	0	0	0	2
Hurt	1	2	2	0	0	3	2	0	0	0	0	2	1	1	4	0
Ice	0	0	0	1	1	0	0	0	0	0	0	0	0	1	0	3
Impossible .	0	0	0	0	0	0	0	2	0	1	0	0	0	0	0	0
Light	0	2	1	1	1	3	0	0	0	1	0	0	0	0	2	1
Long	0	0	2	0	1	0	0	0	0	0	1	0	0	0	0	2
Marble . . .	0	0	0	0	0	0	0	0	0	0	2	0	0	1	1	0
Mean	0	0	0	0	0	0	0	1	0	0	2	0	1	0	1	2
Metal . . .	0	0	0	0	0	2	3	0	0	0	1	1	1	1	4	0
Nail	0	0	0	0	1	0	3	0	0	0	0	1	0	3	4	4
Not easy . . .	2	1	1	0	1	1	0	0	0	1	0	1	0	0	0	0
Not soft . . .	3	0	2	0	2	0	1	3	0	2	0	0	0	1	0	0
Pencil	0	0	0	0	0	0	0	0	0	0	0	0	0	2	3	3
Rock	11	11	17	12	25	26	21	14	18	20	31	22	25	18	30	33
Rocks	0	0	0	0	0	0	0	1	1	3	2	0	0	0	1	0
Rough . . .	10	11	12	18	14	17	15	11	13	7	6	2	2	6	5	5
School	0	0	1	0	0	0	1	1	2	2	1	0	1	0	0	1
Sharp	0	0	0	0	0	0	0	0	0	0	2	0	0	0	1	0
Smooth . . .	4	2	3	5	6	2	1	1	1	1	3	2	2	2	5	6
Soft	90	98	76	95	84	91	118	116	119	120	110	118	130	136	290	295
Solid	6	2	4	3	7	6	5	5	2	4	1	4	2	0	1	2
Steel	2	1	2	3	4	0	4	1	5	1	3	1	4	0	3	5
Stiff	0	2	5	0	1	0	0	0	0	0	0	0	0	0	0	0
Stone	1	3	1	1	2	2	4	1	1	3	2	0	3	3	7	3
Strong	1	1	0	2	2	3	0	1	3	0	0	1	0	0	0	1
Surface . . .	0	1	0	2	1	0	2	0	0	0	0	0	0	1	0	1
Table	0	2	0	0	0	2	0	9	0	6	0	2	2	1	0	3
Terrible . . .	0	3	0	0	0	0	0	0	0	0	0	0	0	0	0	0
Test	0	1	0	0	3	1	1	0	1	0	0	3	0	1	0	1
Thick	0	0	0	0	2	0	0	0	0	0	1	0	0	0	0	0
Tough	3	3	7	6	2	3	2	8	7	1	1	3	1	3	3	2
Trouble . . .	1	1	0	0	0	2	1	0	0	0	0	0	0	0	0	0
Uncomfortable	1	1	0	0	0	1	0	1	0	1	0	1	1	1	4	2
Uneasy . . .	1	1	1	0	2	0	0	0	0	0	0	0	0	0	0	0
Wood	2	4	5	5	3	7	6	8	2	5	6	10	2	6	5	11
Work	25	26	33	22	18	16	7	10	10	14	10	4	5	3	11	8
Working . . .	2	2	1	4	3	1	1	1	0	0	0	0	1	0	1	0

76. HARDLY

Response Word	M	F	M	F	M	F	M	F	M	F	M	F	M	F	M	F
Able	0	0	0	0	1	0	0	0	0	0	2	1	2	1	1	2
All	1	0	0	0	0	2	1	2	1	3	1	1	0	0	2	2
Almost . . .	5	6	4	4	5	1	5	2	-2	5	3	2	5	1	9	4

Response Word	4th M	4th F	5th M	5th F	6th M	6th F	7th M	7th F	8th M	8th F	10th M	10th F	12th M	12th F	College M	College F
								HARDLY								
Alot	0	0	0	0	0	0	2	1	1	1	0	0	0	0	0	0
Always ..	1	0	2	2	0	0	2	3	3	3	0	4	4	5	6	7
Any	6	9	5	2	3	5	6	7	5	8	3	12	4	15	26	45
Anything ..	3	2	0	0	1	0	0	0	1	1	1	1	0	0	1	2
At	3	3	1	0	1	0	2	1	3	0	0	0	0	0	2	4
At all ...	1	0	1	0	0	1	1	1	0	1	2	0	1	0	1	5
Barely ..	8	10	4	11	11	16	16	19	5	11	10	13	15	13	28	15
Be	0	0	0	0	0	1	1	0	0	0	0	0	0	0	2	0
Because ..	0	0	1	2	1	0	0	1	0	0	0	4	2	0	3	3
Boy	0	1	1	0	2	1	1	2	1	0	0	0	0	0	0	0
But	0	0	0	0	1	0	0	1	0	0	2	1	1	1	2	2
Can	2	2	5	4	5	4	4	3	3	2	18	10	11	4	12	13
Can't....	0	3	1	6	2	4	4	5	1	3	6	5	4	0	6	9
Care	0	0	0	0	2	0	0	1	0	1	0	0	0	0	1	0
Cat	2	0	0	0	1	0	0	0	0	0	0	0	0	0	0	0
Chance ..	0	0	0	2	0	0	0	0	0	0	0	0	0	0	0	0
Cold	0	0	2	0	0	0	0	0	1	0	0	0	0	0	0	0
Could ...	1	3	3	2	3	1	0	1	3	2	0	0	1	2	3	1
Couldn't ..	1	2	1	1	0	2	0	0	0	0	3	0	1	0	0	0
Do	3	0	0	0	0	0	0	0	0	0	0	0	0	0	0	0
Did	3	0	0	0	1	1	0	0	0	1	0	0	0	0	0	0
Difficult ..	0	1	0	0	0	0	1	0	0	0	0	0	0	0	0	2
Done	2	0	2	2	2	0	0	0	2	0	1	0	0	0	1	0
Doubt ...	0	2	1	0	0	0	0	0	0	2	0	1	4	0	0	1
Easier ..	0	1	0	3	0	0	0	0	0	0	1	0	0	0	0	0
Easily ...	0	0	2	2	3	3	3	4	5	2	1	2	1	0	4	1
Easy	1	4	5	5	4	4	4	2	3	6	3	3	2	1	1	2
Enough...	4	1	2	3	3	4	4	4	4	12	9	8	7	9	10	7
Even	2	1	1	0	6	2	2	3	0	2	1	2	0	2	4	2
Ever	7	7	4	7	12	7	12	18	12	21	17	29	31	47	83	122
Every ...	0	0	0	2	0	0	0	0	0	1	0	0	0	0	0	1
Faint.....	0	0	0	0	0	0	2	0	0	0	0	0	0	0	0	0
Far	0	0	0	2	0	1	0	0	0	0	0	0	0	0	0	0
Fast	3	2	4	3	3	3	3	3	2	1	1	1	0	0	0	1
Fat.....	0	2	2	0	1	0	0	0	2	1	1	0	0	0	0	0
Few	0	0	2	0	1	2	1	5	0	1	0	2	1	5	7	5
Find	0	2	4	0	2	1	0	1	0	0	0	0	0	0	0	0
For	0	0	1	0	0	0	0	0	0	0	0	0	0	0	2	0
Funny ...	0	0	0	1	2	0	0	0	0	0	0	0	0	0	1	0
Gone	0	0	0	1	1	0	0	0	1	0	1	0	1	0	2	0
Good ...	2	5	7	6	3	1	3	2	1	0	0	0	0	0	0	0
Had	0	0	0	1	3	0	0	0	2	2	0	0	1	0	2	1
Hand ...	1	4	1	0	2	1	0	0	0	2	1	0	0	0	1	0
Handy ...	1	0	0	0	1	0	0	0	0	0	3	0	0	0	0	0
Happen ..	0	2	0	0	0	1	0	0	0	0	0	0	0	0	1	0
Happy ...	0	1	0	0	0	0	0	0	0	0	1	2	0	0	0	0
Hard	41	51	51	39	25	41	21	18	17	11	12	5	5	5	9	4
Hardy ...	0	0	0	1	1	1	0	0	0	0	1	0	2	0	0	0
Haven't ..	0	0	0	2	0	0	0	0	0	0	0	0	0	0	0	0

Response Word	4th M	4th F	5th M	5th F	6th M	6th F	7th M	7th F	8th M	8th F	10th M	10th F	12th M	12th F	College M	College F
								HARDLY								
Heavy . . .	2	0	1	4	0	1	3	0	0	0	0	0	0	0	0	0
Hot.	0	0	0	1	2	0	0	0	0	0	0	0	0	0	0	0
However .	0	0	0	0	1	0	0	0	0	0	0	0	0	2	0	0
I	0	0	2	0	0	0	1	0	0	0	0	0	0	0	0	0
Impossible	1	0	0	0	1	1	1	2	0	2	6	3	0	2	1	1
Is	0	0	0	0	0	0	1	0	0	1	1	1	2	0	0	2
It	1	3	0	0	1	0	1	0	0	0	0	0	0	0	1	1
Just	1	0	0	0	1	0	1	1	1	0	1	0	0	0	2	0
Knew . . .	3	0	0	1	1	1	0	0	0	1	0	0	1	0	0	2
Know . . .	0	1	0	0	2	2	1	0	1	1	1	0	1	1	0	0
Laurel . . .	0	0	0	0	0	0	0	0	1	0	2	0	0	0	0	0
Least . . .	0	0	0	0	0	0	1	0	0	0	2	0	0	1	0	1
Less	0	0	2	0	1	0	0	0	0	0	1	0	0	1	1	0
Light . . .	1	0	2	0	1	0	0	0	0	0	0	0	0	0	0	0
Likely . . .	0	0	0	0	1	1	1	0	1	1	3	1	0	3	1	2
Little . . .	4	7	0	3	2	3	5	7	3	8	2	3	3	5	4	6
Lots	0	0	0	0	0	1	2	0	0	0	0	0	0	1	0	0
Many . . .	0	1	1	0	1	1	0	2	1	0	1	0	0	0	0	0
Maybe . . .	2	2	1	0	1	2	2	3	2	2	2	3	1	5	5	2
Me	0	1	2	0	3	0	2	0	0	1	0	0	0	0	0	0
More . . .	0	0	0	0	0	0	0	0	2	0	0	0	0	0	1	0
Much. . . .	2	0	1	2	1	1	0	2	0	1	0	0	0	0	0	2
Nearly . . .	0	0	0	0	0	1	1	1	3	0	0	1	1	0	6	4
Never . . .	2	2	8	6	9	13	22	19	23	21	22	34	32	42	71	90
Nice	1	1	2	0	0	0	0	0	1	0	0	0	0	0	0	0
No	4	4	4	12	5	4	6	7	3	3	3	7	1	8	9	5
None	2	0	2	3	0	0	2	4	3	5	3	9	1	7	3	14
Not . . .	12	8	11	9	15	7	10	10	13	12	8	7	5	7	15	8
Not at all .	0	0	0	0	0	0	0	0	1	0	0	0	0	1	0	2
Nothing . .	2	4	2	1	1	0	0	0	1	1	2	1	0	0	2	2
Not likely .	0	0	0	0	0	0	1	3	0	0	2	0	1	0	1	1
Not quite. .	0	0	0	0	0	1	2	1	2	4	0	1	1	0	0	0
Now	1	0	0	1	2	1	2	0	0	1	0	1	1	0	4	1
Often . . .	1	1	1	0	0	3	0	2	0	0	1	0	0	2	1	0
One	1	0	0	1	0	2	0	1	1	0	0	0	0	0	0	0
Only	1	0	1	0	1	0	0	1	3	1	0	0	0	1	0	0
Or	3	0	0	0	0	0	0	0	1	0	0	0	0	0	0	1
Possible . .	0	1	0	0	0	0	0	1	1	0	0	1	1	1	3	1
Possibly . .	0	0	0	0	0	0	1	0	2	0	0	1	0	0	3	0
Quite . . .	1	0	1	0	0	1	2	0	1	0	2	1	2	1	2	2
Rarely . . .	0	0	0	0	0	0	0	1	1	2	0	1	2	2	3	1
Really . . .	1	0	0	0	0	2	0	0	0	2	0	1	0	2	0	1
Rock	0	2	0	2	0	0	1	0	0	0	1	0	1	0	0	0
Rough . . .	0	0	0	0	0	0	1	2	0	0	0	0	0	0	0	0
Scarcely . .	0	0	0	0	2	2	2	2	0	0	4	14	4	9	16	22
See.	0	4	1	1	0	0	1	0	1	0	1	0	1	0	1	0
Seems . . .	0	0	0	0	0	0	0	0	0	0	0	0	1	1	2	0
Seen	0	0	0	0	1	0	0	0	0	0	0	0	0	0	0	2
Seldom . .	0	1	2	2	1	2	1	4	1	0	4	0	2	4	4	9

Response Word	4th M	4th F	5th M	5th F	6th M	6th F	7th M	7th F	8th M	8th F	10th M	10th F	12th M	12th F	College M	College F
								HARDLY								
Sick	2	0	0	0	0	0	0	1	1	0	1	0	1	0	0	0
Slightly . .	0	0	1	0	0	1	0	1	1	0	2	0	0	0	0	1
Slow	1	1	1	0	0	0	1	1	2	2	0	0	0	0	0	0
Slowly . . .	1	1	0	0	0	2	0	0	0	0	0	0	0	2	0	0
Small . . .	0	2	0	0	1	3	1	0	0	0	0	0	2	0	4	0
So	1	0	0	3	1	0	1	0	0	1	0	0	0	0	0	1
Soft	8	4	6	6	9	10	8	9	5	8	0	4	3	2	4	2
Softly . . .	4	3	3	5	6	10	8	7	17	15	10	0	12	3	9	3
Some	1	0	0	2	0	0	1	0	0	1	0	0	1	0	0	3
Sometimes	1	1	0	0	1	0	0	0	1	0	0	2	1	1	0	2
Stone	0	0	0	0	0	0	0	0	2	0	0	0	0	0	0	0
Strong . . .	3	0	0	0	0	0	0	0	0	1	0	0	0	1	0	0
Surely . . .	0	0	0	0	0	0	0	1	1	1	0	3	0	0	2	0
Than	0	0	0	0	0	0	0	0	1	0	2	1	0	0	0	0
That	1	1	0	3	0	0	1	0	0	0	1	1	0	0	1	0
The	1	0	2	0	0	0	1	0	0	0	0	0	0	0	0	0
Then . . .	1	0	2	0	1	0	0	0	1	0	0	0	0	0	4	0
There . . .	3	0	1	0	0	1	0	1	0	0	0	0	0	1	0	1
Thought . .	0	0	0	1	0	0	0	0	0	0	0	0	0	0	2	0
Time	0	0	0	0	0	2	0	0	0	0	0	3	0	0	1	0
True	1	1	3	0	0	0	0	0	0	1	0	1	0	0	1	1
Unlikely . .	0	0	1	0	0	2	3	0	0	0	2	0	4	0	0	1
Very	1	1	1	0	1	1	6	1	0	1	1	1	1	0	0	0
Wait	5	11	2	4	1	6	0	2	1	2	3	1	5	1	2	2
Was	1	0	0	1	1	1	1	0	1	1	1	0	1	0	0	3
What	1	0	1	0	1	0	0	0	1	0	0	0	2	0	0	0
Why	0	1	2	0	0	1	0	0	0	0	0	1	0	1	0	0
Work . . .	5	2	1	3	0	0	0	1	0	0	0	0	1	0	0	0
Worth . . .	0	0	0	0	0	0	0	0	0	0	0	0	0	0	2	0
Yes	0	0	0	0	1	0	0	2	0	0	0	0	0	0	1	0
Yet	0	0	0	0	0	0	0	0	1	0	1	0	1	0	2	2
You	0	2	4	0	2	1	0	3	2	0	1	0	0	0	1	0
Yours . . .	0	0	0	0	0	0	0	0	1	2	0	0	1	0	0	0
							77.	HAVE								
A	14	7	10	6	9	0	5	1	2	1	0	0	1	1	4	2
Already . .	1	0	0	0	1	0	2	0	0	0	0	0	0	1	0	1
An	0	0	1	1	1	0	0	0	1	0	2	0	0	0	0	0
Any	2	0	0	1	0	2	0	1	1	0	0	2	0	2	3	1
Are	2	0	1	0	0	0	0	0	0	0	0	0	0	0	0	1
Been . . .	2	0	3	1	1	2	3	1	2	5	6	6	3	2	6	9
Belong . . .	0	0	0	1	2	0	2	1	1	0	0	0	0	1	0	4
Bought . . .	0	1	1	1	0	0	1	0	2	1	2	1	0	0	0	0
Buy	0	1	1	1	0	0	1	0	1	0	0	0	0	2	0	3
Can	0	2	0	1	1	1	0	0	1	0	0	0	0	1	0	0
Coke	0	2	0	0	0	1	0	0	0	0	0	0	0	0	0	0
Come . . .	1	2	0	1	0	3	0	1	2	1	0	0	1	1	1	4
Do	1	1	2	1	2	2	0	0	1	0	1	0	0	1	1	0
Done	1	3	6	1	1	3	0	2	1	6	5	3	4	2	6	7

141

Response Word	4th M	4th F	5th M	5th F	6th M	6th F	7th M	7th F	8th M	8th F	10th M	10th F	12th M	12th F	College M	College F
								HAVE								
Don't....	1	3	1	3	1	0	1	0	2	2	0	1	2	1	2	1
Eat	0	2	0	0	0	0	0	0	0	0	0	0	0	0	0	0
Enough ..	0	0	0	0	0	0	1	0	0	0	0	0	0	1	0	2
For	0	2	0	0	1	0	0	0	0	0	1	0	0	0	0	0
Fun	2	1	1	3	1	4	2	2	2	1	3	6	1	1	3	10
Gave	2	4	2	0	0	0	1	2	3	1	1	2	1	0	1	0
Get	1	2	1	4	1	4	5	2	4	4	5	1	1	6	5	15
Give	3	2	4	4	2	10	2	5	1	6	3	4	0	3	9	5
Given ...	0	0	0	1	0	0	1	2	1	0	0	0	0	0	0	0
Go	1	0	0	0	1	0	1	1	2	0	0	0	0	0	3	1
Gone	1	5	0	3	3	3	7	3	5	5	9	6	5	4	12	4
Good	1	0	0	1	2	0	0	0	0	0	0	0	0	0	0	0
Got.....	13	15	8	15	21	23	20	20	14	15	19	18	24	25	37	25
Gotten ...	0	1	0	0	0	0	0	0	1	1	1	0	1	1	5	1
Gun ...	1	2	2	2	4	1	2	0	0	1	4	1	6	3	6	5
Had	11	14	9	21	7	24	35	50	36	54	43	46	37	35	58	87
Half	0	0	0	0	0	0	0	2	0	0	1	0	0	0	1	0
Hand	2	0	0	0	0	0	0	0	0	0	0	0	0	0	0	0
Has	2	2	3	2	0	2	9	18	15	20	7	13	11	15	16	17
Have	0	1	0	0	3	0	0	0	0	0	0	0	0	0	0	1
Have not ..	1	1	1	0	1	1	1	0	1	1	0	0	2	1	3	3
Haven't ..	4	4	8	8	5	7	12	10	8	3	7	10	13	5	20	21
Having ...	1	1	2	0	0	1	0	1	1	0	1	0	1	0	0	0
He	2	1	0	1	1	0	1	0	0	0	0	0	0	0	0	0
Heard ...	0	0	1	0	1	0	1	0	0	2	0	0	0	0	0	0
Her	0	0	0	0	0	0	1	0	1	1	2	0	0	0	0	0
Here	0	3	1	1	1	1	2	3	1	3	1	0	0	1	1	1
Him ...	2	1	4	2	3	0	0	0	2	0	1	0	1	0	0	2
His	1	0	1	1	2	0	0	1	0	2	0	0	0	1	0	0
Hold	1	0	0	1	2	0	0	4	4	9	3	6	4	8	12	14
Hope	0	2	0	1	0	0	0	0	0	0	0	0	0	1	0	0
House ...	0	0	0	1	0	0	1	0	0	0	0	0	0	1	0	2
I	3	3	1	4	1	0	1	5	1	0	0	1	0	1	3	2
Is	0	1	1	1	1	2	0	1	0	3	0	1	1	1	1	0
It	11	11	11	10	12	7	7	1	4	4	4	2	2	3	15	4
Just	0	0	0	1	0	0	0	0	0	0	0	0	0	0	0	2
Keep	1	4	1	3	1	5	2	1	0	0	1	0	2	0	1	2
Loose ...	0	0	0	0	0	0	0	0	0	0	0	2	0	0	0	0
Lose	1	0	1	0	0	0	0	0	0	0	1	0	0	0	2	0
Lost	2	0	0	0	0	2	0	1	0	0	0	1	0	4	2	1
Lot.....	0	0	0	0	0	0	0	0	0	0	2	0	0	0	0	0
Love	0	0	0	0	0	0	0	2	0	0	0	1	1	0	1	0
Many....	1	3	0	0	0	0	1	0	2	1	1	4	0	2	2	3
Me	5	7	8	3	2	3	0	0	1	1	1	0	0	2	0	0
Mine	5	5	2	5	1	2	1	3	3	4	4	0	1	2	4	2
Miss	0	0	0	0	0	0	0	0	0	0	0	2	0	0	0	0
Money ...	1	0	0	0	1	2	4	2	2	2	2	5	6	3	3	6
Much....	0	0	0	1	0	0	0	0	0	0	2	1	1	1	2	1
My	1	0	1	2	2	1	0	0	0	0	0	0	1	0	2	0

Response Word	4th M	4th F	5th M	5th F	6th M	6th F	7th M	7th F	8th M	8th F	10th M	10th F	12th M	12th F	College M	College F
							HAVE									
No	4	3	2	0	4	0	3	0	0	1	1	2	0	0	1	1
None	1	0	0	0	0	0	0	0	0	0	1	2	4	2	4	2
Not.	15	13	11	15	16	7	19	17	13	10	14	13	23	16	86	67
Nothing . .	0	3	1	1	2	1	0	0	1	1	0	2	0	3	1	2
Now	1	3	2	0	2	2	1	1	0	2	1	0	0	0	1	2
Obtain . . .	0	0	0	0	0	0	0	0	0	0	0	0	0	2	2	5
One	0	2	2	4	4	1	0	1	3	0	1	1	0	2	2	4
Only	3	0	0	0	0	1	1	1	0	1	1	2	0	1	2	0
Ours	0	0	0	0	0	0	0	0	0	0	0	0	0	2	1	0
Own	5	4	6	6	4	8	5	11	6	5	8	15	8	8	20	29
Plenty . . .	0	0	0	0	0	0	0	0	0	0	2	0	0	0	1	0
Possess . .	0	1	0	0	0	1	1	1	0	0	0	2	1	1	14	9
Possession	0	0	0	0	1	0	2	0	0	0	2	0	1	0	1	3
Quick . . .	0	0	2	0	0	1	1	0	0	0	0	0	1	0	0	0
Quickly . .	1	0	1	0	0	0	0	0	0	0	0	0	0	0	2	0
Quit	0	0	2	0	0	0	0	0	0	0	0	0	0	0	0	0
Same. . . .	0	0	0	2	0	0	0	0	0	0	0	0	0	0	0	0
Save	3	0	2	2	1	0	1	0	0	0	0	0	0	1	0	0
Seen	0	0	0	0	1	0	0	3	1	0	1	0	2	1	1	0
Some. . . .	2	3	4	3	4	3	0	5	0	2	2	3	5	2	4	9
Something .	6	8	3	4	3	5	2	0	4	1	0	3	2	3	1	2
Take	3	2	4	6	4	2	3	6	2	5	6	2	2	2	4	5
Taken . . .	0	0	0	0	0	0	0	0	3	0	1	1	0	1	0	0
That	4	1	2	1	0	1	1	1	1	0	1	0	0	0	0	0
The	6	4	2	0	6	1	1	0	0	0	0	0	2	0	1	0
Them . . .	2	1	0	1	1	0	1	0	2	2	0	1	0	0	1	1
Then	0	1	3	1	2	0	1	0	1	0	1	0	0	0	0	0
There . . .	1	0	0	2	0	0	1	0	0	0	1	0	0	0	0	0
They	2	4	3	3	1	2	2	1	1	0	1	0	4	1	2	0
Things . . .	1	0	0	0	1	0	0	0	0	0	1	2	1	0	1	1
This	2	0	1	2	0	0	0	0	1	3	0	0	0	1	1	2
To	1	2	3	2	5	2	2	0	0	2	1	0	2	2	1	3
Told	0	0	0	0	0	0	0	0	0	0	0	0	0	0	2	0
Toys	0	1	2	0	0	1	0	1	0	0	0	0	0	0	0	0
Us	1	0	5	1	0	1	1	1	3	0	1	1	1	2	0	2
Verb	0	0	0	0	0	0	0	0	0	1	0	0	0	0	2	1
Want	2	1	0	0	1	2	0	3	0	1	1	5	4	1	2	5
Was	0	0	0	0	1	0	0	0	2	0	1	0	0	0	0	0
We	4	1	3	3	4	3	8	4	3	4	1	1	4	0	4	3
What	1	0	2	0	1	1	2	1	4	1	3	1	3	2	5	2
When. . . .	0	2	0	0	1	0	1	0	1	0	0	0	0	0	0	0
Will	2	0	1	3	1	0	1	0	0	0	0	0	1	0	4	1
Yes	1	0	1	0	0	2	0	0	0	0	1	0	0	0	0	0
You	27	26	33	38	38	40	21	19	35	25	14	22	28	26	33	30
Your	0	1	0	0	0	0	2	0	1	0	0	0	0	0	1	0
Yours . . .	0	1	0	3	0	0	0	1	1	0	0	0	0	1	0	0

Response Word	4th M	4th F	5th M	5th F	6th M	6th F	7th M	7th F	8th M	8th F	10th M	10th F	12th M	12th F	College M	College F

78. HE

Response Word	4th M	4th F	5th M	5th F	6th M	6th F	7th M	7th F	8th M	8th F	10th M	10th F	12th M	12th F	College M	College F
Bee	0	0	0	0	0	0	1	0	0	0	0	0	2	0	0	0
Boy	25	48	33	50	26	40	12	44	10	30	18	27	7	28	12	27
Boys	0	0	0	0	0	0	0	0	0	3	0	1	0	0	0	0
Cute	0	0	0	0	0	0	0	1	0	0	0	2	0	1	0	0
Darrone	0	0	0	0	0	2	0	0	0	0	0	0	0	0	0	0
Dave	0	0	0	0	0	0	0	1	0	0	0	2	0	0	0	0
Did	2	1	2	3	3	0	2	0	3	0	0	1	2	0	2	3
Girl	2	0	0	1	2	1	1	0	0	0	1	0	0	0	2	0
God	0	0	0	0	0	0	1	0	0	0	3	0	1	2	1	4
Had	2	0	0	0	0	0	2	0	1	0	0	0	0	0	0	0
Has	3	0	1	0	1	0	0	0	0	0	2	0	0	2	0	0
Her	29	43	35	33	33	35	39	31	29	25	27	15	28	18	27	21
Here	0	0	1	0	1	0	2	0	1	0	0	0	0	0	0	0
Him	25	13	31	20	33	31	33	25	24	15	33	18	32	23	41	24
Himself	2	0	1	0	0	0	0	1	0	0	0	0	0	0	0	0
His	5	8	5	5	6	3	4	2	3	2	1	1	6	1	6	5
I	0	1	2	1	3	0	3	0	0	2	1	0	1	0	0	0
Is	15	6	11	7	18	10	6	2	19	9	9	7	19	14	27	12
It	1	1	2	0	2	0	5	1	2	1	0	0	0	0	6	6
Jerry	0	0	0	0	0	0	0	0	0	0	0	0	0	0	0	2
Jim	0	0	0	0	0	0	0	0	0	0	2	1	0	0	0	3
Male	1	0	1	1	5	2	5	1	1	0	1	1	0	2	2	2
Man	12	11	9	8	13	15	9	5	7	4	7	7	8	5	18	17
Me	16	6	19	8	13	6	13	8	11	12	7	11	8	6	18	14
Person	6	3	9	5	4	7	1	2	1	1	3	1	0	0	1	0
Pronoun	0	0	0	0	0	1	0	0	0	1	0	0	0	0	2	0
Said	2	0	1	2	2	3	0	1	0	2	0	0	0	1	0	1
Saw	0	0	1	0	0	1	0	0	0	0	0	0	0	0	2	0
She	61	90	49	88	55	77	86	115	105	119	111	128	11	123	294	318
Someone	0	0	1	0	0	2	1	0	0	0	0	0	0	0	0	0
Steve	0	0	0	0	0	0	0	0	0	2	0	0	0	0	0	0
Tall	0	0	0	0	0	3	0	0	0	0	0	0	0	1	0	0
The	0	0	2	0	2	0	0	0	0	0	0	0	0	0	2	0
They	2	1	1	0	1	1	1	0	7	1	2	2	0	2	9	5
Was	4	3	3	0	6	1	7	1	6	1	6	1	1	1	3	3
We	1	1	1	0	1	0	1	0	0	0	1	0	0	1	2	0
Went	4	2	1	1	2	1	0	0	0	0	0	1	2	1	1	0
Will	2	2	0	0	0	0	1	0	3	1	1	1	1	1	1	1
You	6	0	4	2	4	0	1	0	4	2	1	1	2	1	3	4

79. HEAD

Response Word	4th M	4th F	5th M	5th F	6th M	6th F	7th M	7th F	8th M	8th F	10th M	10th F	12th M	12th F	College M	College F
Ache	0	0	0	0	1	0	5	2	7	7	2	6	8	6	5	11
Arm	4	10	3	3	5	6	5	9	1	5	5	3	1	3	4	9
Arms	1	4	1	1	2	1	1	1	0	0	0	0	0	1	1	0
Back	0	1	2	0	1	2	0	0	1	1	1	0	1	1	0	0
Bald	0	0	0	0	0	0	1	0	2	0	0	0	0	0	1	0
Ball	2	0	1	0	0	0	1	0	0	1	0	0	0	0	0	0
Bed	1	2	2	3	2	0	1	1	0	1	1	0	0	0	0	0
Big	0	0	3	1	0	0	1	2	1	4	0	5	1	10	3	2

Response Word	4th M	4th F	5th M	5th F	6th M	6th F	7th M	7th F	8th M	8th F	10th M	10th F	12th M	12th F	College M	College F
							HEAD									
Body	29	34	35	38	35	40	31	27	16	14	17	25	7	12	19	27
Boy	1	0	1	0	1	0	1	0	1	2	0	0	0	0	0	0
Brain . . .	32	16	23	18	29	20	40	28	25	24	18	9	15	13	20	17
Brains . . .	4	4	4	9	3	5	5	5	9	8	6	6	1	4	6	4
Cabbage . .	2	0	0	0	3	1	2	0	1	1	3	0	2	1	2	2
Cap	0	0	0	0	1	0	1	0	0	0	0	0	1	0	2	0
Cattle . . .	0	0	1	0	0	2	0	0	0	0	0	0	0	0	0	0
Center. . . .	0	0	0	0	0	0	0	0	0	0	1	0	0	0	2	0
Cheese . .	0	0	0	0	0	0	0	0	0	0	0	0	1	1	2	2
Cold	0	0	0	0	0	0	0	0	1	0	0	0	0	1	2	0
Dog	0	0	0	0	0	0	0	0	0	0	0	0	2	0	0	0
Ear	8	2	0	0	4	3	0	1	1	3	0	0	1	0	3	0
Ears	0	0	2	0	0	0	4	1	2	2	1	0	0	1	1	1
Empty . . .	0	0	0	0	0	0	0	0	0	2	1	0	0	0	1	0
Eye	9	4	5	2	2	1	5	2	5	1	1	3	2	3	6	5
Eyes	17	22	12	23	10	21	11	17	8	20	14	16	11	11	14	26
Face	5	8	7	7	2	6	7	12	5	12	7	10	9	9	19	24
Fat.	1	0	0	0	0	0	1	0	3	0	0	0	0	0	0	0
Feet	14	8	3	6	3	0	7	3	7	6	6	5	4	5	7	5
First . . .	0	0	0	0	2	0	0	0	1	0	0	0	0	0	0	1
Foot	7	7	7	10	0	9	10	7	22	9	13	12	12	14	26	34
Forehead .	0	0	0	0	0	0	0	0	0	0	0	0	0	0	2	0
Front . . .	0	0	0	0	0	0	0	0	0	0	2	0	0	0	2	0
Glove . . .	0	0	0	0	0	0	0	0	0	0	0	0	0	0	2	0
Hair	5	19	19	28	19	37	16	35	25	37	39	50	38	32	87	107
Hand	10	16	8	13	6	9	2	3	4	4	4	3	5	5	11	14
Hands . . .	0	0	0	0	0	1	0	0	1	0	1	1	0	2	1	1
Hard	3	3	4	2	1	4	4	3	6	0	3	6	4	7	7	6
Hat.	0	1	0	1	3	2	0	2	0	2	3	3	5	5	17	21
Hear	2	1	0	1	0	0	0	0	0	0	0	0	0	0	0	0
Heard . . .	0	0	0	1	2	0	0	0	0	0	0	0	0	0	0	0
Heart . . .	0	0	0	0	1	0	0	3	0	0	1	1	1	1	6	11
High	0	1	0	0	0	0	0	1	1	0	0	1	2	3	1	3
Hollow . . .	0	0	0	0	0	2	0	0	0	0	0	0	0	0	0	0
Human . . .	0	0	0	0	0	2	0	0	0	0	2	0	1	0	1	0
Hunter . . .	0	0	0	0	2	1	2	0	1	0	0	0	1	2	2	1
Intelligence	0	0	0	0	0	0	0	0	0	0	0	0	0	0	1	3
Large . . .	0	0	0	0	1	0	0	1	0	0	1	0	1	0	2	0
Leader . .	1	0	1	0	0	0	0	1	0	0	0	0	2	2	0	1
Leg	4	4	1	4	4	0	4	0	5	0	0	1	0	0	0	0
Lettuce . .	0	1	1	0	0	1	1	1	0	1	2	1	5	1	3	4
Looks . . .	0	0	0	0	0	0	0	1	1	0	1	0	0	0	2	0
Man	1	0	3	1	2	0	5	0	3	1	6	2	7	0	12	3
Me	0	0	0	2	1	0	0	1	0	0	0	1	1	1	1	0
Mind	2	3	6	3	10	3	2	1	4	2	1	0	3	3	6	7
Mine	1	0	1	3	2	0	0	1	1	0	0	0	0	1	1	0
Mouth . . .	3	2	1	0	2	1	2	0	2	2	2	0	2	0	1	0
Neck	9	11	11	5	0	10	7	15	15	6	20	20	11	18	35	21
Nose	3	2	1	2	1	0	2	3	4	1	4	2	4	3	4	1

Response Word	4th M	4th F	5th M	5th F	6th M	6th F	7th M	7th F	8th M	8th F	10th M	10th F	12th M	12th F	College M	College F

HEAD

Response Word	4th M	4th F	5th M	5th F	6th M	6th F	7th M	7th F	8th M	8th F	10th M	10th F	12th M	12th F	College M	College F
Oval	1	0	0	0	0	0	0	0	0	2	0	1	0	0	0	0
People	1	2	6	0	1	1	2	0	1	1	1	2	0	3	0	1
Person	3	5	6	1	7	2	1	3	3	5	4	4	3	4	5	4
Pin	0	0	0	0	0	0	0	0	0	0	0	1	0	0	2	0
Pretty	0	0	0	0	0	1	0	1	1	0	0	0	0	4	0	1
Round	6	5	8	6	3	4	6	12	4	8	6	3	2	4	5	10
Scarf	0	0	0	0	0	0	0	0	0	0	0	0	0	2	0	3
See	1	3	1	0	0	0	0	0	0	1	0	0	0	0	0	0
Shoulder	0	1	1	1	3	0	2	7	5	4	2	3	2	1	15	5
Shoulders	1	2	0	2	4	4	2	4	6	6	5	5	9	11	14	27
Skull	1	1	0	0	2	1	5	1	0	0	0	1	1	0	4	1
Small	0	0	1	0	1	1	0	1	0	2	1	1	1	1	0	1
Smart	0	0	3	1	0	1	3	0	1	2	1	1	3	2	0	1
Soft	0	0	1	1	3	1	0	0	1	0	2	0	1	0	1	1
Square	0	0	0	0	1	0	0	1	3	0	0	0	0	0	0	0
Stomach	0	0	0	1	0	0	1	0	0	1	0	0	1	2	1	1
Stove	0	0	0	0	1	0	0	0	0	1	0	0	0	0	2	1
Strong	1	0	0	0	0	0	0	0	0	1	0	0	2	0	2	2
Tail	0	0	1	1	1	1	0	0	1	0	1	2	0	1	8	4
Thing	2	0	5	1	2	0	0	1	0	0	0	0	0	0	0	0
Think	10	24	10	22	16	15	2	11	5	11	6	6	8	5	13	12
Thinking	0	0	0	0	0	1	1	0	1	0	0	3	0	1	0	1
Thought	0	1	0	0	0	0	0	1	0	1	1	0	0	0	1	3
Thoughts	0	0	0	0	0	0	0	0	0	0	0	0	0	2	0	0
Toe	2	1	2	1	2	3	5	1	8	4	2	2	8	2	8	11
Toes	1	2	0	1	2	0	1	0	0	0	0	0	1	0	2	2
Toilet	0	0	0	0	0	0	0	0	0	0	1	0	2	0	2	0
Top	1	1	0	0	1	4	1	2	1	0	4	8	6	3	10	10
Waiter	0	0	0	0	0	0	0	0	0	0	0	0	0	0	2	0
Water	0	0	2	0	0	0	0	0	0	0	0	0	0	0	0	0
Woman	0	0	0	0	0	0	0	0	0	0	0	0	0	0	2	0

80. HEALTH

Response Word	4th M	4th F	5th M	5th F	6th M	6th F	7th M	7th F	8th M	8th F	10th M	10th F	12th M	12th F	College M	College F
Apple	0	0	0	0	0	1	0	1	1	1	0	1	0	4	1	3
Bad	3	4	5	3	2	2	1	4	2	2	0	2	1	0	1	1
Body	10	6	9	13	15	12	8	8	9	1	6	6	5	8	5	6
Book	1	1	0	2	1	1	0	1	0	0	2	3	0	0	2	0
Boy	1	2	3	1	2	0	1	1	1	0	1	1	2	0	0	0
Care	0	0	0	2	1	0	0	1	0	0	0	1	0	0	0	0
Center	0	0	0	0	1	0	0	0	0	0	0	0	0	1	4	1
Class	0	0	0	0	0	0	0	0	0	2	10	7	0	1	0	2
Clean	7	9	4	6	4	10	5	3	3	1	0	1	0	1	1	2
Cold	0	0	0	1	3	1	2	1	1	0	2	2	0	1	3	3
Comfort	0	0	0	0	0	0	1	0	0	0	0	0	2	0	0	1
Condition	0	1	1	2	1	4	3	4	4	1	1	3	1	1	1	1
Dead	0	3	2	0	1	0	1	0	0	1	0	0	0	0	1	0
Death	0	0	0	0	0	0	0	0	1	1	0	1	0	0	0	2
Dentist	1	3	1	1	1	0	1	0	0	0	0	0	0	1	0	0
Disease	0	0	0	0	1	0	0	0	2	0	1	0	1	1	1	3

Response Word	4th M	4th F	5th M	5th F	6th M	6th F	7th M	7th F	8th M	8th F	10th M	10th F	12th M	12th F	College M	College F
						HEALTH										
Doctor	19	14	10	15	13	13	9	17	6	18	9	12	16	7	23	19
Dr.	0	1	1	0	0	1	1	0	0	0	0	2	0	0	0	0
Eat	4	4	5	1	1	2	0	0	0	0	0	1	2	0	0	0
Education	0	0	0	0	2	1	0	0	0	0	0	0	1	1	1	0
Energy	0	1	0	1	0	2	0	2	1	0	0	0	0	1	0	1
Exercise	0	0	1	2	0	0	2	1	2	1	1	3	2	0	1	0
Feel	1	0	4	1	0	1	1	0	1	1	0	0	1	0	1	3
Feeling	0	0	0	0	1	1	1	3	1	0	0	1	1	0	3	1
Fine	0	0	0	0	2	1	3	0	0	1	0	0	0	0	3	0
First aid	0	0	0	0	0	0	1	0	0	0	0	0	4	2	1	0
Fit	0	0	0	0	0	0	1	1	0	0	2	0	0	1	2	1
Fitness	1	0	2	0	0	1	1	0	0	0	3	0	1	1	2	0
Food	6	7	5	7	4	5	7	2	4	6	9	1	1	2	9	5
Fresh air	0	0	0	0	0	0	0	0	0	0	0	0	0	2	0	0
Fruit	2	1	0	0	0	0	1	0	1	1	0	1	0	0	0	0
Fun	1	0	0	0	0	0	1	1	1	0	3	2	4	0	0	2
Girl	0	1	0	4	0	0	0	0	2	1	0	0	1	0	0	0
Good	45	41	49	26	36	35	25	14	10	21	18	26	23	40	50	38
Good condition	0	0	0	0	0	1	2	0	0	0	1	1	0	0	0	0
Great	0	0	0	0	0	0	0	0	0	0	0	0	0	0	0	2
Gym	0	0	0	1	0	0	2	0	4	2	1	1	0	0	0	0
Habits	0	0	0	0	0	1	1	1	0	1	0	2	0	0	0	0
Happiness	0	0	0	0	1	1	0	2	1	4	3	6	5	5	19	26
Happy	5	2	3	2	2	4	3	7	4	7	3	12	8	7	13	33
Heal	3	0	0	0	0	1	0	0	1	0	0	0	0	0	0	0
Healthy	4	5	4	8	5	8	5	3	2	1	0	5	4	1	1	0
Heart	0	0	0	3	1	0	0	0	1	0	2	0	0	0	0	0
Help	2	0	0	0	0	0	0	0	0	0	0	0	0	1	0	0
Hope	0	0	0	0	0	0	0	0	0	0	0	0	0	0	0	2
Hospital	0	0	1	0	1	0	0	0	0	1	2	3	1	2	6	11
Ill	5	5	5	8	6	8	5	7	6	11	6	6	6	8	9	9
Illness	0	0	1	0	1	2	0	3	2	4	3	5	4	2	17	21
Important	0	1	1	0	0	0	2	0	0	0	1	0	0	1	0	2
Joy	0	0	0	0	0	0	0	0	0	0	0	0	1	0	2	1
Life	1	0	0	0	0	1	1	3	2	0	0	0	1	5	1	2
Live	0	0	2	2	1	1	0	0	0	0	0	0	0	0	1	0
Living	0	1	0	0	1	0	1	0	0	0	2	2	1	0	0	0
Me	3	0	2	0	1	0	1	1	2	0	2	1	1	1	2	0
Medicine	1	1	3	1	1	0	0	0	0	0	0	0	1	1	3	4
Mental	0	0	0	0	0	1	2	0	0	0	3	1	0	0	0	0
Milk	1	3	4	1	1	1	1	1	0	0	0	1	0	0	0	0
Nice	1	0	0	0	0	2	0	0	0	0	1	0	0	1	0	0
Nurse	2	2	0	2	1	2	1	2	1	4	0	3	1	2	2	5
OK	3	0	0	1	0	0	0	0	0	0	0	0	0	0	2	0
Pain	0	0	0	0	0	0	0	0	0	0	0	0	0	0	0	2
People	1	2	0	0	1	0	0	3	1	1	2	1	2	1	0	1
Person	1	0	1	0	1	1	2	2	0	1	2	2	1	0	1	2
Physical	0	0	0	0	0	1	4	1	1	1	0	0	1	2	0	0
Pills	1	0	0	0	2	0	0	1	0	2	0	0	1	0	0	0

Response Word	4th		5th		6th		7th		8th		10th		12th		College	
	M	F	M	F	M	F	M	F	M	F	M	F	M	F	M	F

HEALTH

Response Word	M	F	M	F	M	F	M	F	M	F	M	F	M	F	M	F
Play	2	0	1	0	0	0	2	0	0	0	1	0	0	0	1	0
Poor	0	0	2	0	0	1	0	0	1	3	0	0	1	0	2	0
Public . . .	0	0	0	0	0	0	0	0	0	0	0	0	0	0	0	3
Rosy	0	0	0	0	0	0	0	0	0	0	0	0	0	1	3	0
Run	0	0	0	1	1	0	0	0	0	2	0	0	0	0	0	0
Safety . . .	1	5	10	7	1	2	0	1	0	1	0	1	0	1	0	1
Sanitary . .	0	0	0	0	0	0	0	0	0	0	3	0	0	0	0	0
School . . .	0	5	0	0	0	2	2	1	1	0	2	4	3	2	0	1
Science . .	0	0	0	0	1	0	3	1	3	1	0	0	0	0	0	1
Service . .	0	0	0	0	0	0	0	0	0	0	0	0	0	0	5	4
Shape . . .	0	0	0	1	2	1	0	0	1	1	0	0	1	0	0	0
Sick	24	26	20	35	25	34	47	38	61	55	37	34	41	38	64	60
Sickness . .	1	3	3	2	6	11	21	24	32	35	29	34	22	38	117	113
Sleep	0	0	0	0	3	0	0	1	1	2	0	1	1	1	1	3
Sports . . .	0	1	0	0	0	0	0	0	0	0	1	0	1	2	3	0
Strength . .	1	3	3	1	0	0	2	1	2	2	2	0	2	0	4	1
Strong . . .	12	19	15	15	8	8	12	3	5	4	7	3	9	1	7	3
Subject . .	0	0	0	0	0	0	0	1	1	0	3	1	1	0	0	0
Teacher . .	0	0	0	0	1	0	0	0	0	0	3	1	0	0	0	0
Teeth . . .	19	22	17	14	14	13	0	2	0	3	1	3	0	1	0	0
Trim . . .	0	0	0	0	2	0	0	0	0	0	0	0	0	0	0	0
Unhealthy .	1	0	0	1	2	1	2	4	3	1	1	3	1	0	1	0
Vigor . . .	0	0	0	0	0	0	0	1	0	0	0	0	1	0	3	1
Vitality . .	0	0	0	0	0	0	0	0	0	0	1	0	1	0	2	1
Vitamins .	0	1	1	0	0	0	1	0	0	0	0	1	0	0	0	2
Weak	3	1	2	2	1	2	1	1	10	1	0	0	0	1	0	0
Wealth . . .	1	1	0	1	2	1	2	5	4	3	3	3	8	10	17	14
Welfare . .	0	0	1	0	2	0	0	0	2	0	3	0	0	2	4	1
Well	6	16	8	17	6	17	7	23	10	12	7	14	13	15	14	30
Well being .	0	0	0	0	0	0	0	1	1	0	0	1	0	0	1	3
Wonderful .	0	0	0	0	0	1	1	0	0	0	0	0	0	1	0	4
Work . . .	0	0	0	1	0	0	0	1	0	0	3	0	2	0	0	0

81. HEAVY

Response Word	M	F	M	F	M	F	M	F	M	F	M	F	M	F	M	F
Back	0	0	0	0	2	0	1	0	0	0	0	1	0	0	0	0
Barbells . .	0	0	0	0	0	0	2	0	1	0	0	0	0	0	0	0
Big	12	3	6	5	9	9	6	6	4	4	9	10	2	4	5	9
Blanket . .	0	1	0	1	0	0	0	0	0	1	0	0	0	1	0	2
Book	0	0	0	1	0	1	0	0	0	0	0	1	0	1	2	4
Books . . .	0	0	0	0	0	1	0	0	0	3	0	7	0	0	2	6
Boulder . .	0	0	0	0	0	0	0	0	0	2	0	0	0	0	0	2
Box	0	1	0	2	1	2	0	2	1	1	2	2	1	4	2	8
Brick . . .	0	0	0	0	0	1	1	3	2	0	1	1	1	1	2	0
Burden . .	0	0	0	1	1	4	3	0	1	0	1	1	1	5	2	5
Burdensome	0	0	0	0	0	0	0	0	1	0	0	1	1	2	0	0
Car	1	3	1	1	2	2	2	0	2	3	3	2	3	2	2	1
Carry . . .	3	7	0	8	0	2	0	0	0	2	0	1	0	1	0	1
Chair . . .	0	1	0	0	0	1	0	0	0	4	1	0	1	1	0	0
Coat	0	1	0	1	0	3	0	1	0	1	5	0	1	2	0	1

Response Word	4th		5th		6th		7th		8th		10th		12th		College	
	M	F	M	F	M	F	M	F	M	F	M	F	M	F	M	F

HEAVY

Response Word	M	F	M	F	M	F	M	F	M	F	M	F	M	F	M	F
Dark	0	0	0	1	0	1	0	1	2	1	0	2	1	1	2	1
Drop	0	0	0	0	0	0	0	1	0	0	0	1	2	0	1	0
Dull	0	0	0	0	0	0	0	0	0	0	0	0	0	0	0	3
Elephant . .	0	2	2	0	0	1	0	3	0	3	1	0	0	1	0	0
Eyes	1	0	0	1	0	0	1	0	0	1	0	2	0	0	0	1
Fall	2	0	1	0	0	0	0	0	0	0	0	0	0	0	0	0
Fat	1	3	4	2	1	2	3	3	3	7	4	4	4	6	22	29
God	0	1	0	0	0	2	0	0	0	1	0	0	0	0	0	0
Going . . .	2	0	0	0	0	0	0	0	0	0	0	0	0	0	0	0
Good	0	1	3	0	1	0	0	1	0	0	0	0	0	0	0	0
Hammer . .	0	0	2	1	0	0	0	0	1	2	1	0	0	0	0	2
Hand	1	0	0	0	0	0	0	0	0	0	0	0	0	0	2	2
Hard	31	42	40	35	40	33	30	33	20	16	17	29	17	24	25	35
Head	0	0	1	0	2	1	0	1	0	2	1	0	2	0	0	1
Heat	2	0	0	0	0	0	0	0	0	0	0	1	0	0	0	0
Hold	1	0	0	1	1	1	0	0	0	0	0	1	0	1	0	2
House . . .	0	0	0	0	1	2	0	2	0	0	0	0	0	0	0	0
Huge	1	1	1	1	1	3	0	0	0	0	0	0	1	0	0	0
Iron	2	0	0	3	0	1	1	2	3	5	3	2	2	1	4	4
Laden . . .	0	0	0	0	0	0	0	0	0	0	0	2	1	0	0	2
Large . . .	4	7	6	1	3	5	0	3	3	3	3	3	0	2	7	3
Lead	1	3	6	4	1	2	10	5	2	4	4	6	6	4	10	10
Left	1	0	0	0	0	0	0	0	2	0	0	0	0	0	0	0
Lift	6	6	8	6	7	4	3	2	1	2	7	3	6	5	10	6
Light	83	77	70	85	79	72	86	88	109	107	86	97	109	111	213	209
Load	6	18	14	20	16	13	12	15	10	7	10	10	9	17	25	29
Log	0	0	1	0	3	0	0	1	1	1	0	0	0	0	0	0
Logs	0	0	0	0	0	0	0	0	0	2	0	0	0	0	0	0
Loud	4	3	4	1	2	2	1	0	1	0	1	1	0	1	1	0
Man	0	2	0	0	0	0	0	1	0	1	0	0	2	2	2	3
Me	0	1	0	0	0	1	0	0	1	2	0	0	0	1	0	0
Nice	0	0	1	1	0	2	0	0	0	0	0	0	0	0	0	0
Not light .	1	0	3	0	0	0	0	1	0	0	1	1	0	0	0	0
Pull	0	0	0	0	0	0	0	0	0	2	0	0	0	0	0	0
Purse . . .	0	0	0	0	0	0	0	0	0	0	0	2	0	0	0	0
Rain	0	0	0	0	2	0	1	0	0	0	0	0	0	0	0	0
Rock	1	1	0	3	2	3	3	1	1	5	2	4	4	1	7	4
Rocks . . .	2	0	0	0	0	0	0	0	1	1	1	1	0	0	2	1
Sleep . . .	2	0	0	0	1	0	0	1	1	0	1	0	1	0	2	4
Smoke . . .	0	0	0	0	0	0	3	0	1	0	1	1	1	2	1	2
Smoker . .	0	0	0	0	0	0	0	0	0	0	2	0	1	0	0	0
Soft	1	5	2	10	1	5	7	9	9	7	4	2	6	3	10	11
Solid	0	0	0	0	1	1	0	0	0	0	0	0	0	0	0	3
Steal	0	0	2	1	0	0	0	0	0	0	0	0	0	0	1	0
Steel	1	0	2	0	2	2	2	1	2	0	1	0	5	1	5	0
Stone . . .	1	2	1	0	0	0	1	0	1	1	1	1	0	1	1	2
Strain . . .	0	0	0	0	0	0	0	0	3	0	5	0	0	0	1	1
Strong . . .	6	2	4	5	3	3	2	1	1	1	1	1	2	3	6	2
Suitcase . .	1	0	0	0	0	0	0	0	0	0	0	0	1	0	0	2

Response Word	4th		5th		6th		7th		8th		10th		12th		College	
	M	F	M	F	M	F	M	F	M	F	M	F	M	F	M	F

HEAVY

Response Word	4th M	4th F	5th M	5th F	6th M	6th F	7th M	7th F	8th M	8th F	10th M	10th F	12th M	12th F	College M	College F
Table	1	0	0	0	0	1	0	5	0	1	0	1	1	0	0	0
Thick	0	1	0	0	0	1	0	0	2	1	0	1	0	0	1	1
Tired	1	1	0	1	2	1	0	0	1	2	2	5	1	1	3	4
Ton	3	2	3	5	7	6	8	5	2	5	2	2	0	1	4	1
Top	0	0	0	0	0	0	0	0	0	0	0	0	0	0	2	0
Tough	1	0	0	1	0	0	1	1	2	1	0	0	2	0	1	0
Trouble . . .	0	0	0	0	0	0	0	0	0	0	0	0	0	0	0	2
Truck	0	2	1	1	1	0	0	0	0	0	0	2	1	0	1	2
Uncomfortable	0	0	0	0	0	2	0	0	0	0	0	0	0	0	0	1
Water	2	0	0	0	0	0	0	0	0	0	0	1	0	0	1	0
Weak	1	0	0	0	0	0	2	2	3	0	0	0	1	0	1	0
Weigh	1	0	1	0	0	1	1	0	2	0	0	1	0	0	1	0
Weight	14	10	20	5	17	13	25	20	19	13	22	8	13	5	39	23
Weights . . .	0	0	0	0	0	1	2	0	5	2	2	1	7	2	5	2
Weighty . . .	0	0	0	0	0	0	0	0	0	0	0	0	0	0	2	0
Wheat	0	0	2	0	0	0	0	0	0	1	0	0	0	0	0	0
Work.	0	2	2	0	4	0	1	0	5	0	9	2	11	1	13	6

82. HERE

Response Word	4th M	4th F	5th M	5th F	6th M	6th F	7th M	7th F	8th M	8th F	10th M	10th F	12th M	12th F	College M	College F
A	0	0	0	0	3	0	0	0	0	0	0	0	0	0	0	0
Am	3	0	1	1	1	3	0	0	2	0	1	1	1	1	3	0
Are	17	16	13	11	15	8	12	8	10	8	18	8	15	14	22	23
Beer	2	0	1	0	0	1	0	0	1	0	0	0	0	0	0	0
By	5	1	2	1	0	1	1	2	2	1	0	0	0	0	0	0
Cat	0	0	0	2	0	1	0	0	0	0	0	0	0	0	0	0
Class	0	0	0	0	0	0	0	0	0	0	0	0	0	0	2	0
Close	0	0	0	1	0	2	1	0	0	0	1	0	0	0	0	1
Come	4	5	3	6	5	8	3	2	4	3	4	3	2	0	2	2
Comes	2	3	2	4	6	1	1	2	1	2	2	1	1	1	3	1
Ear	1	0	0	1	1	1	3	1	0	1	2	0	0	0	0	1
Ears	0	2	0	0	0	0	0	0	0	0	1	0	1	0	0	0
Fear	0	0	0	0	0	0	0	2	0	0	0	0	0	0	0	0
For	1	0	0	2	1	0	0	0	1	0	0	0	0	0	0	1
Fun	2	0	0	0	0	0	0	0	0	0	0	0	0	0	0	0
Give	1	1	1	3	1	1	1	0	1	0	0	0	0	1	0	0
Go	2	1	3	0	3	1	0	0	2	0	0	0	0	1	2	0
Goes	3	3	2	4	0	2	3	0	1	2	2	4	4	3	5	1
Have	1	1	0	2	0	0	1	0	0	0	0	0	0	0	0	0
He	3	1	2	0	1	2	0	0	1	1	0	0	0	0	0	0
Hear	4	6	6	11	8	11	5	4	3	1	4	2	3	3	4	0
Heard	1	0	0	1	1	2	1	1	0	0	0	0	0	0	0	0
Her	5	1	2	1	0	0	3	2	2	2	0	0	1	1	2	0
Him	1	0	1	0	0	0	2	0	0	0	0	0	0	0	0	0
His	0	0	3	0	0	2	1	1	0	0	1	0	0	0	0	0
Home	0	1	0	1	0	3	0	1	1	0	0	2	0	3	2	1
House	1	1	0	0	4	1	0	2	0	0	2	0	0	1	0	2
How	0	1	2	0	1	0	0	1	1	0	0	0	0	1	0	0
I	3	0	3	3	6	3	4	2	1	1	0	2	1	3	2	1
Is	27	18	27	13	30	15	19	18	13	12	16	11	28	17	33	25

Response Word	4th M	4th F	5th M	5th F	6th M	6th F	7th M	7th F	8th M	8th F	10th M	10th F	12th M	12th F	College M	College F
							HERE									
It	1	2	3	4	4	3	2	0	2	1	0	0	2	1	1	4
It is	1	0	0	1	0	0	0	0	2	0	0	0	0	0	0	0
Lies	0	0	0	0	0	0	0	0	0	0	1	0	1	2	0	1
Location . .	0	0	0	0	0	0	1	0	0	0	0	0	0	0	2	1
Me	3	2	3	1	1	1	1	3	3	0	0	1	0	1	1	0
Near	1	1	2	1	1	0	1	0	1	1	0	0	0	0	5	1
Now	6	9	5	10	5	12	8	8	12	11	12	13	6	9	33	26
One	0	2	0	0	0	0	0	0	0	0	1	0	0	0	0	0
People . . .	0	0	0	0	0	0	0	0	0	1	2	0	0	0	0	0
Place . . .	6	4	7	8	10	13	2	6	2	6	8	3	5	4	10	3
Present . .	0	0	0	0	1	0	0	0	0	0	0	2	0	3	2	1
Right	1	2	0	0	0	3	0	0	0	0	0	0	0	0	1	0
School . . .	0	0	1	0	0	1	1	2	1	2	3	6	1	5	4	3
She	1	1	0	2	2	0	0	0	0	1	1	0	0	0	0	0
Some . . .	0	0	1	0	0	0	2	0	0	1	0	0	0	0	0	0
Spot	1	0	1	2	1	0	0	0	0	0	2	0	1	0	0	0
Stay	2	1	0	0	0	0	0	0	0	0	0	0	0	0	0	0
Table . . .	0	0	0	0	0	0	0	0	1	2	0	0	0	0	0	0
Take	0	1	3	2	0	2	0	1	0	0	2	0	0	0	0	1
That	2	1	1	1	1	0	0	1	2	0	0	0	0	1	0	0
The	0	1	2	0	8	0	1	0	1	0	1	0	0	0	0	0
Their . . .	4	3	5	5	5	3	1	1	0	0	1	3	0	0	0	0
Then . . .	0	0	0	0	0	1	1	0	0	0	0	1	2	0	0	2
There . . .	62	101	82	105	79	97	124	147	134	162	124	162	130	149	302	367
They	2	4	3	2	0	2	1	0	1	2	2	1	3	1	3	1
This	1	0	0	1	0	4	1	2	0	0	4	2	0	0	1	0
To	0	1	0	2	0	0	1	1	0	0	0	0	1	0	0	0
Today . . .	0	0	0	1	0	0	0	0	0	1	0	0	0	1	2	0
Us	1	3	2	1	1	0	2	0	2	0	0	0	0	0	0	0
Was	2	1	1	0	2	0	3	1	1	1	4	1	1	0	3	0
We	8	6	4	5	4	3	5	2	4	3	3	3	5	4	9	6
We are . .	0	1	0	1	0	0	0	0	2	1	0	0	1	0	0	0
Were . . .	2	0	2	1	3	0	0	2	0	1	0	0	0	0	0	0
Where . . .	8	8	3	5	2	8	9	10	8	5	5	2	8	9	14	9
Word . . .	0	0	2	0	0	1	0	0	0	0	0	0	0	0	1	0
You	5	4	1	1	6	3	2	0	3	1	2	0	3	0	2	0
						83.	HIGH									
Above . . .	0	2	0	1	1	1	1	1	1	0	1	0	0	1	1	1
Air	1	2	0	2	1	1	2	1	0	0	2	1	0	0	0	2
Airplane . .	1	0	3	1	0	0	0	2	4	0	2	1	2	1	3	1
Altitude . .	0	0	5	0	4	1	1	0	4	2	0	2	1	1	1	1
Bar	0	0	0	0	0	0	0	0	0	0	2	0	0	0	0	0
Big	3	7	7	4	2	3	4	2	0	2	4	2	2	1	1	1
Bridge . .	0	0	0	0	0	0	0	0	0	0	0	0	1	1	7	2
Building . .	1	1	1	1	0	4	2	2	4	2	7	4	9	4	16	12
Buildings .	0	0	0	0	0	0	0	0	2	1	0	0	0	0	1	0
By	2	0	0	0	0	0	0	1	0	0	0	0	0	0	0	0
Chair . . .	0	1	1	0	0	0	0	0	0	1	0	0	0	3	3	5

Response Word	4th M	4th F	5th M	5th F	6th M	6th F	7th M	7th F	8th M	8th F	10th M	10th F	12th M	12th F	College M	College F
							HIGH									
Cliff	0	1	1	0	0	1	1	0	1	0	0	0	2	1	5	1
Climb ...	0	1	0	1	2	0	0	0	0	0	0	0	0	1	1	0
Clouds ...	0	1	1	0	0	2	0	0	0	0	0	0	2	0	3	1
Deep	1	1	3	3	3	0	1	1	1	1	3	1	0	3	2	3
Dizzy ...	0	0	2	3	0	4	3	1	1	0	3	1	1	0	4	1
Down ...	2	1	2	0	3	2	1	1	0	1	0	0	0	0	0	0
Drunk ...	0	0	0	0	0	0	0	0	2	0	1	0	3	0	1	0
Fall	2	1	1	1	3	2	1	0	3	0	0	2	1	0	2	1
Falling ..	0	0	0	0	0	0	1	0	0	0	0	0	0	0	2	0
Far	5	4	5	2	7	5	7	0	2	0	2	1	2	0	0	2
Far up ...	0	0	0	0	0	0	1	0	0	0	0	2	0	0	0	0
Feet	0	0	0	0	0	0	2	0	0	0	0	0	0	0	0	0
Fence ...	0	0	0	0	0	0	0	0	0	2	0	0	0	1	1	1
Fly	1	1	1	0	1	0	0	0	2	0	0	0	0	0	1	0
Hard	0	1	1	1	0	0	0	0	0	0	0	3	0	0	0	0
Heel	0	0	0	0	0	0	0	0	0	1	1	0	0	0	2	1
Heels ...	0	0	0	0	0	0	0	1	0	2	1	1	2	2	3	1
Height ...	2	0	1	3	3	1	2	3	0	0	2	3	2	1	0	0
Higher ...	1	1	0	0	0	0	1	1	2	0	1	0	0	0	0	0
High school	0	0	1	2	0	1	1	0	0	0	0	0	0	0	0	0
Hill	4	6	0	6	1	3	0	3	2	1	2	1	4	4	5	11
House ...	2	1	0	0	0	1	0	0	0	0	1	1	0	0	0	0
Jump ...	0	0	1	1	1	1	2	2	1	3	3	0	4	0	3	1
Ladder...	1	2	0	2	0	4	4	6	0	2	2	9	2	10	11	13
Large ...	0	1	1	0	3	1	0	0	1	0	1	0	0	0	0	1
Light....	0	1	2	0	0	0	0	0	0	0	1	0	1	1	0	0
Long	1	3	4	1	3	1	1	0	2	1	0	0	0	0	1	0
Look	1	2	0	0	0	0	0	0	0	0	0	0	0	0	0	0
Low	129	127	109	123	104	111	110	120	139	139	107	115	125	128	271	297
Mighty ...	0	1	0	0	0	1	1	1	2	0	0	1	3	0	1	2
Mountain .	12	8	14	23	21	18	21	22	15	15	34	23	24	15	28	40
Mountains .	2	4	1	1	3	3	3	0	1	1	1	2	3	1	0	0
Mt.	0	1	0	1	2	0	0	1	0	0	0	0	0	2	1	2
Mts.	0	0	0	2	0	0	0	0	0	1	0	0	1	0	0	0
Not low ..	2	0	0	0	0	0	0	0	0	0	0	0	0	0	0	0
Plane ...	1	0	1	0	1	0	1	0	0	0	2	0	2	1	2	1
Pole	1	0	0	1	0	0	0	0	0	0	0	0	0	0	0	2
Roof	0	0	0	0	1	0	0	1	0	1	0	2	0	0	0	2
Scared ...	1	0	2	0	0	2	1	0	0	0	0	0	0	2	2	1
Scary ...	1	1	0	1	1	1	1	0	0	0	1	2	0	0	0	2
School ...	3	4	3	5	8	8	7	11	10	6	10	9	14	5	13	5
See.....	1	0	1	1	0	0	0	0	0	0	0	2	0	0	0	0
Short ...	0	1	0	2	1	0	0	1	3	2	1	1	0	1	2	3
Sky	6	2	4	3	2	5	4	5	6	4	3	5	2	11	9	4
Sky scraper	0	1	0	0	1	0	1	0	0	2	1	1	0	0	1	1
Small ...	0	1	1	1	1	0	0	2	1	0	1	0	1	1	0	0
Space ...	2	0	0	0	0	0	0	0	0	0	0	0	0	0	0	1
Steep ...	3	4	3	0	2	4	7	6	5	2	0	3	0	3	3	0
Tall	16	27	25	19	19	21	20	28	10	20	16	16	15	9	20	24

Response Word	4th M	4th F	5th M	5th F	6th M	6th F	7th M	7th F	8th M	8th F	10th M	10th F	12th M	12th F	College M	College F
							HIGH									
Thin	0	0	0	0	0	0	0	1	0	0	0	2	1	0	0	0
Top	4	3	2	1	1	2	0	0	0	0	1	1	0	1	1	6
Tower	2	0	2	0	1	0	2	0	2	4	5	1	3	3	4	6
Tree	0	0	0	0	0	1	0	0	0	2	2	1	0	2	2	4
Up	14	10	16	13	23	15	10	11	8	7	7	5	5	4	16	10
Wall	0	0	0	0	0	0	2	0	0	1	0	0	0	1	2	2
Way up	0	0	0	0	0	0	2	0	3	0	0	0	0	0	0	0
Wide	0	0	0	0	0	0	0	0	1	1	0	1	0	2	1	4
Windy	1	0	0	0	0	0	0	0	0	0	2	0	0	0	0	0
Wire	0	0	1	0	0	1	0	0	0	0	0	0	1	0	2	0
							84. HIM									
And	0	0	0	0	3	1	0	0	0	1	1	0	0	1	0	1
Are	2	1	0	1	0	0	1	0	1	0	0	1	0	0	0	2
Boy	17	25	16	27	13	27	4	24	5	16	11	18	1	12	5	16
Boys	0	0	0	0	0	0	0	0	0	2	0	0	0	0	0	0
Can	0	0	0	0	1	1	0	0	0	0	0	0	2	0	0	0
Dave	0	0	0	0	0	0	0	1	0	0	0	3	0	0	0	1
Dick	0	0	0	0	0	0	0	0	0	0	0	0	1	2	0	0
Down	0	0	0	0	0	0	0	0	0	0	2	0	0	0	0	0
Father	1	1	1	0	0	1	1	0	0	0	0	2	0	0	0	2
God	0	0	0	0	0	1	1	1	0	2	1	3	1	2	10	14
Have	0	0	2	0	1	0	0	0	0	0	0	0	0	0	0	1
He	23	14	23	21	7	22	20	18	18	7	24	11	23	25	40	36
Her	80	121	81	110	103	117	124	152	135	157	132	153	145	134	298	329
Hers	0	0	2	2	1	1	3	1	4	1	1	0	1	1	5	4
Here	3	1	4	0	4	4	2	1	2	1	3	0	0	2	2	1
Hi	1	0	0	1	2	0	0	0	0	0	0	0	0	0	0	0
Himself	0	2	0	1	1	0	0	0	0	0	0	0	0	0	1	0
His	8	7	8	10	10	10	9	10	7	13	5	6	11	15	15	9
Hymn	0	0	2	2	1	0	0	0	0	0	0	0	0	0	0	0
I	2	1	5	0	2	0	0	1	0	0	2	0	1	1	0	0
In	1	2	0	0	0	0	0	0	0	0	0	0	0	1	0	0
Is	4	5	1	2	2	2	3	1	4	1	4	1	6	0	3	2
It	2	2	4	0	4	1	3	0	3	0	4	1	0	0	4	3
Jim	1	0	0	1	1	0	2	0	0	2	1	0	0	0	3	1
John	0	0	0	0	0	0	0	1	0	0	1	1	0	0	2	1
Love	0	0	0	0	0	0	0	0	0	1	0	2	0	5	0	0
Male	3	0	1	1	1	0	1	1	1	0	1	0	0	0	1	0
Man	7	8	4	5	7	7	3	1	0	2	4	4	1	5	9	10
Me	14	9	19	4	15	5	13	3	14	9	11	11	7	8	9	18
Mine	0	0	0	0	0	0	0	0	0	0	0	0	0	1	0	2
Not	0	0	0	2	3	0	0	0	0	0	0	0	0	0	0	0
Now	2	0	0	0	0	0	2	0	0	1	0	0	0	0	2	0
Person	4	1	5	4	9	3	2	0	1	0	2	0	3	0	7	0
Pronoun	0	0	0	0	0	0	0	0	0	4	0	0	0	0	0	0
Quietly	0	0	0	0	0	0	0	0	2	0	0	0	0	0	0	0
Self	0	2	4	1	5	1	1	1	4	0	3	0	0	2	5	0
She	10	19	14	18	3	15	11	10	10	8	8	8	10	3	16	13

Response Word	4th M	4th F	5th M	5th F	6th M	6th F	7th M	7th F	8th M	8th F	10th M	10th F	12th M	12th F	College M	College F
							HIM									
So	0	0	0	2	0	1	0	0	0	0	0	0	0	0	0	0
Song	1	0	0	1	1	0	0	0	0	0	2	0	0	0	0	0
That	1	0	2	0	1	0	0	0	0	1	0	0	0	0	0	0
The	0	0	1	0	6	0	1	0	0	0	0	0	0	0	0	0
Them . . .	3	2	2	2	4	1	3	2	5	2	0	2	8	3	3	1
They	0	0	2	1	0	2	4	0	3	0	1	0	3	3	9	0
There . . .	0	0	1	0	3	0	0	0	1	0	0	0	0	0	1	0
To	0	0	2	1	3	0	2	1	0	0	0	0	0	0	0	2
Too	0	0	0	1	0	0	1	0	0	1	1	0	0	0	2	0
Us	1	0	1	1	2	3	2	1	3	0	2	2	1	0	1	0
We	1	0	1	0	0	0	2	0	0	0	1	0	0	0	2	1
Who	0	0	0	0	0	0	1	1	1	0	0	0	0	1	3	0
You	10	2	6	11	4	2	7	1	6	2	3	0	4	2	7	4
						85.	HIS									
Ankle . . .	0	0	0	0	0	0	0	0	0	0	2	0	0	0	0	0
Are	0	0	0	0	0	0	0	0	0	0	0	0	1	0	0	2
Arm	1	1	0	2	0	2	2	0	1	1	0	1	2	4	1	1
Ball	0	0	0	0	0	2	0	0	2	1	0	1	0	0	2	0
Belong . . .	0	1	0	2	0	1	1	1	0	0	0	0	0	0	1	0
Belonging .	0	0	0	1	0	0	0	0	0	0	1	0	0	0	2	1
Belongs . .	0	0	0	0	0	0	1	1	0	0	2	1	0	0	1	0
Bike	0	0	1	0	0	0	0	1	1	0	1	2	0	0	2	0
Boat	0	0	0	0	0	0	0	1	1	0	0	0	0	2	2	0
Book	0	0	2	0	0	0	0	0	0	1	3	0	0	2	3	3
Books . . .	0	0	0	0	0	0	0	1	0	0	0	0	2	0	0	0
Boy	10	19	7	12	8	16	2	11	5	8	2	9	0	6	2	7
Boys . . .	0	0	1	1	0	4	1	1	0	1	0	0	0	0	1	0
Brother . .	1	2	0	0	1	0	0	0	1	0	0	0	2	0	0	0
Cake	0	0	2	0	0	0	0	0	0	0	0	0	0	2	1	0
Car	2	0	2	0	0	0	0	0	2	2	5	3	7	6	7	13
Cat	0	0	1	0	1	0	2	0	1	0	0	0	0	1	1	0
Coat	1	0	1	0	0	0	1	0	0	3	0	3	1	3	5	5
Come . . .	0	0	2	1	0	1	0	0	0	0	0	0	0	0	0	0
Dad	0	0	3	0	0	1	0	0	1	0	1	0	0	0	1	0
Dog	0	1	2	1	2	0	5	0	2	1	3	1	1	4	7	5
Eyes . . .	0	0	0	0	0	0	0	0	0	0	2	0	0	0	0	0
Face	2	0	0	0	2	0	0	0	1	2	1	1	0	0	4	2
Father . . .	2	4	3	2	1	1	3	0	1	0	1	0	1	0	0	0
Feet	1	0	0	1	1	0	0	0	2	0	0	0	2	0	3	0
Foot	2	0	3	0	1	0	0	0	0	1	0	0	2	1	1	0
Friend . . .	0	1	2	0	0	0	1	0	0	2	2	0	0	1	0	2
Girl	0	2	1	1	2	0	0	3	3	3	5	0	7	0	2	2
Girls . . .	0	0	0	0	0	0	0	0	2	0	0	0	0	0	0	0
God	0	0	0	0	0	0	0	0	0	1	0	2	0	1	1	2
Hair	0	0	0	2	0	0	0	1	4	1	2	2	0	3	0	0
Hand	1	3	0	2	3	1	1	2	3	5	4	7	6	4	4	5
Hands . . .	0	0	1	0	0	0	0	0	0	0	3	1	0	1	1	1
Hat	3	1	4	0	3	2	1	0	4	1	2	3	8	1	5	7

154

Response Word	4th M	4th F	5th M	5th F	6th M	6th F	7th M	7th F	8th M	8th F	10th M	10th F	12th M	12th F	College M	College F
							HIS									
He	8	6	9	13	0	10	5	7	2	5	7	0	2	3	7	4
Head	0	0	1	0	1	0	1	1	0	0	1	1	2	1	1	1
Heart	2	0	0	0	1	0	0	0	0	0	0	0	0	2	0	0
Her	36	67	36	60	40	62	50	62	36	61	35	43	45	61	100	101
Here	2	0	1	0	1	0	0	0	0	0	0	1	0	0	1	0
Hers	50	56	55	70	69	71	91	99	110	103	97	122	94	84	223	256
Him	14	13	18	13	13	14	14	15	5	8	8	6	6	8	4	1
His	2	0	0	0	2	1	0	0	1	0	0	0	0	0	0	0
Horse	0	0	1	1	1	0	0	0	0	0	0	1	0	0	0	2
House	0	2	2	0	3	0	0	2	1	0	0	0	1	1	1	1
Is	14	9	8	6	5	2	5	1	2	1	3	1	0	7	1	1
It	1	2	0	2	0	1	2	0	0	0	2	0	1	0	0	0
Its	0	0	0	0	0	0	0	0	0	0	1	0	0	0	2	0
Leg	0	0	0	1	0	0	0	0	0	0	2	0	0	0	0	0
Majesty	0	0	0	0	0	0	0	0	1	1	0	0	0	0	2	0
Make	0	1	0	3	1	0	0	0	0	0	0	0	0	0	0	0
Man	5	4	5	7	2	9	4	4	1	0	2	3	1	2	2	4
Mans	0	0	0	1	2	1	0	0	0	0	0	0	0	0	1	0
Me	7	1	7	0	1	1	2	0	0	0	0	0	0	0	0	0
Mind	0	0	1	1	1	0	0	1	2	0	0	1	2	0	0	0
Mine	10	5	8	2	8	3	10	7	3	8	4	4	3	6	16	12
Mistake	1	0	0	0	0	1	1	2	0	0	1	1	5	1	2	0
Money	0	0	0	1	0	1	2	0	1	0	0	0	0	0	1	1
Mother	6	3	5	3	4	1	4	2	5	1	2	1	3	0	5	3
My	1	0	2	1	3	0	0	2	1	0	1	0	0	0	1	0
Name	2	5	6	4	9	8	1	4	4	4	4	3	5	8	2	3
One	2	0	0	0	0	0	0	0	0	0	0	0	0	0	0	0
Own	1	2	2	3	3	3	3	1	2	0	1	2	5	3	9	5
Ownership	0	0	1	0	0	0	0	0	0	0	2	0	0	0	0	1
Person	1	1	1	1	3	1	1	0	0	0	1	1	0	0	1	0
Pocket	0	2	0	0	0	0	0	0	0	0	0	0	0	0	0	0
Possession	0	0	0	0	0	0	1	1	0	0	1	0	0	1	5	3
Pronoun	0	0	0	0	0	0	0	0	0	2	0	0	0	0	0	1
Ring	0	0	0	0	0	0	0	0	0	3	0	0	0	0	0	3
She	7	11	4	5	0	6	1	1	2	1	3	0	1	2	0	2
Shirt	0	0	1	0	1	0	1	0	0	0	1	1	2	0	2	3
Shoe	1	0	0	1	0	2	1	1	0	0	1	0	2	3	5	2
Shoes	1	0	4	0	1	0	1	1	0	0	1	1	0	0	3	5
Sister	3	3	1	1	0	0	0	0	1	2	0	1	0	0	0	0
Sweater	0	0	0	0	0	0	0	0	0	0	2	0	0	0	0	0
The	0	0	2	1	2	0	0	0	0	0	0	0	0	0	0	0
Theirs	0	2	0	1	0	0	1	0	0	1	0	0	4	1	1	1
There	1	0	0	0	0	0	0	0	0	0	2	0	1	0	0	0
Thing	1	0	2	0	1	0	0	0	0	0	1	0	0	0	1	0
Three	2	0	0	0	0	0	0	0	0	0	0	0	0	0	0	0
Tie	1	0	0	0	0	1	0	0	1	0	0	1	0	3	1	0
Towel	0	0	0	0	1	0	0	0	0	0	0	3	2	1	3	5
Toy	4	1	2	0	2	1	0	0	0	1	0	0	0	0	1	0
Voice	0	0	0	0	2	0	0	0	0	0	0	0	0	0	0	0

Response Word	4th M	4th F	5th M	5th F	6th M	6th F	7th M	7th F	8th M	8th F	10th M	10th F	12th M	12th F	College M	College F
HIS																
Was	0	1	0	0	0	0	0	0	4	0	0	0	0	0	1	0
Wife	0	0	2	1	0	1	3	0	1	0	1	0	0	0	0	0
Yours . . .	1	1	1	1	2	0	0	0	1	0	0	1	0	0	1	3
86. HOTTER																
Animal . .	0	0	0	0	2	1	0	0	0	0	0	1	0	0	0	0
Bath	0	0	0	0	0	0	0	0	0	0	2	0	0	0	0	0
Better . . .	0	0	1	1	0	0	0	0	0	1	1	0	2	0	0	0
Boil	1	4	3	2	3	3	0	2	0	2	0	1	1	0	0	1
Boiling . .	3	2	2	5	3	8	3	1	2	1	1	2	1	0	0	0
Burn	6	4	5	9	3	13	8	6	5	4	7	7	5	6	7	2
Burning . .	0	2	0	1	0	1	2	0	0	0	1	0	0	0	0	0
Coat	0	0	0	0	2	0	0	0	0	0	0	0	0	0	0	0
Coffee . . .	0	0	0	0	0	0	0	0	0	1	0	0	0	2	0	1
Cold	52	51	45	30	48	39	42	38	46	27	30	34	46	38	74	56
Colder . . .	47	60	39	64	33	62	65	91	84	95	70	80	94	86	227	263
Cool	3	0	5	4	10	1	3	4	6	5	1	4	3	2	6	1
Cooler . . .	5	6	1	9	9	7	7	8	11	21	9	8	1	8	11	15
Day	0	1	0	1	2	0	2	1	0	0	2	0	0	1	2	2
Fire	5	1	3	1	5	6	7	4	5	5	5	1	3	4	5	14
Flame . . .	0	0	0	0	0	1	0	0	0	0	0	0	0	0	0	2
Food	0	0	2	1	1	1	0	0	0	0	0	0	1	1	0	0
Furnace . .	0	0	0	0	0	0	0	0	0	0	2	2	0	0	3	0
Girls . . .	0	0	0	0	0	0	0	0	0	0	0	0	1	1	2	0
Heat	3	4	10	1	15	5	8	6	6	4	7	2	7	3	10	11
Heater . . .	0	0	0	1	0	2	0	0	1	0	0	2	0	0	0	1
Hell	0	0	0	0	0	0	0	0	3	1	1	2	6	1	13	11
Hold	2	0	0	0	0	0	2	0	0	0	0	0	0	0	1	0
Horse . . .	0	0	3	0	2	1	0	2	0	0	0	0	0	2	0	0
Hot	36	23	28	25	24	20	26	14	9	4	10	7	11	3	10	5
Hottest . .	0	0	0	0	2	0	2	1	3	5	6	4	5	4	5	5
House . . .	0	2	0	0	0	0	0	0	1	0	0	0	0	0	0	0
Hurt	1	0	0	0	0	0	0	0	0	0	0	2	0	0	0	0
Iron	0	0	0	1	0	1	0	0	1	1	1	2	0	1	1	1
Lighter . .	0	0	0	0	0	0	0	0	0	2	0	0	0	0	0	0
Ouch	2	1	1	1	0	2	0	2	4	3	2	2	0	1	2	1
Oven	3	2	1	5	2	5	4	1	2	4	1	1	3	2	4	1
Pain	0	0	0	0	0	0	1	0	0	0	0	0	1	0	0	2
Pan	3	1	2	2	0	0	3	1	2	3	3	3	1	0	5	3
Place . . .	0	0	2	0	0	0	0	0	0	0	0	0	0	0	0	0
Plate . . .	0	0	0	0	0	0	0	0	0	1	0	0	0	0	2	0
Pot	1	2	4	2	0	1	0	2	0	1	0	0	0	0	0	0
Potato . . .	0	0	0	0	1	0	0	0	0	1	1	0	0	0	2	0
Potter . . .	2	0	1	1	1	0	0	3	0	0	0	0	0	1	1	0
Red	2	1	4	1	0	2	1	2	1	1	7	6	1	1	7	4
Redder . .	2	0	0	0	0	0	0	0	0	0	0	0	0	0	1	0
Roasting . .	0	0	2	1	0	0	0	0	0	0	0	1	0	0	0	0
Roof	0	0	0	0	0	0	0	0	0	0	1	0	0	0	0	2
Softer	0	0	0	0	0	0	0	0	0	0	0	1	0	0	0	2

Response Word	4th		5th		6th		7th		8th		10th		12th		College	
	M	F	M	F	M	F	M	F	M	F	M	F	M	F	M	F

HOTTER

Response Word	4th M	4th F	5th M	5th F	6th M	6th F	7th M	7th F	8th M	8th F	10th M	10th F	12th M	12th F	College M	College F
Steam ...	0	5	3	4	3	5	1	5	0	0	2	1	0	0	1	1
Steaming..	0	0	0	1	1	2	0	0	0	0	0	0	0	0	0	0
Stove ...	5	10	9	12	11	9	8	7	8	9	17	23	10	8	22	31
Summer ..	2	7	1	2	3	4	3	6	2	8	4	10	1	18	7	9
Sun	2	4	8	7	3	4	2	4	3	5	5	4	7	7	5	7
Sweat ...	1	5	2	1	0	2	1	4	5	1	2	1	3	2	2	1
Than ...	0	0	0	2	1	0	0	0	6	1	3	3	3	1	8	7
Totter ...	0	0	0	0	0	0	0	1	1	1	0	0	2	0	0	1
Warm ...	15	10	20	17	19	14	10	8	7	10	13	8	8	11	10	9
Warmer ..	6	8	7	4	1	5	5	2	4	2	6	6	3	8	6	5
Water ...	2	0	1	0	2	0	0	0	0	1	1	1	3	2	3	2
Weather ..	0	0	0	0	0	2	0	1	0	2	0	3	0	1	5	1
Wet	0	0	0	0	1	1	0	0	2	0	0	0	0	1	1	0
Yell	0	0	0	0	2	1	0	0	0	0	0	0	0	0	0	0

87. HOUSE

Response Word	4th M	4th F	5th M	5th F	6th M	6th F	7th M	7th F	8th M	8th F	10th M	10th F	12th M	12th F	College M	College F
Animal...	0	0	0	1	0	2	0	0	0	0	0	0	0	0	0	0
Apartment .	0	1	1	2	0	1	0	0	2	1	1	2	0	1	0	2
Back	2	0	0	1	0	0	0	0	0	0	1	0	0	0	1	1
Barn	9	4	7	10	3	6	3	5	6	8	4	4	4	6	11	6
Beautiful .	0	0	0	0	0	0	0	1	1	0	0	2	0	1	0	2
Bed	1	0	2	0	0	1	1	2	0	4	4	0	2	0	0	0
Big	11	13	7	18	18	15	11	16	3	12	16	17	6	15	13	14
Black ...	0	1	0	0	0	0	0	1	0	1	0	0	0	0	2	4
Block ...	0	0	0	1	0	0	1	1	0	1	0	0	2	2	1	3
Blue	0	1	1	1	0	1	0	0	0	1	1	2	0	0	0	0
Boat	0	0	1	0	0	0	0	1	1	0	1	1	6	2	9	5
Boy	1	1	1	0	1	0	0	0	1	0	0	0	0	0	0	3
Brick ...	2	1	3	1	2	0	3	5	2	6	3	6	4	6	14	12
Brown ...	0	0	1	1	0	1	0	1	0	0	0	2	0	1	2	1
Build ...	0	0	0	0	0	0	0	0	0	0	2	0	0	0	1	0
Building ..	11	8	10	7	4	5	9	5	9	8	4	6	4	3	9	3
Cabin ...	5	5	1	2	2	2	1	0	3	1	2	0	0	0	0	1
Car	1	0	0	1	0	0	4	5	14	10	10	4	12	13	17	10
Cat	0	0	2	0	1	1	0	1	2	2	1	1	2	1	4	0
Cave ...	0	0	0	0	0	3	0	0	1	1	0	0	1	0	0	0
Chair....	2	2	0	1	0	1	1	2	3	2	1	0	1	2	2	5
Chimney ..	1	2	0	4	1	6	0	1	3	1	1	2	4	1	5	7
Clean ...	1	2	0	0	0	0	0	0	0	0	0	1	0	0	0	0
Coat	0	0	0	0	0	2	0	0	0	0	0	0	2	0	2	1
Comfort ..	1	0	0	0	1	1	1	0	0	1	2	1	2	1	5	3
Comfortable	0	1	0	2	0	0	0	0	0	0	0	0	0	0	0	2
Cottage ..	2	2	1	2	1	4	1	3	2	1	0	2	1	2	0	2
Dark	0	0	3	0	0	1	2	0	0	1	1	2	2	0	7	2
Dog	3	0	2	1	1	4	2	0	3	1	5	3	1	1	6	5
Door	8	10	6	14	14	6	8	12	12	14	8	5	10	10	39	35
Family...	0	0	1	0	2	2	1	1	1	3	4	8	3	7	9	18
Farm ...	0	0	1	0	1	1	0	1	1	2	0	0	0	0	0	0
Fence ...	1	0	0	0	0	0	1	1	0	1	2	4	0	2	0	1

Response Word	4th M	4th F	5th M	5th F	6th M	6th F	7th M	7th F	8th M	8th F	10th M	10th F	12th M	12th F	College M	College F
						HOUSE										
Furniture .	2	3	1	2	2	1	2	5	1	3	0	6	0	4	2	2
Gable . . .	0	0	0	0	0	0	0	0	0	0	0	0	0	0	2	0
Garage . .	7	10	3	9	16	3	20	13	22	9	16	8	20	14	20	16
Garden. . .	1	1	1	0	0	1	2	0	0	2	0	1	0	1	0	0
Green . . .	0	1	2	0	0	1	0	1	0	1	2	0	2	3	1	2
Ground . .	0	0	2	0	0	1	0	0	0	0	0	0	0	0	0	0
Haunted . .	0	0	1	0	0	0	0	0	2	0	0	0	0	0	0	0
Hill	0	0	1	0	0	1	0	1	0	3	0	1	0	0	4	5
Hole	1	0	0	0	0	0	1	0	2	0	1	0	0	0	0	1
Home . . .	52	52	56	50	55	48	55	46	40	37	49	46	59	50	106	124
Homes . .	0	1	0	0	0	0	2	0	0	0	0	0	0	0	0	0
Horse . . .	2	0	1	3	2	3	0	1	0	0	1	0	0	2	0	0
Hotel . . .	2	2	1	1	0	1	1	0	0	0	0	0	0	1	3	0
Hut	4	1	0	1	0	1	1	2	0	3	0	1	0	1	2	2
Lady	0	0	0	0	0	2	0	0	0	0	0	0	0	0	0	0
Large . . .	1	1	0	1	0	3	2	3	1	4	5	2	0	3	3	3
Lawn . . .	0	0	0	0	0	0	2	0	0	0	1	0	0	0	0	0
Life	2	0	0	0	1	0	0	1	0	0	0	0	0	0	0	1
Little . . .	0	1	1	0	2	1	0	0	1	1	0	1	0	0	0	0
Live	9	20	16	20	13	20	9	12	4	8	5	6	1	5	13	5
Live in . .	3	1	1	0	0	1	0	1	1	0	0	0	0	0	0	0
Living . . .	1	4	1	3	5	0	1	1	2	1	1	1	1	2	2	2
Long	0	0	0	0	2	0	0	0	0	0	0	0	0	0	0	0
Love	0	0	0	0	0	0	0	1	0	0	0	0	0	0	1	2
Man	1	1	0	1	1	0	1	1	0	0	1	2	0	0	4	1
Mansion . .	0	0	0	0	2	0	1	0	0	3	0	0	1	0	2	1
Marriage .	0	0	0	0	0	0	0	0	0	0	0	0	0	0	1	2
Mine . . .	0	2	0	0	0	0	2	1	0	0	0	0	0	1	1	4
Modern . .	0	0	0	0	0	0	0	0	0	0	0	0	0	1	0	2
Money . . .	0	0	0	0	0	0	0	0	0	0	0	0	0	0	3	0
Mother. . .	1	0	0	1	1	0	0	0	0	0	0	1	0	0	2	3
Mouse . . .	2	10	7	7	8	3	3	3	5	5	2	1	4	0	5	4
New	0	0	0	0	0	0	0	0	0	0	0	0	0	0	1	2
Nice	3	2	2	2	1	1	0	1	0	1	0	2	1	0	1	0
Paint . . .	1	0	0	0	0	0	0	0	1	2	0	0	2	1	8	1
People . .	4	8	5	6	1	5	3	6	4	9	3	4	4	9	6	6
Place . . .	3	2	10	4	1	6	2	3	1	1	0	1	1	0	2	0
Place to live	0	0	0	0	0	0	2	1	0	0	0	0	0	0	0	0
Pretty . . .	0	0	1	2	1	2	0	1	0	1	0	0	0	0	0	0
Protection .	0	0	0	0	0	0	0	0	0	2	0	0	1	0	1	0
Rambler . .	0	0	0	0	0	0	0	1	0	2	0	0	0	0	2	1
Red	2	0	0	2	2	1	3	1	0	3	1	2	1	2	2	4
Roof . . .	8	8	9	1	2	5	7	8	6	7	8	13	5	7	13	12
Room . . .	2	2	4	4	2	4	6	9	2	4	3	5	4	4	11	7
Rooms . .	1	2	2	5	3	2	0	1	3	2	0	3	1	0	0	4
School . . .	0	0	0	0	0	0	2	2	0	0	1	0	1	0	1	0
Security . .	0	0	0	0	0	0	0	1	0	0	0	0	2	1	3	0
Shack . . .	8	4	5	3	3	1	4	3	4	3	4	1	3	0	3	1

Response Word	4th M	4th F	5th M	5th F	6th M	6th F	7th M	7th F	8th M	8th F	10th M	10th F	12th M	12th F	College M	College F
							HOUSE									
Shed	3	2	0	0	0	0	0	0	2	1	2	0	2	1	0	1
Shelter...	7	6	6	3	9	6	11	6	7	1	6	1	5	5	2	2
Shutter...	0	0	1	0	0	0	0	0	0	0	0	0	0	0	2	0
Sleep ...	1	2	1	1	1	0	1	1	3	0	1	2	1	0	2	0
Small ...	0	0	3	1	2	2	2	3	0	2	0	0	0	0	0	1
Square ...	0	0	0	2	0	2	0	2	0	2	2	1	1	0	2	1
Steps....	0	1	0	1	0	0	0	0	2	0	0	0	1	2	0	0
Store....	1	0	0	0	1	2	1	1	0	0	1	1	0	0	0	0
Street ...	0	2	0	1	1	1	1	1	1	2	2	2	3	6	0	4
Stucco ...	0	0	0	0	0	2	0	0	0	1	0	1	0	1	1	1
Table ...	2	1	2	1	0	1	0	0	1	1	0	0	1	0	1	0
Tall ...	2	1	0	0	0	2	1	0	0	0	0	0	0	0	0	0
Tent ...	4	1	0	1	0	1	0	0	1	0	0	0	0	0	0	0
Top	0	0	1	0	0	0	0	0	0	0	2	1	1	0	7	1
Tree	0	0	0	0	0	0	0	0	0	2	1	1	1	0	1	6
TV	0	0	0	0	2	0	0	0	0	0	0	0	0	0	0	0
Wall ...	0	0	0	0	0	2	0	0	0	0	0	0	1	0	2	1
Warm ...	11	7	10	9	8	10	4	3	4	3	2	1	7	4	6	6
Warmth ..	0	0	1	1	0	0	1	0	0	1	2	1	0	0	1	2
White ...	2	1	0	2	1	4	2	5	2	7	14	15	8	16	27	47
Wife	0	0	0	0	0	0	0	0	0	0	0	0	1	0	0	2
Window ..	1	2	0	0	5	3	4	1	5	2	2	4	4	2	9	12
Windows ..	0	0	1	0	0	1	1	0	2	1	1	0	1	2	2	3
Wood ...	2	2	5	3	7	3	5	2	4	2	4	6	0	3	4	5
Yard ...	2	5	4	7	3	4	7	2	4	5	5	9	4	2	5	6
						88.	HOW									
About ...	4	0	0	2	3	0	0	2	2	0	0	0	2	1	1	5
Answer ..	0	0	0	0	0	0	0	0	0	0	0	0	0	0	2	0
Anyway ..	0	1	0	0	0	1	0	0	0	1	0	0	0	0	2	0
Are	6	5	1	5	5	3	1	4	5	2	1	1	4	3	7	6
Ask	0	4	0	7	1	4	2	0	0	2	1	0	0	0	1	0
Bad	0	0	0	1	0	2	0	0	0	0	1	0	1	0	0	0
Because ..	0	0	3	0	1	1	1	2	2	1	2	1	3	2	5	2
But	0	0	1	0	1	0	0	1	0	0	2	0	0	0	0	1
By	2	0	1	0	0	1	0	1	0	0	0	0	0	0	1	0
Can	4	8	9	7	2	5	1	4	3	1	4	4	3	5	2	8
Car	0	0	0	0	0	1	1	0	1	0	6	2	1	0	0	1
Come ...	7	4	1	10	9	6	7	10	11	12	11	21	10	21	31	28
Could ...	2	1	0	0	2	0	2	0	0	0	0	0	0	0	0	1
Cow ...	7	2	0	2	1	0	3	1	0	4	2	3	0	2	2	4
Did	6	4	10	4	12	5	6	3	1	1	4	0	4	1	3	2
Do	19	21	17	18	22	15	5	7	7	4	12	16	8	8	13	13
Does	0	3	1	1	0	0	1	1	0	1	2	0	0	0	0	0
Done	0	1	1	0	2	0	0	0	1	2	0	0	0	1	1	0
Do you do .	0	2	0	0	0	0	0	0	0	1	0	0	0	0	0	0
Easy	2	0	2	0	1	2	3	2	4	1	2	4	4	3	5	7
Else	0	0	0	0	0	0	0	0	0	0	0	0	0	0	0	3
Ever ...	11	19	17	14	12	11	11	15	12	6	12	11	19	3	31	16

Response Word	4th M	4th F	5th M	5th F	6th M	6th F	7th M	7th F	8th M	8th F	10th M	10th F	12th M	12th F	College M	College F
							HOW									
Every	2	1	3	2	0	0	0	0	0	0	0	0	0	0	0	0
Explain . . .	0	0	0	0	0	2	0	2	0	0	0	1	0	3	1	2
Far	1	0	1	1	2	0	1	0	1	1	3	1	1	0	3	1
Fast	1	3	2	1	5	3	1	1	3	2	6	6	6	2	4	3
For	0	0	0	0	0	2	0	0	0	0	0	0	1	0	1	0
Go	4	6	2	2	4	1	1	0	1	0	0	1	0	0	0	0
Good	3	2	7	1	4	2	1	1	3	0	0	0	1	1	0	0
Had	0	0	0	0	0	1	0	0	2	0	0	1	0	0	0	0
Hard	2	1	3	3	2	4	3	3	0	3	1	0	2	0	1	1
Have	0	0	0	0	0	0	3	0	0	0	1	0	0	0	1	0
He	1	0	0	0	1	0	3	0	0	0	1	0	1	0	0	0
Hello . . .	0	2	0	1	1	1	2	0	2	1	1	0	1	1	2	0
Ho	2	0	1	0	0	0	1	1	0	0	0	0	0	0	0	0
However . .	3	2	0	0	0	2	3	0	1	1	0	0	6	2	7	0
I	0	2	0	0	0	0	0	1	0	0	0	0	0	0	0	0
Indian	6	7	5	8	4	10	9	7	7	7	14	8	14	10	5	13
Indians . . .	0	0	0	1	2	0	1	2	0	1	1	3	2	0	1	0
Is	5	4	3	2	1	4	3	3	2	2	4	0	3	5	3	4
It	2	3	3	0	4	2	1	0	1	0	0	0	1	1	1	0
Know	2	5	4	3	4	6	1	1	2	2	0	0	1	0	2	0
Later	0	0	0	0	0	0	2	0	0	0	0	0	0	0	1	0
Like	0	2	0	2	0	1	0	1	1	2	0	1	1	1	0	2
Long	0	2	0	1	7	5	3	0	1	5	3	4	2	5	1	2
Low	0	0	0	0	2	0	0	0	0	0	0	0	0	0	0	0
Many . . .	4	1	2	2	1	3	3	3	2	2	3	5	1	3	10	7
May	0	0	0	3	0	0	0	0	0	0	0	0	0	0	0	0
Maybe	0	0	3	0	0	0	0	0	0	0	0	0	0	0	0	0
Me	0	1	2	0	2	0	0	1	0	0	0	0	0	0	0	0
Means	0	0	0	0	0	0	0	0	0	0	0	0	0	2	2	0
Method	0	0	0	0	0	0	1	0	0	0	0	0	0	1	6	0
Much	1	0	2	3	1	3	9	10	6	11	11	10	6	9	21	22
Never	1	1	0	0	1	3	0	2	3	0	0	0	3	2	1	1
Nice	1	0	2	1	0	0	1	0	0	2	0	0	0	0	1	0
No	6	1	4	1	2	1	2	0	0	1	0	1	1	0	0	1
Not	2	2	2	3	0	0	0	0	1	0	2	0	0	2	5	3
Now	22	25	34	30	23	25	35	34	44	42	36	27	46	33	112	109
Now brown cow	0	0	0	0	0	0	0	0	0	0	1	0	0	0	1	3
Often	0	0	1	0	0	0	1	0	2	2	1	0	0	1	1	0
Old	0	0	0	0	2	0	0	0	0	1	0	0	1	1	0	0
Out	0	0	0	0	0	0	0	0	0	0	0	0	0	10	0	1
Ow	0	1	1	0	2	0	0	0	0	0	0	0	0	0	0	0
People . . .	2	0	0	0	1	0	0	0	0	0	0	0	0	0	0	0
Pow	1	1	2	0	1	0	0	0	0	0	1	0	0	0	0	0
Problem . .	0	0	0	0	0	0	0	1	0	0	0	0	1	0	2	0
Procedure . .	0	0	0	0	0	0	0	0	0	0	0	0	0	0	0	2
Question . . .	4	7	6	10	7	16	10	10	11	11	6	20	11	23	27	28
Questions . .	0	0	0	2	0	0	0	0	0	0	0	0	0	0	0	0
Reason . . .	0	1	0	0	0	0	0	1	1	0	1	0	0	0	3	0
Run	0	0	0	0	2	0	1	0	0	1	0	0	0	0	0	0

Response Word	4th M	4th F	5th M	5th F	6th M	6th F	7th M	7th F	8th M	8th F	10th M	10th F	12th M	12th F	College M	College F
							HOW									
See	2	0	0	0	0	0	0	0	0	0	0	0	0	0	0	1
Should . . .	1	1	0	2	0	0	0	1	0	0	0	1	1	0	0	0
Show	0	1	0	2	1	0	1	0	1	3	1	0	0	1	2	2
Slow	2	0	1	1	0	0	2	0	2	1	1	0	0	0	2	0
So	0	0	0	1	0	0	0	2	0	0	0	0	0	0	0	0
Something .	0	1	2	0	0	1	0	0	0	0	1	0	0	0	0	0
That	0	2	1	1	0	0	0	2	0	0	1	1	1	0	1	0
The	1	2	3	0	4	0	0	0	2	0	0	1	1	0	0	0
Then . . .	0	1	4	2	2	2	2	1	1	1	0	0	1	0	1	3
There . . .	1	1	1	1	2	2	0	0	0	2	0	0	0	0	0	0
Think . . .	0	3	0	0	0	0	1	0	0	0	0	0	0	0	0	0
This	0	0	1	2	0	0	1	1	1	1	1	1	1	0	1	3
To	11	4	5	4	7	2	7	1	5	2	8	3	6	4	9	15
To do . . .	0	2	0	0	0	2	0	1	0	1	1	0	0	0	0	0
Too	0	0	1	1	0	0	2	0	0	0	0	0	0	1	0	0
Ugh	0	0	0	1	0	0	0	0	2	0	0	0	2	0	2	0
Walk . . .	0	0	0	0	0	0	0	1	1	1	0	2	1	2	2	0
Was	1	2	0	2	1	1	1	2	1	0	0	0	0	0	0	0
Way	0	1	1	1	0	1	2	0	0	1	1	0	2	3	5	7
We	0	0	0	0	0	0	2	2	0	0	0	1	0	0	0	0
Well	1	0	0	0	0	1	0	2	0	0	1	3	0	1	1	0
Were . . .	0	0	0	1	1	0	0	2	1	0	0	1	1	1	0	1
What . . .	7	7	3	10	6	9	7	8	8	13	7	7	2	8	12	10
When . . .	3	6	5	4	7	11	7	15	15	18	12	12	7	11	36	31
Where . . .	3	2	1	2	0	2	1	6	3	5	3	4	2	5	9	6
Who	4	0	3	3	1	3	9	7	7	2	2	2	1	0	3	1
Why	13	6	14	18	12	19	25	31	22	31	25	42	27	26	54	80
Will	2	2	0	2	3	0	2	0	2	2	0	0	2	1	1	1
Wonder . .	1	0	0	2	0	1	0	0	0	0	0	0	0	1	0	0
Word . . .	0	1	1	1	2	0	1	0	0	0	0	0	0	0	1	0
Wow	0	2	0	1	1	0	0	0	0	0	0	0	1	0	0	0
Yes	1	1	0	2	0	0	0	0	0	0	0	0	0	0	0	0
You	4	4	2	2	5	2	1	1	5	1	0	1	2	0	0	0
						89.	HOWEVER									
Also	2	1	1	0	5	3	4	3	4	6	9	6	4	7	7	6
Although . .	0	1	1	0	1	4	1	2	0	3	1	5	5	1	7	5
Always . .	1	3	2	1	0	1	3	10	2	5	1	1	2	2	1	1
And	2	0	3	1	1	3	2	1	1	2	1	6	0	4	7	6
Any	1	0	1	0	0	0	0	1	0	0	0	0	0	0	2	0
Anyhow . .	0	2	0	0	1	1	2	1	0	1	0	1	1	1	0	0
Anyway . .	4	2	4	6	6	8	6	7	2	6	5	8	4	2	2	6
As	0	0	0	0	0	0	0	0	0	0	1	0	0	2	1	2
Be	0	0	2	1	1	1	1	0	2	0	0	0	1	1	0	0
Because . .	2	0	1	1	0	1	2	6	2	5	3	3	5	10	11	20
Before . . .	0	0	1	0	0	0	2	0	0	2	0	0	1	0	1	1
Besides . .	0	0	1	0	0	0	0	4	1	2	0	2	3	5	3	3
Big	1	2	0	0	0	0	0	0	0	0	0	0	3	0	0	0
But	9	3	10	6	11	8	22	24	21	28	13	18	19	18	70	95

Response Word	4th M	4th F	5th M	5th F	6th M	6th F	7th M	7th F	8th M	8th F	10th M	10th F	12th M	12th F	College M	College F
								HOWEVER								
Can	4	1	0	1	2	1	0	0	0	1	1	0	1	1	0	0
Can't	0	3	0	2	0	0	0	0	0	0	0	0	0	0	0	0
Come	0	1	0	1	0	3	0	0	0	0	0	1	0	0	1	0
Comma . . .	0	0	0	0	0	0	1	0	1	0	1	1	1	6	4	3
Conjunction .	0	0	0	0	0	0	0	0	0	0	1	0	0	2	2	0
Did	3	2	3	1	0	0	0	0	0	0	0	0	0	0	0	0
Different . .	0	0	0	0	0	0	0	1	3	0	1	1	1	0	1	0
Do	4	4	5	2	5	2	0	0	1	0	1	0	0	0	0	0
Doubt	0	0	0	0	0	0	0	0	0	0	0	0	0	0	0	2
English . . .	0	0	0	0	0	0	1	0	2	0	0	0	0	0	0	1
Even	0	2	0	0	1	1	4	2	0	1	0	1	0	1	0	1
Ever	12	16	18	12	18	15	13	4	9	7	2	4	6	3	5	4
Every	3	3	1	3	2	1	3	1	1	4	1	0	1	0	0	0
Everywhere .	0	0	0	2	0	0	0	0	0	0	0	0	0	1	0	0
Except . . .	0	1	0	0	0	1	1	1	2	0	0	1	2	1	0	1
Exception . .	0	0	0	0	0	0	0	0	0	1	2	0	1	1	0	0
Excuse . . .	0	1	0	0	0	0	0	0	0	0	0	1	1	1	1	3
Fast	0	0	0	1	0	1	0	1	0	0	2	2	1	0	0	0
For	0	0	1	0	2	1	0	2	1	1	0	0	1	0	1	1
Forever . . .	0	1	0	3	2	0	1	2	4	6	2	3	1	2	2	8
Furthermore	0	0	0	0	0	0	3	0	0	0	0	1	1	0	2	1
Going	0	0	0	2	0	0	0	0	0	0	0	0	0	0	0	0
Good	3	5	5	3	1	0	1	0	2	0	1	1	2	0	0	0
He	1	1	4	0	3	2	2	0	2	0	1	1	0	1	2	0
Him	0	0	0	0	2	0	0	0	0	0	0	0	0	0	0	0
How	24	19	23	13	14	12	11	12	9	6	3	2	3	4	4	1
I	0	4	1	1	2	0	1	1	2	0	1	1	4	1	6	2
If	2	2	2	2	0	4	1	1	1	2	1	2	6	3	14	8
Is	4	2	0	0	2	0	0	1	0	0	1	2	2	0	1	4
It	3	3	4	2	5	4	3	0	2	2	0	1	3	1	3	8
Know	0	0	1	1	1	2	0	2	0	0	0	0	0	0	0	0
Long	1	1	0	0	2	2	1	0	0	0	0	0	1	2	1	1
Man	2	0	1	1	0	0	0	1	0	0	1	1	0	0	1	0
Many	1	0	0	3	0	0	0	1	0	0	0	1	0	1	0	0
May	0	1	1	2	0	0	0	2	1	0	0	1	0	2	0	1
Maybe	3	5	6	7	2	2	3	6	7	6	9	7	0	3	4	0
Me	0	0	1	0	3	2	0	1	0	0	0	0	1	1	0	2
Might	0	2	0	1	1	0	0	0	0	0	0	0	0	1	0	0
More	0	0	0	0	0	0	1	2	4	3	1	1	3	0	2	3
Moreover . .	0	0	0	0	0	0	0	0	0	0	5	5	4	2	8	9
Much.	0	0	0	0	0	2	0	1	0	0	0	1	1	0	2	2
Near	0	0	0	0	2	0	0	0	0	0	0	0	0	1	2	0
Never	13	13	8	16	12	18	24	29	30	29	33	27	29	25	71	47
Nevertheless	0	0	0	0	0	0	0	1	0	1	2	1	1	5	8	23
Nice	0	2	2	1	0	1	1	0	1	1	0	1	1	0	1	0
No	3	2	3	1	2	5	2	2	2	3	3	3	2	3	3	7
None	0	0	0	0	0	0	2	0	1	0	1	0	0	0	0	0
Not	2	1	0	2	2	3	2	2	4	0	1	2	1	3	6	6
Not ever . . .	1	0	0	2	0	0	0	0	0	1	0	0	0	0	0	0

Response Word	4th M	F	5th M	F	6th M	F	7th M	F	8th M	F	10th M	F	12th M	F	College M	F

HOWEVER

Response Word	4th M	4th F	5th M	5th F	6th M	6th F	7th M	7th F	8th M	8th F	10th M	10th F	12th M	12th F	College M	College F
Now	12	8	9	15	13	8	8	11	10	13	10	5	3	8	15	16
No where	0	0	0	0	0	0	0	2	0	1	1	1	1	1	1	0
Of course	0	0	0	0	0	0	0	2	1	0	0	0	1	0	0	0
One	0	0	0	2	1	0	1	0	0	0	0	0	0	0	0	0
Only	0	0	2	1	1	1	2	0	2	1	1	1	3	0	4	1
On the other hand	0	0	0	0	0	0	0	0	1	0	0	0	0	0	1	2
Or	1	0	0	0	0	0	0	0	0	1	1	0	0	0	3	0
Pause	0	0	0	0	0	0	0	0	0	0	2	1	0	0	0	1
Person	0	1	0	0	0	2	0	0	0	0	1	0	0	0	0	0
Pig	2	0	0	0	0	0	0	0	0	0	0	0	0	0	0	0
Possible	1	0	0	0	0	0	2	0	0	0	0	0	0	0	0	0
Question	1	0	1	0	2	2	0	0	0	1	0	0	0	1	1	0
Really	0	2	0	0	0	0	0	1	0	0	0	0	0	0	0	1
Reason	0	0	0	0	1	0	0	0	0	0	1	2	0	1	0	0
See	3	3	0	0	2	1	1	1	0	0	0	0	0	1	0	0
She	0	0	0	2	1	1	0	1	0	0	2	2	2	0	2	2
Since	0	0	0	0	0	0	0	0	0	0	0	3	1	0	1	4
Small	1	0	0	0	0	0	0	0	0	0	0	0	0	0	3	0
So	4	5	4	4	1	10	2	5	2	4	2	8	2	4	7	11
So ever	0	2	0	0	0	0	0	0	1	0	0	0	0	1	2	1
Some	1	1	4	0	1	1	2	0	0	0	3	0	0	0	1	1
Something	2	5	4	2	1	0	0	0	0	1	2	1	1	0	0	0
Sometime	0	0	1	1	1	1	0	0	0	2	0	0	0	0	0	0
Sometimes	0	0	1	0	0	2	3	1	2	1	1	2	3	2	2	3
Somewhat	0	0	0	0	0	0	0	0	0	1	0	0	0	0	0	4
Soon	0	0	0	1	2	2	0	1	0	0	1	0	1	2	0	2
Stop	0	0	0	0	0	0	0	0	1	0	2	0	1	0	0	0
Strange	0	0	2	0	0	0	0	0	0	0	0	0	0	0	0	0
Surely	1	0	0	0	0	0	0	0	0	0	0	2	0	0	0	0
Talking	1	0	0	2	1	1	0	0	0	0	0	0	0	0	0	0
Teacher	0	0	0	0	0	1	2	0	0	0	1	2	0	1	1	0
Tell	0	2	1	0	0	2	0	0	0	0	0	0	0	1	0	0
Than	0	0	0	0	3	0	0	0	0	1	0	1	1	0	0	1
That	3	5	3	5	1	1	4	1	1	2	1	3	3	1	0	3
The	1	1	4	0	3	1	0	1	0	0	2	0	0	2	2	2
Then	0	2	2	3	2	2	1	1	4	1	2	4	0	3	7	4
There	0	2	4	1	0	3	2	1	1	1	1	0	0	2	4	1
Therefore	1	0	0	0	2	2	1	5	4	4	4	7	3	15	27	44
They	0	1	2	1	0	2	0	0	2	0	1	1	1	3	0	1
Thing	1	0	2	2	3	1	0	0	0	0	0	0	0	0	0	0
Think	1	1	2	3	0	3	0	0	1	0	0	0	0	0	0	0
This	1	1	1	1	1	0	1	1	0	1	1	1	1	2	6	0
Though	1	1	0	3	5	3	4	4	1	1	2	0	0	1	1	3
Thus	0	0	0	0	0	2	0	0	0	0	0	1	2	0	4	10
True	0	0	0	0	0	0	0	0	0	0	0	0	0	1	0	2
Very	0	3	1	5	1	0	1	0	0	0	0	0	0	0	0	0
Very well	2	0	1	0	0	0	0	0	0	0	0	0	0	0	0	0
Wait	0	0	0	0	2	1	0	0	0	0	0	0	0	0	0	0
Was	0	1	0	0	2	1	0	1	0	0	1	0	0	0	1	0

Response Word	4th M	4th F	5th M	5th F	6th M	6th F	7th M	7th F	8th M	8th F	10th M	10th F	12th M	12th F	College M	College F
							HOWEVER									
Way	0	1	0	0	0	0	2	0	0	1	1	1	0	0	0	0
We	6	3	1	2	1	1	1	2	1	3	1	2	0	1	4	3
Well	1	1	1	2	0	4	3	4	1	2	0	6	1	0	2	0
Went . . .	0	3	1	0	0	0	0	0	0	0	0	0	0	0	0	0
Were . . .	1	0	0	0	1	0	0	0	2	0	0	0	0	0	0	0
What . . .	3	2	5	6	4	1	0	2	2	4	3	5	2	2	7	1
Whatever .	2	1	0	1	1	1	1	1	2	2	3	3	1	1	4	1
When . . .	2	4	4	8	4	11	9	5	12	10	11	9	5	2	6	6
Whenever .	0	2	2	5	3	2	10	10	8	8	11	5	8	11	10	11
Where . . .	2	1	3	4	1	2	1	1	3	1	1	0	2	0	2	3
Wherever .	3	2	1	0	2	0	2	4	2	4	0	0	3	4	4	5
Whether . .	0	0	0	0	0	0	0	0	0	0	0	2	0	1	0	0
Who	0	3	0	0	1	0	0	0	2	1	4	0	2	0	2	0
Whoever . .	1	1	1	2	1	0	3	2	1	0	3	0	2	1	1	2
Why	1	0	3	1	2	0	5	0	3	1	2	2	0	2	9	4
Word . . .	8	3	2	4	1	5	1	3	1	0	2	2	1	1	0	0
Yes	1	3	1	1	1	3	3	0	2	1	1	1	1	1	4	1
Yet	0	0	0	1	0	0	0	0	0	0	0	1	0	0	6	8
You	9	8	9	10	11	3	6	9	6	4	6	4	11	4	9	0
Yours . . .	0	0	0	0	0	0	0	0	0	0	0	0	2	0	1	0
							90. **HUNGRY**									
Ache . . .	0	0	0	0	1	2	2	0	0	0	2	0	1	1	5	1
Always . .	0	0	0	0	0	0	0	0	0	0	0	2	1	0	1	0
Angry . . .	0	2	0	1	0	0	0	0	0	1	0	0	0	0	1	0
Animal . .	0	0	0	0	0	1	0	0	1	0	0	0	2	0	1	1
Appetite . .	0	0	1	0	1	0	0	0	2	2	0	0	2	2	2	1
Apple . . .	0	1	0	0	1	1	0	2	0	0	0	0	0	0	0	1
Ate	3	1	0	1	0	2	1	0	0	0	0	0	1	0	0	0
Bear . . .	2	0	2	0	0	0	1	0	0	0	0	1	0	0	1	1
Boy	1	2	1	1	2	3	1	1	1	0	2	2	1	0	1	1
Bread . . .	2	2	1	1	1	1	1	0	0	0	0	0	1	0	0	0
Child . . .	0	0	0	0	0	0	0	0	0	2	2	0	1	0	0	1
Children . .	0	0	0	0	0	0	0	0	0	2	0	2	0	2	0	2
Chocolate .	0	0	0	0	0	0	0	0	0	0	0	0	0	2	0	0
Cold	0	0	0	0	1	0	0	0	1	0	2	0	0	2	1	1
Country . .	1	1	2	1	3	1	2	1	3	3	6	2	7	4	7	7
Cow	0	0	0	0	0	0	2	0	0	0	0	0	0	0	0	0
Cry	0	0	0	0	0	1	0	0	0	2	0	0	1	0	0	0
Dinner . .	0	0	0	1	1	0	0	0	0	1	1	1	0	0	2	6
Eat	71	76	42	67	48	57	30	38	21	36	39	32	37	36	91	83
Eating . . .	1	3	3	3	3	3	1	2	2	4	0	3	1	2	2	4
Empty . . .	2	1	0	1	0	3	0	1	1	1	1	2	1	0	1	3
Eye	0	0	0	0	0	0	0	0	0	0	0	0	0	0	2	1
Famished .	1	0	0	0	0	0	0	2	2	4	1	0	1	3	0	4
Fat	0	0	1	0	0	1	4	0	0	1	0	1	1	1	2	2
Food	78	63	91	74	99	98	87	94	110	96	101	110	91	113	198	215
Full	4	7	10	12	11	8	15	7	20	9	8	8	7	8	22	16
Girl	0	1	0	0	0	1	0	0	1	0	0	0	2	0	0	0

Response Word	4th		5th		6th		7th		8th		10th		12th		College	
	M	F	M	F	M	F	M	F	M	F	M	F	M	F	M	F

HUNGRY

Response Word	M	F	M	F	M	F	M	F	M	F	M	F	M	F	M	F
Good	2	4	3	4	3	3	2	0	1	0	0	0	0	0	1	0
Growl	0	0	1	0	0	0	0	0	0	0	0	0	0	1	1	3
Hungary	0	0	0	0	0	0	0	0	0	0	0	0	1	0	3	1
Hunger	2	1	0	1	0	1	1	1	1	0	0	1	0	0	2	0
Hurt	0	0	2	2	1	0	2	3	1	1	1	1	1	0	2	0
I	0	0	0	0	0	0	0	0	0	0	0	0	4	0	6	2
Ice cream	0	0	0	0	0	0	0	0	0	0	0	0	0	0	0	2
Lunch	0	2	1	0	2	1	1	3	0	5	2	5	2	3	0	2
Man	0	0	0	0	0	0	0	1	0	0	0	0	2	0	4	1
Me	2	1	1	1	1	2	2	2	1	1	4	2	3	1	2	2
Meat	3	0	2	0	3	0	0	0	1	0	1	0	0	0	0	0
Not	0	0	1	1	2	0	0	0	0	0	0	0	0	0	1	0
Pain	0	0	0	0	1	0	3	1	3	1	3	4	6	5	14	12
Pains	0	0	0	0	1	0	2	0	0	0	1	0	1	0	0	3
Peasants	0	0	0	0	0	0	0	0	0	0	0	0	0	0	0	2
People	1	2	0	0	2	1	1	2	1	1	4	4	3	0	2	3
Person	0	1	1	1	0	0	1	1	0	2	0	0	0	0	0	1
Poor	0	0	2	0	0	1	0	1	1	0	0	0	0	0	0	0
Sandwich	0	1	1	0	1	0	0	1	0	0	0	0	0	0	1	4
Satiated	0	0	0	0	0	0	0	0	0	0	0	0	0	0	0	2
Satisfied	0	0	0	0	0	0	0	0	0	1	0	0	0	0	3	0
Sick	0	0	0	0	1	0	0	1	1	2	0	0	0	0	3	2
Starvation	0	0	0	0	0	0	2	0	0	0	0	0	1	1	0	0
Starve	12	14	13	8	10	11	11	11	4	8	4	3	5	4	4	6
Starved	8	9	12	20	12	17	16	15	12	18	7	17	14	7	10	10
Starving	8	6	6	5	4	7	10	16	10	11	8	5	4	4	2	4
Steak	0	0	0	0	0	0	1	0	0	0	0	0	1	0	1	2
Stomach	4	2	3	2	1	6	8	16	17	13	14	15	12	16	23	25
Stomach ache	0	0	0	0	0	0	2	0	0	1	0	1	0	0	0	0
Table	0	2	0	1	0	0	0	0	0	0	2	0	0	0	2	0
Taste	0	2	1	0	4	0	0	1	0	0	0	0	0	0	2	0
Thirst	0	0	1	0	0	0	0	4	2	1	1	0	1	3	5	2
Thirsty	7	7	8	10	7	7	8	7	3	7	10	5	1	4	16	19
Tired	0	1	1	1	0	0	0	1	0	0	4	1	1	1	6	5
Want	1	0	1	1	1	1	0	0	0	0	0	0	0	0	2	0
Yes	0	0	0	0	2	0	0	0	1	0	1	1	0	1	0	0
Yum	0	0	0	2	0	0	0	0	0	0	0	0	0	0	0	0

91. I

Response Word	M	F	M	F	M	F	M	F	M	F	M	F	M	F	M	F
A	3	3	3	4	3	2	2	1	0	0	0	0	0	0	1	0
Am	20	20	21	7	22	10	9	7	18	13	11	9	17	15	44	33
An	1	1	1	3	0	0	1	0	1	1	0	0	1	0	1	1
Blank	0	0	0	0	0	0	0	0	0	0	0	0	0	0	0	2
Bob	0	0	0	0	0	0	0	0	0	0	0	0	0	0	2	0
Boy	1	1	1	1	0	0	1	0	0	0	1	0	1	0	3	0
Can	3	4	2	5	3	3	3	0	4	0	5	2	6	1	2	2
Desk	2	0	0	0	0	0	0	0	0	0	0	0	0	0	0	0
Did	4	0	1	0	2	0	1	0	0	0	0	2	0	0	0	1
Do	1	0	1	0	0	1	0	0	1	1	2	1	0	0	0	3

Response Word	4th M	4th F	5th M	5th F	6th M	6th F	7th M	7th F	8th M	8th F	10th M	10th F	12th M	12th F	College M	College F
							I									
Don't ...	0	2	0	0	0	0	0	0	0	0	1	0	1	0	0	0
Eye	1	3	0	5	1	4	1	3	1	2	0	1	2	1	0	0
Get	0	0	0	0	2	0	0	0	0	0	0	0	0	0	0	0
Girl	0	0	0	1	0	0	0	0	0	1	0	0	0	3	0	7
Go	2	1	1	0	1	1	0	0	1	0	0	2	3	0	8	1
God	0	0	0	0	0	0	0	0	0	0	1	0	0	0	0	2
Going ...	0	0	0	0	2	0	0	0	0	0	0	0	0	0	0	0
Had	1	1	0	2	0	0	0	0	2	2	0	0	0	0	0	0
Have	1	0	4	1	3	1	0	1	1	0	2	1	1	0	4	1
He	2	0	0	0	0	1	7	6	8	4	6	7	3	8	9	7
Her	0	1	2	2	1	0	0	3	4	1	3	0	3	1	1	0
Him	4	0	1	0	4	3	5	9	6	3	3	5	3	3	1	5
If	7	4	4	2	2	3	4	0	0	0	0	0	0	0	0	0
I'll	1	1	0	0	0	0	2	2	0	0	0	0	0	0	0	0
I'm	3	2	4	2	2	3	2	0	2	1	2	0	1	0	1	0
Is	3	2	4	1	0	1	1	0	1	0	0	0	0	0	0	0
It	6	6	1	6	4	2	7	0	1	1	1	0	1	1	7	1
J	0	0	0	0	0	0	2	0	1	0	0	0	0	0	0	0
Jim	0	0	0	0	0	0	1	0	0	0	0	0	0	0	2	0
Know ...	2	1	1	2	1	1	1	0	1	1	1	0	1	1	0	0
Letter ...	0	1	1	1	3	0	0	1	0	0	0	0	0	0	0	0
Like ...	1	1	4	0	3	1	1	1	0	2	0	1	1	3	0	1
Love	0	1	1	0	1	0	0	1	0	1	0	0	2	2	2	3
Me	89	97	104	114	100	108	108	123	89	107	94	123	105	99	187	196
Mom	0	0	0	0	0	2	0	0	0	0	0	0	0	0	0	0
My	3	1	2	2	2	4	3	2	0	2	0	0	2	0	0	4
Myself ...	5	12	8	17	9	26	8	12	10	3	8	10	10	12	19	19
No	0	2	1	0	0	0	0	0	0	0	0	0	0	1	0	0
Not	1	0	2	0	0	0	1	0	0	0	0	0	0	0	0	0
Now	0	2	0	1	0	0	0	0	0	0	0	0	0	0	0	0
One	0	1	2	1	0	0	0	0	0	0	1	0	0	0	1	0
Person ..	1	5	1	3	2	5	5	0	1	1	3	1	1	2	1	1
Play	2	2	3	0	1	0	0	0	0	0	0	1	0	0	0	0
Pronoun ..	0	0	0	0	0	0	1	0	0	2	0	0	0	1	0	0
Ran	0	1	0	0	0	0	0	1	2	2	1	0	2	0	0	0
Run	0	1	0	0	0	0	1	0	0	0	0	0	0	0	0	2
Said	0	1	0	0	0	2	0	0	0	0	0	0	0	0	0	0
Saw	1	0	0	0	0	1	0	0	2	0	2	1	3	0	0	0
See.....	1	4	1	2	1	1	3	0	2	4	1	1	1	0	1	2
She ...	1	1	0	0	2	1	3	0	0	0	0	0	5	3	4	3
Them ...	1	0	0	1	1	3	1	1	3	1	0	1	2	0	4	0
There ...	2	0	0	0	0	0	0	0	0	0	0	0	0	0	0	0
They ...	0	0	2	1	2	2	3	2	1	2	3	0	1	2	8	3
Think ...	2	2	0	1	0	0	3	2	1	1	0	0	0	1	2	2
To	0	1	2	0	1	0	0	0	0	0	0	0	0	0	0	0
Us	0	1	0	1	2	2	0	0	1	0	1	0	0	0	0	2
Want ...	1	2	1	1	1	0	3	1	0	0	0	2	1	0	3	3
Was	1	4	6	2	13	3	7	2	9	2	10	0	5	1	8	3
We	1	0	0	0	1	1	2	2	1	1	0	1	1	3	16	8

166

Response Word	4th M	F	5th M	F	6th M	F	7th M	F	8th M	F	10th M	F	12th M	F	College M	F
							I									
Well	1	0	1	0	2	1	0	0	0	0	0	0	0	0	0	0
Went	2	1	4	1	1	1	1	2	2	2	3	2	2	1	3	3
Were . . .	0	0	0	2	0	0	0	0	0	0	0	0	0	0	0	0
Will	10	4	2	7	5	4	2	1	6	3	4	4	7	3	7	3
Would . . .	2	1	3	2	1	0	1	0	0	0	2	0	1	0	1	0
You	24	27	19	29	15	32	21	44	46	70	52	52	39	70	118	159
							92. IF										
A	2	1	2	2	1	0	1	0	0	0	0	0	0	0	3	1
Also . . .	1	1	0	1	1	0	0	0	0	0	0	1	2	1	0	1
An	0	0	0	0	0	0	0	0	0	1	1	0	0	0	2	1
And	2	0	0	3	2	1	1	4	1	0	1	3	5	2	13	7
Are	1	0	0	0	1	2	2	0	0	1	2	0	0	0	2	1
As	0	0	0	0	0	1	0	0	0	1	0	1	0	0	2	3
Ask	0	2	0	0	0	0	0	0	0	0	0	1	0	2	0	0
At	3	0	0	0	0	2	0	1	2	3	0	3	0	3	3	2
Because . .	0	0	1	1	1	1	2	3	2	4	2	5	7	6	9	18
Big	0	0	0	0	0	0	0	0	0	0	2	0	4	0	2	0
But	10	19	13	14	9	21	15	14	8	6	5	7	3	6	25	19
By	0	0	0	0	0	0	0	2	0	1	0	0	0	0	0	0
Can	0	3	5	2	0	3	1	4	1	1	4	2	2	5	5	2
Car	0	0	0	0	0	0	0	0	0	0	2	0	1	0	0	1
Come . . .	0	2	0	1	1	1	0	2	1	1	2	0	0	0	5	2
Condition .	0	0	0	0	0	1	0	0	0	0	0	1	0	1	1	5
Could . . .	4	1	5	2	1	1	1	2	1	0	1	0	0	1	0	2
Do	2	1	1	1	1	0	0	1	0	0	0	0	0	0	0	1
Don't . . .	0	0	2	1	2	0	0	0	0	0	0	0	0	0	0	0
Doubt . . .	0	1	0	0	1	0	0	0	0	1	0	0	0	0	2	1
Even	0	0	0	0	0	0	0	0	0	0	1	2	0	0	1	0
Ever	0	0	0	0	0	0	0	0	0	2	2	1	1	1	1	4
Except . .	0	0	1	0	0	0	0	2	0	1	0	1	1	0	0	0
Excuse . .	1	1	0	0	0	2	1	0	0	1	1	0	0	0	0	0
Fit	0	0	0	0	0	0	2	0	0	0	0	0	0	0	0	0
For	0	0	0	0	0	0	0	0	0	0	1	0	0	0	2	2
He	6	6	5	0	6	3	4	4	2	3	9	5	8	5	6	10
Her	0	0	0	0	0	2	0	0	0	0	0	0	0	0	0	0
How	2	1	2	3	2	0	0	0	3	2	0	3	2	0	0	5
However . .	0	0	0	0	0	0	0	0	0	0	0	1	0	0	3	6
I	39	29	35	36	38	30	19	25	15	13	23	16	28	13	34	28
Ifs	0	0	0	0	0	0	0	2	0	0	0	0	0	0	0	0
In	1	2	3	0	2	0	1	1	1	1	1	0	0	1	2	1
In case . .	2	0	0	0	1	0	0	0	0	0	0	0	1	0	0	0
Instead. . .	0	0	0	0	0	0	0	1	0	2	0	0	0	0	0	0
Is	10	11	11	11	0	5	2	13	6	3	1	1	5	5	7	2
It	32	42	37	41	31	28	37	25	27	29	29	25	19	18	52	43
Lift	3	0	2	0	0	0	1	0	0	2	0	0	0	0	0	1
Like	0	3	0	0	0	0	0	0	0	0	0	0	0	0	0	1
May	0	0	1	1	2	0	0	0	0	0	1	0	0	0	2	0

Response Word	4th		5th		6th		7th		8th		10th		12th		College	
	M	F	M	F	M	F	M	F	M	F	M	F	M	F	M	F

IF

Response Word	M	F	M	F	M	F	M	F	M	F	M	F	M	F	M	F
Maybe	3	11	5	18	6	21	13	20	14	27	13	25	19	25	26	34
Me	2	2	2	1	3	1	2	2	0	2	0	0	0	0	0	0
Might	3	2	0	0	0	2	0	0	0	0	0	0	0	0	0	0
My	0	2	0	0	0	0	1	0	0	0	0	0	0	0	0	0
Never	0	0	0	0	0	0	0	0	1	1	0	2	2	3	3	1
No	1	3	3	3	0	1	3	5	4	1	0	1	2	0	1	0
Not	6	5	9	9	12	6	8	9	7	5	7	10	6	14	29	22
Not sure	0	0	0	0	1	2	0	0	0	0	0	0	0	0	0	0
Now	0	1	0	1	1	3	0	0	2	0	0	2	1	0	1	2
Of	2	4	2	5	1	1	6	3	1	4	3	2	0	1	2	4
Off	1	1	0	0	0	2	0	0	1	1	0	0	0	0	0	1
On	0	3	1	3	3	0	0	1	0	0	0	0	0	0	0	1
One	0	0	2	0	0	0	0	0	0	0	0	3	0	1	0	0
Only	2	1	0	0	0	2	0	3	0	1	0	1	4	1	2	3
Or	0	1	0	1	0	3	3	3	5	3	3	3	1	3	4	5
Out	0	0	0	0	0	0	0	0	2	0	0	0	0	0	1	0
Perhaps	0	0	0	0	0	0	0	0	0	0	1	0	0	2	2	4
Possibly	0	0	0	1	0	0	0	0	0	1	1	0	2	0	2	0
Preposition	0	0	0	0	0	0	0	0	0	0	0	0	0	2	2	1
Question	1	6	3	4	1	4	4	1	5	4	3	6	7	14	21	16
Questionable	0	0	0	0	0	0	0	0	0	0	0	0	0	2	0	0
Reason	0	0	1	0	1	0	0	1	0	1	1	3	2	1	2	2
See	0	1	0	0	0	2	0	0	1	0	0	0	0	0	0	0
She	0	1	0	3	0	1	1	2	2	2	4	0	0	3	2	1
Should	1	1	0	0	0	0	1	0	0	0	0	2	0	0	0	2
Since	0	0	0	0	0	0	0	0	0	0	0	0	0	0	2	3
So	1	1	0	2	1	7	4	5	2	5	1	2	3	4	6	23
Some	1	0	3	0	0	0	1	0	0	0	0	0	0	0	0	0
Someone	0	0	0	0	0	0	0	0	0	0	1	2	0	1	0	0
Something	1	2	1	2	2	1	0	0	1	2	1	0	0	0	0	0
Than	0	0	0	0	0	0	0	0	0	1	0	0	0	0	0	2
That	4	3	1	1	4	0	2	1	3	1	4	0	0	2	1	4
The	3	0	3	1	6	2	2	0	1	1	1	0	0	3	1	2
Then	0	0	2	0	0	0	2	2	2	2	2	2	0	2	18	18
There	2	1	2	0	2	2	3	0	0	1	0	0	0	0	0	1
They	10	4	7	11	12	14	20	8	22	8	13	10	22	9	24	16
Want	0	0	0	0	0	2	0	1	1	0	0	0	0	0	0	0
Was	0	0	0	0	1	0	1	2	1	1	0	0	0	2	1	3
We	3	5	2	1	2	2	4	3	5	7	7	3	1	6	9	14
Were	1	1	0	1	0	0	1	1	0	0	0	0	1	0	2	2
What	8	8	11	5	11	12	10	11	16	21	19	15	10	13	22	13
When	2	2	0	2	4	2	6	4	4	8	5	13	4	6	20	23
Where	1	0	0	0	2	0	0	0	0	1	0	2	1	1	0	0
Whether	0	0	0	0	0	0	0	0	0	0	0	0	0	3	1	2
Who	3	0	1	1	3	2	2	0	2	0	1	0	0	0	0	0
Why	0	3	2	5	6	10	8	5	6	6	15	14	11	15	29	25
Word	1	2	5	3	2	1	0	0	0	0	1	0	1	1	1	0
Yes	2	1	0	1	1	1	1	1	0	0	1	0	0	0	1	2
You	27	22	28	17	28	15	18	22	37	28	28	22	29	14	30	29

Response Word	4th M	4th F	5th M	5th F	6th M	6th F	7th M	7th F	8th M	8th F	10th M	10th F	12th M	12th F	College M	College F
								93. IN								
A	7	5	3	2	1	2	4	0	2	2	0	2	1	1	2	1
And	0	0	0	0	2	0	0	0	0	0	0	0	0	0	1	0
At	1	1	2	3	1	4	4	1	1	3	1	2	4	3	6	4
Bed	0	0	1	0	0	0	0	0	1	1	2	0	0	0	3	0
Between . .	0	0	0	0	0	0	0	1	0	1	1	0	1	0	2	1
Box	0	0	0	2	0	3	0	5	0	0	3	3	1	1	2	6
Building . .	0	0	0	0	0	0	0	0	1	0	0	0	0	0	3	1
By	0	0	0	0	0	0	0	2	0	0	0	0	0	0	1	1
Car	0	0	0	1	0	1	3	1	0	4	3	1	3	2	1	7
Chair . . .	1	1	0	0	1	0	3	0	0	1	0	1	0	0	1	2
Come . . .	5	2	0	3	2	0	0	0	0	0	1	0	0	0	0	1
Contain . .	0	0	0	0	0	0	0	0	0	0	0	0	0	0	3	1
Door . . .	3	1	1	0	6	5	2	2	2	1	4	3	1	2	1	2
Doors . . .	1	1	1	2	3	1	1	2	2	2	0	3	1	2	3	1
Down . . .	0	0	0	0	0	0	0	0	1	0	0	1	0	0	2	0
Enclosed .	0	0	0	1	0	0	0	1	1	0	0	0	0	0	1	2
Food	2	0	0	0	0	0	0	0	0	0	0	0	0	0	0	0
Go	0	1	2	1	3	0	4	0	2	0	1	2	0	0	1	0
Good . . .	1	0	2	0	0	0	0	0	0	0	0	0	0	0	0	0
Her	0	0	1	0	0	0	0	0	0	0	1	0	3	1	1	0
Here . . .	2	4	2	1	4	2	2	0	3	3	3	1	2	1	3	7
His	0	0	0	0	1	0	0	1	0	0	0	0	2	0	0	0
Home . . .	2	2	1	4	2	0	0	4	1	1	1	0	0	2	0	0
House . . .	13	28	21	32	13	22	16	18	18	32	25	28	21	21	18	22
Indoors . .	0	2	0	0	0	2	2	2	0	0	0	0	0	0	0	0
Inn	0	1	1	3	2	6	3	1	0	3	1	0	3	0	0	0
Inside . . .	17	8	12	12	12	16	19	17	9	15	11	15	13	12	23	25
Interior . .	0	0	0	0	0	0	0	0	2	0	0	0	0	0	0	0
Into	2	0	2	0	4	2	2	3	2	4	7	2	3	7	7	5
Is	1	4	1	2	2	3	0	1	1	0	0	1	1	0	1	0
It	37	26	28	27	22	17	15	7	10	3	8	7	8	10	15	14
May	0	0	0	2	0	0	0	0	0	0	0	0	0	0	0	0
Me	0	3	0	0	0	0	0	0	0	0	0	0	0	1	0	0
Nice	2	0	0	0	0	2	0	0	0	0	0	0	0	0	0	0
No	1	0	0	0	2	0	0	0	0	0	0	0	0	0	0	0
Not	0	1	0	2	1	0	0	1	0	1	0	0	0	16	0	1
Now	0	0	1	0	0	0	0	0	0	0	2	0	0	1	0	0
Off	0	2	0	0	0	0	0	0	0	2	0	0	0	1	1	0
On	6	9	6	5	5	12	10	16	12	8	10	19	12	13	41	58
Out	52	74	82	73	78	75	89	103	120	104	85	84	100	76	200	185
Outside . .	1	1	1	0	0	1	1	0	1	1	1	1	0	0	2	1
Over	0	2	0	1	0	0	0	0	0	1	0	0	0	0	1	1
Pin	0	0	0	0	1	2	0	0	0	0	0	0	0	0	0	0
Place . . .	3	0	3	4	5	7	2	3	1	4	1	2	2	3	5	1
Preposition	0	0	0	0	0	0	0	0	0	0	1	1	1	1	2	2
Put	0	0	0	0	0	0	0	0	0	0	0	0	0	0	1	3
Room . . .	1	1	0	1	2	1	2	0	0	1	2	1	1	3	4	5
Sat	2	0	0	1	0	0	1	0	0	0	0	0	0	1	0	0
School . . .	1	0	0	0	0	3	2	2	0	1	5	3	0	0	0	2

Response Word	4th M	F	5th M	F	6th M	F	7th M	F	8th M	F	10th M	F	12th M	F	College M	F
							IN									
Side	14	15	8	19	15	12	16	10	7	9	9	16	8	10	33	29
Sit	3	5	0	2	2	1	0	1	1	0	0	1	0	0	1	1
Something	1	0	2	0	1	0	1	0	0	1	0	0	0	1	0	0
Spin	2	0	0	0	0	0	0	0	0	0	0	0	0	0	0	0
Stead	0	1	0	0	0	0	0	0	0	0	0	0	0	0	0	2
That	3	0	1	1	0	1	0	1	0	0	1	2	3	1	5	7
The	13	15	14	16	25	19	15	12	13	9	16	14	16	15	28	26
There	3	6	9	3	9	8	7	7	8	5	12	14	8	15	20	22
Time	1	0	1	0	0	0	1	0	0	0	0	1	0	0	2	2
To	0	1	1	2	1	2	0	0	1	3	3	1	4	3	5	7
Town	0	0	0	0	0	0	0	1	0	1	0	0	0	0	1	2
Tune	0	0	0	0	0	0	0	0	0	0	0	0	0	0	0	2
Under	0	0	0	1	0	0	0	3	1	0	1	0	1	1	0	0
Us	0	0	0	0	0	0	0	1	0	0	0	0	0	2	0	0
Warm	1	0	1	1	1	2	0	0	0	0	0	0	1	0	1	2
Were	0	0	0	0	2	0	0	0	0	0	0	0	0	0	0	0
What	4	1	1	3	1	1	1	0	1	1	4	0	1	0	3	3
Where	1	0	1	0	0	0	0	2	3	2	1	0	1	3	4	1
Which	0	0	0	0	0	0	0	1	0	0	0	1	0	0	2	0
Winter	0	0	0	0	0	0	0	0	0	0	0	2	0	0	0	1
Within	0	0	0	0	0	0	0	0	1	0	0	0	1	0	2	1
Word	1	2	4	0	0	1	1	0	0	0	0	0	0	0	0	0
							94. IS									
A	10	6	9	3	8	0	9	2	4	1	5	2	1	1	4	4
Ain't	0	0	1	0	2	0	2	0	1	3	0	1	2	0	3	0
Always	0	1	3	2	0	1	3	2	0	1	3	0	1	1	4	2
Am	1	1	0	0	0	0	1	2	7	6	2	5	4	1	4	7
An	0	1	1	1	1	2	1	1	1	2	1	0	0	0	1	2
And	2	1	3	1	1	2	1	2	2	0	2	3	3	4	8	5
Ant	0	0	2	0	0	0	0	0	0	0	0	0	0	0	0	0
Are	2	8	4	5	7	5	10	9	11	22	15	9	29	21	46	57
Aren't	1	1	0	0	0	2	0	1	1	1	0	0	0	0	2	0
As	2	0	2	4	0	4	4	1	2	2	1	2	5	1	5	5
At	3	8	9	5	8	15	8	10	12	21	10	17	16	14	37	34
Be	0	1	0	0	1	0	0	1	0	1	1	4	0	3	5	6
Being	0	0	0	0	1	0	0	2	3	0	2	2	2	2	5	4
Boy	0	0	2	0	0	0	0	0	0	0	2	0	1	0	1	1
But	0	0	0	0	1	0	1	0	1	0	1	0	0	1	5	0
By	0	0	0	0	0	1	1	0	0	3	0	2	0	0	0	1
Can	2	2	1	0	0	1	0	0	0	0	1	1	0	0	0	2
Could	0	2	0	0	0	0	0	0	0	0	0	0	1	0	0	0
Dog	0	0	1	0	1	0	0	2	0	0	0	0	0	0	0	0
Doing	0	0	1	0	2	1	0	0	0	0	0	0	0	0	0	0
Esta	0	0	0	0	0	0	0	0	0	0	0	0	0	0	0	2
Exist	0	0	0	0	0	1	1	0	0	0	0	0	0	2	1	0
Exists	0	0	0	0	0	1	0	0	0	1	0	0	1	2	9	2
Fizz	0	0	0	0	0	0	0	2	0	0	0	0	1	0	1	0
For	1	0	0	0	0	0	0	0	1	1	0	1	1	0	2	0

Response Word	4th M	4th F	5th M	5th F	6th M	6th F	7th M	7th F	8th M	8th F	10th M	10th F	12th M	12th F	College M	College F
							IS									
Fun	2	0	0	0	0	1	0	0	0	1	0	1	0	0	1	0
Girl	0	0	0	1	0	0	1	0	0	0	0	0	0	0	2	0
Go	0	0	0	0	2	1	0	0	0	0	0	0	0	0	0	0
Going ...	0	0	1	1	0	3	1	1	1	1	1	2	0	1	2	1
Good	2	1	2	0	1	1	1	0	1	1	4	1	1	0	2	3
Hard ...	0	0	0	2	0	0	0	0	0	0	0	0	0	0	0	0
He	1	3	6	1	11	6	3	2	2	2	3	2	1	1	7	2
Hear	0	2	0	1	0	0	0	0	0	0	0	1	0	0	0	0
Here	2	3	1	3	4	3	3	3	1	5	1	4	1	7	7	8
Him	1	2	0	0	0	1	0	0	0	0	1	1	1	0	0	1
His.....	2	2	1	2	1	1	3	2	1	0	2	3	4	14	4	3
Home ...	0	0	0	0	0	0	0	1	0	1	2	0	0	0	0	0
Hot	1	0	0	1	0	1	1	0	1	1	0	0	1	2	0	0
How	0	1	0	0	0	0	1	1	0	0	0	0	0	0	1	2
I	2	2	5	1	2	1	0	1	1	0	1	0	0	0	0	0
If	1	0	0	1	2	1	2	0	0	3	0	0	2	0	1	2
In	6	3	3	7	3	3	3	2	10	2	3	5	3	2	3	3
Is not ...	2	0	0	0	1	0	0	0	1	0	0	0	0	1	2	0
Isn't	11	14	17	15	11	24	24	43	23	20	22	20	17	16	42	51
It	46	52	49	60	39	48	34	47	27	29	25	28	19	30	43	50
Like	1	1	0	2	0	1	1	0	1	0	2	1	0	0	0	3
Me	2	0	0	2	0	1	0	0	0	1	0	0	1	1	4	0
Mine ...	1	1	0	1	1	2	0	1	1	0	1	3	0	0	2	0
Move ...	0	0	0	0	0	0	0	0	0	0	0	0	0	0	2	0
My	1	2	2	1	3	0	1	0	0	1	0	0	0	0	0	0
Never ...	0	0	0	0	0	0	1	1	0	1	2	2	2	1	0	2
Nice	3	1	2	0	0	2	0	0	0	3	0	0	0	1	3	0
No	0	0	4	2	1	1	0	1	1	0	1	0	0	0	1	0
Not	39	31	22	21	28	18	19	21	31	21	21	14	22	30	47	42
Now	0	3	1	1	5	1	4	4	5	3	3	8	0	5	8	7
Nuts	0	0	0	0	0	0	0	0	0	2	0	0	0	0	0	0
Of	0	0	0	0	0	1	4	2	5	0	1	0	1	0	5	4
On	9	6	6	4	7	3	7	2	5	3	2	4	4	3	5	4
One	1	2	1	3	0	0	1	1	3	2	2	1	1	0	1	0
Only	2	4	3	2	1	2	1	0	0	0	0	2	1	1	1	0
Or	0	1	0	0	1	1	1	0	1	0	1	0	0	1	2	2
Out	0	0	0	0	1	0	1	2	2	0	1	0	2	2	0	1
Over ...	2	0	0	0	0	0	0	0	0	1	0	0	1	0	2	0
Person ..	0	0	1	0	0	0	0	0	1	0	2	1	0	0	0	2
Question ..	0	2	1	1	0	2	1	1	0	0	0	2	1	2	1	1
Quick ...	1	0	3	0	0	0	1	0	1	1	0	1	2	0	1	1
Quickly ..	0	1	1	0	0	1	0	0	0	0	0	0	0	0	3	0
Right ...	0	1	0	3	1	2	1	2	0	0	1	0	1	0	1	2
She	1	2	1	4	2	2	0	2	1	1	1	1	3	0	2	1
Small ...	2	0	0	0	1	0	0	0	0	0	0	0	0	0	0	0
So	2	0	0	0	1	2	1	0	0	0	2	1	1	1	0	3
Some ...	1	0	2	0	0	0	0	0	0	0	0	0	0	0	0	1
Something .	5	4	3	1	1	5	3	4	0	2	5	0	1	0	1	1
That	14	15	11	19	19	8	13	9	12	10	15	13	9	6	24	25

Response Word	4th M	4th F	5th M	5th F	6th M	6th F	7th M	7th F	8th M	8th F	10th M	10th F	12th M	12th F	College M	College F
							IS									
The	4	3	3	2	8	8	6	3	4	3	5	5	4	3	3	9
Then	0	0	1	0	1	0	1	0	1	0	2	0	0	1	1	0
There ...	1	3	6	6	6	6	5	10	11	7	11	7	8	7	10	10
They	2	0	0	0	1	0	0	0	0	0	0	0	0	0	1	0
Thing ...	2	4	4	1	3	0	1	1	0	0	2	1	1	0	0	0
This ...	4	2	4	6	3	6	5	6	4	3	3	3	4	2	2	9
Time....	1	0	0	0	0	0	1	0	0	0	0	1	0	2	0	0
To	1	2	0	2	2	1	2	0	2	2	0	0	3	3	3	5
Too	0	0	0	0	0	0	0	0	0	0	0	0	0	0	0	3
True ...	0	1	1	1	2	1	1	1	2	0	0	0	0	2	0	1
Verb....	0	0	0	0	1	0	1	2	4	6	1	3	3	8	7	4
Very....	1	0	2	0	0	1	0	0	0	0	0	1	0	0	0	1
Was ...	0	2	1	3	5	5	5	6	8	12	10	13	11	11	42	49
Well	0	0	0	0	0	0	0	0	0	0	0	0	0	0	0	3
Were ...	0	0	0	0	0	0	0	0	0	0	0	1	3	0	0	0
What ...	5	1	1	2	1	2	3	3	2	3	8	2	4	5	10	3
Where ...	0	0	1	0	1	0	1	2	0	0	0	2	1	2	2	0
White ...	0	0	0	0	0	0	0	0	0	0	0	0	0	0	0	2
Whiz....	0	0	0	0	0	0	0	0	0	0	0	0	0	0	2	0
Who	0	1	0	0	0	0	0	2	0	0	0	0	0	0	0	0
Will	0	0	0	2	1	2	1	1	1	0	0	3	1	0	1	2
Wise ...	2	0	0	0	0	0	0	0	0	0	0	0	0	0	0	0
Word....	3	2	8	5	3	8	2	0	2	4	3	0	0	1	0	0
Yes	1	3	1	4	2	0	1	0	0	2	0	1	3	1	1	0
You	0	2	0	2	2	0	2	2	3	1	0	1	3	0	0	1
Your ...	1	0	1	0	0	0	0	0	0	0	0	0	2	0	0	0
Yours ...	0	0	0	2	0	1	0	0	1	1	0	0	0	1	0	1
						95.	IT									
A	1	2	1	1	0	0	0	1	2	1	2	1	0	0	1	1
Ain't....	0	0	0	0	0	0	0	0	0	0	0	0	0	0	2	0
An	1	0	3	1	1	1	1	2	0	0	0	0	0	0	0	0
And	1	1	0	0	1	2	1	1	2	0	1	0	1	0	2	0
Animal ..	0	1	1	0	0	0	1	2	1	1	5	2	2	3	1	4
At	2	1	1	3	3	5	5	2	4	4	0	1	2	24	1	17
Baby....	0	0	0	1	0	1	0	2	1	0	0	0	1	2	0	1
Big	0	0	0	0	0	0	0	0	0	1	0	0	1	0	0	2
Book....	0	0	0	0	0	0	0	0	0	0	2	0	0	0	0	0
Box	0	0	0	0	0	0	0	0	0	0	0	0	0	0	0	2
Boy	1	0	0	0	0	1	0	1	0	2	0	1	0	0	0	0
Came ...	0	0	1	0	1	0	1	1	1	1	0	0	0	0	1	2
Can	0	2	2	2	1	3	4	1	3	3	3	0	3	2	3	5
Car	0	0	0	0	0	0	1	0	1	2	1	0	2	0	2
Cat	0	0	0	0	0	1	2	2	0	1	1	4	1	4	1	3
Child ...	0	0	0	0	0	0	0	1	1	0	0	0	0	0	2	0
Could ...	2	0	1	0	1	1	0	0	0	0	1	1	0	0	0	1
Do	2	0	0	2	1	1	0	0	0	0	0	0	0	1	0	0
Dog	0	2	2	1	1	1	0	3	3	5	6	7	3	4	4	8
Fish	0	0	0	0	2	0	0	0	0	0	0	0	1	0	0	0

Response Word	4th		5th		6th		7th		8th		10th		12th		College	
	M	F	M	F	M	F	M	F	M	F	M	F	M	F	M	F

IT

Response Word	M	F	M	F	M	F	M	F	M	F	M	F	M	F	M	F
Fit	0	0	0	0	3	0	0	2	0	0	1	0	0	0	0	1
Fun	2	2	3	0	0	1	1	1	0	0	1	0	0	0	0	0
Get	1	0	2	0	1	0	0	0	1	0	0	0	0	0	0	0
Girl	1	0	0	0	0	0	1	1	2	0	0	0	0	0	0	0
Had	0	1	0	0	1	1	0	0	0	0	1	0	1	0	2	0
Happened	0	1	3	0	1	0	0	0	0	0	0	0	0	0	2	0
Has	3	0	0	3	4	1	1	4	0	0	0	2	1	3	6	0
He	0	0	0	1	1	1	1	3	3	2	7	5	1	2	7	14
Her	0	1	0	1	1	2	1	0	3	1	0	2	1	0	1	2
Him	0	0	2	1	1	1	4	2	3	2	2	0	2	3	1	4
His	1	1	0	0	0	0	0	0	0	0	0	2	0	0	1	0
Hit	1	1	0	0	2	0	0	0	0	0	1	0	0	0	0	0
I	3	2	1	1	1	1	2	0	2	1	2	0	1	0	0	0
If	1	2	3	4	1	3	1	0	0	0	0	0	0	1	3	1
In	23	20	9	16	13	12	5	2	1	2	1	2	1	3	1	2
Insect	0	0	0	0	0	0	0	0	0	0	0	0	0	0	2	0
Is	72	81	88	88	70	71	70	98	63	70	74	80	89	88	179	184
Isn't	0	0	3	1	2	1	2	0	3	1	0	1	2	0	2	1
It	1	0	0	0	2	0	0	0	0	0	0	0	0	0	0	0
Item	0	0	0	1	0	0	0	0	0	0	0	0	1	0	0	2
Its	5	2	3	2	6	3	8	4	6	2	3	2	6	5	1	2
Man	0	0	0	0	0	0	2	0	0	0	0	0	1	0	0	0
Me	1	1	2	2	3	1	0	0	1	0	2	0	0	1	1	2
Monster	0	0	0	0	1	0	2	0	2	3	2	1	2	1	3	1
Neuter	0	0	0	0	0	0	0	1	0	0	2	0	1	2	1	4
Nice	2	1	0	1	0	0	0	0	0	0	0	0	0	0	0	0
Not	2	1	0	2	1	0	1	0	0	0	0	0	1	0	1	0
Nothing	0	0	0	0	0	0	0	0	0	1	0	1	0	0	1	2
Now	0	1	2	0	0	1	1	1	0	0	1	0	1	0	0	1
Object	1	0	0	3	2	1	0	2	0	1	2	1	2	1	7	9
Of	0	0	0	0	0	0	1	0	2	1	0	0	0	0	0	0
On	2	1	1	1	2	2	1	0	0	0	0	0	0	0	0	1
One	0	1	1	3	1	1	2	1	0	3	4	1	1	4	3	3
Person	1	0	0	1	0	1	0	3	1	3	1	3	0	0	1	1
Pronoun	0	0	0	0	0	0	1	1	0	2	0	1	0	1	1	3
Ran	0	2	2	1	2	0	0	0	2	1	0	1	0	2	1	0
Runs	0	0	0	2	0	0	0	1	0	0	0	0	1	0	0	1
Sat	0	2	0	0	0	0	0	0	0	0	0	0	0	0	0	0
Seems	0	0	0	0	0	0	0	0	0	1	0	0	0	1	1	3
She	0	1	0	0	0	1	4	5	2	5	5	4	3	0	9	11
Should	0	0	0	0	0	0	0	1	0	2	0	0	0	0	0	2
Sit	4	2	2	4	1	1	1	3	0	2	0	0	1	0	3	4
Small	0	2	0	0	0	0	0	0	0	0	0	1	0	1	2	1
Something	8	4	2	7	3	5	3	3	9	9	1	7	1	2	2	5
Spit	2	0	0	0	0	0	0	0	1	0	0	0	0	0	0	0
That	15	17	16	10	11	19	24	22	16	16	23	14	21	13	43	40
The	1	3	3	1	4	5	4	2	2	4	1	3	3	4	3	9
Them	0	0	1	0	1	0	1	0	1	3	4	1	4	1	6	5
Then	0	1	0	1	1	1	0	1	0	2	2	1	0	2	2	1

Response Word	4th		5th		6th		7th		8th		10th		12th		College	
	M	F	M	F	M	F	M	F	M	F	M	F	M	F	M	F

IT

Response Word	4th		5th		6th		7th		8th		10th		12th		College	
There . . .	1	2	2	1	1	2	3	0	3	1	1	2	1	1	2	1
They	0	0	0	0	2	1	0	1	2	4	2	5	5	3	17	13
Thing . . .	5	8	13	16	23	21	26	21	27	30	31	30	22	23	39	36
This	2	0	5	0	0	0	1	4	3	2	0	1	0	1	9	4
Unknown . .	0	0	0	0	0	0	0	0	0	0	0	0	2	0	1	0
Was	32	34	25	28	35	33	25	18	35	26	22	26	34	20	68	40
Went	0	0	0	0	2	0	0	0	0	0	0	0	0	0	1	0
What . . .	2	0	2	2	2	0	1	2	3	1	3	3	2	1	4	4
When . . .	1	2	1	0	0	0	0	0	1	0	0	1	0	0	0	0
Will	2	4	2	2	0	2	0	1	2	2	1	1	1	0	2	2
With	0	0	2	0	1	0	0	0	0	0	0	0	0	0	0	0
Word . . .	3	2	5	3	3	1	1	1	0	0	1	1	0	0	1	0
You	0	1	2	0	0	1	1	1	0	2	3	3	2	1	1	1

96. JOY

Response Word	4th		5th		6th		7th		8th		10th		12th		College	
Anger . . .	0	0	0	1	0	0	1	0	0	2	3	0	1	1	1	3
Baby	0	0	0	2	1	1	1	1	0	1	0	1	1	3	1	3
Bad	2	0	2	0	3	1	4	1	1	0	2	0	2	0	0	0
Bells . . .	0	0	0	1	0	0	0	0	0	0	1	0	0	0	2	0
Boy	8	5	1	2	1	3	1	1	2	1	0	0	1	0	0	0
Car	0	0	0	0	0	0	1	0	0	0	0	0	2	0	0	0
Cheer . . .	0	0	0	0	0	0	1	0	0	0	0	0	0	2	1	0
Cheerful . .	0	0	0	0	0	0	0	0	0	0	0	0	0	2	0	0
Child . . .	0	0	0	0	0	1	0	0	0	0	1	0	0	0	3	1
Christmas .	4	7	4	8	5	6	4	5	6	7	4	5	4	4	14	21
Dishes . . .	0	0	0	0	1	0	0	0	1	0	1	0	2	1	2	0
Elation . .	0	0	0	0	0	0	0	0	0	0	0	0	0	0	2	0
Enjoy . . .	1	2	2	0	1	0	1	0	0	0	0	0	0	0	0	0
Fear	0	0	0	0	0	0	2	0	2	3	0	1	3	1	10	1
Food	0	0	0	0	0	0	0	0	0	1	0	0	2	0	0	0
Full	4	2	3	1	2	0	1	0	4	1	0	0	1	0	0	0
Fun	37	15	29	16	34	23	23	13	26	13	37	8	23	8	16	11
Gay . . .	2	2	1	3	1	0	1	2	0	2	1	1	1	1	0	0
Girl	0	4	0	3	1	1	2	1	2	0	5	4	6	1	10	3
Girls	0	0	0	0	0	0	2	0	3	0	0	0	0	0	0	0
Glad	9	8	3	7	10	7	5	4	2	4	5	1	6	3	8	5
Gladness .	0	0	0	0	0	0	0	2	1	3	0	2	1	1	3	4
Good	6	1	4	4	7	1	4	1	0	2	4	6	2	0	3	3
Grief . . .	2	0	0	0	0	0	0	0	2	1	2	2	9	2	8	7
Happiness .	4	4	7	6	6	10	10	25	13	28	18	46	34	38	81	105
Happy . . .	102	143	130	144	112	142	113	120	98	107	85	96	66	90	132	128
Hate	1	0	0	0	0	0	0	0	0	0	0	2	0	1	0	2
Home . . .	1	0	0	0	0	0	0	0	0	0	0	0	0	0	0	2
Hope	0	0	0	1	0	0	0	0	1	0	0	0	1	0	2	0
Jesus . . .	0	0	0	0	0	0	0	0	0	0	0	0	0	0	2	0
Joyful . . .	3	1	1	0	2	2	2	1	0	0	1	0	1	0	0	0
Jump . . .	0	0	0	0	2	0	1	0	0	0	2	0	2	0	3	3
Jumping . .	0	0	0	0	0	0	0	0	0	0	2	0	0	0	0	1
Lady	0	2	0	0	0	0	0	0	0	0	0	0	0	0	0	0

Response Word	4th		5th		6th		7th		8th		10th		12th		College	
	M	F	M	F	M	F	M	F	M	F	M	F	M	F	M	F

JOY

Response Word	4th M	4th F	5th M	5th F	6th M	6th F	7th M	7th F	8th M	8th F	10th M	10th F	12th M	12th F	College M	College F
Laugh	1	5	3	2	1	2	1	4	1	4	1	4	1	0	7	8
Laughing	0	1	0	0	1	0	0	0	0	0	0	0	0	0	1	2
Laughter	0	1	1	0	1	0	2	0	4	0	0	4	1	2	7	5
Life	0	1	0	0	0	0	0	0	0	0	0	0	1	2	2	2
Like	0	2	0	1	1	0	0	0	0	0	0	0	0	0	0	0
Love	1	1	2	3	1	2	1	4	3	2	3	5	3	8	3	12
Mad	1	2	2	0	2	2	0	0	4	0	3	2	2	0	2	0
Marriage	0	0	0	0	0	0	0	0	0	0	0	0	0	2	0	0
Merry	0	0	0	1	0	0	0	0	0	0	0	0	0	2	0	0
Money	0	0	0	0	0	0	1	0	2	0	0	0	0	0	0	0
Music	0	0	0	0	0	1	0	0	0	0	0	0	0	2	3	0
Name	0	1	2	2	0	1	1	0	1	0	0	1	0	0	0	0
Nice	3	1	2	1	0	1	2	0	1	0	0	0	1	1	1	0
Party	0	0	0	0	2	0	0	1	0	0	1	0	0	0	0	0
Peace	1	0	0	0	1	2	0	1	1	1	3	2	1	6	8	7
Play	2	1	2	0	1	0	2	0	0	0	0	0	0	0	0	0
Pleasant	0	0	0	0	0	0	0	0	0	0	0	0	0	0	0	2
Pleasure	0	0	1	0	0	0	0	0	0	0	0	0	0	0	1	2
Ride	0	0	0	0	0	0	1	0	1	1	2	0	2	1	2	1
Sad	9	8	10	14	9	8	17	13	19	17	11	10	10	12	16	12
Sadness	0	0	1	0	0	2	2	4	10	5	10	11	2	8	9	19
Scared	0	0	0	0	2	0	0	0	0	0	0	0	0	0	0	0
Smile	0	0	0	0	0	1	0	1	0	0	1	0	0	1	4	7
Soap	3	1	3	2	0	1	4	1	2	0	2	1	6	1	4	2
Song	1	1	1	2	0	0	0	0	0	1	0	1	1	2	1	1
Sorrow	1	1	0	2	0	2	8	14	12	18	6	12	14	24	72	62
Sweet	0	0	0	0	0	0	0	2	0	0	0	0	0	0	1	1
Tears	0	0	0	0	0	0	0	1	0	0	1	2	1	1	2	1
Thrill	0	0	0	0	0	0	1	0	0	0	0	0	0	0	0	2
To	1	1	0	0	3	1	0	0	0	0	0	0	0	0	0	0
Toy	4	0	1	0	2	1	1	0	0	0	0	0	1	0	0	0
Unhappiness	0	0	0	0	0	0	1	2	1	0	0	1	0	0	0	1
Unhappy	2	2	0	1	1	1	2	7	3	1	0	2	0	0	1	0
Wedding	0	0	0	0	0	0	0	0	0	2	0	0	0	0	0	4
Winning	0	0	0	0	0	0	0	0	0	0	0	0	1	0	2	0
Woman	0	0	0	0	0	0	2	0	0	0	0	0	0	0	1	0
Wonderful	0	1	2	0	2	4	1	1	1	0	1	1	1	3	2	0
World	0	5	2	1	3	4	1	0	1	0	2	0	4	0	2	2
Xmas	0	0	0	0	0	0	0	0	0	0	0	0	0	0	2	1

97. JUMP

Response Word	4th M	4th F	5th M	5th F	6th M	6th F	7th M	7th F	8th M	8th F	10th M	10th F	12th M	12th F	College M	College F
Action	0	0	0	0	0	0	0	0	0	2	0	0	0	0	0	0
Air	1	3	1	2	1	0	0	1	0	1	1	0	0	0	0	0
Basketball	0	0	0	0	0	0	0	1	0	0	2	0	0	0	1	0
Big	0	2	0	0	1	0	0	0	0	0	0	0	0	0	0	0
Bounce	1	0	0	0	0	0	1	0	2	0	0	0	0	1	1	3
Bridge	0	0	0	0	0	0	0	0	0	0	0	0	0	0	0	2
Broad	0	0	0	0	0	0	0	0	0	0	0	0	2	1	1	0
Bump	7	3	4	0	3	0	4	1	2	1	0	0	0	0	0	0

175

Response Word	4th M	4th F	5th M	5th F	6th M	6th F	7th M	7th F	8th M	8th F	10th M	10th F	12th M	12th F	College M	College F
							JUMP									
Candle . . .	0	0	0	0	0	0	0	0	0	0	1	0	0	0	0	2
Children . .	0	0	0	0	0	0	0	0	0	0	0	2	0	1	0	1
Climb . . .	0	0	0	0	2	0	0	1	1	3	0	2	1	1	2	4
Crawl . . .	0	0	0	0	0	0	1	1	3	0	2	0	3	1	4	1
Down . . .	7	1	5	5	13	5	2	2	7	3	3	3	8	5	11	10
Exercise .	0	0	0	0	0	0	0	0	0	0	0	0	0	1	3	0
Fair	0	0	0	0	0	0	0	0	2	0	0	0	0	0	0	0
Fall	2	1	3	0	3	4	4	4	15	4	6	0	8	6	17	4
Far	1	0	2	0	2	1	0	0	0	0	3	0	0	1	4	2
Fast	1	4	5	2	1	3	1	2	1	1	3	3	2	1	5	4
Feet	1	1	1	1	2	0	1	0	0	0	1	0	0	0	0	0
Fence . . .	2	4	1	3	1	3	0	1	1	2	1	0	1	1	1	4
Field day .	0	0	0	0	0	2	0	0	0	0	0	0	0	0	0	0
Fly	2	1	0	0	0	0	1	1	1	1	3	1	1	1	3	0
For joy . .	0	0	0	0	0	0	0	0	0	0	0	0	0	0	2	0
Fun	2	0	0	0	0	1	0	0	1	0	1	0	0	0	0	1
Gate	0	0	0	0	0	0	0	0	0	0	0	0	0	0	0	2
Go	1	1	3	0	0	0	0	0	0	0	0	0	0	0	0	0
Good . . .	0	0	0	0	2	0	0	0	0	0	0	0	0	0	0	0
Height . . .	1	1	3	1	3	1	0	0	0	0	2	0	2	0	0	2
Here	1	0	0	2	2	0	0	0	0	0	0	0	0	0	0	0
Hi	1	1	2	0	2	0	0	0	0	0	0	0	0	0	0	0
High	66	70	76	71	66	67	65	63	55	55	57	55	48	57	82	82
Higher . . .	0	0	0	0	1	0	0	1	0	2	1	4	1	0	3	1
Hill	0	2	0	0	0	0	0	0	1	0	0	0	2	0	1	0
Hop	9	17	5	26	11	26	15	29	5	18	13	23	10	23	20	39
Hope	0	2	0	2	0	0	1	0	1	0	0	0	0	0	0	0
Horse . . .	0	2	0	2	0	0	0	1	0	2	0	1	0	3	2	2
Hump . . .	2	0	1	0	1	0	1	1	0	0	0	0	0	0	1	1
Hurdle . . .	0	1	0	1	0	1	1	1	0	0	0	0	0	0	3	0
Hurdles . .	1	0	0	0	0	0	0	0	0	0	3	0	0	0	0	1
In	2	3	3	2	2	1	2	0	1	0	0	1	1	0	2	0
Into	0	0	0	1	1	0	0	0	0	0	2	1	1	0	0	0
It	1	1	3	1	2	0	1	0	0	0	1	0	0	0	0	0
Jim	0	0	0	2	1	0	0	0	0	0	0	0	0	0	0	1
Joy	0	0	0	0	0	0	0	0	0	0	0	0	0	0	5	1
Jumped . .	3	2	4	2	1	3	4	1	11	0	1	0	4	2	2	2
Jumper . .	0	2	0	2	0	0	0	1	0	0	0	0	1	0	1	0
Jumping . .	2	2	3	4	1	4	2	0	2	1	1	1	0	1	2	1
Kick	0	0	2	0	0	0	0	0	0	1	0	2	0	1	0	3
Land	0	0	0	0	0	1	1	0	0	1	0	0	0	1	2	0
Lay	0	0	0	0	0	0	2	0	1	0	0	0	0	0	0	0
Leap	6	0	5	0	6	6	10	10	3	2	6	7	12	10	21	17
Like	0	3	0	0	0	0	0	0	0	0	0	0	0	0	0	0
Low	1	2	1	2	0	0	0	1	1	2	0	0	0	0	0	0
Lump . . .	1	0	1	0	2	0	0	1	0	0	0	0	0	0	0	0
Me	0	0	0	0	2	0	2	0	0	0	0	0	1	0	0	0
Move . . .	0	0	1	0	2	0	0	1	0	0	1	0	1	0	1	2
My	2	1	1	1	0	0	0	0	0	0	0	0	0	0	0	0

Response Word	4th		5th		6th		7th		8th		10th		12th		College	
	M	F	M	F	M	F	M	F	M	F	M	F	M	F	M	F

JUMP

Response Word	M	F	M	F	M	F	M	F	M	F	M	F	M	F	M	F
Now	0	2	2	0	1	1	0	0	0	1	0	0	1	0	1	0
Off	1	0	0	0	1	0	1	0	1	1	1	0	3	0	2	3
On	0	0	0	2	1	0	0	0	2	0	1	0	1	0	1	1
Out	2	0	0	1	1	1	0	1	0	0	1	0	0	0	3	0
Over	12	18	16	14	15	7	17	11	17	9	14	15	19	10	39	33
Parachute	0	0	0	0	0	0	0	0	0	0	0	0	0	0	2	0
Play	0	0	1	3	0	0	0	0	1	3	1	0	1	0	0	0
Put	2	0	0	0	0	0	0	0	0	0	0	0	0	0	0	0
Quick	0	0	1	1	0	0	2	0	1	0	0	1	0	2	1	4
Quickly	0	0	0	0	0	0	1	1	2	0	0	0	0	0	1	2
Rabbit	0	0	2	1	3	1	1	0	0	1	4	2	1	0	0	0
Ran	0	0	1	1	0	0	1	2	2	3	2	0	0	2	5	0
Rope	4	8	3	7	1	13	3	6	3	9	2	9	4	14	8	18
Run	8	7	8	8	9	17	21	28	21	40	36	34	24	23	55	67
Sit	0	2	1	1	1	2	7	5	15	7	6	4	8	8	13	16
Ski	0	0	0	0	0	1	0	0	0	0	1	0	2	0	0	0
Skip	2	11	2	14	1	13	10	17	9	14	5	11	3	15	18	34
Slow	2	0	3	0	1	0	0	2	0	0	0	0	0	0	1	0
Slowly	0	0	1	0	1	0	0	1	3	0	2	0	1	1	1	1
Spring	0	1	0	0	0	0	0	0	1	1	2	0	2	0	1	0
Stamp	0	0	0	0	0	0	0	0	0	0	0	2	0	0	0	0
Stand	3	1	1	3	1	2	2	4	3	3	2	3	1	3	3	9
Step	2	1	1	0	0	0	1	0	0	0	0	1	1	0	2	0
Stoop	0	0	0	0	0	0	0	2	1	1	1	0	0	0	0	0
Stop	0	0	2	0	1	1	0	0	0	0	0	0	0	1	0	1
The	0	0	1	0	3	0	0	0	1	0	1	0	0	0	1	0
To	1	1	0	1	1	1	1	0	0	1	0	0	0	0	2	0
Track	0	0	0	0	0	0	0	0	2	0	2	1	1	0	0	0
Up	39	32	37	30	36	34	19	18	18	25	22	34	31	36	89	70
Walk	2	5	7	7	3	5	11	7	6	12	5	6	8	3	12	19
You	3	0	1	0	0	0	0	0	0	0	0	0	0	0	0	0

98. JUSTICE

Response Word	M	F	M	F	M	F	M	F	M	F	M	F	M	F	M	F
Apple	3	0	0	0	0	1	0	0	0	1	0	0	0	0	0	0
Bad	1	3	3	0	2	1	1	2	1	2	1	1	1	0	1	0
Badge	3	0	0	0	0	0	0	0	0	0	0	0	0	0	0	0
Blindfold	0	0	0	0	0	0	0	0	0	0	1	0	0	0	0	2
Boy	0	0	1	2	0	0	0	0	0	0	0	0	0	0	0	0
Cold	0	2	3	0	0	1	0	0	0	0	0	0	0	0	0	0
Cop	2	0	1	1	3	0	1	1	4	1	1	1	1	0	2	0
Cops	0	0	0	0	1	0	2	0	3	0	4	1	2	0	0	0
Court	25	27	29	33	20	34	24	17	28	34	27	28	40	24	54	43
Courtroom	0	0	0	0	0	1	1	0	2	0	0	0	0	0	2	1
Courts	0	0	0	0	0	0	0	0	0	2	1	3	3	0	5	2
Cow	2	0	0	0	0	0	0	0	0	0	0	0	0	0	0	0
Crime	0	1	0	0	1	0	4	1	1	2	5	1	1	2	9	2
Democracy	0	0	0	0	0	0	0	0	0	0	0	0	1	1	4	3
Drink	6	3	1	3	1	2	0	1	0	0	1	1	0	0	0	0
Duty	1	1	0	0	0	0	0	0	0	1	0	2	0	1	0	3

Response Word	4th		5th		6th		7th		8th		10th		12th		College	
	M	F	M	F	M	F	M	F	M	F	M	F	M	F	M	F

JUSTICE

Response Word	4th M	4th F	5th M	5th F	6th M	6th F	7th M	7th F	8th M	8th F	10th M	10th F	12th M	12th F	College M	College F
Eat	3	1	1	1	0	0	0	0	0	0	0	0	0	0	0	0
Equal	0	0	0	0	0	0	0	0	0	0	0	0	1	3	0	1
Equality	0	0	0	0	0	0	0	9	1	0	0	0	1	0	5	2
Equity	0	0	0	0	0	0	0	0	0	0	0	0	0	0	2	0
Evil	0	0	0	0	0	0	0	1	0	0	0	1	2	0	0	0
Fair	0	1	0	2	1	2	2	5	1	6	1	6	4	7	7	7
Fairness	0	0	0	0	0	0	0	1	0	1	0	0	0	2	5	3
Food	1	3	1	0	0	0	0	0	0	0	1	0	0	0	0	0
Free	0	0	0	0	1	0	1	1	0	0	0	2	0	1	0	0
Freedom	1	3	1	1	0	0	1	2	2	1	0	1	0	5	3	0
Fuzz	0	0	0	0	0	0	1	0	2	0	0	0	0	0	0	0
God	0	0	0	0	0	1	1	1	1	0	0	0	1	0	1	4
Good	9	8	5	7	4	4	9	16	6	5	8	11	4	9	15	9
Goodness	0	0	0	0	0	0	0	0	0	0	0	0	0	0	0	3
Government	0	0	0	1	0	0	1	1	0	1	1	0	2	1	0	2
Health	0	0	0	0	0	0	0	0	0	0	0	0	0	0	0	2
Help	0	0	0	2	1	0	0	1	0	0	0	0	0	0	0	1
Honesty	0	0	0	0	0	1	0	1	0	0	0	0	0	2	2	1
Honor	0	2	0	0	0	0	1	2	0	1	1	0	1	1	3	1
Ice	3	5	5	2	2	0	0	0	0	0	0	0	0	0	0	0
I'm	2	0	0	0	0	0	0	0	0	0	0	0	0	0	0	0
Injustice	0	0	0	0	0	0	0	2	7	3	3	3	6	5	14	18
Jail	1	1	2	2	5	2	0	1	2	0	2	3	0	0	3	1
Judge	5	13	12	28	10	31	23	29	27	38	31	39	16	26	61	65
Juice	0	2	0	0	0	0	0	0	0	0	0	0	0	0	0	0
Jury	2	1	0	1	0	1	2	5	0	2	4	3	1	3	2	4
Just	5	3	2	1	1	1	4	1	0	0	0	0	1	0	0	0
Lady	0	0	0	0	0	0	0	0	0	0	0	0	0	0	0	2
Law	71	27	74	40	82	54	62	37	49	37	63	35	54	46	132	111
Laws	1	2	1	0	2	3	0	0	1	1	2	1	0	0	0	0
Lawyer	0	0	0	1	0	0	1	0	3	0	2	1	0	2	2	2
Liberty	1	1	0	0	1	0	0	2	3	2	2	3	1	1	3	6
Loyal	0	0	0	0	0	0	0	0	0	2	0	0	0	0	0	1
Man	1	4	6	6	3	2	1	1	0	1	0	1	0	2	8	0
Marriage	1	1	0	0	0	0	0	1	1	4	2	4	0	3	0	3
Married	0	0	1	1	0	2	0	0	0	1	1	0	1	0	0	0
Marry	0	4	1	1	0	0	0	0	0	0	0	0	0	1	0	1
Mercy	0	0	0	0	0	0	0	0	0	0	0	0	0	1	1	4
Nice	3	2	1	0	0	0	1	0	2	0	1	0	1	0	0	0
Obey	0	1	2	2	0	2	0	0	0	0	0	1	0	0	0	1
Of peace	0	0	0	1	0	0	0	0	1	1	0	0	0	3	2	2
Of the peace	0	0	0	0	0	0	0	0	3	1	1	1	2	0	0	2
Orange	0	1	1	0	0	0	1	0	2	1	0	3	0	1	0	0
Order	1	5	2	3	0	2	1	7	1	4	1	2	2	4	1	2
Peace	37	56	38	57	52	60	47	62	35	42	32	61	43	53	63	105
Peach	0	2	0	0	0	0	0	0	0	0	0	0	0	0	0	0
People	0	1	2	1	0	2	0	0	0	0	0	0	0	0	0	0
Pest	0	0	2	1	0	0	0	0	0	0	0	0	0	0	0	0
Piece	0	3	2	2	0	2	1	0	0	0	0	0	0	0	0	0

Response Word	4th M	4th F	5th M	5th F	6th M	6th F	7th M	7th F	8th M	8th F	10th M	10th F	12th M	12th F	College M	College F

JUSTICE

Response Word	4th M	4th F	5th M	5th F	6th M	6th F	7th M	7th F	8th M	8th F	10th M	10th F	12th M	12th F	College M	College F
Police	5	1	7	5	12	5	3	3	11	2	8	1	9	2	11	3
President	0	2	0	1	1	0	0	2	0	0	0	0	0	0	0	0
Right	1	4	3	4	6	5	16	7	6	18	8	8	11	13	15	19
Righteousness	0	0	0	0	0	0	0	0	0	0	0	2	0	0	2	0
Rights	0	1	1	1	0	1	1	0	0	4	1	0	1	2	0	2
Rule	1	0	0	2	0	0	0	0	0	0	0	0	0	0	0	0
Scale	0	0	0	0	0	0	0	0	0	0	0	0	1	0	3	1
Scales	0	0	0	0	0	0	0	0	0	1	0	0	0	0	3	1
Supreme court	0	0	0	0	0	0	0	0	0	0	1	0	0	0	2	0
Table	0	0	0	0	0	2	0	0	0	0	0	0	0	0	0	0
Thing	2	1	0	0	0	0	0	0	0	0	0	0	0	0	0	0
Think	1	2	1	0	0	0	0	0	0	0	0	0	0	0	0	0
Trial	0	2	0	1	2	1	2	2	1	1	1	1	3	1	0	2
Trouble	0	0	0	0	1	2	1	0	4	1	0	1	0	0	0	0
Truth	3	1	3	2	1	1	4	5	3	6	3	1	3	2	1	3
US	0	0	0	0	0	0	0	0	0	0	0	0	1	1	0	2
USA	0	0	0	0	0	0	0	0	0	0	0	0	0	0	1	2
Unfair	0	0	0	0	2	0	0	0	0	0	0	0	0	1	0	0
Unjust	0	0	0	0	0	0	0	2	1	0	2	0	0	0	0	0
Virtue	0	0	0	0	0	0	0	0	0	0	0	0	0	0	0	2
War	0	0	0	0	2	0	0	0	0	0	0	0	0	1	0	2
Water	1	2	1	1	1	0	0	1	0	0	0	0	0	0	0	0
What	2	0	0	0	0	0	0	0	0	0	0	0	0	0	0	0
Wrong	0	0	0	0	0	0	1	0	0	0	2	1	0	0	0	0

99. KING

Response Word	4th M	4th F	5th M	5th F	6th M	6th F	7th M	7th F	8th M	8th F	10th M	10th F	12th M	12th F	College M	College F
Alfred	0	0	0	0	0	0	0	0	0	0	0	0	0	0	0	2
And I	0	0	0	0	0	0	0	0	0	0	0	1	2	0	0	0
Arthur	0	0	0	0	1	1	3	2	0	0	1	0	1	1	0	0
Authority	0	0	0	0	0	0	0	1	0	0	0	0	0	0	3	1
Bad	2	0	0	0	1	0	0	0	0	0	0	1	1	0	0	0
Big	5	2	2	0	1	0	1	1	0	0	2	2	0	1	0	1
Boss	1	1	2	1	1	0	0	1	0	0	0	0	0	0	0	0
Boy	0	0	0	0	2	1	0	0	0	0	0	0	0	0	0	1
Cards	0	0	0	0	0	0	0	0	0	1	0	0	2	0	3	1
Castle	6	3	3	6	6	3	5	5	1	2	1	2	4	0	3	1
Charles	0	0	0	0	0	0	0	0	2	1	1	0	1	1	1	0
Cheese	1	0	0	0	1	0	0	0	1	0	1	0	0	0	2	0
Chess	0	0	0	0	0	0	0	0	1	0	2	0	0	0	2	1
Cole	0	1	0	2	1	0	2	1	2	3	2	0	3	3	3	3
Corn	0	0	0	0	0	0	0	0	2	0	0	0	1	0	0	2
Cotton	0	0	0	0	0	0	0	0	0	2	0	0	0	0	0	0
Country	3	0	0	1	1	1	0	0	0	0	3	1	4	0	4	1
Crown	9	15	7	15	12	6	9	8	3	9	8	10	6	3	19	19
David	0	0	0	1	0	0	0	0	0	0	0	0	0	1	1	2
Dictator	0	0	0	0	0	0	1	0	1	0	1	0	2	0	1	0
Dog	1	0	0	0	0	1	2	0	0	0	0	0	0	0	0	0
Elvis	0	0	0	0	0	0	0	0	0	0	0	2	0	0	0	0
Emperor	1	0	2	0	0	3	3	2	0	0	0	0	1	0	0	0

Response Word	4th M	4th F	5th M	5th F	6th M	6th F	7th M	7th F	8th M	8th F	10th M	10th F	12th M	12th F	College M	College F
							KING									
England	0	0	2	1	0	2	1	1	2	3	4	7	10	2	5	9
Farouk	0	0	0	0	0	0	0	0	2	0	0	0	3	0	2	0
Fish	0	0	0	0	1	0	1	0	0	1	0	0	0	0	2	0
George	0	0	1	0	1	0	0	1	3	1	7	5	2	4	3	8
George third .	0	0	1	0	0	0	0	0	0	0	0	2	0	0	0	0
Go	2	0	0	0	0	0	0	0	0	0	0	0	0	0	0	0
God	0	0	0	0	0	1	0	1	0	0	1	1	0	2	0	1
Gold	1	0	1	2	0	0	0	0	1	0	0	0	0	1	2	0
Good	0	2	3	1	0	0	0	0	0	0	0	0	1	0	0	0
Government ..	0	0	0	0	0	0	0	0	0	0	0	0	0	0	2	0
Great	2	0	0	0	0	0	1	1	0	0	1	1	0	0	0	0
Green	1	1	1	2	0	0	0	0	0	0	0	0	0	0	0	0
Head	2	2	4	0	1	2	3	3	0	0	1	0	0	0	5	1
Henry	0	0	0	0	0	0	1	0	0	0	0	0	0	1	1	4
High	0	0	3	2	1	2	0	1	2	1	1	4	1	4	0	2
Highest	0	0	0	0	4	1	0	0	0	0	0	0	0	0	0	0
History	0	0	0	0	0	0	1	0	0	0	0	1	0	0	0	2
Horse	0	0	0	1	1	0	1	0	0	0	0	2	0	0	0	2
I	0	0	0	0	0	0	0	0	0	0	1	0	0	0	2	0
James	0	0	0	0	0	0	0	0	1	1	1	0	2	0	2	1
Jewels	0	2	1	0	1	1	0	2	1	0	0	0	0	0	0	1
John	0	0	0	0	0	0	1	1	0	0	2	1	0	0	1	1
Kennedy	0	0	0	0	0	0	1	0	0	0	0	0	2	0	0	0
Kingdom	1	0	0	0	4	1	0	1	1	2	0	1	1	1	2	0
Knight	0	0	0	0	0	0	2	0	1	0	0	0	0	0	3	1
Koil	0	0	0	0	0	0	0	0	2	0	0	0	0	0	0	0
Kong	0	0	0	0	2	0	3	1	7	1	2	0	4	2	8	3
Korn	0	0	0	0	0	0	0	0	0	0	0	0	1	2	1	2
Land	0	0	0	0	0	0	1	0	0	0	1	0	2	0	0	0
Leader	6	3	0	2	5	5	0	0	3	1	3	1	1	2	2	1
Lear	0	0	0	0	0	0	0	0	0	0	0	0	0	0	3	2
Lion	1	0	0	1	3	1	2	0	3	0	0	2	4	0	3	0
Lord	0	0	0	0	2	0	0	1	0	0	1	0	0	0	0	0
Louis	0	0	0	0	0	1	0	0	1	0	2	0	0	0	0	0
Macbeth	0	0	0	0	0	0	0	0	2	0	0	0	0	0	0	0
Majestic ...	0	0	0	0	0	0	0	0	2	0	0	0	0	0	0	0
Majesty	1	0	1	2	2	2	0	0	0	1	0	0	0	0	0	2
Man	13	6	21	8	14	11	4	4	6	4	7	6	7	5	7	5
Master	3	0	3	1	0	1	1	2	1	2	2	1	1	0	0	0
Me	1	0	2	0	1	0	2	0	3	0	0	0	2	0	3	0
Men	0	0	0	1	3	0	0	0	0	0	0	0	0	0	1	0
Midas	0	0	0	0	0	0	0	0	0	0	0	0	1	1	0	2
Mighty	0	0	0	0	1	1	0	2	0	0	0	0	1	0	0	0
Monarch ...	0	0	1	0	0	0	2	0	0	0	2	0	2	1	3	2
Money	2	1	1	1	0	0	0	0	1	0	3	1	0	0	0	0
Nice	1	2	1	0	0	1	0	1	0	0	0	0	0	0	0	0
Night	1	0	2	0	0	0	0	0	0	0	1	0	0	0	0	0
Noble	0	0	0	0	0	0	2	1	0	0	1	0	0	0	1	0
Order	0	0	0	2	0	0	0	0	1	0	0	0	0	0	0	0

Response Word	4th M	4th F	5th M	5th F	6th M	6th F	7th M	7th F	8th M	8th F	10th M	10th F	12th M	12th F	College M	College F
							KING									
Palace . . .	5	3	0	4	2	5	3	0	1	1	1	1	2	1	1	0
People . . .	0	0	2	1	1	0	1	0	1	0	0	0	1	0	1	0
Person . .	2	2	7	1	2	3	1	1	2	2	0	0	0	2	1	0
Pin	0	0	0	0	0	0	0	0	0	0	1	0	1	0	4	1
Power . . .	0	0	0	0	3	0	0	0	0	1	4	1	0	2	2	4
President .	2	1	1	1	3	1	2	0	0	0	3	0	3	1	0	0
Prince . . .	6	3	3	3	6	2	4	3	0	1	1	1	1	0	4	0
Princess .	1	1	1	3	1	1	1	0	0	0	0	1	0	0	0	0
Queen . . .	101	152	102	146	96	138	122	153	133	164	122	149	129	155	301	350
Queens . .	0	0	0	0	0	0	0	0	0	0	0	0	0	0	0	2
Reign . . .	0	0	0	0	0	0	0	0	1	0	0	0	0	2	0	0
Rich	1	2	3	6	5	5	1	2	0	1	2	1	2	1	0	1
Ring	3	0	0	1	0	0	0	1	1	0	0	0	0	0	0	0
Robe	0	0	0	0	0	0	1	0	0	0	0	0	0	0	3	1
Royal . . .	2	2	0	2	2	3	3	3	4	4	0	1	1	1	2	2
Royalty . .	0	2	1	1	1	0	2	1	0	0	2	2	0	2	8	3
Rule	2	1	1	3	1	2	2	5	1	1	3	2	0	3	4	3
Ruler . . .	14	10	14	8	25	15	19	18	13	16	14	12	10	8	8	13
Size	1	0	0	0	0	0	0	2	1	0	1	0	1	2	1	2
Solomon . .	0	0	0	0	0	0	0	0	0	0	0	0	0	2	2	0
Teacher . .	0	0	0	0	0	0	2	0	1	1	0	0	0	0	0	0
Throne . .	2	2	5	4	2	3	4	2	4	3	7	4	1	1	8	3
						100. KITTENS										
Animal . .	7	6	8	4	6	6	2	4	1	3	0	0	0	1	0	0
Animals . .	3	11	13	8	10	5	3	3	0	3	1	4	0	3	5	1
Are	3	0	4	4	4	0	3	1	4	0	4	1	7	0	5	0
Babies . . .	4	5	4	4	2	2	1	2	2	2	0	3	2	1	2	1
Baby	3	7	3	7	2	6	0	0	4	0	0	1	0	2	1	1
Bite	0	0	0	0	2	0	0	0	0	0	0	0	0	1	0	0
Cat	100	93	95	106	100	99	102	103	90	101	104	89	100	82	181	169
Cats	42	42	30	38	32	44	51	62	77	62	68	62	71	81	194	179
Cry	0	0	0	0	0	0	1	0	0	0	1	0	1	0	2	0
Cute	1	2	1	5	1	4	4	9	0	6	5	13	3	8	4	7
Dog	6	3	3	3	9	4	2	0	6	4	1	1	3	1	0	2
Dogs	12	10	10	9	8	7	11	8	16	13	11	12	11	9	10	14
Fluffy . . .	0	0	0	1	0	0	0	0	0	0	0	1	2	0	0	2
Food	0	0	2	0	0	0	1	0	1	0	1	0	0	0	0	0
From . . .	0	0	0	0	2	0	0	0	0	0	0	0	0	0	0	0
Fun	0	0	1	0	1	1	1	0	0	0	0	0	0	0	2	0
Fur	2	3	1	1	6	0	2	1	2	2	4	4	1	3	7	8
Furry . . .	0	1	0	0	1	2	0	0	0	0	0	2	0	3	2	5
Fuzzy . . .	0	1	1	0	0	3	0	1	0	1	1	2	0	0	1	0
Is	2	1	0	0	0	1	0	0	1	0	0	0	0	0	0	0
Ish	0	0	0	0	0	0	0	0	0	0	0	0	0	0	0	2
It	0	0	2	0	1	0	0	0	0	0	0	0	0	0	0	0
Kit	3	3	2	1	1	2	3	0	1	0	0	0	0	0	0	0
Kitten . . .	2	2	0	1	3	1	1	0	2	0	1	0	0	0	0	0
Kitty	1	3	1	3	1	1	1	0	0	0	0	0	0	0	0	0

Response Word	4th M	4th F	5th M	5th F	6th M	6th F	7th M	7th F	8th M	8th F	10th M	10th F	12th M	12th F	College M	College F
	M	F	M	F	M	F	M	F	M	F	M	F	M	F	M	F

KITTENS

Response Word	4th M	4th F	5th M	5th F	6th M	6th F	7th M	7th F	8th M	8th F	10th M	10th F	12th M	12th F	College M	College F
Little ...	5	7	1	2	4	3	2	2	2	1	2	3	1	3	4	7
Many ...	0	0	1	0	0	0	0	0	0	0	2	0	0	0	0	0
Meow ...	0	5	1	7	3	5	5	7	1	8	4	8	3	6	12	18
Mew	2	0	0	0	0	0	0	0	0	0	0	0	0	0	0	5
Mice	0	1	2	0	0	2	5	1	2	0	1	2	2	1	13	5
Milk	0	1	2	0	1	0	1	2	1	0	0	2	2	0	0	2
Mittens ..	7	5	14	10	6	6	7	3	8	4	3	4	4	8	9	9
Mom	2	0	0	0	0	0	0	0	0	1	0	0	0	0	0	0
Mother ..	1	1	2	0	4	2	2	1	0	2	0	1	2	1	0	0
Mouse ...	0	0	1	0	0	0	0	0	1	1	1	0	0	0	0	2
Nice	1	1	1	0	0	1	0	1	0	0	0	2	1	0	1	0
Now	0	0	0	0	2	0	0	0	0	0	0	0	0	0	0	0
Pet	1	2	4	1	1	2	0	2	0	1	0	0	0	0	0	1
Pets	0	1	1	1	1	0	0	2	0	2	1	0	2	2	2	1
Play	0	0	0	3	1	0	2	1	1	0	0	1	0	1	0	3
Pretty ...	0	2	1	1	0	0	0	1	0	0	0	0	1	1	0	0
Puppies ..	1	1	2	3	1	5	6	6	4	6	1	5	3	3	4	8
Puppy ...	0	1	0	2	0	0	0	0	0	1	0	0	1	0	1	0
Pups	1	1	1	0	0	0	0	3	1	0	0	0	0	0	0	0
Purr ...	0	0	2	0	0	1	0	0	0	1	0	1	0	2	3	3
Small ...	0	1	1	0	4	0	1	1	2	5	3	1	5	2	6	1
Soft	2	8	3	4	1	6	2	6	1	7	2	14	4	11	14	21
Stove ...	0	0	2	0	0	0	0	0	0	0	0	0	0	0	0	0
String ...	0	0	0	1	0	0	0	0	0	0	2	0	0	0	0	0
Sweet ...	0	0	0	1	0	2	0	0	0	0	0	1	0	0	0	1
Ten	0	1	1	0	2	0	1	0	0	0	0	0	0	0	0	1
Yarn ...	0	0	0	0	0	0	2	0	1	1	1	2	0	1	0	0

101. LAMP

Response Word	4th M	4th F	5th M	5th F	6th M	6th F	7th M	7th F	8th M	8th F	10th M	10th F	12th M	12th F	College M	College F
Am	0	2	0	1	0	0	0	0	0	0	0	0	0	0	0	0
Animal ..	8	3	2	0	4	4	2	3	0	1	1	0	1	0	0	0
Black ...	0	0	0	0	0	0	0	0	0	0	0	0	6	0	1	0
Bright ...	1	1	5	3	2	1	1	6	1	3	4	1	3	4	6	2
Brightness	0	0	0	0	0	0	0	0	0	0	0	0	0	0	1	2
Bulb	4	5	3	3	5	5	11	5	10	6	9	4	8	3	16	8
Burn	2	0	0	1	1	0	0	1	0	0	1	0	1	0	0	0
Cat	0	2	0	0	0	0	0	0	0	0	0	0	0	0	0	0
Chair ...	4	3	1	1	1	3	0	1	1	3	4	2	0	3	0	1
Cord	0	0	3	2	2	0	1	1	7	0	3	1	3	3	7	1
Cow	0	0	0	0	0	0	0	0	2	0	0	0	0	0	0	0
Dark ...	0	1	1	0	1	0	2	1	2	0	0	0	2	1	3	0
Desk	0	0	0	0	0	0	1	0	1	0	0	1	1	1	5	8
Electricity	1	0	0	0	0	0	2	0	4	0	1	0	1	0	1	0
Fire	1	0	0	0	2	0	0	0	0	0	0	0	0	0	1	0
Floor ...	0	0	1	0	1	0	0	1	1	2	1	1	0	0	2	2
Food	0	0	1	1	0	0	2	0	0	1	0	0	0	0	0	0
Fur	0	2	0	1	0	0	0	0	0	1	0	0	0	0	0	0
Furniture .	0	1	0	0	0	0	0	1	0	1	0	4	2	0	0	0
He	2	0	0	0	0	0	0	0	0	0	0	0	0	0	0	0

Response Word	4th M	4th F	5th M	5th F	6th M	6th F	7th M	7th F	8th M	8th F	10th M	10th F	12th M	12th F	College M	College F
						LAMP										
Heat	2	0	1	1	0	0	0	1	0	0	0	0	1	0	0	0
High	0	0	0	0	0	1	0	2	0	0	0	0	0	0	0	0
Hot	3	0	4	1	1	0	0	2	0	0	0	1	1	1	0	0
House . . .	0	0	0	3	1	1	2	0	1	0	1	1	0	1	0	1
Lamb . . .	3	2	1	2	0	1	0	0	1	0	0	0	0	0	0	0
Lame . . .	0	1	3	1	0	0	0	0	0	0	0	0	0	0	0	0
Light . . .	147	172	153	163	163	194	170	168	150	168	174	176	162	197	346	360
Light bulb .	1	0	0	2	0	0	2	4	2	0	1	1	0	2	1	0
Lighter . .	1	0	0	0	0	0	1	1	0	0	1	0	2	0	5	0
Limp	0	0	0	0	1	0	0	0	2	0	0	0	0	0	0	0
Living room	0	0	0	1	0	2	0	1	0	0	0	0	0	0	0	0
Meat	1	1	0	1	0	0	0	3	0	1	0	0	0	0	0	0
Oil	1	3	3	0	1	0	0	0	0	0	1	0	1	1	0	0
Post	1	0	0	1	7	1	3	3	3	3	5	4	8	2	7	3
Pretty . . .	0	0	0	2	0	0	0	0	0	0	0	0	0	0	0	0
Road	0	0	0	0	0	0	0	2	0	0	0	0	0	0	0	0
Room . . .	0	1	0	0	0	1	0	1	0	0	0	0	0	0	2	1
Round . . .	0	0	0	2	0	0	0	0	0	0	0	0	0	0	1	0
See	0	1	0	0	0	0	0	0	0	3	0	0	0	0	1	1
Shade . . .	13	11	17	25	15	20	14	20	20	21	6	23	25	18	52	47
Sheep . . .	8	6	9	3	5	1	4	0	1	3	1	1	1	0	0	0
Socket . . .	0	0	1	0	0	0	0	0	3	0	0	0	0	0	0	0
Soft	0	2	0	1	0	0	0	0	1	2	0	0	0	0	0	1
Study . . .	0	0	0	0	0	0	0	0	0	0	0	0	0	0	3	1
Switch . . .	0	1	0	0	0	0	0	1	2	1	0	0	0	0	0	0
Table . . .	8	13	8	9	8	9	5	7	11	11	16	20	10	9	18	37
Tree	0	1	0	1	0	0	0	0	1	1	0	0	0	2	0	0
Wood . . .	0	0	0	0	0	0	4	0	0	0	0	0	0	1	0	0
Wool	0	2	2	2	3	0	0	0	1	0	2	0	1	0	0	0
Yellow . . .	1	0	1	0	0	0	0	0	0	2	0	0	1	0	1	3
						102. LIFT										
A	0	0	2	0	1	0	1	0	0	0	0	0	1	0	1	0
Air	0	2	1	0	1	1	0	0	0	0	0	0	0	1	0	1
Arm	0	1	1	0	1	0	1	2	0	0	1	0	0	0	1	1
Bed	0	0	0	0	0	0	0	0	0	0	0	2	0	0	0	0
Books . . .	0	0	0	0	0	0	0	0	0	1	0	1	0	2	0	1
Box	1	3	1	0	0	2	0	0	1	0	1	0	0	5	2	4
Boy	0	0	3	0	0	1	0	0	0	0	0	1	0	0	0	0
Bra	0	0	0	0	0	0	0	0	0	0	0	0	0	0	2	0
Car	1	0	1	1	0	1	1	1	0	0	2	0	1	0	0	2
Carry . . .	10	20	12	26	12	25	32	44	25	46	45	60	43	49	78	130
Chair . . .	0	1	1	1	0	0	1	2	0	3	3	0	0	4	5	7
Dead	1	2	1	0	1	1	0	1	1	0	0	0	0	0	0	0
Down . . .	3	7	5	5	1	4	2	4	3	8	2	1	1	3	2	4
Drop	8	3	4	1	5	11	20	12	27	14	9	9	19	9	43	25
Elevator . .	0	0	0	0	0	0	0	0	1	0	1	3	3	0	7	12
Fall	1	0	1	0	2	0	0	1	3	1	0	0	0	1	1	1
Force . . .	0	0	0	0	0	0	0	0	0	0	0	0	0	0	2	0

Response Word	4th M	4th F	5th M	5th F	6th M	6th F	7th M	7th F	8th M	8th F	10th M	10th F	12th M	12th F	College M	College F
							LIFT									
Gift	1	0	2	2	0	2	1	2	0	0	0	1	0	0	1	0
Go	0	2	1	0	1	1	1	0	0	0	1	0	0	0	0	0
Grunt	0	0	0	0	0	0	0	0	0	0	0	0	0	0	2	0
Hand	1	4	2	3	1	2	1	0	0	0	0	0	0	0	0	0
Hard	4	2	5	3	2	4	3	1	3	3	3	0	5	0	5	4
Have	0	2	1	0	0	0	0	0	0	0	0	0	0	0	0	0
Head	0	0	0	1	0	0	0	0	0	0	1	0	1	0	2	0
Heave	0	1	3	1	2	0	2	1	2	1	2	0	0	1	3	3
Heavy	57	52	54	65	59	59	29	41	31	31	36	51	33	45	60	58
Height	0	0	0	1	2	0	0	0	0	1	0	0	2	0	0	1
Help	0	0	0	0	1	0	0	0	1	1	0	1	0	0	2	0
Her	0	0	0	0	1	0	0	0	0	0	2	1	2	0	0	0
Here	0	2	1	0	1	0	0	0	0	1	0	0	0	0	1	0
High	14	17	9	13	11	14	8	6	6	8	8	9	9	12	17	24
Him	0	0	1	0	0	1	1	0	1	0	1	1	2	0	1	0
Hoist	0	0	0	0	0	0	2	0	0	0	0	0	0	0	3	1
Hold	3	12	5	7	2	9	3	11	4	6	7	3	0	5	6	12
Home	1	2	0	0	1	0	0	1	0	0	0	0	0	0	0	0
If	2	4	2	0	0	1	0	0	0	0	0	0	0	1	0	0
In	1	0	0	0	4	0	0	0	1	0	0	0	0	0	0	0
Is	0	0	2	0	0	0	0	0	0	0	0	0	1	0	0	0
It	9	9	6	7	10	8	6	6	9	5	6	5	10	8	20	10
Lay	0	0	0	2	0	0	0	2	3	2	1	0	3	2	0	1
Leave	1	1	1	0	0	4	1	0	3	0	0	1	2	1	0	4
Left	2	2	2	1	2	1	2	1	10	5	0	4	3	2	7	1
Let	1	0	1	1	1	0	0	3	0	1	0	3	2	2	1	1
Let go	0	0	0	0	0	0	0	2	0	0	0	0	0	0	1	0
Lie	2	0	0	0	0	0	0	0	1	0	1	0	0	0	0	0
Life	3	0	4	1	1	1	1	1	1	0	0	0	0	0	2	1
Lifted	0	0	0	0	1	0	5	0	2	3	3	0	0	1	0	1
Light	6	6	2	10	3	8	3	4	4	4	0	1	0	2	1	2
Little	0	4	0	0	1	0	0	1	0	0	0	0	0	0	0	0
Live	6	4	2	9	9	4	1	3	1	3	0	1	1	2	0	1
Load	2	1	3	4	0	3	2	2	3	0	4	3	1	1	13	7
Love	0	1	0	0	0	2	0	0	0	0	2	0	0	0	0	0
Lower	1	0	0	0	1	0	1	3	2	1	1	2	1	2	3	5
Man	0	0	2	0	0	0	0	0	1	0	0	0	0	0	2	0
Me	8	4	5	6	5	2	4	1	2	2	1	3	2	2	4	2
Move	0	1	0	0	0	1	2	0	0	1	0	0	0	0	1	1
Muscle	0	1	0	0	0	1	0	0	2	0	0	0	0	0	0	0
Not	2	1	0	0	0	0	0	0	0	0	0	0	1	0	0	0
Object	0	0	0	0	0	0	0	0	0	0	0	0	0	0	2	2
Off	0	1	0	0	0	0	1	2	1	0	0	0	1	1	2	0
Out	0	0	0	0	1	1	1	0	3	0	3	0	2	0	4	3
Over	0	0	1	0	1	0	3	1	1	0	0	0	0	0	0	1
Package	0	0	0	1	0	1	0	0	0	0	0	2	0	0	1	1
Pick	3	1	1	2	1	3	4	1	0	2	1	2	0	0	1	2
Pick up	5	1	2	2	2	1	1	5	3	5	0	3	4	2	4	3
Place	0	0	0	0	0	0	0	0	0	0	0	1	0	0	1	2

Response Word	4th M	4th F	5th M	5th F	6th M	6th F	7th M	7th F	8th M	8th F	10th M	10th F	12th M	12th F	College M	College F
							LIFT									
Plane . . .	0	0	0	0	0	0	3	0	0	0	0	0	0	0	0	0
Pull	0	0	1	2	4	1	2	4	1	2	4	3	1	5	5	3
Push . . .	0	2	1	0	0	0	0	0	1	2	1	0	0	0	2	2
Put	0	2	1	3	2	1	3	4	2	5	0	4	1	5	0	5
Put down .	0	0	0	0	1	0	1	2	1	0	0	1	0	0	0	1
Raise . . .	0	0	1	0	1	0	0	2	0	1	5	6	4	11	22	23
Ride	0	1	0	1	0	3	0	2	0	0	1	3	1	2	0	0
Right . . .	15	10	14	12	12	5	2	7	1	4	3	0	3	0	1	0
Rise	0	0	0	0	0	0	2	1	0	1	2	2	1	3	3	1
See.	2	0	0	0	0	0	0	0	0	0	0	0	0	0	1	0
Set	1	0	1	1	2	0	4	6	7	10	1	3	8	7	4	10
Shop	0	0	0	0	0	0	0	0	2	0	0	0	0	1	0	0
Sit	1	4	0	1	0	2	0	0	0	2	1	2	0	1	2	0
Something .	0	0	1	0	1	2	0	0	0	1	0	0	0	0	0	0
Stand . . .	0	1	1	1	0	0	0	0	0	0	1	1	0	0	1	2
Steal . . .	0	0	0	0	0	0	0	0	1	0	2	0	0	0	0	0
Strain . . .	0	0	0	0	0	0	0	0	0	0	0	1	2	0	2	1
Strength . .	0	0	0	0	1	0	1	0	1	0	4	0	1	0	1	0
Strong . . .	2	0	0	0	0	0	5	2	1	0	1	1	1	0	1	2
Swift . . .	1	0	0	0	0	0	2	1	0	0	0	0	0	0	0	0
Take	2	2	1	2	0	1	1	4	1	2	3	1	1	0	6	1
That	2	0	1	1	1	1	1	1	2	2	1	2	1	3	3	0
The	2	0	0	0	3	1	4	0	2	0	1	1	0	1	1	3
Them . . .	0	0	2	0	1	0	0	0	0	0	0	0	0	0	0	0
Thing . . .	0	0	0	2	0	1	0	1	0	0	1	0	1	0	0	0
Throw . . .	0	0	0	0	0	1	0	1	1	0	1	0	0	1	3	6
Truck . . .	0	0	0	0	0	0	0	0	1	0	0	0	1	0	3	0
Up	20	22	29	24	28	29	24	18	26	33	20	25	21	23	60	52
Weight . .	1	1	5	3	9	0	9	1	6	3	12	3	12	2	21	10
Weights . .	1	1	0	0	0	0	2	0	2	1	3	0	2	2	2	0
What	1	0	1	0	0	0	0	0	2	0	3	0	0	1	0	1
Work . . .	0	0	0	0	1	0	1	1	1	0	4	0	1	0	8	1
You	2	0	1	1	1	1	0	1	1	1	1	1	1	0	0	0
Your . . .	0	0	0	0	0	0	1	0	2	0	0	0	1	0	1	0
						103.	**LIGHT**									
Air	0	0	0	2	0	0	0	1	1	1	0	0	0	2	0	2
Airy	0	0	0	0	0	0	0	1	0	0	0	1	0	0	2	0
Beam . . .	1	0	0	0	0	0	1	0	1	0	0	0	0	0	2	1
Black . . .	2	0	2	1	1	0	2	1	6	1	1	1	0	2	6	1
Blue	0	1	0	0	0	0	1	0	1	0	1	0	0	0	2	2
Bright . . .	15	30	25	25	28	28	16	17	8	18	15	11	16	10	18	30
Brightness	0	0	0	0	1	0	0	1	0	0	0	1	0	1	1	2
Brown . . .	0	1	0	0	0	1	1	0	1	0	1	0	1	0	2	0
Bulb . . .	3	4	10	5	5	7	4	0	7	2	8	4	10	3	9	5
Candle . .	2	1	1	0	2	1	0	0	0	0	1	0	0	0	3	4
Clear . . .	1	0	3	0	1	0	0	1	1	1	0	1	0	0	0	0
Color . . .	1	1	1	0	1	0	1	1	1	1	1	1	1	0	1	3
Dark	74	76	78	100	71	75	94	108	128	124	110	111	127	126	240	248

Response Word	4th M	4th F	5th M	5th F	6th M	6th F	7th M	7th F	8th M	8th F	10th M	10th F	12th M	12th F	College M	College F
								LIGHT								
Darkness .	0	0	0	0	2	0	0	0	0	2	1	4	1	2	7	7
Day	11	8	10	6	2	18	10	15	10	14	17	18	6	20	18	20
Dim	1	0	0	0	2	1	0	0	0	0	0	0	2	0	0	1
Feather . .	2	0	0	0	0	1	2	2	3	0	6	2	0	0	1	2
Fight. . . .	0	2	1	1	0	0	1	0	0	0	0	0	0	0	0	0
Fire	1	1	1	0	2	1	0	0	0	1	1	0	0	0	2	0
Flash . . .	0	0	0	0	0	0	0	0	1	0	0	0	2	0	2	0
Glare . . .	0	0	0	0	0	0	1	0	0	0	0	0	0	0	2	0
Green . . .	0	0	0	1	0	0	2	0	0	1	0	0	0	1	0	1
Hair	0	0	1	0	0	3	0	0	0	2	0	0	0	1	0	0
Hard . . .	0	0	0	0	0	0	0	1	0	0	1	0	0	1	2	1
Hearted . .	0	0	0	0	0	0	0	1	0	0	0	0	0	0	0	2
Heat	1	0	1	1	0	1	1	1	2	2	1	2	0	0	4	3
Heavy . . .	0	0	0	0	1	0	9	6	4	5	6	6	3	1	14	9
Hot	0	0	2	3	0	0	0	0	1	0	0	0	0	0	1	0
House . . .	1	1	3	1	3	1	1	0	3	1	0	0	1	1	2	4
Knowledge .	0	0	0	0	0	0	0	0	0	0	0	0	0	0	0	2
Lamp . . .	67	65	57	53	62	59	36	29	30	25	22	23	18	24	35	47
Life	0	0	0	0	2	0	0	0	0	0	0	0	0	0	1	0
Light . . .	0	1	0	0	2	1	0	0	0	0	0	0	0	0	0	0
Light bulb .	1	0	0	1	0	0	2	1	1	0	1	0	0	0	0	1
Match . . .	0	0	0	0	1	0	0	0	0	1	1	1	0	1	3	1
Morning . .	0	2	1	0	1	1	0	1	0	0	0	1	0	0	2	1
Night. . . .	13	4	5	2	4	1	1	0	0	0	2	1	2	3	1	2
Ray	1	0	0	0	0	0	0	1	0	0	1	0	0	0	2	0
Rays	0	0	1	0	0	0	0	0	0	0	0	0	0	0	2	1
Read . . .	1	2	1	3	2	1	0	1	0	2	1	2	1	2	3	2
Red	0	0	0	0	0	1	0	0	2	0	1	0	0	0	0	0
Right . . .	1	1	0	0	0	0	1	0	0	0	0	0	0	0	2	0
Room . . .	0	1	0	0	0	2	1	0	0	0	0	0	0	2	1	0
Security . .	0	0	0	0	0	0	0	0	0	0	0	0	0	0	2	0
See	7	8	8	5	9	3	2	7	5	6	3	9	8	5	8	13
Seeing . . .	0	0	0	0	0	0	0	0	0	1	1	2	1	1	2	2
Shade . . .	1	2	1	0	1	1	0	0	2	0	1	0	0	0	3	1
Shadow . .	0	0	0	0	1	0	0	0	0	0	1	0	0	1	2	0
Shine. . . .	1	4	3	1	0	2	0	0	1	1	0	0	0	0	0	3
Sight	0	0	0	0	0	0	0	2	0	0	1	0	3	0	2	1
Sky.	2	1	0	1	0	0	0	0	0	0	1	0	0	2	0	1
Soft	0	0	0	0	1	1	0	1	1	0	2	1	4	3	6	2
Study . . .	0	0	0	0	0	0	0	0	0	0	0	0	0	0	2	0
Sun	8	4	6	15	12	13	19	15	9	9	13	21	13	11	37	28
Sunshine .	0	0	0	0	2	0	0	2	0	0	0	0	0	0	0	1
Switch . . .	1	1	0	0	0	1	0	0	1	2	0	0	1	0	0	0
White . . .	1	5	7	2	2	7	6	7	4	3	4	4	4	4	4	5
Window . .	0	0	0	1	1	1	2	1	2	0	2	3	2	2	0	8
Yellow . . .	1	3	2	4	2	4	5	3	2	3	1	2	2	2	3	8

Response Word	4th		5th		6th		7th		8th		10th		12th		College	
	M	F	M	F	M	F	M	F	M	F	M	F	M	F	M	F

104. LION

Response Word	M	F	M	F	M	F	M	F	M	F	M	F	M	F	M	F
Afraid . . .	1	0	0	1	2	0	0	0	0	0	0	1	0	0	0	0
Africa . . .	0	0	1	1	0	0	1	0	0	2	3	0	4	2	4	2
Anger . . .	0	0	0	0	0	2	0	0	0	0	0	2	0	0	1	0
Angry . . .	0	1	0	0	0	0	1	1	0	5	0	3	1	0	0	2
Animal . . .	59	64	65	53	54	68	57	50	44	47	51	22	23	38	48	70
Animals . .	0	2	2	0	2	1	1	3	0	0	1	0	0	1	0	0
Bad	0	5	2	2	1	1	0	0	2	1	0	0	2	1	0	1
Bear	5	2	2	1	2	2	2	0	2	1	4	3	4	2	5	4
Beast . . .	4	2	6	3	3	10	1	8	2	2	0	1	3	1	13	4
Big	6	4	11	12	10	5	2	4	4	4	10	12	7	4	11	16
Bite	1	1	1	0	2	0	1	1	0	1	0	1	0	0	1	0
Boy	0	2	1	0	2	2	0	0	0	0	2	0	1	0	1	0
Brave . . .	0	0	0	0	0	0	0	0	0	2	1	1	2	0	1	3
Cage	5	4	4	8	7	3	2	2	4	4	5	8	4	8	7	10
Cat	16	7	17	8	25	14	24	9	21	9	26	17	17	14	29	21
Circus . . .	1	4	1	1	2	2	4	0	4	3	2	4	1	2	1	1
Cub	3	3	2	3	2	5	9	4	2	5	13	7	8	6	13	9
Cute . . .	0	0	0	0	0	0	0	1	0	0	0	2	0	0	0	0
Danger . .	0	0	0	0	0	1	0	0	0	0	1	1	0	1	3	2
Dangerous .	0	1	1	0	1	0	0	1	1	0	0	2	3	2	0	2
David . . .	1	0	0	0	1	0	1	2	0	0	0	2	0	0	0	0
Den	0	1	0	1	1	1	2	2	4	5	1	1	8	3	8	14
Dog	2	1	4	1	2	0	0	0	1	1	1	0	2	0	1	2
Duck . . .	0	0	0	0	0	0	0	0	2	0	0	0	0	0	0	0
Eat	2	0	3	5	5	1	4	0	2	5	2	4	5	0	5	1
Fear . . .	1	0	1	0	0	0	0	1	1	1	1	4	0	3	1	2
Ferocious .	2	1	0	2	2	0	1	1	2	4	4	0	0	2	2	1
Fierce . .	4	4	1	6	4	5	1	5	6	7	1	5	3	6	9	10
Fur	0	1	1	1	1	1	1	1	1	1	1	2	0	2	2	4
Furry . . .	0	0	0	0	0	1	0	0	0	0	0	0	0	0	2	1
Growl . . .	2	4	0	5	0	4	3	1	1	7	1	3	0	8	4	8
Gun	0	0	0	0	0	0	0	0	0	0	1	0	2	1	0	0
Hair	0	4	1	3	1	1	0	2	1	0	3	1	0	5	7	3
Hairy . . .	1	0	0	0	1	2	1	1	0	0	1	0	1	0	0	0
Head	0	0	0	0	1	0	0	0	0	0	0	0	0	0	4	2
Heart . . .	0	0	0	0	0	0	0	0	0	0	0	4	1	1	0	2
Hearted . .	0	1	1	1	1	0	1	0	2	0	3	0	3	0	8	5
Hungry . . .	1	0	3	1	0	1	2	3	1	1	0	0	0	0	3	1
Hunt	0	0	0	0	3	0	0	0	1	0	0	0	1	1	2	1
Jungle . .	1	3	2	8	1	2	7	3	2	6	8	8	10	2	10	8
Kill	1	0	0	1	2	1	1	1	4	0	0	0	1	0	0	0
King . . .	4	1	3	2	5	2	10	3	8	6	6	5	8	4	11	9
Lamb . . .	0	0	0	1	0	1	0	0	2	3	0	1	0	1	3	10
Large . . .	0	0	0	0	0	1	0	0	0	1	1	0	1	2	3	0
Leo	0	0	1	0	1	0	0	0	0	1	0	1	3	2	1	1
Leopard . .	0	0	2	0	0	0	0	0	1	1	1	2	0	0	0	1
Lioness . .	0	0	0	2	1	0	2	2	1	1	0	1	1	1	2	4
Loud	7	2	2	4	0	3	1	2	1	4	0	3	1	3	4	3
Mad	2	1	2	2	2	0	0	2	0	4	0	0	0	0	0	0

Response Word	4th M	F	5th M	F	6th M	F	7th M	F	8th M	F	10th M	F	12th M	F	College M	F

LION

Response Word	4th M	F	5th M	F	6th M	F	7th M	F	8th M	F	10th M	F	12th M	F	College M	F
Man	1	0	1	1	2	0	0	0	2	0	0	2	0	0	1	0
Mane	0	0	0	0	1	3	1	3	3	2	3	4	5	3	12	12
Mean	2	6	2	2	2	5	1	5	1	3	2	5	0	6	5	3
Meat	0	0	3	0	1	0	3	0	4	1	0	0	1	0	4	0
Monkey	2	0	0	4	0	0	1	2	0	0	0	0	0	0	0	0
Mouse	6	1	0	1	4	3	2	3	6	2	3	0	2	1	1	5
Mouth	1	0	0	1	2	0	0	0	2	1	2	1	1	0	1	0
Movie	0	0	0	0	0	0	0	0	0	0	0	0	1	0	2	0
Noisy	0	0	0	0	0	0	0	0	0	2	0	0	0	0	0	0
On	0	2	0	0	0	0	0	0	0	0	0	0	0	0	0	0
Power	0	0	0	0	0	0	0	0	0	0	1	0	0	0	0	3
Powerful	0	0	0	0	0	0	2	0	0	0	0	0	0	0	0	0
Proud	0	0	0	0	0	0	0	0	0	0	0	0	0	0	1	2
Roar	9	19	8	13	13	10	11	22	15	11	4	17	12	15	34	65
Rough	0	0	0	0	1	1	1	2	0	0	0	2	0	1	0	0
Run	0	0	2	0	0	1	0	2	0	0	0	1	0	0	0	0
Scare	0	0	0	0	0	0	0	0	0	0	0	0	0	0	2	0
Scared	1	2	0	0	1	1	0	1	0	0	0	2	0	1	0	1
Scary	0	0	0	0	0	2	0	1	0	0	0	0	0	0	0	1
Sheep	0	0	0	0	1	0	0	1	0	0	1	0	0	0	6	2
Strength	0	0	0	0	0	0	0	0	0	0	0	0	0	1	4	1
Strong	1	1	0	0	1	0	4	0	2	1	3	1	2	2	8	11
Tame	0	1	0	0	0	0	1	0	1	0	1	0	4	1	4	1
Tamer	4	1	0	2	2	3	0	2	1	4	5	2	7	2	8	2
Tarzan	0	0	0	0	0	0	2	0	0	1	0	0	0	0	0	0
Teeth	3	4	0	3	1	2	2	5	3	2	3	0	0	1	2	2
Tiger	52	57	56	54	38	45	50	56	57	51	40	52	57	54	118	98
Tigers	2	0	0	0	0	0	0	0	0	0	0	0	0	0	0	0
Tough	0	0	2	0	0	0	0	0	1	0	0	0	0	0	0	0
Trainer	0	0	0	1	0	0	0	1	0	0	0	1	0	0	0	2
Vicious	0	0	1	1	0	1	0	1	0	0	2	0	2	6	0	2
Wild	0	1	1	3	0	3	3	2	0	0	0	1	0	1	2	1
Wolf	0	2	0	0	0	0	0	0	0	0	0	0	0	0	1	0
Yellow	0	0	1	0	0	1	0	3	0	0	1	1	0	2	2	6
Zoo	2	3	4	4	4	7	4	4	1	8	1	10	4	7	10	10

105. LIVE

Response Word	4th M	F	5th M	F	6th M	F	7th M	F	8th M	F	10th M	F	12th M	F	College M	F
Alive	13	14	12	24	10	18	14	9	1	6	4	8	6	6	7	10
Alone	0	0	0	1	0	0	0	0	2	0	0	0	0	1	1	2
Animal	0	0	0	0	0	0	2	0	2	2	1	0	3	1	5	0
At	0	0	1	0	3	0	3	2	3	3	0	1	1	1	1	1
Ate	0	0	0	0	3	0	0	0	0	0	0	0	0	0	0	0
Bait	0	0	3	0	1	1	0	0	3	2	2	4	6	2	7	1
Be	1	1	0	1	1	1	1	1	0	1	1	0	1	0	4	3
Believe	0	0	0	2	0	0	0	0	0	0	0	0	0	0	1	0
Better	0	1	1	0	1	0	1	0	1	0	3	1	3	1	5	1
Breath	1	1	0	1	0	0	1	2	2	3	3	1	4	3	2	1
Breathe	1	0	0	0	0	1	1	2	0	1	1	5	1	0	4	9
By	0	0	0	0	0	0	0	1	0	0	3	3	0	1	3	0

Response Word	4th M	4th F	5th M	5th F	6th M	6th F	7th M	7th F	8th M	8th F	10th M	10th F	12th M	12th F	College M	College F
							LIVE									
City	0	0	0	1	0	0	1	0	0	0	0	0	0	2	1	0
Dead . . .	22	19	17	13	19	18	25	21	41	19	24	12	21	13	35	25
Death . . .	0	0	2	0	0	0	2	4	3	0	0	1	3	1	4	1
Did	0	2	0	0	1	0	1	0	0	0	1	0	1	0	0	0
Die	22	28	33	28	17	39	55	54	70	71	54	56	68	60	163	169
Died	4	0	6	1	6	2	3	3	10	4	1	0	1	1	0	0
Dog	0	0	0	1	2	1	1	0	0	0	0	0	0	0	5	0
Dwell . . .	0	0	0	0	1	0	0	0	0	0	1	2	0	2	1	1
Earth . . .	0	1	0	1	0	1	2	0	1	0	0	0	0	0	0	0
Eat	1	0	0	0	2	1	1	2	0	0	1	0	0	0	7	3
Egg	2	0	0	0	0	0	0	0	0	0	0	0	0	0	0	0
Enjoy . . .	0	0	0	0	0	0	0	0	0	0	0	0	0	0	0	2
Exist . . .	0	0	0	0	1	1	0	0	1	0	1	1	1	3	5	15
Fast . . .	0	0	0	0	0	0	0	0	0	0	1	0	0	0	3	1
Fish	0	1	2	0	2	0	0	0	1	1	1	1	3	3	2	3
For	0	0	0	0	1	0	0	1	0	0	0	0	0	1	4	0
Forever . .	1	0	0	0	0	0	1	2	0	0	0	1	0	1	0	1
Fun	0	0	1	0	0	0	0	1	2	0	2	2	3	7	3	3
Give	2	0	1	0	0	0	0	0	1	0	0	1	0	0	0	2
Good . . .	2	3	2	1	0	0	0	1	0	0	1	1	1	2	2	2
Happy . . .	0	0	1	2	0	2	0	1	0	3	0	4	1	3	0	2
Hear	0	3	1	0	0	1	0	0	0	0	0	0	0	0	0	0
Here . . .	7	8	4	8	7	1	1	4	2	4	5	4	4	4	1	8
Home . . .	18	20	13	15	6	9	5	13	3	8	6	5	7	7	5	9
House . . .	29	47	23	46	38	45	10	33	12	28	18	31	9	19	16	45
Human . .	2	1	1	0	0	1	0	0	0	1	0	0	0	1	0	1
I	1	2	0	1	1	0	0	0	0	0	0	0	0	0	0	0
In	6	4	5	3	6	4	5	0	2	1	2	1	1	3	3	5
Is	0	1	0	2	0	0	0	0	0	0	0	0	0	1	0	1
It	2	0	1	0	0	0	0	1	0	0	1	0	0	0	1	1
Learn . . .	0	0	0	0	0	0	0	2	0	0	0	0	1	2	1	1
Leave . . .	1	0	2	0	0	0	0	1	0	0	0	0	0	0	0	0
Let	0	0	0	0	0	0	0	1	0	0	0	0	0	0	4	4
Life	27	26	33	44	48	45	42	42	33	43	44	38	42	38	72	62
Like	4	6	2	0	1	2	3	2	1	0	0	0	4	1	2	3
Live	0	0	0	0	6	2	0	0	0	0	0	0	0	0	0	0
Lived . . .	4	0	1	1	2	0	6	1	1	1	4	0	3	2	2	0
Lively . . .	0	0	0	0	0	0	1	0	0	1	1	0	1	0	1	3
Lives . . .	1	1	0	0	1	1	1	0	4	1	0	1	0	0	1	2
Living . . .	8	5	5	4	3	4	5	4	1	2	3	1	1	1	1	1
Long	0	3	0	3	5	1	0	3	3	2	3	3	5	8	13	10
Longer . .	0	0	0	0	1	0	0	0	1	0	0	0	1	2	3	3
Look	0	0	0	0	0	0	2	0	1	0	0	1	0	0	0	0
Love	2	3	3	7	2	2	2	3	1	4	1	9	4	5	23	22
Man	1	0	2	0	1	0	1	0	0	0	0	0	0	0	0	0
Me	3	0	3	0	2	0	1	1	4	1	0	2	0	1	0	1
Near	4	1	0	0	0	0	1	0	0	0	1	0	1	2	0	2
Next door .	0	0	0	0	0	0	0	0	0	0	0	0	0	0	0	2
Nice	3	0	1	0	1	1	0	0	1	2	0	1	0	0	1	0

Response Word	4th M	4th F	5th M	5th F	6th M	6th F	7th M	7th F	8th M	8th F	10th M	10th F	12th M	12th F	College M	College F
							LIVE									
Now	1	2	0	0	1	1	0	0	2	2	3	1	0	2	4	2
On	1	2	0	0	1	0	2	0	1	1	1	1	3	0	4	4
Out	0	0	0	2	0	0	0	0	0	0	0	0	0	2	0	0
People . .	8	5	6	1	0	6	4	2	5	2	8	9	2	1	3	0
Person. . .	1	1	2	0	0	0	1	1	0	2	2	0	0	1	0	0
Place . . .	0	0	3	0	2	0	0	0	0	0	0	1	0	0	0	1
Reside . .	0	0	0	0	0	0	0	0	0	0	0	0	0	0	0	5
Right . . .	0	0	0	1	3	0	0	0	1	0	0	0	0	0	0	0
See	0	0	1	0	0	0	0	1	0	0	0	0	1	0	0	2
Street . . .	0	0	0	1	0	2	0	1	1	1	0	1	0	0	0	0
Survive . .	2	0	0	0	0	0	0	0	0	0	0	0	0	1	1	0
There . . .	1	2	4	2	2	1	2	1	1	1	1	1	1	1	0	0
Today . . .	0	0	1	1	0	0	0	0	1	0	1	0	0	2	1	0
Together .	1	0	0	1	2	3	3	1	3	0	3	2	3	1	10	4
Well . . .	0	0	0	0	0	0	0	0	1	0	0	0	0	0	1	2
What . . .	0	0	1	0	2	1	0	0	0	0	0	1	0	0	0	0
Where . . .	1	1	0	2	1	2	3	0	1	1	0	2	3	3	4	1
Wire	0	0	0	0	2	0	1	0	0	0	0	0	0	0	1	0
Work . . .	0	0	0	1	0	0	0	0	0	0	1	1	0	0	2	2
You	2	1	0	0	0	0	1	0	0	0	0	0	0	0	0	0
						106.	LONG									
Ago	5	2	5	1	1	5	0	0	1	0	1	0	0	2	1	0
Arm	0	0	0	0	0	0	0	0	1	1	1	1	0	0	2	1
Away . . .	2	0	0	0	1	1	1	0	0	0	1	0	0	0	1	0
Big	11	1	8	7	8	4	3	3	3	5	3	1	1	1	4	1
Block . . .	0	0	0	0	2	0	0	0	0	1	2	0	1	2	0	0
Board . . .	0	1	1	0	1	0	1	2	0	0	1	1	1	1	0	0
Boat	0	0	0	0	0	1	0	0	0	0	0	0	0	1	2	1
Book . . .	0	0	0	0	0	0	0	0	0	0	0	0	0	2	0	0
Broad . . .	0	0	0	0	0	2	0	1	0	0	0	0	0	1	0	0
Day	1	0	1	0	0	0	0	0	0	1	1	0	0	1	2	3
Desire . .	0	0	0	0	0	0	0	0	0	0	0	0	0	1	0	3
Distance .	2	1	2	2	2	1	3	1	1	0	3	0	3	2	6	5
Distant . .	0	1	0	0	0	0	2	0	0	1	1	0	0	0	1	0
Dog	0	0	2	0	1	0	2	0	1	1	0	1	0	0	1	0
Endless . .	0	0	0	0	0	0	2	1	0	1	0	0	1	0	0	1
Far	16	12	15	2	20	10	13	4	8	4	10	10	7	2	11	4
Fast	1	2	1	2	0	0	1	0	2	0	0	0	0	0	1	1
Fat	0	0	0	0	0	0	0	0	2	0	0	0	0	0	1	0
Feet	0	2	2	0	1	0	0	0	2	0	0	1	0	0	0	0
Fellow . . .	0	0	1	0	2	0	1	0	1	0	0	0	0	0	0	0
Foot	1	1	0	1	0	1	1	0	0	0	2	0	1	0	0	0
Forever . .	0	0	0	0	0	0	0	0	0	1	0	2	0	0	1	0
Gone	1	0	1	2	0	0	0	0	0	0	0	0	2	0	1	0
Great . . .	0	0	0	0	0	0	0	0	0	0	0	0	2	0	0	0
Hair	0	2	0	2	1	1	0	3	2	8	1	2	3	4	4	3
Hard . . .	0	0	3	0	0	0	2	2	0	0	0	0	0	1	3	1
High	1	3	3	1	1	2	2	2	2	1	0	1	0	0	0	0

Response Word	4th M	4th F	5th M	5th F	6th M	6th F	7th M	7th F	8th M	8th F	10th M	10th F	12th M	12th F	College M	College F
							LONG									
Hour	0	1	0	2	0	0	0	0	0	0	0	0	0	0	0	0
Island	0	0	0	0	0	1	0	1	0	1	4	2	1	0	1	0
John	1	0	0	0	1	0	0	0	0	1	0	0	0	0	3	0
Lake	0	0	0	0	3	1	0	0	1	0	0	1	2	0	1	0
Large	0	0	0	0	1	0	2	0	0	0	0	1	0	1	0	0
Leg	0	0	0	2	0	1	0	1	1	0	0	0	0	0	1	0
Legs	2	2	1	0	1	0	1	2	0	2	3	2	2	0	1	0
Length	1	1	2	2	4	11	1	7	3	2	5	0	2	0	5	4
Lengthy	0	0	0	0	0	0	1	2	1	0	2	0	0	0	1	0
Life	0	0	0	0	1	1	0	0	0	0	0	1	1	1	0	2
Line	0	2	1	1	0	1	1	4	1	1	0	1	0	1	2	11
Little	0	2	0	2	2	0	0	1	1	2	1	0	0	0	0	0
Lone	2	0	0	0	0	0	0	0	0	0	0	0	0	0	0	0
Low	0	0	0	0	0	1	0	0	1	2	3	4	0	0	0	0
Man	0	0	0	1	0	0	0	0	0	0	0	0	0	0	2	1
Mile	3	8	3	2	5	2	3	2	5	4	4	1	3	4	0	2
Miles	2	0	2	1	0	0	1	0	1	0	0	0	0	0	0	1
Narrow	1	3	2	5	5	3	2	3	1	8	8	5	5	6	4	11
Nose	0	0	0	0	0	0	1	0	1	1	0	0	0	0	2	0
On	0	2	0	0	0	0	0	0	0	0	0	0	0	0	0	0
Pencil	0	0	2	0	1	1	0	2	1	0	0	1	1	0	3	1
Pole	1	0	1	0	1	0	3	2	1	1	1	0	4	0	2	0
Range	1	0	0	0	0	0	0	0	0	0	2	0	5	0	0	0
Reach	0	0	0	0	0	1	0	0	0	0	0	0	0	0	2	0
Ribbon	0	1	1	2	0	0	0	0	0	0	0	0	0	0	0	1
Rifle	0	0	0	0	0	0	0	0	0	0	0	0	0	0	3	1
River	0	0	0	0	0	1	2	5	1	1	3	4	6	3	5	4
Road	2	3	2	4	3	0	4	6	4	7	6	9	6	8	14	10
Rope	2	1	1	1	1	4	3	1	1	1	3	0	0	1	1	2
Ruler	1	1	1	1	0	3	0	0	0	0	0	1	0	1	6	2
School	0	0	0	0	0	0	2	0	1	1	0	0	1	0	0	0
See	0	0	0	0	2	0	0	0	0	0	0	0	0	0	0	0
Short	114	99	106	129	103	111	130	131	156	145	129	138	143	162	308	326
Shot	3	5	4	0	1	1	0	2	1	0	0	0	1	0	0	0
Shout	0	0	0	0	0	2	0	1	0	0	0	0	0	0	0	0
Skinny	1	4	0	1	3	0	2	3	0	3	1	4	0	0	1	0
Slender	0	0	0	0	0	0	0	0	0	0	1	2	0	0	1	0
Slim	0	1	0	0	0	1	1	1	1	0	0	2	1	0	1	1
Slow	1	3	0	1	3	1	0	1	0	0	0	0	0	0	0	2
Small	3	4	3	3	3	1	0	1	1	0	0	0	0	0	0	0
Snake	0	0	3	1	0	1	1	0	1	2	1	2	0	0	0	1
Sort	4	4	6	1	2	0	0	1	0	0	0	0	0	0	0	0
Spaghetti	0	0	0	0	0	0	0	0	0	1	0	0	1	1	0	2
Stem	3	0	0	0	0	0	0	0	0	0	1	0	0	1	2	1
Stick	0	1	0	1	3	1	0	1	0	0	2	1	1	0	3	2
Stockings	0	0	0	0	1	0	0	0	0	0	0	2	0	0	0	0
Store	0	2	0	1	0	0	0	0	0	0	0	0	0	0	0	0
Story	0	3	0	0	0	0	1	1	1	0	0	0	1	1	0	2
Straight	1	6	2	1	3	3	1	0	1	0	1	2	0	0	1	0

Response Word	4th M	4th F	5th M	5th F	6th M	6th F	7th M	7th F	8th M	8th F	10th M	10th F	12th M	12th F	College M	College F

LONG

Response Word	4th M	4th F	5th M	5th F	6th M	6th F	7th M	7th F	8th M	8th F	10th M	10th F	12th M	12th F	College M	College F
Street	0	0	0	1	1	0	0	0	1	1	1	1	2	1	0	0
Stretch . . .	6	2	5	2	4	5	2	0	0	0	1	2	0	1	0	1
String	1	2	0	1	3	5	1	3	1	1	3	1	2	1	2	7
Swift	0	0	2	0	0	1	0	0	0	0	0	0	0	0	0	0
Table	0	0	0	1	0	0	3	0	1	1	1	0	0	0	0	0
Tall	11	16	6	11	7	6	5	6	3	2	7	7	3	6	11	8
Thin	2	1	4	3	2	2	1	4	1	4	4	5	0	0	5	10
Thread . . .	0	0	0	1	0	0	0	0	0	0	0	0	1	0	1	3
Time.	6	3	7	5	4	6	2	1	1	2	1	0	3	3	3	7
Tired	0	0	0	0	0	0	0	0	1	0	0	1	0	0	2	1
Tiresome . .	0	0	0	0	0	1	0	2	0	1	0	0	0	1	0	0
Train	0	0	1	0	0	0	0	0	0	0	0	2	0	1	0	1
Tree	0	0	1	0	2	1	0	0	0	0	0	0	0	0	0	0
Trip	1	0	1	0	0	0	0	0	0	0	1	0	0	2	2	2
Wait	1	2	1	0	1	2	0	0	0	0	0	0	0	1	2	0
Walk	0	1	1	1	0	2	0	1	0	0	1	2	1	2	1	1
Want	0	0	0	0	0	0	0	0	0	0	0	0	1	0	2	1
Way	2	2	1	0	0	0	0	1	0	0	0	0	0	2	0	0
Wide	2	6	3	3	0	9	3	5	2	1	1	2	4	2	2	4
Width	0	0	0	0	0	0	2	0	0	1	0	0	0	0	0	0
Worm	0	0	0	0	0	0	0	0	0	0	1	3	0	0	0	2
Yardstick . .	0	0	0	0	0	0	0	0	0	2	1	0	0	0	1	0

107. LOUD

Response Word	4th M	4th F	5th M	5th F	6th M	6th F	7th M	7th F	8th M	8th F	10th M	10th F	12th M	12th F	College M	College F
Annoying. . .	0	0	0	0	0	0	0	0	0	0	0	0	0	1	3	0
Bang	0	0	0	0	1	1	2	2	1	0	1	3	2	1	9	6
Bell	0	0	0	0	0	0	0	0	0	0	0	0	0	0	1	3
Big	3	3	1	2	1	0	0	0	0	0	2	2	1	0	1	0
Blast	0	0	0	0	0	1	2	0	0	0	0	0	1	1	0	1
Boisterous .	0	0	0	0	0	0	0	0	0	1	1	0	1	2	2	2
Boom	0	0	1	1	0	0	0	0	0	0	0	0	0	0	0	2
Boy	0	0	0	1	1	2	0	0	0	0	0	0	1	0	2	0
Boys	0	0	0	0	1	0	0	1	0	1	0	1	0	2	0	0
Brother . . .	0	0	0	0	2	0	2	0	1	0	0	0	0	0	0	0
Call	2	1	3	0	0	0	0	0	0	0	0	0	0	0	0	0
Clap	0	0	0	0	0	0	0	0	0	0	0	0	0	0	0	2
Clear	2	2	4	3	3	4	2	0	1	2	2	2	3	6	5	5
Crash	0	2	0	0	0	0	0	0	0	2	0	0	0	2	0	2
Crowd	0	0	1	0	0	0	0	0	0	0	0	1	1	0	2	1
Cry	0	0	0	1	1	1	0	1	0	0	0	1	1	0	0	2
Deaf	0	0	0	0	1	0	0	0	0	0	0	0	0	0	3	1
Drum	1	0	0	2	0	1	1	0	0	0	0	0	1	1	0	1
Ear	1	1	4	3	2	0	3	1	1	0	5	2	1	1	5	4
Ears	0	0	0	0	0	1	1	4	3	0	3	2	1	1	0	1
Firecrackers .	0	0	0	0	0	0	0	0	0	2	0	0	0	0	0	0
Girls	0	0	0	0	0	0	0	0	1	1	0	2	0	0	0	0
God	0	1	3	1	5	1	0	1	0	0	0	0	0	0	0	0
Good	0	0	2	0	0	0	0	0	0	1	0	0	0	0	0	0

Response Word	4th		5th		6th		7th		8th		10th		12th		College	
	M	F	M	F	M	F	M	F	M	F	M	F	M	F	M	F

LOUD

Response Word	M	F	M	F	M	F	M	F	M	F	M	F	M	F	M	F
Hammer . .	1	0	1	1	0	3	0	1	1	0	0	0	0	0	0	0
Hard	5	2	1	2	1	1	4	3	1	0	1	1	1	1	1	1
Harsh . . .	1	0	1	0	0	0	1	2	0	0	0	3	0	1	3	4
Hear	3	3	4	4	3	0	0	1	0	1	2	0	0	0	2	0
Heavy . . .	5	1	2	1	8	1	0	1	0	0	1	0	1	1	0	0
Hi-fi . . .	0	1	0	0	0	0	0	0	1	0	1	1	0	0	4	1
High	0	1	2	1	1	1	1	0	2	0	0	0	0	0	0	0
Holler . . .	1	1	2	0	1	2	2	0	1	1	0	0	1	0	0	0
Horn	0	1	3	0	1	0	3	1	1	4	1	0	2	4	0	3
Hurt	0	1	1	1	0	0	0	0	0	0	1	0	0	2	1	3
Laugh . . .	0	1	0	1	0	0	0	0	0	0	0	2	0	2	0	1
Lion	2	0	0	0	0	0	0	0	0	0	1	1	0	0	0	0
Long	0	0	1	2	2	1	0	1	0	0	2	1	1	2	1	1
Louder . .	1	0	0	0	0	1	1	0	0	0	1	0	2	0	1	0
Low	4	6	2	3	6	6	3	1	0	1	1	1	0	0	1	1
Man	0	0	0	0	0	0	0	0	1	0	0	1	2	1	2	0
Mouth . . .	10	2	3	4	3	3	3	1	11	4	4	2	3	1	2	1
Music . . .	0	1	1	0	1	0	0	1	1	0	2	0	1	2	5	4
Nice	1	0	2	0	0	0	0	0	0	0	0	0	0	0	0	0
Noise . . .	38	45	51	36	47	45	50	37	25	33	50	44	45	41	119	112
Noisy . . .	13	13	11	15	10	21	15	24	15	12	12	24	10	13	20	21
Nose	2	2	1	0	1	1	0	0	0	0	0	0	0	0	0	0
Ouch . . .	0	0	0	1	0	0	0	0	0	0	0	0	0	0	3	0
People . .	0	0	0	0	0	0	0	0	0	0	0	1	0	0	1	3
Quiet	5	12	3	5	4	6	5	3	6	7	6	9	15	8	24	19
Quit	0	0	1	0	2	0	1	0	0	0	1	0	0	0	0	0
Quite . . .	1	1	2	1	1	0	0	1	1	0	1	3	1	2	4	0
Scream . .	3	11	8	7	4	6	1	1	1	6	0	1	0	0	1	3
Sharp . . .	0	0	1	0	1	2	0	0	0	0	0	1	0	1	1	2
Short . . .	1	0	3	0	2	1	0	0	1	0	1	0	0	0	0	1
Shot	2	0	0	0	1	0	0	0	0	0	0	1	0	0	0	0
Shout . . .	13	21	10	17	7	14	6	10	2	10	5	4	5	5	6	5
Shouting . .	0	1	0	0	0	0	0	0	0	3	1	0	0	0	0	1
Shrill . . .	0	0	0	0	0	0	1	2	4	1	0	0	0	0	3	1
Silent . . .	1	0	0	0	2	0	0	1	0	0	0	2	0	0	0	0
Siren . . .	0	0	0	0	0	0	1	0	1	1	2	0	0	1	0	0
Soft	68	65	48	80	53	75	91	105	124	109	92	93	96	118	195	228
Softly . . .	0	1	1	0	0	0	0	2	0	0	0	0	0	0	0	1
Sound . . .	9	3	9	3	6	2	8	0	2	1	2	1	2	1	14	9
Speak . . .	1	0	1	2	1	1	0	1	1	0	1	0	0	0	1	0
Stereo . .	0	0	0	0	0	0	0	0	0	0	1	0	2	0	0	0
Strong . . .	0	0	2	0	0	0	4	11	3	3	1	0	0	0	1	3
Talk . . .	5	2	3	7	8	4	0	1	0	2	0	0	2	0	0	0
Talking . .	1	1	0	0	1	0	0	0	2	2	0	2	0	1	0	0
Teacher . .	0	0	0	0	0	0	1	2	0	0	0	0	1	0	0	0
Thunder . .	1	0	0	0	0	1	0	0	0	0	1	2	0	1	2	5
Voice . . .	1	8	6	1	4	8	1	1	6	2	4	0	6	4	4	1
Water . . .	1	0	0	0	2	0	0	0	0	0	0	0	0	0	0	0

Response Word	4th M	4th F	5th M	5th F	6th M	6th F	7th M	7th F	8th M	8th F	10th M	10th F	12th M	12th F	College M	College F

LOUD

Response Word	4th M	4th F	5th M	5th F	6th M	6th F	7th M	7th F	8th M	8th F	10th M	10th F	12th M	12th F	College M	College F
Whistle	2	0	1	1	0	0	1	0	0	1	0	0	3	1	3	1
Yell	4	5	2	8	12	13	7	1	4	1	6	2	3	3	3	3
Yelling	0	0	0	0	0	1	0	0	0	0	2	0	0	0	1	1

108. MAKE

Response Word	4th M	4th F	5th M	5th F	6th M	6th F	7th M	7th F	8th M	8th F	10th M	10th F	12th M	12th F	College M	College F
A	8	2	8	2	3	0	0	0	0	0	1	0	0	0	1	0
Ache	0	0	0	0	1	0	4	1	0	0	0	0	0	0	0	0
Art	0	1	1	4	0	2	0	0	0	2	0	1	0	0	0	0
Bake	4	10	3	5	2	6	0	3	3	5	2	3	0	6	0	10
Bed	0	0	1	0	0	0	1	1	2	1	2	1	1	0	0	3
Believe	0	1	0	5	3	1	0	1	1	0	2	0	3	4	7	9
Bought	0	0	0	0	0	0	0	2	1	2	0	0	0	0	0	1
Brake	0	1	0	0	0	0	0	0	1	2	1	0	2	0	2	2
Bread	1	0	0	0	1	0	1	0	0	0	0	0	0	0	1	2
Break	1	1	3	0	0	1	4	1	7	6	5	10	8	5	28	20
Broke	0	0	0	0	0	0	0	1	0	2	0	0	0	1	0	0
Build	2	3	14	4	5	4	17	2	8	4	11	3	15	6	42	16
Buy	1	2	1	3	1	3	6	11	4	10	4	14	2	7	5	11
Cake	17	16	20	18	2	19	8	13	9	11	9	13	12	10	2	15
Car	0	0	0	1	0	0	1	1	0	0	0	0	3	2	8	1
Cause	0	0	0	0	0	0	0	0	0	0	0	0	0	0	2	0
Chair	0	0	0	0	0	0	0	0	0	0	0	0	0	1	2	0
Choice	0	0	0	0	0	0	0	0	0	0	0	0	0	2	2	2
Choose	0	0	0	0	0	0	0	1	1	0	0	1	0	1	0	2
Clear	1	0	0	0	0	0	0	1	1	0	3	0	1	6	7	5
Closer	1	2	0	0	1	0	1	0	1	1	0	0	1	0	1	0
Clothes	1	3	2	1	1	1	0	0	2	2	0	6	0	3	0	4
Construct	0	0	1	0	0	0	4	2	1	0	4	2	1	0	8	5
Cook	0	2	0	3	4	0	0	1	2	0	1	4	0	0	1	1
Cookies	1	1	0	1	0	2	0	0	1	0	1	0	0	1	1	2
Create	0	0	2	7	3	6	5	12	5	5	8	6	5	11	23	32
Cut	0	1	0	1	0	2	2	0	0	0	0	1	0	1	0	1
Destroy	1	0	1	2	0	2	3	2	7	3	3	3	5	2	11	8
Did	0	0	0	0	2	0	0	2	0	0	0	1	1	0	0	2
Do	11	13	5	14	10	17	10	8	7	11	9	31	6	33	30	63
Doing	0	0	1	0	3	0	0	0	0	0	0	0	0	0	0	0
Done	1	0	0	0	0	3	0	0	1	0	0	1	0	0	1	0
Don't	0	0	2	0	0	0	1	0	0	0	0	1	0	0	0	0
Dough	1	0	0	0	0	0	0	0	0	1	0	0	0	2	0	0
Draw	0	1	0	0	1	1	0	5	1	1	2	2	0	0	2	1
Dress	0	1	0	0	0	0	0	1	0	1	0	2	0	1	0	3
Easier	0	1	0	0	0	0	0	0	1	0	0	1	0	0	3	2
Easy	0	0	0	0	0	0	0	0	0	1	1	1	1	1	2	0
Fabricate	0	0	0	0	0	0	0	0	0	0	0	0	0	0	2	0
Fashion	0	0	0	0	0	0	0	0	0	0	0	0	2	0	0	0
Fast	0	0	0	1	0	0	0	1	0	0	0	0	0	1	2	0
Find	0	0	0	0	0	0	1	1	0	0	0	0	0	0	2	0
Fix	1	0	0	0	4	0	0	1	0	1	2	3	0	0	4	2
Food	0	0	1	1	1	0	1	1	1	0	3	1	1	1	1	1

Response Word	4th M	4th F	5th M	5th F	6th M	6th F	7th M	7th F	8th M	8th F	10th M	10th F	12th M	12th F	College M	College F
							MAKE									
Form	0	0	0	2	0	0	0	0	0	0	1	0	3	0	0	1
Fun	1	0	0	0	1	4	1	0	0	1	1	0	1	0	2	0
Get	0	0	1	0	0	0	0	1	0	0	0	0	0	2	4	4
Girl	0	0	0	0	0	0	0	0	0	0	1	0	2	0	5	0
Give	0	0	0	0	0	3	0	1	0	1	0	0	0	0	0	0
Go	0	0	0	0	3	0	1	0	0	0	0	1	0	0	2	2
Good	2	0	4	0	3	1	1	2	2	1	4	3	2	2	5	3
Hammer . . .	2	0	1	0	0	0	0	0	0	0	0	0	0	0	0	0
Hands	0	1	0	2	1	0	0	0	0	1	2	1	0	2	2	0
Hard	2	0	0	0	0	0	0	0	0	0	0	0	1	0	2	0
Haste	0	0	0	0	0	0	0	0	1	0	0	0	2	0	2	1
He	0	2	0	0	0	0	0	0	0	0	0	0	0	0	0	0
Her	4	0	0	0	1	3	0	1	0	0	1	0	0	0	5	1
Him	5	6	4	3	8	5	2	0	2	4	0	2	6	1	4	3
His	2	1	1	0	1	0	2	0	0	0	0	1	0	0	0	0
Homemade .	0	0	0	0	0	0	0	2	0	0	0	0	0	0	0	0
House	1	0	0	0	1	0	0	0	2	1	0	0	1	0	0	1
Is	0	2	2	0	1	1	0	0	0	0	0	0	0	0	0	0
It	22	14	22	15	20	10	12	6	10	5	9	13	11	4	30	19
Kiss	0	0	0	0	0	0	0	0	1	0	0	0	1	0	2	0
Leave	0	0	0	0	0	0	0	0	0	1	1	0	0	2	0	0
Like	1	0	0	2	1	0	1	0	1	0	1	0	0	0	1	0
Lose	0	0	0	0	0	0	1	0	0	0	0	0	2	1	1	4
Love	0	0	1	0	0	2	1	0	0	0	0	2	2	3	10	11
Made	20	27	19	36	14	24	30	47	33	43	15	11	19	22	24	24
Maker	0	0	0	0	0	0	1	2	0	0	0	0	0	0	1	1
Makes	1	2	1	0	0	1	1	0	1	1	1	0	1	1	0	0
Making . . .	2	4	2	0	1	4	2	0	2	1	0	1	0	1	2	0
Manufacture .	0	0	2	0	2	1	3	1	1	1	0	2	2	0	2	3
Me	18	14	15	13	30	16	15	13	13	17	11	12	25	11	24	13
Mike	0	0	1	0	1	0	1	0	0	0	0	0	0	1	2	0
Mine	1	0	0	0	2	1	0	2	4	3	6	3	4	5	4	7
Mistake . . .	0	0	0	2	0	0	1	4	1	0	2	0	0	1	4	0
Mistakes . .	0	0	0	0	0	0	0	0	0	0	0	0	0	0	2	0
Mix	2	0	1	1	0	0	0	0	0	2	0	1	0	1	0	2
Model	0	1	0	0	2	0	1	1	0	0	2	0	4	1	2	0
Mold	1	0	0	0	1	0	2	0	0	1	0	3	1	0	2	1
Money	0	0	0	0	0	0	0	2	1	0	1	1	2	0	4	3
More	0	0	0	0	0	1	0	0	1	0	1	0	2	2	0	2
My	1	1	2	1	0	0	1	1	0	0	0	0	0	0	0	0
New	0	2	0	1	0	0	0	0	0	0	1	1	0	0	0	0
Noise	0	0	0	0	1	0	0	1	0	2	3	1	3	1	1	0
Out	0	0	0	0	0	0	9	3	17	22	11	2	10	2	21	13
Over	0	0	0	1	0	0	0	0	0	0	0	1	1	1	0	2
Paper	1	1	0	0	0	2	0	1	0	0	0	1	0	1	0	0
Picture . . .	0	0	2	1	1	0	0	0	0	0	0	0	0	0	0	0
Pie	0	0	0	1	0	3	0	1	0	0	2	1	1	1	1	1
Play	1	1	0	3	0	1	2	0	3	0	0	0	0	0	0	3
Prepare . . .	0	0	0	0	0	0	0	0	0	1	0	1	1	1	0	3

Response Word	4th M	4th F	5th M	5th F	6th M	6th F	7th M	7th F	8th M	8th F	10th M	10th F	12th M	12th F	College M	College F
							MAKE									
Produce	0	0	2	2	1	2	0	0	0	2	1	0	0	0	6	4
Put	0	0	0	0	0	0	1	2	0	0	1	2	1	0	2	2
Ready	0	0	0	0	0	0	0	0	0	0	0	0	2	0	2	0
Room	1	0	0	0	0	1	1	0	0	0	1	1	0	0	3	0
Ruin	0	0	1	1	0	1	0	2	0	0	0	1	1	0	0	0
Sell	0	0	0	1	0	1	0	0	0	0	2	0	1	1	0	1
Sense	0	0	0	0	0	0	0	0	0	0	0	2	0	0	0	0
Sew	0	3	0	2	1	1	0	7	0	4	1	10	0	10	2	12
Sex	0	0	0	0	0	0	0	0	0	0	0	0	0	0	2	0
Shake	0	0	0	0	1	0	0	0	0	0	1	0	1	1	2	0
Shape	1	0	0	0	0	1	0	0	0	0	0	0	2	0	1	0
Some	3	4	4	4	1	0	1	0	0	1	1	1	1	0	0	1
Something	9	13	7	9	5	6	3	2	1	0	2	2	1	0	2	4
Stake	0	0	1	0	1	0	1	0	1	0	0	0	0	0	0	2
Sure	0	0	0	0	1	1	1	0	0	0	2	1	1	0	1	3
Take	8	7	6	15	8	11	10	13	5	9	14	8	7	11	17	20
That	2	0	2	1	2	1	2	0	1	0	1	0	0	0	0	0
The	6	5	5	4	7	3	2	0	2	0	4	0	0	2	2	2
Them	0	0	3	0	1	2	4	1	2	1	1	0	0	0	3	3
Thing	2	1	1	3	3	1	0	1	0	0	1	0	0	1	1	0
Things	2	1	2	1	0	2	1	0	0	0	1	0	1	0	0	0
This	2	2	1	1	1	0	0	0	0	0	0	0	1	0	2	0
To	1	0	1	0	1	0	0	0	0	1	0	0	2	0	0	0
Toy	0	2	1	0	0	3	0	1	0	1	0	0	1	0	1	3
Unmake	0	0	0	3	0	0	0	0	0	0	0	0	1	0	0	2
Up	3	11	9	3	15	10	11	6	5	12	5	10	7	9	17	26
Us	0	1	2	0	1	1	2	0	1	0	2	2	0	2	2	2
Use	2	1	0	0	2	0	1	1	1	1	1	0	2	1	2	3
Wake	1	0	0	1	2	0	0	0	0	0	0	0	0	0	0	0
What	0	0	1	0	0	1	0	0	0	1	2	1	0	1	4	3
With	0	0	0	0	0	1	0	0	0	0	0	0	0	0	0	2
Wood	2	1	0	0	2	0	3	0	1	1	2	1	1	0	0	0
Work	1	0	4	1	5	1	2	3	3	2	5	1	2	1	4	2
Wreck	1	0	1	1	1	0	1	1	1	2	1	0	1	0	0	0
You	2	4	3	4	1	0	0	3	10	1	2	1	4	1	2	1
Your	0	1	1	1	2	0	0	1	1	0	0	1	0	1	0	0
Yours	1	0	0	0	0	0	0	0	1	0	0	0	0	1	2	0
							109. MAN									
Beast	1	0	0	0	0	0	0	0	2	0	0	0	0	0	0	0
Big	16	12	8	13	10	11	6	11	1	3	10	8	7	6	7	9
Body	1	0	0	0	0	0	2	0	0	0	0	0	0	1	2	0
Boy	27	23	24	18	21	35	27	26	15	25	26	40	24	36	36	45
Boyfriend	0	0	0	0	0	0	0	2	0	0	0	0	0	0	0	0
Boys	0	0	0	1	0	0	0	0	1	2	0	0	0	0	0	0
Car	1	0	0	0	2	0	1	0	1	0	0	1	1	0	0	0
Child	2	2	0	1	1	1	0	0	0	0	0	1	2	1	0	2
Clothes	1	0	2	0	0	0	0	0	1	0	2	0	0	0	2	0
Coat	3	7	9	11	4	2	2	2	3	2	1	2	0	1	2	0

Response Word	4th M	4th F	5th M	5th F	6th M	6th F	7th M	7th F	8th M	8th F	10th M	10th F	12th M	12th F	College M	College F
							MAN									
Cute	0	0	0	0	0	0	0	2	0	0	0	1	0	0	0	0
Dad	0	3	3	3	3	6	0	3	1	5	2	1	3	1	1	4
Daddy	0	4	0	1	0	0	0	0	0	1	0	0	0	0	0	0
Dark	0	1	0	0	0	0	0	0	0	1	1	1	0	1	1	3
Deep	1	0	0	0	0	0	0	1	0	0	0	0	1	0	0	2
Dick	0	0	0	0	0	0	0	0	0	0	1	1	0	1	0	2
Dog	1	1	2	0	1	1	4	4	4	3	4	3	7	3	10	5
Father	2	6	2	2	3	8	2	6	2	7	1	5	2	3	2	6
Female	0	0	0	0	0	0	0	0	0	0	0	0	1	0	2	0
Gentleman	2	0	0	0	0	1	0	0	0	0	0	0	0	0	0	0
Girl	6	7	8	8	10	8	4	9	11	16	14	13	16	8	17	16
Good	0	0	0	0	1	1	0	0	0	0	0	0	0	1	3	1
Hair	0	0	0	0	0	3	0	2	1	1	0	1	0	0	0	0
Handsome	0	0	1	0	0	0	1	4	0	4	0	6	0	4	0	3
Hat	8	1	7	7	8	5	2	4	4	4	1	4	3	2	4	6
Head	0	0	1	0	0	0	0	1	1	0	1	2	0	0	0	0
Human	4	2	7	2	9	4	1	3	2	1	2	2	0	1	3	0
Husband	1	0	0	1	1	2	0	0	0	0	0	1	0	1	0	1
Lady	16	26	11	20	14	17	8	15	4	8	1	14	1	7	2	14
Love	0	1	0	0	0	0	0	4	0	2	0	4	0	1	0	3
Mail	0	0	2	0	0	0	0	0	0	0	1	0	0	0	0	0
Male	7	3	3	2	14	5	14	8	8	5	2	0	1	1	2	2
Masculine	0	0	0	0	0	2	0	0	0	0	0	1	0	0	1	0
Me	1	1	2	0	0	1	3	0	1	0	3	0	0	0	0	0
Men	6	2	8	8	6	3	4	1	1	2	3	1	0	0	2	1
Mouse	0	0	0	0	0	0	0	0	0	0	3	0	1	0	0	1
Mr.	2	0	2	1	0	0	0	1	0	0	0	0	0	0	0	0
Muscles	0	0	0	0	0	0	0	0	2	0	1	0	0	0	0	1
Nice	0	0	2	0	1	0	0	1	0	2	1	2	0	1	0	1
Old	1	0	3	0	1	0	0	0	0	4	2	1	0	0	2	1
Pants	0	0	0	0	2	0	0	0	0	1	0	0	1	0	0	1
People	3	5	1	0	4	2	0	1	2	3	0	0	0	0	1	1
Person	22	22	30	23	24	21	11	11	5	3	1	2	1	0	2	3
Sex	3	1	1	2	1	2	2	1	1	0	1	1	0	0	2	2
Shoes	2	0	0	0	0	0	0	0	0	0	0	0	0	0	0	0
Son	0	0	0	0	0	0	1	0	0	0	0	1	0	0	0	2
Sports	0	0	0	0	0	0	0	0	2	0	0	0	0	0	0	0
Strength	0	0	0	0	0	0	0	0	1	0	1	1	0	0	3	0
Strong	1	2	2	3	2	0	1	1	4	1	5	0	5	1	4	4
Tall	4	15	12	19	12	18	15	16	3	11	11	9	3	9	7	13
Tan	0	0	0	0	2	0	0	0	1	0	0	0	0	0	1	0
Teacher	0	0	0	1	0	0	0	0	0	4	0	1	0	0	0	0
Walk	0	0	2	0	1	1	1	0	0	0	1	0	0	1	0	0
Wife	0	1	0	2	0	0	0	0	0	2	1	0	0	0	3	1
Woman	44	39	42	52	52	48	81	73	108	92	87	80	107	114	320	304
Women	38	38	24	33	22	25	27	25	37	28	43	24	48	29	30	17
Work	1	1	0	3	0	2	1	0	0	0	1	0	2	0	0	1

Response Word	4th M	F	5th M	F	6th M	F	7th M	F	8th M	F	10th M	F	12th M	F	College M	F

110. <u>ME</u>

Response Word	4th M	F	5th M	F	6th M	F	7th M	F	8th M	F	10th M	F	12th M	F	College M	F
Am	3	0	2	1	0	2	1	0	0	0	0	0	0	0	1	0
And	4	0	0	2	8	1	3	0	3	1	2	1	2	2	6	1
Are	1	0	1	0	0	0	1	0	0	0	1	0	3	0	0	0
Boy	4	0	8	0	6	0	1	1	2	0	4	0	2	0	4	0
Cat	0	1	0	0	0	1	2	0	0	0	0	0	0	0	0	0
Fat	0	0	0	0	0	0	0	2	0	0	0	0	0	1	0	1
Girl	0	0	1	4	0	4	0	4	1	4	0	2	1	5	0	7
He	7	5	5	1	6	4	9	6	5	4	5	2	4	3	3	5
Her	1	0	4	2	4	7	3	2	7	5	7	2	5	1	5	2
Him	12	5	5	2	10	2	8	6	14	7	10	9	8	13	4	5
Home	0	0	0	0	1	0	0	0	2	0	2	0	1	0	0	0
How	0	2	0	0	3	1	1	0	0	0	0	0	0	0	0	0
Human	0	1	0	0	0	2	0	0	1	0	0	0	0	0	0	1
I	36	52	48	49	38	58	39	32	24	22	29	21	30	26	46	51
Is	3	2	1	1	2	3	1	0	0	0	1	0	1	0	2	0
It	4	0	1	0	0	2	2	1	0	1	1	0	0	0	1	0
King	0	0	0	0	0	0	0	0	0	0	0	0	0	0	2	0
Know	0	3	0	0	0	0	1	0	0	0	0	0	0	0	1	1
Men	0	0	1	0	0	0	0	0	0	0	0	0	2	0	0	0
Meow	0	2	0	1	1	2	0	1	0	0	1	0	1	1	5	2
Mine	1	0	0	0	1	1	2	2	2	0	1	0	2	2	5	6
Mother	1	0	0	0	0	0	1	0	0	1	0	0	0	0	0	2
My	9	3	5	17	5	8	15	12	4	8	8	2	8	10	21	16
Myself	16	27	25	26	29	32	19	16	13	8	14	22	15	8	16	12
Name	1	1	2	0	0	0	0	0	0	1	0	0	0	0	0	0
No	0	1	2	2	2	1	0	0	0	0	0	0	0	0	1	0
Now	8	4	9	2	1	1	1	1	0	2	0	1	0	3	5	0
One	0	0	2	0	0	0	0	0	0	0	0	0	0	0	0	0
Out	1	0	0	0	0	0	2	0	0	0	1	0	0	0	0	0
Ow	0	1	2	1	0	0	0	0	2	0	2	1	1	0	2	0
Pam	0	0	0	0	0	2	0	0	0	0	0	0	0	0	0	0
People	1	1	1	0	2	0	0	0	0	0	0	0	0	0	0	0
Person	2	2	4	4	9	3	5	2	2	5	5	7	3	2	4	2
Pretty	0	2	0	0	0	0	0	1	0	1	0	0	0	0	0	0
See	5	2	2	1	2	1	0	1	2	0	1	0	0	1	1	1
Self	0	2	1	2	0	0	0	0	0	0	0	0	0	0	3	2
She	4	1	1	2	0	0	7	5	5	4	7	3	4	0	12	5
Someone	0	1	2	0	0	0	0	0	0	0	0	0	0	0	0	0
The	2	0	2	0	2	0	0	0	1	0	0	0	0	0	0	0
Them	1	1	1	2	2	5	2	3	3	2	4	1	4	0	4	2
They	2	0	0	3	2	4	4	2	6	1	2	2	6	1	22	6
To	2	1	0	0	2	1	0	0	1	0	1	1	0	1	2	0
Too	0	0	1	1	1	0	0	1	2	1	1	1	2	1	6	6
Ugly	0	0	0	0	0	0	0	2	0	1	0	0	0	0	0	0
Us	0	1	1	2	1	0	2	2	0	0	0	2	0	3	3	2
We	4	3	1	0	3	1	0	0	1	1	1	0	1	1	6	1
Who	3	2	1	1	2	2	0	2	1	0	1	0	0	1	1	1

Response Word	4th M	4th F	5th M	5th F	6th M	6th F	7th M	7th F	8th M	8th F	10th M	10th F	12th M	12th F	College M	College F
							ME									
Word	2	0	0	0	0	0	0	0	0	0	0	0	0	0	0	0
You	76	104	85	108	81	86	98	117	130	152	118	142	122	146	288	336
Yourself	0	1	2	0	0	0	0	0	0	0	0	0	0	0	0	0
						111.	MEMORY									
Amnesia . . .	0	0	0	0	0	1	1	0	1	0	4	1	1	0	2	1
Back	2	0	1	3	0	0	1	0	1	1	0	0	0	0	0	0
Bad	1	1	2	3	3	4	3	5	10	7	14	7	8	8	6	8
Blank	0	0	1	1	0	0	1	0	4	0	3	1	2	1	2	1
Book	1	3	0	4	2	4	1	1	0	0	0	2	1	3	3	8
Boy	1	2	2	0	4	0	0	0	0	0	0	3	1	0	1	3
Brain	9	6	8	9	12	9	16	8	10	6	8	3	5	9	14	13
By heart . . .	0	0	0	2	0	0	0	0	0	0	0	0	0	0	0	0
Car	0	2	0	1	0	0	0	0	0	0	0	0	0	0	0	0
Cemetery . . .	1	0	0	0	1	0	0	0	2	0	0	0	0	0	0	0
Chemistry . .	0	0	0	0	0	0	0	0	0	0	0	0	0	0	2	0
Child	0	0	0	0	0	0	0	0	0	0	0	0	2	1	0	1
Childhood . . .	0	0	0	0	0	0	0	0	0	0	1	3	0	2	2	5
Church	0	2	0	1	2	1	0	0	0	0	0	0	0	0	0	0
Dad	2	1	0	0	0	0	0	0	0	0	0	0	0	0	0	0
Dark	0	0	0	0	0	0	0	0	2	0	0	0	0	2	1	1
Day	1	4	2	1	2	0	1	0	0	0	0	0	0	0	0	0
Dead	0	2	3	2	2	1	5	0	3	4	1	0	1	0	0	0
Diary	1	3	0	1	1	4	0	1	0	1	0	0	0	0	0	1
Died	2	0	0	1	0	0	0	1	0	0	0	0	0	0	0	0
Dim	0	0	0	0	0	0	0	0	1	0	0	0	1	2	0	0
Do	0	0	1	0	0	0	0	0	0	0	0	0	0	0	0	2
Dog	1	0	0	0	0	0	0	0	1	1	0	0	2	0	0	0
Dream	5	1	8	8	2	9	4	7	3	5	7	8	4	7	7	9
Dreams	1	0	1	0	0	0	0	1	0	2	1	1	1	3	3	2
Dumb	0	0	0	0	2	0	0	0	0	3	0	0	0	0	0	1
Elephant	0	0	0	0	1	2	3	1	2	2	1	2	7	1	2	5
English	0	0	0	0	0	0	0	0	0	0	1	1	0	2	0	0
Events	0	0	0	0	0	0	0	0	0	0	0	0	0	0	0	3
Facts	0	0	0	0	0	0	0	0	0	0	1	0	0	1	2	1
Far	0	1	2	1	0	0	0	0	0	0	0	0	0	0	0	1
Fast	0	1	2	0	0	0	0	0	0	0	0	0	0	0	0	1
Father	0	1	0	0	0	0	0	1	1	1	0	2	2	0	0	0
Fond	0	0	0	0	0	0	0	0	0	0	0	0	0	0	1	2
Forget	7	1	3	4	4	9	13	13	13	9	13	8	16	10	29	33
Forgetful . . .	0	0	0	0	0	0	1	0	4	3	1	0	1	1	2	2
Forgetfulness .	0	0	0	0	0	0	0	2	2	0	2	2	1	1	4	11
Forgot	3	1	1	1	2	0	3	1	2	2	1	0	1	1	0	1
Forgotten . . .	0	0	1	0	0	0	0	0	1	1	1	0	2	0	0	1
Fortune teller .	0	0	0	0	0	0	0	0	0	2	0	0	0	0	0	0
Fun	1	0	1	0	0	0	1	3	1	1	5	6	4	4	3	6
Girl	0	0	0	0	1	0	0	1	2	0	0	0	0	0	3	0
Girls	0	0	0	0	0	0	1	0	1	0	0	0	2	0	0	0
Good	4	4	5	12	10	10	3	7	3	6	6	15	7	7	17	18

Response Word	4th M	4th F	5th M	5th F	6th M	6th F	7th M	7th F	8th M	8th F	10th M	10th F	12th M	12th F	College M	College F
							MEMORY									
Grades ...	0	0	0	0	0	0	0	0	0	0	0	1	0	0	2	1
Grandmother	0	1	0	0	0	0	0	0	0	1	0	0	0	0	0	3
Grave	1	0	1	1	3	0	2	0	1	0	0	0	0	0	0	0
Happiness ..	0	0	0	0	0	0	1	0	0	3	2	2	1	1	1	1
Happy	0	3	0	2	0	0	0	2	0	4	0	1	2	2	0	6
Hard	1	0	0	1	1	0	0	0	1	0	1	0	2	0	1	0
Head ...	4	5	4	6	4	6	2	5	0	1	0	1	1	0	2	3
Hear	0	0	0	0	2	0	0	0	0	0	0	0	0	0	0	0
Heart	1	2	1	3	1	1	0	0	0	1	0	2	0	0	0	0
History ...	1	1	0	0	0	0	3	0	0	0	0	0	1	0	1	1
Holiday ...	0	0	2	0	0	0	0	0	0	0	0	0	0	0	0	0
Home	0	0	0	0	0	1	0	1	0	0	0	1	0	0	1	2
Hope	0	0	0	0	0	0	0	1	0	2	0	0	0	2	0	0
Idea	0	0	0	0	0	1	0	1	0	0	0	0	2	0	3	2
Intelligence .	0	0	0	0	0	0	0	0	0	0	0	3	0	0	1	0
Jog	0	0	0	0	0	0	0	0	0	0	0	1	5	1	0	0
Killed	0	0	1	0	2	0	0	0	0	0	0	0	0	0	0	0
Know	2	3	1	2	2	3	2	1	1	0	1	1	0	2	0	2
Knowledge .	0	0	0	0	0	0	0	0	0	0	1	0	1	0	2	0
Lane	0	0	0	0	0	0	0	0	0	0	0	0	0	0	1	2
Lapse	0	0	0	0	0	0	0	0	0	0	0	0	0	1	2	1
Learn	3	3	0	3	2	3	0	2	1	2	0	0	0	0	1	6
Learning ..	0	0	0	0	0	0	0	0	0	0	0	0	0	0	1	2
Lesson ...	0	0	0	0	2	0	0	2	0	0	0	0	0	0	0	1
Life	0	0	0	0	0	0	0	0	0	0	0	0	0	0	2	0
Like	0	1	0	0	0	0	0	0	0	2	0	0	0	0	1	0
Long	3	1	3	2	5	3	0	1	0	2	3	2	2	0	2	4
Long ago ..	0	0	2	1	0	0	0	2	0	1	1	1	0	1	1	0
Loss	0	0	0	0	0	0	0	0	0	0	1	0	2	0	0	3
Lost	0	0	1	0	1	0	0	2	0	1	0	2	1	0	0	1
Love	0	1	0	0	0	3	1	2	1	0	0	2	0	1	1	3
Maker	0	0	0	0	0	0	0	0	0	0	0	0	0	0	2	0
Me	1	0	2	0	0	0	0	0	0	0	0	0	0	1	0	0
Memories ..	0	1	0	1	2	0	0	0	0	1	1	0	0	0	1	3
Memorize ..	1	1	1	2	2	2	2	0	2	1	1	0	0	2	3	1
Men	2	2	1	0	0	0	0	0	0	0	0	0	0	0	0	0
Mind	25	31	29	33	36	28	30	22	25	29	31	22	35	24	67	50
Mine	0	2	1	1	1	0	0	0	0	2	1	1	1	0	0	0
Money	2	0	1	0	0	1	0	0	0	0	0	0	0	0	1	0
Mother ...	0	0	0	0	0	0	0	2	2	1	2	0	0	0	0	5
Music	2	0	0	0	0	0	0	0	0	0	1	0	0	2	0	1
Nice	0	1	0	1	2	1	1	0	0	0	1	0	2	0	1	5
None	0	0	0	0	0	0	0	0	5	1	0	1	0	0	3	0
Now	2	0	0	0	0	0	0	0	0	0	0	0	0	0	0	0
Of	0	0	0	0	1	0	0	0	0	0	0	0	2	0	0	0
Old	1	0	1	1	0	1	3	2	0	2	0	1	0	0	0	1
Paper	1	1	0	0	0	2	0	1	0	0	0	0	0	0	0	0
Past	2	3	2	1	2	2	7	4	5	6	7	9	8	6	15	10
People	1	1	1	0	0	1	2	0	1	1	3	1	0	1	1	0

Response Word	4th M	4th F	5th M	5th F	6th M	6th F	7th M	7th F	8th M	8th F	10th M	10th F	12th M	12th F	College M	College F
								MEMORY								
Person . . .	1	0	1	2	0	0	0	2	0	0	0	0	0	1	0	0
Pleasant . . .	0	0	0	0	0	0	0	0	0	2	1	0	0	3	1	6
Poem	0	0	1	0	0	0	1	2	1	0	0	2	1	0	0	1
Poems . . .	0	0	0	0	0	1	0	1	0	0	1	2	0	2	0	1
Poor	0	0	0	0	0	0	2	0	1	1	1	0	0	4	8	3
Pop	1	2	0	0	0	0	0	0	0	0	0	0	0	0	0	0
Recall	0	0	0	0	0	0	1	2	2	1	1	1	1	0	4	3
Remember .	42	37	38	39	27	42	35	30	30	26	19	22	19	28	39	42
Remembering	1	1	0	0	1	2	1	3	1	2	2	0	0	1	1	0
Remembrance	0	0	0	0	2	1	1	1	0	0	0	0	0	0	0	0
Remind . . .	3	2	0	1	1	3	1	0	0	0	1	0	0	1	0	0
Sad	0	0	0	2	0	2	1	2	3	0	0	2	2	1	1	3
Sadness . . .	0	0	0	0	0	0	0	0	0	0	0	0	0	0	0	2
School	3	2	1	4	3	0	3	2	0	6	3	5	3	0	10	7
Short	1	0	0	0	0	0	0	0	0	0	0	2	0	2	3	2
Sick	0	0	0	0	0	0	0	1	2	0	0	0	0	0	0	0
Sleep	1	1	0	0	4	0	1	1	2	1	4	0	3	0	12	6
Smart	0	0	0	0	0	0	0	2	0	2	1	0	0	2	1	2
Song	1	2	1	1	1	1	0	2	0	0	0	0	1	0	3	0
Stories . . .	0	1	0	1	0	0	0	0	0	0	0	0	0	0	0	2
Story	1	1	1	0	2	3	1	0	0	0	0	0	0	0	0	1
Studies . . .	0	0	0	0	0	0	0	0	0	0	0	0	0	0	2	0
Study	0	0	1	0	0	0	0	4	0	0	1	0	0	1	2	5
Studying . . .	0	0	0	0	0	0	0	0	0	0	0	0	0	0	0	2
Sweet	0	0	0	0	1	0	0	1	0	0	0	2	0	3	1	1
Terrible . . .	0	0	0	0	0	1	0	0	0	0	2	2	0	0	0	0
Test	0	0	0	0	0	0	0	0	0	2	0	1	1	2	8	5
Tests	0	0	0	0	0	0	0	0	0	0	0	1	0	1	1	4
The past . .	0	0	0	0	0	0	0	2	0	0	0	0	0	1	0	0
Thick	0	0	2	0	0	0	0	0	0	1	0	0	0	0	0	0
Thing	1	1	1	1	8	1	0	0	1	0	1	0	0	0	0	0
Things . . .	0	1	1	1	1	0	0	1	1	1	1	1	2	1	0	1
Think	32	40	35	35	23	20	25	23	23	21	13	19	11	19	51	40
Thinking . . .	1	3	3	0	2	2	1	2	2	5	6	2	3	2	5	2
Thought . . .	1	2	7	3	8	8	5	8	15	5	13	9	15	11	19	13
Thoughts . .	0	0	1	1	1	1	0	1	4	0	5	2	4	3	5	6
Time	0	1	2	2	1	1	0	0	0	0	3	0	0	1	0	2
Verse	3	5	0	6	1	1	1	1	1	0	1	1	1	0	2	2
Vision	0	0	0	0	0	0	0	0	0	2	0	0	0	0	0	1
Wish	0	0	0	0	0	0	0	0	0	3	0	2	1	0	1	3
Wonderful . .	0	0	0	0	0	0	0	1	0	2	0	2	0	1	1	1
Word	0	0	0	0	0	0	0	2	0	0	0	0	1	0	0	0
Words	0	0	0	0	0	1	1	0	0	0	0	1	1	0	2	1
Work	1	5	1	0	4	5	2	3	1	3	2	1	2	3	1	2
							112.	MOON								
Astronomy .	0	1	0	0	0	0	2	0	1	1	0	0	0	0	2	2
Ball	1	0	1	0	1	0	0	0	0	0	2	0	1	0	0	0
Beam	1	0	1	0	0	1	2	0	1	0	0	0	2	2	9	4

Response Word	4th M	4th F	5th M	5th F	6th M	6th F	7th M	7th F	8th M	8th F	10th M	10th F	12th M	12th F	College M	College F
							MOON									
Beautiful .	0	1	0	0	0	1	0	1	0	3	1	1	0	4	1	3
Big	3	3	5	1	7	1	2	5	1	6	3	5	1	3	0	7
Blue	0	0	0	0	1	0	2	2	1	7	4	2	1	2	4	5
Boy	0	0	0	0	0	0	0	0	0	3	0	2	0	1	0	0
Bright . . .	2	9	4	16	5	10	2	16	6	10	8	8	8	8	15	12
Car	0	0	0	0	0	0	1	0	0	0	2	1	0	1	0	0
Cheese . .	0	3	2	2	5	3	6	4	7	8	2	6	2	1	5	2
Cold	0	0	0	1	1	1	0	2	0	1	4	0	0	0	2	2
Cow	0	0	0	0	3	0	1	0	0	0	0	0	0	0	1	0
Crater . .	2	0	0	0	1	0	4	0	2	0	1	0	1	2	2	0
Craters . .	2	0	4	0	2	1	1	0	1	1	2	0	0	0	3	0
Crescent .	0	0	0	0	1	0	0	0	0	1	1	0	1	0	2	1
Dark	1	4	0	3	2	1	0	2	1	3	1	3	1	4	2	1
Earth . . .	17	6	6	10	8	4	19	9	23	4	5	2	12	0	17	5
Face	0	0	0	0	1	0	0	0	0	0	2	0	0	0	1	1
Far	4	0	5	3	2	1	2	1	3	2	1	1	4	2	3	0
Full	0	1	1	0	0	2	1	1	0	4	4	5	5	4	3	7
Fun	0	0	0	0	0	0	0	0	0	0	2	0	1	0	0	0
Girl	0	1	0	0	0	0	2	0	1	0	2	0	1	0	1	0
Girls . . .	0	0	0	0	1	0	2	0	3	0	0	0	0	0	0	0
Glow	0	0	0	0	0	0	0	0	0	0	0	1	2	0	12	5
Golden . .	0	0	0	0	0	0	0	0	0	0	0	0	0	0	2	0
Goon	1	0	3	1	0	0	0	0	0	0	0	1	0	0	0	0
Green . . .	0	1	0	1	0	1	0	1	1	0	0	1	1	1	1	2
Half	0	0	1	0	0	1	0	0	1	0	0	0	0	0	0	2
High	1	1	2	3	0	2	1	0	0	0	2	2	0	1	3	3
Lake . . .	0	0	0	0	0	0	0	1	0	0	0	0	0	1	2	2
Light . . .	20	16	19	17	22	14	14	11	7	14	15	4	18	12	34	18
Lonely . .	0	0	0	0	0	0	0	0	0	0	0	0	0	0	0	2
Love	0	0	0	1	3	1	0	5	0	2	5	4	8	5	5	7
Lunar . . .	1	0	0	0	0	0	1	0	0	0	0	0	0	0	2	0
Man	4	0	5	4	3	1	4	0	4	3	3	1	4	1	3	1
Mars . . .	4	0	4	1	3	1	2	0	2	4	1	0	1	2	1	1
Men	1	0	2	0	0	0	0	0	2	0	0	0	0	1	1	0
Missile . .	0	0	0	0	0	0	1	0	0	0	0	0	1	0	2	0
Nice	1	1	0	0	1	0	2	1	0	0	1	0	1	2	0	0
Night . . .	5	14	8	20	13	24	9	20	15	21	23	27	25	25	44	58
Noon . . .	2	0	2	1	0	1	0	0	1	1	0	0	2	0	0	0
On	0	2	0	0	0	0	0	0	0	0	0	0	0	0	0	0
Planet . . .	16	10	22	7	15	7	21	5	19	4	8	2	5	2	7	3
Plant . . .	3	0	6	0	2	1	0	0	0	0	0	0	1	0	0	0
Pretty . . .	0	1	0	0	0	1	1	2	0	1	0	5	1	3	2	4
Reflect . .	0	2	0	0	0	0	0	0	1	0	0	0	0	0	0	0
Reflection .	0	1	0	0	0	0	0	0	0	1	0	0	1	0	2	0
Rock . . .	0	0	0	2	1	0	0	0	1	0	0	0	1	0	1	0
Rocket . .	1	1	3	2	2	0	5	3	3	4	7	2	6	0	2	1
Rockets . .	0	0	0	1	1	0	0	0	0	2	0	0	0	0	2	1
Romance .	0	0	0	0	1	0	0	1	1	0	3	7	1	8	5	3
Romantic .	0	0	0	0	0	0	0	0	1	0	1	2	1	2	1	1

Response Word	4th M	4th F	5th M	5th F	6th M	6th F	7th M	7th F	8th M	8th F	10th M	10th F	12th M	12th F	College M	College F

MOON

Response Word	4th M	4th F	5th M	5th F	6th M	6th F	7th M	7th F	8th M	8th F	10th M	10th F	12th M	12th F	College M	College F
Round . . .	2	2	9	4	3	6	5	10	0	3	3	5	3	7	13	17
Satellite . .	0	0	1	0	1	0	3	0	3	0	0	3	2	0	3	2
Science . .	0	0	0	0	1	0	0	0	0	2	0	0	0	0	0	1
Shine . . .	1	4	4	2	6	10	9	8	19	5	10	5	14	11	15	20
Shines . . .	0	3	0	1	1	0	0	1	0	0	1	0	0	0	1	0
Shiny . . .	0	0	0	0	1	1	1	0	0	3	0	1	0	0	0	0
Shot	0	0	0	0	0	0	0	0	0	0	0	0	2	0	2	0
Silver . . .	0	0	0	0	0	1	0	0	1	0	1	2	0	3	1	4
Sky	8	23	15	12	11	13	7	22	7	14	9	14	8	12	25	23
Son	2	0	0	0	1	1	0	0	0	0	0	0	0	0	1	0
Soon	1	1	2	0	1	1	0	0	0	0	0	0	0	0	1	0
Space . . .	13	6	10	5	9	5	8	5	8	0	9	2	6	0	6	0
Spoon . . .	0	0	1	0	1	0	0	0	0	0	0	0	1	0	1	2
Star	36	47	32	49	42	47	46	36	27	43	43	53	29	55	87	149
Stars . . .	3	1	0	3	0	2	1	4	0	0	2	2	1	1	0	3
Sun	54	57	46	52	29	49	37	45	39	40	23	33	32	26	45	49
Telescope .	1	0	0	0	0	0	2	0	0	0	0	0	0	0	0	0
Tide	0	0	0	0	0	0	0	0	0	0	0	0	0	0	2	0
Universe .	0	0	0	0	2	0	0	0	2	0	1	0	0	0	1	2
Up	0	0	0	1	0	0	0	0	0	0	0	0	1	0	3	0
Watch . . .	0	0	0	0	1	0	0	0	0	0	0	0	0	0	2	0
White . . .	3	5	5	2	2	3	0	6	6	2	7	2	1	6	9	17
Yellow . .	3	5	1	5	4	8	1	7	2	4	7	16	5	12	27	22

113. MOUNTAIN

Response Word	4th M	4th F	5th M	5th F	6th M	6th F	7th M	7th F	8th M	8th F	10th M	10th F	12th M	12th F	College M	College F
Alps	1	0	0	1	1	0	0	0	0	1	1	1	0	1	1	2
Beautiful .	0	0	0	0	0	0	0	1	0	1	1	4	0	4	3	2
Beauty . . .	0	0	0	0	0	1	0	0	0	0	0	0	0	1	0	2
Big	6	4	13	10	10	13	5	5	4	8	10	6	8	7	15	9
Big hill . .	0	2	1	0	0	0	0	0	0	0	0	0	0	0	0	0
Black . . .	0	0	0	0	0	0	0	1	0	0	0	0	0	0	0	2
Blue	0	0	0	0	0	0	1	0	0	0	0	1	1	2	0	1
Brown . . .	0	2	0	1	1	0	0	0	0	0	0	0	0	0	0	0
Cliff	2	1	0	1	0	0	1	0	0	3	1	1	0	1	3	1
Climb . . .	8	8	5	8	7	3	4	6	8	9	6	8	9	14	25	28
Climber . .	0	0	1	0	0	2	1	0	2	2	5	2	7	2	6	6
Climbing .	3	5	2	3	0	2	0	2	9	10	4	3	6	3	14	15
Clouds . . .	0	0	0	0	0	0	0	0	1	0	2	1	1	0	1	0
Cold	1	0	1	0	1	1	1	1	2	0	0	2	0	0	3	1
Colorado .	0	0	0	0	0	1	1	0	1	0	1	1	0	0	2	0
Cool	0	0	0	0	0	2	0	0	0	0	0	2	0	0	0	0
Deep	2	1	0	1	0	0	0	0	0	0	0	0	0	0	1	0
Desert . .	0	0	0	0	0	0	2	1	0	2	0	0	0	2	0	0
Dirt . . .	1	0	2	0	1	0	0	0	1	0	1	1	0	0	0	0
Everest . .	0	0	0	0	1	0	3	0	1	0	1	0	0	2	0	1
Forest . . .	0	0	0	0	0	0	0	1	0	1	0	0	0	1	2	0
Fountain . .	1	2	0	0	1	0	1	1	1	0	1	0	0	0	0	0
Glacier . .	0	0	0	0	0	0	0	0	0	0	0	0	1	0	2	1
Goat	0	1	2	1	2	1	1	1	2	0	4	1	4	2	11	8

Response Word	4th M	4th F	5th M	5th F	6th M	6th F	7th M	7th F	8th M	8th F	10th M	10th F	12th M	12th F	College M	College F
							MOUNTAIN									
Grass . . .	0	1	0	0	1	1	3	0	0	2	0	2	0	0	1	2
Green . . .	0	0	2	1	0	0	0	1	1	0	1	2	0	1	2	4
Greenery .	0	0	0	0	0	0	0	0	0	0	0	0	0	0	2	0
Ground. . .	0	1	0	0	0	0	0	1	0	2	0	0	0	0	0	0
Height . . .	0	2	2	3	1	2	2	4	2	1	5	2	2	1	5	3
Hi	3	0	1	0	0	0	0	0	0	0	0	0	0	0	0	0
High	55	78	64	85	76	78	53	67	44	69	44	73	34	45	72	108
Hill	97	77	81	67	65	67	87	81	83	65	64	59	67	66	128	85
Hills	9	2	3	4	2	4	5	4	5	6	3	1	4	4	0	1
Hilly	0	0	0	1	0	2	1	0	0	0	0	0	0	0	0	0
Hole	0	0	0	0	0	0	1	0	2	0	1	0	0	0	0	1
Horse . . .	0	0	0	1	0	0	1	1	0	0	0	0	1	0	3	5
House . . .	1	1	1	0	0	0	0	2	1	0	1	0	0	0	1	0
Huge	0	1	0	0	1	2	1	1	0	0	3	0	2	0	0	1
Ice	1	0	0	0	0	0	1	0	0	0	0	2	0	0	0	3
Lake . . .	1	1	0	1	0	1	2	0	2	0	3	2	1	3	3	3
Land	1	1	1	2	0	0	0	0	1	0	1	0	0	0	0	0
Large . . .	0	1	2	0	1	1	2	2	0	0	2	3	1	2	3	1
Lion . . .	0	0	2	0	0	0	0	0	0	0	0	0	1	0	2	0
Low	1	0	2	0	1	0	0	0	0	0	0	0	0	0	0	0
Man	0	0	1	0	0	1	1	2	3	0	2	0	9	3	10	2
Mike	0	0	0	0	0	0	0	0	0	0	0	0	2	0	0	0
Mole hill .	0	1	1	0	1	1	2	0	6	1	0	2	6	2	7	6
Mount . . .	0	0	3	1	1	0	0	0	0	0	0	0	1	0	0	0
Mountainous	0	2	0	0	0	0	0	0	0	0	0	0	0	0	0	0
Peak . . .	1	2	5	1	6	2	6	4	5	4	6	3	2	1	8	8
Peaks . . .	0	1	0	1	0	2	1	0	0	0	0	0	0	1	0	2
Pike's Peak	0	1	0	0	0	0	0	0	0	0	2	1	0	0	0	0
Plain . . .	0	0	0	1	0	1	1	1	0	0	3	2	0	4	3	0
Plains . . .	0	1	0	0	1	1	1	1	2	1	0	0	0	0	1	1
Plateau . .	0	0	0	0	3	0	1	1	0	1	0	0	0	0	0	0
Purple . .	0	0	0	1	0	0	0	0	0	0	0	0	1	1	1	9
Range . . .	0	0	1	0	0	0	2	0	1	2	2	0	1	0	1	1
River . . .	2	1	1	0	3	1	1	0	2	4	3	7	4	2	4	4
Road . . .	0	0	0	2	1	0	0	0	0	0	0	0	0	2	3	1
Rock	5	5	5	2	6	4	8	3	5	3	1	2	3	1	10	9
Rocks . . .	2	1	3	1	0	4	0	1	2	3	3	3	3	3	6	1
Rocky . . .	0	1	0	1	1	0	2	0	1	0	3	0	0	0	1	2
Rough . . .	1	1	0	1	0	0	1	0	0	2	0	0	0	0	0	1
Sea	0	0	0	0	0	0	0	0	0	0	1	1	0	1	2	3
Sharp . . .	2	0	0	0	0	0	0	0	0	0	0	0	0	0	0	1
Skiing . . .	0	0	0	1	0	0	0	0	0	3	0	0	1	3	1	4
Sky	0	1	0	0	0	0	0	1	1	0	1	2	1	2	5	2
Slope . . .	1	0	0	0	0	1	0	1	2	0	0	0	1	1	0	1
Snow	1	3	3	4	5	6	6	12	9	4	20	10	17	24	28	44
Steep . . .	3	7	4	4	0	4	1	3	2	5	0	1	1	0	3	2
Stream . .	0	0	0	0	0	0	1	0	2	3	4	1	5	3	7	12
Sun	0	0	0	0	0	0	0	1	0	1	0	0	0	0	0	2
Tall	4	7	1	11	2	5	1	7	1	4	4	0	0	3	6	5

Response Word	4th M	F	5th M	F	6th M	F	7th M	F	8th M	F	10th M	F	12th M	F	College M	F
MOUNTAIN																
Top	1	1	0	4	5	2	1	1	4	1	0	7	8	2	23	16
Train ...	3	3	3	1	1	2	0	1	0	0	0	1	0	1	0	0
Tree	0	0	0	1	0	0	0	0	1	0	1	1	0	0	0	3
Trees ...	0	0	1	0	1	0	0	0	1	0	1	2	1	1	2	1
Valley ...	3	1	3	6	9	5	12	6	11	6	7	5	13	7	25	23
View	0	0	0	0	0	0	0	0	0	0	0	0	0	0	2	0
Water ...	0	0	0	0	0	1	1	0	0	1	1	1	1	3	0	0
West	0	0	0	0	0	0	0	0	0	0	0	0	2	0	0	1
114. MUSIC																
Accordian .	0	0	1	2	1	1	0	0	0	0	0	0	0	0	2	1
Art	0	1	0	0	1	1	1	0	2	0	1	0	2	0	0	2
Awful ...	0	0	0	0	0	1	0	1	2	0	0	0	0	0	0	0
Bach	0	0	0	0	1	0	1	1	1	1	0	0	1	0	6	5
Band	2	4	4	3	5	1	10	2	12	8	9	9	9	4	10	4
Beat	1	0	1	0	0	0	0	0	2	1	0	0	0	0	0	1
Beautiful .	0	0	1	1	3	2	1	2	0	2	1	1	2	2	2	2
Beethoven .	1	0	0	0	0	0	0	0	1	0	0	1	0	1	8	4
Book	3	6	1	3	1	2	2	0	0	2	0	0	3	0	1	1
Bore	0	0	0	0	0	0	2	0	0	0	0	0	0	0	0	0
Box	0	0	0	0	0	0	0	0	0	1	2	0	1	0	1	4
Chair ...	1	0	0	0	1	0	0	0	1	0	0	0	0	1	2	0
Choir ...	0	0	0	0	0	0	0	2	0	0	1	2	0	2	1	1
Chord ...	0	0	0	0	0	0	0	0	0	0	0	0	0	1	0	2
Chorus ..	0	0	0	0	0	0	2	2	1	4	0	0	1	0	0	0
Clarinet ..	1	1	1	0	0	1	1	1	1	0	2	0	1	1	1	6
Composer .	0	0	0	0	0	0	2	0	0	0	1	0	0	0	0	2
Dance ...	3	6	1	3	3	3	2	1	3	4	3	8	2	10	5	3
Dancing ..	2	1	0	1	0	2	1	2	2	1	1	0	0	0	1	2
Drum ...	0	3	1	1	1	1	2	0	2	1	3	0	5	0	0	0
Drums ..	0	1	1	0	0	0	0	0	1	1	5	0	2	0	0	0
Ear	2	0	0	1	0	0	0	0	0	0	0	0	0	0	2	1
Elvis ...	0	0	0	0	0	0	0	0	0	1	0	2	1	0	0	0
Flute ...	1	0	1	2	0	1	0	2	0	0	1	2	0	1	1	3
Fun	3	4	3	2	5	3	1	2	3	1	1	1	1	0	0	2
Gay	1	0	0	2	0	2	0	1	0	2	0	0	0	0	0	3
Good ...	1	0	0	1	2	0	0	0	0	0	1	1	0	1	3	1
Guitar ...	0	0	0	0	1	0	1	0	0	0	0	0	2	1	2	0
Happiness .	0	0	0	0	0	0	0	0	0	0	0	0	0	0	2	0
Happy ...	1	0	2	1	0	2	0	0	0	0	1	3	0	2	0	2
Harmony .	0	0	0	0	0	1	1	1	0	0	2	0	1	1	1	1
Hate	0	0	0	0	0	1	1	0	2	0	0	0	0	0	0	2
Hear ...	1	4	2	1	2	1	1	0	1	1	0	0	0	0	2	2
Hi-fi	0	0	0	0	0	0	0	0	0	0	0	0	0	0	2	3
Horn ...	3	2	8	2	9	1	4	1	2	4	9	5	7	2	15	2
Instrument	5	4	7	7	13	6	2	4	3	2	6	5	4	1	11	2
Instruments	4	1	3	0	2	1	0	0	0	0	4	0	1	0	0	0
Ish	0	0	0	0	0	0	3	0	1	0	0	0	0	0	0	0
It	0	0	2	0	0	0	0	0	0	0	0	0	0	0	0	0

Response Word	4th		5th		6th		7th		8th		10th		12th		College	
	M	F	M	F	M	F	M	F	M	F	M	F	M	F	M	F

MUSIC

Response Word	M	F	M	F	M	F	M	F	M	F	M	F	M	F	M	F
Jazz	2	0	1	1	0	0	1	2	5	0	7	2	2	4	6	3
Joy	0	0	0	0	0	0	0	1	0	0	0	0	0	0	0	2
Leader	0	0	0	0	0	0	0	0	0	0	0	0	2	0	0	0
Lesson	1	0	0	1	1	2	0	0	0	0	0	1	1	0	0	1
Lessons	0	2	1	0	0	1	0	0	0	0	0	0	0	0	1	0
Like	0	2	0	0	0	0	0	0	0	0	0	0	0	0	0	0
Listen	0	2	1	2	2	0	1	1	0	1	0	0	0	0	1	2
Loud	3	2	2	3	2	1	0	3	0	0	2	0	0	1	1	0
Love	0	0	0	0	2	0	0	0	0	0	0	1	2	0	1	1
Lovely	0	2	0	2	1	0	0	1	0	1	0	0	0	0	0	1
Madrigals	0	0	0	0	0	0	0	0	2	0	0	0	0	0	0	0
Man	0	1	1	0	2	1	0	0	0	0	3	1	3	3	9	9
Melody	2	3	2	1	1	5	3	2	0	0	2	1	2	2	3	3
Miss Powell	0	0	0	0	0	0	3	3	0	0	0	0	0	0	0	0
Miss Smith	0	0	0	0	0	0	0	3	2	3	0	0	0	0	0	0
Mozart	0	0	0	0	0	1	0	0	0	0	0	2	0	0	1	0
Mr. Mendenhall	0	0	0	0	0	0	0	2	0	1	0	0	0	0	0	0
Nice	2	3	4	1	2	1	1	0	1	1	1	0	1	0	1	3
Noise	7	6	11	7	10	4	8	3	9	1	11	3	10	2	14	2
Note	3	10	6	15	9	12	8	13	11	14	11	14	12	13	38	56
Notes	23	19	19	28	14	18	17	19	25	12	12	12	12	18	21	28
Orchestra	0	0	1	1	0	2	1	2	0	0	0	0	0	1	3	3
Organ	0	0	0	1	0	1	0	0	1	1	1	0	0	2	0	0
Paper	0	0	1	0	0	0	0	0	0	0	0	0	2	1	0	0
People	0	1	0	1	1	0	0	1	0	2	0	0	0	0	0	0
Piano	12	15	8	6	3	12	4	13	9	20	5	30	9	29	21	57
Play	6	4	0	2	2	1	1	2	0	1	1	0	1	1	3	0
Playing	0	0	0	0	2	0	0	0	0	0	1	0	1	0	0	0
Powell	0	0	0	0	0	0	0	0	3	0	0	0	0	0	0	0
Pretty	2	5	7	10	4	3	4	5	1	1	0	2	2	5	6	6
Quiet	1	0	1	0	0	0	1	1	0	0	0	0	0	0	2	0
Radio	1	0	0	0	2	0	0	2	2	2	5	4	3	2	2	1
Record	1	0	0	1	0	0	1	0	2	2	0	5	6	2	0	0
Records	0	0	0	0	0	0	0	0	2	3	2	1	1	1	2	0
Rhythm	1	1	1	1	0	2	1	0	1	0	2	1	0	1	2	1
Rock and Roll	0	0	0	0	0	1	0	0	0	5	3	2	0	0	0	0
Rock 'n' Roll	0	0	0	0	0	0	2	0	0	0	0	0	0	0	0	0
Sad	1	0	0	0	0	0	0	0	2	0	0	0	0	0	0	1
Saxophone	0	0	0	0	0	1	0	0	1	0	2	0	1	0	0	2
Scale	0	0	0	1	0	1	0	0	1	0	1	1	1	0	0	2
School	1	1	0	0	0	0	0	2	0	2	2	0	0	0	0	0
Score	0	0	0	0	0	0	0	0	0	0	0	0	0	2	1	2
Sheet	0	0	0	0	1	1	0	0	0	0	1	2	1	2	0	1
Sing	33	38	22	42	21	38	20	21	11	28	8	17	8	18	11	16
Singer	0	0	0	0	0	0	0	0	0	0	0	0	0	3	1	4
Singing	6	11	11	15	7	11	5	15	6	21	2	6	3	7	5	4
Smith	0	0	0	0	0	0	0	2	3	2	0	0	0	0	0	0
Soft	3	4	0	4	0	8	1	1	2	5	4	3	6	4	18	7
Song	36	22	35	28	28	35	37	47	39	41	38	38	45	52	80	84

Response Word	4th M	4th F	5th M	5th F	6th M	6th F	7th M	7th F	8th M	8th F	10th M	10th F	12th M	12th F	College M	College F
							MUSIC									
Songs ...	4	5	4	5	4	4	7	3	3	6	0	2	3	1	4	0
Sound ...	18	18	31	19	33	19	24	24	18	11	22	22	16	13	87	74
Sounds ..	2	0	1	0	0	0	2	0	1	0	0	0	0	0	0	0
Staff	0	0	1	0	0	0	1	2	1	1	0	0	1	1	0	3
Stand ...	0	0	0	0	0	0	0	0	0	0	0	0	2	0	3	0
Sweet ...	4	2	2	3	4	1	8	3	1	2	2	3	3	3	4	5
Symphony .	0	0	1	1	0	1	1	0	0	0	0	1	3	2	3	7
Teacher ..	0	0	0	0	1	0	5	1	3	4	0	4	3	0	3	0
Tone	3	0	2	1	2	3	1	1	0	0	1	1	2	0	2	2
Treble clef	0	0	0	0	0	0	0	2	1	0	0	0	0	0	0	0
Trombone .	0	1	0	0	2	0	1	0	0	0	1	1	2	0	0	0
Trumpet ..	2	0	5	0	0	0	0	1	1	0	8	0	5	1	1	0
Tune	6	1	0	1	3	4	1	1	1	3	1	1	2	0	2	3
Violin ...	2	4	2	2	4	3	2	2	2	0	5	5	6	2	6	5
Voice ...	0	0	0	0	0	0	0	0	1	1	1	0	0	1	3	5
						115.	MUTTON									
Animal ..	0	2	1	1	0	2	1	0	0	6	1	2	1	5	4	8
Beef	0	1	0	0	0	0	3	1	2	2	0	2	4	3	14	11
Big ...	1	0	1	2	2	2	0	0	0	0	1	1	0	0	0	0
Biscuit ..	0	0	0	1	1	2	0	0	0	1	2	0	1	0	0	0
Black ...	1	0	0	1	2	0	0	1	0	0	0	1	0	0	0	0
Blue	1	2	1	0	1	1	1	0	2	0	0	0	1	1	0	0
Bone	0	0	0	1	2	0	1	0	0	1	0	0	0	0	1	1
Boy	0	1	0	2	0	0	0	0	0	1	0	0	0	0	0	0
Bread ...	2	1	2	0	3	0	2	3	5	1	2	2	3	3	1	0
Brown ...	2	1	0	1	0	1	1	1	0	0	1	0	0	0	0	0
Bun	0	0	1	0	0	0	2	0	0	0	0	0	0	0	0	0
Butter ...	2	0	0	0	1	0	0	0	0	0	0	0	0	0	0	0
Button ...	31	32	16	28	17	31	15	14	7	10	13	11	2	5	5	3
Buttons ..	0	2	0	0	0	0	0	0	0	0	0	0	0	0	0	0
Cake	0	0	0	3	1	0	1	0	0	0	1	0	0	0	0	0
Calf	0	0	2	0	0	0	0	0	0	0	0	0	0	0	0	0
Cat ...	5	3	1	3	0	2	1	1	3	1	1	3	0	2	0	0
Cats	0	2	0	0	0	0	0	0	0	0	0	0	0	0	0	0
Cereal ...	0	1	0	0	0	0	1	0	0	0	0	3	0	0	0	0
Chicken ..	0	0	0	0	0	0	0	0	2	0	1	0	0	0	0	1
Chop	1	0	0	2	0	0	0	1	1	0	0	2	0	2	6	8
Chops ...	1	1	0	0	0	1	0	0	0	3	0	0	1	1	4	5
Clay	0	0	0	0	0	2	0	0	0	0	0	0	0	0	0	0
Cloth ...	2	2	3	1	1	1	0	1	1	0	0	0	1	0	0	0
Coat	3	7	5	4	3	3	1	2	2	3	1	2	2	1	0	1
Cold	1	3	2	0	3	0	1	0	0	0	0	0	2	1	0	1
Comfort ...	2	0	0	1	0	0	0	0	0	0	1	0	0	0	0	0
Cotton ...	5	3	0	3	2	1	3	2	1	0	3	1	4	1	1	1
Cow	1	0	1	0	0	0	1	1	0	0	1	1	1	1	2	1
Dark	1	1	0	1	0	2	0	0	1	0	0	0	0	0	0	0
Deer	1	0	1	0	0	2	5	1	1	0	3	3	0	1	3	2
Dinner ..	1	0	0	0	0	0	0	0	0	0	0	0	1	0	2	0

Response Word	4th M	4th F	5th M	5th F	6th M	6th F	7th M	7th F	8th M	8th F	10th M	10th F	12th M	12th F	College M	College F
							MUTTON									
Dog	6	10	5	12	11	7	2	2	5	3	1	4	3	9	7	2
Eat	3	3	7	6	6	4	2	2	4	2	3	2	4	1	8	4
Eating ...	1	2	1	0	0	0	0	0	0	0	0	2	0	0	0	1
England ..	0	0	0	0	0	0	0	0	0	0	0	0	0	0	0	2
Fat	1	0	1	0	0	0	2	1	0	2	2	1	3	2	3	4
Fish	1	1	1	2	3	0	0	2	3	0	0	1	1	0	1	1
Food ...	13	10	20	13	18	19	28	26	40	21	33	30	36	18	42	26
Fun	0	1	0	0	2	0	0	0	0	0	0	0	0	0	0	0
Fur	1	0	1	0	1	2	0	0	0	1	0	0	1	0	0	1
Glove ...	7	3	8	5	6	2	7	2	2	1	3	0	1	0	1	0
Gloves ..	0	0	2	0	0	1	2	1	1	1	0	0	0	0	0	0
Glutton ..	0	0	0	0	0	0	1	0	1	1	1	0	1	0	1	2
Goat	1	0	0	0	1	0	0	0	3	1	1	2	2	0	2	1
Good	5	4	4	5	4	5	1	2	0	0	1	0	1	0	1	0
Ham	1	0	0	0	0	0	0	1	0	0	2	0	0	0	0	0
Hand	3	1	4	3	0	2	1	1	1	0	0	0	0	0	0	0
Hands ...	1	1	0	2	0	1	0	0	0	0	0	0	0	0	0	0
Hard ...	2	2	1	1	2	1	1	0	0	0	0	0	0	0	0	0
Hat	0	2	2	1	1	0	0	2	1	0	1	0	0	0	0	0
Head	0	0	0	0	0	1	4	0	2	0	0	0	0	1	1	1
Hot	0	2	0	0	1	1	1	0	0	0	1	0	1	1	1	0
House ...	1	1	1	2	1	0	1	0	0	0	1	0	1	0	0	0
Insect ...	0	0	0	2	0	0	1	0	0	0	0	0	0	0	0	0
Ish	0	0	0	0	1	0	0	0	1	1	0	1	0	2	0	1
Jeff	0	0	0	0	0	0	1	0	0	0	4	2	6	3	8	4
John	2	0	0	0	0	0	0	0	0	0	0	0	0	0	0	0
Kitten ...	3	1	1	1	0	0	0	2	0	0	0	0	0	0	0	0
Lamb	9	13	9	9	20	23	34	52	49	78	35	50	41	59	130	187
Lamp ...	0	0	0	0	1	2	2	0	0	0	0	0	1	1	0	0
Leg	0	0	0	0	1	0	2	3	0	0	0	2	0	1	7	4
Light ...	0	1	1	0	1	2	0	1	0	0	0	0	0	0	0	0
Meal	0	0	0	0	1	1	0	0	0	0	2	0	0	0	0	0
Meat	7	5	5	12	14	15	16	33	26	38	16	25	17	27	42	47
Meet ...	1	0	0	0	1	2	0	0	0	0	0	0	0	0	0	0
Mitten ...	9	11	4	13	3	5	2	2	2	1	5	4	2	1	0	0
Mud	3	2	2	1	1	0	2	1	0	0	0	0	1	0	0	0
Muff	0	1	0	2	0	1	0	0	0	0	0	0	0	0	0	0
Muffin ...	2	0	1	0	1	0	0	0	0	0	1	0	0	1	0	0
Mush ...	0	0	1	1	0	0	2	0	3	3	2	1	1	0	0	1
Mut	0	0	0	2	0	0	0	0	0	0	0	0	0	0	0	0
Mutt	5	0	3	0	1	1	1	1	1	0	0	0	0	0	0	0
Name ...	1	1	0	3	0	0	1	0	0	0	0	0	0	0	0	0
Nice	2	2	2	2	1	0	0	0	0	1	1	0	0	0	0	0
Nothing ..	2	0	0	0	1	0	0	1	1	0	0	0	0	1	0	0
Odd	0	0	1	0	0	0	0	2	0	0	0	0	0	0	0	0
On	0	2	2	1	0	0	0	0	0	0	0	0	0	0	0	0
Pancake ..	0	0	2	0	0	0	0	0	0	0	0	0	0	0	0	0
Pie	0	0	1	0	1	2	1	0	1	0	0	0	0	1	0	0
Pig	0	0	0	1	0	0	0	1	0	0	1	3	1	1	2	1

Response Word	4th M	4th F	5th M	5th F	6th M	6th F	7th M	7th F	8th M	8th F	10th M	10th F	12th M	12th F	College M	College F
							MUTTON									
Pork	0	0	0	0	0	0	1	0	0	0	0	0	0	0	2	0
Pudding . .	0	0	0	0	0	0	1	0	0	0	0	0	0	2	0	0
Roll	0	0	0	0	0	1	0	0	1	0	2	0	0	0	0	1
Round . . .	1	2	0	1	0	0	0	0	0	0	0	0	0	0	1	0
Scarf . . .	0	2	0	1	0	1	0	1	0	0	0	0	0	0	0	0
Sheep . . .	11	9	6	3	17	16	23	21	23	35	50	46	56	46	155	133
Soft	3	6	10	6	6	6	1	6	1	0	3	1	1	1	1	0
Something .	0	1	0	0	1	0	2	0	0	0	0	0	0	0	0	0
Soup	1	1	1	0	0	0	1	4	2	2	5	7	5	9	2	1
Steak . . .	0	0	0	0	0	0	1	0	0	1	0	0	0	0	2	1
Stew	0	0	0	0	1	2	4	3	3	0	4	4	1	5	11	8
Sweet . . .	4	0	0	0	0	0	0	0	0	0	0	0	0	0	0	0
Table . . .	0	0	0	0	0	2	0	0	0	0	0	1	0	0	0	0
Talk	0	1	0	2	0	1	1	1	0	0	0	0	0	0	0	0
Taste . . .	0	1	0	0	0	0	0	0	0	0	0	0	0	0	2	0
Ton	0	2	1	0	0	0	0	0	0	0	0	0	0	0	0	0
Veal	0	0	0	0	0	0	1	1	0	0	2	0	1	0	3	1
Warm . . .	7	10	12	8	8	12	1	1	1	0	2	0	2	1	0	1
Wear . . .	1	0	2	4	1	0	0	0	0	0	1	0	0	0	0	0
Were . . .	0	0	0	0	2	0	0	0	0	0	0	0	0	0	0	0
White . . .	1	0	0	3	0	0	0	0	0	0	1	0	0	1	0	0
Wool	2	0	1	2	2	3	2	1	4	2	0	2	5	0	5	5
Worm . . .	2	0	1	0	0	0	0	0	0	0	1	0	0	0	0	0
Yellow . .	0	0	0	0	0	0	0	0	2	0	0	0	0	1	0	0
							116. MY									
And	2	0	0	0	0	0	0	0	0	0	0	0	0	0	0	0
Aunt	0	0	0	0	0	0	0	0	0	0	2	0	0	0	0	0
Baby	0	0	3	0	0	0	0	0	0	1	1	0	0	0	0	0
Ball	0	1	2	1	1	0	0	0	2	1	0	0	0	0	2	0
Belong . . .	1	0	0	2	1	1	0	1	0	1	0	0	1	1	2	0
Book . . .	0	4	1	0	1	1	1	1	1	4	4	2	0	4	5	9
Books . . .	0	0	0	0	0	0	0	0	0	0	0	1	0	0	3	1
Boy	2	0	0	3	0	0	0	2	1	5	1	2	3	0	2	1
Brother . .	1	2	1	2	2	2	4	4	4	1	0	4	3	2	4	1
By	4	0	1	2	0	1	1	0	0	1	0	0	1	0	0	0
Car	0	1	2	1	0	0	1	0	0	0	3	0	8	2	13	5
Cat	1	4	4	3	2	3	2	0	0	0	0	0	3	0	5	2
Coat	0	0	0	0	0	0	0	2	0	1	0	0	0	1	2	2
Dad	1	0	1	2	1	0	1	0	1	0	1	0	0	0	1	0
Dear . . .	3	1	1	0	1	0	0	1	0	1	0	1	0	0	1	3
Dog	12	5	2	9	4	9	10	4	8	7	4	10	2	9	14	17
Doll	0	3	2	1	0	2	0	0	0	1	0	0	0	0	1	0
Dress . . .	0	0	0	0	0	0	0	0	0	2	0	1	0	4	0	2
Face	1	0	0	0	2	0	0	1	0	0	0	0	0	0	1	1
Fast	0	0	0	0	0	0	2	0	0	0	0	0	0	0	0	0
Father . . .	3	1	5	7	6	1	2	3	2	1	3	1	0	1	3	0
Feet	0	0	0	1	2	0	0	0	1	1	1	1	2	0	1	1
Foot	0	0	0	0	1	1	0	0	4	1	2	0	2	0	0	2

Response Word	4th M	4th F	5th M	5th F	6th M	6th F	7th M	7th F	8th M	8th F	10th M	10th F	12th M	12th F	College M	College F
							MY									
Friend . . .	2	5	3	3	4	6	3	2	3	2	6	4	10	8	4	4
Friends . .	0	0	0	1	0	0	2	0	1	0	3	1	0	1	0	2
Girl	3	2	0	0	3	2	1	1	2	0	5	1	6	2	9	1
Glasses . .	0	0	0	0	0	0	0	0	0	0	0	0	0	0	2	0
God	0	0	0	0	0	0	0	0	1	0	0	0	0	1	3	1
Good	2	1	3	1	1	1	1	0	0	0	0	0	0	0	1	0
Goodness .	1	3	0	1	1	4	0	5	1	4	0	9	4	5	10	13
Gosh . . .	1	2	0	1	0	1	0	1	1	2	0	0	0	1	4	1
Gun	1	0	0	0	2	0	1	0	0	0	1	0	1	1	2	0
Hair	1	0	0	2	2	0	1	0	0	1	1	2	2	3	1	1
Hand . . .	2	1	3	0	1	1	0	1	2	0	1	2	0	0	3	2
Hat	1	0	5	5	0	1	2	2	2	2	1	5	7	3	3	6
He	5	1	2	0	0	0	6	1	0	0	0	0	0	0	1	3
Head . . .	1	4	1	2	2	0	0	0	2	0	4	1	0	3	4	1
Heart . . .	0	0	0	0	1	0	0	0	2	1	1	2	0	0	1	1
Her	1	1	2	3	0	5	3	4	2	4	4	5	1	1	4	1
Hers . . .	0	1	0	1	0	6	2	6	3	3	1	3	3	5	4	3
Hi	3	1	0	1	1	1	2	1	0	1	0	0	1	0	1	0
High	2	0	0	0	1	0	1	0	1	1	0	0	0	0	1	0
Him	0	4	2	1	3	1	0	0	0	2	1	0	0	2	0	0
His	11	7	11	5	15	6	13	14	18	7	24	10	11	14	22	13
Home . . .	3	4	1	0	0	1	0	0	0	3	0	2	0	2	2	4
House . . .	4	3	6	3	8	4	3	3	3	9	3	6	3	5	5	11
I	5	11	3	4	7	8	9	5	2	1	7	6	6	2	3	5
Is	7	5	1	3	1	1	1	1	0	0	0	1	1	0	0	1
It	1	1	1	1	2	1	2	0	0	1	1	1	0	0	2	1
Kite	0	0	0	0	0	0	0	2	0	0	1	0	0	0	0	0
Kitten . . .	0	1	1	1	2	1	0	0	0	0	1	0	0	0	0	1
Land	0	0	0	0	0	1	1	0	0	0	0	0	0	0	2	0
Legs . . .	2	0	1	1	0	0	0	0	0	0	0	0	0	0	0	0
Life	0	0	0	0	1	1	0	1	0	0	1	0	0	1	0	3
Lips	0	0	0	0	0	0	0	0	0	1	0	0	0	0	2	0
Little . . .	3	1	0	1	2	0	0	0	2	1	0	0	1	0	0	0
Love . . .	0	0	0	1	0	1	0	0	0	0	1	0	2	1	0	1
Man	2	0	2	0	1	0	0	0	1	0	0	1	0	0	1	1
May	0	0	0	0	0	0	2	0	1	0	1	0	0	0	0	1
Me	31	36	46	45	28	37	41	49	25	30	23	29	28	38	36	42
Mine	21	18	11	32	17	47	39	47	33	38	27	30	21	37	69	74
Mom	4	0	2	0	2	0	2	0	0	4	0	0	0	1	0	0
Money . . .	0	0	0	0	0	0	0	0	0	0	2	1	0	0	1	0
Mother . .	3	2	4	3	5	2	11	4	13	3	8	5	7	4	5	5
My	0	0	1	0	2	2	0	0	0	0	0	0	0	0	6	0
Myself . . .	2	2	8	6	3	5	0	3	2	4	3	0	2	2	3	1
Name . . .	1	6	1	2	3	5	0	1	2	2	1	2	1	7	3	1
Not	0	0	0	0	2	0	0	0	0	0	0	0	0	0	0	0
Oh	0	3	2	1	1	2	0	1	1	2	3	1	1	0	4	7
One	0	1	2	0	0	0	0	0	0	0	0	0	0	0	0	0
Our	0	0	0	0	0	0	0	1	0	0	0	0	0	1	4	0
Ours	0	1	0	0	2	1	1	1	1	0	0	3	0	0	4	7

Response Word	4th M	4th F	5th M	5th F	6th M	6th F	7th M	7th F	8th M	8th F	10th M	10th F	12th M	12th F	College M	College F
								MY								
Own	5	8	7	5	9	8	4	1	4	3	1	9	5	2	18	17
Owner	0	0	0	0	1	0	1	0	0	0	0	1	2	0	0	0
Pal	0	0	2	0	1	0	0	0	0	0	0	0	1	0	1	0
Pen	0	0	0	0	0	0	0	0	1	0	0	0	0	1	1	5
Pencil	0	0	0	0	0	0	1	0	1	0	0	0	0	0	2	1
People	1	0	0	0	0	0	0	0	2	0	0	0	1	0	0	0
Person	2	0	0	1	1	0	1	0	0	0	1	0	0	0	0	0
Personal	0	0	0	0	0	0	0	0	0	0	0	1	1	0	2	0
Pie	2	1	1	0	1	0	0	0	0	0	0	0	0	1	0	0
Possession	0	0	0	0	0	0	0	2	0	0	1	1	1	3	7	1
Ring	0	0	0	0	0	1	0	0	0	0	0	0	0	0	0	2
Self	8	4	11	8	17	15	3	1	5	3	11	7	12	3	11	7
She	0	0	0	0	0	2	1	0	0	1	0	1	2	0	0	0
Shirt	0	0	0	0	0	0	1	0	0	0	0	0	0	0	2	0
Shoes	0	1	3	0	3	0	2	0	3	1	1	3	1	0	2	1
Shy	0	0	0	0	0	0	0	0	2	0	0	0	0	0	0	0
Sin	0	0	0	0	0	0	0	0	0	0	0	1	1	1	2	0
Sister	1	9	6	4	5	4	5	6	7	5	4	6	12	7	7	8
Skirt	0	0	0	0	0	0	0	2	0	1	0	2	0	0	1	1
Son	0	1	0	0	1	0	0	0	1	0	0	1	1	0	0	2
Sweater	0	0	0	0	0	0	0	0	0	0	0	1	0	0	0	2
That	0	0	0	0	2	0	1	0	0	0	0	0	0	0	0	0
The	1	2	5	0	2	0	0	0	0	0	0	0	0	0	0	0
Their	0	0	1	1	1	1	1	1	0	1	1	0	0	2	1	1
Theirs	0	0	2	1	0	0	0	1	0	2	1	2	2	1	1	0
They	0	0	0	1	0	1	1	1	1	1	1	1	3	1	2	4
Thing	1	2	1	1	1	1	0	0	0	0	1	0	1	0	4	0
Things	0	0	0	1	0	1	0	0	0	0	2	1	0	0	1	0
This	2	2	1	1	0	1	1	1	0	0	2	2	1	1	1	4
Thoughts	0	0	0	0	0	0	0	0	0	0	0	0	1	0	2	0
Toy	4	0	4	2	0	0	0	0	0	0	1	0	0	0	0	0
Watch	0	0	0	0	0	0	0	0	0	0	0	1	0	1	2	1
Way	0	0	0	0	2	0	0	0	0	0	0	0	0	0	0	0
We	1	0	0	1	1	0	1	0	3	1	1	0	0	0	2	2
What	1	1	2	1	0	2	1	0	0	1	5	0	0	0	1	0
Why	1	1	0	2	2	0	5	0	1	0	1	2	1	1	0	0
Wife	0	1	0	0	1	0	0	0	2	0	0	0	2	0	2	0
Will	1	0	0	0	0	0	0	1	0	0	1	1	0	0	2	1
Word	1	1	2	1	2	0	0	2	1	3	3	1	1	0	2	3
You	10	5	6	6	6	3	7	9	9	13	9	6	6	7	11	18
Your	1	7	1	4	3	2	3	5	2	12	8	7	9	11	30	51
Yours	4	14	6	9	5	13	4	17	19	24	11	18	9	18	42	63
						117.	NEEDLE									
Beetle	1	0	3	0	1	0	0	0	0	0	0	0	0	0	0	0
Blood	0	0	0	0	1	0	0	0	1	2	0	0	0	0	0	1
Cloth	2	0	2	0	2	0	0	1	3	0	0	2	2	0	1	2
Eye	3	4	2	5	2	5	2	12	3	4	1	6	10	9	42	26
Fun	0	0	0	0	0	0	0	2	0	0	0	0	0	0	0	0

Response Word	4th M	4th F	5th M	5th F	6th M	6th F	7th M	7th F	8th M	8th F	10th M	10th F	12th M	12th F	College M	College F

NEEDLE

Response Word	4th M	4th F	5th M	5th F	6th M	6th F	7th M	7th F	8th M	8th F	10th M	10th F	12th M	12th F	College M	College F
Hay	0	0	0	1	2	0	2	2	2	0	2	1	1	1	2	3
Haystack	0	0	1	0	0	1	6	0	7	4	3	4	7	2	13	9
Heart	2	0	0	0	0	0	0	0	0	0	0	0	0	0	0	0
Help	3	0	0	0	0	0	1	0	0	0	0	0	0	0	0	0
Hole	0	4	3	6	3	0	0	2	1	0	1	0	1	1	2	2
Hurt	2	0	3	6	5	3	3	0	2	2	1	0	0	2	2	2
Long	1	1	2	1	0	0	0	0	1	0	2	0	0	0	2	0
Mother	1	0	0	0	0	0	0	0	0	0	2	0	0	0	0	0
Nail	2	0	1	0	0	0	0	0	0	0	0	0	0	0	0	0
Need	3	4	3	1	0	1	0	0	0	0	0	0	0	1	0	0
Nose	0	0	0	0	0	0	0	0	2	0	1	0	1	0	1	0
Ouch	1	1	4	2	6	3	1	3	7	1	4	0	3	1	1	0
Pain	0	0	0	1	0	0	0	0	0	0	1	0	1	2	5	1
Pen	2	1	1	1	1	1	2	0	2	1	0	0	1	0	0	1
Pick	0	0	0	1	0	2	1	0	0	0	0	0	0	0	1	1
Pin	42	40	46	29	30	22	37	30	41	28	24	24	27	20	44	41
Pins	0	0	0	0	0	0	0	0	0	2	1	0	0	0	0	1
Point	6	5	7	7	8	11	12	3	11	5	19	10	13	3	32	10
Pointed	3	1	1	1	0	2	1	0	0	0	1	1	0	0	3	0
Poke	0	2	1	0	1	0	0	0	1	0	0	0	0	0	0	0
Prick	2	0	1	8	1	5	2	2	0	1	2	4	3	3	7	3
Sew	17	26	9	31	15	32	5	29	8	11	10	29	10	34	29	58
Sewing	3	11	6	4	6	9	9	11	7	17	9	10	5	8	12	15
Sewing machine	0	0	0	0	0	0	0	0	0	1	0	0	0	0	0	2
Sharp	49	25	53	26	50	30	51	32	31	42	55	25	45	25	76	45
Shot	1	0	0	0	1	0	0	0	5	0	4	1	1	0	2	1
Skinny	0	0	2	1	0	0	1	0	0	0	0	0	0	0	0	0
Small	1	3	3	1	0	2	1	1	0	2	1	1	1	0	0	0
Spool	0	0	0	0	2	0	1	0	0	0	0	0	0	0	2	0
Steel	4	0	0	0	2	1	0	0	0	1	2	1	0	0	0	0
Stick	0	3	2	4	1	4	2	3	3	6	1	0	0	2	4	4
Sting	0	0	0	1	1	0	0	2	0	0	0	0	0	0	0	0
String	3	1	0	1	1	2	1	1	1	0	1	0	2	0	1	0
Syringe	0	0	0	0	0	0	0	0	0	0	0	0	0	0	2	0
Thimble	0	0	0	1	0	0	1	1	0	1	0	0	0	0	2	1
Thin	0	3	3	1	1	1	0	0	1	1	1	0	0	0	0	0
Thread	56	96	54	88	83	95	90	103	82	107	93	125	99	126	196	261
Tick	3	0	0	0	0	0	0	0	0	0	0	0	0	0	0	0
Tree	2	0	0	0	1	0	1	0	0	0	0	0	0	0	1	0
Work	0	1	2	1	0	0	0	0	0	0	0	0	0	1	0	0
Yarn	2	1	1	1	0	2	1	0	2	0	0	0	0	0	0	0

118. NOW

Response Word	4th M	4th F	5th M	5th F	6th M	6th F	7th M	7th F	8th M	8th F	10th M	10th F	12th M	12th F	College M	College F
After	1	4	5	3	1	2	0	4	3	3	1	1	1	1	1	1
Always	0	0	0	1	0	0	0	1	0	3	0	1	1	2	2	6
And	1	0	0	0	1	0	0	0	0	0	0	0	1	0	2	2
Are	1	2	3	1	2	1	1	0	2	0	2	0	0	1	0	0
Away	2	0	1	1	1	0	0	0	0	0	1	0	0	0	1	2
Before	1	0	1	0	0	1	1	3	2	2	0	2	1	0	4	3

Response Word	4th M	4th F	5th M	5th F	6th M	6th F	7th M	7th F	8th M	8th F	10th M	10th F	12th M	12th F	College M	College F
							NOW									
Begin	0	0	0	0	0	0	0	0	0	0	0	0	0	0	2	0
Being	0	0	0	0	0	2	0	0	1	0	0	0	0	0	0	0
Brown	0	0	0	1	0	1	1	1	0	0	0	0	0	1	2	0
Can	1	1	4	0	1	1	0	1	0	0	0	2	0	0	1	0
Come	0	4	5	5	1	2	2	0	0	3	2	1	0	0	1	3
Cow	5	2	5	6	2	0	3	1	1	5	2	3	2	1	1	3
Do	3	1	2	3	2	3	1	0	1	0	1	0	0	0	0	1
Ever	0	0	0	1	0	1	2	2	1	0	2	1	2	0	3	3
For	0	0	1	0	0	0	0	0	1	0	0	0	0	0	2	0
Forever . . .	0	0	0	0	0	0	0	2	3	6	1	7	2	4	3	4
Go	7	6	5	3	4	3	4	4	2	2	6	6	4	2	3	2
He	2	0	0	0	2	0	1	1	2	0	1	0	1	0	0	0
Hear	2	1	1	1	3	0	1	2	0	0	0	0	0	0	0	1
Here	8	5	12	10	11	16	6	7	8	5	8	7	3	9	18	24
House	2	0	1	0	1	0	0	0	0	0	0	0	0	0	0	0
How	26	18	21	27	16	21	24	19	15	6	12	5	16	11	17	17
Hurry	0	0	0	0	0	0	1	0	0	0	1	2	0	0	0	1
I	9	3	2	1	5	1	2	2	4	1	3	1	2	0	4	2
If	1	2	2	3	0	0	0	0	1	0	0	0	0	1	1	0
I'm	0	0	0	2	0	0	0	0	0	0	0	0	0	0	0	0
Immediate .	0	0	0	0	0	0	0	0	0	0	0	0	1	0	0	2
Immediately .	0	0	5	1	0	3	1	4	4	1	3	5	4	11	8	8
Instant . . .	2	3	0	1	1	1	2	2	2	1	1	0	0	1	2	0
Instantly . .	0	0	0	0	0	0	0	0	1	1	0	0	0	0	2	2
Is	3	2	4	0	2	4	0	2	2	2	1	2	2	1	7	3
It	2	0	2	3	3	4	3	0	1	2	0	1	1	0	2	2
Know	5	4	3	3	4	5	3	3	3	1	2	0	2	0	0	0
Later	6	6	6	13	9	9	20	18	17	22	11	14	11	19	23	17
Latter	0	1	3	1	2	0	0	0	0	0	1	2	0	0	0	1
Let	0	0	0	2	3	0	1	0	0	0	0	0	0	0	0	0
Lets	0	2	0	0	1	0	0	0	0	1	0	0	0	0	1	1
Look	3	0	2	0	0	3	1	2	0	1	0	0	0	0	0	0
Me	7	1	6	2	2	1	2	0	3	1	1	1	0	1	1	0
Meanwhile .	0	0	0	0	0	0	0	0	0	0	0	0	0	0	0	2
Minute . . .	1	7	2	2	1	6	1	4	0	1	1	2	0	5	0	3
Minutes . . .	0	0	0	2	0	0	0	0	0	1	0	0	0	0	0	0
Moment . . .	1	0	1	3	2	2	0	0	2	2	2	1	1	0	1	1
Near	0	0	0	1	0	0	1	2	0	0	0	0	0	0	0	1
Never	1	4	2	4	8	11	19	26	26	37	24	30	36	29	53	81
New	1	2	1	2	0	2	4	1	1	1	1	0	0	2	3	0
No	3	4	7	7	1	6	1	1	1	1	2	1	5	2	2	0
Not	0	1	0	1	1	1	2	0	1	0	0	0	0	1	1	0
Now	0	0	0	0	0	2	0	0	0	0	0	0	0	0	0	0
On	1	2	0	1	0	0	0	0	1	0	1	0	0	0	0	0
Or	1	0	1	0	0	0	0	0	0	0	0	0	0	3	2	0
Ow	2	0	1	0	1	0	0	0	0	0	0	0	0	0	0	0
Plow	1	0	1	2	0	0	0	0	0	0	0	0	0	0	0	0
Present . . .	3	0	1	2	4	2	6	5	4	6	8	5	5	4	20	16
Presently . .	0	0	0	0	0	0	0	0	0	0	0	0	0	0	2	1

Response Word	4th M	4th F	5th M	5th F	6th M	6th F	7th M	7th F	8th M	8th F	10th M	10th F	12th M	12th F	College M	College F
								NOW								
Quick	1	2	0	0	0	1	0	0	0	0	2	1	0	1	3	0
Right	3	16	8	10	6	6	1	3	3	1	2	7	4	1	3	3
Right away	0	2	1	2	0	1	0	2	0	0	0	3	2	1	1	1
Second	1	3	1	0	1	0	0	1	0	0	0	0	0	0	0	0
See	12	29	12	11	16	10	6	12	6	9	5	7	9	6	17	8
Some	2	0	0	0	0	2	0	0	0	0	0	0	0	0	1	0
Soon	1	0	0	1	1	1	0	0	1	2	2	1	1	2	4	6
Start	1	5	0	1	0	1	0	0	0	2	0	0	2	0	1	0
Stop	0	1	0	0	0	0	0	0	3	0	0	0	0	0	1	0
Than	0	0	2	1	0	2	0	2	1	3	1	1	1	0	2	1
That	2	0	0	3	1	0	0	2	1	0	0	0	0	0	5	0
The	1	1	2	0	6	2	0	0	0	0	0	0	0	1	1	0
Their	0	0	0	2	0	0	0	0	0	0	0	0	0	0	0	0
Then	30	24	26	34	38	40	51	55	56	62	57	75	58	74	186	192
There	2	2	6	1	2	0	0	0	2	0	1	0	1	0	5	2
They	1	3	0	1	2	1	0	1	3	0	2	0	2	0	1	2
Think	1	2	0	0	1	0	0	0	0	0	0	0	0	0	0	1
This	0	1	1	5	1	2	0	0	0	0	0	1	0	1	0	0
This minute	0	1	0	0	1	1	2	0	0	1	1	1	0	0	0	0
Time	13	10	10	10	7	11	6	6	7	5	10	12	10	7	10	17
Today	3	2	2	1	1	4	3	1	1	0	4	0	1	3	2	2
Us	0	0	0	0	0	0	0	2	1	0	1	1	1	0	1	0
We	3	8	3	1	9	4	8	2	5	1	6	1	2	1	5	3
What	5	3	1	1	4	1	2	0	2	2	1	1	1	1	3	2
When	11	9	6	7	7	8	17	14	12	17	17	12	16	12	26	18
Where	1	4	2	1	2	0	1	1	2	2	0	0	1	1	0	1
Who	1	4	0	0	0	0	2	1	0	0	0	0	1	1	0	0
Why	1	0	1	1	2	2	2	1	1	1	4	2	4	2	2	1
Will	0	2	0	0	0	0	1	0	0	0	0	0	0	0	0	0
Word	2	0	3	0	1	1	0	0	0	0	0	0	0	1	0	0
Wow	0	1	0	0	1	3	1	0	0	0	0	0	0	1	0	0
Yes	1	0	2	0	1	0	0	0	2	0	1	1	0	2	1	0
Yesterday	0	0	1	0	1	0	1	2	1	2	0	0	0	1	2	0
You	8	3	4	9	6	10	3	3	6	2	5	1	3	1	3	3
						119.	NUMBERS									
Add	4	0	0	2	1	1	2	1	0	0	0	2	1	1	8	6
Age	0	0	0	0	0	0	0	1	0	1	0	1	0	3	0	0
Algebra	0	0	0	0	0	0	0	0	2	0	1	4	1	2	4	1
All	0	0	0	0	0	0	0	0	0	0	0	0	0	0	2	0
Alphabet	1	0	1	2	1	2	3	0	1	1	0	0	0	1	2	1
Amount	0	0	0	0	0	0	1	0	0	0	0	0	2	2	0	0
Arabic	0	1	1	2	0	1	2	0	0	0	0	0	1	0	2	1
Are	3	1	6	4	4	1	1	0	3	2	5	1	14	2	6	0
Arithmetic	14	24	17	21	13	25	7	7	1	3	1	8	2	2	4	11
Bible	0	0	0	0	0	0	0	0	1	0	0	0	0	0	2	0
Book	0	0	0	0	0	0	1	0	0	0	2	0	0	0	1	0
Calculus	0	0	0	0	0	0	0	0	0	0	0	0	0	0	2	2

Response Word	4th M	4th F	5th M	5th F	6th M	6th F	7th M	7th F	8th M	8th F	10th M	10th F	12th M	12th F	College M	College F
						NUMBERS										
Can	2	0	0	0	0	1	0	0	0	0	1	0	0	0	0	0
Cards	0	0	0	0	0	0	0	0	0	0	1	0	1	1	2	3
Come	0	0	0	0	1	1	0	0	2	0	0	0	2	0	1	0
Count	13	13	15	8	10	11	7	7	4	5	10	10	7	13	20	22
Counting . .	1	0	0	0	0	0	0	0	2	2	0	1	0	1	1	1
Decimals . .	0	0	0	0	2	0	1	0	0	0	0	0	0	0	0	0
Digits	0	0	0	0	3	1	0	1	4	6	1	3	2	4	25	10
Eight	0	2	1	4	0	0	2	5	3	0	2	1	2	2	3	6
Eleven . . .	0	0	0	0	3	1	0	1	1	0	0	1	0	1	0	0
Facts	1	5	2	0	0	0	0	0	0	0	0	0	0	0	0	0
Fast	1	1	2	0	1	1	0	0	0	0	0	0	0	0	1	1
Fifteen . . .	1	0	0	0	0	0	1	0	0	0	1	2	0	0	0	0
Figure	2	1	1	0	1	0	1	1	1	0	0	2	0	0	3	0
Figures . . .	0	1	3	1	3	5	4	10	7	7	7	7	5	20	21	35
Fingers . . .	0	0	0	0	0	0	0	1	0	3	0	1	0	2	1	0
Five	17	5	8	7	12	3	8	5	9	9	4	5	7	3	7	6
For	0	1	2	0	1	1	0	0	0	0	0	0	0	0	0	0
Four	9	3	4	6	4	8	5	4	5	8	3	4	2	2	5	8
Fractions . .	0	0	0	4	0	0	0	0	0	0	1	0	0	0	1	1
Functions . .	0	0	0	0	0	0	0	0	0	0	0	0	2	0	0	0
Gambling . .	0	0	0	0	0	0	0	0	0	0	0	0	2	0	0	0
Game	0	0	0	0	0	0	1	0	0	0	0	0	2	1	14	4
Games . . .	0	0	0	0	0	0	0	0	0	0	0	0	0	2	6	2
Geometry . .	0	0	0	0	0	0	0	0	0	0	5	4	0	0	0	0
Go	1	1	0	0	1	0	0	0	0	0	0	0	0	0	2	0
Good	2	1	1	0	1	0	0	0	0	0	0	0	0	0	0	0
Hard	0	0	0	0	0	0	1	1	0	0	0	1	0	3	0	0
Hundred . . .	0	2	0	1	1	0	0	0	0	0	0	0	0	0	0	0
Hundreds . .	0	0	0	0	0	0	0	0	0	0	0	0	0	0	0	2
Integers . . .	0	0	0	0	0	0	0	0	0	0	0	0	0	0	5	0
Large	0	0	0	0	0	0	0	0	0	0	1	0	1	0	2	0
Learn	0	2	0	0	0	0	0	0	0	0	0	0	0	0	0	0
Letter	2	5	4	6	2	1	6	2	3	5	2	0	3	0	3	0
Letters . . .	25	30	25	41	17	23	55	53	44	61	46	60	45	54	85	105
Like	0	1	1	2	0	0	0	0	0	0	0	0	0	0	0	0
Long	1	0	0	0	0	0	0	1	0	0	0	2	0	0	0	0
Man	1	0	2	0	0	0	1	0	0	0	0	1	0	0	0	0
Many	0	1	2	0	2	2	1	3	1	2	4	8	8	13	12	14
Math	0	0	1	3	3	4	22	17	15	21	14	19	21	10	43	40
Mathematics .	0	0	0	0	0	1	2	2	0	0	1	0	0	0	4	2
Money	0	0	0	0	1	0	0	1	0	0	2	0	2	3	5	2
Name	0	2	1	1	0	1	0	0	0	0	0	0	0	0	0	0
Names . . .	1	0	0	0	0	0	0	0	2	0	0	0	0	1	1	2
Nine	6	3	2	2	2	1	2	3	3	3	0	0	3	2	1	1
No	0	0	0	0	0	0	2	0	1	0	1	0	0	0	0	0
Now	2	0	1	0	0	0	0	0	0	0	0	0	2	0	0	0
Numb	0	3	1	1	1	1	1	1	0	0	0	0	0	0	0	0
Number . . .	10	5	8	6	5	11	4	2	6	2	1	2	0	1	4	1
Numeral . .	0	0	1	0	0	0	2	1	0	1	0	1	1	0	0	1

Response Word	4th M	4th F	5th M	5th F	6th M	6th F	7th M	7th F	8th M	8th F	10th M	10th F	12th M	12th F	College M	College F
						NUMBERS										
Numerals	3	2	2	1	5	9	11	7	11	0	8	6	3	3	8	15
Of	3	0	2	2	5	2	3	2	2	2	2	0	2	1	3	2
One	35	48	40	38	46	58	20	41	22	39	26	31	25	27	61	71
Ones	0	0	0	0	0	0	1	1	0	0	0	0	0	1	0	2
One two	1	0	0	0	0	0	1	1	0	2	1	0	0	1	0	2
One two three	1	4	1	2	3	1	2	2	4	1	1	1	1	6	1	4
One two three four	1	1	1	0	1	0	0	1	1	1	0	0	0	0	2	0
One two three four etc.	0	0	0	0	0	0	0	0	0	0	0	0	0	0	0	3
One two three four five	0	0	0	0	0	1	0	0	2	0	0	0	0	0	0	0
One two three four five etc.	0	0	0	0	0	0	0	0	0	0	0	2	0	0	0	0
People	0	0	0	0	0	0	0	0	1	0	1	2	4	1	0	2
Please	0	0	1	1	0	1	3	0	3	3	4	1	1	0	0	0
Prison	0	0	0	0	0	0	0	0	0	0	2	0	0	0	0	0
Problems	0	0	0	0	0	0	0	0	0	0	0	0	0	0	2	4
Racket	0	0	0	0	1	0	0	0	4	1	6	2	13	1	7	1
Roman	1	1	0	4	2	1	1	1	0	1	2	1	1	0	3	1
Roman Numerals	0	0	1	2	0	2	0	0	0	1	0	1	0	0	0	0
Seven	0	0	2	1	4	4	2	1	4	3	5	1	2	3	6	3
Six	6	3	3	3	2	4	4	4	5	1	4	1	0	0	3	2
System	0	0	0	0	0	0	0	0	0	0	0	0	0	0	2	0
Talk	0	0	0	2	0	0	0	0	0	0	0	0	0	0	0	0
Telephone	0	2	0	0	1	0	0	0	0	4	0	1	0	3	1	2
Ten	6	6	9	14	7	4	6	3	12	4	11	9	4	8	11	17
The	2	0	0	0	1	0	2	1	0	0	0	0	0	0	0	0
Think	0	0	2	1	0	1	0	0	1	0	0	1	0	0	0	1
Thirteen	0	0	0	0	0	0	0	0	3	0	0	0	1	0	0	0
Three	0	4	5	2	9	10	1	8	3	1	7	6	2	5	7	5
Time	0	0	0	1	0	0	0	3	0	1	0	1	2	0	1	0
Twelve	1	0	0	0	1	0	6	3	1	3	0	0	3	1	0	4
Two	8	15	17	11	24	15	4	8	16	11	6	3	5	4	13	16
We	2	1	1	1	2	1	1	1	0	0	0	0	0	0	0	0
Word	4	1	0	3	1	0	0	0	0	0	0	0	0	0	0	0
Words	2	8	1	3	4	2	2	2	2	4	3	4	5	3	8	12
Work	1	0	1	1	0	0	0	0	0	0	0	1	2	1	1	0
Write	1	0	3	3	2	1	0	1	0	1	1	0	0	1	1	1
You	3	1	1	1	0	1	1	0	0	0	0	0	1	0	0	0
Zero	0	0	0	0	0	0	0	0	0	0	0	0	0	0	2	4
						120. OCEAN										
An	0	2	0	0	0	0	0	0	0	0	0	0	0	0	0	0
Atlantic	2	1	3	2	4	2	3	7	4	6	8	6	9	7	5	14
Big	4	5	3	4	3	5	5	5	3	8	14	12	9	17	13	10
Blue	7	11	6	14	9	17	10	23	18	37	10	28	16	21	41	60
Boat	0	1	1	1	4	1	0	1	1	1	1	2	0	2	2	11

Response Word	4th M	4th F	5th M	5th F	6th M	6th F	7th M	7th F	8th M	8th F	10th M	10th F	12th M	12th F	College M	College F
							OCEAN									
Boats . . .	0	0	0	1	0	0	0	0	0	0	0	0	0	0	2	1
California .	0	0	0	0	0	0	0	1	0	0	1	2	0	0	0	1
Cool	0	0	0	0	0	0	0	3	0	0	0	0	0	0	1	1
Deep . . .	0	1	0	3	2	4	3	2	3	3	6	7	7	10	22	24
Eleven . .	0	0	0	0	0	0	0	0	3	1	1	0	5	0	10	1
Fish	5	2	2	1	1	1	3	2	5	0	2	2	3	1	1	1
Floor . . .	1	0	0	0	1	0	1	1	1	0	0	1	0	2	3	1
Green . . .	0	0	0	0	0	1	0	0	0	0	0	2	3	1	3	3
Huge	0	0	0	0	0	0	0	0	0	1	1	3	0	0	0	2
Indian . . .	0	0	0	0	1	1	0	0	2	0	1	0	0	0	1	0
Lake . . .	17	20	21	16	9	12	12	15	24	7	9	6	3	7	6	3
Lakes . . .	0	0	2	0	0	0	0	1	0	0	0	0	0	0	0	0
Land	0	0	0	0	1	0	0	1	1	2	0	1	0	2	1	2
Large . . .	0	0	0	0	0	0	1	4	1	2	3	4	2	2	8	6
Liner . . .	1	0	0	0	2	0	1	0	0	0	2	1	2	0	3	0
Oh	2	0	0	0	0	0	0	0	0	0	0	0	0	0	0	0
Pacific . .	4	1	0	3	6	4	7	9	7	10	15	7	7	6	17	11
River . . .	4	10	4	8	3	8	4	5	3	5	0	4	0	1	6	9
Rough . . .	0	1	0	0	0	0	1	0	0	0	0	0	0	0	0	2
Salt	6	2	0	7	3	3	6	4	2	0	4	3	5	2	6	4
Salt water .	1	0	1	0	2	0	0	1	0	1	0	1	1	0	0	1
Salty . . .	0	0	0	0	0	1	1	1	0	1	0	0	1	3	1	0
Sand	0	0	0	0	0	0	0	0	1	2	0	0	0	0	0	1
Sea	73	67	57	73	50	62	62	48	42	45	35	45	31	38	83	72
See	0	3	0	0	1	1	0	0	0	0	0	0	1	0	0	0
Ship	1	3	4	1	3	1	3	1	2	2	4	5	5	3	4	8
Ships . . .	0	0	0	0	1	0	0	0	1	0	1	0	2	1	1	3
Sky	0	0	0	0	1	0	0	0	0	0	1	0	0	0	2	0
Swim . . .	0	2	0	3	5	0	2	2	3	2	1	5	1	0	2	1
Swimming .	0	4	0	0	0	1	0	2	0	1	0	0	0	3	0	0
Vast	0	0	1	0	0	0	0	0	0	0	2	1	1	1	7	3
Vastness .	0	0	0	0	0	0	0	0	0	0	0	0	1	0	3	0
Water . . .	98	95	124	94	123	106	107	91	103	97	109	76	107	93	183	179
Wave . . .	1	0	0	1	2	1	0	0	0	1	0	0	0	1	4	4
Waves . .	1	5	2	4	1	6	3	5	0	8	2	5	1	6	17	22
Wavy	0	0	0	0	0	0	0	0	0	2	0	0	0	1	0	0
Wet	1	0	1	0	0	1	2	1	3	2	2	1	2	1	5	2
Wide . . .	0	0	1	4	1	1	1	2	0	2	2	6	8	5	5	10
							121. OF									
A	1	4	1	3	4	0	2	2	4	1	1	1	4	1	3	2
About . . .	0	1	0	0	1	1	0	1	1	0	1	0	2	2	4	1
After . . .	0	0	0	0	0	0	0	0	0	2	0	0	0	0	0	1
Ah	0	0	0	0	0	0	0	0	0	0	0	0	0	0	2	0
All	0	0	1	1	0	4	3	1	1	1	0	1	3	3	1	2
Am	0	0	0	0	0	0	0	2	0	0	0	0	0	0	0	0
An	0	0	1	4	2	0	2	0	0	1	1	0	1	0	1	2
And	0	0	2	2	2	3	1	3	2	1	3	3	2	2	8	4
At	1	1	3	2	1	3	8	11	7	7	7	10	1	5	6	18

Response Word	4th M	4th F	5th M	5th F	6th M	6th F	7th M	7th F	8th M	8th F	10th M	10th F	12th M	12th F	College M	College F
								OF								
Because . .	0	0	0	1	1	2	1	4	0	4	1	4	3	5	1	11
Before . .	0	0	0	0	0	0	0	0	0	1	0	0	1	0	2	0
Belong . . .	1	2	2	0	0	1	2	1	2	1	1	1	0	1	5	1
Belonging .	0	0	0	1	0	0	0	1	1	1	0	0	1	0	2	2
Between . .	0	0	0	0	0	0	1	0	0	0	0	0	0	0	0	2
Book	0	2	0	0	0	4	0	0	1	0	0	1	0	0	0	0
By	0	0	1	0	0	0	0	1	1	1	0	1	1	3	9	4
Car	0	2	0	0	0	1	0	0	0	0	0	0	1	0	1	0
Cat	2	0	0	0	1	0	0	0	0	0	0	0	0	0	0	0
Course . .	15	10	16	16	17	21	16	23	22	35	21	33	16	26	61	59
De	0	0	0	0	0	0	1	0	0	0	0	0	0	0	2	1
Did	0	2	0	1	0	0	0	0	0	0	0	0	0	0	0	0
Dove . . .	0	0	1	0	0	0	2	1	0	0	0	0	2	0	1	0
Fell	2	2	0	1	0	0	0	0	0	0	0	0	1	0	1	0
For	0	0	1	0	1	2	0	6	0	2	3	1	4	3	7	14
From . . .	0	1	2	2	2	3	0	1	1	2	4	4	7	0	18	13
German . .	0	0	0	0	0	0	0	0	0	0	0	2	0	0	0	0
Get	0	0	1	0	0	2	0	0	0	0	0	0	0	0	0	0
Go	0	2	2	0	4	0	1	1	1	0	1	0	0	1	0	0
Good . . .	0	1	2	0	1	0	0	0	0	0	1	1	0	0	1	0
Have . . .	0	0	0	0	0	0	0	0	0	0	0	2	1	0	1	0
He	1	0	1	2	1	2	2	1	0	0	1	0	0	0	1	0
Her	0	2	1	0	2	3	0	1	0	2	2	0	3	2	0	2
Him	1	2	4	0	2	1	2	2	4	2	2	1	5	3	3	1
His	1	0	2	2	0	1	3	1	4	0	2	1	2	0	8	3
House . . .	0	0	1	2	0	0	0	0	1	0	1	0	1	0	0	0
How	0	0	1	0	2	1	0	1	0	0	1	1	0	0	0	1
If	3	5	1	4	1	6	6	2	3	2	2	1	3	1	5	11
In	1	4	2	1	2	1	2	5	1	3	3	0	3	4	6	4
Is	0	2	2	4	5	4	3	4	4	3	4	1	4	0	3	7
It	14	7	16	18	13	13	12	13	18	10	7	6	10	6	22	13
Kind	0	0	1	1	2	0	0	1	0	0	1	0	0	1	0	0
Light . . .	0	0	3	1	1	0	1	0	1	0	0	0	0	0	0	0
Love . . .	1	0	1	1	0	0	0	0	0	1	0	0	1	0	2	0
Many . . .	0	0	1	0	1	0	0	0	0	0	2	1	0	0	2	1
Me	4	2	3	3	2	3	1	1	3	4	2	3	2	3	0	2
Men	0	0	0	0	0	1	0	0	0	0	1	0	0	0	1	2
Mice . . .	0	1	0	0	0	0	0	0	0	0	1	1	0	1	1	2
Mine . . .	0	2	2	2	1	0	1	0	0	1	0	0	0	1	1	2
Most . . .	1	0	0	0	0	0	0	0	0	0	0	2	0	0	0	0
My	0	0	0	0	0	0	1	0	0	2	0	0	0	1	4	1
Name . . .	0	2	0	1	0	1	0	0	0	0	0	0	0	0	0	0
Not	1	2	0	3	1	2	0	1	1	1	1	2	1	1	2	4
Nothing . .	1	0	0	0	0	0	0	0	0	2	0	0	0	0	0	1
Now	2	3	1	2	1	2	1	1	2	2	0	3	2	0	2	5
Of	0	0	0	0	2	0	0	0	0	0	0	0	0	0	0	0
Off	38	31	29	37	23	26	51	40	40	40	30	36	41	27	34	38
Often . . .	2	4	2	0	0	1	2	2	3	3	4	2	3	0	2	1
Oh	3	1	1	3	3	1	1	0	0	0	0	1	1	0	0	1

OF

Response Word	M	F	M	F	M	F	M	F	M	F	M	F	M	F	M	F
OK	0	2	0	0	0	1	0	0	0	0	0	0	0	0	0	0
On	31	34	31	26	32	17	26	31	35	12	26	22	18	14	29	35
One	2	4	3	2	2	3	2	1	1	1	1	1	3	2	2	1
Only	0	1	0	0	0	0	0	0	0	2	0	0	2	0	1	1
Onward	0	0	0	0	2	0	0	0	0	0	0	0	0	0	0	0
Or	1	1	2	0	1	3	1	0	3	1	1	1	2	3	4	4
Out	1	1	0	1	1	1	1	3	0	0	1	0	2	1	0	1
Oven	1	0	1	0	0	3	0	0	0	0	0	0	0	0	0	0
Over	1	2	0	0	1	0	0	0	0	1	0	0	0	1	2	1
Part	1	0	1	1	3	1	1	1	1	1	2	0	1	1	5	2
People	1	2	1	2	0	2	0	0	2	0	3	3	1	1	3	1
Person	0	1	0	0	0	1	1	0	0	0	0	0	2	1	0	0
Place	1	0	0	0	1	2	0	1	0	0	0	0	0	0	0	0
Preposition	0	0	0	0	0	0	1	0	1	7	4	6	4	14	7	9
Say	0	0	0	2	0	0	0	0	0	0	0	0	0	0	0	0
Sentence	0	0	0	1	0	2	0	0	0	0	0	0	0	1	0	0
So	0	0	0	1	0	1	0	0	0	0	0	1	0	2	2	2
Some	3	2	0	0	1	0	1	2	0	1	2	1	0	0	0	2
Something	2	6	2	4	4	6	3	1	2	0	1	3	1	0	2	2
Studies	0	0	0	0	0	0	0	0	0	0	0	0	0	0	0	2
That	8	8	13	12	10	9	8	7	5	9	17	13	10	12	23	28
The	9	16	8	8	13	13	8	11	9	3	7	4	9	16	32	28
Thee	0	0	0	0	0	0	1	0	0	0	0	0	0	0	4	2
Their	1	0	1	0	2	0	0	0	1	0	1	0	0	0	1	1
Them	6	7	3	7	4	2	9	3	9	8	8	8	1	6	26	28
Then	8	7	4	3	2	4	2	5	3	6	3	3	4	4	14	10
There	0	2	2	4	1	2	0	0	2	1	2	3	0	1	2	2
They	0	0	1	0	0	2	0	0	0	0	0	0	1	0	0	0
Thing	5	2	2	3	3	2	0	1	1	1	1	2	0	1	0	0
Things	1	0	0	0	0	0	0	2	1	0	0	2	0	1	0	0
Think	0	1	1	0	0	2	0	0	0	0	0	0	0	0	0	0
This	2	1	0	1	1	2	0	3	3	0	1	3	3	3	8	12
Those	0	0	1	0	0	0	0	0	0	0	0	0	1	1	0	2
Three	0	0	0	0	0	0	0	0	0	0	0	0	0	0	0	2
To	1	1	4	1	2	1	3	2	5	4	3	6	1	5	10	16
Us	2	0	0	1	0	0	0	0	1	1	0	0	0	0	2	3
What	9	2	2	5	6	4	3	6	7	10	11	7	5	20	17	7
When	2	1	0	2	0	1	2	2	2	0	1	0	2	1	1	2
Where	0	2	0	0	0	0	1	0	0	2	0	0	1	1	3	1
Which	0	0	1	0	0	0	0	0	0	2	0	1	1	0	4	4
Whom	0	0	0	0	0	0	0	1	0	1	0	1	0	0	3	1
With	0	0	0	0	0	2	3	1	0	1	0	0	0	0	1	2
Word	0	2	6	2	6	3	1	1	1	2	1	0	0	3	1	1
Yes	1	0	0	0	2	1	1	0	0	0	1	0	0	0	0	0
You	6	6	5	4	3	3	3	7	4	3	5	3	6	2	6	7
Yours	0	0	1	0	1	1	0	0	0	2	0	0	1	0	0	2

Response Word	4th		5th		6th		7th		8th		10th		12th		College	
	M	F	M	F	M	F	M	F	M	F	M	F	M	F	M	F

122. OH

Response Word	M	F	M	F	M	F	M	F	M	F	M	F	M	F	M	F
A	3	0	2	3	2	3	2	2	2	0	0	1	1	0	4	0
Ah	1	1	2	6	4	9	12	16	12	18	8	16	19	15	54	46
All	0	0	0	0	2	0	0	0	0	0	0	0	0	0	0	1
And	0	0	1	2	0	0	1	1	0	0	0	0	0	0	1	2
Are	0	0	0	1	0	1	0	0	2	0	0	0	0	0	0	0
Bad	0	2	2	2	0	5	1	0	0	0	0	0	0	0	0	1
Be	0	1	2	0	1	0	0	0	0	0	0	0	0	0	0	1
Boy	1	1	1	4	0	1	3	4	0	2	1	6	5	4	5	8
Boys	0	0	0	0	0	0	0	0	0	0	0	0	0	2	0	0
Brother	0	0	0	0	0	1	0	0	0	0	0	0	0	0	2	0
But	0	0	1	0	0	0	1	0	4	0	0	1	0	0	3	5
Cry	1	2	2	2	3	2	1	1	1	0	2	6	2	1	4	5
Darn	0	0	0	0	0	0	0	0	0	1	0	0	0	1	2	0
Dear	2	4	1	9	5	14	5	9	1	6	3	1	1	4	0	7
Dog	0	0	0	0	0	0	0	0	1	0	0	0	0	2	0	0
Excited	2	3	1	1	1	3	0	2	0	0	1	1	2	1	2	0
Excitement	0	0	0	0	0	1	0	1	0	2	5	3	1	0	2	0
Exclaim	0	0	0	0	1	2	3	5	1	2	2	4	4	4	5	8
Exclamation	1	0	0	0	1	4	3	6	1	4	4	3	2	9	12	8
Exclamation point	0	0	0	0	0	0	0	0	0	0	0	0	0	0	2	0
Expression	1	1	2	1	1	4	1	2	0	2	0	1	2	5	1	2
Fear	0	0	0	0	0	0	0	0	0	0	2	0	0	1	1	0
Forgot	2	2	0	0	0	3	0	1	0	0	1	0	0	0	0	0
Fright	1	1	0	0	2	0	0	0	0	0	0	0	1	0	6	0
Fun	1	1	1	0	1	0	0	1	2	1	0	0	1	1	0	0
Funny	0	1	0	0	0	0	0	1	0	0	0	1	0	2	0	0
Gee	0	0	1	1	1	0	2	3	2	1	1	0	0	1	2	1
Girl	0	1	0	0	1	1	0	0	0	0	1	0	0	0	2	0
Go	0	1	0	1	1	1	3	0	0	0	0	1	0	0	0	0
Good	1	2	3	2	0	1	2	0	0	1	2	1	1	0	0	2
Good grief	0	0	0	0	0	0	0	0	0	2	0	0	0	0	0	0
Goodness	0	1	0	1	0	1	0	0	0	0	0	2	0	2	2	0
Gosh	0	1	1	0	0	0	1	1	1	3	1	0	0	0	0	0
Ha	0	1	1	0	4	3	3	1	0	3	1	1	1	2	2	4
Happened	0	3	0	0	0	0	0	0	0	0	0	0	0	0	0	0
Happy	0	0	0	1	2	1	1	0	1	3	0	1	0	1	0	0
Have	0	0	0	2	0	0	0	0	0	0	0	0	0	0	0	0
Hay	1	2	0	0	0	0	1	0	0	0	0	0	0	0	0	0
He	2	1	3	3	3	2	3	0	1	0	1	1	2	0	1	0
Heck	0	0	0	0	0	0	0	0	2	0	0	0	1	0	1	1
Hell	0	0	0	0	0	0	0	0	0	0	0	0	0	0	5	0
Hello	1	2	1	0	2	1	0	0	1	0	0	0	0	0	1	0
Help	0	2	2	0	1	1	2	0	3	2	0	0	0	0	0	4
Henry	0	0	0	0	2	0	0	0	0	0	0	0	0	0	1	0
Hey	0	1	2	0	0	0	0	0	0	0	0	0	0	0	0	0
Hi	6	4	5	4	5	1	2	4	2	4	5	0	0	1	3	1
Him	0	1	0	0	1	1	1	1	2	0	0	0	0	0	0	0
Ho	5	1	5	3	0	1	4	1	1	0	0	0	1	0	1	3

Response Word	4th M	4th F	5th M	5th F	6th M	6th F	7th M	7th F	8th M	8th F	10th M	10th F	12th M	12th F	College M	College F
								OH								
Hot	0	0	0	0	2	0	1	0	1	0	1	0	0	1	0	0
How	11	6	4	3	7	6	3	8	5	1	5	2	1	2	3	2
Hum	0	0	0	0	0	0	0	0	1	0	0	0	2	0	0	0
Hurt	0	1	1	5	2	0	2	1	1	0	3	0	5	2	5	1
I	2	0	3	0	1	1	4	1	1	0	0	0	1	1	5	0
If	0	0	1	1	0	0	0	0	1	0	1	0	0	0	2	1
Is	1	3	0	1	0	0	1	0	0	1	0	1	0	0	0	0
Ish	0	1	0	0	0	0	0	2	0	1	0	1	0	1	0	1
It	3	3	1	1	3	3	2	0	0	1	0	1	0	0	1	1
Joy	0	0	0	0	0	0	0	1	1	3	0	2	0	1	0	1
Know	2	3	1	1	0	1	0	1	0	0	0	0	0	0	1	1
Laugh	1	1	2	0	1	1	0	2	0	0	0	0	1	1	1	2
Look	5	2	2	3	3	0	2	2	0	2	2	1	1	1	0	2
Low	1	0	3	0	0	0	0	0	0	0	0	0	0	0	0	0
Mad	0	0	0	0	2	1	1	0	0	0	0	0	1	0	0	0
Man	0	0	0	0	0	0	0	1	2	0	1	1	0	0	2	2
Me	5	1	6	1	9	4	2	7	2	6	7	6	7	3	19	16
Mistake	0	1	0	0	3	0	0	1	0	0	0	1	0	0	0	1
Mouth	0	0	0	2	0	0	0	1	0	0	0	0	0	0	1	0
My	17	17	21	21	18	23	21	31	16	35	25	31	25	34	77	93
Never	0	0	0	0	0	0	1	1	2	0	0	1	0	0	3	1
Nice	0	1	1	2	0	1	0	0	0	1	0	0	0	2	0	0
No	43	40	45	37	45	33	34	35	47	48	49	70	54	65	68	88
Not	3	0	1	2	2	0	0	0	0	1	1	0	0	2	2	0
Now	0	3	1	1	1	0	0	0	1	1	0	0	0	1	4	2
Nuts	0	0	0	0	1	1	1	1	1	0	0	0	0	0	2	3
O	1	0	2	0	0	0	0	0	1	0	0	0	0	1	2	0
Of	0	0	0	1	0	0	3	1	0	2	0	0	0	0	0	0
Off	0	1	0	0	0	0	1	0	2	1	0	0	0	0	0	0
Oh	1	1	0	0	2	4	0	0	0	0	0	0	0	0	0	2
OK	2	1	1	1	1	0	0	0	1	1	0	0	0	2	0	0
Okay	0	0	0	1	0	3	1	0	0	0	1	0	0	0	0	1
On	7	4	2	7	3	3	4	1	3	0	3	0	0	0	2	2
One	0	0	2	1	1	1	0	0	0	0	0	0	0	0	0	0
Ouch	2	0	0	0	6	1	11	5	11	2	6	4	7	1	10	13
Out	2	0	1	0	0	1	0	1	0	0	0	0	0	0	0	0
Ow	0	0	0	0	0	1	1	1	3	1	3	1	0	0	2	1
Pain	0	0	0	0	0	0	0	0	0	0	0	0	0	1	7	1
Question	0	0	1	0	0	0	2	2	1	1	0	0	3	0	0	0
Really	1	1	1	1	0	3	0	2	0	1	2	3	4	3	1	7
Remark	0	0	1	0	0	0	1	0	0	0	0	0	0	2	0	0
Run	2	2	2	1	0	1	0	0	2	1	1	0	0	0	0	0
Said	3	1	1	0	1	0	0	0	0	0	0	0	0	0	0	0
Say	3	0	0	3	1	0	1	0	2	1	0	1	1	0	2	0
Scared	1	1	0	1	1	0	2	2	1	2	1	1	0	0	1	0
Scream	0	0	0	0	0	0	0	0	1	0	0	0	2	1	1	2
See	1	4	1	4	2	6	0	3	2	1	0	1	0	1	0	3
Sentence	0	0	0	0	0	0	0	0	0	0	0	2	0	0	0	0
Shock	0	0	0	0	0	0	0	0	1	0	2	2	0	1	0	2

Response Word	4th M	F	5th M	F	6th M	F	7th M	F	8th M	F	10th M	F	12th M	F	College M	F

<u>OH</u>

Response Word	4th M	F	5th M	F	6th M	F	7th M	F	8th M	F	10th M	F	12th M	F	College M	F
Shout	0	1	1	0	2	1	1	0	0	0	1	2	0	0	0	1
Sigh	0	0	1	0	0	0	1	0	0	1	0	1	1	5	1	1
So	1	0	2	5	0	1	2	1	2	3	0	2	0	0	1	6
Something	3	4	2	0	0	1	0	0	0	1	0	0	0	0	0	0
Startled	1	1	2	1	0	0	2	0	0	1	0	0	1	1	0	0
Stop	0	0	1	0	0	0	0	0	0	0	2	0	1	0	3	1
Sudden	0	0	0	0	0	2	0	0	0	1	0	0	0	0	0	0
Surprise	3	12	5	12	2	10	9	7	7	17	10	17	13	6	21	24
Surprised	4	4	1	8	4	6	0	0	2	2	3	1	2	1	0	0
Susanna	0	0	0	0	2	0	0	1	0	0	0	0	0	0	0	1
Talk	0	0	0	0	0	2	0	0	0	0	0	0	0	1	0	0
That	7	2	2	2	0	1	1	1	2	2	3	1	4	0	3	6
The	0	1	2	0	2	0	2	0	2	2	1	0	1	2	4	2
Then	0	0	0	0	0	0	0	0	1	0	0	0	0	0	2	0
There	0	0	1	0	1	2	0	0	1	0	1	0	0	0	0	0
This	1	0	0	0	0	0	0	0	0	0	0	0	0	0	2	0
Trouble	1	1	0	2	0	1	1	2	0	1	0	0	0	0	0	0
Understand	0	1	0	0	1	2	1	0	0	0	0	0	0	0	0	0
We	0	1	0	0	0	0	0	2	0	0	0	0	0	0	1	0
Well	2	0	1	0	0	1	3	3	2	1	1	3	2	4	6	4
What	4	3	4	5	0	6	4	3	7	3	2	2	4	1	15	6
When	0	1	0	1	0	0	0	0	0	0	0	1	0	1	2	1
Who	0	0	1	1	0	0	0	2	0	0	1	0	0	0	0	0
Why	1	1	3	3	4	3	1	1	6	4	4	5	6	2	5	11
Word	2	3	2	2	4	2	2	0	0	1	2	0	0	1	0	0
Wow	0	0	0	0	1	0	0	2	1	1	0	2	0	1	3	1
Ya	0	0	1	0	0	0	0	0	2	0	1	1	1	0	2	1
Yea	0	0	0	0	0	0	0	0	0	2	2	0	2	0	1	1
Yeah	1	0	2	0	3	1	0	0	2	1	2	0	0	0	1	1
Yes	9	11	12	10	12	3	8	6	15	8	12	6	9	11	22	36
You	7	3	9	6	7	3	6	4	5	5	11	2	11	3	15	2

123. <u>ON</u>

Response Word	4th M	F	5th M	F	6th M	F	7th M	F	8th M	F	10th M	F	12th M	F	College M	F
A	3	2	1	0	0	0	0	0	1	0	0	0	1	1	2	0
Aboard	0	0	2	0	0	0	0	1	0	0	0	0	0	0	0	0
Above	0	0	0	2	0	0	0	0	1	2	2	0	0	1	8	4
And	0	0	0	0	0	0	0	0	0	0	1	0	0	0	2	0
At	0	1	0	4	1	3	4	7	8	2	2	3	1	7	12	19
Back	2	2	1	1	2	0	0	1	0	0	0	0	0	1	0	0
Bed	1	0	0	1	0	0	2	0	0	1	2	1	0	0	0	1
Before	0	0	0	0	0	0	0	0	0	0	0	1	1	0	1	2
Bike	0	0	1	2	0	0	0	0	0	0	0	0	0	0	1	0
Boat	0	0	0	0	0	0	0	0	0	0	2	0	0	1	1	0
By	0	0	0	0	1	0	1	2	1	0	1	1	0	1	3	7
Chair	0	1	1	1	1	0	0	1	0	1	1	4	0	0	0	2
Clothes	0	0	0	0	0	1	0	1	0	0	0	3	1	2	0	1
Day	0	2	0	0	0	1	0	0	0	0	1	0	0	0	0	0
Dot	0	0	0	0	0	0	2	0	0	0	0	0	0	0	0	0
Down	0	0	0	0	1	1	1	2	0	1	0	0	0	0	0	0

	4th M	4th F	5th M	5th F	6th M	6th F	7th M	7th F	8th M	8th F	10th M	10th F	12th M	12th F	College M	College F

ON

Response Word	4th M	4th F	5th M	5th F	6th M	6th F	7th M	7th F	8th M	8th F	10th M	10th F	12th M	12th F	College M	College F
Electric	0	0	0	0	0	0	2	0	0	0	0	0	0	0	0	0
Fire	1	1	1	0	1	0	0	0	1	1	2	1	2	0	5	0
Floor	0	2	0	0	0	1	0	1	0	0	1	1	1	1	0	2
Forward	1	0	0	1	1	0	0	0	0	0	0	1	2	0	0	1
Gas	0	0	2	0	0	0	0	0	0	0	0	1	2	0	0	0
Get	1	2	0	0	0	0	0	0	0	0	0	0	0	0	0	0
Go	5	3	3	2	2	0	2	0	1	0	3	1	1	0	0	0
Going	1	1	1	0	1	2	2	0	0	0	0	1	0	0	0	0
Gone	0	0	0	1	0	0	2	0	0	0	0	0	0	0	0	0
Heat	2	0	0	0	2	0	1	0	0	0	0	0	0	1	0	0
Here	1	2	0	1	1	0	0	2	0	0	2	0	0	0	0	1
High	0	2	1	0	0	0	0	0	0	1	1	0	0	0	0	1
Hill	0	1	0	2	0	1	0	0	0	0	0	0	0	2	0	0
His	0	1	0	0	1	0	0	0	2	0	0	0	2	0	0	0
Horse	2	0	1	2	2	1	2	1	1	2	3	1	0	1	2	2
Hot	3	0	2	1	1	0	0	0	0	0	1	0	0	0	1	0
House	0	1	0	1	0	0	0	0	0	0	0	0	2	0	0	0
In	8	6	9	7	9	15	15	16	16	9	17	14	20	25	45	57
Is	7	6	4	4	0	3	0	1	2	1	2	2	0	0	1	0
It	12	13	10	12	11	10	3	3	6	2	4	8	5	5	10	10
Light	3	2	3	2	5	2	6	4	1	1	5	0	3	1	1	0
Lights	0	0	0	0	0	0	1	1	2	0	0	1	1	0	1	0
Me	3	1	0	1	0	1	1	0	1	1	0	0	0	1	0	0
My	0	0	2	0	0	0	0	0	0	0	0	0	0	0	0	0
Near	0	1	0	0	0	0	1	0	0	0	0	2	0	1	0	1
No	5	4	3	1	1	0	0	0	0	0	1	0	0	0	0	0
Now	0	1	1	1	0	0	0	0	0	0	0	0	0	0	0	2
Of	5	7	2	5	5	5	3	2	3	1	3	2	4	1	3	0
Off	88	91	105	81	95	88	118	115	138	119	103	99	135	101	211	212
One	0	3	1	0	1	0	1	0	0	1	0	0	0	0	0	0
Only	1	1	0	2	0	1	0	0	0	0	0	0	0	0	0	0
On top	1	1	1	3	4	0	2	1	1	1	0	2	2	1	0	1
Or	0	0	1	0	0	0	0	0	1	0	0	0	0	1	2	1
Out	1	1	0	2	4	1	1	0	3	2	1	0	2	1	2	2
Oven	0	0	2	1	0	2	1	0	0	0	0	0	0	2	0	0
Over	3	3	1	2	2	3	3	6	8	7	9	7	6	5	9	7
Place	1	0	1	1	2	2	1	1	0	2	1	0	1	1	0	1
Put	2	1	2	5	1	3	0	0	1	2	2	1	3	0	1	1
Ride	1	1	0	3	3	3	0	2	0	0	0	1	1	0	0	0
Road	2	0	0	0	0	0	0	0	0	0	0	1	0	0	1	0
Roof	0	1	0	0	0	1	1	0	1	0	4	2	3	0	1	0
Sat	0	1	1	1	1	0	0	1	0	0	1	0	2	0	1	0
Set	0	1	3	1	1	3	1	2	1	1	1	0	0	1	0	0
Sit	2	3	5	5	3	10	5	5	3	2	3	6	0	3	5	0
Sitting	0	2	0	2	0	3	1	0	0	2	2	0	0	0	1	2
Something	3	4	2	4	2	4	3	1	0	2	0	2	0	0	0	0
Stage	0	0	2	0	0	0	0	0	0	1	0	1	1	0	0	1
Stand	0	0	0	1	0	0	2	0	0	0	0	0	0	0	0	0
Step	0	1	0	0	0	2	0	0	0	0	0	1	0	0	0	0

Response Word	4th M	F	5th M	F	6th M	F	7th M	F	8th M	F	10th M	F	12th M	F	College M	F
							ON									
Stove	1	3	5	5	2	2	5	4	0	5	6	1	0	2	6	7
Street	0	0	1	1	1	0	0	0	0	2	0	0	0	1	0	0
Switch	2	1	1	2	0	1	1	1	1	0	2	2	0	0	4	0
Table	3	2	2	1	0	6	2	8	6	8	5	6	1	7	11	18
Tap	0	0	0	0	1	0	0	0	0	0	0	0	0	0	0	2
That	2	0	2	5	2	0	0	3	0	1	1	1	3	0	3	3
The	5	3	6	4	9	1	6	2	3	2	1	5	3	4	14	7
Them	0	0	0	0	0	0	0	0	0	0	0	0	0	0	2	0
There	4	2	1	0	0	2	1	2	1	0	1	0	2	0	2	0
Thing	0	2	3	1	0	1	1	0	0	0	0	0	0	0	0	0
This	5	3	2	1	4	2	0	0	2	0	1	1	1	1	4	1
Time	1	0	0	0	1	0	1	0	0	3	0	2	2	2	5	4
To	0	1	2	2	3	0	1	1	3	0	1	3	2	3	3	9
Top	21	12	16	18	16	26	13	17	15	28	24	18	11	18	57	50
Turn	0	2	0	1	0	0	2	0	0	0	0	0	0	0	3	1
TV	0	2	1	1	2	0	0	0	0	0	1	0	0	0	0	0
Under	1	2	0	0	0	2	2	4	1	2	0	2	1	3	3	8
Up	2	2	2	2	4	2	1	2	1	1	0	5	0	1	1	4
Upon	2	1	2	3	3	7	3	8	2	7	1	6	4	5	6	8
Ward	0	0	0	0	2	0	0	0	0	0	0	0	0	0	0	1
Way	0	2	0	2	1	0	0	0	0	0	0	0	0	0	1	0
Wear	0	1	0	0	0	0	0	0	0	0	0	0	0	2	1	0
What	0	0	0	0	0	0	0	0	1	3	2	0	0	3	3	1
With	0	0	0	0	0	0	0	0	0	1	0	0	0	2	1	0
Word	1	0	2	1	1	1	0	0	0	0	1	1	0	0	0	2
You	0	1	1	0	0	0	0	0	1	1	1	0	1	0	3	0
						124.	ONLY										
All	1	0	0	2	2	3	1	4	4	2	1	5	3	4	8	15
Alone	2	2	6	5	4	8	5	6	5	2	7	8	12	12	18	25
Also	1	0	0	0	1	0	2	1	0	1	0	0	0	0	1	0
Always	4	2	1	6	2	4	2	2	4	8	4	7	2	6	7	11
At	0	0	0	0	0	0	0	0	0	0	1	0	1	0	3	0
Because	4	0	2	3	3	5	1	0	3	5	1	0	3	1	8	6
Before	0	0	0	0	0	0	0	0	0	0	0	0	1	0	2	0
Boy	2	2	1	0	2	0	0	0	0	1	1	2	0	0	1	1
But	1	0	0	0	2	3	0	3	4	2	3	5	2	0	11	13
Car	0	0	0	0	1	0	0	0	0	0	0	0	0	0	3	0
Child	0	1	0	2	1	3	1	5	1	2	1	3	0	2	2	3
Children	0	0	0	0	0	0	0	2	0	0	0	0	0	0	0	0
Do	3	0	1	1	1	0	0	0	0	0	0	0	0	0	0	0
Does	0	2	0	0	0	0	0	0	0	0	0	0	0	0	0	1
Door	2	0	1	0	1	0	0	0	1	0	0	1	0	0	4	1
Ever	0	0	0	0	0	1	0	1	0	0	1	1	1	1	4	3
Every	1	0	1	0	0	2	2	2	0	2	1	0	0	0	0	2
Everyone	0	0	0	1	0	0	0	0	0	3	0	0	0	0	0	0
Everything	0	0	0	1	0	0	0	0	2	0	0	0	0	0	0	0
Except	0	0	0	0	0	1	0	1	2	0	0	0	0	1	0	0
Exclusive	0	0	0	0	0	0	0	0	1	0	0	1	0	0	2	0

Response Word	4th M	4th F	5th M	5th F	6th M	6th F	7th M	7th F	8th M	8th F	10th M	10th F	12th M	12th F	College M	College F
							ONLY									
Few	1	1	1	2	3	1	2	0	4	1	4	3	1	0	2	11
First . . .	1	0	0	0	1	0	0	0	0	0	0	0	0	1	0	2
For	0	0	0	0	0	0	0	1	0	0	0	1	1	1	4	3
Forever . .	0	0	0	1	0	0	0	1	0	3	2	0	0	0	0	1
Girl	1	0	0	1	0	0	1	1	0	1	2	0	3	0	0	0
Got	0	2	0	0	0	0	0	0	0	0	0	0	0	0	0	0
Had	0	1	0	0	0	0	2	0	1	0	0	0	0	0	0	0
Her	0	1	0	2	0	1	1	0	0	0	0	1	1	0	1	0
Him	2	0	1	0	3	1	0	1	1	2	0	2	2	0	1	0
House . . .	2	2	0	0	1	1	0	0	2	0	0	1	0	0	1	1
I	0	1	0	2	1	1	0	0	1	1	0	0	0	0	0	0
If	2	3	0	2	0	0	3	0	0	0	0	2	2	0	7	3
Is	0	2	0	1	0	0	0	0	1	0	0	0	0	0	2	0
It	1	1	2	0	0	0	1	1	0	0	0	0	1	0	2	0
Just	2	3	7	8	1	7	3	3	2	0	6	5	2	3	5	7
Know . . .	0	2	0	0	1	0	0	0	0	0	1	0	1	0	0	0
Last	1	1	1	1	0	0	0	0	0	0	0	0	0	0	2	0
Little . . .	2	0	0	0	1	1	0	0	0	0	1	0	1	1	0	1
Lonely . . .	5	4	3	0	5	5	6	8	3	5	3	5	8	4	15	14
Lonesome .	0	1	0	0	0	0	0	0	0	0	2	0	2	0	1	1
Lot	0	0	2	0	0	1	1	0	0	0	0	0	0	0	0	0
Lots	2	0	1	0	0	0	0	0	1	0	0	0	0	0	0	0
Love	1	0	1	0	0	0	0	0	0	0	1	0	1	1	2	1
Many . . .	0	0	1	0	0	3	3	1	4	4	3	1	1	6	7	5
Maybe . . .	1	0	0	1	0	0	0	0	0	1	2	1	0	0	2	0
Me	4	5	4	4	3	4	4	10	4	8	5	2	4	6	9	9
Men	0	0	0	0	0	0	0	0	0	0	2	0	0	1	1	0
Mine . . .	1	1	1	0	1	1	0	1	2	0	1	0	0	0	1	0
Money . . .	1	0	0	0	1	1	0	0	1	0	2	0	1	0	0	0
More . . .	1	1	0	1	1	1	0	2	1	1	1	1	0	2	0	1
My	0	0	1	1	0	0	1	1	1	1	0	0	0	1	2	0
Never . . .	1	4	1	3	4	2	7	4	6	9	4	10	9	7	23	23
Nice	1	2	1	0	0	0	0	0	0	0	0	0	0	0	0	0
No	2	0	0	1	3	2	0	0	0	0	1	0	2	3	1	0
None . . .	0	0	1	1	2	0	1	1	4	1	4	2	5	1	3	8
Not	4	3	1	6	0	1	4	1	0	1	2	1	1	3	8	4
Nothing . .	0	1	0	0	2	1	0	0	0	0	0	1	1	0	0	1
Now	1	4	5	4	3	2	5	4	9	4	5	6	5	2	13	20
Oh	2	1	0	0	0	0	0	0	0	0	0	0	0	0	0	0
On	13	6	9	8	6	2	2	1	1	1	1	1	1	0	0	0
Once	6	8	10	10	2	11	5	5	3	3	4	4	2	4	10	16
One	104	103	104	99	116	110	127	122	111	109	108	117	91	118	173	186
Ones	0	1	1	0	0	0	0	2	0	0	0	0	0	0	0	0
Only	0	0	0	0	2	1	0	0	0	0	0	0	0	0	0	0
Open . . .	0	0	0	0	2	0	1	0	0	1	0	0	0	0	0	0
Other . . .	1	1	1	1	0	0	1	0	0	0	0	0	0	0	2	0
Ours	1	0	0	0	1	0	2	1	0	0	1	0	1	0	1	0
Out	0	0	1	1	1	1	1	0	1	0	0	1	2	0	1	2
Own	1	2	1	0	0	1	1	0	0	0	0	0	0	0	0	0

Response Word	4th		5th		6th		7th		8th		10th		12th		College	
	M	F	M	F	M	F	M	F	M	F	M	F	M	F	M	F

ONLY

Response Word	M	F	M	F	M	F	M	F	M	F	M	F	M	F	M	F
People	2	2	1	1	1	0	0	0	1	0	0	0	0	0	0	1
Person	0	0	1	3	0	1	1	0	2	2	2	2	0	0	0	0
Single	0	0	1	2	1	0	8	3	2	4	1	1	3	3	4	4
Solely	0	0	0	0	0	0	0	0	0	0	0	0	0	0	2	2
Solo	0	0	0	0	0	0	0	0	0	0	0	0	1	0	3	3
Some	1	3	3	1	2	1	1	0	1	0	1	1	0	1	4	8
Something	2	0	0	1	1	0	1	1	0	0	0	0	0	0	0	0
Sometimes	0	1	1	2	0	1	1	0	1	1	1	3	0	0	2	0
Still	0	0	0	0	0	0	0	0	0	0	0	0	0	0	2	0
That	5	2	6	5	2	3	1	3	1	2	3	2	3	2	1	2
The	0	2	2	0	2	2	4	0	1	0	1	1	2	0	4	3
Then	0	1	2	0	1	1	0	1	0	0	0	1	2	2	4	1
There	0	1	2	1	1	2	0	0	0	0	0	0	0	0	0	0
Thing	1	3	1	3	2	0	0	1	2	1	0	1	1	0	0	0
This	1	0	0	0	2	0	0	1	0	3	2	3	2	0	5	4
To	0	1	0	1	0	0	0	0	0	0	1	0	2	0	1	0
Today	0	0	0	2	0	0	0	0	0	0	0	0	0	0	0	0
Together	0	0	0	0	0	0	0	0	0	0	0	1	0	0	2	1
Two	3	1	3	1	1	0	2	0	2	1	0	0	1	0	0	1
Well	0	0	0	0	0	0	0	0	0	0	0	0	0	0	2	0
What	1	0	0	0	0	0	0	0	1	1	0	0	1	0	2	0
When	0	1	1	0	2	0	3	3	0	0	1	2	1	1	2	2
White	0	0	0	0	0	0	0	0	0	0	0	0	0	0	0	2
Why	1	2	1	1	0	0	0	1	0	1	0	0	1	3	1	0
With	0	0	1	0	1	1	1	0	0	2	0	0	0	0	0	1
Without	0	0	0	0	0	0	0	0	0	0	2	0	2	0	0	0
Word	0	0	2	2	2	1	0	0	0	1	0	0	0	0	1	0
Yes	2	1	1	0	0	0	0	1	0	1	1	0	0	0	1	1
Yesterday	0	0	0	0	1	0	0	0	0	1	0	0	0	1	1	3
You	4	12	7	6	9	5	2	4	13	16	14	14	21	20	37	25
Yours	0	2	0	1	3	0	3	2	2	3	4	0	3	0	2	1

125. OR

Response Word	M	F	M	F	M	F	M	F	M	F	M	F	M	F	M	F
A	2	5	4	2	3	2	1	2	1	1	3	1	0	0	1	3
Also	1	0	0	1	3	3	7	6	6	0	2	1	3	7	3	6
Alternative	0	0	0	0	0	0	0	0	1	0	0	0	0	1	7	0
Am	1	1	0	0	0	0	1	0	1	1	1	0	2	0	3	0
An	1	1	3	0	2	3	1	1	0	2	3	0	1	1	1	2
And	7	16	10	17	9	21	32	29	24	25	22	29	28	24	68	61
Another	2	0	2	3	2	2	1	1	2	0	3	6	5	1	3	0
Anyway	1	0	1	0	0	0	0	2	0	0	0	0	0	0	0	0
Are	4	3	4	3	6	4	4	1	3	0	2	0	7	2	6	6
As	1	0	0	4	0	1	0	0	0	0	0	0	1	1	1	3
At	0	1	1	0	2	3	0	1	2	3	2	3	1	1	5	1
Baby	1	0	0	0	0	0	0	2	1	0	0	0	0	0	0	0
Be	1	0	0	2	0	0	1	0	0	0	1	0	1	0	1	0
Because	3	2	1	0	2	1	1	1	3	1	1	3	2	0	0	2
Besides	0	0	0	0	1	0	1	0	1	0	1	0	1	3	1	0
Boat	2	1	4	2	7	5	8	1	2	1	9	3	6	3	3	6

Response Word	4th M	4th F	5th M	5th F	6th M	6th F	7th M	7th F	8th M	8th F	10th M	10th F	12th M	12th F	College M	College F
							OR									
Bore	0	0	2	0	0	0	0	1	1	0	0	0	2	0	0	1
But	1	0	0	1	2	1	6	10	9	17	6	5	5	12	14	20
By	1	0	0	1	0	1	2	1	0	0	0	0	0	1	0	0
Can	0	2	0	1	0	0	0	0	0	0	0	0	0	0	3	2
Choice	0	0	1	0	0	0	1	0	0	4	0	1	3	2	3	3
Conjunction	0	0	0	0	0	1	0	0	0	1	1	3	1	1	1	1
Correct	0	0	0	0	0	2	0	0	0	0	0	0	0	0	0	0
Could	1	0	0	0	0	2	1	0	0	0	1	0	0	1	1	0
Did	2	1	2	0	1	0	2	1	2	0	0	1	1	0	0	0
Different	0	2	0	2	2	5	0	1	0	0	1	0	1	0	2	1
Do	1	1	0	2	0	2	1	0	0	0	0	0	0	0	0	2
Door	2	0	2	0	3	0	2	1	0	1	1	0	2	1	2	3
Either	1	2	1	2	2	0	7	7	3	10	5	18	6	21	33	56
Else	10	9	7	8	3	16	11	9	8	7	6	9	8	11	13	15
Etc.	0	0	0	0	0	0	0	2	0	1	0	0	0	0	0	0
Even	0	1	0	0	0	0	1	1	0	2	2	1	0	0	1	0
Ever	0	0	0	0	0	0	0	0	0	1	0	0	0	1	2	0
Example	0	0	0	0	0	0	0	0	0	2	0	0	0	0	0	0
For	0	4	5	8	3	2	3	2	3	0	2	1	0	2	8	4
Girl	1	0	0	0	0	1	0	2	0	0	0	0	0	0	1	0
Good	2	0	0	0	0	0	0	0	0	0	0	0	0	0	0	0
Had	2	0	1	1	2	0	0	0	0	0	1	1	1	0	0	0
Hard	2	1	3	1	0	0	0	0	0	2	1	0	1	0	0	0
Hardly	1	3	0	0	0	0	0	0	1	0	0	1	0	0	2	0
Have	0	2	0	0	0	0	0	0	0	0	0	1	0	1	1	2
He	6	3	4	5	5	4	4	3	2	0	4	0	2	2	6	0
Her	2	1	2	1	1	1	2	1	0	1	2	0	2	0	1	0
Him	4	0	1	0	3	0	4	3	5	1	5	2	1	4	1	2
How	0	0	4	2	2	1	1	1	2	1	1	0	0	1	0	2
I	3	1	2	1	0	0	0	1	3	0	2	1	0	0	1	0
If	3	5	3	3	3	3	5	5	4	5	4	9	5	6	17	18
Instead	0	0	0	0	0	3	1	1	0	1	0	1	1	1	2	3
Iron	0	2	3	0	1	2	2	0	1	0	3	0	3	0	2	0
Is	4	4	4	7	8	4	5	3	5	4	7	5	7	4	12	4
It	3	4	5	6	5	2	2	1	1	5	3	3	2	2	1	5
Man	1	0	0	2	0	1	0	0	0	0	0	1	0	0	0	0
Many	0	0	1	0	0	1	0	0	0	0	0	0	1	0	2	1
May	0	0	0	1	0	1	0	0	2	0	0	0	0	1	0	0
Maybe	9	15	9	12	11	9	7	14	7	15	7	14	9	4	10	9
Me	10	6	12	3	2	7	7	8	2	3	5	1	4	1	3	1
Mine	0	0	0	2	0	0	0	0	1	0	0	0	1	0	1	0
Money	0	0	2	1	1	1	0	0	0	0	0	0	0	0	0	0
More	4	2	2	2	3	2	0	1	0	6	1	2	2	2	1	2
My	1	1	3	1	0	1	2	1	1	1	1	0	0	0	1	1
Neither	0	0	0	0	0	0	2	0	1	1	0	2	5	2	4	5
Never	0	0	0	0	0	0	0	0	2	2	3	1	2	3	5	9
No	1	7	3	1	2	1	2	2	0	0	0	1	5	0	2	0
Nor	0	1	1	4	1	4	8	9	23	33	15	25	28	43	85	106
Not	7	14	11	14	13	12	4	8	4	4	6	8	7	8	17	21

227

Response Word	4th		5th		6th		7th		8th		10th		12th		College	
	M	F	M	F	M	F	M	F	M	F	M	F	M	F	M	F

OR

Response Word	4th M	4th F	5th M	5th F	6th M	6th F	7th M	7th F	8th M	8th F	10th M	10th F	12th M	12th F	Coll M	Coll F
Now	2	3	1	2	2	1	2	3	2	1	0	2	3	2	4	4
Oar	1	0	0	2	2	3	3	2	0	4	3	0	3	1	0	1
Of	5	6	2	9	5	7	2	7	5	4	3	4	1	1	8	4
Off	0	2	2	0	0	0	2	0	0	1	0	0	0	0	1	0
Oh	0	0	0	2	0	1	2	1	0	0	0	0	1	0	0	0
On	5	7	6	3	3	1	1	2	5	1	3	2	1	1	7	5
One	0	1	1	2	0	2	0	0	0	0	1	0	0	2	0	0
Only	1	0	0	0	2	0	0	0	0	0	1	0	0	0	4	2
Opposite	0	0	0	2	0	1	0	0	1	0	0	0	0	1	0	1
Order	0	0	0	0	0	0	0	1	1	0	1	0	1	0	1	2
Ore	12	6	8	7	6	4	13	8	4	3	4	3	3	1	7	4
Other	2	0	5	2	1	2	0	1	4	6	2	4	3	2	9	4
Otherwise	0	2	0	2	0	1	0	1	1	0	0	3	1	0	1	2
Our	0	1	3	2	1	0	5	0	0	0	0	0	0	0	0	0
Over	0	0	1	1	0	1	0	1	0	0	0	2	0	0	1	0
Perhaps	0	0	0	0	0	0	0	0	0	1	1	0	0	0	1	2
Plus	0	0	1	0	0	2	1	0	0	0	1	0	0	0	1	0
Poor	1	0	1	0	1	1	0	2	0	0	1	0	0	0	0	0
Question	0	0	0	0	0	1	0	0	0	0	0	0	0	1	3	1
Rather	0	0	1	0	0	0	0	1	1	2	0	0	0	3	0	1
Reason	0	2	0	0	0	0	0	0	0	0	1	0	0	0	1	1
Rock	1	0	0	0	0	0	1	0	0	0	2	0	0	0	0	0
Row	0	1	1	1	2	1	2	0	0	0	1	0	0	0	0	1
See	1	0	0	0	2	2	0	0	0	0	0	0	0	0	0	1
She	0	3	1	1	3	2	1	0	3	1	3	2	3	1	3	1
So	1	2	0	1	1	1	0	2	0	0	1	1	0	0	1	1
Some	0	0	1	3	2	0	0	0	0	0	1	0	0	0	0	1
Something	5	3	1	2	9	6	4	1	2	3	1	1	0	1	0	0
Something else	1	2	0	0	0	1	0	0	0	0	0	0	1	1	0	0
That	7	5	5	3	6	6	6	1	6	3	7	8	3	2	6	6
The	6	2	4	0	6	0	0	0	1	2	2	2	0	2	4	2
Them	0	0	0	1	1	0	0	1	2	0	2	1	1	1	2	1
Then	1	1	1	0	2	2	1	2	1	0	0	2	0	1	4	4
There	0	0	0	1	3	1	0	0	3	0	2	1	0	2	1	1
They	0	0	0	2	0	2	2	0	3	5	4	0	2	1	3	0
Thing	2	1	1	1	1	1	0	0	0	0	1	0	0	0	0	0
This	2	4	1	1	2	4	3	3	2	3	0	3	1	0	5	2
To	1	1	2	0	1	0	1	1	1	0	0	0	1	1	0	1
Too	0	0	0	0	0	0	1	0	0	1	0	0	0	0	1	2
Two	1	2	1	3	0	0	0	0	2	0	2	0	1	1	1	1
Was	3	4	4	2	3	0	1	4	3	2	4	3	1	2	5	1
Wasn't	2	3	3	1	0	2	0	0	0	0	0	0	0	0	0	0
We	0	0	0	0	1	0	0	1	1	0	0	1	0	0	2	0
What	3	1	6	2	4	5	3	7	5	3	7	8	2	5	13	3
When	0	0	0	0	3	0	3	3	1	0	2	2	1	2	0	1
Where	1	0	0	0	0	0	0	1	0	1	2	0	1	0	0	2
Who	0	0	2	0	0	0	0	1	1	0	0	2	0	0	0	0
Why	5	5	1	3	2	8	3	3	1	1	2	1	3	4	3	3

Response Word	4th M	4th F	5th M	5th F	6th M	6th F	7th M	7th F	8th M	8th F	10th M	10th F	12th M	12th F	College M	College F
								OR								
Will	1	0	0	0	1	1	0	2	3	1	0	0	1	0	0	5
Word . . .	0	1	3	1	2	1	1	0	0	0	1	0	1	0	0	0
Work . . .	0	2	0	0	0	0	0	0	0	0	0	0	0	0	0	0
Yes	0	2	2	1	1	1	0	1	2	0	0	0	0	0	1	0
Yet	0	0	0	1	0	0	0	0	0	0	0	1	0	0	0	2
You	15	9	5	5	13	4	5	6	4	6	3	2	3	1	3	1
Your . . .	1	0	1	2	1	2	0	1	0	0	0	0	1	0	0	1
						126.	OVER									
A	2	0	0	0	1	0	0	0	0	0	0	0	0	0	0	0
About . . .	0	0	0	0	0	0	0	0	0	0	1	1	0	0	2	0
Above . . .	1	1	1	3	1	0	4	3	3	2	6	2	3	5	15	39
Across . .	2	1	1	0	0	0	0	3	1	2	0	2	0	2	2	3
Again . . .	1	1	2	2	2	8	3	3	0	2	1	3	2	1	6	12
Against . .	0	0	0	0	0	0	0	0	0	0	0	0	0	2	0	0
Ahead . . .	0	0	0	0	0	0	0	2	0	0	0	1	0	0	0	0
Air	2	0	1	1	2	0	0	0	0	0	0	0	0	0	0	0
All	0	1	1	0	2	0	1	0	0	0	0	2	3	3	0	2
And	3	1	2	2	3	0	2	0	1	0	3	0	0	1	2	4
And over .	0	0	0	0	0	0	0	0	0	0	0	0	0	0	2	0
Around . .	0	2	2	2	2	0	1	0	5	2	3	6	2	1	7	2
A top	0	0	0	0	0	0	0	0	0	0	0	0	1	0	2	0
Away . . .	0	1	0	0	0	0	0	0	1	0	0	0	0	1	2	0
Back . . .	0	1	0	2	0	3	1	3	0	0	1	0	0	0	2	0
Ball	0	2	0	0	0	1	0	0	0	0	0	0	0	0	0	1
Beyond . .	0	0	0	0	0	0	0	1	0	0	1	1	0	1	1	5
Bridge . . .	1	2	0	1	0	1	0	3	0	0	2	3	2	2	7	4
By	0	1	0	0	2	0	0	3	0	1	0	0	0	0	1	1
Closer . . .	0	0	0	0	0	2	0	0	0	0	0	0	0	0	0	0
Clover . .	2	1	0	1	1	0	0	0	0	0	0	0	0	0	1	0
Come . . .	3	1	1	1	3	5	0	0	0	0	0	1	0	0	2	2
Cover . . .	3	3	1	2	0	2	1	2	0	0	0	1	0	0	0	0
Done	0	1	1	3	2	2	0	3	4	2	0	2	1	3	3	2
Dover . . .	0	0	1	0	0	0	0	0	0	0	0	0	0	0	0	2
Down . . .	4	0	4	1	5	3	1	5	3	5	3	0	1	0	1	0
Easy . . .	0	0	1	0	0	0	1	0	1	0	0	0	2	0	1	0
End	0	0	0	0	0	0	0	0	1	0	0	0	0	0	1	2
Fall	0	0	2	0	0	0	0	0	0	1	0	0	0	0	0	0
Far	1	2	0	0	1	3	0	0	0	1	0	0	0	0	1	2
Fast	1	1	1	1	1	0	0	1	0	0	0	2	0	0	0	0
Fence . . .	1	1	2	0	4	8	3	6	1	7	1	6	6	4	7	20
Go	2	2	0	0	1	0	0	0	1	0	0	0	0	0	0	0
Going . . .	0	2	1	0	1	0	0	0	0	0	0	1	0	0	0	0
Gone . . .	0	0	0	1	0	1	0	1	2	0	1	0	0	0	0	0
Head . . .	3	3	0	2	3	2	1	2	0	1	0	2	2	0	0	1
Hear . . .	0	2	1	0	0	2	0	1	0	0	0	0	0	0	0	0
Here	5	11	5	12	11	10	10	4	5	8	6	7	6	5	11	9
High	4	6	5	3	1	5	5	1	2	0	4	1	0	0	2	3
Hill	9	12	8	8	8	18	14	10	8	3	6	10	11	11	14	15

Response Word	4th		5th		6th		7th		8th		10th		12th		College	
	M	F	M	F	M	F	M	F	M	F	M	F	M	F	M	F

OVER

Response Word	M	F	M	F	M	F	M	F	M	F	M	F	M	F	M	F
Him	0	0	4	0	0	0	0	0	0	0	1	0	1	0	0	0
Hurdle . . .	0	0	0	0	0	0	1	0	0	0	0	0	0	0	1	3
In	2	2	0	1	3	2	0	0	0	0	1	0	0	0	2	1
It	3	2	3	4	3	1	4	0	4	0	1	1	2	1	5	1
Joyed	0	0	0	0	0	0	0	0	0	0	0	0	0	0	5	0
Jump	8	15	8	8	9	4	9	9	5	6	5	9	7	4	6	8
Look	0	0	0	2	0	0	0	1	0	0	1	0	2	0	0	0
Me	5	2	5	2	5	2	0	1	0	0	0	0	0	0	0	0
Moon	0	0	0	0	1	0	0	0	2	0	0	0	0	0	3	0
More	0	0	0	0	0	0	0	0	0	0	0	0	2	0	0	0
Mountain . .	1	0	2	2	0	0	0	0	0	0	1	0	1	1	1	0
Mountains . .	0	0	1	0	0	0	0	2	1	0	0	0	0	0	0	0
Move	0	1	0	2	0	0	0	0	0	0	0	0	1	0	0	0
My	0	2	0	0	2	0	0	0	0	0	0	0	0	0	0	0
Near	0	0	0	1	0	0	0	0	0	1	0	1	0	0	2	0
Night	2	0	0	0	0	0	0	1	0	0	0	0	0	0	0	0
Not.	2	0	0	1	0	0	0	0	0	0	0	0	0	0	0	0
Now	2	2	2	2	3	3	3	2	1	3	3	1	4	1	4	1
On	4	4	3	3	5	3	8	5	7	3	1	3	2	1	10	10
On top	0	2	1	2	1	2	0	1	1	0	2	2	1	0	0	3
Other	2	2	0	2	2	1	1	0	0	2	0	2	0	0	1	1
Out	0	0	1	1	1	1	0	7	0	2	2	0	0	1	8	7
Oven	3	4	1	2	1	0	2	2	0	0	0	0	0	0	0	0
Over	2	1	0	0	2	1	0	0	0	0	0	0	0	0	0	0
Page	0	0	0	1	0	1	0	0	1	0	0	0	0	0	2	0
Rainbow . . .	0	0	0	0	0	0	0	0	0	0	0	1	1	0	1	3
River	0	1	0	1	0	0	0	0	1	0	0	0	0	0	4	0
Roll	0	1	2	1	0	2	2	0	0	0	0	0	2	0	2	1
Round	1	0	0	2	0	1	0	0	0	0	0	0	0	0	0	0
Rover	1	1	0	1	3	0	2	0	0	0	1	0	0	0	1	1
Sea	2	1	0	1	0	1	0	1	0	0	0	0	0	0	0	0
Side	1	2	2	4	4	0	0	0	2	1	0	1	2	1	1	1
Sky	1	1	0	0	0	1	0	0	1	0	2	0	0	0	0	0
Slow	4	2	0	0	0	0	0	0	2	0	0	1	0	0	1	0
Slowly	2	1	0	3	0	0	0	0	0	0	2	0	3	0	4	2
Some place .	0	0	1	2	0	0	0	0	1	0	0	0	0	0	0	0
Take	0	0	0	0	0	0	2	0	0	1	0	0	0	0	1	0
Ten	0	0	1	0	0	2	0	0	0	0	0	0	0	0	0	0
That	2	1	1	0	0	1	1	0	0	0	1	0	0	0	1	0
The	16	5	16	11	22	5	8	2	3	3	5	1	5	3	13	3
Their	4	1	1	1	3	1	1	0	0	0	1	1	0	0	1	0
Them	0	2	0	1	0	0	1	0	0	0	0	0	0	0	0	0
There	28	21	49	42	35	25	26	27	51	43	52	39	57	48	78	59
They	0	0	0	2	1	1	0	0	1	0	0	0	0	0	0	0
Throw	0	0	0	0	2	0	0	0	0	0	0	0	0	0	1	0
To	3	2	0	2	3	3	2	1	1	1	1	1	1	1	0	1
Top	3	1	4	2	1	3	6	2	4	3	3	4	3	2	11	3
Turn	6	11	8	19	11	13	9	7	4	11	8	13	9	8	13	4
Under	29	43	35	28	28	54	83	97	78	99	82	90	71	112	173	214

Response Word	4th M	F	5th M	F	6th M	F	7th M	F	8th M	F	10th M	F	12th M	F	College M	F

OVER

Response Word	4th M	F	5th M	F	6th M	F	7th M	F	8th M	F	10th M	F	12th M	F	College M	F
Up	8	4	4	4	2	6	4	2	8	5	4	7	1	2	4	9
Upon	1	1	1	1	0	0	0	4	1	0	2	0	1	0	0	1
Upside down	0	0	0	0	1	0	0	0	1	0	0	0	1	2	0	0
Wall	3	1	2	1	2	2	0	0	2	1	0	0	1	0	3	2
We	1	2	0	1	0	0	0	0	0	0	0	0	0	0	0	0
What	0	0	0	0	0	0	0	0	2	1	1	0	0	0	1	0
Where	0	0	0	0	1	1	0	0	0	0	2	1	1	2	2	2
Yon	0	0	0	0	0	0	0	0	0	0	0	0	0	0	2	0
You	0	1	4	1	2	1	1	0	1	2	1	0	2	0	1	0

127. PEOPLE

Response Word	4th M	F	5th M	F	6th M	F	7th M	F	8th M	F	10th M	F	12th M	F	College M	F
Adults	0	0	0	0	0	1	0	2	0	0	0	1	0	1	1	0
All	0	0	0	0	0	0	0	0	0	0	1	2	0	2	1	0
Animal	0	2	1	3	2	2	0	3	1	2	0	1	1	0	2	0
Animals	1	10	3	7	3	4	8	15	12	18	7	15	9	13	18	23
Apple	0	0	2	0	0	0	0	0	0	0	0	0	0	0	0	0
Are	5	3	2	3	3	0	1	3	7	1	5	5	18	4	26	10
Baby	1	1	1	2	0	1	0	0	2	1	0	0	0	0	0	0
Beings	0	0	0	0	0	0	1	0	0	0	0	1	0	0	2	2
Big	1	2	1	1	0	1	0	0	0	0	2	1	0	0	0	0
Body	0	1	0	0	2	0	0	0	0	0	0	0	0	0	0	0
Boy	9	6	8	1	5	3	3	0	4	3	2	0	1	2	2	0
Boys	1	3	2	0	3	0	3	4	3	9	1	13	0	2	1	4
Came	0	0	0	0	1	0	1	0	0	0	0	0	1	1	2	0
Can	2	0	0	1	2	1	0	0	1	0	0	0	1	1	1	0
Cars	0	0	1	1	0	0	2	0	0	2	2	1	1	2	4	1
Cats	0	0	0	0	0	0	0	2	0	1	2	0	0	0	1	0
Child	3	6	3	7	1	2	1	2	1	0	1	0	1	0	0	0
Children	9	26	6	16	4	10	7	16	8	11	5	5	4	5	3	10
Citizen	2	0	2	1	0	0	0	1	2	1	0	0	2	0	0	1
Citizens	0	2	0	0	1	1	2	5	1	3	0	3	0	2	2	2
City	4	1	0	1	1	1	2	3	4	3	3	4	0	1	1	5
Class	0	0	0	0	0	0	0	0	0	0	0	0	0	0	2	1
Clothes	1	0	1	0	1	1	0	1	2	0	1	0	3	1	0	1
Come	0	0	0	0	0	1	0	0	0	0	1	0	1	1	2	2
Country	1	0	0	0	0	0	0	0	0	1	0	1	2	2	2	1
Crowd	3	4	4	4	3	3	8	11	8	8	18	27	20	23	56	83
Crowds	1	0	0	0	0	1	0	0	1	2	1	1	2	1	4	7
Cry	0	0	0	0	1	0	0	0	1	0	0	0	0	0	2	0
Did	0	0	0	0	0	0	0	0	0	0	0	0	0	0	2	0
Do	1	0	0	0	0	0	0	0	0	0	0	0	0	1	2	0
Does	0	0	0	0	0	0	2	0	0	0	0	0	0	0	0	0
Dog	3	1	0	2	3	1	1	0	2	0	0	0	0	0	0	0
Dogs	2	4	0	5	1	1	2	4	4	4	4	6	2	3	6	3
Earth	0	0	1	1	0	0	0	0	0	1	1	1	2	0	0	0
Eat	1	2	0	0	0	1	0	0	0	0	0	0	2	0	1	1
Everybody	1	2	0	0	0	0	0	0	0	0	0	0	0	0	0	0
Faces	0	0	0	0	0	0	0	2	0	1	0	5	0	3	3	10
Family	0	1	1	3	0	1	1	1	0	1	1	1	0	0	0	1

Response Word	4th M	4th F	5th M	5th F	6th M	6th F	7th M	7th F	8th M	8th F	10th M	10th F	12th M	12th F	College M	College F
							PEOPLE									
Find	0	0	2	0	0	0	1	0	0	0	0	0	0	0	0	0
Food	0	0	0	0	0	0	0	2	0	0	0	1	0	0	0	0
Friend	0	0	0	0	0	1	0	0	2	0	0	0	0	0	0	0
Friends	0	0	1	1	0	1	1	2	3	0	2	4	2	3	6	4
Fun	1	1	0	0	0	0	0	1	0	0	1	1	0	2	4	1
Funny	1	3	1	0	1	1	1	0	2	1	1	0	8	3	8	4
Girl	6	4	2	10	5	9	2	3	4	1	1	1	0	0	1	1
Girls	0	4	1	5	3	2	2	1	3	5	8	4	3	3	4	1
Go	1	1	0	1	3	0	1	0	2	0	1	0	0	0	2	7
Good	2	1	2	1	0	1	1	0	1	0	0	1	0	0	2	1
Group	0	0	0	2	0	1	1	1	0	3	8	2	5	6	11	13
Groups	0	0	0	0	0	1	0	0	0	0	0	0	0	0	2	1
Happy	0	2	0	0	0	0	0	2	0	1	0	0	0	1	0	0
He	0	0	2	0	2	0	0	1	3	1	0	0	0	1	0	1
Heads	0	0	0	0	0	0	0	0	0	0	2	0	1	0	2	1
Help	1	0	0	2	0	0	0	0	0	0	0	0	0	0	0	0
Her	1	1	1	0	0	2	0	0	0	0	0	0	0	0	1	0
Him	1	0	0	2	1	0	1	0	0	0	0	0	1	1	1	0
Horses	0	0	0	0	0	0	0	0	0	0	0	0	0	0	2	0
House	0	1	0	0	0	2	0	1	0	2	0	1	0	1	0	1
Human	10	4	15	7	13	8	6	4	5	4	8	7	7	5	7	8
Human beings	0	1	1	0	0	0	0	0	0	0	0	0	0	2	0	1
Humans	5	0	4	4	9	7	13	10	9	15	17	10	14	16	16	11
If	2	0	0	0	0	0	0	0	0	0	0	0	0	0	0	0
Individuals	0	0	0	0	0	0	0	0	0	0	0	0	0	0	0	2
It	0	0	0	0	1	0	0	2	1	1	0	0	0	0	0	0
Kids	0	2	2	3	0	0	1	1	2	2	0	2	2	1	1	2
Know	0	0	0	0	0	0	0	0	0	0	0	0	0	2	0	0
Ladies	0	3	0	0	0	1	0	0	0	0	0	0	0	0	0	0
Lady	1	2	1	1	0	2	0	0	0	0	0	0	0	0	0	0
Land	0	0	0	0	0	0	0	0	0	2	0	0	0	0	0	0
Large	0	0	0	1	0	0	0	0	0	0	0	2	0	0	2	0
Laugh	1	4	1	2	2	1	0	1	0	3	1	2	5	5	8	2
Life	0	0	0	0	0	0	0	0	0	1	0	0	0	0	2	0
Like	1	2	1	0	0	0	0	0	1	0	0	1	1	0	1	2
Live	1	0	0	3	1	1	2	1	0	0	1	0	1	1	2	1
Lot	0	0	1	0	2	0	1	0	0	0	0	0	1	0	0	0
Lots	0	0	2	2	2	0	0	1	1	0	0	0	0	1	0	1
Love	0	0	0	0	0	0	0	1	0	1	0	1	0	2	0	0
Mammals	0	1	0	0	1	0	2	0	0	0	0	0	0	0	0	0
Man	15	10	16	8	12	10	6	5	11	4	5	2	2	8	9	12
Many	0	5	3	5	1	7	2	2	4	3	5	5	0	13	17	20
Mass	0	0	0	0	0	0	0	0	0	0	1	0	0	0	4	5
Me	4	8	4	2	3	2	11	5	4	6	6	2	5	1	3	2
Men	13	5	15	7	12	7	18	10	16	11	6	8	6	15	24	20
Mob	0	0	0	0	0	0	0	0	0	0	0	1	0	0	1	2
Monsters	0	0	0	0	0	0	0	0	3	0	0	0	0	0	0	0
Mother	0	0	1	0	0	0	1	0	2	0	0	0	0	0	0	0
Negroes	0	0	0	0	1	3	0	0	0	0	0	0	0	0	0	1

Response Word	4th M	4th F	5th M	5th F	6th M	6th F	7th M	7th F	8th M	8th F	10th M	10th F	12th M	12th F	College M	College F

PEOPLE

Response Word	4th M	4th F	5th M	5th F	6th M	6th F	7th M	7th F	8th M	8th F	10th M	10th F	12th M	12th F	College M	College F
Nice	1	2	0	0	0	3	0	0	0	1	0	1	1	2	0	1
Paper	0	0	2	0	0	0	0	0	0	0	0	0	0	0	0	0
Peoples	0	0	2	1	1	0	0	0	0	0	0	0	0	0	0	0
Person	46	52	52	62	46	60	57	54	33	46	19	16	25	25	37	31
Persons	12	9	8	11	15	20	13	13	10	10	14	8	14	5	23	21
Place	0	0	0	1	0	0	3	1	0	1	4	3	0	0	2	6
Places	0	1	1	2	4	4	5	5	9	4	7	6	12	7	27	38
Population	1	0	0	0	0	1	3	0	2	1	0	0	0	0	1	2
Pupils	0	2	0	0	1	0	0	0	0	0	0	0	0	0	0	0
Purple	1	0	0	0	2	0	0	0	0	0	0	1	0	1	0	0
Race	0	0	0	0	0	0	0	1	1	1	3	0	0	0	3	0
Run	0	0	0	0	1	0	0	0	0	0	0	0	0	1	2	0
Say	0	0	1	0	0	0	0	1	0	0	0	0	0	1	2	3
School	0	0	0	1	0	1	0	0	0	1	2	0	0	0	0	0
See	0	1	1	0	2	0	0	0	0	0	1	3	2	1	1	3
Sex	0	0	0	0	2	1	0	0	0	0	0	0	0	0	1	0
Should	0	0	0	0	0	0	0	0	1	0	1	2	0	0	1	0
So	0	0	0	0	0	0	0	0	0	0	0	0	0	0	0	2
Somebody	1	0	2	0	0	0	0	0	0	1	0	0	0	0	0	0
Steeple	0	0	0	0	0	0	0	0	0	0	0	0	0	0	2	1
Street	0	0	0	0	0	1	1	1	0	1	0	2	0	0	0	1
Students	0	0	0	0	0	0	0	0	1	0	0	0	1	0	2	2
Talk	0	0	0	2	0	0	0	0	0	0	0	0	0	1	1	6
Talking	0	0	0	0	0	0	0	0	0	2	0	0	0	0	0	0
Teachers	0	0	0	0	0	1	0	0	2	0	0	0	0	0	0	0
Them	1	0	1	1	0	0	1	0	1	0	2	1	0	0	1	2
They	0	0	1	0	0	2	0	2	0	1	4	4	3	1	6	3
Thing	0	0	0	0	0	0	2	0	0	0	0	0	0	1	0	0
Things	1	0	0	1	4	0	1	0	4	1	3	7	4	0	2	8
Think	1	0	0	1	0	0	0	1	1	3	0	0	1	0	1	0
Town	0	0	1	1	0	1	0	0	0	0	1	2	0	2	0	2
Us	1	0	1	4	2	2	2	1	1	2	4	6	1	3	3	7
Walk	0	3	0	1	0	1	1	1	0	1	2	0	0	1	1	1
Walking	0	0	0	0	0	0	1	1	0	0	0	0	0	0	2	0
We	0	0	0	0	0	1	0	1	0	0	1	0	0	1	3	3
Were	0	0	0	0	0	1	0	0	0	0	0	0	1	0	1	2
What	0	0	0	0	0	0	0	0	1	0	0	0	0	0	0	0
Where	1	0	0	0	0	0	0	0	0	0	2	0	0	0	0	0
White	0	0	0	0	0	1	0	0	0	0	1	2	0	1	1	1
Who	0	0	1	0	0	0	1	1	1	1	0	1	3	0	5	5
Woman	0	4	0	0	0	1	1	0	0	0	0	1	3	0	1	1
Women	0	1	1	2	0	3	2	1	1	3	3	2	0	1	4	1
World	0	0	0	1	0	1	1	1	0	0	0	1	0	0	0	3
You	5	1	3	5	2	1	1	2	1	3	1	2	4	1	2	2

128. PLAYING

Response Word	4th M	4th F	5th M	5th F	6th M	6th F	7th M	7th F	8th M	8th F	10th M	10th F	12th M	12th F	College M	College F
Around	1	0	0	0	2	0	1	0	2	2	1	1	0	1	5	0
Ball	13	9	22	25	29	14	21	23	12	16	24	16	8	10	22	23
Baseball	3	1	3	0	5	0	6	5	9	3	3	2	7	0	2	0

233

Response Word	4th M	4th F	5th M	5th F	6th M	6th F	7th M	7th F	8th M	8th F	10th M	10th F	12th M	12th F	College M	College F
								PLAYING								
Basketball .	1	0	0	0	1	0	1	0	0	0	2	1	3	0	0	0
Bat	2	0	0	0	1	0	0	0	0	1	0	0	0	0	0	0
Bed	0	0	0	0	0	0	0	0	2	0	0	0	0	0	0	0
Bored . . .	0	0	0	0	0	0	0	0	0	0	0	0	0	0	0	2
Boy	2	0	0	0	1	0	0	0	1	0	0	0	1	0	1	0
Boys . . .	0	0	0	0	0	0	1	0	0	3	0	3	0	1	1	2
Card . . .	0	1	0	0	0	0	0	1	0	0	0	0	0	1	0	2
Cards . . .	0	0	1	1	3	3	6	1	5	5	14	10	18	23	22	36
Cars	0	0	0	0	2	0	1	0	0	0	1	1	0	0	0	0
Cat	0	0	0	1	0	0	0	0	0	0	0	0	0	1	2	0
Cats	0	0	0	0	0	0	0	0	0	0	0	0	0	0	3	0
Child . . .	0	0	0	0	1	0	0	0	1	0	1	4	2	0	1	6
Children .	0	1	0	1	0	1	0	3	0	4	4	13	6	15	26	24
Cry	0	0	0	0	0	0	0	0	2	0	1	0	0	0	0	0
Crying . .	0	0	0	0	1	0	1	1	1	1	1	0	0	0	2	5
Dancing . .	0	1	0	0	0	0	0	0	0	2	0	0	0	1	1	0
Doing . . .	0	0	0	0	2	1	1	0	0	1	0	0	0	0	1	1
Doll	0	2	0	1	0	1	0	1	0	0	0	0	0	0	0	0
Dolls . . .	0	4	0	1	1	3	1	1	0	3	0	4	0	2	2	5
Don't . . .	0	0	0	0	0	1	0	0	2	0	0	0	0	0	0	0
Eating . . .	0	0	0	0	0	0	0	0	0	0	0	0	0	0	1	2
Enjoyment .	0	0	0	0	0	0	0	0	0	0	2	0	1	0	0	0
Fast	0	3	4	1	1	1	0	2	0	0	2	0	1	1	2	1
Fight . . .	1	0	1	2	0	0	1	1	2	1	0	0	0	0	1	2
Fighting . .	5	5	5	3	2	3	1	5	8	3	3	7	3	2	8	5
Fooling . .	0	0	0	0	0	1	0	0	1	0	1	0	1	0	2	1
Football . .	3	1	6	1	3	0	0	1	1	0	2	1	0	0	4	0
Fun	33	48	42	47	54	62	42	43	36	38	43	45	40	58	56	58
Funny . . .	2	0	0	1	0	0	0	0	0	1	0	0	0	1	0	0
Game . . .	8	8	7	10	5	11	4	6	6	8	4	2	6	5	9	12
Games . .	5	7	6	10	8	13	4	7	7	11	7	12	12	12	41	58
Girls . . .	0	0	0	0	0	0	1	0	2	0	0	0	2	0	0	0
Giving . .	0	0	0	0	0	0	0	0	0	0	0	0	0	0	0	2
Go	0	0	2	0	1	0	1	0	0	0	2	0	0	0	0	1
Golf	0	1	0	0	0	0	0	0	0	0	1	2	0	0	1	0
Good	1	1	1	0	2	0	1	0	0	0	0	1	0	0	1	1
Ground . .	0	2	2	0	0	0	2	0	2	0	1	1	1	0	0	2
Guns	1	2	2	0	0	0	1	0	0	0	1	0	0	0	0	1
Happy . . .	3	4	2	2	2	1	0	0	2	0	0	0	1	0	3	0
Hard . . .	7	3	5	9	8	4	7	4	5	3	9	4	9	9	18	9
Home . . .	1	0	1	0	0	0	0	0	0	2	0	0	0	0	0	0
House . . .	2	2	1	0	3	1	1	3	1	4	2	1	1	0	2	5
I	3	3	2	1	1	0	0	0	0	0	0	0	0	1	0	0
In	2	0	2	0	1	0	1	0	0	0	1	0	0	0	1	1
Is	2	0	0	0	2	0	0	0	0	0	0	0	0	0	0	1
It	0	0	2	0	1	0	0	0	0	0	0	0	1	0	0	0
Jump . . .	0	0	0	2	0	0	1	1	1	3	0	0	1	2	2	0
Jumping .	0	0	1	2	1	0	1	0	0	1	0	2	0	1	1	4
Jump rope .	0	0	0	2	0	0	0	0	0	0	0	0	0	0	0	0

234

Response Word	4th M	4th F	5th M	5th F	6th M	6th F	7th M	7th F	8th M	8th F	10th M	10th F	12th M	12th F	College M	College F
							PLAYING									
Kids	1	0	1	0	0	0	0	0	1	1	2	1	3	3	5	2
Laughing	0	0	0	1	0	0	1	1	0	1	1	1	1	1	1	2
Lazy	0	0	0	0	0	0	1	0	3	0	0	0	0	0	0	0
Loafing	0	0	0	0	0	0	0	1	0	0	0	0	0	1	2	0
Marbles	0	0	0	0	0	0	1	0	0	0	0	0	1	1	0	2
Me	2	1	0	1	1	1	1	0	0	1	0	0	0	1	0	0
Nice	2	2	4	3	0	0	1	0	0	1	0	1	0	0	0	0
Not	1	4	0	0	1	1	0	0	0	0	0	0	0	0	0	0
Now	2	1	2	0	2	0	0	0	0	2	0	0	0	0	0	0
On	1	1	0	0	0	0	0	0	1	0	0	0	0	0	2	0
Out	0	4	3	0	2	0	2	2	1	0	1	0	0	0	0	0
Outside	3	2	1	4	0	3	2	1	0	2	1	2	2	0	1	0
Piano	0	1	0	1	1	3	1	3	1	1	2	4	2	1	3	10
Play	45	31	28	21	16	28	24	19	15	7	11	7	9	4	7	5
Played	2	0	4	7	1	1	4	6	12	6	3	4	9	2	11	4
Player	0	0	1	0	0	0	0	2	0	0	2	1	0	0	2	0
Playground	0	0	1	0	0	0	0	0	3	0	0	0	0	0	0	0
Poker	0	0	0	0	0	0	0	0	1	0	2	0	0	0	0	0
Record	2	0	0	0	0	0	0	0	0	0	0	0	0	0	1	0
Records	0	0	0	0	0	0	0	0	0	2	0	0	0	0	2	1
Rest	0	0	1	0	0	0	0	0	0	0	0	0	0	0	2	0
Resting	0	1	0	1	0	0	0	2	0	4	1	2	0	2	0	4
Romping	1	0	0	0	0	0	0	0	0	0	0	0	0	0	2	2
Rough	0	1	0	0	0	0	1	1	0	2	0	0	1	0	0	0
Run	3	2	4	5	4	1	4	2	1	2	2	1	3	0	0	1
Running	4	0	1	6	7	1	4	7	4	4	7	7	1	3	13	18
Sand	2	1	0	0	1	2	0	1	1	2	0	1	4	0	6	2
Sand box	0	0	0	0	0	0	0	0	0	2	2	1	1	0	1	5
Saying	1	1	0	0	0	1	0	3	2	0	1	0	0	3	2	0
Serious	0	0	0	0	0	0	0	0	0	0	0	0	1	1	2	0
Singing	1	0	0	0	0	0	0	1	1	1	0	0	0	0	1	6
Sitting	0	0	0	1	1	1	2	2	5	1	1	3	0	2	0	3
Sleeping	0	2	0	3	0	1	3	4	3	1	2	2	2	4	2	9
Staying	0	1	0	0	0	0	0	0	0	2	0	0	0	0	1	0
Stop	1	2	2	0	1	3	1	0	1	1	2	0	0	0	1	0
Studying	0	0	0	0	0	1	1	0	1	0	0	0	0	0	1	2
Swing	2	1	0	1	0	0	2	0	0	0	1	0	0	0	1	2
Tag	0	3	1	2	1	0	0	2	0	1	1	0	1	0	0	3
Talking	0	0	0	1	0	1	0	0	0	1	0	1	0	1	2	0
Tennis	0	0	0	0	0	0	1	0	0	2	1	0	0	1	0	0
Time	0	0	1	0	0	0	0	0	0	0	2	0	0	0	1	1
Tired	1	0	1	3	1	0	0	0	0	0	0	0	1	0	0	0
Together	0	0	1	0	0	0	0	0	0	0	0	1	0	0	4	0
Toy	1	1	1	1	1	3	1	0	0	0	0	0	2	1	2	0
Toys	1	2	1	3	2	4	1	4	1	3	2	7	1	5	7	13
Violin	0	0	0	0	0	0	0	2	1	0	0	0	0	0	0	0
Walking	0	0	0	0	0	0	1	1	1	2	0	0	0	1	0	1
What	0	0	0	0	1	0	0	0	2	0	2	0	1	0	0	0
With	3	3	4	3	6	3	9	2	8	6	6	1	12	5	9	7

Response Word	4th M	F	5th M	F	6th M	F	7th M	F	8th M	F	10th M	F	12th M	F	College M	F
						PLAYING										
Work . . .	10	14	8	12	8	9	12	10	15	14	4	7	9	5	18	6
Working . .	17	24	16	21	11	19	25	33	18	22	17	26	24	23	73	69
Yard	0	0	0	1	1	1	0	1	0	0	0	1	0	0	2	1
						129. **PRIEST**										
Altar . . .	0	1	0	1	0	0	0	0	0	0	0	1	0	0	0	2
Animal . .	0	2	0	1	0	0	0	0	0	0	0	0	0	0	0	0
Bible . . .	24	12	16	7	14	7	5	4	6	2	11	3	5	0	6	0
Bishop . .	1	0	1	0	1	0	2	1	1	0	0	0	0	0	2	3
Black . . .	0	1	0	0	0	1	1	2	0	1	3	0	7	8	19	22
Brother . .	0	0	0	0	0	0	0	0	0	0	0	0	0	2	0	0
Cassock .	0	0	0	0	0	0	0	0	0	0	0	0	0	0	2	1
Catholic . .	2	3	1	0	1	9	10	15	11	20	22	39	23	44	82	103
Catholic Church .	0	0	1	0	0	0	1	0	0	0	0	1	2	0	0	1
Catholicism	0	0	0	0	0	0	0	0	0	0	0	0	0	0	1	6
Catholics .	0	0	0	0	0	0	0	1	1	2	0	2	2	4	5	7
Christ . . .	1	0	0	0	1	0	1	2	1	0	0	0	0	0	0	1
Church . .	45	80	59	69	67	86	64	65	70	70	78	90	81	75	99	126
Clergy . . .	0	0	0	0	0	0	0	0	0	0	0	1	0	0	2	2
Confession .	0	0	0	0	0	0	0	0	0	0	0	1	0	1	1	2
Desk	0	0	0	0	2	0	0	0	0	0	0	0	0	0	0	0
Doctor . .	1	0	0	2	1	0	0	1	0	0	0	0	0	0	0	2
Eat	1	2	0	0	0	0	1	0	0	0	0	0	0	0	0	0
Father . .	5	5	5	8	5	13	7	6	7	10	13	18	14	12	25	12
Flat	1	0	2	0	1	0	0	0	0	0	0	0	0	0	0	0
Food . . .	0	3	0	0	0	1	1	0	0	0	0	0	0	0	0	0
God	6	5	8	7	16	9	8	6	12	8	15	14	13	8	22	15
Good . . .	1	2	6	2	5	2	0	3	0	1	6	1	5	2	3	4
Goodness .	0	0	0	0	0	0	0	0	0	0	0	0	0	0	3	1
Hard . . .	2	3	0	0	2	1	4	0	0	0	0	0	0	0	0	0
Hear . . .	3	0	1	0	0	0	0	0	0	0	0	0	0	0	0	0
Here . . .	0	0	2	0	0	0	0	0	0	0	0	0	0	0	0	0
High	1	1	2	0	1	0	0	0	2	3	0	0	2	0	2	1
Holy	1	2	4	2	5	7	4	2	5	3	2	2	6	3	4	2
Hood . . .	0	0	0	0	0	0	0	0	0	0	0	0	1	0	3	0
Hoodlum .	0	0	0	0	0	0	1	0	3	1	0	0	0	0	0	0
Iron	0	2	0	1	1	0	1	0	0	0	0	0	0	0	0	0
Jesus . . .	0	0	1	2	0	0	1	0	0	1	0	0	0	0	0	0
Kind . . .	1	0	0	0	1	0	0	0	0	2	0	0	0	2	0	0
Leader . .	1	0	0	0	1	1	0	1	1	1	1	0	1	0	2	0
Lord . . .	1	0	1	0	2	0	0	1	1	1	0	0	0	0	0	0
Man	22	12	31	28	14	20	14	18	12	16	10	11	10	19	37	29
Marriage .	0	0	0	0	0	0	0	0	0	1	0	1	0	2	0	0
Mass . . .	1	0	0	0	1	0	0	1	0	1	0	0	0	1	5	11
Minister .	20	34	25	42	28	37	46	49	30	35	19	22	14	15	23	16
Missionary	0	2	0	1	1	1	1	0	0	0	0	0	0	0	0	0
Money . . .	2	0	1	0	0	0	0	0	0	1	0	0	1	0	1	1
Monk . . .	0	0	0	0	0	1	1	0	0	0	0	2	1	1	0	2

Response Word	4th M	4th F	5th M	5th F	6th M	6th F	7th M	7th F	8th M	8th F	10th M	10th F	12th M	12th F	College M	College F
						PRIEST										
Mother ..	2	0	0	0	0	0	0	0	0	0	0	0	0	0	0	0
Nice	2	1	1	1	1	1	0	2	2	1	0	0	0	0	0	0
Nothing ..	0	0	0	1	0	0	0	0	2	0	0	0	0	0	0	0
Nun	0	1	0	0	0	0	0	2	0	0	0	2	1	5	3	9
Ocean ...	2	0	0	0	0	0	0	0	0	0	0	0	0	0	0	0
Parson ..	0	0	0	0	1	0	0	0	0	0	0	0	1	0	0	2
Pastor ..	8	6	6	13	12	11	13	12	13	7	14	14	10	8	3	7
People ..	1	0	2	1	2	1	0	0	0	0	0	0	0	0	0	0
Person ..	5	2	4	2	4	2	0	3	4	1	4	0	2	2	2	0
Pope ...	0	1	1	1	0	1	1	0	0	2	1	1	3	0	3	2
Pray ...	3	0	0	3	1	6	0	2	1	1	0	0	0	1	2	5
Praying ..	0	0	0	2	0	0	0	0	0	0	0	0	0	0	0	0
Preach ..	0	2	0	1	1	0	1	0	1	1	0	0	2	0	2	2
Preacher .	2	4	1	2	5	4	11	3	3	3	4	0	2	0	1	0
Pretty ...	1	3	0	1	0	1	0	0	0	0	0	0	0	0	0	0
Push	0	0	2	0	0	0	1	0	0	0	0	0	0	0	0	0
Rabbi ...	0	0	2	0	0	1	9	7	15	10	2	1	0	2	12	7
Religion .	0	2	4	3	4	5	9	10	9	16	13	5	9	10	55	40
Religious .	0	1	0	0	0	0	2	0	0	1	0	3	2	0	6	1
Rev.	0	0	1	1	0	0	0	3	0	0	0	0	0	0	0	0
Reverend .	0	0	0	2	1	1	2	2	2	2	2	0	1	1	2	0
Robe	0	0	1	0	1	0	0	0	1	1	1	0	1	2	2	6
Robes ...	0	0	0	0	0	0	0	0	0	0	0	0	0	0	4	1
Roman Catholic	0	0	0	0	0	0	0	0	1	0	0	0	0	0	0	2
Sacrifice .	0	0	0	0	0	0	0	0	0	0	0	0	0	0	2	0
Sermon ..	0	0	0	0	0	0	0	2	4	3	1	0	1	1	0	0
Sick	2	0	0	0	0	0	0	0	0	0	0	0	0	0	0	0
Sin	0	0	0	0	0	0	0	0	0	0	0	0	0	0	0	2
Sister ...	0	1	1	0	0	1	0	0	0	0	0	1	0	1	0	2
Sunday ..	2	1	1	1	1	1	0	0	0	0	0	0	0	0	0	0
Talk	2	0	0	1	1	0	0	0	0	0	0	0	1	0	0	0
Teach ..	3	1	2	3	2	0	0	0	0	0	1	1	1	1	0	0
Teacher ..	4	2	3	0	3	3	2	3	1	1	1	0	0	1	0	0
White ...	0	0	0	2	0	0	1	0	0	0	0	0	0	0	0	0
Worship ..	1	2	1	0	2	0	0	0	0	0	0	0	0	0	0	0
						130. QUICKLY										
A	2	1	0	0	1	0	0	0	0	0	0	0	0	0	0	0
At	1	0	1	0	1	0	0	0	2	0	0	0	0	0	0	0
Away ...	0	2	0	0	1	0	0	0	0	0	1	0	0	0	1	0
Bob	0	0	0	0	0	0	0	0	0	0	2	0	0	0	0	0
Car	0	0	0	0	0	1	0	0	1	1	1	0	2	0	0	0
Cat	0	0	0	0	1	0	0	1	0	0	0	0	2	0	2	1
Come ...	0	0	0	1	0	0	0	0	0	0	1	1	0	2	4	2
Done ...	0	1	1	0	4	0	2	0	0	2	0	0	0	0	3	1
Fast ...	127	130	142	140	135	145	129	124	87	103	121	122	108	103	193	223
Faster ..	1	2	1	1	0	3	1	3	0	1	3	0	1	0	2	1
Fastly ..	1	0	0	0	0	0	0	0	1	0	0	3	0	0	1	2

Response Word	4th M	4th F	5th M	5th F	6th M	6th F	7th M	7th F	8th M	8th F	10th M	10th F	12th M	12th F	College M	College F
QUICKLY																
Fox	0	0	0	0	0	0	0	0	0	0	0	1	0	1	0	2
Go	2	0	2	0	3	1	0	1	2	0	1	1	4	8	2	3
Gone	0	0	0	1	0	2	0	0	2	0	0	0	0	0	0	0
Good	2	2	0	1	0	0	1	0	0	0	0	0	1	0	0	0
Happy	0	2	0	0	0	0	0	0	0	0	0	1	0	0	0	0
Hurriedly	0	0	0	1	0	0	0	0	0	1	0	0	0	0	2	1
Hurry	6	9	5	13	8	9	6	4	3	7	3	5	2	6	6	6
Jump	0	0	0	0	0	1	2	0	0	0	2	2	1	0	2	1
Move	0	0	0	0	1	0	0	0	0	1	1	0	2	0	4	0
Never	0	0	0	0	0	0	0	0	0	2	0	0	0	1	1	2
Now	2	2	1	1	2	3	3	1	1	1	3	2	2	1	12	2
Quick	10	14	10	4	3	6	3	2	2	3	1	0	2	1	3	0
Quiet	1	1	2	1	1	1	2	1	0	3	0	0	1	0	0	0
Quietly	3	2	1	2	2	1	5	9	5	6	4	9	12	6	4	5
Quit	1	1	1	3	0	0	0	0	0	0	0	0	0	0	0	0
Quite	0	0	1	1	0	2	1	0	0	1	0	0	0	0	0	0
Rabbit	1	0	2	0	0	1	2	0	0	1	2	1	2	6	2	0
Ran	2	0	2	2	1	0	0	0	1	1	2	1	2	1	4	0
Rapid	2	0	0	0	0	0	1	2	0	0	0	1	1	0	3	2
Rapidly	0	0	0	0	0	2	3	2	0	1	0	2	0	0	3	6
Run	6	11	4	8	5	4	3	8	6	14	17	16	8	18	20	26
Runner	0	0	0	0	0	0	0	0	0	0	0	0	0	0	2	0
Running	0	1	0	2	0	0	0	0	0	0	1	0	0	1	1	1
Short	0	0	0	0	0	0	0	0	0	2	0	0	0	0	1	0
Shortly	0	0	0	0	0	0	0	0	0	0	0	0	0	0	2	0
Slow	32	24	23	21	26	19	27	24	50	28	16	13	21	24	48	37
Slowly	13	18	8	17	18	24	34	38	58	49	37	47	49	46	106	123
Soft	0	1	0	2	1	0	0	0	1	1	0	0	0	0	0	0
Softly	0	0	0	0	0	0	0	2	0	4	0	0	0	0	0	1
Soon	0	2	1	0	1	0	0	0	0	0	0	1	0	2	5	3
Speed	1	0	1	0	1	0	0	1	3	1	4	2	1	3	6	4
Speedily	0	0	0	0	2	0	0	1	0	0	0	0	0	0	0	0
Start	0	1	1	0	0	0	0	0	1	0	0	0	2	1	1	0
Stop	0	0	2	1	0	1	0	1	2	0	0	0	1	1	0	1
Swift	1	2	1	1	1	3	3	2	1	3	2	0	1	0	4	3
Swiftly	0	0	0	0	3	0	1	2	2	4	3	1	1	2	7	6
Test	0	3	1	2	0	1	0	1	0	0	0	0	0	1	0	2
Think	2	2	1	1	3	1	0	1	1	0	0	1	1	0	1	0
Turn	0	0	0	0	0	0	0	0	0	0	0	0	0	0	1	2
Went	0	0	0	0	0	0	0	0	0	0	0	0	0	1	0	2
Where	0	0	0	0	0	0	0	0	0	0	0	0	0	0	2	0
Write	0	0	0	1	0	0	1	1	0	0	1	2	1	0	0	2
You	1	0	0	0	2	1	0	0	0	0	0	0	0	0	1	0
131. QUIET																
Alone	0	0	0	0	0	0	0	0	0	1	2	0	0	0	0	0
Baby	1	2	2	1	1	3	0	1	1	0	2	1	2	0	0	1
Be quiet	2	0	1	0	1	0	0	1	0	0	0	0	0	0	0	0
Calm	1	0	1	1	4	1	2	0	0	1	2	3	0	2	1	4

Response Word	4th		5th		6th		7th		8th		10th		12th		College	
	M	F	M	F	M	F	M	F	M	F	M	F	M	F	M	F

QUIET

Response Word	M	F	M	F	M	F	M	F	M	F	M	F	M	F	M	F
Cat	1	2	0	0	0	0	1	0	1	0	0	0	0	0	2	0
Church	0	0	0	2	0	0	0	0	0	0	0	1	1	2	0	2
Dark	0	0	0	0	0	0	0	1	0	0	3	3	1	0	1	2
Evening	0	0	0	0	0	0	0	0	0	0	0	0	0	0	2	1
Fast	2	1	1	0	0	2	1	1	0	0	0	0	0	1	0	0
Girl	1	1	0	0	1	1	0	2	1	0	0	0	0	1	0	0
Good	4	3	3	0	0	0	1	4	1	0	0	2	0	1	0	1
Hear	0	0	1	1	1	0	0	3	0	0	0	0	0	0	1	0
Home	1	0	0	0	0	0	0	0	0	0	0	1	0	0	2	0
Hospital	0	1	4	2	6	3	6	6	1	8	12	9	15	9	25	26
Hours	0	0	0	0	0	0	0	0	0	0	0	0	0	0	2	1
House	0	0	2	0	0	0	1	0	0	2	0	0	2	1	0	2
Hush	0	1	1	2	2	2	0	2	0	1	0	2	1	0	0	0
Lake	0	0	0	1	0	0	0	0	0	2	0	2	1	1	0	3
Library	1	1	0	3	1	0	2	2	2	1	10	5	8	3	12	6
Listen	1	0	2	1	0	2	0	0	0	0	0	0	0	1	0	0
Load	1	4	0	1	0	1	0	2	0	0	2	1	1	0	0	0
Lonely	1	0	0	0	1	0	0	1	0	0	0	0	0	2	0	0
Loud	56	43	53	69	72	47	68	52	104	68	61	50	62	67	134	119
Low	0	0	1	2	0	1	2	0	1	0	0	0	0	1	0	0
Me	0	0	1	0	2	1	1	1	0	0	0	0	0	0	1	0
Mouse	0	0	0	0	1	2	0	0	0	0	0	0	0	5	0	1
Music	0	0	0	0	0	0	1	2	1	0	0	0	1	0	1	1
Nice	5	7	5	4	2	4	4	2	1	4	2	4	2	0	1	2
Night	1	5	1	2	2	5	6	7	5	4	3	9	6	6	10	16
No	2	0	0	0	2	0	0	0	1	0	0	1	0	0	0	0
Noise	35	29	32	25	29	12	24	26	23	16	24	16	24	13	48	39
Noiseless	0	0	1	1	4	3	3	4	3	4	2	3	2	1	4	2
Noisy	7	18	11	15	11	22	20	12	13	20	16	21	14	21	45	42
No noise	1	2	0	1	0	1	1	0	2	0	1	0	1	0	0	0
Nose	0	5	2	0	0	0	0	0	0	0	0	0	0	0	0	0
Not loud	1	1	0	0	0	0	0	0	0	2	0	0	0	0	0	0
Now	1	1	1	0	0	0	0	1	0	0	2	0	0	0	0	0
Ocean	0	0	0	0	0	0	0	0	0	1	0	1	3	1	1	0
Peace	1	2	1	3	2	5	3	6	4	13	7	13	9	17	23	30
Peaceful	1	0	2	3	5	6	1	6	4	8	6	16	4	10	9	17
Person	2	0	0	0	0	0	0	0	0	1	0	0	0	0	0	0
Pleasant	0	0	0	0	0	1	0	0	0	0	0	0	0	0	2	1
Please	1	2	2	2	1	0	1	0	3	2	0	1	1	0	1	1
Rest	0	0	0	4	1	1	0	0	0	0	1	1	4	4	5	5
Restful	0	0	0	0	1	0	0	2	0	1	0	2	1	1	3	4
Room	0	3	4	0	2	2	0	1	0	0	3	5	2	2	8	9
School	1	0	0	0	0	2	0	0	0	2	0	0	2	0	0	0
Serene	0	0	0	0	0	0	0	1	0	0	1	1	1	2	3	4
Sh	4	7	0	0	0	11	0	2	2	0	1	0	0	0	0	2
She	0	1	0	0	2	2	0	0	0	0	0	0	0	0	0	0
Shh	0	0	2	7	5	0	1	0	0	2	0	0	0	0	1	0
Short	2	0	0	0	0	0	0	0	0	0	0	0	0	0	0	0
Shout	2	3	0	0	0	0	0	0	0	2	0	0	1	0	0	0

Response	4th		5th		6th		7th		8th		10th		12th		College	
Word	M	F	M	F	M	F	M	F	M	F	M	F	M	F	M	F

QUIET

Shut up ..	3	1	2	1	0	0	3	2	4	1	1	0	0	0	0	2
Shy	0	0	1	0	0	0	0	4	0	0	1	2	0	1	0	0
Silence ..	6	3	5	4	3	10	10	15	2	5	4	6	4	7	7	3
Silent ...	3	9	5	9	3	12	4	2	5	6	2	4	5	4	9	5
Sleep ...	5	14	12	13	8	14	7	5	14	12	22	19	21	21	33	39
Sleeping ..	0	1	0	0	0	0	0	0	2	2	2	2	0	0	0	1
Sleepy ...	2	0	0	1	1	0	0	1	0	0	0	0	0	0	0	1
Slow ...	1	1	1	0	0	2	0	0	0	0	0	0	0	1	1	0
Snow ...	1	0	0	0	0	0	0	0	0	0	2	0	0	0	0	0
Soft	15	15	9	20	5	21	28	20	17	20	18	21	19	14	33	30
Softly ...	0	1	0	0	1	1	2	2	1	0	1	1	2	1	0	0
Sound ...	5	8	13	5	11	12	9	0	3	2	8	1	2	2	6	7
Soundless .	1	2	1	2	0	2	1	2	1	2	0	0	0	1	0	1
Speak ...	2	0	0	0	0	0	2	0	0	1	0	0	0	0	0	0
Still	1	1	4	4	4	3	3	9	1	7	3	6	2	1	7	15
Stillness .	0	0	0	0	0	0	0	2	1	1	1	3	0	0	0	2
Stop	4	0	4	0	2	0	1	2	1	1	1	0	1	2	0	0
Street ...	0	0	0	0	0	0	0	0	0	0	0	0	0	0	2	0
Study....	0	0	0	0	0	0	0	0	0	0	0	0	1	0	7	8
Talk	2	4	2	1	2	0	1	2	1	0	1	1	0	1	1	0
Tired ...	0	1	0	0	1	0	0	0	0	0	0	2	1	0	0	0
Unnoisy ..	1	0	0	0	3	2	0	0	0	0	0	0	0	0	0	0
Village ..	0	0	0	0	0	0	0	0	0	0	0	0	2	0	1	0
Whisper ..	1	4	1	2	1	0	0	1	0	0	0	0	0	0	0	1
White ...	1	0	0	0	0	0	0	0	0	0	0	0	0	0	0	2
Work ...	1	2	0	0	0	1	1	0	0	0	0	0	0	0	0	0
Yell	0	0	0	1	2	0	1	0	3	0	0	0	0	0	0	0
You	0	0	1	0	2	0	0	0	0	0	0	0	0	0	0	0

132. QUIETLY

And	2	0	0	1	0	0	0	0	0	0	0	0	0	0	0	0
Baby ...	0	0	0	0	0	1	1	0	0	1	0	2	0	1	0	0
Be	0	1	2	1	1	0	1	0	0	0	0	0	0	0	0	0
Cat	0	0	1	0	0	1	0	0	0	0	0	2	1	0	0	2
Come ...	1	0	2	1	0	3	0	0	1	1	1	0	1	1	2	0
Creep ...	1	0	0	0	0	0	0	0	2	0	0	0	0	0	0	0
Do	1	1	3	0	0	0	1	0	0	0	1	0	0	0	0	0
Don't ...	2	0	1	0	0	0	0	0	0	0	0	0	0	1	0	0
Down ...	2	0	0	0	1	1	1	0	0	0	1	0	0	1	0	0
Fast ...	17	19	28	11	17	16	8	7	6	4	8	5	5	6	3	4
Faster ..	2	1	1	0	1	0	0	3	0	1	0	0	0	0	0	0
Go	2	1	1	3	0	0	0	1	3	2	1	0	3	1	4	1
Gone ...	0	0	2	0	0	0	0	0	0	1	0	0	3	1	2	0
Good ...	2	2	2	1	2	0	0	0	0	0	0	0	0	0	0	0
Hard ...	1	3	0	0	0	0	0	0	0	0	0	0	0	0	0	0
Have ...	1	2	2	1	1	1	1	0	1	0	0	0	0	0	0	0
Here ...	0	1	0	0	2	0	1	0	0	0	1	0	1	0	0	0
Him	1	1	1	0	1	0	0	1	3	0	1	0	0	0	0	0
Hospital ..	0	0	1	0	1	3	1	0	2	2	3	5	7	6	10	10

Response Word	4th		5th		6th		7th		8th		10th		12th		College	
	M	F	M	F	M	F	M	F	M	F	M	F	M	F	M	F

QUIETLY

Response Word	M	F	M	F	M	F	M	F	M	F	M	F	M	F	M	F
Hush	0	0	0	0	0	1	1	1	0	1	1	2	0	1	0	2
I	0	0	0	0	2	0	2	0	0	0	0	0	0	0	1	0
Is	0	0	2	0	0	0	0	0	0	1	0	0	1	0	0	0
It	1	0	0	0	2	1	0	0	1	0	0	0	0	0	0	0
Kill	0	0	0	0	0	0	0	0	0	0	1	0	0	0	2	0
Library	0	0	0	0	0	0	0	0	0	0	2	1	0	0	1	1
Load	0	2	0	1	2	0	1	0	2	1	1	2	0	0	0	0
Loud	12	15	12	20	19	15	20	27	45	32	16	20	26	30	47	20
Louder	0	0	0	1	1	1	1	1	2	2	0	0	2	0	2	0
Loudly	9	11	6	13	4	9	20	28	38	26	14	27	13	46	62	80
Me	0	0	0	0	4	0	0	1	0	0	0	0	0	0	0	0
Mouse	0	0	0	1	1	0	1	0	0	0	2	1	0	1	1	1
Move	1	0	0	0	1	2	0	0	1	0	0	0	1	1	1	1
Nice	1	0	1	0	0	2	0	1	0	0	0	0	0	0	0	1
Night	0	0	0	0	1	0	1	0	1	1	0	1	1	1	1	4
No	0	1	1	0	2	0	0	0	0	0	0	0	0	0	0	0
Noise	16	19	14	12	17	15	22	19	25	9	12	12	15	12	43	27
Noiseless	1	0	0	0	2	1	0	0	1	0	1	1	2	1	0	1
Noiselessly	0	0	0	0	0	1	1	2	0	2	1	0	1	1	2	1
Noises	0	0	1	1	0	0	0	2	1	0	0	0	0	0	0	0
Noisily	2	1	6	8	2	5	13	15	7	13	21	18	17	5	25	29
Noisy	7	6	6	12	4	16	11	20	10	19	9	13	12	13	21	37
Nose	1	0	0	0	2	1	0	0	0	0	1	0	0	0	0	0
Not	3	1	1	2	0	0	0	0	0	0	0	0	0	0	0	0
Now	2	2	2	2	4	1	2	0	1	0	2	1	4	0	4	0
One	0	0	1	1	0	0	2	0	0	0	0	0	0	0	0	0
Peace	0	0	0	0	0	1	0	1	1	0	1	1	0	2	0	3
Peaceful	0	0	1	0	0	0	0	0	0	0	0	3	0	0	0	0
Peacefully	0	0	0	0	0	1	0	0	0	0	1	0	0	2	1	3
Please	0	0	0	2	0	1	2	2	2	2	0	1	1	0	2	1
Quick	2	6	2	4	1	4	4	3	1	1	1	0	1	1	1	2
Quickly	2	4	3	7	3	3	6	11	1	8	7	12	8	4	12	20
Quiet	36	41	27	29	18	26	17	11	10	9	8	3	7	7	8	4
Quietest	0	0	0	0	0	0	0	0	0	0	0	0	0	0	2	0
Quit	2	2	5	1	1	1	2	0	1	1	0	1	0	0	0	0
Quite	3	0	3	2	2	3	3	1	1	0	0	1	0	1	1	0
Ran	1	1	0	1	0	0	0	0	0	0	2	0	0	0	0	1
Rest	0	0	0	0	0	0	0	0	0	0	0	0	0	3	2	0
Room	0	0	1	0	2	0	0	0	0	0	0	0	0	0	1	1
Run	1	1	1	1	0	0	0	0	1	0	3	2	1	2	3	0
Sat	0	0	0	0	0	0	0	1	0	0	0	0	0	0	3	0
Sh	0	5	1	5	6	0	0	4	0	0	0	4	0	0	5	8
She	1	0	1	0	0	2	1	0	0	0	0	0	0	0	0	0
Shh	3	0	0	0	0	13	1	0	1	0	0	0	0	0	0	0
Shut up	1	0	0	0	0	1	3	0	2	1	1	0	0	0	0	0
Shy	0	0	0	0	0	0	0	1	0	0	0	0	0	0	0	2
Sight	0	0	2	0	0	0	0	0	0	0	0	0	0	0	0	0
Silence	1	1	0	0	1	0	2	3	0	3	1	1	2	2	5	2
Silent	4	4	6	5	10	3	2	3	0	5	5	8	5	4	14	13

Response Word	4th M	4th F	5th M	5th F	6th M	6th F	7th M	7th F	8th M	8th F	10th M	10th F	12th M	12th F	College M	College F

QUIETLY

Response Word	4th M	4th F	5th M	5th F	6th M	6th F	7th M	7th F	8th M	8th F	10th M	10th F	12th M	12th F	College M	College F
Silently ..	3	0	1	2	2	3	3	2	2	1	2	3	5	2	10	8
Sing	0	0	0	0	0	0	0	1	0	3	0	0	0	0	1	0
Sit	0	1	0	1	0	1	0	0	1	1	2	1	0	1	0	1
Sleep ...	0	5	2	4	2	4	2	3	3	2	5	7	3	10	7	8
Sleeping ..	1	2	1	3	1	0	0	0	0	1	0	3	0	1	0	1
Slow ...	9	6	13	9	7	6	1	2	8	3	2	5	2	1	3	6
Slowly ..	5	5	2	6	6	6	7	7	5	7	8	7	1	2	13	8
Sneak ...	0	0	0	0	0	1	0	0	0	0	2	0	1	1	4	2
Soft	7	8	6	12	15	15	12	17	7	19	14	14	15	16	19	35
Softly ...	5	6	11	10	10	16	22	25	16	33	25	34	25	27	64	91
Sound ...	1	4	3	4	3	3	3	1	1	0	3	0	9	1	0	1
Soundless .	1	3	1	1	0	1	2	1	0	1	1	0	0	0	1	0
Speak ...	1	0	0	0	0	0	0	0	2	0	1	0	3	4	7	5
Still	0	2	0	0	1	0	0	1	0	1	0	3	1	0	1	3
Stop	1	0	1	0	1	0	0	0	0	0	1	0	0	0	2	0
Sweetly ..	0	0	0	0	0	0	0	0	0	0	0	0	2	1	0	1
Talk ...	2	3	1	1	0	0	3	0	0	4	1	1	0	1	1	6
Than ...	0	0	0	0	1	0	0	0	2	0	0	0	2	0	0	0
The	0	0	1	0	5	0	0	0	0	0	0	0	0	0	0	0
They ...	2	0	0	0	1	0	0	0	2	0	1	0	0	0	1	0
Think ...	0	0	0	0	0	0	0	0	0	1	1	1	0	0	0	2
Tip toe ..	0	4	0	3	1	4	0	1	0	1	3	1	0	3	2	0
To	2	1	1	1	2	0	0	0	0	1	1	0	0	0	2	0
Walk ...	0	1	1	0	2	0	1	0	3	1	3	1	0	0	5	3
We	1	0	1	1	0	0	3	0	0	0	0	0	0	0	0	0
Well ...	0	0	0	0	0	0	0	0	2	0	0	0	0	0	0	0
Went ...	1	0	0	0	0	0	0	0	0	0	1	1	1	0	2	0
Whisper ..	1	1	0	3	2	4	3	3	0	0	0	3	1	0	2	3
Work ...	2	0	0	1	0	0	0	0	0	1	0	0	0	0	1	0
Yes	1	2	0	0	0	0	0	0	0	0	0	0	0	0	0	0

133. RED

Response Word	4th M	4th F	5th M	5th F	6th M	6th F	7th M	7th F	8th M	8th F	10th M	10th F	12th M	12th F	College M	College F
Anger ...	1	0	0	0	0	1	0	0	0	0	0	1	1	0	2	2
Angry ...	0	0	0	0	0	0	1	0	0	0	0	0	1	3	0	2
Apple ...	0	3	2	1	1	2	6	7	4	4	1	3	0	4	4	7
Ball	0	0	2	1	0	0	0	0	0	0	0	0	0	0	1	1
Barn ...	0	0	0	0	0	2	1	0	2	0	0	0	2	2	1	2
Beautiful .	0	0	1	2	2	0	1	0	0	0	0	0	0	0	0	0
Bed	3	5	4	4	3	1	1	0	2	1	1	0	1	0	0	0
Black ...	12	9	19	14	16	18	18	17	26	7	27	34	29	27	65	74
Blanket ..	1	0	0	0	0	0	0	0	0	0	0	0	0	0	2	0
Blood ...	6	6	6	9	12	8	19	13	13	26	19	8	14	18	27	33
Blue	48	45	32	42	36	39	34	43	46	39	21	28	21	32	56	71
Blush ...	0	0	0	0	0	0	0	2	0	1	0	0	0	0	0	1
Book	0	1	0	1	0	0	0	0	0	1	0	0	0	0	0	2
Bright ..	8	5	14	16	14	22	23	16	13	23	14	21	6	11	11	20
Brown ...	4	2	2	3	1	1	1	0	4	1	1	2	0	1	0	0
Bull	0	0	1	0	3	0	4	1	2	0	1	2	4	4	8	9
Cap	0	0	1	0	0	2	0	0	0	1	4	1	0	0	3	0

Response Word	4th M	4th F	5th M	5th F	6th M	6th F	7th M	7th F	8th M	8th F	10th M	10th F	12th M	12th F	College M	College F
							RED									
Car	0	0	0	0	0	2	1	2	1	2	8	6	12	0	5	0
Christmas .	0	0	1	2	1	0	0	1	0	1	0	1	0	0	0	1
Cloth	0	2	0	1	0	0	0	0	0	0	2	0	1	0	2	3
Coat	2	3	3	2	3	5	0	4	1	4	6	13	1	7	7	10
Color	68	83	68	60	64	78	44	35	39	27	30	16	14	14	39	26
Colorful . . .	1	0	2	1	1	0	0	0	0	0	1	0	0	0	0	1
Colors . . .	0	1	1	1	4	0	1	0	0	0	0	0	0	0	0	0
Communist .	0	1	0	0	0	0	0	0	0	1	0	0	1	0	4	2
Crayon . . .	1	2	1	0	0	2	1	0	1	0	0	0	0	0	0	0
Danger . . .	0	0	0	0	0	0	0	0	0	0	1	0	1	1	3	1
Dark	1	5	6	10	3	3	5	2	1	1	2	0	0	3	0	1
Dog	0	0	0	1	0	0	0	0	0	0	0	0	1	0	2	0
Dress	0	2	0	1	1	1	0	2	0	2	0	8	0	4	1	13
Embarrassed	0	0	0	0	0	0	0	0	0	0	2	1	1	0	0	0
Fire	0	1	2	1	4	2	4	5	3	2	9	7	3	6	10	5
Fire engine .	0	1	0	1	0	1	0	1	3	0	3	2	4	0	0	0
Flag	2	2	1	2	1	0	2	1	0	1	2	2	1	2	5	4
Green	9	10	9	6	18	5	13	10	16	15	15	11	17	13	30	22
Hair	0	2	0	1	1	0	1	3	1	0	1	1	3	5	4	4
Hat	1	1	0	2	1	3	0	0	0	0	0	0	1	0	1	1
Head	0	0	0	1	0	0	0	0	3	0	0	0	1	1	2	2
Hot	2	3	3	3	2	2	3	3	2	11	4	4	8	3	7	9
House	3	1	1	2	1	0	0	2	0	0	1	0	0	1	1	0
Hunting . . .	0	0	0	0	1	0	0	0	0	0	0	0	0	0	2	0
Indian	0	2	0	0	1	0	0	0	1	1	0	1	0	0	1	0
Light	1	1	1	0	1	2	3	1	2	1	3	2	3	3	9	6
Lips	0	0	0	0	0	0	0	2	0	2	0	0	1	0	0	0
Lipstick . .	0	0	0	0	0	0	0	0	0	0	0	1	0	2	0	1
Mad	0	0	0	0	0	0	0	0	0	0	0	1	1	0	1	2
Orange . . .	2	0	2	2	3	0	3	4	5	6	1	2	1	6	4	0
Paint	0	1	0	0	2	0	0	0	0	1	0	0	1	0	1	2
Pink	2	0	3	4	1	3	0	3	0	1	1	4	1	1	1	4
Pretty	5	3	4	1	2	4	2	5	1	4	2	2	0	0	2	0
Purple . . .	0	0	1	0	0	1	1	2	0	0	1	0	0	0	0	0
Read	0	2	0	0	0	0	0	1	0	0	0	0	0	1	0	0
Red	0	0	0	0	2	1	0	0	0	0	0	0	0	0	0	0
Riding . . .	1	0	0	0	0	0	0	0	0	0	0	0	0	0	2	0
River	0	1	1	0	0	0	1	0	3	0	1	1	7	1	3	3
Rose	0	1	0	1	0	2	0	0	0	1	2	0	1	1	1	6
Rough	0	0	0	0	0	0	0	0	0	0	0	0	0	0	2	0
Russia . . .	0	0	0	0	0	0	0	0	0	0	1	0	2	0	0	0
Sea	0	0	0	0	0	0	0	0	0	0	1	0	1	0	2	1
Shirt	0	3	0	2	3	0	1	2	0	1	0	0	0	0	1	0
Shoe	0	0	0	1	0	0	0	0	0	1	0	0	0	0	2	0
Sore	0	0	0	0	0	0	0	0	0	0	0	2	0	0	0	0
Stop	2	0	3	0	1	0	0	0	2	2	3	2	7	4	4	9
Sun	0	0	0	0	0	0	1	0	0	0	1	0	0	0	2	0
Sunset	0	0	0	0	0	0	2	0	0	0	0	0	0	1	0	1
Sweater . . .	0	0	1	1	0	0	0	1	0	1	1	1	1	1	4	9

Response Word	4th M	4th F	5th M	5th F	6th M	6th F	7th M	7th F	8th M	8th F	10th M	10th F	12th M	12th F	College M	College F

RED

Response Word	4th M	4th F	5th M	5th F	6th M	6th F	7th M	7th F	8th M	8th F	10th M	10th F	12th M	12th F	College M	College F
Velvet	0	0	0	0	0	0	0	0	0	0	0	0	0	0	1	2
Wagon	0	0	0	1	1	1	1	2	0	1	1	0	0	1	0	0
Warm	0	0	0	0	1	1	0	0	0	2	0	4	1	0	2	3
White	28	19	24	22	15	9	29	23	26	23	31	26	37	40	94	69
Yellow	9	8	3	7	3	2	5	9	7	7	5	3	9	3	4	8

134. RELIGION

Response Word	4th M	4th F	5th M	5th F	6th M	6th F	7th M	7th F	8th M	8th F	10th M	10th F	12th M	12th F	College M	College F
Are	0	0	0	2	0	0	0	0	0	0	0	0	0	0	0	0
Atheist	0	0	0	0	0	0	0	0	1	0	1	0	1	0	0	2
Baptist	0	1	1	1	1	2	3	4	1	2	2	1	1	2	1	2
Belief	1	0	4	1	0	1	10	11	5	4	12	7	7	9	12	11
Believe	2	1	1	3	1	1	5	3	1	1	0	2	3	0	3	0
Bible	13	10	10	15	11	14	13	14	16	9	20	4	12	6	25	18
Big	0	2	0	0	0	0	0	0	0	0	0	0	0	0	0	0
Book	1	2	0	0	1	0	0	0	0	1	2	0	1	0	0	3
Catholic	7	13	5	8	8	17	9	9	6	8	11	15	9	14	24	30
Christ	2	2	2	2	2	2	2	1	0	2	2	3	1	4	7	5
Christian	4	1	2	2	0	2	8	7	8	4	1	2	0	2	1	5
Christianity	0	0	0	0	0	0	1	2	1	0	0	0	0	1	2	2
Church	50	62	67	74	83	81	52	58	66	57	67	82	56	45	93	115
Come	1	0	2	0	0	0	0	0	0	0	0	0	0	0	0	0
Congregationalist	0	0	0	0	0	0	0	0	1	2	0	0	0	0	0	0
Controversy	0	0	0	0	0	0	0	0	0	0	0	0	0	0	0	2
Corn	2	0	0	0	0	0	0	0	0	0	0	0	0	0	0	0
Country	1	1	0	0	1	0	2	0	0	0	0	0	0	0	0	0
Cousin	2	3	2	1	1	0	0	0	0	0	0	0	0	0	0	0
Covenant	0	2	0	1	0	0	0	1	0	1	0	0	0	0	0	0
Creed	0	0	0	0	0	0	0	0	0	0	1	0	2	0	0	1
Cross	0	0	0	0	0	1	0	0	0	0	1	0	0	0	3	1
Different	0	0	0	0	0	0	0	2	0	1	0	0	0	1	0	0
Episcopal	0	0	0	0	1	0	0	0	0	1	0	0	0	0	0	2
Faith	5	5	10	6	11	16	19	10	13	17	8	8	13	11	12	9
False	0	0	0	0	0	0	0	0	0	0	0	0	0	0	2	0
Father	1	0	0	1	1	0	0	0	1	1	0	0	0	1	1	2
Freedom	0	0	2	3	0	0	0	1	0	2	1	0	1	1	0	0
Friend	2	2	1	1	0	0	0	0	0	0	0	0	0	0	0	0
Go	1	0	0	2	0	0	0	0	0	0	0	0	0	0	0	0
God	16	13	15	11	26	17	24	35	30	33	44	62	51	63	109	129
Good	3	3	7	7	6	3	3	4	6	2	3	3	5	5	13	7
Hindu	0	0	0	0	0	0	1	0	0	2	0	0	0	0	0	0
Holy	0	3	1	1	2	2	9	3	5	0	1	3	1	2	2	1
Hope	0	0	1	0	0	0	0	1	0	0	0	0	2	0	1	2
House	0	0	2	0	1	0	0	0	0	0	0	0	0	0	0	0
Idea	0	0	0	0	0	0	0	0	0	0	0	0	0	0	0	2
Important	0	0	0	0	0	0	0	0	0	4	0	0	1	1	0	1
Jesus	0	3	3	1	0	2	1	6	0	2	2	5	0	1	2	3
Jew	1	0	0	0	0	0	3	2	3	3	1	0	0	0	1	0
Jewish	1	2	2	2	0	1	14	10	9	11	0	2	0	2	8	8

Response Word	4th		5th		6th		7th		8th		10th		12th		College	
	M	F	M	F	M	F	M	F	M	F	M	F	M	F	M	F

RELIGION

Response Word	4th M	4th F	5th M	5th F	6th M	6th F	7th M	7th F	8th M	8th F	10th M	10th F	12th M	12th F	College M	College F
Kind	0	1	2	1	0	0	1	0	1	0	0	0	0	0	0	0
Know	0	2	0	0	1	0	0	0	0	0	0	0	0	0	0	1
Land	2	0	3	1	1	0	0	0	0	0	0	0	0	0	0	0
Law	2	0	2	0	0	0	1	0	0	0	1	0	0	0	0	0
Life	1	0	0	0	0	0	0	0	0	1	0	0	1	0	4	5
Light	0	2	0	0	0	0	0	0	0	0	0	0	0	0	0	0
Lord	0	0	2	1	3	0	1	0	0	0	0	0	1	0	0	0
Love	1	1	0	0	0	0	0	1	1	0	0	0	0	2	4	2
Lutheran	7	14	8	16	15	26	12	16	13	12	12	26	12	19	13	26
Man	1	0	1	0	0	0	0	0	1	1	1	1	3	1	6	3
Me	0	2	1	2	1	1	1	0	0	0	0	0	0	0	2	1
Methodist	0	3	0	0	1	2	1	3	3	8	4	1	1	2	2	5
Mine	0	0	0	0	0	0	0	1	1	0	1	1	2	1	2	3
Minister	0	0	1	2	2	0	0	0	0	5	2	1	0	5	2	8
Myth	0	0	0	0	0	0	0	0	0	0	1	0	0	0	2	0
Nice	2	3	1	3	2	1	0	0	0	0	0	0	0	0	0	0
None	0	0	0	0	0	0	0	0	0	1	0	2	0	0	2	1
Pastor	0	0	0	0	3	1	3	0	1	0	2	2	4	0	2	1
Peace	0	0	2	1	0	1	0	1	0	0	0	0	1	1	0	0
People	2	1	5	8	2	4	3	5	1	7	2	2	1	0	3	0
Person	2	3	1	5	0	1	1	0	0	2	2	0	1	1	0	0
Philosophy	0	0	0	0	0	0	0	0	0	0	0	0	1	2	2	1
Place	1	1	1	2	0	0	0	0	0	0	0	0	0	0	0	0
Politics	0	0	0	0	0	0	0	0	0	0	0	0	0	0	3	0
Pray	1	2	2	2	2	2	1	1	2	1	2	0	2	0	4	4
Prayer	1	0	0	1	1	0	1	1	0	1	0	0	1	0	4	3
Preacher	0	0	0	0	0	0	0	1	1	1	1	0	1	0	3	0
Presbyterian	0	0	0	0	0	2	2	2	0	1	1	1	0	0	0	0
Priest	4	4	11	4	14	5	5	3	6	8	10	6	5	5	20	3
Protestant	0	1	1	0	1	1	1	1	3	1	2	2	2	3	5	4
Race	0	0	0	0	2	0	2	1	2	0	0	0	0	0	1	0
Religious	1	2	1	1	0	0	2	1	0	0	1	0	0	0	0	0
Rule	2	0	1	0	2	0	0	0	0	0	0	0	0	0	0	0
School	8	5	1	1	0	1	0	0	1	1	0	0	1	1	1	1
Something	1	0	3	0	0	0	0	0	0	0	0	0	0	0	0	0
Sunday	3	2	1	2	0	1	0	1	1	1	0	0	3	1	0	2
Sweet	0	0	0	0	0	0	0	0	0	0	0	0	0	0	2	0
Teach	2	0	0	1	0	0	0	0	0	0	0	0	0	0	0	0
Theology	0	0	0	0	0	0	0	0	0	0	0	0	0	0	0	2
Thing	0	1	2	0	2	0	0	1	0	0	0	0	1	0	0	0
Thought	0	0	0	0	0	0	0	0	0	0	0	0	0	0	2	0
Training	2	3	0	0	0	1	0	0	0	0	0	0	0	0	0	0
Truth	0	0	0	1	0	0	0	0	0	0	0	1	2	0	2	1
War	0	0	2	1	0	0	1	0	0	0	0	0	0	0	0	0
Way	2	1	1	0	0	0	0	0	0	0	0	0	0	0	0	1
Worship	0	0	2	3	3	4	1	1	3	2	4	0	2	4	5	6

Response Word	4th		5th		6th		7th		8th		10th		12th		College	
	M	F	M	F	M	F	M	F	M	F	M	F	M	F	M	F

135. <u>RIVER</u>

Response Word	M	F	M	F	M	F	M	F	M	F	M	F	M	F	M	F
Amazon ..	1	0	0	0	2	1	0	0	0	0	0	0	0	0	0	0
Bank ...	0	0	0	1	0	0	3	0	1	0	0	0	1	0	5	7
Beautiful .	1	1	1	0	0	2	0	0	0	1	0	0	0	0	1	1
Bed	2	1	1	1	2	4	3	3	3	1	3	5	1	4	9	8
Bend ...	0	0	0	1	1	0	0	1	1	0	0	1	0	1	1	2
Big ...	0	0	3	0	0	1	0	0	0	1	1	1	1	0	0	1
Black ...	0	0	0	0	2	0	0	1	0	0	0	0	0	0	1	1
Blue ...	2	2	1	2	1	6	3	2	1	4	4	5	1	7	12	11
Boat ...	0	1	4	0	2	2	1	2	2	6	5	2	10	2	11	15
Bridge ..	0	1	0	0	0	0	0	0	0	0	0	0	4	1	1	2
Brook ...	2	0	0	2	0	1	2	0	1	0	1	1	0	0	1	0
Brown ..	0	0	0	0	0	1	0	0	0	0	0	3	0	0	0	0
Canoe ...	0	0	0	0	0	0	0	0	0	0	0	0	0	0	0	2
Cold	0	0	0	0	0	1	0	1	0	1	2	1	1	0	1	4
Cool	0	0	0	3	1	0	1	1	0	1	0	1	1	2	1	2
Creek ..	3	0	7	4	1	1	9	1	3	0	4	2	4	4	3	6
Current ..	0	0	0	0	0	0	0	0	0	0	0	1	1	0	1	2
Dark ...	0	0	0	0	0	0	0	1	0	0	0	0	0	2	0	1
Deep ...	1	5	6	2	0	5	5	3	1	2	6	9	3	4	11	14
Drown ..	0	0	1	0	3	0	0	0	0	0	0	0	1	0	0	0
Falls ...	0	0	0	0	0	0	0	0	1	0	1	0	2	0	0	1
Fast	0	3	1	2	4	1	0	1	1	1	2	3	5	2	6	3
Fish ...	3	4	2	3	3	3	3	0	9	1	3	1	4	1	4	4
Fishing ..	1	0	0	0	3	0	1	0	2	1	0	1	0	1	0	0
Float ...	0	1	0	0	1	0	0	0	0	2	0	0	0	0	1	0
Flow	7	0	6	7	5	11	6	3	0	3	4	4	3	5	17	20
Flowing ..	0	2	0	2	1	2	0	0	4	0	2	2	2	0	0	1
Go	0	1	0	2	0	0	0	0	0	0	0	0	0	0	0	0
Green ..	0	0	0	0	0	0	0	0	0	0	1	0	0	0	1	2
Lake	66	71	43	69	40	49	49	40	56	49	36	32	33	43	36	44
Lakes ...	1	1	0	2	0	0	0	0	0	0	0	0	0	0	0	0
Long ...	0	1	4	3	7	5	3	9	1	3	6	4	2	4	7	7
Mississippi	2	5	9	4	10	13	11	12	10	17	20	23	22	22	42	47
Mountain .	1	0	0	0	0	1	1	1	1	0	1	1	1	0	0	3
Mud	0	0	0	0	1	0	0	1	0	0	0	1	3	0	0	2
Muddy ..	0	0	0	0	0	0	0	0	1	2	0	1	0	1	2	2
Ocean ...	1	3	1	0	1	0	1	1	4	5	1	2	1	2	2	2
Ohio ...	0	0	0	0	1	0	0	0	1	0	2	0	0	1	0	0
Pond ...	0	0	0	0	1	0	1	0	0	2	0	0	0	0	1	0
Pretty ..	0	0	0	0	0	0	0	0	0	0	0	1	0	0	2	2
Rapids ..	0	0	0	0	0	0	1	0	0	0	0	0	0	0	3	2
Red	0	0	0	0	0	0	0	0	0	0	0	0	2	1	1	1
Road ...	0	0	0	0	0	0	0	1	0	0	0	0	1	1	3	1
Run ...	0	1	1	1	1	1	3	0	0	2	3	5	1	4	9	4
Running ..	0	1	0	0	0	0	1	1	0	1	1	0	0	2	1	0
Sea	0	1	0	1	0	1	1	1	1	4	1	0	0	2	1	2
Shells ...	0	2	0	0	0	0	0	0	0	0	0	0	0	0	0	0
Side	0	0	0	0	0	0	0	0	0	0	1	0	0	1	0	2
Slow	0	0	0	1	0	0	2	0	0	0	0	0	1	0	3	1

Response Word	4th		5th		6th		7th		8th		10th		12th		College	
	M	F	M	F	M	F	M	F	M	F	M	F	M	F	M	F

RIVER

Response Word	M	F	M	F	M	F	M	F	M	F	M	F	M	F	M	F
Spring . . .	0	0	0	1	0	0	0	0	0	2	0	0	0	0	0	0
St. Croix .	0	0	0	0	0	0	0	0	0	0	0	0	0	0	0	2
Steam . . .	3	0	2	0	0	0	0	0	0	0	0	0	0	0	0	0
Stream . .	48	46	31	35	34	39	50	52	47	41	28	33	32	27	79	75
Swanee . .	0	0	0	0	0	0	0	2	1	0	0	0	0	0	0	0
Swift . . .	0	0	0	1	1	0	2	2	0	1	3	0	0	0	4	2
Swim . . .	1	2	3	2	4	0	1	3	2	0	1	3	1	1	4	5
Swimming .	0	1	1	1	1	2	1	1	0	2	1	1	0	2	0	0
Thames . .	0	0	0	0	0	0	0	0	0	0	0	0	0	2	0	0
Valley . . .	0	0	1	0	1	1	0	2	1	4	2	0	1	0	1	0
Water . . .	77	72	88	72	95	74	61	78	67	62	77	68	71	66	156	130
Wet	2	1	2	3	3	2	4	1	8	2	4	5	4	5	5	11
Wide . . .	1	2	4	4	2	1	0	4	1	4	5	10	6	3	12	9
Wild . . .	0	0	1	0	0	0	0	0	0	0	1	0	1	0	2	1
Wind . . .	0	0	0	0	0	0	1	2	0	0	1	0	0	0	0	0
Winding . .	0	0	1	1	0	0	0	1	3	1	1	1	1	1	2	2
Wish . . .	2	0	0	0	0	0	0	0	0	0	0	0	0	0	0	0

136. ROUGH

Response Word	M	F	M	F	M	F	M	F	M	F	M	F	M	F	M	F
Bad	0	2	2	1	1	0	1	0	0	0	3	0	1	0	2	0
Bark . . .	0	0	0	0	1	0	0	3	0	2	1	0	0	1	0	2
Bear . . .	0	0	0	0	0	0	0	0	2	0	0	0	0	0	0	0
Beard . . .	0	0	0	0	0	0	0	1	0	0	2	0	3	1	2	0
Board . . .	0	0	1	1	0	1	1	0	0	0	0	0	2	0	2	5
Boy	0	2	0	0	2	3	0	2	3	2	2	2	0	1	1	1
Boys . . .	0	2	0	1	0	0	1	2	0	3	0	2	1	0	0	0
Bump . . .	2	6	3	2	2	2	0	2	0	0	1	0	0	0	0	0
Bumps . .	2	3	1	1	1	1	0	0	1	0	0	2	0	0	0	1
Bumpy . .	19	16	8	11	14	16	9	5	1	9	3	9	2	2	5	11
Cheese . .	0	0	0	0	0	2	0	0	0	0	0	0	0	0	0	0
Coarse . .	1	0	1	0	2	1	4	1	5	1	6	2	6	0	8	5
Coat	0	0	0	0	0	0	0	0	0	0	0	0	0	0	0	2
Course . .	0	0	1	0	0	1	1	2	3	1	3	2	3	0	1	0
Cowboy . .	0	0	0	1	0	0	0	0	0	0	0	4	1	0	1	2
Crude . . .	0	0	1	0	0	0	0	0	0	0	0	1	0	1	0	4
Desk . . .	0	0	0	0	0	2	0	0	0	0	1	0	0	0	0	0
Dirty . . .	0	0	0	0	0	0	0	0	0	0	0	0	0	0	2	0
Dog	2	0	0	1	2	1	0	0	0	0	0	0	1	3	3	2
Dry	0	0	0	0	0	0	0	0	1	0	0	0	0	0	0	2
Easy . . .	1	2	0	2	4	0	1	0	2	1	1	1	1	0	1	1
Edge	0	1	0	0	1	1	0	1	0	1	2	0	0	0	2	2
Edges . . .	0	1	0	0	0	0	0	0	0	0	0	0	0	0	2	0
Field . . .	0	0	0	0	0	0	0	0	0	0	0	0	0	0	2	0
Fight . . .	0	3	2	1	3	2	1	0	1	0	0	0	1	1	0	0
File	1	1	0	0	0	0	0	0	0	0	4	0	3	0	3	1
Floor . . .	1	3	0	0	1	0	1	1	0	0	0	1	1	0	0	0
Football . .	0	0	0	0	0	0	0	0	1	0	1	0	1	0	3	0
Golf	0	0	0	0	1	0	0	0	0	0	4	0	2	0	3	0
Good . . .	2	0	3	0	1	0	0	0	0	0	0	0	0	0	0	0

Response Word	4th M	4th F	5th M	5th F	6th M	6th F	7th M	7th F	8th M	8th F	10th M	10th F	12th M	12th F	College M	College F
							ROUGH									
Goon	0	0	2	0	0	0	0	0	0	0	0	0	0	0	0	0
Grass	0	0	0	0	0	0	0	0	1	1	1	0	1	0	1	3
Gravel	0	0	0	0	0	1	0	0	0	3	0	1	1	2	0	4
Gravel road	0	0	0	0	0	0	0	0	0	0	0	0	1	0	0	2
Ground	0	0	2	2	0	3	1	0	2	0	5	2	3	0	7	7
Guy	0	0	0	0	0	0	0	0	2	1	0	0	0	0	0	0
Hand	3	0	0	0	0	0	0	2	0	0	0	1	1	2	0	6
Hands	0	0	0	1	0	0	0	0	0	2	1	2	1	3	1	7
Hard	31	50	46	55	36	51	31	35	33	22	31	39	20	28	38	32
Harsh	0	0	0	0	0	0	1	2	0	1	1	3	0	0	3	3
Hill	0	0	0	0	1	0	0	3	0	0	1	0	0	2	2	0
Hills	0	0	2	0	0	1	0	0	0	0	0	0	1	0	1	0
Hilly	0	0	0	2	1	0	0	0	1	0	1	1	0	0	0	0
Hood	0	0	0	0	0	0	0	0	0	0	1	0	0	0	1	2
Horse	0	0	1	0	1	0	1	0	0	0	0	2	0	0	0	0
Hurt	1	0	0	2	1	0	0	0	1	0	2	1	0	0	2	0
Ice	0	2	0	0	0	0	0	0	0	0	0	1	0	0	0	0
Jagged	1	0	4	1	1	5	2	1	4	0	3	2	1	0	1	3
Light	1	0	1	0	0	2	0	0	0	0	0	0	0	0	0	0
Log	0	0	0	0	0	0	0	0	0	0	0	0	0	0	2	0
Man	0	0	0	0	1	0	2	0	1	1	0	1	1	0	4	5
Me	0	2	0	0	0	0	1	0	0	0	0	0	0	0	0	0
Mean	3	3	3	0	4	6	0	1	2	2	0	2	2	2	1	4
Mountain	3	0	3	3	2	5	3	3	0	5	1	2	3	1	4	4
Mountainous	0	0	0	0	0	0	2	0	0	0	1	0	0	0	0	0
Mountains	2	0	0	2	2	1	2	1	1	1	0	1	0	1	3	1
Neat	1	0	0	0	0	0	0	0	2	0	0	0	0	0	0	0
Nice	0	3	2	2	1	2	0	0	0	0	1	0	0	0	0	0
Not smooth	2	2	1	0	1	0	0	1	0	0	0	0	0	0	0	0
Ocean	0	0	0	0	0	0	0	0	0	0	0	1	0	0	0	2
One	0	2	0	0	0	0	0	0	0	0	0	0	0	0	0	0
Paper	0	0	2	0	1	0	0	0	0	0	0	0	0	0	0	1
Ragged	0	1	1	0	1	0	1	2	0	1	1	0	0	0	0	4
Ready	0	0	0	0	0	0	0	1	0	1	1	2	3	1	7	9
Red	0	0	0	0	0	0	0	0	0	4	0	2	0	1	1	1
Ride	0	2	1	0	0	0	0	0	0	0	1	1	2	0	2	0
Rider	0	0	0	0	0	0	1	0	1	0	3	0	6	5	5	0
Riders	1	0	0	0	3	0	2	1	4	1	2	0	5	0	5	4
Road	2	2	4	3	6	2	4	5	3	2	10	11	18	20	29	20
Rock	3	5	3	4	3	1	3	0	3	6	1	2	0	2	0	5
Rocks	3	1	1	4	1	3	1	3	1	11	1	2	3	1	1	1
Rocky	0	4	6	8	5	2	0	0	0	1	0	0	0	1	2	2
Rode	1	1	1	0	2	1	0	0	0	0	0	0	0	0	0	0
Rough	0	0	2	0	0	0	0	0	0	0	0	0	0	0	0	0
Rough Riders	0	0	0	0	0	0	0	0	0	0	2	0	0	0	0	0
Rug	0	0	0	0	2	1	0	0	0	1	0	0	0	0	0	2
Rugged	2	0	2	4	7	7	3	2	3	0	5	4	1	3	1	3
Sand	0	0	3	2	0	1	4	1	1	4	4	5	2	3	8	5
Sandpaper	1	1	1	0	0	0	14	5	8	9	13	15	12	9	43	26
Saw	0	0	0	0	0	0	0	0	0	0	0	0	0	0	2	0

Response Word	4th M	4th F	5th M	5th F	6th M	6th F	7th M	7th F	8th M	8th F	10th M	10th F	12th M	12th F	College M	College F

ROUGH

Response Word	4th M	4th F	5th M	5th F	6th M	6th F	7th M	7th F	8th M	8th F	10th M	10th F	12th M	12th F	College M	College F
School	0	0	0	0	1	0	1	0	0	0	0	0	2	0	1	0
Scratch	0	0	0	0	1	0	0	0	0	0	0	0	0	1	0	2
Scratchy	0	0	0	0	0	0	0	1	0	2	0	2	1	0	1	4
Sharp	1	0	1	1	2	0	0	2	1	1	0	2	1	1	4	2
Shave	0	0	0	0	0	0	0	0	0	0	0	0	0	3	0	0
Sidewalk	0	1	0	0	0	0	0	2	0	2	0	0	0	1	0	1
Skin	0	0	1	0	0	0	0	1	0	2	0	0	0	0	1	4
Smooth	55	35	40	50	50	43	71	67	82	79	60	61	68	81	145	159
Soft	13	13	19	15	10	7	15	16	20	15	15	14	17	18	34	22
Stiff	0	1	2	0	0	0	0	0	0	0	0	0	0	0	0	0
Stone	0	0	0	1	2	0	2	0	0	2	1	2	0	0	2	3
Stones	2	0	0	1	0	0	2	0	0	0	0	0	0	1	1	3
Street	0	0	0	0	0	0	0	0	0	0	0	2	0	1	0	1
Strong	1	0	2	0	2	0	0	1	1	0	0	0	2	0	1	0
Surface	0	0	2	1	1	0	1	4	0	0	0	1	1	2	3	1
Test	0	0	0	0	0	0	1	0	0	0	1	0	0	0	0	2
Texture	0	0	0	0	0	1	0	2	0	1	1	1	0	0	0	1
Tough	13	15	18	19	18	25	14	20	25	10	16	2	8	9	26	19
Tree	1	1	0	0	0	1	0	0	0	0	2	1	0	0	0	1
Uncomfortable	0	0	1	0	0	0	0	2	0	0	0	0	0	0	0	0
Uneven	1	2	0	0	0	1	3	2	0	1	0	1	2	0	1	1
Unsmooth	1	2	0	0	1	0	0	0	0	0	0	1	0	0	0	0
Walk	0	1	2	0	0	0	0	1	0	0	0	0	0	0	0	0
Water	0	1	1	1	0	0	0	1	1	0	0	1	2	3	0	2
Waves	2	0	0	0	0	0	0	0	0	0	0	0	0	0	1	1
Weather	0	0	0	0	0	0	0	0	0	0	0	1	0	2	0	2
Whiskers	0	0	0	0	0	0	0	0	0	0	0	0	0	0	0	2
Wood	1	0	1	3	0	2	2	5	1	5	2	2	1	3	5	7
You	2	1	0	0	0	0	0	0	0	0	0	0	0	0	0	0

137. RUNNING

Response Word	4th M	4th F	5th M	5th F	6th M	6th F	7th M	7th F	8th M	8th F	10th M	10th F	12th M	12th F	College M	College F
After	0	0	0	0	0	0	0	0	0	0	0	0	0	0	2	0
Around	0	0	0	1	0	0	1	0	0	1	0	0	0	0	2	1
Away	0	4	1	1	2	1	4	1	4	5	8	4	3	2	7	8
Back	2	0	0	0	0	0	0	0	1	0	0	1	0	0	1	0
Bear	1	1	0	1	2	1	6	4	7	9	4	8	7	4	12	0
Board	0	0	0	0	0	0	0	0	0	0	1	1	2	1	1	1
Book	0	0	0	0	0	0	0	2	0	0	0	0	0	0	0	0
Boy	1	0	0	0	0	0	1	0	0	0	3	2	0	2	9	10
Breath	0	0	2	1	1	0	2	0	0	0	1	0	3	0	0	2
Came	0	0	1	0	1	0	0	0	0	0	0	0	1	0	0	2
Car	0	0	0	1	1	0	0	0	2	1	0	1	0	1	0	1
Catch	0	0	0	2	0	0	0	0	0	0	0	0	0	0	1	1
Child	0	1	0	0	0	0	0	0	0	0	0	0	0	0	0	2
Crawling	0	0	0	0	0	0	1	0	1	0	2	1	0	0	0	1
Deer	0	0	0	0	0	0	0	0	0	2	1	0	0	0	1	6
Dog	1	0	0	0	1	2	1	2	0	2	1	2	0	2	4	6
Down	0	0	3	0	1	0	0	0	1	0	1	1	1	0	0	0
Exercise	0	0	0	0	0	0	0	0	0	0	0	2	2	0	2	0

Response Word	4th M	F	5th M	F	6th M	F	7th M	F	8th M	F	10th M	F	12th M	F	College M	F
							RUNNING									
Fall	1	3	0	2	1	1	0	2	0	1	0	3	1	3	1	1
Fast	86	88	100	89	95	102	86	66	53	55	76	78	61	75	123	119
Faster	0	1	0	0	0	0	0	0	1	1	0	0	0	3	2	2
Feet	1	3	1	2	2	3	0	2	0	2	3	2	1	1	9	9
Gear	0	0	0	0	0	0	0	0	0	0	0	0	2	0	0	0
Go	1	1	1	2	1	1	0	1	2	1	0	0	0	1	2	3
Going	1	2	1	2	1	1	0	0	0	0	2	1	0	1	3	1
Hard	2	2	2	1	3	2	2	0	2	1	3	1	4	1	5	1
Home	0	0	0	1	4	1	0	1	1	2	1	2	2	1	3	4
Hopping	0	2	0	1	1	1	0	1	0	0	0	0	0	0	0	0
Horse	1	0	1	0	0	1	1	0	1	1	0	1	0	0	1	2
Hot	0	0	2	1	0	0	1	1	2	1	0	0	1	0	1	3
Hurry	0	3	1	1	4	2	0	1	1	0	1	4	0	4	1	3
Hurrying	1	0	1	1	0	0	0	0	0	0	1	1	0	2	1	1
Jump	2	1	2	3	1	4	2	7	3	7	6	1	1	0	7	6
Jumping	2	3	1	6	3	5	5	4	6	7	6	7	8	7	16	21
Laughing	0	0	0	1	0	0	0	0	0	0	1	0	0	1	0	2
Leaping	0	0	0	0	0	0	1	0	0	0	0	0	1	2	0	1
Legs	5	2	0	4	7	3	1	1	0	2	2	2	3	4	6	7
Man	1	0	0	0	0	0	2	0	0	0	0	0	0	0	0	1
Mate	0	0	0	0	0	0	0	0	0	0	0	0	0	0	5	1
Move	0	1	0	1	0	0	0	2	0	1	0	0	0	0	1	0
Moving	0	2	0	0	3	1	0	1	0	2	1	0	2	2	2	2
On	0	0	0	0	0	0	1	0	0	2	0	1	0	0	0	0
Panting	0	0	0	1	0	0	2	1	3	0	0	1	0	0	0	2
Playing	0	1	0	1	0	0	0	0	0	0	0	0	0	1	3	3
Quick	0	1	1	1	1	0	0	1	1	0	0	2	0	1	1	4
Quickly	0	0	0	1	0	0	0	0	0	0	2	0	0	1	1	0
Rabbit	0	0	2	2	0	0	0	0	0	1	0	0	0	0	0	0
Race	2	5	1	5	1	5	3	2	1	3	1	1	1	0	8	6
Racing	0	0	0	1	0	1	0	2	0	1	0	0	0	0	0	0
Ran	8	8	15	13	9	19	12	17	7	7	7	4	13	8	12	11
Run	35	21	24	18	18	12	9	5	5	3	5	2	4	1	3	1
Scared	0	0	0	0	0	0	1	2	0	1	0	0	0	2	0	0
Shoes	0	0	0	0	0	0	0	0	2	0	0	0	0	0	0	0
Singing	0	0	0	0	0	0	0	0	0	0	0	0	0	0	2	1
Sitting	0	0	0	0	0	0	0	0	0	0	0	0	1	0	2	1
Skip	1	1	3	3	0	0	0	0	1	0	0	0	1	0	0	2
Skipping	2	3	1	8	0	4	1	3	0	5	0	6	2	4	1	8
Slow	2	5	4	6	5	4	1	1	5	1	0	0	3	3	3	1
Slowly	1	0	0	1	0	0	0	1	0	1	0	0	0	1	2	1
Speed	2	0	5	2	1	0	2	2	2	0	6	1	4	3	5	5
Sprint	0	0	0	0	0	0	0	0	0	0	0	0	0	0	2	0
Standing	0	0	0	0	0	0	0	0	0	1	0	0	1	0	2	0
Stop	4	5	9	4	5	3	9	5	8	8	3	1	5	2	10	7
Stopping	0	2	0	0	2	2	1	1	3	2	1	0	2	4	1	4
Sweat	0	0	0	0	0	0	1	0	0	0	0	0	2	0	2	0
Swift	2	0	0	0	1	1	1	1	0	0	0	0	1	1	1	1
There	0	0	0	0	1	0	1	0	0	0	0	0	0	2	0	0

Response Word	4th M	4th F	5th M	5th F	6th M	6th F	7th M	7th F	8th M	8th F	10th M	10th F	12th M	12th F	College M	College F

RUNNING

Response Word	4th M	4th F	5th M	5th F	6th M	6th F	7th M	7th F	8th M	8th F	10th M	10th F	12th M	12th F	College M	College F
Tired ...	3	0	0	0	1	1	2	4	3	2	5	3	4	0	8	4
Track ...	0	0	0	0	0	0	3	2	2	1	5	0	6	2	10	2
Trotting ..	0	0	1	0	1	1	1	2	0	0	1	0	0	0	1	0
Walk ...	27	25	16	16	11	17	24	26	26	27	23	15	14	16	28	25
Walking ..	23	29	20	28	23	26	38	54	52	49	28	53	40	42	102	116
Water ...	1	0	3	1	3	6	1	5	14	16	8	13	12	11	12	21
Wild ...	0	1	0	2	0	0	0	1	2	2	2	0	3	1	6	10
You	1	1	0	0	2	0	0	0	0	0	0	0	0	0	0	0

138. SALT

Response Word	4th M	4th F	5th M	5th F	6th M	6th F	7th M	7th F	8th M	8th F	10th M	10th F	12th M	12th F	College M	College F
Apple ...	0	0	0	0	0	0	0	0	0	1	1	0	1	0	0	3
Bad	0	0	2	0	1	1	1	1	0	0	0	0	0	0	0	0
Beer ...	0	0	0	0	0	0	0	0	0	0	0	0	0	0	3	0
Bitter ...	1	5	6	10	12	6	20	15	11	11	9	6	6	4	18	15
Block ...	0	0	0	0	0	0	0	0	0	0	0	0	0	0	1	2
Bread ..	0	0	0	0	1	0	1	1	0	0	0	1	1	0	1	2
Celery ..	0	0	1	0	1	0	0	1	0	0	0	2	0	1	0	1
City	0	0	0	0	0	1	0	0	0	0	0	0	0	0	2	0
Cook ...	0	0	0	1	0	0	0	1	0	0	0	1	0	0	0	2
Cooking ..	0	0	0	0	0	0	0	2	0	0	0	1	1	1	0	0
Corn ...	0	1	0	0	1	0	1	1	1	0	0	0	0	2	1	0
Cracker ..	0	0	0	0	0	0	0	0	0	0	0	0	0	0	2	1
Crystal ..	0	2	0	3	1	0	1	0	1	0	1	0	0	0	0	2
Dry	2	0	2	0	1	1	1	0	1	0	2	0	0	0	1	0
Eat	12	10	10	11	6	1	6	1	4	6	4	2	4	3	9	3
Egg	0	1	0	2	1	1	0	0	0	0	1	0	1	0	1	1
Eggs ...	0	2	0	1	0	1	0	1	0	1	1	0	1	0	0	0
Fish ...	2	0	0	0	0	0	1	0	0	0	0	2	0	3	0	0
Flavor ..	0	0	0	1	1	0	0	6	1	2	1	4	1	2	3	7
Flavoring .	0	0	0	0	0	2	0	2	2	0	0	0	1	0	0	1
Flour ...	0	0	0	0	0	2	0	0	0	0	0	0	0	0	0	0
Food ...	27	12	30	14	16	19	15	13	11	9	16	11	10	8	19	19
Good ...	4	7	6	5	2	2	5	0	2	3	3	5	3	4	2	3
Grain ...	1	0	1	0	0	1	0	2	0	1	0	0	0	0	0	1
Grains ..	1	0	0	0	0	0	0	0	0	0	0	1	0	0	0	2
Grapes ..	0	0	0	0	0	0	2	0	0	0	0	0	0	0	0	0
Hard ...	0	0	0	0	1	0	1	0	1	0	0	0	0	2	0	1
Hot	1	1	1	1	2	0	2	1	2	1	0	0	0	1	0	0
Hurt ...	0	0	0	0	0	0	2	0	0	0	0	0	2	0	0	0
Ice	0	0	1	0	0	0	0	0	0	0	1	1	2	0	0	0
Is	0	2	0	0	1	0	0	0	0	0	0	0	0	0	0	0
Lake ...	1	0	5	2	5	1	7	0	7	3	5	2	4	0	8	0
Lick	0	0	3	0	0	1	0	0	1	1	0	0	1	0	6	1
Little ...	0	3	0	1	0	0	0	0	0	0	0	0	0	0	0	0
Meat ...	2	1	0	4	1	5	3	2	0	2	5	3	5	3	7	8
Mine ...	1	0	0	2	1	0	1	0	1	0	0	0	2	1	1	0
Mineral ..	1	0	1	1	0	0	3	0	0	0	2	1	0	0	0	0
Mines ...	0	0	0	0	0	0	1	0	3	0	0	0	1	0	1	0
NaCl....	0	0	0	0	0	0	0	0	0	0	0	0	6	1	7	1

Response Word	4th M	4th F	5th M	5th F	6th M	6th F	7th M	7th F	8th M	8th F	10th M	10th F	12th M	12th F	College M	College F
							SALT									
Ocean . . .	5	1	4	3	10	7	12	13	6	6	9	6	9	10	15	2
Paper . . .	2	2	1	0	0	1	0	1	0	1	0	0	0	0	0	0
Peanuts . .	0	1	0	0	0	0	0	0	0	0	0	0	2	0	0	0
Pepper . .	82	108	73	102	72	119	64	95	84	117	65	110	62	106	147	261
Peter . . .	0	0	1	0	0	0	0	0	0	0	0	0	1	0	3	1
Popcorn .	1	1	0	0	1	0	0	0	0	0	1	1	0	1	2	3
Pork . . .	0	1	1	0	1	0	4	0	0	0	0	1	3	0	2	5
Potatoes .	0	1	0	0	1	1	0	0	0	1	2	3	1	0	1	3
Pour . . .	0	0	0	1	0	0	0	0	0	0	0	0	0	0	0	2
River . . .	0	0	0	0	2	0	0	0	0	1	0	1	0	0	0	0
Rock . . .	0	0	0	1	3	0	0	0	2	0	2	0	0	0	2	0
Salty . . .	1	1	2	1	2	0	2	2	1	6	2	2	2	2	6	2
Sea	3	1	4	5	1	4	6	4	3	1	1	7	5	7	14	12
Season . .	0	0	0	0	1	0	2	1	0	0	1	0	0	4	2	1
Seasoning .	0	1	0	1	1	3	1	4	4	8	3	2	2	5	5	8
Shake . . .	1	3	0	0	2	0	0	0	1	0	0	0	0	0	0	0
Shaker . .	3	0	1	2	1	1	1	4	5	4	5	2	7	6	17	12
Sharp . . .	0	0	0	0	0	0	0	0	0	0	0	0	0	0	2	2
Small . . .	0	1	0	1	0	0	0	0	0	0	3	0	0	0	0	0
Sodium . .	0	0	0	0	0	0	0	0	0	0	0	0	0	0	3	0
Soup	0	0	0	0	0	2	0	0	1	0	0	0	0	0	0	0
Sour . . .	5	5	4	5	3	4	8	3	6	4	3	1	2	2	11	2
Spice . . .	1	2	2	2	7	3	5	3	1	2	2	0	5	1	3	3
Steak . . .	0	0	0	0	0	0	0	2	1	1	1	0	1	0	1	0
Street . . .	0	0	0	0	1	0	1	0	1	0	0	1	3	2	1	0
Strong . .	1	2	2	0	0	0	1	1	1	0	1	0	0	1	1	0
Sugar . . .	17	14	15	20	22	20	21	18	32	14	23	14	17	17	32	21
Sweet . . .	2	1	4	1	3	1	3	2	3	3	5	0	4	2	8	1
Table . . .	0	0	0	1	1	0	0	1	0	1	2	2	3	2	4	4
Taste . . .	7	3	12	3	8	2	6	9	2	8	15	11	7	6	39	20
Tasty . . .	0	1	0	1	1	2	0	4	0	2	0	0	0	2	1	3
Thirsty . .	1	1	0	1	2	1	0	2	0	0	1	2	2	2	1	2
Tomato . .	0	0	0	0	0	0	0	0	0	0	0	1	0	0	2	1
Tomatoes .	0	0	0	0	0	0	0	0	0	2	0	0	0	0	0	0
Water . . .	11	9	15	10	22	2	14	9	22	5	17	15	31	15	30	21
White . . .	9	12	7	12	7	15	7	6	7	5	7	3	4	5	6	5
						139.	SALTY									
Air	0	0	0	0	0	0	0	0	0	1	0	0	2	0	3	2
Awful . . .	1	0	2	0	2	2	0	1	0	0	0	0	1	0	0	0
Bad	8	4	6	2	4	2	2	1	1	0	1	2	2	0	1	1
Better . . .	0	0	1	0	1	1	0	2	2	0	0	0	0	0	1	1
Bitter . . .	3	6	9	5	11	10	25	18	7	10	18	8	3	11	21	22
Boy	1	0	0	0	0	0	0	0	0	0	0	0	0	0	2	0
Bread . . .	0	2	0	1	3	1	0	0	0	0	0	0	1	0	0	0
Brine . . .	0	0	1	0	0	0	1	0	1	0	0	0	1	0	7	4
Bring . . .	0	0	0	0	0	0	0	0	0	0	0	0	0	0	2	0
Butter . .	0	1	1	1	0	0	2	0	0	0	0	0	0	0	0	1
Candy . . .	0	1	1	2	0	0	0	1	4	0	0	0	0	2	0	0

Response Word	4th M	4th F	5th M	5th F	6th M	6th F	7th M	7th F	8th M	8th F	10th M	10th F	12th M	12th F	College M	College F
							SALTY									
Cheese ...	0	0	0	0	0	0	0	0	0	0	0	0	0	0	2	0
Clear	1	0	1	0	0	0	1	0	0	0	2	0	0	0	0	0
Cracker ..	2	0	0	0	0	1	1	0	0	3	1	1	4	4	9	10
Crackers ..	2	1	3	0	2	1	1	2	4	7	4	4	3	12	24	16
Crisp	0	0	0	0	0	0	0	0	2	0	1	0	0	0	1	0
Crispy ...	0	0	0	0	0	0	0	0	0	0	1	0	0	0	2	0
Cry	0	1	0	1	0	0	0	0	1	0	0	0	0	0	3	4
Dog	1	0	0	0	1	0	0	0	0	1	0	0	0	1	2	1
Dry	1	1	1	2	2	1	4	0	4	4	4	7	5	3	13	11
Eat	3	1	0	0	0	0	1	0	0	0	0	0	0	0	1	2
Faulty ...	0	0	0	0	0	0	0	0	0	0	0	0	0	0	2	0
Fish	0	2	0	2	2	5	2	3	0	13	4	9	1	7	9	15
Flavor....	1	0	1	1	0	1	0	1	1	2	1	2	1	4	2	1
Food	7	10	9	11	9	7	2	2	6	4	9	9	6	5	8	8
Fresh	2	0	0	0	1	2	2	0	3	0	1	1	1	0	1	2
Good	8	5	5	7	6	2	5	1	3	4	1	1	1	3	3	3
Ham	0	0	0	0	0	1	0	1	0	1	1	2	1	2	0	0
Hot	3	1	4	1	1	2	7	1	4	1	1	1	0	0	3	0
Ick	0	0	0	0	0	1	1	1	0	0	2	0	0	0	0	0
Ish	3	1	2	1	0	3	1	1	1	0	0	1	2	2	0	1
Ishy	2	0	1	2	2	4	0	0	0	1	0	0	0	0	0	0
Lake	4	2	4	1	8	4	3	0	2	2	2	3	4	1	3	2
Meat	4	3	5	2	4	6	3	4	5	4	7	12	7	8	7	6
Much	1	2	0	2	1	0	0	0	0	0	0	0	0	0	0	0
NaCl	0	0	0	0	0	0	0	0	0	0	0	0	0	0	2	0
Name	0	0	1	2	0	0	0	0	0	0	0	0	0	0	0	0
No	2	0	1	0	0	0	0	0	0	0	0	0	0	0	0	0
Not good ..	1	2	1	0	0	0	0	0	0	0	0	0	0	0	0	0
Not salty ..	0	0	0	0	0	0	0	2	3	0	0	0	0	0	0	0
Nuts	1	1	2	0	1	0	0	0	2	0	0	1	2	4	2	2
Ocean ...	5	4	6	8	12	22	23	26	12	11	9	16	16	8	12	12
On	0	2	0	0	0	0	0	0	0	0	0	0	0	0	0	0
Peanut ...	2	0	0	1	0	0	0	0	0	0	1	0	0	1	1	3
Peanuts ...	0	2	0	2	0	1	0	1	4	1	1	2	1	3	4	11
Pepper ...	29	48	19	39	26	30	27	27	24	34	16	17	7	12	18	24
Peppery ..	4	14	7	17	7	9	6	14	11	10	7	12	1	8	9	20
Peppy	0	0	0	0	0	0	0	0	1	3	0	0	0	0	0	0
Popcorn ...	0	1	0	2	0	1	0	0	0	2	1	2	1	2	2	7
Pork	0	0	0	0	2	0	1	0	1	0	0	0	2	0	1	5
Potato chip .	0	2	0	0	0	0	0	0	0	0	0	0	0	0	0	0
Potato chips	0	2	1	0	0	0	1	1	0	0	0	1	0	2	0	0
Potatoes ..	1	1	0	1	0	4	0	0	0	2	0	1	0	1	0	1
Sailor	0	0	0	0	0	0	0	0	0	0	1	0	4	0	6	0
Saline	0	0	0	0	0	0	0	0	0	0	0	0	0	0	2	0
Salt	28	31	41	28	22	22	19	10	14	15	10	8	5	4	22	11
Sandy	1	0	0	0	0	0	1	0	1	0	4	1	0	1	1	1
Sea	6	4	6	8	6	4	6	16	14	13	15	16	25	18	43	34
Shaker ...	0	0	0	0	0	0	0	0	0	0	1	1	1	0	3	1
Sharp	0	0	0	0	0	0	0	0	0	0	0	0	0	0	2	0

Response Word	4th		5th		6th		7th		8th		10th		12th		College	
	M	F	M	F	M	F	M	F	M	F	M	F	M	F	M	F

SALTY

Response Word	M	F	M	F	M	F	M	F	M	F	M	F	M	F	M	F
Soft	0	0	0	1	0	0	0	0	0	0	0	0	0	0	0	2
Soup	0	1	0	0	0	0	0	0	2	0	0	1	0	0	0	1
Sour	8	3	3	4	7	10	12	10	10	6	5	10	5	11	13	16
Spice	2	2	0	1	0	0	0	3	1	3	0	1	2	0	1	0
Spicy	0	1	0	1	1	0	4	1	1	2	2	1	1	0	4	4
Stale	0	0	0	0	0	0	0	0	1	2	1	0	0	0	1	1
Street	0	0	0	0	2	0	2	0	0	1	0	1	1	0	0	0
Streets	0	0	0	0	0	0	0	0	0	0	2	0	1	0	0	0
Strong	1	3	1	2	1	0	0	2	1	0	2	2	1	0	0	0
Sugar	9	7	10	5	9	8	6	9	7	4	9	5	5	5	6	11
Sugary	1	2	1	2	0	1	0	4	6	2	0	0	0	4	2	5
Sweat	0	1	0	0	1	0	2	0	0	0	1	0	1	0	0	0
Sweet	10	7	4	11	11	10	15	12	20	23	18	12	21	20	53	54
Taffy	0	0	0	0	1	0	0	1	1	1	2	1	1	3	2	4
Tangy	1	0	0	0	1	2	1	2	1	1	0	2	1	0	0	1
Tart	0	0	0	0	0	0	0	0	0	0	0	1	0	0	0	2
Taste	11	11	30	18	14	11	14	15	6	9	15	15	23	17	61	38
Tasteless	0	0	0	1	0	0	0	0	1	0	0	0	0	0	2	0
Tasty	2	2	2	2	3	3	9	7	3	4	3	4	5	2	15	4
Tear	0	0	0	0	0	0	0	0	0	0	0	0	0	1	1	3
Tears	0	1	0	0	0	0	1	3	0	0	1	4	5	2	11	19
Thirst	0	0	0	0	0	0	0	0	0	1	0	0	2	1	0	0
Thirsty	2	0	0	1	1	2	0	0	0	1	1	2	1	2	2	0
Tongue	0	0	0	0	0	0	0	0	0	0	0	0	1	0	0	2
Unsalty	0	0	0	0	1	0	0	2	0	2	0	1	0	0	0	0
Water	11	11	15	23	19	22	14	19	26	19	31	29	38	34	35	48
Wet	0	0	2	0	1	0	0	1	1	0	0	0	3	3	0	7
White	1	3	0	3	0	2	1	1	0	0	2	2	0	1	1	2

140. SCISSORS

Response Word	M	F	M	F	M	F	M	F	M	F	M	F	M	F	M	F
Big	2	0	1	0	1	0	0	0	0	0	0	0	0	0	0	0
Blood	0	0	0	0	0	0	0	0	0	0	0	0	0	0	0	2
Boy	1	0	0	0	2	0	0	0	0	0	0	0	0	0	0	0
Cloth	0	1	1	4	2	2	4	7	8	4	3	10	4	3	14	21
Cut	115	153	125	169	125	162	160	161	151	161	150	150	159	154	352	326
Cute	0	0	1	0	1	2	1	1	0	0	0	0	0	0	0	0
Cuts	2	1	0	1	0	0	0	0	0	0	0	1	1	2	1	0
Cutter	1	0	0	0	0	1	2	0	0	0	0	0	0	0	0	0
Cutters	0	0	2	0	1	1	3	1	0	0	1	0	0	0	0	0
Cutting	0	5	3	2	6	0	8	4	8	5	10	5	7	6	9	3
Doctor	1	0	2	0	0	0	0	0	0	0	0	0	0	0	0	0
Father	0	2	0	0	0	0	0	0	0	0	0	0	0	0	0	0
Girl	2	0	0	0	1	0	0	0	0	0	0	0	0	0	0	0
Go	0	0	0	1	4	0	0	0	0	0	0	0	0	0	0	0
Good	1	0	3	3	3	2	0	0	1	0	0	0	0	0	0	0
Hair	0	0	2	0	0	2	0	0	0	0	1	0	2	1	1	1
Hard	2	0	0	0	0	0	1	0	0	0	0	0	0	0	0	0
Hurt	0	0	1	1	2	0	0	0	1	0	0	0	0	0	0	0
Joy	0	0	0	0	2	1	0	0	0	0	0	0	0	0	0	0

Response Word	4th M	4th F	5th M	5th F	6th M	6th F	7th M	7th F	8th M	8th F	10th M	10th F	12th M	12th F	College M	College F

SCISSORS

Response Word	4th M	4th F	5th M	5th F	6th M	6th F	7th M	7th F	8th M	8th F	10th M	10th F	12th M	12th F	College M	College F
Knife	4	4	10	3	7	7	11	3	19	2	6	6	6	7	9	5
Man	1	1	4	0	2	0	0	0	1	0	0	0	1	0	0	0
Material	0	1	0	0	0	0	0	3	0	7	0	10	0	9	0	13
Me	0	1	0	0	2	0	0	0	0	0	0	0	0	0	0	0
Men	0	1	2	0	0	0	0	0	0	0	0	0	0	0	0	0
Metal	0	0	0	0	0	1	0	1	1	0	1	0	0	1	2	1
Moon	3	0	1	0	1	1	0	0	0	0	0	0	0	0	0	0
Needle	0	0	0	0	2	0	0	2	1	1	1	0	1	0	4	2
No	2	1	1	0	0	0	0	0	0	0	0	0	0	0	0	0
Pair	0	0	0	0	0	0	0	0	0	2	0	0	1	0	0	0
Paper	15	14	11	14	12	8	12	9	11	10	15	12	14	11	16	23
Paste	2	2	0	0	0	2	0	1	0	0	0	0	0	0	0	0
People	1	1	3	1	1	3	0	2	1	0	2	0	0	0	0	0
Person	0	0	0	0	3	0	1	0	0	0	0	0	0	0	0	0
Point	0	0	0	0	0	0	0	0	0	0	2	0	0	0	0	0
Science	0	0	0	0	0	2	0	0	0	0	0	0	0	0	0	0
Sew	0	0	0	2	1	0	0	0	0	0	0	3	1	2	3	13
Sewing	0	0	0	0	0	2	0	7	5	0	1	4	3	8	2	10
Sharp	10	9	17	13	14	17	12	29	21	33	36	37	24	32	53	51
Shears	0	0	0	0	0	0	1	4	1	7	1	0	0	0	2	1
Shiny	0	0	0	0	0	0	0	0	0	0	0	0	0	0	2	0
Silver	0	0	0	1	0	2	0	1	1	0	0	1	1	2	1	0
Sky	0	2	0	0	0	0	0	0	0	0	0	0	0	0	0	0
Snip	0	0	1	1	0	0	1	1	0	0	0	1	1	1	3	1
Steel	0	1	1	0	1	0	0	0	2	0	0	0	0	0	2	2
Sun	0	0	2	0	0	0	0	0	0	0	0	0	0	0	0	0
Thing	0	0	3	0	1	0	0	0	0	0	0	0	0	0	0	0
Thread	0	3	1	0	0	1	1	3	1	1	2	3	1	5	8	11
Tool	2	2	3	1	0	3	0	2	0	0	1	0	1	0	0	0
You	2	1	0	0	0	0	0	0	0	0	0	0	0	0	0	0

141. SEE

Response Word	4th M	4th F	5th M	5th F	6th M	6th F	7th M	7th F	8th M	8th F	10th M	10th F	12th M	12th F	College M	College F
A	1	1	2	0	0	0	0	0	0	0	0	0	0	0	1	0
Airplane	0	0	0	0	0	0	0	0	0	0	0	0	0	0	2	0
Appear	0	1	1	0	0	0	0	0	1	0	0	1	0	0	1	3
Bee	0	1	0	0	2	0	1	1	0	0	0	0	0	0	0	0
Bind	0	0	0	0	0	0	0	2	0	0	0	0	0	0	0	0
Bird	0	0	1	1	0	0	0	0	0	2	0	1	1	0	1	1
Blind	9	8	14	10	7	9	15	20	15	11	11	16	10	19	23	23
Can	0	2	1	0	2	1	1	0	0	0	0	0	0	0	0	0
Can't	1	2	0	4	0	0	1	0	1	1	0	0	1	0	0	0
Car	0	0	0	0	0	0	1	0	0	0	2	0	1	1	0	1
Clear	0	1	2	0	0	0	0	0	0	0	0	0	0	2	0	1
Cliff	0	0	0	2	0	0	0	0	0	0	0	0	0	0	0	0
Color	0	0	0	0	0	0	0	0	0	0	0	0	2	0	1	0
Colors	0	0	0	0	0	0	0	0	0	0	0	0	1	0	0	2
Dark	0	0	0	1	0	0	0	0	0	1	2	0	0	0	1	0
Do	2	1	0	0	0	1	0	0	0	0	0	0	0	0	1	0
Dog	0	0	0	0	0	1	0	0	0	1	1	0	0	2	1	1

Response Word	4th M	4th F	5th M	5th F	6th M	6th F	7th M	7th F	8th M	8th F	10th M	10th F	12th M	12th F	College M	College F
							SEE									
Don't ...	0	2	1	1	0	2	1	0	0	0	0	0	0	0	0	0
Eye	11	5	5	1	8	8	8	10	7	6	11	9	4	4	19	24
Eyes ...	16	21	11	17	15	30	18	30	11	13	19	21	10	32	20	33
Far	3	0	6	0	3	1	6	3	4	1	2	4	0	0	3	2
Farther ..	0	0	0	1	0	0	0	0	0	0	2	0	0	0	1	0
Fast	1	0	2	0	0	1	0	0	2	0	2	0	1	0	3	0
Feel	0	0	0	0	0	0	0	0	0	0	0	0	0	0	1	3
Girl	0	0	0	0	0	0	1	0	1	2	1	0	0	0	2	0
Glasses ..	0	1	1	1	0	2	1	2	1	0	1	3	3	3	1	2
Go	1	1	0	1	1	2	0	1	1	1	1	1	0	0	0	0
Good ...	1	1	0	0	0	0	0	0	1	0	1	1	0	0	1	2
He	4	4	4	0	1	1	3	1	0	1	0	0	0	0	0	0
Hear ...	3	2	3	3	4	6	3	8	8	8	5	11	7	14	29	48
Her	4	3	1	2	1	2	2	4	3	7	3	3	6	2	4	2
Here ...	3	4	1	1	1	2	3	3	2	2	1	7	1	1	17	14
Him	7	6	6	3	6	5	6	1	5	3	4	4	3	4	4	1
House ...	0	0	0	1	0	0	0	0	0	0	1	2	0	0	0	0
How	2	5	3	2	3	1	3	0	2	1	3	0	2	4	2	3
If	6	3	2	4	2	1	3	0	3	2	1	1	2	1	4	3
It	5	11	11	10	11	5	11	2	10	5	13	6	16	4	34	14
Lee	0	1	2	0	0	0	0	0	0	0	0	0	0	0	0	0
Light ...	0	0	0	0	0	0	0	1	0	0	0	0	0	0	7	4
Look ...	42	40	34	56	36	44	19	38	23	41	40	54	29	41	65	86
Me	28	31	35	29	27	25	23	6	13	9	14	8	12	11	17	14
Not	2	2	0	0	0	1	0	0	0	1	0	0	1	0	0	1
Now ...	4	5	3	5	3	4	0	2	5	1	1	1	5	2	0	0
Observe ..	0	0	0	0	0	0	1	0	0	0	1	0	0	0	5	2
Ocean ...	0	0	0	0	0	0	0	0	0	0	0	0	1	1	2	0
Peek ...	1	0	0	0	0	0	0	0	0	2	0	0	0	0	0	0
Perceive .	0	0	0	0	0	0	0	0	0	0	0	0	0	0	2	1
Picture ..	0	0	0	0	0	0	0	0	0	0	0	0	1	0	0	3
Plane ...	0	0	0	0	0	0	0	0	0	0	0	0	0	1	2	1
Read ...	0	2	2	0	0	0	0	1	0	0	0	0	0	0	0	0
Run	0	0	0	0	0	0	0	0	0	0	0	0	0	0	2	3
Saw	9	18	20	30	16	24	55	64	70	68	35	47	60	64	95	116
Sea	10	9	9	15	10	11	9	4	3	1	10	1	2	2	4	2
Seen ...	4	3	4	6	4	5	3	5	5	5	3	1	4	1	4	3
Show ...	0	0	0	1	0	0	2	0	0	2	1	0	0	0	0	1
Sight	1	1	1	3	5	2	4	3	6	3	6	1	6	3	8	5
Sky	0	0	0	0	0	0	0	0	0	0	3	1	1	1	1	3
Smell ...	0	0	0	0	0	0	0	1	1	1	0	0	0	0	1	3
Something .	0	4	0	0	0	1	0	0	0	0	0	0	1	0	2	0
Spot	0	0	0	1	0	1	0	0	1	0	0	1	0	0	0	4
Taste ...	0	0	0	0	0	0	0	0	0	0	0	0	0	0	0	3
That ...	11	4	3	3	8	4	3	2	3	4	5	7	2	3	3	2
The	5	5	3	2	8	3	3	3	2	2	3	0	2	1	3	3
Their ...	2	0	0	0	0	0	0	0	0	0	0	0	0	0	0	0
Them ...	1	1	3	0	3	3	2	0	3	4	1	1	4	5	9	3
There ...	0	2	1	1	6	1	1	1	1	0	1	2	1	0	4	4

Response Word	4th M	4th F	5th M	5th F	6th M	6th F	7th M	7th F	8th M	8th F	10th M	10th F	12th M	12th F	College M	College F

SEE

Response Word	4th M	4th F	5th M	5th F	6th M	6th F	7th M	7th F	8th M	8th F	10th M	10th F	12th M	12th F	College M	College F
They	2	0	1	1	1	0	0	0	0	0	0	0	0	0	0	0
Thing	1	0	0	2	2	0	0	0	0	0	1	0	0	0	2	0
Things	0	0	0	0	0	0	1	0	0	0	1	0	1	1	3	0
This	0	0	1	0	0	0	1	0	1	1	1	1	1	0	3	1
Tree	0	0	0	4	0	0	0	1	0	2	0	0	0	0	1	0
Us	1	1	1	0	3	2	1	1	2	0	1	2	1	1	4	2
View	1	0	0	0	0	0	0	0	1	0	0	0	0	0	4	2
Vision	0	0	2	0	1	0	1	1	1	2	0	3	0	0	4	2
Visualize	0	0	0	0	0	0	0	0	0	0	0	1	0	0	2	2
Watch	0	0	0	1	0	0	1	0	0	1	0	0	1	1	1	3
We	3	0	1	2	4	0	1	1	0	0	0	0	1	0	0	0
What	3	1	6	1	4	0	2	1	4	3	1	2	4	5	11	3
When	0	2	0	0	0	0	1	0	0	0	0	0	0	0	0	0
Where	0	1	0	2	0	0	1	0	2	1	2	0	1	1	1	0
Who	1	0	0	1	0	1	0	0	0	0	1	0	0	0	2	0
You	4	4	6	5	18	7	7	3	10	13	13	0	11	3	15	7

142. SELL

Response Word	4th M	4th F	5th M	5th F	6th M	6th F	7th M	7th F	8th M	8th F	10th M	10th F	12th M	12th F	College M	College F
Apple	1	0	4	0	0	0	0	0	0	1	2	0	0	0	0	0
Apples	1	2	1	3	0	0	0	1	0	0	0	0	0	2	0	2
Away	1	3	0	1	1	0	0	0	0	0	0	0	0	0	0	0
Bell	0	4	5	2	2	2	1	4	4	1	1	0	1	0	3	2
Boat	0	0	0	0	2	0	0	0	0	0	0	0	0	0	1	0
Book	1	0	0	0	0	1	1	2	0	1	1	1	2	1	0	2
Books	0	0	2	1	0	0	0	1	0	0	4	2	0	0	9	12
Bought	3	0	1	2	0	3	3	1	8	6	2	1	3	3	0	0
Brush	0	0	0	0	0	0	0	0	0	0	0	0	0	0	0	2
Buttons	0	0	0	0	0	0	0	0	0	0	0	0	0	0	0	4
Buy	84	91	86	110	86	99	111	104	121	111	119	126	139	111	276	288
Buying	0	0	0	0	0	1	0	0	2	0	0	0	0	0	0	0
Buys	0	0	1	0	0	0	0	0	0	0	0	2	0	0	0	1
By	5	5	10	3	8	5	4	5	0	0	5	1	2	0	3	0
Candy	1	2	5	0	1	0	4	5	5	2	5	6	0	6	1	3
Car	1	1	1	0	1	1	1	1	2	0	3	0	5	2	6	3
Cars	0	0	0	0	0	0	0	0	0	0	1	2	1	0	6	1
Cat	0	3	0	0	0	0	0	0	0	0	0	0	0	0	0	0
Cell	0	0	0	1	0	0	1	2	1	0	0	0	0	0	0	0
Clothes	0	1	0	1	0	1	0	3	1	5	1	1	1	7	9	15
Clothing	0	0	0	0	0	0	0	0	0	0	0	0	0	1	1	2
Cloths	0	0	0	0	0	0	0	0	0	0	0	2	0	0	0	0
Cookies	0	1	1	1	0	0	0	2	0	2	2	1	0	0	0	1
Cost	1	0	0	0	0	0	2	0	0	0	1	0	0	1	0	1
Dark	2	0	0	0	0	0	0	0	0	0	0	0	0	0	0	0
Do	0	0	0	2	2	0	0	0	0	0	0	0	0	0	0	0
Dog	1	2	1	1	1	1	2	0	0	2	0	0	0	0	0	0
Dogs	0	1	0	1	0	0	0	0	2	0	0	0	0	0	1	1
Fell	1	1	2	0	1	0	0	1	0	0	0	0	0	0	0	0
Fish	0	0	0	1	2	0	0	0	0	0	0	0	0	0	0	0
Flowers	0	0	0	0	0	0	0	0	0	0	0	0	2	0	0	1

Response Word	4th		5th		6th		7th		8th		10th		12th		College	
	M	F	M	F	M	F	M	F	M	F	M	F	M	F	M	F

SELL

Response Word	4th M	4th F	5th M	5th F	6th M	6th F	7th M	7th F	8th M	8th F	10th M	10th F	12th M	12th F	College M	College F
Food	8	11	10	7	9	8	3	3	3	7	3	12	4	10	9	3
Fruit	0	0	0	1	0	1	0	0	0	2	0	0	0	0	0	0
Gas	0	0	0	0	1	0	0	0	0	0	0	0	2	0	0	0
Get	4	1	2	3	1	1	0	1	0	0	0	0	0	0	0	1
Give	8	8	8	3	6	16	3	3	3	0	0	5	1	0	1	2
Go	0	0	1	2	2	0	0	1	0	0	0	0	0	0	1	0
Gone	2	2	1	0	0	1	0	0	0	0	0	0	0	0	0	0
Good	2	0	2	0	2	1	1	0	0	0	1	2	1	1	0	0
Goods	0	0	0	1	0	4	2	0	3	2	6	4	2	6	14	7
Groceries	0	0	0	0	0	0	0	2	0	0	1	4	0	0	0	0
Hard	0	0	0	0	0	0	0	0	0	0	0	1	1	0	2	0
Hats	0	0	0	0	0	2	0	0	0	0	0	0	0	0	0	0
House	0	0	1	0	1	2	0	4	2	6	1	1	2	5	4	3
It	1	2	1	0	0	0	2	1	0	0	0	2	1	2	2	1
Jail	1	0	0	1	5	0	3	1	1	3	0	0	0	0	0	0
Keep	2	1	0	0	1	0	0	1	0	0	0	1	0	0	0	1
Lemonade	0	0	0	0	0	0	0	2	0	0	0	0	0	0	0	0
Magazines	0	0	0	0	0	0	0	0	0	0	1	0	0	0	0	2
Man	0	2	0	0	3	2	1	0	0	0	2	4	1	2	1	5
Market	1	1	1	0	1	2	0	1	0	0	0	0	1	0	0	0
Me	1	0	2	1	3	1	3	0	1	1	0	1	0	2	1	2
Mell	0	2	0	0	1	0	0	0	0	0	0	0	0	0	0	0
Merchandise	1	0	0	1	0	0	0	2	0	0	2	2	2	0	4	6
Merchant	1	0	0	0	1	0	0	2	0	0	0	0	0	0	0	1
Money	14	10	14	7	18	9	14	8	8	4	18	12	7	6	12	14
Now	0	1	0	0	0	0	0	0	0	0	0	0	2	0	1	0
Out	0	0	0	2	1	0	1	0	0	0	3	1	0	0	1	1
Paper	1	0	0	1	1	2	0	0	0	1	0	0	0	0	0	1
Papers	0	0	0	0	0	0	0	1	1	0	3	1	1	0	0	0
Pay	1	1	0	2	0	2	0	0	1	1	0	0	0	2	0	0
Peddle	0	0	0	0	0	0	2	0	0	0	0	0	0	0	0	1
People	0	0	0	0	0	0	0	0	1	0	0	0	2	0	0	0
Pots	0	0	0	0	0	0	0	0	0	0	0	0	0	1	2	2
Price	0	0	0	0	1	0	2	1	0	0	1	0	0	0	0	1
Prison	0	0	0	0	1	1	2	0	1	0	0	0	0	0	0	0
Product	0	0	1	0	1	0	0	0	0	1	1	1	1	1	2	2
Products	0	0	0	0	0	0	0	0	0	2	0	2	1	0	2	1
Purchase	0	0	0	1	1	2	3	1	0	0	1	0	0	1	0	0
Sale	2	2	4	4	6	5	4	3	5	6	1	5	2	5	9	7
Salesman	1	2	1	0	0	3	1	3	2	3	3	0	1	4	11	5
Salesmen	0	0	1	1	0	0	1	0	1	0	0	0	1	0	2	0
Sea	1	4	2	1	2	1	1	1	1	2	1	0	0	0	4	0
See	2	1	1	0	0	0	1	0	0	0	1	0	0	0	0	0
Seller	0	0	0	1	0	0	0	0	0	0	0	1	0	0	2	0
Selling	1	2	3	0	1	0	1	0	1	1	1	0	0	2	1	0
Shell	3	0	2	2	0	0	2	2	0	0	1	3	1	0	0	1
Shells	0	0	0	0	0	0	0	2	0	0	0	0	0	2	1	0
Shoes	0	0	0	0	0	1	0	0	0	0	1	0	2	4	6	3
Smell	1	0	2	0	1	1	2	0	2	0	2	0	2	0	1	1

Response Word	4th M	4th F	5th M	5th F	6th M	6th F	7th M	7th F	8th M	8th F	10th M	10th F	12th M	12th F	College M	College F
							SELL									
Sold	19	16	15	19	17	22	19	30	30	23	10	11	16	19	21	17
Something .	4	2	0	1	2	0	1	0	0	2	0	0	0	0	0	0
Steal . . .	0	0	0	0	0	0	0	0	1	1	0	0	0	0	2	2
Store . . .	9	11	5	13	7	15	13	12	4	13	6	12	5	9	9	20
Swell . . .	1	1	0	0	0	0	0	0	0	0	0	0	0	0	2	0
Tea	0	0	2	0	0	0	0	0	0	0	0	0	0	0	0	0
Them . . .	1	0	0	0	0	0	0	0	1	2	0	1	1	1	0	0
Thing . . .	2	1	2	1	2	0	0	0	0	1	0	0	0	0	1	0
Things . .	0	2	2	2	4	2	0	1	1	2	0	0	0	2	4	3
Toys	1	2	2	0	3	0	0	0	0	0	1	0	0	2	2	3
Vegetables	0	3	0	0	0	0	1	0	0	0	0	0	0	0	0	0
Vendor . .	0	0	0	0	0	0	0	0	0	1	0	0	0	0	2	0
Ware . . .	0	0	0	0	0	0	0	0	0	0	0	0	0	0	0	2
Water . . .	2	0	0	1	0	2	1	1	0	0	0	1	0	0	0	0
Well	0	1	0	2	1	0	1	1	2	2	1	0	1	0	2	2
What . . .	0	0	0	0	0	0	0	0	2	2	2	1	0	1	1	1
Work . . .	0	0	1	1	0	0	0	0	0	0	0	0	0	4	1	2
You	0	0	0	1	0	0	0	0	1	0	0	0	1	0	2	0
						143.	SHEEP									
Animal . .	55	30	42	35	37	46	31	45	28	51	45	25	28	37	56	49
Animals .	4	12	1	1	6	5	6	5	6	5	4	3	3	9	7	6
Awake . . .	1	4	1	2	2	1	1	1	3	1	1	1	0	0	1	1
Baa	3	3	0	1	1	2	1	1	3	2	2	0	4	1	7	4
Baa baa . .	0	1	0	0	0	0	0	0	2	1	0	0	0	0	0	1
Ba ba . . .	0	0	0	2	1	0	0	0	0	0	0	0	0	0	0	0
Baby	0	1	0	2	0	1	0	0	0	0	0	0	0	1	0	0
Bed	6	2	5	3	3	4	1	2	3	0	2	1	2	1	2	0
Black . . .	1	0	1	1	0	2	2	3	2	1	3	2	1	2	7	10
Calf . . .	0	1	0	0	0	1	2	0	0	2	0	0	0	0	0	0
Cattle . .	2	5	2	2	10	5	5	4	6	5	5	6	3	3	7	9
Cloth . . .	2	1	1	1	0	1	0	1	1	0	1	0	0	0	0	0
Clothing . .	0	0	0	0	2	0	0	1	0	0	0	0	0	0	0	0
Coat	0	0	2	0	0	0	0	0	0	0	1	0	1	1	1	0
Count . . .	2	2	1	2	1	0	0	1	2	4	0	2	2	1	5	2
Counting .	0	1	0	0	0	1	0	3	1	3	0	0	1	0	0	0
Cow	4	4	2	2	3	3	3	1	9	4	4	7	6	4	6	13
Cows . . .	1	0	2	0	1	3	1	1	0	3	4	3	1	1	4	4
Cute . . .	0	0	0	0	0	0	0	0	0	0	0	2	0	1	0	0
Deep . . .	0	1	0	2	0	1	0	0	0	0	0	0	0	0	0	0
Dip	0	0	0	0	0	0	0	0	0	0	0	0	0	0	2	0
Dog	9	6	6	2	8	2	8	6	11	2	5	7	15	6	22	10
Dogs . . .	0	1	0	0	0	1	1	0	1	0	0	1	3	0	2	0
Dream . .	4	1	1	2	0	2	3	2	5	1	1	2	2	2	1	0
Dumb . . .	0	0	0	0	0	0	2	0	0	0	0	0	1	0	0	1
Eat	2	0	0	0	2	0	1	0	0	2	0	0	1	0	2	0
Ewe . . .	0	0	0	0	0	0	0	0	0	0	1	0	0	2	2	4
Farm . . .	2	2	2	4	2	1	3	2	4	4	6	10	5	13	1	10
Fence . . .	0	0	0	1	1	0	0	1	1	0	1	0	2	2	7	2

Response Word	4th M	4th F	5th M	5th F	6th M	6th F	7th M	7th F	8th M	8th F	10th M	10th F	12th M	12th F	College M	College F
SHEEP																
Field . . .	1	0	0	0	2	0	1	0	0	0	2	0	3	0	0	2
Fleece . .	0	0	0	0	0	1	0	2	1	0	0	0	0	1	1	0
Flock . . .	2	0	0	1	0	1	2	1	2	1	4	2	2	4	8	2
Fluffy . . .	0	0	0	0	0	0	0	0	2	0	0	1	0	1	0	0
Food . . .	0	1	2	0	2	0	1	0	1	2	6	5	3	1	2	2
Fur	1	3	2	1	0	0	1	0	1	1	1	1	1	2	2	1
Fuzzy . . .	0	0	0	0	0	1	0	1	0	1	0	2	0	1	2	1
Goat	3	5	4	5	4	4	11	8	4	8	6	0	11	8	15	17
Goats . . .	0	0	0	1	1	0	2	4	2	0	1	3	2	3	6	6
Grass . . .	0	0	2	0	1	1	2	2	2	0	1	0	1	0	2	3
Graze . . .	0	0	0	0	0	1	0	1	0	0	1	0	0	0	1	4
Grazing . .	0	0	0	0	1	0	0	0	2	0	0	0	0	0	1	0
Hair	2	0	1	1	0	0	0	0	0	0	0	0	0	0	0	1
Heap . . .	0	0	2	0	0	0	0	0	0	0	1	0	0	0	0	0
Heard . .	2	2	1	1	2	0	0	0	0	0	1	0	0	0	0	1
Herd . . .	3	0	3	1	4	3	4	0	3	1	4	1	3	5	21	10
Herder . .	0	1	1	1	1	0	0	0	0	0	0	0	3	0	5	1
Hill	0	0	0	1	0	0	0	1	0	0	0	0	0	0	0	2
Horse . . .	0	2	0	0	2	1	1	0	0	0	0	0	0	0	1	0
Lamb . . .	34	53	47	52	38	40	39	41	48	63	22	52	35	40	79	103
Lamb chops	0	0	0	0	0	0	0	0	2	0	0	0	0	0	0	1
Lambs . .	0	0	1	3	2	1	5	5	6	3	1	7	2	5	10	20
Lame . . .	0	0	2	1	0	1	0	1	0	0	0	0	0	0	0	0
Lamp . . .	3	5	6	8	3	6	1	0	0	0	0	2	0	0	3	0
Lanolin . .	0	0	0	0	0	0	0	0	0	0	0	2	0	0	0	0
Meat . . .	1	2	0	1	1	0	2	1	1	0	0	0	1	0	2	0
Mutton . .	3	4	4	7	9	7	7	6	14	5	17	7	14	8	27	17
Night . . .	1	1	2	1	1	4	1	3	0	1	0	0	1	0	0	0
Pasture . .	1	6	2	2	2	4	2	1	0	3	4	7	2	5	11	12
Peep . . .	1	2	0	0	0	0	0	0	0	0	0	0	0	0	0	0
Pigs . . .	0	0	0	0	0	0	1	0	0	0	0	1	1	0	2	0
Rest . . .	1	0	1	2	0	1	1	1	0	0	2	0	0	3	0	0
Run	1	0	0	0	0	0	0	0	0	0	0	0	0	0	0	2
Shear . . .	0	1	0	0	2	0	2	1	0	0	0	0	0	0	1	1
Shepherd .	3	7	3	2	2	5	5	0	4	3	2	1	6	3	6	11
Sleep . . .	10	6	9	8	8	6	7	7	8	6	6	4	6	7	9	15
Smell . . .	0	0	0	1	0	0	0	0	0	1	0	0	1	0	2	1
Soft	1	3	0	3	2	4	1	5	1	2	1	1	0	2	3	7
Tired . . .	2	0	2	0	0	0	1	1	0	0	0	1	0	0	0	1
White . . .	7	9	7	12	9	13	5	8	2	1	7	9	4	20	10	17
Wolf . . .	1	1	1	1	0	0	2	1	5	1	1	0	4	0	2	1
Wool . . .	33	41	39	46	43	51	43	46	25	37	49	48	46	26	95	92
Woolly . .	0	2	0	0	0	0	0	2	0	0	0	0	0	0	0	2
Wooly . . .	0	0	1	2	1	0	1	0	2	6	0	2	0	2	0	0
144. SHOES																
Are	3	2	4	5	5	3	4	1	5	0	3	0	7	0	8	1
Big	0	1	0	0	1	1	0	1	1	1	0	0	0	2	2	0
Black . . .	1	4	0	0	1	3	5	1	5	2	12	7	6	11	8	8

Response Word	4th M	4th F	5th M	5th F	6th M	6th F	7th M	7th F	8th M	8th F	10th M	10th F	12th M	12th F	College M	College F
							SHOES									
Blue	0	0	0	0	0	1	0	0	0	3	0	1	0	0	2	0
Boats . . .	1	0	0	2	0	1	0	0	0	1	0	0	0	0	0	1
Boot	2	1	1	0	0	1	4	0	3	1	0	0	1	0	2	0
Boots . . .	9	6	9	5	9	4	15	4	8	2	11	3	7	6	4	5
Brown . .	1	2	1	1	4	5	1	0	1	2	2	3	3	2	13	6
Buckle . .	0	0	0	1	0	0	0	0	0	0	0	2	0	0	1	0
Buy	1	0	1	0	1	0	0	0	0	0	0	0	2	0	0	0
Clean . . .	0	2	0	0	0	1	0	0	0	1	0	1	0	0	0	1
Cloth . . .	0	1	0	0	0	2	1	1	1	0	0	0	0	0	0	0
Clothes . .	5	7	7	4	5	5	0	2	5	3	4	1	3	1	2	4
Clothing .	1	3	1	0	2	0	2	0	0	0	0	1	0	0	0	1
Coat	0	0	2	2	0	0	1	0	1	0	0	0	0	1	1	2
Cold . . .	0	0	0	0	0	0	0	0	0	0	0	0	1	0	0	2
Cute . . .	0	0	0	0	0	0	0	2	0	0	0	0	0	0	0	0
Feet . . .	39	62	53	72	54	58	64	68	76	81	72	84	70	90	184	174
Fit	1	4	1	6	4	2	2	3	0	7	6	7	8	4	22	9
Flats . . .	0	0	0	0	0	0	0	2	0	2	0	1	0	2	0	3
Foot . . .	8	9	9	4	6	1	9	6	7	9	6	2	2	4	9	7
Gloves . .	2	0	1	0	0	0	0	0	1	0	0	1	1	0	1	0
Go	0	2	2	0	0	0	0	0	0	0	0	0	1	0	0	0
Hat	3	0	1	0	0	1	0	3	0	0	0	1	1	0	1	0
Hats . . .	0	0	0	2	0	0	0	0	0	0	0	1	0	1	0	0
Head . . .	2	0	0	0	0	0	0	0	0	0	0	0	0	0	0	0
Heel	0	0	0	0	0	0	0	2	2	0	2	0	0	0	0	0
Heels . . .	0	0	0	0	0	1	0	2	0	2	0	3	2	1	0	10
Hole . . .	2	0	0	0	1	0	1	0	1	1	1	1	0	0	0	0
Holes . . .	0	0	1	0	0	0	0	0	1	0	0	1	2	0	1	1
Home . . .	0	0	0	0	0	2	0	0	0	0	0	0	0	0	0	0
Hose . . .	0	0	3	1	0	0	0	0	0	0	0	1	0	0	0	0
Hurt . . .	0	0	1	0	0	0	1	0	0	1	1	1	2	2	2	2
Lace . . .	2	2	2	2	6	1	1	4	2	1	1	3	1	0	2	2
Laces . . .	4	4	4	7	2	3	7	8	6	7	3	6	8	6	21	17
Leather . .	4	0	9	4	9	6	3	4	5	3	4	3	5	6	16	5
Many . . .	0	0	0	0	0	0	0	0	0	0	0	3	0	0	0	0
Me	6	0	0	0	1	0	0	0	0	0	0	0	0	0	0	1
My	0	0	1	0	0	2	0	0	0	0	0	0	0	0	1	0
New	4	1	1	3	0	4	2	1	0	4	6	2	0	2	2	6
Off	0	0	1	0	0	0	1	0	1	0	2	1	1	0	1	0
Old	0	1	0	0	1	0	0	0	0	0	0	1	1	0	1	2
On	4	2	2	1	5	2	2	0	1	1	1	0	0	0	4	0
Pair	2	1	1	2	2	2	0	1	1	0	0	0	1	0	0	0
Pants . . .	0	1	1	0	0	0	1	0	2	0	0	0	1	0	0	0
People . .	3	0	0	0	0	0	0	0	0	0	1	0	0	0	1	0
Pointed . .	0	0	0	0	0	0	0	2	0	1	0	0	0	2	0	0
Polish . .	0	1	1	1	0	0	0	0	0	0	3	3	1	0	0	0
Pretty . .	0	0	2	2	0	1	0	2	0	0	0	0	0	0	0	1
Red	0	0	0	0	0	0	0	3	0	2	0	1	0	0	0	1
Shine . . .	2	4	2	0	6	1	2	4	0	1	12	4	8	12	9	4
Shiny . . .	0	0	0	0	0	0	0	0	0	0	0	0	0	2	0	0

Response Word	4th M	4th F	5th M	5th F	6th M	6th F	7th M	7th F	8th M	8th F	10th M	10th F	12th M	12th F	College M	College F
							SHOES									
Shoe	15	9	6	5	7	9	5	0	6	0	3	3	2	0	7	2
Shoe laces .	0	0	0	0	0	0	0	0	0	0	0	3	2	0	1	0
Shoe strings	0	1	0	0	0	0	0	0	1	0	1	0	1	2	0	0
Show	0	2	2	1	0	0	0	0	0	0	0	0	0	0	0	0
Skirt . . .	0	0	0	0	0	0	0	0	0	2	0	0	0	0	0	0
Slippers . .	2	1	1	0	0	3	2	3	5	0	2	0	0	1	0	3
Small . . .	0	0	0	0	0	0	0	1	0	0	1	1	2	2	0	0
Sock	3	3	1	2	5	1	2	3	4	0	0	1	3	0	1	3
Socks . . .	6	13	9	12	12	21	18	34	23	41	16	32	19	32	59	76
Sole	1	1	1	2	1	1	5	2	4	3	4	1	3	0	0	1
Soles . . .	2	1	1	2	3	0	4	2	2	3	4	3	7	4	8	8
Sox	1	0	0	1	0	0	0	1	2	2	1	1	0	0	2	3
Squeak . . .	0	0	0	0	0	0	0	0	0	2	0	0	0	0	0	0
Stocking . .	2	2	2	3	3	3	3	4	0	0	1	3	0	1	2	3
Stockings .	6	6	1	13	6	17	6	13	8	19	13	15	7	7	14	38
Stocks . . .	0	2	0	1	0	1	1	2	2	0	1	0	0	0	0	0
Store . . .	1	0	0	1	2	2	0	1	2	0	0	1	0	0	0	0
String . . .	4	2	1	0	1	2	0	0	4	0	2	2	2	0	3	4
Strings . .	2	1	3	0	3	2	1	0	3	3	1	2	4	1	5	4
Tennis . .	0	0	1	0	0	0	1	1	0	2	2	1	1	1	0	6
Tie	2	6	2	4	4	6	4	4	4	4	4	8	5	4	12	8
Tied . . .	1	0	0	0	0	0	0	0	0	0	1	0	0	1	2	0
Ties	0	0	0	0	0	1	0	2	1	0	0	1	0	3	0	6
Tight . . .	0	1	3	0	0	0	2	3	0	1	0	1	0	3	3	2
To	0	1	1	2	2	0	0	0	0	0	0	0	0	0	0	0
Toe	1	0	6	1	0	1	3	1	1	0	0	0	1	0	0	0
Toes . . .	2	2	1	4	1	5	8	2	4	0	2	1	4	1	2	3
Tongue . .	0	0	1	0	0	0	0	0	1	0	0	0	0	0	2	0
Two	3	2	2	4	1	3	1	1	1	0	0	0	0	0	0	0
Walk . . .	5	8	5	5	2	12	1	3	6	6	5	4	6	9	10	13
Wear . . .	23	26	25	27	17	18	16	19	8	4	4	5	7	6	4	7
Were . . .	2	3	3	2	4	2	3	0	0	0	0	0	0	0	0	0
Where . .	3	1	2	1	2	0	2	0	0	1	0	0	0	0	0	0
White . . .	0	0	0	0	0	1	1	0	0	0	0	2	0	1	0	3
Whose . .	1	0	0	0	2	0	0	0	0	0	0	0	0	0	2	0
Worn . . .	0	0	1	0	0	0	0	0	0	0	1	0	0	1	2	0
You	0	2	0	2	1	1	0	0	0	0	0	0	0	0	0	0
						145.	SHORT									
Baby . . .	1	2	0	2	1	0	1	0	0	1	0	0	0	1	0	0
Big	5	7	3	2	1	4	1	0	2	0	2	0	0	0	0	2
Boy	4	0	1	0	1	1	1	1	0	2	1	0	3	1	8	5
Cut	0	0	1	0	0	1	1	0	0	0	0	0	1	0	2	1
Dress . . .	0	1	0	1	0	1	0	0	0	0	0	0	0	0	0	2
Dwarf . . .	0	0	0	0	0	0	0	0	0	0	0	0	0	0	0	2
Fat	2	7	5	7	7	12	5	34	14	28	26	36	14	40	60	75
Feet . . .	2	0	1	0	0	0	0	0	0	0	0	0	0	0	0	0
Funny . . .	0	1	2	0	0	0	0	1	1	0	0	0	0	0	0	1
Fur	0	0	0	0	0	0	0	0	0	2	0	0	0	0	0	0

Response Word	4th M	4th F	5th M	5th F	6th M	6th F	7th M	7th F	8th M	8th F	10th M	10th F	12th M	12th F	College M	College F
							SHORT									
Girl	0	0	1	1	0	1	0	1	0	4	3	4	2	8	5	5
Gun	2	0	0	1	1	0	0	0	0	0	0	0	1	0	0	0
Hair	0	3	1	2	1	4	0	3	4	2	2	5	5	5	5	9
Hand	0	0	0	2	0	0	0	0	1	1	0	1	2	0	1	0
Hard	1	0	2	1	1	1	1	4	2	0	1	0	2	0	1	0
High	2	2	2	0	3	0	1	1	3	1	1	0	0	0	2	0
Large	0	1	1	2	1	1	0	0	0	0	0	0	1	0	0	1
Length	0	1	2	1	1	1	1	1	1	1	0	0	0	0	0	0
Line	0	0	1	2	0	0	0	0	0	0	0	0	0	0	0	0
Little	15	23	16	11	10	19	8	9	2	7	4	15	6	3	3	14
Long	100	74	81	72	82	71	76	58	77	50	70	54	81	56	128	77
Low	2	1	0	0	1	1	1	1	3	0	1	0	0	0	2	0
Man	2	0	1	2	3	1	1	1	1	1	9	2	3	1	11	6
Me	1	0	0	0	0	1	0	2	0	3	1	4	1	3	1	3
Midget	0	3	0	1	5	0	5	2	1	1	5	1	2	2	2	1
Not long	3	1	2	1	0	1	1	1	0	0	0	0	0	0	0	0
Or	0	2	0	1	0	0	0	0	0	0	0	0	0	0	0	0
Pants	0	0	0	0	1	0	1	0	3	0	1	0	1	1	3	0
Pencil	0	1	2	0	2	0	1	0	3	0	2	0	0	0	1	0
Person	0	2	1	1	0	3	0	1	0	2	0	1	1	1	2	3
Puny	0	0	0	0	0	0	2	0	0	0	0	0	0	0	0	0
Separate	0	0	0	0	0	0	0	0	0	0	2	0	0	0	0	0
Shirt	0	0	0	0	0	0	0	0	0	0	0	0	0	0	2	0
Shorts	0	0	0	1	0	1	0	0	1	3	2	2	4	0	3	2
Skinny	1	0	1	0	2	2	1	0	0	1	0	0	0	0	1	0
Skirt	0	0	1	0	0	1	1	5	0	3	1	8	3	4	1	5
Small	31	43	46	53	46	44	39	27	18	16	19	11	13	12	21	10
Stick	1	0	0	1	0	0	0	0	0	1	1	0	1	0	0	2
Stocky	2	1	0	0	2	0	3	0	2	1	2	1	0	1	3	2
Stop	0	0	0	1	1	3	0	1	0	0	1	0	1	0	0	2
Stout	0	3	0	1	2	2	2	3	1	2	0	0	0	0	2	3
Stub	0	0	0	1	0	0	2	0	0	0	0	0	1	0	1	0
Stubby	3	3	4	1	7	8	10	8	6	2	3	6	1	0	2	4
Tall	32	40	34	48	34	43	58	64	74	91	63	79	82	92	180	231
Thin	0	1	2	0	0	1	1	1	0	0	1	0	0	0	1	1
Time	0	1	2	1	2	0	0	0	1	0	0	0	0	0	1	1
Tiny	0	3	3	3	0	2	3	2	1	4	0	3	0	1	0	1
						146.	SICKNESS									
Ache	0	0	2	0	0	1	0	1	0	0	0	0	0	0	2	0
Awful	0	0	0	2	1	3	0	0	1	0	0	2	0	0	0	0
Bad	15	7	13	3	12	5	7	4	2	3	5	2	3	2	4	4
Bed	15	22	20	17	15	10	18	18	13	14	27	31	23	21	40	37
Chicken pox	2	0	0	0	2	1	4	0	1	1	0	1	0	0	0	0
Cold	21	13	14	8	19	4	8	8	12	13	16	10	7	8	8	13
Colds	0	0	0	0	0	0	0	2	0	1	1	0	0	0	0	0
Cough	1	1	1	1	0	0	0	1	2	1	0	1	2	2	1	0
Dead	0	2	1	1	1	2	5	1	5	2	2	1	3	0	1	1
Death	0	1	1	0	0	3	11	6	8	10	18	20	25	12	61	41

Response Word	4th M	4th F	5th M	5th F	6th M	6th F	7th M	7th F	8th M	8th F	10th M	10th F	12th M	12th F	College M	College F
							SICKNESS									
Die	1	0	1	0	2	1	0	2	0	0	0	2	0	0	1	4
Disease . . .	4	5	11	3	8	8	11	8	5	8	7	2	4	3	11	9
Doctor	3	2	2	5	1	2	4	3	4	1	7	6	6	8	12	10
Dr.	2	1	1	1	0	0	0	0	0	1	0	0	0	0	1	0
Faint	0	0	0	0	0	0	0	0	0	0	0	0	0	2	0	0
Feel	2	1	2	6	1	3	1	1	0	0	0	0	1	0	0	0
Feel bad . .	2	0	0	1	0	0	0	0	0	0	0	0	0	0	0	0
Fever	2	1	1	2	4	0	1	7	3	2	4	2	2	1	0	3
Flu	1	3	0	4	5	2	1	6	0	7	6	7	4	4	7	6
Food	0	0	0	0	2	0	0	1	0	0	0	0	2	0	0	0
Girl	1	2	0	1	1	2	0	1	0	0	0	0	0	1	0	0
Good	4	2	0	1	4	0	1	1	1	0	1	0	1	0	0	0
Green . . .	0	0	0	0	0	0	0	0	1	0	0	1	0	0	1	2
Happy	0	0	0	0	0	0	0	0	2	0	0	0	0	0	0	0
Headache . .	1	0	0	3	1	0	0	1	1	0	0	1	1	1	0	1
Health	1	7	6	10	6	18	29	25	44	36	37	47	66	69	199	170
Healthy . . .	2	3	1	1	0	3	3	1	4	4	4	3	3	1	1	0
Help	2	1	0	1	1	0	0	0	0	0	0	0	0	0	0	0
Home . . .	2	1	0	0	2	1	1	1	2	0	1	0	0	0	1	1
Hospital . . .	1	0	4	1	4	4	0	2	4	3	5	7	5	7	8	17
Hurt	2	6	5	1	0	3	1	1	2	0	2	1	1	0	0	2
Ill	59	69	71	98	85	98	63	72	54	66	43	47	40	45	60	84
Illness . . .	3	3	3	6	1	9	9	11	7	14	9	10	8	14	11	13
Mad	1	0	0	0	0	0	0	0	4	1	0	0	0	1	0	0
Man	1	0	2	1	0	0	0	0	0	0	0	0	1	0	2	1
Me	0	0	0	0	0	0	0	1	0	0	0	0	0	2	1	1
Measles . . .	2	1	3	5	2	9	5	3	1	8	2	3	2	2	0	3
Medicine . .	1	1	1	2	1	0	2	1	1	0	0	3	1	2	0	3
Mental . . .	0	0	0	0	0	0	3	0	1	0	0	1	0	0	0	0
Misery . . .	0	0	0	1	1	0	0	0	0	0	2	0	1	0	1	2
Mumps . . .	2	1	1	2	0	2	2	7	4	2	0	0	2	1	1	0
Nausea . . .	0	0	0	0	0	0	0	0	0	0	0	1	0	0	2	1
No	2	0	0	0	0	0	0	0	0	0	0	0	0	0	0	1
Not well . .	3	0	0	0	2	1	0	3	0	0	0	0	1	0	0	0
Nurse	0	0	0	0	0	0	0	0	1	0	0	1	0	1	1	5
Ouch	0	0	0	0	0	0	0	0	2	0	0	0	0	0	0	0
Pain	1	2	2	2	2	2	2	2	4	3	1	3	2	7	2	6
Pale	0	0	0	1	0	1	1	0	0	1	1	0	0	3	1	0
People . . .	2	0	1	0	0	0	0	0	0	0	0	3	1	0	2	0
Person . . .	0	0	1	1	0	1	1	0	0	0	2	0	1	1	1	0
Pills	0	0	0	0	1	1	0	0	1	1	0	0	0	0	3	1
Pneumonia .	0	1	1	0	0	0	0	0	2	0	2	1	0	1	0	1
Poor	0	0	0	0	1	0	1	0	0	0	2	0	0	0	1	0
Sad	0	2	2	3	2	4	2	2	2	2	2	2	0	0	5	5
Sadness . . .	2	1	0	0	0	0	2	2	1	0	2	0	1	0	0	6
School	0	0	0	0	0	0	0	0	4	0	1	0	0	0	0	1
Sick	20	17	17	8	9	8	7	4	2	3	2	4	1	0	0	0
Temperature	0	1	0	0	0	0	0	0	0	2	0	3	1	0	2	1
Terrible . .	0	2	2	0	0	0	0	0	0	1	0	0	0	0	0	0

Response Word	4th M	F	5th M	F	6th M	F	7th M	F	8th M	F	10th M	F	12th M	F	College M	F

SICKNESS

Response Word	4th M	F	5th M	F	6th M	F	7th M	F	8th M	F	10th M	F	12th M	F	College M	F
Vomit	0	0	0	0	0	0	1	0	0	0	1	0	1	0	3	1
Weak	0	2	0	2	4	2	1	4	1	2	3	2	0	3	1	0
Weakness ..	0	0	1	0	0	0	1	2	1	1	0	0	0	0	0	0
Weary	0	0	3	0	0	0	0	0	0	0	0	0	0	0	0	0
Well	23	35	21	25	16	12	19	13	16	14	7	12	13	9	16	18
Wellness ..	0	4	2	0	0	0	0	0	1	0	0	0	0	0	0	0

147. SIT

Response Word	4th M	F	5th M	F	6th M	F	7th M	F	8th M	F	10th M	F	12th M	F	College M	F
Baby	3	1	0	4	1	1	1	2	1	0	0	0	0	0	1	0
Bend	0	0	0	0	0	0	0	2	0	0	0	0	0	0	0	0
Bit	2	1	0	0	0	0	0	1	0	0	0	0	0	0	0	0
Chair	40	49	40	48	31	47	35	39	24	39	47	43	26	26	38	45
Couch	0	1	0	1	0	2	0	0	0	1	1	0	1	0	0	0
Down	62	58	76	82	104	69	62	43	67	58	63	76	70	54	132	139
Fit	2	1	0	0	2	0	0	0	0	0	0	0	0	0	0	0
Get	0	0	2	1	0	0	0	0	0	0	0	0	0	0	0	0
Hear	0	0	2	0	1	0	0	0	0	0	0	0	0	0	0	0
Here	4	1	2	1	0	1	2	2	3	0	4	3	2	4	6	3
In	5	6	0	1	4	4	1	0	1	0	3	0	0	0	2	1
It	6	6	2	3	2	1	0	2	0	0	0	0	0	0	0	1
Lay	2	0	3	2	1	2	1	2	1	2	3	3	1	2	4	4
Lie	1	0	1	0	0	0	2	0	0	1	1	2	1	1	4	5
Longer....	0	0	0	0	0	0	0	0	0	1	2	0	0	0	0	1
Of	2	0	0	0	0	0	0	0	0	0	0	0	0	0	0	0
On	17	6	10	1	7	7	10	0	9	2	4	0	7	5	9	12
Out	0	0	0	0	0	0	0	0	1	0	0	0	0	0	0	2
Position ..	0	1	0	0	0	0	1	2	0	0	0	0	0	0	1	0
Quiet	0	0	0	1	0	0	0	0	0	0	0	0	2	0	0	0
Relax	0	1	0	0	2	1	2	0	1	0	0	3	0	2	4	4
Rest	0	1	2	1	0	3	1	2	2	2	5	2	8	4	13	7
Run	0	1	1	2	0	0	0	0	0	0	0	0	1	0	2	0
Sat	26	31	32	35	22	33	60	55	59	44	44	24	50	63	91	65
Seat	4	4	5	1	2	4	2	0	0	2	0	1	1	1	2	0
Set	1	5	7	4	2	4	1	3	6	3	11	4	12	12	7	11
Sit	0	0	0	0	2	0	0	0	0	0	0	0	0	0	0	0
Sitter	0	0	1	1	0	0	2	0	1	0	0	0	0	0	0	0
Sitting ...	1	5	4	0	3	0	1	0	1	0	2	1	1	0	1	0
Stand	25	30	20	35	25	42	39	64	44	60	34	64	28	41	109	148
Still	1	2	3	2	2	4	0	3	0	4	5	2	3	7	9	20
Stool	0	0	1	0	2	0	0	2	1	1	0	0	1	0	1	1
Stoop	0	0	0	0	0	0	1	1	2	1	0	1	0	0	0	0
Talk	0	0	0	0	0	0	0	1	2	0	0	0	0	0	2	0
The	2	1	1	0	0	0	0	0	0	0	0	0	0	0	0	0
There ...	2	6	1	2	4	1	2	1	5	4	6	5	9	4	6	3
Tight	0	1	0	0	0	0	0	2	1	0	1	0	2	0	9	1
Tired	0	0	0	1	0	0	1	0	0	0	1	2	0	1	2	2
Together ..	0	0	0	0	0	0	0	4	1	0	3	2	0	3	13	1
Up	3	3	1	0	1	2	2	0	2	3	1	2	1	2	1	1
Upon	0	0	0	0	0	2	1	1	0	0	0	0	0	0	1	0

Response Word	4th M	4th F	5th M	5th F	6th M	6th F	7th M	7th F	8th M	8th F	10th M	10th F	12th M	12th F	College M	College F
							SIT									
Walk . . .	0	1	0	1	0	0	1	0	1	1	0	1	0	1	1	4
Where . .	0	0	0	0	0	0	0	0	1	1	0	0	0	0	2	2
You	2	0	0	1	0	0	0	0	0	0	1	0	0	0	0	0
Your . . .	1	0	3	0	0	0	1	0	0	0	0	0	0	0	0	0
						148.	SLEEP									
Anger . . .	1	0	0	0	0	0	0	0	0	0	0	1	0	0	2	0
Awake . .	41	56	34	36	33	34	26	40	42	36	23	16	18	18	48	42
Awaken . .	1	0	0	1	1	1	0	3	2	0	0	0	0	1	2	1
Awoke . .	1	1	2	0	0	0	0	0	1	0	0	0	0	0	1	0
Bed	43	43	38	42	37	35	38	38	50	36	56	62	59	47	96	117
Close . . .	0	3	0	2	1	1	1	0	1	0	0	0	0	0	0	0
Comfort .	2	1	4	0	3	3	3	6	6	8	11	5	11	9	15	14
Comfortable	2	1	2	2	3	3	5	0	2	1	0	2	2	1	2	2
Dark . . .	1	0	2	3	4	1	6	2	1	0	0	0	4	0	3	6
Dead . . .	0	0	1	0	1	0	1	0	2	1	0	0	0	0	0	0
Deep . . .	0	4	0	1	2	4	3	1	2	1	1	0	2	0	13	6
Do	0	0	0	1	2	0	0	0	0	0	0	0	0	0	0	0
Doze . . .	0	0	0	1	3	1	1	1	1	1	1	1	2	0	5	1
Dream . .	3	5	6	8	11	16	20	17	12	19	13	13	14	12	26	37
Dreams . .	2	3	1	1	1	1	2	2	1	2	0	4	2	2	1	2
Drowsy . .	2	2	1	1	1	2	1	2	0	0	0	1	0	0	1	3
Eat	2	1	0	1	2	0	2	1	3	2	1	7	2	2	6	3
Eyes . . .	3	3	0	2	2	3	1	7	1	5	0	1	0	1	0	2
Fall	0	0	0	0	3	1	0	0	0	0	0	0	0	0	0	0
Fast . . .	0	1	0	1	2	1	0	1	0	0	0	0	0	0	0	1
Fun	0	1	1	0	0	0	0	0	0	1	2	0	1	1	2	1
Go	2	0	0	0	3	1	0	0	0	0	0	0	0	0	0	0
Good . . .	3	0	7	4	0	1	2	2	2	1	4	0	3	0	6	5
Hours . . .	0	0	0	0	0	0	0	0	0	0	0	0	0	1	1	2
Lamb . . .	1	0	0	0	0	0	0	0	0	0	0	0	0	0	0	2
Lamp . . .	0	0	2	0	0	0	0	0	0	1	0	0	0	0	0	0
Lay	1	3	2	3	1	3	4	0	2	1	3	1	0	0	0	0
Lazy . . .	1	0	1	1	0	2	3	4	2	2	1	1	1	0	3	1
Leap	0	0	2	0	0	0	0	1	0	0	1	0	0	1	0	0
Leep . . .	0	2	0	0	0	0	0	0	0	0	0	0	0	0	0	0
Lie	0	1	0	0	1	0	0	0	1	0	0	0	0	1	2	0
Light . . .	0	0	2	0	0	1	0	1	0	0	0	0	1	0	0	0
Long . . .	2	1	0	0	0	1	0	1	1	0	0	1	4	0	3	0
Morning . .	1	0	0	0	2	0	0	1	0	0	0	0	1	0	0	0
Nap	1	1	0	2	0	0	2	0	0	0	0	0	1	1	1	4
Nice . . .	2	2	1	0	3	3	1	2	1	2	7	2	2	6	6	6
Night . . .	27	24	23	20	18	28	19	20	9	26	11	22	10	13	19	23
Peace . . .	0	0	0	0	0	0	1	0	0	0	0	1	2	2	6	7
Peaceful .	0	0	0	1	0	0	1	0	0	0	0	1	0	2	1	2
Pillow . . .	0	1	5	5	2	2	0	2	7	3	4	3	4	1	10	14
Pleasant .	0	0	0	0	0	0	0	0	0	0	0	0	0	1	0	3
Quiet . . .	2	3	1	1	0	2	2	0	2	2	2	5	1	3	6	6
Quite . . .	0	1	0	0	1	0	0	1	0	0	2	0	0	0	0	0

Response Word	4th M	4th F	5th M	5th F	6th M	6th F	7th M	7th F	8th M	8th F	10th M	10th F	12th M	12th F	College M	College F

SLEEP

Response Word	4th M	4th F	5th M	5th F	6th M	6th F	7th M	7th F	8th M	8th F	10th M	10th F	12th M	12th F	College M	College F
Relax	0	0	0	0	0	1	2	3	0	0	3	1	3	2	7	4
Relaxing	0	0	1	0	0	0	0	2	1	1	1	1	1	0	1	0
Rest	2	11	17	25	26	20	26	20	21	20	28	18	29	24	62	42
Restful	0	0	0	0	0	2	0	0	0	0	0	0	0	1	0	1
Resting	1	0	0	0	1	0	0	2	1	1	0	0	0	0	0	0
Sheep	8	2	5	6	5	2	0	0	2	2	2	0	0	0	2	0
Sleeping	1	3	0	0	2	0	0	0	0	0	0	0	0	0	0	0
Sleepy	2	2	2	0	0	1	0	0	1	0	0	0	0	0	0	0
Slept	3	1	2	1	0	2	2	1	1	0	0	0	1	0	0	0
Slumber	0	2	2	2	3	2	2	1	3	4	1	0	1	2	6	7
Snooze	0	0	1	3	0	1	1	1	1	0	1	0	0	0	2	1
Snore	5	3	6	7	7	4	10	3	7	4	7	6	6	6	14	8
Snoring	2	0	0	0	0	0	0	0	0	0	0	0	0	0	0	0
Soft	2	2	1	1	3	1	2	1	0	0	4	0	0	0	4	7
Sound	3	3	5	1	3	5	0	2	0	0	4	3	3	3	9	8
Soundly	0	1	0	0	0	0	0	0	0	0	0	0	0	0	2	0
Study	0	0	0	0	0	0	0	0	0	0	0	0	0	0	0	2
Tight	0	0	1	1	2	0	0	0	1	1	0	2	6	1	4	1
Tire	0	0	0	0	1	0	0	0	0	1	0	2	0	0	0	0
Tired	15	14	20	21	13	23	24	24	21	33	21	47	18	50	38	55
Unconscious	1	0	0	0	1	0	3	0	1	0	1	0	1	1	0	0
Up	1	0	3	0	1	0	0	0	0	0	0	0	0	0	0	0
Wake	14	11	9	22	9	9	11	13	10	10	5	4	7	8	12	15
Wake up	2	0	1	0	0	2	1	0	1	0	1	0	0	0	0	0
Walk	1	0	1	0	0	2	0	1	0	4	0	1	3	3	3	1
Walker	0	0	0	0	0	0	0	0	0	0	0	0	0	2	0	1
Warm	0	1	2	0	1	0	0	0	0	0	1	0	0	0	3	4
Well	0	0	2	0	1	0	0	0	0	0	0	0	0	0	2	1
Wool	0	0	0	0	1	2	0	0	2	0	0	0	1	0	0	0

149. SLOW

Response Word	4th M	4th F	5th M	5th F	6th M	6th F	7th M	7th F	8th M	8th F	10th M	10th F	12th M	12th F	College M	College F
Bad	1	0	0	0	0	0	0	0	0	0	1	0	0	0	2	0
Behind	1	1	1	0	1	2	0	1	0	0	0	0	0	0	0	0
Boat	0	0	0	0	0	0	0	0	0	1	0	0	0	1	2	2
Buses	0	0	0	0	0	0	0	0	0	0	0	0	0	2	0	0
Car	3	2	4	0	8	4	5	1	7	3	20	15	12	7	19	8
Careful	0	0	1	0	1	0	0	0	0	0	0	2	0	1	2	1
Cars	0	0	0	0	0	0	0	1	1	0	1	2	0	0	1	0
Clumsy	0	0	0	0	2	0	0	1	0	0	0	0	0	0	0	0
Cold	3	0	1	0	1	2	3	0	1	2	2	0	0	1	0	0
Crawl	0	1	0	0	0	1	0	0	3	0	1	0	0	0	0	2
Creep	0	0	0	0	1	2	0	0	0	0	0	0	1	0	0	2
Donkey	0	0	1	1	0	0	0	2	0	0	1	0	0	0	0	0
Down	1	1	0	0	1	0	1	0	1	0	0	0	3	1	6	1
Drag	1	1	2	2	3	1	0	0	1	1	0	1	0	0	0	1
Dragging	0	0	0	0	0	0	2	0	1	0	0	0	0	0	0	0
Drive	0	0	0	0	1	1	0	0	0	1	0	1	1	1	3	2
Driver	0	0	0	0	1	0	0	0	0	0	1	1	0	1	3	1
Drivers	0	0	0	0	0	0	1	0	0	0	0	1	0	2	1	0

Response Word	4th M	4th F	5th M	5th F	6th M	6th F	7th M	7th F	8th M	8th F	10th M	10th F	12th M	12th F	College M	College F
								SLOW								
Driving	0	0	0	1	0	0	0	0	0	0	0	2	2	0	0	2
Dumb	0	0	0	0	0	0	0	1	0	0	0	1	0	1	1	2
Easy	0	1	0	0	1	1	2	1	1	0	4	2	1	1	1	0
Fast	122	130	121	137	130	126	142	132	158	142	132	135	159	157	307	327
Fat	0	0	0	0	1	1	0	1	1	0	1	0	2	0	2	1
Go	3	2	3	3	2	3	2	1	1	0	1	1	0	0	1	0
Hard	1	1	1	2	3	0	0	1	0	0	0	0	0	0	0	1
How	1	0	0	0	0	0	2	0	0	0	0	0	0	0	0	0
Hurry	0	0	0	1	0	1	0	0	0	0	0	2	0	0	0	2
Ice	2	0	3	0	0	0	1	0	0	0	1	0	0	1	0	1
Late	0	0	1	2	0	1	0	0	0	1	0	2	0	0	1	0
Lazy	1	1	0	1	1	3	2	3	1	1	2	4	1	3	1	2
Little	0	2	0	0	0	0	0	0	0	0	0	0	0	0	0	0
Long	1	4	4	0	0	5	0	2	1	1	1	0	0	0	0	0
Low	1	2	2	0	1	0	0	0	0	0	0	0	0	0	0	0
March	2	0	0	0	0	0	0	0	0	1	0	0	0	0	0	0
Me	0	1	0	0	1	2	0	1	0	1	0	1	2	4	2	5
Molasses	0	0	0	0	0	0	0	0	0	1	0	0	2	2	0	2
Move	4	1	2	3	4	4	2	1	2	0	1	1	1	1	0	1
Moving	0	0	2	1	3	0	1	0	0	0	0	0	0	0	1	1
Mule	0	0	0	0	0	0	0	0	0	2	0	0	0	0	0	0
No	2	0	0	0	0	0	0	0	0	0	0	0	0	0	0	0
Not fast	7	1	5	1	5	2	3	4	3	0	1	0	0	0	0	0
Old	0	0	1	0	0	0	0	0	0	0	0	1	1	1	1	3
Pause	0	0	0	0	0	0	0	2	0	0	0	0	0	0	0	1
People	0	1	0	0	0	2	0	0	0	2	0	2	0	0	0	0
Poke	2	5	1	3	1	2	0	2	0	0	0	0	0	0	3	1
Pokey	6	9	6	10	5	10	4	4	0	6	0	7	0	2	1	7
Quick	0	0	0	0	0	0	1	4	0	2	1	0	1	2	2	4
Rain	1	2	0	1	1	1	1	2	2	1	1	0	0	0	0	0
Road	0	0	0	0	0	0	0	0	0	0	0	0	0	0	2	0
Run	1	1	1	3	4	1	1	1	1	1	0	1	2	1	4	0
Running	0	1	1	0	0	0	0	3	0	1	0	0	0	0	1	0
School	0	0	0	0	1	0	1	1	0	0	0	0	0	2	0	1
Short	2	1	1	1	0	0	0	1	0	0	0	1	0	0	0	0
Sign	0	3	0	0	0	2	2	2	1	2	0	1	1	2	12	7
Slowly	2	1	1	0	0	1	0	0	0	0	0	1	0	1	0	0
Sluggish	0	0	0	0	1	0	2	0	0	0	0	0	0	0	1	1
Snail	0	1	0	1	4	8	4	3	1	6	5	4	3	3	4	7
Snow	2	2	0	0	0	0	0	0	0	0	3	0	1	0	0	0
Speed	2	0	2	0	2	0	2	3	2	0	2	0	4	3	4	12
Start	0	0	0	1	1	0	0	0	0	0	0	0	1	0	3	1
Steps	0	0	0	0	0	0	0	0	0	2	1	0	0	0	0	0
Stop	24	5	12	13	11	10	7	4	4	4	13	4	7	8	8	12
Stupid	0	0	0	0	0	0	0	0	0	0	0	1	0	0	1	2
Swift	0	0	0	0	0	0	0	2	0	0	1	0	0	0	0	0
Time	0	0	3	2	1	1	1	2	0	0	1	2	0	2	0	0
Tired	1	2	1	2	0	2	0	2	0	0	1	1	0	1	3	0
Traffic	0	0	1	1	0	1	0	1	0	2	1	5	4	3	4	9

Response Word	4th		5th		6th		7th		8th		10th		12th		College	
	M	F	M	F	M	F	M	F	M	F	M	F	M	F	M	F

SLOW

Response Word	M	F	M	F	M	F	M	F	M	F	M	F	M	F	M	F
Train ...	0	0	0	0	0	0	0	0	1	0	0	0	0	2	3	1
Trot ...	0	0	0	2	1	0	0	0	0	0	0	0	0	0	0	0
Turtle ..	9	12	13	11	5	14	24	27	16	33	13	22	8	10	18	18
Walk ...	6	14	12	15	5	11	5	4	6	6	6	5	3	3	10	9
Walking ..	0	5	0	1	0	1	1	1	2	2	0	0	0	1	1	1
White ...	0	0	1	0	2	0	1	0	0	1	1	0	0	1	2	0
Work ...	0	0	2	0	2	0	0	0	0	0	0	0	1	0	0	0

150. SLOWLY

Response Word	M	F	M	F	M	F	M	F	M	F	M	F	M	F	M	F
And	3	0	0	0	0	0	0	0	0	0	1	0	0	0	0	0
But	0	0	2	0	0	2	0	0	0	0	0	0	0	1	5	0
By	0	1	0	0	0	0	0	0	0	0	0	0	2	0	1	0
Car	1	0	0	2	2	0	2	1	1	0	2	3	0	1	4	2
Clumsy ..	0	0	0	0	0	0	2	0	0	0	0	0	0	0	1	0
Come ...	2	1	1	2	1	0	2	1	2	0	0	2	2	0	3	3
Crawl ...	0	0	1	1	0	0	1	1	0	0	1	0	1	1	3	6
Creep ...	0	2	0	0	0	0	0	0	0	0	1	2	0	1	6	3
Down ...	5	0	4	2	3	3	3	0	1	0	2	1	3	1	3	0
Drag ...	0	0	0	0	0	1	3	0	0	0	1	0	1	0	1	1
Drive ...	0	0	0	0	0	0	0	0	0	0	1	0	2	4	4	1
Easy ...	0	0	0	0	0	0	0	0	1	0	1	1	0	0	1	2
Fast	80	95	98	87	93	103	98	88	99	114	86	80	87	91	162	185
Faster ..	17	34	12	30	14	33	36	52	45	59	36	54	34	49	61	94
Fastly ...	6	6	3	3	2	3	6	8	10	3	3	1	1	4	9	4
Go	3	1	3	2	5	2	3	4	4	1	1	1	2	1	3	4
Going ...	1	0	3	0	0	0	0	0	0	0	0	1	0	1	0	0
He	2	0	0	1	3	2	0	0	0	0	0	0	0	0	2	0
Here ...	2	0	0	0	0	0	1	0	0	0	0	0	0	0	0	0
In	0	0	0	0	3	0	0	0	0	0	0	0	0	0	1	0
Jump ...	5	0	9	3	4	2	1	8	9	4	7	3	6	1	15	4
Jumped ..	0	0	0	0	0	0	0	0	1	1	0	1	0	0	2	0
Lazy	0	0	0	0	0	1	0	1	0	0	0	0	0	0	2	1
Less ...	0	0	0	0	0	0	2	0	0	0	0	0	0	0	0	0
Let	0	0	0	0	0	0	0	0	0	0	0	0	0	0	0	2
Me	2	0	2	0	3	0	0	0	0	0	1	1	0	0	0	0
Move ...	2	1	2	1	0	2	0	0	0	1	2	2	2	0	9	8
Movement .	0	0	0	2	0	0	0	0	0	0	2	0	0	0	0	0
Not	4	0	0	0	0	0	0	0	0	0	0	0	0	0	0	0
Not fast ..	1	0	0	0	2	1	1	0	0	1	0	0	1	0	0	0
Now	1	3	1	2	6	1	1	0	2	0	3	1	1	1	3	1
Over ...	1	1	0	1	1	2	0	0	1	0	0	0	1	0	1	0
Please ..	0	0	2	0	0	0	0	0	1	0	0	0	1	0	1	1
Poke	0	1	2	0	0	2	0	0	0	0	0	0	0	0	1	0
Pokey ...	1	4	1	3	3	5	1	1	0	0	0	0	0	0	0	1
Quick ...	1	0	0	0	1	0	2	3	0	2	0	2	2	2	2	2
Quicker ..	0	0	0	0	0	0	0	0	1	0	0	0	0	0	0	2
Quickly ..	1	0	0	2	1	1	4	8	7	5	9	13	11	17	42	60
Quietly ..	0	1	0	0	0	1	0	1	0	0	1	0	0	0	0	2
Ran	0	0	1	0	0	1	0	1	0	1	1	1	0	0	2	0

Response Word	4th M	4th F	5th M	5th F	6th M	6th F	7th M	7th F	8th M	8th F	10th M	10th F	12th M	12th F	College M	College F

SLOWLY

Response Word	4th M	4th F	5th M	5th F	6th M	6th F	7th M	7th F	8th M	8th F	10th M	10th F	12th M	12th F	College M	College F
Rapidly	0	0	0	0	0	0	1	2	0	1	0	0	0	0	6	3
Run	2	1	1	5	1	3	0	2	5	3	7	2	3	8	10	1
Sign	0	0	0	0	0	0	0	1	0	1	0	1	0	2	0	0
Silent	0	1	0	0	0	0	0	0	0	0	0	2	0	0	0	0
Slow	36	37	38	30	30	36	19	21	16	13	15	10	5	7	23	10
Slower	5	3	3	2	2	3	2	4	3	2	1	1	7	2	4	1
Sluggish	0	0	0	0	0	0	0	0	0	0	0	0	0	0	2	1
Snail	0	0	2	1	0	0	0	1	1	2	3	1	2	2	1	2
Snow	0	1	0	0	0	2	0	0	0	0	0	0	0	0	1	0
Softly	0	0	0	0	0	0	2	1	0	0	0	2	1	0	0	1
Speed	0	1	2	0	0	0	1	0	0	0	2	0	1	0	3	2
Speedily	0	0	0	0	1	0	0	0	0	0	2	0	2	0	0	2
Stop	4	1	6	2	3	2	6	0	1	1	5	0	2	4	4	5
Surely	0	0	1	0	0	1	0	2	1	0	1	1	2	0	2	1
Swift	0	0	1	0	0	0	2	0	0	0	0	1	0	0	0	1
Swiftly	0	0	0	1	0	1	1	3	1	0	0	1	0	2	4	3
Than	0	0	0	1	1	0	0	0	0	0	0	0	2	0	0	1
The	0	0	0	0	2	0	0	0	0	0	0	0	0	0	0	0
Time	0	0	0	0	0	0	0	0	0	0	0	1	2	0	1	0
Tired	1	1	0	1	0	0	1	0	0	0	0	2	0	3	2	2
Traffic	0	0	0	0	0	0	0	0	0	0	0	2	1	0	0	0
Trot	2	0	0	0	0	0	0	0	0	0	0	0	0	0	1	0
Turtle	4	5	2	3	4	6	7	9	2	6	6	7	9	3	3	2
Up	5	1	3	3	4	1	3	1	2	2	3	2	1	5	5	1
Walk	5	13	8	19	14	10	7	8	5	5	11	16	8	9	25	22
Walking	0	3	0	0	0	0	0	0	2	1	1	0	2	2	2	0
We	3	0	2	2	1	0	0	1	1	1	4	0	0	0	2	0
Went	0	0	0	0	0	0	2	0	1	0	1	0	0	0	0	0
Word	0	0	1	0	2	0	0	0	0	0	0	0	0	0	0	0
Worm	0	0	0	0	0	0	0	0	0	0	0	0	0	0	0	2

151. SMOOTH

Response Word	4th M	4th F	5th M	5th F	6th M	6th F	7th M	7th F	8th M	8th F	10th M	10th F	12th M	12th F	College M	College F
Bed	0	3	0	0	1	1	0	0	0	1	1	0	0	0	1	0
Board	1	1	0	2	2	0	0	0	1	0	0	0	2	1	0	2
Bumpy	9	7	4	8	3	3	3	3	0	4	1	1	1	0	1	3
Butter	0	1	0	1	0	0	1	0	2	2	4	0	1	2	3	1
Car	1	0	0	0	2	0	0	0	0	0	4	1	2	0	1	2
Clean	0	0	1	0	2	0	2	2	1	0	1	1	0	1	2	0
Cloth	1	0	2	0	0	0	1	0	1	0	0	0	1	1	1	2
Coarse	0	0	0	0	0	0	1	1	1	0	1	1	1	1	2	0
Cold	1	0	0	0	0	0	0	0	0	0	0	0	0	0	1	2
Cream	0	0	0	0	0	2	0	1	1	1	1	3	2	2	2	5
Creamy	6	1	4	3	11	2	7	7	8	6	6	2	5	3	5	5
Desk	3	1	0	0	0	1	0	0	0	0	1	4	0	1	0	0
Easy	2	1	2	1	2	1	1	0	0	1	3	2	1	3	4	0
Even	0	2	2	0	2	2	6	3	4	0	2	1	1	0	3	6
Face	0	0	0	0	1	0	1	0	1	3	1	2	0	1	1	1
Fast	0	0	1	0	2	0	1	1	0	0	1	0	0	0	1	1
Fine	0	0	0	0	0	1	0	1	1	0	3	1	0	0	1	1

Response Word	4th M	4th F	5th M	5th F	6th M	6th F	7th M	7th F	8th M	8th F	10th M	10th F	12th M	12th F	College M	College F

SMOOTH

Response Word	4th M	4th F	5th M	5th F	6th M	6th F	7th M	7th F	8th M	8th F	10th M	10th F	12th M	12th F	College M	College F
Finish	0	0	0	0	0	0	1	0	0	0	0	0	0	0	2	0
Flat	19	11	13	9	26	17	10	3	6	2	4	3	1	0	8	7
Floor	0	2	2	1	0	0	0	0	0	1	0	0	0	0	1	0
Flush	0	0	0	0	0	0	6	0	0	0	0	0	0	0	0	0
Frosting . .	0	0	0	0	0	0	0	0	0	2	0	0	0	0	0	0
Fur	0	0	1	1	0	0	0	0	0	0	0	0	0	0	0	3
Gentle . . .	1	0	0	0	2	0	0	1	0	1	0	0	1	1	0	0
Glass	0	1	0	2	3	2	8	3	7	5	5	4	6	1	13	8
Good	0	1	1	0	2	0	0	0	0	0	0	0	1	0	0	0
Hair	1	1	1	0	0	0	0	2	2	2	0	2	2	2	2	3
Hand	0	4	3	3	2	1	1	3	0	4	0	1	1	4	9	21
Hands . . .	0	0	0	1	0	0	0	0	0	1	0	3	0	2	1	2
Hard . . .	18	32	20	24	27	15	11	17	26	22	24	13	19	15	61	47
Highway . .	1	0	0	1	0	0	0	0	0	0	0	0	2	0	1	1
Ice	0	1	0	1	0	2	1	1	1	1	1	2	2	3	3	6
Ice cream . .	0	0	0	0	0	0	0	0	1	1	0	1	0	0	0	2
Land	0	0	0	0	2	0	0	0	1	0	0	0	0	0	1	0
Level	2	0	5	1	2	2	0	2	0	2	1	0	0	0	2	3
Light	2	0	2	0	0	0	0	0	0	0	2	0	1	2	0	1
Long . . .	1	4	1	2	0	0	0	2	0	0	0	1	0	0	1	1
Lumpy . . .	1	0	0	0	0	2	0	1	1	0	0	0	0	0	0	0
Mellow . . .	0	0	0	0	0	0	0	0	0	0	0	0	0	0	0	2
Metal	0	0	0	0	0	1	1	0	0	1	0	1	0	0	3	0
Moo	0	0	2	1	0	0	0	0	0	0	0	0	0	0	0	0
Music . . .	0	0	0	0	0	0	0	0	0	0	0	2	0	1	0	0
Nice	4	7	9	6	3	13	4	5	4	0	3	2	2	2	1	5
Not rough . .	2	0	0	0	0	0	1	0	0	0	0	0	0	0	0	0
Paper	1	1	1	1	0	1	2	1	1	1	0	2	0	1	2	2
Peanut butter	0	1	0	1	1	1	0	1	3	0	2	1	1	0	2	2
Plain	1	0	0	0	0	0	0	0	0	0	0	1	0	2	0	0
Plane	1	0	0	0	0	1	2	0	0	0	0	0	0	0	2	0
River	0	0	0	0	0	0	0	0	0	0	0	2	0	0	0	0
Road . . .	0	3	1	2	4	0	0	1	1	0	1	2	3	1	2	3
Roof	0	1	0	1	2	0	1	0	0	0	0	0	0	0	0	0
Rough	58	23	41	44	39	34	81	61	87	77	53	63	74	70	132	111
Round	0	0	1	0	1	0	0	1	0	0	2	1	0	0	4	2
Sand	0	1	0	0	0	0	0	0	0	0	0	0	0	3	0	1
Sandpaper .	0	0	0	0	0	0	2	0	0	0	0	0	2	0	0	0
Satin	1	0	0	0	0	0	1	0	0	1	0	0	0	1	1	8
Sharp	0	0	1	0	0	1	0	2	0	0	2	1	2	0	1	0
Shiny	2	0	0	1	1	3	2	3	0	4	3	5	1	1	4	3
Short	1	0	0	0	0	0	2	0	0	0	0	0	0	0	0	0
Silk	2	5	2	4	0	3	1	12	3	7	6	7	7	2	25	28
Silky	0	0	0	0	2	1	0	1	1	0	0	0	1	1	1	4
Skin	1	1	0	0	1	0	4	0	2	3	1	3	5	7	7	6
Sleek	0	0	0	0	0	0	1	1	0	1	0	0	0	2	1	0
Slippery . .	0	1	0	0	1	2	1	2	0	1	1	0	0	3	1	1

Response Word	4th M	F	5th M	F	6th M	F	7th M	F	8th M	F	10th M	F	12th M	F	College M	F

SMOOTH

Response Word	4th M	F	5th M	F	6th M	F	7th M	F	8th M	F	10th M	F	12th M	F	College M	F
Slow	0	0	0	0	0	0	1	0	0	0	0	0	0	0	0	2
Soft	63	90	62	94	62	94	45	68	42	52	68	70	66	71	116	121
Stone ...	0	0	0	0	0	0	0	0	0	1	0	0	0	1	1	2
Straight ..	4	9	7	5	3	7	1	2	0	2	0	2	0	1	1	2
Surface ...	1	0	1	0	0	0	1	1	0	0	0	1	1	1	3	0
Table ...	2	0	5	4	2	3	4	4	2	6	5	1	3	5	5	8
Table top .	0	0	0	0	0	0	0	0	0	0	0	0	0	0	3	1
Thick ...	0	0	0	0	0	0	0	1	2	0	0	0	0	0	0	0
Tough ..	0	0	0	1	0	0	0	1	0	0	2	0	0	1	0	0
Velvet ...	0	0	0	0	0	2	2	0	0	1	1	4	2	1	3	3
Warm ...	0	0	0	0	0	0	0	0	1	0	0	0	0	1	2	0
Water ...	0	0	0	0	0	2	2	1	2	2	2	1	3	1	2	3
Wood ...	1	0	5	0	0	0	7	0	1	0	1	2	0	0	1	0
Wrinkle ..	0	0	0	0	0	2	0	0	0	0	0	1	0	0	0	0

152. SO

Response Word	4th M	F	5th M	F	6th M	F	7th M	F	8th M	F	10th M	F	12th M	F	College M	F
A	1	0	1	3	1	2	0	0	0	0	0	0	0	0	0	0
Ah	0	2	2	1	1	0	5	1	7	2	6	3	4	2	7	1
Aha	0	0	0	0	0	2	0	0	0	0	0	0	0	0	0	0
Ah so ...	0	0	0	0	0	0	0	2	0	0	0	0	0	0	0	0
Also ...	1	0	0	1	1	1	2	5	1	1	1	1	2	6	3	2
Am	0	1	3	3	3	1	1	1	1	0	0	0	1	1	0	0
And	2	0	2	3	0	4	1	4	3	2	1	4	3	2	7	7
Anyway ..	0	1	2	1	1	0	0	1	0	0	1	1	0	0	0	0
Are	0	0	0	1	1	1	0	2	0	0	1	0	0	2	2	1
As	1	2	2	1	0	4	3	2	2	2	1	9	0	2	3	19
At	2	0	0	0	0	0	1	0	0	0	0	0	1	0	0	0
Be	1	2	0	0	0	1	2	0	0	1	1	0	2	1	3	6
Because .	2	0	2	0	0	0	2	2	2	4	2	7	4	8	4	11
Big	2	0	0	1	0	1	1	0	0	1	3	1	1	3	2	1
Blow ...	1	0	0	0	3	0	1	0	0	0	0	0	0	1	0	1
But	0	1	2	0	1	2	0	0	1	2	0	2	1	0	3	3
Buttons ..	0	0	1	0	1	0	0	0	2	0	0	0	2	0	1	0
Can	1	3	0	3	3	2	0	1	0	0	0	1	0	1	0	1
Close ...	0	2	1	0	0	1	0	1	1	1	6	1	2	1	3	0
Cloth ...	0	0	0	0	0	0	1	0	0	0	2	1	1	0	0	0
Come ...	1	1	0	2	0	0	0	0	0	0	1	1	1	0	0	0
Condition .	0	0	0	0	0	0	0	0	0	0	0	0	0	0	0	2
Did	3	1	0	1	0	0	0	0	0	0	0	0	0	1	0	0
Do	2	6	3	3	2	3	3	2	1	0	4	4	1	3	2	6
Even ...	0	0	0	0	0	1	0	0	0	0	1	2	0	0	0	0
Far	3	3	5	5	5	3	8	5	6	10	2	6	6	6	13	23
Fast ...	3	5	3	3	2	2	1	2	2	0	2	1	9	2	4	1
Fine	0	0	0	0	1	0	1	0	0	1	0	0	2	1	1	0
For	0	1	1	1	0	0	0	1	1	2	0	1	1	0	1	3
Forth ...	0	0	0	0	0	0	0	0	2	0	0	0	0	1	1	3
Fun	0	1	0	1	0	0	1	0	1	0	2	0	0	0	0	0
Girl	0	0	0	0	0	2	0	0	0	0	0	0	0	0	0	0
Go	0	3	0	3	1	2	3	2	5	4	2	2	2	1	4	3

Response Word	4th		5th		6th		7th		8th		10th		12th		College	
	M	F	M	F	M	F	M	F	M	F	M	F	M	F	M	F

SO

Response Word	4th M	F	5th M	F	6th M	F	7th M	F	8th M	F	10th M	F	12th M	F	College M	F
Good	5	4	3	1	1	2	3	1	2	3	2	1	1	1	4	3
Hard	0	0	0	1	2	0	1	0	0	0	0	1	0	0	0	0
He	5	4	4	3	2	5	3	2	3	1	5	1	3	0	1	0
Here	2	1	0	1	1	1	0	1	0	2	1	0	0	1	0	1
Him	3	1	3	0	0	0	0	0	1	0	0	0	0	0	0	0
Ho	3	1	2	1	1	2	1	1	1	0	0	0	0	0	2	0
How	2	1	1	1	1	0	2	0	0	2	0	1	0	2	1	1
I	8	9	8	5	6	2	6	3	3	1	4	2	1	0	4	1
If	2	1	3	3	2	4	3	2	3	5	3	6	6	8	12	13
I'm	0	0	0	0	2	0	0	0	0	0	0	0	0	0	0	0
In	0	0	0	0	0	0	0	2	1	0	0	0	0	0	0	0
Is	2	4	5	7	3	6	3	4	2	3	1	3	8	8	10	11
It	7	12	10	10	12	6	4	3	7	5	2	6	2	1	8	1
Know	0	1	0	0	0	2	0	0	1	0	0	0	0	0	0	0
Long	0	2	2	1	0	2	3	1	1	5	2	0	2	1	1	0
Low	0	0	0	1	2	0	0	1	0	0	0	0	0	0	0	0
Many	0	1	3	3	1	1	4	4	2	4	4	2	6	7	3	7
Maybe	1	1	0	0	0	1	1	0	0	0	2	2	0	0	1	0
Me	10	2	12	3	4	4	6	1	0	1	2	1	1	0	0	1
Mold	2	0	1	0	0	0	0	0	0	0	0	0	0	0	0	0
Much	2	3	0	2	4	1	6	3	2	3	5	4	5	3	11	9
Near	0	0	0	0	1	0	1	2	1	0	2	0	1	1	1	0
Needle	1	2	1	1	2	3	1	0	1	0	3	3	0	1	0	0
Nice	1	0	1	0	2	0	2	0	0	3	2	0	0	2	0	0
No	11	9	4	6	3	4	4	9	3	3	4	1	1	2	2	3
Not	0	0	1	1	2	0	4	0	2	0	0	1	2	0	2	0
Now	2	3	5	3	9	4	3	8	3	3	4	7	5	3	9	11
Oh	5	2	3	1	4	2	0	1	0	1	2	3	0	1	4	4
OK	0	0	0	3	0	0	0	0	0	0	0	1	0	0	1	0
On	0	5	4	0	3	2	3	4	3	2	5	5	1	5	8	6
One	0	2	0	0	0	0	0	0	0	0	0	0	0	0	0	0
Question	0	0	0	0	0	0	1	0	0	0	1	1	1	2	5	2
Rare	0	0	0	0	0	0	0	0	0	0	2	0	1	0	0	0
Really	1	0	0	0	0	0	0	1	0	0	0	0	2	0	0	1
Reason	0	0	1	1	1	0	0	1	0	2	0	0	1	0	4	1
Result	0	0	0	0	0	0	0	0	0	0	0	0	0	0	2	0
Sad	0	0	0	2	0	0	0	0	0	0	0	0	0	0	0	0
Sat	0	0	1	0	0	0	0	0	0	0	0	0	0	0	2	1
Saw	0	0	0	0	0	1	2	4	2	2	3	0	1	0	2	0
Say	1	1	1	1	0	0	2	0	0	1	0	0	0	0	0	0
See	1	2	4	2	1	4	5	2	3	3	4	0	0	1	0	5
Sew	4	7	10	17	8	27	9	18	7	18	6	9	12	12	12	13
Sewing	1	0	0	0	0	1	0	0	0	2	0	1	0	0	0	0
She	0	0	0	2	1	1	0	2	0	0	0	0	1	1	0	1
Since	0	0	1	0	0	0	0	0	0	0	0	0	0	0	0	2
Sit	1	2	0	0	0	1	0	0	1	0	0	0	0	0	1	1
Slow	1	2	2	0	2	0	1	0	1	2	1	0	0	2	1	0
Small	2	0	0	0	0	0	0	0	0	0	0	0	0	0	0	0
So	1	0	0	0	0	4	0	0	0	0	0	0	0	0	0	0

Response Word	4th M	F	5th M	F	6th M	F	7th M	F	8th M	F	10th M	F	12th M	F	College M	F

SO

Response Word	4th M	F	5th M	F	6th M	F	7th M	F	8th M	F	10th M	F	12th M	F	College M	F
Soft	0	0	0	0	0	0	0	0	1	0	0	0	0	1	0	2
Sole	1	0	0	0	0	1	0	0	2	0	0	0	0	0	0	0
Some	5	0	4	2	0	1	4	3	0	6	0	1	2	0	2	2
Son	1	0	0	0	0	0	0	0	2	0	0	0	0	0	0	0
Soo	1	2	0	1	1	1	2	1	0	0	0	0	0	0	1	0
Soon	3	4	2	14	7	4	4	11	7	3	3	3	8	4	2	3
Sow	1	0	1	1	1	4	3	0	3	1	4	0	2	0	0	0
So what	0	0	1	0	0	1	0	0	3	1	0	0	0	0	0	0
Still	0	0	0	0	0	0	0	0	0	0	0	1	0	0	0	2
That	6	2	4	4	3	4	6	3	1	4	4	6	2	9	15	29
The	8	5	4	5	8	0	4	2	1	1	1	1	2	1	2	2
Then	2	0	2	2	2	4	0	1	1	5	4	3	3	2	12	18
There	2	4	3	7	9	3	1	10	1	5	8	10	5	6	17	23
Therefore	0	0	1	0	0	0	0	3	1	1	1	1	1	7	10	12
They	2	2	2	1	2	1	2	2	1	0	1	1	1	1	3	0
This	0	0	0	0	0	0	0	1	0	0	0	1	0	1	1	3
Thread	0	0	1	0	0	1	0	1	0	1	1	1	0	0	2	0
Thus	0	0	0	0	0	0	0	0	0	0	0	0	0	1	10	6
To	1	2	4	5	1	5	3	0	0	2	2	1	2	1	4	5
Too	0	0	0	0	0	0	0	0	0	0	0	2	0	0	0	2
Us	0	1	1	0	2	0	0	0	0	1	0	0	0	0	0	0
Very	0	0	0	1	0	0	0	0	1	0	2	1	1	0	1	1
Was	0	1	0	0	2	0	2	0	1	0	0	1	0	0	7	3
We	7	3	3	1	1	4	1	2	7	2	4	1	0	0	3	3
Well	0	1	0	4	1	1	1	1	2	3	1	3	1	3	0	2
What	28	25	22	24	42	31	39	49	56	64	54	60	50	57	156	130
When	0	3	0	2	0	2	3	0	3	3	1	1	1	1	1	3
Who	1	0	0	1	4	0	0	0	1	0	0	0	0	0	1	0
Why	4	1	1	2	3	4	8	4	2	3	3	5	2	3	8	10
Will	0	3	0	1	0	0	1	0	0	0	0	2	1	0	1	0
Word	2	3	5	4	2	2	0	0	0	0	0	0	0	3	0	0
Yes	1	1	0	1	0	0	1	0	2	1	1	0	0	1	2	4
You	16	17	18	8	11	8	4	6	8	7	7	5	12	4	11	1

153.   SOFT

Response Word	4th M	F	5th M	F	6th M	F	7th M	F	8th M	F	10th M	F	12th M	F	College M	F
Baby	0	0	1	0	0	0	0	0	0	0	0	0	1	2	0	2
Ball	0	0	0	0	0	0	2	0	0	0	0	0	0	0	0	0
Bed	9	10	4	7	11	7	13	9	15	6	19	5	11	9	27	13
Blanket	1	2	1	1	2	0	1	1	1	2	1	5	2	3	0	3
Blue	0	0	0	0	0	1	0	0	0	1	1	2	0	0	0	2
Bounce	0	2	0	0	0	2	1	0	0	0	0	0	0	0	0	0
Bouncy	2	1	2	0	1	0	1	0	0	0	0	0	0	0	0	0
Bunny	0	0	0	0	0	1	0	0	0	0	0	0	0	0	0	2
Cat	0	0	1	3	0	1	0	1	0	2	1	1	0	1	2	4
Chair	1	0	1	1	0	3	0	0	0	0	2	3	1	1	3	2
Cloth	2	0	2	0	0	3	0	0	0	0	1	0	1	1	1	1
Comfort	1	0	0	1	3	1	2	0	1	0	1	1	0	0	1	0
Comfortable	8	7	10	10	9	15	8	4	5	2	3	6	0	2	1	7

Response Word	4th M	4th F	5th M	5th F	6th M	6th F	7th M	7th F	8th M	8th F	10th M	10th F	12th M	12th F	College M	College F

SOFT

Response Word	4th M	4th F	5th M	5th F	6th M	6th F	7th M	7th F	8th M	8th F	10th M	10th F	12th M	12th F	College M	College F
Cotton	9	10	9	9	7	4	10	13	4	9	9	10	5	8	13	15
Couch	0	0	0	0	0	0	1	0	1	0	2	0	3	1	2	0
Cozy	2	4	1	2	1	4	1	0	0	1	0	0	0	1	0	0
Cuddly	0	0	1	3	1	4	1	1	0	1	0	3	0	1	3	7
Cushion	1	3	0	2	1	0	3	2	2	2	4	0	3	3	1	1
Dark	0	0	0	0	0	1	0	2	0	0	0	1	1	0	0	1
Deep	2	0	0	0	0	1	0	0	0	2	1	0	0	0	0	3
Drink	0	0	0	0	0	0	0	0	0	0	0	0	2	0	0	0
Earth	0	0	0	0	0	0	0	0	0	0	0	0	2	0	1	0
Easy	1	0	3	0	2	0	1	1	1	0	1	1	1	1	5	1
Egg	0	0	0	0	0	0	0	0	0	1	0	0	0	0	2	1
Feather	0	1	2	1	1	2	1	4	2	2	3	2	2	1	3	6
Feathers	1	6	1	2	1	1	2	3	5	4	0	3	0	2	3	3
Feathery	0	0	0	0	1	2	0	0	0	0	0	0	0	1	0	0
Feel	1	1	0	3	2	0	0	0	0	0	0	0	1	0	0	0
Fluffy	10	9	7	11	12	17	11	9	7	7	4	7	1	5	7	9
Fur	1	2	1	6	4	2	4	2	1	0	3	5	3	3	6	13
Furry	0	1	2	1	0	3	0	1	0	0	0	2	1	1	3	8
Fuzzy	0	2	0	1	1	0	0	1	1	1	2	1	0	2	1	2
Gentle	1	2	1	2	2	1	0	3	0	1	1	0	3	3	0	4
Girl	0	0	0	0	1	0	0	0	0	0	1	0	3	0	1	0
Good	2	0	4	1	0	1	0	1	0	0	0	0	1	0	0	0
Hair	0	0	0	0	0	1	0	0	0	0	1	1	1	2	6	2
Hand	0	2	1	0	0	0	0	0	0	1	1	0	0	0	0	0
Hard	87	82	77	81	81	56	94	67	104	83	77	56	85	75	168	136
Harsh	0	0	0	0	0	0	0	2	1	2	0	0	0	0	1	1
Hear	1	0	0	0	0	0	0	0	0	0	0	0	0	0	0	2
Heard	0	0	2	0	1	0	0	0	0	0	0	0	0	0	0	0
Heavy	0	0	3	1	0	2	1	7	5	3	0	4	0	4	2	6
Herd	0	0	2	0	0	0	0	0	0	0	0	0	0	0	0	0
High	0	0	0	0	0	2	0	0	0	0	1	0	0	0	0	2
Kitten	0	1	0	3	0	3	0	1	0	4	1	7	0	6	4	16
Light	30	13	18	18	10	26	14	14	11	13	24	18	17	14	34	28
Lights	0	0	0	0	0	0	0	0	0	0	0	0	0	0	2	0
Little	2	0	0	0	0	0	0	0	0	0	1	0	0	0	1	0
Loft	0	0	1	0	2	0	0	0	0	0	0	0	0	0	1	0
Loud	1	2	1	3	1	2	5	6	7	13	0	6	5	3	8	9
Lovely	1	0	0	2	0	0	2	0	1	0	0	1	0	0	0	1
Low	0	0	0	0	0	2	0	2	0	0	0	0	0	0	0	5
Mud	0	0	2	0	0	0	0	0	0	0	0	0	0	0	0	0
Mushy	0	0	0	0	0	0	0	0	0	3	0	0	0	0	0	0
Music	0	2	0	0	0	1	2	3	2	4	3	3	4	2	12	16
Nice	5	13	13	11	14	11	8	10	6	4	6	6	1	4	6	3
Not hard	3	0	0	0	0	0	1	0	1	0	0	0	0	0	0	0
Pillow	11	23	19	16	24	12	19	25	28	34	38	38	38	29	54	50
Pink	0	0	0	0	0	0	1	0	0	1	0	3	0	3	0	1
Plush	0	0	0	0	0	0	0	1	0	1	0	2	0	0	0	0
Pretty	0	0	0	1	0	4	0	2	0	0	0	1	0	1	1	1
Quiet	2	3	0	0	0	1	2	1	0	1	1	0	0	1	1	1

Response Word	4th M	4th F	5th M	5th F	6th M	6th F	7th M	7th F	8th M	8th F	10th M	10th F	12th M	12th F	College M	College F
							SOFT									
Rough ...	1	3	2	3	3	4	2	1	3	3	0	0	2	1	3	1
Round ...	0	0	0	0	0	0	0	0	0	0	1	0	0	0	0	2
Satin ...	0	0	0	0	0	0	2	1	0	1	0	1	0	1	0	0
Silk	0	0	2	1	0	0	2	2	1	1	1	1	4	3	2	4
Skin	0	0	0	0	0	0	0	0	1	0	0	1	0	2	1	3
Sleep ...	3	0	2	0	3	2	0	0	0	0	0	1	0	0	1	1
Smooth ..	8	14	7	13	7	12	8	13	6	5	7	11	5	14	15	19
Snow ...	1	0	0	1	0	0	0	0	0	0	0	3	0	1	3	1
Sofa	0	1	0	0	0	0	1	0	0	0	0	0	2	0	1	0
Sound ...	0	0	0	0	0	0	0	0	0	0	0	0	0	0	2	2
Sponge ..	2	0	1	0	2	0	0	0	3	0	0	0	1	0	0	0
Squishy ..	0	0	0	0	0	0	0	0	0	0	0	0	0	0	1	2
Strong ...	1	1	0	0	1	0	0	1	1	0	2	0	1	1	1	0
Sweater ..	0	0	0	0	0	0	0	0	0	1	0	3	0	2	2	2
Sweet ...	1	0	0	1	0	2	1	3	2	4	1	1	1	2	3	5
Tender ..	0	0	0	1	0	2	0	1	0	0	0	0	2	0	3	1
Tissue ..	0	0	0	0	0	0	0	0	0	0	0	0	1	0	2	0
Touch ...	0	0	0	0	1	0	0	2	0	0	1	1	2	0	5	3
Velvet ..	1	0	0	1	0	1	0	0	0	0	2	0	1	4	2	3
Warm ...	2	3	6	9	8	2	1	4	2	4	4	7	4	6	21	24
Water ...	0	0	0	0	0	0	0	0	1	0	1	0	1	0	3	1
White ...	1	0	1	1	1	0	0	0	1	3	2	0	1	1	2	3
Woman ..	0	0	0	0	0	0	0	0	0	0	0	0	2	0	0	0
Wool ...	0	0	0	0	0	0	0	2	0	0	0	1	0	0	1	0
Yellow ..	0	0	0	0	0	0	0	0	0	0	0	1	1	1	3	1
						154.	SOLDIER									
Air Force .	1	0	0	0	0	0	0	0	0	1	0	0	1	1	0	3
American .	0	0	0	0	0	0	0	0	2	1	0	0	0	0	0	0
Arm	2	3	0	0	4	0	0	1	1	0	2	0	2	0	1	0
Armed Forces .	0	0	0	0	0	0	0	1	0	0	0	0	0	2	0	0
Armor ...	0	0	0	0	1	0	2	2	0	0	0	0	1	0	0	0
Army ...	41	43	51	37	44	46	65	46	52	56	56	40	48	39	64	85
Attention .	1	0	0	1	0	1	3	0	0	0	0	0	0	1	0	0
Bad	0	0	0	2	0	0	0	0	0	0	0	0	1	0	1	0
Bang ...	0	0	1	0	0	0	0	0	2	0	0	0	0	0	0	0
Battle ..	0	0	0	1	1	0	1	1	0	0	3	0	0	0	1	2
Big	0	0	1	2	2	1	1	0	0	1	1	0	0	0	0	0
Blue ...	0	2	0	0	0	0	0	0	0	1	0	0	0	0	0	3
Boy	2	5	1	3	3	7	2	2	4	10	2	12	4	12	17	26
Boys ...	0	0	0	0	0	0	0	0	0	2	0	0	0	1	0	0
Brave ...	0	2	1	3	0	2	2	1	2	2	3	2	1	5	3	3
Brother ..	0	0	0	0	0	1	1	0	1	0	1	1	2	2	0	1
Brown ...	0	0	0	0	0	0	0	0	0	0	0	0	1	0	4	0
Captain ..	1	1	1	1	0	1	0	1	0	0	0	2	0	1	2	1
Citizen ..	1	0	0	2	2	1	3	2	7	1	2	0	1	2	4	0
Civilian ..	1	2	0	0	2	0	2	2	4	2	0	1	0	1	2	2
Cold	0	2	0	0	0	0	0	0	0	0	0	0	0	0	0	0

Response Word	4th M	4th F	5th M	5th F	6th M	6th F	7th M	7th F	8th M	8th F	10th M	10th F	12th M	12th F	College M	College F
						SOLDIER										
Command .	0	1	1	2	1	1	0	2	0	3	1	0	0	1	3	4
Country ..	0	0	0	0	0	0	0	0	0	0	1	0	0	2	3	0
Courage ..	0	0	0	0	0	0	0	0	0	0	0	0	0	0	3	2
Cute	0	0	0	0	0	0	0	1	0	1	0	3	0	0	0	1
Death ...	0	0	0	0	0	0	0	0	0	0	0	0	0	1	2	1
Don	0	0	0	0	0	0	0	0	0	0	0	0	0	0	0	2
Draft ...	0	0	0	0	0	0	0	0	1	0	0	0	0	0	2	0
Enemy ..	0	0	0	0	0	0	0	0	1	0	1	0	0	0	2	1
Fight ...	14	10	4	12	10	8	8	6	8	5	15	5	13	6	34	21
Fighter ..	9	2	7	1	3	3	8	2	4	1	4	1	7	3	6	0
Fighting ..	2	1	4	1	2	1	2	0	2	3	1	1	7	2	3	1
Foot	1	0	0	0	0	0	0	0	1	0	1	1	2	1	4	1
Fort	2	0	0	0	0	0	0	0	0	0	0	0	0	0	0	1
Fortune ..	0	0	0	0	0	1	0	0	1	0	0	1	0	0	5	1
Friend ..	0	0	1	0	0	0	0	0	0	1	0	0	0	0	2	0
Fun	0	0	1	0	0	1	0	0	2	0	0	0	1	0	0	0
General ..	3	0	0	0	3	0	2	1	2	3	2	0	0	0	2	0
GI	0	0	1	0	1	0	1	0	0	0	2	0	1	0	4	1
Girl	1	0	0	0	0	1	0	1	0	0	0	2	0	0	0	1
Good ...	2	3	6	0	1	2	1	0	0	1	0	2	0	2	2	0
Green ...	0	0	0	0	0	0	0	0	1	2	1	3	0	1	1	4
Guard ...	1	5	2	3	2	4	2	2	2	1	1	1	0	0	0	0
Gun	10	8	7	8	14	3	18	9	18	5	14	21	22	4	50	39
Guns ...	3	0	3	2	3	1	0	0	4	1	0	1	0	3	1	1
Handsome .	0	0	0	0	0	0	0	0	0	1	0	3	0	3	0	1
Hard ...	4	3	2	3	0	1	1	0	0	0	0	0	0	0	1	1
Head ...	1	1	1	0	2	0	0	0	0	0	0	0	0	0	0	0
Helmet ..	0	0	0	0	2	0	0	1	1	0	1	0	1	0	2	1
Hero ...	0	0	0	0	1	1	0	0	1	0	1	0	2	0	1	0
Infantry ..	0	0	0	0	0	0	0	0	2	0	1	1	0	0	0	1
Infantryman	0	0	1	0	0	0	0	0	2	0	0	0	0	0	0	0
Iron	2	0	0	0	0	0	0	0	1	0	1	0	0	0	0	0
Kill	0	0	0	0	0	0	0	0	1	0	0	0	0	0	2	0
Knife ...	0	2	1	0	0	0	0	0	0	1	0	0	0	0	1	1
Larry ...	0	0	0	0	0	0	0	0	0	1	0	0	0	0	0	2
Man	51	62	67	69	55	74	39	60	34	59	37	56	39	61	81	96
March ..	7	6	3	8	3	8	3	9	0	7	4	1	1	5	7	8
Marching .	0	2	1	2	3	1	0	0	1	1	0	1	1	1	1	1
Marine ..	0	0	2	0	1	0	1	1	6	2	3	2	5	2	11	3
Marines ..	0	0	0	2	0	0	0	0	0	2	1	0	1	0	0	0
Men	6	5	4	6	7	6	3	2	4	4	1	9	0	1	3	1
Military ..	0	0	0	1	0	1	2	2	1	1	2	4	0	2	5	1
Navy ...	3	1	0	3	1	3	1	2	3	2	2	3	2	4	2	4
Nice	0	1	3	0	0	1	0	1	0	0	0	1	0	0	0	0
Officer ..	1	0	1	0	2	1	0	4	4	1	2	1	0	0	0	1
Old	0	0	0	2	1	0	0	0	1	0	0	1	0	0	0	0
Order ...	0	0	0	1	1	0	0	0	0	0	0	0	0	0	2	0
Peace ...	0	0	0	0	2	0	0	0	0	0	0	0	0	0	0	0
Person ..	3	2	4	4	2	5	6	3	2	2	2	0	0	2	2	0

Response Word	4th M	4th F	5th M	5th F	6th M	6th F	7th M	7th F	8th M	8th F	10th M	10th F	12th M	12th F	College M	College F

SOLDIER

Response Word	4th M	4th F	5th M	5th F	6th M	6th F	7th M	7th F	8th M	8th F	10th M	10th F	12th M	12th F	College M	College F
Private	0	0	1	0	0	0	0	2	2	0	1	0	0	0	3	1
Rifle	1	0	0	0	2	0	1	0	0	1	3	0	3	0	11	2
ROTC	0	0	0	0	0	0	0	0	0	0	0	0	0	0	4	0
Sailor	1	1	0	1	0	3	1	3	3	3	2	4	11	8	18	19
Sergeant	0	1	0	1	0	0	2	1	2	1	0	0	1	0	3	0
Shoot	0	1	1	0	0	0	0	0	0	0	1	1	2	0	1	1
Sold	4	10	5	1	1	4	0	0	1	0	0	0	0	0	0	0
Steve	0	0	0	0	0	0	0	0	0	0	0	2	0	0	0	0
Stiff	0	1	0	1	0	1	0	4	0	1	0	2	0	0	0	0
Straight	1	1	0	3	3	1	1	1	0	2	0	0	0	2	0	2
Strong	0	1	2	2	0	0	1	1	0	0	1	3	0	0	1	3
Tall	0	1	0	1	0	2	0	1	0	1	1	2	0	0	0	1
Tin	1	0	0	2	1	1	2	1	1	4	0	2	0	0	1	2
Tough	0	0	0	1	0	0	1	0	0	0	0	1	2	0	1	1
Toy	0	0	1	4	1	0	0	0	0	0	0	1	0	0	0	0
Trouble	0	0	0	0	0	0	1	0	1	0	0	0	2	0	0	0
Uniform	0	3	3	2	0	5	7	9	5	4	7	7	7	15	20	42
Walk	0	1	0	0	0	0	0	0	0	0	0	0	0	0	2	1
War	11	12	15	13	19	16	21	29	19	25	25	20	27	30	45	65
Warrior	0	0	0	0	2	0	0	1	0	1	0	0	0	0	3	0
Work	1	2	2	0	3	2	0	1	0	0	3	0	2	0	1	0

155. SOUR

Response Word	4th M	4th F	5th M	5th F	6th M	6th F	7th M	7th F	8th M	8th F	10th M	10th F	12th M	12th F	College M	College F
Acid	0	0	0	0	1	0	0	0	0	0	2	0	0	0	4	2
Anger	0	2	0	1	0	1	0	0	1	1	1	0	1	0	0	0
Angry	0	1	2	0	0	0	0	0	0	0	0	0	0	0	0	0
Apple	1	1	0	0	2	2	0	2	7	1	2	3	3	2	9	12
Apples	0	0	0	0	0	1	0	0	1	0	0	0	1	4	4	2
Awful	1	6	8	2	7	7	2	3	3	0	2	2	1	1	0	0
Bad	11	6	12	12	4	5	8	3	4	3	8	5	2	1	7	2
Bad taste	0	1	0	0	0	0	1	0	0	2	0	0	0	0	0	0
Bitter	10	3	7	12	15	18	26	19	14	15	17	21	20	21	33	28
Buttermilk	0	0	0	1	0	0	0	2	1	1	3	0	0	0	0	0
Cream	6	12	6	14	12	14	9	10	3	11	17	24	22	27	31	46
Cut	3	0	3	1	6	0	2	1	0	0	0	0	0	0	0	0
Dough	0	0	0	0	0	0	0	0	1	0	1	0	4	0	2	2
Eat	0	0	0	1	1	1	1	0	2	0	1	1	0	0	0	0
Fast	2	1	0	0	1	0	0	0	0	0	0	0	0	0	0	0
Fly	1	0	0	0	2	0	0	0	0	1	1	1	1	0	0	0
Food	2	3	2	0	0	0	2	0	0	0	0	0	2	2	0	0
Foot	3	1	1	1	0	0	0	0	0	0	0	0	0	0	0	0
Fresh	1	1	1	0	0	1	0	0	0	0	0	0	0	0	0	1
Fruit	1	1	0	0	0	0	1	0	0	1	2	0	0	1	1	0
Good	11	6	10	8	2	8	5	1	5	1	1	2	0	0	1	0
Grape	1	2	0	0	4	0	0	0	2	2	2	4	0	3	7	5
Grapefruit	0	0	2	1	1	1	0	2	3	0	4	5	0	1	1	0
Grapes	0	1	1	2	2	2	4	2	2	3	3	2	8	8	18	15
Happy	0	0	2	2	1	0	0	1	1	0	0	1	1	0	0	0
Hard	1	0	1	0	2	0	0	0	0	0	1	0	0	0	0	0

Response Word	4th M	4th F	5th M	5th F	6th M	6th F	7th M	7th F	8th M	8th F	10th M	10th F	12th M	12th F	College M	College F
							SOUR									
Heart . . .	2	2	0	0	2	1	1	0	1	0	1	0	1	0	0	0
High	0	2	0	0	0	0	0	1	1	0	0	0	0	0	0	0
Hole . . .	1	0	2	0	0	0	0	0	0	0	0	0	0	0	0	0
Hurt	9	8	13	9	17	8	6	3	2	1	2	1	4	1	0	0
Ick . . .	0	1	1	0	3	3	1	1	1	0	4	1	0	0	1	0
Icky . . .	1	3	1	2	0	1	0	0	1	1	0	0	0	0	0	0
Ish . . .	0	3	1	2	2	3	3	3	1	3	3	2	2	0	0	2
Ishy . . .	2	1	3	4	4	4	0	0	1	1	0	3	0	0	1	0
Juice . . .	1	2	0	0	1	0	1	1	1	0	1	0	0	1	0	0
Lemon . .	13	17	16	16	11	13	25	15	24	30	22	24	24	20	58	47
Lemons . .	0	0	0	1	0	0	2	1	4	1	0	1	0	0	1	1
Like	2	1	0	0	1	0	0	0	0	0	0	0	0	0	0	0
Mad . . .	5	2	3	4	5	5	1	2	1	1	3	0	0	0	0	0
Man	2	0	1	0	0	0	0	0	0	0	0	0	0	0	0	0
Mean . . .	1	0	0	1	0	0	0	2	0	1	1	0	0	0	0	0
Milk	7	17	12	9	10	12	5	20	7	18	12	19	25	26	28	27
Nice	0	3	2	2	1	1	0	0	1	0	1	0	0	0	0	0
No good . .	2	1	3	0	4	0	1	0	0	0	2	0	0	0	0	0
Not	1	0	0	0	2	0	0	0	0	0	0	0	0	0	0	0
Not good .	2	2	5	2	0	2	0	0	0	1	0	0	0	0	0	0
Not sweet .	5	0	0	0	0	0	1	2	1	1	0	0	0	0	0	0
Old	0	0	0	1	0	2	0	1	0	0	0	1	0	0	0	0
Orange . .	1	1	0	0	0	0	1	0	0	0	0	0	0	1	2	2
Ouch . . .	2	2	0	0	0	0	2	1	0	0	0	0	0	0	0	0
Our	1	4	1	1	1	1	0	1	0	0	0	0	0	0	0	0
Pain . . .	0	0	1	0	2	1	1	0	0	0	0	0	0	0	1	0
Pickle . . .	0	2	0	0	2	2	3	1	1	2	5	4	1	2	4	8
Pickles . .	0	0	0	0	0	0	0	1	1	2	0	0	2	0	2	4
Pop	0	0	0	1	0	0	0	0	2	2	0	0	0	0	0	0
Pucker . .	0	1	0	0	0	0	0	0	0	2	0	0	0	0	2	1
Puss . . .	1	0	1	0	1	0	0	0	1	0	0	0	2	0	4	1
Rhubarb . .	0	0	0	0	0	0	0	0	1	0	0	0	0	0	1	2
Right . . .	2	0	0	1	1	0	0	0	0	0	0	0	0	0	0	0
Rotten . .	2	0	1	1	2	2	1	1	2	1	1	0	1	0	0	0
Sad	0	2	0	0	1	1	0	0	0	0	0	0	0	0	0	0
Salt	1	0	0	1	0	0	0	0	0	1	1	0	0	0	3	0
Sauerkraut .	0	1	0	0	0	0	0	0	2	0	1	0	0	0	0	1
Smell . . .	1	3	1	1	0	2	2	1	0	0	0	0	1	0	1	1
Soap	0	2	0	0	0	0	0	0	0	0	0	0	0	0	0	0
Soft	0	0	0	0	0	1	0	0	2	0	0	1	0	0	1	0
Soup . . .	2	1	2	1	0	0	0	0	2	0	0	0	1	1	2	2
Sour	0	0	0	0	0	2	0	0	0	0	0	0	0	0	0	0
Spoiled . .	0	2	0	1	0	1	0	0	0	0	1	1	0	3	0	1
Stale	0	0	0	0	0	2	0	0	1	1	0	0	0	0	0	0
Strong . . .	0	2	0	1	2	0	0	2	1	0	0	0	0	0	0	1
Sweat . . .	2	1	0	0	0	1	0	0	1	1	2	0	1	3	0	1
Sweet . . .	55	54	53	70	56	65	88	102	107	106	87	105	93	100	232	255
Taste . . .	1	4	11	6	8	7	5	8	4	6	6	4	3	4	9	5
Terrible .	3	3	2	6	1	2	2	0	1	1	1	0	2	1	1	0

Response Word	4th M	4th F	5th M	5th F	6th M	6th F	7th M	7th F	8th M	8th F	10th M	10th F	12th M	12th F	College M	College F
							SOUR									
Ugly	0	0	0	1	0	2	0	1	0	1	0	1	2	0	0	0
Unsweet . .	1	1	0	1	1	2	0	4	1	0	0	1	0	0	0	0
Vinegar . .	1	0	0	1	1	1	2	1	0	3	0	1	1	0	2	6
Water . . .	2	2	3	2	1	1	0	0	0	0	0	0	1	1	0	0
Whiskey . .	0	0	0	0	0	0	0	0	0	0	0	0	0	0	2	0
Wine . . .	0	0	0	1	0	0	0	0	0	0	0	0	0	0	2	0
Yes	1	2	0	0	0	0	0	0	0	0	0	0	0	0	0	0
							156. SPEAK									
Aloud . . .	0	0	2	0	1	0	0	1	0	0	0	0	0	0	2	1
Clear . . .	1	3	4	0	2	1	0	1	0	1	1	0	0	0	0	1
Clearly . .	1	1	5	1	2	1	2	2	2	1	0	3	2	2	3	7
Cry	0	0	0	0	0	0	0	0	1	0	0	0	0	1	1	2
Deaf	1	0	0	0	0	0	0	0	0	0	0	0	0	0	2	1
Dog	2	0	1	0	4	0	1	1	3	0	3	0	1	0	3	1
Done . . .	0	0	0	0	0	0	2	0	0	0	0	0	0	0	0	0
Don't . . .	2	0	0	1	0	0	0	0	1	0	0	0	0	0	0	0
Dumb . . .	0	0	0	0	0	0	0	0	2	2	0	0	0	1	1	0
Easy . . .	0	0	0	0	0	0	0	0	1	0	5	1	7	0	16	3
Eat	0	2	0	0	0	0	0	0	0	1	0	0	0	0	0	0
Eek	0	0	0	0	0	0	2	0	0	0	0	0	0	0	0	0
English . .	0	1	1	4	3	1	1	2	2	1	0	1	0	0	0	1
Fast	2	1	2	0	6	2	2	0	0	4	6	2	4	6	7	1
Fluently . .	0	0	0	0	0	0	0	0	0	0	1	0	1	2	0	0
From . . .	2	0	0	0	0	0	0	0	0	0	0	0	0	0	0	0
Good . . .	0	1	2	0	0	1	1	0	0	0	1	1	1	0	0	0
Hear . . .	2	3	0	1	2	2	4	2	2	3	1	2	3	6	11	15
Heard . . .	0	1	2	1	0	0	0	0	0	0	0	0	0	0	1	0
Here . . .	3	1	1	0	2	1	1	0	0	0	0	0	2	0	1	0
Him	0	2	0	0	0	0	0	0	0	0	0	0	0	0	0	0
It	2	0	0	1	1	0	0	0	0	0	0	0	0	0	2	0
Language .	0	1	5	5	4	3	0	1	1	0	2	0	1	0	2	2
Laugh . . .	0	1	0	1	0	1	1	1	0	1	0	1	0	1	1	3
Listen . .	0	1	0	2	0	3	0	1	0	1	2	4	3	2	10	12
Load	1	2	0	0	0	1	0	1	0	0	1	0	0	0	1	0
Look . . .	0	1	0	0	0	0	0	0	1	0	2	1	0	0	0	1
Loud . . .	13	18	12	1	17	15	10	7	8	9	11	12	9	5	13	23
Louder . .	0	2	3	2	0	1	0	3	1	4	3	5	3	3	2	6
Loudly . .	0	1	0	1	2	2	1	0	2	1	1	1	2	0	3	4
Low	0	1	0	0	0	1	0	0	0	0	0	0	1	1	5	4
Man . . .	0	0	3	1	0	0	1	0	0	0	0	0	1	0	0	0
Me	1	2	1	1	1	2	1	0	2	2	1	1	0	0	0	2
Mouth . . .	2	16	4	6	7	6	7	6	5	6	4	7	0	3	7	7
Mute . . .	0	0	0	0	0	0	0	0	0	0	0	0	0	1	0	2
My	1	0	0	0	0	1	0	0	0	0	0	0	0	0	0	0
Nice . . .	2	2	1	0	0	0	0	0	0	0	0	0	0	0	0	0
No	2	1	0	1	0	0	0	0	0	0	0	0	1	0	0	1
Noise . . .	1	0	0	1	2	1	1	1	1	0	2	2	0	0	4	3
Not	1	1	2	1	0	1	1	0	0	0	0	0	0	0	1	1

Response Word	4th M	4th F	5th M	5th F	6th M	6th F	7th M	7th F	8th M	8th F	10th M	10th F	12th M	12th F	College M	College F
SPEAK																
Now	4	2	2	0	2	1	2	0	1	3	0	1	0	2	7	5
Of	1	1	3	3	4	1	2	0	1	1	2	0	5	0	3	1
Out	0	2	1	0	2	0	1	0	0	0	2	0	0	0	2	2
Peak . . .	3	3	3	5	2	4	3	0	1	0	0	0	0	0	0	0
People . .	1	0	0	0	0	1	0	0	0	1	0	2	0	0	0	0
Play	0	1	0	0	2	0	0	0	0	0	1	0	0	0	0	1
Quiet . . .	1	1	0	1	1	0	3	5	5	5	1	8	3	4	4	12
Rapid . . .	0	0	0	0	0	0	0	0	2	0	0	0	0	0	0	0
Said	2	0	2	0	2	0	1	1	0	0	0	0	0	1	1	1
Say	5	5	5	4	2	6	1	5	7	5	4	5	4	6	21	28
Scream . .	0	0	0	0	0	0	0	0	0	0	0	0	0	2	1	1
See	2	0	0	0	0	0	0	0	0	1	0	0	0	1	1	0
Seek . . .	0	0	4	0	0	0	1	0	0	0	0	0	0	0	1	0
Shout . . .	1	1	1	0	1	0	1	3	3	2	2	1	1	2	2	8
Shut up . .	0	0	0	0	0	0	0	0	1	2	0	1	0	1	0	1
Silence . .	1	0	0	0	0	0	0	0	0	1	0	1	0	1	4	5
Silent . . .	0	0	0	0	1	4	1	2	0	1	0	0	0	2	2	6
Sing	0	0	0	0	0	1	1	3	0	2	0	2	1	1	2	5
Slow . . .	0	0	1	0	1	0	1	0	1	1	1	1	2	0	0	4
Slowly . .	0	0	0	0	0	0	0	0	0	2	1	2	2	1	5	8
Soft	0	0	0	0	1	1	4	1	2	5	4	6	0	2	6	4
Softly . . .	0	0	0	1	0	0	0	1	2	5	5	3	14	20	29	18
Sound . . .	1	1	2	0	2	1	1	2	2	0	1	0	2	2	1	1
Spake . . .	0	0	0	0	1	0	0	0	4	0	0	0	0	0	0	1
Speaker . .	0	3	1	2	0	1	1	0	2	1	3	3	4	4	5	1
Speaking .	1	0	0	0	0	2	3	1	0	0	1	0	0	0	2	0
Speech . . .	1	5	3	4	1	2	1	4	2	0	6	2	4	6	6	5
Spoke . . .	6	10	10	11	9	12	41	49	67	53	29	20	37	32	84	56
Spoken . .	1	0	1	0	0	3	5	6	7	8	3	7	13	10	15	10
Spook . . .	0	1	0	2	1	0	0	0	0	0	0	0	0	0	1	1
Take	1	1	6	2	2	0	1	0	0	0	0	0	0	0	1	1
Talk . . .	97	100	89	115	93	122	94	108	57	84	93	107	75	77	119	133
Teacher .	0	0	0	0	0	0	0	0	1	2	0	0	0	0	1	0
Tell	1	0	2	0	0	1	1	0	1	1	0	0	0	2	1	2
The	1	0	1	2	2	0	0	1	0	0	1	0	0	0	0	0
There . . .	2	0	0	1	0	0	0	0	0	0	0	1	0	0	0	0
Think . . .	0	0	0	0	0	0	0	0	0	0	3	0	0	0	0	0
To	5	4	8	4	6	5	3	3	5	4	3	2	2	4	10	7
Tongue . .	1	0	0	0	1	1	1	0	1	0	0	0	2	2	2	1
Up	10	7	4	4	6	1	2	0	4	1	4	1	3	5	5	4
Voice . . .	1	2	4	2	3	4	2	2	1	4	3	4	2	5	6	10
Week . . .	0	0	2	0	1	0	0	0	0	0	0	0	0	0	0	0
Well	1	0	3	1	0	0	0	1	3	0	0	1	2	1	1	0
When . . .	0	0	0	2	1	0	1	0	1	1	1	0	1	0	1	0
Where . .	1	0	0	1	0	0	0	0	0	0	0	0	0	0	2	0
Whisper . .	0	1	2	0	0	0	0	0	0	1	0	0	0	1	0	5
With . . .	0	0	0	0	0	0	2	0	3	0	0	0	0	0	0	0
Word . . .	4	1	3	2	4	4	0	0	1	0	0	2	1	0	2	5
Words . .	1	1	1	2	3	3	1	0	1	1	2	2	2	7	3	5

Response Word	4th M	4th F	5th M	5th F	6th M	6th F	7th M	7th F	8th M	8th F	10th M	10th F	12th M	12th F	College M	College F

SPEAK

Response Word	4th M	4th F	5th M	5th F	6th M	6th F	7th M	7th F	8th M	8th F	10th M	10th F	12th M	12th F	College M	College F
Write	0	0	0	0	0	0	0	0	1	0	0	1	3	0	2	3
Yell	0	0	0	0	0	0	7	2	1	2	1	3	4	0	5	3
You	2	0	1	1	2	1	1	0	0	0	1	0	2	0	2	2

157. SPIDER

Response Word	4th M	4th F	5th M	5th F	6th M	6th F	7th M	7th F	8th M	8th F	10th M	10th F	12th M	12th F	College M	College F
Afraid	0	1	0	3	0	1	0	0	0	0	0	1	0	2	0	0
Animal	10	9	12	12	9	14	11	5	9	8	6	6	4	3	8	6
Ant	2	4	5	7	3	2	2	5	5	3	1	6	2	3	8	6
Arachnid	0	0	0	0	0	0	1	0	1	0	0	0	0	0	3	0
Arachnida	0	0	0	0	0	0	0	0	0	0	0	0	0	0	3	0
Awful	0	1	0	1	0	5	0	0	0	0	0	0	1	2	0	2
Bad	0	1	2	0	3	0	1	0	1	0	3	0	0	1	3	2
Basement	0	0	0	0	0	0	0	0	0	0	2	0	0	0	0	0
Bee	3	0	0	0	0	0	0	1	1	0	1	0	1	1	0	0
Big	2	1	3	1	1	0	2	1	0	0	2	1	0	1	0	0
Bird	0	1	1	0	0	0	0	2	0	0	0	0	1	0	0	0
Bite	0	1	1	0	0	1	1	2	0	1	2	2	1	1	3	1
Bites	0	0	0	0	0	0	2	0	0	0	0	0	0	0	0	0
Black	3	8	10	13	7	9	6	13	4	15	12	19	11	23	15	40
Black widow	0	0	2	0	1	0	1	1	1	1	3	0	2	1	2	3
Bug	36	35	32	31	13	43	21	32	25	35	24	30	36	39	63	73
Bugs	0	0	0	1	0	2	0	0	1	0	0	0	1	3	2	4
Butterfly	0	1	2	3	0	0	1	0	2	0	0	0	0	0	1	0
Centipede	0	1	1	0	0	0	1	2	1	0	1	1	0	1	1	1
Cider	0	0	0	0	0	0	0	0	0	0	2	0	0	0	0	0
Climb	0	2	0	0	0	0	1	0	0	0	0	0	0	0	0	0
Crawl	0	4	0	2	2	5	4	1	2	3	2	2	5	4	8	9
Crawling	0	0	1	0	2	0	0	1	1	0	0	0	0	0	1	1
Creature	2	0	4	1	1	0	0	0	0	1	0	0	0	1	0	1
Creepy	0	0	0	1	1	1	0	0	1	1	0	2	0	1	0	1
Dirty	1	0	0	0	0	0	0	0	0	0	2	0	0	0	0	0
Dog	0	1	0	1	0	0	2	1	1	0	1	0	0	0	0	0
Eek	0	0	0	2	0	0	0	0	0	1	0	1	0	1	0	0
Eight	4	1	0	0	0	2	1	2	0	0	0	0	0	0	3	0
Eight legs	1	1	0	0	2	0	3	1	0	0	2	0	0	0	1	1
Fast	2	0	3	1	1	0	0	0	1	0	0	0	0	0	0	0
Faster	0	2	0	0	0	0	0	0	0	0	0	0	0	0	0	0
Fear	0	0	0	0	0	0	1	0	0	1	2	4	2	7	0	4
Feet	0	0	1	0	2	1	1	1	0	1	0	0	0	2	0	0
Fish	0	1	2	0	0	0	0	0	1	0	0	0	1	0	0	0
Fly	6	3	5	3	6	3	7	4	7	7	4	7	4	4	21	11
Foot	1	0	2	1	1	1	1	0	1	0	0	1	1	1	2	0
Fright	0	0	0	0	0	0	0	0	0	0	0	2	0	1	1	2
Girl	2	0	1	0	2	0	0	0	0	0	1	0	0	0	0	0
Good	0	1	2	0	2	0	0	0	0	0	0	0	0	0	0	0
Horrible	0	0	0	0	0	1	0	0	0	1	0	3	0	1	0	3
Hurt	1	0	1	3	1	1	0	0	0	0	0	1	0	0	0	0
Icky	0	0	1	2	2	1	0	2	0	0	0	1	0	1	1	0
Insect	47	35	34	33	52	58	74	60	62	56	49	30	35	34	69	49

Response Word	4th M	4th F	5th M	5th F	6th M	6th F	7th M	7th F	8th M	8th F	10th M	10th F	12th M	12th F	College M	College F
								SPIDER								
Insects ..	0	2	0	0	2	0	1	2	3	1	1	1	1	0	0	0
Ish	1	3	1	2	0	5	0	6	2	5	1	13	1	15	0	11
Ishy ...	0	0	1	1	2	4	0	2	0	4	0	5	0	3	0	1
Kill	0	0	0	1	2	0	0	0	1	0	2	0	0	1	0	1
Leg	1	0	0	1	2	0	1	0	1	0	1	1	1	0	0	2
Legs ...	9	13	7	12	10	9	6	10	15	10	18	10	17	10	26	25
Long ...	0	1	3	1	2	0	0	1	0	1	1	0	0	0	2	1
Monkey ..	0	0	0	0	2	1	0	0	1	0	2	0	0	0	3	0
Monster ..	1	0	1	0	0	1	2	0	1	0	0	0	0	0	1	0
Needle ..	2	0	0	0	0	0	0	0	0	0	0	1	0	0	0	0
Nest	0	2	0	0	0	0	0	0	0	0	0	1	0	0	0	0
Net	0	0	0	0	0	1	0	0	1	1	0	1	0	0	2	7
Octopus ..	0	0	0	0	2	0	0	0	0	0	0	0	0	0	0	0
On	2	0	0	0	0	0	0	1	0	0	0	0	0	0	0	0
Poison ...	1	0	1	0	2	0	1	1	0	1	2	2	0	1	2	1
Run	0	0	0	2	1	0	0	2	1	1	0	1	0	1	1	2
Scare ...	0	2	1	0	0	0	0	0	1	0	0	0	1	0	0	0
Scared ..	1	0	0	3	1	1	0	3	0	5	1	5	1	1	1	0
Scary ...	0	3	0	1	0	1	0	1	0	2	0	0	0	0	0	1
Scream ..	0	0	2	1	0	1	0	1	0	2	1	0	0	1	0	3
Shiver ...	0	0	0	0	0	2	0	0	0	0	0	0	0	0	0	1
Shoe ...	0	3	2	0	2	1	0	0	2	0	0	0	0	0	0	0
Shoes ...	0	0	2	0	0	1	0	2	0	1	0	0	0	0	0	0
Six ...	0	0	0	0	1	0	0	2	0	0	0	1	0	0	0	0
Slow ...	1	0	2	0	0	0	0	0	0	0	0	0	0	0	0	0
Small ...	0	1	2	1	1	0	0	0	0	1	3	0	2	0	1	0
Snake ...	0	0	0	1	1	0	1	1	1	2	1	1	0	1	2	5
Spin	0	3	0	0	0	0	0	0	0	0	1	0	1	1	0	0
Sting ...	0	0	0	0	0	0	2	1	0	1	0	0	0	1	0	0
Tarantula .	0	0	0	1	0	0	13	3	7	2	3	0	0	0	3	1
Terrible .	0	1	0	1	0	3	0	0	0	0	0	0	0	1	2	1
Thing ...	0	0	1	0	0	1	0	0	2	0	0	0	0	1	0	0
Ugh	0	1	0	0	0	1	0	2	0	2	1	0	0	0	0	3
Ugly ...	1	4	6	6	1	3	3	3	1	8	2	14	11	7	4	7
Wall	0	0	0	0	0	0	0	0	0	0	0	0	0	2	0	0
Web	44	50	37	44	53	33	39	33	45	42	61	51	77	45	203	175
Webs ...	0	0	0	2	0	0	1	0	1	1	0	0	2	1	0	0
Widow ..	0	1	0	0	0	0	2	1	0	0	1	0	0	0	0	0
Wood ...	1	0	2	1	3	0	1	2	1	0	4	0	0	0	0	0
Worm ...	1	1	1	0	0	1	0	0	1	1	1	0	0	2	2	1
							158.	SQUARE								
Algebra ..	0	0	0	0	0	0	0	0	0	0	0	3	0	0	1	1
Angle ...	0	0	1	0	0	1	1	1	1	0	1	0	0	0	4	0
Animal ..	4	0	0	1	3	1	0	0	0	0	0	0	0	0	0	0
Are	0	2	0	1	0	0	0	0	0	0	0	0	0	0	0	0
Arithmetic .	0	0	0	0	2	1	0	0	0	1	0	0	0	0	0	0
Around ..	0	1	0	1	3	0	1	0	0	0	0	1	0	0	0	0
Beat	0	0	0	0	0	0	0	0	0	0	0	0	0	0	0	2

Response Word	4th M	4th F	5th M	5th F	6th M	6th F	7th M	7th F	8th M	8th F	10th M	10th F	12th M	12th F	College M	College F
								SQUARE								
Beatnik ..	0	0	1	0	1	1	2	0	0	1	0	0	0	0	0	1
Big	0	1	4	3	0	1	1	0	0	1	0	0	0	0	0	1
Black ...	0	0	0	0	0	0	2	0	1	0	1	1	0	0	1	1
Block ...	20	21	21	27	25	10	32	28	21	20	29	16	21	24	47	47
Blocks ..	0	0	0	0	0	0	0	0	1	1	2	1	0	1	1	0
Board ...	1	0	0	0	0	0	0	0	0	1	0	0	0	0	5	1
Book ...	0	0	0	3	0	0	0	1	0	1	0	1	1	0	0	0
Box	27	41	19	27	15	21	1	22	4	11	7	13	8	7	19	19
Boy	0	1	0	1	0	3	0	0	1	0	1	2	2	0	0	1
Bryant ...	0	0	3	0	0	1	0	0	0	0	0	0	0	0	0	0
Building ..	0	0	0	0	0	1	1	0	1	1	0	0	1	1	1	2
Butter ...	1	0	0	0	0	0	0	0	0	1	0	0	0	1	1	3
Candy ...	0	0	0	1	0	1	0	0	0	1	0	0	0	2	0	0
Carpenter .	0	0	0	0	0	0	0	0	0	0	0	0	2	0	1	1
Center ..	0	0	0	0	0	0	0	0	0	0	1	0	2	0	2	0
Chocolate .	0	0	0	0	0	0	0	1	1	2	0	0	0	1	0	2
Circle ...	31	41	25	36	23	32	23	40	33	37	23	29	24	39	72	71
City	3	2	1	0	2	0	1	1	2	1	3	0	1	5	7	6
Corner ..	0	1	3	0	2	3	0	3	2	0	4	3	3	0	4	2
Corners ..	2	5	1	3	3	7	0	0	1	2	2	6	0	0	1	5
Cube ...	0	0	2	0	0	5	20	6	13	8	12	11	14	11	14	10
Dance ..	4	7	3	6	3	4	0	2	0	5	1	0	1	2	12	18
Dancing ..	0	2	0	0	0	0	0	0	0	0	0	0	0	0	0	0
Deal	0	0	0	0	0	0	0	0	0	0	0	0	3	0	2	0
Desk ...	0	0	0	0	0	1	0	0	0	0	0	0	2	0	0	0
Equal ...	0	0	0	0	0	0	1	0	0	0	3	1	0	0	1	1
Even	1	0	0	0	1	2	1	0	0	2	0	1	0	0	0	1
Feet	0	0	0	0	0	2	0	1	0	0	1	0	0	0	0	0
Figure ..	0	0	2	0	0	0	2	2	2	3	0	0	0	1	3	2
Flat	1	2	1	0	0	0	1	1	0	0	2	0	0	0	1	0
Fool ...	0	2	3	3	3	1	3	1	0	3	0	1	3	3	2	0
Four ...	2	0	0	1	4	2	0	1	3	2	1	2	1	0	2	2
Four sides	0	0	0	0	0	1	2	4	0	0	4	0	0	0	1	1
Garden ..	0	0	0	0	2	0	0	1	1	0	1	0	2	0	0	1
Geometry .	0	0	0	0	0	0	1	2	1	0	14	9	7	2	7	9
Girl	0	0	2	0	1	0	1	0	0	0	0	0	0	0	0	0
Grass ...	0	0	1	2	0	1	0	0	0	0	1	0	0	0	0	0
Head ...	1	1	5	4	8	5	7	2	12	4	5	3	3	0	4	3
House ...	0	0	0	0	5	2	1	3	0	0	0	0	3	0	1	2
Ice cube ..	1	0	1	0	1	0	0	1	0	2	0	0	0	1	0	0
Inch	0	0	0	1	1	2	1	0	0	0	0	0	0	0	2	1
Jerry ...	0	0	0	0	0	0	0	0	0	0	0	2	0	0	0	0
Line ...	3	1	1	0	2	0	0	0	0	0	0	0	0	0	0	0
Lines ...	1	2	1	1	1	4	0	0	0	1	0	0	0	0	3	0
Long ...	0	1	3	1	2	3	1	0	0	1	0	0	1	1	2	1
Man	1	0	0	0	1	0	0	1	0	0	2	1	2	0	2	0
Market ..	0	0	0	0	0	0	0	0	0	0	0	0	0	0	0	2
Math ...	0	0	0	0	1	1	2	4	2	6	1	0	3	4	1	3
Mile ...	2	1	7	4	5	1	1	1	1	1	2	5	2	2	2	1

Response Word	4th M	4th F	5th M	5th F	6th M	6th F	7th M	7th F	8th M	8th F	10th M	10th F	12th M	12th F	College M	College F
							SQUARE									
Miles	1	2	1	2	2	1	0	0	0	0	0	0	0	0	0	0
New York	0	0	0	0	0	0	0	1	1	1	0	1	1	0	2	0
Ninety degrees	0	0	0	0	0	0	0	0	0	0	1	0	0	0	2	0
Nut	0	1	0	0	0	0	2	0	2	0	0	0	0	0	1	0
Nuts	2	0	1	0	0	0	0	0	0	0	0	0	0	0	0	0
Object	0	0	0	0	1	1	5	4	1	2	0	0	0	0	1	0
Oblong	0	1	0	0	1	2	0	2	0	2	2	1	0	2	2	1
Odd	0	0	0	0	1	0	1	0	0	1	1	0	0	2	2	0
Odd ball	0	0	0	0	0	0	0	1	0	0	0	0	0	0	0	2
Oval	0	0	0	0	2	0	0	2	0	1	0	1	0	1	1	1
Paper	0	0	1	0	1	2	0	0	2	0	0	1	0	0	0	0
Park	2	1	3	3	0	4	1	0	1	1	1	2	5	3	4	10
Peg	0	0	0	0	0	0	0	0	0	0	0	0	0	0	1	3
People	0	0	0	0	1	0	1	2	0	2	0	3	5	3	1	1
Person	0	0	2	1	2	4	0	1	4	0	3	5	2	0	5	2
Plaza	0	0	0	0	1	3	1	1	1	0	0	1	0	0	0	4
Point	0	0	0	0	2	0	0	0	0	0	0	0	0	0	0	0
Quadrilateral	0	0	0	0	0	0	0	0	0	0	1	2	0	0	0	0
Queer	1	0	0	3	0	0	1	0	0	1	0	0	0	1	0	0
Rectangle	2	3	4	1	7	4	11	8	9	5	10	6	4	7	6	10
Root	0	0	0	0	0	0	2	2	4	3	0	1	1	0	4	4
Round	53	47	53	51	42	47	44	51	53	57	66	71	68	72	146	169
Ruler	0	0	0	0	0	0	0	0	0	0	0	0	0	0	0	2
Shape	12	7	14	10	7	9	8	5	0	5	1	1	1	0	0	2
Shapes	2	0	0	0	0	0	0	0	0	0	0	0	0	0	0	0
Sharp	0	0	0	0	0	0	0	0	0	0	2	3	0	0	2	3
Sides	0	0	0	0	0	1	2	2	1	1	1	0	0	1	1	1
Sidewalk	0	0	0	0	1	2	0	0	0	0	0	0	0	3	0	0
Small	0	0	0	0	0	0	0	0	1	1	0	2	0	0	1	0
Street	0	0	0	0	1	1	0	0	1	1	0	1	1	1	2	1
Table	0	1	0	0	1	1	2	2	1	0	0	1	1	3	4	3
Teacher	0	0	0	0	1	0	1	0	1	1	0	0	4	0	0	1
Teachers	0	0	0	0	0	0	0	0	2	0	2	0	1	0	0	0
Time	0	0	0	0	0	0	0	1	0	0	2	0	1	1	2	0
Times	0	0	0	0	0	0	1	0	0	1	1	0	0	3	2	1
Tool	0	0	0	0	0	0	0	0	0	0	2	0	0	0	1	0
Town	0	3	2	3	5	2	4	3	1	1	3	2	2	1	4	4
Town square	0	0	0	0	0	0	0	0	0	0	0	0	0	0	2	0
Trafalger	0	0	0	0	0	0	0	0	0	0	0	0	0	2	0	0
Tree	2	2	1	0	1	0	1	0	1	0	0	0	0	0	0	0
Triangle	9	7	3	6	7	8	14	5	8	12	1	3	6	7	13	7
Village	0	0	0	0	1	1	0	1	1	2	0	2	1	0	1	2
Window	0	0	0	2	1	0	0	0	0	0	0	0	0	0	0	0
Wood	1	0	1	0	0	0	0	0	2	0	0	1	1	1	2	1
Yard	1	0	0	0	2	1	2	4	1	0	0	2	1	0	1	1
You	2	1	0	1	2	0	0	2	2	0	0	0	1	0	0	0

Response Word	4th M	4th F	5th M	5th F	6th M	6th F	7th M	7th F	8th M	8th F	10th M	10th F	12th M	12th F	College M	College F

159. <u>STAND</u>

Response Word	4th M	4th F	5th M	5th F	6th M	6th F	7th M	7th F	8th M	8th F	10th M	10th F	12th M	12th F	College M	College F
Alone	0	1	1	0	0	1	1	0	0	1	3	5	5	5	2	3
And	11	9	5	4	2	0	0	0	0	0	0	0	0	0	0	0
Around	0	0	0	0	1	0	1	0	2	0	0	0	0	0	0	0
At	0	0	1	0	2	0	0	0	0	0	0	0	0	0	1	1
Away	0	1	0	1	1	0	0	0	0	0	2	1	0	0	3	0
Back	1	1	1	0	0	0	0	0	0	0	3	0	1	0	1	0
Band	2	0	1	1	1	0	2	2	0	0	0	0	0	0	0	1
Bus	0	1	0	0	0	0	0	0	0	0	1	0	0	2	1	0
Buy	3	0	0	0	1	0	0	0	0	0	0	0	0	1	0	0
By	25	14	18	18	18	11	18	6	23	14	8	5	13	10	27	17
Chair	0	0	1	1	0	0	2	1	0	0	0	0	0	0	0	0
Close	1	0	2	2	0	0	2	0	2	0	2	0	2	0	4	0
Corner	0	0	1	2	2	0	1	1	0	2	1	1	1	0	1	0
Dirt	0	0	1	1	3	0	0	0	1	0	0	0	1	0	0	0
Erect	0	0	0	0	0	0	0	0	1	0	0	0	2	1	3	0
Fall	0	1	0	0	1	1	1	0	1	1	0	0	0	1	3	2
Fast	0	0	0	0	0	0	0	0	0	0	1	0	2	0	9	0
Feet	9	10	5	13	16	11	3	6	4	3	9	9	4	8	7	9
Fence	0	0	0	0	0	0	0	0	0	2	0	0	0	0	0	0
Floor	1	1	2	2	0	1	0	1	1	0	2	0	0	1	2	1
Foot	1	0	2	0	0	1	1	0	0	0	0	0	0	0	2	0
Go	0	1	0	0	0	0	2	0	1	0	1	0	0	0	0	1
Good	0	0	3	0	0	2	0	0	0	0	0	0	0	0	0	0
Hand	4	2	1	1	0	0	0	1	0	0	0	0	0	0	1	0
Head	0	1	0	0	0	0	0	2	0	0	0	0	1	1	0	0
Hear	1	1	1	0	1	2	1	1	0	0	0	0	0	0	0	0
Her	0	2	0	1	0	0	0	0	0	0	0	0	0	0	0	2
Here	10	18	9	12	19	9	7	7	3	11	13	5	14	8	23	15
High	2	2	2	0	2	0	0	3	0	1	1	0	0	0	0	1
His	2	2	1	2	2	1	0	0	0	0	0	0	0	1	0	0
Hot dog	2	0	0	0	0	1	0	0	0	0	1	0	1	0	0	0
In	2	0	0	1	1	1	0	0	5	0	1	1	1	0	4	1
It	1	2	3	1	1	1	0	0	1	0	0	0	0	0	1	0
Jump	0	0	0	0	1	0	1	0	2	0	0	0	0	0	0	0
Kiss	0	2	0	0	0	0	0	0	0	0	0	0	0	1	0	0
Land	3	1	1	0	0	0	0	1	0	0	0	0	0	0	2	0
Lay	0	0	0	2	0	2	1	1	3	0	2	0	0	0	0	0
Leg	1	0	0	0	0	0	0	0	0	0	0	0	0	0	3	0
Legs	5	1	3	1	2	3	1	1	2	1	4	1	1	0	6	0
Lie	0	0	0	0	0	0	0	0	0	1	1	2	0	0	0	0
Line	0	1	0	0	0	0	0	0	0	0	0	2	0	0	0	0
Little	0	0	0	0	0	0	0	0	2	0	0	0	0	0	0	0
Look	0	1	0	1	1	0	0	0	0	1	1	0	1	0	0	2
Man	1	0	0	0	1	1	1	0	3	0	0	0	0	0	0	1
Near	1	0	2	3	0	1	0	1	2	1	5	1	3	3	2	0
Off	1	0	0	0	0	0	0	0	1	0	0	0	2	0	4	0
On	2	3	4	1	3	3	1	2	2	2	0	0	5	1	7	2
Over	0	0	0	0	0	0	3	0	1	1	1	0	1	0	0	1
Pat	0	0	0	0	0	0	0	0	0	0	0	1	0	0	4	0

Response Word	4th M	F	5th M	F	6th M	F	7th M	F	8th M	F	10th M	F	12th M	F	College M	F

STAND

Response Word	4th M	F	5th M	F	6th M	F	7th M	F	8th M	F	10th M	F	12th M	F	College M	F
People . . .	1	1	1	0	1	0	0	1	0	0	0	2	0	0	1	0
Person . .	0	0	0	0	1	1	0	0	0	2	0	0	0	0	0	2
Place . . .	0	0	1	0	0	0	0	1	0	0	2	0	0	0	1	0
Play	2	0	0	1	0	0	0	0	0	0	0	0	0	0	0	0
Please . .	0	2	0	0	0	0	0	1	0	0	1	0	0	0	1	0
Pop . . .	1	0	0	0	1	0	0	0	0	0	1	0	1	0	2	1
Pop corn .	0	0	0	1	0	0	0	1	0	0	1	2	0	0	0	0
Position . .	0	0	0	0	0	0	0	2	0	0	0	0	0	0	1	0
Run	1	0	1	2	1	1	0	0	0	0	3	2	1	1	0	0
Sand . . .	6	1	3	3	0	1	1	2	2	0	0	0	0	0	0	0
Sat	1	0	1	0	0	0	3	0	1	1	2	0	0	0	0	0
Sell	0	0	0	0	0	0	0	0	1	0	1	0	0	2	0	0
Set	2	1	1	0	0	2	2	3	1	1	1	0	0	1	2	1
Side . . .	0	0	2	0	0	0	0	1	0	0	0	0	0	0	0	0
Sit	36	47	29	64	42	62	83	106	90	109	70	101	70	88	153	230
Sitting . .	0	0	0	0	0	0	0	1	2	0	0	0	0	0	0	0
Soldier . .	0	0	0	0	0	0	0	0	0	0	0	0	0	0	2	0
Speak . . .	0	1	0	0	0	1	0	0	0	0	0	0	0	0	2	0
Standard .	0	1	0	0	1	0	1	0	0	0	1	0	2	0	0	0
Standing . .	1	0	2	0	2	1	1	0	2	2	1	1	2	0	0	0
Stay	0	4	0	1	1	2	1	2	1	1	1	1	0	0	0	0
Still	3	17	9	11	20	25	21	18	7	20	18	27	32	41	65	69
Stood . . .	7	4	14	11	5	11	23	19	15	15	11	4	10	14	26	16
Stool . . .	2	1	0	0	0	0	0	0	0	0	0	0	1	0	0	0
Stoop . . .	0	1	0	0	2	0	1	1	1	1	1	1	2	0	0	0
Straight . .	3	16	7	9	3	10	3	6	2	3	11	11	6	4	7	12
Tall	4	6	7	2	0	4	2	3	1	1	2	5	1	4	5	6
Their . . .	1	0	1	0	0	2	0	0	0	0	0	0	0	0	0	0
There . . .	8	4	12	1	14	6	12	4	10	7	12	4	4	5	3	3
Tired . . .	1	0	1	0	1	1	1	2	0	2	0	4	2	5	5	2
Up	35	29	28	32	28	29	20	18	23	24	18	28	23	22	50	49
Wait . . .	0	3	1	0	1	1	0	0	0	0	2	0	3	1	3	2
Walk . . .	5	8	7	12	3	9	6	4	3	7	6	5	3	5	10	14
Where . .	0	1	1	1	0	1	1	0	2	0	1	2	1	1	1	4
With	1	1	1	1	0	0	0	0	0	0	0	0	2	1	1	0

160. STEM

Response Word	4th M	F	5th M	F	6th M	F	7th M	F	8th M	F	10th M	F	12th M	F	College M	F
Air	1	2	3	2	2	0	2	4	1	0	0	2	0	2	0	0
Apple . . .	0	1	0	0	0	0	1	0	2	0	1	0	2	1	4	1
Base . . .	0	0	0	0	0	0	0	0	0	0	0	0	2	0	2	0
Bath . . .	0	1	0	0	0	2	1	0	0	0	1	0	0	1	0	0
Beginning .	0	0	1	0	0	0	0	0	0	0	0	0	0	0	2	0
Biology . .	0	0	0	0	0	0	0	0	0	0	0	0	0	0	0	2
Boat	2	2	3	6	5	2	0	1	1	1	0	0	0	0	0	0
Bottom . .	0	1	0	1	0	0	1	1	0	1	1	0	2	0	2	0
Brain . . .	0	0	0	0	0	0	0	0	0	0	0	0	0	0	2	0
Branch . .	5	2	7	8	11	4	5	2	8	1	4	1	10	6	18	7
Bright . . .	0	0	0	2	0	0	0	0	0	0	0	0	0	0	0	0
Brown . . .	0	0	0	0	0	0	0	0	0	0	0	0	0	2	0	0

Response Word	4th M	4th F	5th M	5th F	6th M	6th F	7th M	7th F	8th M	8th F	10th M	10th F	12th M	12th F	College M	College F
									STEM							
Bud	0	0	1	0	0	2	1	0	0	0	1	0	0	1	0	3
Cloud ...	0	2	0	1	0	0	2	0	0	0	0	0	0	0	0	0
Cold	3	1	1	0	1	0	0	0	0	0	0	0	0	0	0	0
Dream ..	2	0	0	0	0	1	0	0	0	0	0	0	0	0	0	0
End	1	0	1	0	2	0	0	0	2	1	2	1	1	0	1	1
Engine ..	0	0	1	2	1	2	0	0	0	0	0	0	1	1	0	0
Fast ...	0	0	2	0	0	0	0	0	0	0	0	0	1	0	0	0
Fire	0	2	1	0	1	0	0	1	1	0	0	0	0	0	0	0
Flower ..	47	78	47	93	43	102	76	102	51	123	85	148	79	139	162	236
Flowers ..	0	0	1	0	0	0	0	0	1	2	0	0	0	0	0	0
From ...	0	0	0	0	0	0	0	0	0	0	0	0	1	1	2	0
Fruit ...	0	0	0	0	0	0	1	0	0	0	0	0	1	0	5	0
Glass ...	0	0	0	0	0	0	0	0	0	0	0	1	0	0	2	2
Good ...	1	0	1	0	0	2	0	1	1	0	0	0	0	0	0	0
Gray	1	0	0	2	0	0	0	0	0	0	0	0	0	0	0	0
Green ...	7	12	6	7	3	13	2	8	6	4	4	4	2	4	4	9
Grow ...	1	1	0	0	0	0	0	0	0	0	1	0	0	0	2	0
Hat	1	0	1	1	0	0	1	2	0	0	0	1	0	0	0	0
Heat ...	3	2	5	3	4	3	2	3	1	2	3	1	2	2	0	2
Hot	27	25	26	28	25	13	5	7	3	5	5	1	0	4	1	0
Iron	0	1	2	0	3	2	0	0	0	0	1	1	0	0	1	0
Lamp ...	0	1	0	0	1	2	0	0	1	0	1	0	2	0	5	6
Leaf	5	3	10	7	5	5	20	23	33	26	17	15	17	13	54	66
Leave ...	5	2	2	1	2	6	0	2	0	0	3	4	0	0	5	13
Leaves ..	0	0	0	1	1	1	5	5	5	5	0	1	2	2	1	4
Leg	0	0	0	0	0	0	1	0	0	1	0	2	0	1	0	0
Limb ...	1	0	1	0	1	2	4	1	2	0	1	0	0	0	0	0
Line	1	1	1	2	1	2	0	0	0	0	0	0	0	0	0	1
Long ...	6	6	8	6	6	4	3	6	2	2	2	2	5	2	7	1
Mushroom .	1	0	0	0	0	0	0	0	0	0	0	0	0	0	2	2
My	0	1	0	2	0	0	0	0	0	0	0	0	0	0	0	0
Neck ...	0	0	0	0	0	0	0	0	3	0	0	0	0	0	1	0
Pipe	1	0	0	2	0	2	0	0	0	0	0	0	2	0	4	1
Plant ...	26	25	29	20	39	32	47	35	51	40	54	36	62	39	109	92
Root	2	5	4	2	7	3	13	6	13	6	8	9	11	7	14	9
Rose ...	0	0	0	0	0	1	1	3	0	1	0	1	1	1	3	9
Ship	2	0	0	0	0	0	0	0	0	0	0	0	0	1	1	0
Smoke ...	19	18	7	7	8	4	3	3	0	0	1	2	0	0	0	0
Stalk	0	0	0	0	1	1	1	1	1	1	0	0	1	0	3	2
Steam ...	0	0	1	1	1	2	1	2	1	0	1	0	0	0	1	0
Stern ...	0	0	1	0	0	0	1	0	9	0	2	1	5	1	9	3
Stick ...	4	2	4	1	1	1	3	1	0	1	0	0	1	1	0	0
Stove ...	0	2	0	0	1	2	1	0	0	0	0	0	0	0	0	0
Stream ..	0	2	1	0	0	0	0	0	1	0	1	0	0	0	1	0
Tall	0	0	0	0	0	0	0	0	0	0	0	0	0	1	0	2
Thin ...	0	0	0	0	0	0	0	0	0	2	0	1	1	0	1	1
Train ...	1	3	1	1	0	0	0	0	0	0	1	1	1	0	0	0
Tree ...	10	2	15	5	16	6	6	3	18	1	20	6	15	2	26	7

Response Word	4th M	F	5th M	F	6th M	F	7th M	F	8th M	F	10th M	F	12th M	F	College M	F

STEM

Trunk	0	0	0	0	2	0	2	2	1	0	0	0	0	0	3	0
Tulip	0	0	0	0	0	0	0	0	0	0	0	0	0	2	1	2
Twig	0	0	1	1	0	0	0	0	1	1	1	0	0	0	2	0
Vapor	1	0	1	0	2	2	1	2	1	0	1	0	1	1	1	0
Vine	0	1	1	0	0	0	3	0	2	0	0	0	0	0	0	0
Watch ...	0	0	0	0	0	0	0	0	0	0	0	0	1	0	4	1
Water	5	9	8	7	9	5	5	2	3	4	3	2	3	0	0	0
Wood	0	0	0	0	0	0	0	0	0	0	0	0	0	0	2	0

161. STOMACH

Abdomen ..	0	0	0	0	0	0	0	2	3	3	0	1	3	2	1	3
Ache	8	26	21	36	26	25	28	25	26	46	24	36	38	37	68	91
Acid	0	0	0	0	0	0	1	0	4	0	1	0	2	1	5	1
Anatomy ..	0	0	0	0	0	0	0	0	1	0	1	0	0	1	2	2
Arm	0	2	1	0	3	0	0	0	1	2	0	1	0	0	1	0
Aspirin ...	0	0	0	0	0	0	1	0	0	0	0	0	3	1	1	0
Back	2	1	1	2	1	3	2	2	1	2	1	1	0	0	0	0
Bad	0	0	0	0	0	0	2	0	0	0	0	0	0	0	0	0
Belly	10	3	8	4	11	1	10	2	7	0	0	0	1	0	2	1
Big	1	2	6	2	3	1	0	2	1	2	1	4	0	1	1	3
Biology ...	0	0	0	0	0	0	0	0	0	0	1	1	0	0	0	3
Body	33	42	33	40	23	55	25	23	11	28	10	18	5	8	17	12
Bones ...	2	1	0	0	0	0	0	0	0	0	0	0	0	0	0	0
Bottom ...	0	2	0	0	0	0	0	0	0	0	0	0	0	0	0	0
Brain	0	2	2	0	0	0	0	0	0	0	1	0	0	0	0	2
Bread basket	1	0	0	0	2	0	0	0	0	2	0	0	0	0	0	0
Butterflies .	0	0	0	0	0	0	0	0	1	2	0	0	0	0	1	0
Cells	0	0	0	0	0	0	0	2	0	0	0	0	0	0	0	0
Chest	10	3	4	4	1	1	1	0	0	0	0	0	1	0	1	0
Digest ...	3	0	1	1	3	1	1	1	1	0	1	0	1	0	3	2
Digestion ..	1	0	0	0	0	0	4	0	3	0	2	2	3	3	12	15
Digestive system .	0	0	0	0	0	0	0	0	0	0	0	0	0	0	0	2
Duodenum ..	0	0	0	0	0	0	0	0	0	0	0	0	0	0	1	2
Eat	9	10	10	12	14	13	13	15	12	10	15	15	13	18	51	35
Eating ...	1	1	2	0	2	1	2	2	0	2	2	2	0	2	4	2
Empty	0	0	0	0	1	1	0	1	0	1	3	7	5	7	4	4
Esophagus .	0	0	0	0	0	0	0	1	0	0	2	1	2	2	2	0
Face	0	1	1	0	0	2	0	0	0	0	0	0	0	0	0	0
Fat	4	7	4	4	1	1	0	8	2	2	5	2	0	0	0	0
Feed	2	0	0	0	0	0	0	0	1	0	0	0	0	0	1	0
Flesh	0	2	0	0	0	1	0	0	0	0	0	0	0	0	1	0
Flu	1	1	0	0	1	0	0	1	0	0	0	1	2	1	5	3
Food	20	23	24	30	63	49	61	55	76	47	91	75	91	71	122	120
Full	0	4	0	1	2	4	3	4	2	5	4	1	2	5	7	5
Good	1	0	2	3	3	1	0	0	0	0	0	0	0	0	0	0
Growl	0	0	0	0	1	1	1	1	0	0	0	0	1	0	1	4
Growling ..	0	0	0	0	0	0	0	0	0	0	0	0	0	0	2	1
Gut	0	0	0	0	0	0	4	0	5	0	0	0	2	1	3	0

STOMACH

Response Word	4th M	F	5th M	F	6th M	F	7th M	F	8th M	F	10th M	F	12th M	F	College M	F
Guts	0	0	1	0	0	0	2	0	3	1	0	0	2	0	3	0
Hand ...	2	0	0	0	1	0	0	1	0	0	0	0	1	0	1	1
Hard ...	2	1	1	1	1	0	0	0	2	0	0	0	1	1	1	2
Head ...	9	7	7	12	4	7	2	3	12	7	2	3	2	2	0	0
Health ...	0	1	2	1	0	0	0	0	0	0	0	0	0	0	1	0
Heart ...	4	4	7	5	4	4	7	9	3	6	2	1	1	0	4	4
Human ..	0	1	0	0	2	0	1	1	1	0	2	0	0	1	2	0
Hunger ..	0	2	0	2	0	1	1	3	2	4	4	3	7	6	14	21
Hungry ..	4	2	3	6	7	7	7	15	5	11	7	22	7	16	16	34
Hurt	1	4	2	4	3	4	2	1	1	1	0	4	3	2	1	6
Hurts ...	0	1	0	0	0	1	0	0	0	0	0	1	0	2	1	1
Ill	0	0	0	2	0	0	0	0	0	0	0	0	0	0	0	0
Indigestion	0	0	0	1	0	1	0	1	1	1	0	1	0	0	2	1
Inside ...	6	2	5	8	2	4	1	1	2	0	3	0	0	2	1	0
Insides ..	3	3	6	1	4	3	4	1	2	1	0	0	0	0	0	0
Intestine .	0	0	4	1	2	1	5	3	5	0	15	9	3	7	15	20
Intestines .	0	0	0	0	1	0	4	3	3	5	2	5	6	4	5	9
Ish	0	0	0	0	0	0	0	0	0	2	0	0	0	1	1	0
Kidney ..	0	0	1	0	0	1	1	0	3	0	0	1	0	0	0	1
Large ...	0	0	0	2	0	0	0	0	0	0	0	0	1	0	0	0
Lining ..	0	0	0	0	0	0	0	0	0	0	0	0	0	2	1	0
Liver ...	0	0	2	1	0	1	1	0	2	5	2	0	0	1	2	1
Lungs ...	1	0	0	0	0	0	3	1	1	0	1	0	0	0	1	0
Man	3	2	2	0	1	0	2	1	1	0	2	0	1	0	1	2
March ..	2	0	0	0	0	0	0	0	0	0	0	0	0	0	0	0
Middle ..	2	1	0	0	0	0	0	0	0	0	0	0	0	0	0	0
Mine ...	0	0	1	0	0	0	0	1	1	0	0	0	0	0	0	2
Mouth ...	2	3	0	2	2	1	2	3	5	1	2	1	2	0	6	1
Muscle ..	0	0	0	0	0	0	0	1	0	0	1	0	0	0	0	2
Muscles ..	0	0	0	0	0	0	0	0	0	0	0	0	0	1	2	0
Organ ...	0	0	1	0	2	1	6	2	2	2	4	2	1	2	9	11
Oval ...	0	0	0	0	0	0	2	0	0	0	0	0	0	0	0	0
Pain	1	1	2	1	0	3	1	3	1	3	1	2	4	2	7	8
Pains ...	0	0	0	0	0	0	0	0	0	0	0	0	0	1	2	1
Part of body	0	1	1	0	0	0	0	2	0	2	0	0	1	0	0	0
People ...	2	1	2	0	0	1	0	1	1	2	0	0	0	1	0	0
Person ..	2	4	4	2	4	3	1	4	2	2	1	3	3	1	2	1
Place ...	0	0	1	2	0	0	1	0	0	0	0	0	0	0	0	0
Pump ...	0	0	0	0	0	0	0	0	0	1	0	0	0	0	3	2
Red	0	0	0	1	1	0	1	0	2	0	1	0	0	0	0	0
Round ...	5	4	1	3	0	4	0	1	0	0	0	2	0	1	5	1
Science ..	0	0	0	0	0	0	2	1	1	2	0	0	0	0	0	0
Sick	1	4	1	2	1	0	1	1	2	0	6	3	4	5	4	7
Sickness .	0	0	2	0	0	0	0	0	1	0	0	0	0	1	0	0
Skin	2	1	1	2	0	2	1	1	0	1	0	0	0	0	2	1
Small ...	1	1	0	0	0	0	0	2	0	2	3	0	0	0	0	0
Soft	1	0	1	5	3	0	0	1	0	3	0	1	0	0	2	2
Sore ...	0	1	1	0	0	2	0	0	0	0	0	2	3	2	0	1
Sour	0	0	0	0	1	0	0	0	0	0	1	1	0	0	4	0

Response Word	4th M	4th F	5th M	5th F	6th M	6th F	7th M	7th F	8th M	8th F	10th M	10th F	12th M	12th F	College M	College F

STOMACH

Response Word	4th M	4th F	5th M	5th F	6th M	6th F	7th M	7th F	8th M	8th F	10th M	10th F	12th M	12th F	College M	College F
Stomach ache	0	0	0	2	1	0	0	2	1	3	0	0	0	0	1	0
Stop	2	1	0	0	0	0	0	0	0	0	0	0	0	0	0	0
The	0	0	0	0	2	0	0	0	0	0	0	0	0	0	0	0
Thin	0	0	0	2	0	1	0	0	0	0	0	0	0	0	0	0
Thing	1	0	3	0	1	1	0	0	0	0	0	0	0	0	0	0
Throat	2	0	0	0	0	0	1	0	1	0	0	0	0	1	2	1
Trouble	0	0	0	0	0	0	0	0	0	0	1	0	0	0	3	3
Tummy	11	10	2	10	4	4	0	2	0	2	1	0	0	1	0	1
Ulcer	0	0	0	0	0	0	0	0	0	0	1	2	2	1	9	10
Ulcers	0	0	0	0	0	0	0	0	0	0	0	0	1	0	7	4
Upset	0	0	1	0	0	1	2	3	2	2	0	1	1	1	4	3
Vomit	0	0	0	0	1	0	0	0	3	0	0	0	0	0	1	0
Weak	0	0	2	0	0	0	0	0	0	0	0	0	0	0	0	0

162. STOVE

Response Word	4th M	4th F	5th M	5th F	6th M	6th F	7th M	7th F	8th M	8th F	10th M	10th F	12th M	12th F	College M	College F
Appliance	0	0	0	0	0	1	2	1	1	0	0	1	0	0	1	0
Bake	0	2	2	0	0	2	0	1	1	3	0	0	1	0	1	2
Black	2	3	0	0	2	0	2	2	1	2	4	5	6	6	14	9
Bolt	0	0	0	0	1	0	0	0	0	0	0	0	3	0	1	0
Burn	2	2	0	4	4	2	2	1	1	0	2	2	0	1	2	3
Burner	0	2	1	1	0	1	2	2	0	4	0	1	0	2	5	2
Burners	0	0	0	2	0	1	0	0	0	1	0	1	0	0	1	2
Chair	0	3	0	2	0	0	0	1	0	1	0	0	1	0	1	1
Chimney	0	0	0	0	0	1	1	0	0	0	0	0	2	1	1	1
Coal	0	0	0	0	0	2	0	1	2	0	2	1	2	0	2	0
Coffee	0	0	0	2	0	0	0	0	0	0	0	0	0	1	0	0
Cook	27	42	26	49	14	44	24	40	27	35	16	26	15	26	33	64
Cooking	2	9	2	2	5	6	6	8	4	6	5	5	3	12	6	7
Dinner	0	1	0	0	0	0	1	0	0	0	0	2	0	0	0	0
Eat	2	0	4	3	1	0	1	1	2	0	1	1	1	1	1	1
Fire	29	18	17	24	27	24	18	15	13	23	14	10	16	10	27	33
Floor	0	2	1	0	0	0	0	0	0	0	0	0	0	0	0	0
Food	5	7	9	3	19	15	15	9	22	14	14	21	17	19	20	28
Furnace	1	0	1	1	0	1	1	1	5	1	3	1	1	1	4	1
Gas	3	2	5	4	7	5	5	5	2	1	3	0	1	3	4	3
Heat	16	13	30	22	42	18	27	16	37	15	49	21	57	40	111	57
Heater	1	0	1	0	1	0	2	0	0	0	0	0	1	0	0	0
Hot	70	60	59	46	41	42	50	56	48	48	52	71	34	51	104	122
House	0	0	0	1	1	2	2	1	0	1	0	0	0	1	1	0
Icebox	0	1	0	1	1	2	0	2	0	0	0	0	0	0	1	1
Iron	3	2	3	0	1	0	3	0	1	0	0	1	0	0	5	2
Kettle	1	0	0	1	0	1	0	0	1	2	0	0	0	0	0	1
Kitchen	3	6	2	4	6	5	6	3	5	4	5	1	3	3	6	8
Lid	0	0	2	0	0	0	0	0	0	0	0	0	0	0	0	0
Light	4	1	1	2	2	1	5	2	0	4	2	2	1	0	3	3
Long	0	2	0	0	0	0	0	0	0	0	0	0	0	0	0	0
Metal	1	0	1	0	0	0	2	0	0	0	0	0	0	0	0	0
New	0	0	0	0	0	0	0	0	0	0	0	0	0	2	0	0

Response Word	4th M	4th F	5th M	5th F	6th M	6th F	7th M	7th F	8th M	8th F	10th M	10th F	12th M	12th F	College M	College F
										STOVE						
Oven	23	35	25	30	17	26	22	34	22	38	10	22	9	16	13	24
Pan	3	2	2	3	1	0	0	1	0	4	2	0	1	1	1	5
Pans	0	1	0	0	0	1	0	0	0	2	0	2	0	0	0	0
Pipe	3	1	11	9	16	11	13	11	11	12	29	26	30	17	55	43
Place	0	0	2	1	0	0	0	0	0	0	0	0	0	0	0	0
Pot	1	3	2	0	0	1	0	2	0	1	0	1	1	0	3	2
Range	0	0	1	4	0	1	5	1	5	2	1	1	0	2	4	1
Refrigerator	1	1	1	1	0	3	2	0	5	0	0	2	2	4	2	7
Rock	2	0	0	0	0	0	0	0	0	0	0	0	0	0	0	0
Shove	0	0	0	0	0	0	2	0	0	0	0	0	0	0	0	0
Sink	1	2	0	2	0	2	2	4	2	3	0	1	3	3	1	2
Smoke	2	0	1	1	0	0	2	0	2	0	0	0	1	0	1	0
Steel	0	0	1	0	0	0	1	0	2	0	0	0	0	0	0	0
Store	0	0	0	0	0	0	0	0	2	0	0	0	0	0	0	0
Table	1	2	0	0	0	0	0	0	0	0	0	0	0	0	1	0
Thing	0	0	0	0	2	0	0	0	0	1	0	0	0	0	0	0
Top	0	0	0	0	0	0	0	0	0	0	0	0	0	0	0	2
Warm	7	7	8	6	8	11	5	8	4	7	19	9	13	13	27	21
Warmth	0	0	0	1	3	4	6	5	1	2	5	3	6	5	11	15
White	2	0	1	0	0	1	0	0	0	0	0	1	0	0	0	1
Wood	2	0	2	0	3	0	3	2	4	2	4	2	3	1	7	7
							163.	STREET								
Address	2	1	0	1	1	2	0	0	1	0	0	2	2	2	4	1
Aldrich	0	0	1	1	2	0	0	2	0	0	0	0	0	0	0	0
Alley	4	3	1	4	4	4	3	7	5	2	6	6	7	4	7	9
Ave.	10	4	15	9	3	4	6	2	6	6	7	1	4	0	6	1
Avenue	11	4	11	13	16	21	41	33	30	35	49	44	52	50	38	42
Big	1	1	1	1	0	2	1	0	0	0	0	0	0	0	0	0
Black	10	6	2	6	6	5	1	1	0	3	7	3	3	4	5	5
Block	5	2	3	2	5	2	0	2	3	2	3	3	2	4	7	2
Busy	0	0	0	1	0	0	0	0	0	0	0	1	0	4	0	1
Car	26	25	23	30	21	19	17	14	22	18	24	17	16	19	50	49
Cars	12	22	10	14	14	14	8	14	9	18	10	20	12	19	25	34
Cement	0	0	1	0	1	1	1	0	3	4	0	1	2	0	1	3
City	8	9	4	8	2	6	8	5	5	7	11	11	2	1	26	10
Clean	0	0	0	0	1	2	0	2	0	2	1	0	0	1	4	3
Cleaner	0	0	1	1	2	0	1	1	0	0	4	2	3	1	5	7
Concrete	0	0	0	0	0	0	0	0	0	0	0	0	0	0	2	0
Corner	0	1	3	0	0	3	4	5	3	2	6	5	6	10	8	8
Cross	1	0	0	2	0	1	1	2	0	1	1	2	1	3	5	1
Crossing	0	0	0	0	0	0	0	0	0	0	1	0	0	0	3	1
Curb	1	1	0	0	1	0	0	0	1	1	0	1	4	0	1	3
Curbing	0	0	0	0	0	0	0	0	0	0	0	0	0	0	0	2
Dark	0	0	0	0	0	1	0	1	3	2	1	3	2	2	2	0
Dirt	0	0	1	0	0	0	0	0	1	1	0	0	2	0	1	0
Dirty	0	0	0	1	0	0	2	1	0	1	0	0	0	0	1	2
Drive	0	1	2	0	0	1	0	1	1	1	0	0	8	2	7	3
DuPont	0	0	0	0	0	0	1	0	0	2	0	0	0	0	0	0

Response Word	4th M	4th F	5th M	5th F	6th M	6th F	7th M	7th F	8th M	8th F	10th M	10th F	12th M	12th F	College M	College F
						STREET										
Fight	0	0	0	0	0	0	0	0	1	0	2	0	2	1	4	1
Gang . . .	0	0	0	0	0	0	0	0	0	0	0	1	0	0	4	1
Garfield . .	0	0	0	2	0	0	0	0	0	0	0	0	0	0	0	0
Hard . . .	1	0	0	0	2	1	2	1	0	0	0	0	0	0	1	1
Highway . .	3	3	1	3	2	3	2	2	3	1	0	0	1	1	2	1
Home . . .	1	0	1	0	2	1	1	0	3	1	1	1	1	2	2	2
House . . .	3	6	6	5	3	10	3	4	10	7	8	10	5	7	5	17
Houses . .	0	1	0	1	0	1	0	2	0	1	0	2	2	4	2	7
Hurry . . .	0	0	0	0	0	0	0	0	0	0	0	0	0	0	2	0
Kenwood .	0	0	0	0	0	2	0	0	0	0	0	0	0	0	0	0
King	1	1	0	0	2	2	0	0	0	0	0	0	0	0	0	0
Knox . . .	0	0	0	0	0	0	0	3	0	0	0	0	0	0	0	0
Lake	1	1	0	1	0	1	1	0	0	0	2	0	1	0	2	0
Lamp . . .	1	0	1	3	0	0	4	3	1	2	3	1	1	0	2	7
Land . . .	0	0	0	0	2	0	0	0	0	0	0	0	0	0	0	0
Lane . . .	0	1	1	0	1	4	3	7	0	1	0	2	2	0	4	5
Leaves . .	0	0	0	0	0	0	0	0	0	0	0	0	0	0	0	2
Light . . .	6	4	4	2	12	5	5	7	9	8	8	11	11	8	29	19
Lights . .	0	0	0	1	0	0	0	3	1	2	0	1	0	1	1	8
Line	1	2	2	0	0	0	0	0	0	0	0	1	1	0	1	2
Live	4	1	1	2	3	1	2	0	1	1	3	1	2	2	5	5
Logan	0	0	0	2	0	0	0	0	0	1	0	0	0	0	0	0
Long . . .	4	9	6	2	9	1	5	5	2	4	7	3	1	5	4	4
Lyndale . .	0	0	0	2	0	0	0	0	0	0	0	0	0	0	0	0
Main . . .	0	0	0	2	1	0	1	0	0	1	0	1	1	0	0	2
Mine . . .	0	0	1	0	0	0	0	0	0	0	0	0	2	0	1	0
Name . . .	0	0	0	0	1	0	0	0	0	2	0	0	0	0	3	1
Narrow . .	0	0	0	0	0	0	0	2	1	0	1	0	0	4	1	2
Night	0	2	0	2	0	1	0	1	0	1	0	1	0	0	1	0
Noise . . .	0	0	0	0	0	0	0	0	0	0	0	0	1	1	2	5
Noisy . . .	0	0	0	0	0	0	0	0	0	2	0	1	0	0	0	0
Number . .	1	1	0	0	0	5	2	0	0	0	0	3	1	1	4	0
Path	1	0	0	0	0	1	0	1	0	0	0	0	0	0	0	4
Paved . . .	0	0	0	0	0	0	0	0	1	3	1	0	0	0	1	1
Pavement .	0	0	3	2	1	1	3	1	1	0	1	3	1	4	7	8
People . .	0	0	0	0	1	1	0	1	0	0	0	0	0	0	5	2
Place . . .	0	0	4	3	2	1	4	1	2	3	2	1	0	0	0	1
Play	0	1	1	0	0	0	0	0	0	0	0	0	1	0	1	3
Post	0	0	0	0	1	0	1	0	2	0	0	0	0	0	0	1
Ride	2	5	2	1	2	0	1	2	1	0	0	1	1	0	0	0
Road . . .	50	62	70	48	51	47	53	44	56	26	26	25	26	26	58	60
Rode . . .	3	0	2	1	4	1	0	0	0	0	0	0	0	0	0	0
Rough . . .	0	0	0	0	0	0	0	0	0	1	0	0	1	2	0	0
Run	0	0	0	0	0	0	0	0	0	2	1	0	1	0	1	0
Russell . .	0	0	0	0	0	0	0	0	2	0	0	0	0	0	1	1
Scene . . .	0	0	0	0	0	0	0	0	0	0	0	0	0	0	3	1
Side	4	0	0	0	0	0	0	0	1	0	1	0	1	0	0	0
Sidewalk .	8	23	11	15	12	14	6	19	9	17	5	12	4	11	7	19
Sidewalks .	0	0	0	0	0	0	0	0	0	0	0	0	0	0	0	2

Response Word	4th M	4th F	5th M	5th F	6th M	6th F	7th M	7th F	8th M	8th F	10th M	10th F	12th M	12th F	College M	College F
							STREET									
Sign	2	1	2	1	1	2	4	3	2	4	1	2	4	4	7	16
Signs	0	0	0	0	0	0	0	0	0	1	0	0	0	0	0	2
Sixteen	0	0	0	0	0	0	2	0	0	0	0	0	0	0	0	0
Snow	0	0	0	0	0	0	0	0	0	0	0	0	0	2	0	0
Song	0	0	0	0	0	0	0	1	0	0	0	0	1	0	2	1
Sour	0	2	1	0	0	0	2	0	1	0	0	0	1	0	1	2
Street lamps	0	0	0	0	0	0	0	0	0	0	0	0	0	0	0	2
Sweet	1	0	2	0	0	1	0	0	1	0	0	0	0	0	0	0
Tar	9	3	11	2	8	8	6	2	6	5	7	2	8	1	10	5
Taylor	0	0	0	2	1	0	0	0	0	0	0	0	0	0	0	0
Thirty eighth	0	0	0	0	0	0	0	0	0	0	1	0	0	2	0	0
Three	0	0	0	0	0	2	0	0	0	0	0	0	0	0	0	0
Town	3	2	3	2	5	4	7	2	1	2	9	2	2	1	8	10
Traffic	0	0	0	0	0	0	1	0	0	0	0	0	0	1	2	1
Trees	0	0	0	0	0	0	0	1	0	0	0	1	1	1	1	2
Walk	6	12	8	11	7	14	6	7	8	11	2	13	4	8	23	27
Walker	0	0	0	0	0	0	0	0	0	0	0	0	0	0	4	0
Washington	0	0	0	1	0	0	0	0	0	0	0	0	0	0	2	1
Wide	0	1	0	1	0	1	0	1	1	1	0	1	2	2	3	2
Yard	0	1	2	1	1	0	0	1	0	0	0	0	1	0	0	1
						164.	SWEET									
Apple	2	1	3	1	1	0	0	0	3	2	0	0	1	0	0	4
Awful	0	2	1	0	3	0	0	1	2	0	0	0	0	0	0	0
Bad	2	1	1	0	1	1	1	0	1	1	1	0	0	0	0	0
Beautiful	1	2	1	1	1	1	0	0	0	1	0	0	0	0	0	0
Better	0	1	0	1	1	0	0	0	2	0	0	0	1	0	1	0
Bird	0	0	1	1	2	0	1	0	1	0	0	0	1	0	2	1
Bitter	5	4	6	8	4	5	17	7	14	7	17	12	13	8	24	11
Boy	0	0	0	0	0	2	0	0	0	3	0	4	1	1	0	0
Cake	1	2	0	1	1	2	0	0	1	1	1	1	1	4	0	2
Candy	28	22	32	26	30	28	31	40	22	37	45	52	43	51	63	96
Charming	0	0	0	2	0	0	0	0	0	0	2	0	0	0	0	0
Chocolate	0	0	0	0	1	0	2	1	0	2	5	4	4	4	3	4
Cider	0	0	0	0	0	1	0	0	0	0	0	0	0	1	2	0
Delicious	0	0	0	2	0	0	0	0	0	0	0	0	0	0	0	0
Eat	1	3	1	1	0	0	0	1	0	0	1	1	0	0	1	0
Flower	1	1	0	0	0	3	1	0	1	2	0	0	0	0	0	0
Flowers	2	0	0	2	0	0	0	0	0	0	0	1	0	0	0	0
Food	2	1	0	0	1	1	2	0	2	0	0	1	0	0	4	2
Fruit	2	2	0	3	0	0	2	1	1	2	0	0	0	0	0	1
Gentle	0	0	0	0	0	1	0	2	0	0	0	0	0	0	0	2
Girl	2	1	4	1	6	2	3	1	7	4	10	4	8	4	12	3
Girls	0	1	0	0	1	0	1	0	5	0	2	1	2	0	0	0
Good	29	21	50	20	31	33	24	24	12	6	22	15	17	8	15	19
Hard	0	1	1	2	3	3	1	0	3	2	0	1	0	0	1	2
Harsh	0	0	0	0	0	0	0	3	1	1	0	1	2	1	0	1
Honey	6	0	4	5	9	0	4	3	0	4	2	4	6	1	4	10
Horrid	0	2	0	0	0	0	0	0	0	1	0	0	0	0	0	0

Response Word	4th M	4th F	5th M	5th F	6th M	6th F	7th M	7th F	8th M	8th F	10th M	10th F	12th M	12th F	College M	College F
							SWEET									
Hot	0	0	0	2	1	0	0	0	1	0	0	1	0	1	0	0
Ice cream .	0	0	0	0	0	0	0	0	0	0	2	0	0	1	2	0
Kind	3	6	1	5	2	3	0	1	2	2	0	2	1	4	0	1
Kiss ...	3	0	0	0	0	0	0	0	0	0	0	0	1	0	1	0
Lemon ..	0	0	0	0	0	0	0	0	1	1	2	0	0	0	0	1
Loud	0	0	0	0	1	1	1	2	0	1	0	0	0	0	0	1
Love ...	1	5	4	4	1	2	0	3	1	1	0	0	0	0	0	2
Loveable .	0	0	0	0	0	0	0	0	0	0	0	1	0	0	2	0
Lovely ...	4	1	2	6	3	3	1	3	3	1	0	2	0	1	1	1
Low	0	0	0	1	0	2	0	0	0	2	0	2	1	5	1	6
Mad	1	1	1	0	3	1	0	1	0	1	0	0	0	0	0	0
Mean ...	3	4	2	3	2	2	0	4	1	1	2	3	1	0	0	1
Mellow ..	0	0	0	0	0	0	1	0	2	1	0	0	1	0	0	2
Melody ..	0	0	0	0	0	0	0	0	0	0	0	0	0	0	2	0
Mother ..	0	2	1	0	1	2	0	0	0	0	0	0	0	0	0	0
Music ...	2	1	1	3	4	6	6	12	8	6	6	10	8	17	26	30
Nice	32	55	26	30	15	35	15	30	18	28	8	7	9	8	8	15
Orange ..	0	0	0	0	0	0	2	1	1	0	0	1	0	0	0	1
Pie	1	0	0	0	0	0	0	0	1	1	0	1	2	0	2	1
Pretty ..	1	4	2	2	1	3	3	5	1	5	0	0	0	2	2	4
Roll	0	0	0	1	0	0	0	0	0	0	0	0	0	0	2	0
Rotten ..	0	0	2	0	0	0	0	0	1	0	0	0	0	0	0	0
Salt	1	0	0	0	0	0	0	0	0	0	0	0	0	0	0	2
Sidewalk .	2	0	0	0	0	0	0	0	0	0	0	0	0	0	0	0
Smell ...	2	6	4	6	3	1	2	1	1	0	3	5	2	1	4	2
Smooth ..	2	0	1	0	0	0	0	0	0	0	0	0	0	1	0	0
Soft	4	1	1	7	4	8	12	7	5	8	6	7	7	6	22	18
Song ...	0	1	1	0	0	1	0	0	0	0	0	0	2	1	6	4
Sour	37	19	33	31	34	41	53	58	76	72	60	67	67	73	191	163
Sticky ...	0	0	0	0	0	0	0	0	0	0	0	0	0	0	2	0
Sue	0	0	0	1	0	0	0	0	0	2	0	0	0	0	0	0
Sugar ...	24	22	25	25	40	25	30	16	25	21	30	26	30	20	54	49
Sugary ..	0	1	0	0	0	1	0	2	0	0	0	0	0	0	0	0
Talk ...	0	1	0	0	0	0	0	0	0	0	0	0	0	1	0	2
Taste ...	2	3	4	4	3	2	7	3	2	1	4	1	6	0	16	2
Tasty ...	1	1	2	1	0	0	1	1	0	0	3	0	0	1	1	0
Teeth ...	2	0	1	1	1	0	0	0	0	0	1	0	1	0	0	0
Terrible .	0	0	0	0	1	1	2	0	0	0	0	0	0	0	0	0
Tooth ...	0	0	1	1	0	1	0	1	0	0	0	2	2	1	5	5
Tweet ...	0	2	1	1	0	0	0	0	0	0	0	0	0	0	0	0
Ugly	1	0	2	4	0	0	0	0	2	0	1	0	0	0	0	0
Woman ..	1	0	1	0	0	0	2	0	0	0	0	0	0	0	0	0
Work ...	0	0	2	0	0	0	0	0	0	0	0	0	0	0	0	0
						165.	SWIFT									
Arrow ...	0	0	0	0	1	0	0	0	0	2	1	0	3	0	3	0
Bacon ...	1	1	2	0	0	0	0	0	0	0	1	1	3	1	3	5
Bird ...	1	2	0	1	2	1	1	1	2	3	4	3	5	3	10	3
Birds ...	0	0	0	0	0	0	0	1	0	2	0	0	0	0	1	0

Response Word	4th M	4th F	5th M	5th F	6th M	6th F	7th M	7th F	8th M	8th F	10th M	10th F	12th M	12th F	College M	College F
								SWIFT								
Boat	0	0	1	0	0	0	1	0	0	1	1	0	0	1	1	2
Book ...	0	0	0	0	1	0	0	0	0	0	0	0	0	0	1	2
Boy	1	0	3	0	1	0	1	0	0	0	0	1	0	0	0	1
Broom ..	0	2	0	0	0	0	0	0	0	0	0	0	0	0	0	0
Car	1	2	1	0	0	2	2	1	1	0	2	1	2	1	4	2
Cheese ..	6	5	5	3	5	1	1	1	1	0	0	0	1	1	1	0
Company .	1	1	0	0	0	0	3	0	0	0	0	0	0	1	4	0
Current ..	1	0	4	2	6	3	3	2	4	0	2	4	2	5	5	22
Deer ...	1	0	0	4	1	3	3	2	3	4	1	7	3	0	4	5
Dog	0	0	0	0	0	1	0	1	0	0	1	1	2	0	1	1
Eagle ...	0	0	0	0	0	0	0	0	0	0	0	3	1	0	3	4
Easy ...	0	0	0	0	0	0	0	1	0	0	0	3	0	1	0	0
Fast	124	122	124	136	137	156	142	159	100	124	127	129	114	137	224	228
Fleet ...	0	0	0	0	0	0	0	0	1	0	0	0	1	0	1	4
Flour ...	0	0	0	0	1	2	0	0	0	0	0	0	0	0	0	0
Fly	0	0	0	1	0	2	0	1	1	0	0	0	0	0	1	4
Food ...	2	2	1	0	2	1	1	0	1	0	2	0	0	1	2	0
Foot	0	1	0	0	1	0	0	0	0	0	0	0	1	0	2	0
Go	2	0	0	0	1	0	0	0	1	0	0	0	0	0	0	0
Good ...	3	0	0	1	0	1	1	0	1	0	0	0	0	1	0	0
Ham	1	2	0	0	0	3	0	0	1	0	2	2	0	1	0	1
Hard ...	2	2	1	1	0	0	2	0	0	1	0	1	0	0	0	0
Horse ...	0	1	2	0	0	4	0	3	1	3	1	4	3	1	1	8
Hurry ...	0	3	0	2	1	1	0	3	1	3	1	0	0	2	0	3
Indian ...	0	0	0	0	0	0	0	0	0	0	0	1	0	0	1	2
John	0	0	0	0	0	0	0	0	0	1	0	0	0	0	2	0
Jonathan .	0	0	0	0	0	0	0	0	0	0	0	0	4	3	5	5
Kick	0	0	0	0	0	0	1	1	1	0	2	0	0	1	1	2
Lake ...	0	1	0	0	2	1	0	0	0	0	0	1	0	0	1	0
Light ...	1	1	1	3	0	1	1	0	0	5	0	0	0	0	1	0
Lightning .	0	0	0	0	0	0	0	0	0	0	0	0	0	0	0	3
Meat	4	5	8	2	3	2	4	2	9	10	7	1	11	6	11	8
Meats ...	0	0	0	0	0	0	0	0	2	0	1	0	0	0	1	0
Mighty ..	0	0	0	0	0	0	2	0	0	0	0	0	0	0	0	0
Nice	2	2	0	1	0	0	1	1	0	0	0	1	0	0	0	0
Plane ...	0	0	0	0	0	0	0	0	0	0	0	0	0	0	2	0
Premium .	0	0	1	0	0	0	0	0	3	0	1	0	1	1	1	1
Product ..	0	2	1	0	0	0	0	0	0	0	0	0	0	0	0	0
Quick ...	0	3	4	1	4	0	1	3	4	3	4	6	2	0	7	7
Quickly ..	1	0	1	1	0	1	0	0	0	0	0	2	0	0	0	2
Rabbit ...	0	0	2	0	0	0	1	0	1	1	0	2	2	0	2	0
Race	0	0	0	0	0	0	0	0	0	0	0	1	0	0	2	1
Rapid ...	0	0	0	0	0	1	0	3	1	1	1	0	1	1	2	2
River ...	4	6	4	4	7	3	10	5	11	8	18	14	13	9	23	16
Run	10	10	5	8	10	7	5	1	2	4	7	6	6	7	11	24
Runner ..	0	0	1	1	1	1	0	0	2	1	1	3	0	2	9	2
Running ..	1	2	1	1	3	1	0	0	2	3	0	1	0	0	1	5
Shortening .	0	0	0	0	0	1	0	0	1	0	1	2	3	2	0	0
Slow	19	12	19	12	17	13	22	16	53	34	32	29	41	32	85	70

Response Word	4th M	4th F	5th M	5th F	6th M	6th F	7th M	7th F	8th M	8th F	10th M	10th F	12th M	12th F	College M	College F
							SWIFT									
Slowly . . .	0	1	0	0	0	0	0	0	0	0	0	0	0	1	0	2
Smooth . .	6	11	9	9	5	6	5	7	4	4	0	1	0	2	1	0
Soft	2	2	1	2	0	1	0	2	1	0	1	1	0	0	1	1
Speed . . .	0	1	1	0	3	1	0	1	0	2	1	0	0	4	6	3
Speedy . .	0	0	0	0	0	0	0	2	1	0	1	1	1	0	2	3
Stream . .	1	2	0	4	1	2	7	1	2	3	4	2	2	0	6	6
Strong . . .	1	0	0	4	1	0	3	2	0	2	0	0	0	0	2	1
Sure	0	0	0	0	0	0	0	1	0	0	0	0	2	0	6	0
Swallow . .	0	0	0	0	0	0	0	0	0	0	0	0	0	0	0	2
Tom . . .	0	0	0	0	1	0	0	0	2	0	0	0	1	0	1	2
Water . . .	5	2	5	5	4	4	5	5	5	9	2	4	2	1	4	4
Wind . . .	2	3	5	2	2	3	0	1	1	1	1	1	0	1	0	1
Wing	0	0	0	0	0	0	0	0	0	0	0	0	0	0	2	0
Writer . .	0	0	0	0	0	0	0	0	0	0	0	0	0	2	0	1
						166.	TABLE									
Able	1	1	1	3	0	1	0	0	0	0	0	0	0	0	0	0
Big	4	3	3	1	4	4	1	1	1	0	7	4	0	1	1	0
Board . . .	1	0	0	2	0	1	0	0	0	0	0	0	0	0	0	0
Book . . .	0	0	0	0	0	0	2	1	0	0	1	0	0	0	1	0
Brown . . .	2	3	0	2	2	6	0	0	1	2	2	2	0	2	2	2
Cards . . .	0	0	0	0	0	0	0	0	0	0	0	0	0	0	2	0
Chair . . .	108	108	89	107	88	110	121	148	131	155	114	154	155	175	325	366
Chairs . .	2	1	2	4	5	1	2	6	3	5	2	4	2	3	1	1
Cloth . . .	9	10	8	5	4	4	3	2	4	3	11	3	9	6	16	13
Cup	0	0	0	0	3	0	1	1	0	1	0	0	0	0	0	0
Dark . . .	1	0	0	0	1	0	0	2	1	0	0	0	1	0	1	1
Desk . . .	5	5	16	7	9	8	17	6	12	7	14	17	12	12	17	16
Dinner . .	1	3	2	1	1	2	0	1	1	1	2	3	0	0	2	2
Dish	1	1	3	5	2	1	1	1	0	1	0	1	3	0	2	6
Dishes . .	1	2	0	7	1	4	1	3	2	3	1	1	3	3	0	4
Eat	30	40	24	43	20	27	19	16	7	15	8	7	10	6	15	8
Eating . .	3	6	2	1	3	2	5	5	2	0	4	0	1	0	1	1
Flat	4	3	2	1	8	10	2	1	2	2	1	1	0	0	3	0
Floor . . .	1	0	2	0	1	0	1	0	2	0	0	0	0	0	1	1
Food . . .	22	23	26	25	35	32	32	23	56	33	36	20	18	19	35	24
Fork . . .	0	0	0	0	1	0	0	0	0	1	1	0	0	2	0	5
Furniture .	2	3	3	1	4	2	1	0	1	0	0	2	0	0	0	0
Glass . . .	0	0	2	1	0	0	1	2	0	0	3	0	1	0	0	0
Hard	0	2	3	2	2	0	1	2	0	1	1	1	0	0	0	0
Hat	0	0	2	0	0	0	0	0	0	0	0	0	1	0	0	0
High . . .	1	0	2	0	0	2	0	0	0	0	0	0	0	0	0	0
Kitchen . .	1	1	0	0	0	0	1	3	1	1	6	1	1	2	4	2
Lamp . . .	0	1	0	1	0	1	3	0	1	1	1	0	1	1	4	4
Large . .	0	0	0	0	0	0	0	1	0	0	2	0	0	0	1	0
Leg	1	1	0	0	1	0	2	1	3	2	1	2	3	1	9	2
Legs . . .	3	2	2	1	6	1	1	3	2	3	1	2	2	0	4	3
Maple . . .	0	0	0	0	1	0	0	0	0	0	0	0	0	1	2	0
Plate . . .	2	2	0	0	2	0	0	0	0	0	1	2	1	0	0	3

Response Word	4th M	4th F	5th M	5th F	6th M	6th F	7th M	7th F	8th M	8th F	10th M	10th F	12th M	12th F	College M	College F
							TABLE									
Red	1	0	2	0	1	0	0	0	0	0	0	0	0	0	0	0
Room	0	0	0	0	0	0	0	2	0	0	0	0	0	0	0	0
Round	1	0	1	1	0	2	1	0	0	1	0	1	1	0	2	0
Salt	0	0	1	0	0	0	2	0	0	0	0	0	2	0	3	1
Set	0	1	2	2	0	0	0	0	1	1	0	1	0	0	1	2
Silverware	0	2	0	0	0	0	0	0	0	0	1	0	0	0	1	0
Sit	3	3	1	3	0	2	0	0	0	0	0	1	0	1	1	0
Smooth	0	0	0	3	0	0	0	0	0	0	1	0	0	0	0	0
Something to eat at	0	0	0	0	0	0	0	0	2	0	0	0	0	0	0	0
Spoon	0	3	7	3	1	1	0	0	0	1	0	1	0	1	4	1
Square	0	0	0	0	2	0	1	0	0	0	0	2	0	0	0	0
Supper	0	0	2	0	0	1	1	0	0	0	0	0	0	0	0	0
Table cloth	0	1	1	0	0	0	3	0	0	0	0	1	2	2	1	2
Tennis	0	0	0	0	0	0	0	0	0	0	2	0	0	0	1	1
The	0	0	2	0	1	0	0	0	0	0	0	0	0	0	0	0
Top	0	1	2	0	10	4	2	3	2	1	4	3	8	2	20	10
Wood	9	1	9	5	8	9	10	6	6	1	7	3	3	4	2	5
						167.	TAKE									
A	0	1	0	0	1	0	1	0	0	1	0	1	0	0	2	0
Along	0	2	2	6	1	3	0	1	0	0	1	1	0	2	4	7
Ask	0	0	0	0	0	0	0	2	0	1	0	0	0	0	0	0
Away	13	10	9	9	6	6	6	5	4	6	3	9	3	2	10	13
Back	1	0	3	2	0	2	0	1	0	0	0	0	1	0	0	0
Bake	1	1	2	2	0	1	1	3	0	0	0	0	0	0	1	0
Book	0	0	0	0	0	0	0	0	0	1	0	0	0	0	0	2
Books	0	0	0	0	0	0	0	1	0	0	0	0	0	0	2	1
Borrow	0	0	0	0	0	0	1	2	1	0	0	1	0	1	2	1
Bring	3	5	6	7	4	7	4	8	6	8	38	46	20	35	7	36
Buy	1	1	1	0	0	1	3	1	6	4	0	1	1	2	4	7
Cake	2	3	2	2	1	1	0	1	0	1	0	1	1	0	0	1
Candy	1	2	1	0	2	0	1	0	0	0	0	1	0	1	2	1
Care	8	9	18	9	10	12	4	8	10	10	9	10	11	6	12	9
Carry	4	2	0	3	2	5	0	7	4	7	1	3	0	4	5	14
Come	0	0	0	1	1	0	0	0	0	2	0	0	1	1	1	0
Cookie	0	1	0	0	0	0	0	2	0	0	0	0	0	0	1	0
Don't	0	1	0	1	0	2	2	0	0	0	0	0	0	0	0	0
Easier	0	0	0	0	2	0	1	0	0	0	0	0	0	0	0	0
Easy	2	2	1	2	2	2	3	4	1	7	4	6	5	7	26	19
Eat	1	0	0	0	2	0	0	1	0	2	0	0	0	0	1	2
Five	0	0	0	0	0	0	0	0	0	0	0	0	2	0	0	0
From	0	0	1	0	3	0	3	0	2	1	2	1	0	0	3	0
Gave	0	0	1	0	0	2	1	0	0	1	0	0	0	0	0	0
Get	2	5	6	8	3	6	2	7	4	6	3	5	3	7	18	26
Gift	0	0	0	1	0	0	0	0	0	0	0	0	0	0	0	3
Give	17	13	15	15	16	24	17	28	22	28	13	31	23	27	46	70
Given	0	0	0	0	0	2	0	0	0	0	0	1	0	0	0	0
Go	7	7	1	8	7	6	1	3	4	4	7	5	4	11	3	9

Response Word	4th M	4th F	5th M	5th F	6th M	6th F	7th M	7th F	8th M	8th F	10th M	10th F	12th M	12th F	College M	College F
							TAKE									
Good	0	2	1	0	0	0	0	0	0	0	0	0	0	0	1	0
Got	1	1	0	1	0	2	2	0	0	2	0	0	0	0	0	0
Grab	1	7	1	5	7	5	7	4	6	8	2	4	3	4	10	9
Hand	0	1	0	0	1	0	1	0	0	0	0	0	1	0	2	3
Have	0	2	1	5	1	3	1	1	0	0	3	2	0	4	6	3
Her	3	6	2	9	3	1	4	0	5	0	6	0	3	1	3	2
Here	1	2	1	0	0	0	0	0	0	1	1	1	0	0	0	0
Him	3	2	4	2	6	4	0	2	2	3	1	0	3	1	2	1
Hold	1	2	0	0	0	3	2	0	1	0	3	0	0	0	4	2
Home	0	1	0	3	1	4	4	3	2	4	1	0	0	3	5	7
How	2	0	0	0	0	1	1	0	0	0	0	0	0	0	0	0
In	0	1	0	1	1	3	1	1	4	0	3	1	1	3	2	4
It	28	21	15	17	28	19	13	9	11	6	13	22	20	22	64	40
It easy	1	0	0	0	0	0	1	0	0	0	0	1	0	0	1	2
Keep	2	1	1	4	1	6	0	3	0	2	0	0	1	3	2	8
Leave	1	5	3	8	6	4	7	11	9	8	5	8	5	10	26	18
Lift	0	0	0	0	1	0	1	2	1	0	0	0	0	0	1	1
Live	1	1	0	0	0	0	0	2	0	0	0	0	0	0	0	0
Look	1	0	2	0	0	0	0	0	0	0	1	0	1	0	0	0
Lose	0	0	0	0	1	0	0	0	0	2	0	0	0	0	2	0
Make	8	3	3	6	1	1	1	3	1	0	0	0	1	0	2	4
Me	10	11	17	9	6	8	8	8	8	11	11	7	9	8	7	9
Money	0	0	0	0	0	0	0	1	1	2	3	3	1	0	2	3
More	0	1	0	0	0	0	0	0	0	2	0	0	0	0	0	0
My	1	2	0	1	1	1	0	0	0	0	0	0	0	0	0	0
Not	0	2	0	0	0	0	0	0	0	0	0	0	0	0	1	0
Now	1	0	0	0	2	1	0	0	0	0	0	1	0	0	0	1
Obtain	0	0	0	0	0	0	0	0	0	0	0	0	1	1	3	0
Of	0	2	2	0	1	1	0	0	0	0	0	0	0	0	1	0
Off	2	3	1	1	4	1	4	1	7	4	0	0	5	0	11	2
On	1	0	1	1	1	0	0	0	0	0	0	0	0	0	1	2
One	3	3	4	8	3	1	2	3	4	3	1	4	2	2	2	2
Out	1	4	3	3	4	1	6	4	9	4	6	1	8	4	9	7
Over	0	2	2	2	4	2	1	1	4	3	4	3	7	3	9	7
Pick	0	0	0	0	0	0	0	0	1	0	0	1	0	0	3	1
Pick up	0	0	0	0	0	2	0	0	0	1	1	0	0	3	1	1
Place	1	0	1	0	1	2	1	0	0	0	0	1	1	0	2	1
Possess	0	0	1	0	0	0	0	0	0	0	0	0	0	0	2	0
Pull	0	0	2	0	0	0	1	0	0	0	0	0	0	0	0	0
Put	0	1	1	1	0	3	4	2	0	4	1	0	2	3	7	3
Receive	0	1	0	1	0	2	3	4	1	1	0	1	4	2	1	3
Remove	0	0	0	0	0	0	1	0	1	0	0	1	1	0	3	1
Replace	0	0	0	0	0	0	0	0	0	2	0	0	0	0	0	0
Return	0	0	0	0	0	0	0	0	0	1	0	0	0	0	2	0
Some	0	2	0	1	1	1	2	2	1	0	1	0	1	1	1	3
Someone	0	0	0	2	0	0	0	0	0	0	0	0	0	0	0	0
Something	1	0	5	5	3	4	2	1	0	0	0	1	0	0	1	0
Steal	11	9	15	16	21	23	32	21	17	21	23	24	17	14	39	20
Steel	0	0	2	2	1	2	0	0	0	0	0	0	0	0	0	0

Response Word	4th M	4th F	5th M	5th F	6th M	6th F	7th M	7th F	8th M	8th F	10th M	10th F	12th M	12th F	College M	College F
							TAKE									
Stole	0	1	2	0	1	0	0	2	0	3	0	0	0	0	0	1
Swipe	0	0	0	0	2	0	2	0	3	0	4	2	2	0	1	0
Taken	4	0	1	2	2	2	4	2	6	3	8	2	8	2	9	3
Takes	0	0	2	0	0	0	0	0	0	0	0	0	0	0	0	0
Taking	2	0	0	0	0	1	0	0	0	0	1	0	0	0	0	0
Talk	2	5	0	2	2	1	3	1	0	1	0	0	0	0	0	0
That	3	2	7	0	2	3	3	3	3	0	4	3	3	3	2	2
The	6	2	2	0	6	0	1	0	0	0	3	0	2	1	0	0
Them	0	0	1	0	0	0	0	0	3	0	0	0	2	0	0	1
There	1	0	0	0	3	0	1	0	0	0	0	0	0	0	0	0
They	0	0	0	0	2	0	0	0	0	0	0	0	0	0	0	0
This	4	5	0	4	2	2	0	0	0	3	5	3	2	2	3	4
Time	0	1	0	1	1	0	1	0	0	1	0	1	2	0	1	3
To	0	1	2	0	0	0	0	1	0	0	2	0	3	0	0	2
Took	10	9	11	10	9	11	31	36	39	32	9	8	23	16	42	41
Us	1	1	1	1	0	2	0	1	0	0	1	2	2	0	0	1
Wake	2	2	1	1	1	0	1	1	0	0	0	0	0	0	0	0
Walk	2	0	1	0	0	0	0	1	0	0	1	0	0	0	1	0
Want	1	0	3	0	1	0	1	0	0	1	1	0	2	0	0	0
Was	0	0	0	2	0	1	0	0	0	0	0	0	0	0	0	0
What	0	0	0	0	2	1	0	0	2	0	1	0	2	3	5	0
Where	0	0	1	1	0	0	0	0	0	0	2	0	1	1	1	0
With	15	15	7	7	8	7	9	10	3	1	9	4	4	2	3	9
Yes	2	0	0	0	0	0	0	0	0	0	0	0	0	0	0	0
You	2	6	5	2	4	1	1	0	1	0	0	2	0	0	3	1
Your	3	5	1	1	0	0	2	0	2	0	1	1	2	0	1	1
						168.	TELL									
A	2	0	3	4	0	1	1	0	0	0	0	0	0	0	0	0
All	1	1	0	0	0	1	0	2	1	0	0	1	4	2	9	13
An	0	3	0	1	1	0	0	0	0	0	0	0	0	0	0	0
Apple	0	0	0	0	0	0	0	0	0	0	0	0	1	0	3	0
Ask	2	3	3	2	3	2	2	4	1	0	1	1	1	3	5	5
Bell	3	1	0	2	1	1	4	1	0	0	1	0	0	0	1	0
Book	1	0	0	0	0	0	0	0	0	0	0	0	2	0	0	0
Ear	0	0	1	0	0	0	0	0	0	0	0	1	0	0	0	2
Explain	0	0	0	1	0	1	1	0	0	2	2	0	1	2	2	4
Fell	2	1	0	2	0	0	0	1	0	1	0	0	0	0	0	0
Give	0	0	0	1	0	0	3	0	0	1	0	0	0	0	0	0
Gossip	0	0	0	0	0	0	0	1	2	1	0	2	1	1	0	3
Hear	1	0	0	1	1	4	0	3	1	0	1	3	1	5	8	2
Hello	2	0	0	0	0	0	0	0	0	0	0	0	0	0	0	0
Her	2	2	2	2	2	7	2	5	5	7	8	6	6	3	10	6
Him	13	8	8	11	13	7	10	9	10	6	25	9	12	15	25	11
How	0	0	0	3	0	1	0	0	3	3	2	1	0	0	0	0
Ill	0	1	0	0	0	2	0	0	0	0	0	0	0	0	0	0
Inform	0	0	0	0	0	0	0	0	0	0	0	1	2	1	1	0
It	2	3	2	4	0	0	2	0	2	1	0	0	0	2	5	1

Response Word	4th M	4th F	5th M	5th F	6th M	6th F	7th M	7th F	8th M	8th F	10th M	10th F	12th M	12th F	College M	College F
							TELL									
Joke	0	0	0	0	0	0	0	0	0	0	0	0	0	0	0	2
Keep	0	0	0	0	0	2	0	0	0	1	1	1	1	1	2	3
Lie	0	0	0	1	2	0	2	2	1	0	2	3	1	1	7	2
Listen	2	1	0	2	1	3	2	2	0	1	2	3	3	2	10	12
Me	77	77	88	64	83	63	65	48	74	67	53	47	69	51	134	117
Mouth	0	1	0	1	1	0	0	0	0	0	0	0	0	0	0	2
Off	1	0	0	0	0	0	0	0	0	0	0	0	2	0	0	0
People	0	0	0	0	0	0	0	0	0	0	0	0	0	1	2	0
Phone	1	0	2	0	0	0	1	0	0	0	1	0	0	0	1	0
Quiet	0	1	0	0	0	0	0	1	1	0	0	6	1	1	1	3
Relate	0	0	0	1	0	0	0	0	0	2	2	3	1	2	7	8
Repeat	1	0	0	0	0	0	0	1	0	0	0	1	0	0	0	3
Said	0	0	0	0	0	1	2	0	2	0	0	1	0	0	0	0
Say	2	8	5	3	1	6	10	11	2	14	8	18	9	11	22	40
Secret	1	2	0	0	0	3	0	4	1	2	3	6	3	13	5	11
See	1	1	0	1	0	0	1	1	0	0	0	0	1	0	3	0
Sell	0	1	2	1	1	2	1	1	0	0	0	1	1	2	0	2
Short	0	0	0	0	0	0	1	0	0	2	0	0	0	0	0	0
Shout	0	0	0	0	0	1	0	0	0	0	1	0	0	2	1	1
Show	2	1	0	0	0	2	1	0	1	1	0	1	1	1	1	5
Silence	0	0	0	0	0	0	0	0	0	0	0	0	0	0	1	2
Some	0	1	0	0	2	0	0	0	0	0	0	0	0	0	0	0
Something	2	2	1	2	1	2	1	0	0	0	0	1	0	0	0	1
Speak	1	7	3	5	9	9	8	11	11	11	8	10	14	16	37	38
Squeal	0	0	0	0	1	0	0	0	2	0	0	0	1	0	1	0
Stories	1	1	1	0	0	1	0	2	0	0	0	0	0	1	1	0
Story	11	24	14	24	13	21	11	17	11	18	13	19	15	22	28	44
Take	2	1	1	1	1	1	0	0	1	0	1	0	0	0	0	0
Tale	1	3	2	6	2	3	1	3	0	0	1	3	2	1	3	3
Talk	34	23	27	28	36	48	37	27	19	24	40	43	23	26	36	47
Tall	1	1	5	3	1	2	3	1	1	1	1	0	0	1	0	0
Tattle	0	0	4	3	1	2	0	0	0	1	3	1	2	0	1	0
Telephone	0	0	0	2	2	1	0	1	0	1	2	1	0	0	0	1
Telling	3	0	1	1	1	1	0	4	2	0	0	1	0	0	0	0
That	3	0	0	0	1	0	0	0	2	0	0	1	0	0	0	1
The	3	5	3	2	3	0	3	0	1	0	1	0	0	1	0	0
Them	1	1	3	2	2	1	3	2	6	0	4	2	2	4	9	8
Then	0	0	0	0	1	0	0	0	1	0	0	0	3	0	0	1
This	2	0	2	0	0	1	0	1	0	0	0	0	0	0	1	0
Time	0	0	0	1	1	1	1	0	0	0	0	0	0	0	2	2
Told	8	18	8	13	3	14	26	34	28	38	17	12	19	21	39	35
Truth	1	0	2	4	4	3	4	6	2	5	5	6	4	7	6	6
Us	6	7	7	2	4	5	7	4	4	2	2	4	4	3	5	5
Well	4	3	2	8	6	0	5	3	2	2	1	0	0	1	1	0
What	4	3	3	2	3	1	2	5	6	6	5	2	4	0	9	8
Whisper	1	1	0	1	0	0	0	2	0	1	0	3	0	0	2	5
Who	0	1	1	1	0	0	1	1	0	1	1	0	1	1	3	2
Whom	0	0	0	0	0	0	0	0	0	0	0	0	0	0	2	0
Why	0	1	3	2	3	0	0	2	6	4	1	3	3	1	7	1

Response Word	4th M	4th F	5th M	5th F	6th M	6th F	7th M	7th F	8th M	8th F	10th M	10th F	12th M	12th F	College M	College F
							TELL									
William ..	0	0	1	0	0	0	3	0	0	0	1	4	2	0	5	3
Word ...	0	0	2	1	0	0	0	0	0	0	0	0	0	0	0	0
Yell	1	1	0	0	1	0	1	0	2	0	4	0	2	1	1	0
You	4	1	5	4	4	0	3	5	10	6	8	2	4	2	9	8
						169.	**THAT**									
A	0	0	3	0	0	0	0	0	0	0	0	0	0	0	1	0
Also ...	0	1	0	0	0	0	0	0	0	0	0	0	0	2	1	1
Always ..	0	0	0	0	1	0	0	0	0	0	1	2	1	0	0	0
And	3	3	1	6	3	3	5	2	3	2	3	1	4	0	5	0
Apple ...	0	2	0	0	0	0	0	0	0	0	1	0	0	0	0	0
At	5	1	4	6	6	6	4	2	4	3	1	1	1	2	0	1
Bat	0	1	2	1	0	1	2	1	1	2	1	1	1	0	1	3
Because ..	1	1	1	0	0	0	2	0	1	0	0	1	0	1	1	3
Book ...	1	0	1	0	0	0	1	1	0	0	1	1	0	1	2	1
Boy	3	5	3	3	6	4	1	2	4	2	4	5	7	2	9	9
But	1	0	0	0	0	0	0	1	0	2	0	0	0	1	1	1
Can	3	2	2	3	0	1	1	1	1	1	0	0	0	1	1	2
Car	2	3	1	1	0	2	3	2	4	3	4	5	3	4	8	1
Cat	5	5	6	6	10	8	6	13	7	5	6	3	11	4	17	11
Certain ..	0	0	0	0	1	0	0	0	0	2	0	1	0	2	0	1
City ...	0	1	3	2	4	1	0	0	2	3	4	0	2	1	4	1
Come ...	1	2	0	0	2	0	0	0	2	0	0	0	0	0	0	1
Could ...	0	0	3	0	0	0	0	0	0	0	0	0	1	0	1	1
Day	0	0	1	0	0	0	0	0	1	0	0	1	0	0	0	2
Did	2	1	0	0	0	0	0	0	0	1	0	0	0	0	0	0
Do	1	4	0	0	0	0	0	1	0	0	0	0	0	0	0	0
Dog	3	5	4	7	8	3	6	6	4	4	1	4	1	3	6	9
Door ...	0	0	0	0	0	0	0	1	0	0	0	0	0	0	1	2
Fat	2	2	1	0	3	0	1	0	0	1	0	0	0	0	0	2
For	0	0	0	1	0	0	0	0	1	2	1	0	4	2	1	3
Girl	0	2	0	0	1	0	2	2	1	2	3	2	0	2	7	5
Good ...	3	0	0	2	0	0	0	0	0	0	0	0	0	1	0	0
Guy	0	0	0	0	0	1	0	0	0	0	1	1	2	1	0	0
Hat	12	10	19	10	3	7	7	10	2	5	5	2	5	1	9	3
He	2	1	4	0	4	2	0	1	3	2	1	2	3	1	4	1
Her	0	0	0	0	0	2	0	2	0	0	0	0	0	0	1	1
Here ...	4	2	0	0	2	2	2	1	0	1	0	0	0	0	1	2
Him ...	0	0	2	1	2	0	4	0	4	0	1	3	0	2	1	0
His	0	0	0	0	1	1	1	0	1	1	1	1	2	0	1	0
House ...	2	2	1	2	5	4	2	1	3	5	6	4	1	2	3	8
I	2	1	1	2	0	0	0	0	0	0	0	0	1	0	1	0
Is	22	20	13	18	15	11	14	17	15	14	11	22	28	27	54	54
It	10	4	9	7	18	10	21	15	18	15	18	12	15	11	21	16
Letters ..	2	0	0	0	0	0	0	0	0	0	0	0	0	0	0	0
Man	2	2	2	2	3	1	0	2	3	2	0	2	1	3	7	6
Mat	2	0	0	0	3	1	1	1	0	1	1	1	0	1	2	2
Me	2	0	1	1	0	1	1	0	1	0	0	0	1	1	0	0
Money ...	0	0	0	0	0	0	0	0	0	0	2	0	0	0	0	0

Response Word	4th M	4th F	5th M	5th F	6th M	6th F	7th M	7th F	8th M	8th F	10th M	10th F	12th M	12th F	College M	College F
							THAT									
My	0	0	0	0	0	0	0	0	0	0	0	0	0	0	2	0
No	2	1	0	1	0	0	1	0	0	0	1	0	1	1	0	0
Now	0	0	0	0	0	0	0	1	1	0	0	0	0	1	0	3
Object	0	0	0	1	1	1	2	0	0	0	3	2	1	1	3	2
One	1	1	0	2	0	0	3	0	0	3	3	6	1	4	4	12
Or	0	0	0	0	0	0	1	0	0	0	0	0	0	0	2	1
Over	0	0	1	0	3	0	0	0	1	0	0	1	0	0	0	0
Over there	0	0	0	0	0	1	0	2	0	0	0	2	0	1	1	0
Particular	0	0	0	0	0	0	0	0	0	0	0	0	0	0	2	0
Person	2	1	1	0	0	5	2	3	5	1	3	0	1	1	1	1
Piece	0	2	0	0	0	0	0	0	0	0	0	0	0	0	0	0
Place	2	2	1	2	0	2	1	4	1	6	6	2	2	0	2	2
Point	1	1	2	1	1	0	0	0	0	1	0	3	1	0	0	1
Rat	1	1	3	3	0	0	0	0	1	0	0	0	3	1	2	2
Sat	1	1	1	0	0	2	1	0	1	1	0	0	0	0	2	0
See	4	0	1	2	1	0	1	0	1	0	0	0	1	0	0	0
So	1	1	0	2	0	5	0	2	0	0	1	1	1	3	3	6
Something	4	6	2	5	3	5	5	0	1	1	5	0	1	0	1	0
Teacher	0	0	0	0	0	0	0	0	0	3	0	0	0	0	0	0
Than	2	2	1	3	1	0	0	0	0	0	1	1	0	1	1	1
That's	1	1	4	0	0	1	1	0	3	0	0	0	0	1	0	0
The	11	10	7	9	11	9	12	7	9	6	8	3	5	5	6	10
Their	1	0	5	4	1	4	1	4	0	3	3	1	1	0	3	0
Them	1	1	2	0	1	2	4	1	2	0	6	2	4	4	1	1
Then	4	5	2	5	2	3	2	5	4	6	2	1	7	3	3	5
There	10	18	19	16	20	21	18	21	26	23	28	28	24	19	33	42
These	0	0	0	0	0	0	1	1	0	2	0	1	1	0	3	2
They	2	9	4	8	4	6	6	3	5	0	3	1	11	5	9	3
Thing	27	23	29	24	34	33	12	17	18	16	21	14	16	20	23	12
This	9	22	12	18	12	23	29	40	34	44	30	45	19	37	107	146
Those	1	0	0	1	1	2	5	6	8	6	5	10	6	11	14	11
Though	0	0	0	0	1	1	0	0	1	3	0	0	0	0	3	2
Till	0	0	0	0	0	0	0	0	0	0	0	0	0	0	2	0
Time	0	0	0	2	1	0	1	2	0	0	1	0	0	1	1	0
To	1	0	2	0	0	1	0	1	0	0	1	0	1	0	2	2
Too	0	1	0	0	0	0	0	1	0	0	0	0	0	2	0	3
Was	5	4	4	3	4	3	3	2	4	6	7	5	5	2	5	14
Way	2	1	1	2	0	1	1	3	3	3	3	0	2	0	4	5
We	0	1	1	0	1	0	0	0	0	1	0	2	2	0	1	4
Went	0	0	0	0	0	0	0	0	0	0	0	0	0	0	0	2
Were	1	0	0	1	3	0	0	0	0	0	0	1	0	0	0	0
What	10	8	13	12	12	12	16	5	4	10	2	9	7	10	11	7
When	0	2	2	0	0	2	2	1	1	0	1	2	0	1	2	1
Where	2	1	1	0	2	0	1	1	4	1	1	0	0	3	0	1
Which	0	0	0	1	0	3	3	1	1	3	2	10	6	11	21	17
Who	1	0	1	0	0	0	1	1	1	0	0	0	0	2	1	1
Why	0	1	3	2	0	0	1	1	1	2	0	2	1	2	3	1

Response Word	4th M	4th F	5th M	5th F	6th M	6th F	7th M	7th F	8th M	8th F	10th M	10th F	12th M	12th F	College M	College F
							THAT									
Will	2	2	1	0	1	2	0	2	0	1	0	0	0	1	3	2
Word . . .	1	4	7	5	3	1	2	1	1	1	2	2	0	1	0	1
You	0	1	1	3	2	3	2	1	3	2	1	0	2	1	2	2
					170.		THE									
A	4	5	4	2	0	1	2	4	4	14	5	9	6	13	27	49
Adjective .	0	0	0	0	1	0	2	2	1	3	0	1	8	6	3	3
An	0	0	0	0	0	0	0	1	0	5	0	4	1	0	5	7
And . . .	3	2	6	1	3	1	2	2	1	1	5	1	3	3	6	18
Apple . . .	0	0	0	0	0	0	0	0	0	0	0	0	0	0	3	2
Article . .	0	0	0	0	0	0	0	1	0	1	1	3	3	3	14	15
At	1	0	0	0	2	0	0	0	1	0	0	0	0	1	2	3
Baby . . .	2	10	2	5	5	0	3	3	6	6	2	2	2	1	1	1
Ball	0	0	3	2	2	1	1	2	0	1	1	1	1	1	2	1
Be	0	2	0	1	1	0	0	0	0	0	0	0	0	0	0	0
Beginning .	0	1	0	1	0	0	1	0	1	1	0	3	1	0	4	2
Best	1	1	0	0	1	0	2	0	0	0	1	0	0	1	1	0
Big	1	0	2	0	1	1	2	0	0	0	0	1	1	0	0	0
Bird . . .	1	0	1	0	2	1	0	0	0	1	0	1	1	1	3	2
Boat	0	0	0	0	1	1	0	0	0	0	0	2	1	0	1	2
Book . . .	1	1	1	0	1	2	0	5	1	2	3	7	1	3	10	8
Boy	28	21	40	26	39	27	20	24	31	26	42	35	42	41	85	44
Boys . . .	0	0	2	2	2	1	2	4	2	3	7	5	4	1	0	5
By	1	5	3	2	1	2	1	0	1	0	0	2	0	0	0	0
Car	0	0	0	0	0	0	0	1	0	0	2	2	7	4	3	3
Cat	1	1	7	2	5	6	11	7	6	6	6	3	7	4	8	10
Child . . .	0	0	0	0	0	1	0	0	0	2	0	0	0	0	0	1
Children .	0	0	0	0	0	0	0	0	2	0	0	2	0	0	0	0
Could . . .	2	0	0	0	1	0	0	0	0	0	0	0	0	0	0	0
Cow	0	0	0	0	3	1	1	0	1	0	2	0	0	0	1	0
Day	0	1	0	0	1	1	1	0	0	0	0	2	0	2	1	5
Dog	3	1	3	3	2	5	7	9	7	11	8	9	12	12	16	26
Doll . . .	0	0	0	2	1	0	0	0	0	0	0	0	0	0	0	0
Door . . .	1	0	0	0	0	2	2	0	1	0	1	2	0	0	1	10
End	6	11	9	17	5	13	4	16	8	15	8	13	12	12	15	18
English . .	0	0	0	0	0	0	3	0	0	0	0	0	0	0	1	0
Fat	0	0	0	0	2	0	0	0	0	0	0	0	0	0	0	0
Floor . . .	2	0	0	0	0	0	0	0	0	0	0	0	0	0	0	0
For	0	2	0	1	0	0	0	0	0	0	0	0	0	0	0	0
Fun	2	0	0	0	0	0	0	0	0	0	0	0	0	0	1	1
Game . . .	0	0	1	0	0	0	0	0	0	0	0	0	0	0	2	1
Girl	3	1	0	3	3	3	0	1	7	1	1	5	5	3	7	5
Go	0	0	0	1	2	0	1	0	0	0	0	0	0	0	0	0
Hat	0	0	0	0	0	1	0	1	0	0	0	2	0	0	1	2
He	4	9	7	4	4	8	5	2	5	2	6	0	2	2	2	2
Hear . . .	2	0	0	0	0	0	0	0	0	0	0	0	0	0	0	0
Here	0	1	0	2	0	0	0	1	0	0	0	0	0	0	0	0
Him	6	0	2	1	3	1	2	1	1	1	0	1	0	0	0	0
His	1	1	0	1	0	0	1	0	2	0	0	0	0	0	1	0

Response Word	4th M	4th F	5th M	5th F	6th M	6th F	7th M	7th F	8th M	8th F	10th M	10th F	12th M	12th F	College M	College F
							THE									
Home	0	3	0	0	0	0	0	0	1	1	0	0	0	0	0	0
Horse	0	2	0	0	1	0	3	2	1	0	0	1	1	1	0	3
House	4	6	7	5	8	6	5	5	5	8	4	4	4	8	9	17
If	1	1	0	0	2	3	0	0	1	0	0	0	0	0	0	0
In	1	2	0	0	0	0	0	0	0	0	0	0	0	0	0	0
Is	1	9	3	3	2	4	2	5	0	4	4	1	1	4	5	5
It	13	8	13	18	13	17	30	21	31	22	19	29	19	26	59	53
Lake	0	0	0	0	0	2	0	0	0	0	0	0	0	1	0	1
Little	0	0	0	0	1	1	0	0	0	0	0	0	2	0	0	1
Man	2	4	2	5	8	8	6	2	1	4	2	5	2	5	18	11
Me	3	3	2	1	3	2	2	0	2	0	0	0	0	0	1	0
Name	3	1	0	2	0	0	0	0	0	0	0	0	0	1	0	1
Nice	0	2	0	0	0	0	0	0	0	0	0	0	0	0	0	0
Not	2	0	0	0	0	1	0	0	0	0	0	0	0	0	1	0
Object	0	0	0	0	0	0	0	0	0	1	5	2	2	0	5	2
One	1	0	1	1	0	2	1	5	2	7	4	3	1	2	9	9
Only	0	0	0	0	0	0	1	0	0	0	4	1	2	0	2	2
People	2	2	4	1	2	5	0	2	1	3	4	2	2	2	1	1
Person	3	2	2	2	0	3	1	5	1	0	1	2	2	2	1	1
Pig	0	0	2	0	0	0	0	0	0	0	0	1	0	0	1	0
Place	1	0	1	0	1	2	0	0	0	0	0	0	0	0	0	0
School	0	0	0	1	0	0	0	0	0	0	0	0	0	2	1	1
Sea	0	0	0	0	0	0	0	0	0	0	0	0	0	0	2	0
See	0	1	0	2	0	0	0	0	0	0	0	0	0	0	0	0
Sentence	0	2	0	1	0	3	1	1	2	1	0	2	1	2	2	3
She	0	0	0	0	1	0	1	0	0	0	0	0	0	0	2	0
Shoe	0	0	1	0	0	0	0	0	0	0	2	0	1	1	0	2
Something	5	4	1	4	3	2	0	1	1	3	1	0	1	0	0	0
Store	0	0	0	0	0	0	1	0	0	2	1	0	1	0	1	0
Story	0	3	3	4	2	3	2	2	0	6	3	2	1	0	1	2
Sun	0	0	0	2	0	0	0	0	0	0	0	0	0	0	0	0
Table	0	1	0	0	0	0	1	0	1	0	0	0	1	0	0	2
That	10	9	4	8	3	7	11	7	9	6	10	8	5	3	14	21
The	0	0	0	0	0	4	0	0	0	0	0	0	0	0	0	0
Thee	3	0	4	5	3	9	5	9	4	3	3	3	3	1	7	4
Their	1	0	0	1	0	2	0	1	1	0	0	1	0	1	0	0
Them	4	4	3	2	3	7	6	4	8	7	1	3	3	3	4	2
Then	3	7	4	5	2	3	5	7	8	6	3	5	4	5	3	4
There	5	5	6	5	4	3	3	6	3	3	2	3	0	2	3	2
They	30	25	20	23	22	22	25	15	22	11	12	3	10	10	12	7
Thing	11	9	14	9	21	9	13	5	8	6	12	8	12	3	11	15
Things	0	0	0	0	2	0	0	1	0	1	0	0	0	1	0	0
This	3	5	0	1	0	0	3	8	3	5	4	4	3	1	7	8
Those	0	0	0	0	0	0	1	2	1	1	0	1	1	2	4	2
Thought	0	0	0	0	0	0	0	0	2	0	0	0	0	0	0	0
Thy	1	4	3	4	4	4	3	4	1	3	3	0	4	0	1	2
Time	1	2	0	0	1	1	0	2	0	1	0	3	2	1	0	1
Title	0	0	3	2	1	3	1	0	1	0	0	1	0	0	0	1
To	1	1	2	1	0	1	1	0	0	0	0	0	1	0	1	1

305

Response Word	4th M	4th F	5th M	5th F	6th M	6th F	7th M	7th F	8th M	8th F	10th M	10th F	12th M	12th F	College M	College F
							THE									
Tree	1	0	0	0	0	0	1	0	0	0	1	1	0	3	1	4
Water	0	0	1	0	0	0	2	0	0	1	0	0	0	0	0	0
Way	0	1	2	1	0	3	0	3	0	2	2	1	0	2	0	4
We	0	0	1	1	1	1	3	0	0	2	0	1	0	0	1	0
What	0	1	1	2	0	3	1	3	1	1	2	0	0	3	8	0
When	0	2	0	0	0	1	0	1	0	0	0	1	0	1	0	0
Who	2	0	0	1	0	0	1	0	1	0	0	0	0	0	0	0
Woman	0	0	0	0	2	0	0	0	0	0	0	0	0	0	0	1
Word	4	6	6	8	4	5	5	0	1	2	2	6	0	7	5	4
You	2	3	1	1	2	0	1	1	0	0	0	0	1	0	1	1
							171. THEN									
A	0	0	2	0	0	1	1	0	0	0	0	0	0	0	0	0
After	0	1	1	5	3	3	3	2	3	0	2	5	2	0	9	3
Again	0	0	0	1	0	0	2	1	0	1	2	0	0	0	0	0
Ago	1	1	0	0	4	0	1	0	1	1	0	1	0	0	1	0
All	0	2	2	0	0	0	0	0	0	0	0	0	0	0	0	0
Also	0	0	0	0	0	0	1	0	0	1	0	0	0	0	2	0
Always	2	1	0	3	1	0	1	0	3	1	0	4	1	0	1	4
And	2	1	0	1	0	1	0	0	0	1	0	1	0	0	2	3
Anything	2	0	0	0	0	0	0	0	0	0	0	0	0	0	0	0
Are	1	0	0	0	0	0	0	0	0	0	0	0	0	0	1	3
At	1	0	0	0	1	2	0	1	0	1	2	0	1	0	1	2
Back	0	0	0	0	0	0	0	0	0	0	2	1	1	0	0	0
Be	0	0	0	0	0	1	0	0	0	0	0	0	0	0	2	0
Because	2	0	0	0	0	0	1	0	0	1	1	0	0	0	1	2
Before	1	2	1	1	2	3	4	6	0	3	2	1	2	4	5	4
But	0	0	0	0	0	0	0	0	0	0	1	0	0	0	3	0
Came	0	0	0	0	0	0	0	0	1	2	2	0	0	2	0	0
Can	0	1	0	0	0	0	0	0	0	0	1	0	0	2	0	1
Come	0	2	0	0	1	0	1	1	0	0	1	0	1	1	0	1
Do	1	1	2	1	0	0	0	0	0	1	1	0	0	0	0	0
For	0	1	0	0	0	0	0	0	1	0	0	0	0	0	2	0
Go	1	2	1	2	2	1	0	2	2	0	0	2	3	0	3	2
Good	2	0	1	0	0	0	0	0	0	0	0	0	0	0	0	0
Happen	0	3	0	0	2	1	0	2	0	1	0	0	2	2	0	0
Happened	1	0	2	3	2	6	1	0	0	1	0	1	0	0	0	0
He	9	15	15	8	9	10	7	2	12	4	8	4	3	7	9	5
Hen	6	7	4	5	6	4	2	0	0	1	0	0	0	0	1	0
Her	1	0	2	0	2	0	0	0	0	0	0	0	0	0	2	0
Here	1	1	1	0	1	1	0	0	1	1	0	0	0	2	1	2
Him	1	1	0	1	2	0	0	2	2	0	0	0	0	0	0	0
Home	2	0	0	0	0	0	0	0	0	0	0	0	0	0	1	0
House	0	0	0	0	0	0	0	0	0	0	2	0	0	0	0	1
How	2	1	3	1	2	0	1	0	2	1	1	0	0	0	1	1
I	2	1	2	1	2	2	2	0	1	0	0	0	0	1	3	1
If	1	0	1	0	1	0	0	0	0	1	0	2	0	0	1	2
Is	0	1	1	1	0	1	0	0	0	1	1	0	2	0	2	3
It	7	2	1	5	7	5	0	2	1	1	1	0	3	3	6	0

Response Word	4th M	4th F	5th M	5th F	6th M	6th F	7th M	7th F	8th M	8th F	10th M	10th F	12th M	12th F	College M	College F
								THEN								
Just	0	3	0	1	1	0	0	0	0	0	0	1	0	0	0	0
Know	1	0	1	0	1	1	1	1	0	1	3	0	1	0	0	0
Later	1	2	1	4	1	2	3	1	2	1	0	1	3	1	2	6
Look	0	0	2	1	0	0	0	0	0	0	0	1	0	0	0	0
Man	2	0	1	0	0	0	0	0	0	1	0	0	0	0	0	0
Me	1	1	2	2	2	0	1	0	0	0	0	0	0	2	0	0
Men	0	0	1	0	1	0	0	1	0	0	0	0	0	0	2	1
More	0	0	0	0	0	0	0	0	1	2	0	0	0	0	0	1
Never	0	0	0	2	0	2	1	1	2	4	0	2	1	1	3	2
Next	1	0	3	2	1	1	0	0	1	2	2	0	0	4	1	1
No	0	0	0	0	0	0	0	0	0	1	0	0	3	0	0	1
Now	21	26	31	31	38	37	41	48	57	64	56	69	56	58	164	196
Of	3	2	2	1	1	1	1	1	1	0	1	0	0	2	1	1
Oh	0	1	0	0	1	1	0	0	0	2	0	0	0	0	0	0
On	0	0	2	0	0	0	1	1	0	0	0	1	0	1	0	0
Once	1	0	0	0	0	1	0	0	0	0	0	1	0	0	0	2
Only	0	0	0	0	2	0	1	0	0	0	1	0	1	1	4	0
Past	1	0	1	1	0	2	0	0	0	2	3	1	1	2	7	1
Pen	0	0	2	4	0	0	0	0	0	0	0	0	0	0	0	0
People	6	5	8	2	2	6	1	0	0	0	3	0	1	2	0	0
Place	0	1	1	0	1	1	0	0	0	0	2	2	0	0	0	0
Right	2	0	1	2	2	0	0	0	0	0	0	0	0	0	0	0
See	1	1	0	1	0	1	0	0	0	0	0	2	0	0	0	0
She	0	1	1	1	0	4	0	2	1	5	0	1	0	0	2	2
So	0	1	0	0	0	2	0	0	1	0	0	1	0	1	2	3
Something	1	1	1	3	0	0	0	0	0	0	0	0	0	0	0	0
Sometimes	0	0	0	0	0	0	2	0	0	0	0	0	1	0	0	0
Soon	2	0	0	0	0	1	0	1	2	0	0	0	0	0	0	1
Sudden	0	0	1	0	2	0	0	1	1	0	0	0	0	0	0	0
Suddenly	0	1	2	0	0	0	4	0	0	0	0	0	0	0	1	0
Than	3	4	3	8	0	4	5	9	7	8	8	8	10	34	13	30
That	8	18	8	12	3	8	5	9	11	10	10	8	4	3	12	15
The	11	6	9	2	15	3	6	1	6	1	4	2	2	0	5	3
Their	2	2	0	1	1	3	3	7	3	0	2	0	4	0	1	0
Them	10	5	9	9	3	7	9	11	16	8	4	2	6	0	5	2
There	18	28	25	28	29	28	23	34	25	29	32	30	21	23	49	51
Therefore	0	0	0	0	0	0	0	0	0	0	0	0	0	0	0	2
They	9	13	7	16	7	8	12	10	7	5	7	8	15	5	15	4
This	1	4	0	1	1	1	2	1	1	0	5	2	1	0	3	0
Those	0	0	0	0	0	0	1	1	1	3	1	1	0	3	5	2
Though	0	0	0	1	0	0	0	1	3	1	0	1	0	0	2	1
Time	7	4	3	4	7	3	13	4	4	5	10	5	11	2	8	10
To	0	1	1	1	0	1	1	0	0	0	0	0	1	3	1	0
Tomorrow	0	0	0	0	0	0	0	1	0	0	2	0	0	1	0	0
Too	0	0	0	0	0	0	0	2	0	0	1	0	2	0	3	0
Two	0	0	1	0	0	0	0	0	2	0	0	0	0	0	0	0
Was	0	0	0	1	2	2	2	1	1	0	1	2	1	0	1	6
We	5	5	3	3	6	3	7	2	4	1	5	6	4	2	15	9
Well	0	0	0	0	0	0	0	0	0	0	0	0	2	0	1	0

Response Word	4th M	4th F	5th M	5th F	6th M	6th F	7th M	7th F	8th M	8th F	10th M	10th F	12th M	12th F	College M	College F

THEN

Response Word	4th M	4th F	5th M	5th F	6th M	6th F	7th M	7th F	8th M	8th F	10th M	10th F	12th M	12th F	College M	College F
Went . . .	2	1	0	0	1	1	0	0	0	0	0	0	0	0	1	0
Were . . .	1	0	1	2	0	0	1	1	0	0	0	0	1	0	0	0
What . . .	3	2	0	3	2	3	2	1	1	3	0	1	2	3	3	4
When . . .	26	29	34	26	29	34	43	49	29	48	40	51	45	51	61	78
Where . .	2	3	4	3	2	1	1	4	3	0	1	0	2	0	3	0
Why	1	0	1	1	0	1	1	0	3	0	0	1	0	2	5	2
Will	1	1	0	1	0	0	0	0	1	0	0	1	0	0	2	3
Word . . .	0	1	2	3	2	0	1	1	0	0	0	0	0	1	1	0
Yesterday .	0	0	0	0	0	1	0	1	1	0	0	0	1	2	0	1
You	9	4	3	6	5	2	0	2	6	3	0	1	6	2	5	1

172. THERE

Response Word	4th M	4th F	5th M	5th F	6th M	6th F	7th M	7th F	8th M	8th F	10th M	10th F	12th M	12th F	College M	College F
After . . .	0	0	1	0	0	0	0	0	2	0	0	0	0	0	0	0
Are	14	6	4	5	9	4	8	10	12	11	11	3	21	10	32	22
At	1	0	3	0	0	1	1	4	3	2	2	3	3	2	3	3
Away . . .	1	0	0	1	0	2	1	1	0	1	1	2	0	1	6	1
Because .	0	0	0	2	0	1	0	0	2	0	0	0	0	1	1	0
By	0	0	0	0	0	1	1	2	0	0	0	1	0	0	0	0
Car	1	1	0	2	0	1	0	0	0	0	1	0	1	0	0	1
Care . . .	0	1	1	0	0	0	0	2	0	0	1	1	0	1	0	0
Cat	0	2	2	0	0	0	1	0	0	0	0	0	1	0	1	1
Chair . . .	0	0	2	0	0	0	0	0	1	0	0	1	0	0	0	0
Corner . .	0	0	0	0	1	0	0	0	2	0	0	0	0	0	0	0
Far	2	1	2	1	0	0	0	1	0	0	1	1	1	0	2	2
For	1	2	1	1	3	1	0	0	3	2	3	0	2	1	5	2
Fore . . .	0	0	0	0	4	1	0	0	1	2	1	1	3	1	5	5
Get	2	4	1	0	2	3	1	0	0	0	1	0	0	1	2	0
Go	6	12	3	12	2	4	2	1	1	1	0	2	4	1	9	1
Goes . . .	4	8	4	6	9	2	2	1	3	8	3	4	6	7	11	3
Going . . .	0	1	2	0	0	0	0	0	1	0	0	0	0	0	0	0
Gone . . .	0	0	2	1	1	1	0	0	0	0	0	0	1	1	0	0
Hair	1	0	0	0	1	0	2	1	0	0	0	0	1	0	2	0
He	4	2	3	2	4	2	0	0	5	0	1	1	0	0	0	1
Hear . . .	4	2	5	3	3	2	5	0	0	0	1	1	0	0	1	0
Her	1	0	0	0	2	1	0	1	0	1	0	1	3	1	2	4
Here . . .	47	44	48	51	61	66	73	86	71	89	67	85	61	78	164	204
Hill	0	0	0	1	1	0	0	0	0	0	0	0	0	0	2	0
Hire . . .	0	0	2	0	0	0	0	0	0	0	0	0	0	0	0	0
Home . . .	0	1	3	1	0	1	0	1	0	2	1	2	2	1	1	1
House . . .	1	3	1	5	0	3	1	1	1	3	4	0	0	3	0	0
If	0	1	0	0	0	0	0	0	0	0	0	1	0	0	1	2
In	1	2	0	0	0	0	1	1	0	0	2	0	0	0	1	0
Is	19	14	14	13	20	10	14	15	16	9	19	15	20	22	62	57
It	0	4	2	4	3	2	4	1	1	2	1	3	1	0	5	2
Look . . .	0	2	3	1	0	0	0	0	0	0	2	0	0	0	0	0
May	0	0	2	0	0	0	0	0	0	0	0	0	0	0	0	0
Me	0	0	1	2	0	1	0	0	0	0	0	1	1	0	0	1
More . . .	0	0	0	0	2	0	0	0	0	0	0	0	0	0	0	0
Now	2	4	2	3	1	2	0	6	6	1	2	4	3	4	10	9

Response Word	4th M	4th F	5th M	5th F	6th M	6th F	7th M	7th F	8th M	8th F	10th M	10th F	12th M	12th F	College M	College F
							THERE									
On	0	0	0	0	0	0	2	0	0	0	0	1	0	0	0	0
Over	12	11	6	11	5	8	12	7	5	7	8	7	8	10	3	6
Over there	0	1	0	0	2	0	0	0	0	0	0	0	1	1	0	0
People	1	1	2	1	0	0	0	0	0	0	0	0	1	0	0	0
Place	14	10	10	13	13	29	7	10	10	9	19	11	8	15	28	20
Places	1	1	0	0	0	0	0	0	1	0	0	0	2	0	0	0
Point	1	0	1	1	2	1	1	0	0	0	2	4	1	0	3	4
Position	0	0	0	0	0	0	0	0	0	2	0	1	0	0	1	0
Right	1	0	0	0	1	2	0	0	0	0	0	0	0	0	0	0
School	0	2	0	0	0	0	0	0	1	1	0	0	0	0	0	1
See	1	3	3	2	1	3	0	1	0	0	2	0	0	0	2	0
She	0	0	2	1	1	0	0	0	1	2	1	1	3	1	0	0
So	0	0	0	0	0	0	0	2	0	0	0	0	0	0	1	0
Some place	1	3	1	1	2	1	2	2	0	0	2	0	0	0	1	0
Somewhere	0	1	1	1	0	1	3	1	0	2	0	2	1	0	0	0
Spot	0	0	1	0	2	0	0	0	0	0	0	0	1	0	1	1
Street	0	0	0	0	0	0	1	2	0	0	0	0	0	0	0	0
Table	0	1	1	0	0	0	0	1	0	0	0	1	0	2	1	0
Than	1	0	1	0	0	0	0	0	1	2	0	0	0	1	0	0
That	5	6	2	5	4	3	4	5	3	6	10	8	3	5	12	11
The	3	0	5	2	5	0	0	0	0	1	0	0	0	0	1	1
Their	14	18	17	26	10	22	19	21	15	9	10	10	19	19	13	12
Them	0	0	0	1	1	1	2	1	2	0	1	2	0	0	0	0
Then	6	11	5	7	3	7	4	8	7	7	12	10	6	5	14	17
There	0	0	0	0	2	0	0	0	0	0	0	0	0	0	3	0
There's	0	0	3	0	0	0	0	1	2	0	0	0	1	0	0	0
They	4	3	2	1	5	3	2	2	3	2	1	0	0	1	2	1
This	0	2	2	2	2	1	1	0	2	0	3	1	1	1	3	6
Three	1	2	0	0	0	0	0	0	0	0	0	0	0	0	0	0
Tree	2	0	0	0	1	0	0	0	0	0	1	0	0	0	0	0
Was	2	5	9	5	8	5	10	2	14	6	4	3	8	1	9	7
We	1	1	1	0	2	0	0	1	1	0	0	0	0	0	3	0
Were	6	2	9	4	3	6	1	3	9	1	3	2	0	2	1	3
What	2	1	0	2	1	0	0	0	0	0	0	0	0	0	0	0
When	1	1	1	0	0	0	1	0	0	1	3	2	1	0	1	0
Where	21	13	20	16	20	18	30	23	25	39	23	27	29	41	38	55
Will	0	0	0	3	0	1	1	0	1	0	0	0	0	0	1	1
Word	0	1	1	0	2	0	0	0	0	0	1	0	0	0	0	0
You	1	2	1	2	0	2	0	2	3	0	0	1	1	0	1	2
						173.	THEREFORE									
A	2	0	1	0	0	0	0	0	0	0	0	0	0	0	0	0
After	0	0	1	0	1	1	5	3	5	0	10	5	2	3	3	1
Afterward	0	0	0	0	0	0	0	0	0	2	0	0	0	0	0	0
Again	0	0	1	0	0	0	0	0	0	0	0	2	1	0	2	0
Also	1	0	0	3	2	3	9	3	5	1	8	13	6	10	7	5
Although	0	1	0	1	1	0	2	0	0	1	1	1	1	2	3	3
Always	0	0	0	1	0	0	0	0	0	1	0	1	0	2	1	1
And	3	1	1	3	1	6	3	3	1	0	3	6	3	4	3	5

Response Word	4th M	4th F	5th M	5th F	6th M	6th F	7th M	7th F	8th M	8th F	10th M	10th F	12th M	12th F	College M	College F
							THEREFORE									
And so	0	0	0	0	1	0	1	1	0	0	0	0	0	0	1	2
Another . .	0	0	0	1	0	0	1	0	2	0	1	0	0	0	0	0
Anyhow . . .	0	1	0	0	1	0	0	0	0	1	0	2	0	0	0	0
Anyway . . .	0	0	0	3	0	2	0	3	0	2	1	1	0	0	1	1
Are	1	1	1	3	2	1	2	2	2	0	1	1	4	3	3	2
Argue	0	0	0	0	0	0	0	0	0	0	0	0	0	0	2	0
As	0	2	0	0	1	0	0	2	1	0	1	0	3	0	1	3
At	2	0	0	0	0	0	0	0	0	0	0	0	0	0	0	0
Be	5	1	1	1	2	0	0	1	0	0	1	0	0	0	0	1
Because . .	6	6	6	11	6	6	19	28	14	22	22	37	30	38	99	104
Because of .	0	0	0	0	0	0	0	1	0	0	1	0	0	0	2	1
Before . . .	2	5	8	6	6	1	4	9	6	7	1	1	2	4	3	2
Besides . . .	0	0	1	0	0	0	0	0	0	1	1	3	3	2	0	1
But	0	2	0	0	1	0	1	1	1	3	0	1	1	3	3	1
Can	1	2	1	0	0	0	0	0	0	1	0	0	2	0	0	0
Come	1	4	1	1	1	6	1	2	0	1	1	0	1	0	0	0
Comma . . .	0	0	0	0	0	0	0	0	0	0	0	0	0	3	1	1
Commas . .	0	0	0	0	0	0	0	0	0	0	0	0	0	3	0	0
Conclusion .	0	0	0	0	1	0	1	2	1	0	1	0	6	2	4	5
Consequently	0	0	0	0	0	0	0	0	0	0	1	0	1	2	6	6
Court . . .	0	0	0	0	0	0	0	0	2	0	0	0	0	0	0	0
Do	2	0	2	2	0	0	0	0	0	0	0	0	0	0	1	1
English . . .	0	0	0	0	0	0	1	0	0	2	0	0	0	0	0	1
Etc.	0	0	0	0	0	0	1	1	0	0	0	3	2	1	3	0
For	12	18	7	5	8	8	5	5	1	3	0	0	3	2	1	2
Fore	9	5	12	15	1	8	8	3	4	3	0	0	0	1	1	0
Forever . .	1	1	0	0	0	0	0	0	0	1	0	0	1	1	0	2
Four	3	5	3	7	3	5	2	2	0	0	1	1	2	0	0	0
From	0	0	0	0	0	3	0	1	1	1	1	0	0	1	1	0
Fun	2	0	0	0	0	1	0	1	0	0	0	0	0	0	0	0
Furthermore	0	0	0	1	0	1	0	0	0	0	1	1	1	2	4	1
Go	1	0	2	5	0	0	1	3	5	2	5	1	1	2	10	4
Golf	0	0	0	0	0	0	0	1	0	0	2	0	0	0	0	0
Good	0	0	3	0	0	0	0	1	0	0	0	1	0	0	0	0
Have	0	3	1	0	1	1	1	1	0	3	0	0	0	1	1	1
He	6	5	6	1	8	6	2	2	2	1	3	1	3	1	3	1
Hence	0	0	0	0	0	2	0	0	0	1	0	0	1	0	3	7
Henceforth .	0	0	0	0	0	0	0	0	0	0	1	1	0	0	2	0
Her	0	0	0	1	0	0	1	0	0	0	0	0	2	0	0	0
Here	8	4	7	14	7	6	6	12	8	7	2	7	4	0	2	3
Hereafter . .	0	0	0	0	0	0	0	2	1	1	0	2	1	0	2	3
Here fore . .	2	1	4	3	4	2	5	4	13	7	3	3	3	4	4	3
Heretofore .	0	0	0	0	0	0	0	0	0	1	0	0	2	2	2	3
Him	0	2	3	0	2	0	0	0	3	0	0	2	0	0	0	0
How	1	0	0	1	2	1	1	1	1	1	0	0	1	0	2	1
However . .	2	1	0	1	2	4	1	4	2	10	3	8	2	16	22	66
I	15	10	10	7	13	5	4	0	3	4	9	4	6	6	13	4
If	0	1	1	2	0	1	3	0	1	0	0	1	2	2	7	5
Is	6	2	3	0	5	3	4	1	3	4	2	2	4	2	1	3

Response Word	4th M	4th F	5th M	5th F	6th M	6th F	7th M	7th F	8th M	8th F	10th M	10th F	12th M	12th F	College M	College F
It	6	2	4	5	7	2	4	3	3	1	2	2	2	1	9	7
Know	0	0	0	0	0	0	0	0	1	1	0	0	0	0	0	2
Maybe	0	2	1	0	0	0	1	3	0	0	0	2	1	0	2	0
Me	8	6	2	3	1	3	2	3	1	0	1	1	1	2	1	0
Moreover	0	0	0	0	0	0	0	0	0	0	1	0	0	2	2	1
My	1	0	0	1	0	1	1	1	2	0	0	0	0	0	1	0
Never	1	2	0	1	0	1	2	3	2	6	0	3	3	6	8	5
Nevertheless	0	0	0	0	0	0	0	0	0	1	0	0	1	0	6	7
No	0	0	0	0	1	0	0	1	0	1	0	2	3	0	0	0
Not	0	3	0	3	3	0	0	1	2	0	0	0	2	0	1	1
Nothing	3	0	0	2	1	0	0	0	2	1	0	1	0	1	0	0
Now	4	5	11	11	6	7	4	4	7	12	4	7	6	3	14	13
Of	0	0	0	0	3	4	0	0	0	0	0	1	0	0	1	0
OK	0	2	0	0	2	0	0	1	0	1	0	1	0	0	0	0
On	0	1	2	0	0	0	0	0	0	0	0	0	0	0	0	0
Over	1	0	2	0	1	0	0	1	0	0	0	0	0	0	0	1
People	2	0	0	2	0	0	0	0	0	1	0	1	0	0	0	0
Play	0	2	0	0	0	0	0	1	0	0	0	1	0	0	0	0
Reason	1	0	1	0	1	0	1	0	0	1	2	3	5	4	7	4
Result	0	0	0	0	0	0	0	0	0	0	0	1	0	0	4	3
Shall	0	1	0	1	0	0	0	0	0	2	1	0	0	1	0	0
She	0	0	0	0	1	1	0	0	0	0	2	0	1	0	0	0
Since	0	0	2	0	0	0	0	1	0	2	0	1	1	1	6	5
So	5	8	9	8	5	21	12	20	5	13	7	18	8	19	26	53
Something	1	2	0	1	1	0	0	0	0	1	0	2	0	0	0	0
Speech	0	0	0	2	0	1	3	1	0	1	1	1	0	1	0	0
Talking	0	1	0	2	1	2	0	0	0	0	0	0	0	0	0	0
Teacher	0	0	0	0	0	0	0	0	0	0	1	2	1	0	0	1
Tell	1	1	0	1	2	1	0	0	1	0	2	0	0	3	0	0
That	2	1	1	1	0	0	4	0	0	0	1	0	0	2	2	3
The	3	1	1	2	5	1	0	1	1	1	4	1	1	0	1	0
Their	0	1	2	0	0	2	2	0	0	0	0	1	0	0	1	0
Them	0	1	2	1	1	0	2	0	1	0	2	0	0	1	0	0
Then	2	5	1	2	3	5	6	3	3	5	7	4	5	2	8	11
There	19	26	26	22	19	17	13	12	21	14	12	4	1	7	5	1
Thereafter	0	1	1	0	1	1	2	4	4	3	5	6	3	2	1	0
There as	0	0	0	0	0	0	1	0	2	0	0	0	0	0	0	0
Therefore	0	0	0	0	1	0	0	0	0	0	0	0	0	0	2	0
There is	1	0	0	0	1	0	0	0	2	0	0	1	0	0	1	0
Thereof	1	1	4	0	1	2	3	5	5	10	1	4	0	1	2	0
They	1	2	2	2	2	3	1	0	0	1	0	0	2	0	4	2
This	0	0	0	1	0	1	1	0	2	0	2	1	0	0	2	2
Thus	0	0	0	0	2	0	0	1	1	3	0	1	1	1	12	16
To	2	0	2	0	1	1	1	0	1	0	3	0	2	0	1	0
Us	0	1	3	2	4	1	4	1	1	0	3	3	2	1	0	0
We	14	14	19	15	20	15	20	10	23	14	21	15	18	9	36	31
Were	0	0	0	0	2	0	2	1	1	1	1	0	0	0	0	0
What	3	4	4	0	2	2	4	2	4	2	7	2	2	1	2	3
What fore	0	0	0	0	0	0	0	0	1	0	2	0	0	0	2	0

Response Word	4th M	F	5th M	F	6th M	F	7th M	F	8th M	F	10th M	F	12th M	F	College M	F

THEREFORE

Response Word	4th M	F	5th M	F	6th M	F	7th M	F	8th M	F	10th M	F	12th M	F	College M	F
When	2	1	0	1	0	4	3	1	5	0	0	1	3	2	5	3
Where	1	0	0	0	2	0	0	3	5	5	1	2	1	0	1	1
Whereas	0	0	0	0	0	0	0	1	0	0	0	0	0	0	2	3
Wherefore	0	0	1	2	0	2	3	3	2	8	3	3	5	8	6	7
Who	0	0	1	1	1	0	0	0	0	1	0	0	0	0	0	2
Why	1	1	2	0	6	3	2	2	8	2	4	3	4	3	18	6
Why not	0	0	0	0	0	0	0	0	0	1	0	0	0	0	4	0
Will	3	0	0	2	0	0	0	0	1	0	0	1	1	0	0	1
Word	1	2	1	1	4	2	0	1	0	0	1	0	1	2	0	0
You	14	15	8	8	10	4	9	9	10	3	4	4	9	2	9	4

174. THEY

Response Word	4th M	F	5th M	F	6th M	F	7th M	F	8th M	F	10th M	F	12th M	F	College M	F
All	3	1	0	0	1	1	0	1	0	2	1	0	1	1	1	0
Are	28	27	21	16	23	13	18	11	23	15	17	13	33	18	46	40
Aren't	0	0	0	0	0	0	2	0	0	0	0	0	0	0	0	0
Boys	1	0	2	1	1	1	0	1	0	2	1	1	0	1	1	0
Came	2	4	0	2	4	0	2	2	0	0	0	2	2	1	3	3
Can	3	1	1	4	2	2	6	4	2	0	5	3	3	5	10	4
Children	2	3	2	4	0	0	1	1	0	0	0	0	0	0	0	1
Come	5	2	2	0	1	1	0	1	1	1	0	2	3	4	2	3
Could	0	1	3	0	0	0	0	0	1	0	0	0	0	0	0	2
Crowd	0	0	0	0	1	1	0	2	0	1	1	0	3	0	5	2
Did	5	2	3	3	3	0	2	0	0	2	2	1	2	1	3	0
Do	0	1	0	0	1	0	0	0	0	0	0	1	0	0	3	4
Friends	0	1	0	1	0	1	0	0	0	0	0	2	1	2	1	3
Girl	0	1	0	2	1	0	0	0	0	0	0	0	0	0	0	0
Girls	0	0	1	0	0	1	1	1	3	0	2	0	3	1	0	2
Go	2	3	2	5	5	3	3	3	7	7	8	9	5	9	22	13
Gone	0	0	1	0	1	0	2	0	0	0	1	0	0	0	0	0
Got	0	2	3	0	1	0	1	1	1	0	0	0	1	0	2	0
Group	0	3	0	1	3	4	0	1	0	1	5	0	7	1	8	8
Guys	0	0	0	0	0	0	0	0	0	0	2	0	0	1	0	0
Had	1	1	1	2	1	3	2	0	1	0	0	0	0	0	1	1
Have	4	0	4	2	3	3	2	2	3	0	4	1	0	1	3	2
Hay	1	0	2	0	2	0	0	1	1	0	0	0	1	0	0	0
He	4	1	1	3	1	1	4	5	1	5	5	3	1	3	0	3
Her	0	0	1	0	0	1	0	1	0	0	0	1	0	2	0	0
Here	2	0	0	0	2	0	0	0	0	0	1	0	0	0	1	0
Hey	5	2	4	2	1	1	0	2	1	0	0	0	0	0	0	0
Him	6	2	7	2	2	4	3	2	2	1	3	1	1	1	1	1
I	1	2	0	0	1	1	1	0	0	0	1	0	0	0	0	0
In	0	2	0	0	1	0	1	0	0	0	0	0	0	0	0	0
Is	0	2	1	0	0	1	1	0	0	0	0	0	0	0	2	0
It	0	0	1	1	2	1	0	0	0	2	1	1	0	0	0	0
Kids	0	3	0	1	0	0	0	2	0	1	1	1	0	2	0	0
Lots	0	0	0	2	0	1	0	0	0	0	0	0	0	0	1	0
Man	0	0	0	0	0	2	0	0	0	1	0	0	0	0	0	0
Many	1	4	2	3	5	5	0	3	2	3	1	4	4	3	6	7
May	1	2	1	2	0	1	2	0	0	0	0	0	1	0	1	0

Response Word	4th M	4th F	5th M	5th F	6th M	6th F	7th M	7th F	8th M	8th F	10th M	10th F	12th M	12th F	College M	College F

THEY

Response Word	4th M	4th F	5th M	5th F	6th M	6th F	7th M	7th F	8th M	8th F	10th M	10th F	12th M	12th F	College M	College F
Me	13	5	7	6	5	4	3	3	4	3	1	2	1	0	2	1
More	0	3	1	1	0	1	1	1	1	0	0	1	0	1	0	0
Must	0	0	0	0	0	0	0	1	1	1	2	0	1	0	0	0
Now	0	0	1	1	2	0	0	0	0	0	0	0	0	0	0	0
One	0	0	2	0	0	0	1	0	0	0	0	0	0	0	1	0
Others	0	0	0	1	0	1	0	1	0	0	0	1	0	1	4	2
People	21	30	24	29	23	24	7	15	11	17	23	31	17	29	40	37
Person	0	0	0	0	1	2	0	1	0	0	1	0	0	0	0	0
Persons	2	0	0	1	0	2	0	3	1	2	0	0	0	0	1	1
Plural	0	0	0	0	1	0	0	0	0	0	0	0	0	3	2	0
Pronoun	0	0	0	0	0	0	0	0	0	2	0	0	0	1	0	1
Ran	0	0	0	0	2	0	0	0	2	2	1	1	0	0	2	0
Run	0	0	0	0	0	0	0	0	2	0	0	2	0	1	1	3
Said	0	2	1	0	0	3	0	1	0	1	0	1	0	1	0	2
Say	0	0	1	0	1	0	1	1	0	0	0	0	0	0	3	1
She	0	1	0	1	0	1	1	0	1	1	1	0	0	4	3	5
Should	0	0	0	0	1	0	0	0	1	2	0	1	1	0	0	1
Some	0	1	2	0	0	0	0	2	0	0	0	0	0	0	2	1
Someone	1	2	2	0	2	0	0	0	0	0	0	0	1	0	0	0
That	1	1	5	3	3	2	0	4	4	1	1	0	0	2	0	0
The	9	8	8	2	6	4	4	0	2	0	1	0	0	0	0	0
Their	2	2	2	6	1	4	3	6	4	1	1	3	2	2	3	1
Them	36	38	50	46	58	73	92	79	78	81	81	89	87	79	153	155
Then	2	9	2	8	2	1	5	3	2	2	3	2	3	5	1	2
There	11	6	4	11	7	7	3	5	2	5	0	1	2	1	0	2
This	0	2	0	0	0	0	0	0	1	0	1	0	0	0	0	0
Those	1	0	1	2	1	0	1	2	4	3	4	3	2	2	3	10
Together	0	0	0	0	0	0	0	1	0	2	0	0	0	0	0	0
Two	0	5	1	6	4	7	2	0	2	1	3	1	1	1	5	2
Us	5	7	10	10	7	8	9	14	18	17	7	18	5	15	33	37
Was	1	0	0	0	0	0	2	0	1	0	0	0	0	0	0	0
Way	0	0	1	2	2	0	0	0	0	1	0	0	0	0	0	1
We	10	15	8	12	12	16	11	19	7	24	10	14	12	19	56	79
Went	3	2	5	3	5	6	4	5	6	6	3	5	7	6	15	11
Were	5	6	6	6	8	6	11	6	8	7	7	7	11	9	8	10
Where	4	1	0	1	2	0	0	1	1	0	0	0	0	0	0	1
Who	1	2	2	1	1	2	2	3	3	2	6	1	1	1	10	4
Will	3	4	3	3	2	2	6	4	8	2	5	4	6	3	7	8
You	5	5	4	4	1	4	1	3	2	4	1	4	0	1	5	5

175. THIEF

Response Word	4th M	4th F	5th M	5th F	6th M	6th F	7th M	7th F	8th M	8th F	10th M	10th F	12th M	12th F	College M	College F
Bad	16	11	19	11	15	9	11	14	6	7	8	11	13	13	11	15
Bandit	0	0	2	1	0	3	3	1	1	0	1	0	2	1	4	2
Bank	2	1	0	0	0	0	0	0	0	2	0	0	0	1	0	0
Black	0	0	0	0	1	0	0	1	0	0	2	0	0	0	1	2
Boy	2	0	0	0	0	0	0	0	0	0	1	0	0	0	0	1
Burglar	9	18	11	17	13	18	25	21	23	20	18	16	18	9	15	12
Burglary	0	1	0	0	0	0	0	0	0	0	0	0	0	2	1	1
Catch	0	0	0	0	0	0	0	0	0	1	0	0	2	2	4	1

| | 4th | | 5th | | 6th | | 7th | | 8th | | 10th | | 12th | | College | |
Response Word	M	F	M	F	M	F	M	F	M	F	M	F	M	F	M	F

THIEF

Response Word	M	F	M	F	M	F	M	F	M	F	M	F	M	F	M	F
Caught	1	0	0	0	1	0	0	0	0	0	0	0	1	0	5	1
Cheat	0	0	0	0	0	0	0	0	1	1	1	0	0	2	1	1
Chief	3	4	2	0	0	3	2	0	1	1	1	2	0	0	1	1
Cop	1	0	0	0	2	0	1	0	4	1	4	1	1	0	6	0
Crime	0	0	1	1	0	0	1	1	3	1	1	1	0	1	1	2
Criminal	0	2	0	0	0	0	2	0	1	4	4	2	4	3	11	14
Crook	15	5	10	5	7	7	17	6	14	7	24	6	28	7	52	10
Cup	0	2	0	0	0	0	0	0	0	0	0	0	0	0	0	0
Dark	0	0	0	0	0	0	0	0	1	1	0	1	0	1	4	1
Dishonest	0	0	0	0	0	0	0	0	1	1	0	0	0	0	1	4
Dishonesty	0	0	0	0	0	0	0	0	0	0	1	0	0	1	2	0
Fast	4	2	5	3	2	3	1	0	2	1	1	2	1	0	0	0
Fear	0	0	0	0	0	0	0	0	0	0	0	0	0	2	0	0
Gold	0	1	0	2	0	0	0	0	1	0	0	0	0	0	1	2
Good	2	0	6	6	5	2	1	1	0	0	0	1	0	0	1	0
Gun	0	0	0	1	2	1	1	0	3	1	3	3	1	0	1	1
Handkerchief	0	0	0	0	0	0	0	0	0	0	0	0	0	0	0	2
Honest	0	0	1	2	1	0	2	1	1	2	0	0	0	1	2	1
House	1	2	0	0	0	1	1	1	0	1	1	0	1	0	2	2
In	0	0	2	0	0	0	0	0	0	0	0	0	0	0	0	0
Jail	0	0	0	0	0	0	1	3	1	5	3	1	6	0	2	7
Jewelry	0	0	1	1	0	3	1	1	1	4	2	2	1	3	3	4
Jewels	0	2	0	3	1	2	0	3	1	5	1	6	1	2	3	11
Justice	0	0	0	0	0	0	0	0	0	0	0	0	0	1	4	2
Kill	0	0	0	1	0	2	0	0	1	0	0	0	0	0	0	0
Killer	1	1	0	0	2	0	0	0	0	1	0	0	0	0	1	0
Law	0	0	1	0	0	0	0	0	1	1	1	3	0	0	3	2
Long	0	1	0	2	0	0	0	0	0	0	0	0	0	0	0	0
Loud	0	0	0	0	0	0	0	2	0	0	0	0	0	0	0	0
Man	3	7	6	9	3	9	3	7	3	4	6	11	4	5	8	13
Mask	0	0	0	0	0	1	0	1	0	1	0	1	1	0	8	5
Mean	2	3	1	1	0	1	0	1	0	3	0	4	0	1	0	0
Money	6	10	7	12	15	13	11	12	8	8	11	21	4	9	19	28
Murder	1	0	2	3	1	1	2	2	1	2	2	0	0	1	0	2
Murderer	0	0	0	0	0	1	1	0	0	0	0	1	1	2	0	0
Naughty	0	0	0	2	0	1	0	0	0	1	0	1	0	0	0	0
Night	0	0	0	0	1	1	1	0	0	0	3	2	1	1	5	8
Paul	0	0	0	0	0	0	0	0	2	0	0	0	0	0	0	0
Person	2	2	2	1	4	0	2	1	1	3	1	0	0	1	2	2
Police	3	1	1	2	3	1	2	3	4	2	11	6	10	2	16	7
Policeman	0	0	1	1	0	0	0	0	1	1	1	1	0	0	0	2
Prison	0	0	0	0	0	0	0	0	1	0	1	1	2	0	2	2
Purse	0	0	0	0	1	1	0	0	0	0	0	1	0	2	0	0
River	0	2	0	0	1	0	0	0	1	0	2	0	2	0	5	0
River Falls	0	0	0	0	0	0	0	0	0	0	1	0	2	0	0	0
Rob	7	3	8	7	7	8	8	5	6	5	6	7	5	4	16	14
Robber	49	46	46	41	47	37	43	43	45	33	36	34	31	41	71	77
Robbery	0	2	0	0	3	2	1	1	2	1	2	2	5	5	4	12
Run	0	0	0	2	1	2	1	0	0	1	2	1	0	5	7	5

Response Word	4th M	4th F	5th M	5th F	6th M	6th F	7th M	7th F	8th M	8th F	10th M	10th F	12th M	12th F	College M	College F
							THIEF									
Running	0	0	0	0	0	0	0	0	0	0	0	0	0	0	2	1
Save	0	2	0	3	3	0	1	0	0	0	0	0	0	0	0	0
Scoundrel	0	0	0	0	0	0	2	0	0	0	0	1	0	0	0	0
Silver	0	0	0	0	0	0	0	1	0	0	0	1	0	0	0	2
Slow	0	1	1	2	0	0	0	0	2	0	0	0	0	0	0	0
Sly	0	0	0	0	0	0	0	0	0	0	0	0	0	1	2	1
Sneak	0	0	0	0	0	1	1	0	0	0	2	0	0	1	1	1
Steal	35	34	35	46	43	48	41	49	43	64	40	58	54	73	114	150
Stealer	8	8	10	6	3	15	4	13	3	2	1	2	0	4	1	1
Stealing	1	3	0	1	3	0	0	2	4	4	2	4	1	4	1	6
Steals	0	1	0	0	0	0	2	1	1	0	0	0	0	0	0	0
Stealth	0	0	0	0	0	0	0	0	0	0	0	0	0	0	3	0
Stealthy	0	0	0	0	0	0	0	0	0	0	0	0	0	0	0	2
Steel	0	4	1	1	2	2	0	0	0	0	0	2	0	0	0	0
Stole	8	9	9	4	8	4	6	5	6	8	2	3	5	8	2	7
Stolen	3	2	3	4	1	1	6	6	3	10	2	2	9	10	8	8
Stop	0	0	0	0	0	0	0	0	0	0	0	1	1	0	2	0
Store	0	0	0	0	1	0	1	0	1	0	2	0	0	0	1	1
Tack	0	0	2	0	0	0	0	0	0	0	0	0	0	0	0	0
Take	4	7	8	4	5	10	2	9	1	7	2	3	1	1	5	8
The	1	0	0	0	2	0	0	0	1	0	0	0	0	0	0	0
Theft	1	0	0	0	0	1	5	1	0	0	0	0	2	0	0	1
Thug	0	0	0	0	0	0	0	0	2	0	0	0	0	0	0	0
Vandal	0	0	0	0	0	0	1	0	2	0	0	0	2	0	0	0
Wrong	0	0	0	1	0	1	1	0	0	0	1	2	0	2	2	2
You	2	2	0	0	0	0	0	0	1	0	0	0	0	0	0	0
						176.	**THINNER**									
Bigger	1	1	1	2	2	2	2	2	0	1	1	0	0	0	0	0
Bones	0	0	0	0	0	0	3	1	0	1	0	1	0	0	1	0
Bony	0	0	0	0	0	0	1	0	0	0	0	0	0	2	0	1
Boy	1	0	0	1	0	2	0	0	1	1	0	1	0	1	1	0
Bread	0	2	0	0	0	0	0	0	1	0	0	0	0	0	0	0
Broad	0	0	0	0	0	0	0	0	1	0	2	0	0	0	0	0
Broader	0	0	0	0	0	0	0	3	7	3	4	1	1	1	1	3
Diet	0	0	0	1	0	1	0	1	1	3	0	4	0	6	2	7
Dinner	5	2	0	1	1	0	0	1	0	0	0	0	0	0	0	0
Dog	1	1	1	0	1	0	1	0	0	1	0	2	0	0	0	0
Fat	32	43	22	36	35	43	20	28	32	41	21	27	18	38	40	55
Fatter	31	42	19	42	18	46	25	75	42	88	32	77	38	63	113	208
Food	1	0	3	0	0	0	0	0	1	1	2	0	0	2	1	1
Girl	0	1	0	0	0	1	0	0	0	3	1	1	0	5	4	2
Girls	0	0	0	0	0	0	0	0	0	0	0	1	0	2	0	0
Good	0	2	2	0	0	0	0	0	0	0	0	0	0	0	0	0
Hair	0	0	1	0	0	0	0	0	1	0	0	1	0	0	0	2
Hard	0	1	2	0	2	0	0	0	0	0	0	1	0	0	0	0
Heavier	0	0	1	0	1	1	1	6	1	2	1	3	3	5	3	3
Heavy	1	1	1	1	2	0	1	2	1	2	0	1	2	2	1	1
Ice	1	2	0	1	1	1	1	0	1	0	1	0	1	0	1	1

Response Word	4th		5th		6th		7th		8th		10th		12th		College	
	M	F	M	F	M	F	M	F	M	F	M	F	M	F	M	F

THINNER

Response Word	M	F	M	F	M	F	M	F	M	F	M	F	M	F	M	F
Knife	0	0	0	0	0	0	0	0	0	0	0	0	0	0	2	0
Lean	0	0	0	0	0	0	0	0	0	1	0	0	0	0	0	3
Leaner	0	0	0	0	0	0	0	0	0	0	0	0	0	0	0	2
Less	0	0	1	0	0	0	2	0	0	0	1	1	0	0	0	0
Light	0	3	3	4	2	1	2	1	1	1	0	2	1	0	2	0
Lighter	2	0	1	1	1	2	2	1	1	1	0	1	0	0	1	0
Liquid	0	0	1	0	4	1	0	1	0	1	0	0	0	0	0	1
Little	1	1	3	1	2	0	1	1	0	0	3	3	0	0	0	1
Long	0	0	0	3	1	0	0	0	0	0	1	1	0	0	1	0
Longer	1	2	0	0	1	0	1	0	1	0	0	0	0	0	1	0
Man	0	0	0	0	2	0	0	0	2	0	3	0	2	2	2	2
Me	0	2	0	1	1	0	3	1	0	0	0	0	0	1	1	1
Narrow	0	0	3	2	2	0	0	0	0	1	2	3	1	3	2	3
Narrower	0	0	0	0	0	0	0	0	0	0	0	0	0	1	2	4
Nice	2	1	0	0	1	0	0	0	0	0	0	0	0	0	1	0
Paint	19	6	41	15	28	8	30	5	18	3	29	4	46	8	45	10
Paper	2	2	3	1	0	2	2	0	1	0	1	1	2	1	3	1
Person	1	0	2	0	0	0	0	0	1	1	0	2	1	0	1	0
Sick	0	1	0	0	0	0	0	0	0	0	0	1	0	1	0	3
Skin	1	2	0	1	1	1	0	0	0	1	0	0	0	1	0	1
Skinnier	3	1	1	4	0	2	6	4	2	2	3	5	0	2	4	4
Skinny	22	43	21	39	17	49	20	35	20	28	16	37	16	24	27	39
Slender	0	0	0	0	0	1	1	0	0	2	0	0	0	0	1	2
Slight	0	0	0	0	0	0	0	0	0	0	0	0	0	0	0	2
Slim	1	2	0	5	5	3	0	2	1	2	2	4	3	2	6	10
Slimmer	0	0	0	0	0	1	1	2	1	0	0	1	2	1	1	6
Small	2	0	5	1	7	1	2	5	1	1	1	2	3	5	3	2
Smaller	0	2	2	1	1	1	2	3	0	1	2	2	0	1	1	1
Smell	0	0	0	0	0	0	0	0	0	0	2	0	0	0	0	0
Soup	1	0	0	0	0	0	0	0	1	0	0	0	0	0	2	0
Stick	0	0	2	0	0	0	1	2	0	1	0	0	2	0	3	0
Sticky	0	0	0	0	0	0	0	0	0	0	0	0	0	0	2	0
String	0	2	0	1	1	1	1	0	0	1	1	0	0	0	0	0
Strong	1	0	1	0	0	0	0	0	0	0	0	0	2	1	0	1
Tall	0	0	0	0	0	0	0	3	0	1	0	2	0	0	3	4
Taller	1	0	0	0	1	0	0	0	1	2	0	3	1	3	4	2
Than	3	0	3	2	10	2	8	1	8	2	10	3	11	7	26	6
The	2	0	0	0	2	1	0	0	0	0	0	0	0	0	0	0
Then	5	1	4	3	3	1	1	2	2	1	0	0	1	0	1	1
There	0	0	2	0	0	0	1	0	0	0	1	0	0	0	0	0
Thick	6	6	12	8	9	10	21	6	15	9	10	7	13	5	15	11
Thicker	10	13	9	11	11	12	30	21	33	14	29	13	23	18	72	38
Thin	25	26	20	13	12	19	12	9	5	5	14	5	9	3	11	1
Think	1	0	0	0	2	0	0	0	0	0	0	0	0	0	0	0
Thinnest	0	0	0	1	0	0	1	0	2	0	4	0	2	0	5	2
Time	1	0	2	0	0	0	0	0	0	0	0	0	0	0	0	0
Tin	1	0	3	0	0	0	0	0	0	0	0	0	0	0	0	0
Turpentine	0	0	0	0	3	0	0	1	1	0	3	1	1	0	2	1
Water	1	0	3	2	4	2	3	1	5	0	3	1	4	3	7	2

Response Word	4th M	4th F	5th M	5th F	6th M	6th F	7th M	7th F	8th M	8th F	10th M	10th F	12th M	12th F	College M	College F
						THINNER										
Watery	0	0	0	0	1	0	1	0	0	0	3	0	1	0	0	0
Weak	1	1	1	0	0	1	0	0	1	0	0	0	1	1	2	1
Weaker	0	0	0	0	1	0	0	0	0	0	1	0	0	0	2	0
Weight	1	1	1	0	0	0	0	0	0	0	0	3	0	2	2	6
Wide	2	0	2	3	0	1	2	0	1	1	1	2	1	1	3	0
Wider	4	3	3	5	3	2	4	7	10	6	5	6	11	10	18	12
Winner	0	0	0	2	0	0	0	0	0	0	0	0	2	0	0	0
					177.	THIRSTY										
Beer	0	0	0	0	3	1	0	0	3	0	4	0	5	1	8	0
Booze	0	0	0	0	0	0	0	0	1	0	0	0	2	0	0	0
Boy	1	0	2	0	0	0	0	0	0	0	1	1	1	0	0	0
City	2	0	0	0	0	1	0	0	0	0	0	0	0	0	0	0
Coffee	0	0	0	0	0	0	0	0	0	0	0	0	0	1	0	2
Coke	0	1	0	0	0	0	0	3	1	3	0	1	0	1	2	4
Cold	1	0	0	0	3	1	1	0	0	0	2	0	0	0	2	2
Desert	1	0	1	1	0	0	6	1	1	4	3	0	3	1	2	3
Drink	67	66	48	68	58	67	59	63	41	56	59	63	79	70	147	142
Drought	0	0	0	0	0	0	0	0	3	0	0	1	1	0	1	0
Drunk	1	0	1	0	1	0	2	0	4	0	1	0	2	0	1	0
Dry	15	10	12	11	14	17	23	18	24	16	21	18	20	16	59	46
Eat	1	0	0	2	1	0	0	0	0	0	0	0	0	0	0	0
Fast	1	2	3	1	2	0	1	0	0	0	2	0	0	0	0	0
Food	0	1	0	0	0	2	0	1	1	0	2	2	0	1	0	1
Full	0	2	1	0	0	2	2	0	2	0	1	1	1	1	2	2
Glass	0	2	3	1	1	2	0	0	0	0	1	1	1	1	3	2
Good	0	2	2	0	1	2	2	0	1	0	0	0	0	0	0	0
Hard	0	0	1	0	2	0	0	0	0	0	0	0	0	0	0	0
Hot	4	4	3	0	1	2	0	2	2	3	1	0	1	2	5	3
Hunger	1	0	1	3	1	1	0	0	3	0	0	0	3	0	1	4
Hungry	13	13	16	20	6	11	16	16	13	14	14	10	2	6	24	22
Is	0	2	0	0	0	0	0	0	0	0	0	0	0	0	0	0
Juice	0	0	0	0	0	0	0	1	0	0	0	0	0	1	2	0
Kind	0	0	0	0	2	0	0	0	0	0	0	0	0	0	0	0
Lemonade	0	0	0	0	0	0	0	0	2	2	0	0	0	0	1	1
Liquid	1	0	1	0	0	0	1	0	0	0	0	0	0	2	0	0
Liquor	0	0	0	0	0	0	0	0	2	0	0	0	1	0	0	0
Man	2	0	1	2	0	0	0	0	0	0	0	0	3	0	0	0
Me	0	0	1	0	1	1	3	0	0	0	1	1	0	0	1	0
Milk	0	2	1	2	3	3	0	2	1	0	0	1	1	2	2	3
Money	0	0	2	0	0	0	0	0	0	0	0	0	0	0	0	0
One	0	2	0	1	1	0	0	0	0	0	0	0	0	0	0	0
Parched	0	0	0	0	0	1	0	1	0	2	0	0	0	1	0	1
Pepsi	0	0	0	0	0	0	1	1	1	0	0	0	0	0	2	0
Pop	1	1	0	0	1	2	3	5	4	2	4	4	3	3	4	2
Quench	0	0	1	0	1	0	0	0	1	2	0	0	1	1	2	0
Sad	0	0	0	0	1	0	0	0	0	0	0	2	0	0	0	0
Summer	0	0	0	1	0	0	0	0	0	0	0	0	0	0	0	2
Throat	1	1	3	2	0	0	0	1	0	2	0	0	0	1	2	0
Tired	0	0	0	0	1	0	0	0	0	1	3	0	0	1	3	2

Response Word	4th M	4th F	5th M	5th F	6th M	6th F	7th M	7th F	8th M	8th F	10th M	10th F	12th M	12th F	College M	College F

THIRSTY

Response Word	4th M	4th F	5th M	5th F	6th M	6th F	7th M	7th F	8th M	8th F	10th M	10th F	12th M	12th F	College M	College F
Turn	0	0	2	1	0	0	1	0	0	0	0	0	1	0	0	0
Warm	0	0	0	2	0	0	0	0	1	0	0	0	0	0	0	0
Water	90	107	107	106	118	115	103	112	116	127	116	134	101	128	198	234
Wet	2	3	3	0	2	1	4	0	2	4	0	3	0	1	4	1
Whiskey	0	0	0	0	0	0	2	0	5	1	4	0	2	0	2	0
White	0	0	0	2	0	0	0	0	0	0	0	0	0	0	0	0

178. THIS

Response Word	4th M	4th F	5th M	5th F	6th M	6th F	7th M	7th F	8th M	8th F	10th M	10th F	12th M	12th F	College M	College F
All	1	0	4	1	1	0	1	0	1	0	0	1	0	1	2	0
And	1	2	1	0	0	1	0	0	0	0	0	0	0	0	1	0
Ball	0	1	1	1	1	0	2	2	0	3	1	0	1	1	2	3
Book	0	1	0	1	1	3	1	3	0	1	3	4	2	3	4	6
Boy	1	0	0	1	1	2	1	0	0	2	0	0	2	0	4	2
Can	2	0	2	3	1	0	1	1	0	0	0	1	1	0	1	0
Car	0	0	0	1	0	0	0	0	2	1	4	5	3	1	3	3
Cat	1	0	2	1	0	2	2	1	0	1	2	0	1	0	2	1
Class	0	0	0	0	0	0	0	0	0	0	0	0	0	0	3	1
Day	0	1	0	0	0	0	0	0	0	1	1	0	1	2	3	0
Desk	0	0	1	0	0	0	0	0	0	0	2	1	0	0	0	0
Dog	0	0	0	2	1	0	1	2	0	2	0	5	0	1	0	1
Fall	0	0	0	0	0	0	0	1	0	0	1	3	1	0	3	2
Girl	1	2	0	0	1	1	0	1	1	1	2	0	1	2	2	1
Hat	0	0	0	1	0	0	1	0	0	1	2	0	1	0	0	4
He	3	0	2	0	0	3	0	1	0	0	1	0	0	0	0	0
Heart	0	0	0	0	0	0	0	0	0	0	0	0	0	0	0	2
Here	3	2	2	4	3	6	1	6	3	6	3	11	2	4	11	10
His	6	7	7	7	4	7	11	4	6	6	4	1	1	1	1	0
House	0	0	1	2	0	0	3	0	6	3	4	2	2	2	3	1
Hurt	0	0	0	0	0	0	0	0	0	0	0	0	2	0	0	0
Is	93	100	105	91	99	88	74	78	59	58	67	44	87	73	128	104
It	6	2	9	8	10	8	5	7	9	10	4	3	1	6	11	6
Kiss	3	0	1	0	0	0	1	1	0	1	0	0	0	0	0	0
Man	2	1	1	0	0	1	1	0	1	1	0	2	2	0	1	1
Me	1	1	1	1	0	1	2	0	0	0	1	0	1	0	0	0
Mine	3	0	2	1	2	0	2	1	0	4	2	2	1	0	3	2
Miss	2	1	2	2	1	1	0	1	2	0	0	0	0	1	2	0
My	2	4	1	3	0	1	2	0	0	0	0	0	0	1	0	0
Name	0	0	0	0	0	2	0	0	0	1	0	0	0	0	0	0
Now	1	0	0	2	0	1	1	1	0	1	0	1	0	0	0	1
Object	2	0	1	1	0	1	2	1	0	0	4	1	1	2	6	2
Old	0	0	0	0	0	0	0	0	0	0	1	0	0	0	2	0
One	0	1	1	1	1	1	1	1	1	2	5	4	1	2	4	9
Paper	0	0	0	0	0	1	0	0	0	3	1	4	1	0	3	7
Pen	0	0	0	0	0	0	0	0	0	0	1	0	1	1	0	2
Pencil	0	1	0	0	0	1	0	0	3	1	0	0	1	0	2	0
Person	0	0	0	0	0	0	0	0	2	0	1	0	1	0	0	0
Place	0	1	0	0	0	0	2	0	0	2	1	0	2	0	2	0
School	0	0	0	0	1	0	0	0	0	0	0	2	0	0	0	0
Seat	0	0	0	0	0	0	0	0	0	0	0	0	0	0	0	2

Response Word	4th M	4th F	5th M	5th F	6th M	6th F	7th M	7th F	8th M	8th F	10th M	10th F	12th M	12th F	College M	College F
							THIS									
See	1	0	2	1	0	0	0	0	0	0	0	0	0	0	0	0
She	0	2	0	0	0	0	0	0	0	0	0	0	0	0	0	0
Something	3	8	2	1	3	2	1	0	2	1	1	2	1	0	0	0
Story	1	0	1	1	0	1	0	2	1	3	3	5	0	1	2	1
Table	0	0	0	0	0	0	1	0	2	0	0	1	1	0	1	0
Tall	0	0	0	0	0	0	0	0	0	0	0	0	0	2	0	0
Tell	3	1	0	1	1	1	1	1	0	0	0	0	1	0	1	0
Tells	2	1	1	0	0	0	0	2	0	0	0	0	0	0	0	0
Test	0	2	0	0	0	0	0	0	1	1	0	3	1	4	3	1
Than	0	0	1	0	0	0	2	0	0	0	0	0	0	0	0	0
That	18	41	23	38	25	49	71	60	58	77	72	99	65	93	188	256
The	12	7	5	3	7	5	2	3	6	5	2	0	1	1	1	0
Their	1	0	1	0	2	1	0	2	0	1	0	0	0	0	0	0
Theirs	0	0	0	0	0	0	0	0	2	0	0	0	2	0	1	2
Them	1	1	0	4	2	0	1	2	4	2	0	1	0	0	1	0
Then	0	5	1	3	1	1	1	3	0	0	0	0	0	2	4	1
There	1	3	4	2	2	2	2	4	3	4	4	3	3	2	5	3
These	0	0	1	0	0	1	2	2	2	0	2	0	3	3	3	6
They	0	0	3	3	1	0	4	3	6	1	1	0	2	2	1	1
Thing	11	10	20	13	20	19	7	19	12	9	19	4	9	6	21	10
This	2	0	0	0	0	0	0	0	0	0	0	0	0	0	0	3
Those	0	0	1	0	0	1	1	2	4	1	0	2	1	3	5	5
Time	5	2	1	1	2	2	2	0	1	5	1	2	3	5	2	1
To	0	0	0	2	1	1	0	0	0	0	0	0	0	0	0	0
Tree	1	0	0	0	0	0	0	0	0	2	0	1	0	2	0	0
Wall	1	0	0	0	2	0	1	0	1	0	1	0	0	0	0	0
Was	1	1	0	1	3	1	4	2	3	2	3	2	4	1	8	4
Way	0	0	4	1	0	1	1	2	0	2	1	2	2	0	4	1
Well	0	2	2	2	3	0	1	0	2	0	2	1	1	1	2	0
What	1	2	1	0	0	3	0	2	4	0	0	0	0	2	3	0
Will	4	3	2	4	6	2	5	3	3	4	1	3	7	2	3	3
Word	2	2	4	2	1	1	0	0	0	0	0	0	0	0	0	0
Year	0	0	0	0	0	2	0	0	3	1	0	3	1	0	0	3
Yours	0	0	0	0	0	0	0	0	0	0	1	0	0	0	0	2
						179.	TO									
A	1	1	2	0	3	1	1	1	0	0	1	0	0	0	1	0
Also	1	1	3	0	2	3	1	4	0	3	1	3	3	5	11	10
Am	4	2	0	2	1	1	0	0	0	0	0	0	0	0	2	1
And	0	0	0	0	0	1	0	2	0	0	0	0	0	2	3	2
Ann	1	0	0	2	0	0	0	0	0	0	0	0	1	0	0	0
Another	0	0	1	0	0	0	0	0	1	0	2	0	1	0	0	0
As	1	2	0	1	1	0	1	0	1	0	0	0	2	0	1	1
At	0	0	0	1	1	0	0	2	4	1	1	2	1	2	7	11
Away	0	0	0	0	0	0	0	0	0	1	0	1	0	0	5	5
Bad	0	0	0	0	1	1	1	0	2	0	0	2	0	0	0	0
Be	1	2	0	0	1	0	1	0	2	4	4	4	8	2	14	6
Big	1	1	0	1	0	1	1	0	0	0	0	0	2	0	0	0
By	0	0	0	0	0	0	0	0	0	0	0	0	1	0	0	2

Response Word	4th M	4th F	5th M	5th F	6th M	6th F	7th M	7th F	8th M	8th F	10th M	10th F	12th M	12th F	College M	College F
TO																
Came ...	0	0	0	0	0	0	0	0	0	2	0	0	0	0	0	0
Come ...	4	3	4	1	3	0	1	2	2	2	3	3	0	2	7	9
Day	2	1	1	0	1	0	0	0	1	0	2	0	1	1	3	0
Do	3	3	4	5	4	3	3	0	1	3	3	0	1	3	3	3
Far	1	2	0	1	1	0	0	1	0	0	0	0	0	0	0	0
Fast ...	0	1	3	0	0	0	0	0	0	0	2	0	0	0	1	0
For	0	2	0	3	0	1	1	5	7	3	2	5	0	1	3	5
Four ...	0	0	0	0	0	0	1	1	1	0	3	0	0	1	1	0
Fro	0	0	0	0	0	0	1	4	1	2	4	0	2	0	6	5
From ...	22	42	26	57	26	62	39	69	37	45	37	66	42	49	88	132
Get	0	0	0	1	0	0	1	1	1	0	1	0	1	1	2	3
Gether ..	0	1	0	0	1	0	1	0	0	1	1	0	1	0	2	4
Give	3	2	1	0	1	0	0	3	2	1	1	2	0	2	3	3
Go	10	13	17	21	14	10	17	22	23	29	23	24	28	35	48	49
Going ..	2	1	0	1	0	1	1	2	1	0	2	1	1	1	2	4
Good ...	1	0	0	0	0	2	0	0	0	0	0	0	0	0	1	0
Hard ...	1	2	0	0	1	0	0	0	0	0	0	0	0	0	1	1
He	1	0	2	0	0	0	3	0	0	0	1	0	0	0	0	0
Heavy ...	0	0	2	0	0	0	0	0	0	0	0	0	0	0	0	0
Her	0	1	0	0	1	0	4	4	3	2	2	4	2	0	6	1
Here ...	4	2	0	1	1	4	3	3	0	6	2	4	2	1	7	1
Him	4	5	8	2	8	3	4	1	7	4	5	8	10	6	8	6
Home ...	2	0	0	1	1	2	0	2	1	2	2	0	2	1	2	4
House ...	0	1	0	0	0	1	0	1	0	4	2	1	1	2	2	1
How	2	0	0	0	3	0	1	0	1	0	0	0	0	0	0	0
I	0	1	2	1	1	0	0	0	0	1	0	0	0	0	0	0
If	0	1	2	1	0	3	0	0	0	0	0	0	0	0	0	0
In	0	2	2	0	0	0	0	0	1	0	0	1	0	1	0	1
It	7	5	5	4	8	3	4	2	7	2	3	0	1	1	10	7
Letter ..	0	3	0	2	1	4	0	0	1	0	1	0	0	2	2	1
Long ...	0	0	0	2	0	0	0	0	0	0	0	0	0	0	0	0
Love ...	1	0	0	0	0	0	0	1	0	0	0	0	0	0	2	0
Many ...	1	1	2	2	0	0	1	0	4	0	3	1	3	2	1	1
Me	28	23	31	24	20	21	16	27	22	17	20	17	19	10	28	22
Moo ...	1	1	0	0	2	0	0	0	0	0	0	0	0	0	0	0
Mother ..	0	0	1	0	0	1	1	0	0	2	0	0	0	0	0	0
Much ...	1	2	3	1	4	0	1	3	1	2	2	1	3	1	1	0
My	5	3	2	1	4	0	0	1	0	1	2	1	0	0	0	0
New	2	0	0	0	0	0	0	0	0	0	0	0	0	0	0	1
No	0	0	0	0	2	0	0	0	0	0	0	0	0	0	0	0
Now	3	0	0	1	0	0	0	1	0	0	2	1	0	0	1	0
Number ..	2	0	2	3	2	3	0	2	0	2	1	2	0	0	0	0
Of	1	1	1	0	0	0	0	0	2	1	0	0	0	0	0	0
On	0	0	2	0	0	0	0	0	0	0	0	1	0	0	1	0
One	0	4	1	0	1	2	0	1	0	0	0	1	0	0	0	0
People ..	0	1	2	0	1	2	1	0	1	0	0	0	0	0	0	0
Person ..	1	4	0	0	1	0	1	0	0	0	0	1	0	1	0	1
Place ...	3	2	0	2	6	2	2	4	3	2	1	4	2	2	6	4
Preposition	0	0	0	0	0	0	0	0	0	0	1	1	3	4	2	5

Response Word	4th M	4th F	5th M	5th F	6th M	6th F	7th M	7th F	8th M	8th F	10th M	10th F	12th M	12th F	College M	College F
							TO									
Run	0	1	0	0	0	0	1	1	0	0	1	0	0	0	2	2
School . . .	0	1	0	0	0	0	3	3	0	1	0	2	1	2	2	6
See	1	1	0	0	0	0	0	2	0	0	2	1	3	0	2	1
Send . . .	1	1	0	2	1	2	0	0	0	1	0	1	0	0	0	0
Shoes . . .	1	0	0	2	1	2	0	0	0	0	0	0	0	0	0	0
Sleep . . .	0	0	0	0	0	0	0	0	0	0	0	2	0	0	0	0
Someone .	1	3	1	1	0	1	0	0	0	0	1	1	0	0	0	1
Store . . .	1	1	3	2	0	3	3	1	1	5	5	4	0	3	3	5
Take . . .	0	1	0	0	0	0	0	2	0	0	2	3	0	0	1	1
Talk	0	0	0	0	0	0	0	0	0	0	2	1	0	0	0	0
That	1	0	2	0	0	1	0	0	0	0	0	0	0	0	0	0
The	7	8	7	7	25	9	6	2	3	4	5	3	3	10	8	11
Them . . .	2	1	3	0	2	0	3	3	5	7	7	6	7	2	9	8
Then . . .	0	1	0	2	1	1	0	2	0	1	0	1	0	0	1	1
There . . .	6	6	5	0	4	5	14	6	9	7	12	8	6	11	18	17
This . . .	0	0	0	0	0	0	1	1	0	1	0	0	0	0	1	3
Three . . .	1	1	3	0	3	1	0	0	2	1	1	0	1	2	2	0
Toe	0	0	0	0	1	0	1	0	0	1	2	0	1	0	1	0
Together .	0	1	0	0	0	0	1	0	2	1	0	0	1	0	1	1
Too	10	12	8	13	4	8	12	6	8	10	4	2	12	14	16	9
Toward . .	0	0	0	0	1	0	2	1	6	2	0	0	2	2	15	14
Towards .	0	0	0	0	0	0	0	0	0	0	0	2	0	0	3	2
Town . . .	0	0	0	0	0	0	0	0	0	0	2	0	0	0	2	2
Two	14	7	7	13	18	22	18	9	12	5	5	10	10	7	5	9
Us	0	1	2	0	0	1	2	1	5	1	0	0	1	4	2	2
We	2	0	0	0	0	0	0	0	0	0	0	0	1	0	0	0
Were . . .	0	0	0	0	2	1	0	0	0	0	0	0	0	0	0	0
What . . .	1	0	1	0	0	0	0	0	3	0	7	1	4	1	4	3
When . . .	2	0	0	0	0	0	0	0	1	1	0	0	0	0	0	0
Where . .	0	2	3	0	3	4	8	4	4	6	7	3	5	4	21	14
Who	3	2	3	2	4	2	2	0	1	2	4	1	2	0	3	2
Whom . . .	0	0	0	1	0	0	0	0	1	2	1	1	7	5	8	9
With	0	0	0	0	0	0	1	2	0	0	0	0	0	1	0	0
Word . . .	0	4	2	1	2	0	0	0	0	0	0	1	0	0	0	0
You	28	24	31	31	18	20	19	10	23	26	15	21	17	17	35	37
						180.	**TOBACCO**									
Awful . . .	0	0	1	0	0	0	0	1	0	1	0	1	1	2	0	0
Bad	1	0	2	0	5	0	4	3	1	0	5	3	5	4	4	4
Bitter . . .	0	0	0	0	0	0	0	3	0	1	0	1	0	1	2	0
Brown . .	2	6	5	4	3	0	1	3	0	3	1	2	1	4	9	7
Cancer . .	0	0	0	0	0	0	4	0	0	0	2	0	5	0	5	1
Chew . . .	3	6	7	9	6	6	4	10	7	8	3	8	4	2	4	11
Chewing . .	0	0	0	0	0	0	2	0	2	1	0	0	0	0	0	0
Chews . .	0	0	2	0	0	0	0	0	0	0	0	0	0	0	0	0
Cigar . . .	13	11	15	19	18	21	21	18	21	18	12	10	4	6	9	9
Cigarette .	41	39	34	36	37	39	48	55	47	43	36	41	31	56	68	106
Cigarettes .	3	2	11	4	11	11	10	7	25	17	19	20	11	19	11	33
Cigars . . .	0	0	0	1	0	0	3	3	2	5	0	1	3	3	0	2

Response Word	4th M	4th F	5th M	5th F	6th M	6th F	7th M	7th F	8th M	8th F	10th M	10th F	12th M	12th F	College M	College F
						TOBACCO										
Coffee ...	1	0	0	0	0	0	2	0	0	0	0	0	0	0	0	1
Corn ...	0	0	0	3	0	0	0	0	0	0	0	0	0	0	0	0
Crop ...	0	0	3	1	1	1	0	0	1	0	0	0	0	0	0	0
Dad	0	0	0	1	2	0	1	0	0	0	0	0	0	0	0	0
Eat	5	5	2	5	2	1	1	1	0	1	0	0	0	0	0	1
Farm ...	0	0	1	2	0	0	1	0	0	0	0	1	0	0	1	0
Field ...	0	1	1	2	2	0	1	1	0	0	0	0	0	2	1	0
Filter ...	1	2	0	0	0	0	0	0	0	0	0	0	0	0	0	0
Fish ...	2	0	0	0	0	0	0	0	0	0	0	0	0	0	0	0
Food ...	2	1	6	0	1	1	1	3	1	0	0	0	0	0	0	0
Good ...	1	4	0	1	1	1	1	0	0	0	2	0	5	1	1	0
Grasshopper	0	2	0	0	0	1	0	0	0	0	0	0	0	0	0	0
Habit ...	0	0	0	0	0	0	0	0	0	0	2	0	0	0	0	0
Ish ...	1	1	0	0	0	2	0	0	1	2	0	2	0	2	0	1
Ishy ...	0	0	0	0	2	0	0	0	0	0	0	0	0	0	0	0
Juice ...	1	1	0	0	1	0	0	0	2	1	1	2	1	2	11	1
Leaf ...	1	0	3	5	4	2	1	5	1	1	0	0	1	2	1	3
Leaves ..	4	1	2	4	1	1	2	1	2	0	0	1	0	0	2	0
Light ...	3	0	0	0	0	0	2	0	0	1	1	0	0	0	2	0
Man	2	1	0	0	0	3	0	0	0	0	0	0	0	0	0	0
Marlboro .	0	0	0	0	0	0	0	0	0	0	0	0	2	0	1	0
Matches .	0	0	0	0	0	0	0	0	0	0	0	0	0	0	0	2
Mouth ...	0	0	0	2	1	0	0	0	0	0	0	0	0	0	0	0
Nicotine .	0	0	0	0	0	1	0	0	2	0	0	0	1	0	1	1
Pipe ...	30	31	15	29	17	25	17	18	9	23	11	8	8	12	21	30
Pipes ...	0	1	0	0	0	0	0	0	0	0	0	2	0	0	0	0
Plant ...	2	5	14	3	8	2	3	5	1	2	3	2	0	1	2	2
Pouch ..	0	0	0	0	0	0	0	1	0	0	0	0	0	0	1	2
Road ...	1	1	0	0	0	1	1	0	2	0	1	1	5	2	10	3
Seed ...	0	0	3	0	0	0	0	0	0	0	0	0	0	0	0	0
Sick	0	0	0	2	0	0	0	0	0	0	0	0	0	0	0	0
Sled	0	2	0	0	0	0	0	0	0	0	0	0	0	0	0	0
Smell ...	1	2	1	0	1	2	1	2	1	3	0	5	2	6	6	15
Smells ..	0	0	0	0	0	0	0	1	0	0	0	1	0	0	2	2
Smelly ..	0	0	0	0	0	1	0	1	0	1	0	2	0	3	0	0
Smoke ...	69	74	80	79	93	97	93	87	86	97	115	111	133	96	256	226
Smokes ..	0	0	0	0	0	0	0	1	0	0	4	0	0	0	0	0
Smokey ..	0	0	0	0	0	2	0	2	0	0	0	0	0	0	0	0
Smoking .	4	0	6	6	3	3	6	1	10	11	7	8	8	11	17	13
Snuff ...	3	0	1	0	0	2	0	0	0	0	1	0	0	0	0	1
Sour	0	0	0	0	0	0	0	0	0	0	0	0	0	0	2	0
Spit	2	0	0	0	0	2	0	1	0	1	0	1	2	0	1	0
Stain ...	0	0	0	0	0	0	0	0	1	0	1	0	1	1	7	2
Stains ...	0	0	0	0	0	0	0	0	0	0	0	0	0	0	0	2
Strong ..	0	1	0	1	0	1	1	1	1	1	1	2	1	1	2	2
Taste ...	2	3	1	1	1	0	0	0	0	2	0	1	2	0	2	1
Terrible .	2	0	0	0	0	0	0	1	0	0	1	1	0	0	0	0
To	2	0	0	2	0	0	0	0	0	0	0	0	0	0	0	0

Response Word	4th M	4th F	5th M	5th F	6th M	6th F	7th M	7th F	8th M	8th F	10th M	10th F	12th M	12th F	College M	College F
						TOBACCO										
Weed ...	0	0	0	0	1	1	2	0	2	1	0	0	0	0	2	2
Weeds ..	0	0	0	0	0	0	2	0	3	0	2	0	0	0	1	0
Winston ..	0	0	0	0	0	0	0	0	2	0	2	0	0	0	0	2
					181.	TROUBLE										
Accident .	1	0	0	0	0	1	1	0	0	1	0	1	0	0	5	3
Afraid ..	2	1	0	2	1	3	1	1	3	0	1	0	0	1	1	0
Always ..	0	0	1	0	0	0	0	0	0	0	0	1	1	2	1	1
Anger ...	1	3	5	4	5	7	7	4	6	4	6	8	3	5	12	13
Angry ..	7	8	3	1	1	2	1	1	2	1	0	0	1	1	2	0
Anxiety ..	0	0	0	0	0	0	0	0	0	0	0	1	0	2	7	7
Avoid ...	0	0	0	0	0	0	0	0	0	0	0	0	0	0	0	2
Awful ...	0	0	2	1	0	4	1	4	0	2	0	0	1	0	1	0
Baby ...	0	0	0	0	0	0	0	0	0	0	0	0	0	0	0	2
Bad	52	45	50	44	37	43	35	38	26	31	30	33	32	20	50	57
Big	0	0	2	0	0	0	0	1	0	0	1	0	0	0	1	0
Bother ..	0	0	0	0	0	0	1	0	0	0	0	0	1	1	3	2
Boy	3	2	2	1	4	0	2	4	1	2	3	5	3	6	5	6
Boys ...	0	0	1	0	2	2	1	0	3	6	0	3	0	2	1	1
Break ...	0	0	0	1	0	0	2	0	0	0	0	0	0	1	0	0
Broke ...	0	2	0	0	0	0	1	0	0	0	0	0	0	0	0	0
Brother ..	0	1	0	2	2	2	0	1	0	2	1	0	0	1	0	0
Bubble ..	0	2	1	0	1	1	0	0	0	0	1	0	1	0	0	1
Calm ...	0	0	0	0	0	0	0	0	0	0	0	0	0	0	2	1
Car	0	1	0	1	0	0	0	1	0	1	1	1	7	1	2	3
Comfort .	0	0	0	0	0	0	0	1	0	1	0	0	2	0	1	1
Confusion .	0	0	0	0	0	0	0	0	0	1	1	0	2	0	0	0
Cop	0	0	0	0	0	0	1	0	1	0	1	0	1	0	2	0
Cops ...	0	0	0	0	2	0	4	0	3	2	8	3	5	2	5	1
Cry	0	1	0	0	0	0	0	0	0	0	0	2	0	1	0	4
Cuba ...	0	0	0	0	0	0	1	2	0	0	0	0	0	0	0	0
Danger ..	6	5	11	7	2	17	11	8	7	7	9	15	4	14	24	18
Dangerous .	0	0	0	0	1	0	2	0	0	0	0	0	0	0	0	0
Delinquent .	0	0	0	0	0	0	0	0	0	1	0	0	1	2	2	1
Delinquents	0	0	0	0	0	0	0	0	0	0	0	1	0	1	0	2
Difficult ..	0	0	0	0	0	0	1	1	0	0	0	1	0	0	2	0
Difficulty .	0	0	0	0	0	1	0	2	2	1	3	0	2	1	2	2
Disaster ...	0	0	0	0	0	0	0	0	0	3	0	1	1	1	0	1
Discomfort	0	0	0	0	0	0	0	1	0	0	0	0	0	1	2	1
Distress .	0	0	0	0	0	0	0	0	0	1	0	2	0	0	2	0
Dog	1	0	0	0	0	1	0	1	0	0	0	0	0	2	0	0
Double ..	0	1	0	1	2	0	0	0	1	3	0	2	1	1	7	1
Ease ...	1	0	0	0	0	0	0	0	0	1	1	0	1	1	4	2
Easy ...	2	1	5	0	1	4	2	4	3	4	3	3	3	1	6	3
Fear ...	2	1	1	6	4	2	5	0	1	2	6	5	8	6	19	15
Fight ...	16	4	7	7	13	6	11	8	3	9	9	7	8	5	20	8
Fighting ...	0	1	1	0	2	0	1	0	1	0	0	0	0	1	0	0
Fine ...	1	0	2	0	2	0	0	0	0	0	0	0	0	0	0	0

Response Word	4th M	4th F	5th M	5th F	6th M	6th F	7th M	7th F	8th M	8th F	10th M	10th F	12th M	12th F	College M	College F
	M	F	M	F	M	F	M	F	M	F	M	F	M	F	M	F

TROUBLE

Response Word	4th M	4th F	5th M	5th F	6th M	6th F	7th M	7th F	8th M	8th F	10th M	10th F	12th M	12th F	College M	College F
Fix	1	0	0	1	0	1	0	1	0	0	0	0	0	0	3	1
Friend	0	1	0	0	2	1	0	0	1	0	0	0	1	1	1	0
Friends	0	0	0	0	0	0	0	2	0	0	0	0	0	0	0	0
Frightened	0	0	0	0	0	0	0	0	0	2	0	0	0	0	0	0
Fun	2	2	4	6	1	8	4	3	6	4	5	3	2	2	3	3
Fuzz	0	0	0	0	0	0	1	0	2	0	1	0	1	0	0	0
Gangs	0	0	0	0	0	0	0	0	0	0	0	0	0	2	0	0
Girl	0	1	0	0	0	0	0	0	0	1	3	0	0	1	1	2
Girls	0	0	1	0	0	0	0	0	1	0	0	0	2	0	0	0
Good	2	5	6	4	4	1	5	3	8	4	7	6	1	2	0	1
Guns	0	0	0	0	0	0	0	0	0	0	0	0	0	0	0	2
Happiness	1	0	0	0	1	0	0	3	0	2	1	1	1	1	6	2
Happy	1	4	3	1	3	0	2	4	6	4	1	2	0	4	1	5
Hard	7	10	12	15	6	14	11	13	2	5	4	3	3	3	10	9
Hardship	0	0	0	1	2	2	2	1	1	1	2	1	0	0	1	3
Harmony	0	0	0	0	0	0	0	0	0	0	0	0	0	0	3	0
Harry	0	0	0	0	0	0	0	0	0	0	0	0	0	0	2	0
Hate	0	0	0	0	0	0	0	0	1	0	0	0	0	1	2	1
Help	7	8	6	4	10	8	4	4	3	4	6	4	8	4	11	6
Hide	0	0	1	1	0	0	0	0	2	0	0	0	0	0	0	0
Hope	0	0	0	0	0	0	0	0	2	0	0	0	0	0	0	0
Hot water	1	0	0	0	0	0	2	0	0	0	0	0	0	0	0	0
Hurt	3	3	0	4	3	0	1	1	1	0	1	2	2	2	1	3
Ill	0	0	0	0	0	0	0	0	0	0	0	0	0	1	2	1
In	1	3	1	1	1	1	1	0	0	0	1	0	1	0	1	0
Innocent	0	0	0	0	0	0	0	0	2	0	1	2	0	0	0	0
Jail	0	0	2	1	0	1	1	1	0	2	5	2	1	3	4	6
Jam	1	0	0	0	1	2	1	0	0	0	2	0	0	1	0	1
Laughter	0	0	0	0	0	0	0	0	0	0	0	0	0	0	0	2
Law	0	0	0	0	0	0	2	0	0	0	3	1	0	0	6	1
Life	0	0	0	0	0	0	0	0	0	0	0	0	2	0	0	2
Look out	1	0	0	0	0	0	0	0	2	1	0	0	0	0	0	0
Mad	10	14	10	15	8	9	3	7	7	5	4	7	2	4	7	9
Make	0	1	0	2	0	0	0	0	0	0	0	0	0	0	0	0
Maker	0	1	3	2	1	1	0	1	3	4	0	1	3	0	5	4
Man	0	2	0	0	1	0	0	1	0	0	0	1	1	0	2	2
Me	1	0	1	0	2	1	0	0	4	1	3	0	1	4	1	1
Mean	1	7	4	4	2	7	4	0	2	3	2	1	1	1	0	2
Meanness	0	0	0	2	0	0	0	0	0	0	0	0	0	1	0	0
Men	0	1	0	0	0	0	0	0	0	1	0	0	0	0	0	6
Mess	0	0	1	1	0	0	1	3	1	1	2	0	2	2	0	2
Mind	0	0	0	0	0	0	1	0	0	0	0	0	0	1	0	2
Mischief	5	1	6	6	3	3	4	3	4	2	0	5	0	0	0	6
Misery	0	0	0	0	0	0	0	0	0	1	1	1	1	2	0	0
Misfortune	0	0	0	0	0	1	0	0	0	0	0	0	0	0	2	0
Mistake	0	0	4	0	1	1	0	1	0	0	0	1	0	2	0	0
Money	0	0	0	0	0	0	0	1	1	1	0	2	0	0	8	0
Mother	0	0	0	1	0	0	0	0	1	0	1	1	2	0	0	1
Much	0	0	0	0	0	0	0	0	0	0	0	0	0	1	2	0

Response Word	4th M	4th F	5th M	5th F	6th M	6th F	7th M	7th F	8th M	8th F	10th M	10th F	12th M	12th F	College M	College F
								TROUBLE								
Naughty	0	1	0	1	0	4	0	1	0	0	0	1	0	1	0	0
Nervous	0	0	0	1	0	0	1	0	0	0	0	0	2	1	0	0
Nervousness	0	0	0	0	0	0	0	0	0	0	0	0	0	0	0	2
Never	0	0	0	0	1	0	0	0	0	0	1	0	0	0	0	2
Nice	8	4	2	0	1	3	0	0	2	1	0	1	0	1	1	0
Night	0	0	1	0	0	0	0	0	0	0	2	0	0	0	0	0
No	3	0	2	3	0	0	1	1	0	1	0	0	0	0	2	1
Not	0	0	0	0	1	1	2	0	0	0	0	0	0	0	0	0
Not trouble	2	0	0	0	0	0	0	0	0	0	0	0	0	0	0	0
Oh oh	1	2	4	2	2	2	1	1	0	1	0	0	1	1	0	0
OK	1	0	2	1	0	0	0	0	0	0	0	0	0	0	1	0
Out	1	2	1	0	1	0	1	0	1	0	0	0	0	0	0	0
Pain	0	0	0	0	0	0	0	0	0	1	1	1	0	1	4	9
Parents	0	0	0	0	0	0	0	0	0	0	1	2	0	0	1	0
Peace	0	0	0	0	1	1	0	2	3	1	1	2	0	1	5	4
People	0	2	0	0	0	0	0	3	0	3	4	3	0	3	1	0
Person	0	0	1	1	1	1	0	0	2	1	3	0	1	0	1	0
Police	4	1	6	2	6	2	7	3	16	6	19	8	21	9	34	19
Poor	0	0	0	0	0	0	0	0	0	0	0	0	0	0	2	0
Pregnant	0	0	0	0	0	0	0	0	0	0	0	0	0	0	2	0
Principal	1	1	0	0	0	0	1	0	0	2	0	0	2	0	0	0
Problem	1	3	0	1	2	8	1	4	2	5	1	12	3	7	6	14
Problems	0	0	0	0	1	0	0	2	0	5	2	8	2	2	6	8
Punishment	0	0	0	0	1	0	1	0	0	2	1	1	1	0	1	3
Quarrel	0	0	0	0	0	0	0	0	0	0	0	0	0	2	1	0
Red	0	0	0	0	0	0	0	0	0	0	0	0	0	0	0	2
Rough	0	2	0	0	1	0	2	0	0	0	1	0	0	0	1	0
Run	4	1	3	1	2	0	1	3	0	0	3	3	2	2	5	0
Sad	1	2	1	2	1	0	1	2	0	2	1	1	0	4	1	9
Sadness	0	0	0	0	0	0	0	0	1	0	1	0	0	1	0	5
Safe	4	1	0	2	1	0	0	1	1	1	1	0	0	1	0	0
Scared	2	5	3	2	3	6	3	0	3	2	2	2	0	4	2	2
School	0	1	0	1	2	0	1	2	3	6	4	6	12	3	4	4
Serious	1	0	1	0	0	0	1	0	1	2	0	0	0	0	2	0
Shoot	0	0	0	0	0	0	0	0	0	0	0	0	0	0	2	0
Shooter	0	0	0	0	1	0	1	0	1	0	3	0	11	1	17	6
Sick	0	0	0	0	1	0	0	1	1	1	2	1	0	0	1	4
Sickness	0	0	0	0	0	0	0	2	1	1	0	2	1	1	1	4
Sinister	0	0	0	0	0	0	0	0	0	0	0	0	0	0	2	0
Sister	0	0	0	0	0	2	0	0	0	1	0	0	1	2	0	0
Some	0	0	0	0	0	0	0	2	0	0	0	0	0	0	1	1
Song	0	0	0	0	0	0	0	0	0	0	0	0	0	0	0	2
Sorrow	0	1	0	2	1	0	2	10	1	2	2	7	2	8	10	24
Sorry	0	4	0	1	1	1	0	1	0	0	1	1	0	0	0	2
Spanking	0	3	0	2	1	0	0	1	0	0	0	0	0	0	0	0
Spot	0	0	0	0	0	0	0	0	2	0	0	0	0	1	0	1
Steal	1	0	0	1	1	0	1	0	2	3	1	1	0	0	1	0
Strife	0	0	0	0	0	0	0	0	0	0	0	0	0	0	0	3
Teacher	1	0	0	0	0	1	1	2	0	0	1	2	0	0	0	1

Response Word	4th		5th		6th		7th		8th		10th		12th		College	
	M	F	M	F	M	F	M	F	M	F	M	F	M	F	M	F

TROUBLE

Response Word	M	F	M	F	M	F	M	F	M	F	M	F	M	F	M	F
Teachers .	0	0	0	0	0	0	0	0	0	2	0	0	0	0	0	0
Terrible .	2	2	2	3	1	4	0	0	0	1	1	1	1	1	0	2
Test . . .	0	0	0	0	0	0	0	0	0	0	0	0	0	1	1	2
Thing . . .	2	0	0	0	2	0	0	0	0	0	1	0	0	0	0	0
Tough . . .	0	0	2	1	1	1	1	1	0	2	0	0	0	0	0	0
Unhappiness	0	0	0	0	0	0	0	1	0	0	0	1	0	0	0	3
Unhappy . .	0	1	0	2	0	3	0	0	0	1	1	2	1	2	0	1
Unpleasant	0	0	0	0	0	0	0	0	0	0	0	0	0	0	1	2
Upset . . .	0	0	0	0	1	2	0	0	0	0	0	0	0	0	0	1
Us	0	0	0	0	0	0	0	0	2	0	0	0	0	0	0	0
Violence .	0	0	0	0	0	0	2	0	0	0	0	0	0	0	1	0
War	0	0	1	1	4	1	3	1	1	1	0	2	0	1	1	4
Window . .	1	1	0	0	1	0	2	0	0	0	0	1	0	0	0	0
Windows .	0	0	0	0	0	0	2	0	0	0	0	0	0	0	0	0
With . . .	0	0	0	0	1	0	0	0	0	0	0	0	0	0	2	1
Women . .	0	0	1	0	0	0	0	0	0	0	2	0	1	0	0	0
Work . . .	0	0	2	2	1	1	6	0	1	0	1	0	3	6	2	2
World . . .	0	0	0	0	0	0	0	1	0	0	0	0	0	1	2	0
Worried . .	1	3	1	2	0	2	1	4	0	2	1	2	2	2	0	1
Worries . .	0	0	0	0	0	0	2	0	0	0	0	0	0	0	0	1
Worry . . .	2	4	0	4	2	1	1	7	2	3	1	5	6	4	7	20
Wrong . .	4	6	2	5	4	4	5	5	1	4	0	0	2	2	3	3
Yes	2	0	0	0	1	0	0	0	0	0	0	1	0	0	1	0

182. US

Response Word	M	F	M	F	M	F	M	F	M	F	M	F	M	F	M	F
All	0	0	4	2	3	4	2	3	0	0	0	1	1	2	1	2
And	1	1	0	5	2	0	0	0	0	2	0	0	0	0	0	0
Are	9	5	0	0	0	4	2	2	2	1	1	1	5	1	3	0
As	0	1	0	3	1	1	1	0	0	0	0	0	0	0	0	0
Both . . .	1	2	1	1	0	1	0	1	0	0	0	0	1	3	0	1
Boys . . .	0	0	0	0	1	0	1	1	2	1	3	1	5	2	4	0
Bus	5	0	2	0	0	2	1	2	0	1	0	0	0	0	2	0
Can	0	1	2	2	0	0	0	1	1	0	1	0	0	0	0	0
Children .	0	1	0	3	1	0	0	1	1	0	1	0	0	0	0	1
Couple . .	0	0	0	0	0	0	0	0	0	0	0	0	0	1	2	2
Crowd . .	0	0	0	0	0	1	0	0	0	0	0	0	0	0	1	2
Do	3	0	0	0	0	0	0	0	0	0	1	0	0	0	0	0
Family . .	0	2	0	1	0	0	0	0	0	0	0	0	0	0	1	0
For	1	2	0	1	3	0	0	0	0	0	0	1	0	1	1	0
Friends . .	0	0	0	0	1	1	1	1	0	0	1	1	1	2	1	5
Fun	0	0	0	0	0	0	0	0	0	0	1	2	1	0	1	2
Fuss . . .	1	0	0	0	2	0	2	0	0	0	0	0	0	0	0	0
Girls . . .	0	0	0	0	0	0	0	2	0	2	2	2	0	5	0	1
Go	1	1	2	1	2	0	0	0	0	0	2	1	0	1	1	1
Group . .	0	1	1	3	2	3	0	0	1	2	2	1	4	1	11	5
He	0	1	2	0	0	1	1	1	1	0	0	0	0	0	0	0
Her	0	3	0	0	1	1	0	1	1	0	1	0	0	0	2	0
Him	6	1	2	1	3	0	7	1	4	1	0	1	1	0	0	0
I	1	1	0	3	0	2	0	2	0	1	0	0	0	0	1	0

Response Word	4th M	F	5th M	F	6th M	F	7th M	F	8th M	F	10th M	F	12th M	F	College M	F
							US									
Is	5	3	8	4	5	2	2	0	1	1	3	0	0	0	1	1
It	4	1	2	0	1	3	1	0	0	0	1	0	0	0	2	0
Kids . . .	0	1	0	0	0	0	0	1	0	0	4	2	3	2	1	2
Love . . .	0	1	0	0	0	0	0	1	0	0	0	1	0	0	1	2
Many . . .	0	1	2	0	1	2	0	4	0	1	2	0	1	2	1	0
Me	18	19	22	15	14	14	16	9	10	6	4	2	2	1	4	4
Now . . .	5	1	1	1	2	0	1	0	1	0	0	0	1	0	0	1
Our	2	1	0	1	0	0	0	0	2	0	0	1	0	0	0	1
Ours . . .	0	0	0	0	1	0	1	0	0	0	0	1	1	0	1	2
Ourselves .	0	1	0	0	0	2	0	0	0	0	2	0	1	0	1	0
Out	1	0	0	0	2	0	0	0	0	0	0	0	0	0	0	0
People . .	12	9	14	6	16	7	7	3	5	5	6	6	6	2	11	5
Person . .	0	2	0	1	0	0	0	0	0	0	0	0	0	0	0	0
See	0	2	0	0	0	0	0	0	0	0	0	0	1	0	0	0
She	0	0	0	0	0	2	0	0	0	0	0	0	0	0	0	0
That . . .	3	0	1	0	0	0	0	0	0	0	0	0	0	0	0	0
The	1	0	2	2	4	0	0	0	0	0	1	0	0	0	0	0
Them . . .	10	13	16	13	13	23	26	32	38	25	28	29	22	23	60	58
Then . . .	0	1	2	1	1	0	2	0	3	0	3	2	0	1	2	0
There . .	1	0	2	2	1	1	1	1	1	1	0	0	0	0	0	0
These . . .	0	0	2	0	0	0	0	0	0	0	0	0	0	0	0	0
They	6	7	7	9	10	9	17	17	19	19	13	18	16	19	67	40
This . . .	2	0	0	1	0	1	0	0	0	1	0	0	1	0	0	0
Those . .	1	0	0	0	0	0	0	0	2	0	0	1	0	0	0	0
Three . .	0	2	1	1	0	0	0	1	0	0	0	0	0	1	0	2
To	1	2	2	0	6	3	1	0	1	2	1	1	2	0	2	1
Together .	3	2	0	5	2	4	1	6	1	3	6	3	4	8	11	14
Too	0	0	0	3	0	1	0	0	0	3	1	0	0	0	2	0
Two	1	6	2	3	4	8	1	4	2	0	1	2	3	1	2	3
US	0	1	2	0	2	1	0	0	0	0	0	0	0	0	0	2
USA . . .	1	1	0	1	0	2	0	0	0	0	1	0	0	0	1	0
United . .	0	0	0	2	0	0	0	0	0	0	0	0	0	0	0	0
Up	0	1	0	0	2	0	0	0	0	1	0	0	0	0	0	0
Use	7	5	6	8	5	3	5	4	1	1	2	0	1	0	4	0
Used . . .	1	0	2	0	0	0	2	0	0	0	0	0	0	0	0	0
Was	0	0	0	0	2	0	1	0	1	0	0	0	2	0	0	0
We	40	48	49	61	59	76	91	89	81	100	115	121	128	126	235	275
Were . . .	0	1	1	0	0	0	1	0	1	2	0	1	3	1	1	2
Who	0	0	0	0	0	0	1	0	0	1	1	0	0	0	2	1
Why	0	1	0	0	0	0	0	0	0	0	0	2	0	0	0	0
Word . . .	0	0	1	0	2	0	0	0	0	0	0	0	0	0	0	0
Yes	2	0	0	1	0	0	0	0	0	0	0	0	1	0	0	0
You	50	57	47	60	32	44	27	45	48	48	19	23	16	28	33	43
You and me	0	0	0	0	0	1	0	0	0	0	0	3	0	1	0	0
Your	0	1	2	0	0	0	1	0	0	1	0	0	0	0	1	0

Response Word	4th M	4th F	5th M	5th F	6th M	6th F	7th M	7th F	8th M	8th F	10th M	10th F	12th M	12th F	College M	College F
							183. VERY									
Adjective .	0	0	0	0	0	0	0	0	0	0	0	0	0	2	0	1
Adverb . .	0	0	0	0	0	0	0	1	0	0	0	0	0	2	2	1
All	0	0	0	0	0	0	1	0	0	0	0	1	0	0	2	0
Alot . . .	3	1	1	4	1	2	3	8	4	11	2	4	1	3	2	2
Also . . .	1	0	0	1	1	1	0	2	1	1	0	0	0	1	1	1
Always . .	0	0	1	1	1	1	6	4	4	3	2	6	4	4	4	6
And	0	0	1	0	0	1	1	2	0	0	0	0	0	0	0	1
Appealing .	0	0	1	0	0	0	1	0	0	0	0	0	0	0	2	1
Awfully . .	0	0	0	0	0	0	1	1	0	0	0	0	0	0	0	2
Bad	4	3	2	2	0	1	0	1	3	1	0	0	1	0	1	4
Berry . . .	1	0	0	1	1	1	0	1	0	0	2	1	0	1	0	0
Big	4	0	2	2	1	4	0	1	0	1	3	0	1	1	0	2
But	1	0	0	0	0	0	1	0	0	0	0	1	0	1	2	0
Can	0	0	0	1	0	0	0	2	0	0	0	0	0	0	1	0
Careful . .	0	0	1	0	0	2	0	0	0	0	0	0	0	0	1	0
Carry . . .	1	0	1	0	0	0	4	2	0	2	1	1	0	0	0	1
Change . .	0	0	0	0	1	0	1	0	0	0	0	0	0	0	2	0
Clear . . .	1	0	1	0	0	0	0	0	0	0	0	1	0	0	2	4
Close . . .	0	0	0	1	1	0	1	0	2	0	1	1	1	2	1	0
Cold . . .	6	1	4	4	2	1	1	0	10	1	4	0	3	4	8	4
Come . . .	2	0	0	0	1	0	0	0	0	0	0	0	0	0	0	0
Cool . . .	0	0	0	0	0	0	0	0	3	0	0	0	0	0	0	0
Dairy . . .	0	0	0	0	0	0	0	0	0	0	0	2	0	0	0	0
Day	3	0	0	0	0	0	0	0	0	0	0	0	0	0	0	0
Dear . . .	0	0	0	0	0	0	1	0	0	0	0	0	0	0	2	0
Different .	0	0	2	0	1	1	3	1	1	0	4	2	0	0	0	1
Ever . . .	1	0	2	1	1	1	1	0	4	0	2	0	0	1	2	0
Every . . .	5	5	11	11	9	0	4	8	2	2	5	5	1	2	4	3
Extreme .	0	0	1	0	0	1	1	1	2	1	2	0	0	0	0	3
Extremely .	0	0	1	0	0	2	3	4	3	1	4	3	9	3	2	7
Far	0	0	0	0	0	0	0	0	0	0	0	0	2	0	1	1
Fast . . .	13	12	15	10	17	7	9	6	14	8	8	7	11	4	20	13
Fat	0	0	0	0	0	0	0	0	1	1	0	0	0	2	0	1
Few	0	0	2	1	2	0	4	2	4	0	2	5	3	3	4	11
Fine . . .	0	1	1	0	0	0	0	0	1	0	2	1	1	0	3	0
Fun	1	2	0	0	0	0	0	0	0	0	0	0	0	0	1	0
Funny . . .	0	3	0	1	0	0	0	0	0	0	1	0	0	0	0	2
Glad	0	0	0	0	0	2	0	1	0	0	1	1	1	2	0	0
Good . . .	35	52	36	41	44	48	18	23	25	27	25	22	24	29	57	24
Great . . .	0	0	0	0	0	0	0	1	0	0	0	0	2	0	0	2
Hairy . . .	0	0	1	0	3	0	1	0	0	0	0	0	0	0	1	0
Happy . . .	12	8	4	8	12	12	6	8	4	5	11	4	7	7	4	4
Hard . . .	2	8	6	6	9	11	5	4	0	5	0	2	7	1	4	1
Heavy . .	1	1	2	0	1	1	2	2	0	0	1	1	1	0	0	1
Hot	2	4	8	3	2	1	9	4	1	4	5	1	1	1	12	5
However .	0	2	0	1	0	0	0	0	0	0	0	0	0	0	0	0
Important .	1	1	2	1	2	4	1	1	1	2	4	0	2	5	2	2
In	1	0	0	0	0	0	0	0	0	0	0	0	0	0	2	0
Is	2	0	1	1	0	1	0	0	0	1	0	1	0	1	1	0

Response Word	4th M	4th F	5th M	5th F	6th M	6th F	7th M	7th F	8th M	8th F	10th M	10th F	12th M	12th F	College M	College F

VERY

Response Word	4th M	4th F	5th M	5th F	6th M	6th F	7th M	7th F	8th M	8th F	10th M	10th F	12th M	12th F	College M	College F
Large	2	0	0	1	0	0	0	0	0	1	1	1	0	1	2	1
Light	0	1	1	0	1	1	1	1	2	0	3	2	2	0	0	0
Like	0	2	0	2	0	1	0	1	0	0	0	0	0	1	0	2
Likely	0	0	0	1	0	0	0	1	0	2	1	0	3	1	2	3
Little	6	5	1	3	8	6	6	12	9	8	4	7	7	11	11	11
Long	0	1	1	0	2	0	0	0	0	0	0	0	1	0	0	1
Lot	0	2	3	3	1	1	4	1	0	3	0	0	0	1	1	3
Lots	0	2	2	1	0	0	0	2	0	0	0	2	0	0	0	0
Mad	0	1	2	2	1	0	1	0	1	1	0	0	2	0	0	0
Many	0	3	2	3	5	3	6	9	4	3	6	5	2	0	5	6
Maybe	0	0	0	0	0	0	0	0	0	1	2	0	0	0	0	0
Me	0	0	0	0	1	0	2	0	0	0	0	0	0	0	0	0
Merry	0	0	1	2	0	0	1	1	0	2	1	1	2	1	2	4
Most	1	0	0	0	0	0	0	0	0	2	1	0	0	3	4	2
Much	18	23	20	28	19	25	34	43	33	48	28	55	34	45	111	160
Near	0	0	0	1	0	1	0	1	0	2	1	1	0	1	18	4
Nearly	0	0	0	2	0	0	0	0	0	1	0	0	4	1	1	4
Neat	0	0	0	0	0	0	0	0	0	0	0	0	1	0	5	1
Never	0	0	0	1	0	1	3	2	3	3	1	1	3	5	4	12
New	1	0	0	1	0	0	0	0	0	0	0	0	0	0	2	0
Nice	22	23	14	16	10	13	12	10	11	17	11	10	9	9	17	19
Not	1	3	0	1	1	1	1	1	1	3	2	2	0	1	0	3
Now	0	1	1	1	0	0	0	0	2	0	0	1	1	0	1	2
Often	1	0	2	2	1	2	2	4	2	5	5	10	4	7	14	11
Old	1	0	3	0	1	0	1	1	1	1	3	0	1	1	1	0
One	2	1	1	1	0	0	2	1	1	0	1	0	0	0	0	0
Only	2	0	0	0	0	0	0	2	0	0	1	2	0	2	2	2
Pleasant	0	0	0	0	0	0	0	2	0	0	0	1	0	0	1	0
Poor	0	1	3	2	2	2	2	2	2	0	5	2	3	1	0	2
Pretty	2	8	1	5	3	7	1	1	3	4	3	2	2	9	1	2
Quick	3	5	2	2	2	0	4	1	1	2	1	0	5	0	3	2
Quickly	0	2	3	0	0	1	1	1	1	0	1	0	1	2	4	1
Quiet	2	1	1	0	2	0	0	2	1	2	0	0	0	0	0	0
Quietly	0	0	0	0	0	0	0	0	0	2	0	0	1	0	0	0
Quit	1	0	0	0	2	0	0	0	0	0	0	0	0	0	0	0
Quite	0	1	0	1	0	1	1	0	1	2	2	3	1	2	7	9
Real	1	0	1	0	2	0	1	1	0	0	1	2	2	2	1	3
Really	0	1	0	2	0	0	0	2	1	1	0	1	2	2	0	3
Sad	2	8	2	1	1	0	0	2	4	6	0	2	1	3	0	1
Same	0	0	0	1	0	0	2	4	0	0	1	0	0	0	1	0
Seldom	0	0	0	0	0	0	3	2	2	0	1	0	2	1	5	4
Sharp	0	0	0	0	0	0	0	0	0	0	0	0	1	0	3	0
Size	0	0	0	0	2	0	0	0	0	0	0	0	0	0	0	0
Slow	5	1	5	3	5	4	3	2	6	6	4	5	4	2	13	5
Slowly	0	0	0	1	0	0	0	1	0	2	2	1	0	0	1	0
Small	2	2	2	1	1	5	3	3	8	2	4	5	5	3	3	3
Smart	1	1	0	2	1	0	0	1	0	0	0	0	0	1	1	2
Smooth	0	0	0	0	0	0	0	0	0	1	0	0	0	0	2	1
So	0	2	0	1	1	1	0	0	1	2	0	0	1	0	4	2

Response Word	4th M	F	5th M	F	6th M	F	7th M	F	8th M	F	10th M	F	12th M	F	College M	F

VERY

Response Word	4th M	F	5th M	F	6th M	F	7th M	F	8th M	F	10th M	F	12th M	F	College M	F
Soft	0	0	1	1	1	0	0	0	4	1	0	0	0	2	4	3
Some . . .	0	0	0	1	0	2	0	0	1	0	0	0	0	2	0	0
Soon	5	4	5	5	2	8	5	8	1	2	5	6	5	10	21	28
Special . .	1	0	1	0	3	1	0	0	0	1	0	0	0	0	2	1
Sure	2	0	0	2	0	2	1	0	2	0	0	2	1	1	1	2
The . . .	0	0	2	0	1	0	0	0	0	0	0	0	0	0	1	1
There . . .	0	0	1	1	0	0	0	0	1	0	2	0	1	0	0	0
Thing . . .	2	1	4	1	2	0	0	1	0	0	0	0	1	0	0	0
Too . . .	0	1	0	0	0	0	0	0	0	1	0	1	2	0	1	3
True . . .	0	0	0	1	0	1	0	0	1	0	1	2	0	1	0	2
Truly . . .	0	0	0	0	0	0	0	1	2	0	0	4	1	3	1	3
Vary . . .	0	0	0	0	0	1	2	0	0	1	3	0	1	1	1	0
Verily . .	0	0	0	0	0	1	0	0	0	0	0	0	3	2	1	0
Warm . . .	0	0	0	0	0	2	0	1	1	1	0	3	0	0	1	1
Well	5	2	7	4	8	5	8	4	7	4	10	4	13	4	10	11
When . . .	0	0	0	0	1	0	0	2	0	0	0	0	0	1	1	0
Word . . .	0	1	3	1	3	0	0	0	1	0	0	0	0	0	0	0
Yes	3	0	0	2	2	0	1	0	0	0	0	0	1	0	0	4
You	3	0	0	0	1	0	0	0	0	0	0	0	0	0	0	0

184. WAS

Response Word	4th M	F	5th M	F	6th M	F	7th M	F	8th M	F	10th M	F	12th M	F	College M	F
A	6	1	4	2	2	1	0	1	0	1	0	0	0	0	1	1
After . . .	1	1	1	0	0	2	0	0	0	1	0	0	0	0	0	0
Ago	1	1	0	2	1	2	0	0	0	0	0	0	0	0	1	0
Almost . .	0	0	1	0	2	0	0	0	0	0	0	0	0	0	0	0
Already . .	0	1	0	0	0	1	1	2	0	0	0	0	0	0	0	0
Am	0	0	0	0	1	0	0	1	2	0	1	1	0	1	2	2
Are . . .	0	0	0	0	0	0	0	0	1	0	0	0	0	0	2	0
As . . .	7	9	4	7	6	5	6	3	1	2	0	0	0	1	0	2
At	0	0	1	2	1	1	0	2	2	2	0	1	1	0	3	1
Be	0	0	0	0	0	0	2	0	0	1	2	0	0	2	0	0
Because .	1	1	0	0	2	0	0	1	0	0	1	0	0	2	0	0
Been . . .	0	0	0	0	0	0	0	1	0	2	0	0	1	1	0	1
Before . .	2	5	2	7	5	5	2	3	4	4	2	11	3	3	7	3
Boy	0	2	0	0	0	0	0	1	0	0	0	0	0	0	0	0
Bus	0	0	4	0	0	0	0	0	0	0	0	0	0	0	0	0
Car	0	0	2	1	0	0	0	0	0	0	0	0	1	0	0	0
Cause . . .	1	0	1	2	0	0	0	3	1	0	0	1	0	0	0	1
Could . . .	2	0	0	0	0	0	0	0	0	0	0	1	0	0	1	0
Dead . . .	0	0	0	0	0	0	1	0	0	0	0	0	0	0	1	2
Did	0	0	1	2	3	4	0	0	1	1	1	1	2	0	1	2
Do	2	0	0	0	1	0	0	0	0	0	0	0	0	0	0	0
Does . . .	0	0	0	2	1	0	0	0	1	0	1	0	1	0	0	0
Done . . .	0	0	0	0	0	0	0	0	0	0	0	0	0	0	2	1
Ever . . .	0	0	0	2	0	1	0	1	0	0	0	0	0	1	1	0
Fast	0	0	0	2	0	0	1	0	0	0	1	0	0	0	0	1
For	3	3	4	1	1	2	1	1	1	2	1	1	1	1	0	1
Going . . .	2	1	1	1	1	1	0	1	1	0	1	2	2	1	2	4
Gone . . .	2	2	4	0	3	4	0	0	3	2	0	4	3	3	4	3

Response Word	4th M	4th F	5th M	5th F	6th M	6th F	7th M	7th F	8th M	8th F	10th M	10th F	12th M	12th F	College M	College F
								WAS								
Good	3	2	4	2	2	0	0	1	1	1	1	0	0	1	0	0
Had	3	2	1	3	1	2	1	2	0	0	0	1	1	0	2	1
Happen	0	1	0	1	0	0	1	0	0	2	1	0	0	0	0	1
Happened	1	0	0	1	0	2	1	0	0	2	1	0	1	1	0	0
Happy	1	1	0	0	1	3	0	0	0	0	0	0	0	0	0	0
Has	3	2	1	7	1	4	5	2	0	3	5	2	3	3	4	2
Has been	0	0	0	0	0	0	1	0	0	3	0	1	0	0	2	1
He	9	11	8	9	20	8	5	8	13	5	17	13	22	9	34	14
Her	0	0	2	1	0	1	1	0	0	0	1	1	1	0	0	0
Here	1	6	4	4	5	7	3	8	4	8	11	9	5	4	5	15
Him	1	1	2	0	2	1	0	0	0	0	1	0	2	2	0	0
His	1	0	0	0	3	1	3	1	1	0	2	1	0	3	0	0
Home	0	0	0	0	0	2	0	0	0	0	2	1	0	0	1	0
Hurt	0	0	0	0	0	0	0	0	0	1	0	0	0	0	2	0
I	2	4	0	3	1	0	1	2	1	1	0	0	0	4	4	1
In	1	0	2	2	2	2	2	0	1	0	0	1	0	4	1	2
Is	8	14	18	11	8	15	19	19	27	33	32	34	34	40	119	129
Isn't	0	2	2	1	1	1	0	1	1	1	2	1	0	0	1	4
It	26	29	20	23	26	24	19	12	19	18	12	28	21	26	53	50
Its	0	0	0	0	0	0	0	0	0	0	0	0	0	0	2	0
Me	2	2	1	0	0	0	2	0	0	0	1	0	0	1	0	1
Mine	0	1	1	1	0	0	0	2	1	2	0	0	0	0	0	0
My	2	0	0	1	0	0	0	0	0	0	1	0	0	1	0	0
Never	1	0	1	0	0	1	2	1	3	2	3	0	2	1	7	4
Nice	2	1	0	0	2	2	0	0	0	3	0	1	0	0	0	0
No	3	0	1	0	0	0	1	0	1	0	1	1	0	0	0	0
Not	28	15	13	17	14	12	9	8	16	7	12	9	10	10	24	25
Now	0	2	2	4	3	1	1	7	2	3	1	3	0	1	3	3
Of	0	0	1	2	0	0	0	0	2	0	1	0	2	1	1	0
Off	0	0	2	0	1	0	1	0	0	0	0	0	0	0	1	0
Old	0	0	0	1	0	0	2	0	0	1	0	0	0	0	0	0
On	1	2	3	2	4	1	3	0	3	0	1	0	2	0	1	1
Once	2	2	2	1	2	3	2	0	1	3	0	1	0	1	0	1
Only	3	2	4	1	0	0	1	1	1	2	2	1	0	0	1	4
Or	5	0	2	2	0	0	2	0	1	0	0	0	0	0	0	0
Our	1	0	0	1	2	0	0	0	0	0	0	0	0	0	0	0
Out	0	0	1	0	1	0	0	2	0	0	1	0	0	1	0	0
Over	0	1	0	1	3	0	1	0	2	0	0	1	1	0	0	0
Passed	0	0	0	2	0	0	0	0	0	0	0	0	0	0	0	0
Past	1	0	0	1	1	5	3	4	4	2	11	2	3	4	17	22
Question	0	3	0	4	0	2	0	1	0	0	2	2	1	0	2	0
Reason	0	1	0	0	0	0	0	1	0	0	0	0	2	0	0	0
Saw	6	10	7	3	8	3	5	5	2	2	2	2	1	0	0	1
Sea	0	0	2	0	0	0	0	0	0	0	0	0	0	0	0	0
She	0	5	1	2	1	5	1	5	0	2	5	5	5	3	6	4
So	0	1	1	1	4	0	0	1	0	1	0	0	0	0	0	1
Some	2	0	0	0	0	0	0	1	0	0	0	0	0	0	0	0
Something	7	2	0	2	0	1	0	0	0	0	0	0	0	0	0	1
That	6	11	9	5	3	8	5	10	8	5	7	10	7	6	19	4

Response Word	4th M	4th F	5th M	5th F	6th M	6th F	7th M	7th F	8th M	8th F	10th M	10th F	12th M	12th F	College M	College F
							WAS									
The	1	1	1	1	5	3	2	0	1	0	3	0	0	0	0	1
Their . . .	1	1	0	1	1	2	1	0	0	1	0	0	0	1	0	0
Then . . .	3	3	1	3	2	4	5	4	1	2	7	3	3	1	7	2
There . .	13	10	18	18	26	17	15	12	10	19	6	14	9	8	10	15
They	0	0	1	0	1	1	0	0	3	0	0	0	1	0	0	1
Thing . . .	0	0	0	0	2	1	0	0	0	0	0	1	0	0	0	1
This . . .	1	1	0	0	0	1	0	2	0	1	2	1	2	1	3	2
Time . . .	1	0	0	0	0	0	2	0	0	1	1	0	1	0	0	0
To	0	0	1	3	1	1	1	0	1	1	1	0	1	1	0	3
Ugly . . .	0	0	0	0	0	0	0	0	0	0	2	0	0	0	0	0
Us	0	2	2	0	0	0	2	0	1	0	0	0	0	0	1	0
Use	0	0	0	0	0	0	0	2	0	0	0	0	0	0	0	0
Used to . .	0	0	0	0	1	0	1	0	0	2	0	1	0	1	1	0
Used to be .	0	0	1	0	0	1	0	0	1	0	0	0	1	0	2	0
Verb . . .	0	0	0	0	0	0	0	0	1	5	2	5	3	6	9	2
Very	0	0	0	0	0	0	0	0	0	0	0	2	0	0	1	1
Want . . .	0	1	0	2	0	0	1	0	0	0	0	0	0	0	1	0
Was	0	0	0	0	1	2	0	0	0	0	0	0	0	0	0	0
Wasn't . .	8	12	15	7	6	13	12	9	10	8	7	5	8	9	14	13
We . . .	0	0	0	0	0	0	2	0	0	0	0	0	0	0	0	0
Went . . .	0	0	1	2	0	2	0	0	1	0	0	0	1	0	0	0
Were . . .	1	3	7	5	4	8	28	45	36	42	24	33	37	39	64	103
What . . .	4	2	4	5	2	0	5	6	3	7	8	9	5	7	6	3
When . . .	3	4	2	4	2	8	10	10	7	6	3	5	3	5	5	6
Where . .	3	3	3	2	6	4	6	4	9	2	3	1	3	4	3	3
Who	1	0	1	0	1	0	1	1	1	1	0	1	0	0	3	0
Why	1	0	1	5	0	4	2	1	0	0	2	0	1	4	1	1
Will	0	4	1	2	1	4	6	1	1	1	0	1	0	0	1	0
With . . .	0	0	0	1	0	0	1	1	2	0	0	0	1	0	0	0
Word . . .	0	2	4	0	0	1	1	0	0	0	0	0	0	1	0	0
Yes	0	2	1	1	0	0	0	0	0	0	1	0	0	0	0	0
Yesterday .	0	1	2	0	0	1	1	1	1	0	0	0	0	2	0	0
You . . .	3	4	1	1	5	2	1	0	3	3	4	1	2	0	2	1
						185.	WE									
All	6	2	6	2	2	4	3	2	1	2	2	1	0	3	1	1
And . . .	2	1	2	1	0	1	0	0	0	0	0	0	0	0	0	0
Are	26	43	39	37	41	40	24	20	34	23	27	17	38	28	54	53
As	0	0	1	0	0	0	1	3	0	0	1	0	0	0	0	0
Both . . .	0	3	0	1	0	1	0	1	0	0	0	1	0	1	1	2
Boys . . .	2	0	0	0	0	0	0	1	0	0	2	0	2	0	2	0
Came . . .	1	0	0	0	1	0	2	0	0	0	0	1	0	0	0	0
Can	5	2	6	8	6	1	2	2	1	0	4	1	3	3	6	2
Can't . . .	1	1	0	0	0	0	2	0	0	1	0	0	0	1	1	0
Come . . .	2	2	0	2	0	0	0	0	0	0	1	1	1	1	0	2
Could . . .	1	1	0	0	0	4	0	0	1	0	0	0	0	0	1	0
Do	5	2	1	0	1	2	1	0	2	1	3	0	0	1	0	5
Don't . . .	0	0	0	2	0	0	0	0	0	0	0	0	0	0	0	0
Family . .	0	0	0	1	0	0	0	0	0	0	0	0	0	0	2	0

Response Word	4th M	F	5th M	F	6th M	F	7th M	F	8th M	F	10th M	F	12th M	F	College M	F
							WE									
Friends	0	1	0	0	0	0	0	0	0	0	0	2	0	0	0	1
Girls	0	0	0	1	0	0	0	0	0	0	0	1	0	2	0	0
Give	0	0	2	0	0	0	0	0	0	0	0	0	0	0	0	1
Go	9	6	7	7	6	3	6	4	3	4	5	4	3	3	6	8
Got	0	0	1	0	2	0	0	0	0	0	0	0	0	0	0	0
Group	0	2	0	0	1	2	0	0	0	2	1	0	5	0	10	4
Had	0	0	0	1	0	0	3	0	0	0	0	0	0	0	1	0
Have	11	2	13	2	8	5	5	1	0	1	3	0	2	2	7	0
He	8	3	3	3	2	2	5	2	2	0	3	0	0	1	3	0
Him	3	2	0	1	2	1	1	3	2	3	0	0	0	0	0	0
Hope	0	0	0	0	0	0	0	0	0	0	0	0	2	0	0	0
How	0	0	2	0	0	0	0	0	0	0	0	0	1	0	0	0
I	7	6	4	5	2	3	4	3	3	2	1	0	0	1	0	0
It	0	0	1	1	2	0	0	0	0	0	0	0	0	0	0	0
Know	1	1	1	0	2	2	1	0	0	0	0	1	1	0	0	0
Like	1	0	0	0	2	1	0	1	0	1	0	0	1	3	1	0
Look	0	0	1	2	0	0	0	0	0	0	0	0	0	0	0	0
Love	0	1	0	0	0	0	0	0	0	1	0	3	2	3	1	0
Make	2	0	0	0	0	0	0	0	0	0	0	0	0	0	0	0
Many	2	1	0	0	0	2	0	2	1	0	1	0	0	0	1	0
Me	8	13	18	12	7	9	6	10	6	7	4	1	3	2	2	2
More	0	3	1	1	0	2	0	0	0	0	0	0	0	0	0	0
Must	0	1	0	0	0	0	0	1	1	2	0	0	0	0	0	1
My	1	2	0	0	0	0	1	0	0	0	0	0	0	0	0	0
Never	1	0	0	0	0	0	0	0	0	0	1	0	0	1	5	1
No	2	0	0	0	1	0	1	0	0	0	0	0	0	0	0	0
Now	5	1	2	2	1	2	0	0	0	0	0	0	1	0	0	0
Ought	0	0	0	0	0	0	0	0	0	0	1	0	2	0	2	0
Our	2	2	3	0	4	0	4	2	4	2	0	2	1	2	5	5
Ours	0	1	0	0	0	0	0	0	1	1	0	2	0	0	0	0
Ourselves	1	2	0	0	0	1	1	1	1	0	2	0	2	2	2	0
Owe	0	0	0	0	1	0	0	0	0	1	0	1	3	1	3	0
People	7	9	10	8	10	5	4	3	3	4	8	9	7	6	5	3
Person	1	0	0	2	0	0	0	0	0	0	0	1	0	0	0	0
Persons	1	0	1	0	2	1	0	0	0	0	0	0	0	0	0	0
Plural	0	0	0	0	1	0	0	0	0	0	0	0	0	1	2	0
Saw	1	0	0	1	0	0	0	0	0	0	2	0	0	1	1	0
See	3	3	6	1	0	1	1	1	0	0	0	1	1	0	2	1
Several	0	0	0	0	0	0	0	0	0	0	0	0	0	0	0	2
She	1	1	2	0	0	0	1	3	0	0	1	0	2	0	1	2
Should	0	0	0	1	1	0	0	0	2	1	0	2	0	0	3	2
The	1	1	2	1	1	0	0	1	1	0	0	1	0	0	1	1
Them	0	6	3	7	5	10	10	10	15	22	10	16	10	9	24	15
Then	0	1	1	1	0	0	0	1	0	0	1	0	0	0	3	1
They	12	19	7	16	10	25	32	27	29	41	49	49	53	61	165	190
Think	0	2	0	1	0	0	0	1	0	0	0	2	0	0	0	2
Three	2	3	0	2	0	0	1	0	0	0	0	0	1	1	2	1
Together	0	4	1	0	4	3	0	2	2	1	5	2	2	5	6	5
Two	1	4	6	7	1	7	1	2	2	0	5	3	4	3	4	3

Response Word	4th M	4th F	5th M	5th F	6th M	6th F	7th M	7th F	8th M	8th F	10th M	10th F	12th M	12th F	College M	College F

WE

Response Word	4th M	4th F	5th M	5th F	6th M	6th F	7th M	7th F	8th M	8th F	10th M	10th F	12th M	12th F	College M	College F
Us	36	36	45	62	52	61	68	87	53	62	64	75	49	55	81	108
Use	0	1	1	0	2	1	1	1	2	0	0	0	0	0	0	0
Want	2	0	1	0	2	0	1	1	0	0	0	0	0	1	1	0
Was	0	0	0	0	0	0	0	0	3	1	1	0	1	0	1	0
We're	0	0	0	0	0	1	0	2	0	1	0	0	0	0	0	0
Went	5	2	1	2	4	5	0	0	1	5	0	5	3	2	4	2
Were	4	5	10	12	6	9	17	11	22	6	6	2	9	13	6	7
What	2	0	2	0	1	1	0	0	0	0	0	0	0	0	0	0
When	0	1	0	0	1	2	1	1	0	0	0	1	0	1	0	0
Where	1	0	0	0	5	0	2	0	2	1	1	0	1	0	1	0
Who	0	0	0	0	1	1	0	1	1	1	3	0	0	0	1	0
Will	4	2	5	6	4	2	4	2	8	5	4	1	10	1	3	3
Won	0	0	0	0	1	0	2	0	2	0	0	1	1	0	3	0
Work	1	0	0	1	2	0	0	0	0	0	0	0	0	1	0	0
You	14	14	9	6	11	6	9	21	18	30	14	22	10	13	36	43

186. WHAT

Response Word	4th M	4th F	5th M	5th F	6th M	6th F	7th M	7th F	8th M	8th F	10th M	10th F	12th M	12th F	College M	College F
A	2	0	1	1	3	0	1	2	0	0	0	0	0	2	2	1
About	0	0	0	0	0	2	0	0	0	0	0	0	1	0	1	0
Although	0	1	0	0	2	0	3	1	2	0	0	1	0	0	0	0
Answer	1	0	0	2	0	2	1	3	1	1	3	1	0	1	1	1
Are	5	5	2	2	3	1	1	3	6	1	2	0	9	3	6	3
Article	0	0	0	0	0	0	0	0	0	0	0	0	0	0	0	2
Ask	2	4	3	6	1	1	1	3	0	0	1	0	0	1	0	0
Asking	0	0	0	2	0	0	0	0	0	0	0	0	0	0	0	0
At	3	5	1	1	1	0	1	1	1	0	0	0	1	0	0	0
Because	1	0	0	1	0	2	0	0	0	2	0	0	0	0	0	1
Boy	0	1	0	0	0	0	1	0	0	0	0	2	1	0	0	0
Can	5	0	1	3	1	2	0	0	1	1	0	2	2	1	3	5
Car	0	0	1	0	0	0	0	1	2	0	0	1	1	0	0	1
Cat	0	0	0	2	1	1	0	0	2	1	0	1	0	2	0	0
Did	6	7	7	3	5	5	4	1	1	0	1	3	3	5	4	0
Do	6	3	2	2	5	4	1	1	1	0	0	1	2	0	2	4
Dog	0	2	1	0	0	0	0	0	0	2	0	0	0	0	0	0
Don't	0	0	0	0	1	0	2	0	0	0	0	0	0	0	0	0
Ever	3	6	9	4	7	7	4	2	6	5	12	10	8	6	19	16
Every	0	2	0	0	1	0	0	0	1	0	0	0	1	0	0	0
Exclamation	0	0	0	0	0	1	1	2	0	0	0	0	1	0	0	1
Explain	0	0	0	0	0	0	0	0	0	2	0	0	0	0	0	0
For	1	0	0	0	0	0	0	2	1	1	1	3	1	2	13	11
Girl	0	1	0	0	2	0	0	1	0	0	0	0	1	0	1	1
Guess	1	0	0	0	0	0	0	0	0	2	0	0	0	1	0	1
Ha	1	0	0	1	0	2	1	2	0	1	0	0	0	0	0	0
Happen	1	2	2	2	1	1	0	0	0	2	1	1	2	1	0	0
Happened	3	0	3	2	4	6	3	3	4	4	2	3	1	1	4	3
Happens	0	0	0	0	0	0	0	0	0	0	0	0	0	0	0	2
Hat	8	5	7	0	5	6	4	2	2	4	0	2	1	0	0	0
Have	1	3	2	2	2	0	1	3	1	2	4	2	0	3	2	1
He	0	0	2	3	0	1	0	1	0	0	1	0	0	0	1	0

Response Word	4th		5th		6th		7th		8th		10th		12th		College	
	M	F	M	F	M	F	M	F	M	F	M	F	M	F	M	F

WHAT

Response Word	4th M	4th F	5th M	5th F	6th M	6th F	7th M	7th F	8th M	8th F	10th M	10th F	12th M	12th F	College M	College F
Hear	4	5	2	4	2	2	0	0	2	0	3	4	5	0	1	3
Here . . .	0	4	1	0	0	0	0	1	0	1	0	0	0	1	2	2
Hot	0	0	1	0	2	0	1	1	0	0	0	0	0	0	0	0
House . . .	0	0	0	0	0	1	0	2	0	0	2	1	0	0	1	0
How	7	4	5	6	6	2	5	7	4	4	7	1	3	6	5	11
Huh	2	2	0	0	0	4	2	2	1	3	2	1	1	1	5	3
I	1	1	3	0	2	0	2	1	1	0	0	0	1	0	0	0
If	3	0	0	1	0	0	4	1	1	5	3	3	8	10	24	17
In	1	1	1	0	0	2	1	0	0	0	1	0	0	0	1	0
Is	21	19	19	22	16	15	15	16	11	14	11	17	18	23	49	44
Is it . . .	0	2	2	0	0	0	1	0	0	0	0	0	0	0	0	1
It	4	0	2	2	4	3	3	1	7	3	1	4	1	2	3	4
Kind . . .	2	0	1	0	0	1	2	0	2	2	0	1	0	2	1	0
Life	0	2	0	0	2	0	0	0	0	0	0	0	2	0	1	1
Live	1	4	2	1	3	1	0	0	0	0	0	1	0	0	1	0
Me	3	1	0	0	2	1	0	0	0	1	1	2	0	1	0	0
Mother . .	0	2	0	0	0	0	0	0	0	1	0	0	0	0	0	0
Mr. Engle .	0	0	0	0	0	0	0	0	2	0	0	0	0	0	0	0
Never . . .	1	0	0	1	0	0	0	1	0	0	0	1	0	2	1	3
No	2	2	2	1	0	1	2	0	2	0	2	1	1	2	0	1
Not	0	0	0	1	0	1	2	2	0	2	1	1	0	2	3	4
Nothing . .	1	0	2	0	0	0	0	0	0	1	0	0	1	0	0	2
Now	0	1	2	2	1	1	3	4	2	1	6	4	3	2	16	10
Nut	0	0	2	0	2	1	1	0	0	0	0	0	0	0	0	0
Object . .	0	0	0	0	0	0	0	1	0	0	0	0	0	0	2	1
Of	1	0	1	0	0	1	1	1	5	2	4	3	4	4	4	9
Oh	3	1	2	3	0	0	1	0	0	0	2	0	0	0	2	2
Pardon . .	0	1	0	1	0	3	0	2	1	0	1	0	1	0	1	0
Place . . .	0	2	0	0	0	0	0	1	0	0	0	0	0	0	0	0
Question .	8	17	8	23	19	46	24	25	23	26	25	36	32	39	66	44
Question mark .	1	0	0	0	1	1	3	1	1	2	1	1	0	0	3	0
Repeat . .	0	0	0	1	0	0	3	1	1	1	0	0	1	1	1	0
Said	1	3	0	1	2	0	0	1	1	0	0	0	0	0	0	2
Say	1	4	0	4	1	0	1	1	2	1	0	1	1	0	3	3
See	1	0	0	1	0	2	1	1	0	0	2	0	1	0	1	1
She	0	0	0	0	0	1	1	0	0	1	1	0	2	1	0	0
So	0	0	1	1	2	0	0	0	0	0	1	1	0	0	0	1
Some . . .	1	0	1	0	2	0	0	0	0	0	0	0	0	0	0	0
Something .	1	5	4	1	2	2	0	1	0	1	1	0	0	1	0	0
Surprise . .	0	0	0	2	1	0	1	1	0	1	3	0	2	1	0	3
Surprised .	0	0	0	2	0	0	0	0	0	0	0	0	0	0	0	0
That . . .	27	14	27	24	16	17	20	16	14	19	22	13	12	10	25	31
The	1	0	3	0	6	1	1	1	7	0	1	0	4	1	9	4
Then . . .	4	2	3	0	0	2	2	0	0	1	2	0	1	0	3	3
There . . .	0	1	2	2	3	2	1	0	1	0	0	0	0	0	1	0
They	0	0	3	2	1	1	0	0	3	0	0	0	1	0	0	1
Thing . . .	4	2	3	4	6	2	6	1	4	0	4	1	2	3	2	4
This	0	0	1	0	0	1	1	1	0	1	2	1	1	1	5	6

Response Word	4th M	4th F	5th M	5th F	6th M	6th F	7th M	7th F	8th M	8th F	10th M	10th F	12th M	12th F	College M	College F
WHAT																
Time	0	1	0	1	0	0	0	0	0	0	1	0	0	2	0	0
To	0	0	3	1	0	0	0	0	1	0	0	0	0	0	0	2
Want	5	6	2	3	2	3	0	1	0	3	1	0	1	0	1	0
Was	1	2	4	2	1	0	4	2	3	1	6	1	2	1	3	3
We	3	4	2	3	4	5	4	1	2	3	0	2	4	0	1	2
Went	3	1	1	0	0	0	0	0	0	0	0	0	1	0	0	0
Were	3	1	5	2	1	1	1	2	3	1	1	1	1	2	1	0
What	0	0	0	1	1	0	0	0	0	0	0	0	0	0	2	0
When	2	13	7	11	8	12	21	18	23	22	15	25	15	17	32	47
Where	13	23	12	26	26	20	19	33	22	28	31	22	19	30	46	50
Which	1	0	0	0	0	0	3	0	3	4	5	4	3	1	13	11
Who	1	3	4	0	2	4	9	4	8	9	7	10	7	4	16	22
Why	11	12	8	10	16	15	17	23	17	25	13	31	16	18	40	42
Will	2	1	2	3	2	1	2	3	2	3	0	1	5	1	3	5
With	0	0	2	0	1	0	1	1	2	1	1	0	1	1	1	1
Word	1	3	4	1	2	1	1	0	0	0	1	0	0	0	0	0
Yes	0	0	0	1	3	1	3	1	1	2	1	1	3	1	3	2
You	5	4	2	3	2	1	0	5	2	2	2	1	3	0	3	2
187. WHERE																
Am	2	3	2	1	3	0	0	1	1	0	2	1	2	0	0	0
Anywhere	0	0	0	0	0	0	1	1	0	0	0	1	0	0	2	1
Are	17	16	19	13	16	11	12	6	14	13	13	10	20	14	28	19
Are you	0	2	0	0	0	0	1	0	0	0	0	0	0	0	2	1
As	2	1	1	2	1	1	1	2	4	0	5	0	0	1	3	6
Ask	0	0	0	2	1	0	0	1	0	0	0	0	0	0	0	0
At	1	0	0	1	2	0	1	2	5	1	3	1	4	2	8	4
Away	2	0	0	0	0	0	1	0	0	0	0	1	1	0	1	1
Boys	0	0	0	0	0	0	0	0	0	1	1	2	0	1	0	0
Can	0	2	0	0	0	0	0	2	0	0	0	0	0	0	2	1
Country	0	0	0	0	0	0	0	0	0	1	2	1	0	0	0	0
Did	2	4	1	3	3	1	2	0	1	1	1	0	2	1	1	0
Direction	0	0	0	0	0	0	0	0	0	0	0	0	0	2	0	0
Distance	0	0	0	0	0	0	1	0	0	0	0	0	0	1	2	1
Does	0	0	1	2	0	0	1	1	0	0	0	0	0	0	0	1
Downtown	0	0	0	0	0	0	0	0	0	0	0	0	0	0	0	2
Ever	2	2	1	1	1	1	1	1	0	1	2	1	1	2	3	5
Find	2	2	2	4	2	1	3	1	1	2	0	2	1	3	0	2
For	0	0	0	0	1	0	0	0	1	0	0	0	1	0	3	0
From	3	1	0	0	0	2	0	3	0	0	1	1	1	0	3	5
Go	1	2	0	5	0	4	0	0	1	1	2	4	0	3	2	2
Going	1	0	3	2	1	1	0	0	0	1	0	2	1	3	1	0
Gone	0	1	0	1	0	2	0	0	0	0	0	0	0	0	0	0
Hair	1	1	1	2	3	1	2	0	0	0	1	0	0	0	1	0
He	2	1	4	0	1	0	0	0	2	1	1	0	1	1	1	1
Hear	3	1	3	0	0	2	1	1	0	0	0	0	0	1	0	0
Her	3	0	1	0	1	0	0	0	0	1	1	0	2	0	0	0
Here	35	40	31	35	32	43	36	45	41	52	37	44	38	28	90	97
Hide	1	2	0	1	1	1	0	0	0	0	0	0	0	0	0	0
Home	0	1	1	2	1	1	0	0	0	1	0	0	0	1	3	1

Response Word	4th M	4th F	5th M	5th F	6th M	6th F	7th M	7th F	8th M	8th F	10th M	10th F	12th M	12th F	College M	College F
							WHERE									
House	0	0	0	2	0	1	0	3	2	1	1	2	0	0	1	3
How	2	1	3	2	2	0	2	0	4	0	0	1	0	3	0	4
I	0	3	2	1	3	0	0	0	1	0	1	0	0	1	1	0
Is	30	19	30	20	33	24	18	19	20	15	17	14	19	17	43	38
It	3	2	2	3	2	3	0	0	2	0	0	0	1	0	2	4
Lake	0	0	0	0	0	0	0	0	0	0	0	1	0	2	0	0
Location	0	0	0	0	0	1	0	1	0	1	0	1	2	0	3	3
Look	0	0	3	0	1	0	3	1	0	0	1	1	0	1	1	1
Lost	1	0	0	1	0	0	0	0	0	1	0	2	2	0	0	3
Me	0	2	2	1	0	3	0	0	1	0	0	0	0	1	0	0
Near	0	0	0	0	0	0	2	0	0	0	0	0	0	0	0	1
Not	2	0	0	0	2	0	0	0	0	0	0	0	1	0	0	0
Now	1	1	3	2	2	0	0	1	3	0	1	0	0	5	1	1
No where	0	0	0	0	0	0	0	0	1	2	0	0	0	0	0	1
Out	0	0	0	0	2	0	0	0	0	0	0	0	1	1	0	0
Over	0	2	0	0	2	0	1	0	0	0	1	1	0	0	1	0
Over there	0	0	0	0	0	1	0	0	0	1	0	0	0	2	1	1
Place	9	9	13	11	11	15	5	7	3	7	14	7	9	13	14	20
Position	0	0	0	0	0	0	0	0	0	0	0	0	0	0	2	0
Question	2	9	1	11	6	14	7	3	1	1	7	8	6	7	16	9
School	0	0	0	0	1	1	2	2	2	1	1	2	0	1	0	0
Someplace	1	3	0	4	1	1	1	0	1	1	2	1	0	1	1	0
Somewhere	1	1	0	0	0	1	0	1	0	2	0	0	0	0	0	0
The	0	1	1	0	5	0	2	1	0	1	2	0	0	0	1	0
Their	3	0	2	4	0	4	1	1	0	0	2	0	0	0	0	0
Then	0	2	1	0	0	0	0	1	2	1	0	0	1	0	3	0
There	41	38	39	42	33	39	54	53	53	54	56	62	58	64	95	110
They	3	2	2	2	2	3	2	0	0	1	0	0	2	1	1	0
To	1	1	2	2	3	1	1	4	0	3	4	8	6	1	16	12
Was	1	6	5	0	8	0	6	9	8	1	9	3	3	1	8	8
We	2	1	2	0	0	3	0	0	1	0	0	1	0	0	0	1
Wear	1	1	0	1	0	0	2	0	1	1	0	0	1	1	0	0
Went	0	0	0	0	0	0	0	1	2	2	0	0	0	1	1	0
Were	3	6	9	4	6	3	10	7	5	9	7	2	10	10	7	3
What	9	8	6	6	7	7	3	2	4	5	5	1	3	0	15	6
When	8	14	9	24	13	21	31	39	26	37	22	36	25	35	70	88
Which	0	0	0	0	0	0	1	0	0	0	1	1	0	0	0	2
Who	3	2	5	4	2	1	1	2	4	1	3	1	0	0	4	2
Why	2	1	3	3	2	3	4	6	6	3	2	3	5	2	7	7
Will	0	2	0	0	0	0	1	0	3	1	1	1	1	0	0	1
Word	0	0	2	0	2	1	0	0	0	0	0	0	0	0	0	0
You	4	5	2	4	2	2	2	0	4	2	1	2	2	0	1	3
						188.	WHISKEY									
Alcohol	1	1	3	2	8	3	15	8	10	10	18	4	14	15	18	17
Awful	0	2	1	0	0	1	0	0	0	1	0	0	0	1	0	2
Bad	4	2	2	8	7	2	10	12	8	9	11	15	10	6	11	12
Bar	0	0	4	2	2	0	0	1	0	0	0	1	0	0	0	1
Bear	0	2	1	1	0	1	0	0	0	0	0	0	0	1	0	0

Response Word	4th		5th		6th		7th		8th		10th		12th		College	
	M	F	M	F	M	F	M	F	M	F	M	F	M	F	M	F

WHISKEY

Response Word	M	F	M	F	M	F	M	F	M	F	M	F	M	F	M	F
Beer	34	24	21	25	35	29	22	20	22	21	17	23	12	14	17	16
Beverage	1	0	0	0	0	0	0	1	2	1	2	1	2	0	1	1
Bitter	0	0	0	0	0	1	0	0	1	0	0	1	0	1	2	1
Blow	2	0	0	0	0	0	0	0	0	0	0	0	0	0	0	0
Booze	2	2	3	1	0	0	9	0	5	0	10	5	10	3	18	4
Bottle	4	7	4	6	14	9	1	6	3	6	7	5	9	6	28	25
Bourbon	0	0	1	0	0	0	4	2	6	1	4	1	0	1	10	9
Brandy	0	2	0	0	1	1	2	0	1	2	0	1	0	0	0	1
Brown	0	0	0	0	0	2	1	0	0	1	2	0	1	2	2	2
Cat	2	2	0	0	0	0	0	1	0	0	0	0	0	0	0	0
Corn	0	0	0	0	0	0	0	0	1	0	0	0	1	0	3	0
Dad	0	0	0	0	0	0	1	0	3	0	0	0	0	0	0	0
Delicious	0	0	0	0	0	0	0	0	0	0	1	0	2	0	0	0
Dog	1	1	0	2	1	1	0	0	0	0	0	0	0	0	0	0
Drank	0	0	3	1	0	1	1	0	1	1	1	0	0	0	0	0
Drink	67	97	86	98	80	90	63	88	49	74	51	70	71	83	154	174
Drinking	0	1	2	2	2	2	2	0	4	2	3	3	1	1	4	10
Drug	0	0	0	0	0	2	0	0	0	1	0	0	0	0	0	0
Drunk	27	12	33	12	31	21	42	31	46	50	40	41	46	31	57	53
Drunkard	0	0	0	0	0	0	1	1	1	2	0	2	1	0	0	3
Drunkenness	0	0	0	0	0	0	0	0	0	0	3	1	3	1	3	0
Drunks	0	0	0	0	1	0	2	0	1	0	0	1	1	0	1	0
Fast	1	10	3	7	2	3	0	0	0	0	0	0	0	0	0	0
Four Roses	0	0	0	0	0	0	0	1	0	0	1	1	0	2	1	1
Fun	0	1	0	0	1	0	1	0	1	0	0	0	2	0	3	3
Gin	3	2	1	1	2	0	5	5	6	4	5	4	1	5	1	8
Glass	0	1	1	1	0	3	0	1	2	1	1	1	2	0	4	7
Good	2	0	3	2	1	0	2	0	10	2	13	3	12	1	17	10
Hair	1	0	2	0	0	0	0	0	0	0	0	0	0	0	0	0
Hate	0	0	0	0	0	0	0	1	0	0	0	0	0	2	0	0
Headache	0	0	0	0	0	0	0	0	0	0	1	0	0	0	2	0
Hiccough	0	0	0	2	0	0	0	0	1	0	0	0	0	0	0	0
Hiccup	0	0	0	0	0	0	0	2	0	0	0	0	0	0	0	0
Hick	0	0	0	0	0	0	2	0	0	0	0	0	0	0	0	0
Horse	2	2	1	1	1	0	0	0	0	0	0	0	0	0	0	0
Hot	0	0	0	0	0	1	2	0	0	0	2	1	0	1	0	1
Ice	0	0	1	0	0	0	0	0	0	1	0	0	1	0	2	1
Ice cubes	0	0	0	0	0	0	0	0	0	0	0	0	0	0	0	2
Inebriate	0	0	0	0	0	0	0	0	0	0	0	0	0	0	2	0
Intoxicating	0	0	0	0	0	0	0	0	0	2	1	1	0	0	0	0
Ish	2	0	0	0	0	0	2	1	2	1	1	4	2	4	0	3
Jug	0	0	0	0	0	0	0	1	0	0	1	0	0	0	3	1
Key	1	4	2	3	2	0	0	0	0	0	0	0	0	0	0	0
Liquid	0	0	3	0	0	0	1	0	0	1	4	1	0	0	3	1
Liquor	12	13	9	9	14	17	26	23	18	20	17	14	4	21	19	33
Long	0	2	0	1	0	1	0	0	0	0	0	0	0	0	0	0
Man	1	2	1	0	2	2	0	1	0	0	0	1	0	0	1	0
Name	0	0	0	4	0	0	0	0	0	0	0	0	0	0	0	0

Response Word	4th M	F	5th M	F	6th M	F	7th M	F	8th M	F	10th M	F	12th M	F	College M	F

WHISKEY

Response Word	4th M	F	5th M	F	6th M	F	7th M	F	8th M	F	10th M	F	12th M	F	College M	F
Old Crow	0	0	0	0	0	0	0	0	3	0	0	0	0	0	0	0
Pop	2	2	3	2	2	0	2	1	2	1	0	1	0	0	0	0
Rebellion	0	0	0	0	0	0	0	0	0	0	0	0	1	0	3	0
Rum	5	2	2	1	1	1	0	2	1	1	0	3	0	2	6	3
Rye	0	0	0	0	0	0	0	0	0	0	0	1	0	0	2	3
Scotch	0	0	0	0	0	0	0	0	0	0	2	1	1	0	2	1
Seven Up	0	0	0	0	0	1	0	0	0	0	1	0	0	0	0	2
Shot	0	0	0	0	0	0	0	0	0	0	0	0	0	1	2	1
Sick	0	0	0	0	0	0	0	0	1	1	0	0	2	1	2	0
Smell	0	0	0	0	1	0	0	1	1	0	0	1	0	2	1	6
Sour	0	0	1	1	0	0	1	2	1	1	2	3	2	6	28	23
Spirits	0	0	0	0	0	0	0	0	0	1	0	0	1	0	1	2
Strong	1	1	2	0	0	0	2	2	2	1	1	4	4	2	1	6
Terrible	0	0	0	0	0	0	0	0	1	1	0	2	0	2	0	0
Thirsty	0	0	0	0	0	0	0	1	3	0	0	0	0	0	0	1
Vodka	1	0	0	0	0	0	1	1	1	1	1	2	0	1	0	4
Warm	0	0	0	0	0	0	0	0	0	0	0	0	1	0	0	3
Water	3	3	7	3	2	0	1	1	0	0	0	0	1	2	5	3
Wet	0	0	0	0	0	0	0	0	0	0	0	0	0	0	2	0
Wine	11	14	12	15	7	16	8	10	3	7	7	6	3	1	3	3

189. WHISTLE

Response Word	4th M	F	5th M	F	6th M	F	7th M	F	8th M	F	10th M	F	12th M	F	College M	F
Air	0	3	1	1	2	0	1	0	1	0	0	1	1	0	1	1
Bell	0	0	0	1	0	0	1	1	0	0	0	3	0	1	1	2
Bird	3	1	4	0	2	1	2	0	1	2	3	2	2	3	1	6
Black	0	0	0	0	0	2	0	0	1	0	0	0	0	0	0	0
Blew	0	1	0	1	2	0	1	0	0	0	0	2	1	0	0	0
Blow	39	32	29	35	37	32	22	25	24	22	18	22	16	17	34	26
Boat	0	0	0	0	0	0	0	0	1	0	3	0	0	0	1	1
Boy	3	2	1	2	4	3	0	8	0	33	5	25	6	21	3	34
Boys	0	0	1	0	0	0	0	1	0	6	0	2	1	2	0	3
Call	1	4	1	1	4	2	4	4	1	3	4	5	3	1	1	4
Come	0	0	1	1	2	1	0	2	0	0	0	0	1	0	2	3
Cop	0	0	0	0	0	0	0	0	1	0	3	0	6	1	11	2
Cute	0	0	0	0	0	0	0	0	0	0	0	2	0	0	0	0
Dixie	0	0	0	0	0	0	0	0	2	0	3	1	0	0	0	0
Dog	0	0	1	2	3	5	2	3	7	4	10	9	9	4	5	13
Drink	0	0	0	0	1	0	2	0	0	0	0	1	2	0	0	0
Eat	2	0	0	0	0	0	0	0	0	0	0	0	0	0	1	0
Flute	0	0	0	0	0	2	1	1	1	0	1	0	0	0	0	0
Fun	0	2	3	1	0	0	0	1	0	0	1	0	0	0	0	0
Gay	0	0	0	2	0	0	0	0	0	0	0	0	0	0	0	0
Girl	0	0	0	0	4	1	6	2	6	2	19	8	33	8	35	8
Girls	0	0	1	0	0	0	2	0	5	0	4	0	9	1	5	0
Go	0	1	2	0	0	0	2	0	1	0	0	0	1	0	0	0
Gym	0	0	0	0	0	1	0	0	0	2	0	0	0	2	0	0
Happy	2	0	0	2	2	2	1	0	1	3	0	2	1	2	3	6
Hard	0	2	0	0	1	0	0	1	0	0	0	0	0	2	0	0
Harsh	0	0	0	0	0	0	0	0	0	1	1	2	0	0	0	0

Response Word	4th		5th		6th		7th		8th		10th		12th		College	
	M	F	M	F	M	F	M	F	M	F	M	F	M	F	M	F

WHISTLE

Response Word	4th M	F	5th M	F	6th M	F	7th M	F	8th M	F	10th M	F	12th M	F	College M	F
Hear	2	0	4	2	3	0	0	1	0	1	0	1	0	0	1	6
High	0	0	0	0	1	0	0	2	0	1	0	2	2	1	2	5
His	0	2	1	1	0	0	0	0	0	0	0	0	0	0	0	0
Holler	0	0	0	0	0	1	0	0	0	1	2	1	0	0	2	0
Horn	1	4	2	3	1	1	1	0	2	5	6	2	9	4	5	1
Howl	0	0	0	0	0	0	0	0	0	0	0	1	0	0	2	0
Hum	2	2	0	2	1	3	3	5	3	2	2	4	1	3	4	3
Large	0	0	0	2	0	0	0	0	0	0	0	0	0	0	0	0
Laugh	1	0	0	2	0	1	0	1	1	1	0	0	0	2	0	1
Lips	1	5	2	1	1	0	2	3	2	1	5	4	1	4	11	7
Long	0	0	1	1	0	0	0	0	0	0	0	0	0	2	0	0
Look	0	0	1	1	0	0	0	1	0	0	0	0	0	2	3	0
Loud	22	16	21	17	25	23	19	16	17	14	18	13	7	8	22	18
Man	1	2	2	1	3	1	1	2	1	1	2	5	1	2	3	14
Mother	0	0	0	0	0	0	0	0	0	0	0	0	0	0	2	4
Mouth	6	9	9	6	8	6	7	6	6	7	4	5	2	5	6	12
Music	13	16	5	9	8	11	9	7	6	2	5	5	5	1	5	6
Noise	31	25	36	29	36	35	32	24	21	16	22	23	16	20	24	42
Noisy	2	3	2	0	0	1	2	0	0	0	0	0	2	0	0	0
Nose	3	3	6	2	3	1	0	0	0	0	0	0	1	0	0	0
Note	0	1	0	2	0	3	1	0	2	0	0	0	1	1	2	3
Notes	0	0	0	0	0	0	0	1	2	1	0	0	0	0	0	0
Piercing	0	0	0	0	0	0	0	0	0	0	0	1	0	0	0	3
Police	1	0	0	3	2	0	0	0	2	1	2	1	3	2	7	6
Policeman	1	1	1	1	1	1	1	1	0	1	2	7	2	4	8	9
Policemen	0	0	0	0	0	1	0	0	1	0	1	0	2	0	0	0
Pop	0	0	0	0	0	0	1	0	0	0	1	0	4	0	3	0
Pretty	1	2	1	3	0	1	0	0	0	1	0	0	0	0	0	0
Referee	0	0	0	0	0	0	0	0	1	1	0	2	2	0	2	0
Scream	2	0	0	1	1	1	0	2	6	1	1	0	1	3	6	2
Sharp	0	1	0	0	0	1	0	1	1	0	0	2	1	2	6	7
Shout	3	0	1	0	2	0	2	0	3	0	0	1	0	2	3	0
Shriek	0	0	0	0	0	0	2	0	2	3	0	1	0	5	1	0
Shrill	0	4	2	3	4	5	11	10	4	5	4	2	7	10	11	19
Sing	16	15	11	20	8	13	14	28	20	21	10	14	6	12	18	36
Siren	0	0	0	0	0	0	1	0	0	0	0	0	1	0	4	1
Soft	0	2	1	1	0	0	0	0	0	0	0	0	0	0	1	0
Song	3	5	6	5	3	8	11	16	6	8	6	4	2	15	21	16
Sound	14	27	26	20	12	20	21	16	16	9	18	7	10	10	36	25
Stop	0	0	0	1	1	1	1	3	0	1	3	5	5	3	34	25
Talk	3	1	3	8	0	2	8	3	9	3	2	0	1	2	0	2
Teeth	1	0	0	0	0	0	0	0	0	0	2	0	0	0	1	0
Tone	1	2	0	3	2	2	2	0	1	0	0	0	0	1	1	2
Toot	2	3	3	2	3	2	2	0	1	2	0	3	2	1	3	0
Toy	0	1	1	0	0	0	0	1	1	3	0	1	0	1	1	1
Train	4	3	6	2	3	2	3	1	2	1	7	11	17	15	57	49
Tune	3	15	12	14	7	17	2	15	2	18	5	4	8	10	15	17
Tweet	0	0	0	1	1	0	2	2	1	0	3	0	0	0	0	0

Response Word	4th M	F	5th M	F	6th M	F	7th M	F	8th M	F	10th M	F	12th M	F	College M	F

WHISTLE

Response Word	4th M	F	5th M	F	6th M	F	7th M	F	8th M	F	10th M	F	12th M	F	College M	F
Wet	1	0	0	0	1	1	0	1	2	0	0	0	0	0	0	0
Whisper	0	0	0	1	2	1	0	1	0	1	0	1	1	1	0	1
Will	0	0	0	0	0	2	0	0	0	0	0	0	0	0	0	0
Wind	4	1	0	0	2	1	0	1	1	2	1	2	0	0	2	0
Wink	0	2	0	0	0	0	1	0	1	2	0	0	0	0	0	0
Wolf	0	0	0	0	0	0	3	0	5	2	2	2	1	3	10	13
Woman	0	0	1	0	1	0	1	0	0	0	3	0	1	1	5	0
Women	0	0	0	0	0	0	1	1	0	2	2	0	1	0	3	0
Work	0	1	1	0	0	2	0	1	4	0	4	1	6	0	2	5
Yell	2	0	3	3	3	0	7	6	12	2	8	0	3	1	8	4

190. WHITE

Response Word	4th M	F	5th M	F	6th M	F	7th M	F	8th M	F	10th M	F	12th M	F	College M	F
Back	1	0	2	0	1	0	0	0	0	0	1	0	0	0	0	0
Bear	0	0	0	0	0	0	1	0	0	0	3	0	1	2	4	3
Beautiful	2	2	1	0	1	2	1	1	1	2	0	1	0	1	3	0
Black	107	90	101	107	89	91	115	95	130	114	103	99	122	123	247	253
Blank	0	0	1	0	1	0	0	2	0	0	0	0	0	0	0	1
Blouse	0	0	0	0	0	0	0	0	0	1	1	4	0	1	0	0
Blue	1	5	2	5	3	2	3	4	6	2	1	2	2	4	4	5
Bride	0	1	0	0	0	0	0	3	0	1	1	3	0	2	0	4
Bright	1	3	3	5	6	6	5	3	3	2	2	1	2	2	3	2
Brown	2	2	2	0	4	2	1	1	1	1	0	0	2	1	2	0
Car	0	0	0	0	0	0	1	0	1	0	2	0	2	1	2	0
Cat	1	2	0	0	0	0	0	1	0	0	0	0	1	0	2	0
Christmas	0	0	2	0	1	0	0	0	1	0	0	0	0	0	2	1
Clean	4	5	3	2	3	3	5	10	2	7	1	9	2	7	4	6
Clear	0	1	2	6	4	1	2	3	2	0	1	0	1	3	1	1
Cloth	0	0	0	0	0	0	0	0	1	1	1	0	1	0	3	1
Cloud	2	0	1	0	0	1	2	5	0	1	3	3	2	5	2	1
Clouds	2	1	0	0	0	1	0	1	0	2	2	1	0	2	0	1
Coat	0	0	0	3	3	1	0	1	1	1	2	0	0	1	0	1
Cold	0	0	0	0	1	0	0	0	0	0	0	1	0	0	1	4
Color	40	33	39	26	33	33	19	17	13	12	9	13	10	4	9	2
Colorless	0	0	0	0	0	1	1	1	1	0	0	1	0	0	2	0
Cotton	0	0	0	2	0	1	1	0	0	0	1	1	0	0	0	0
Dark	4	3	8	10	15	5	5	9	9	8	16	6	13	5	21	6
Day	0	0	0	0	0	1	0	0	1	0	2	1	0	0	1	1
Dog	0	0	0	1	0	0	0	0	0	0	2	0	0	0	3	0
Dress	1	0	1	0	1	1	1	5	1	1	2	4	2	5	2	10
Frosting	0	0	0	0	0	0	0	2	0	0	0	0	0	0	0	0
Gown	0	0	0	0	0	0	0	1	0	4	0	0	0	3	0	2
Green	0	1	2	1	0	2	1	0	2	0	1	2	0	1	0	2
Hair	0	0	1	0	0	0	0	3	2	0	0	0	0	2	1	3
Hard	0	0	0	0	0	1	1	0	0	0	0	0	0	0	2	0
Home	0	0	0	0	0	2	0	0	0	0	0	0	0	0	0	0
Horse	0	1	0	0	0	0	0	0	1	2	1	0	0	0	1	3
Hospital	0	0	0	0	0	0	0	1	0	0	0	0	2	1	0	0
House	7	2	2	1	4	6	2	0	4	3	13	5	6	0	8	6

Response Word	4th M	4th F	5th M	5th F	6th M	6th F	7th M	7th F	8th M	8th F	10th M	10th F	12th M	12th F	College M	College F
							WHITE									
Kite	0	2	0	1	0	0	0	0	0	0	0	0	0	0	0	0
Light ...	24	29	21	34	18	31	36	32	17	27	21	15	10	5	11	9
Man	0	0	1	0	1	0	2	0	0	0	0	0	0	0	1	0
Mountain .	0	0	0	0	1	0	0	0	0	0	0	0	0	0	2	0
Nice	1	1	2	0	0	0	1	0	0	0	0	0	1	0	1	0
Nurse ..	0	0	0	0	0	1	0	0	0	0	0	2	0	0	2	1
Paint ...	3	1	1	0	0	0	0	0	1	1	0	0	1	0	1	2
Paper ...	1	1	3	1	5	2	4	1	1	2	5	1	2	2	4	2
People ..	0	1	0	0	2	0	2	0	1	0	0	0	0	0	1	0
Pillow ..	0	1	0	1	0	0	1	1	1	0	0	0	0	0	1	2
Pink	1	0	0	0	2	1	0	0	0	0	0	0	0	1	0	0
Plain ...	1	0	0	2	0	1	0	1	1	0	1	0	1	0	0	0
Pretty ..	2	8	5	2	2	5	3	2	1	2	1	0	0	2	1	0
Pure ...	1	2	0	0	0	3	0	5	0	0	3	7	4	6	8	17
Purity ..	0	0	0	0	0	0	0	0	0	0	0	1	0	1	2	2
Rain ...	0	0	0	1	0	0	0	0	0	0	0	0	0	1	2	0
Red	4	7	2	1	1	2	3	5	2	3	2	3	0	2	2	4
Sheet ...	0	1	1	0	1	0	5	2	2	1	4	3	3	2	2	7
Shirt ...	0	2	0	0	2	0	0	0	0	0	2	1	2	0	1	0
Snow ...	15	23	16	22	20	24	12	18	22	26	25	35	35	36	98	92
Soft	2	1	4	3	2	2	2	2	0	0	2	0	3	1	3	0
Sweater ..	0	0	0	0	0	0	0	0	0	0	0	0	0	0	2	0
Uniform .	0	0	0	0	0	0	0	0	0	0	0	0	0	0	0	2
Wedding ..	0	0	0	0	0	0	0	0	0	5	0	1	0	3	1	5
Yellow ..	2	3	1	0	1	0	0	0	1	0	0	2	1	0	0	0
						191.	WHO									
Am	1	2	0	0	1	0	1	0	0	0	0	0	0	0	0	1
Are	7	12	8	11	12	7	2	3	7	3	4	3	8	4	10	4
As	2	0	0	0	0	0	1	0	0	0	0	0	0	0	0	0
Ask	0	1	1	3	0	1	0	0	0	0	0	1	0	0	1	0
Boo	1	2	1	2	0	0	1	0	0	0	0	0	0	0	0	0
Boy	1	1	0	0	0	3	1	0	0	0	0	3	0	1	0	0
Came ...	0	1	0	0	1	0	0	1	0	0	2	0	0	1	1	3
Can	0	1	3	0	0	0	0	0	3	0	2	2	1	1	2	4
Cares ...	0	0	0	0	1	0	0	0	0	1	1	0	0	0	3	1
Comes ..	1	0	0	0	0	0	0	0	0	0	0	0	0	0	0	2
Did	6	3	6	5	10	2	4	5	3	4	3	5	9	3	7	3
Do	0	0	0	0	0	0	1	2	0	0	0	0	0	1	1	0
Does ...	0	0	0	0	0	0	0	0	2	1	1	0	3	1	2	2
Else ...	1	0	0	0	0	0	0	0	1	0	1	2	0	1	1	0
Ever ...	0	1	1	3	0	0	0	1	1	0	2	2	0	1	6	1
Girl	0	1	1	1	0	0	1	2	0	0	1	0	0	1	1	0
Guess ..	0	2	0	1	1	1	0	1	0	1	0	0	0	0	1	1
He	2	3	1	0	6	5	3	5	4	4	8	3	1	2	10	19
Her	1	0	1	1	0	2	5	4	3	2	1	5	6	3	3	3
Him	12	5	12	1	15	5	10	8	13	3	10	12	12	11	11	10
His	0	0	0	0	0	1	1	0	2	0	0	0	0	1	0	0
Ho	1	3	1	1	1	0	3	0	0	0	0	0	0	0	0	0

Response Word	4th M	4th F	5th M	5th F	6th M	6th F	7th M	7th F	8th M	8th F	10th M	10th F	12th M	12th F	College M	College F
							WHO									
How	5	5	5	3	6	5	6	5	8	3	2	0	0	0	5	3
I	1	3	1	1	0	0	3	0	0	1	0	1	0	0	1	0
If	4	1	1	1	2	1	3	0	0	0	0	0	0	0	0	0
Is	23	24	18	13	22	15	26	15	22	16	22	10	26	17	66	62
Is it	0	1	1	0	0	0	1	0	0	0	0	0	0	0	0	2
It	6	2	3	2	0	4	1	0	3	4	1	3	1	2	2	1
John	0	0	0	0	0	0	0	0	0	0	2	0	0	0	0	0
Knows	0	0	0	0	1	0	0	0	0	0	1	1	1	0	2	2
Man	0	0	1	0	0	1	2	0	1	0	1	2	2	0	2	1
Me	28	20	25	27	25	30	23	29	19	31	16	24	14	14	34	31
Moo	1	0	0	1	0	1	0	1	0	0	0	0	0	0	0	2
Name	0	2	0	0	0	0	0	0	0	0	0	0	0	0	0	0
No	0	2	1	1	0	1	0	0	0	0	0	1	0	0	1	0
Now	1	2	0	0	0	1	0	1	1	1	0	0	0	1	2	1
Oh	2	1	3	0	0	0	0	0	0	0	0	0	0	0	0	0
One	0	1	2	1	1	1	0	0	0	0	0	0	1	0	0	1
Owl	6	14	8	19	13	22	2	9	5	8	11	11	6	8	11	6
People	0	3	2	2	4	2	3	1	4	5	3	9	5	7	6	6
Person	4	7	6	13	7	15	3	12	4	9	8	5	8	10	16	19
Pronoun	0	0	0	0	0	0	0	0	0	0	0	0	0	1	0	2
Question	4	18	4	8	5	17	7	6	4	11	10	10	9	10	17	16
Said	0	2	0	0	0	1	0	1	0	1	1	0	1	2	2	1
Says	0	0	0	0	0	0	0	1	0	0	0	0	0	0	2	1
She	0	0	0	1	0	0	1	2	1	3	1	1	1	3	9	7
Shot	1	0	0	0	1	0	0	0	0	0	0	0	0	0	2	0
Somebody	1	2	2	1	3	0	1	0	0	0	0	0	0	0	0	0
Someone	7	8	6	3	0	4	2	2	1	1	2	1	2	1	3	1
That	3	4	2	5	2	3	1	1	2	0	0	1	0	0	2	0
The	0	1	1	0	3	0	1	1	0	0	1	0	0	1	1	0
Them	4	2	5	3	3	5	14	13	6	12	12	10	5	8	16	12
Then	1	0	0	1	1	0	1	0	1	0	2	0	0	0	0	1
There	4	7	1	1	2	3	0	1	2	0	0	0	0	2	2	1
They	0	5	6	4	5	5	9	12	11	9	11	14	12	12	25	32
Us	1	0	0	4	1	0	1	1	2	1	3	1	0	1	6	3
Was	6	1	9	6	8	6	16	7	11	11	14	2	10	10	28	22
We	0	0	3	2	0	0	1	1	0	1	0	1	2	1	2	4
Well	0	0	0	0	0	2	0	0	0	0	0	0	0	0	0	0
Went	2	0	0	0	1	0	1	0	4	0	1	0	2	0	0	2
Were	0	0	0	1	0	0	2	3	1	1	0	0	1	0	0	0
What	17	13	16	19	23	20	19	19	20	15	16	14	15	17	35	36
When	3	6	1	2	8	1	1	4	5	4	3	6	3	1	8	9
Where	7	11	4	7	8	3	6	10	7	6	4	8	3	5	13	14
Which	0	0	1	0	0	1	3	1	1	1	3	4	1	1	6	3
Whom	0	0	5	3	3	5	3	12	13	20	13	33	37	37	43	46
Who's	0	0	0	0	0	1	1	0	2	1	0	0	1	1	0	0
Whose	0	0	2	1	0	0	5	4	1	1	1	3	2	3	4	4
Why	5	6	8	5	7	4	5	6	6	4	11	12	4	5	11	22

Response Word	4th		5th		6th		7th		8th		10th		12th		College	
	M	F	M	F	M	F	M	F	M	F	M	F	M	F	M	F
WHO																
Will	4	2	2	4	0	1	0	5	3	4	2	5	5	1	4	2
Word	1	1	2	0	1	0	0	0	0	0	0	0	0	0	0	1
You	29	20	36	38	12	22	18	18	21	33	20	9	16	15	24	37
192. WHY																
Answer	1	1	4	5	2	1	1	1	3	1	2	4	1	1	1	1
Are	4	5	2	3	1	2	5	3	3	1	0	0	7	1	3	3
Ask	3	10	3	9	3	8	4	4	1	3	4	4	2	3	6	6
Asking	0	1	0	1	1	0	0	0	2	0	0	0	0	0	0	0
Be	0	0	0	0	0	0	0	0	0	0	0	0	0	0	2	0
Because	20	42	41	38	34	47	43	40	33	60	35	59	47	59	76	120
Boy	0	2	0	0	0	0	0	1	0	0	0	0	0	0	1	0
By	0	0	0	2	0	1	1	1	1	0	0	0	0	0	0	1
Can	1	0	0	2	0	0	1	1	0	0	0	0	1	0	0	1
Cause	1	0	1	1	1	1	0	3	0	0	0	1	0	1	1	0
Children	0	0	0	0	0	0	0	0	0	0	0	2	0	0	0	0
Cry	1	0	6	2	1	1	1	3	3	1	1	0	1	1	1	0
Did	10	9	10	1	6	1	1	3	2	1	4	1	0	2	4	1
Do	5	2	2	2	2	1	1	3	2	1	0	5	0	3	3	7
Does	0	1	1	1	0	0	0	1	0	1	0	0	0	0	0	2
Don't	1	2	4	1	2	3	1	2	0	4	1	0	0	0	1	0
Doubt	0	0	0	0	0	0	0	0	0	0	0	0	0	0	2	0
For	6	2	4	2	2	1	2	1	4	6	5	3	1	1	17	9
Get	2	0	0	2	1	0	0	2	0	0	0	0	0	0	0	0
Go	1	0	1	0	1	2	0	0	0	0	1	0	1	0	3	3
Good	0	2	1	0	0	0	0	0	0	0	0	0	0	0	0	0
Hi	4	1	2	0	2	1	2	1	0	1	1	0	0	0	0	0
High	1	0	0	0	0	0	1	0	1	0	0	0	0	0	2	0
House	1	2	0	0	0	0	0	0	0	0	0	0	0	0	0	0
How	5	7	12	10	8	5	12	8	3	4	12	10	9	11	17	29
How come	5	1	1	3	3	5	5	6	4	4	7	2	5	0	3	2
Huh	0	0	0	0	0	0	2	0	0	0	0	0	0	0	0	0
I	0	1	3	0	0	2	2	0	0	0	0	0	0	0	2	0
I don't know	0	0	0	0	0	0	0	0	0	2	1	0	0	0	0	0
If	0	0	0	0	0	0	0	0	0	1	0	0	1	1	0	2
Is	7	4	7	7	6	6	4	3	1	2	1	6	4	5	12	7
It	3	1	0	1	1	1	1	0	0	0	0	0	1	0	1	0
Know	1	1	0	3	3	4	0	2	1	1	0	1	2	0	2	1
Me	0	2	2	2	1	2	2	0	1	1	2	2	2	4	1	0
Must	0	0	0	0	0	1	0	1	0	0	0	0	0	0	0	2
My	3	0	1	1	2	1	0	0	0	0	0	0	0	0	0	0
Never	0	0	0	0	0	0	0	0	0	0	0	0	2	0	1	1
No	5	6	4	4	3	2	4	3	1	0	1	1	1	1	3	0
Not	41	46	34	42	58	34	33	24	50	32	53	41	56	49	100	85
Now	4	0	3	1	0	2	0	0	2	1	2	3	1	3	6	5
Of	2	0	0	0	0	0	1	0	0	0	0	1	0	0	0	1
Oh	0	2	0	1	0	0	1	0	1	0	1	0	0	1	0	0
Question	12	22	12	27	27	47	29	35	23	36	29	34	34	41	80	74

344

Response Word	4th M	4th F	5th M	5th F	6th M	6th F	7th M	7th F	8th M	8th F	10th M	10th F	12th M	12th F	College M	College F

WHY

Response Word	4th M	4th F	5th M	5th F	6th M	6th F	7th M	7th F	8th M	8th F	10th M	10th F	12th M	12th F	College M	College F
Question mark	1	1	1	0	0	1	2	1	3	0	0	0	2	0	3	1
Reason	2	1	0	0	1	2	0	2	4	2	5	5	4	7	13	11
She	0	0	1	2	0	2	0	1	0	0	1	0	0	0	0	1
Should	3	0	3	3	2	6	4	2	1	3	2	0	3	2	1	2
Shy	0	1	0	1	0	1	2	1	2	0	0	0	0	0	1	0
So	1	0	0	1	0	0	1	0	0	4	1	1	3	0	2	3
That	1	2	3	1	1	0	0	0	4	0	1	0	0	0	4	1
The	3	0	2	0	2	0	3	0	0	0	0	0	0	1	1	0
Then	0	0	0	1	0	0	0	1	1	1	0	0	0	0	1	2
There	0	0	2	0	0	0	1	0	1	1	0	0	0	0	0	0
They	1	1	0	2	0	1	0	0	1	0	0	0	0	1	0	0
Thing	0	0	0	2	0	0	0	0	0	0	0	0	0	0	0	0
Think	1	2	0	0	0	0	0	0	0	0	0	0	1	1	1	1
Try	0	0	0	0	1	0	0	0	0	0	0	0	0	0	0	2
Was	0	0	2	0	3	0	1	0	2	1	1	0	1	0	1	1
Way	2	1	2	0	2	0	0	0	0	0	0	0	0	0	0	0
We	1	0	0	2	0	0	1	1	0	0	0	0	0	0	2	0
Were	0	1	0	2	2	0	1	0	2	2	0	0	1	0	0	0
What	22	18	15	14	14	16	20	26	21	15	12	14	6	10	25	28
What for	0	2	0	0	1	0	1	2	3	0	1	1	1	0	0	1
When	2	8	6	6	5	10	12	17	19	19	16	20	16	11	34	27
Where	2	3	6	3	1	1	4	9	8	12	5	6	3	4	20	24
Wherefore	0	0	0	0	0	0	0	0	0	0	1	0	2	0	0	6
Which	1	0	0	0	0	0	1	1	0	0	1	0	1	0	4	1
Who	5	2	6	7	3	3	4	10	6	4	4	9	2	6	7	2
Why not	1	1	1	0	0	1	1	0	3	0	2	0	1	2	2	1
Will	0	1	0	0	0	0	1	1	1	0	1	0	0	0	0	2
Wonder	1	0	0	2	1	0	0	0	0	0	0	1	0	0	1	0
Word	0	1	1	0	2	0	1	0	0	0	0	0	0	0	0	0
Would	0	1	2	1	2	0	0	0	0	0	1	0	0	0	0	0
Yes	3	3	2	1	0	0	0	1	3	1	2	0	2	0	3	1
You	5	5	3	5	7	4	6	1	6	5	2	0	2	1	0	2

193. WINDOW

Response Word	4th M	4th F	5th M	5th F	6th M	6th F	7th M	7th F	8th M	8th F	10th M	10th F	12th M	12th F	College M	College F
Air	4	4	3	0	2	3	2	4	1	4	2	0	2	5	1	7
Big	0	3	1	1	3	1	1	2	0	1	3	1	0	1	0	0
Box	0	1	0	0	0	0	0	0	0	0	2	1	0	1	0	1
Break	2	2	1	0	1	0	0	0	4	1	3	1	2	0	0	0
Breeze	0	0	0	0	0	0	0	0	1	0	0	1	0	0	0	3
Broke	1	0	0	0	2	0	0	0	2	0	1	0	0	0	0	0
Broken	1	0	0	0	3	0	1	2	7	0	1	0	2	2	0	1
Car	0	0	0	0	0	1	2	0	0	0	1	1	0	0	0	1
Chair	0	1	0	0	0	0	0	0	0	0	0	0	0	0	4	1
Class	2	3	2	0	3	0	0	0	1	0	0	0	0	0	0	0
Clean	1	0	1	1	0	2	2	1	2	1	0	0	2	2	4	3
Cleaner	0	0	0	0	1	0	0	0	0	1	0	0	0	0	2	0
Clear	4	3	9	6	8	6	15	11	8	7	9	9	10	4	17	10
Close	1	1	1	2	0	1	0	0	0	0	0	0	0	0	1	0

Response Word — WINDOW

Response Word	4th		5th		6th		7th		8th		10th		12th		College	
	M	F	M	F	M	F	M	F	M	F	M	F	M	F	M	F
Cold	1	1	1	0	0	2	0	1	0	1	0	1	0	0	0	0
Cool	0	0	0	0	0	0	2	1	0	0	0	0	0	0	0	0
Curtain	0	0	1	3	0	1	2	5	0	2	0	5	0	4	1	12
Curtains	0	0	1	2	0	0	1	0	0	2	0	1	0	2	0	5
Dark	0	0	0	0	0	0	0	0	2	0	0	0	0	0	0	0
Dirty	0	0	0	0	1	0	0	1	0	1	0	4	0	2	2	2
Door	35	35	22	39	18	29	32	43	50	44	30	28	29	33	54	58
Flower	1	1	1	0	0	0	0	2	1	0	0	0	0	0	0	1
Frame	1	0	1	2	2	0	2	2	0	4	1	3	6	0	6	5
Frost	0	1	1	0	0	0	2	0	0	0	0	0	0	1	0	2
Glass	83	61	84	55	90	71	84	57	75	63	74	63	67	58	123	93
High	0	2	0	0	1	0	0	1	0	2	0	1	0	2	0	2
Hole	2	0	2	0	1	2	1	1	3	0	2	1	0	0	3	0
Home	0	0	0	0	1	0	0	0	2	0	0	0	0	1	0	1
House	10	6	3	7	9	6	4	13	13	10	16	10	12	8	18	24
Ice	0	2	0	0	0	0	0	0	0	0	0	0	0	0	0	0
Large	0	0	0	1	0	0	0	0	1	0	1	2	0	1	2	0
Ledge	0	0	0	0	0	0	0	0	0	0	1	1	3	2	7	4
Light	4	3	2	6	3	1	4	7	5	6	11	11	7	14	24	34
Look	6	28	19	33	19	17	7	12	5	8	9	8	8	10	18	15
Looking	0	5	1	0	2	1	0	1	1	0	0	1	1	0	0	0
Look out	0	1	1	1	1	2	0	0	0	1	0	1	1	2	0	0
Look through	0	0	0	0	0	0	2	0	0	0	0	0	0	0	0	0
Man	0	0	0	0	0	1	0	0	0	0	0	0	0	0	1	2
Mirror	0	0	0	0	1	1	2	1	0	0	1	0	0	2	0	0
Mother	0	0	0	0	0	0	0	0	0	0	0	0	0	0	2	0
Open	4	6	1	3	3	5	2	9	4	5	1	5	3	9	14	14
Opening	0	0	1	1	1	6	0	3	1	1	1	0	0	0	2	2
Out	0	1	1	1	1	2	0	1	0	0	0	2	0	0	5	2
Outdoors	1	1	0	0	2	2	1	0	0	1	0	0	0	1	0	1
Outside	4	1	4	3	3	5	3	3	3	1	5	6	3	4	3	7
Pain	0	2	3	2	9	8	0	0	0	0	0	0	1	0	2	0
Pan	0	0	2	0	0	0	0	0	0	0	0	0	0	0	0	0
Pane	28	17	16	20	11	16	27	16	15	29	20	18	29	20	36	61
Peek	0	0	0	0	0	0	0	0	2	0	0	0	0	1	0	0
Picture	0	0	0	2	1	0	0	0	0	0	1	1	1	0	2	4
Rain	0	1	1	0	0	3	0	1	1	2	0	0	1	0	2	1
Room	0	0	0	1	0	0	0	1	0	0	0	0	1	0	2	1
Sash	0	0	1	0	0	0	0	0	0	0	0	0	2	1	3	2
Scene	0	0	1	2	1	0	0	0	0	0	1	1	1	0	3	6
Scenery	0	0	0	0	1	2	0	2	0	1	2	1	1	1	1	3
School	0	0	0	0	0	0	2	0	0	0	1	0	0	1	0	0
Screen	0	0	0	0	1	1	1	2	0	0	1	2	2	0	5	3
Seal	0	0	0	0	1	1	0	0	0	0	0	2	0	0	0	0
Seat	0	0	0	0	0	0	0	0	0	0	0	0	0	0	2	1
See	12	12	13	8	6	16	10	14	4	8	5	11	7	13	31	23
See through	0	0	0	0	0	1	1	2	2	0	0	0	0	1	0	0
Sell	0	1	1	0	0	2	0	0	0	0	0	0	0	0	0	0

Response Word	4th M	4th F	5th M	5th F	6th M	6th F	7th M	7th F	8th M	8th F	10th M	10th F	12th M	12th F	College M	College F

WINDOW

Response Word	4th M	4th F	5th M	5th F	6th M	6th F	7th M	7th F	8th M	8th F	10th M	10th F	12th M	12th F	College M	College F
Shade . . .	4	2	2	3	5	4	3	6	6	6	7	9	8	8	12	10
Shelf . . .	0	1	0	0	0	0	1	0	0	0	0	0	2	0	0	0
Sill	3	6	4	5	7	7	6	3	5	7	6	6	6	9	22	26
Sky	1	0	2	1	1	0	1	0	0	1	3	2	1	1	0	2
Snow . . .	1	0	1	2	1	0	0	0	0	2	0	1	0	0	1	2
Square . .	0	1	1	0	0	3	1	1	0	0	0	0	0	0	1	1
Sun	1	2	0	0	0	0	0	2	0	1	1	1	0	3	2	3
Through .	0	0	0	0	0	0	0	0	0	0	0	0	0	0	2	0
Transparent	0	0	0	0	0	0	4	0	2	0	3	1	3	2	1	0
Tree . . .	0	0	0	5	0	0	0	1	0	1	1	1	0	0	1	1
View . . .	0	0	1	2	0	0	0	1	0	1	1	3	1	2	12	7
Wall	0	4	1	3	0	0	1	2	0	2	1	1	1	0	1	2
Wash . . .	1	1	0	1	0	1	0	0	0	0	1	0	0	0	5	2
Washer . .	0	0	0	0	0	1	1	0	1	1	1	0	4	0	0	0
Well	0	0	0	0	0	0	0	0	1	0	0	0	2	0	1	1
Win	0	0	2	2	0	0	0	0	0	0	0	0	0	0	0	0
Wind . . .	2	4	5	1	1	2	0	0	1	0	0	0	0	0	0	1
Woman . .	0	0	0	0	0	0	0	0	0	0	1	1	0	0	3	0

194. WISH

Response Word	4th M	4th F	5th M	5th F	6th M	6th F	7th M	7th F	8th M	8th F	10th M	10th F	12th M	12th F	College M	College F
Anything .	1	0	0	0	2	0	0	1	0	0	0	0	0	0	0	0
Ask	3	2	2	4	6	1	2	1	1	1	3	0	0	0	2	1
Bike . . .	0	2	1	1	2	1	1	0	0	1	0	0	0	0	0	0
Birthday .	0	0	0	3	2	2	4	3	3	5	3	5	2	1	8	15
Boat	0	0	1	0	0	0	3	0	0	0	0	0	2	0	0	0
Bone . . .	1	1	2	6	5	1	3	3	3	3	5	6	10	8	16	29
Can	2	0	0	0	0	0	0	0	0	0	0	0	0	0	0	0
Candle . .	1	0	0	1	1	0	0	0	2	1	0	1	1	0	1	0
Candles . .	0	0	0	0	0	0	0	0	0	0	1	0	0	0	2	0
Candy . . .	2	0	0	0	1	0	0	0	0	0	0	0	0	0	0	0
Car	1	0	1	1	1	0	2	1	0	1	6	7	3	2	1	1
Chicken . .	0	0	0	0	0	0	0	0	0	0	0	0	0	0	2	0
Christmas	1	1	0	2	1	0	0	0	0	0	0	0	0	0	0	0
Clean . . .	0	2	1	0	4	0	1	0	3	0	1	0	1	1	0	0
Come true .	3	4	2	1	1	1	1	1	0	0	1	0	0	3	0	0
Command .	1	1	1	0	3	2	0	1	2	3	2	0	2	4	5	0
Could . . .	1	2	5	6	7	1	0	0	0	0	0	0	3	1	1	0
Desire . .	0	1	0	0	1	1	2	1	1	4	3	4	7	13	28	33
Dime . . .	0	0	1	0	2	0	0	0	0	0	0	0	0	0	0	0
Dirty . . .	2	0	0	1	0	0	0	0	0	0	0	0	0	0	0	0
Dish . . .	3	3	4	3	3	0	3	1	3	1	2	0	4	0	1	0
Dishes . .	1	2	0	0	1	0	1	1	0	0	0	0	0	0	0	0
Do	0	2	1	2	3	2	0	0	0	0	0	1	1	0	1	2
Dog	0	1	2	0	0	3	0	1	0	0	0	0	0	0	0	0
Doll . . .	0	2	0	2	0	0	0	0	0	0	0	0	0	0	0	0
Dream . .	14	7	12	10	20	18	37	35	21	29	19	29	26	36	54	95
Dreaming .	0	0	0	0	0	0	0	0	0	0	0	2	0	0	0	0
Dreams . .	0	0	1	0	0	0	0	0	0	0	1	2	2	0	1	0
Dry . . .	1	0	1	1	0	0	1	3	2	1	0	0	0	0	1	0

Response Word	4th M	4th F	5th M	5th F	6th M	6th F	7th M	7th F	8th M	8th F	10th M	10th F	12th M	12th F	College M	College F
							WISH									
Fairy ...	6	11	4	5	3	7	6	2	2	1	0	2	4	3	3	5
Fairy tale .	0	0	0	0	0	0	0	0	0	0	0	0	0	0	2	2
Favor ...	0	0	0	1	0	0	1	1	0	0	0	0	0	0	2	0
Fish ...	4	8	2	3	3	3	1	0	1	0	1	0	0	0	3	0
Food ...	2	1	0	0	1	0	0	0	0	1	0	0	0	0	0	0
For	0	1	0	0	2	1	0	0	0	0	0	0	0	0	1	0
Fun	1	0	0	2	1	2	0	0	0	1	0	0	1	0	1	2
Genie ...	0	0	1	0	1	0	0	1	0	0	0	0	0	0	2	0
Get	2	5	6	2	0	1	2	1	2	2	4	1	6	0	6	1
Gift	0	0	1	0	0	2	0	1	1	0	1	0	0	2	2	2
Girl	1	0	0	0	0	0	0	0	3	0	0	0	0	0	0	0
Gold ...	0	0	0	0	0	0	0	0	0	0	0	0	0	0	0	2
Good ...	4	1	6	1	5	2	2	2	1	2	2	3	1	0	4	5
Grant ...	0	0	2	0	1	2	0	1	0	1	0	0	2	0	2	0
Granted ..	0	0	0	0	0	0	2	1	0	0	3	0	0	0	2	2
Guess ...	0	1	1	1	1	0	5	3	1	2	0	1	1	0	2	0
Had	5	3	4	3	6	2	2	0	2	1	0	0	1	0	0	0
Happiness .	0	0	0	0	1	0	0	0	0	2	1	0	1	0	0	3
Happy ...	3	1	3	1	0	2	2	3	0	3	1	1	0	2	2	2
Hard ...	1	1	1	6	3	3	0	0	0	2	0	1	0	1	2	0
Have ...	0	0	1	0	2	4	3	5	1	3	2	0	3	2	0	1
Hop	2	0	0	0	0	1	0	0	0	0	0	0	1	0	0	0
Hope ...	24	27	30	36	26	36	34	29	44	43	38	39	30	27	50	38
Hopeful ..	0	0	1	0	0	0	0	0	2	2	0	0	0	0	0	0
Hoping ..	1	2	0	1	0	0	0	0	2	0	0	0	0	1	0	1
Horse ...	0	1	3	0	4	1	0	4	0	1	0	0	0	1	0	0
I	2	1	1	0	0	2	2	1	0	0	1	0	1	1	2	0
Idea ...	1	0	0	0	0	1	0	4	0	0	1	0	1	0	0	0
Impossible	0	0	1	0	0	1	0	0	0	1	0	0	0	0	0	2
Is	0	1	2	1	1	0	0	0	0	0	0	0	0	0	0	0
King ...	0	0	0	2	0	0	0	0	0	0	0	0	0	0	0	0
Like ...	3	1	4	0	1	1	0	0	0	1	0	0	0	0	2	2
Long ...	0	0	0	0	0	0	1	0	0	0	2	0	0	1	0	2
Love ...	0	1	1	2	0	0	0	0	0	0	0	1	0	0	1	3
Luck ...	0	1	0	0	0	1	0	1	3	2	3	0	0	2	3	0
Magic ...	2	3	1	0	0	1	0	0	0	0	1	0	0	0	0	2
Make ...	0	0	0	1	1	3	1	0	0	1	0	0	1	0	0	0
Marriage .	0	0	0	0	0	0	0	0	0	0	0	1	1	2	0	0
Me	0	0	0	1	0	0	0	2	1	0	0	0	0	0	1	0
Mind ...	0	0	0	0	0	0	2	0	0	0	1	0	1	0	1	0
Money ..	2	1	5	2	1	2	4	0	4	1	7	5	6	3	11	5
Never ...	1	0	1	1	2	0	1	0	1	0	4	1	0	1	0	1
Nice	1	2	1	6	2	2	1	2	0	1	0	1	0	0	0	0
One	0	0	0	0	0	0	0	0	0	0	2	0	0	0	0	0
Penny ...	0	1	1	1	0	0	1	5	0	5	0	0	2	0	0	1
Pond ...	0	1	0	0	0	0	0	2	0	0	0	0	0	0	1	0
Pray ...	0	0	0	1	1	0	3	2	0	2	0	0	1	1	1	2
Prayer ..	0	0	0	0	0	0	0	0	0	1	0	0	0	0	2	1
Promise .	0	1	0	1	0	1	1	0	0	0	3	0	0	2	1	4

Response Word	4th M	4th F	5th M	5th F	6th M	6th F	7th M	7th F	8th M	8th F	10th M	10th F	12th M	12th F	College M	College F

WISH

Response Word	4th M	4th F	5th M	5th F	6th M	6th F	7th M	7th F	8th M	8th F	10th M	10th F	12th M	12th F	College M	College F
Receive	0	0	0	0	0	1	0	0	0	0	1	0	1	1	2	0
Ring	0	0	0	2	1	0	0	1	0	3	0	2	0	1	1	9
River	0	0	0	0	0	1	0	1	0	0	0	1	1	1	2	0
Sleep	0	0	0	1	2	0	0	0	0	0	0	0	0	0	0	1
Something	5	1	3	2	2	5	1	0	1	1	0	0	1	0	0	1
Star	1	6	4	4	2	8	4	5	4	12	10	20	7	21	8	28
Stars	0	0	0	1	0	1	0	0	3	0	0	2	2	0	1	0
Surprise	1	0	0	0	0	0	0	0	0	1	0	2	0	0	0	0
Talk	0	1	0	0	0	0	0	0	2	0	0	0	0	0	0	0
Tell	0	1	0	1	0	0	0	0	2	1	1	0	0	0	1	1
Thing	2	1	0	0	3	1	0	0	1	0	1	0	0	0	0	0
Think	11	7	5	16	6	8	16	12	16	11	21	13	21	14	24	21
Thinking	0	0	1	0	0	0	0	1	0	0	0	1	0	1	5	2
Though	0	1	0	1	0	0	0	0	2	0	0	1	1	0	0	0
Thought	0	4	7	3	2	4	3	6	11	5	5	6	4	4	10	6
Three	3	0	0	1	2	0	0	1	0	1	1	2	0	3	1	2
True	13	18	7	14	6	13	5	9	3	6	1	5	2	8	12	7
Truth	0	0	1	0	0	0	0	0	2	0	0	0	1	0	3	1
Turkey	1	0	0	0	2	0	0	0	1	1	0	1	1	2	0	1
Wall	0	1	2	1	0	0	0	0	0	0	1	0	0	0	0	0
Want	24	28	19	20	25	37	19	28	18	27	20	26	21	23	60	66
Wash	5	2	2	0	0	3	5	0	5	2	5	2	6	1	14	9
Water	2	2	2	0	1	0	1	0	0	0	0	0	1	0	0	0
Well	19	18	9	10	9	8	21	13	22	21	20	16	21	11	41	29
Wet	0	0	0	0	0	0	2	0	0	0	0	0	0	0	0	0
Will	0	2	0	1	0	1	0	2	0	1	0	0	0	1	4	1
Wish	0	2	0	0	0	0	0	0	0	0	0	0	0	0	0	0
Wishbone	1	1	2	3	1	2	3	3	1	0	2	3	1	3	3	6
Wishing	2	1	0	1	1	0	2	0	0	0	0	0	1	0	0	0
Wishing well	1	0	0	2	0	4	1	1	1	0	1	2	1	1	1	1
Wonder	6	7	8	4	5	3	1	2	4	3	5	3	1	1	1	3
Yes	1	0	0	0	0	0	0	0	0	0	0	0	0	0	2	0
You	0	2	0	0	1	0	0	0	0	0	0	0	0	0	0	0

195. WITH

Response Word	4th M	4th F	5th M	5th F	6th M	6th F	7th M	7th F	8th M	8th F	10th M	10th F	12th M	12th F	College M	College F
A	4	2	1	1	2	0	3	0	1	0	0	0	0	0	3	0
Accompanied	0	0	0	2	0	0	0	0	0	0	0	0	0	0	0	0
Accompany	0	0	0	0	0	1	1	0	0	0	1	0	1	1	1	2
All	0	1	1	0	1	0	0	0	0	0	0	0	1	1	1	4
Alone	0	0	0	2	1	1	2	3	5	10	2	8	5	0	6	7
Along	3	3	5	5	7	1	7	12	5	6	9	8	5	9	19	25
Also	1	1	1	1	2	3	4	3	2	3	0	3	2	2	1	7
Among	0	0	1	0	1	0	0	0	0	0	1	0	0	1	2	2
And	2	1	0	1	1	1	1	1	0	2	0	1	1	0	2	2
Another	1	1	0	1	1	2	0	0	0	1	1	0	0	0	0	0
At	1	1	0	1	0	2	0	1	3	1	1	0	0	1	1	0
Away	1	1	1	0	0	0	0	0	0	1	1	2	0	0	1	1
Be	0	0	0	1	0	0	0	0	0	0	0	0	0	0	2	0
Belong	0	0	0	1	0	0	0	0	0	0	0	1	2	1	0	0

Response Word	4th M	4th F	5th M	5th F	6th M	6th F	7th M	7th F	8th M	8th F	10th M	10th F	12th M	12th F	College M	College F
							WITH									
Beside	0	0	0	0	0	0	2	1	1	0	0	1	1	1	7	6
Besides	0	0	0	0	0	0	0	0	0	0	2	0	1	1	0	0
Boy	0	0	2	1	0	0	0	3	0	2	0	0	0	2	0	1
Boys	0	0	0	0	0	0	0	2	0	0	0	0	0	0	0	0
Bring	0	0	0	0	0	2	0	1	0	0	0	0	0	0	0	0
By	4	0	0	0	2	3	2	1	2	1	7	3	2	1	10	5
Care	2	1	0	0	0	2	0	0	0	0	2	0	0	1	5	2
Companion	0	0	0	0	1	1	0	0	0	0	1	1	3	1	0	4
Cum	0	0	0	0	0	0	0	0	0	0	0	1	0	1	0	2
Dog	0	0	0	2	0	0	1	0	0	0	0	0	1	0	0	0
Food	2	0	0	0	0	0	0	0	0	0	0	1	0	0	0	0
Friend	0	2	1	0	0	1	0	0	0	1	2	1	1	1	0	0
Friends	0	0	0	0	0	0	0	1	0	0	0	2	0	0	0	0
Girl	1	0	0	1	0	0	4	2	2	1	6	0	0	0	5	1
Girls	0	0	0	0	0	0	0	1	2	0	0	0	1	0	0	0
Give	0	0	0	0	0	0	2	0	0	0	0	0	0	0	0	0
Go	2	0	2	6	5	3	1	1	2	1	1	2	0	1	2	3
Going	0	0	1	1	2	0	0	1	1	1	1	1	1	1	0	0
Gone	1	1	0	0	1	1	2	0	0	1	0	0	0	0	0	1
Group	0	0	0	0	0	0	0	0	0	0	1	0	0	0	2	0
Have	0	3	1	0	2	1	2	3	0	0	1	1	0	1	3	5
He	2	0	1	1	2	1	0	0	0	0	0	0	0	0	0	0
Hear	0	0	2	0	0	0	0	0	0	0	0	0	0	0	0	0
Her	2	3	3	3	4	4	1	3	3	2	11	3	8	3	13	8
Here	3	0	0	0	1	1	0	4	0	0	0	0	1	0	0	1
Him	17	7	15	6	13	9	11	7	19	11	10	12	18	22	11	15
Hold	2	0	0	0	1	1	0	1	0	0	1	0	0	0	2	0
In	3	8	6	7	7	7	10	8	6	10	15	3	6	4	7	8
It	19	14	16	17	10	9	8	4	7	4	4	6	5	6	18	10
Like	0	2	0	0	0	0	0	0	0	0	0	0	0	0	0	0
Man	0	0	2	0	1	0	0	0	0	0	0	0	0	0	0	1
Many	0	0	0	1	0	0	0	0	0	0	0	0	0	0	0	2
Me	17	22	22	16	16	22	10	13	11	12	9	22	11	16	24	27
More	0	0	0	0	0	0	0	0	0	0	0	3	0	0	0	1
My	0	1	0	1	1	0	2	0	0	1	0	0	2	0	0	0
Not	5	5	0	3	1	3	1	3	1	1	1	0	1	0	3	2
Now	0	0	0	1	2	0	0	1	0	0	1	0	0	0	2	0
Of	0	0	0	0	0	0	1	0	2	0	0	0	1	0	0	1
On	0	0	1	1	1	1	0	2	0	0	1	1	0	0	0	0
Or	1	0	1	0	1	0	0	0	0	0	0	0	0	0	0	2
Other	0	0	0	1	0	0	2	0	0	1	0	1	0	0	0	0
Out	19	17	15	21	36	16	19	18	27	25	17	25	35	27	64	73
People	0	4	2	1	2	1	0	0	0	1	1	1	1	4	3	3
Person	2	2	3	1	0	0	0	0	1	1	1	2	1	0	0	1
Place	0	0	0	0	0	2	0	0	0	0	0	0	0	0	0	0
Preposition	0	0	0	0	0	0	0	0	0	0	1	0	0	2	3	3
Somebody	1	1	0	1	1	5	0	1	0	0	1	1	1	0	0	0
Someone	2	6	5	7	5	9	5	5	3	3	7	1	2	1	3	0
Something	4	0	0	3	0	0	0	0	0	0	0	1	0	2	0	0

Response Word	4th M	4th F	5th M	5th F	6th M	6th F	7th M	7th F	8th M	8th F	10th M	10th F	12th M	12th F	College M	College F
							WITH									
Take	12	16	11	5	10	7	5	4	0	6	7	7	2	1	0	5
That	6	3	0	3	0	0	4	3	1	1	3	5	3	2	12	3
The	8	5	8	1	8	5	3	0	2	1	0	0	1	4	8	5
Them . . .	5	1	4	1	7	6	2	0	4	1	3	8	1	4	10	9
Then	1	1	0	2	0	0	0	2	0	0	1	0	1	0	0	0
There . . .	1	0	2	1	0	2	2	0	0	0	0	0	0	0	0	0
This	1	0	0	3	0	0	0	0	0	0	2	0	1	1	2	2
To	0	0	0	1	0	0	1	1	3	1	0	0	0	0	3	3
Together . .	2	2	3	7	10	12	11	9	8	18	6	14	16	20	37	27
Togetherness	0	0	0	0	0	0	0	0	1	2	0	0	0	0	0	0
Too	0	0	0	1	2	2	0	1	0	0	1	1	0	1	0	2
Took	2	0	0	0	0	0	0	0	0	0	0	0	0	0	0	0
Two	0	5	4	2	2	3	4	2	3	1	5	1	2	3	1	2
Us	2	1	3	1	2	4	2	2	2	0	5	8	0	7	9	8
Want	1	2	1	0	0	0	2	1	0	0	0	0	0	0	0	0
Was	1	2	2	2	0	1	3	0	2	2	2	0	1	0	2	0
We	1	0	0	0	0	1	0	2	0	0	0	0	0	0	0	1
What	2	1	4	9	2	9	5	8	9	7	4	2	6	8	17	23
When	1	2	0	4	0	1	2	1	2	1	2	0	1	0	1	0
Where . . .	0	1	2	0	1	0	1	1	2	1	1	0	0	1	1	0
Who	2	1	3	3	2	2	4	4	4	1	7	0	3	7	4	2
Whom	0	0	0	0	0	1	1	0	1	3	2	1	4	4	8	6
Why	1	0	0	0	0	2	0	0	2	0	0	2	0	0	0	0
Wit	1	0	0	0	3	0	1	0	1	0	0	0	0	0	0	0
With	0	0	0	1	2	0	0	0	0	0	0	0	0	0	0	0
Within . . .	1	0	1	1	1	2	3	3	7	1	2	0	2	0	1	2
Without . . .	11	23	16	23	9	19	41	54	46	55	38	39	43	33	86	95
Word	0	0	3	0	2	1	0	0	0	0	0	0	0	0	0	0
You	20	38	31	22	26	17	19	17	23	25	19	22	18	15	34	42
Young	2	0	1	0	0	0	0	0	0	0	0	0	0	0	0	0
Your	1	1	0	0	0	1	2	0	0	1	0	0	0	1	0	1
						196.	WOMAN									
Baby	1	1	1	0	1	0	3	1	1	0	0	0	1	2	1	8
Beautiful . .	0	0	0	2	0	2	2	1	5	4	0	4	8	4	1	1
Beauty . . .	0	0	0	0	0	0	1	0	1	1	3	3	3	2	5	3
Blonde . . .	0	0	0	0	0	0	0	0	0	0	2	0	0	0	0	0
Boy	0	1	1	0	0	3	1	2	1	3	3	3	0	1	2	2
Child	0	1	3	4	0	3	2	7	6	3	7	10	5	9	18	32
Children . . .	0	1	0	0	0	1	1	1	0	2	2	2	0	1	0	1
Clothes . . .	0	0	1	1	0	0	0	0	2	3	3	6	2	3	4	8
Coat	2	1	0	2	1	2	0	0	0	0	0	0	0	0	1	0
Curves . . .	0	0	0	0	0	0	0	0	0	0	0	1	0	0	2	0
Cute	0	1	0	0	0	0	2	0	1	0	2	0	0	0	0	0
Dress . . .	2	4	4	5	5	6	1	8	6	4	9	11	3	0	13	18
Dumb	0	0	0	0	0	0	2	0	0	0	0	0	0	0	0	0
Eve	0	0	0	1	0	0	0	0	0	0	0	0	0	1	0	2
Face	0	0	0	0	0	1	0	1	1	0	0	2	0	0	1	0
Fat	1	0	3	0	0	2	0	2	0	1	1	0	0	0	1	1

351

Response Word	4th		5th		6th		7th		8th		10th		12th		College	
	M	F	M	F	M	F	M	F	M	F	M	F	M	F	M	F

WOMAN

Response Word	M	F	M	F	M	F	M	F	M	F	M	F	M	F	M	F
Female	5	3	4	3	16	6	13	11	11	5	3	1	3	4	5	4
Feminine	0	0	0	0	0	0	1	2	0	0	2	1	1	0	1	1
Figure	0	0	1	0	0	0	0	1	0	3	0	0	2	1	3	0
Fine	0	0	0	0	0	0	0	0	0	0	0	0	0	0	2	0
Fun	0	0	0	0	0	0	0	0	2	0	2	0	2	0	0	0
Gentle	0	0	0	2	0	1	0	0	0	0	1	1	0	5	1	1
Girl	14	23	15	32	28	32	27	26	26	26	28	36	28	26	50	44
Girls	0	0	0	1	0	0	1	0	3	2	0	0	0	0	0	0
Good	0	0	0	0	2	0	0	0	1	0	1	0	0	0	2	1
Hair	1	1	4	1	2	3	2	0	1	1	1	1	1	1	0	3
Hat	1	1	1	2	1	1	3	4	2	3	2	3	3	3	1	1
Human	1	1	5	0	3	0	1	0	0	0	0	0	0	1	0	0
Kind	0	1	0	0	1	2	1	1	0	1	0	1	0	1	1	0
Lady	36	46	33	34	17	31	11	15	8	9	6	12	2	12	11	16
Legs	0	0	1	0	0	0	0	0	0	0	0	0	2	0	2	0
Love	0	0	2	0	0	0	1	5	2	0	0	0	6	2	7	2
Lovely	0	0	0	0	0	0	0	0	0	0	0	0	0	1	1	3
Man	132	111	107	106	99	96	123	109	127	319	116	99	131	124	265	263
Me	0	0	0	1	0	1	0	0	0	0	0	1	0	1	0	2
Men	2	4	3	5	3	3	1	3	2	4	2	2	4	1	2	0
Mom	1	2	1	3	2	1	1	3	2	2	1	2	1	2	0	1
Mother	3	8	6	5	10	12	2	7	7	15	10	9	4	13	11	32
Neat	0	0	0	0	0	0	1	0	1	0	0	0	0	0	2	0
Nice	0	4	2	1	2	5	5	0	4	1	5	3	5	1	8	1
Old	0	2	2	0	1	0	4	1	0	1	1	3	2	3	8	6
People	2	1	0	0	2	1	0	0	2	0	0	0	0	0	1	0
Person	14	9	18	13	18	7	8	6	3	1	0	0	0	0	1	0
Pretty	1	4	5	3	3	4	1	10	1	7	5	16	2	6	8	12
Sex	4	1	1	1	1	3	2	1	2	1	2	1	1	1	4	1
Short	0	2	1	0	0	3	1	0	1	0	1	1	0	0	1	0
Slow	0	0	2	0	0	0	0	0	0	0	0	0	0	0	0	0
Small	0	0	0	3	0	1	1	0	0	0	2	0	1	0	1	1
Soft	1	0	0	1	0	0	0	0	0	0	0	0	1	0	3	0
Talk	0	0	1	0	0	0	2	0	0	0	0	1	1	0	0	0
Tall	0	2	0	2	2	1	1	2	1	0	2	2	0	2	0	2
Teacher	0	1	1	0	0	0	0	1	1	2	0	0	0	3	0	1
Whistle	0	0	0	0	1	0	1	0	0	0	1	1	3	1	3	0
Wife	1	0	0	1	1	0	1	1	0	1	0	2	2	1	8	2
Women	0	0	2	1	4	1	2	1	1	0	1	1	1	0	0	1
Work	2	0	1	0	0	1	0	0	0	0	0	0	0	0	0	0
Wow	0	0	0	0	0	0	1	0	2	0	3	0	2	0	2	0

197. WORKING

Response Word	M	F	M	F	M	F	M	F	M	F	M	F	M	F	M	F
Arithmetic	0	2	2	1	0	0	0	0	0	0	0	0	0	0	0	0
Build	3	0	1	0	0	0	0	0	0	0	0	0	0	0	0	0
Building	1	2	1	0	0	0	0	0	0	0	0	0	0	0	0	0
Busy	2	7	1	5	3	5	3	5	3	7	5	7	2	5	6	10
Class	0	0	0	0	0	0	0	0	0	0	0	0	0	0	2	0
Cleaning	1	0	2	2	0	0	0	1	0	1	0	0	0	1	0	1

Response Word	4th		5th		6th		7th		8th		10th		12th		College	
	M	F	M	F	M	F	M	F	M	F	M	F	M	F	M	F

WORKING

Response Word	M	F	M	F	M	F	M	F	M	F	M	F	M	F	M	F
Dad	0	2	1	2	2	1	1	1	0	0	0	0	0	1	0	0
Day	0	1	0	0	0	0	0	0	0	1	3	1	0	0	4	3
Digging . .	0	0	0	0	0	0	1	0	1	0	0	1	0	0	2	1
Dishes . .	0	0	0	1	2	2	0	1	0	3	1	0	1	0	0	0
Do	3	2	1	2	0	1	0	1	0	0	0	0	0	0	0	1
Doing . . .	6	3	6	5	4	3	7	2	0	1	1	1	2	0	1	1
Done	1	0	1	2	0	0	1	0	1	0	0	0	0	0	0	0
Drug store	0	0	0	0	0	0	0	0	0	0	0	0	0	2	0	0
Earning . .	0	0	0	1	0	1	1	0	0	1	0	1	0	2	1	2
Easy	0	1	3	0	0	0	0	0	2	0	1	0	0	0	0	1
Effort . . .	0	0	0	0	0	0	0	0	0	0	0	0	0	1	0	3
Energy . .	0	0	0	0	0	0	0	0	1	0	2	1	0	1	0	0
Factory . .	0	0	0	0	1	0	0	0	1	2	1	0	0	0	1	0
Fast	5	0	0	4	3	3	0	3	1	3	6	5	4	5	3	5
Father . .	0	2	1	0	1	3	0	4	0	0	1	1	0	0	0	1
Fun	0	2	1	1	2	1	0	2	2	1	1	1	2	2	2	3
Girl	0	0	0	1	0	0	1	2	0	2	1	0	0	2	4	5
Good . . .	0	0	3	0	0	0	0	0	0	0	1	0	0	0	1	3
Had	0	0	0	0	0	2	0	0	0	1	0	0	0	0	0	0
Hammer .	2	3	1	0	1	0	0	0	1	0	0	1	0	0	1	1
Hand . . .	0	0	0	0	0	0	0	0	0	0	0	0	0	0	2	0
Hard . . .	62	76	86	90	78	93	65	54	39	54	43	53	54	56	77	69
Hate	0	1	0	0	0	0	0	1	0	0	0	1	3	0	1	1
Help . . .	0	2	3	0	0	1	0	0	0	0	0	0	0	0	0	0
Hospital . .	0	0	0	0	0	0	0	0	0	0	0	0	0	0	1	5
Hot	2	0	1	1	0	0	2	1	1	2	1	0	0	0	2	0
Hour . . .	0	0	0	0	0	0	0	1	0	0	0	0	1	0	2	1
Hours . . .	0	0	0	0	0	0	1	0	0	2	0	0	8	0	3	2
House . . .	3	0	0	1	0	1	0	0	0	0	0	0	0	0	0	1
Idle	0	0	0	0	1	0	0	0	0	0	0	0	0	0	3	0
Ish	0	0	0	0	1	0	0	0	1	2	0	0	0	2	0	1
Job	7	5	5	6	7	13	3	10	11	9	8	9	6	11	19	26
Labor . . .	3	0	4	0	15	13	9	7	6	8	5	8	11	5	27	15
Laboring .	0	0	0	2	1	1	1	1	1	1	0	0	1	2	2	1
Laying . . .	0	0	0	1	0	0	2	0	1	0	0	0	0	0	0	1
Lazy . . .	6	5	4	4	7	5	15	17	21	20	16	12	8	14	18	18
Leisure . .	0	0	0	0	0	0	0	0	0	0	0	2	0	0	1	2
Loaf	0	0	0	0	0	0	2	1	4	1	1	1	0	2	0	2
Loafing . .	1	0	1	1	5	1	9	4	21	12	15	5	18	10	31	27
Long	0	0	0	0	0	0	1	0	0	0	0	0	0	0	1	3
Mad	0	0	0	0	0	2	0	0	0	0	0	1	0	0	0	0
Man	6	6	3	8	8	3	3	2	3	11	8	9	11	5	25	27
Me	0	2	1	0	0	0	1	0	0	2	0	0	2	0	0	0
Men . . .	5	2	4	8	7	4	5	0	1	2	1	7	2	2	12	6
Money . .	1	2	5	2	4	4	3	4	6	7	17	17	21	14	24	33
Moving . .	0	0	0	0	0	0	0	2	0	0	0	1	0	0	0	1
No	4	0	0	0	1	0	0	0	0	0	0	0	1	0	0	0
Not	2	2	0	0	0	0	0	0	0	0	0	0	0	0	0	0
Nothing . .	0	0	0	0	0	0	1	0	2	1	0	0	0	0	0	0

Response Word	4th M	4th F	5th M	5th F	6th M	6th F	7th M	7th F	8th M	8th F	10th M	10th F	12th M	12th F	College M	College F
							WORKING									
Not working .	0	0	0	0	2	0	1	3	0	0	0	0	0	0	0	0
Office	2	0	0	0	1	1	0	0	0	2	0	0	0	0	0	2
Out	0	0	0	0	2	0	0	0	0	0	1	0	0	0	1	0
Pay	0	0	1	0	0	0	0	0	0	0	1	0	0	2	4	1
Pencil . . .	0	1	0	0	0	1	1	0	0	0	0	0	0	0	2	0
People . . .	0	2	0	0	0	0	0	1	1	1	0	0	0	1	1	1
Person . . .	0	0	0	0	0	0	0	0	0	0	0	0	2	0	0	0
Play	15	13	8	7	7	10	4	5	3	3	2	2	3	1	5	3
Playing . . .	27	24	20	24	18	12	17	18	12	13	5	16	7	10	24	25
Pleasure . .	0	0	0	0	0	0	0	0	2	0	0	0	0	0	0	0
Railroad . .	0	0	0	0	0	0	0	0	0	1	0	0	0	0	2	2
Reject . . .	0	0	0	0	0	0	0	0	2	0	0	0	0	0	0	0
Relax	0	0	0	0	0	0	0	0	1	0	1	0	0	1	2	2
Relaxing . .	0	0	0	1	1	0	1	0	0	0	1	0	0	0	2	2
Rest	3	0	3	0	1	2	3	0	3	1	1	3	1	1	7	2
Resting . . .	2	2	0	2	4	2	2	4	3	11	1	7	3	5	13	8
Retired . . .	0	1	0	0	0	0	0	0	2	0	0	0	0	0	0	0
Saw	1	2	0	0	0	0	0	0	0	0	0	0	0	0	0	0
School . . .	0	3	4	8	6	5	8	7	15	6	6	6	4	6	3	7
Sears	0	0	0	0	0	0	0	0	0	0	0	0	0	2	0	0
Secretary . .	0	0	0	0	0	0	0	1	0	1	0	2	0	0	0	0
Shovel . . .	0	0	1	1	1	0	0	0	0	1	1	1	0	0	1	2
Shoveling . .	0	0	0	0	0	0	1	2	1	0	0	0	1	0	0	0
Sitting . . .	1	3	1	1	0	0	1	0	1	2	1	1	0	2	1	1
Slave	0	0	0	0	2	3	1	2	1	0	2	3	3	2	1	3
Slaving . . .	1	1	1	0	1	3	1	9	4	1	6	1	0	0	1	1
Sleep	2	1	1	2	0	2	2	2	3	2	2	0	1	3	5	6
Sleeping . . .	2	2	3	1	3	2	13	8	17	8	15	12	11	10	32	26
Slow	3	3	0	1	1	2	1	0	1	0	1	1	0	0	4	0
Something . .	1	2	1	0	0	1	0	0	0	0	0	0	0	0	0	0
Stop	5	5	1	3	0	3	1	1	0	1	1	0	0	0	1	1
Stopping . .	2	0	0	0	0	0	1	0	0	0	0	0	0	0	0	1
Store	0	0	0	1	0	1	1	0	0	0	2	0	2	1	1	1
Study	0	0	0	0	0	2	0	2	1	0	0	0	0	0	3	4
Studying . .	0	0	0	1	0	2	0	1	0	0	0	0	1	1	2	8
Summer . .	0	0	0	0	0	0	0	0	0	0	1	0	0	1	2	1
Sweat . . .	1	2	3	0	4	0	7	5	9	0	8	2	10	3	26	10
Sweating . .	0	0	0	0	0	0	2	1	2	0	2	0	1	1	2	3
Test	0	2	0	0	0	0	2	0	1	0	0	0	0	0	0	0
Thinking . .	0	1	0	0	0	1	0	1	0	0	2	1	0	1	0	2
Time	0	0	0	0	0	0	0	0	0	0	2	0	1	1	1	2
Tired	2	2	2	2	2	5	3	3	2	3	4	3	5	8	14	18
Toil	0	2	0	1	0	1	1	0	1	0	1	1	1	0	1	1
Tools	0	0	0	0	0	0	1	0	1	0	0	0	0	0	3	0
Trying . . .	0	0	0	0	0	0	0	0	0	1	0	0	1	1	0	2
Typing . . .	0	0	0	0	0	0	0	0	0	0	0	1	0	1	0	5
Unemployed .	0	0	0	0	0	0	0	0	1	0	0	0	0	0	2	0
Walking . . .	0	0	0	0	0	1	0	0	1	1	1	0	0	2	1	0

Response Word	4th M	4th F	5th M	5th F	6th M	6th F	7th M	7th F	8th M	8th F	10th M	10th F	12th M	12th F	College M	College F
							WORKING									
Wood ...	5	1	1	0	0	0	0	0	0	0	0	0	1	0	0	0
Work ...	14	16	21	5	10	12	9	7	0	2	9	1	2	1	0	2
Writing ..	1	0	2	1	0	0	0	0	0	0	0	1	2	0	0	2
						198.	YELLOW									
Afraid ..	0	0	0	1	0	0	2	0	3	0	0	0	1	0	2	2
Balloon ..	0	0	0	0	2	0	0	1	0	0	0	0	0	1	0	0
Banana ..	3	1	1	2	1	3	5	10	5	11	7	5	10	2	8	7
Beard ...	0	0	0	0	0	0	0	0	0	0	0	0	0	2	0	1
Beautiful .	0	0	0	0	0	0	0	0	0	2	0	0	0	0	0	0
Bed	0	0	0	0	0	0	0	0	0	1	0	0	1	0	0	2
Bee	0	0	0	0	0	1	0	0	1	0	0	1	0	0	4	2
Bile	0	0	0	0	0	0	0	0	0	0	0	0	0	0	2	2
Bird ...	0	0	2	1	1	3	4	6	1	7	9	11	6	15	26	39
Black ...	18	5	25	13	20	8	18	6	26	4	19	6	22	9	32	28
Blue	14	24	14	14	16	11	10	12	26	23	9	14	27	16	40	35
Book ...	1	0	0	0	0	1	0	0	1	0	2	0	0	0	0	0
Bread ..	2	0	0	0	0	0	0	0	1	0	0	0	0	0	1	1
Bright ..	7	15	16	13	14	20	19	11	8	10	8	12	7	13	12	19
Brown ..	3	6	6	7	13	5	5	6	10	0	4	4	2	4	10	15
Butter ..	2	3	0	4	2	1	2	7	2	4	2	7	3	12	13	21
Buttercup .	0	0	0	0	0	0	0	0	0	0	0	0	0	0	0	2
Butterfly .	0	2	0	0	0	2	1	2	0	0	1	2	2	3	3	9
Cab	0	0	0	0	0	0	0	0	1	0	0	0	2	0	3	0
Canary ..	0	0	0	0	0	1	2	0	0	1	0	2	1	4	6	6
Car	0	0	0	0	1	1	1	0	0	0	5	1	7	3	3	1
Cat	0	0	2	0	1	0	0	0	0	0	0	0	2	0	1	0
Cheerful .	0	0	0	0	0	0	0	1	0	0	0	0	0	0	0	2
Cheese ..	0	0	0	0	0	0	0	0	0	0	0	0	0	0	0	2
Chicken .	2	1	2	0	3	2	11	8	6	6	6	2	3	1	3	2
Chinese ..	0	0	0	0	0	0	1	0	0	0	1	0	2	0	3	0
Coat	1	0	1	0	0	2	0	0	1	0	0	0	0	2	0	1
Color ...	101	95	98	104	86	107	48	56	46	45	51	31	29	25	56	36
Colors ..	1	4	0	0	3	0	0	1	1	0	0	0	0	0	0	0
Coward ..	1	0	0	0	0	0	1	1	3	3	8	1	5	4	12	2
Crayon ..	2	2	0	0	0	1	3	0	0	0	1	1	0	0	4	0
Daffodil ..	0	0	0	1	0	0	0	0	0	0	0	2	0	0	0	0
Daisy ...	0	0	0	0	0	1	1	1	0	0	1	3	0	4	3	3
Dandelion .	1	0	0	0	0	0	1	0	1	2	0	0	0	0	1	3
Dark ...	1	1	1	0	1	1	1	1	0	0	0	0	0	0	2	0
Dog ...	0	0	0	0	2	0	0	0	1	0	0	1	8	0	3	2
Dress ...	0	3	1	1	0	4	1	2	0	1	0	8	1	8	2	10
Duck ...	0	1	0	1	0	2	0	0	0	0	0	0	0	0	0	0
Dull ...	0	0	0	0	0	0	0	0	0	2	0	1	0	0	0	0
Egg	0	0	0	0	0	1	0	0	0	0	0	1	0	1	2	1
Fear	0	0	0	0	0	0	0	0	0	0	0	0	1	0	0	2
Fellow ..	0	4	0	1	0	1	0	0	0	0	0	0	1	1	0	0
Fever ...	0	0	0	0	0	1	3	0	3	1	2	0	6	1	5	2
Flower ..	0	1	2	1	3	2	0	7	2	5	12	10	4	15	22	16

Response Word	4th M	4th F	5th M	5th F	6th M	6th F	7th M	7th F	8th M	8th F	10th M	10th F	12th M	12th F	College M	College F
								YELLOW								
Flowers . .	0	1	0	0	0	0	1	0	0	2	0	2	0	1	0	0
Fruit . . .	0	2	0	0	0	0	0	0	0	0	1	0	0	0	0	1
Gold	0	0	1	1	0	3	1	1	5	0	0	3	1	2	8	6
Golden . .	0	2	0	0	0	0	0	0	0	0	0	0	0	0	0	0
Green . . .	5	6	6	10	11	9	9	11	10	15	11	16	15	15	21	32
Hair	1	0	1	2	0	1	3	3	3	5	3	2	3	6	5	8
Hat	0	0	0	0	0	2	0	0	0	0	1	0	0	0	0	0
Hay	0	0	0	0	0	2	0	0	0	0	0	0	0	0	0	0
House . .	1	0	1	1	1	0	2	0	1	1	0	0	0	0	2	0
Jacket . .	0	0	0	0	0	0	2	0	0	0	1	0	1	0	2	1
Lazy . . .	0	0	0	0	0	0	0	0	0	0	0	0	0	2	0	0
Lemon . .	1	1	0	1	1	0	2	1	1	4	0	1	0	3	4	8
Light . . .	3	5	9	8	6	5	16	8	4	6	9	6	4	0	16	12
Moon . . .	0	0	0	1	0	0	0	0	2	0	1	2	0	0	0	3
Orange . .	3	1	2	3	2	2	2	11	5	4	5	7	4	9	9	5
Pear . . .	0	0	0	0	0	0	0	0	0	0	2	0	0	0	2	3
Pencil . .	1	1	1	1	0	0	0	0	1	0	0	2	1	0	0	0
Pink	7	0	0	5	1	4	1	4	2	3	4	2	1	3	2	1
Pretty . .	0	2	1	3	0	3	0	0	0	3	1	4	1	1	2	2
Purple . .	1	2	2	1	0	1	3	4	2	7	1	2	1	1	2	5
Red	29	30	29	18	25	12	24	14	23	16	18	13	21	16	42	27
Ribbon . .	0	0	0	0	0	0	0	3	0	2	1	1	0	1	3	3
River . . .	0	0	0	0	0	0	2	0	2	1	3	2	1	1	3	2
Rose . . .	0	0	0	0	1	0	0	0	0	2	0	0	0	1	5	6
Scared . .	1	0	1	1	0	0	0	0	1	0	3	0	1	1	2	0
Shirt . . .	1	0	0	0	0	0	1	0	0	0	0	0	0	0	2	0
Sick	0	0	0	0	0	0	0	1	1	0	0	0	0	2	2	1
Skirt . . .	0	0	0	0	0	0	0	0	0	1	0	2	0	0	0	1
Soft . . .	0	0	1	0	0	0	2	2	1	3	1	2	2	2	1	4
Stain . . .	0	0	0	0	0	0	0	0	0	0	0	0	0	0	2	0
Streak . .	0	0	0	0	0	0	0	0	1	0	0	0	1	0	3	0
Sun	0	7	1	8	6	10	7	20	5	20	6	23	6	13	18	33
Sunlight . .	0	0	0	0	0	0	0	0	0	0	0	0	0	0	0	2
Sunshine .	0	1	0	0	0	0	0	1	0	0	0	2	0	0	0	2
Sweater . .	0	0	0	0	0	2	0	0	0	0	0	1	0	1	4	5
Teeth . . .	0	0	1	1	0	0	0	0	1	2	1	0	2	0	3	0
The	2	0	0	0	0	0	0	0	0	0	0	0	0	0	0	0
Ugly . . .	0	0	0	0	0	0	0	0	0	0	0	0	1	0	2	1
Wall . . .	0	0	0	0	0	0	0	0	0	0	0	0	1	0	1	2
Warm . .	0	0	0	0	0	0	0	0	0	3	0	1	0	0	0	4
White . . .	7	6	6	7	2	5	5	3	6	2	8	6	7	4	8	11
							199.	YOU								
Always . .	0	0	0	0	0	0	0	0	0	0	2	0	0	0	1	0
And	3	1	4	1	4	2	2	1	3	2	4	3	1	2	10	4
Are	16	11	11	13	17	13	8	8	14	5	13	9	23	13	28	22
At	2	0	1	0	0	0	0	0	1	0	0	0	0	0	0	0
Beautiful .	0	0	0	2	0	0	0	0	0	0	0	0	0	0	0	0
Boy	4	3	5	0	1	1	4	0	2	2	1	3	2	1	1	1

Response Word	4th M	4th F	5th M	5th F	6th M	6th F	7th M	7th F	8th M	8th F	10th M	10th F	12th M	12th F	College M	College F
							YOU									
Can	4	5	3	3	5	2	0	2	0	0	1	0	8	3	5	4
Could	1	0	0	2	0	0	0	0	0	0	0	0	0	0	0	0
Do	1	1	1	1	0	0	0	0	0	0	1	0	1	0	2	3
Friend	0	1	0	0	0	1	0	0	0	0	1	0	0	0	0	2
Girl	0	1	1	1	1	2	1	4	1	3	2	2	3	2	2	1
Go	0	0	1	0	2	0	0	0	1	0	1	0	0	0	1	2
Have	3	0	0	0	0	0	0	0	1	0	0	0	1	0	1	0
He	2	1	1	0	3	1	4	2	4	1	5	2	2	3	11	13
Her	0	4	1	2	2	2	6	4	3	1	7	3	4	3	5	2
Here	0	0	0	0	0	0	0	0	0	0	0	0	0	0	2	0
Him	7	6	7	6	10	7	12	4	16	10	9	7	9	4	10	8
I	14	22	17	15	8	18	13	14	12	12	20	10	18	16	42	33
It	2	0	1	0	0	0	5	0	4	2	2	1	1	1	0	0
Know	3	1	0	0	2	0	0	0	0	0	0	1	0	0	0	2
Like	0	1	1	2	0	0	0	0	0	0	0	0	0	0	0	0
Love	0	2	0	1	0	0	0	0	0	1	0	0	1	0	1	0
Man	1	1	1	0	2	0	0	0	0	0	1	1	0	0	3	0
May	1	0	1	0	0	0	0	1	2	0	0	0	1	0	0	0
Me	95	126	124	139	130	131	130	159	123	167	133	178	126	150	282	326
Myself	1	7	3	7	3	5	1	1	2	3	2	2	1	0	1	0
Nice	0	0	1	1	0	0	0	0	0	1	0	0	1	0	2	0
No	2	1	0	1	2	1	0	0	0	0	0	0	0	0	1	0
One	1	0	2	2	0	0	0	1	0	1	0	0	0	0	0	0
People	1	2	0	1	1	0	1	1	3	1	1	0	1	2	1	2
Person	10	10	9	10	8	20	3	7	3	7	8	7	6	7	6	5
Said	0	0	2	0	0	1	1	0	0	0	1	1	0	0	1	0
Say	1	3	0	0	0	0	1	1	0	1	0	0	0	0	1	0
See	2	1	1	0	2	1	1	2	0	0	2	0	0	0	0	1
Self	4	0	1	0	1	0	0	0	0	0	0	1	2	0	1	1
She	2	1	0	0	1	0	1	1	1	0	3	1	4	2	4	5
Should	3	3	1	1	1	1	0	1	2	1	0	0	1	0	2	1
Someone	5	1	0	1	2	2	1	1	0	0	0	0	0	0	1	0
Them	0	0	1	1	0	1	2	2	6	2	4	1	2	1	3	4
There	0	0	0	0	1	0	0	0	1	0	0	0	1	0	3	0
They	1	0	1	0	2	0	1	1	5	4	3	1	6	2	17	12
Too	0	0	0	0	1	0	0	0	0	2	1	0	0	1	0	0
Us	1	4	2	2	1	2	2	3	5	0	3	2	0	0	7	2
We	0	0	0	0	0	1	1	1	1	1	0	0	0	0	2	4
Where	0	0	0	0	2	0	0	0	0	0	0	0	0	0	0	0
Will	2	0	1	3	4	0	7	0	2	2	0	1	2	1	5	4
You'll	0	0	2	0	0	0	0	0	0	0	0	0	0	0	0	0
Your	12	7	10	5	6	4	10	7	6	3	4	4	5	18	2	11
Yours	0	0	2	1	1	0	2	0	4	1	1	0	2	1	3	8
Yourself	5	6	5	8	2	8	8	5	1	0	1	2	1	1	0	0
						200.	YOUNGER									
Age	2	3	3	3	2	3	3	2	2	2	2	2	2	2	9	5
Baby	5	7	5	11	8	10	11	14	3	8	2	9	3	5	4	8
Boy	13	3	10	2	7	3	3	2	5	0	4	4	3	0	3	1

Response Word	4th M	4th F	5th M	5th F	6th M	6th F	7th M	7th F	8th M	8th F	10th M	10th F	12th M	12th F	College M	College F
								YOUNGER								
Brother	5	3	1	6	12	5	16	11	10	8	20	5	24	13	22	25
Brothers	0	0	1	0	0	0	0	0	1	0	0	0	0	0	2	0
Child	12	14	21	25	17	29	13	30	15	25	20	23	13	24	25	49
Children	2	15	5	5	4	15	3	7	2	14	11	20	6	16	11	23
Days	0	0	0	0	0	0	0	0	0	0	0	0	0	0	2	1
Earlier	0	0	0	0	0	0	0	0	0	0	0	0	0	0	0	2
Elder	0	0	0	2	0	0	1	0	0	1	0	0	0	1	1	0
First	0	0	0	0	2	0	0	0	0	0	0	0	0	0	0	0
Generation	0	0	0	1	1	2	3	3	4	4	1	1	3	1	4	2
Girl	2	2	1	0	1	0	1	1	2	2	4	0	2	2	3	0
It	0	0	2	0	0	0	0	0	0	0	0	0	0	0	0	0
Kid	1	3	3	1	1	0	5	3	3	2	6	2	0	0	3	2
Kids	0	0	0	0	1	0	1	0	3	2	2	3	2	1	1	1
Little	6	10	12	17	7	10	1	8	1	9	3	10	3	7	5	7
Littler	3	1	0	2	3	3	4	1	0	0	1	2	0	0	0	2
Man	4	0	2	0	4	1	0	0	1	0	2	0	0	0	3	2
Me	0	0	1	1	1	1	1	1	0	0	1	0	3	3	0	0
Men	0	0	0	0	0	2	0	0	1	0	0	0	1	0	1	0
New	1	0	0	0	0	0	0	0	0	0	0	0	0	0	2	0
Old	22	22	31	19	24	15	21	10	23	8	9	4	11	10	15	18
Older	63	71	58	72	57	69	90	93	111	103	89	104	101	101	249	276
Oldest	2	0	0	0	1	0	0	1	0	0	2	0	1	0	1	0
One	0	2	0	2	0	0	0	0	0	0	0	0	0	0	0	0
People	4	3	3	3	1	2	1	0	1	1	4	1	1	1	8	2
Person	1	1	2	2	1	0	0	0	1	0	1	2	3	1	2	0
Set	0	1	0	0	0	0	0	0	0	1	0	0	1	2	1	1
Sex	0	0	0	0	2	0	1	0	0	0	1	0	0	0	0	0
Sister	2	7	3	9	8	5	4	8	3	7	4	17	10	14	12	15
Small	5	15	7	11	9	13	3	11	6	6	5	5	9	9	12	4
Smaller	6	7	9	10	13	17	11	17	2	12	14	6	7	8	8	7
Son	0	0	1	0	0	0	0	0	0	0	0	0	1	0	2	0
Spring	0	0	0	0	0	0	0	0	0	1	0	2	0	0	0	3
Stronger	0	0	0	0	1	0	0	0	1	0	1	0	4	0	0	2
Ten	0	0	2	0	0	0	0	0	0	1	0	1	0	0	0	0
Than	4	4	0	3	6	2	8	2	13	7	7	7	10	5	31	13
Then	4	2	4	2	4	0	0	0	4	0	0	0	2	0	2	0
Years	0	0	0	0	0	0	0	0	0	0	1	1	1	0	2	0
You	6	3	2	2	1	2	3	2	0	0	0	0	0	0	0	0
Young	30	21	29	19	23	18	17	6	9	7	6	0	2	4	7	3
Youngest	1	0	0	1	1	1	3	1	2	4	5	2	4	2	12	2
Youngster	1	0	0	1	1	0	0	2	0	1	0	1	0	0	0	0
Youth	1	0	4	0	1	2	2	3	3	1	2	1	3	5	7	4

IDIOSYNCRATIC RESPONSES

A

A baby, Abbreviation, ABC, ABC's, Ache, Act, A dog, Afraid, Again, Airplane, Alice, All right, Alone, Also, Always, Amen, A name, Animals, Ant, Any, Anything, Apply, Around, Art, Ask, A thing, Atom, Away, Awe

Back, Banana, Baron, Bat, Bay, Bean, Because, Bed, Beginning, Bell, Best, Better, Bicycle, Bid, Big, Big cat, Block, Board, Body, Bone, Box, Bridge, Bug, Buggy, Bunch, Bus, Butt, Button, Buy

Cap, Capital, Capitol, Carry, Cars, Cat or dog, Cats, Certain, Chair, Cherry, Child, Chill, Cigarette, Circle, City, Color, Come, Conjunction, Connect, Cry

D, Daddy, Dare, Day, Deer, Describe, Describing, Dictionary, Did, Dish, Do, Doll, Dolls, Don't, Dope, Drip, Dumb, Dummy, Dump

E, Ear, Eat, Egg, EIOU, Eye

Fact, Fair, Fairy, Fan, Farm, Fast, Fat, Few, First letter, Fish, Food, For, Fox, Friend, Fuel, Fun

Game, Girls, Give, Go, Goofed, Got, Grades, Grammar, Grass, Green, Guy

Hair, Happy, Hay, He, Heard, Help, Her, Here, Hi, Him, Hit, Hog, Hold, Hole, Home, Huh, Hurry

If, Impossible, Infinitive, Interest

Jeep, Jet, Job

Key, Kid, Knob

La, Lamp, Last, Late, Latter, Laugh, Lay, Letter A, Letters, Light, Like, Load, Long, Lot, Lots

Math, May, Mean, Men, Mice, Mine, Minute, Monkey, Moon, More, Mother, Move

Never, Nite, No, Noise, Nose, Note, Nothing, Number

Once, One letter, One thing, Or, Orange, Own

Paper, Paragraph, Particular, Pat, Pay, Peanut, Pear, Pen, Pet, Piano, Pigeon, Pink, Plan, Plural, Pop, Puzzled

Quick

Rabbit, Radio, Rat, Ray, Reading, Reason, Ride, Rug, Ruler, Run

Same, School, Sea, Seven, She, Short, Sidewalk, Singular, Sky, Sled, Slow, So, Somebody, Song, Soon, Sound, Spoon, Sport, Start, Stay, Steep, Store, Story, Stream, Student, Study, Stutter, Subject, Superior

Table, Talk, Teacher, Teepee, Test, Than, Their, They, Things, This, Thought, Thy, Time, Tings, Tongue depressor, Top, Tower, Toy, Toys, Train, Trap, Tree, Two

U, Us, Use

Very

Wall, Want, Weigh, Well, While, Who, Will, Window, With, Wolf, Woman, Won't, Words, World

Yes, You, Your

Z

AFRAID

A, Accept, Accident, Accidents, Afraid, After, Aid, Alarmed, Alphabet, Always, An, Ants, Anxiety, Ape, Asked, Ate, Avoid, Aware, Away, Awful

Baby, Back, Back up, Bare, Bashful, Bat, Be, Beast, Beginning, Believe, Birds, Bitter, Black, Blackness, Blood, Blue, Bo, Bogey men, Bomb, Boo, Boogie man, Boom, Boys, Braid, Bravery, Bread, Brother, Bugged, Bull

Came, Car, Card, Cared, Carolyn, Carry, Cats, Cautious, Cave, Challenge, Children, Chills, Chose, Chrianson, Class, Cliff, Cliffs, Cold, Confidence, Continent, Cops, Cowardice, Cower, Craig L., Crazy, Criminals, Cringe, Crowd, Crying, Cute

Dad, Dangerous, Dare, Daring, Dart, Dead, Dear, Death, Dentist, Director, Distressed, Dread

Eagle, Easy, Egg, Emotion, Exam, Exams, Excited, Eyes

Failure, Faith, Fast, Father, Fearsome, Field, Fighting, Fire, Flashlight, Floor, Flower, Fool, Foolish, Forest, Fraid, Free, Frightful, Front, Frown, Frustrated, Frustration, Fun, Funny

Get, Ghost, Ghosts, Giant, Girl, Girls, Glad, Go, God, Going, Goodby, Green, Guerilla, Gun

Hair, Happiness, Hard, Harm, Harmless, Hate, He, Head, Heart, Hell, Heroism, Hide, High, High bar, Hit, Horrible, Horrified, Horror, Horror pictures, Hot, Humorous

Ick, Ill, Illness, Indian, Insect, Insects, Intimidate, Is, It

Jim, John, Joy, Juggle, Jungle, Justice

Kids, Kill, Killer, King, Know, Knowledge

Lady, Land, Large, Lets, Life, Lightning, Like, Little, Loneliness, Lonely, Long, Look-out, Looks, Lost, Loud, Love, Loved

Machine, Made, Maniac, Martians, Men, Met, Mice, Might, Miserable, Miss Newharth, Mom, Money, Monster, Moose, Morning, Mother, Mouse, Movie, Mummy, Murder, Music, Mystery

Name, Natives, Nerves, Nice, Nightmare, Nightmares, Nighttime, Noisy, Nope, Not brave, Not good, Nothing, Not me, Not nice, Not possessing confidence, Now, Nut

Of, Of the dark, Of you, Oh, Oh oh, Open, Out

Page, Pain, Pale, Pall, Panicky, People, Person, Plane, Plans, Pleasure, Poland, Police, Pretty, Protected, Psychology

Quiet, Quit, Quite, Quivering

Raid, Ran, Respect, Revenge, Rick, Rising, Risk, Robber, Robbers, Romeo and Juliet, Running, Russia

Sacked, Safety, Said, Scare, Scardy cat, Scent, School, Scram, Secure, Security, Sew, Shake, Shaking, Shaky, Shiver, Shock, Shook, Shout, Show, Sick, Silly, Sinister, Skyscraper, Slug, Small, Smart, So, Soared, Sometimes, Soon, Sore, Sorry, Spook, Spooks, Spooky, Square, Stare, Stared, Startle, State, Stay, Stiff, Still, Stop, Storms, Strength, Sure, Sweet, Swift, Sword

Tear, Ten, Terrible, Terrier, Terrify, Test, That, The, Thief, Thing, Think, This, Thunder, Tiger, Timid, Tired, Tomorrow, Too bad, Tough, Trembling, Truck, Truth, TV

Ugly, Unbalanced, Uncertain, Unexpected, Unfriendly, Unhappiness, Unknown, Unsafe, Unwelcome, Unwilling

Vampire

Walk, Wall, Wary, Water, Weak, Welcome, When, Whimper, Whistle, Who me, Why, Wild animal, Window, Witch, Women, Woods, Work, Wrong

Yell, Yellow chicken, Yike, You, Yourself

AH

Ache, Admiration, Admire, Afraid, Africa, After, Again, Age, Aha, Ah ah, Ah ha, Ahhh, Ahs, All, Allah, All right, Also, Amazed, Amen, Ann, Answer, Ant, Anything, Anyway, Art, Ask, Astonished, Astonishment, At, At last, Aw, Away, Awe,

A word

Ba, Baa, Baby, Bah, Bashful, Basketball, Bat, Bath, Bay, Be, Beauty, Because, Bed, Beer, Believeable, Bet, Bit, Blob, Boat, Bologna, Bomb, Boom, Bored, Boys, Breath, Bright, Burglar, Burn, Burp, Butter, By

Can, Candy, Can't, Careful, Cat, Catch, Caught, Cha cha, Cheerleader, Children, China, Cho, Choose, Chu, Chuck, Clean, Clear, Clearer, Cold, Comb, Come, Come on, Comfortable, Comic, Comment, Contempt, Content, Contentment, Cough, Cry

Darn, Darrone, Daughter, Dear, Deen, Delicious, Delight, Did, Didn't, Dinner, Disappointment, Discovered, Disgust, Do, Doc, Doctors, Dog, Done, Donny, Don't known, Dope, Dopey, Doubt, Down, Dr., Dumb

Each, Ease, Easily, Eat, Ecstasy, Ee, Em, Enough, Er, Excellent, Excitement, Exclamatory, Excuse, Explanation

Fa, Face, Fair, Fall, Fast, Fat, Father, Feet, Felt, Find, Finish, Finished, Fooey, Foolish, Football, Fooy, For, Found, Friday, Fright, Frog

Game, Gasp, Girl, Girls, Going, Goodness, Goofed, Gosh, Got, Grandmother, Grime, Groan, Grown, Guess, Gum, Gun

Ha ah, Hack, Ha ha, Has, Hat, Hear, Heck, Hell, Hello, Help, Hemm, Her, Hey, Him, His, Hit, Hmm, Hmmm, Ho ho, Holler, Hop, Hot, House, How come, Howl, Humbug, Hummer, Hurrah, Hurt

Ice cream, Ick, Idea, If, Ill, In, Interjection, Ishy

Ja

Kind, King, Know

La, Lady, Lah, Lake, Last, Laughed, Laughter, Lets, Lie, Light, Like, Lips, Little, Lo, Lone, Lost, Louder, Lovely, Lung

May, Maybe, Mean, Meat, Mine, Mmm, Moan, Mom, Mother, Mud, Music, My goodness

Neat, Never, New, Noise, No no, Not true, Nut

Oak, Objection, Oh boy, Oh oh oh, OK, Old, On, Once, One, Or, Ought, Over, Ow

Pa, Page, Paper, Pause, Paw, Peace, Person, Phil, Pie, Pig, Pleasant, Please, Pleasing, Pooh, Pop, Pshaw

Quiet

Rah, Rats, Really, Refresh, Refreshed, Refreshment, Relaxation, Relaxed, Relaxing, Relieve, Relieved, Remark, Reply, Response, Rest, Right, Roar, Rotten

Sad, Safe, Same, Satellite, Satisfactory, Satisfy, Saved, Saying, Scale, Scary, School, Scream, Screaming, See it, Seem, Sentence, Sex, Shack, Shame, She, Sheep, Shh, Ship, Shock, Shocks, Shoo, Shoulder, Shout, Shucks, Shut, Si, Sick, Sign, Sing, Six, Skunk, Sky, Sleepy, Slow, Sly, Smell, Smile, Smooth, Soap, Sob, Soft, Sol, Some, Song, Sooth, Soothing, So what, Speak, Spy, Statement, Stick, Stop, Stuck, Stutter, Sum, Sun, Sure, Suspicious, Sweet

Tall, Taste, Tea, Teacher, Tell, Than, Thanks, Them, Theme, Then, They, Thing, Things, Think, Thinking, This, Those, Thought, Through, Tiny, Tongue, Tonsils, Too, Touch, Tree, Tried, Trouble

Uh, Uhh, Umm, Understand, Understanding, Up

Voice, Voice sound

Wah, Wait, Warm, Warmth, Was, Waste, Water, Way, We, Where, Whew, Wicked, Wieners, Wilderness, Will, Win, Woe, Women, Wonder, Wonderous, Words

Yah, Yawn, Yawned, Yay, Ye, Yea, Yeah, Yell, Yip, Your, Yum, Yummy

ALTHOUGH

A, Abbreviation, Able, About, Across, Actually, Add, Adverb, Afraid, After, Afterwards, Age, Albeit, All done, All over, All right, All there, All through, All time, Alone, Along, Already, Alter, Alternative, Altogether, Although, Although we are nice, Alway, An, And sign, And then again, Anger, Answer, Any, Anything, Apart, Apple, Apt, Are, Aren't, Argue, Ate, At once, Away

Baby, Bad, Badly, Because of, Become, Bees, Begin, Be good, Bell, Below, Beside, Between, Big, Blackboard, Blank, Body, Book, Both, Brought, Building, Bunch, But then, By

Cage, Cake, Called, Came, Can, Car, Care, Cars, Cat, Catch, Cause, Chair, Change, Cheer, Child, Christmas, Clause, Clean, Clear, Close, Cloth, Coal, Cold, Color, Come, Coming, Comma, Comment, Conclude, Conclusion, Condition, Connect, Connecting, Contrary, Correction, Could, Could be, Course, Cow, Crazy, Cries, Crowds, Crying

Dame, Day, Days, Dear, Dec, Den, Despite, Did, Didn't,

Difference, Different, Dog, Door, Dough, Down, Due to, Dumb

Else, Every, Everything, Excuses, Expect, Explanation, Expression, Extra

Fact, False, Fast, Fat, Fault, Fight, Find, Finest, Finish, Finished, Fire, Food, Forever, Four, From, Fulcrum, Full, Funny

Game, Gang, Gate, Give, Going, Gone, Grammar, Grass, Great, Green, Group

Hair, Happened, Happening, Happy, Hard, Hardly, Has, Hate, Have, Health, Help, Her, Here, Hesitating, High, His, Hole, Holy, Home, Hot, Houses, How, How come, Hut

Illustrated, I'm, Including, Increase, In spite of, Into, Isn't, It happened, It is, Its

Jax, Jerry, Just

Kid

Ladies, Lady, Laugh, Less, Let, Letter, Like, Little, Live, Look, Lost

Mad, Male, Matter, May, Meanwhile, Meat, Men, Mice, Middle, Mine, Miss, Mistake, Money, Monkey, More, Moreover, Most, Mother, Movie, Music, My, Myself

Nearly, New, Next, Niger, None, Nonetheless, No say, Not always, Not there, Not often, Not only, Not slow, Nut

Objection, Of, Office, Of it, Often, Oh, OK, On, Once, One, Or, Other, Otherwise, Other words, Over

Paint, Pass, Passage, Passed, Past, Picture, Pie, Piece, Pop, Possible, Prefer, President, Pretty, Prob, Puzzled

Quite

Rain, Rather, Ready, Really not, Reasons, Red, Reservation, Restriction, Restrictive, Right, Room, Rough, Round

Said, Salt, Same, Sat, Say, School, Scientist, Scold, Second, Seem, Seldom, Shall, She isn't home, She's, Should, Show, Sick, Sing, Sissy, Smart, Smell, Smoke, Somehow, Someone, Some people, Some place, Something else, Somewhat, Soon, Sorry, So what, Speech, Speak, Spell, Spelling, Spoken, Spring, State, Statement, Steel, Stop, Story, Strict, Subject, Such, Surely

Teacher, Teachers, Tease, Telephone, Tell, Telling, Test, Than, The day, Their, Them, The night, Things, Thorough, Those, Throughout, Thoughts, Throw, Thru, Till, Tired, Today, Togetherness, Tomorrow, Tonight, Tooth, Tough, Toward, Town, Train, Transition, Tree, Tried, Trouble, Trough, True, Trueness, Try, Tunnel, Twin, Two

Uncertain, Undecided, United, Unless, Us

Very

Wait, Want, Was, Wee, We eat, Week, Went, Were, What fore, Where, Where upon, Wherever, Whether, Which, While, Who cares, Whole, Wild, Will, Window, Winner, Wish, With, Without, Won't, Wood, Woods, Words, Work, World, Wow, Wrong

Ya, Yeah, Year, Yesterday, Yours

ALWAYS

A, About, Absent, Act, Adventures, Adverb, Al, Alike, All time, Alone, Along, Alot, Already, All right, Also, Always, Am, Amber, And, Angry, Any, Anywhere, Afraid, Are, Around, Aways

Back, Bad, Become, Been, Begin, Behind, Belong, Black, Book, Books, Bore, Bibles, Big, Bill, Birthdays, Boy, Boyfriend, Boys, Brothers, Busy, But, Buyer

Came, Card, Care, Careful, Cars, Certainly, Clean, Clear, Come back, Comes, Coming, Command, Completely, Consent, Consistent, Consistently, Continuously, Continual, Continually, Continue, Could, Cross, Cry, Custom

Dave, Day, Daylight, Days, Dear, Depend, Does, Dog, Dogs, Doll, Donny, Don't, Dose, Diamonds, Different, Direction, Down, Drink

Earth, Eat, End, Endeavor, English, Enough, Eternal, Eternally, Everlasting, Everything, Everywhere, Except

Fair, Fairy tale, Few, Following, Forevermore, Forget, Fight, Fighter, Fighting, Find, Finish, First, Fish, Frequently, Friend, Friends, From

Get, Goodby, Goodbye, Girl, Girls, Grass, Green, Guy

Had, Handy, Happen, Happening, Happens, Happy, Hay, He, Hear, Heaven, Help, Hers, Homework, House, High, How, Hurry

I, I always do good work, Immediately, In, Indefinite, In way, It

Just

Keeps, Kept, Know, Known, Kind, Kiss

Land, Lasts, Laugh, Lawful, Leave, Lone, Lot, Lots, Life, Light, Like, Live, Loving

Man, Marriage, May, Maybe, Mean, Men, Money, More, Most often, Most of the time, Most times, Mother, Move, Movie, Much, Music

Name, Nearly, Neat, Need, Night, Nimmer, None of the time, Not always, Noting, No ways, No where

O, Ocean, Omnipresent, On, Once, One, Only, On time, Over, Owl

Past, Peace, People, Perpetual, Persistent, Pet, Place, Places, Plane, Plant, Playing, Pleased, Positive, Positively, Prayer, Present, Promise, Put

Quick, Quickly

Rain, Rainy, Reader, Red, Regular, Remind, Road, Roads, Right away, Ring, Runaway, Running

Said, Samething, Sample, Saw, Say, Sea, Seashore, See, Seem, Seen, Sell, Semper, Sleep, Slow, Smart, Some place, Some thing, Songs, Sidewalk, Siempre, Sinatra, Sincere, Sincerely, Stars, Steak, Still, Stop, Store, Street, Streets, Such, Sudden, Sun, Sweetheart, Swimming

Talk, Tests, That, That way, Their, Them, They, Things, Think, This, Till, Times, Tired, Tree, Truly, To, Today, Tomorrow, Top, Tough, Toujours

Up, Use, Usual

Very

Wagon, Wait, Walk, Walk out, Walks, Water, Waves, Weekly Readers, Went, Work, What, Whenever, Where, Wherever, Whole, Win, Write

Yeah, Year, Yell, Yellow, Yet, Yours forever

AM

Able, About, Act, Aims, Ain't, A letter, All, Alone, Am, Amber, Ambition, Ambulance, Amen, Ammy, Am not, Ample, Ams, Amy, Angry, Another, Ant, Any, Apple, Arms, Army, Art, Asking, Aunt

Bam, Ban, Because, Become, Belong, Bigger, Bin, Black, Blame, Blue, Body, Bold, Book, Both, Bought, By

Cam, Came, Car, Cat, Catch, Certain, Certainly, Chair, Character, Cheer, Cheerful, Child, Christmas, Church, Clearer, Clever, Clock, Close, Coming, Contraction, Cow, Crack, Cut

Dam, Damm, Dead, Do, Dog, Done, Don't, Dry

Easy, English, Ever, Existence, Explaining

Fair, Far, Fast, Fine, Food, Fool, For, Forget, Foul, Four, Free, From, Funny

Ghosts, Girl, Glass, Glove, Go, God, Goes, Going to, Gone, Got, Grade, Grammar, Grass, Great, Gum, Guns

Had, Hammer, Hand, Hard, Have, Hear, His, Ho, Hoarse, Horse, Hoses, Hot, House, Hungry, Huts

If, I'll, Ink, Inn

Jam, Jonkh

Knock

Lake, Lamb, Leader, Legs, Letter, Like, Little, Live, Living, Lonesome, Long, Look, Looking, Louder, Love, Lovely, Lucky

Ma, Mad, Madame, Make, Male, Mam, Mind, Mother, Move, Much, Muscle, Must, My

Name, Nearly, Never, New, Night, No, Nothing, Nuts

Ohm, OK, Old, Only, Or, Ore, Out, Oven, Own

Pan, Pan American, Past, People, Perfect, Permanent, Personality, Pilot, Place, Pleasant, Positive, Prepare, Preposition, Present, Pretty, Put

Quick, Quiet, Quite

Ram, Real, Reply, Ride, Rifle, Right, Root

Sad, Saw, Say, School, Scout, Sea, Self, Sentence, Shall, Shame, Shoot, Short, Should, Shout, Si, Sigh, Sight, Silly, Sincerely, Singular, Slam, Slow, Small, Smart, Something, Sorry, Sour, Stand, Start, State, Statement, Stay, Staying, Strong, Student, Studying, Sure, Sweet

Talk, Tame, That, Them, Then, Thin, Thing, Think, Thinking, Three, Tom, Too, Too or also, True, Trying, Two

Um, Uncle, Under, Useful

Walking, Want, Way, Well, Went, Wet, When, Which, White, Who, Will be, Willing, Window, Winter, Women, Word after, Work, Working, Write, Writing

Yes, Young, Younger, Your

AN

About, Accident, Accordian, Ace, Acre, Add, Adjectives, Adventure, Adverb, Advertising, Afternoon, Again, A girl, Ain't, Air, All, Alphabet, Amateur, American, Andrew,

And sign, Angle, Annie, Anniversary, Anomaly, Ante, Antelope, Anvil, Ape, Apology, Apples, Apply, Apron, Arabian, Aren't, Arm, Armadillo, Army, Art, As, Ass, Attendance, Author, Automobile, Away, Awfully, Ax, Axe

B, Baby, Bad, Bear, Bed, Beet, Before, Beginning, Being, Bell, Besides, Bicycle, Big, Bike, Bird, Black, Blanket, Boat, Body, Boo, Boys, Butter, Buying

Cart, Certain, Children, Coat, Come, Coming, Continue, Contraction, Cool, Course, Cow

Dan, Date, Day, Did, Doe, Doll, Don't, Door, Dope, Double, Drink

Each, Easter, Eat, Else, Encyclopedia, Ending, Engine, English, Ennui, Episode, Erasure, Etc., Even, Evening out, Excellent, Exception, Exciting, Excuse, Eye

Fan, Father, Few, Fix, Floor, Flower, Food, For, Friend, From, Fun

Game, Get, Goat, Going, Good

Ha, Hair, Hand, Harmony, Has, Have, Heal, Hear, Heart, Hero, Hers, His, Hole, Huh

Icicle, Idea, Ill, Image, Imbecile, Important, Indian, Infant, Ink, Insect, Instrument, Interesting, Item, Its

Jane, Jill, Joe, Joke

Kite, Know

Land, Leave, Leg, Let, Letter, Life, Lion, Listen, Little, Look, Love

Make, Mary, Maybe, Mean, Met, Middle, Mine, Minute, Mom, Monkey, More, Mother, Mouse, Mrs. Jolly, Mug, Mush

Near, Nell, Nice, None, Not, Note, Nother, Nothing, Noun, Number, Nut

O, Oak, Oar, Objection, Object, Octopus, Off, Offering, Older, Onion, Only, Open, Opera, Order, Organ, Ostrich, Others, Ounce, Out, Outboard, Oven, Overpowering, Overture, Owl, Ox, Oyster

Party, Pay, People, Phone, Pick, Place, Plane, Play, Pop, Preposition, Pronoun, Purse

Quantity

Rabbit, Ran, Randy, Rat, Really, Reason, Red, Right, Run,

Said, Same, Sand, Saw, Schroeder, See, Self, Sell, Send, Sentences, She, Shock, Shoot, Should, Shout, Show, Sick, Single, Singular, Ski, Sloppy, Slouch, Snack, Sock, So forth, Some, Someone, Something else, Son, Soon, Speaking, Specific, Spelling, Spend, Star, Stick, Store, Surprise

Table, Talking, Tan, Teacher, Telephone, Television, Tell, Ten, Test, Think, Thought, Three, Threw, Thus, Time, Together, Tom, Toy, Tree, Truck, Twins, Two

Umbrella, Until, Unusual, Uproar, Us

Vowels

Waffle, Wall, Wam, Wan, Want, Was, Way, Were, When, White, Who, William, Women, Worm

Year, Yours

AND

Abbreviation, About, Above, Ad, Adjective, After, Ah, Almost, Along, Although, Am, And I said it, And sign, Another thing, Answer, Ant, Any, Anyhow, Are, Arithmetic, Around, Article, As, Aunt, Away

Baby, Back, Bad, Ball, Bear, Beauty, Beet, Began, Beginning, Behave, Being, Betty, Big, Bill, Boat, Boy, Boys, Bread, Breathe, Brother, Bud, By

Candy, Car, Clothes, Color, Coma, Compound, Conclude, Conj., Connect, Connection, Continuation, Continue, Continued, Continuing, Could, Could be, Cow, Crave, Cry

Dad, Dan, Desk, Did, Dog, Dogs, Doing, Done, Don't, Dumb

E. g., Elephant, Et cetera, Even, Every, Everything, Except, Expression

Fan, Far, Father, Finish, First, First grade, Fish, Food, Fore, Forever, From, Front, Fun

Get, Girl, Give, Gone, Got, Go to the store, Grab, Grammar

Had, Hair, Happen, Has, Hat, Have, Hello, Help, Hem, Hide, His, Home, Honk, Horse, Horses, Hot

I do, I'm, Include, Including, Inquire, Interjection, Its

Joe, John, Join, Jump, Just

Keeping, Kindness

Lamb, Land, Last, Later, Leave, Left, Less, Lets, Letter, Long

Mad, Make, Man, Mand, Many, March, Math, Maybe, Middle, Mine, Money, Monkey, Mother, Mouth, Movie

Naue, New, Next, Nice, Night, No more, None, Nor, Nothing

O, Occasion, Off, Oil, On, One, Only, Out, Over

Pan, People, Period, Person, Pie, Pig, Place, Play, Please, Pronoun, Put

Rand, Remember, Repeat

Sat, Saw, School, Schools, Sea, Sell, Send, Sentences, Sheep, Sign, Sing, Sister, Small, Some more, Someone, Something else, Sometime, Sometimes, Sours, Speech, Spelling, Stand, Start, Stay, Stop, Story, Stutter, Sue, Suppose, Sure

Talk, Teacher, Teeth, Than, Their, The last, Them, Thin, Things, Thou, Thought, Thoughtful, Through, Throw, Thy, Tie, Togetherness, Tom, Tree

Uh, Um, Uncle, Und

Walk, Want, Warm, Way, Whatever, Where, Will, Win, Without, Wood, Work, World

Yet, Your

ANGER

Ache, Actor, Afraid, Age, Airplane, America, And, Angel, Angels, Angle, Anguish, Animal, Ant, Anxiety, Argue, Argument, Arouse, At, Awful

Baby, Badness, Bad shot, Baseball, Bear, Beat, Beat up, Beautiful, Become, Bed, Bee, Better, Big, Bike, Bill, Bird, Bitter, Bitterness, Black, Blow up, Blush, Boiling, Book, Bottle, Boy, Boys, Brother, Brothers, Bull

Cake, Car, Cards, Carpet, Cat, Cause, Caution, Chance, Charm, Chart, Cheer, Cheerful, Child, Choir, Choleric, Christmas, Clam, Clean, Close, Coat, Comma, Command, Conflict, Confusion, Contempt, Contentious, Cool, Court, Crab

Dad, Dangerous, Dark, Darn boy, Death, Deep, Delight, Despair, Destruction, Detest, Disappointed, Disease, Disgusted, Dislike, Disposition, Disrupt, Disturbed, Disturbing, Dog, Dogs, Doll, Door, Dread

Eager, Eat, Eileen, Emotions, Enemies, Enemy, Excited, Expression, Extreme

Fake, Fast, Fat, Feeling, Feelings, Ferocity, Fiery, Fine, Firm, Fish, Fist, Flare, Flower, Flush, Flustered, Flying, Food, Fool, Forgiveness, Free, Frenzy, Friendly, Friendship, Frown, Fume, Fun, Funny, Funny face

Gaiety, Gay, Gentleness, Get, Ghost, Girl, Girls, Gladness, Go, Goal, God, Golf, Green, Gripe, Grouch, Grouchy, Growl, Grumpy, Guilt

Happily, Harp, Haste, Hat, Hateful, Hath, Haven, Head, Heart, Heat, Height, Her, Herald, Hi, High, High blood pressure, Hive, Holler, Hollo, Home, Homely, Horrid, Horrified, Horror, Hostility, Howard, Huffy, Humbug, Humor, Hungry

In anger, Insect, Ish, It

Jane, Jealous, Jealousy, Joyful, Justice

Karen, Kill, Kindness, Knife

Lad, Laugh, Laughing, Laughter, Leg, Level, Lightning, Lion, Listen, Little brother, Little kids, Lone, Loving

Machine, Madden, Mad look, Mad sad, Manger, Meanness, Men, Michele, Mike, Mild, Mind, Mine, Miss, Moaned, Mom, Monkey, Monster, Mood, More than, Mother-in-law, Mouth, Mr. Patterson, Mr. Roberts, Murder, Mystery

Name, Nasty, Naughty, Neat, Nervous, New, Niceness, Noise, Noisily, Noisy, Not, Not angry, Not mad, Not nice, Not round, Now, Nut

Obnoxious, One, Or, Outrageous, Over

Parents, Party, Peaceful, Pencil, Perturbed, Pillow, Pity, Plane, Pleasant, Pleased, Pleasure, Polite, Pretty thing, Pride, Provoke, Punish, Punishment, Purple, Purse

Quarrel, Quick, Quiet

Rag, Ranger, Rash, Red hair, Redness, Regret, Remorse, Resent, Respect, Response, Rid, Ridicule, Right, Roar, Rod Egen, Rough, Rumble, Russia

Sadness, Said, Sandy, Satiety, School, Scolding, Scorn, Self control, Serene, Severe, Sharon, Ship, Should, Sick, Side, Sight, Silent, Silly, Sin, Skin, Slap, Sleep, Slug, Smart, Smiling, Smooth, Soft, Solitude, Someone, Song, Sooth, Sore, Sorry, Spit, Star, Start, Steve, Stick, Stop, Strong, Stupid, Sugar, Sun, Swear, Sweet, Swift, Sympathy

Tantrum, Tantrums, Taught, Teacher, Teachers, Tear, Teeth, Temperament, Tempers, Tempter, Ten, Tense, Tension, Terrier, Terrified, Terror, The, Then, There, They, Thing, Thought, Thoughtfulness, Thoughts, Threat, Threaten, Threatening, Three, Throw, Throwing, Tired, To, Tom, Too, Tried, Trouble, Turn, Turtle

Ugly, Unhappiness, Unhappy, Unnecessary, Unnice, Unreasonableness, Used

Vase, Verse, Violence, Violent, Voice, Vulgar

Wait, Wants, War, Warmth, Watch, Water, Weakness, Weep, Wept, White, Window, Wings, Wit, Wolf, Woman, Women, Wonderful, Wood, Work, Worry, Wrath dad, Wrong

Yelling, Yes, Yesterday, You

APPEAR

A, Above, Absent, Add, Agree, Air, Airpower, Alive, All, Also, Am, And, Angels, Angry, Announce, Ants, Ape, Apparently, Apparition, Appeal, Appearing, Appears, Apples, Apply, Apprehend, Approve, Arise, Arms, Arose, Arrived, Assent, At home, Awake, Awful

Bat, Bear, Beauty, Became, Becomes, Bed, Begin, Behind, Behold, Belt, Beneath, Better, Big, Bill, Black, Blank, Blind, Blonde, Blurry, Book, Books, Bottle, Boy, Bride, Briefly, Bunch, By

Calm, Can, Can't, Carry, Cats, Child, Children, Christmas, Class, Closer, Clothed, Clothing, Cloud, Come forth, Come forward, Come out, Comes, Come to, Coming, Confront, Cool, Cot, Court, Cow, Cry, Cut

Dawn, Dear, Dilute, Dirty, Disappears, Dissolve, Distant, Dodo, Does, Don't, Door, Doorway, Dressed, Drowsy, Dumb

Easy, Eat, Eating, Envision, Erscheinen, Eye, Eyes

Faded, Faint, Fairy, Fangs, Fat, Fear, Feature, Fin, Fine, Flower, Focus, Food, Foot, Forgotten, Frequently, Fright, Front, Fun, Funny, Fuzzy

Ghosts, Ghost stories, Girls, Glance, Glass, Glasses, Glow, God, Graceful, Great, Green, Ground, Grow, Guilty

Hair, Hand, Handsome, Happened, Happier, Hat, Have, Hazy, He, Head, Healthy, Heard, Help, Her, Herd, Hi, Hid, Hide, High, Horizon, Hot, How

Ill, Imagination, Imagine, Immediately, In, In dress, Instant, Invisible man

Jack Paar, Jean, Jensen, Job, Judge, Jump

Know, Known

Lady, Large, Later, Lazy, Leprechaun, Less, Lest, Little, Lonely, Looked, Looking, Looks as if, Loose, Lose, Lost, Loud, Lousy, Lovable, Lovely, Lowly

Mad, Make, Make believe, Man, Marriage, Mask, Materialize, May, Mean, Menace, Mind, Mine, Minor, Moon, More, Mouse, Move, Movie, Music, My

Neatness, Need, Nervous, New, Nicely, Night, Nightly, Noise, Non appear, Not appear, Not here, Not there

Obscure, Odd, Off, Often, Oh, OK, Old, Older, Once, One, Out, Outdoors, Oven, Over

Pair, Paper, Pare, Part, Peace, Peak, Pears, Peep, Peer, Pen, People, Pepper, Performance, Perish, Persons, Pet, Phoney, Picture, Pig, Placed, Plainly, Play, Pleasant, Point, Poof, Presence, Produce, Public

Queer, Question, Quick, Quit, Quite

Rabbit, Read, Ready, Realize, Reappeared, Rear, Red, Relaxed, Remain, Restless, Ride, Ridiculous, Right, Rise, Rose

Sad, Sat, Satisfactory, Scared, Scene, Screen, Seat, Secret, Sees, Seldom, Sentence, Set, Sexy, Shape, Sharp, She, Shear, Shine, Shoe, Shoes, Should, Shoved, Shows, Show up, Shy, Sick, Silently, Silly, Slim, Slippers, Slop, Sloppy, Slowly, Smart, Smoke, Snow, Sociable, Someplace, Spear, Spirit, Spook, Stand, Stands, Star, Stars, Stay, Stood, Stop, Street, Subscribe, Subtract, Sudden, Sun, Surprise

Talk, Taste, TB, Teacher, Tear, Television, The, Them, They, Thing, Things, Think, Though, Tight, Time, Today, Together, To look like, To me, Tonite, Too, Took, Torn, To see, Transparent, Tree, True, Try, Turn up, Twins, Two

Unappear, Unappeared, Unclean, Unexpected, Unhappy, Unless, Upside, Us

Vanished, Very, Visualize

Warm, Watch, Wear, Weird, Welcome, Were, Wet, What, Which, White, Who, Will, Wind, Wish, Witch, Wonderful, Work

Yellow, Yes, You appear nice, Young

AS

About, Acknowledge, Adze, After, Ah, Alike, All, Along, Although, Any, Anyone, Apple, Asbestos, Ash, Asked, As not, As of, Asphalt, Asthma, As though

Back, Bad, Balloon, Base, Bass, Bat, Because of, Bed, Bee, Been, Being, Be quiet, Better, Bible, Big, Blank, Blue, Boy, Butt

Came, Cat, Cause, Certain, Child, Cig, City, Clean, Close, Compare, Comparing, Comparison, Condition, Conjunction, Contraction, Course

Dark, Demonstrate, Describe, Desk, Dew, Did, Different, Doing, Donkey, Don't, Don't know, Down

Easy, Either, End, English, Equal, Even, Every, Example, Exception, Explain

Facsimile, Fact, Fare, Flower, Fly, Food, Forever, Four, Friend, From, Fun

Glass, Goes, Gone, Gradually, Grammar, Grass

Happy, Hard, Have, Head, Her, Here, Hi, Hid, His, Hold, Hole, House, However

If I knew, I'm, In between, Introductory, I see it, Isn't, It is, Its

Jazz, Jim, Jump, Just then

Keep

Land, Leaf, Leave it, Letters, Likely, Little, Look, Lots, Love

Ma, Maine, Mama, Man, Mass, May, Maybe, Meanwhile, Moment, Mother, Must, My, Myself

Nail, Near, New, News, Next, No comment, Noise, North, Nothing

Off, Oh, Okay, Old, Once, Only, Opposed, Other, Others, Out, Over

Park, Pass, Past, Pay, Perhaps, Person, Play, Please, Plus, Prep, Preposition, Present, Pretend, Pronoun, Propeller, Purse

Quick, Quickly, Quit

Record, Red, Resemble, Result, Rhythm, Right, Right away, Roman, Run

Said, Same form, Saw, Say, Says, See, Seen, Sentence, Shall, Shoe, Shoes, Short, Show, Showers, Shown, Side, Sing, Small, Smoke, Somebody, Someone, Sometime, Speaking, Speech, Standard, Store, Stories, Stout, Street, Study, Suddenly, Sure, Sweet

Table, Taken, Talk, Talking, Tell, Telling, Text, Their, Therefore, Thou, Thought, Through, Tie, Time, Today, To-gether, Too, To that, Towards, Transmission, Trash, Two

Up, Usual, Ut

Verb

Walking, Want, Way, Well, Went, Which, Whom, Will, Wonder, Wood, Words, Working, Would, Wrong

Yes, Yet, You are, Your, Yourself, You see

AT

Above, Across, Act, Add, Adult, After, Against, Aim, Along, Also, Alter, Always, Am, Among, An, Anyplace, Anywhere, A place, Are, Aren't, Art, As, Ask, At a place, Atlas, At someone's house, Attack, Attend, Attention, Attic, Attica

Back, Bad, Ball, Bats, Beach, Bed, Begin, Beginning, Behind, Beside, Big, Book, Both, Boulevard, Boy, Brushes, Bulbs, Bunch, Bus

Call, Came, Car, Cats, Church, Circus, Corner, Cost, Cousins

Dawn, Dayton's, Do, Dog, Dogs, Doll, Don't, Down, Dusk

Ease, English, Even, Everyone

Fall, Family, Far, Fast, Find, First, Foot, Friend, Friends

Game, Get, Girl, Goes, Good, Got, Grandma, Grandma's

Had, Hand, Have, He, Her, Hi, Hide, Homes, Houses, How

I, If, Ill

Lake, Landmark, Large, Lat, Least, Letter, Location, Long, Look, Lunch

Mail, Man, Many, Maps, Mary's, Mate, Mean, Meat, Met, Mint, Money, Most

New York, Nine, No, Noon, Nut

OK, One, Our, Out, Own

Park, Pat, Peace, People, Play, Point, Position, Pronoun, Put

Reader, Reason, Relatives, River, Round, Rum

Said, Sale, Salesman, Seen, Sell, Sentence, Shell, Short, Shot, Side, So, Someone, Something, Soon, Spat, Spelling, Still, Stop, Story, Sundown

Table, Tack, Tell, Ten, That's, The house, The word, They, Three, Through, Throw, Tick, Too, Towards, Town, Trip, Two

U, Under, Up, Us

Verb, Visit, Visiting

Went, Wet, Which, Whom, Why, Within

Yell, Yet, Your

Zoo

BABY

Adorable, Allen, Animals

Babe, Babies, Baby sit, Baby sitter, Ball, Barbara, Bath, Beads, Beauty, Becky, Bib, Big, Billy, Birth, Blankets, Bobby, Body, Bonnet, Boo, Book, Bother, Bottles, Boy or girl, Boys, Breast, Brenda, Brian, Bundle, Bunting, Butch, By

Care, Carol, Carry, Cheryl, Child and love, Chris, Cigar, Close, Cow, Crawl, Cribs, Cried, Cuteness

Daddy's, Dave, Dave Lindberg, David, Day, Delicate, Dicky, Doctor, Doug, Dribble

Face Nelson, Fall, Fat, Fish, Fragile, Friend, Funny

Giant, Giggles, God, Gone, Goo-goo, Greg, Ground, Grow, Grown-up, Grown-ups, Gurgle

Ha, Happiness, Hat, Hate, He, Heat, Him, Hold, Holding, Home, Homely, Hugging, Human being, Hurt, Husband

Innocence, Innocent, It

Jackie, Janet, Jesus, John, John Olsen, Juvenile

Karen, Kathy, Kind

Lady, Lamb, Laugh, Lay, Learn, Life, Like, Likeable, Linda, Litter, Little and cuddly, Little child, Little cousin, Little kid, Little one, Lori, Lotion, Lovable, Lovely, Lullaby

Mama, Man woman, Many, Married, May, Mess, Michael, Mike, Milk, Mine, Mischief, Misery, Mommy, Mon, Money, Moon, Mouth, My brother, My cousin

Name, Nancy, Nephew, New born, Nice to have, Nine months, No, Noisy, Noon, Nose, Nursery, Nut, Nuts

Oh, Oil, Old, One, Our baby sleeping

Parent, Pat, Paul, Peter, Picture, Pin, Play, Playful, Play pen, Pleasant, Powder, Power, Precious

Quiet, Quit, Quite

Rabbit, Ralph, Rattles, Rest, Ricky, Riddle, Robin, Rock, Ron, Ronnie, Roommate

Sand, School, Sex, She, Shelly, Shoe, Shoes, Shoot, Shrimp, Sing, Sit, Small kid, Smile, Smiley, Smoke, Smooth, Snooks, Softness, Soft small, Soft sweet, Someone, Son, Sort, Spot, Steven, Stomach, Such, Sue, Sweetness

Talk, Tears, Teeth, Thing, Time, Toes, Tooth, Tranquility

Ugly, Underwear, Up

Waaaaa, Warm, Warmth, Wee, Weiner, Wet, White, Wife, Window, With, Wonderful, Word

Youth

BATH

Acts, Age, Alive, At, Ate

Baby, Bano, Bar, Bass, Bat, Bathed, Bathesphere, Bathing, Bath salts, Bath water, Beauty, Beth, Bird, Both, Boy, Breath, Brush, Bubble bath

Call, Care, City, Cleaness, Clean feeling, Cleaning, Clear, Close, Cloth, Cologne, Comforting, Cook

Date, Day, Deep, Deodorant, Do, Dog, Down, Dress, Drink, Dry

Ears, Eat

Faucet, Fight, Filth, Flower, Foam, Food, Fragrant, Freshness, Friday, Fun

Gas, Gay, Get, Get clean

Hair, Hard, Hat, Hate, Have, He, Head, Healthy, Help, Helps, Home, Hound

Ick, Ish

June

Keen

Lady of, Lake, Land, Laughed, Light, List, Long

Math, Me, Metal, Minister, Mon, Morning, Mother

Need, Night, Nightly, No like, Note, Nut

Ocean, Oh, Out

Pan, Peg, People, Plastic, Play, Pool

Quick

Radio, Refresh, Relax, Rest, Restful, Robe, Rooms

Salt, Salts, Sat, School, Scum, Sea, See, Shop, Show, Showers, Sitting, Sleep, Smell, Soak, Soaking, Soap bubbles, Soap suds, Soft, Song, Soothing, Soup, Sour, Spell, Steam, Suds, Sudsy, Sun, Supper, Sweat, Sweet, Swimming, Swimming hole

Table, Taking, Talk, Terrible, The, Tile, Toilet, Top, Turkish

Walk, Wars, Wash good, Watch, Water and tub, We, White, Women, Wonderful, Won't, Wrap

Yellow, You

BEAUTIFUL

Admirable, Agate, A girl, Alone, Anger, Angry, Animals, Awesome, A woman

Baby, Ball, Banner, Be, Beast, Beaut, Beauteous, Bed, Birds, Birds sing, Black, Blind, Blonde, Blonde hair, Blouse, Body, Book, Books, Boy, Boys, Brave, Bride, Brown, Bug, Build-ing, Butter

Cake, California, Camping, Cars, Cat, Chair, Cheryl, Chick, Cinderella, Clean, Clear, Cloth, Clouds, Cold, Colorado, Colored, Colors, Come, Complexion, Connie, Contest, Country, Country side, Creative, Cross, Crumb, Crummy

Damask, Darling, Dear, Diamond, Diamonds, Diane, Dingy, Dirty, Dogs, Draw, Dreamer, Dreamy, Dump, Dwight

Eagle, Easy, Eliz Taylor, Enjoy, Envious, Ethics, Evergreen,

Evergreens, Everything, Exquisite

Face, Fair, Fairy, Fine, Fish, Flabbergasted, Flag, Food, Force, Forest, Forests, Friend, Fruit

Garden, Gay, Gayful, Gentle, Gift, Girlfriend, Glad, Glamorous, Glorious, Go, God, Gold, Golden, Good looks, Goofy, Gown, Gracious, Grand, Grass, Great, Green, Greens, Gully

Happy, Hat, Heat, Heaven, Her, Hills, Him, Hit, Horrid, Horses

Icky, Ish, Ishy

Jayne Mansfield, Joan

Kathy, Kind, Kiss, Kitten

Lace, Lacy, Lad, Ladies, Land, Landscape, Lavender, Leg, Like, Little, Lonely, Long, Look, Look good, Looking, Lora, Loveliness

Madonna, Magnificent, Maine, Majestic, Man, Manner, Mary, Meadow, Mean, Men, Mess, Mess up, Mice, Mine, Mink, Miss, Model, Mom, Money, Moon, Morning, Movie, Movie star, Mt., My, My country, My dog

Nancy, Nice looking, Niece, Night, No, No good, Nose, Not beautiful, Not ugly

Ocean, Ohio, Old, One, Ought, Out of doors, Outside

Pale, Pants, Party, Pat, People, Pink, Plain, Pleasant, Poised, Poor, Precious, Prettier, Putter

Quite

Radiant, Rain, Rainbow, Relative, Restful, Ribbon, Right, Ring, Roberta, Room, Rotten, Ruti

Sad, Sand, Sandi, Sandy, Satisfying, Scarf, Sea, See, Shadow, Sharon, She, She's, Shining, Shiny, Shoes, Sick, Sight, Skating, Slow, Smart, Smile, Smooth, Snowflake, Snow White, So, Something, Something pretty, Sorrow, Splendid, Spoon, Spring, Star, Stars, Stay, Strange, Stream, Striking, Strong, Stunning, Sun, Swan, Sweaters

Tender, Terrible, The, Thing, Things, Think, Tress

Ugh, Unbeautiful, Unbelievable, Under, Unicorn

Valley, Vase, Venice, Venus, Very, Very good, Very nice

Wait, Warm, Waterfall, Waterfalls, We, Weather, White, Wild, Wish, World, Wow

Year, Yellow, Young, Young girl

BECAUSE

A, Accident, Advise, Afraid, After, After all, Again, Alibi, Along, Already, Alright, Alternative, Although, Am, An, Another, Answered, Answers, Ant, Anything, Appeal, Apple, Are, Around, As if, Ask, Away

Bad, Been, Bees, Begin, Be gone, Being, Believe, Belong, Be not, Beside, Bet, Better, Between, Beware, Blue, Boat, Book, Bought, Broke, Brown, Bug, Bump, Bus

Canoe, Car, Cat, Causation, Certain, Chile, Chose, Clause, Coming, Comma, Condition, Conj., Connection, Consequence, Consequently, Convict, Could, Couldn't, Course, Cry

Davis, Death, Definition, Desk, Destiny, Didn't, Disease, Dog, Dogs, Done, Do not, Don't know, Don't known, Doubt, Dress, Due to

Earth, Else, End, English, Etc., Even though, Ever, Except, Excuses, Exist, Expect

Fact, Faint, Fast, Fear, Feel, Fight, Finish, Flower, For a while, Forever, Forget, Forgot, Found, Friend, From

Girl, Go, Going, Gone, Goodbye

Handsome, Happen, Hard, Has, Have to, Heck, Hello, Her, Here, Hesitation, Hi, Him, His, Horse, Hot, How come, Hurry

I like you because you're nice, In, In as much as, I no, In other words, Instead, Intelligence, Isn't, Its, It's that way, I want to

Jeeps, Just because

Late, Laugh, Let, Letters, Lie, Like, Little, Long, Look, Lots

Mad, Making, Man, Manger, Many, Matter, May, Means, Might, Mike, Mine, Mother, Mouse, Murder, Music, Muss, Must

Naturally, News, Nit, None, Nostril, Not because, Nothing, Nuts

Of course, Off, Of it, Of it he got into trouble, Often, OK, Ole, On account, Once, Order, Or else, Otherwise, Ouch, Own

Park, People, Person, Pig, Place, Plan, Please, Plus, Positive, Pro, Promise

Reading, Really, Rease, Red, Riding, Right, River, Rules, Run, Running

Sad, Said so, Salty, Saw, Say, School, Second, Sent, Seven, She wanted it, Should, Shouldn't, Sick, Side, Simply, Sing, Slow, Smart, Snotty, Soft, Sometime, Sometimes, Soon,

So that, So what, Speed, Spelling, Statement, Still, Store, Street, Stutter, Such, Suggestion, Suppose, Sure, Swim

Table, Talk, Telling, Than, That's, That's why, That way, Their, Them, Thing, Things, Thinking, Those, Thought, Throw, Time, To do, Told, Too, Trouble, Truck, True, Try, Tubs

Uncertain, Until, Us

Verb, Very

Ware, Went, Were, Where, Whereas, While, Who, Why not, Will, With, Woman, Words, Work, Write

You're, Yours

BECOME

Able, About, Accustomed to, Accustomed, Achieve, Active, Actor, Actress, Addict, Adjusted, Adult, Advance, After, Again, Age, Aged, Aggravated, Agree, Ahead, Aid, Air, Alike, Alive, All, Almost, Along, Already, Also, Always, Ambition, Ambitious, A member, An, Anger, Angry, Animal, Animals, Annoyed, Another, Anxious, Ape, Apparent, Approach, Approximate, Aren't, Around, Arrived, Artist, Assume, Astronomer, At, A tiger, Attractive, Away

Baby, Bat, Beauty, Became is, Became teacher, Bee, Been, Bees, Beget, Begin, Beginning, Behave, Behold, Believe, Belong, Below, Besides, Beyond, Bigger, Bird, Board, Bored, Born, Brave, Bright, Broader, But

Came in, Can't, Cat, Cause, Chained, Changed, Changing, Child, Citizen, Clean, Close, Clothes, Club, Cold, Come as, Comely, Comes, Comfortable, Continue, Cow, Crazy, Create, Created, Cuase, Cute

Dark, Deaf, Dentist, Descend, Didn't, Die, Dig, Dirty, Disappeared, Disappointed, Distract, Dog, Done, Don't know, Do something, Down, Dragon, Dress, Due, Duke, Dumb

Earth, Easy, Eat, Educated, Elephant, Eligible, Emerge, End, Ends, Engaged, Engineer, Enter, Exception, Excuse, Existence, Eye

Fact, Fade, Fail, Fairy tale, Faker, Familiar, Fan, Far, Farm, Fascinated, Fatter, Fiend, Finally, Find, Finish, Finished, Firm, First, Fit, Five, Flat, Flatter, Flatters, Flower, Fluid, Flyer, For, Former, Fourth, Free, Friend, Fun, Funny, Furniture

Gang, Girls, Give, Goal, Goes, Going to be, Good looking, Got, Graduate, Green, Grown, Grown-up, Growth, Guiet, Gun

Had, Happens, Hazard, Hazy, Health, Healthy, Heavy, Hero, Hers, High, Himself, Hired, His, Hold, Homesick, Hopeless, Horse, How, Hum, Human, Hummy, Hurry, Hurt, Husband, Hysterical

Icing, I don't know, If, I'm, Immuned, Important, Improve, Income, Increase, Inherit, Inquire, Instant, Interested, Invalid, Involved, Its

Jerk, Join, Just

Kid, Kill, Kind, Knew, Know

Lady, Land, Larger, Late, Later, Lava, Lawyer, Lazy, Learn, Legend, Let, Lets, Lie, Life, Lift, Live, Lonely, Lonesome, Long, Longer, Looking, Look nice, Loose, Lose, Lost, Loud, Louder, Lovely, Low, Lucky

Magic, Manage, Marriage, Master, Mature, May, Maybe, Mean, Member, Might, Mild, Misty, Model, Mold, Money, Monster, More, Moron, Mother, Must

Name, Nauseated, Near, Neater, Neighbor, Nervous, Never, Next, Nicer, Noise, None, Non-fiction, Note, Nothing, Notice, Noun, Numb, Nun

Obtain, Off, Of it, Oh, OK, On, Originate, Origin, Over, Overcome, Overnight

Painter, Part, Pass, Peaceful, People, Persons, Pilot, Place, Please, Pleasing, Popular, Poser, Position, Presence, Present, Presented, Priest, Profession, Progress, Prominent, Put, Put down

Quiet, Quit

Reach, Real, Realize, Reason, Red, Result, Results, Run

Same, Satisfied, Saw, Say, Seen, Sensible, She, Sheep, Shoes, Shoot, Should, Show, Shy, Shyer, Silent, Silly, Skater, Slim, Slower, Smaller, Soft, Softer, Soldier, Somebody, Sometime, Somewhere, Sooner, Sour, Stable, Stand, Stand out, Star, State, Stiff, Still, Stood, Stop, Stopped, Stranded, Strive, Strong, Stronger, Student, Stupid, Style, Success, Successful, Sudden, Suddenly, Surprise, Sweeter

Take, Tall, Tangle, Teacher, Ten, That, Their, Thing, Things, Think, Thinner, This, Those, To come, To go, To me, Tomorrow, Too, Torn, Transformed, Tried, True, Try, Turned, Two

Unbecoming, Understand, Unhappy, Until, Up, Upset, Us
Vaccinated, Victorious, Visible, Visit
Want, Warm, Way, We, Weak, Wealth, Wealthy, Well, Wet,
    What happened, What he, What's, Who, Wife, Will come,
    Window, Wish, Witch, With, Within, Woman, Worried,
    Would
Yet, Young, Younger, You're, Yours, Yourself

BED

Ahhhh, A place to sleep
Baby, Bad, Bed bug, Bed clothes, Bed love, Bed spread, Bed
    time, Bell, Bellow, Blue, Bouncy, Bowl, Bracelet, Bread,
    Brick, Buggy, Bunk, By
Child, Children, Circle, Clean, Cloth, Clothes, Cold, Cot, Cozy,
    Crackers, Cradle, Crib, Crumby
Dark, Dead, Deed, Desk, Diver, Doctor, Door, Double, Drawer
Early, Electric blanket, Exhaustion
Feather, Feathers, Feed, Fellow, Fer, Fire, Flat, Fluffy,
    Food, Four poster, Frost, Fun, Fun with girl
Gee, Geno, Girls, Glass, Go, Good night, Ground, Guess
Hand, Have, Hay, Help, Hen, Hope, Horse, Hot
Ick, It
Jonkh, Joy, Jump, Jungle
Lad, Lake, Lamp, Large, Lead, Leg, Legs, Lie down, Life,
    Linens, Lines, Little, Long, Loud, Lounge, Lying
Made, Make, Mate, Me, Mine, Mink, Mit, Money, Movie, Music,
    My
Nap, Narrow, Need, News, Night time
OK
Person, Pillows, Place, Place to sleep, Play, Pleasure, Pole
Quiet
Read, Rectangle, Relaxation, Relaxing, Rock, Rug, Run
Sack, Said, School, Sh, Sickness, Side, Sit, Slap, Sled, Sleepi-
    ness, Slept, Slippers, Slumber, Smooth, Snore, Snow, Snug,
    Sofa, Soft comfortable, Sold, Some, Sores, Speed, Spring,
    Springs, Square, Stead, Steel, Steep, Story, Sun
Ted, Ten o'clock, The, Tonight
Utility
Warmth, Wet, What, Whip, Why, Window, Wood, Worn

BIBLE

Able, A book, About God, Adam, A good book, Always, Ancient,
    Around, Atheist, Atheists
Baby, Bad, Balloon, Be, Believe, Best, Best book, Bib, Bible
    stories, Big, Black and gold, Black book, Blasphemy, Book
    about God, Book mark, Books, Boy, Bread, Bubble, Bust
Came, Christian, Christianity, Church book, Comfort, Command-
    ment, Commandments, Comments, Cover, Creation, Cross
David, Desk, Devotion, Do, Donkey
E. Gantry, Eternity
Fable, Fear, February, Fraud, Full of truth like
Genesis, Girl, Glad, Glory, Go, God and his love, God Jesus,
    God's book, Gold, Golden rule, Good book, Goodness, Gospel,
    Gospels, Great, Great book, Guesses, Guide, Gush
Ha, Heaven, Hell, Help, Helpfulness, Hi, Him, Hold, Holiness,
    Holy book, Home, Honor, Hope
I, Important, Inspiration, Inspiring
Jacob, Jehovah, Jerusalem, Jesus is the Son, Jews, Jo, Job,
    John, Just, Justice
King James, Kiss, Knowledge, Koran
Lamp, Large, Law gospel, Laws, Legend, Lesson, Letters,
    Liable, Library, Light, Like, Literature, Long, Lovely
Marker, Mass, Masses, Matthew, Me, Mean, Meat, Meditation,
    Memory, Mention, Missal, Morals, My, Myth
Name, Neat, Necessary, New, News, Night stand, None, Novel
OK, Old, Old Testament
Page, Pages, Parable, Part, Passage, Pay, Peace, People, Pious,
    Playing, Prayer book, Prayers, Praying, Preach, Preacher,
    Precious, Propaganda, Prophet, Prophets, Prose
Question, Quiet
Reading, Red, Region, Religious book, Religious training, Remem-
    brance, Reverence, Reverend, Reverent, Ribbon, Ridiculous,
    Right, Righteous, Ritual, Ruth
Sad, Said, Salvation, Satisfaction, Scripture, Scriptures, Silly,
    Sing, Sixty-six books, So, Sock, Spelling, Store, Story of God,
    Stove, String, Sunday School, Sunday School book, Swear,
    Synagogue
Table, Tale, Tales, Talk, Talmud, Teach, Tell, Temple, Ten
    Commandments, Testimony, The, They, Thing, Think, Time,
    Told, Torah, Two

Very
Water, Wish, Word of God, Work, Worship, Writing, Wrong
Yellow, You

BITTER

Alive, Almond, Almonds, A nut, Arctic, Ash, Asparagus,
    Aspirin, Ate
Baby, Bad date, Badder, Bad food, Bad taste, Baking chocolate,
    Bead, Bear, Beat, Bed, Belt, Berry, Best, Birch, Bird,
    Biting, Bitterly, Bitters, Bittersweet, Black, Blue, Blurt,
    Boy, Boys, Brandy, Brown, Bud, Buttermilk
Calm, Candy chocolate, Caraway, Caster oil, Chair, Champagne,
    Child, Children, Choice, Choke cherries, Crunchier, Ciga-
    rettes, Clean, Cocoa, Colder, Cooking, Cooking chocolate,
    Crab apple, Crabby, Cranberry, Cream, Crime, Crisp, Cross,
    Cup, Cynic
Dandelion, Dark, Dead, December, Different, Disappointment,
    Disappointed, Distasteful, Do, Dog, Dr. Rossel, Dry, Dull
Earth, Easy, Eating, End, Even, Ex-lax, Experience, Expression
Face, Fair, Far, Fast, Fear, Feelings, Fight, Filling, Fish,
    Flat, Flinch, Fly, Frown, Fuming, Fun
Gall, Garlic, Gay, Geno, Get, Glad, Grape, Grapes, Grass,
    Green, Green apple
Ham, Hammer, Happiness, Hardened, Harmony, Hateful,
    Health, His, Hitter, Homework, Honor, Horrid, Horse,
    Horse radish, Hostility, Hot, House, Hunger, Hydro-ride
Israel
Janet, Joy, Juice, Jump, Junk
Kind, Knife
Lack, Lad, Lemons, Lemon sour, Lime, Lime water, Liquor,
    Litter, Little, Long, Look, Lovely
Made, Madness, Make, Mankind, May, Melt, Memories, Memory,
    Men, Mice, Mild, Milk, Mind, Minute, Misunderstood, Mitter,
    Mixer, Molasses, Mouth, Mrs. O'Connell, Mustard, My
Nasty, Naughtier, No, No good, Nonsweet, Nose, Not, No taste,
    Not like, Not nice, Not so much, Not tasty, Nut, Nuts
Odd, OK, Old, On, Onion, Ouch, Outlook
Pain, Pat, Peaches, Peach seed, Peanut hearts, Pear, People,
    Pepperoni, Person, Pessimist, Phosphate, Pill, Plant, Plate,
    Poor, Pop, Pucker
Radish, Resent, Resentful, Rhubarb, Roar, Romance
Sadness, Sage, Salivia, Salty, Sandwich, Sauce, Sauerkraut,
    Saw, Screw, See, Sharp, Sick, Sit, Slime, Small, Smell, Smoke,
    Smooth, Soar, Soda, Softness, Sore, Sorrow, Sorrowful,
    Sorry, Soup, Sour cream, Sourer, Sour milk, Spicy, Spinach,
    Spit, Start, Step, Stern, Sticky, Stings, Store, Stove, Sue,
    Sugar, Sure, Sweetened, Sweeter, Syrup
Table, Taffy, Tang, Task, Taste awful, Tasteful, Tastes, Tasting,
    Tea, Tears, Teeth, Temper, Tender, Terribly, Test, Than,
    Thing, Things, Thirst, This, Thought, Tight, Timber, Tin,
    Titter, To, Tomato, Tongue, Torn, Tough, Tub
Ugh, Unhappy, Unpleasant, Unsweeten, Unsweetened, Up
Vanilla, Vanilla flavoring, Vodka
Warm, Wasp, Water, Weak, Well, What, Winter, Witch, Women,
    Wood, Words, Worse, Wrong, Wry
Yeast, Yellow, You

BLACK

Abyss, A cave, Ace, A color, Alley, Ate
Bag, Ball, Bark, Bat, Bear, Beatnik, Beauty, Bee, Big, Bird,
    Black, Black board, Black paper, Blow, Blown, Book, Boot,
    Bottom, Box, Boy, Broad
Cape, Carpet, Cave, Cavern, Child, Clear, Close, Clothes,
    Collar, Colorless, Cotton, Cow, Crayon, Crow, Curtains
Dale, Dan, Danger, Dark car, Dark color, Dark room, Dark
    very dark, Dart, Day, Dead, Depth, Devil, Door, Dot, Dreary,
    Duck, Dull
Eat, Eats, Empty, Evil, Eye
Face, Fear, February, Fight, Front
Gangster, Gloomy, Gloves, Go, Goat, Gold, Grass, Grave, Grease
Hard, Head, Hear, Hearse, Heavy, Hole, Hook, Horror, Hot,
    House, Houses, Hut
Ink, Insecure, Ish
Jack, Jacket
Kitten
Lack, Lamb, Large, Leather, Like, Lock, Lonely, Lost, Love it
Mad, Make, Mean, Meat, Monkey, Montana, Morbid, Mother,
    Mountain, Mouse, Mr. Black, Mud, Mysterious
Nack, Nice, Noise, Not, Nun
Old, Open, Orange, Our, Out

Pack, Paint, Pants, Paper, Park, Paul, Pencil, People, Piano keys, Pig, Pit, Pitch, Place, Preacher, Purple
Ribbon, Rich, Right
Sad colors, Sake, Satin, Scare, Sea, Shade, Sharon, Sharp, Sheet, Shiny, Shirt, Shoe, Shoes, Sick, Sin, Sky, Slacks, Sleep, Smoke, Smooth, Soft, Soot, Sorrow, Space, Spooky, Square, Stone, Storm, Stove, Street, Suit
Table, Tack, Tar, Teacher, There, Thing, Through, Thursday, Too dark, Tree, Trees
Ugly, Umbrella
Very
Wait, Warm, Water, What, Which, While, Widow, Wife, With, Wool, Write
Yard

Pain, Painting, Pale, Pansy, Pants, Pastel, Pay, Peace, Peaceful, Pen, Picasso, Pine, Plane, Plate, Pleasant, Pleasing
Racer, Rainbow, Record, Red and white, Relaxing, Rest, Restful, Ribbon, Ridge, Ripple, River, Ronnie, Room, Rooms, Rug
Sadness, Scarf, Scarab, Scheme, Seat cover, Shade, Shoe, Shoes, Sick, Silver, Ski, Skies, Snow, Soap, Something, Song, Sore, Sorrow, Sorry, Space, Sparrow, Stair, Star, Steel, Story, Straight, Streak, Stripes, Sue, Suit, Sun, Sweet
Tango, Tears, Terrance, Texture, The, Tie, Tired, To, Train, Trouble, True, Two
Uniform
Vase, Veins, Velvet, Violets
Wall, Walls, Wedding, Wind, Window
Yes, Yonder, You, Your

BLOSSOM

Afraid, Air, Am, Animal, Anything, Appearance, Apple and peach, Apple trees, Arm, Ask
Baby, Bar, Be, Bean, Beauty flower, Bee, Bees, Berry, Big, Bird, Birds, Blooming, Blow, Bob, Body, Boom, Boss, Branch, Break, Breast, Bring, Bubble gum, Buds, Bug, Bulb, Burst, Bus, Bush, But, Butter, Buzzy
Cabbage, Can, Cattle, Cheese, Cherries, Cherry blossoms, Child, China, Close, Colorful, Come out, Country, Cow, Crown, Cuff
Daisy, Dandelion, Dearie, Deary, Deck, Dew, Die, Do, Dream
Falls, Fat, Fell, Field, Fields, First, Fish, Five, Flow, Flower bed, Flower bud, Flowered, Flowery, Fog, Follow, For, Fragile, Fragrant, Fresh, Friend, Fun
Garden, Go, God, Green, Grow
Hair, Hard, Hat, He, High school, Hot
In
Japan, Junk
Kid, Knife
Lake, Leaf, Leave, Life, Like a petal, Lilacs, Lily, Little, Long, Lose, Lost, Lotus, Loud, Love, Lovely
Maybe, Mean, Men, Money, Moon, Moon glory, Mother, Mouse, Music
Nature, Needed, New, News, Nice
Oh, OK, Old, On, Open, Orange juice, Orange trees, Orchards, Orchid, Out, Own
Part, Party, Peach, Pear, People, Perfume, Petals, Petty, Petunia, Plants, Play, Plum, Preachers, Pulps, Purple, Putter
Queen
Rain, Reddest, Rose bud, Roses
Sad, See, Seed, Sell, Set, Skunk, Small, Smells, Smile, Some, Speared, Spread, Start, Stink
Thief, Thing, Tom, Tow
Ugly, Up
Vegetables, Violet
Weather, Wilt, Wind, Wither, Woman, Wonderful, Work, Worm
Yeast

BLUE

A, A color, Aloof, Amethyst, Angels, Anger, Angle, Angry, Aqua, Army, Art, Away, Azure
Back, Balloon, Bark, Beautiful, Beautiful color, Beauty, Bedroom, Berries, Best, Bike, Blanket, Bleach, Bless, Block, Blow, Blueberry, Bluebird, Blue water, Bluing, Body, Bowl, Bruise, Bugged, Bugle
Calm, Cap, Cat, Cheese, Clear, Clouds, Collar, Colorful, Corvette, Craft, Crayon, Cry
Dared, Dark blue, Day, Dead, Deep, Denim, Dependable, Depressed, Depression, Dew, Door, Down sad, Dreary, Due, Dull, Dye
Eagle, Eagles, Envy, Eye
Face, Favorite color, Feeling, Feelings, Feet, Flight, Flowers, Food, Foot, From, Fun, Fungi
Girls, Gloomy, Glory, Glue, Going, Good color, Gorgeous, Gown, Grass, Grotto
Happy, Hay, Haystack, Her, High, Hill, Honor, Horizon, Hot
Indigo, Ink, Is, It, Ivory
Jacket, Jay, Jean, Joy
Lace, Land, Leaving, Light blue, Light dark, Little, Little Boy Blue, Lonesome, Long, Love, Lovely
Man, Margarine, Material, Me, Meet, Melancholy, Mild, Mist, Mother
Navy and Angles, New, Night, No, North, Nose, Note, Now
Ox

BOY

A, Active, Adolescent, Adventurer, Adventurous, Airplane, Anger, Animal, Animals, Arm, Athletic, Athletics, Awkward
Bard, Barefoot, Basketball, Bat, Beanie, Bee, Being, Bill, Blond, Boat, Boats, Bob, Bobby, Bold, Bolts, Books, Both, Box, Boy, Boyfriend, Boy Scout, Brain, Brat, Bright, Brought, Brown, Buddy, By
Candy, Cap, Cat, Children, Chuck, Church, Clod, Clothes, Clumsy, College, Considerate, Country lad, Cousin, Cow, Craig, Crazy, Cry
Dad, Dark, Darrone, Deer, Denny, Dick, Dirt, Do, Dogs, Don, Donkey, Doug
Eagle, Eleven, Eyes
Farm, Fast, Fat, Father, Feet, Female, Fight, Fighting, Fights, Fish, Flag, Flight, Foot, Football, Frank, Freckles, Friends, Frog, Frogs, Funny
Games, Garland, Gary, Gentlemen, Girl love, Glasses, Go, Good news, Great, Gun, Guy, Guys, Gym
Hair cut, Hand, Hands, Happy, Hard, Hate, He, Heard, Hello, Herman, Hokey, House, Husband
Infant, Innocence, Intelligent, Interest, Is, Ish, It
Jack, Jacket, James, Jean, Jerry, Jim, Jimmy, Job, John, Joy, Juvenile, Juvenile delinquent
Kiss, Kite
Lady, Large, Larry, Last, Laughing, Leg, Legs, Lollipop, Long, Long hair, Looks, Loves girl
Mail, Man brat, Marbles, Mark, Marriage, Marry, Masculine, May, Mike, Mischief, Mischievous, Mitten, Money, Monster, Mood, Mother, Mud, Muddy feet, My, Myself
Name, Native, Neat, Nephew, News, Nice and handsome, Nothing, Now, Nuts
Oh, OK, On, One, Outdoors, Outside
Paints, Pal, Party, Pat, Paul, Persons, Playful, Playing, Power, Pretty, Punk, Pupil
Ran, Ray, Read, Red, Rest, Rocks, Rod, Romance, Ron, Rugged
Sam, School, Scouts, Set, Shirts, Short, Short hair, Sight, Six year old child, Slacks, Sling shot, Snakes, Snowball, Soldier, Somebody, Someone, Sport, Standing, Steve, Stones, Street, Stubborn, Student, Stupid, Sweater, Sweet, Sweetheart, Swift, Swim
Tail, Teenager, Terry, Tie, Time, Tom, Tommy, Tough, Toys, Tree, Trike, Truck
Ummm, Unmature
Wagon, Was, Watch, Whistle, Why, Woman, Women, Wonderful, Work, Worker, Wow
Yellow, Yes, You, Young man, Youth, Youthful, Yummy

BREAD

Acid taste, And water, Apple, Are, Ask
Bacteria, Bad, Baked, Baker, Bakery, Base, Basket, Bead, Bear, Beatnik, Bed, Better, Big, Bird, Birds, Biscuit, Black, Blue, Board, Bomb, Bought, Boy, Bread board, Bread box, Break, Breakfast, Bun
Cage, Calories, Carbon dioxide, Chamatz, Chewy, Chipmunk, Church, Clay, Coffee, Communion, Cook, Cookie, Cookies, Corn, Cracker, Cram, Cream, Crumby
Daily, Dead, Do, Doe, Dog, Donuts, Doughy, Dressing, Drink, Dryness
Eater, Eats, Egg, Eggs, El pan, Existence
Face, Factory, Far, Fat, Fattening, Fatting, Feed, Fish, Five, Floor, Flower, Food sandwiches, Four
Ginger, Gluten, God, Grain, Grains, Gravy, Great, Green
Hamburgers, Hand, Harp, Have, Health, Heavy, Holely, Holes, Holsum, Home, Honey, Horse, Hot
Indian, Is
Jim, Juicy

Kind
Lettuce, Light, Line, Loaves, Long
Mad, Made, Maker, Mammon, Man, Marmalade, Master,
   Masters, Meal, Meals, Men, Mill, Mix, Moldy, Mole, Mom,
   Money, Moose, Mother, Mouth, Mucky, Mush, Mutton, My
New, Nourishing, Nut
Oat, Oats, Odor, Old ladies
Paper, Peace, Peanuts, People, Pickles, Pie, Pink, Place,
   Plate, Play, Pop, Potato, Potatoes, Pudding
Raisin, Rectangular, Rest, Rice, Rise, Rough, Russian
Said, Salad, Sand, Sandwiches, Sauce, Saw, Seed, Share, Slice,
   Slices, Snack, Solid, Some, Something to eat, Sour, Spread,
   Stale, Steam, Store, Stuff, Supper, Support
Table, Tasteless, Thread, Toaster, To milk, Tread
Unleavened
Warm, Warmth, What, Where, Whiskers, Whole wheat
Yellow, Yum

BROADER

Aboard, Abroad, Aces, Airplane, A line, And, Ape, Appear, Are,
   Area, Arithmetic, At, Atom, Avenue, Axe
Back, Bake, Banding, Barrier, Bath, Batter, Bay, Be, Beater,
   Been, Beetle, Behind, Belt, Better, Better build, Between,
   Beyond, Bird, Block, Blue, Boards, Board walk, Boast, Boil,
   Bold, Bonnet, Boo, Book, Boot, Bored, Bother, Boulder,
   Bound, Boy, Bra, Brad, Bragger, Brat, Brazil, Breast, Bride,
   Bright, Brilliant, Bring, Broader countr, Broad jump, Broad-
   way, Broiler, Brood, Brooder, Build, Buildings, Bust line,
   But, Butt
Can, Cannons, Car, Care, Case, Cat, Cats, Center, Chair,
   Chase, Cherry, Chicken, Children, China, Church, Clear,
   Clearer, Close, Closer, Clothes, Coast, Coat, Cocoa, Collie,
   Cord, Corner, Cornering, Cost, Cotton, Countries, County
   line, Course, Cow, Crazy, Create, Crocked, Crossing, Crow,
   College
Dad, Dam, Dame, Dark, Daughter, Day light, Death, Deep,
   Desert, Dick, Did, Die, Dive, Divide, Dog, Doll, Done, Door,
   Doors, Down, Dress, Driveway, Drown, Due
Eagle, Eat, Eater, Edges, Egg, Eraser, Escape, Even, Exit,
   Explain, Eye
Face, Faster, Field, Fields, Figure, Fine, Finish, Firmer,
   Fish, Flood, Food, Football, For, Ford, Forehead, Four,
   Frailer, Frame, Fuller, Fun, Future
Gate, General, Get, Go, Goal, Grader, Grand, Grass, Greater,
   Grow
Hammer, Handsome, Hanky, Happy, Hard, He, Head, Hear,
   Heavier, Hem, Her, High, Higher, Hill, Him, Hips, History,
   Hoarder, Hold, Hole, Home, Hot, Houses, How, Hurt, Husky
I, Idea, If, In, Inside, Iowa, Is, It
Jim
Know
Lace, Lad, Ladder, Lady, Lakes, Lawn, Leader, Leaves, Legs,
   Lend, Length, Lesser, Let, Life, Lighter, Like, Liner,
   Lines, Lining, Lord
Machine, Maker, Manager, Mansfield, Map, Marilyn Monroe,
   Mark, Material, Mean, Measure, Measurement, Mexican,
   Middle, Minded, Minn., Minnesota, Minute, Mississippi, Money,
   More, More life, More of, Muscular, My, My sister
Name, Near, Nearer, New York, Next to, Nice, Nicer, Night,
   No, Not fat, Nothing, Now
Obese, Odd, Off, OK, Older, On, Ohh la la, Order, Out, Outside,
   Over, Own, Owner
Paper, Passenger, Passport, Pay, Perspective, Picture, Piece,
   Pig, Plain, Plainer, Plains, Plank, Plant, Police, Print,
   Purple, Put
Range, Reader, Red, Reef, Renter, Resident, Ridge, Rim, Rise,
   Rivers, Rock, Rooming, Rough, Round, Route, Row, Rubber,
   Run, Runner
Safe, Sandwiches, Say, School, Seam, See, Sent, Sewing, Shallow,
   Shallower, Shape, Sharp, She, Shinier, Shiny, Shore, Should,
   Side, Sidewalk, Simplier, Sing, Sister, Sit, Sitter, Skin,
   Skirt, Sky, Sleep, Sleeve, Slow, Slower, Smooth, Snake, So,
   Soft, Softer, Some, Something, Son, Sooner, Sound, Soup,
   South Pacific, Sow, Space, Stairs, Stander, Star, Stare, State
   line, Stay, Staying, Stays, Steep, Step, Stern, Stick, Stiff,
   Stop, Stouter, Straighter, Stream, Streets, Strength, String,
   Strings, Stripe, Stroke, Strong, Stubby, Stupid, Sulky, Surround,
   Surrounded
Table cloth, Take, Taken, Tale, Tall, Taller, Teacher, Ten,
   Than me, Their, Them, There, Thick, Thing, Three, Through,

Tie, Tilt, Time, Tine, To, Too, Tractor, Train, Travel, Tree,
   Trim, Trimming, Truck, Turkey
Unexplainable, United States, Upstairs
Vacancy, Vast, Vine, Visitor
Waist, Walk, Walker, Wall, Wallpaper, Walls, War, Was, Washer,
   Waste, We, Weaker, Wear, Weave, Weights, Were, Where,
   Which, Why, Widen, Wife, Wild, Wildest, Wire, Wiser,
   With, Words, Would, Wow
Yard, Yes, You, Young

BUT

Aber, About, Accept, After, Against, Ah, All, Alley, Almost,
   Alternative, An, And or, And so on, Another, Answer, Any,
   Any how, Anyways, Argue, Arguing, Argument, Arm, As if,
   Ask, A talk
Back ender, Bang, Batting, Bear, Beat, Beater, Beauty, Bee,
   Been, Belong, Ben, Bereavement, Better, Bite, Bitter, Black,
   Blank, Bold, Boo, Book, Boot, Bottom, Bought, Bow, Boys,
   Bring, Bud, Bull, Bum, Bun, Bundle, But, But nut, Butter-
   field, Butterfly
Came, Care, Cat, Catch, Cause, Chair, Change, Chemical,
   Chicken, Child, Choir, Cigarettes, Clues, Come, Comma,
   Command, Comment, Common, Compact, Connect, Connecting
   word, Continue, Contract, Contraction, Contradict, Contra-
   diction, Contrast, Correction, Could be, Course, Cow, Cup
Day, Desperation, Dick, Did, Didn't, Disagree, Disappointed,
   Disappointment, Dog, Donkey, Do not, Didn't known, Dope,
   Down, Drop
Either, Enough, Escape, Etc., Even, Even though, Every,
   Exceptions, Exclaim, Excuses, Explain, Explaining, Explanation,
   Expression, Extra
Face, Fake, Fanny, Fast, Fat, Feel, Fence, First, Fore, Forever,
   Forgot, From, Front, Fun, Fuss
Gate, Gat, Girl, Girls, Goal, God, Goes, Got, Guess, Gut
Ha, Had, Ham, Hardly, Have, Head, Heavy, Her, Here, Hesitate,
   Hesitation, His, Ho, Home, Honey, Horns, Horse, Horses, House,
   How come
If only, I'm, I mean, Inquire, Interjection, Interrupt, Isn't
Jim, Join, Jump, Just
Lady, Later, Laugh, Leave, Less, Lie, Light, Like, Line, Live,
   Lonely, Look, Loud, Luck
Mais, Mary, Meant, Might, Might change mind, Mine, Mink, Mom,
   Moment, Monday, More, Moreover, Mountain, Move, Mud,
   Mut, Mutton
Neither, Net, Never mind, Nevertheless, Nice, None, Not like,
   Not sure, Nuts
Obligation, Off, OK, On, One, Other, Otherwise, Our, Out
Pants, Part, Perhaps, Person, Pig, Play, Pleading, Plus,
   Premise, Preposition, Protest
Qualify, Questioning, Questions, Quiet
Remark, Result, Round, Run, Rust, Rut
Said, Same, Sat, Saved, Say, Scare, School, Seal, Sed, Seldom,
   Send, Sentence, Sheep, Should, Shovel, Shut, Side, Silly,
   Sir, Skip, Slow, Slut, Soe, Somebody, Someone, Something
   else, Soon, Sorry, Sow, Sputter, Stall, Stammer, Stand, Start,
   Static, Stay, Stomach, Stumble, Sure, Surprised, Swim
Talking, Teacher, Telling, Their, Those, Thought, Threw, Thus,
   Time, To do, Toilet, Ton, Too, Tool, Tow, Trees, Trouble,
   Tummy, Tut, Two
Understand, Undue, Unless, Unsure, Up, Us, Use, Ut
Very
Wasn't, Water, Way, Went, Were, Whatever, What I mean, With-
   out, Women, Won, Wonder, Words, Wreath, Wrong
Y, Yeah, Your

BUTTER

And, Animal, Art, Arterie, Ate, Awful
Ball, Be, Bead, Biscuit, Biscuits, Blue, Bowl, Box, Braid,
   Bred, Breed, Bun, Burn, Butt, Buttercup, Butter dish, Butter-
   milk
Cake, Calorie, Calories, Came, Candy, Car, Carrots, Cat,
   Cheer, Cholesterol, Christanson, Coat, Coffee, Come, Cook.
   Cooking, Cool, Corn, Cotton, Cows, Creamery
Dairy product, Die, Dinner, Doctor, Dog, Door, Dread, Dry
Ears, Eating, Egg
Face, Fair, Farm, Fats, Fatting, Fatty, Feet, Field, Fifty nine
   cents per lb., Fingers, Fluffy, Foot
Gold, Grain
Handle, Hands, He, Health, Hill, Horse, Hot, House
Ice, Ice cream, Ish

Jelly, Job
Late, Lick, Liquid, Litter, Locker, Love, Lubber
Ma, Maker, Man, Me, Meat, Melted, Melts, Melty, Messy, Mild, Mill, Moist, Mom, Money, Mushy, Mutter
Nice, Nut, Nuts
Oily, OK, Old
Pancake, Pancakes, Pap, Pat, Peanuts, Peas, Pepper, Pig, Plate, Poop, Pop, Popcorn, Potatoes, Pound, Products
Rancid, Read, Refrigerator, Roll, Rolls, Runny
Salty, Sandwich, Scotch, Shortening, Shutter, Side, Sledge, Slice, Slimy, Slip, Slosh, Small, Smear, Some, Spoon, Square, Sticky, Store, Stories, Story
Table, Taste, Telephone, Test, The, Toaster, Tread, Trouble, Two
Ugly, Utter
Vacuum
Wait, Want, Warm, Wars, Whiskey, White, Woman
Yellow soft, You, You put it on bread

BUTTERFLY

A creature, Airplane, Alive, An animal that flies, Angle worm, Arm, Art, Arthropods, Awful
Bag, Banana, Bat, Bear, Beetle, Beetles, Better, Big, Biology, Birds, Black, Black and orange, Blue, Breeze, Brid, Bride, Bright, Brown, Bud, Bumble bee, But, Butt, Buttermilk
Cake, Can, Car, Catching, Cecropia, Chloroform, Chris, Cloak, Colored, Cow, Crazy, Cricket, Cute
Dance, Date, Deer, Deerfly, Dizzy, Dots, Dove, Dragonfly
Eagle, Eat, Egg, Eyes
Fast, Field, Fish, Flap, Flea, Fleeing, Flighty, Fling, Flits, Floor, Flour, Flutter, Fluttering, Flutters, Flyer, Fragile, Frog, Fun, Funny, Furry
Gay, Gentle, Get, Giraffe, Girl, Glitter, Gnat, Go, God, Goes, Gold, Golden, Good, Goodbye, Gorgeous, Graceful, Grass, Ground
Hand, Happiness, Hat, Heart, Helicopter, Hemoptera, Hill, Hobby, Holy, Honey, Horse, Horsefly, House, Housefly, Hummingbird, Hunt
Ice cream, Into
Japan, Jar
Kiss, Kite
Lake, Land, Larva, Larvae, Leech, Lion, Little, Lizard, Lofty, Lovely
Madame, Mammal, Mate, Math, Me, Meat, Messy, Milk, Milkweed, Monarch butterfly, Monarchy, Monitor, Month, Moose, Mosquito, Moths, Movie, Music
Neat, Need, Nerves, Nervous, Nest, Nice, No
Offer, One, Orthropoda, Outside, Over
Papalon, Park, Pastel, Patty, Peanuts, Pencil, Pigeons, Pink, Plane, Play, Ply, Pod, Pollen, Powder, Pretty ode, Purple
Queen, Quiet
Rabbit, Rat, Reptile, Ride, Right, Roast duck, Roll
Sail, Scared, Scarlet, Secropia, See, Short, Sick, Size, Small bird, Smoke, Smooth, Snail, Something that can fly, Something that flies, Song, Species, Spoon, Spot, Spots, Star, Stroke, Swallow tail, Sweet
Table, Tall, Thats, Thing, Tiny, Toy
Valve
Waltz, Watch, Willow, Wind, Window, Winged, Winged insect, Winning, Wood, World, Worms
Zebra, Zoology

BUYING

Acquire, All, An, Animals, Any, Apple, Apples, Are, Arrows, Articles, Avarice
Baby, Ball, Banana, Baseball, Bat, Be, Bear, Because, Bee, Begun, Being, Best, Bid, Big, Bills, Bird, Blouse, Blouses, Boat, Bonds, Book, Boot, Bough, Boy, Bringing, Broke, Brother, Brown, Build, Bunny, Bus, Business, Butter, Buyed, Buying, Buys, Bye
Cake, Came, Can, Career, Cart, Cats, Cent, Cents, Change, Cheap, Cheat, Chemistry, Chickens, Child, Close, Clothe, Clothing, Clutch, Coats, Coffee, Coin, Coins, Collect, Compare, Consumer, Consuming, Cookies, Costs, Cottage, Counter, Cows, Cream, Cut
Dad, Dance, Day, Discount, Dog, Dogs, Doll, Dresses, Drying
Eat, Eating, Eggs, Electric, Everything, Expensive
Fabric, Fare, Fast, Fastest, Fence, Find, Finding, Fingers, Fish, Flew, Flower, Flowers, Flying, Football, Fruits, Frying, Fun, Fund

Game, Gas, Get something, Girl, Girls, Give, Given, Giving, Gloves, Go, Going, Goodby, Goodies, Got, Grain, Grocery, Gum, Gun, Guns
Hair, Ham, Hand, He, Hear, Hello, Help, Her, Highing, His, Homes, Hope, Horse, Houses, How, Hurry
Ice cream, In, Is, Items
Jump
Keeping, Know, Known
Land, Leave, Leaving, Lettuce, Lifting, Like, List, Looking, Loose, Lose, Losing, Lot, Lots, Lunch, Lying
Ma, Make, Making, Market, Material, Meats, Merchant, Milk, Mine, More, Mother, My
Ness, Nice, No, No buying, Nothing
Objects, Obtain, Of, Ooning, Opener, Oranges, Ordering, Owe, Owning
Package, Paid, Papers, Partner, Paul, People, Perfume, Person, Pie, Piece, Please, Pop, Powder, Power, Powers, Present, Presents, President, Product, Products, Profit, Purchases, Purse, Purses
Receive, Receiving, Ring, Rings, Rocket, Roy, Run
Sales, Salesman, Salt, Save, Saving, Scarf, School, See, Seeing, Seems, Seller, Send, Set, Sewing, Shipping, Shirt, Shirts, Shop, Shop lifting, Shot, Show, Shows, Shying, Sighing, Sing, Sit, Skirt, Skirts, Slippers, Soap, Socks, Soon, Spree, Spuds, Square, Stand, Staring, Staying, Steer, Stiff, Stockings, Stole, Stone, Stool, Storing, Stove, Streak, Strong, Suit, Suits, Supplies, Swapping, Sweaters
Table, Tack, Tacking, Talking, Tell, Telling, Ten, Test, Their, These, They, Thin, Those, Though, Three, Thrift, Ticket, Tickets, Time, To, Trade, Trading, Travel bag, Try, Two
Up, Us, Use, Using
Verb
Want, When, Where, Who, Why, Will, With, Worth
Yes

BY

Across, Adios, After, Air, All, Alligator, Alone, Am, An, Another, Answer, Ant, A place, As, A store, A tree
Back, Ball, Bank, Barbara, Bay, Become, Bed, Bee, Been, Beer, Before, Behind, Below, Beneath, Best, Beyond, Bicycle, Bill, Bird, Bite, Black, Blew, Bo, Boat, Boo, Book, Both, Bough, Box, Bread, Bring, Brought, Budge, Bug, Building, Bury, Bus stop, Buying, By birdie, By gone, By pass, By stander
Came, Came past, Candy, Cat, Certain, Chair, Chairs, Charlene, Chicken, Close to, Clothes, Composer, Conjunction, Cracky, Cry
Dad, David, Day, Death, Depart, Did, Die, Dog, Don, Done, Don't, Duties
End, English, Enlarge, Eraser, Eye
Farewell, Farther, Fat, Fear, Few, Floor, Fly, Football, Forever, Friend, From author, Front
George, Girl, Girls, Glass, Go by, God, Going away, Gones, Gosh, Grandmother, Ground, Gum, Guy
Hah, Ham, Happen, Hard, Hater, Hay, He, Hey, Hollow, Holly, Honey, Hope
I, If, Including, Island
Jane, Jerry, Joan, John Hancock, Jove
Know
Lamp, Land, Larger, Lay, Leaving, Ledge, Lend, Letter, Lie, Light, Line, Lions, Live, Long, Look, Lot, Loud, Low, Lullaby
Made, Magic, Mail, Make, Man, Mat, Means, Method, Mike, Mine, Mon, Move
Nash, Nearby, Never, New stand, Nine, No, Noon, North, Nothing
Ocean, Oh, OK, One, Or, Other, Ourselves, Out, Out house, Over, Over there, Own
Paper, Park, Parting, Passed, Passing, Pay, Peace, Person, Pig, Places, Plane, Pole, Pond, Prep, Preposit, Preposition, Present, Presented, Process, Producer, Put
Ready, Really, Reason, Recede, Respond, Right, Right next, Rise, Run
Sad, Said, Sally, Sam, Sand, Sat, Saturday, Saw, Say, Saying, School, Seashore, See you, Self, Selling, Set, She, Shoes, Showing, Shy, Si, Sister, Sky, Slept, Slow, Sold, Some, Someone, Soon, South, Spend, Stair, Standard, Standers, Standing, Stars, Stay, Still, Stop, Story, Straight, Strait, Summer, Sweet
Table, Take, Teacher, Than, The by, Their, The sea, Thing,

Three, Thy, Times, Together, Tòmorrow, Tool, Towards, Town, Toy, Trap, Travel, Tree, Trees, Truck, Try
Up, Used
Veronica, Via
Walked, Wall, Want, Was, Water, Waving, Were, Wind, Window, Within, Wolf, Work, Would, Written
Yard, Ye, Young, Your, Yours, Yourself

CABBAGE

A ball of cabbage, A food, Asparagus, Ate, A vegetable
Baggage, Bags, Bake, Baked, Ball, Bay, Beans, Beef, Beer, Beige, Big, Bite, Boil, Boiling, Bologna, Bones, Book, Box, Boy, Bug, Bunny, Butter, Buy
Cabbage rolls, Cabbage slaw, Cabin, Caboose, Cans, Car, Cards, Carry, Cat, Catch, Catty, Chard, Charge, Chew, Circle, Climb, Cold, Come, Cooking, Corn beef an, Corn bread, Counselors, Crab, Cream, Crisp, Crop, Crunch, Crunchy
Delicious, Did, Dinner, Dirt, Dirty, Dog, Dressing, Dump
Each, Earth, Eater, Eats, Egg, Encamped
Farm, Farmer, Fat, Finger, Flies, Flour, Flower, Food eating, Foot, For, Fun, Funny
Gabble, Game, Garage, Garbage can, German, Girl, Gone, Good taste, Grass, Green head, Green leaves, Greens, Ground, Grove, Grow, Guess, Gunk
Hair, Ham, Hate, Hater, Head of, Healthful, Healthy, Heart burn, Hearts, Herb, Hog, Home, Horrible, Hot, Hot dogs, House, Hunger, Hungry
Ich, Ishy
Jean, Junk, Just
Kennedy, Kings, Knife, Kohl rabi, Kraut, Kraut and potatoes
Lake, Land, Lard, Leafed, Leafy, Left, Left overs, Leg, Lemon, Letters, Like, Little, Lousy, Love
Mad, Me, Meat, Meat balls, Mess, Might, Milk, Mix, Money, Music, My nickname
New, Nice, Night, No good
O boy, Odor, Onion, Onions, Orange
Page, Pea, Peach, Peas, Peelings, Pencil, People, Pepper, Pig, Pineapple, Poop, Poor, Potato, Potatoes, Produce, Push
Rabbit food, Raw, Red, Rice, Ride, Rope, Rotten, Rough, Roughage, Rubbers, Run
Salary, Sandwich, Sauce, Sausage, Scraps, Sharp taste, Shoot, Shredded, Simple, Sister, Skins, Skunk, Slop, Small, Smells, Smelly, Smooth, Sneak, Soft, Solid, Soot, Spaghetti, Spinach, Square, Squash, Steam, Stinks, Stop, Store, Street, Strong, Stuffed, Suitcase, Supper, Sweet, Swell
Table, Tasty, Taxi, Teach, Teacher, Ten cents per lb., The, Thing, Throw up, Tomatoes, Track, Train, Tree, Trick, Truck, Turnip, TV, Two
Ugly
Vains, Veg, Vet, Vinegar, Vitamin C
Waste, Waste food, Weed, Went, Window, Wire, Woman, Women, Work, Worm

CARPET

Animal, Arabia, Are, Armstrong, A rug
Bad, Barefoot, Be, Beautiful, Bed, Beetle, Beggar, Beige, Bellows, Bird, Black, Blanket, Book, Books, Bounce, Bug, But
Cap, Carpet bagger, Carpeting, Ceiling, Chairs, Chart, Church, Cleaner, Cleaning, Coat, Color, Comfort, Comfortable, Correct, Couch, Cozy, Cushion
Dad, Design, Desk, Dining room, Dirty, Dogs, Don't let sparks burn it, Door, Dough, Dust, Duty
Earth, Eat, Expensive
Fall, Fat, Fire, Fish, Fix, Flat, Floor covering, Flooring, Floor rug, Floors, Flour, Flower, Flowered, Flowers, Foamy, Food, Fool, Fooled, Fort, Friend, Fun, Fur, Furnace, Furry, Fuzz, Fuzzy
Genie, Girl, Globe, Go, Gold, Good, Got, Grey, Ground
Hammer, Hard, Hate, Her, Hide out, High, Hole, Hose, House pet
Ink
Kid
Lamp, Large, Lawn, Lay, Layer, Lies, Light, Like, Linoleum, Looms, Loud, Lush
Mad, Magic carpet, Material, Me, Meat, Men, Middle, Mohawk, Move
Nails, Nap, Net, No, None, No shoes on, Nut
One, Oriental, Ours, Oven
Pad, Padding, Paper, Pen, People, Phone, Pile, Pillow, Pink,

Plane, Play, Playing, Pork, Pretty, Puppy, Purple, Put feet on, Putt
Rage, Rags, Rat, Ride, Rig, Ripped, Road, Robber, Roll, Roof, Root, Rouge, Rub, Rugged
Saw, Sea, Set, Shake, Shock, Shoe, Shoes, Sit, Skill, Sleep, Slip, Slow, Small, Snoop, Soft and smooth, Softness, Soft plush, Soil, Spill, Spilt, Spongy, Spot, Stained, Stairs, Stamp, Step, Step on, Store, Surface, Swept
Table, Tacks, Taj Mahal, Tan, Television, Texture, Thickness, Thing, Thread, Tile, Too little, Tooth, To step on, Toys, Truck
Upstairs
Vacuum cleaner, Velvet
Wake, Walking, Walk on, Wall to wall, War, Ward, Warmth, Wealth, Wean, Wear, Weaver, White, Why, Wide, Wipe feet, Wood, Woolen, Woolly, Wool rug, Working
Yarn, Yellow, Yes

CARRY

Above, Across, Addition, All, Alone, Always, An, And, Animal, Answer, Ant, Apple, Apples, Are, Arithmetic, Astronomy
Banana, Barry, Bat, Bearing, Bed, Being, Bicycle, Bill, Bird, Blanket, Boat, Borne, Borrow, Bought, Bowl, Bowling, Bread, Bricks, Bride, Brief case, Broke, Broom, Brought, Buckets, Buggy, Build, Bundles, By
Cage, Came, Can, Canary, Cane, Cans, Cared, Carefully, Carriage, Carrier, Carries, Carry on, Carry over, Carry things, Cars, Carve, Case, Cat, Chair, Chicken, Child, Choose, Class, Clothes, Coat, Cold, Come, Conversation, Convey, Could, Cow, Coy, Crawl, Crayon, Cried
Daddy, Dairy, Dale, Deliver, Deport, Disease, Do, Doing, Doll, Donkey, Don't, Doorstep, Doug, Drive, Dropped, Drudgery
Eggs
Fair, Fall, Fat, Feel, Fell, Fetch, Fever, Find, Fireman, Floor, Flow, Flowers, Fly, For, Ford, Fore, Fruit, Fun, Fur
Garbage, Gary, Girls, Golf, Good, Got, Grab, Grandma, Green, Grocery
Hairy, Hall, Hand, Hand bag, Hands, Hat, Have something, He, Head, Heavily, Heel, Held, Here, Hide, High, His, Hit, Holding, Hop, Hopper, Hot, House, Hover, Hug, Hunch, Hurt
I, In, Indian, Item
Jerry, Jug, Jump
Keep, Know
Labor, Ladder, Laden, Larry, Lead, Letters, Life, Lifted, Lifting, Lifts, Lit, Llama, Loading, Log, Long, Loose, Loss, Lost, Loud, Low, Lower, Luggage
Men, Merry, Messenger, Milk, Milkman, Miss, Mother, Moved, Movement, Muscle
Nay, Never, Newspaper, Nice, Not, Not carry, Nothing, Now
Object, Of, Oh, On load, On nurse
Pal, Pan, Parcel, Parcels, Parry, Patch, Peas, People, Person, Pie, Pigeon, Piggy back, Play, Plus, Pole, Portage, Portare, Porter, Porto, Pound, Pregnant, Pure, Put, Putting
Quick
Ran, Red, Relief, Rest, Roll, Route
Sack, Sad, School, See, Self, Sell, Send, Set, Shop, Shoulders, Shove, Sit, Sled, Sling, Slow, Someone, Sorry, Spill, Stand, Steal, Stick, Stop, Store, St. Paul, Strain, Strap, Sun, Support, Sweater
Table, Take out, Tear, Tears, Terry, Their, Thing, Those, Threshold, Through, Time, Tired, Tom, Took, Tow it, Travel, Traverse, Tray, Trays, Tree, Trunk, Try, Tug
Umbrella, Unhappy, Unload, Up, Use
Very, Virginia
Wagon, Walked, Walking, Wary, Was, Way, Wet, Wheel, Where, Who, Will, Woman, Wood, Word, Worship
Your

CARS

Accidents, Air, Airplane, Airplanes, Alot, And, Animals, Antique, Apple, Are, As, Assembly, Atom, Austin
Back seat, Bang, Bar, Beauty, Beep, Bills, Bit, Blondes, Blood, Body, Books, Boy, Brakes, Broke, Broken, Brother, Buggies, Buggy, Bump, Bumper, Bumpers, But, Buys, By
Cab, Cabs, Can, Cards, Care, Cares, Car hop, Car lot, Carriages, Carrots, Carry, Cars, Cart, Carts, Car wash, Chain, Chairs, Chevrolets, Chevs, Child, Children, Chrome,

City, Clean, Colors, Come, Compact, Conformism, Convertible, Convertibles, Core, Corvair, Crack, Cry, Customer, Cycle

Dad, Dads, Danger, Dangerous, Dark, Date, Dates, Dave, DeSoto, Detroit, Die, Dirty, Docks, Doctor, Dodge, Dodges, Dog, Dope, Drag, Dragster, Dragsters, Driven, Driver, Drives

Europe, Expense

Fact, Feet, Fenders, Fiat, Fins, Floors, Force

Garages, Gasoline, Gears, Girl, Glass, Goats, Go cart, Go carts, Goes, Going, Gone, Good

Hard, Hat, Hats, Have, Headlight, Her, Highway, Highways, Him, Hit, Homecoming, Hood, Hoods, Horns, Horse power, Hot, Hub caps, Hurt

Impala, Imperial, Is

Jack, Jag, Jars, Jeeps, John, Junk

Kaiser, Keys, Kids, Knob

Lake, Large, Length, License plates, Light, Lights, Like, Lincoln, Lines, Little, Load, Long, Look, Loud, Love, Low

MG, Make, Makes, Man, Mans, Mars, Me, Men, Merc, Mercury, MGs, Might, Mike, Mobil, Mobile, Model A, Models, Model T, Modern, Monkey, More, Mr., My

Neat, Night, Nineteen sixty one

Oil, OK, Old, Olds, One, One nine six one, Ours, Over

Park, Parking lot, Parks, Pass, Peoples, Pet, Phil, Pigs, Pink, Pipes, Play, Playing, Plymouth, Plymouths, Polish, Porche, Prestige, Pretty, Price

Quick

Races, Rack, Rambler, Ran, Rat, Red car, Rice, Rid, Rides, Riding, Roar, Rode, Roll, Rolls Royce, Roof, Rubber, Running, Runs, Rush, Rust

Sale, Sales, Seat, Sedan, Seed, Self, Sharp, Shell, Shining paint, Should, Shut, Sick, Signs, Sirens, Sit, Sixty one, Slow, Smash, Smoke, Something that moves, Soon, Sport, Sport car, Sport cars, Sports car, Sports cars, Stall, Stars, Start, Steal, Steer, Sure

Table, Tanks, Taste, T Bird, Thank, That, There, Thing, Things, Thing to drive, Three, Thunderbird, Tin, Tin cans, Tire, To, Todd, Top, Tow, Town, Towns, Toy, Track, Tracks, Tractors, Trade, Trailer, Trailers, Trait, Tree, Trees, Tricks, Trip, Trolleys, Trunks, Truth

Ugly, Um, Used

Vehicle, Volkswagon, Volkswagons

Walk, Walks, Want, Washed, Way, What, Whiles, White, Will, Window, Windows, Wish, Women

Yellow, You

Zoom

CHAIR

Age, Airplane, And, Anger, Arm rest, Arms, Ass

Barber, Bare, Bear, Bike, Black, Blue, Boat, Bridge, Broken

Can't, Car, Care, Cat, Check, Child, Choir, Close, Coach, Command, Cool, Corn, Cover, Covering, Cupboard, Cushions

Dad, Dare, Dark, Deep, Dinner, Dog, Door, Down

Ease, Easy chair, Eat, Eating, English, Every

Fair, Fall, Far, Feet, Flat, Flood, Flour, Flower, Fly, Food, Footstool, Fortune, Four, Four legs, Fun

Garage, Girl, Girls, Grandma, Green, Ground

Hand, Hat, He, Head, Hear, Heavy, High chair, Him, Home

Lamp, Large, Lily, Link, Livingroom, Loud, Lounge, Love seat, Low, Lumpy

Mahogany, Maple, March, Me, Modern, Mother, Mouse, Movies, Mug

Near, New, Nice

Oak

Pair, Patch, People, Pink, Plushy, Point, Poor, Post

Recline, Relaxation, Resting, Rock, Rocking chair, Rough, Round, Run

Sat down, Sating, School, See, Sell, Send, Shot, Show, Sitable, Sit down, Sit down in it, Site, Sit on, Sit sitting, Sitting down, Sitting object, Sit upon, Sleep, Slow, Small, Smooth, Sort, Sow, Square, Stair, Stand, Stare, Steady, Steak, Steel, Stiff, Stood, Stoop, Strait, Strong, Stuffed, Sweet, Swing

Tan, Television, Thing, Tip, Tired, Together, Top, To sit in, Turn

Uneasiness

Velvet

Wall, Warm, Was, Water, Wear, Were, What, Where, White, Woke, Woman, Wooden, Wooden straight backed, Wood hard, Woody, Worn, Would, Write

Yellow

CHEESE

Age, Aged, Aid, Alps, Alright, And bacon, Apple, Ate, A thing to eat, Awful

Baby, Bad, Bead, Beef, Beer, Big, Biscuit, Blah, Block, Blossom, Blow, Blue cheese, Blue horn, Board, Boat, Bongards, Book, Boom, Boy, Bred, Breed, Breeze, Brick, Brown, Burglar, Butter solids, Button

Camembert, Camera, Candy, Cats, Cave, Celery, Cheese, Cheeseburger, Chest, Choose, Chop, Chose, Churn, Churning, City, Coffee, Color, Cottage cheese, Craft, Creamed, Creamy, Crickets, Crummy, Cut, Cutter

Dark, Dave is one, Delicious, Did, Dip, Dislike, Don't like it, Dreams, Dressing

Egg, Eggs, English, Expensive, Eyebrows

Factory, Family, Fat, Father, Fattening, Fees, Flavor, Floor, Fold, Fork, Formosa, Fruit, Fun

Game, Go, Goat, Goats, Grade, Grated, Grilled

Hamburger, Hard, Head, Her, Highness, Holds, Holler, Holy, Home, Honey, Hunger

Ice, Ice cream, Ick, Ill smelling, Is

Jack, Japanese

King, Kiss, Knees, Kraft, Kuwana Club

Lake, Lettuce, Like, Little, Lumber, Lumps, Lunch

Man, Mart, Meals, Mellow, Melt, Might, Mike, Mines, Mom, Moonglow, Moose, Mother, Moved, Mushy, Mutton, My,

Name, Noon, Not, Not good, Nut

Odor, Old, Onion, Orangish

Peas, People, Person, Pickets, Picture, Pictures, Pink, Plate, Pop, Pretzels, Product

Queen, Quiet

Red, Refrigerator, Religion, Rich, Ritz, Roast, Ronald, Ronnie, Room, Round, Rye krisp

Salad, Salami, Salt, Sandy Balchunas, Scared, Sheep, Sick, Slab, Slice, Slimy, Smells, Smelly, Smile, Smoked, Smooth, Snacks, Soup, Sour cream, Spelling, Spice, Square, Stale, Starch, Stink, Stinky, Supper, Sweet, Swift cheese, Swiss cheese

Table, Take, Tasteless, Taster, Tastes, Teeth, Terrible, Texture, The, These, Thing, Think, Toast, Toasted, Tobacco, Tomato

Ugh

Wet, What, White, White rat, Whiz, Whole, Wine, Work

Yea, Yellowish, Yum

CHILD

Adorable, Adults, Angry, Animal, Arm, At, Average child

Babe, Baby sit, Baby sitter, Baby sitting, Ball, Bear, Better, Big, Bike, Bill, Body, Bonnie, Booties, Bother, Bottle, Box, Boy and girl, Boy girl, Bracelet, Brain, Bratty kids, Brothers, Brothers and sisters

Camper, Candy, Carefree, Carriage, Cathy, Chatter, Cheerful, Cherished, Cherub, Child, Childish, Chill, Christ, Chubby, Cindy, Clean, Clod, Cool, Cradle, Crawl, Crib, Crying, Cuddly, Cuteness

Dad, Daddy, Dangerous, Darling, Daughter, Dave, David, Dead, Death, Debbie sister, Delinquent, Desire, Diaper, Diapers, Dirt, Dirty, Do, Doll, Dolls, Dress, Drug, Drunk

Elder, Enjoy, Eyes

Face, Fair, Fam, Families, Fat, Father, Fear, Five, Flesh, Food, Fool, Foolish, Fragile, Frail, Frank, Friend, Friends, Funny

Games, Garden, Gentle, Giggle, Girl boy, Girl or boy, Girls, Glad, Gladys, Gold, Grow, Grows, Grow up, Guidance

Hair, Hat, Hay, He, Health, High, Hill billy, Honest, Hood, Hope, Hopeful, Hospital, Hot, House, Human being, Humanity, Hungry, Hurry, Hurt, Husband

Infantry, Inquisitive

Jerk, Jerry, Jesus, Jodie, Joe, John, Johnny, Joy, Joyful, Julie

Key, Kind

Lady, Laughter, Life, Like, Little boys, Little brat, Lona, Long, Look, Loud, Lovable

Male, Male or female, Manger, Maniac, Mary, Memory, Merry, Mike, Milk, Minor, Mischief, Mischievous, Mitten, Mom, Monster, Monsterous, Mothers, Myself

Naive, Name, Nasty, Naughty, Need, Nephews, Nick, Niece, None, Not, Not a grown up, Nuisance, Nursery

Offspring, OK, One, One five years, Oops, Outside

Patience, Peg, Persons, Pest, Pests, Peter, Pick, Pill, Pink, Playful, Playing, Pleasing, Pre-adolescent, Precious, Pregnant, Pretty, Problems, Propagation, Psychology, Pupil

Ramsey, Randy, Rascal, Read, Responsibility, Rick Perry, Ricky, Rough neck, Run

Sad, Schools, Scottie, Scream, Self, She, Shoes, Short, Short and small, Six, Slave, Sleep, Slow, Small boy, Small person, Smart, Smell, Softness, Sometimes me, Spoiled, State, Stupid, Sue, Susy, Sweetness

Taker, Talk, Tantrum, Teen, Three, Tom, Two, Two year old, Tyke

Unadult, Under twelve, Under twenty one, Ungrown, Unlearned, Up

Warm, What, Wild, Wimp, Wonderful, Wondering

Yard, Yes, You, Young person

CHILDREN

A, Accident, Adorable, All, All of us, Always, Angry, Animal, Animals, Answer, Arithmetic, At

Babe, Baby sitting, Becky, Bed, Bird, Birds, Bob, Bodies, Body, Boys and girls, Boys girls, Bratlings, Bread, Brothers, Brother sister, Bryce, Bus, Busy, Butch

Came, Candy, Car, Care, Cars, Cats, Chicken, Childhood, Children, Children are nice, Chinese, City, Class, Classes, Clean, Clods, Close, Coat, Color, Come, Cottage, Couple, Cripple, Crippled, Crossing, Crowd

Daddy, Darling, Den, Diane, Did, Dirt, Dirty, Do, Dog, Dolls, Don't, Dope, Down, Dresses, Dumb

Earth, Eat, Eggs, Eight, Enough, Eraser, Everyone

Faces, Fast, Fat, Faye, Find, Fingernail, First, Five, For, Four, Friendly, Friends, Funny

Games, Gather, Get, Gladys, Go, Goats, Going, Gone, Grand-parents, Gripe, Grow

Had, Hair, Hand, Handy, Hard, Hate, Hats, Have, Headache, Helpless, Hide, High, Hood, Horses, Hour, House, Human being, Humans, Husband

In, Is, Ish, It, Its, I wonder

Joy, Jump

Kenny, Kind, Kinder, Kindergarten, Kindness, Kiss, Kittens

Ladies, Lady, Laughter, Left, Level, Liberi, Life, Linda Smith, Little girls, Little people, Lively, Look, Lost, Lot, Loud

Mad, Married, May, Mean, Menace, Mess, Mice, Mike, Mind, Mischief, Mom, Money, Monsters, More, More than one, Mothers, Myself

Nice, No, None, Noun, Nurse, Nuts

Of, Older, One, One plus one equals three, Our

Park, Parks, Peds, Pest, Pests, Pet, Piggy, Pigs, Playful, Playground, Plot, Plural, Potty, Preadolescent, Pregnant, Punk, Pupil, Puppies

Questions

Ramsey, Ran, Rascals, Read, Red, Rim, Roy, Running

Said, Sand, Sandy, Saw, Say, Says, School room, Schools, Scream, Screamed, See, Seen, Set, Seven, Sex, She, Shield, Shoe, Shortness, Should, Shouting, Siblings, Signs, Sing, Sister, Six, Sleep, Slow, Snake, Snow, Soft, Son, Sons, Soon, Squirt, Start, Steph, Story, Stove, Stupid, Sweet, Swing, Swings

Tables, Teachable, Teachers, Teenagers, Ten, Tender, There, They, Think, Thoughts, Three, Threw, Toddlers, Tommy, Tot, Toy, Two, Two hundred seven

Unadult

Very

Wait, Walk, Want, Was, We, Went, What, Who, Wife, Wild, Will, Wimps, Wives, Woman, Won't, Wren, Write

Young adults, Younger, You or me

CITIZEN

Act, Adult, African, A good person, Alamo, Anarchist, And, Anger, Animal, Answer, Any, Apathy, Army, At

Babbitt, Baby, Bad, Baseball, Bead, Beatnik, Belonger, Belong-ing, Big, Bird, Blown, Boat, Book, Born, Boy Scout, Brave, British, Building, Bum, Business man

Canadian, Cannibal, Care, Carry, Cars, Cat, Catholic, Chair, Chicken, Children, Christian, Church, Cite, Cites, Citizenness, Civics, Civilian, Civilization, Clean, Clod, Club, Coat, Cold, Come, Command, Communist, Communists, Comrade, Conform, Conscientious, Constitution, Convict, Cop, Council, Countries, Country or city, County, Court, Criticism

Dad, Days, Democrat, Democratic, Descent, Dickens, Doctor, Dog, Dollar sign, Dope, Dr., Duties, Duty

Eat, Elder, Elderly, Election, Emigrant, European, Everyone, Ex-patriot

Fail, Fair, Family man, Farmer, Father, Feel, Feet, Fellow, Fellowship, Fine, Fish, Five, Floor, Food, Fool, Foot, Forgivers, Four, France, Frank, Freedom, Free man, French, Frozen, Fugitive

Game, General, Gentleman, George Washington, Geo. Washington, German, GI Joe, Girls, Going, Gone, Good one, Good people, Good person, Good worker, Governor, Gov't, Grand mom, Great, Greece, Group, Growing, Grown up, Guy

Hard, Hat, Hay, Health, Help, Helper, Helpful, Hermit, Hobo, Honest, Honorable, Honored, House, Human being, Hungarians, Hunting, Hurt

Immigrate, In, Individual, Informed, Inhabitant, Ish, It

J.F.K., Jail con, Japan, J.Kennedy, Job, John Doe, Judge

Kane, Keeper, Kid, Kitchen

Ladder, Lady, Lake, Land, Large, Latin, Law, Laws, Leader-ship, League, Leg, Like, Lincoln, Listened, Live, Living, Liz Steffenson, Loyalist, Loyalty

Mad, Male, Manners, Man or woman, Many, Meat, Membership, Minn., Minneapolis, Minnesota, Moscow, Mpls., Mr., Much, My country

Name, Nation, Nationalist, Naturalization, Naval man, Nazi, Negro, Newspaper, New York, No, Noble, Non, Not, Not citizen, Nut, Nuts

Obedient, Obey, Of, Of a town, Officer, Old man, Organization, Over

Paper, Papers, Parents, Part of a state, Patron, Peace, Peoples, Persons, P.K. Peterson, Place, Platonic, Plebian, Police, Politician, Polk, Poll, Poor, Population, Positive, Pretty, Privilege, Proud, P.T.A., Public, Publican, Purse

Quiz

Radio, Rebel, Red, Refugee, Religion, Republic, Resident, Respectable, Responsibility, Responsible, Ride, Right, Rights, Road, Robber, Rome, Run, Russia, Russian

Sad, Salt, Senator, Sentence, Set, Shop, Sister, Slave, Slow, Smart, Smith, Sociology, Socrates, Soldiers, Somebody, Someone how is, Something, Special, Spider, Sport, Spy, Stand, Start, Staunch, Stop, Store, Street, Subject, Suit, Sun, Sweden

Taxes, Tax payer, Teacher, Terrible, The United States, Thing, Thirty, Thoughtful, Time, Told, Towns, Towns folk, Townsman, Traitor, Tramp, Trash, True American, Trust, Trusted, Truthful, Twenty-one

U.S. male, Uncitizen, Uncle, Uniform, Unkind, Up, Up side down, Upstanding, U.S.A., U.States

Visitor, Voting

Wait, Wash, Watch, Well adjusted, Western, What, White, Will, Window, Woman, Women, Work

Yes, You, Young

Zone

CITY

Activity, Air, Albert Lea, Area, Austin

Berkley, Big and dirty, Big and nice, Black, Blocks, Bob, Boston, Box, Boy, Brooklyn Center, Buena Park, Bum, Bus, Buses, Bustle, Bustling

Cab, Cake, California, Cambridge, Camp, Canada, Capital, Capitol, Cares, Cement, Child, Children, Church, Circle, Cite, Citizens, City, City's, City square, Civilian, Clean, Clothes, Color, Comfrey, Complex, Confusion, Cops, Cottage, Could, Council, Crowd, Crowds, Cumberland

Dassel, David, Day, Dense, Dish, Dislike, Doctor, Dog, Don't, Down, Down town, Drive, Dumaguete City, Dump, Dust, Dusty

Edifice, Ely, Enormous, Evil, Excitement

Far, Fast, Fig, Food, Fosston, Friends, Fun

Garage, Gas, Girl, Glass, Go, God, Grandpa's house, Grand Rapids, Green, Group, Gutter

Hard, Heaven, Here, Hill, Hills, Home city, Homes, Hong Kong, Hopkins, Hotel, Houston, Huge, Hurry, Hustle

Jail, Judge, Justice

Kansas, Kansas City, Kitten

Lake, Lakes, Land, Lawn, Light, Like, Limit, Limits, Little, Live in, Living, Lonely, Long, Los Angeles, Los Angles, Loud

Machine, Mad, Madison, Madness, Man, Many, Masses, Massive, Maze, Mc Intosh, Mecca, Metropolitan, Miami, Mild, Million, Mississippi, Move, Municipal

Naked, Name, Nation, Near, Night life, Noisy, Not a town

Ocean, Oh, Ohio, Olympus, Omaha, Our, Oxboro

Pad, Paris, Parks, Pavement, Peace, Pencil, Perham, Person, Pink, Pittsburg, Place to live, Play, Playground, Plumbing, Police, Pooh, Population, Public, Pump

Ride, Right, Road, Roads, Rochester, Rome, Row

School, Sea, Service, Side, Sidewalks, Sit, Sky, Skyscraper, Slicker, Small, Smell, Smelly, Smog, Smoke, Smoky, Something, Soot, Space, Squad, Stadt, Start, States, Stay, Store, Suburban

Tall, The, They, To, Toe, Tomorrow, Tone, Travel, Tree, Trees, Truck

Ugly

Valley, Virginia, Vote

Waconia, Wadena, Want, We, Where live, Wide, Window, Woman, Wonderful, Woods, World

Yukon

Zone

CLEARER

Ahead, Aid, All, All right, Am, An, And, Ann, Apparent, Appear, Appearance, Are, As, At, Away

Baby, Bad, Barely, Baseball, Bath, Be, Bean, Beater, Beauty, Bee, Beer, Before, Bell, Bible, Bigger, Bitter, Blank, Bleary, Blemish, Blind, Block, Blond, Blood, Bloody, Blurrier, Blurring, Boat, Boo, Book, Boy, Bring, Broad, Bull dozer

Call, Can, Can see, Can't, Can't see, Cat, Cats, Caught, Cellophane, Certain, Cheer, Clarify, Classes, Clause, Cleanest, Cleaning, Cleans, Cleanser, Clearasil, Cleared, Clearer, Clearing, Clearness, Clever, Climb, Clogged, Cloggy, Close, Cloth, Clothes, Cloud, Clouded, Clouds, Clutter, Coats, Color, Come, Completion, Complexion, Concise, Confusing, Cool, Cooler, Corner, Could, Cut

Dear, Dearer, Deer, Definite, Den, Dew, Diamond, Did, Different, Difficult, Dish, Distincter, Distinctive, Distinctly, Distorted, Dizzier, Dizzy, Do, Does, Dog, Done, Don't, Dow, Drab, Dreary, Dress, Drier, Drill, Dry, Dryer, Dug, Dust, Dustier, Dusty, Duty

Easily, Easily seen, Enunciate, Evening, Explain, Explanation Eye sight

Face, Faded, Fading, Fail, Fair, Far, Fat, Fatter, Fearer, Field, Field glasses, Fill, Finer, Fire, First, Fizzy, Fluid, Food, For, Fore, Forgotten, Fort, Fresh, Fresher, Frog, Frosty, Full, Fun, Fuss, Fussy, Fuzzier

Get, Get away, Girl, Gloomier, Glossy, Go, Go away, Goes, Gray, Ground, Gun

Ha, Hair, Hand, Have, Hay, Haze, Hazey, Hazily, Head, Health, Hearer, Heavier, Help, Here, Hi, Home, Horizon, House, How, Hurry

I, I can see better, Ice, Ill, Image, In, Indistinct, Invisible, It Know

Learn, Leather, Legible, Less, Let, Letter, Library, Like, Liquid, Little, Long, Loud, Low

Made, Man, Me, Meat, Mess, Messier, Mind, Mirror, Mist, Mix, Modified, Mom, More, More clear, More vague, Mornings, Move out of way, Movie, Much, Mucky, Muggy, Murky, Musty, My

Natural, Nebulous, Net, Never, New, Noise, Non clear, No one, Not clear, Not clearer, Not dirty, Notes, Not hazy, Nothing

Obscure, Obstructed, Obvious, Ocean, Of, Off, Office, Oh, Oil, OK, Older, One, Open, Or, Outside, Oven

Paint, Painter, Pale, Pane, Path, Peak, Pear, Pencil, Pig, Pimple, Pipe, Plan, Play, Please, Pool, Post, Precise, Premise, Prettier, Pretty, Print, Problem, Pure, Purer, Puzzled

Radio, Ran, Real clear, Refresh, Relief, Road, Room, Rougher, Rug

Safer, Sand, Say, Scared, Scene, School, Scribble, Sea, Seeable, See better, See it, Seek, See through, Set, Shabbier, Shade, Shallower, Shimmery, Shine, Shinier, Shining, Shoe, Shout, Shovel, Show, Short, Sign, Silk, Simple, Simpler, Sink, Skies, Sleep, Slow, Smart, Smearer, Smeary, Smile, Smog, Smoggy, Smoother, Smudged, Snow, So, Soap, Sober, Some, Sound, Space, Sparkle, Sparkling, Speaking, Specify, Speck, Speed, Spoken, Spotless, Spotty, Star, Still, Stop, Stormy, Straight, Strong, Subjects, Sun

Take, Talk, Teeth, Telescope, Television, Test, Than mud, That, Their, Them, There, They, Thinker, Thinner, Thorough, Though, Thought, Three, Throat, Through, Thru, Time, Today, Tone, Too, Top, Too see, Tree, Trees, True, TV,

Two

Unclean, Understanding, Undistorted, Unobstructed, Up

Vaguely, Vast, View, Vivid, Voice, Void

Wait, Wall, Was, Washer, Washing, Wax, Weaker, Wear, Well, Went, Were, What, When, Where, Wherever, Whites, Whose, Wider, Widow, Will, Windows, Windy, Winter, With, Woods, Word, Words

Year, Yes, Yet, Your

CLOSER

A, Action, Adjacent, Afraid, Again, Age, Ah, Almost, Along side, Alot, Am, And, Animal, Apart, Appear, Approach, Are, Arms, As

Baby, Backer, Bad, Base, Be, Behind, Besides, Between, Bigger, Bill, Bird, Black, Block, Board, Boys, Bring, Brother, Building, Bump, Bus, But, Buy

Cake, Call, Camera, Cars, Cat, Chase, Cheese, Chose, Clause, Clean, Cleaner, Clear, Clearance, Clock, Closer, Closer still, Closes, Close to, Closing, Cloth, Coat, Comes, Comfort, Companion, Confined, Cozier, Cozy, Crammed, Crept, Crowded, Crowds, Cuddle, Cut

Dance, Dare, Dark, Desk, Dick, Distant, Do, Does, Done, Don't, Dose, Down, Draw, Dress, Drive

Earth, Easier, Easy, Embrace, Even, Ever, Every, Exposed, Eye

Face, Fan, Faraway, Farther away, Fat, Fatter, Feel, Feeling, Fell, Fight, Finish, Fish, Fit, Floor, Food, Forward, Fought, Friends, Friendship, Fright, From, Fun

Game, Get, Get close, Ghost, Girls, Glasses, Glove, God, Going, Gone, Good, Ground, Guy

Hair, Handier, Hands, Harder, Hat, Have, Hay, He, Heard, Heart, Heat, He came, Higher, Him, Home, Honey, Hoser, Hug, Huge, Human, Hurry

I, I come, If, Ill, Impact, Inch, Inside, Is

Jim, Join, Joining, Jump

Lady, Lake, Larger, Left, Let, Light, Like, Little, Loose, Loser, Lost, Lovely, Lower

Make up, Meet, Mind, Miss, Mit, Moon, More, Mother, Move in, Moving, My

N, Narrow, Narrower, Nearby, Nearest, Nearly, Nearness, Nears, Neat, Neck, Neighbor, Never, New, Nicer, Night, Not

Of, Off, Old, On, Or, Out, Over, Owl

Page, Paper, Party, Pig, Place, Plane, Police, Pop, Position, Pressed, Pure

Quick, Quite

Race, Races, Real, Real close, Red, Relation, Relaxation, Ride, Room, Rounded, Run, Running, Run with

Safety, Said, Same, Sand, Sat, Scared, Seat, Sex, Shake, She, Shoe, Shoes, Short, Shorter, Shot, Shout, Shove, Show, Shower, Silver, Sir, Size, Slim, Slow, Slowly, Small, Sneak, Snuggle, Softer, Some, Something, Song, Soon, Sooner, Space, Square, Squashed, Squeeze, Squirm, Standing, Start, Stay, Stopper, Store, Stork, Sudden, Sun, Sweater

Take, Taller, Tar, Target, Teacher, Teens, Tell, Tender, Tension, Terror, Test, That, That's, The end, Their, Them, There, They, Thicker, Thing, Through, Today, Toes, Togetherness, To him, To it, To me, Top, Touching, Toward, To you, Train, Tree, Trees, Try, Two

Ugly, Us

Vent, Very, View

Walls, Wanted, Warmer, Water, Way, We, Wear, Welcome, Well, What, Where, Wide, Wider, Wife, Will, Winner, With, Within, Woman, Word, Worm

Yes

COLD

A drink, Alaska, Arctic, Art

Baby, Beer, Better, Biting, Bleak, Blizzard, Blow, Blowing, Boiling, Bold, Boys, Bread, Breeze, Breezy, Brisk, Bundle, Burning, Burr, Burrrr

Car, Chatter, Chilling, Chills, Climate, Clothes, Cloud, Coal, Coats, Cold, Coldness, Covering, Curl

Days, Deep, Discomfort, Disease, Dog, Dreary, Dristan, Dry, Dull

Eye

Feel, Feeling, Fever, Fine, Fire, Flu, Friday, Friends, Frost bite, Frosty, Fur

Girls, Given, Glove, Gloves, Going, Good, Grey

Hair, Hand, Handkerchief, Hands, Handky, Hat, Head, Help, Hold, Holy, Home, Horrible, How, Hungry, Hunt, Hurt

Ice cream, Icicles, Icy, Illness, Ishy, It
Light, Long, Low
Man, Mass, Meat, Met, Milk, Minnesota, Mirror, Miserable,
  Mittens, Mold, Money, Morning, Music, Mutton
Naked, Night, Nippy, North Pole, Not hot, Not nice
Ouch, Out, Outdoors
Pain, Pop
Rain, Ran, Raw, Refrigerator, Rehearsal, Roasting, Rosy,
  Rush
Scarf, Shell, Shivers, Shivery, Short, Shoulder, Show, Shrill,
  Sigh, Sinusitis, Sit, Skiing, Slaw, Sleigh riding, Slow, Sneezes,
  Sniff, Sniffle, Sniffles, Snow or rain, Snowy, Sold, Sore,
  Sore throat, South, Storm, Straw, Suffer, Sun, Swimming
Temp, Temperature, Terrible, Thermometer, Thick clothes,
  Throat, Tired
Ugly, Unfavorable, United, Unpleasant
Very, Virus
War, Ware, Warmth, Wear, Wild, Window, Woman, Women,
  Wool, Worn, Would

COME

A, Accompany, Action, Advance, Afghanistan, Again, Alone,
  Also, Although, Always, Am, And, Appear, Approach, Are,
  Arms, As, Ask, Asking, At, Attend, Attract, Away
Be, Beckon, Beckoning, Bed, Before, Begin, Blank, Blue,
  Brown, But, By
Call, Calling, Can't, Cat, Cats, Children, Church, Comb, Come
  here, Comes, Come to, Company, Cone
Dance, Date, Day, Dear, Deer, Desk, Do, Dog, Done, Donny,
  Door, Drive
Early, Easier
Faster, Find, Finger, Fluid, For, Forth, Friendship
Gather, Gee, Girl, Go away, Goes, Got, Go there, Go with,
  Greet
Hand, Hate, He he, Hey, Hire, His, Hospital, How, Hum
I, If, Indians, Invite, Invited, Is, It
Join
Keep, Know
Late, Later, Lest, Let, Lets, Lick, Little, Live, Long, Love
Make, Man, Many, May, Meet, Mother, Motion, Mountain,
  My, My name
Nearer, Never, Next to, Not, Nothing, Nut
Of, Oh, Only, Or, Orange, Order, Outside
Party, Person, Places, Plans, Play, Plead
Quicker
Retire, Riding, Right, Road
Same, Saw, Saying, Seduction, She, Sink, Sit, Six, Slow, Smash,
  Someday, Someplace, Sometime, Son, Song, Sooner, Star,
  Start, Step, Store, Street, Supper
Take, Telephone, Telling, That, The, Their, They, Thither,
  Thought, Thru, Time, To bed, Today, To me, Tomorrow,
  Tonight, Towards, Travel, Trot
Under, Us
Verb, Visit
Walls, Want, Was, Way, We, Were, What, When, Who, Why,
  Will, Women, Won, Would
Yes, Yesterday, You

COMFORT

Able, Ache, Afflicted, Afterwards, Agony, Aid, Airplane, Alone,
  Always, Armchair, Arms, Asleep, Awake
Baby, Back, Bad, Bar, Beer, Below, Better, Big, Black,
  Blue, Book, Bouncy, Boy, Bug, Bumpy, By
Calm, Came, Camp, Care, Casual, Cat, Chain, Chairs, Cheer,
  Clam, Class, Cliff, Close, Cloth, Coach, Coal, Coat,
  Comfortable chair, Comfortably, Comforter, Comforting,
  Comfy, Concise, Condolence, Confer, Connie, Content,
  Convenience, Conveniences, Cow, Crying, Cushion, Cutlery
Dad, Darkness, Death, Delightful, Dick, Disability, Disease,
  Distress, Disturb, Disturbing, Do, Dog, Driving
Eased, Easiness, East, Easy going, Enjoy, Enjoyable
Family, Far, Fast, Fear, Feathers, Feelings, Feels good,
  Feet, Fell, Fill, Finger, Fire, Fire place, Food, Foot,
  Foot stool, Ford, Forget, Form, Friend, From, Fur,
  Furniture
Gentle, Gently, Gentry, Girl, Girls, Glad, Gofort, Gone,
  Good feeling, Goodness, Green, Ground
Had, Handy, Hardships, Hat, Hate, Head, Headache, Healthy,
  Hearth, Heavy, Heel, Hell, Helpful, Her, Here, Hold, Homely,
  Horse, Hose, Hospitality, Hurt

Ill, Ill at ease, Illiterate, Important, Incomfort, Index, Injury,
  Iritable, Is, Island, It
Jacket, Joy, Jump, Just right
Kind, Kiss, Knife, Korea
Laid, Land, Laugh, Laying, Lazily, Less, Lie, Lie down,
  Life, Light, Lion, Liquor, Live, Living, Loaf, Long, Lounge,
  Lounging, Lousy, Loving, Lunch, Luxuries, Luxurious,
  Lying, Lying back
Mad, Magazine, Mansion, Marge, Mattress, Me, Men, Mice,
  Miss, Mississippi, Mix, Mom, Mountain, Myself
Name, Nap, Need, Neglect, Nervous, Never, Night, No,
  No comfort, Non comfort, Not, Not comfort, Not comfortable,
  No work, Nut
Old, Or, Ouch, Out
Painless, Past, Peaceful, Pencil, People, Person, Pillows,
  Please, Pleased, Pleasing, Plush, Poor, Put
Quite
Radio, Ran, Read, Realizing, Release, Relics, Relieve,
  Restful, Restless, Right, Rocking chair, Room, Rough,
  Roughness, Run
Sad, Sadness, Safe, Sag, Salad, Satisfaction, Satisfied, School,
  Seat, Secure, Set, Settled, Share, Shelter, Shoes, Shorts,
  Shout, Shower, Sickness, Sigh, Silence, Silent, Silk, Sink,
  Slacks, Sleepy, Slept, Slipper, Slippers, Small, Smooth,
  Snow, Snug, Sock, Soft chair, Softly, Some, Song, Soothing,
  Soreness, Sorry, Southern, Spoil, Spring, Station, Sticky,
  Still, Stop, Stove, Style, Swank, Sweet, Sweetness, Swim,
  Swimsuit, Swing, Sympathize
Tall, Tears, Television, Tell, Tension, Tent, The, Thing,
  Thunderbird, Tidy, Tired, To, Together, Tough, TV, Two
Ugly, Um, Uncomfortably, Uncomforted, Uneasiness, Unfit,
  Unhappy, Unrest, Unsatisfied, Us
Vacation, Velvet, Very
Walk, Want it, Was, Water, Weak, Wear, Whistle, Wide, Widow,
  Wife, Wonderful, Wool, Words, Work, Worm
Yellow, Yes, You

COMMAND

A, Ace, Act, Advise, After, Aggressive, Air command,
  Airplane, Along, Always, Anger, Angry, Argue, Arm,
  Armed Forces, Asked, Attack, Authoritarian, An order to do
  something, Awful
Base, Basement, Beg, Behest, Bible, Big, Bitter, Black,
  Blue, Bold, Bomb, Book, Bossing, Both, Buddy, Bus, Button
Call, Came, Camp, Can, Castro, Cat, Chain, Chair, Challenge,
  Church, Cigarette, Clouds, Colonel, Commandment, Commando,
  Commands, Common, Compelled, Complete, Cone, Connect,
  Convince, Corpse, Cpl., Cruel, Cry, Cry out, Custer
Dad, Dare, Dark, Decide, Decommand, Decree, Defeated,
  Demanding, Deodorant, Describe, Dick, Dictate, Dictator,
  Did, Different, Directions, Discharge, Discipline, Discommand,
  Disobedience, Do as you wish, Doing, Do it now, Dominant,
  Domineer, Domineering, Don't, Dot, Do this, Do what he says,
  Down, Dumb
Easy, Eat, Egg, Engineer, English, Ensign, Excitement, Exclaim,
  Exclamation
Face, Fast, Fight, Finger, Fired, Flag ship, Flight, Follower,
  For, Forget, Formal, For the man, Forward, Four, Fourth,
  Friend, Fun
Game, Generals, Given, Gob, Going, Govern, Greet, Gripey,
  Grouch, Grown, Grown up, Growth, Gruff, Guard, Guess,
  Gun, Guy in boat, Gym
Hair cream, Hair oil, Hair spray, Handed, Harbor, Harshness,
  Hat, Hate, Have to, He, Head, Head of, Heartless, Help,
  Helpful, Her, Here, Hide, Hide out, Highest, Hilton, Hit,
  Hitler, Hold, Home, Horrible, Horse, Hoye, Human being,
  Hurry up
Imperative, Important, In garage, Instruction, Is, It
Jesus
Khrushchev, Known
Land, Language, Late, Led, Lesson, Lie, Like, Line up, Lone,
  Long, Look, Lose, Love
Main, Major, Make you do it, Marine, Marines, Mark, Me,
  Meanness, Metal, Mine, Mom, Move, Movie, Mr. Berg,
  Mr. Berg teacher, Mr. Swanson, Must, Must do
Natural, No command, Noise, Non command, None, Norway,
  Not, Note, Not like, Not new, NROTC, Nut
Obedience, Obeying, Object, Odor, Office, Officer in Navy, OK,
  Old, Order to give order, Ornery, Others, Ouch, Out,
  Overbearing

Parents, Paul, People, Perfect, Person, Picnic, Pig, Pilot, Plan, Plane, Plea, Please, Police, Policeman, Post, Present, President, Prince, Prison, Private Mulvaney, Proud, Put

Question, Quick, Quiet

Rain, Rank, Reaction, Read, Receive, Recommended, Record, Redeem, Regent, Regular, Regulate, Reject, Remain, Remember, Requested, Respond, Responsibility, Right away, Risk, Roof, Rough, Rules, Ruling, Run

Said, Sailor, Same, Sand, Sarge, Sat, Saying, Say so, Scared, Scold, Scout leader, Scream, Sea, Sense, Sentence, Servant, Service, Services, Set, Sharpness, Shave, Shoot, Short, Shot, Silence, Silly, Sing, Sit, Sixteen, Slave, Slow, Small, Smart, Smoke, Smooth, Song, Sound, Spanish, Speech, Spoken, Spot, Stand, Start, Steep, Still, Story, Straight, Strengthen, Stress, Strictness, Struggle, Suggestion, Suit, Suitable, Sunday School, Superlative, Supervisor, Sweet, Sword

Tale, Talkative, Talking, Tall, Task, Teach, Tension, They, Thing, Things, This, Threaten, To do, To do something, Top, Tough, Tree, Trees, Troop, Trouble

Uncommon, Uniform, Us, Useful

Valor, Verb

Walk, Want, Wanting, War, Warden, Warn, Well, Whistle, Wife, Will, Willing, Wise guy, Wish, With, Woman, Worn, Write

Yelling, Yes, Yes sir

COTTAGE

A, Add, A home, Air, Also, Amery, A place to stay, Ate, Away

Bad, Ball, Bath, Bathing, Be, Beautiful, Beauty, Bed, Big Lake, Book, Books, Bought, Boy, Boys, Boys and girls, Bright, Brown, Building, Butter

Cabbage, Cane, Canoe, Car, Carry, Castle, Chair, Chick, Chimney, Clean, Cliff, Cloth, Coffin, Cold, College, Colt, Comb, Comfort, Comfortable, Cool, Cove, Cow, Cream, Creamy, Creek, Cup, Curtain, Curtains

Day, Dog, Doll, Downs, Dream, Dreams, Dreamy, Drive in

Ease, Education, Eight hundred eighty one, Enjoyment, Excuse, Explain

Far, Faster, Feather, Fields, Fill, Flower, Foot, Forest Lake

Garden, Gate, Geese, Get, Girl, Go, Good, Got, Grade, Graduate, Grandma, Grandmother, Grantsburg, Grave, Ground, Guess

Had, Happiness, Hat, Hay, Heaven, Helpful, Hi, Hidden, High, Hill, Home away from home, Home fun, Home lake, Homey, Hose, Hot, Hotel, Hour, House by lake, Houses, How, Hunt, Hunting

Ice, Inn, In the woods, Is, It

Kitchen, Knife

Lack, Lakeside, Lamp, Lattice, Lawn, Lean, Learn, Life, Like, Little cabin, Little house, Living, Loafing, Lodge, Log cabin, Lone, Long, Lumber

Ma, Make, Married, Mary, Meadow, Men, Miles, Milk, Mine, Money, Moss, Mountain, Movie, My boat

Name, Neat, Newly weds, Night, North

Ocean, Of, Off, OK, Old, Outdoors

Pace, Peaceful, Peaceful home, Pebbles, People, Picket fence, Pillow, Pine, Pink, Place on lake, Pleasure, Poor

Quiet, Quite

Raining, Recreation, Red, Refreshing, Relax, Relaxation, Remote, Retire, Rich, River, Roads, Roof, Rooms

Sauk Centre, Scene, Sea, Seashore, Security, Sheep, Shelter, Shingles, Shore, Short, Sick, Skiing, Sky, Slave, Small house, Snow White, Snug, Soft, Sold, Solid, Song, Soup, Splinter, Spring, Stay, Stone, Store, Stove, Stream, Summer home, Summer vacation, Sun, Surf, Sweep, Sweet

Tag, Take, Teepee, Thatched, Thatched roof, Tin, To, Tony, Top, Town, Tranquility, Tree, Trip, Two

Use

Vacations, Valuable, Vegetable, Villa, Vine covered

Warm, Warmth, Water and straw house, Water fall, Water skiing, Wedding, Weekend, While, White fence, White house, Wind, Window, Witch, Wool, Work

Yacht, Yellow

CRY

A, Above, Ah, Ain't, Angry, At, Awake

Baa, Baba, Bag, Bald, Bawl baby, Bay, Bear, Because, Bed, Beg, Be still, Big, Blow, Blubber, Blue, Boil, Boo, Boys, Brave, Bring, Brother, Bubble, Bug, Bull, Bus, Bye

Call, Car, Carolyn, Case, Cat, Chant, Chatter, Cheer, Children, Christ, Cities, Clear, Come, Country, Coward, Crabby, Crayon, Cries, Crime, Crow, Crown, Crumbly, Cry, Cry baby, Cry out, Cup, Cut

Despair, Do, Does, Dress, Drink, Drop, Drops, Drown, Dye

Emotions, Everyone cries, Eye, Eyes

Fast, Fear, Fierce, Fight, Fingers, Flings, Fly, Food, For happy, Fry, Fun, Funeral, Funny

Gay, Get, Girls, Good, Goodbye, Guilt

Ha, Hag, Hail, Hand, Handkerchief, Happily, Have, Havoc, He, Head, Hear, Heart, Heart break, Heavy, Her, Here, Hide, High, His, Hobo, Hollow, Hope

I, In, Is

Kid, Kill, Kookie

Laughed, Lie. Lift, Little, Live, Load, Long, Louder, Loudly

Mate, Maudlin. Mean, Meow, Mind, Minn., Miserable, Moan, Mom, Monday, Moon, Mope, Mother, Mouth, Mumble, Myself

Never, Nice

On, Onion, Ouch, Over

Pear, People, Pie, Pig, Please, President, Pry, Put

Quiet

Rain, Read, River, Run, Rut

Sadly, Sadness, Said, Salt, Sam, Same, Sax, Scare, Scared, See, Select, Seven, Shame, She, Shriek, Shrill, Shut up, Sick, Sighing, Sight, Silent, Silly, Sin, Sit, Small, Smell, Smiling, Sneeze, Sniff, Sniffle, Snot, Soar, Sobbed, Sobbing, Sober, Sobs, Soft, Something, Song, Soon, Spank, Spanking, Speak, Squeal, State, Stop, Street, Sulk, Sun, Sway, Swear, Sweet, Swore, Sy

Tap, Teacher, Test, The, Thing, Think, Tie, Ties, Tire, Tired, To, Today, Tomorrow, Towel, Town, Tries, Trouble

Un

Voice

Wa, Waa, Waawaa, Wah, Wailed, Want, Warm, Weak, Web, Weeping, Wept, What, When, Whimpered, Whining, Who, Wild, Win, Wipe, Wire, Women, Work, Worry, Wrap, Wreath, Wring, Wrong

Yellow, Yes, You

DARK

A, Ages, Air, Alone, Ark, Art, Ate

Bat, Be, Bedroom, Beer, Blackness, Black or brown, Blank, Blind, Block, Boo, Boy, Bread

Camera, Candle, Candles, Can't, Can't see, Car, Cat, Cave, Chair, Class, Classic, Clock, Close, Cloth, Clouds, Coat, Colors, Corner, Cozy, Crawl, Creek

Dale, Damp, Danger, Dark, Darker, Dark room, Dart, Deep, Dick, Dim, Dirt, Do, Dog, Door, Dreary, Drop, Dull

Ebony, Eek, Evening, Eyes

Face, Fright, Frighten, Frightened, Fun

Gee, Ghosts, Girl, Glass, Glasses, Gloom, Green

Hall, Handkerchief, Hard, Hat, Heart, Help, Hid, Hideous, Horrible, Horse, Hum

Jane, Job, Jungle

Lamp, Land, Lark, Late, Light bulb, Lighter, Lightless, Lights, Like, Lit, Lonesome, Lover's Lane

Man, Mark, Mary, Me, Mean, Meet, Men, Midnight, Might, Mom, Moody, Moonlight, Moose, Mouse, Movie, Movies, Murder, Mysterious

Negro, Ness, Nice, Night cloud, Night time, No light, Noon, Nothing, Not light

Obnoxious, Outside

Park, Pencil, Pictures, Pink, Pit, Place, Pop, Pretty

Ray, Romantic

Scar, School, Shade, Shadow, Shadows, Shoes, Shows, Side, Sightless, Silence, Silent, Sleeping, Slipper, Smart, So, Solo, Space, Spark, Stair, Star, Stares, Stars, Start, Stick, Still, Street, Stumbling, Suit, Sun

Table, Tall, Ten, Theatre, Thick, Tight, Time, Tom, Tree, Try

Up, Upstairs

Vast, Very

Weird, Wilderness, Window, Witch, Without light, Wood, Work

DEEP

Abyss, Afraid, Alot, And, At, Away

Bad, Bed. Beg, Beyond, Boat, Bottom, Bowl, Boy, Bread, Brown

Castle, Cat, Cavern, Cavernous, Cellar, Cello, Chair, Cleft,

Cliff, Close, Coat, Color, Cool, Cozy, Creep, Crevasse, Crevice, Cup, Curve, Cut
Danger, Darkness, Dart, Dear, Death, Debt, Deep, Deeper, Deepness, Dense, Dept, Dig, Dirt, Distance, Dive, Dizzy, Dog, Drear, Dreary, Drift, Drop, Drown, Drowned, Drowning, Dry, Dug, Dungeon
Ear, Elevator, Encaved
Fall down, Far down, Farness, Fee, Feet, Fish, Flat, For, Full
Gay, Get away, Girl, Glass, Go, Gorge, Great, Green, Growl, Grump
Hall, Hay, Heat, Height, Here, Hill, Hold, Hole pit, Hope, Horse, House, How, Huge, Hungry, Hurt
Inches, In ground
Jar, Jeep
Keep
Land, Large small, Law, Leap, Length, Lets, Load, Loft, Lone, Long down, Long ways, Love
Man, Meat, Middle, Mine, Moments, Money, Mysteries, Mysterious
No, Not deep, Nothing
Often, Open, Over
Pool, Potatoes, Purse, Put
Quite
Ravine, Really, Reap, Rich, Rivers, Roar, Rock, Rocky, Round, Rut
Scare, Scared, See, Seep, Set, Shadows, Shall, Shovel, Silence, Sink, Sky, Slick, Slope, Slumber, Smooth, Something, Song, Sorrow, Sort, Sound, South, Step, Still, Sudden, Swallow, Swamp, Swimming
Tall, The, There, Thin, Thorough, Though, Thought, To, Top, Ugly, Underground, Unknown
Vacation, Very
Warm air, Waves, Way down, Ways, We, Wet, White, Whole, Width, Will, Wonderful, Wood, Wow
You

DOCTOR

A, Accident, Ache, Adkins, Aid kit, Ambition, A person who helps you, Appendix, Arlander, Artist, Aurness
Babies, Back, Bandage, Band aid, Belzer, Benjamin, Birth, Black, Blind, Blue, Bob, Body, Brill, Brother, Brown, Bugs Bunny, Bull, Butter
Cable, Cadillac, Call, Called, Calling, Cares, Carlson, Carry, Case, Chair, Chats, Check, Chest, Chief, Citizen, City, Clean, Cold, Compulsory, Confidence, Consult, Corpse, Creep, Curer, Cut
Dad, Daddy, Dead, Dean, Death, Decorate, Dennis, Dentists, Denton, Died, Diet, Dislike, Distinguished, Dock, Doctor, Dog, Done, Doolittle, Dope, Dr., Dr. Booth, Dr. Brown, Dr. Hom, Drill, Dr. Leland, Dr. Petit, Dr. Reiley, Duff, During
Education, Eilers, Einstein, Emergency, Enemy, Erickson, Esenten, Exam, Examination, Examine, Eye, Eye phones, Eyes
Family, Faust, Fear, Feel, Fixed, Fix you, Floor, Fool, Frey, Fried, Friendly
Gentle, Gentleness, Germs, Get well, Girl, Girls, Glasses, Go, Gold, Gonzalez, Good Joe, Grandfather, Grandma, Great, Guts, Guy
Hall, Hammer, Hard, Harry, Harsh, Hat, Hate, Head, Healing, Heals, Heel, Held, Helping, Helps cure, Help someone, Help us, Help you, Here, Hi. Him, Hippocrates, His, Honest, Hours, Hunt, Hurts you, Hypo, Hypodermic
I, Ick, Impatient, In, Injury, Instruments, Intelligence, Intern
Jacket, Jay, Jeckel, Jerry, Jew, Job, Joel Seltz, John
Keeping, Kick, Kindness, Knee, Knowledge, Kosiak
Lad, Lady, Lake, Lamp, Land, Large, Larson, Law, Lawyer Uncle Stick, Layer, Learned, Like, Linner, Listen, Live, Look, Lower
Machine, Mad, Magnificent, Make, Mankind, Man or help, McMurtrie, Md. Doctor, Mean shots, Measles, Medical care, Medicine man, Meland, Men, Meyers, Mine, Minister, Mister, Mold, Mother, Mustache, My dad, My uncle he's a doctor
Nasty, Near, Nelson, Nest, No, No no, Nose, Note, Now, Nueman, Nut
O, O'clock, October, Odor, Oh, Oh no, Operate, Orders, Orthodontist, Ott. Ow
Panasuik, Patch, Patience, Patients, Pediatrician, Pencil,

Physic, Physical, Pin, Practition, Pre-med, Prickle, Priest, Procter, Professional
Quist
Rat, Respect, Respected, Ricky my cousin, Robb, Robes, Room, Ross, Runquist
Safe, Said, Save, Saw bones, Says, Scale, Scare, Scared, Scent, Science, See, Sergeant, Shaperman, She, Sheep, Shirt, Shoot, Short, Shorts, Shragg, Sickly, Siperstein, Sir, Sister, Smart, Smell, Smiley, Smith, Snake, Soft, Sore, Special, Specialist, Spoch, Spock, Spocks, Stairs, St. Cyre, Stick, Stub name, Survivial, Sweet
T.D. Wright, Teeth, Television, Terrible, Test, The, Thief, Thompson, Tongue, Tooth, Town, Tractor, Treat, Tree doctor, Trouble, Trow
Uncle, Understanding, Uneasy, Uniform, Uselessness
Virgil, Vital
Went, Which, White chalk, White coat, White uniform, Will, Wise, Woman, Wonderful, Wonders, Word, Worker, Wort, Wound
You, Y.T. Johnson
Zinter

DOGS

Alot, Arf, Art, At
Baa, Bag, Barked, Barks, Bay, Beagles, Bears, Beau, Becky, Bell, Bird, Bitch, Bitches, Bites, Blackie, Block, Body, Bog, Book, Boots, Bowl, Bowser, Bow wow, Boxer, Britt, Brow, Brownie, Brutus, Bull, Bull dog, Buster, By
Calf, Canine, Canines, Cap, Cast, Catch, Chain, Charles, Children, Chinkie, Chubby, Cindy, Coat, Cocker, Cockers, Cocker spaniel, Collar, Collars, Collies, Come, Cookie, Cool cats, Cow
Dachshund, Dads, Dalmatian, Dane, Danny, Dashhound, Days, Dirty, Dixie, Do, Doggy, Door, Down, Drive, Duchess, Dug, Duke, Dukie, Dumb
Ears, Eat
Feathers, Feet, Fleas, Foot, Freckles, French poodle, Friendly, Friends, Frogs, Furry, Fury
Germans, German shepherd, Gigi, Girl, Girls, Good, Got, Grass, Gray, Ground, Growl, Gun
Hat, Have, Head, Hear, Her, Hit, Hog, Holly, Home, Honey, Horse, Horses, Hot dogs, Hound, Hounds, Houses, Humans, Hunt
Ish
Jug, Jump
Kelly, King, Kip, Kitten, Kittens, Kitties
Lady, Lassie, Lawn, Leg, Legs, Like, Little, Logs, Lot, Lots, Loud, Love, Loyal, Lucky
Male, Mammal, Man, Mascots, Me, Mean, Meat, Men, Messy, Mice, Mike, Mimi, Mine, Mittens, Mogs, Moon, Mother, Mud, Mutts
News, Nipper, Noise, Noisy, Noodles, Not, Nutrena
OK
Pack, Paw, Paws, Pen, Penny, People, Pepper, Pig, Pigs, Piles, Plutos, Poddles, Pointers, Pond, Poodles, Poopsy, Pound, Pretty, Prince, Pup
Rabies, Raggs, Raw meat, Rebel, Red, Rex, Running
Sally, Sammy, Sandy, Satin, Scotty, Setters, Shepherd, Showmanship, Sick, Sit, Small, Smoky, Smudge, Sox, Spaniel, Spot, Spots, Sweet
Taffy, Take, Tammy, Tasso, Teachers, Teddy Martin, Teeth, Ten, Terrier, Terriers, Thing, Thor, Thump, Tip, Toy, Train, Tree, Tummy, Turds, Two
Veterinarian
Weiners, Wild, Wolf, Wolves, Wonderful, Woof, Wow, Wuffty
Yard

DOORS

Air, Aluminum, And, Apartment, Arch, Are, At, Auto
Baby, Ball, Bang, Bar, Barn, Barriers, Bedroom, Between, Bills, Black, Blue, Board, Bolts, Boo, Boor, Boors, Bore, Bores, Boy, Broad, Broken
Cabinet, Cane, Ceiling, Church, Clowns, Cold, Come, Confused, Corridor, Cottage, Could, Cowboy, Creaking, Crummy, Curtain, Curtains
Dell, Depth, Dianne, Digits, Docks, Doctor, Doctors, Dog, Donaldson's, Doorbells, Door handle, Doors, Doorway, Doubt, Down, Draw, Drawers
Elevators, Enclosure, End, Entry, Eye
Feet, Fence, Fingers, Flaps, Flat, Folding, Foot, Four, Frame,

French, Front
Games, Give
Halls, Hall way, Hard, Hat, Hats, Head, Heavy, Help, High,
  Hold, Holes, Homes, Hooks, Horse, Hose, Hospital, Hurt
Inside, Is, It, Ivy League
Jam
Key, Key holes, Kitchen, Know
Later, Lawn, Left, Letter, Lettuce, Lights, Locker, Long,
  Look, Lot, Lots, Louvre, Luck, Luncheon
Mad, Man, Many, Me, Men, Metal, Mine, Mirror, Money,
  Moor, Moors, Mops, More, Move, My
Nail, Nails, Neatness, Never, No, Nokomis, Nor, Not, Now
Oak, Oars, Oh, On, One, Only, Opens, Opportunity, Opportunities,
  Or, Orange, Outdoor
Pair, Paneled, Panels, Passage, Passage ways, Path, Pathway,
  Pathways, People, Person, Phones, Pills, Pipe, Place,
  Play, Poor, Poors, Porch, Porte, Post, Prize, Puerta, Push
Quit
Rags, Rain, Ramsey, Rang, Rat, Rectangle, Revolve, Rugs
Sash, Seat, Sex, Shatter, Sheet, Shelter, Shoes, Shout, Shutter,
  Sidewalk, Sidewalks, Sill, Sills, Six, Slams, Slide, Sliding,
  Smash, Smell, Smooth, Soar, Soars, Something to open,
  Speak, Spin, Spores, Squeak, Squeeze, Stares, Stars, Steeple,
  Step, Stop, Store, Stores, Streets, Sun, Swing open
Table, Tall, Tan, That, The, Thing, Things, Those, Three,
  Thresholds, Through, To, Too, Top
Upon
Very
Wagon, Wall, Wars, Way out, Weather, Welcome, Where, White,
  Whores, Why, Winder, Winds, Woman, Worm
Yellow, You, Yours

DREAM

Adventure, Air, Alike, Along, Am, Amusement, Angel, Angels,
  Anger, Anything, Ask, At, Awaken, Away, Awful
Bad sad happy, Band, Bat, Beam, Bean, Beauty, Berry, Big,
  Bill, Birds, Black, Boot, Bout, Bow, Boy friend, Brain,
  Bring, Brown, Bubble
Came true, Candy, Carol, Carpet, Child, Cloudy, Cold, Color-
  ful, Colors, Come, Come true, Comfort, Comforting,
  Concussion, Confused, Conscious, Cool, Could, Crackers,
  Crazy, Crow, Cup, Curt
Damp, Dance, Darkness, Day dream, Days, Day time, Daze,
  Dear, Death, Deep, Delight, Delightful, Desire, Desires,
  Did, Different, Dim, Do, Dog, Don, Dram, Dreamboat,
  Dreamed, Dreaming, Dreams, Dreamt, Drum
Ear, Eat, Enchanting, Ending, Enjoyment, E.S.P., Ethereal,
  Exciting
Fake, Falling, False, Fanciful, Fantasies, Far, Faraway, Fear,
  Feeling, Fight, Figment, Fire, Flower, Flowers, Flowing,
  Flying, Foggy, Food, Fool, Foot, Football, Forest, Frank,
  Frightened
Game, Gary, Gay, Gaze, Geno, Ghost, Giant, Gleam, Glory
  Goblins, Green, Grow, Guess
Had, Hair, Happen, Happening, Happiness, Hard, Have, Haze,
  Hazy, Heaven, Heavenly, Help, High, Him, Hopes, Horrible,
  Horror, Horses, Hot, House, Houses, Hurt
Ice, Ice cream, Ideal, Idealism, Illusions, Image, Imaginary,
  Imagination, Impossible, Interesting, In your sleep, Is, Ish
Jack, Jeanie, Jerry, Joyce, June
Kathy, Ken, Kids, Kind, King, Kiss, Kitten, Knives
Lake, Lame, Last, Laugh, Lean, Let, Life, Light, Like, Little,
  Live, Loaf, Long ago, Look, Loud, Lover, Lynne
Make, Make believe, Make up, Mare, Marriage, Mary Lou,
  Mean, Meat, Mellow, Memory, Men, Mental, Mice, Mind,
  Mine, Miss, Mist, Misty, Monster, Mother, Music, My,
  Mystery, Myth
Nancy, Nancy L., Neat, Nice dream, Nick, Niece, Nightmares,
  None, Nonsense, Nostalgia, Not, Not clear, Nut, Nuts
Odd, Of, Old, On, Onion, Out of space, Over
Peace, Person, Peter, Phantasy, Phil, Pictures, Pillows,
  Pink, Place, Pleasure girls, Ponder, Poor, Prayer, Pretend,
  Prince
Queer, Quiet
Race, Read, Relax, Relaxation, Remember, Restful, Resting,
  Restless, Rich, Right, Rim, River, Romantic, Room, Running
Sad, Sat, Say, Scheme, School, Scream, Seconds, Seem, Seem
  when sleep, Seen, Sense, Sent, Sequence, Shadow, Short,
  Show, Silence, Silly, Sky, Slap, Slept, Slow, Smile, Smoke,
  Smooth, Snore, Soda, Softly, Softness, Something that you

have when you, Song, Sorrow, Sound, Speak, Spooks, Stair,
  Star, Stare, Stars, Steam, Steep, Stem, Steve, Stories,
  Subconcious mind, Sue, Surealism, Swim
Table, Tale, Teak, Technicolor, Ten, That, The, Things,
  Think of, Though, Tired, Tomorrow, Trouble, Troubled,
  Truthful, TV, Two
Unconscious, Unconsciousness, Unhappiness, Unhappy,
  Unreality, Untrue, Upon, Useless, Utopia
Vacation, Vague, Ville, Visions, Voice
Wander, Want, Wear, Weather, Wheat, While, Whip, Widow,
  Wild, Window, Wishes, Witch, With, Woman, Wonderland,
  Wonders, Work, Wow
Yellow, Yes

EAGLE

A bird, Age, Air Force, Airplane, Alert, American flag,
  American symbol, An, An animal, Anger, Angle, Army,
  As in gulf
Baby, Bad, Badge, Bait, Bald eagle, Balded, Bald head,
  Bald red tailed, Ball, Band, Banner, Barn, Bat, Beast,
  Beautiful, Bend, Bid, Big bird, Bird of U.S.A., Bite, Black,
  Blue, Blue bird, Blue jay, Bold, Book, Boy, Boy Scouts,
  Boys some, Bred, Brick, Brown, Buzzard
Candle, Cap, Car, Cars, Cat, Catfish, Chicken, Child, Clock,
  Cloud, Country's bird, Cow, Crest, Crow, Cruel, Curve
Danger, Dark, Devil, Dog, Don, Dove, Duck
Eager, Eaglet, Earth, Earthy, Edge, Eggs, Electricity, End,
  Europe
Face, Falcon, Fall, Fierce, Fifty cents, Finger, Fish, Flat,
  Fleet, Flew, Flies, Flower, Food, Free, Freedom, Friendly,
  Fun
Giggle, Girl, Gliding, Going, Gold, Golf, Good, Graceful,
  Gracefulness, Grand, Great, Green
Had, Hard, Hark, Haven, Head, Heat, Homely, Honor, Horse,
  Hot, House, How, Hunt, Hunting
Insignia, Intelligence, It
Jungle
Keen, Kill, King
Lake, Land, Large, Late, Leg, Liberty, Light, Line, Lodge,
  Lofty, Look
Mad, Magnificent, Majesty, Make, Mammal, Man, Me, Mean
  look, Meanness, Meat, Men, Mighty, Mouse
Name, Nat. emblem, Nationalism, Nat'l. crest of America,
  Neck, Nigeria, Nine, None, Nose, Now, Nuts
Of, Old, One, Os prey, Owl
Parakeet, Parrot, Past, Patriotic, Pendent, Pheasant, Pig, Pin,
  Pinion, Plume, Point, Prairie, Pretty, Prey, Proud, Punch
Quarter, Quarters, Quick
Rabbit, Range, Red, Regal, Repulsive, Right, Rock, Rod Egen,
  Roman, Rough
Sale, Same, Scar, Scared, Scary, Scouting, Scouts, Serpent,
  Sharpness, Sheep, Shoot, Silver dollar, Smart, Smash, Snake,
  Soft, Sore, Sour, Sparrow, Speed, Spider, Spread, Spring,
  Springs, Square, Squirrel, Stand, State, Steam, Stern, Stomach,
  Stop, Stork, Stove, Straight, Strength, Swoop, Symbol of
  strength
Tall, Talon, Talons, Ten, Tent, Then, Tooth, Tough, Tree,
  Triangle, Two
U.N., U.S. flag, United, United States symbol, US
Watch, Who, Wicked, Wide, Wiggle, Wind, Wisdom, Wolf,
  Woman, Word, Work, Working, Worm

EARTH

America, American, Angle, Angle worms, A place, Are
  Art, Astronomy, Aviation, Awaken, Axis
Bake, Beautiful, Bigness, Big step, Birth, Block, Boat, Bones,
  Book, Both, Bound, Bountiful, Boy, Brake, Bread, Buck,
  Bug, Bumpy
Cabin, Can't, Carry, Cave, Center, Clay, Clean, Cloud, Cold,
  Color, Continents, Cool, Core, Corruption, Countries,
  Country, Cow, Crumble, Crust
Damp, Deep, Dense, Die, Different, Dig, Divit, Domain, Dry,
  Dust
Eagle, Earthquake, East, Enormous, Entire, Equator, Everything
Fall, Farmer, Farming, Fire, Firm, Flat, Floor, Flower,
  Flowers, Food, Form
Giant, Gold, Goodness, Gravitation, Gravity, Great circle,
  Grow, Grown, Growth
Hearth, Here, Hills, Hope, Hot, House, Humus
I, Inner core, Irregular

Jupiter
Late, Layers, Leg, Like, Ling, Little, Live on, Living,
Loam, Long, Love, Lunar
Magna, Map, Mars candy bars, Marvelous, Mass, Mater,
May, Me, Men, Mercury, Merry, Mine, Mined, Minerals,
Minneapolis, Moan, Mole man, Mountains, Move, Moves,
Moving, Muddy, Music
Nat Sci, Nice, Night, North, Not, Now
Ocean, On, Orange, Orbit
Peace, Pear, Pebble, Physical, Pineapple, Planet from
sun, Planets universe, Plants, Plenty, Pluto, Polar ice
caps, Pot, Pretty, Problems
Quack, Quakes, Quick
Ran, Red, Revolving, Rich, Rock, Rocket, Rockets, Rotation,
Rough, Round ball, Round small, Round sphere, Run, Russia
Sad, Sail, Sandy, Seen, Seven, Shovel, Slow, Small, Smell,
Smooth, Sod, Soft, Soil or planet, Solar, Solar system,
Sorrow, Sound, Sour, Spare, Spear, Spin, Spinning, Spire,
Spy, Stability, Stand on, State, Steep, Stone, System
Table, Terra firma, The, Thing, This, Till, Time, To live,
Top, Town, Tree, Trees, Tremble, Troubles, Turn, Turning
U.S., U.S.A., United, United States, Universal, Up, Up high,
Upons
Vacation, Valley, Variety, Volcano
Walk, We, West, Wet, What, White, Whole, Will, Woman,
Women, Wonderful, Wood, World, Work, World planet,
Worth, Would

EASIER

Action, Adverb, All, Always, Answer, As, Away
Baby, Bad, Balance, Bananas, Basket, Be, Because, Bed,
Best, Bicycle, Big, Board, Book, Boy, Breeze, Breezier,
Bubby, But, Buy
Call, Can, Car, Carry, Cash, Chalk, Cheating, Choke, Christ-
mas, Cinch, Classes, Clean, Climb, Color, Come, Comfort,
Complicated, Confidence, Convenient, Correct, Cover up
Dictionary, Died, Dive, Does, Dog, Doing, Don't, Door,
Driving, Dumber
Each, Early, Easier, Eater, Efficiency, Efficient, Effortless,
Enjoyable, Erase, Ever, Examples, Execution
Face, Facile, Fair, Few, Fewer, Finding, Fine, First,
Fish, Food, Football, For, Friend, From, Funner,
Funnier, Funny
Game, Gas, Getting, Girl, God, Gone, Grades, Grease
Halloween, Handier, Handle, Handy, Happier, Hardest,
Hardier, Hardly, Hard non, Hat, Hay, Hear, Heavy, Help,
Helpful, Hen, Here, Hi, Him, History, Hit, Hold, Homework,
Hotter, House
I, If, Is, Its
July
Keep, Kindergarten, King, Kiss, Kitchen, Know
Lake, Last, Late, Lay, Lazier, Laziest, Learn, Leisure,
Lesson, Less work, Lest, Let, Lie, Listen, Little, Living,
Loaf, Longer, Look, Lost, Lot, Love, Luck, Lucky
Machines, Mad, Match, May, Maybe, Moment, Money, More,
Mouse, Much, My
Nails, Name, Neater, Nicer, No work
Of, Off, Oil, OK, On, One, Out, Over
Park, Party, Pat, Pattern, Peace, Pen, Pie, Place, Play,
Pleasant, Pleasanter, Please, Pleasier, Pleasing, Pleasure,
Plentiful, Plenty, Possible, Psych, Push, Puzzled
Quiet
Rapid, Ready, Relax, Rest, Ride, Rite, Roller, Rougher
Safe, Safer, Said, Scrubbing, Sell, Sharp, She, Shoe, Shopping,
Similar, Simply, Singing, Sister, Sit, Sitters, Skiing, Skip,
Sleep, Slide, Sling, Slip, Slippery, Sloppy, Sloth, Slowly,
Small, Smaller, Smart, Smarter, Smile, Snow, So, Some,
Someone, Soon, Sooner, Spend, Standing, Start, Still, Stub,
Summer, Sunday, Supple
Teacher, That, Them, There, Things, Thought, Three, Thus,
Today, To do, To go, Too, To rest, Tough, Tougher, Trick,
Trouble, Truck, Two, Type
Under, Undifficult, Us, Use
Vacation
Walk, We, Went, West, What, When, Whiz, Who says, Why,
Word, Words, Worse, Write, Writing
Yellow, Yes, Yet, You, Younger

EATING

Acting, All, Alot, Appetite, Apples, Are, At, Awful

Baby, Bad, Banana, Beans, Beating, Bird, Bite, Biting, Boot,
Bought, Brown, Bull, Bun, But
Carrots, Celery, Cheese, Chewed, Chicken, Chocolate,
Choking, Chomp, Chomping, Cliff, CN, Coffee, Coke,
Comfort, Comfortable, Consuming, Contentment, Cooking,
Corn, Cottage cheese, Crackers, Crunch, Cry
Dancing, Dark, Delicious, Devour, Devouring, Dietary, Digest,
Digestion, Dine, Diner, Dining, Dinner place, Dishes,
Dissolve, Do, Dog, Doing, Don, Don't, Donut, Doors, Dorm,
Dress, Drive in, Drunk, Dying
Eaten, Eating, Egg, Eggs, Enjoy, Enjoyable, Enough
Family, Famine, Famish, Faster, Fasting, Fat person,
Fattening, Feasting, Fed, Feed, Feel, Feet, Fill, Filling,
Fine, Finish, Flower, Food and pizza, Food bread dishes,
Foot, Fountain, Fruit
George, Getting full, Glad, Glutton, Gluttony, Go, Going, Gorge,
Great, Gulp, Gulping
Had, Ham, Hamburgers, Happy, Hard, Has, Hat, Health,
Healthful, Hog, Home, Hope, Horse, Hot fudge sundae, House,
Hungrier, Hurt
In, Indigestion, Indulge, Instinct
Kitchen, Knife
Late, Lemons, Lie, Light, Like, Liking, Lime, Living, Look,
Lot, Love, Lunchroom
Making, Me, Meant, Meet, Meeting, Mmm, Money, More,
Motion, Much, Munch, Music
Nice, Noise, None, Not, Nourishing, Nourishment, Now,
Nowhere, Nutrition
Obese, Okay, Oranges, Over stuffed
Pain, Pancakes, Pastries, Peach, Peanuts, People, Person,
Pies, Place, Plant, Play, Playing, Pleasurable, Pleasure,
Popcorn, Potato, Potato chips, Potatoes, Pray, Praying,
Prunes, Psychology, Put things into your mouth
Raisins, Reading, Refreshing, Refrigerator, Relaxing, Restaurant,
Resting, Rice, Run, Running
Salad, Sat, Scrounging, Seat, Sew, Sewing, Sharp, She's, Sick,
Silk, Silverware, Sit, Sitting, Slop, Sloppy, Slow, Slurp,
Smoking, Snack, Soap, Soft, Something, Sowing, Spaghetti,
Spitting, Stack, Stake, Stare, Stark, Start, Starvation, Starved,
Stubbed, Stuff, Stuffing, Sucking, Swallow, Swallowing
Tastes good, Tasty, Teeth, Television, The, Thin, Through,
Tired, Too much, Tubby, Turkey
Vegetables, Vomit, Vomiting
Washing, Water, Watermelon, Well, What, Win, Work
You, Yummy, Yum yum

FARTHER

A, Adult, Adverb, After, Airplane, Alaska, All, Am, An, And,
Are, At, At length, Authority, Away from
Backward, Ball, Bark, Baseball, Because, Beer, Before,
Behind, Best, Better, Big, Blank, Blurry, Board, Boss, Boy,
Boys, Broader, Bud, Building, But
Cabin, Caesar, Calif, Came, Can't, Car, Carl, Chair, China,
Church, Cities, Clear, Climb, Closely, Closes, Cloud,
Come, Comparisance, Corn ball
Dam, Dead, Deep, Deeper, Dig, Diverse
Eating, End, Europe, Even, Extent, Extra, Extreme
Family, Fan, Far as, Fare, Farer, Farmer, Farmers, Farther,
Farthing, Fastest, Fat, Fatter, Few, Fish, Flower, Fly,
Food, For, Foremen, Forest, Friend, Fun, Fur
Get, Gin, Girl, Glasses, Goes, Golden, Goon, Great, Greater,
Grey hair, Guardian
Hammer, Hard, Harder, Harther, Hat, Hate, Head, Hearer,
Her, Hide, Highway, Hill, Hills, Him, Hit, Horse, Hot,
Hurry, Husband
If, Interior, Its
Japan, Journey, Jump
Kind, King, Kite
Lake, Land, Last, Late, Laugh, Layer, Length, Less, Lesser,
Lift, Like, Little, London, Lonesome, Long distance, Longest,
Long way, Look, Lost, Love
Ma, Many, Mars, Me, Mean, Men, Mine, Moon, Mountains,
Move, Much, My, My daddy
Name, Nearby, Neared, Nearest, Nears, Never, None, Nore,
North, Now, No where
Ocean, Oceans, Off, Old, Onward, Or, Ouch
Pa, Paint, Past, Path, Place, Please, Pop, Pops, Priest, Push
Quick, Quicker, Quickly
Race, Radio, Ran, Regress, Remember, Restriction, Rivers
bend, Roam, Running, Russia

Said, San Francisco, Say, Sea, Searching, Seeing, Seek, Shoes,
Shot, Sister, Sky, Sleep, Small, Smaller, Smokey, So, Soft,
Softer, Some, Soon, Sooner, Sorrow, South, Sow, Space,
Spain, Spank, Spark, Speaking, Speed, Spoke, Square, Stars,
Step, Street, Stretch, Strict, Strong, Sun, Sunset
Table, Take, Talk, Tall, Tea, Teacher, That, The, Them, There,
They, Threw, Through, Time, Tired, To go, Toward, Train,
Trip, Trot
Vanish
Walking, Water, Way, Ways, Weaker, Weather, Went, West,
What, Where, Why, Wife, Will, Wonderful, Word, Work,
Worse, Would
Yonder

FASTER

Acceleration, Again, All, Am, Andre, Are, As, Ask her,
Aster, A stop, Away
Back, Baseball, Be, Bed, Beat, Because, Before, Best, Better,
Bicycle, Bird, Blurry, Boat, Boys, Bunny, Burry
Can't, Caster, Christ, Clean, Cow, Come, Constitution, Could,
Crazy
Dance, Dart, Dead, Dear, Death, Do, Dog, Done, Down,
Drive
Eat, East, Eastern, Easy, Egg, Eggs, End, Even, Ever, Extreme
Far, Fail, Fall, Farthest, Faster, Feet, Fester, Fewer, Fix,
Find, Flies, Floor, Ford, Fred, Fright, Further
Gas, Gain, Game, Gas pedal, Get, Gears, Glide, Goes, Go
faster, Go go go, Gone, Grew, Greyhound, Gun
Hat, Happy, Hardly, Hastily, He, Her, Heavy, Help, Hit, High,
Hill, How, Holiday, Holly, Horse, Hot rods, Hotter, Hurrying,
Hustle
I, If, Immediately
Jets, John
Kite, Know
Last, Later, Legs, Lighter, Lightning, Lively, Low, Look, Lost
Man, Marbles, Master, Merry, Mississippi, Mister, More,
Mother, Moving, Much, My
Native, No, Not, Not slow
On, One, Out
Pain, Paint, Past, Paste, Pastor, Pedal, Pell mell, Pencil,
People, Place, Playing, Please
Quickness
Rabbit, Racer, Racing, Raft, Raod, Rapid, Rapidly, Rat, Rice,
Ride, Right away, Rocket, Rockets, Roll, Rush
Scared, School, Sea, See, Seem, Shiny, Shiver, Short, Shorter,
Shower, Sister, Skate, Skating, Skiing, Sleek, Slowed, Slowest,
Small, Smoother, Sow, Soft, Softer, Sold, Sole, Soled,
Something, Soon, Sound, Space, Sped, Speeder, Speedily,
Spot, Start, Still, Stop, Store, Sun, Sundae, Sunday, Swing
Taste, Test, That, There, Thin, Thing, Think, Time, Tired,
Tops, Track, Travel, Tree, Turtle
Unslow
Very, Very fast
Wagon, Walk, Walking, Water, We, Who, Wheels, When, Wide,
Wind, With, Work
Yet, Yes, You
Zoom

FIND

Acquire, Ad, Again, All, Always, Another, Ant, Any, Apartment,
Appear, Apple, Arduous, Are, Article, At
Baby, Bad, Basket, Billfold, Bind, Bird, Blind, Bob, Books,
Box, Boy, Brought, Brown, Bug, Bury, Button
Candy, Can't, Capture, Car, Caught, Cave, Chase, Clever,
Cognate, Coin, Collect, Color, Come upon, Coop, Corner,
Cuase
Day, Diamond, Dig, Dime, Din, Dirt, Disappear, Discovered,
Discovery, Dish, Do, Doll, Dollar, Do something, Drop
Easy, Encounter, End, Enough, Everything, Excited, Excitement,
Experiment, Explore
Fact, Fault, Fear, Fetch, Fill, Fin, Finder, Find not, Find out,
Find something, Fine, Finish, Finland, First, Fix, Follow,
Food, Forest, Fortune, Fought, Friend, From, Fund, Fuzz
Game, Getting, Gift, Girl, Give up, Glad, Glove, Gloves,
Going, Gone, Got it, Grass, Ground, Guess
Hand, Handkerchief, Happy, Hard, Hat, Have, Hear, Hen,
Hey, Hidden, Hiding, Hind, His, Hold, Hole, Home, Horse,
House, How, Hunting
I, Invent, Investigate, Item
Jewel

Keeper, Keepers, Kept, Key, Kitten, Knife, Know
Last, Lets, Letter, Level, Lift, Like, Lint, Location, Long,
Look for, Looking, Loser, Losers, Love, Luck, Lucky
Man, Many, Map, May, Mine, Mitten, Mouse, Mud, My,
Mystery
Necklace, Needle, Nest, Nickel, Night, Nine, Nothing, Now,
Nut
Off, Oil, On, One, Only, Open, Operate, Ore, Other, Own
Placed, Package, Peanut, Pen, Pencil, Penny, Pick, Piece,
Place, Playing, Pocket, Present, Prize, Purse, Put
Quick, Quickly, Quit
Rabbit, Rainbow, Rate, Receive, Rescue, Reward, Rock, Run,
Runaway, Running
Sand, Secret, Seen, She, Shell, Shoe, Show, Sign, Silk, Sit,
Skirt, Sold, Someone, Something lost, Sorry, Sought, Source,
Spot, Spy, Stones, Surprise, Swat
Tag, Then, They, Throw, Time, Timed, Treasurer, Tree, Try
Under, Upon, Us
Valuable
Wallet, Want, Weight, Well, Who, With, Woman, Wonderful
Yellow pages, Yes, You find things, Yours

FINGERS

A, ABC, Am, And, Appendage, Appendages, Away
Ball, Be, Bigger, Blind, Bone, Bonnie Kittleson, Bowls, Boy,
Break, Bring, Broken, Burn, Burned, But, Butter, By
Carr, Cats, Cello, Chew, Chocolate, Clap, Claw, Clean,
Clippers, Close, Cold, Come, Construct, Could, Crayon,
Crook
Day, Delicate, Desk, Digitals, Dip, Dirt, Do, Does, Dog,
Don't, Down
Ear, Eight, Else, Enjoyment, Everywhere, Exercise, Exercises
Fabrics, Fan, Far, Farther, Feathers, Fig, Fight, Figures,
Finder, Fine, Fingering, Finger nail, Finger paints, Finger
prints, First, Fish, Fist, Fit, Flanges, Flash, For, Fore,
Fought, Four, Freed, Freeze, From, Fumble, Fun
Get, Girl, Girls, Glad, Going, Got, Grab, Grasp, Guns
Ha, Had, Hail, Handy, Hang, Have, He, Heart, Hide, Higher,
Hold, Hole, Hot, How many
I, If, Is, Itch, Itching
Jack, Joint, Joints, Jump
Keepers, Kid, Kite, Know, Knuckle, Knuckles
Lady, Lady fingers, Lakes, Last, Leg, Let, Lick, Lift, Limber,
Limbs, Lingers, Lips, Little, Live, Lost, Lots, Love
Make, Male, Man, Manipulation, Marchetti, McGee, McLain,
Men, Messy, Milk, Mind, Mine, Mit, More, Movable, Move-
ment, Moving, Much, Mud, Music
Nail Polish, Name, Narrow, New, Nice, Nimble, Nine, Noise,
Nose, Not, Number
Of, Off, OK, On, One, Our, Out
Paint, Paints, Palm, Palms, Panties, Parts, Paws, Pencil,
Pencils, People, Person, Pick, Pie, Pin, Place, Playing,
Please, Polish, Prehensile, Print, Project, Projections,
Pudding, Putting
Quite
Really, Red, Ringers
Safe, Said, Saw, School, Sell, Sex, Sharps, Shoes, Shoot, Sing,
Sings, Skates, Slim, Slip, Slippery, Snap, Soft, Some,
Something, Soon, Sore, Sores, Sound, Spoon, Squeeze,
Squirrel, Stay, Steal, Stick, Sticky, Stiff, Stop, Store, Strong,
Stubby, Swell, Swim
Tack, Tanned, Tentacles, That, Thief, Thin, Thing, Think,
This, Things, Those, Though, Thump, Tight, Tired, To,
Too, Took, Tools, Touched, Tower, Town, Toy, Toys,
Trumpet, Tuck, Tune, Two, Type
Under, Used, Useful, Using, Utility
Was, We, Were, Where, Whose, Why, Wiggle, Will, Wings,
With, Women, Wrong
Your

FOOT

A big foot, Ache, Always hurts, Answer, A part of your body,
Appendature, Arch, Athlete, Athletes
Barefoot, Beet, Blister, Bones, Book, Boot, Boots, Boy, Broken,
Brown
Cabbage, Canter, Car, Chair, Clam, Clean, Club, Cool man,
Corns, Crusty, Cup, Cut
Dance, Deep, Dig, Dirty, Dog, Door
Ear, Eat, Elbow, End, Examination, Extremity, Eye
Fall, Fast, Fat, Feed, Feel, Feet shoe, Felt, Fight, Finger,

Fingers, Five toes, Flange, Flesh, Floor, Food, Foot man, Fruit

Gear, Girl, Go, Good, Grandmother, Gym

Had, Hands, Hard, Hat, Heal, Hear, Heart, Hell, High, Hill, Hold, Hoot, Horn, Hot, Huge, Human, Hurts

Ill, In, Inches, Injury

Jump

Kathy

Ladder, Lag, Led, Left, Length, Let, Little, Look, Loose, Low

Magic, Make, Mans, Mark, Math, Me, Measurement, Meeting, Meter, Mile, Mine, Moth, Mountain, Move, Myself

Near ankle, Necessity, Nice, Night, Nose

Object, One, One feet, Oranges, Over shoes

Part of body, Part of human body, Path, Ped, Pedal, People, Persons, Piece of body, Pink, Print, Put

Red, Rest, Right, River, Rode, Rotten, Rule, Runner, Running

Scratch, Series, Seven, Shape, Shoot, Shore, Short, Shoulder, Shove, Sidewalk, Size, Size thirteen, Sleep, Socks, Soft, Sole, Something, Sores, Sox, Specialist, Spilling, Spindle, Spine, Stand, Stand on, Steep, Step on, Steps, Stick, Stocking, Stomp, Stool, Stretch, Strong, Swollen

Table, Tarsals, The, Tickle, To, Toe nail, Toe nails, Told, Tongue, Too, Toot, Tooth, To step on, Track, Trouble, Trouser, Twelve, Twelve in.

Use, Useful

Wait, Walking on, Walk on, Warm, Wart, Wart on foot, Warts, Water, Wear, Web, Women, Work

Yds., You

Zoo

FOR

Able, About, Adverb, Affirmative, Aft, After, Aid, Along, Also, Although, Answer, Anything, Are, Ask, As much, Avail, Away

Baby, Basket, Became, Because of, Bed, Being, Belong, Belonging, Belongs, Big, Birds, Birthday, Blood, Boar, Book, Boy, Boys, Bring, Brought, Buy

Can, Candy, Car, Card, Cars, Cast, Cause, Certain Christmas, Church, Clerk, Cold, Come, Considering, Crime

Day, Days, Death, Dodo, Dog, Dogs, Do it, Dollar, Dollars, Dress, Due

Each, Else, English, Errand, Every, Everyone, Explanation

Fad, Fair, Fall, Fare, Fast, Fat, Favor, Fear, Fetch, Fever, Fight, Film, Find, Fingers, Fit, Floor, Flower, Flowers, Foe, Food, For, Force, Ford, Forest, Forfeit, Forget, Forgetting, Forgot, For his own good, Form, Former, For not, Forth, Fortitude, Fortunate, For what, For you, Found, Fourth, Free, Friend, Fright, Front

Gift for, Girl, Girls, Giving, Glass, Golf club, Gone, Goodness sake, Gore, Got for, Grandma, Green

Hair, Happy, Hard, Hat, Have, Heaven, Heavens, Heaven sake, Heck, Hell, Help, Hers, He's, Hold, Honor, Hop, House, However

I, Important, In, In order, Instance, Intend, Intended, Isn't, Its

Jane, John, Just

Keep, Keeps, Knew, Know

Land, Life, Little, Live, Long, Look, Loose, Love, Luck, Lucky, Lying

Magic, Many, Maybe, Mead, Meant, Mine, Minutes, Mom, Mommy, Money, Morning, Mother, Mumber, My, Myself

Name, Naught, Neat, Need, New, Nice, Night, No, Not for, Nought, Numbers

Of course, Off, Often, On, Once, Only, On to, Ore, Others, Our, Ours, Ow, Owner, Ownership

Package, Peace, Pencil, Per, Pet, Pipe, Place, Please, Possess, Presents, Pro, Provide

Question

Racoon, Ralph, Reading, Reasons, Response, Rose

Saw, Say, School, Shame, Shore, Short, Sitting, Six, Sore, Sour, Space, Special, Stop, Store, Studying, Sure

Table, Take, Team, Tell, Ten, That reason, Theater, Their, Therefore, They, They're, Thieves, Thing, Those, Thus, To give, Too, Tore, Toward, Try

Use, Used

Versus

War, Way, We, Week, Well, Went, Were, What for, Where, While, Whiskey, Wise, Women, Won't, Woo, Wore

Years, Your, Yours

Zion

FROM

About, Above, Across, Address, Afraid, Against, Alan, Alaska, All, Always, Among, And, A person, Are, Arizona, Army, Around, Arrived, As, Aunt

Babies, Back, Because, Bed, Been, Before, Begin, Beginning, Behind, Between, Birds, Blue, Born, Box, Boy, Boy friend, Bridge, Brought, Bull, Bum, Button, Bye

California, Can, Canada, Car, Card, Cat, Chair, China, Christmas, Circle, Clothes, Come from, Comes, Come to, Cook, Copy, Cord, Cottage, Could, Cow

Daryl, De, Death, Delivered, Depart, Derived, Distance, Do, Dog, Dome, Door, Down, Drum, Duluth

Earth, Eat, Egg, England, English, Eternity, Europe, Ever, Ex

Fast, Fat, Fear, Find, Flat, Food, Fore, Foreign, Found, Four, France, Friend, From us, Front, Froth

Garage, Gave, Georgia, Gerald, Girl friends, Girls, Given, Glare, God, Good, Go out, Got, Grandma, Grand mother, Grandpa, Greg, Ground, Guess

Had out, Hails, Ham, Has, Hat, He, Heaven, Hell, Hello, Helping, Here to there, Her house, High, Highway, Hit, Home town, Hope, Horse, Hum, Hunger

I, If, Ill, Inside, Iowa, Ish, Island, Its

Jean, Jim, Joanie, Join

Kansas, Keep, Key, Kid, Kite, Kitten, Know

Lake, LaVonne, Leave, Leaving, Left, Legs, Lemon, Less, Let, Light, Like, Lips, Live, Location, Look, Lot, Luck, Lynne

Made, Mail, Man, Men, Mexico, Mice, Mike, Mind, Minn., Minneapolis, Mom, Moom, Moon, More, Mother, Movie, Moving, Mower, Mpls., My

Never, New, New York, Next, Nice, No, Noon, North, Norway, Nothing, Numb, Nun, N.Y.

Off, Office, Off of, Oh, One, Or, Others, Our house, Ours, Outside, Over there, Oz

Package, Paint, Pals, Pan, Parcel, Parents, Park, Peace, Pen, Perfect, Persons, Places, Planet, Practice, Prep, President, Pretty, Proceed, Prom, Put

Rebecca, Rodney, Rome, Roof, Root, Roots, Round, Rum, Russia

Sad, Santa, Santa Claus, Schools, Sea, Send, Sender, Shape, She, Sheet, Shore, Short, Sister, Sit, Skinny, Sky, Small, Some, Someplace, Something, Somewhere, Source, South, Spot, State, States, Stay, Stop, Stove, Street, Stronger

Tall, Teacher, Term, Terrace, Than, Thank you, Thence forth, These roots, The store, They, Thing, Thither, Those, Thumb, Time, Together, Tom, Took, Tough, Towards, Travel, Tree

Uncle, Up

Visitor

Walk to, Ware, Was, Water, We, Wear, Well, West, What's, Where came, Which, Window, Woman, Womb, World

Yellow, Your, Yours, Yours truly

Zoo

FRUIT

Acid, All, All colors, Appeal, Appetite, Apple orange peach, Apply

Back, Ball, Bean, Bear, Bee, Bell, Berries, Big, Billy, Bite, Black, Blow, Book, Boot, Box, Boy, Bread, Breakfast, Bright colors, Bug, Bugs, Bunch, By

California, Canned, Chain, Chair, Cherries, Choice, Cocker spaniel, Cock tar, Cold, Color, Colorful, Cookie, Corn, Cream

Dairy, Desk, Dessert, Diet, Dinner, Door, Dress, Drink pop, Drip

Eating object, Eden, Egg, Eight, Enjoyment

Fairy, Farmer, Father, Feet, First, Fish, Flavor, Florida, Fruit flies, Fruit fly, Fruits, Fry, Full

Garden, Girl, Glass, Go, Gone, Good tasting, Grass, Green, Gum

Hair, Hand, Hay, Health, High, His, House, Hunger, Hungry

Iron, It, Itch

Jello, Jelly, John, Joy

Last, Lemons, Light, Like, Lunch, Luscious

Mark, Market, Mate, May, Me, Melon, Milk, Mind, Monkey, Much

News, Nice, Noon, Nuts
Oddball, On
Pair, Parrot, Patty, Pea, Peaches, Peas, People, Persimmon,
Pick, Picker, Plant, Plentiful, Plum, Potato, Proteins,
Pumpkin
Ripe, Ripened, Root, Rotten, Rough, Round
Salty, Sauce, Save, Saw, Scratch, Seed, Seeds, Shoot, Sight,
Small, Smooth, Solid, Some, Soup, Spinach, Spoil, Spoon,
Stand, Still life, Stock, Stomach, Store, Strawberries,
Strawberry, Summer, Sun, Sweets, Swell
Take, Tangerine, Tangerines, Tasty, Ten, The, Think, Three,
To, Toe nail, Toot, Tropics
Vitamin C, Vitamins
Was, Water, Watermelon, Went, When
You eat, Yum

GET

A bone, About, Achieve, Across, After, Ahead, A horse,
Along, Also, Any, Apple, Apples, Ask, Ate, Attain
Bat, Baby, Be, Beat, Beat it, Become, Beg, Bent, Be sure,
Bet, Big, Blue, Board, Borrow, Bought, Boy, Bq, Bread,
Bridge, Brought, Bucket, Bug, Busy, But, Bye
Can, Candy, Can't, Carrots, Cars, Cart, Caught, Chair,
Chippewa, Clothes, Cold, Control, Cookies, Cops, Cry
Desire, Dog, Dogs, Done, Dress, Drop, Drunk
Ease, Eat, Effect, Errand, Even
Fat, Feel, Few, Fit, Flow, Foot, Forgot, From, Fund
Gas, Gate, Gather, Gave, Gee, Get, Get away, Get out, Gets,
Get something, Girl, Git, Given, Gnat, Go after, Goat, Goes,
Gotten, Gotton, Grasp, Greedy, Green, Groceries, Gives,
Gun
Hand, Hanged, Happy, Has, Hat, Hide, His, Hoe, Horse, Hot,
House, How, Hunt, Hurry
I, Inside, Is
Killed, Kit
Last, Letter, License, Like, List, Long, Look, Love
Make, Many, Matter, Mean, Meat, Mine, Model, Mother,
Movement, Muscles, Myself
Near, Need, Net, Never, New, Newspaper, No
Obey, Object, Open, Or, Order, Over there, Own
Paid, Pail, Paper, Pearls, Phone, Pick up, Pie, Pigs, Place,
Poison, Police, Possess, Possession, Presents, Put
Quick, Quickly
Ran, Rat, Received, Reserve, Retrieve, Return, Rid, Ride,
Right, Road
Sat, Save, Search, See, Seek, Seize, Sell, Send, Shoes, Show,
Sick, Sidewalk, Sig, Sir, Sister, Six, Skin, Slacks, Slave,
Sleep, Smart, Smokes, So, Soft, Sold, Someplace, Somewhere,
Soon, Started, Stay, Stick, Still, Strong, Surprise
Tack, Taste, Tell, Thee, Their, Then, There's, They, Thin,
Thing, Things, Those, Three, Throw, Tired, Together,
To have, Toy, Trouble
Under, Understand
Very
Walk, Was, Water, We, Wear, Went, Were, When, Will, Win,
Wise, With, Word, Worth
Yes, Yet, You, Your, Yours

GIRL

Afraid, Aha, A human being, A lady, Animal, Ann, Are, A
small person, Av beautiful nice, Awful
Bab, Barbara, Bashful, Beads, Bed, Betty, Bev, Big, Binnie,
Black, Blond, Blouse, Blue, Box, Boy friend, Boy love,
Broad, Brown, Brunette, Bud, Build
Cap, Card, Cat, Charming, Cheryl, Children, Class mate,
Climbing, Close, Coat, Coats, Co-ed, Connie, Cook, Cool,
Cousin, Crazy, Creep, Cry, Curl, Curls, Curve
Dame, Dance, Dances, Darling, Dates, Daughter, Dave, Diana,
Different, Dog, Dolls, Dope, Dorm, Dresses, Dressy, Dumb
Eh, Eighteen, Eileen, Enemy, Enjoyment, Eyes
Face, Fair, Faith, Faye, Feet, Fellow, Field, Fine, Five,
Flower, Fool, Foolishness, Fox, Funny, Fur, Fuss
Gal, Garbage, Gentle, Giggle, Girl, Girl friend, Glasses,
Good looking, Gray, Great, Grill, Guy
Hands, Happiness, Happy, Hard, Hate, Heaven, High, High
heels, High school, Holly, Hot, Human being
Ick, Icky, Idiot, Immature, Innocent, Ish, It
Jackie, Jane, Janet, Janice, Jealous, Joan, Joyce, Jump rope
Karen, Kathie, Kathy, Kind, Kiss, Kissing, Kitten, Know
Ladies, Lanina, Lassie, Laughter, Leg, Legs, Leslie, Less

tall, Light, Like, Linda, Lipstick, Long, Look, Lora,
Lovely, Lynne
Magazine, Male, Marilyn Monroe, Meat, Men, Mild, Mine,
Miss, Misses, Money, Moon, Mother, Moving, Myself
Name, Nancy, Necklace, Next to me, Nice lady, Noisy, Nothing,
Now, Nurse, Nut, Nuts
Oh, OK, Okay, Out, Outdoors, Ow
Parties, Party, Passion, Patty, Perfume, Pig tail, Pig tails,
Pink, Play, Playful, Plays, Pleasure, Ponytail, Pretty
ugly, Purse
Quit
Rat, Red, Red hair, Ribbon, Rings, Rope, Running, Ruti
Sally, Sandra, Sassy, Scarf, Scouts, Selfish, Sew, Shape,
Sharon, She, Sheep, Sheila, Shoe, Shoes, Short, Show,
Shows, Silly, Sing, Skinny, Slow, Smart, Smooth, Snot,
Softie, Somebody, Someone, Someone young, Sonia, Student,
Stupidity, Sue, Sugar, Superb, Susan, Sweet and homely,
Sweetheart, Swell
Table, Take, Talk, Teacher, Teenage girl, Teenager,
Tender, Thing, Thirty-six twenty-four, Thrill, Tiny, Tom,
Tot, Twelve
Ugh, Ugly
Walk, Walking, Want, Warmth, Where, Whirl, Whistle,
Whistling, Who, Why, Wife, Will, Wolf, Work
Yikes, Young female, Young lady, Young lady or a miss,
Young woman, Youth

GO

A, Abroad, Accelerate, Action, Along, Ancestor, And, Anger,
Around, At
Bad, Beat it, Because, Become, Begin, Be gone, Between,
Bicycle, Bike, Blow, Boat, Bow, Brain, Bring, Bull dog,
Bus
Can, Casey, Cat, Chair, Close, Confidence, Crazy
Day, Dentist, Depart, Die, Dig, Do, Dog, Don't, Don't go,
Drive
Ever, Extremely
Farther, Fat, Fetch, Fishing, Flow, Fly, Foe, Follow, Foot,
Forth, Forward, Further
Game, Gas, Get along, Get out, Getter, Give, Goal, Goat,
Go cart, Goes, Go fast, Go go, Going gone, Gown, Gun
Hall, Hard, He, Head, Him, Hit, Ho, Honey, Horse Power,
House, Hunt, Hurry, Hurt
I, Immediately, Inside, Into, Is
Jimmy, Joe, Joel
Kind
Later, Let, Live
Man, March, Me, Meat, Mo, Moe, More, Movie, Moving, Mow
Near, Nice, Not
Of, Off, Oh, One, Outer, Outside, Over
Pass, Past, Permission, Person, Play, Please, Pole, Power,
Progress
Ran, Ride, Riding, Road, Round, Row, Running
Said, Sat, Say, Scat, Schmo, School, See, Seek, Send, She,
Shoe, Show, Side, Sincerely, Sit, Sleep, Slower, Slow stop,
Snow, Soft, Some, Somewhere, Son, Soon, South, Spot,
Stand, Stop light, Stopping, Stop sign, Straight, Street, Sun,
Supper, Swift, Swing
That, The, Then, They, Thing, Though, Through, Throw,
Time, To hell, To it, Tow, Toward, Traffic, Traffic light,
Trip, Turn
Up
Verb, Visit
Wait, Walking, Want, Was, Watch, Way, Were, West, When,
Why, Wild, Will, Word, Work, Wow
You, You know
Zoo, Zoom

GREEN

Acid, A color, Apples, Art, Awful
Back, Bacon, Bed, Bedroom, Blow, Blush, Boat, Boy, Bread,
Brightness, Bush
Cabbage, Calm, Candy, Cats, Celery, Chair, Christmas,
Cloak, Cloth, Clothes, Clover, Cold, Collar, Colorful,
Color grass, Coloring, Come, Comfort, Complexion, Coolness,
Cooper, Court
Dark color, Day, Dead, Deep, Depressed, Different, Door,
Drown, Dull
Embarrassed, Emerald, Emeralds, Evergreen, Eyes
Farm, Fat, Favorite, Fence, Flow, Flower, Folder, Forest,

Fresh, Freshmen

Garden, Giant, Girl, Gland, Glass, Goats, Goblin, Gold, Golf course, Golfing, Go light, Good, Go youth, Gray, Green, Green beans, Green house, Greens, Grey, Ground, Grow, Growing, Gum

Had, Happy, Harsh, Hate, Help, Hide, Hill, Hills, Horn

Ivy

Jim

King

Lady, Land, Lay, Lean, Life, Like, Lime, Litchfield, Little, Lizard, Loud, Love, Lovely

Make, Mars, Martian, Material, Me, Meadow, Mean, Middle, Mint, Mittens, Moldy, Moss, Mossy, Mother, Mountain, Mountains, Mr. Green

Nature, Nice, Noise, Noon

Olives, OK, One, Orchard, Outside, Oxygen

Paint, Paper, Park, Pastime, Pea, Pear, Pen, Pencil, People, Peppers, Persimmon, Picket, Pickle, Pleasant, Pleasing, Point, Pop, Potato, Protection, Put

Quiet

Read, Restful, Ribbon, Ring, Ripe, River, Robin, Rock, Roof, Room, Rose, Rug

Saint Patrick's Day, Sale, Screen, Seasick, Seaweed, Seen, Shamrock, Shelf, Shirt, Shoes, Shower, Sickening, Sickness, Silk, Sky, Slack, Slippers. Smell, Smoke, Socks, Solid, Spearmint, Spinach, Spoon, Spring, Stain, Stamp, Stamps, Stars, Stems, Stick, Stocks, Stone, Stop light, Stop sign, St. Patrick, St. Patrick's, St. Patrick's day, St. Pat's Day, Straw, Street, Sublime, Swamp, Sweater

Table, Teacher, Tie

Uniform

Valley, Veg, Vegetable, Vegetables, Verdant

Wall, Waves, Way, Wear, While, Willow, With, Word

Wow

X-mas

Yard, You

There, They, Things, Three, Timber, Time, To, Toe, Tommy, Tonto, Too, Took, Tool, Town, Travel, Triggers, Trouble, Trucks, Try, Tweety's, Twelve inches, Twenty-two caliber, Twenty-two cal

Ugly, Unhappy, Up, Us

Violence

Wall, Was, Water, We, Will travel, Winchester, Wood, Woods, Wrap, Wrong, Wyatt Earp

You

GUNS

A, Across, Ah, Aim, Airplane, Alfonse Capone, Aloud, Alvin, Ammunitions, Animal, Animals, Annie, Arrow, As, At, Automatic

Bag, Balls, Ban, Band, Bandit, Bangs, Bank, Banks, Battle, Battles, BB, Bears, Bebe, Bee, Belts, Big, Bing, Bird, Blame, Blew, Blonde, Boats, Bolt, Bomb, Bombs, Boots, Bow, Bows, Boy, Broke, Brother, Brown, Built, Bull, Bum, But, Butler, Butter

Can, Candy, Cannons, Cap, Caps, Car, Car hill, Castro, Children, Childs, Choke, Chopper, Clay, Clean, Club, Cold, Colt, Colt forty-five, Cost, Cow, Cow girls

Dad, Day, Deer, Detectives, Die, Died, Dog, Doll, Done, Dose, Doubles, Draw, Drink, Ducks

Eliot Ness, Enemy, Enjoyment, Equipment

Fast, Father, Feet, Fighting, Fights, Fine, Fire, Fire arm, Fired, Fishing, Flame, Food, Fool, For, Forty-five colts, Forty-fours, Forward, Four

Gangster, Gat, Gave, Gene Autry, Get, GI, Girl, Going, Gone, Got, Grease, Great, Green, Grey, Gums, Gunners, Gun powder, Gun show, Gun smith, Gun smoke, Guts, Guys

Hair, Hammer, Hammers, Hat, Have, He, Heavy, Help, Hill, History, Hit, Hobby, Hoodlum, Hook, Horrid, Horse, How, Hunter, Hurts

I, If, Indians, Injury, Iron, Irons, It

Jail, Jam, Joys, Jump

Kids, Killers, Killings, Kills, Kiss, Knife, Knifes

Large, Lead, Let, Little, Live, Loaded, Lock, Long, Look

Machines, Many, Marshall, Maverick, Me, Metal, Mi, Military, Mine, Mitchell, Moon, Mother, Motor, Movie, Movies, Mum, Murder

Naughty, Navy, Nets, New, No, Noisy, Now, Nun

Of, Off, On, One, Ouch, Outlaw, Over

Paul, Pea shooter, Person, Peter, Pets, Pill, Planes, Plate, Pointed, Policeman, Pony, Pop, Powered, Powerful, Powers, Put

Rabbits, Race, Ran, Report, Revolver, Revolvers, Roar, Roared, Robbers, Rod, Rods, Ron, Rounds, Rubbish, Run, Runs

Safety, Salute, Sand, Sheep, Sheriff, Ship, Ships, Shooters, Shore, Shot gun, Shot guns, Shouldn't, Show, Shut, Silver, Six, Six shooter, Six shooters, Smokey, So, Some, Son, Soot, Spot, Sticks, Stock, Stop, Story, Sword, Swords, Syndicate

Talk, Tanks, Tap, Television, Terrible, That, Their, Them,

HAMMER

Am, Animal, Arm and hammer, A tool, Ax

Band, Banging, Banner, Basement, Basket, Bead, Beat, Bed, Bell, Berg, Bet, Big, Bird, Bitter, Black blue mark, Blood, Bludgeon, Boy, Broad, Building

Carpentry, Cart, Chain gang, City, Clammer, Claw, Club, Concrete, Cut, Cycle

Dad, Dark, Do, Dog, Don't, Door, Dress, Drive, Drive-in, Drunk

Ear, Eat, Eight, Equipment

Family, Farmer, Fat, Fathers, Flat, Food, Force, Fork, Four, French fries, Fun

Garage, Girl, Go, Gone, Goon, Got, Grade

Had, Hammer, Handy, Hardware, Harm, Hat, Have, Headache, Health, Hear, Heard, Held, Helpful, Hitting, Hoe, Home, Hot, House, Hurts

I, Implement

Knife

Large, Laugh, Locked, Long, Loud noise

Machine, Mails, Make, Man, Me, Mean, Meat, Metal, Metal nails, Mike, Mill, Monday, Monkey, Muscles

Nailed, Name, Needle, Nick, Nile, Noisy, Nut, Nuts

Object, OK, Old, On, Ow

Pad, Pain, Pan, Percussion, Pet, Picture, Pistol, Piston, Plier, Pliers, Plow, Pond, Pool, Post, Pounder, Powerful, Proud

Radio, Revenge, Right, Rust

Scythe, Shoe, Shovel, Sickle, Sing, Sledge hammer, Smash, Smith, Soft, Something, Sore, Sour, Spear, Star, Stein, Stick, Sting, Stomp, Stone, Stove, Suite, Summer, Swift, Swing

Table, Tack, That, The, Thing, Thistle, Thrower, Toes, Toil, Took, Top, Tottle, Tough, Towel, Toy, Track, T square

U.N., Up, Use

Violence

Weak, Weapon, Wedge, Woodwork, Work bench, Working, Would, Wrench

You

HAND

Alge, A part of your body, Appendage, Armed, Arm or wrist, Ax

Baby brothers, Back, Bad, Bag, Bares, Beautiful, Bed, Bell, Belly, Belongings, Black, Blanket, Bone, Bones, Book, Bottom, Box, Boy, Burn, Butter, Button

Came, Can, Candy, Cap, Capability, Car, Caress, Carry, Cello, Children, Clap, Claps, Claw, Clean, Clock, Close, Clutch, Coat, Cold, Color, Command, Cream, Cripple, Cut

Dad, Dick, Dirt, Dirty, Dishes, Doing, Draw

Elbow, Extended, Extremity, Eyes

Faith, Farm, Fat, Feed, Feeler, Fell, Figure, Figures, Fin, Finder, Fine, Firm, First, Five finger, Five fingers, Flanges, Fool, Fore, Fork, Figure, Friend, Friendly, Friendship, Fruit, Full, Funny

Garden, Gave, Gentle, God, Good, Green, Grenade, Gun

Had, Hair, Hairy, Hammer, Handkerchief, Handle, Hand out, Hands, Handsome, Handy, Heat, Held, Helper, Helping, Helpless, Her, Hip, His, Hit, Hose, Hot, House, Human, Hurt

It

Jeff, Jive

Kathy, Kind, Knife, Knuckles

Lady, Land, Lead, Left hand, Legs, Lift, Lifting, Light, Limp, Long, Lotion, Loud, Love, Lovely

Mad, Made, Manicure, Mano, Man's hand, Meet, Mittens, Moist, Money, Moth, Mother, Mothers, Move, Movement, Moving, Muscle, Mutton, My brother, Myself

Nail polish, Necessity, Neck, None, Nose, Not, Nothing

Object, Or, Organ, Other hand, Out, Over

Pale, Palm of hand, Part of body, Part of person, Pass, Paw,

Pen, Pet, Piano, Pin, Pink, Place, Play, Playing, Plays, Polish, Power, Pretty, Print, Purple
Ram, Reach, Red blue flossy, Rock, Romance, Roots, Rough, Round
Salt, Sam, Sand, Score, Shack, Shaking, Shirt, Shoe, Should, Shoulder, Sine, Size, Skim, Slap, Slapped, Sleeve, Slender, Smooth, Soap, Solid, Something on your body, Sore, Speed, Spoon, Squeeze, Stair, Stand, Stop, Strength, Stroke
Tabb, Table, Take, Tan, Ten, Tender, Than, Thankful, Thanks, The, There, Tight, To do things with, Toes, To hold things, Tough, Towel, To write, Trust, Two
Ugly, Usable
Vains
Ward, Warmer, Washing, Watch, Water, Welcome, Wet, What, Wide, Wipe, Woman, Worker, Working, Work with, Wrinkle, Wrinkled, Write with
Yellow, Yours

HARD

Alot, Apple, Apples, Are, Arithmetic, Awful, Awfully, Awkward
Back breaking, Ball bearing, Bark, Beat, Bee, Black board, Block, Blue, Boiled egg, Bone, Boy, Break, Broke, Brook, Bruise, Bug, Bump, Butter brickle
Cabbage, Can't, Can't do it, Cap, Car, Car body, Card, Carrot, Cast, Cat, Cattle, Chemistry, Chubby, Counter, Course, Cow, Crack, Crackers, Creak, Cruel, Crust
Dark, Day, Deep, Dense, Difficulty, Dirty, Dish, Dishes, Dislike, Do, Dog, Done, Door, Durable, Dust
Eagle, Ear, Eased, Easily, Eat, Egg cooked, Egg shell, Eves, Eye, Eyes
Fall, Fat, Feel, Feeling, Feet, Fight, Fist, Flat, Food, Fragile, Fun
Gay, Girl, Golf ball, Good, Grand, Green, Gum, Guts, Guy, Guys
Had, Hard, Hard ball, Hard boiled egg, Harden, Hardening, Hardness, Hard tack, Hardware, Hat, Hate, Hate to fall on, Headed, Hear, Heard, Heart, Hearted, Her, Herd, Hi, High, Hit, Hockey, Hole, Hollow, House, Hurts
Iron, Ishy, It's not easy
Joe
Keep, Key, Kind, Knife, Knock, Knot
Labor, Large, Lazy, League, League balls, Leather, Let, Lettuce, Liquor, Log, Love, Low, Lump, Lumps
Mad, Make, Man, Marbles, Math, Mats, Medium, Men, Money, Moon, Mother, Mountain, Mud, Munchy, Muscle, Music
Nice, Nickle, No, Nose, Nosed, Not good, Nothing, Nut
Oak, Ouch, Ought, Ow
Pain, Pass, Pavement, Penetrate, People, Person, Physiology, Pillow, Plate, Poor, Potato, Pound, Pour, Problem, Puck, Pull
Rabbit, Radio, Read, Road, Rocky, Rolls, Round, Rugged
Saddle, Said, Salad, Salt, Sawing, School work, Scold, Seat, Shame, Shape, Sheep, Shell, Shiny, Ship, Shoot, Shut, Sidewalk, Sing, Sit, Slow, So, Soon, Sort, Sought, Sound, Sour, South, Spelling, Splinter, Squeeze, Stern, Stool, Stop, Strain, Strenuous, Strict, Struggle, Stuck, Study, Stumped, Sturdy, Suit, Summer sausage, Sweet, Swim
Table top, Tack, Talking, Tap, Tart, Task, Teacher, Tense, Tests, Texture, Thing, Thinking, Through, Tight, Toast, Too, Touch, Tree, Trying, Turtle
Uh, Unbearable, Unbreakable, Understand, Unedible, Unlight, Unsmooth, Unsoft, Unyielding
Very hard
Wall, Water, Wax, Weak, Week, Word, Words, Worker, Wrong
Yolk

HARDLY

A, About, Absent, Advent, Adverb, A faith, Afraid, Ain't, Air, A little, All right, Also, Although, Am, And, Andy, Answer, Anybody, Anyone, Any thing left, Any time, Anyway, Apple, Argue, Ask, Awake, Away
Back, Bad, Bare, Bark, Batter, Bee, Before, Began, Believe, Best, Big, Black, Book, Boys, Brant, Broadly
Calculated, Camel, Cannot, Can wait, Capability, Car, Careful, Carefully, Cares, Carry, Cause, Certainly, Charm, Cheap, Chicken, Child, Children, Chosen, Clay, Clearly, Close, Closets, Cloth, Come, Common, Completely, Correct, Could be, Cow, Cradle
Dandly, Dare, Dark, Dead, Decompressed, Deficient, Definitely, Desk, Didn't, Different, Discover, Distrue, Do, Doesn't, Dog,

Do it, Donkey, Don't, Don't do it, Don't know, Doubtedly, Doubtfully, Doubt it, Doubts, Drive, Dry, Dull, Dumb
Eager, Eat, Eaten, Effort, Egg, Either, Envelope, Exactly, Except, Exception, Excited, Exclamation, Excuse, Expect, Extremely
Faintly, Faithful, Fare, Faster, Fastly, Fear, Feasible, Felt, Fin, Finally, Fine, Finger, Flower, Fly, Food, Forever, Forgot, Frequently, Fun
Generous, Get, Girl, Glove, Go, Going, Going to, Got, Gotten, Greatly, Green, Grown, Guess, Gun, Gym
Hair, Half, Ham, Hammer, Handkerchief, Happening, Harder, Hardest, Hare, Has, Hat, Hate, Have, He, Head, Healthy, Hear, Heard, Heavily, Help, Helper, Her, Here, Him, His, Homework, Honestly, Horrible, Horse, Hour, How, Hurry, Hurt
Idiots, If, I hardly see it, Impossibly, In, Including, Incorrect, Irritable, Irritate, Isn't
Jack, John, Just about, Just make it
Kaum, Keep, Kind, Kindly, Kind of, Kissed, Known
Lake, Lard, Last, Laural, Lazy, Lie, Lightly, Like, Limited, Live, Load, Look, Lot, Loud, Loudly, Love
Mad, Made, Make, Man, Manage, Manly, May, Meal, Merely, Met, Might, Mine, Moorhead, Mostly, Much less, My
Naturally, Near, Neat, Need, Negative, Neither, New, Nicely, Night, No chance, Nor, Not any, Not be, Not done, Not easy, Not enough, Notice, Noticeably, Not many, Not much, Not nearly, Not often, Not quiet, Not really, Not so, Not too much, Not true, Not very, Not very many, Nut
Object, Oddly, Of, Of course, Off, Office, Oh, OK, Old, Once, Out, Over, Ow
Paper, Park, Part, Partly, Pass up, Pen, People, Person, Plenty, Pounded, Practically, President, Probable, Probably
Question, Questionable, Quick, Quickly, Quiet, Quit
Rare, Rather, Ready, Reason, Right, Rocks, Running
Sad, Sadly, Said, Sandy, Sarcasm, Sat, Saw, Say, Scarce, Sea, Seem, Self, Sensible, Sharp, She, Shoes, Short, Short way, Should, Shouldn't, Silly, Simple, Simplicity, Simply, Since, Sincerely, Sit, Six, Skimpy, Slight, Smart, Smooth, Softer, Solemnly, Solid, Something, Sometime, Somewhat, Sooner, Sorrow, Sort, Sort of, Spell, Spoken, Stacked, Stand, Started, Steps, Stop, Stupid, Successful, Sudden, Sunday, Sure
Table, Take, Tardy, Television, Tell, Ten, Their, Theirs, Them, They, Thing, Think, This, Thorough, Thou, Though, Three, Through, Todd, To get, Together, Too big, Tool, Torn, Touch, Touched, Tough, Truth, Two, Type
Unable, Unbeliever, Uncommon, Understanding, Unhardly, Unmentionable, Unoften, Unsoft, Untrue, Us, Usual, Usually
Vaguely, Vary, Verily, Very few, Very often, Visible
Wail, Walk, Walked, Warely, Warm, Way, Weak, Week, Well, Went, Were, Wet, When, Will, Without, Wood, Word, Working, Would, Wouldn't, Wrong
Yardly, Yeah, Yesterday, Your

HAVE

About, Acquire, Acquired, All, Alone, Also, Always, And, Another, Anything, Anyway, Apple, Arithmetic, Arrived, Asked, At, Ate, At thou, Auditorium, Ave
Baby, Bad, Basketball, Bath, Be, Bean, Became, Become, Beer, Before, Begun, Behave, Belonging, Belongs, Bicycle, Big, Bill, Blank, Boat, Bold, Book, Books, Boughten, Boy, Brains, Brave, Bring, Brought, Butter
Cake, Calf, Calve, Came, Candy, Car, Cave, Chair, Chicken, Child, Clean, Clothes, Cold, Company, Concern, Cook, Could, Cow, Curt, Cute
Day, Dick, Did, Does, Dog, Doll, Do not, Down, Drink
End, English, Eve, Ever, Everything
Far, Fast, Figure, Find, Finished, Five, Food, Forest, Forgot, Forgotten, Form, Found
Gain, Garage, Gather, Gently, Gift, Girl, Girl friend, Grown, Guilty, Guns, Gun will travel, Guts
Hadn't, Hardly, Hasn't, Hat, Haven, Have nots, Haves, Have to, Haven't, Hay, Head, Heal, Hear, Heavy, Held, Herd, Hers, Hi, Hill, Hoards, Hole, Home, Horse, How
Ice cream, If, I have, In, Ing, In possession, In possession of, Island, I've
Join
Kissed, Know
Lack, Lady, Lava, Leave, Left, Lend, Less, Let, Light, Like, Little, Live, Long, Looked, Looks, Lots

Mad, Made, Make, Man, May, Men, Met, Milk, Mom, More,
  Move, Mumps, Must
Name, Need, Never, Nice, Niece, Nine, Noon, Nose, Notebook,
  Not own, Not to, Nowhere
Ocean, Of, Of course, Office, Often, Oh, Old, On, Once, Or,
  Over, Owned, Owner, Ownership, Ownings
Paper, Party, Passes, Passion, Patience, Peace, Peanuts,
  People, Pepper, Place, Plan, Please, Pocket, Poor, Position,
  Possessing, Present, Processed, Procession, Property,
  Purchase, Purchased, Purse
Quality, Question, Quiet, Quietly, Quite
Reason, Receive, Received, Ring, Roar
Said, Salve, Sea, Sex, Shave, She, Shoes, Should, Show, Showed,
  Sister, Six, Sky, Slow, Smoke, So, Sold, Soon, Steak, Stole,
  Stopped, Store, Sue, Sun, Supper
Table, Teeth, Tell, Ten, Test, Than, Their, Therefore, Thing,
  Those, Thought, Through, Thy, Time, Toes, To go, To had,
  Too, To own, Touch, Toy, Train, Trucks, Turned, Two
Use
Water, Wave, Way, Wear, Welcome, Welfare, Well, Went,
  Were, Where, Who, Why, Window, With, Without, Won,
  Word, Work, Wow
You gone
Zoo

HE

Ad, Am, Andy, A person, Arrived, At, Ate, Athlete
Bad, Be, Beau, Bill, Bit, Black, Blonde, Blue, Bob, Bought,
  Boyfriend, Bradley, Brother, Brought, Brown, Buy, By
Came, Can, Can't, Car, Cars, Caught, Cause, Circus, Come,
  Comes, Coming, Corn, Could, Curt
Dad, David, Dennis, Denny, Dick, Does, Dog, Donny, Drove
Eyes
Fast, Fat, Father, Fell, Female, Fiancee, Find, Flea, Found,
  Frank, Friend
Gender, Gentle, Go, Goes, Good, Guess
Hair, Hand, Handsome, Hat, Hay, He, Head, Heck, He'd, Hee,
  He he, Hers, He said so, Hit, Home, Hot, How, Hurt
Is a dope, Ish
Jack, Joe, John, Jump
Know
Large, Larry, Lee, Left, Live, Lives, Looked, Lord, Lost,
  Love
Made, Maid, Marines, Marry, Marv, Masculine, May, Men,
  Mike, Mine, Mit, Moon
Name, Never, Nice, No, Not, Noun, Now
Okay, One, Other
Pants, Paul, People, Pete, Point
Ralph, Ran, Richard, Ron, Roommate, Run, Runs
Said so, Sandy, Says, See, Sex, Shall, Sheldon, Shirt, Should,
  Shy, Sink, Small, Somebody, Something, Speed, Start,
  Stopped, Strong, Sweater, Swims
Teacher, Tells, That, Thee, Them, Thought, Tie, Tilt, To,
  Tom, Too, Tough
Us
Vic
Wally, Want, Wants, Well, Who, Win, Wish, Work, Wrote
Yes

HEAD

Above, Ace, Ad, Amy, And, Animal, A part of body, Away
Baby, Band, Bathroom, Bean, Beginning, Behind, Best,
  Between shoulders, Big boy, Biggest, Big wheel, Bird, Block,
  Blond, Blonde, Blood, Board, Body part, Bolt, Bones, Bottom,
  Brand, Bread, Bred, Bright, Bring, Brown, Bump, Bust, But
Can, Capital, Chest, Chief, Chin, Chop, Circle, Club, Coin,
  Colds, Comb, Company, Cow, Cozy, Curly, Cut, Cute
Dad, Dark, Dead, Death, Decapitated, Decent, Deep, Delicate,
  Die, Doctor, Dope, Dream, Dumb
Easy, Eat, Egg, End, Essential, Eyes and brains, Eyes ears
  and nose
Faces, Fact, Fair, Fall, Family, Far, Fast, Faster, Father,
  Fear, Features, Fed, Feel, Finger, Fingers, Firm, Fish,
  Food, Football, Fore, Fragile, From, Full, Funny
Gag, Gay, Glasses, Go, Good, Good looks, Grave, Guillotine
Had, Hade, Haid, Harm, Has, Head, Headache, Headless, Heat,
  Heel, Height, Held, Hi, Hill, Hole, Home, Horse, Horseman,
  Hot, House, Human body, Human head, Hunters, Hurt
Idea, Idiot, In, Indian cannibal, Indians, Inquire, Its
John

Kind, Knee, Know
Land, Last, Lead, Legs, Letters, Light, Like, Limb, Line,
  Lip, Lips, Little, Long, Look, Louis the sixteethth, Lovely
Mad, Made, Marbles, Master, Material, May, Meeting, Mother,
  Move, Myself
Nail, Need, Nice, No, Noggin, Noise, Non, None, Nothing, Nut
Ocean, Odd, Of, On, On body, Organ, Over
Part, Part of body, Persons, Petty, Pillow, Pink, Pope,
  Powerful, President, Psychology, Pull, Pumpkin
Rear, Red, Region, Rock, Rocks, Run
Sailor, Scooter, Screw, Scull, Seem, Shave, Shaven, She, Shell,
  Ship, Shoe, Short, Shrunk, Sick, Size, Skies, Skin, Slow,
  Soldiers, Some, Someone, Something round, Sore, Sort,
  Sound, Spider, Stately, Steam, Stone, Stream, Study, Stupid,
  Swell, Swirl
Table, Taking, Talk, Talking, Teeth, Tender, The, They, Things,
  Think with, Throat, Tip, Tom, Tongue, Torso, Trouble,
  Turn
Ugly, Up, Use, Useful
Warm, Water logged, Way, Went, White, Wig, Wise, Women,
  Wood
Yellow, You

HEALTH

Able, Action, Active, Activity, Age, Ah, Air, Although, Apples,
  Ark, Arm, Aspirin, Ate, Athlete, Athletes, Athletic, Athletics,
  Awake, Awful
Baby, Bad health, Bar, Baseball, Bath, Bath tub, Beautiful,
  Beauty, Bed, Being, Best, Birds, Blake, Blood, Blue,
  Blue cross, Bone, Bones, Bored, Brave, Bread,
  Breath, Bright, Broke, Build, Building, Buoyance
Camp, Can, Cancer, Candy, Car, Carrots, Chair, Chart, Charts,
  Check, Check up, Cheer, Cheers, Child, Children, Class
  room, Cleanliness, Clinic, Club, Come, Complacency, Cool,
  Cooled, Corner, Cough, Country, Course, Cow, Crumb,
  Cut
Dance, Day, Dental, Department, Desk, Die, Diet, Dirt,
  Diseaseless, Diseases, Do, Doc, Doctors, Dog, Dream,
  Drink, Dye
Ear, Eggs, Enjoy, Every, Exam, Examine, Eyes
Fair, Family, Fan, Fast, Fat, Favor, Feeble, Feel good,
  Feeling good, Feelings, Fell, Felt, Fever, Figure, Filling,
  Filthy, Foods, Foot, Fresh, Friendly, Full
Gay, Germs, Glow, Go, God, Golf, Good food, Good grooming,
  Good health, Goodness, Good or bad, Good shape, Grateful,
  Green, Growth, Gun
Habit, Had, Hair, Hands, Hard, Hat, Hate, Head, Health,
  Health class, Healthier, Health service, Heard, Hearty, Heat,
  High, Hit, Home, Hook, Hot, Human, Hungry, Hurt, Hygiene
Ill health, Inch, Institution, Insurance, Intelligent, Is
Joanne, Joyful, Juice, Jump
Keep, Keeping up, Kids
Lane, Large, Last, Let, Like, Lodge, Look, Looking, Looks,
  Love, Luck
Magazine, Man, Meal, Meat, Medical, Mice, Might, Miss Levold,
  Miss Wilbur, Money, Moon, Mother, Motor, Mr. Rau, Mumps,
  Municipal, Muscle, Muscles, Muscular, Myself
Neat, Need, Needed, Needle, Net, No, Non health, Normal,
  Not ill, Not sick, Nursing, Nutrition
Okay, One, Orange juice, Outdoor, Outdoors
P, Peace, Pep, Peppy, Personal, Personality, PhyEd, Physical
  education, Physical help, Physique, Pill, Pink, Poison,
  Polio, Poorly, Posture, Pretty, Problem, Prosperity,
  Protein, Public Health class, Publish, Pure, Push
Radiant, Ran, Ready, Real, Red Cross, Report, Rest, Right,
  Robustness, Running
Safe, Safty, Sake, Sanitation, Sanity, Satisfaction, Seat, Secure,
  Security, Servant, Sex, Shapeless, Sheep, Shot, Shots,
  Sicken, Sickly, Silk, Sink, Sit, Skin, Skinny, Sky, Sleeping,
  Slum, Smart, Smile, Smiling, Smoke, Sniffles, Softly, Soon,
  Sound, Sparkling, Sport, Stamina, Stand, Stealth, Stick,
  Stomach, Stop, Straight, Stronger, Student, Studio, Study,
  Stupid, Sturdy, Sun, Sunshine, Swim, Swimming, System
Table, Taste, Temper, Test, Thermometer, Thing, Three,
  Three period, Tired, Tissues, Today, To feel good, Tool,
  Tooth brush, Trouble
Ugh, Ulcer, Understand, Unfit, Unhealth, Unhealthful, Unsanitary,
  Unsick, Upset
Vegetables, Vital
Warm, Wash, Washing, Weakness, Wealthy, Week, Weep,

Weight, Weight lifting, Weights, White, Why, Will, Wine, Wish, Wishful, Won't, Work out, Worry
Yes, You, Young, Yourself
Zest

HEAVY

A, Ache, Actor, Alot, Anvil, Arm, Article, Ass, Aversion, Awkward, Ax

Back breaking, Bad, Bad character, Ball, Bar bell, Bars, Beautiful, Bed, Bell, Big stone, Black, Block, Board, Boat, Bothersome, Boxes, Boxing, Boy, Boys, Break, Breath, Bricks, Broad, Brother, Brothers, Brown, Burdened

Candy, Can't take it, Carrying, Cars, Cement, Chest, Church, Cigarette, Class, Clean, Cloth, Cloud, Clouds, Coal, Cold, Come on, Cotton bales, Couch, Cover, Covers, Cow, Crate, Crates, Cumbersome

Dave, Dense, Desk, Dew, Diet, Difficult, Dinosaur, Dirt, Dog, Door, Down, Dream, Drinker, Drinking, Drudgery, Drug, Dumbbells, Duty

Ear, Earth, Easy, Eat, Effort, Engine, Eyelids

Far, Farmer, Fat man, Feet, Fight, Fish, Fluffy, Fog, Food, Football, Force, Fun, Fur, Furniture

Giant, Gin, Girl, Girls, Go, Gold, Gravity, Great, Groan, Ground, Grownup, Grunt, Gun

Had, Hair, Hall, Hangover, Hangs, Hard to carry, Hard to lift, Harsh, Have, Hear, Heard, Heart, Heave, Heaven, Heavier, Heavily, Heavy, Height, Help, Helper, High, Hind, Hippopotamus, Honest, Hoof, Horn, Hot, How, Hurry, Hurt, Hurts

I, Iceberg, I'm, Impossible, Is

Jesus, John, Joy, Just

Kathy Grambish, Knife

Ladder, Largest, Laundry, Lazy, Lbs., Leak, Leaving, Lifted, Lighten, Light weight, Loaded, Loaded down, Long, Look, Lot, Lots, Low, Lucky, Lug, Lumber

Machine, Mad, Make, Malted milk, Mark, Mass, Meals, Meat, Mercury, Metal, Milk, Money, Morose, Moth, Mountain, Move, Much, Muscle, Muscles

Not heavy, Now

Obesity, Object, Ocean, Odd, Oh, Oh boy, Old, One hundred lbs., One hundred proof, One ton, Oppressive, Ouch, Over weight, Ox

Pack, Package, Pail, Pain, Papers, Person, Piano, Pig, Pillow, Pin, Place, Pot, Potato in sack, Pound, Pounds

Quiet

Red, Rest, Rough

Sad, Safe, Sand, Scale, Scream, Set, Sheep, Shoe, Shoes, Short, Shoulders, Side, Sky, Slave, Sleepy, Slight, Slow, Small, Smash, Smell, Smokers, Smoking, Smooth, Snow, Something, Sorrow, Space, Stodgy, Stomp, Stones, Store, Stout, Stove, Strength, Sue, Sugar, Suppose, Swear, Sweat, Sweaty, Swell

Task, Thief, Thin, Thing, Though, Thud, Tight, Tiresome, Tobacco, Toil, Tomb, Tons, Too, Tool, Too much, Touch, Tow, Tractor, Train, Trees, Trunk, Tub, Tuba, Tug, Two hundred pounds, Typewriter

Ugh, Unlight

Wait, Warm, Wash, Wax, Way, Weightlessness, Wet, Which, White, Willie, Wire, Women, Wood, Wool

You

HERE

Accident, After, Again, Airplane, Ally, Alone, Already, Anyhow, Anything, Area, As, At, Ate, At home, Away

Baby, Ball, Bare, Be, Bear, Become, Been, Bell, Beside, Birds, Bone, Book, Books, Boy, Bring, Building, But, Buy, Buying

Can, Candy, Car, Cents, Clothes, Corn

Day, Deaf, Deer, Desk, Die, Do, Dog, Doggie, Doll, Dorm, Down, Dumb

Eliot Ness, Else, English, Everywhere

Far, Fast, Fat, Father, Fats, Fer, Figure, Find, Finger, Food, Found, Four, Free, Friend, From

Gail, Gas, Get, Gift, Giving, Glass, Going, Gone, Good

Had, Hair, Hand, Happy, Hard, Hare, Hat, Hearing, Hears, Hello, Help, Herd, Here, Hero, Hers, Hi, High, Hire, Hold, Hot, Hurt

I am, Ice, If, I'm, In, Instant, In the house, Isn't

John

Knee, Know

Lake, Listen, Live, Locations, Look, Love, Lunch room

Man, May, Mean, Merry, Milk, Mirror, Mitzi, Mom, Money, Mother, Mow

Nearby, New, Next, Nice, No, Noise, Nor, Nose, Not

Of, Off, Officer, On, On this spot, Over, Own

Pa, Pear, Pencil, Pet, Places, Point, Put

Queen

Real, Room

See, Self, Separate, She comes, Sit, Sits, Situated, Sky, Small, So, Someplace, Something, Somewhere, Soon, Sound, Speed, Sphere, Stand, Standing, Stands, Stop, Store, Sure, Sweet

Talk, Tall, Tear, Than, Thanks, Them, There and everywhere, These, They are, Thing, This place, Three, Time, Together, Tom, Too, Toy, Tree, Two

Understand, University

Wear, We go, Well, Went, What, When, White, Why, Will, With, Writing

Ye, Yes, Yonder, You are, Your, Yours

HIGH

About, Acropholia, Afraid, Alcohol, And the mighty, Apple

Ball, Beautiful, Below, Bird, Black, Blue, Bold, Bottom, Boy, Bye

Can, Car, Ceiling, Cheek bone, Chimney, Clear, Cloud, Cold, Construction, Cool, Cupboard

Danger, Dangerous, Dart, Depth, Die, Distant, Diving board, Dizziness, Do, Door, Drinking

Elevated, Elevation, Elevator, Empire State Building, Empire State, Enormous, Extended, Extreme

Falls, Far away, Fare, Fear, Feminine, Fire, Flag pole, Flying, For, Foshay, Foshay Tower, Fountain, Fourth floor, Fresh, Fright, Frightening, Fun, Funny

Giant, Girl, God, Going, Good, Grades, Great

Hard to get to, Hat, Head, Heaven, Heightrophobia, Hello, Help, Hey, Hi, High, Highest, High jump, Ho, Hole, Horse, Hug, Huge

Ice, In air, Ionosphere

Jumping, Junior

King, Kite

Lake, Law, Ledge, Leg, Legs, Length, Level, Library, Like, Liquor, Little, Lo, Lofty, Lonely, Lonesome, Long ways up, Looking, Look up, Looped, Lower

Man, Men, Middle, Monster, Moon, Mountain top, Mt. Rushmore, Music

Narrow, Noon, Note

OK, Out

Palne, Person, Pieces, Pinnacle, Pitch, Place, Places, Plain, Planes, Pole vaulting, Pressure, Pretty, Pump

Reach, Road, Roosevelt, Rope

Scaffold, Scarey, Shelf, Shoes, Shy, Sick, Sickness, Side, Silver, Ski, Skirt, Slope, Slopes, Slow, Sly, Smaller, Snow, Socks, Some, Sound, Sport, Stairs, Star, Stars, Steeple, Step, Step ladder, Stool, Story, Straight, Strung, Sun, Swing

Tale, Talk, Tall big large, Tallness, Tell, Temple, Test, Time, Too high, Tor, Towering, Towers, Track, Trees, Two

Unlow

Very tall, Volt

Wade, Water, Way, Way out, What, Why, Width, Wind, Window, Wins, Work, Wow

HIM

A cat, Accuse, Add, After, Again, Ah, Al, All, Alone, Also, And hers, At

Baby, Back, Bad, Basket, Beat, Bed, Beg, Below, Bicycle, Big, Bill, Black, Bob, Bore, Bought, Boy friend, Boy or man, Brother, But, By

Cabin, Calm, Cap, Car, Christ, Church, Clint, Clod, Coat, Coming, Constipation, Crazy, Curt, Cute

Dan, Dark, Darrone, David, Day, Dean, Denny, Dickie, Dim, Do, Doctor, Doll, Doug, Drank, Drunk

Earth, Eat, Ego

Face, Far, Fast, Female, Fight, Floor, Food, For, Frank, Friend, From, Fumble, Fun

Gary, Gentleman, Get, Girl, Give, Go, Going, Gone, Grave, Great, Green, Grin, Guilty, Guy, Guys

Had, Hair, Ham, Harvey, Harry, Has, Hat, Hate, Hay, Hear, Hello, Herself, Him, Home, Hot, Houston, Hum

If, Il, I'm, Intelligent, Ish

Jack, Jerry, Jesus, Jump

Ken, Kind, Kiss, Knife, Know

Land, Larry, Leap, Lift, Life, Like, Lips, Lit, Lonely, Long,

Looked, Lord, Lose, Loud, Lover
Mary, Mate, Men, Mike, Milt, More, Mother, Mow, Mr., Muscular, My, Myself
Name, Neighbor, Nice, No
Of, Off, On, One, Only, Open, Or, Other, Out, Over, Ow, Own
Paleface, Pants, Pat, Paul, People, Persons, Play, Player, Please, Pop
Queer, Quite, Quiet
Read, Remembered, Ricky, Rim, Ron, Room, Run
Said, Sandy, Saw, See, Seem, Sex, Shirt, Shout, Shy, Sink, Sing, Sir, Sleep, Slim, Smart, Somebody, Steve, Steven, Stop, Sun, Swing
Talk, Tall, Taught, Teach, Teacher, Terry, Than, The boy, Then, The one, This, Thing, Think, Thou, Thought, Tie, Tim, Tin, Tom, Tried, Twenty, Two
Ugly, Use
Vim
Walking, Was, Wayne, Well, Went, What, When, Why, Will, With, Woman, Women, Word, Wow

HIS

Am, Anothers, Appetite, Apple, As, At
Back, Bad, Bat, Be, Bed, Belly, Belongings, Best, Bite, Black, Body, Boy friend, Boy or man, Bug, Business, By
Can, Candy, Cap, Care, Catcher, Chair, Chance, Choice, Clock, Clothes, Cow, Cup
Date, Denny's, Dick, Do, Does, Dogs, Donny, Don't, Door, Doug's, Down, Drum
Ear, Ears, English, Eye
Fact, Fast, Fathers, Female, Fingers, Fishing, Fizz, Folks, Food, Found, Fun
Gain, Game, Girlfriend, Glove, Go, Goat, Gods, Good, Grail, Gum, Gun
Hall, Harm, Has, Hate, Hear, Heard, He's, Hi, Himself, His own, Hiss, Hit, Home, Honor, Hot, How, Human, Hysteria
I, If, In, Ish
Jacket, Jim's, Job
Kid, Kind, Kiss, Knife
Lap, Larry's, Legs, Life, Like, List, Look, Love
Maker, Male, Males, Manner, Mark, Marker, Marks, Master, May, Men, Mike, Miss, Mitts, Mom, Mouth, Mr., Must
Nap, Neck, No, Noise, Nose, Not, Not mine, Now
Object, Old, On, Ones, Only, Or, Ours, Over, Owner, Owns
Pants, Paper, Pencil, Penis, People, Personality, Persons, Picture, Pig, Place, Plane, Pop corn, Position, Possession of, Possessions, Property, Purse
Ron's, Room
Sake, See, Seem, Self, Sex, Shine, Shoulder, Show, Shows, Side, Sis, Sit, Skates, Ski, Smoke, Snake, Soap, Some, Someone, Someone's, Something, Son, Song, Soup, Stand, Steven, Steve's, Straight, Suit, Swim
Take, Tall, That, That guy, Their, There's, They, Things, Time, Tis, To, Too, Toothpaste, Towels, Truck
Uncle, Us
Waist, Wallet, Want, Watch, We, Were, West, What, Who, Wise, Woman, Word, Work, Write
Yes, You, Your, You're

HOTTER

Afternoon, Age, Air, Alaska, Angry, Animals
Baby, Backing, Ball, Batter, Be, Belt, Big, Bird, Bitter, Blotter, Blue, Boiled, Book, Bottle, Bow, Bowl, Bread, Bridle, Brighter, Bring, Bug, Butter, By
Cake, Can, Car, Carry, Cat, Chile, Chili, Chill, Clod, Closer, Coal, Coals, Cocoa, Coldest, Colds, Color, Competition, Cook, Cooking, Cooled, Corner, Cottage, Cotton, Could, Cows, Cup
Dad, Dark, Days, Dead, Desert, Different, Dish, Do, Dog, Dogs, Don't, Down, Dry, Dryer
Engine, Enough, Extra
Fast, Faucet, Fine, Fires, Five, Florida, Fluster, Fourteen, Frame, Freezer, Freezing, Fry, Fun
Gas, Getting, Getting hot, Go, Goat, Gold, Good, Grease, Green, Ground, Guess, Gun
Hand, Hat, Hatter, Heated, Heavier, Heavy, Heck, Help, Her, Here, Hi, High, Holder, Home, Hopper, Horn, Hot dog, Hot en tot, Hotter, Houses, Humid, Humidity, Hundred
Ice, In, Is, It
Keep, Kettle, Kill, Kitchen
Later, Laundry, Lips, Little, Loud, Low

Madder, Main, Man, Marilyn Monroe, Mat, Match, Me, Metal, Mile, Miss, More, More hot, Mother, Mouse, Movie, Much, Muggier, Mut
Name, Not colder, Note, Nothing, Notter, Now
Oil, On, Open, Otter, Out, Outside
Pad, Pancakes, Pans, Passion, Pat, Peas, People, Person, Pig, Pistol, Pizza, Plotter, Pot holder, Potters, Pottery, Price, Puff, Putter
Quick
Radish, Really, Red hot, Reigns, Rest, Rice, Roast, Rodder, Room, Run
Sad, Say, Scalding, School, Scott, Scream, Sea, Seat, Sex, Shot, Shots, Shower, Side, Six, Slick, Slip, Slow, Smart, Smell, Smoke, Smooth, Smother, Sod, Soft, Soup, South, Spooks, Stall, Star, Stays, Stem, Still, Sting, Stone, Stop, Stoves, Strange, Surf, Sweating, Swim, Swimming
Take, Talk, Teacher, Tea kettle, Temperature, Then blazes, Than hell, The, Then, Thermometer, They, Thing, Thirsty, ·Toaster, Today, Too hot, Torn, Touch, Tropical, Trotter, Tube
Uncomfortable
Venus, Very, Very hot
Warmest, Was, Well, Were, Wetter, What, Whistler, Winter, Woman, Word, Worm, Wow
Yes, Yet, You

HOUSE

Abode, A home, A place to sleep in, A place where we live in
Baby, Back door, Back yard, Bad, Bake, Bar, Basement, Bedroom, Beg, Bell, Bench, Bib, Bid, Bird, Bleak, Blocks, Board, Boards, Born, Box, Break, Bricks, Broom, Brother, Brothers, Bright, Buick, Buildings, Built, Burn, Burned
Cab, Can, Care, Castle, Children, Church, City, Closet, Colonial, Color, Colors, Come, Conceal, Corner, Cover, Covering, Cow, Cozy, Crazy
Den, Desk, Dim, Dirty, Dog house, Doll, Doll house, Doors, Draw, Duplex, Dwelling
Eat
Fast, Fire, Fireplace, Five seven five one Blaisdell, Float, Floor, Flower, Flowers, Food, Fort, Foundation, Frame, Friend, Friendly, Fun, Funny
Gate, Girl, Good, Got, Grass, Gray, Grey, Grouse, Guest, Gully
Hall, Hamsters, Hand, Happiness, Happy, Hat, Head, Hearth, Heat, Hen, Height, Hi, High, His, Hold, Hold tools, Homey, Hospitality, House, Houses, Huge
In, Inside
Jack
Keeper, Kindness, Kitchen
Lake, Lamp, Land, Larger, Lawns, Light, Like, Living place, Living quarters, Log, Look, Lot, Lots, Louse, Low, Lucky, Lumber, Luxury
Maid, Maison, Mason, Me, Men, Minneapolis, Monkey, More Mand, Motel, Mountain, My home, My house
Neat, Neighbor, Night, Nose, Nothing, Now
Okay, Old, Orange, Our, Ours, Out, Outside, Own
Pad, Palace, Parents, Peak, Pen, Person, Pest, Phone, Picture, Pine Island, Pink, Pink round flat, Places, Place to live in, Plaster, Play, Play house, Plot, Pond, Pony, Pool, Porch, Point
Rake, Ranch, Rain, Rats, Ray, Rent, Responsibility, Rest, Ride, Road, Roomy, Rug, Run
Sack, Saddle, Safe, Safety, Saginaw, Sake, Scream, Shacks, Shake, Shanty, Shape, Side, Sidewalk, Siding, Sister, Six, Size, Sky, Sod, Sold, Something you live in, Split level, Split story, Spook, Spooky, Square frame type, Stairs, Stairway, Stay, Stay or live, Step, Stone, Stop, Stove, Strong, Structure, Sturdy, Swim
They, Thing, This, To live, To live in, Town, Trailer, Trailers, Trees
Underneath, Us
Village
Walk, Walls, War, Wait, Warmer, Warmness, Wax, Where live, White house, White paint, Why, Wide, Work, Worm
Yellow, Yellow house

HOW

A, Ability, Able, About it, Adverb, All, Always, Am, And, An then, Any, Anyhow, Aren't, Are you, Arithmetic, As, Asking

Be able, Become, Been, Before, Begin, Big, Blank, Bought, Bow, Bow wow, Boy, Bright, Build, Bus, By car

Call, Can't, Carry, Cat, Cause, Cave, Chance, Chief, Company, Complicated, Confused, Confusion

Dare, Darrone, Describe, Detective, Did he, Did you, Different, Difficult, Directions, Dog, Doing, Don't, Don't know, Dope, Do something, Doubt, Dow, Down, Do you do it, Drive, Dud, Dye

Eat, Everybody, Example

Fare, Fat, Feel, Feeling, Feet, Find, Fine, Fix, Floor, Food, Forever, Fried, Fun, Funny

Gee, Get, Girl, Going, Good question, Got, Great, Green, Greet, Greeting, Grow, Guess

Ha, Hand, Happen, Happy, Has, Hat, Hay, Heavy, Here, Here's, Hi, High, Highway, Hi Indian, Him, His, Hit, Hoe, Home, Honey, Hope, Horn, Hot, House, How, How come, How did you do it, How do it, How do you do, How not, How now brown cow, How on earth, How's

Idiot, I don't know, If, Impossible, In, Indian chief, Indian talk, Instruct, Instructions, Its

Job, Journalism, Jump, Just

Kind, Knew, Known

Language, Laughs, Lawn, Lazy, Learn, Light, Like this, Limp, Little, Live, Look, Love

Made, Magic, Make, Manner, Mark, Meow, Might, Mind, Minute, Mode, Moo, Mouth, Mow, Must, My

Near, Need, Neither, None, Noon, North, Not easy, Nothing, Not how

Of, Oh, On, One, Or, Our

Peace, Peter, Plan, Plane, Play, Please, Plow, Possible, Pow wow, Pretty, Push, Puzzled

Que modo, Question mark, Quieter

Really, Result, Ribbon, Ride, Right, Right away, Rose, Rules, Rum, Running

School, Seen, Shall, Sharp, She, Sidewalks, Simple, Slower, Slowly, Some, Somehow, Someone, Some way, Soon, Sow, Start, Steal, Stop, Store, Strong, Stupid, Sweet, Swim

Take, Talk, Teach, Teacher, Teepee, Tell, Test, Their, Them, Therefore, Thesis, They, Thing, This way, Though, Thus, Thusly, Today, To do it, Together, To know, To run, Tough, Try, Tub

Uncertain, Understand, Unknown, Us

Very, Village

Wait, Want to know, Ways, Welcome, Went, Whatever, Whenever, Which, Which way, White, Whom, Why fore, Wide, Win, Won, Wondering, Work, World, Would, Write, Wrong

Yeah, Yellow, Young, Your, Yours

Zow

HOWEVER

A, Ad, Add, Addition, After, Afterward, Again, Agree, Alas, Alright, Alway, Am, Amber, Ambition, And so on, And then, Another, Answer, Anyone, Anything, Anyways, Anywhere, Apart, Appear, Apple, Are, Argue, At, At one time, At time

Baby, Bad, Beaver, Beginning, Beside, Best, Bluff, Book, Boring, Boy, Bracelet, Brain, Bridge, Brief, Brought, Bus, By

Came, Candy, Cannibal, Car, Care, Cat, Catch, Cause, Certain, Change, Change mind, Chief, Clause, Clock, Cold, Color, Coma, Commas, Compound, Conclusion, Condition, Connect, Consequently, Considering, Constant, Continue, Contradiction, Contrary, Conversation, Correction, Could, Could never, Could you, Cry

Dam, Daring, Day, Dear, Dearly, Depending, Didn't, Did you, Difficult, Do ever, Dog, Do it, Done, Donna, Donny, Do no, Don't, Doors, Down

Early, Either, Else, Envelope, Even so, Even though, Ever how, Everyone, Everything, Every time, Example, Expect, Explaining, Explanation, Expression, Eyes

Fact, Faithful, Far, Feet, Few, Fine, Flip, Floor, Fog, Fond, Fools, Forget, Four, Friends, Fruit, Fun, Funny

Game, Geometry, Get, Girl, Girls, Glass, Go, Gone, Grammar, Great, Grown ups

Had, Happen, Happened, Happens, Happy, Hard, Hat, Have, Having, Heart, Heavy, Help, Hence, Her, Here, Hesitating, His, Home, Homely, Honest, Horse, Hospital, Hour, House, Hover, How come, How did, However, However I will, How would

I'm, Important, Impossible, In, In addition, In case, Incidentally, Indian, Inside, Inspiteof, Instead, In that case, In the mean time, It is, Its, Itself

Jeepers, Judge, Just

Kathy, Keep, Knew, Knowledge, Known

Lady, Late, Lawyer, Lay, Leave, Lie, Like, Little, Lonely, Look, Lovely, Low

Mainly, Make, Matter, Mean, Meaning, Mean while, Men, Milk, Mine, Money, More ever, More so, Most, Mountain, Mouth, Mow, Mrs., Mrs. Straka, Must, My, Myself

Name, Nearer, Neat, Neater, Neither, Never mind, No ever, No more, None sense, Nonetheless, Non ever, No so, Nothing, Not now, Now ever, Now then, Nurse

Objection, Occasion, Often, Oh, OK, Old, On, Once, Or else, Other, Otherwise, Other words, Over

Paper, Parent is, Past, People, Perhaps, Place, Play, Please, Plus, Possibility, Possibly, Pot, Power, President, Presumptuous, Pretty

Qualify, Questions, Quick, Quickly

Rainbow, Rare, Rather, Read, Real, Red, Rely, Remark, Remember, Reply, Reservation, Result, Right, Right away, Run

Sad, Said, Salve, Same, Say, Saying, Says, School, Scientist, Seem, Seems, Sense, Sentence, She wants it, Shorthand, Should, Sigh, Simple, Sir, Six, Slow, Smaller, So even, So far, So forth, Soon, Somebody, Some day, Some how, Someone, Something else, Something more, Somethings, Somewhere, Sorry, Sound, So what, Speak, Speaker, Speaking, Speech, Spelling, Still, Story, Studious, Stutter, Such, Suppose, Sure, Surprise

Take, Talk, Teaches, Term paper, That is, That's, Their, Them, Theme, There ever, There is one, Things, Thinking, Those, Thou, Thought, Time, To, Today, Too, Trouble, Two, Typing

Undecided, Uneven, Unless, Upon, Usually

Violet, Vowels

Want, Warm, Watch out, Weather, Weaver, What are, What however, Whatsoever, Wheel, Whereas, Which, Whichever, While, Whomever, Why ever, Will, Will be, With, Withever, Wolf man, Woman, Women, Words, Work, Word, Write

Year, You must, Young, Your, Youth

HUNGRY

Africa, After school, Anger, Appreciate, Aren't, At lunch, Austria, Awful

Baby, Bad, Bare, Beast, Bed, Beg, Beggar, Beggars, Belly, Big, Birds, Black, Blew, Blue, Boy friend, Boys, Breakfast, Brother

Cake, Camping, Candy, Car, Care, Carolyn, Cat, Chain, Chemistry, China, Chinese, City, Comfort, Communism, Communist, Concentration camp, Content, Cook, Cookie, Cookies, Corn, County, Crackers, Cramp, Craving, Crying

Dark, Dead, Dear, Delicious, Desire, Diet, Dirty, Discomfort, Dog, Door, Drink, Drunk, Dry, Duck

Eager, East, Eaten, Eat much, Elephant, Emotion, Enough, Europe, Evil

Face, Famine, Fast, Fasting, Feast, Fed, Feed, Feeling, Feet, Fight, Fill, Filled, Fine, Fish, Food or lunch, Foot, Fork, Four, Fowl, French fries, Fruit, Funny, Fur

Girls, Gnawing, Go, Grain, Greece, Green, Grow, Growling, Gut

Hamburger, Happy, Hard, Head, Heal, Health, Help, Herd, High, Home, Horse, Hot, House, Huge, Hung, Hungrier, Hungry, Hunt, Hurry, Hurts

Ill

Jack, Japan

Kids, Kill, Know, Korea, Koreans

Lamb, Land, Light, Like, Lion, Lunch time

Mad, Made, Malnutrition, Meal, Meals, Meek, Men, Meow, Milk, Miserable, Mouth

Nation, Nauseated, Necessity, Need, Needing, Needs, Never, New, Nice, Night, No, No food, Noon, Not full, Not hungry, Now

Ocean, Olives, On, Orange, Order, Ox

Painful, Paper, Peanut butter, Pear, Peasant, Pest, Pheasant, Pie, Pig, Pity, Plate, Play, Plump, Poverty

Rabbit, Ravenous, Red, Refrigerator, Refugee, Relaxed, Revolt, Right, Romania, Rumble, Run, Russia, Russians

Sad, Sadness, Save, School, Serve, Seven starve, Shoes, Slave, Sleep, Sleepy, Slow, Smart, Snack, So, Soft, Soon, Sorry, Soup, Start, Stop, Story, Stove, Stuff, Stuffed, Stump, Suffering, Supper, Swallow

Tantrum, Tasty, Teeth, Terrible, Terror, That's me, Thin, Things, Third period, Toast, Today, Too many, Torture, Travel, Tried, True, Tummy, Turkey

Uncomfortable, Unhappy, Unhungry, Upset

Wait, Waiting for dinner, Wanting, Wants food, Want something to eat, War, Water, Weak, Well fed, Were, Wet, With, Wolf, Woman, Working
Yellow, You

I

Agree, Alone, Alphabet, Always, And, Are, At, Ate
Baseball, Be, Being, Black, Blue, Body, But, By
Cads, Call, Came, Can't, Cat, Chuck, Cold, Come, Conceit, Conceited, Connie, Could, Cry, Cute
Daryl, Didn't, Dog, Down, Dress, Dron, Dummy
Ear, Eat, Ego, Egotist, Ending, Ever, Eyes
Faith, Fat, Father, Fell, Figure, First, Fluff, Forgot, Friend
Gin, Give, Gone, Good, Got, Gymnast
Hair, Hand, Hate, Head, Heard, Herald, Here, Hi, High, His, Home, How, Human, Hurry
I, I'll, I am, Ich, Ick, I'd, Idaho, In, Its, I've, I will
Jack, Jackie, James, Jan, Je, Joyce
Kathy, Ken, Kids, Knew
Lad, Lay, Lazar, Left
Made, Male, Man, Marcia, Marilyn, May, Me question, Might, Mind, Mirror, Must
Nail, Name, Nancy, Never, Nice, Noble, Nose, Nothing, Nut
O, Off, Oh, Only
Pam, Penny, People, Piano, Pie, Playing, Point, Proud, Pure, Put
Quiet
Rather, Realize, Ride, Robin, Rope
Sally, Say, Sea, Seed, Self, Sell, Seven, Shall, Shop, Should, Sigh, Sight, Single, Sky, Small, Smart, So, Someone, Someone else, Something, Space, Speak, Spy, Stop, Study, Subject, Susan, Swam
Talk, Tell, The, Their, Then, This, Those, Thou, Thought, Three, Tie, Time, Tin, Tired, Tom, Tried, Two
Ugly, Understand, Up
Vowel
Walk, Watch, Weep, What, When, Where, Who, Whom, Why, Win, Wish, Wonder, Won't, Word, Work, Writing
Yelled, Yes, Your, Yourself

IF

About, Accident, After, Alternative, Although, Always, Am, Anger, Another, Answer, Ant, Any, Anything, Anyway, Apprehension, Aren't, As if, Asking, As long as, Assume, Ate
Bad, Bat, Be, Besides, Bif, Big word, Blank, Book, Boy, Boys, Button, By chance
Came, Can be, Cannot, Can't, Capital, Cared, Carols, Case, Cause, Cephalopod, Certain, Chair, Chance, Choice, Clause, Cliff, Clues, Come on, Comes, Coming, Complain, Conclusion, Conjunction, Cook, Cool, Correct, Could be, Cow poke, Cut
Day, Decide, Dependent, Dick, Dictionary, Did, Different, Doe, Does, Don't known, Do something special, Do something, Down, Dream
Eight, Even though, Everybody, Example, Exception, Excused, Explanation
Fair, Fall, Faster, Fear, Fibber, Figure, Fish, Fly, Football, Fun, Future
Game, Gift, Girl, Go, God, Going, Gone, Good, Grammar, Guard, Guy
Had, Happen, Happened, Have, Here, Hesitate, Hesitation, Him, His, Hit, Hope, Horse, House, How come, Hypothesis
Ice, I did, I die, I don't know, If clause, If not, If what, Ill, I'm, Isn't, It is, Its
Jif, Just
Kipling, Kiss, Knife, Knit, Know
Laconia, Lamp, Liar, Lie, Light, Line, Little, Lonely, Love
Man, Mat, May I, Mean, Mine, Mint, Misunderstood, Mob, Money, Mother, Much, Myth
Necessary, Nice, Nothing, Not quite, Numbers, Nut
Object, Of course, Oh, OK, Opinion, Opposite, Or else, Other, Otherwards, Otherwise, Our, Over
Parenthetical, Pass, Pause, Pencil, People, Peter, Place, Plank, Play, Please, Pleasure, Poem, Possibility, Possible, Probable, Probably, Problem, Proposal, Proposition, Provided
Qualify, Questioning, Questions
Ran, Rather, Reasons, Referring, Right, Ripe, Roll
Salt, Saw, Say, Sea, Seat, Seen, Sentence, Shall, Short, Si, Sick,

Sift, Six, Small, Snow, Somehow, Sometime, Sometimes, Song, Soon, Speak, Speck, Spring, Stammer, Star, Start, Stiff, Stipulation, Subjunctive, Summer, Suppose, Supposition, Sure, Suspicious, Swif
Take, Talking, Teacher, Thats, Their, Them, Therefore, These, Thing, Things, Think, This, This happens, Though, Time, To, Tree, Try, Twenty, Two
Ukl these, Uncertain, Undecided, Unknown, Unless, Unsure, Until, Us
Variable
Wait, Waiting, War, Water, We can, Well, Went, What if, When if, Wherefore, Which, While, Why not, Wife, Will, Win, Wish, Wishes, With, Wonder, Wood, Work, Would, Wreck
Yet, Younger, Your

IN

About, A can, Again, All, Also, An, Ann, Apple, Around, As, Ask, Awake, Away
Baby, Bar, Barrel, Basement, Bath tub, Be, Bedroom, Been, Beginning, Beside, Beyond, Bin, Blame, Boat house, Bog, Booth, Born, Bowl, Boy, Bucket, But
Cage, Came, Can, Cat, Cave, Cellar, Chairs, Child, Children, China, Church, Citizen, City, Claustrophobia, Closed in, Closet, Club, Corner, Cover, Cozy
Danger, Dark, Day, Deed, Deep, Depth, Did, Do, Drawer, Dumb
Eat, Enclosure, Enter, Entered
Fact, Fast, Few, Fin, Find, Finger, Fishing, For, Foremost, From, Front
Garage, Garden, Get, Girl, Girls, Got in shelter, Guts
Hall, Hat, Hell, Hen, Hers, Hit, Hole, Hoose, Hope, Hose, Hot, Hotel, Hour, Houses, How
I, Ice, If, Imprisoned, In, Indoor, Ink, Inner, Inside of, In something, Instinct, Institute, In the house, Its
Jail
Kiffers
Let, Light, Like, Little, Livingroom, Local, Locked, Look, Love
Mail box, Mantel, Meat, Middle, Mine, Minutes, Move, Movie, My
Near, New York, Nigh, Night, Not out
Oblative, Of, Office, Oh, One, Open, Opposite, Or, Or out, Our, Outdoors
Package, Parade, Pen, Pool, Poor, Porch, Prep
Read, Refrigerator, Respect, Restaurant, Rid, Ride, Roof, Run
Sack, Sand, Sane, Saw, Sea, See, September, Set, Sharing, She, Shelter, Shin, Short, Show, Sides, Sight, Sin, Sir, So, Some, Someplace, Somewhere, Spring, Start, Steal, Store, Such, Suit, Summer, Sun
Take, Tavern, Tent, Their, Them, Then, Thin, Thing, This, Though, Through, Thus, Tin, Too, Top, Touch, Travel, Tree, Trouble, Trunk, Tub, Tuition, Twin
Unseen, Until, Up, Upon
Voice
Wagon, Warmth, Was, Water, Way, White house, Who, Win, Window, With, Would, Write
Yard, Years, You, Your

IS

Able, About, Abbreviation, Action, After, Alive, All, Already, Alright, Also, Another, Anything, Ask
Bad, Because, Been, Bees, Bell, Belonging, Better, Big, Bird, Bobby, Book, Busy
Car, Care, Carry, Cat, Caught, Cause, Chair, Chew, Class, Clear, Clock, Clod, Clothes, Cold, Come, Coming, Cookies, Cool, Crayon, Create, Cute
Dave, Day, Dead, Describing, Desk, Did, Do, Does, Done, Door, Dry, Dumb
Eat, English, Enough, Equals, Ever, Every, Existence
Face, Fact, Far, Fast, Fat, Feet, Fine, Fizzy, From, Funny
Get, Gets, Girls, Going to, Gone, Got, Grammar, Great, Greater, Grill
Happening, Has, Hat, Heavy, He is, Help, Her, Hers, Hi, Hobby, Hog, Hold, Hole, Horse, House, Hurt
Ice, Ill, Immediately, Is gone, Island, Is that a car, Its
Know, Known
Lake, Land, Language, Late, Lay, Let, Lets, Letter, Likely, Little, Live, Lives, Lonesome, Long
Man, Mat, May, Maybe, Mice, Might, Miss, Monkey, Most, Mouse
Name, Neat, Negro, Net, Noise, Nose, Nothing, Number, Numbers
Off, Oh, OK, Okay, Old, Om, Once, Open, Our, Own

Pa, Paper, Part, Pencil, People, Pest, Place, Pope, Position,
  Possible, Preposition, Present, Presently, Pretty
Quiet, Quit, Quite, Quiz
Rat, Ready, Really, Red, Rub, Run, Running
Sad, Salam, Same, Say, See, Sentence, Sentences, Seven, Sew,
  Short, Silly, Sis, Sister, Sit, Slow, Snow, Someone, Soon,
  Stand, Steven, Such, Suppose to, Sure
Talk, Tap, Telling, Than, Thats, Their, Theirs, Think, Tis,
  To be, Together, Toy, Truly, Truth, Try, Twelve, Two,
  Typing
Ugly, Up, Us, Usually
Verbs, Vital
Walking, Wall, Ware, Water, Way, Weak, Wet, When, Whether,
  Which, Why, Win, Wis, With, Wiz, Words, Wow, Wrong
Yet

IT

Abominable, Actor, Also, Always, Andre, Animals, Anonymous,
  Ant, Any, Anything, Appears, Apple, Are, Article, As, Ate,
  A thing, Awful
Bayla, Be, Became, Because, Bee, Being, Beverage, Bird,
  Bit, Black, Blew, Blob, Bob, Boots, Brought, Bug, Building,
  But, Butter
Cabbage, Cadaver, Cannot, Catch, Cats, Certain, Chair, Charles,
  Chicken, Coat, Come, Comes, Cool, Cost, Cow, Crazy,
  Cruel
Day, Dead, Definite, Describing, Desk, Did, Direct, Dish, Does,
  Doesn't, Door, Dorothy, Dumb
Ear, Easy, English, Es, Ever
Far, Fat, Fault, Fine, First, Flit, Flower, Flys, For, Found,
  French, From, Funny
Game, Gender, Ghost, Glasses, Go, Goes, Gone, Good, Grammar
Happen, Happens, Happy, Hard, Hasn't, Hat, Have, Henry, Here,
  Hot, House, How, Hurts
Ill, Indefinite, Inhuman, Inn, Interrupt, Is easy, Isn't here, It is,
  It was nice
Jewels
Kay Larson, Kennedy, Kids, Kit
Lady, Left, Letters, Like, Lips, Lit, Little, Lizard, Look,
  Looks, Loves
Many, Marble, Martian, May, Men, Met, Might, Mine, Mit,
  Money, Moved, Moves, Movie, Must, My
Neutral, Never, No, Nobody, None, Non-human, Noun
Off, Often, Oh, OK, Old, Once, Only, Onward, Or, Other, Out,
  Over
Paper, Pen, Pencil, People, Persons, Pip, Pit, Place, Plays,
  Pro, Project, Pronouns, Puck, Put
Queer
Rags, Rained, Rains, Rather, Reading, Ready, Really, Red,
  Renter, Rosalee, Run
Said, Same, Saw, Say, Scared, School, Sea, See, Seen, Self,
  Sentence, Sex, Sexless, Shall, Shoo, Short, Skit, Smells, So,
  Solid, Some, Somebody, Someone, Spider, Stop, Sun, Surprise,
  Swam
Table, Teachers, Than, That's, Their, The thing, Thieves, Things,
  Those, Three, Tick, Tin, To, Took, Toy, Tree, Turtle, Two
Unearthly, Us
Verb
War, Wasn't, Way, We, Well, Where, White, Who, Why,
  Winner, Wise, Won, Won't, Wood, Work, World, Would,
  Wouldn't, Wrong
Yellow, Yes, Young, Yours

JOY

A, A certain girl, A girl, A name, Angry, Awful
Babies, Ball, Band, Basketball, Beard, Beautiful, Behold,
  Belief, Bell, Bible, Bird, Birth, Birthday, Birthdays, Bitter-
  ness, Bless, Bliss, Blue, Boat, Bob, Bread, Bright, Brother,
  Bubblebath, Bubbles, Butter, By
Cake, Can, Candy, Cat, Charity, Children, Christ, Clown,
  Cousin, Cry
Dance, Day, Death, Delight, Delighted, Delightful, Depression,
  Detergent, Diane, Did, Disaster, Discomfort, Dish, Dish pan,
  Divine, Dog, Dream
Earth, Easter, Eat, Emotion, Enjoyed, Enjoyful, Excited,
  Excitement, Exclaim, Exuberance, Eyes
Family, Fast, Fat, Feed, Feel, Feeling, Feet, Fine, Fishing,
  Fleeting, Flowers, For, Found, Fountain, Friday, Friend,
  Friendly, Friends, Frown, Funny
Glade, Glee, Gloom, God, Good deed, Good time, Gordon,

Grateful, Great, Great feeling, Gutafuson, Gym
Ha, Had, Haha, Hand, Hang, Happen, Happy delightful, Hatred,
  Hay, Head, Health, Heaven, Help, Holiday, Honey, Hot,
  House, Hunting, Hurray
Ire, Ivory
Jack, Jane, Jay, Jim, Joan, Join, Jolly, Joyce, Joys, Jubilation,
  Jug, Juice, Jumble
Kathy, Kindness, King
Lake, Land, Laughed, Laziness, Leap, LeRoy, Light, Lion,
  Liquid, Look, Loud, Loved, Lovely, Low, Luck, Lump
Madness, Man, Marry, Me, Mean, Mist, Moment, Mother,
  Mouse, Murder, My name, My sister
Nancy L., Need, New, New girl friend, New Years, No, Noise
Of, Olsen, Overflowing
Pain, Part, Parties, People, Peppy, Peterson, Picnic, Pink,
  Pious, Place, Playing, Pot, Present, Pretty, Pride, Proud,
  Pump
Rejoice, Relief, Roberta, Run, Rydholm
Said, Sail, Sex, Shout, Shut up, Sick, Side, Silly, Sing, Singing,
  Singing hymns, Sister, Sleigh, Smart, Snow, Soft, Some,
  Songs, Sorrowness, Sound, Soup, Sour, Square, Star, Stream,
  Stupe, Suds, Summer, Sun, Sunshine
Tan, Tarzan, Tell, Terrible, The, Thing, Tide, Tidings, Time,
  Together, Too, To the world, Troubled
Unhappy or sad
Vacation, Valentine, Vibrant
Warm, Wash, Water, What, White, Why, Woe, Word, Work,
  Wow
Yay, Yea, Yeah, Yelling, You

JUMP

A, Across, Ah, Ahead, And, Ankle, Athlete, Away
Back, Ball, Bang, Bar, Barn, Basketball, Bend, Black, Board,
  Bound, Boy, Boys, Broad jump, Broke, Brother, Building,
  Bunny, By
Came, Can, Candlestick, Cars, Cat, Catch, Cheerleader, Child,
  Clap, Cliff, Closer, Come, Cow, Crab, Crash, Crevasse
Dash, Decathlon, Dig, Distance, Dive, Do, Dog, Donny, Drop
Excitement, Exert
Face, Faster, Fastest, Fat, Fell, Fences, First, Fish, Flip,
  Food, For, Fore, Fox, Freeze, Frog, Frogs, From,
  Further
Game, Games, Girl, Good bye, Grasshopper, Ground, Gun,
  Gym
Had, Hair, Hanger, Happy, Hard, Harder, Have, Heap, Hedge,
  Help, Her, Hid, Hide, High jump, Hike, Him, Hint, Hip,
  His, Hit, Home, Hoop, Hopped, Hop scotch, Horses, House,
  Hug, Hurdler, Hurry, Hurt, Hurts
In air, Ing
Jack, Jacks, Jamp, Jan, Jane, January, Jerk, Jip, Joe, Jog,
  Jump, Jumpers, Jumps, Junk
Kangaroo, Kill, Know
Ladder, Leaped, Leaves, Leg, Legs, Let, Lie, Lift, Light,
  Limp, Log, Long, Loud, Lower
Make, Man, Marry, Mice, Mom, Moon, Mother, Motion,
  Mountain, Music
Needle, Nerves, No, Not
Oh, Olympics, One
Paratroopers, Person, Personality, Pig, Plane, Playing, Plump,
  Pogo stick, Pole vaulting, Pounce, Puddle, Pump
Quirk
Raise, Reach, React, Requested, Rest, Revolution, Rise, River,
  Rock, Roll, Ropes, Rough, Rum, Rump, Running
Safety, Said, Sat, Scare, Scared, School, See, Seem, Set, Shake,
  She, Ship, Shoot, Shovel, Show, Sidewalk, Skis, Sky, Sleek,
  Slide, Slop, Sneak, Snow, Some, Soon, Sports, Squat, Started,
  Stay, Steeple chase, Stepped, Stick, Still, Stomp, Stood,
  Strain, Sudden, Sun, Surely, Surface, Swim
Tall, Tell, Tennis shoes, That, There, This, Thought, Through,
  Thump, Tired, Too, Trampoline, Trip, Trot, Turtle
Under, Up and down, Us
Very
Walked, Wall, Was, We, Went, When, Where, Who, Wide, With,
  Word, Work, Wow
Yell

JUSTICE

Action, Agree, Air, A lawyer, All, All right, America, American,
  As, Ate, Attorney, Aw
Be, Beast, Bell, Bergen, Bible, Black, Blind, Blind folded,

Blue, Book, Books, Bread, Bregen, Bride, Brink
Came, Candy, Canteen, Capital punishment, Car, Chair, Charity, Cheat, Chief, Chisanson, Church, Citizen, Clock, Club, Colt forty-five, Command, Communism, Complete, Congress, Constitution, Cookie, Cop fuss, Copper, Corn, Correct, Country, Courage, Court house, Criminal, Crooked, Crooks, Cruel, Cup
Dad, Dead, Decency, Defend, Delinquent, Department, Detective, Dictatorship, Dislike, Disorder, Do, Dog, Done, Dope, Draw, Drinks, Dry, Duties
Ending, Enemy, Even, Expensive
Face, Facts, Fair play, False, Farce, Farm, Fast, Father, Fear, Find, Fine, Fire, Firm, Foolish, Fore, Friend, Fruit, Fun, Funny, Fuss
Gavel, Getting married, Glass, Goose, Gov., Governor, Gov't., Grape, Great, Guilt, Guilty, Gun, Guns
Handle, Hang, Hanged, Hanging, Happy, Hard, Hate, He, Helps, Hill, Holmes, Honest, Horse
Ick, Illegal, Impartial, In, Injury, Integration, Is, It
Jam, Jed Jackson, Joy, Judged, Judges
Keep, Kill, Kind, Kindness, King
Lad, Lake, Law and order, Law breaker, Lawful, Lawlessness, Lawyers, Lay, Leader, League, Legal, Life, Like, Lincoln, Liquid, Low, Loyalty, Lynching
Mad, Magistrate, Magna Carta, Many, Mason, Mayor, Me, Mean, Meat, Mice, Mighty, Milk, Mind, Minister, Ministry, Money, Morality, Mountie, Mr., Murder, Music, My
Name, Needed, News, No, Noble, Noethica community, No fun, Noise, No justice, None, Nonsense, Not, Now
Obeying, Officer, Oh oh, One, Out, Out law, Owner
Pace, Pack, Pare, Parking ticket, Parson, Pastor, Patience, Peace law, Penalty, Perry Mason, Person, Pieces, Pink, Place, Please, Poles, Policeman, Policemen, Police station, Pooh, Poor, Powerful, Prejudice, Press, Priest, Prime Minister, Principal, Prison, Private, Promise, Pulp, Punish, Punishment, Put
Quick, Quiet
Ran, Rank, Red, Religion, Revenge, Right and wrong, Righteousness, Rites, Robber, Robe, Roof, Rules, Ruthlessness
Safety, Scared, Scene, Security, See, Service, Sex, Sheep, Sheriff, Shore, Shot, Sight, Skate, Snow, So, Some, Something done, Sorrow, Speeding, State, Statue, Statue of Justice, Stern, Straight, Strength, Strict, Strong, Supreme, Sweet, Swift
Television, Tell, Test, The, The right thing, Ticket, Tomato, Torch, Trail, Tree, Trials, Triumph, True, Trust, Truthful
Uncle, Understand, Underworld, Unlawful, Up, Us
Victim, Victory, Violence
Want, Warren, Was, Watery, Wedding, Will, Wisdom, Wise, Wish, With, Woman
Yellow, Youth

KING

Above, After, Again, Ahead, Alex, Alice, Almighty, Ancient, Arabia, Army, A ruler, Author
Be, Beast, Bee, Best, Bible, Big man, Big wheel, Bill, Black, Book, Boreas, Bow, Bowdoin, Bowling, Brave, Bread, Britain, Brown
Can, Candy, Captain, Car, Card, Carpet, Ceremony, Chair, Charles the Second, Checkmate, Chief, China, Choose, Christ, Cigarette, City, Class, Clown, Coil, Command, Commander, Commanding, Court, Creole, Cross
Dad, Desk, Dew, Dick, Died, Ding, Divine Right, Dominant, Drill, Drive, Dwight, Dynasty
Edward, Egypt, Elephant, Empire, Eng, Europe, Excellency
Fairy tale, Fat, Father, Fearful, Feruke, First, Food, For a day, France, Funny
George Sixth, George the Third, Germany, Glad, Good man, Got, Grand, Gustav
Hand, Handsome, Hard, Hat, Head of, Height, Henry Eight, Henry IV, Henry the Eighth, Henry the Sixth, Henry the Third, Hierarchy, High class, High man, Highness, High person, High priest, Highway, Home, Home coming, Honor, Honorable, House, Human, Hurry, Husband, Hussein
Important, It
Jack, James the First, Jewel, Jewelers, Jewelry, Joe, Johnson, John the Third, Jones, Joshua, Joy, Justice
Khrushchev, Kind, King Cole, King George, Knights, Kole
Lamumba, Large, Late, Law, Leo, Leonardo, Live good, Loss, Loud, Louis the First, Louis the Fourteenth, Louse, Loyal

Mad, Make, Maker, Mammal, Marie, Mary, Mattress, Mean, Meat, Mens, Mike, Miss King, Mohammed, Mohammed the Fifth, Monarchy, Moses, Mouse, Mr. Brackett
Name, Nation, Nobility, Norway, Not, Nurse, Nut, Nuts
Obey, Of the world God, OK, Olly, Owen, Owner
Palaces, Pare, Peace, Peasant, Philip, Phillip, Place, Play, Pompous, Popular, Powerful, Praise, Pre, Press, Pretty, Price, Priest, Princess, Proud, Purple
Quiet
Rat, Regal, Reigning, Rice, Richard, Richard Five, Richard the Lion Hearted, Riches, Richness, Rings, Road, Robes, Rod, Role, Roll, Rome, Royal stuff, Rube, Ruler authority, Rules
Salmon, Saud, Sceptor, Servant, Servants, Sing, Sit, Sitting, Small, Smart, Snake, Snob, Soldier, Soldiers, Something, Son, Song, Sovereign, Spain, Splendor, Sports, Staff, Stallion, Step, Stories, Story, Street, Strong, Subject, Superior, Supreme, Sweden, Sword
Teller, The, Thing, Throng, Thrown, Tommy, Top, Tops, Town, Treasure, Trouble, Tut, Tutankhamun, Tyranny, Tyrant
Was, Water, Wealth, Wealthy, Wenceslaus, Went, Wild, Wind, Wing, Woman, World, Would
Yes, You

KITTENS

Alive, Animal love, Ape, As, At
Babies, Baby cats, Bad, Ball, Ball of yarn, Barn, Basket, Batch, Beasts, Beautiful, Bedroom, Big, Birds, Black, Blanket, Blind, Book, Boots, Bootsie, Born, Box, Boy, Brown, But
Can, Car, Cart, Cat's babies, Catty, Chair, Chase, Chester, Claws, Color, Come, Comes, Cook, Cubs, Cuddle, Cuddly, Curtains
Darling, Dinner, Doggies, Domestic, Dog
Eat, Elephants, Eyes
Far, Farm, Father, Feed, Feet, Feline, Fetal, Five, Follow, Foods, For, Friends
Garfield, Get, Gigi, Girl, Girls, Go, Goats, Good, Goods, Gray, Green, Grey, Grow
Had, Hat, Hate, Have, Heat, Home, Horse, Hot, House
In, Infant, Its
Kat, Kenny, Kid, Kill, Killed, Kite, Kittens, Kitties, Knit
Lamb, Life, Like, Lion, Lions, Litter, Live, Living, Living room, Look, Lots, Love
Mammals, Manger, Mark, Me, Mean, Meows, Mine, Misty, Mit, Mits, Mitt, Mitten, Moon, More, Moth, Mothers, Move, Mules
Need, Not, Nutty
Of, Oh, On, One, Our, Own
Page, Pair, Party, Paw, Paws, People, Pillow, Pink, Pins, Pioneer, Plant, Playful, Pregnant, Puppies, Pussies, Pussy, Pussy cat
Quit, Quite
Rat, Rats, Ribbon, Riley, Room, Run
Salty, Saw, School, Scratch, See, Several, Sex, She, Siamese, Sink, Sky, Small cats, Smell, Softness, Stop, Stupid
Table, Tammys, Tell, That, The, Them, Those, Three, Tiger, Time, Tiny, Trees, Trouble, TV, Twinkle spot, Two
Was, Wash, Water, Wattle butt, Weakness, Were, Wet, Whine, White, Will, Women, Wooly
Yes, You, Young, Young cats

LAMP

Amp, Animals, At
Base, Bed, Beige, Bey, Big, Blue, Boat, Book, Boy, Brass, Break, Broken, Bulbs, Burning
Camp, Can, Candle, Car, Carpet, Carry, Child, Chop, Close, Coach, Coat, Coffee table, Cold, Color, Come, Coot, Cottage, Couch, Curtain
Damp, Darkness, Deep, Deer, Dim, Do, Dog, Dresser, Drink, Dump
Ear, Eat, Electric, End table, Expense, Exploring, Eyes
Farm, Fast, Fat, Flashlight, Flour, Flower, Flowers, Fool, Front room, Fuel
Gas, Gives off light, Glass, Glow, Go, Goat, Grass, Gray, Green
Hair, Ham, Hearth, Hi, Hill, Home, Horse, Household
Ill, Imp, It
Kerosene
Lamp, Lampshade, Lantern, Large, Light pretty, Lights, Limb,

Lit, Little, Look, Low, Low light
Man, Master, Me, Monkey, Mother, Mutton
Neat, New, Nice, Night, No, Noise, Not
Odd, Off, Oil lamp, Old, Oriental, Oven
Pamp, Pan, Paper, Past time, People, Person, Picture, Pig, Plant, Plug, Pole, Priceless
Radio, Read, Reading, Red, Rug
Sad, Salt, Sand, Sat, Scared, Seep, Sell, Shades, Shark, Shine, Sight, Sit, Sleep, Sleepy, So, Soda, Spanish, Stamp, Stand, Steep, Stew, Stick, Stock, Stone, Studying, Stump, Sugar, Sun, Sunlight, Sweet
Tall, Teacher, Thing, Though, Tight, Time, Tramp, TV
Vase
Wall, Water, Wax, Wet, Whistle, White, Window, Wire, Wood working
Yes, You

LIFT

Above, Age, Ah, Airlift, All, Alone, Along, Am, An, And, Arise, Arms, Away
Baby, Back, Bad, Ball, Bar, Barbells, Basket, Be, Bear, Behind, Bend, Big, Block, Board, Bob, Body, Book, Boxes. Boys, Braw, Bridge, Bring, Bull, Buoyancy, Burden, But, Buy, By
Camshaft, Can, Can't, Care, Carrying, Cart, Carton, Catch, Children, Civil, Close, Come, Convey, Cook, Cow, Crane, Crook
Death, Descend, Desk, Did, Die, Dip, Do, Don't, Door, Drag, Drawer, Drift, Drip, Duluth
Easily, Easter, Easy, Elevate, Energy, Exert, Eyes
Face, Fast, Feet, Fell, Felt, Fine, Foot, For, Forget, From, Front, Fun
Gate, Gently, Get, Girl, Give, Gone, Good, Grass, Groan, Gun
Hair, Hall, Handle, Hands, Hang, Hangers, Hark, Hat, Hauled, He, Hear, Heard, Heart, Heavily, Heavy things, Held, Hi, Hide, Higher, Horse, House, Hunger, Hurt
In air
Jack, Janitor, Jump
Keep, Key, Knee
Lamp, Lane, Laugh, Lazy, Lead, Less, Lever, Lid, Lift, Lifting, Lifts, Like, Like that, Lilt, Lit, Living, Loft, Long, Look, Loose, Lost, Low, Lug
May, Merry, Might, Muscles, My, My mom
Never, Nice, No, Noise, Now
Of, On, One, Only, Open
Pails, Parson, Peek, Pencil, People, Person, Piano, Pig, Pillow, Please, Pry, Pulley
Rain, Reach, Relax, Remove, Rock, Run
Sang, Seat, Send, Set down, She, Shift, Shirt, Shoulder, Shout, Shovel, Show, Side, Sift, Ski, Ski lift, Skirt, Ski tow, Sky, Slow, Slower, Slowly, So, Soft, Some, Soon, Stationary, Stay, Steel, Stiff, Stoop, Struggle, Support, Sway, Swing
Table, Tack, Take up, Thee, Theft, Their, Theme, Then, There, They, Things, This, Though, Through, Till, Tilt, Time, Together, Ton, Tony, Too, Top, Tote, Touch, Towing, Tractor, Try, Tug, Turn
Ugh
Verb
Wait, Was, Way, Weigh, Went, When, Why, Wife, Window, Woman, Write
Year, Yes

LIGHT

Ass
Baby, Bad news, Balloon, Balls, Bark, Beams, Beautiful, Beauty, Bed, Better, Big, Bird, Birth, Bite, Blank, Blind, Blond, Bold, Book, Brilliant, Brush, Bugs
Camp, Car, Carefree, Ceiling, Chair, Cheerful, Christian, Cigarette, Clean, Cloud, Come, Cool, Cord
Dark glasses, Dart, Dawn, Day break, Day light, Day time, Death, Dew, Dine, Draw, Dream, Dress
Early, Earth, Easy, Edison, Electric, Electricity, Eye, Eyes
Face, Fair, Fallen, Far, Fast, Fat, Feather weight, Feathery, Feet, Five, Fixture, Flame, Flew, Fluffy, Foot, Fresh, Friendly, Fright, Fun, Furniture
Girl, Glasses, Glow, Go, God, Good, Got, Gray
Happiness, Happy, Have, Head, Headed, Health, Heart, Heaven, Heavy weight, Height, Her, Hi, High, Horse, Hungry
If, In, Is
Jesus, Joy, Just

Lamb, Lamp post, Lamps, Land, Lantern, Lend, Liberty, Lighter, Light house, Lightness, Lightning, Lingerie, Lit, Little, Long, Look, Love, Lump
May, Meal, Might, Money, Moon, Mother, Mouse
Nice, Nite, Not dark, Not heavy
Off, Oh, On, One lb., Open, Opposite of dark, Out, Outside
Pale, Paper, Pastel, Peace, Pen, Pink, Play, Pleasant, Pleasure, Post, Pretty
Rabbit, Radiance, Ran, Reading, Reflect, Relax, Road
Say, Science, Seeped, Sensation, Shack, Sharp, Shined, Shines, Shining, Shiny, Shirt, Shown, Small, Smooth, Snow, Socket, Sound, Star, Stars, Store, Street, Strong, Sunbeam, Sunlight, Sunny, Sweet, Swift
Table, That, The, The way, Thing, Think, Three X ten ^{10} cm. per sec., Together, Tower, Train, Transparent, Travel, Travels one eight six, Tolley, Truth
Undark
Vegetables, Vision
Warm, Warmth, Watch, Water, Wave length, Way, Weight, Wonderful, World, Worm
Year, Years

LION

A, Adventure, An, Angle, Ant
Bar, Bark, Beard, Beautiful, Bed, Beef, Bend, Bible, Big animal, Big cat, Bird, Bit, Black panther, Blood, Bob, Bob cat, Body, Bold, Book, Books, Braveness, Britain, Brown, Bud, Bug
Carton, Cats, Cattle, Cave, Chain, Chair, Chatter, Cheeta, Chief, Christmas, Claw, Claws, Club, Columbia, Conjure, Courage, Cow, Coward, Creature, Cruel, Cut
Dad, Daniel, Death, Deer, Die, Dirty, Don't, Dungeon
Eag, Eater, Eating, Eats people, Egg, Eight, Elephant, England, Evil
Fearful, Fearless, Feet, Feline, Fierceness, Fight, First, Food, Foot, Forest, Free, Friend, Furious, Fuzz, Fuzzy
George, Girl, Go, Goat, Good, Gorilla, Grass, Great, Greedy, Growling, Growls
Had, Hand, Hard, Harmful, Harold, Hear, Heavy, Help, Hill, Him, Hippopotamus, Horrid, Horse, Hound, House, Huge, Hunger, Hunter, Hunting, Hurt
Ion, Is, It
Jaw, Jaws, Jim Lyons, Joy, Jump, Jungle or zoo
Keeper, Killer, King Leonardo, King of beast, Kitten
Lame, Leader, Learn, Lie, Life bible, Lion, Lion tamer, Load, Loin, Look out, Low
MGM, Mad eater, Majestic, Male, Mammal, Man eater, March, Master, Mate, Me, Meal, Melvin Coshnoski First, Mighty, Mine, Mom, Money, Monster, Movies, Mule
Name, Near, Nest, Noise, Non
Panther, Paw, Paws, Pen, Pencil, People, Person, Pet, Pit, Prayer, Pretty, Prey, Prowl, Purse, Pussy cat
Quadruped, Quiet, Quo Vadis
Rage, Ran, Reading, Richard, Rip, Roaring, Roars, Roy, Rugged
Sad, S Den, See, Shaggy, Share, Shoot, Should, Shout, Show, Simba, Son, Sore, Sphinx, Star, Story, Sweet
Tail, Tale, Teach, Thick, Thing, Toot, Tooth, Toy, Trained, Tree, Two, Tyrant
Violence
We, Weak, Whiskers, Wild animal, Wool, Wooly, World
Yell, Yes, You, Young
Zebra

LIVE

A, Abode, About, Abroad, Again, Age, Air, Aliver, All, Always, And, Animals, Any, Are, Awake, Away
Bacteria, Bad, Bate, Be alive, Bear, Because, Bed, Behind, Being, Biology, Bird, Birth, Blood, Blue, Board, Boat, Body, Book, Border, Born, Boy, Brief, Broadcast, Buy, Bye
Can, Cannibal, Car, Cat, Catch, Cause, Church, Citizen, Civil, Close, Cold, Comfort, Comfortably, Communistic, Correctly, Cost, Cottage, Country, Creature
Dad, Danger, Day, Deadless, Demeurer, Dive, Dogs, Dorm, Down, Drive, Dye, Dying
East, Easy, Entertain, Environment, Eternally, Eve, Ever, Everyday, Evil, Existence
Family, Fan, Fat, Feeling, Few, Find, Fine, Florida, Food, Free, Frog, Functions, Fur
Get, Gift, Girl, Go, God, Grave, Great, Green, Guess
Hair, Happily, Happiness, Hard, Hare, Hate, Have, He,

Health, Heart, Heaven, Hello, Help, Her, Hide, High, Him, Hit, Hive, Homer, Horse, Hospital, Houses, How, Hurry, Hurt

If, Indoor, Indoors, Inhabit, Inside, Intimate, Island, Its

James

Kill, King

Lady, Lap, Laugh, Lay, Lead, Leven, Let live, Lick, Lie, Lifes, Lift, Light, Line, Lined, Liner, Lit, Liver, Lizard, Lobster, Lonely, Lose, Lost, Lot, Loud, Loves, Low

Marriage, Mat, May, Meat, Men, Merry, Migrate, Minneapolis, Miserable, Modern, Money, Moon, Morgue, Motion, Mouse, Move, Moving, Mrs., My

Neighbor, Never, Next, Nicely, Night, No, Nonliving, Not

Of, Off, Oh, OK, Old, Once, Open, Or die, Organic, Own

Party, Peoples, Pets, Plant, Plants, Play, Pool, Poor, Preside

Quietly

Real, Recklessly, Relax, Rent, Rest, Ride, Room

Safety, Salesman, Science, Sea, Seen, Shake, She, Shelter, Show, Sight, Simultaneous, Sit, Site, Sive, Slave, Sleep, Slide, Slowly, Snake, Snakes, Snoring, So, Soap, Soon, Span, Squirm, Stay, Stayed, Stock, Stop, Stream, Strong, Swift

Television, Tell, Tender, The, Thee, Their, They, Thing, Think, Thought, Through, Time, Tonight, Town, Tree

Ugly, Under, Uoi, Up, Us

Vacation

Wagon, Walk, Want, Warm, Water, We, Were, When, Who, Why, Wiggly, Wildly, Window, With, Woman, Wonder, Wonderful, World, Worm

Years, Yes, Yet, Young

LONG

Alley, Alone, Anaconda, Ancient, Arms, Arrow, A year

Beach, Bed, Bedroom, Belt, Bench, Blocks, Body, Bong, Boring, Bow, Bowling alley, Boy, Braids, Branch, Bread, Bridge, Brothers, Building, Bun, Button

Came, Car, Cat, Chair, Chippewa, Church, Cigar, Close, Coat, Cold, Cord, Corn, Couch, Cow, Curly

Dachshound, Dachshund, Dad, Dark, Days, Dean, Deep, Depth, Desk, Dessert, Difficult, Division, Dogs, Dream, Dress, Drive, Driveway, Dry, Dull, Dullness, Durable

Earl, Earth, Elongated, Extended

Fairway, Faraway, Fare, Few, Field, First, Fish, Flat, Flowing, Food, For, Ft.

Gauge, Giraff, Girl, Go, Goat, Going, Good, Graceful, Grass, Gray

Handle, Hard to get, Heavy, Height, Hi, Highway, Highways, Hole, Hope, Horn, Horsetail, Hot, Hot dog, Hot dogs, Hours, House, Huge, Hurry

Immense, Impatience, Inches, Infinity, Inland

Jet, Johns, Journey

Knife

Ladder, Lanky, Lasting, Lean, Leave, Left, Leo, Licorice, Lifetime, Light, Limit, List, Live, Load, Log, Lonely, Lonesome, Long, Long ago, Longer, Longfellow, Longing, Long wave, Long ways, Look, Love

March, Me, Measure, Medium, Men, Minute, Miss, Mississippi, Month, Mud, Music

Nail, Name, Neck, Needle, Never, Nice, Night, No, Not good, Not short

Ocean, One mile

Pale, Pants, Paper, Part, Path, People, Period, Person, Phone, Pier, Pile, Pipe, Pipes, Post, Prairie, Psalm, Pull

Quick

Radio, Rail, Ranger, Rest, Ride, Right, Roads, Roadway, Rod, Round, Run

Sam, Sausage, Saw, Sermon, Shake, Shell, Shells, Shirt, Shoes, Shorter, Short small, Sick, Side, Sidewalk, Siege, Skirt, Sky, Slaw, Sleep, Sleeve, Slick, Smoke, Smooth, So, Soft, Something, Song, Soon, Spoke, Stage, Start, Starve, Steel, Steep, Stocking, Stone, Stop, Strait, Stream, Stream line, Strength, Stretched, Stretched out, Stride, Stringy, Stripe, Strip of road, Strong, Stubby, Stuck, Summer, Sword

Tail, Tale, Tape, Test, Tests, Then, Thick, Thing, Tight, Tiring, Tom, Tomorrow, Ton, Tong, Town, Track, Trail, Trailer, Treacherous, Tread, Trees, Tube, Tunnel

Underwear, Unending

Vacation, Vast, Veil, Very

Wagon, Wake, Wall, Was, Ways, Weiner, Where, While, Whistle, White, Will, Winded, Winding, Winter, Wire, Wiry, Wish, With, Wood, Word, Wrong

Yard, Yards, Yarn, Year, Years, Yes, Young, Yourself

LOUD

A band, Alarm, Almighty, Amplified, Anger, Angry, Awful

Baby, Bad, Band, Banging, Bark, Baseball games, Basketball game, Bible, Big mouth, Bird, Bitter, Black, Blare, Blasting, Blowing, Boat, Bomb, Book, Booming, Booms, Bottom, Bow, Brash, Brenny, Brick, Bright, Bus, Buzzer

Came, Cannon, Car, Care, Castle, Cheering, Cheese, Child, Children, Church, Circus, Cite, Clamor, Clang, Clash, Clothes, Cloud, Clouds, Cod, Cold, Color, Colors, Command, Cook, Cough, Creep, Crying, Cymbals

Dark, Dave, Deafening, Death, Deep, Desk, Detract, Dilapidated, Din, Doctor, Dog, Dogs, Don't, Door, Doorbell, Dormitory, Doug, Down, Dr., Drums

Eardrums, Eat, Effort, Engelbretson, Enough, Explosion, Extreme

Faint, Fast, Ff, Fidelity, Find, Firecracker, Fire engine, Fix, Fog horn, Fore, Friend, Friends, Fun

Game, Games, Get, Girl, Gone, Grandfather, Grief, Guitar, Gun, Gunshot, Guy

Have, Head, Headache, Heard, Hear good, Heart, Heave, Height, Help, Here, Hoarse, Hollering, Horns, Horrible, Hose, Host, Hot, Howl, Hungry, Hurts

Ill bred, Interest, Irritating

Jack, Jean, Jesus, Jet, Jets, Judy

Lad, Land, Large, Laughing, Laughter, Law, Like, Listen, Little, Lo, Load, Lonely, Look, Loquacious, Lord, Lost, Lot, Loud mouth, Loudness, Loud speaker

Mad, Margy, Marlan, Me, Mean, Medium, Mice, Microphone, Milk, Moses, Mother, Mouse, Muffler, My mother

Name, Neat, Niece, Night, Noises, Non-bashful, Not, Not a soft noise, Note, Notes, Not soft, Now

Obnoxious, Oh, On, Oral, Order, Our, Out, Outstanding

Pain, Painful, Party, Paul, Person, Phonograph, Piercing, Pitcher, Play, Pleasure, Pound, Pretty, Public address

Quietly

Radio, Raucous, Record, Record player, Records, Red, Red suit, Ring, Ringing, Roar, Rock and roll, Run

Safe, Saw, Scared, Screaming, Screech, See, Shake, Shatter, Shirt, Show off, Shriek, Shut, Shut up, Shy, Sing, Sister, Sit, Six, Slow, Small, Smash, Smile, Smooth, Sold, Some, Somebody, Song, Sort, So you can hear, Speaker, Squeal, Stand, Stood, Stop, Street, Sweet, Sweeter

Tall, Teachers, Teenager, Telephone, Terrible, The, Them, Thing, Think, Though, Thud, Thunderous, Tie, Tom, Ton, Tone, Tough, Train, Tree, Trouble, Truck, Trumpet, Tuba, TV

Ugly, Unbearable, Uncouth, Unload, Unloud, Unnecessary, Upset

Vibration, Voices, Volume, Vulgar

Wait, Want, Warn, Weight, Whiskey, Whisper, Wild, Win, Wood, Word

Yellow

MAKE

A cake, Accomplish, Achieve, Airplane, Am, An, And, Animal, Apart, Are, Arrange, Arrive, Arrow, Article, Assemble, At

Baby, Back, Bad, Ball, Band, Basket, Become, Beds, Belief, Better, Big, Bigger, Bike, Bird house, Boat, Book, Book case, Box, Boys, Brighter, Bring, Brought, Bug, Building, Built, Bully, Bust, By

Cakes, Can, Candles, Candy, Carry, Cars, Carve, Cat, Chase, Chose, Chug, Circle, Claim, Clay, Clean, Clearly, Close, Cloth, Clown, Coat, Coffee, Cold, Color, Come, Comes, Command, Compile, Complete, Concern, Contact, Control Cooking, Could, Cover, Craft, Craftmanship, Creater, Creation, Creative, Creator, Cry, Cute

Day, Decide, Demand, Den, Describe, Design, Designs, Destroyed, Destruct, Develop, Dike, Dime, Dinner, Direct, Dirt, Discover, Dismake, Doe, Doesn't, Dog, Doll, Dolls, Don't make, Door, Dope, Do something, Dove, Down, Drapes, Drawing, Dream, Drop

Earth, Eat, Empire, Erase, Even, Extra

Faces, Fail, Faire, Fake, Farm, Fasten, Faster, Feathers, Felt, Fight, Finish, Finished, Fit, Fly, For, Force, Ford, Fore, Forts, Found, Friends, From, Fudge

Game, Games, Glow, God, Going, Gone, Guess, Gun, Guns

Had, Hand, Handcraft, Happy, Harm, Hat, Hate, Have, Have to, Hay, Head, Hem, Here, Hers, Herself, History, Hobby, Hold, Home, Hurry, Hurt

Idea, If, In, Instruct, Invent, Invention
Joke
Kill, Kitchen, Knit, Knock, Know, Known
Lake, Laws, Learn, Let, Listen, Little, Lone, Long, Look,
  Loose, Loosen, Lost
Ma, Mack, Mad, Maid, Make, Maked, Make it, Make out,
  Makers, Makeup, Man, Man made, Many, Map, Mark, Market,
  Marks, Material, Mean, Meat, Mend, Merry, Mess, Might,
  Milk, Mind, Miss, Models, Mom, Monkey, Mood, Most,
  Mother, Move, Much, Mud, Must
Nake, Naughty, Near, Neck, Net, Nice, No, None, Not, Nothing,
  Not to, Now
Object, Of, Off, Offer, One, Open, Others, Own
Paint, Pancakes, Paste, Paster, Pencil, People, Persuade,
  Pies, Pizza, Plan, Plane, Plans, Pop, Posters, Potato,
  Presents, Print, Product, Production, Progress, Project,
  Projects, Pull, Puppets, Push, Put together
Quiet
Rack, Rake, Receive, Re-do, Remake, Remodel, Repair, Rich,
  Right, Rocket, Round, Run
Sad, Sake, Same, Sand, Sandwich, Screw, Sculpture, See, Seen,
  Shelf, Shift, Shoe, Shoes, Shop, Show, Sick, Sign, Since,
  Sing, Sit, Skill, Skirt, Smash, Snake, Snow man, So, Soap,
  Soft, Sold, Soon, Sound, Soup, South, Stand, Steel, Stitch,
  Stop, Story, Studies, Stuff, Subject
Table, Tack, Takes, Talent, Talk, Tam, Tape, Tear, Tell,
  Test, Then, There, These, Think, Those, Three, Time,
  Tissue, Together, Too, Took, Tool, Tools, Tore, Tots,
  Touch down, Toys, Try, Two, Two quarts
Undo, Unseen
Valentines, Verb
Wagon, Want, Water, Way, Weave, Went, When, Where, Why,
  Will, Women, Woolen, Word, Words, Working, Wow, Write,
  Writing
Yes, Yourself

MAN

A big, Adam, Adult, Age, Aim, Ambulance, An, Angry,
  Animal, Ann, Ape, A person, Arm
Baby, Bad, Bald head, Band, Beard, Beatnik, Bed, Benilde,
  Bill, Blond, Bob, Boss, Business, Butter
Can, Cap, Children, Chuck, Count, Cow, Croate, Curt
Date, Dave, Day, Delorman, Dennis, Denny, Dense, Do, Doctor,
  Dog woman, Dominant, Don, Done, Doug, Dress
Earth, Eating, Elder, Eye, Eyes
Fast, Fat, Feet, Fellow, Fight, Figure, Flesh, Foot, Fraternity,
  Friend, From
Garland, Gentlemen, Girls, Glad, Glasses, Goes, Good looking,
  Grown, Grown up, Grow up, Guy
Hand, Handy, Hard, He, Healthy, Hear, Heart, Heavy, Him,
  History, Hold, Hole, Homo, House, Huge, Human being,
  Humans, Husky
Intelligent, It
Jack, Jacket, Jim, Job, John
Knowledge
Lad, Land, Large, Lay, Lazy, Leg, Legs, Life, Like, Lindskog,
  Little, Living, Living things
Mad, Mammal, Manage, Mankind, Marriage, Marv Haris, Mean,
  Mighty, Mill, Mister, Model, Money, Mr. Pombeck, Muscle,
  Muscular, Music, Mustache, My dad, Myself
Negro, No, Not woman
Office, Old boy
Paints, Pan, Pans, Parent, Pipe, Play boy, Power, Pretty
Red, Ribs, Rich, Ron, Russ
Sand, Sandy, School, See, Shirt, Shoe, Short, Short hair, Side-
  walk, Size, Skin, Sky, Slacks, Sleep, Small, Smart, Smoking,
  Someone, Stand, Street, Suit
Tall and dark, Tall fat skin, Tar, Terry, The, They, Thin,
  Thing, This, Tie
Ugly, Unfaithful
Walking, Wash, Wayne, Wear, When, Where, White, Who, Will,
  Wolf, Workers, World, Wow, Wrap
Yeti, You, Your

ME

Adele, Adulthood, Afraid, Alan, Alone, Also, Always, An, And
  Mary, Andre, And sign, And you, A person, As, Ate
Bad, Ballerina, Be, Beautiful, Bee, Believe, Big, Bill, Blue,
  Bob, Bonnie, Boys, Brenda, Brother, Bruce, By
Car, Carolyn, Chair, Child, Cloth, Clothes, Coat, Come, Conceit,

Connie, Cow
Daddy, Darlene, Darling, Date, Dave, Desk, Do, Dog, Don't,
  Dress
Eat, Emy, Everyone
Fa, Face, Faith, Family, Farther, Fast, Feeling, Friend,
  From, Fun, Funny, Furry
Genius, Glad, Glasses, Go, Good, Got, Gregg, Grow, Guys
Ha, Had, Hair, Hand, Happy, Hat, Have, Heidi, Hello, Henry,
  Here, His, Horse, Hour, House
Idea, If, I'm, In, Inner, Interested, Into
Jane, Jay, Jeff, Jerry, Jim, Judy
Karen, Kathy, Kay, Ken, Kick, Kiss, Knee, Knew, Known
Lady, Laura, Let, Like, Linda, Little, Long, Look, Lot, Love
Ma, Male, Man, Marcia, Marge, Marilyn, Martha, Mary, Mat,
  Meat, Meet, Mew, Mice, Mike, Milk, Mirror, Mittens, Moe,
  Money, Moo, Mountain, Mouse, Moving, My own
Names, Nancy, Neat, Never, Nice, Nick, Not, Nurse, Nut
Of, OK, Old, On, Opinion, Others, Over, Owl
Paul, Perfection, Pessimist, Pete, Play boy, Plus, Pride,
  Pronoun
Question, Quietly
Rebecca, Red, Rocket, Run
Sad, Sandy, Say, Second, Shadow, Sheryl, Shirt, Short, Show,
  Sick, Sister, Slow, Small, Snot, So, Some, Somebody,
  Strong, Student, Success, Surprise, Susan
Talk, Tall, Tea, Terrible, That, Then, Those, Tired, Tom,
  Tony, Tree, Troubles, Two
Use
Was, Were, What, Where, Why, Will, With, Woman, Women,
  Work, Wow, Writing
Ye, Yes, Young, Your, Yours

MEMORY

Abe Lincoln, A big sheep, Ability, Able, About, Absent, Absent
  minded, Absent mindedness, Accordian, Action, Ago, Aid,
  Amaze, And, Anecdote, Angel, Anger, Animals, Answer,
  Any, Anything, Asked, Asset, Assignment, Aunt, Awareness,
  Away, Awful, Awoke
Baby, Bank, Baseball, Bath, Beautiful, Bed, Before, Belief,
  Bible, Bible verse, Bible verses, Biding, Birthday, Black,
  Boats, Bob, Body, Boy friend, Boy friends, Boys, Brains,
  Brand, Bright, Brother, Bruce, Bud, Building
Calif, Came, Camp, Can't, Can't remember, Cat, Cave, Cell,
  Cents, Chair, Cherish, Children, Class, Clear, Clear mind,
  Close, Cloudy, Coin, Come, Computer, Concentration,
  Confirmation, Conscience, Conscious, Consist, Couch,
  Coward, Cry, Crying, Custom
Dance, Dancing, Dave, Day dream, Days, Death, Deceased,
  Deep, Desk, Details, Dick, Did, Die, Different, Difficult,
  Doctor, Dome, Dreamy, Drum, Duck, Duh, Dull
Easy, Eat, Elephant, Eng. report, Equations, Everything,
  Exams, Exciting, Experience, Experiences
Fable, Fail, Failure, False, Faraway, Farm, Feed back, Fight-
  ing, Find, Finding, Fine, Finger, First grade, Fish, Flag,
  Fly, Foggy, Fondness, Food, Football, Forever, Forfeit,
  Forgetable, Forgetting, Forgiveness, Fred, Friend, Friends,
  Friendship, Funeral, Funny, Future
Gary, Genius, German, Gettysburg address, Glass, Glove, Go,
  Gone, Good sense, Good things, Good time, Good times,
  Grade school, Grandfather, Grandma, Grand parents, Graves,
  Great, Greek, Green, Groceries, Guess, Guide, Guilt
Habit, Had, Hands, Happen, Happenings, Hate, Have, Health,
  Help, Helping, Homework, Honest, Honesty, Honor, Horrible,
  Horse, Hospital, House, How, Hypnosis
I, Ideas, I don't know, Ill, Illusion, Image, Imagination, Improve,
  Incidents, Infinite, Information, Intellect, Intelligent, Intense,
  IQ, It
Jack, Jello, Joan, Job, Jogs, Joy, Judgment
Keen, Keep, Key, Kind, Knew, Know by heart, Know it by heart,
  Know something
Lack, Lack of, Lake, Land, Language, Last, Laugh, Laughs,
  Length, Lessons, Letter, Lies, Light, Lincoln, Line,
  List, Listen, Little, Longing, Look, Lose, Lousy, Loved,
  Lovely, Loving, Luck, Lunch
Man, Mark, Math, Meat, Member, Memo, Memoirs, Memorial,
  Memorization, Memory, Mental, Mercury, Merry, Metamor-
  phic, Mid, Minor, Mom, Moments, Monday, Month, More,
  Moses, Moth, Mt. Rushmore, Mud, My, My elders, Myself
Name, Needed, Neuron, Night, No, No good, No memory, Not,
  Notes, Not good, Nothing, Not nice, Not so good, Not too good,

Nows, Numbers, Nuts

Objectionable, Occasions, Of Christmas, Of kitten, Of past, OK, Okay, Old days, Old times, Optimism, Or

Pad, Park, Parties, Party, Pass, Passed, Pastime, Past time, Peace, Phantom, Phone, Photographic, Picture, Pictures, Piece, Pillow, Placement, Planet, Play, Pleasantness, Pleasant times, Pleasing, Pleasure, Pod, Poetry, Pray, Prison, Prom, Promise, Psalms, Psychology, Put

Quiz

Rain, Rake, Read, Recite, Reciting, Recollection, Record, Red, Reflect, Reflection, Regrets, Relax, Remain, Remembered, Remembers stories, Remembrance, Remembrances, Reminder, Reminds, Reminisce, Reminiscence, Report, Resemble, Response, Retain, Review, Right, River, Room, Rote

Sacred, Sadden, Sandy, Saying, Scholastic ability, Schooling, Scrapbook, Scriptures, See, Seeing, Sense, Senses, Sentiment, Serves, Seventh grade, Shade, Sharp, She, Sheep, Shiny, Shirt, Shock, Sing, Sinner, Sister, Slow, Small, Smartness, Soldier, Soldiers, Somebody, Something, Something good, Sometimes, Soot, Sorry, Soul, Sound, Souvenirs, Span, Speech, Speed, Spelling, Spend, Spice, Star, Start, Statue, Stay, Steve, Stirring, Stone, Stop, Storage, String, Stupid, Subconscious, Suggest, Sum, Summer, Swift, Synopsis, System

Table, Tale, Talked, Teacher, Tear, Tell, Ten, That, The, Things I remember, Things of the past, Think back, Thinking back, Think of, Thinks, Though, Through, Tide, Times, Tombstone, Track, Train, Treasure, Tree, Trip, Trips, Trouble, True, Truth, TV, Two

Ugly, Uncle, Unconscious, Understanding, Unhappy

Vacation, Vague, Vagueness, Verses, Very

War, Warm, Was, We, Weak, Weak memory, Weekend, What, When you remember something, Why, Wise, Women, Write, Wrote

X-mas

Year, Years, Yes, Yesterday, You, Young, Youth, Yukon

Zoo, Zoology

MOON

Above, And six pence, A place, Asteroid, Astronaut, Astronomer, Atmosphere, Autumn, Away

Baby, Balloon, Base, Beams, Beauty, Beyond, Big and shiny, Body, Book, Boy friend, Boy girl, Boys, Brightness, Bun

Canoe, Circle, Circular, Clear, Clear night, Convertible, Cool, Coon, Craig, Cream colored, Creator, Creature, Crest, Croon, Cross, Curves

Darkness, Date, Dave, Day, Dead, Diane's god, Dim, Disc, Discs, Disk, Distance, Distant, Dog, Dream, Drip, Dust

Eclipse, Enjoyment, Ether, Evening

Fair, Far away, Far up, Fast, Fly, Full moon, Full pretty

Gas, Gentle, Girl and boy, Globe, Gloom, Glows, Go, Goal, God, Gold, Green cheese

Happy, Hard, Harvest, He, Heavenly, Heavens, Heavy, Height, Her, Him, Hit, Hole, Holes, Horizon, Huge

Joke, June

Kiss

Lady, Land, Large, Life, Live, Look, Lovable, Lovely, Lovers, Luna, Lunic

Many, Mar, Martian, Mast, Me, Memories, Mercury, M glow, Miami, Might, Miles, Miles away, Missiles, Missle, Missles, Mon, Money, Monster, Months, Moo, Mood, Moon, Moonlight, Moon man, Moon shine, Mountain, Mouse, Mow, Mullins, Mystery

NatSci, Natural science, Near, Neat, Neck, New, Nigh, Nite, Nutty

Object, Ocean, Of, One, Orange, Orbit, Out, Over

Pace, Paint, People, Phil, Pin, Place, Planetoid, Planets, Plants

Quarters

Race, Reading, Red, Relaxing, Ride, Right, Rise, Rocked, Rocketship, Rockets ships, Rocks, Room, Rotation, Run, Russia, Russian, Russians

Sad, Scientist, See, Seen, Set, Sew, Sex, Shape, She, Sheep, Shiner, Shining, Ship, Shoot, Shy, Silver and gold, Sisters, Six pence, Ski, Sleep, Sliver, Small, Soft, Solar, Solar system, Song, Spacemen, Spaceship, Spaceships, Space travel, Sphere, Spots, Sputnik, Stair, Stairs, Stare, Starry, Stars love, Stay, Story, Struck, Sue, Sum, Sun down

Televisions, Thing, Tom, Tonight, Took, Trip, Twilight, Two forty thousand

Vastness, Venus, View,

Walk, Walking with friend, Watcher, Water, Way out, Were-wolf, While, Women, World

Yard, You

MOUNTAIN

A big hill, Air, A large hill, Allegheny, Alp, Alpine, Andes, Animals, Ant hill, Appalachians, Arizona, Atlas mts.

Bake, Baker, Bear, Bed, Berg, Big tall stupendous, Bird, Board, Books, Boy, Breast, Brook, Bump, Bumpy,

Cabin, California, Camping, Canyon, Cap, Caps, Car, Cavern, Caves, Chain, Challenge, City, Cliffs, Climate, Climbed, Climbers, Cloud, Coat, Cooled, Cost, Country, Crag, Creek, Crevice

Dad, Deer, Dew, Dime, Ditch, Down, Drought

Earth, Echo, Elevation, Enormous, Evergreen,

Falling, Falls, Far, Feet, First, Fishing, Flat, Food, Forests, Fun

Garmish, Geography, Girl, Glacier Nat'l Park, Glaciers, Glen, Go, Goats, Gorge, Grey, Grown

Hall, Hard, Health, Heidi, Heights, Hell, Help, High big thing, High cliff, High hill, Hike, Hill tops, Home, Hope, Huge hill, Hunt

I, Ice cream, In, Iron, Iron head, It

Jasper, Jungle

Kathy

Lair, Lamp, Large hill, Lie, Little, Lot, Loud,

Magnificent, Main, Majestic, Many rocks, Massive, Me, Men, Mexico, Minneapolis, Mohammed, Mole, Montana, Moor, Moss, Mountain, Mountain climber, Mountainless, Mountains, Mountain side, Mouse, Mt. Blanc, Mt. Everest, Mt. Hood, Mt. Ranier, Mt. Rushmore, Mt. Vesuvius, Music

Nash's, Nature, Noise, Norway

Ocean, Old, Olympus, Outdoors, Outside

Park, Pass, Path, Peat, Peek, Penn, Pictures, Pine tree, Pioneer, Pit, Place, Point, Pole, Pop, Pretty, Puzzle, Pyrenees

Rack, Rain, Ranges, Ranier, Ravine, Really, Record, Ridge, Rivers, Rockies, Rockies Alps Sierra, Rocky hill, Rocky mountains, Rocky mt., Rocky Mts., Rod Egen, Round, Rugged,

Scene, Scenery, Scenic, Sermon, Shadow, Sheep, Show, Side, Sides, Sierra, Sierras, Sing, Ski, Skiis, Sleep, Slide, Slopes, Small, Smoke, Smokies, Snow cap, Snow covered, Snowy, Soil, Something high, Song, Sooth, Steam, Stomach ache, Stone, Streams, Summer, Summit, Sunset, Swiss, Switzerland,

Table, Take, Tennessee, Tent, Terrain, Teton, There, Too, Topography, Tower, Trail, Travel, Traveler's Palm, Trip, Tub, Tunnel

Up, Up and down

Vacation, Valleys, Vast, Vermont, Vernon, Very, Very large, Volcano

Was, Where, White

Yellow Stone Nat. P.

MUSIC

Air, Album, Alto, Alto horn, Any kind, Appreciation

Back, Bad, Ballet, Bar, Bark, Baroque, Bass, Bassoon, Bat, Baton, Beats, Beautiful thing, Beauty, Bell, Big, Bird, Blue, Blue moon, Bobby Dale, Bond, Books, Bop, Boy, Boys, Bright, Brightness, Brubeck, Bugle

C, Can, Candle, Cat, Cello, Center, Chairs, Chills, Choirs, Chopin, Chorale, Chords, Christmas, Class, Classical, Clef, Clouds, Coat, Cold, Combo, Come, Coming, Composers, Concert, Cornet, Culture, Cye

Death, Director, Do, Dog, Drama, Dumb

Eat, Elvis Presley, Emotion, Enjoy, Enjoyable, Enjoyment, Entertainment, Exodus

Fair, Fast, Feeling, Feeting, Flowers, Flutiphone, For, Free, French horn, Fussy

Girl, Girls' chorus, Glad, Great, Gross, Ground

Hall, Hand, Hard, Harp, Hat, Head, Here, Hill billy, Home, Horns, Horrible, Horror, Hour, House, Hum, Hymn

Invisible

Jail, Junk

KDWB, Key, Keys, Kingston

Lake, Land, Landeen, Laughter, Learn, Liberace, Light, Lights, Lines, List, Listening, Liturgy, Lively, Look, Loudness, Lover, Lyrics

Maestro, Make, Maker, Marches, Mary, Math, Maybe, Me, Mellow, Melodies, Mendenhall, Merry, Money, Mood, Mouse,

Mouth, Movement, Mr. Hutchins, Mr. Kohm, Mrs. Andeen, Mrs. Gross, Mrs. Larson, Mrs. Smith, Mule, Musical, Must, My

New, No, Noises, Noise slowly fast, Noisy, Nose, Nosy, Not, Number, Nuts

Old time, Open air, Opera

Penny, Performance, Person, Phonograph, Piece, Pitch, Player, Playing the piano, Pleasant, Pleasing, Pleasure, Poetry, Poor, Pop, Popular, Pottery, Practice, Practicing, Presley

Quartet

Randr, Read, Red, Rehearsed, Relaxation, Relaxing, Rhapsody in Blue, Ring, Ringing, Rock, Rock in Roll, Rough, Run

Sandeen, Sax, Say, Seat, Sharp, Sheet music, Sick, Sign, Signing, Silence, Singers, Sister, Slice, Slow, Slumber, Sol, Solo, Son, Soothing, Soprano, Soundless, Sour, Speech, Squeak, Stars, Stereo, Stop, Store, Sung, Sweet loud, Sweet music, Sweetness, Swings, Symbols music

Table, Tchaikowsky, Terrible, Test, The, Theater, There, Thing, Time, Tuba, Tunes

Ugh, Us

Verdi, Verse, Vibrations, Vocal, Voices, Vote

We, Wheel, White, Wonderful, Words, Work

MUTTON

Able, Age, A glove, Air, And, Anger, Anything, Appetizing, Approach, Ash, At, Ate, Awful

Baby, Back, Bad, Bag, Ball, Bat, Bed, Bell, Belly, Bill, Bird, Blanket, Blouse, Blubber, Board, Boat, Bottom, Bowl, Bread hoof, Breakfast, Broom, Bum, Burt, Butcher

Cake of meat, Can, Cap, Car, Carcass, Card, Care, Carol, Carrot, Cattle, Cement, Chair, Chap, Cheese, Chill, Clean, Clear, Cliff, Close, Clothe, Clothes, Clothing, Clove, Coal, Cobbler, Collar, Color, Come, Comfortable, Cook, Cool, Corn, Could, Crazy, Creep, Cry, Cupcake, Cute, Cutting

Dead, Dear, Deep, Delicacy, Did, Different, Different word from button, Dig, Dish, Don, Done, Don't, Don't know, Don't known, Don't know word, Door, Drink, Duck, Dull, Dumb

Eskimo, Eyes

Face, Far, Farm, Fast, Father, Feather, Feeling, Feet, Fleece, Flock, Flower, Fluff, Fluffy, For, Forever, Fork, Fort, Forward, Friends, From, Fruit, Full, Funny

Gave, George Washington, Glue, Go, Grass, Gravy, Gray, Grease, Greasy, Green, Guess, Gun

Happy, Have, Hay, Hear, Heat, Heavy, Height, Hello, Help, Hen, Her, Herd, Here, Hibernate, High, Hill, Hog, Hold, Hole, Home, Horrible, Horrid, Horse, Hunting, Hurt, Hut, Hutton

Ick, Icky, I don't know, I don't know what it is, Indians, It

Jacket, Jump

Kill, Know

Lambchops, Lamb leg, Land, Lard, Latin, Left, Leg of lamb, Lie, Liver, Locker, Look, Loud

Mad, Made, Maggots, Man, Math, Me, Mellow, Mice, Milk, Minute, Mit, Mittens, Moist, Mold, Monster, Mother, Mount, Mountain, Mouse, Mule, Mumble, Mummy, Mushy, Music, Muslin, Must, Mute, Mutter, Mutton

Nap, Neat, New, Night, No, Not good, Number, Nut

Oat, Off, Oh, Old, One, Open, Operate, Operetta

Pair, Pancakes, Pasture, Pencil, People, Person, Pillow, Pin, Pink, Place, Plant, Plenty, Poor, Pop, Pork chop, Porridge, Pretty, Puff, Putting, Putton

Queer, Quiet

Rabbit, Race, Ram, Red, Rifle, River, Roast, Role, Rows, Rush

Sad, Scared, School, Serial, Sheep meat, Sheep wool, Sheet, Shirt, Shoe, Shore, Sick, Sickness, Silk, Silly, Sister, Skin, Slant, Sleep, Slimy, Sloppiness, Small, Smell, Smooth, Snow ball, Soap, Softly, Something to eat, Still, Stool, Stop, Story, Strange, Street, Stumble, Stupid, Sup, Supper, Sutton, Sweater

Tail, Talking, Tea, Teeth, Ten, Tender, Terrible, The, Thing, Thread, To, To do with, Top, Tough, Truck, Turkey

Ugh, Understand, Use

Warmth, Warn, Was, Water, Wet, Whale, What, When, Where, Whistle, Window, Winter, Wire, Wolf, Wolves, Wonder, Wonderful, Word, Work, Worn

Yes, You

Zipper

MY

After, Ah, Aim, Air, All, Alone, Am, An, Antonia, Arm, Ass, Astonished, At

Back, Band, Bat, Be, Bear, Because, Bed, Bell, Belonging, Belongings, Belongs, Bicycle, Big, Bike, Bird, Blood, Blouse, Boat, Boots, Bother, Bottle, Boyfriend, But, Buy

Cake, Can, Can't, Cap, Cats, Cause, Chair, Chi, Child, Choice, Chuck, Clothes, Comb, Complex, Cousin, Cry

Darling, Date, Deer, Desk, Dike, Do, Dolls

Ear, Eat, Eight, Elf, Especially, Exclaim, Exclamation, Exclamation mark, Expression, Eye, Eyes

Fair, Family, Farther, Female, Fence, Filling, Finger, Fingers, First, Fist, Fly, Folks, Food, For, Fry

Game, Garage, George, Get, Girl friend, Glove, Go, Goat, Goes, Got, Grow, Grown

Ha, Hands, Happiness, Happy, Hard, Has, Health, Heavens, Here, Hill, Hit, Ho, Hoist, Hope, Horse, How, How come, Hurt, Hy

I am, I'd, If, I'm, In, Isn't, Its

Jack, Jane, Job, Judy, Jump, Just

Knife

Lamb, Lamp, Lands, Lap, Laugh, Lay, Leg, Letter, Lie, Lip, Lord, Luck

Maid, Make, Mammy, Marcia, Mary, Master, Mean, Men, Might, Mind, Mink, Miss, Mistake. Mitten, Mommy, Moo, More, Mouse, Mumps, Music, My own, Mys, Myth

Neck, Noise, Nose, Now

Off, Oh my, Old lady, O Mrs., Only, Over, Ownership, Owns

Pam, Pants, Paper, Parakeet, Parental, Per, Pet, Picture, Plan, Play, Position, Positive, Possess, Precious, Present, Pretty, Problems, Pronoun, Property, Purse

Radio, Really, Reason, Red, Ribbon, Ride, Room, Rope, Ross

Sam, Say, Score, See, Sell, Sentence, Shadow, Shoe, Shower, Side, Sigh, Sign, Sisters, Sit, Sitter, Sky, Sleeve, Slippers, So, Some, Something, Soul, Soup, Spine, Stand, Stars, Stick, Suit, Summer, Super, Supper

Tail, Take, Talk, Talking, Teacher, Tears, Teeth, Telephone, Tell, Temperature, Thanks, Thats, Them, Then, There, Theres, Thigh, Thought, Thought so, Thy, Tie, Time, Tin, Title, Tool, Train, Tree, Try, Tummy, Turn, Twin, Two

Uncle, Us, USA

Valentine

Wall, Want, Was, Weight, When, Where, Who, Whose, Window, Wise, Wish, With, Women, Wonderful, Work, World, Wow, Wrist

Yes, Yet, You're, Yup

NEEDLE

Anger, Art, At, A thing to sew with

Bad, Bee hole, Big, Book, Bowl, Breathe, Brick, Bug, Button

Camel, Candle, Chair, Clock, Clothes, Cloths, Cold, Come, Cushion, Cut

Dan, Darning, Dart, Doctor, Doctors, Dog, Dress, Drip

Eat, Even, Eye needle

Feedle, Find, Finger, Five, Fly, Food, Foot, Fork, For sewing, Girl, Gold, Good, Grandma, Green

Had, Hair, Handy, Hard, Harp, Hat, Hat pin, Having, He, Head, Heard, Hen, Hold, Home, Honk, Hurts

In, Irritate

Jab, Jump

Knees, Knife, Knit, Knitting, Knob

Leaf, Lend, Level, Little, Long and skinny, Look, Lucky

Mable, Machine, Make, Material, Meddle, Metal, Mom, Mouse, Mrs. Happe

Neat, Needed, News, No, Noose, Nosed,

Object, Oh, Ow,

Phonograph, Pie, Pill, Pillows, Pin cushion, Pine, Pink, Pit, Pitch fork, Plastic, Poppy, Pricked, Prickly, Pricks, Puncture, Push

Record player, Red, Report, Ribs, Rough, Round, Rubber,

Sand, Saw, Scared, Scratch, Seed, Sell, Sewing needle, Sewn, Shape, Shark, Sharpy, Shiny, Shirt, Shots, Sick, Silver, Simple, Singer, Skip, Slacks, Sleet, Sleeve, Slick, Sliver, So, Sore, Sparkling, Spindle, Stack, Star, Sticks, Stings, Stitch, Stock, Stop, Straight, Straw, Swear, Swearing

Talk, There, Thing, Third, Thorn, Threaded, Throw, Thumb, Tine, Tiny, Toe, To sew, Tread, Tried,

Up, Use

Wandering, Weapon, Weed, Working

Yarns

NOW

About, Again, Ago, Ah, Already, Am, And then, April, As,

As ever, At, At once, At present, At the time, At this moment, At this time

Bad, Bath, Batter, Be, Because, Bee, Better, Between, Bird, Black, Blue, Bow, But

Came, Candy, Car, Class, Clock, Command, Con, Copper, Could

Dad, Dark, Day, Days, Demand, Desk, Dogs, Doing, Do it, Domineering, Done, Dow

Eat, English, Et cetera, Exact, Exactly

Fame, Far, Fast, Find, First, Flower, From, Fun, Further, Future

Get, Gone, Good, Grass, Gun

Had, Ham, Happening, Hat, Have, Her, Him, His, Hole, Home, Hour

Intelligent, Into, Its

Jan

Knew, Known

Late, Leave, Like, Listen, Lit, Longer, Loud, Love, Low, Lunch room

Mad, Main tenant, Man, Mat, Maybe, Men, Meow, Mew, Momentarily, Money, Mow, Mrs., Much

Navy, Neither, Newer, Nice, Noon, Nothing, No where, Now there

Off, Oh, OK, Okay, Old, Once, One, Only, Order, Or never, Our, Over, Owl, Own

Paper, Pass, Past, Pencil, People, Place, Play, Please, Pow, Power, Pronto

Question, Quickly

Race, Ready, Right now, Right there, Right this moment, Run, Rush

Safe, Said, Saw, School, Seconds, See here, Sell, She, Show, Sigh, Sight, Slow, Snow, So, Something, Sometime, Song, Sow, Spelling, Stamp, Statement, Street, Stupid, Sure, Susan

Table, Take, Talk, Telling, Ten thirty, Ten twenty six, Test, Them, Thin, This moment, This second, This time, To, Tomorrow, Top, Town, Trouble, Two o'clock

Unhappy, Until, Up

Very

Wait, Walk, War, Ware, Was, Water, Way, Well, What now, While, Whom, Won, Wood, Work, Would, Write, Writing

Year, Yet, Your

NUMBERS

A, AB, Added, Adding, Address, After, Again, Aim, Alot, Alphabets, Am, An, A nine, Answer, Answers, Arith, Around, Arrow, At, Attic, Away

Bad, Bar, Bars, Before, Big, Birds, Block, Bookie, Boredom, Boring, Box, Boy, Bumbers, Busy ants, Buttons, By

Calculate, Calendar, Came, Car, Cars, Cartoon, Category, Chair, Change, Checkers, Chemistry, Children, Choose, Classes, Clock, Clothes, Code, Cold, Color, Colors, Complicated, Confuse, Confusion, Counted, Counter, Counts, Court, Crazy, Crowd, Cuantos, Cucumbers

Date, Dates, Decimal, Desk, Deuteronomy, Dial, Dice, Difficult, Digit, Ditto, Divide, Do, Doll, Dollars, Dots, Dueteronomy

Easy, Eat, Eggs, Eighteen, Eight nine ten eleven twelve, Eighty eight, Eleven to twenty two, Enumerate, Etc., Even, Exactness, Exponents

Face, Fact, Fat, Few, Fifteen nineteen, Fifty, File, Find, Fine, Finger, Finish, First, Five ten fifteen twenty, Food, Football, Fore, Forty, Four and five, Four five six, Four four, Fourteen, Fourty six, Fraction, From, Fumble, Fun, Funny

Gamble, Genesis, German, Girls, Gold, Grade, Group, Guns

Hat, Have, He, Her, Hi, High, Him, Hour, House, How many, Hurry

I, If, In, India, Infinity, Is, Ish, It

Jail, Jet, Join

Kids, Kind, Know

Larger, Let, Letters one two three, License, Light, Lights, Line, Lines, Listen, Logarithms, Look, Lots, Lucky, Lumber, Lumbers

Made, Mark, Mass, May, Me, Mean, Measure, Measurements, Members, Men, Millions, Mine, Minute, Minutes, More, Mother, Multiplication, Multiply, Must, My

Naughty, Neat, Nest, Nice, Nine etc., Nines, Nineteen, Non, Not, Nothing, Number facts, Number thirty four, Numbness, Numerator, Numerators, Numerical, Numericals, Numero, Nun, Nut, Nuts

Odds, On, Once, One and two, One hundred, One ten, One thousand, One to nine, One to one hundred, One to ten,

One to zero, One two etc., One two three etc., One two three four five six, Only, Ordinals, Over

Pages, Paper, Past, Pencils, Person, Phone, Pictures, Pig, Pin, Play, Population, Price, Problem,

Quantity, Question, Quick

Rang, Rational, Read, Real, Red, Relate, Right, Ring, Rocket, Rockets, Room, Round

Saw, Say, School, Score, Second, See, Seem, Sequence, Series, Seven nine, Sevens, Seventeen, Several, Shoe, Shoes, Six seven eight nine ten, Sixteen, Sixty one, Sizes, Slow, Slumbers, Small, Smell, So, Song, Spanish, Spatial, Spell, Spelling, Square, Squares, Stamp shop, Stock, Straight, Subject, Subtract, Subtraction, Sums, Symbols

TA five nine one seven, Teacher, Teens, Television, Ten eleven twelve, Tens, Tension, Test, That, Then, They, Thing, Things, Three and four, Three six nine, Thumb, Times, To, Total, Tree, Trig, Tuck, Twenty, Twenty five, Twenty one, Twenty two, Two and three, Two four five six nine, Two four six, Twos, Two six three two, Two three

Ugh, Units, Unto, Up, Us

Visit, Vowels

Want, Well, Were, What, Wheels, When, Where, Whole, Will, With, Wow, Writing, Written, Wrong

Yellow, Yesterday

Zero one two three, Zeros

OCEAN

A big lake, And, Angry, Away

Beach, Beautiful, Beauty, Bed, Been, Belgium, Big huge, Black, Blew, Blue and big, Blue sea, Blue water, Boating, Body of water, Bottom, Boy, Breeze, Breezes, Brief, Broad

Cable, Calf, Can, Chart, Christopher Columbus, Coast, Cold, Continents, Country, Covers three four of world, Crashing, Creature, Cross, Current

Dark roaring, Death, Deeps, Depth, Die, Distance, Distant, Dive, Dock, Down, Drink

England, Europe, Exciting, Expanse

Far, Far away, Fast, Fishing, Float, Florida, Flow, Foam, Food, Frank Sinatra, Free, Front, Fun

Gigantic, Girl, Go, Gray, Great, Gulf

Hawaii, Head, His, Home, Horizon

Ice, In, Island, It

Jelly fish, June

Keep

Lack, Layer, Level, Light house, Line, Long, Lotion, Lots of water, Love, Lovely

Magnificent, Main, Masterful, Memory, Mexico, Mighty

Navy, New York, Nice, Noisy, North Atlantic

Ocean, Oceana, Oceanid, Oceanos, Oceans, Oceans Eleven, Ocean spray, Ographer

Paradise, Pea, Peace, Pearl, Pound, Power, Pretty,

Rabbi, Rain, Red, Reefs, Reptiles, River sea, Roar, Rocks, Roll, Rolling, Run

Sail, Sailing, Salted, Salty water, Seas, Seasick, Shell, Shells, Shore, Sick, Side, Sinatra, Slow, Space, Spray, Steamer, Story, Stream, Submarine, Sun, Surf, Surging, Swift

Tide, Torrent, Transportation, Travel, Trip

Undercurrent

Vacation, Vast deep etc., Voids, Voyage,

Washington, Water area, Water blue, Waters, Water salt, Weather, Whale, White, Wild, Windy, Wit, Woman, Wonderful

OF

Above, Across, Again, Allegiance, Alot, Also, America, Another, Anything, Apple, Apples, Are, Around, Article, As, Ask, Away

Back, Balance, Barn, Be, Become, Becomes, Bed, Beginning, Behind, Being, Belongs, Bird, Black, Blank, Bondage, Bone, Born, Box, Boy, Bread, Bridge, Bud, But, Butter, Button, Buy

Cake, Can, Candy, Care, Cast, Cause, Center, City, Clock, Clothes, Club, Coarse, Coat, Coke, Come, Come from, Composition, Contain, Country, Cow, Cows, Crazy, Cry, Cut

David, Day, Dear, Describing, Different, Dim, Divide, Do, Dog, Door, Doors, Dose, Down

Edge, End, English

Fall, Family, Far, Fast, Find, Fire, First, Fish, Flag, Float, Floor, Flower, Foe, Fold, Food, Football, Fork, Found, Friend, Friends, Full, Fun

Gang, Gas, Girdle, Glass, Glove, Goes, Going, Gold, Gone, Got from, Grammar, Grass, Ground

Half, Hard, Has, Hat, Hatchet, Help, Here, Hers, High, Hold,
   Home, Horse, Hot, Human, Hurt
I, Ice Ideas, Importance, IQ, Isn't, Its
Jean, Jello, Jones, Jump
Knight, Knob, Know
Lands, Last, Late, Lay, Learn, Left, Lets, Liberty, Life,
   Lights, Like, Little, Live, Long, Look, Loose, Lost, Lot,
   Lots, Luck, Lumber
Made, Man, Mane, Maria, Material, Maybe, Mind, Minnesota,
   Missing, Money, More, Mr., Multiply
Nations, Nature, Near, Never, New, Nice, No, Nobody, None,
   Norway, Nose, Not of, Number
Of course, Offer, Office, Of them, Other, Our, Own, Owner
Paper, Part of, Peel, Peep, Pencil, Permission, Pick, Picture,
   Piece, Plain word, Plenty, Possession, Prep, Pronoun, Puff,
   Purse, Push
Race, Ream, Reason, Reasons, Red, Related, Relation, Replace,
   Ride, Ring, Rise, Rocker, Row, Run
Salt, Same, School, Sell, She, Shore, Short, Shot, Shout, Show,
   Side, Sidewalk, Slow, Small, Somebodies, Somebodys, Someone,
   Sort, Start, Stay, Stop, Story, Stove, Street, Such, Sure,
   Switch
Table, Take, Talk, Teacher, Tee, Tell, Than, The book, Thee
   I sing, Theirs, Therefore, These, They're, Thin, Thinking,
   Though, Time, Times, Times sign, Tired, Title, Today,
   Tomorrow, Too, Tough, Town, Toy, Train, Tree, Try, Turn,
   Twice, Two
Unto, Up, Upon, Use
Value, Very
Want, Was, Water, Way, We, Who, Why, Will, Win
Yea, Yet, Your
Zorro

OH

Accident, Ach, Action, Admiration, Afraid, Again, Aha, Alarm,
   Alas, Alphabet, Alright, Also, Always, Am, Amazed, An,
   Answer, Any, Ashamed, Astonish, At, Awe, Awful, A word
Baby, Beach, Beautiful, Because, Be quiet, Big, Birds, Bob,
   Book, Bow, Breath, Burn, By
Call, Came, Can, Candy, Car, Careful, Cats, Cause, Chair,
   Charlie, Cheerios, Child, Circle, Cleary, Come, Comment,
   Comma, Crying
Darling, Delight, Describe, Dick, Did, Didn't, Didn't know, Dim,
   Disappointed, Disappointment, Discovery, Doll, Don't, Don't
   known, Duck
Eee, Eek, Eh, Emphatic, English, Er, Ever, Excite, Excitements,
   Exciting, Exclaimed, Exclaiming, Exclamation mark,
   Exclamatory, Excuse, Exempt, Explanation, Eyes
Face, Faint, Fall, Falling, Feeling, Feels, Feet, Fine, First
   grade, Food, Fool, Foot, For, Fore, Forget, Found, Fright,
   Friend, Frighten, Frightened
Gasp, Gee whiz, Ghost, Glad, God, Goodby, Gracious, Grade,
   Great, Grief, Groan, Guess
Happen, Happiness, Harry, Heat, Heavens, Helps, Henny, Her,
   Here, Hick, High, High time, His, Hit, Holiday, Holler, Hort,
   House, Hungry, Hurrah, Hurry, Hurts
Ice, Ick, Ill, I'm, In, Interjection, I see, Ishy, Is that so, Its
Jane, Jeepers, Jim, Job, Joe, Johnny, Jump
Knew, Knife
Lake, Language, Left, Letter, Lie, Like, Look out, Loud
Mary, May, Maybe, Mew, Middle, Mine, Moe, More, Mother,
   Mothers, Mouse, My gosh, My oh my
Natty, New, Noise, No kidding, Nothing, Notice, Nut
Obey, Odd, Of course, Oh hum, Ohio, Oh is that your dog, Oh
   no, Oh oh, Ohs, Only, Oo, Ooh, Oooh, Oops, Open, Or, Our,
   Over, Owe
Paper, Peel, People, Person, Pig, Pin, Play, Please, Pretty,
   Problem, Punny, Purple
Quickly
Ran, Rats, Read, Reason, Relief, Remember, Reply, Right,
   Ring, River, Road, Row, Running
Sad, Say can you, Saying, Scare, Seen, She, Shoot, Short, Show,
   Shucks, Shut up, Shy, Sign, Slang, Slow, Smart, Snow, Sold,
   Some, Someone, Song, Songs, Soon, Sore, Sorry, Sound,
   Speak, Speed, Spilled, Started, Statement, Story, Sure,
   Surprising, Suzanna, Suzannah, Suzzanna, Swing
Take, Teacher, Ten, Terrible, Terror, Their, Thing, Think,
   Though, Thought, Tired, To, Toe, Took, Tragic, Troubles,
   Two
Um, Unhappy

Vice
Was, Watch, Way, Where, Whoa, Whoops, Will, Window, Woa,
   Women, Wonder, Wonderful, Wondering, Work, Worried,
   Worry, Wrong
Yah, Yeh, Yell, Yikes, Young, Youth

ON

About, Again, Air, Always, Am, An, Angle, Another, Around,
   A thing, A top
Baby, Bad, Ball, Base, Bat, Be, Beach, Beginning, Below,
   Beneath, Beside, Bicycle, Birthday, Body, Bond, Bong,
   Bottom, Boy, Bricks, Bridge, Brush, Building, Burner, Bus,
   Button, Buy, Bye
Can, Car, Cat, Cats, Certain, Cloths, Coat, Coffee, Cold, Come,
   Cover, Cow, Cycles
Days, Desk, Dial, Do, Dock, Dog, Dogs, Donkey, Door, Doors,
   Dress, Dressing
Earth, Eat, Electricity, Ever
Far, Fast, Fasten, Fell, Fence, Find, Firm, First, Flat, Food,
   For, Forever, Form, From, Fun
Grass, Grooved, Ground
Had, Hat, He, Hear, Heating, Heavy, Her, Him, Ho, Horse back,
   Hurt
Ice, If, Ignition, Inside, Iron, Island, Its, Its on something
Knob, Know, Known
Lake, Land, Lay, Laying, Let go, Lie, Light switch, List
Man, Mantel, Material, Mom, Moon, Mountain, Movies
Neat, Next, Not, Nuts
Oh, On, On him, On something, On the way to school, On to, On
   top of, Open, Operating, Operation, Our, Ours
Pan, Paper, People, Pickup, Picture, Pillow, Placed, Place on,
   Plane, Plate, Platter, Pond, Porch, Pot, Program, Push
Radiator, Radio, Rainy, Ready, Record, Red, Refrigerator,
   Rest, Rests, Rid, Ridge, Riding, Rock, Rocks, Run
Sailboat, Sale, Sand, Saturday, School, School days, Seat, See,
   Sell, Setting, Shelf, Shoe, Shoes, Show, Sidewalk, Sled, Slid,
   Slow, So, Sock, Sofa, Some, Someone, Song, Soon, Spelling,
   Spot, Standing, Start, Started, Stay, Steep, Steps, Stone, Stop,
   Street car, Stump, Su, Surface, Sweater, Swim, Swing
Team, Television, Tell, Their, Then, The road, The table,
   Together, Top of, Touch, Train, Travel, Tree, Trail,
   Tuesday, Tune, Two
Us
Wagon, Wards, Water, Went, Were, Where, Will, Winter,
   Wisconsin, Wood, Working, Would
Yes, Young, Your

ONLY

About, Afraid, After, Again, Airplane, Allowed, Almost, Along,
   Alot, Alway, And, Any, Anything, Apple, Are, At all, At
   least, Authentic
Baby, Bad, Baloney, Barely, Be, Become, Bee, Beg, Beginning,
   Behave, Belong, Big, Blue, Bones, Boney, Boo, Book, Born,
   Boss, Both, Boys, By, By self
Can, Candy, Can't, Care, Carry, Cart, Cat, Certain, Cheap,
   Church, Class room, Close, Clothes, Coat, Come, Crazy,
   Crevice, Cross, Crowd, Cry baby, Cure
Dear, Desk, Dick, Different, Dishes, Doctor, Doctors, Dog,
   Dogs, Donny, Don't, Door knob, Doors, Down, Dress, Dumb
Each, Eight, Employees, Enough, Exact, Eyes
Family, Finally, Five, Fool, Fore, Four, Friend, Fun
Gary, Girls, Go, Going, Good, Green
Half, Handle, Hard, Has twenty six calories, Have, He, Heart,
   Heat, Here, Hers, Hi, High, Himself, His, Holy, Home, Horse,
   How, However, Husband
In, Individually, Indoors, Itself, Just one
Left, Left out, Less, Letter, Limited, Linda, List, Live, Load,
   Lone, Long, Lost, Lovely, Low, Lowly
Mad, Majority, Man, May, Members, Merely, Mess, Minute,
   Moon, Mostly, Mother, Mouse, Must, Myself
Near, Neat, Need, Neglect, Neither, New, Night, Nine, Nobody,
   No more, None other, Nonly, No other, Nor, Not much, Not
   only, Nur
Object, Of, Officer, Oily, Old, One hour, One thing, One time,
   One way, Or, Order, Others, Ouch, Our, Outdoors, Oval,
   Over, Owe
Parking, Paul, Pen, Phoney, Picture, Pig, Pigs, Place, Please,
   Plural, Plus, Pony, Poor, Pop, Positive, Pot, Preposition,
   Private
Quiet

Really, Reason, Restricted, Ring, River, Ron, Room, Rule, Ruler, Running

Sad, Said, Same, Say, School, Sea, Secluded, See, Self, Sell, Separate, Settlement, Several, She, Signal, Signs, Similarly, Simple, Sinatra, Singing, Sister, Six, Skate, Skip, Slow, Small, Smell, So, Sold, Sole, Solitary, Solitude, Somebody, Someone, Sometime, Son, Song, Soon, Sorry, Soul, Special, Spell, Stag, Start, Steady, Stop, Street, Stupid, Subject, Sue, Sunday

Take, Ten, Test, Their, The lonely, Them, There is only one, Theres, Thin, Things, Those, Thousands, Three, Through, Thus, Tickets to state basketball, Tie, Time, Tomorrow, Too, Toy, True

Under, Unique, Until, Us

Very

Want, War, Water, Way, WDGY, We, Were, Whatever, Where, While, Who, Win, Wish, Women, Work, World

Yet, Yourself

Zero

OR

About, Again, Air, Alternate, Although, Always, And sign, Another thing, Answer, Answers, Ant, Any, Any how, Anyone, Anything, Apple, Arithmetic, Ask, Ate, Author, Away, Awful, A word

Back, Bad, Badly, Bar, Beautiful, Before, Being, Beside, Between, Beverly, Big, Boat oar, Books, Boor, Boot, Bored, Boy, Boys, Bracelet, Butch, Buy

Can be, Candy, Canoe, Can't, Car, Cat, Cause, Chance, Change, Changeable, Chose, Clean, Clues, Cold, Come, Compare, Comparing, Comparison, Conj., Connect, Connection, Contrary, Core, Could be, Course, Cow, Crop, Crucible

Dad, Dead, Deadly, Deal, Decision, Die, Difference, Differently, Different subject, Docs, Dog, Dogs, Done, Dress, Drive, Dumb, Duwane

Each, Eat, Eight, Either one, Else wise, English, Enough, Except, Exception, Exclamation, Excuse

Family, Far, Fast, Fee, Find, Fine, Fisher, Flag, Floor, Fore, Friend, Fro, Fun, Funny

Gan, Gas, Gay, Get, Go, Going, Gold, Gone, Green, Ground, Gun

Handle, Happen, Happy, Head, Hear, Help, Hen, Here, Him or her, His, Hit, Hold, Horror, Hour, However

In, In between, Instead of, Interjection, Iron ore, Isn't, It'll, Its, Itself

Joe, Just

Key, Kill

Later, Lease, Let, Letters, Light, Lighter, Like, Little, Live, Look, Lost, Low

Man alive, Mary, Mayor, Meat, Meet, Men, Metal, Might, Mike, Mind, Mineral, Mom, Mother, Much, Must

Name, Near, Negative, Next, Nice, Noise, None, Nothing, Nut

O, Oak, Oars, Object, Odd, Odor, Of course, Office, Often, Oil, OK, On the, Or, Oral, Orally, Orange, Oranges, Ordinary, Or else, Oreo, Organ, Originally, Or less, Or not, Orphans, Or this, Or was he mad, Other than, Other words, Out, Owe, Own

Paddle, Penn, People, Pig, Pink, Possibility, Possibly, Preposition, Procrastinate, Purse, Puzzled

Questioning, Question mark, Quickly

Ran, Raw, Really, Reciprocal, Remark, Report, Ride, Right, Ring, Roar, Roll, Rope, Round, Run

Sad, Salt, Same, Sand, Sat, Saw, Say, Scar, Second, Seem, Sentence, Shall, Shoe, Shore, Short, Should, Shout, Sick, Since, Sister, Sit, Sitting, Sixes, Skinny, Small, Snor, Snore, So fun, Somebody, Someone, Someone else, Some other one, Someplace else, Something wrong, Sometime, Sometimes, Son, Soon, Sore, Sour, South, Spelling, Steer, Still, Stone, Stop, Store, Street, Sum, Sure

Table, Tautology, Teacher, Than, The other, Think, This or that, Those, Though, Three, Told, Tore, Tow, Tree, True

Undecided, Undecidedably, Undecisive, Under, Unhappy, Us, Used to

Very

Walk, Want, War, Water, Wave, Way, Well, Were, What else, Whatever, Whether, Which, White, Why not, Wide, Win, Wit, With, Women, Won't, Wore

Yellow, You are

OVER

Action, After, Airplane, Along, Always, An, And out, And under,

Any, At

Back side, Backwards, Be, Become, Bed, Before, Begin, Below, Beneath, Better, Between, Big, Blanket, Board, Boat, Body, Brook, Building, But, Buy

Car, Cards, Cast, Cat, Chair, Channel, Climb, Close, Coat, Cold, Coming, Complete, Confederate, Cool, Country, Cross, Cub

Dale, Dark, Darling, Dea, Dew, Dine, Dirty, Distance, Do, Dog, Don, Don't, Drag, Dress, Drug store

Economy, Egg, Eggs, Ended, Estimate, Ever, Every

Faraway, Farther, Fell, Field, Finish, Finished, Fins, Flat, Flip, Fly, Forty, Forward, Fox, From, Fun

Game, Garage, Giant, Girl, Good, Got, Grandmother, Grass, Ground, Gulf

Had, Hand, Hang, Hard, Has, Haul, Have, He, Heard, Heaven, Height, Hell, Her, Hi, High bar, Higher, Hills, Home, Hop, Horizon, Horse, House, How, Hump, Hundred, Hurdles

Into, Is

Joy, Just

Kiss, Knee, Know

Lag, Land, Leave, Left over, Load, Log, Lots, Low

Made, Man, Many, Meadow, Mit, Mon

Nancys, Never, Next, No, Not over, Not under, November, Nut

Ocean, O'er, Of, Off, Oh, Once, One, On top of, Open, Or, Other side, Ouch, Our, Ovens, Overcome, Over head, Over land, Overly, Over there, Overture

Pages, Pancakes, Paper, Part, Pass, Past, Pencil, Place, Plain, Plane, Play, Please, Plus, Power, Powered, Put

Quickly

Race, Raod, Really, Repeat, Repetition, Reverse, Ridge, Road, Roadway, Roberta, Roof, Rope, Rotate, Run

Same, Seas, See, Send, Seven, She, Sheep, Sheet, Shoe, Shoes, Shoulders, Show, Sick, Sight, Six, Sleep, Slower, So, Soft, Solid, Some, Something, Somewhere, Start, Stay, Still, Stomach, Stone, Stop, Stopped, Stove, Summer, Sure

Table, Test, Than, The fence, The hill, The moon, Then, The rainbow, Thing, This, Though, Through, Times, Today, Town, Try, Tumble, Turned, Turn over, Twenty one, Twice, Twin

Up over on top, Upper, Us

Valley, Very

Wagon, Walk, Was, Water, Wave, Waves, Way, Weight, Went, When, Which, Who, Why, Wider, With, Word

Yard, Yes, Yonder, Your, Yours

PEOPLE

A, Add, Alive, Alot, Always, America, Americans, Amusement, And, And places, Ant, Ants, Apes, Are funny, Arm, Art, Ask, At, Audience, Auditorium

Bad, Bag, Be, Beer, Before, Big and small, Birds, Black, Blue, Bodies, Bought, Boys and girls, Broad, Brother, Brought, Building, Bunch, Bus, Busy

Camping, Car, Carry, Cat, Chair, China, Choise, Church, Cities, Civil, Clan, Classes, Clods, Close, Coat, Coming, Common, Communism, Community, Confession, Conformity, Confusion, Congregation, Cool, Could, Couple, Cows, Crazy, Creature, Creatures, Creek, Crow, Crowded, Crowed, Crown, Cut

Dad, Daddy, Darrone, Days, Different, Dolls, Don't, Down town, Dress, Drug

Each, Eater, Eaters, Enemies, European, Everyone, Every where, Eye

Face, Families, Farm, Fast, Fat, Father, Feet, Fellow, Fellows, Female, Few, Fine, Finger, Fingers, Five, Flesh, Folks, Foreign, Four, Frantic, Freak, Friend, Friendly, Frogs

Game, Gary, Gather, Gathering, Gens, Gentlemen, Gents, Girls boys women men, Gogue, Goose, Gossip, Gossips, Got, Grass, Grown, Grown ups, Guys

Had, Hair, Harm, Hat, Hate, Hats, Have, Head, Heard, Hen, Herds, Here, High, His, His her, Hoe, Home, Hope, Hot, Houses, How, Hum, Human being, Humanity, Humans you and me, Hungry, Hurry, Hurt

I, Ideas, Idiots, I don't dig em, In, Indians, Interest, Interesting, Interests, Is

Japanese, Jerks, Joy

Kathy, Keep, Kill, Kind

Later, Laughed, Laughing, Laughter, Legs, Let, Leute, Little, Living, Look, Loots, Lost

Machine, Mad, Male, Man and woman, Mankind, Marlyce,

Marriage, Mars, Martians, Masses, Mat, Math, May, Mean, Men and woman, Men and women, Mennesker, Men women, Millions, Mine, Mobs, Mom, Money, Monkey, Monkeys, Moon, More, Morons, Mothers, Mountain, Move, Much, Multitude, Multitudes, Must, My

Nation, Nations, Native, Negro, Neighbors, Never, New, New Yorkers, Next door, No, Nobody, Noise, None, No one, Noun, Now, Numbers, Nuts

Of, Off, Officers, Oh, Old, One, On the moon, Or, Other, Others, Over

Pair, Parade, Parents, Parks, Party, Pea, Peasants, Pedestrians, People, People are nice, Pepper, Pessimists, Pets, Pigs, Pink, Playing, Please, Pleasing, Plenty, Pole, Police, Polish, Polynesians, Poor, Pop, Pop corn, Pope, Populace, Popular, Populus, Possessioms, Pot, Prefer, Pretty, Prisoner, Problems, Public, Pupil, Put

Race and creeds, Races, Ran, Rats, Red, Ride, Roman, Room, Running, Rush, Russian

Sad, Said, Sally, Sat, Saw, Scar, Several, Sexes, Shade, She, Sheep, Shnooks, Shoes, Shopping, Show, Sick, Sing, Six, Skin, Small, Smart, Smoke, Society, Some, Someone, Son, Souse, Space, Spain, Speak, Sports, Stable, Start, Steeples, Stem, Steve, Stores, Stupid, Suits, Summer, Sure

Take, Tall, Teacher, Teenagers, Thank, That, The, Then, There, Those, Thought, Thousands, Three, Throng, Through, Time, Today, Todd, Together, Togetherness, Took, Train, Two

U.S., Ugly, Use

Vegetables, Volk

Was, Water, Way, Week, Went, When, Which, Who us, Wife, Will, With, Wonderful, Words, Work

Yes, Young, Youth

Zone

PLAYING

Act, Acting, Action, Acts, After while, Again, All, Alone, Along, An, Argue, Arguing, Army, As, At

Babies, Baby, Back, Back yard, Bad, Balls, Band, Basket, Baying, Beach, Bell, Better, Big, Bikes, Block, Blocks, Board, Boring, Box, Boxing, Brother, Busy, But, By

Came, Can, Car, Carefully, Catch, Catching, Cheating, Checkers, Childish, Clay, Climbing, Clothes, Come, Coming, Cowboy, Cowboys

Dad, Daisy, Dance, Dark, Darts, Dawdle, Day, Dead, Death, Dice, Did, Didn't, Died, Dirt, Dislike, Do, Doctor, Dodge, Dog, Doing things, Donkey, Doodling, Down, Drink, Drive, Dumb, Dying

Easier, Easy, End, Enjoy, Enjoying, Excitement, Exercising, Exhaustion

Failing, Fair, Fall, Fanning, Faster, Feeling, Few, Fiddle, Fiddling, Field, Fields, Find, Fine, Fire, Fitting, Five, Fix, Flags, Flow, Flute, Fly, Flying, Food, For, Fort, Forth, Fought, Found, Friends, Frolic, Frolicking

Get, Girl, God, Going, Goofing, Goofing off, Grabbing, Grounds, Guess, Gum, Gym, Gymnastics

Had, Hammer, Harder, Hardly, Hate, Have, Hay, He, Hear, Heard, Help, Hen, Her, Here, Hiding, High, Hit, Hoar, Hockey, Homework, Hood, Hookey, Hooky, Hop, Hope, Hopscotch, Horn, Houses, How, Hungry, Hunting, Hurry, Hurt, Hurting

Idle, If, I'm, Imagine, Indian, Inside, Instrument

Jacks, Joking, Joy

Kid, Kittens, Knew

Lands, Laugh, Lay, Laying, Learning, Letter, Like, Live, Living, Look, Loudly, Love, Lulling, Lying

Mad, Making, Mate, Merry, Mischievous, Mischief, Missing, Money, Monkey, Mope, Mother, Movies plus girls equals, Music, My

Nap, Naughty, Neglected, Nicely, No, Noise, Nothing, Not play, Not playing

Of, Off, Oh, One, Outdoors

Pan, Pant, Park, Part, Party, Pasty, Pay, Paying, Pen, People, Person, Petting, Pig, Pilots, Pin, Pinochle, Plaid, Plan, Platter, Play boy, Playful, Play house, Play mate, Play pen, Plays, Pleasure, Ply, Plywood, Porch, Practicing, Praying, Pretending, Prying, Puppet, Puppy, Put

Quarreling, Queer, Quick, Quiet, Quietly

Racing, Radio, Ran, Reading, Real, Recreation, Relax, Relaxed, Relaxing, Riding, Roll, Rolling, Romp, Roosevelt, Rope, Rower, Rowing, Runner

Sad, Safe, Safely, Said, Sat, Saw, Say, School, Set, Setting, Sex, She, Shot, Shout, Shouting, Shovel, Shower, Showing, Sick, Side, Sing, Sit, Skating, Skillful, Skipping, Skit, Slaying, Sled, Sleep, Sleeper, Slide, Sliding, Slipping, Slow, Smile, Smoke, Snow, Snowball, Socker, Someone, Something, Sound, Speak, Sports, Squirming, Stay, Still, Stood, Stopping, Street, Streets, Strong, Summer, Sunshine, Swim, Swimming, Swinging, Swings

Table, Teasing, Testing, That, The, Theater, Theatre, Them, Then, There, Things, Thinking, Throw, To, Today, Toddling, Top, Tricks, Trike, Trouble, Trucks, Trumpet, Trying

Us

Vacation, Verb, Vine, Viola, Volleyball

Walk, Want, Was, Waste, Watching, Water, We, Well, When, Where, Wild, Win, Window, With boys, Women, Wonder, Worker, Wow, Writing

Yea good, Yet, You, Young, Youth

PRIEST

Absent, Accident, Acne, A good man, Aid, Aloft, And religion, Anger, Any, A peasant, At

Baby, Back, Bad, Baptism, Bath, Beast, Beauty, Bed, Before, Belgian, Bible teller, Big, Bird, Birthday, Black garb, Black gown, Blank, Bless, Block, Blue, Body, Bone, Book, Books, Boss, Boy, Boy friend, Bud, Buddha, Button

Calm, Can, Card, Cat, Cathedral, Catholic Holy Rollers, Catholic religion, Ceased, Cent, Chair, Child, Christian, Christmas, Citizen, Clean, Clergyman, Clergymen, Closes, Cloth, Cloths, Coach, Coat, Collar, Communion, Confess, Confessor, Convent, Cost, Country, Cow, Cowboy, Crook, Cross, Cutest

Dad, Deacon, Dead, Dear, Death, Decowski, Devil, Devotion, Do, Dog, Don, Don't, Down, Dress, Drop, Druid, Dry, Dumb

Easy, Eggerling, Enjoy, Episcopal

Faith, Faithful, Fake, False, Farce, Farther, Fast, Father church, Father Frank, Fine, Fire, Fish, Fly, Fold, Folded, Fool, For, Fr. Coleman, Fr. Don, Fr. Don Sehneticis, Friend, Friendly, Fr. Kenney, Funny

Gentleness, George, Germs, Get it, Ghost, Gift, Girl, Give, Go, Gone, Good man, Gospel, Gospel man, Got, Gown, Grand, Greek, Grey hair

Had, Hair, Happy, Hardly, Hat, Head, Heard, Height, Hell, Help, Helper, Helpful, Hi, Highest, Holiness, Holy man, Holy one, Holy Rollers, Holy water, Honorable, Hot, Hungry, Hurry

I, Ick, Ill, Inca, Is, Ish, It

Jew, Jewish, Joy, Judas, Judge, Justice

Kenny, King, Kink, Knew

Lake, Lamp, Late, Latin, Laugh, Laura, Learn, Lecturer, Leg, Lesson, Levite, Liar, Life, Like, Like minister, Lite, Long, Long ago, Loud, Love, Low, Loyal, Lutheran

Man of God, Many, Marry, Martin, Master, Maybe, Me, Men, Mere man, Messenger, Ministers, Minsterm Mission, Mister, Mom, Moss, Move, Mr. Bergin

Naughty, Neat, Night, No, Noble, None, Nonsense, Not, Notre Dame, Now, Nut

Oar, Obedience, Officer, Official, Oh, Oh gosh, Olsen, One, Open

Padre, Paper, Party, Past, Pasture, Peace, Penance, Pep, Perfume, Peter, Phony, Pious, Praise, Prayer, Prayers, Preaching, President, Price, Priest, Priestess, Print, Private, Prod, Program, Protestant, Proud, Pulpit, Put

Quiet, Quit

Rabbis, Rage, Ran, Rap, Rector, Red, Region, Relief, Religion God, Religions, Religious man, Repulsion, Rest, Rev. Wallace, Ridiculous, Right, Roman Catholic Church, Room, Rosary

Sacred, Sad, Sanctity, Save, Say, School, Serious, Serve, Service, Show, Sins, Skirt, Skull, Smart, Sneaky, Soft, Solemn, Someone who tells stories about, Soot, Sorry, Speak, Speech, Square, Squeezed, Stately, St. Augustine, Stem, Stomach, Story teller, Stove, Strict, Sunday School, Supper, Surprise, Suspection

Tag, Talker, Talking, Teaches, Tell, Telling, Temple, Test, The, Thing, Think, Time, Treat, Truth

Understanding, Unwed, Up

Verb, Very

Warmth, Water, White collar, Win, Wine, Woman, Women, Won, Word, Words, Write, Wrong

Your

QUICKLY

Accomplish, Accomplished, Act, Adverb, After, Again, Alert, Allied, Always, And, Arrive, As, As can, Ate, At once

Ball, Baseball, Be, Beat, Bee, Black, Blink, Boat, Boy, Boy running, Boys, Briskly, Brown, Bunny, By

Calm, Came, Carry, Cats, Close, Could, Cry

Dad, Danny, Darted, Date, Dear, Deer, Did, Died, Do, Does, Dog, Draw, Dress, Drive, Dry, Duck

Easy, Eat, Eye

Faces, Fall, Fare, Fastest, Fat, Fats, Feet, Find, First, Fleet, For, Four, Fun

Get, Giant, Going, Grasshopper, Gun

Hard, Hardly, Hastily, He, Help, His, Hole, Home, Horse, Hose, Hospital, Hot

Ick, Ik, Immediately, Is

Jeff

Kiss, Know

Last, Left, Leg, Leopard, Light, Lively, Long, Loud, Loudly, Low

Magician, Make, Man, Me, Milk, Mind, Mine, Mistress, Mom, My

New, Nice, No, Noise, Noisy, None, Nut

Of, Old, On, Only, Open, Or, Over

Pencil, People, Person, Planes, Pop, Possible, Prickly

Quaker, Queen, Quicker, Quickest, Quickly, Quitely

Race, Rain, Rate, Read, Red, Reluctant, Responds, Right, Right away, Rite, Runs, Rush

Safe, Said, Sand, Scale, Scatter, Schnell, School teacher, Sea, Seat, See, Sell, Sharp, Shh, Show, Shut, Sick, Sickle, Sickly, Silently, Silver, Sing, Slender, Slept, Slick, Slower, Slowing, Small, Smart, Smooth, Smoothly, So, Sold, Sooner, Soup, Speak, Sped, Speedily, Speedy, Spring, Stairs, Stand, Started, Story, Suddenly, Sure, Surely, Swear

Tell, Than, That, The, There, Thing, This, This test, Thus, Time, To, Too, Train, Tree

Unlikely

Very

Walked, Was, Water, Way, We, Were, What, When, Will, With, Wonders

Zoom

QUIET

A, Abrupt, A closed room, Afraid, All, Apartment, Arithmetic, Arrow, Asleep, Awake

Back, Bad, Barely, Bashful, Be, Bead, Beauty, Because, Bed, Bedroom, Bedrooms, Being, Big noise, Black, Blank, Book, Boot, Boring, Boy, Boys, Bread, Brook, Brush paint, Bug, By

Calmness, Came, Can, Cemetery, Chair, Chapel, Children, Class, Classroom, Clean, Closet, Club, Come, Comfort, Comfortable, Content, Cool, Cop, Cottage, Cotton, Couch, Country, Cow, Cute

Dared, Dave, Day, Dead, Deaf, Death, Deep, Deer, Different, Difficult, Dissolute, Disturb, Do, Dog, Don, Done, Don't talk, Don't want, Dormitory, Down, Dream, Dull

Easy, Eat, Embarass, Empty, Everyone's in bed

Face, Fare, Fat, Fear, Feather, Finish, Fired, Forest, Front, Fun

Game, Garden, Gentle, Giant, Go, Golden, Gone, Grandma's, Grass, Graveyard, Green, Gym

Had, Hall, Happy, Hard, Harsh, He, Heart, Heavy, Here, Holler, Hop, Hospitals, Hospital zone, Hot

Ick, Ill, Isolated, It

Job

King

Lad, Lady, Lakeside, Larger, Lazy, Learn, Less noise, Librarian, Light, Like, Little, Lone, Long, Louder, Loudly, Loudness, Love, Love music

Mad, Man, Meadow, Mean, Mellow, Men, Might, Mile, Milk, Mom, Month, Moody, Moon, Morning, Most, Mountain, Mouth, Moves, Mom, My

Nap, Nature, Neat, Nerves, Night time, Noises, Noisier, Noisily, Non noisy, Nosey, No sound, Not, No talking, Not a sound, Nothing, Not noise, Not noisy, Nursery

Of, Office, On, One, Organ, Out, Outside

Paper, Park, Party, Passive, Peacefully, Pencil, People, Pepper, Pet, Pice, Pin, Pipe down, Place, Prairie, Pretty

Queen, Quick, Quiescent, Quiet, Quieter, Quietly, Quilt, Quinine, Quit, Quite

Read, Reading, Red, Relax, Relaxing, Relief, Remark, Right,

Round

Sad, Salt, Santa, Scared, Scene, Screen, Sea, See, Seems, Serenity, Settled, Seven, Shoo, Show, Shush, Shut, Sick, Sign, Signs, Silence nothing, Silencio, Simple, Sister, Sit, Slumber, Small, Smile, Smooth, Snooze, So, Softness, Soft night, Soft talking, Solace, Solemn, Solitude, Song, Sounds, Sour, Speech-less, Spooky, Spot, Ssh, Start, Stay, Steep, Stone, Storm, Streets, Study hall, Studying, Stupid, Sunny, Sweet

Table, Talking, Tall, Teachers, Test, Thing, Think, Thoughtful, Time, Tip, Tip toe, To, Touch, Tranquil, Trouble, Turn off, TV, Twelve o'clock

Unnoise, Up

Vacuum, Valerie, Valley, Virtue, Voice

Watch, Water, West, Whispering, Williams five, Wind Wish, Woods, Word, Words

Yah, Yelling, Yes

Zone

QUIETLY

A, Adverb, Again, Ah, Alone, Aloud, Always, Am, Annoy, Another, Appear, Are, As, Asleep, At, Ate, Audible

Bad, Bay, Because, Bed, Bed spring, Bee, Been, Be quiet, Better, Big, Bird, Book, Bought, Boy, Breeze, Buy, Buying, Buzz, By

Calm, Calmly, Came, Can, Cautious, Christmas, Church, Class, Classroom, Clear, Close, Closer, Cold, Cotton, Cover, Cow, Crept, Cry

Dark, Dead, Death, Deep, Dentist, Did, Died, Din, Do it, Dolls, Done, Door, Dope, Drinking

Ears, Easily, Easy, Eat, Efficiently, Eyes

Far, Fastly, Feather, Feet, Finally, Fine, Finger, Finished, Firm, First, Foot, For, Fresh, From, Front

Garvey, Gave, Gentle, Germany, Get, Give, God, Going, Got, Grandma, Grandma's

Ha, Had, Happy, Hardly, Harsh, Haven't, He, Hear, Heard, Heavy, Her, He went, Hi, Hidden, His, Hit, Hoe, Home, Homes, Hose, House, Hum, Hunger, Hurry, Hymn

Indians, Inn, Insects, Instrument, Interest, Into, Isn't

Joanne, John, Jump, Junk

Keep, Keep quiet, Kids, Killed, Kiss, Kissed, Know

Lawn, Learn, Learned, Leave, Led, Left, Leisurely, Lesson, Letting, Librarian, Liked, Listen, Little, Loader, Loading, Lonely, Look, Looked, Low, Lowly

Made out, Man, Many, Meekly, Mice, Milk, Moccasin, Money, More, Mum, Music

Name, Near, Nerve, Nerves, Never, Nicely, Noiseless, None, No noise, Nosey, Nosier, No sound, No talking, Not fast, Nothing, Not loud

Of, Off, Outside, Over

Past, Paw, People, Pillow, Pin drop, Plant, Play, Playing, Pleasant, Product, Push, Put

Queen, Quietly, Quiet soft, Quiet tone

Rabbit, Read, Reading, Ready, Remember, Restrained, Reverence, Reverently, Right, River, Rough

Sad, Said, Salt, Saw, Say, School, Secret, Secretly, See, Seen, Sell, Sent, Serene, Serenely, Serenity, Settled, Seven, Shhh, Shoes, Shot, Shout, Shush, Shut, Sick, Sietly, Sign, Sin, Sings, Skip, Sleepily, Sleepy, Slept, Slip, Slipped, Slippers, Slower, Small, Smooth, Smoothly, Sneaky, So, Solemnly, Solitude, Some, Soon, Soundlessly, Soundly, Soup, Speaking, Speechless, Spoke, Spoken, Spot, Squeek, Srrr, Ssh, Stand, Stay, Steal, Stealthily, Steep, Step, Stopped, Study, Stupid, Sung, Sure, Surely, Sweet, Swift, Swiftly, Swim

Take, Taken, Talked, Talking, Talkless, Teacher, Test, Thank, That, Then, There, They went, Thing, Thinking, Thought, Through, Thrown, Time, Timid, Tip toes, Tired, Toes, Together, Tom, Tonight, Tread

Understand, Unloud, Unquietly, Us, Use

Vary, Very, Very quiet, Vibration, Voice

Walks, Was, Watch, We are, Were, What, When, Whispering, Who, Why, Will, Win, With, Word, Write

You

Zone

RED

A color, Afraid, Airplane, An, Animal, A pretty color, Arm, Army, Attractive, Autumn

Badge, Balloon, Bark, Bead, Beard, Beauty, Beet, Beets, Bert, Best color, Bicycle, Big, Bird, Birth, Bishop, Bleed, Blew, Block, Bloody, Blouse, Boot, Boots, Box, Braid, Bred, Bricks,

Bright color, Brightness, Brilliant, Broke, Bull fight, Bulls, Butch, Button

Can, Cannot, Cape, Carpet, Casperson, Cat, Chair, Cheeks, Cherries, Cherry, China, Chuck, Clear, Clothes, Clothing, Clown, Cold, Collar, Coloring, Communism, Cop, Coral, Cost, Covers, Cow, Cows, Crimson, Cross

Dark color, Day, Dead, Death, Deep, Deer, Devil, Dot, Dress shirt, Dull, Dust

Ear, Easy, Embarrass, End, Engine, Excited, Excitement, Exciting, Extra, Eyes

Face, Farm, Favorite, Fear, Feather, Ferreri, Fingernails, Fire hydrant, Fire truck, Five, Flag American, Flame, Flannel, Flashy, Flat, Flower, Four, Fox, Fright, Fun

Gaudy, Ghost, Glare, Glow, Go, Gold, Greed, Grey

Hand, Handkerchief, Hard, Harsh, Hate, Heart, Heat, Hen, Here, Hoarse, Hood, Hunters

In

Jacket

Kite, Knight

Lack, Lake, Leaves, Led, Legs, Life, Light bulb, Like, Loud, Love

Man, Maroon, Mars, Material, Matisse, Medium, Mitten, Mittens, Model, Moscow

Name, Neat, Nice, Nose

One ball, Our, Owl

Pain, Pajamas, Pants, Paper, Patrol, Pen, Pencil, Philosophy, Pick, Pillow, Planets, Plum, Pretty color

Rage, Red Riding Hood, Reduction, Riddle, Ride, Rider, Riding Hood, Ring, Ripe, Robin, Rod, Room, Rosy, Rouge, Round, Ruby, Rug, Russian, Russians, Rust

Said, Santa Claus, Scarf, Scarlet, School, See, See good, Semaphore, Sew, Sexy, Sharp, Shiny, Ship, Shoes, Short, Sign, Signal, Skin, Skin infected, Skirt, Sky, Sleep, Sock, Socks, Soft, Sound, Sox, Soxs, Spider, Spot, Stockings, Stop light, Stop sign, Stove, String, Sucker, Suit, Sun burn

Tape, Texture, Thread, Tie, Tomato, Tongue, Toy, Trouble, Truck

Ugly, Underwear

Valentine, Valentine's Day, Valentines, Violent

Wagner, Want, War, Warmth, Warn, While, White and blue, Whoosh, Wild, Wine, With, Wood pecker, Worm, Wound, Wren, Write

RELIGION

About God, Abstract, Age, Agnostic, Air, Alliance, Altar, American, Ancestor, And, Ant, Antheist, Anxiety, Anything, Argument, Art, Association, Atheism, Atheistic, Atheists, Attention, Aunt

Baby, Background, Bad, Ball, Banker, Baptise, Baptised, Baptism, Bas, Beauty, Because, Bed, Being, Beliefs, Believing, Belong, Best, Bethlehem, Bias, Bible story, Black, Blasphemy, Blew, Boat, Boring, Box, Boy, Brag, Buddha, Buddhism, Buddhist

Can, Cannot, Cap, Care, Cash crop, Cat, Catechism, Catholic faith, Catholic or Lutheran, Catholics, Charity, Chess, Child, Choice, Choir, Chores, Chose, Christian Science, Christians, Christmas, Churches, Church school, City, Class, Close, Club, Code, Cold, Colonies, Color, Comforting, Communism, Confession, Confirmation, Conflict, Confusion, Congo, Convention, Convert, Cookie, Court, Crutch, Custom, Customs

Dad, Day, Dead, Death, Decision, Devotion, Didn't, Difference, Difference of, Disagreements, Discussion, Distasteful, Dog, Dogma, Domestic, Donkey, Don't, Doubt, Dream, Druid, Dull

Earth, Eh, Election, Enjoyment, Epiphany, Episcopalian, Error, Escape, Essential, Evangelist, Everywhere, Evil, Existence

Face, Faithful, Family, Fanatic, Farce, Farm, Fast, Fear, Feeling, Feelings, Few, Fiction, Fight, Fine, Finish, Firm, Follow, Food, Foolish, Foolishness, For, Force, Fore, Forgot, Fort, Free, French, Friends, Friendship, Fruit, Fun

Gas station, Gentile, German, Get, Ghost, Girl, Godliness, Gods, Goodness, Gospel, Got, Grace, Grandfather, Grass, Greek, Group

Ha, Had, Happiness, Happy, Hard, He, Head, Health, Heaven, Hebrew, Hell, Help, Helpful, Hi, High, High school, Highway, Hills, Holiness, Home, Honesty, Hot, How, Human

I, Idol, Ill, Individual, Inspiration, Instruction, Islam, Issue

Jehovah, Jesus Christ, Jews, John, Joy, Judaism, Justice

Kennedy, Key, Kinds, Knew

Lady, Lake, Last, Lawn, Lay, Learn, Learning, Legion, Like, Lion, Little, Live, Long, Look, Lot, Lutherans

Many, Marry, Mass, Math, May, Maybe, Memory, Mike, Milk, Mind, Minnesota, M. Luther, Monk, Morman, Mormon, Mother, Mountain, Must, My, Myths

Name, Nationality, Neat, Necessary, Need, No, No comment, Noise, Non religion, Nonsense, Not, Nothing, Now, Nun, Nuts

Oar, Obey, Obeys, Office, Often, OK, On, Opinion, Opium, Outside, Over, Own

Park, Part, Past, Pastors, Pentecost, Pentecoste, Personal, Pharaoh, Phil, Phony, Pilgrim, Pink, Play, Pooh, Porch, Praise, Prayers, Praying, Prays, Preach, Preachers, Prejudice, President, Pretty, Private, Protestants, Prove it, Punishment

Quakers, Quiet, Quietness

Race people, Ranger, Rat, Read, Reading, Real, Rebel, Red, Refuge, Region, Relay, Relief, Religional, Remember, Report, Republican, Reverent, Revivalists, Right, Ritual, River, Roads, Robes, Roll, Rosary, Rote, Rules

Sacred, Sacrilegious, Sad, Safe, Salvation, Same, Sand, Sarcastic, Satiation, Schools, Sect, Security, See, Seeking, Sermon, Serve, Service, Services, Sex, Sheep, Shore, Shot, Sign, Sing, Sit, Size, Sky, Sly, Small, Smart, Smell, Society, Soldier, Song, Sort, Soul, Speak, Special, Spirit, Star, State, Steeple, Stem, Story, Strength, Strong, Studies, Study, Stupid, Sunday School, Super, Swedish, Sweed, Synagogue

Talk, Teaching, Team, Tell, Temple, Territory, The, Then, Things, Think, Thinking, Thoughts, Three, Time, Tired, To, Together, Tom, Tower, Trinity, Trouble, True, Trust, Truthful, Try, Turkey

Uncle, Universal, Universalist, Us

Valley, Vital, Voted

Waste, Weak, Weight, Wet, What people think, When, Whiskey, Wholesome, Will, Window, Witness, Woman, Women, Wonderful, Word, Work, Worker, Worthy, Wrong

Yes, Young

Zeus

RIVER

Art

Bad, Banks, Barge, Bay, Beard, Beauty, Been, Boating, Boats, Body of water, Bottom, Boy, Broad, Bubbling

Canal, Canoeing, Canyon, Cat, Chippewa, Choppy, Clear, Cloquet, Color, Come, Comfort, Congo, Conn, Cool refreshing, Could, Country, Crooked, Cross, Crossing, Cry, Currents, Curve

Dam, Dangerous, Death, Delaware, Dirty, Distance, Dive, Down, Drink, Drowning, Dry

Elk, Ever

Fall, Fast water, Find, Fist, Floating, Flood, Flower, Flows, Flumen, Fluss, Foam, Forest, Fort, Fresh, Frozen, Fun

Geography, Giver, Gray, Ground, Guy

Ham, Hand, He, Hikes, Hill, House

Ice, Icy, Irrawaddy, Is

Jordan, Jump

Kwai

Lack, Lake like, Land, Large, Late, Lazy, Little, Liver, Loud

Man, Mary, Marylin, Mean, Meander, Minnehaha, Minnesota, Miss, Missouri, Money, Mountains, Mouth, Move, Moving, My home, Mysterious

Narrow, Nice, Nile, Not a lake

Old, Old man

Pad, Path, Pebble, Picture, Place, Po, Pool, Pound, Puddle

Quiet

Rain, Rainy, Rapid, Rat, Ravine, Red River, Refreshing, Rhine, Rhite, Ride, Rio, Ripple, Rippling, River, Rock, Rocks, Roseau, Rough, Running water, Runs, Rush, Rushing

Savannah, Saw, Scene, School, Seine, Shallow, Shore, Silvery, Skinny, Sliver, Small, Smell, Smooth, Snake, Snow, Soil conservation, Song, Sound, Source, Sparkling, Star, Steam boat, Step, St. Louis, St. Mary's, Stones, Straight, Stretch, Summer, Swamp, Swing

Tide, Time, To, Torrent, Travel, Treacherous, Tree, Trees, Tributary, Trickle, Trout, Turbulent

Underwater, Unending

Volga

Wash, Wave, Waves, Waving, Well, Whale, Whistle, White, Windy, Would

Yellow

ROUGH

Abrasive, Abrupt, Age, Although, Angry, Anything, Army, A rowdy, At, Away, Awful

Bank, Bell, Berg teacher, Better, Big, Big holes, Big man,

Biology, Black, Blanket, Block, Boards, Boat, Bony, Bottle, Bough, Bounce, Bouncy, Bow, Boxer, Bracelet, Bread, Breeze, Brick, Broke, Broken, Brother, Brown, Brush, Bug, Bully, Bum, Bumble, Bunch, Bunting, Bush

Cactus, Candy, Car, Carpet, Carved, Cat, Cement, Chair, Chapped, Chase, Cheek, Chemistry, Chicken, Children, Choppy, City, Clad, Class, Claw, Clean, Clear, Climb, Cloth, Cold, Color, Comb, Come, Command, Concrete, Cook, Cook-ed, Cool, Corduroy, Cough, Country, Country road, Courage, Cow, Cowboys, Crevice, Criminal, Crooked, Cruel

Dangerous, Dark, Davenport, Dead, Debby, Delicate, Desert, Deserts, Die, Difficult, Dirt, Displeasing, Disturbing, Ditches, Doll, Door, Dough, Draft, Dream, Driveway, Dull, Dumb

Eagle, Echinoderm, Edgy, Elephant, Emery board, Engine, Enough, Even

Fare, Fast, Fat, Feel, Feeling, Fields, Fighter, Fighting, Fine, Finish, Firm, Fist, Flat, Flooring, Flour, Food, Foot, Forest, Fought, Free, Fright, File, Frog, Front, Frozen

Gagged, Game, Gang, Gangster, Garden, Gently, Get, Gentle, Girl, Glass, Glasses, Go, Goat, Going, Goodby, Gown, Grain, Granite, Green, Grow, Growl, Growth, Grumpy, Gunny sack, Gym

Hair, Hairy, Happily, Hard guy, Hardly, Harp, Heavy, Hew, Hewn, High, Highway, His, Hole, Home work, Horses, Hose, House, Hurts

I, Icky, Irritate, Ishy, Itchy

Jack, Jagged surface, Job, John Wayne, Journey

Kind, Knife

Lake, Land, Lark, Later, Lawn, Lay, Leather, Leave, Legs man's, Line, Logger, Longer, Loud, Lumber, Lumpy

Mad, Mailman, Marine, Material, Meant, Meat, Meek, Men, Mess, Messy, Mild, Muscles

Nail, Nails, Name, Negro, No, Not good, Not rough, Not soft

Oar, Old, Ouch, Outdoors, Outlaw, Outlaws

Paddle, Pail, Pain, Painful, Pass, Path, Pebbles, People, Person, Plane, Plough, Ploughing, Plow, Plush, Puppy

Race, Raft, Rag, Raid, Raiders, Rasp, Rattles, Real tough, Rich, Ridden, Riding, Right, Rigid, Rind, River, Roads, Roar, Robbers, Rod, Roof, Roosevelt, Rope, Rotten, Roughed, Round, Row, Run, Runway, Rustic

Sanding, Sandstone, Sandy, Scaley, Scaly, Scare, Scared, Scout, Scrape, Sea, Shell, Shod, Shoo, Short, Shrubbery, Slate, Sleeve, Sliver, Slivers, Slow, Smaller, Smoother, Smother, Snow, Snow falling, Soldier, Sometimes, Sooth, Sore, Sort, Sour, Splinters, Splintery, Spoiled, Spot, Square, Steve, Stony, Storm, Straightness, Strength, Streets, Stucco, Sweater, Sweet

Table, Talk, Tank, Taught, Teachers, Teaches, Teddy Roosevelt, Terrain, Terrible, Textured, The, Thing, This, Though, Thought, Through, Throw, Tight, Time, Toad, Tongue, Too, Top, Topography, Touch, Tour, Towel, Town, Trail, Travel, Tree bark, Tumble, Turtle, TV, Tweed, Two

Ugly, Unclean, Uneasy, Unfinished, Unkept, Unlevel, Unpleasant, Unstraight, Up

Voice

Wall, Weak, Wear, Weeds, Week, West, Wet, Whip, Wild, Wilder-ness, Willed, Wind, Window, Windy, Winter, Wish, Woman, Women, Woods, Woodsman, Wool, Wool rug, Work, Would, Wrestler, Wrestlers, Wright, Wrinkle

Yellow, Your

RUNNING

A, Across, Action, Advancing, Afraid, Again, Ahead, Along, Alway, Antelope, Asthma, At, Athlete, Autumn

Ball, Bare, Base, Baseball, Beat, Bicycle, Big, Bike, Bill, Block, Boys, Breathe, Breathing, Breathless, Brook, Bruce, Bus

Call, Cars, Cat, Chasing, Church, Climb, Coat, Come, Cops, Copy, Cow, Coward, Crash, Crawl, Creeping, Cross country, Cunning

Danger, Dash, Desk, Disappear, Distance, Dogs, Driving, Dying

Energy, Exertion, Exhausted

Falling, Fanning, Far, Fast movement, Fast walk, Fear, Fell, First, Fleet foot, Flit, Flying, Foot, For, Force, Forest, Free, From, Fun, Funny

Game, Girl, Go fast, Going fast, Gone, Good, Gun, Gym

Have, He, Hear, Heard, Heat, Help, Here, Hi, Hiding, High, Hill, Him, Hither, Hitting, Hop, However, Humming, Hurried, Hurriedly

I, In, Indian, Is, It

Journeying

Kick

Labor, Lake, Late, Laugh, Laying, Leap, Leg, Life, Like, Lion, Long

Mad, Mat, Me, Mile, Motion, My

Never, No, Noise, Nose, Not, Now

Off, Oh, One, Only, Out, Out of wind, Over, Ox

Pace, Pant, Parking, Participle, Past, Peeling, People, Perambulating, Person, Play, Polaway, Prune, Puff, Puffing, Put

Races, Rain, Rapidly, Resting, Riding, Rim, River, Road, Rough, Ruin, Run fast, Runner, Runs, Rush

Same, Sat, School, Screaming, Scurry, Shock, Sidewalk, Sit, Skating, Sleeping, Slip, Slower, Soft, Softly, Some, Song, Sore, Sped, Speeding, Sport, Sports, Spot, Stand, Start, Stay, Still, Stood, Stopped, Street, Stride, Stumble, Summer, Sunning, Sweating, Swiftly, Swim, Swimming, Swing

Talking, Team, Tear, The, Thing, Though, Through, Thru, Tim, Time, To, Track team, Train, Tramp, Travel, Treating, Trees, Trip, Tripping, Trot, Trouble

Up

Verb

Waiting, Wake, Walked, Warm, Where, Why, Wind, With, Working

Yellow, Yes, You are running away

Zoom

SALT

Acid, After, Air, Apples, Arteries, Ate, Atlantic, Awful

Bacon, Bad taste, Bag, Base, Better, Bird, Bits, Black, Blocks, Blue, Born, Bottle, Box, Brine, Burn, Burns, Butter

Cake, Can, Carrots, Carton, Cattle, Caustic, Cave, Chalk, Chemical, Chemistry, Chicken, Clear, Coffee, Cold, Container, Cool, Country, Cow, Cows, Crackers, Crystals, Cube, Cut

Date, Dead Sea, Dear, Deer, Desert, Distasteful, Dog, Dogs

Earth, Eater, Electricity

Face, Fat, Fattening, Favor, Fine, Flakes, Flats, Fly, Foot, Four, Free

Girl, Go, Goiter, Gravel, Green, Grit

Ham, Hamburger, Hamburgers, Harsh, Have, Heart, Help, Helps, Humidity

Icky, Ingredient, Iodine, Iron, Ish

Knife

Lack, Lake City, Lamb, Last, Lemons, Life, Light, Like it, Liquid, Live, Limp

Malt, Man, Me, Mean, Melt, Melting, Milk, Mill, Morton

Necessary, Nice, No, No good, Not sweet

Oceans, Olives, On, On food, Onion

Part, Pasture, Paul, Pay, Peanut, Peep, Peppery, Person, Pet, Pigs, Pillar, Pillar of salt, Piper, Plate, Point, Potato, Potato chips, Preserve, Pretty, Pucker, Purple

Quiet

Radishes, Rain, Rare, Red, Report, Rocks, Russia, Rust, Ryne

Sack, Salt, Salted, Salt Lake City, Salt of the earth, Salt shaker, Salt water, Salty peanuts, Sand, Sat, Saucer, Savor, Seasoner, Seasonings, Seasons, See, Seed, Shape, Shot, Shoulder, Siberia, Sickening, Silt, Sinks, Sister, Sit, Slack, Slat, Sleep, Sleet, Slippery, Sliver, Smell, Sneeze, Snow, Sodium Chloride, Soft, Solid, Solution, Sore, Sparkle, Speck, Spices, Spicy, Spoon, Spray, Sprinkle, Square, S shaker, Stack, Stake, Stew, Sting, Stings, Stone, Stove, Streets, String, Substance, Summer, Surer, Sweat

Tablet, Tablets, Taffy, Take, Tang, Tangy, Tangy taste, Tart, Tasteless, Tastier, Tax, Tears, Terrible, Thing, Thirst, Ton, Tongue, To put on egg, Tray, Two

Us, Utah

Vinegar

Wall, Water eat, Watermelon, Water taffy, While, White pepper, With, Worth, Wounds

SALTY

A, Acid, After, Alot, Always, And, Apple, Aspirins, At, Ate

Bacon, Baldy, Barbecue, Be, Beach, Bird, Bitterly, Black, Bland, Block, Blue, Body, Book, Brisk, Burger, Burn, Buttery, By

Cage, Cake, Captain, Car, Card, Carry, Caustic, Cell, Chicken, Chips, Cigar, City, Clean, Cocoa, Cookie, Cookies, Corn, Cow, Cream, Creamy, Crocks, Crust, Crystal

Dad, Deer, Delicious, Desert, Dirty, Do, Drink, Dull
Ear, Earth, Eating, Egg, Experiment
Fall, Fat, Fatty, Fingers, Fishy, Flake, Flat, Fly, Foods,
   Foul, French fries, Fruity, Fudge, Fun, Funny
Gang, Girl, Go, Goody, Grains, Gravel, Gravy, Grease, Gritty
Hamburger, Happy, Hard, Harsh, Has, Hay, Health, Help, Her,
   Here, Herring, Hi, Him, Hoarse, Horse, Hot ice, How
I, Ice, Icky, Icy, If, Iodine, Is, It
Jar head, Jump, Junk
Known
Land, Lettuce, Lick, Lid, Little, Lots of salt, Low
Malt, Man, Mangos, Map, Me, Meatly, Meet, Milk, Mine,
   Mortons, Mouth water, Mrs., My
Nasty, Nice, Nippy, No good, Non salty, No salt, Not, Not
   sweet, Now, Nut
Ocean water, Oh, Oily, One, Onions
Paper, Pepperish, Peppers, Personality, Pick, Pickle,
   Pickles, Pig, Pinch, Pizza, Plain, Please, Poison,
   Pop, Pork chops, Powder
Quite
Radishes, Rancid, Rat, Rich, River, Road, Rock, Rocks, Rocky,
   Root, Rotten, Run
Sad, Sale, Sally, Salted, Salt Lake City, Salt Lakes, Saltless,
   Salt lick, Salt shaker, Salt water, Salty, Sand, Sandwich,
   Sardines, Sat, Savory, Scare, Scented, Season, Seasoned,
   Seasoning, Sea water, See, Sew, Shade, Shakers, Shiny,
   Shore, Short, Shy, Sick, Sidewalks, Sleep, Slick, Slimy,
   Smart, Smell, Smooth, Sneeze, So, Some, Sore, Sorry,
   Spices, Spot, Spring air, Sprinkle, Sqeege, Starch, Stay,
   Steak, Sticky, Still, Sting, Stingy, Stocking, Stone, Store,
   Story, Strung, Suet, Sweaty, Sweetly, Sweety
Table, Tail, Tang, Tanging, Taste funny, Taster, Tastier,
   Teens, Terrible, Terribly, Test, The, There, This, Tickle,
   To, Toast, Toffee, Tomato, Tomatoes, Too, Too much,
   Tough, Tounge, Track, Train
Ugh, Um, Utah
Very
Warmer, Watery, Weiner, Well, Whitish, Wise, Wormy
Yes, You

SCISSORS

Across, And, Angry, Animal, Anything, At
Baby, Bad, Baseball, Bat, Before, Bitter, Black, Blades, Boat,
   Book, Books, Bore, Brother, Brothers, Bull, Bun, Butter
Cake, Can, Careful, Cat, Chop, Church, Clamp, Clean, Clip,
   Clippers, Close, Clothe, Clothes, Clothing, Cloths, Coat,
   Cold, Comb, Cop, Counter, Crabs, Cross, Cup
Dangerous, Dark, Dead, Discover, Doctors, Don't, Don't known,
   Down, Drawer, Dress
Easier, Easily, Eat, Eek, Equipment, Evil, Explorer
Far, Farm, Fast, Fat, Fingernails, Flat, Flying, Food, Foot,
   For, Fork, Founder, Free, Funny
Game, Gay, Get, Glass, Goodby, Green, Gun
Hair cut, Hammer, Hand, Handy, Have, Hazard, Head, Heart,
   Heavy, Help, Helpers, Helpful, Herald, High, Hill, Him,
   Hole, Hoppe, Horse, Hot
I, Ice, Ice cream, If, Ill, Indian, Instrument, Inventors, Is, It
Junk
Kick, Kit
Lake, Large, Letter, Lever, Light, Like, Listen, Little, Look,
   Looks, Loud, Luck
Mad, Made it, Mars, May, Mean, Merry, Microscope, Missing,
   Money, Monkey, Mother, Mouse
Nail, Narrow, Net, New, News, Nice, None, Nose, Not, Nothing,
   Nut
Object, Ocean, OK, Old, Only, Or, Ouch, Owner
Pain, Pair of, Paper dolls, Papers, Past, Pattern, Pen, Pencil,
   Picture, Pin, Pinking shears, Pins, Plates, Playing, Plier,
   Pointed, Poor, Print, Professor, Prongs
Quick, Quiet
Rabbit, Ranger, Razor, Razor blades, Red, Reflection, Rome
Sailor, Salesman, Salt, Saw, Scalpel, School, Scissor, Scythe,
   Sea, Secret, Sentence, Sever, Sewing tool, Sewn, Share,
   Shared, Shark, Sharpen, Shave, She, Shear, Ship, Shop,
   Short, Shout, Sick, Silent, Sister, Sisters, Six, Skirts, Sleep,
   Slice, Slivers, Small, Smart, Smoke, Snap, Some, Someone,
   Something, Son, Song, Sorry, Space, Spelling, Star, Start,
   State, Street, String, Suck, Sue, Sweet, Swim
Take, Tape, Tear, Tell, That, Thing amabob, Things, Think,
   Thirsty, Thor, Took, Tools, Toy, Trouble, True, Tweezers,

Two
Us, Use, Useful
Warm, Water, Way, Weapon, Wee, Which, White, Wind shields,
   Winning, Work, Worse, Wrestling, Wrist

SEE

Action, After, Ah, All, Along, Animals, Are, As, At, Ate,
   Away
Back, Be, Bear, Beautiful, Beauty, Believe, Better, Blinded,
   Blindness, Blink, Blue, Books, Boy, Boys, Bridge, Bright,
   Brown, Baby, But, Buy, By, Bye
C, Cane, Cannot, Cars, Cat, Cause, Chair, Chickens, Clearly,
   Clouds, Cornea, Country, Cow, Curt
Deer, Desk, Did, Discover, Dogs
Ear, Earth, Eat, Every, Everyone, Evil, Eye sight
Face, Fair, Fare, Faster, Father, Fatter, Fee, Find, Fish,
   Flee, Flower, Flowers, Fly, For, Forever, Forget, Friend,
   Full
Gail, Give, Glad, Glass, Goes, Going, Gone
Hard, Have, Heard, Hi, Hid, Hide, High, Horn, Horse, Hurt
I, Image, In, Intelligent, Invisible, Iris, Is, I saw
Jane, Jim, John, Just
Keep, Key, Kite, Know
Lake, Later, Leave, Lets, Letter, Life, Lift, Like, Line,
   Listen, Locate, Long, Longer, Looking, Lorryane, Love
May, Men, Mexican, Mirror, Miss, Money, Monkey, More,
   Mother, Movies, My
Nee, Neighbors, Night, No, Nothing, Not see
Object, Oh, Or, Out, Outside, Over, Over there
Paper, People, Person, Phil, Place, Playing, Poorly, Pretty,
   Psychology, Puppy
Quickly
Right, Row
Said, Sat, Save, Saw look, Say, Says, Scene, Scenery, School,
   See, Seeing, Seek, Seem, Sell, Sense, Sew, Shall, She, Shoe,
   Shore, Sightless, Sights, Sink, Sir, Site, Skipped, Sleep, Slide,
   Snow, So, Some, Someone, Space, Speak, Speed, Spied, Spy,
   Stare, Stars, Stay, Stop, Store, Straight, Sun
Talk, Tee, Test, Then, Those, Through, To, Took, Touch,
   Trees
Understand, Unseen, Up, Use, Usual
Valley, Visible
Walk, Water, Waves, Way, Wee, Weed, Well, Were, Wet, Why,
   Wide, Will, Window, Wonderful, Word
Ye, Yes, Your

SELL

Advertise, All, All out, Alms, Alone, Always, Any, Anyhow,
   Appliances, Are, Articles, At
Bad, Bake, Ball, Bananas, Bargain, Barter, Be, Because, Bee,
   Beg, Begin, Big, Bike, Bill, Bird, Birds, Biscuits, Block,
   Blood, Blue, Body, Boot, Borrow, Box, Boy, Bread, Bring,
   Brought, Brushes, Brushs, Brush salesman, Bud, Bug, Busy,
   But, Buyer, Bye
Cage, Call, Came, Cards, Carpets, Case, Cashier, Cash
   register, Cats, Celery, Cents, Cheap, Cheat, Chocolate bars,
   Clerk, Clerks, Close, Closet, Cloth, Clother, Cold, Collect,
   Comic, Comics, Con, Consumer, Cosmetics, Counter, Cow,
   Cows, Cream
Dad, Dell, Department, Department store, Dislike, Dolls,
   Donuts, Door, Down, Dress, Drink, Drugs, Dungeon
Eat, Eating, Egg, Eggs
Fast, Fence, Five, Flower, Fly, Foods, Formals, For sale,
   Found, Free, Furniture
Get rid of, Girl, Give away, Giving, Glass, Goodies, Got,
   Grain exchange, Grate, Grocer, Grocery, Grocery store
Hall, Happy, Hat, Haven't, Hay, He, Head, Hear, Heard, Hell,
   Her, Here, Hey, High pressure, Him, His, Hold, Home,
   Horse, Hose, Hot, Hustle
I, In, Ing, Insurance, Item
Job, Juice
Knife, Koolade
Lake, Lamp, Land, Lend, License, Like, Lipstick, Loan, Long,
   Lost, Lumber
Magazine, Make, Male, Mall, Material, Materials, Matter,
   May, Meat, Meats, Medicine, Men, Met, Milk, Mill, Mon,
   Monies, Monkey, Monkeys, Most, Move, Movies, Much, My
Narcotics, Never, Newspaper, No, Nose, Not, Nothing, Nut
Objects, Ocean, Oh, Oil, On, One, Open, Oranges, Order, Own
Package, Packages, Pail, Pans, Peanut, Peanuts, Pie, Pigs,

Pill, Pizza, Place, Plane, Popcorn, Pot, Profit, Puppy
Receive, Records, Roads, Rock, Room, Rooms, Round, Run
Sack, Said, Sail, Salami, Sales, Sales girl, Sales lady, Salt, Save, Say, School, Sea, Seal, Sea shells, Seed, Seeds, Self, Sellings, Send, Set, Shall, Shill, Ship, Shoe, Shop, Shot, Should, Show, Sign, Skunk, Slippers, Small, Snow, Sole, Solicit, Song, Soul, Spell, Spelling, Spend, Stamp, Stamps, Stand, Stay, Still, Stock, Stockings, Stocks, Stole, Stop, Stores, Story, Stuff, Stung, Suit case, Swap, Sweet
Table, Tack, Take, Talk, Talking, Taste, Taxes, Tell, Test, The, Theft, There, Think, This, Thomas, Those, Tickets, To, Tonic, Toy, Trade, Trailer, Traveler, Truck
Ulysses, Under, Up, Users
Vend
Wall, Want, Wares, Was, White, Who, Wholesale, Why, Window, Word, Words, Wore, Worms
Yellow, Yes, You sell things for money
Zell

SHEEP

Ants, Aquiline, Are, Australia
Ba, Baas, Bad, Bah, Barn, Bath, Bee, Ben, Bethlehem, Bible, Bird, Birth of Christ, Blue, Boy, Brothers, Bull calf, By
Camp, Cane, Cat, Cattle or herd, Christ, Clothes, Colt, Come, Comfortable, Conform, Cool, Cottage, Cotton, Country, Cuddly, Curls, Curly, Cut
Dad, Dairy, Dance, Dark, David, Day, Death, Deer, Dirty, Doe, Dogs, Doze, Dreaming, Dreams, Dress, Duck
Eagle, Enough, Ewes, Eyes
Fall, Farmer, Farms, Farm yard, Fast, Fat, Fields, Finger, Fish, Fleecy, Flocks, Flowers, Flute, Fodder, Follow, Followers, Fox, Furry, Fury, Fuzz
Girl, Go, Goal, God, Good, Good shepherd, Got, Gray, Green, Gregarious
Hairy, Half, Hard, Hate, Hay, He, Head, Hear, Help, Herding stick, Herdsmen, Here, High school, Hills, Hill side, Home, Horn, Horns, Horses, House, Hunting
Jesus, Jump, Jumping, Jumping fences
Kid
Lad, Lamb's wool, Lamps, Land, Lay, Leap, Ledge, Leg, Legs, Lice, Light, Lion, Little, Little animals, Live, Livestock, Llama, Long, Look, Lost
Mammal, Man, Many, Mary, Me, Meadow, Memory, Men, Messy, Monkey, Mother, Mountain, My farm, Myth
Nativity, Nice, Nimble, Noise
Old, Oxen
Pace, Pastor, Pastoral, Peaceful, Pen, People, Pig, Pillow, Plains, Pow wow, Pretty
Rain, Ram, Ranch, Relax, Relief, Report, Road
Sap, School, Scissors, Scotland, Seep, Shears, Sheep, Sheep dog, Sheep herder, Shepherds, Shirt, Shop, Shot, Show, Silly, Skin, Sleeping, Slept, Sling, Small, Smooth, Snore, So, Sour, Staff, Steep, Step, Stick, Street, Summer, Sun
Table, Tender, The, Thing, Thread, Tight, Tire, Too, Trouble, Try, Twenty
Unless, Up
Wake, Waken, Walk, Walking, Wall, Warm, Watch, Weak, What, Whish, Winter, With, Woman, Woolen, Work
Yard, Yes, You

SHOES

Ache, Am, Anklets, Arm, As
Baby, Back, Ballet, Barefoot, Baseball, Belt, Bird, Block, Blues, Boat, Body, Book, Books, Booze, Bother, Box, Boy, Breast, Bright, Buckles, But
Can, Can't, Chews, Classes, Cleaner, Clod hoppers, Close, Cloths, Clumsy, Coats, Cobbler, Color, Colt, Come, Comfort, Comfortable, Covering for feet, Cow, Cows, Crock
Dance, Did, Dirt, Dirty, Discomfort, Doc, Dog, Dogs, Door, Down town, Dress, Dresses, Dressing, Dropped
Eat, Eight C, Expensive
Family, Fast, Fat, Fear, Feel, Fill, Flat, Floor, Fools, Foot wear, For, Form, From, Frown
Garments, Get, Girl, Glow, God, Goes, Golf, Gone, Good, Got, Gray, Green, Gum, Gym
Hair, Hand, Hard, Has, Have, Hay, He, Heal, High, High heels, Hi heels, Him, His, Hoe, Hoes, Holland, Horn, Horse, Horse shoes, Hot, House, How, Howl
I, If, I'm, In, Is, It

Kill, Kind, Kinney's, Knew
Ladies, Large, Last, Leave, Leg, Legs, Lesson, Let, Letter, Like, Little, Loafer, Loafers, Long, Look, Loose, Loot, Lose, Loses, Love, Low, Low cuts
Maker, Man, Marriage, Match, Material, Men, Mine, Mitten, Mittens, Money, Moo, Moos, Movie, Musty
Nails, News, Nice, Not, Now, Nylon, Nylons
Ocean, Of, One, On feet, Orange, Ouch, Overshoes, Own, Oxford
Pain, Paper, Parrot, Pink, Plant, Play, Plenty, Points, Policeman, Protect, Protection, Purse, Put, Put on
Really, Right, Right and left, Road, Robbers, Rubber, Rubbers, Run, Running
Saddle, Saddles, Sake, Sales, Sandals, Scarf, Scrape, See, Sell, Set, Seven, Sew, Sharp, She, Shelly, Shining, Shirt, Shock, Shocks, Shod, Shoe lace, Shoes, Shoe store, Shone, Shoot, Shop, Shores, Shot, Should, Shows, Shut, Sidewalk, Sign, Size, Size thirteen, Skates, Skis, Slip, Slipper, Snow, So, Soft, Sold, Sore, Soul, Souls, Sour, Source, Spikes, Spoons, Stacks, Star, Stile, Stink, Stock, Stone, Stop, Stores, Story, Strap, Street, Suit, Sure, Sweater
Take, Talk, Tan, Tear, Tennis shoes, That, They, Things, Those, Tire, Tired, Togs, Too, Torn, Tree, Trees, Trip, Twos, Tying
Up
Wake, Walking, Ware, Warm, Warmth, Was, Wearing, Wet, What, Who, Why, Will, Wing, With, Wood, Wore, Work
Yes

SHORT

Absent, And, Angry, Ant, A short to
Ball, Barb, Baseball, Bermudas, Bill, Bird, Black, Block, Blow, Blue, Blunt, Body, Book, Boys, Brief, Brother, Brothers, Bullet, Burn, By
Carolyn, Cat, Chair, Child, Children, Circuit, Cloth, Clothes, Clothing, Coat, Coffee, Cold, Compact, Cool, Cord, Craig Harris, Crew cut, Cute
Dark, Dash, Day, Dead, Deer, Desk, Distance, Dog, Duck
Early, Easy, Eat, Egg, End, Enough
Far, Fast, Faster, Father, Fat man, Fay, Feather, Find, Finger, Fingers, Fire, Five feet, Five feet tall, Five foot one inch and under, Five foot nine inches, Flat, Flower, Fly, Food, Foot, Full, Fun, Furry, Fuzzy
Game, Gas, Gather, George, Girls, Good, Gown, Grass, Greg, Guy, Gym
Half, Hat, Haul, Head, Heart, Heavy, Height, Hit, Hole, Home, Hot, Hunting, Hurt, Hyphen
Inch, Inches, Inferiority, It
Janice, Jim, John
Karen, Killed, Kind, Kurz
Lag, Lame, Lard, Laura, Lazy, Leg, Lengthy, Letter, Life, Light, Linda, Lode, Log, Lone, Loud
Marvin, Mary, Medium, Midgets, Mike, Mile, Mix, Money, Mort, Mother, Mouse, Mouth, Mr. Courtney basketball coach, Mugs, Myopia, Myself
Nail, Narrow, Never, Night, Not, Not tall, Not too long, Now
One, One inch, Opposite of long, Order
Pen, People, Pig, Pigmies, Pistol, Play, Plump, Poem, Puffy, Punk, Puppy, Put
Quick, Quit
Race, Rapid, Ring, River, Rope, Ruler, Running, Runt
Sad, Sample, Second, Sentence, Shape, Sharon, Sharp, She, Shoot, Shore, Short, Short cake, Shorter, Short hand, Short person, Short stop, Shot, Shout, Show, Shrimp, Shrimpy, Size, Skimpy, Skirts, Slacks, Sleeve, Slight, Slow, Smallest, Small smallest, Smell, Smooth, Snappy, Socks, Some, Something, Sort, Sport, Squat, Squatly, Squatty, Stare, Steel, Step, Stiff, Stool, Stories, Story, Stream, String, Strong, Stubbing, Stuffed, Stuffiness, Stuffy, Stump, Stunted, Subject, Sweater, Sweet
Table, Tail, Tale, Talk, Test, There, Thick, Thing, Thy, Tight, Tough, Tow, Tree, Trouser, Two
Ugly, Unlong, Untall, Up
Vowel
Want, Warm, Water, Way, Wearing, Week, Weigh, Well, Were, Wet, While, Whiskey, Wide, Winter, Wish, Woman, Women, Word, Work

SICKNESS

Accident, Aches, Ail, Alive, Ape, At home, Awake, Awful feeling

Baby, Ban, Bedroom, Belly, Better, Big, Bill, Biting, Black, Blanket, Boil, Bold, Born, Boy
Cancer, Child, Clean, Close, Coat, Coffin, Cold or ill, Comfort, Coughing, Could, Crutches, Crying, Cure
Dad, Danger, Dark, Dark room, Davenport, Depressed, Died, Diet, Diphtheria, Diptheria, Discomfort, Diseases, Dizziness, Dizzy, Do, Doctors, Dog, Don't feel good, Down hearted, Dreary, Dry, Duck, Dull, Dying
Earache, Effect, Epileptic, Evil
Fall, Fat, Feel awful, Feel good, Feeling, Feeling bad, Feet, Fell, Feverish, Filing, First aid, Flag, Flew, Flue, Frightened, Fuel, Full
Germ, Girls, Glass, Glue, Go, Good, Grandmother, Groan, Guy in bed
Ha, Happiness, Happy days, Hard, Hat, Head, Heal, Healing, Heart, Heat, Heave, Heaving, Helpless, Her, Horrible, Horse, Hospitable, Hot, Hot water bag, Humor, Hurts
Ice, Ick, If, Ill diseases sick, Ill feeling, Is, Ish
Kill, Krank
Lad, Lag, Lazy, Leprosy, Lick, Lie, Life, Liveness, Lollypop, Lonely, Look, Looking, Loose, Loud, Love
Mad dog, Malaria, Men, Miserable, Mom, Mommy, Mono, Morbid, Morning, Mother, Mouse, Much
Nests, Non well, Nose, Not, Not good, Not happy, Not normal, Nursing
Of, Oh no, Oh oh, Okay, Old, Old person, Ow
Pail, Painful, Pains, Paleness, Palsy, Pane, Pep, Person in bed, Piano, Pill, Pity, Polio, Pretty, Purse, Presents
Quarantine
Recovery, Red, Restless, Rotten, Run
Saggy, Scared, Shot, Sister, Sleep, Sleepy, Small pox, Smell, Sneeze, Soap, Soft, Someone, Song, Sore, Sorrow, Sorry, Spots, Stethoscope, Stick, Stomach, Stomach ache, Strength, Strong, Stubs, Suffer, Suffering
Temp, The, The lake, There, Themometer, Thick, Thickness, Thing, Throat, Throw up, Tired, Tom Brown, Trouble, Tummy ache
Ugh, Ugly, Uh, Ulcer, Unhappy, Unhealthy, Unpleasant, Unwell, Upset, Us
Very, Virus, Vomiting
Wall, Warm, Wealth, Wet, White, Will, Woman, Worm
Yellow, Yellow slip

SIT
A, Among, Arm, Around, Ass, At
Baby sit, Back, Ball, Bank, Bath room, Because, Bed, Beg, Behind, Bench, Bending, Beneath, Beside, Boat, Boring, Brick, Brother, Bus, Butt, Buy, By
Car, Cards, Cars, Cat, Children, Coach, Comfort, Comfortable, Common, Cramped
Dad, Days, Decline, Desk, Dog, Doing, Donkey, Door, Dope, Downer
Easy, Eat
Far, Fast, Fat, Flat, Floor, For, Fun
Get up, Girl, Glove, Go down, Good
Hard, Hardys, Has, Heard, Her, Hide, High, Him, Hit, Hold, House
Ing, Ing room, Inn, Is, Its
Job, Jump
Kids, Kneel, Knit
Lap, Later, Law, Leg, Legs, Let, Light, Lit, Little, Long, Look, Lounge, Lower
Mate, Me, Meet, Milk, Mit, Mother, Move, My
Name, Near, Nervous, Next, Nice, Notion, Now
Off, On the floor, Ouch
Pant, Parlor, People, Person, Pit, Place, Play, Pot
Quietly
Ran, Read, Recline, Reed, Remain, Repose, Resting, Ride, Right, Rise, Rit, Rock, Room
Sand, Say, School, Seated, Set down, Settle, She, Ship, Shot, Side, Sight, Sister, Sit down, Sits, Six, Sleep, Slid, Small, Sofa, Soft, Someone, Song, Sore, Square, Squat, Stain, Stair, Standing, Stand up, Star, Start, Stay, Stood, Stop, Straight, Stretch
Table, Tease, Terrible, They, Thing, Think, Through, Tiring, To, Toilet, Top, Touch, TV
Under
Verb, Very
Wait, War, Was, Watch, Way, Wet, Why, Wiggle, Wit, With, Wood, Word, Work, Written

Yound, Young, Younger

SLEEP
Active, Acts, Afraid, Ah, Alarm, All, Always, And, Angel, Angry, Animal, Animals, Are, As, Asleep, Awakened, Awareness, Away, Awhile
Baby, Bad, Bag, Bat, Bead, Bedroom, Beds, Bed tired, Beg, Black, Blank, Blanket, Blankets, Bliss, Blue, Boat, Boy
Calm, Can't, Car, Catnap, Cattle, Chair, Closed, Cloth, Coat, Coma, Comfort relaxation, Conscious, Cool, Cough, Cover, Covers, Cow, Cozy, Creep, Crib, Cry
Dad, Darkness, Day, Day dream, Day dreaming, Death, Desire, Dexadrine, Die, Dog, Dormant, Down, Dozy, Dreamed, Dream land, Drink, Drunk
Ease, Easy, Eating, Eight hours, Energy, Enjoyable, Escape, Essential, Exhaustion
Faint, Fine, Fly, Food, Forget, Fur
Get up, Girls, Goat, Goats, Good morn, Good night
Habit, Hangover, Hard, Hate, Hazy, Head, Hear, Herder, Hilly, Him, Hobby, Home, Horse, Hour, House, Hunger
Insomnia
Knocked out, Knock out
Late, Laugh, Lay down, Laying, Leisure, Lie down, Like, Loud, Love, Luxury, Lying
Man, Matin, Me, Meat, Might, Mink, Mood, Mother, Movement, Mutton
Need, Needed, Never, Nigh, Night time, No, No doze, No feeling, Noise, Noon, Nose, No sleep, No sound, Not, Not awake, Not enough, Not moving, Now
Off, Only, Opposite of awake, Out
Pajamas, Pastures, Peacefulness, Peep, Piece, Pills, Play, Provoke
Read, Red, Refresh, Refreshing, Relaxable, Relaxation, Relaxed, Relief, Restlessness, River, Room, Run, Running
Sand, Scarce, School, Seed, Seldom, Sheet, Shepherd, Short, Shut eye, Sick, Silence, Silent, Sit, Sky, Slaughter, Sled, Sleep, Slow, Snow, Snow White, Snooze, Snug, Softly, Somber, Some, Somnia, Sonar, Soothing, Soundless, Squeek, Stand, Star, Steep, Still, Subconscious, Sweet
Talk, Tardy, Tent, Tetsi fly, Think, Thunder, Time, Tiredness, Together, Tonight, Toss, Trance, Tranquil, Tried, Tucked, TV
Under, Unhappy
Waken, Waking, Ware, Warmth, Water, Wear, Weep, White, Why, Wide, Wish, With, Woke, Wolf, Women, Wonderful, Work
Yarn, Yawn, Yellow, Yes
Zzz

SLOW
Acting, Aggravating, Aimless, Air, Almost stop, Also, Amble, Animal, Ann, Ant, A race, Awkward
Baby, Back, Ball, Bank, Basset dog, Beautiful, Beep beep, Bicycle, Big, Bike, Bird, Blow, Bog, Book, Bored, Boring, Bowl, Boy, Boys, Brake, Brother, Bug, Bugs, Bumpy, Bus, By
Call, Calm, Calvin, Camel, Cart, Casual, Cat, Caterpillar, Cautious, Class, Cloddy, Coat, Come, Common, Construction, Cool, Cow, Crash, Creeping, Creepy, Crow
Dance, Danger, Dawdle, Daze, Dead, Death, Deep, Dive, Do, Dog, Door, Droopy, Dry, Dull, Dump
Eating, Elephant, Engine
Fame, Far, Farther, Faster, Father, Fatter, Feat, Feet, Fifty Buick, Fight, Fine, Finish, First, Fish, Fool, Foot, Ford, Friend, Frustration, Fun
Girl, Girls, Glacier, Glow, Going, Go miles an hour, Good, Grade school, Grandpa
Halting, Hand, Harley, Hate, Hates, Hazard, Heavy, Hi, Hill, Hit, Holly, Homework, Horse, Hot, House
Icy, Inclined, Insane, Instating, Intersection, Irritable, Is
Jack, Joan, Job, Jody, Joggy, Jump
Lady driver, Lag, Lagging, Large, Last, Lazily, Laziness, Learner, Learning, Legs, Light, Lonny, Look, Lost, Lower
Mad, Made, Man, Math, Mean, Men, Middle, Middled, Milkes per hour, Most women, Motion, Motionless, Movement, Music, Myself, My sister
Never, Night, Noise, Not, Not moving, Now, Nuts
Obsolete, Oh, Opposite, Opposite of fast
Pace, Person, Pet, Phil, Pig, Pillow, Plodding, Plow, Poking, Policeman, Printing, Progress, Pull

Quiet
Race, Ran, Reader, Real, Reflexes, Relax, Retard, Rhythm,
Rough, Run down, Runner
Safe, See, Show, Sidewalk, Signs, Sign stop, Sings, Sister,
Skiing, Sleep, Sleepy, Slid, Slightly, Sloth, Slow, Slow car,
Slower, Slowest, Slow poke, Slow sign, Sluf, Small, Smooth,
Snails, Snow plow, Snow storm, So, Soft, Something, Speed-
less, Speedy, Spider, Steady, Step, Still, Stong, Stopped,
Stopping, Stop sign, Street, Street car, Street sign, Stuck,
Study, Stumpy, Stupidity, Sue, Summer, Sun, Sunday, Sunday
driver, Sunny, Sure, Susan Murray, Syrup
Table, Tag, Takes long, Tardy, Tell, Test, The, Thick, Thing,
Tie, Tire, Tiring, Today, Torpid, Tortoise, Traffic jam,
Trip, Truck, Trudge, Turtles, Twenty-five
Um, Unfast, Unfinished
Very, Volkswagon, Volkswagons
Wagon, Walker, Walk to school, Waltz, Warm, Water,
Weak, Wheel, Wiggling, Wind, Winter, Woman driver,
Woman drivers, Women, Women drivers, Wood, Worker,
Writer, Writing
Zone

SLOWLY

A, Accelerate, Across, Afraid, Along, Am, Amble, An, Are,
As, At, Away, Awful
Back, Bake, Be, Behind, Ben, Big, Boat, Boots, Bow, Bridge,
Bring, Bump, Buy, Buying
Calculus, Calm, Came, Camera, Can, Care, Carefully, Cars,
Cat, Cause, Caution, Cautious, Cautiously, Children, Christ,
Chugged, Class, Climb, Close, Closer, Club, Comes, Coming,
Consistant, Cow, Cramped, Crash, Crawling, Creepily,
Creeping, Crept
Danger, Dart, Dead, Deer, Dense, Die, Diver, Do, Dodge,
Dog, Doggie, Done, Door, Dragging, Drank, Drivers, Drop,
Drove, Drowsily, Dull, Dumb
Easily, Eat, Even, Evenly
Fall, Farther, Faster and faster, Fasting, Fasty, Fat, Father,
Feet, Fell, First, Flag, Flow, Flower, Foot, Funny
Gain, Get, Girl, Glide, Gradually, Grandpa, Grunt
Had, Happy, Hard, Harder, Hardly, Haste, Hell, High, Highly,
Hill, Hit, Holy, Hop, Horse, Hot, House, Hurry
I, Impatient, Improvement, Is, It, Its
Jumping, Jumps
Kiss, Knead
Land, Last, Late, Lazily, Leap, Learn, Leave, Left, Lie,
Light, Limp, Lion, Little, Long, Longer, Long Sam, Look,
Looking, Lost, Loud, Love, Low, Lowly
Mad, Man, Many, Mind, Mine, Molasses, Mom, More, Motion,
Moving, Mph, Much, My
Never, Nice, No
Of, Old, On, One, Others
Pace, Paddle, Panting, Paper, Patient, Pause, Peaceful,
People, Piece, Plane, Planes, Played, Plodding, Plow,
Pokes, Poor, Pose, Progress, Pull, Pump, Purse
Quiet
Race, Rapid, Rate, Real, Real slowly, Rest, Retardingly,
Rise, Rite, River, Road, Robbs, Running
Sad, Safe, Saunter, Say, School, Sea, Set, Seven, She, Ship,
Short, Shot, Should, Show, Sigh, Sing, Sir, Sit, Six, Ski,
Sleep, Slide, Slip, Slobber, Sloppy, Slouch, Slow down,
Slowed, Slowest, Slow motion, Slug, Sluggishly, Slyly, Small,
Smooth, Sneak, So, Soft, Some, Song, Soon, South, Speak,
Speedier, Speedy, Stalk, Stand, Stand still, Start, Statue,
Steadily, Steady, Stealthily, Stood, Stopping, Story, Strain,
Street, Strong, Struggle, Study, Stump, Stupid, Stupidity,
Sue, Sun, Swim
Table, Talk, Taster, Team, Tedious, Tell, Tempo, Tests, Their,
Then, They, Thick, Thing, This, Threw, Tide, Timidly,
Tin foil, Tiredly, To, Today, Too, Toward, Train, Travel,
Traveling, Trotting, Truck, Truth, Turn, Turns, TV, Two
Under, Undress, Unfast, Unwilling, Us
Waddle, Wake, Walked, Walks, Watch, Water, Weak, What,
Wheel, Where, Who, Why, Width, Will, Wind, Winter, Write,
Writing, Wrong, Wrote
Yes, You, Your

SMOOTH

Air, Airplane, Aluminum, American, An, Anything, Apple, Arm
Baby, Ball, Balloon, Beard, Bee, Beer, Began, Better, Bike,
Black, Black board, Bland, Blank, Blanket, Blankets,

Blonde hair, Boo, Boy, Bright, Bumble bee, Bump, Bumping,
Bumps, Butterfly
Cake, Calm, Candy, Carpet, Casual, Cat, Cement, Chair,
Chocolate, Choice, Chunky, Clay, Clear, Clothes pin, Coat,
Coat fur, Comfort, Comfortable, Cook, Cool, Cordoroy,
Cotton, Counter, Course, Cover, Crayon, Crime, Crooked,
Crude, Cub, Cuddle, Cup, Curve, Curved
Damn, Dark, Day, Delicate, Desert, Desks, Dog, Dress, Drink,
Dull, Dumb
Ease, Easily, Eat, Eating, Egg, Ever, Everywhere
Feather, Feel, Feeling, Fifteen, Fire, Fish, Flowing, Fluffy,
Food, Friction, Fruit, Fudge, Furniture, Furry, Fuzzy
Gads, Girl, Glad, Glide, Glossy, Goat, Going, Golf green,
Graceful, Gracefully, Grain, Grass, Grease, Greasy, Gruff,
Guy
Hand lotion, Handsome, Hare, Harsh, Haul, Head, Heard, Heavy,
Hill, Hilly, Horse, Hungry
If, Ivory
Janet, Jello
Kitten, Knife
Lake, Leather, Leg, Like, Like nice, Line, Linen, Lining,
Lip stick, Lotion, Love, Low, Lump
Malt o meal, Man, Marble, Mice, Milk, Mirror, Money, Moon,
Mooth, Mother, Mountain, Mouth, Muscle
Neat, No bumps, Nose, Not bumpy, Not hard, Nutty
Ocean, Oily, Operator
Paint, Palm, Pen, Pencils, Piano, Pillow, Pink, Plan, Planed
wood, Plastic, Pleasant, Pleasing, Polish, Polished, Pretty,
Pudding, Puddy, Pure
Quick, Quit
Raged, Ragged, Razor, Reflective, Relaxing, Rhythm, Ride,
Rifle, Ring, Roads, Rock, Rocket, Rocky, Rode, Rounded,
Ruffled, Rug, Rugged, Rumple, Run
Sanded, Satiny, Saw, Scrape, Scratchy, Sculpture, Seat, Secret,
See, Set, Shaggy, Shake, Shave, Sheet, Sheets, Shining, Ship,
Shore, Should, Sick, Sidewalk, Silver, Skimp, Skinny, Sky,
Sleep, Slick, Slide, Slim, Slip, Smooth, Snake, Snow, So,
Soap, Soda, Soft hair, Soft pretty very soft, Solid, Sooth,
Soothing, Spread, Steel, Sticky, Stiff, Still, Stomach, Straight-
ness, Strait, Stream lined, Stroke, Strong, Sweater, Sweet,
Swift
Taffy, Talk, Tall, Tanned, Teeth, Texture, Three, Time, To,
Tomato, Too, Tooth, Top, Touch, Tree
Unrough, Unsmooth
Varnish, Velvet like
Walk, Wave, Wax, Well, What, White, Wing, With, Women,
Wonderful, Wool, Worry, Wreath, Wrinkle, Wrinkled,
Wrinkles, Writing
You

SO

Able, About, Abstract, Admonish, After, Ah ah, Ah ha, Air,
Al, All, Almost, Along, Als, Always, An, And so, Angry,
Answer, Ant, Anyhow, Argue, As to do, Ate
Bad, Balloon, Bat, Being, Be it, Belong, Besides, Big deal, Book,
Bow, Boy, Brat, Bring, Button, By
Candy, Care, Careful, Caught, Cause, Cheered, Chinese,
Chunking, Clean, Clear, Closer, Clothes, Cold, Comment,
Complain, Completely, Conjunction, Consequently, Cook,
Cracks, Crash, Crow
Dare, Dead, Debate, Different, Doing, Done, Don't, Dose,
Dough, Dress, Driver
Easy, Elk, Else, Emphasis, Ends, Engine, English, Etc., Ever,
Exclamation, Explanation, Expression,
Fact, Family, Fare, Fat, Fee, Few, Finding, Finer, Finished,
First, Fix, Food, Found, Fourth, Free, From, Fussy
Get, Goes, Going on, Golf, Goodbye, Gophers, Great, Guilty,
Guy
Ha, Had, Happened, Has, Hat, Have, Hear, Height, Hello, Her,
Hesitate, Hi, High, His, Hoe, Hot, How come, However
I'm, In addition, In case, In order, In order to, Instead, Its
Japan, Jealous, Joanne, Just, Just right
Knit
Large, Late, Let, Lets, Like, Likewise, Line, Little, Lo,
Look, Lot, Loud, Love
Machine, Mad, Make, May, Maybe so, Men, Mend, Mi, Mice,
Milk, Mine, Minutes, Moe, Mom, Moo, More, Mother, Mrs.,
Mush, Music, Must, My
Need, Needles, Never, New, Nit, No care, No opinion, Note,
Notes, Nothing, Numbers, Nut, Nuts

O, Of, Often, Okay, Once, Open, Or, Other, Ouch, Out, Over
Paint, Paper, People, Plain, Poke, Position, Pretty
Quite
Reading, Red, Remark, Remember, Right, Rough, Result, Run
Said, Same, Sand, Sassy, Sea, Seed, Seem, Seen, Send, Set,
Seven, Shall, Short, Show, Sigh, Sin, Sing, Single, Sissy,
Slop, Smart, Snob, Snotty, Snow, Soap, Sock, Soe, Sol,
Solo, Someone, Something, Song, So nice, Sore, Sorry, So so,
Sought, Soul, South, Spelling, Statement, Stood, Stop, Store,
String, Strong, Such, Sue, Sun, Surprise, Suspicion, Sweet
Take, Talk, Talking, Tall, Tell, Ten, Than, Thats, Thee, Their,
Them, Thereby, These, They're, Thin, Thing, Those, Thou,
Though, Three, Time, Toe, Told, Tow, Train, True, Two
Under, Until, Up
Want, Warms, Way out, Weave, Went, Were, What of it, Where,
Who cares, Why not, With, Wo, Words, Wrong
Yea, Yet, Young, You're

SOFT

Aches, Ah, Air, Alluring, Apple
Balky, Banana, Beautiful, Bed pillow, Bellow, Below, Big,
Billow, Boy, Bread, Brick, Bright, Brown, Bumpy, Bunnys,
Butter, By
Cake, Car, Caress, Caressing, Cats, Caught, Charmin, Cheek,
Chiffon, Child, Clean, Clinging, Clothes, Cloud, Club, Coarse,
Coat, Cold, Collar, Color, Comforting, Comfortly, Cool,
Cover, Cuddle, Cushioned, Cushiony, Custard
Dainty, Davenport, Delicate, Dog, Down, Downy, Dry, Duck,
Dull
Ear, Eggs, Eight, Enchanting, Eyes
Fat, Feather bed, Feel good smooth, Feeling, Feminine, Fight,
Fill, Fine, Fire, Flabby, Fleece, Fleecy, Flip, Flouncy,
Fluff, Fly, Foam, Foaming, Foam rubber, Fragile, Fully
Gently, Girls, Glass, Go, Going down, Gooey, Gotten, Green,
Grey, Ground
Had, Hands, Have, Heart, Hearted, Heave, Heavily, Height
Ice, Ice cream, In, Iridescent, It
Jan, Jelly, Jumping
Kathy, Kleenex
Laying, Lazy, Leather, Lighter, Liquid, Lo, Loaf, Lock, Lode,
Lovable, Love, Luxurious
Man, Mattress, Mellow, Melt, Mild, Mink, Mist, Mom, Moon,
Mop, Mushrooms
Near, New, Night, Nitrogen, No, Noisy
Ocean, Of, Off, Oh boy, Old, Ooooh, Oozy, Open, Opposite of
hard, Ouch
Paper, People, Pillows, Place, Pleasant, Pliable, Plump,
Plushy, Pop, Powder puff, Puffy, Puppy, Purr, Push
Quilt, Quite
Rabbit, Radiant, Red, Relaxation, Rest, Restful, Robe, Rubber,
Rug
Sand, Sat, Scot tissue, Scratch, Seen, Serene, Sharp, Sheep,
Shining, Show, Sick, Silent, Silky, Silt, Sink, Sister, Sleeping,
Slick, Slow, Slush, Snob, Snug, Snuggly, Soap, Softer,
Softness, Solid, Soothing, Sore, Sour, Spongy, Spring,
Springing, Square, Squashy, Squeeze, Straight, Sweetly
Teddy bear, Texture, The, Thick, Thigh, Thing, Tiny, Tissues,
Toilet paper, Tone, Top, Touching, Tough, Towel
Use
Very
Week, Wet, Whisper, Who, Wool blanket, Wooly
Young

SOLDIER

Ache, Afraid, Ahead, Airman, A man who fights, America,
Anger, Annapolis, Anyone, A part of body, Armed, Armies,
Arms, Army man, Army Navy Marines, Authority
Baby, Badge, Bad guy, Band, Battler, Big bold, Big deal, Bill,
Billet, Bird, Blood, Blue army, Bob, Body, Bone, Books,
Bought, Box, Boy Scout, Brace, Brawl, Brigade, Broad,
Brothers, Buddy, Buy
Cabbage, Cadet, Camp, Castle, Cat, Cavalry, Chicken, Clod,
Colonel, Combat, Come, Commander, Commando, Confederate,
Cop, Corp, Corporal, Courageous, Cousin, Cross, Cuba, Cup,
Cute boy
Dad, Dead, Deep, Defense, Denny, Destroyer, Dick, Did not,
Die, Died, Dies, Dirt, Dirty, Disciple, Do, Doll, Don't, Dress,
Drill, Drink, Drum, Dude, Dusty
Each, Ear, Eat, Eddie, Eisenhower, Elbow, Enlisted
Fat, Father, Feet, Fellow, Fierce, Fife, Fights, Finger, Fire,

Fly, Fly boy, Flyer, Fool, Force, Friends, Fright, Ft. Sill,
Funny
George Washington, German, Glorious, Grave, Great, Grenadier,
Grey, Ground, Guardian, Guards, Gunner
Ha, Had, Hand, Happy, Hard guy, Hard work, Hat, Hate, Heart,
Helper, Helpful, Helps, Him, Holder, Home, Honor, Honorable,
Horse, Hot, House, Houses, How, Hup two three four, Hurt,
Hut
Jerk, John, Jupiter
Kennedy, Kenny, Killed, Killer, Killing, Knight, Knights,
Korea, KP
Ladder, Lady, Lamps, Laos, Law, Lazy, Leader, Leaf, Leather,
Leg, Liberty, Lieutenant, Likeable, Loaded, Lonesome, Lt.
Machine, Mad, Major, Make, Manager, Man important, Man in
battle, Man in war, Many, Marches, Married, Master, Me,
Mean, Melt, Metal, Military forces, Militia, Mind, Misfit,
Missiles, Model, Mold, Monarch, Monkey, Mountie, Movie,
Mud, Muddy
Neat, Neck, Never, Night, No, Not, Now, Number, Nurse, Nut
Of, OK, On, On guard, Orders, Outfit
Patriot, Pay, People, Pete, Pilot, Pioneer, Police, Policeman,
Pop, Power, Precise, President, Priest, Prince, Prisoner,
Protect, Protection, Protector, Proud, Pull
Queen
Radio, Ralph, Ralph war, Rat, Rebel, Reds, Regiment, Regimen-
tation, Regimented, Revolving, Rim, Roar, Roman, Ron,
Rough, Rough Riders, Rugged
Sail, Sailors, Sale, Salute, School, Scout, Sea, Sell, Service,
Seventeen, Sew, Sharp, Ship, Shirt, Shoes, Shouting, Sleep,
Sleeve, Smart, Smooth, Snipe, Soft, Softer, Soldier, Soldier
man, Soon, Sorrow, Sound, Spider, Spoon, Stand, Standing
straight, Station, Statue, Stern, Stomping, Story, Stout, Strait,
Strict, Stripes, Stupid, Suit, Sweat, Swept, Sword
Table, Taller, Tan, The, Thick, Tim, Time, Tin soldier, Tired,
Tony, Toys, Travel, Trench, Troop, Trooper, TV
U.S., Uncle, United States, Unnecessary, U.S. War two
Veteran, Volunteer
WAC, Want, Warfare, Warm, War man, Wars, Was, Wayne,
Weapon, Wear, Web, West Point, What, Wife, Woman, Women,
Won, Wonderful, Wood, Wooden, Worker, Working, Wound,
Wounded
Young man

SOUR

Ache, Air, Airplane, Appeal, Apricots, Arm, Artichokes, Away
Bad face, Bad tasting, Bandage, Band aid, Basement, Bead,
Beautiful, Bed, Bee, Beer, Berry, Better, Black, Blood,
Book, Bottle, Box, Boy, Breath, Browse, Bruise, Bump,
Burn, Bus, Butter, By
Candy, Cheese, Cherry, Citrus, Clabbor, Clean, Corked, Corn,
Cot, Cottage cheese, Crabby, Craig L., Cross, Cry, Crying,
Cup
Dark, Deep, Den, Died, Dill pickles, Dirt, Dislike, Distasteful,
Dive, Do, Dog, Done, Door, Doughnuts, Dr., Drain, Dried
grapes, Drink, Dull
Early, Earth, Eating, Egg, English, Enough
Face, Fall, Far, Feet, Filling, Finger, Flat, Flinch, Flood,
Flu, Fork, Foul, Foul taste, Four, Friend, Frown, Fun,
Funny, Funny face
Game, Garbage, Gin, Girl, Girls, Glad, Glide, Go, Gone, Grape
juice, Grapefruit juice, Grave, Green, Green apple, Gum drop
Ham, Hands, Head, Heat, Heel, Herd, Hit, Horn, Horrible,
Hot, Hour, How, Hurts
Ill
Juicy
Knife, Kool aid, Kraut
Lake, Least, Letter, Lime, Little, Long, Low, Lumpy
Made, Make, Mash, Meat, Mellow, Melt, Met, Mice, Mike, Mix,
Money, Monkey, More, Mr. Downs, Mumps, Music, My
Name, Nauseating, Neuter, Nine, No, Non sour, North, Note,
Nothing, Not sour
Office, Okay, Olives, On, Onions, Orange juice, Oranges
Pan, Pancake, Pancakes, People, Pepper, Pick, Picture, Pine-
apple, Pipe, Place, Plans, Pleasure. Plenty, Plum, Plums,
Point, Poison, Poor, Positive, Pour, Prune, Prunes, Pucker-
ing, Puckery, Pure
Raw, Red, Refrigerator, Repulsive, Rich, Ripe, Rough, Run,
Rutabaga
Sand, Sandy, Sat, Scab, School, Scratch, Semi-sweet, Set,
Shepherds, Ship, Short, Shoulder, Sick, Sickening, Sister, Ski,

Skin, Sky, Sleep, Slurp, Smelling, Smells, Smelly, So,
Soar, Soda, Soiled, Some, Somethings to eat, Sore, Sort,
Soul, Sour cream, Souring, Sour milk, Spat, Spinach, Spit,
Spoil, Squint, Stall, Sting, Stomach, Stop, Store, Strong
tasting, Sugar, Sugarless, Sun, Sweetened, Sweeter, Swept,
Syrup

Table, Tang, Tart, Task, Tasteful, Tasteless, Tastes awful,
Tasting, Tasty, Teacher, Teachers, Terribly, The, Thing,
Tired, Tomatoes, Tonic, Too, Tooth, Top, Traveling, Treble,
Trouble

Ugh, Uh, Uncomfortable, Unfriendly, Ungood, Unlike, Unpleasant,
Unsweetened, Untasting, Untasty, Up

Vomit, Vowels

Wall, Warm, We, Week, Well, Were, Wet, Whee, White, Why,
Wiry, Wish, Wood, Work, Wound, Would, Wrong, Wry

You, Yours

SPEAK

A, Across, Actor, Address, Age, Am, And, Answer, Ant,
Appreciate, Arf, As, Ask, At, Auditorium

Babble, Back, Bad, Bark, Be, Be quiet, Bet, Better, Blab,
Black, Blur, Body, Boredom, Boy, But

Call, Can, Candy, Cat, Check, Class, Clean, Clearer, Command,
Communicate, Contest, Conversation, Correctly, Cough,
Could, Cow, Crowd, Curiosity

Darn, Darrone, Day, Devil, Dirt, Dishes, Distinctly, Dogs, Dot,
Drinks, Drunk

Eagle, Ear, Easily, Ever, Every

Fall, Far, Faster, Fat, Father, Fight, Fine, First, Fly, Food,
For, Framer, Free, French, Friday

Geno, Gently, German, Giggle, Group

Hard, Have, He, Heart, Heat, Hi, Hill, Hit, Ho, Hold, Holler,
Holy, Hop, How, Humphrey, Hush

I, Idea, In, Indian, Is

Kiss, Kittens, Know

Lad, Lady, Large, Later, Leak, Lecture, Lee, Let, Light,
Lips, Long, Lower

Mail, May, Meat, Meek, Meet, Meeting, Microphone, Mike,
Month, More, Moth, Mother, Mrs.

Nervous, Never, Norse, Noses, Notes, Nothing

Oh, OK, On, Only, Oral, Orate

Paper, Parrot, Past, Pat, Pea, Peace, Performer, Person,
Phone, Piece, Pig, Plainly, Plane, Please, Poke, President

Quest, Quick, Quickly, Quietly, Quit, Quite

Radio, Rapidly, Rayburn, Red, Reply, Report, Rostrum, Round,
Running

Sassy, Sat, Saying, Scared, School, Selling, Seven, Sew, She,
Shot, Shut, Sign, Simple, Sioux, Sir, Sit, Sky, Slant, Slap,
Sleep, Slower, Snake, Softer, Someone, Song, Spank, Speakless,
Speaks, Spear, Speck, Speeches, Speed, Squack, Squeak, Squeek,
Stage, Stake, Stand, Stay, Steak, Stop, Stutter, Sue, Sun,
Swear, Swedish, Swimming

Table, Talkative, Talked, Talker, Talking, Talk squeal, Tall,
Teach, That, Their, Them, Then, They, Time, Tired, Today,
Together, Told, To me, Too, Travel, Trees, Truth, Truth-
fully, Twice

Unspoke, Us, Utter

Vocal

Wait, Walk, Wall, Water, We, Weak, What, While, Who, Why,
World

Yelling, Yes, Yourself

SPIDER

Africa, An animal, And, Animals, Anthropod, Ants, Arm, A
small insect, Ate, Aunt

Back, Bag, Bait, Banana, Bananas, Bead, Beautiful, Beetle,
Beets, Belt, Bile, Biology, Bit, Black tarantula, Black widow
spider, Blank, Board, Body, Bog, Book, Boy, Broke, Brother,
Bud, Bunch of legs, Bus, Butter

Camp, Car, Cat, Cats, Cellar, Center, Citizen, Claw, Cloth,
Cobweb, Cobwebs, Cocoon, Cold, Colt, Come, Comfortable,
Corner, Could, Cow, Crawfish, Crawler, Crawls, Crawly,
Creator, Creep, Creeps, Crime, Cringe, Cut, Cute

Daddy long leg, Daddy long legs, Danger, Dangerous, Dark, Day,
Dead, Death, Did, Dinner, Dirt, Dissecting, Dislike, Dust

Eat, Edge, Enemy, Evil

Fall, Fat, Fiendish, Fire, Flies, Floor, Flying, Food, Fork,
Friend, Frighten, Frog, Fun, Funny, Fur, Furry

Gang, Get, Girls, Go, Gone, Grass, Grasshopper, Ground

Hair, Hairy, Hand, Hanging, Hard, Harmful, Hate, He, Head,

Heat, Help, Hid, High, Hill, Hitter, Hold, Hold up, Horrid,
Horror, Horse, House

I, Ice, Ick, If

Jar, Jim

Known

Lady, Large, Life, Light, Like, Little, Little Miss Muffet,
Living, Long legs, Looking, Loria, Luck, Lyropsid

Mad, Made, Make, Mammal, Man, Many, Many legs, Marvel,
Mary, Me, Mean, Men, Microscope, Middle, Miss Muffet,
Money, Month, Mosquito, Moth, Mouse, Mouth, Movie,
Mud, Muffet, Muffin, Musty

Nail, Name, Nasty, Nauseous, Neat, Need, Nice, Nine, Noise,
Not nice, Nuts

Old, Ouch, Out, Over

Pain, Pan, Pants, Part, Pen, Penny, Pest, Pet, Pie, Pill, Pin,
Pin striping, Poems, Possum, Pot, Porridge, Prey

Rabbit, Rain, Rake, Ran, Rat, Ready, Red, Relaxed, Reptile,
Repulsive, Rider, Right, Robe, Rock, Rode, Rough, Round,
Rudder

Sac, Saw, Science, Scorpion, Screams, Sear, Set, Sharp, Shoo,
Shove, Show, Side, Sider, Silk, Silky, Six legs, Skinny, Skip,
Slice, Slide, Slimy, Sliver, Smell, Snail, Snakes, So, Soft,
Something with eight legs, Sore, Spice, Spider, Spiders,
Spider webs, Spied, Spindle, Spindler, Spindley, Spinning,
Spit, Spring, Squirmy, Squish, Steel, Stick, Stool, Stop, Store,
String, Sun, Swimming, Swing

Tacker, Take, Tender, Terror, Thin, Thread, Threatening,
Tickle, Tingling, Top, Tremble

Unclean, Up

Villain

Walk, Warm, Wasp, Water, Weasel, Wed, Weeps, Weird, Wet,
What, Wide, Wider, Window, With, Woman, Women,
Wonderful, Wool, Worker,

Yard, Yarn, Yell, Yes, Yikes

SQUARE

Acre, Activities, A equals S squared, Air, All sides equal, Am,
Angles, Animals, A nut, Anyone, A place, Area, Astronomy

Bad, Ball, Bare, Bat, Bear, Beatniks, Beats me, Bill, Bird,
Black Beauty, Block or cube, Bong, Boom, Bottom, Bowl,
Boxes, Boys, Brat, Brick, Bricks, Brother, Bug, Buildings,
But, Butterfly

Cage, Can, Canton, Car, Cars, Cat, Cats, Cement, Central,
Chess, Church, Circular, Circumference, City square, Class-
room, Climb, Clock, Clod, Cloth, Cold, Color, Columbus,
Common, Common man, Compass, Confine, Cool, Country,
Court, Court yard, Crazy, Creep, Crib, Cross, Crowded,
Cry, Cub, Cubesville, Cubic, Curb

Dad, Dame, Dances, Dark, Dear, Deep, Dense, Design, Diamond,
Dice, Different, Dimension, Dimensions, Dobie Gillis, Dog,
Don't get any place, Door, Dope, Doug, Down, Drawing,
Dull, Dumb, Dump

Eating, Edge, Edges, Egg, Enclosing, England, Engle, English,
Enough, Eraser, E squared, Exactness

Fair, Far, Fast, Fat, Fay, Fellow, Fence, Field, Floor,
Flower, Flowers, Flute, Food, Fool, For, Fore, Fountain,
Four corner, Four corners, Four cornered, Four edges, Four
ends, Four lines, Four side, Four sided, Fraction, Fractions,
Frame, Franklin, Friend, Friends, Fudge, Funny

Game, Geom, Girl friend, Girls, Go, Goof, Grader, Grand,
Grand square, Gray, Green, Guard, Guy Lombardo,

Hair, Half, Hard, Has, Having, Hegna, Her, Hexagon, History,
Hit, Hole, Holland, Home, Honest, Houses

Ice, Ice cubes, Ill, In, Inches, Intersection, In town, Is

Jim Lindman, Jinny Young, John, John Farmer, Jones

Kisling, Knit, Kookie

Lady, Land, Large, Lawrence Welk, Lee, Lester, Light, Like,
Like man, Little, Live, Load, London, Lot, Low

Madison, Madison Sq. Garden, Mall, Many, Market place, Mary,
Math class, Mathematics, Meal, Measure, Measurement,
Measures, Meeting, Memorial, Middle, Milk, Min, Mine,
Minneapolis, Minute, Misfit, More, Moscow, Mouth,
Mr. Engle, Mr. Lery, Mr. Payne

Names, Nation, Neat, New York City, Nice, Ninety, Not, Not
a circle, Not round, Number

Octagon, Old, One, Orderliness, Other boys, Out of mind, Out
of place

Packed, Pair, Pan, Parallelogram, Pare, Parents, Paris,
Parking, Part, Part of city, Payne, Peanut, Pegasus, Pen,
Pepper, Perfect, Perimeter, Phoney, Physics professor,

Piccadilly, Picture, Piece, Pink, Place, Play, Pointed, Points, Polygon, Pooch, Poop, Public
Quick, Quit
Rabbit, Read, Rectangular, Red, Red square, Regular, Rick Scarlet, Right, Right angles, Road, Robot, Rock, Rod, Roll, Room, Roots, Rough, Round house, Rug, Rulers, Run, Russia
Salad, Sally, Same, Sandy Balchunas, Sat, Scare, Scarf, School, Security, Shaped, Sheep, Shooter, Shop, Shut, Side, Simple, Simpleton, Sister, Sit, Slow, Smith, Smooth, Soft, Solid, Somebody, Sound, Southdale, Space, Spain, Spring, Square, Squared, Square head, Squirrel, Stag, Stamp, Station, Statue, Stoop, Straight, Stupid, Sweet, Symmetrical, Symmetry
T, Table top, Tear, Tests, Than, The mall, The middle, There, The teacher, Thing, Tile, Times Square, Toe, Tore, Town center, Toy, Trees, Triangular, Twelve feet, Two
Unsharp, Up
Vile, Villa
Walk, Washington, Watch, Water, Week, Went, Wheel, Where, Wide, Width, Work
Yards, Yd., Yes

STAND

Agony, Ah, All, Along, Apple, Are, Arise, Aside, At ease, Attention
Bad boy, Baseball, Beach, Bears, Before, Beg, Behind, Beside, Bleachers, Board, Bought, Box, Boy
Came, Can, Car, Cart, Chalk, Clear, Click, Cliff, Climb, Closer, Coke, Come, Common, Concrete, Cool aid, Could, Cow, Crest, Crowd, Custer's last, Cutters
Day, Debout, Deer, Describe, Desk, Did, Dive, Do, Dog, Done, Down, Draft
Ease, Ed, Express
Fair, Falling, Fan, Farther, Feat, Fight, Fined, Firm, First, Five, Food, For, Forth, Front, Fruit
Game, Girl, Girls, Glad, Globe, Going, Grade, Grand, Grand stand, Ground, Guard
Ha, Hair, Hands, Hard, Hat, He, Height, Help, Hers, Hill, Him, Hoarse, Holder, Home, Hot dogs, House, How, Hurt
If, Ing, Is, Island
Kneel, Knight
Lake, Laugh, Lean, Leave, Left, Lemon, Like, Lincoln, Long, Looked, Looking, Lye
Make, Me, Men, Mount, Move, Mr. Strand, Music, My
Name, Neck, News, Newspaper, Next, Next to, Nice, No, North, Not, Not sit, Now
Of, On feet, Open, Order, Our, Out, Outside, Owl
Paint, Pan, Paper, Papers, Parade, Party, Peanuts, Pedestal, Pencil, Picture, Platform, Pole, Port, Post, Posture
Quietly
Ran, Refreshment, Relax, Rest, Right, Rise, Road, Rock, Rocks, Root beer
Said, Sank, Say, School, Seat, Second, See, Selling, Shake, She, Shie, Shoes, Shop, Shout, Sill, Site, Sit up, Skip, Slump, Soft, Softly, Solid, Some, Sore feet, Sound, Spand, Speaking, Spot, Stage, Stall, Stan, Stand by, Stands, Stand up, Stare, Stared, Star Spangled Banner, Start, State, Stationary, Statue, Steel, Step, Stole, Stone, Stop, Store, Straight, Strand, Stream, Street, Stretch, Stump
Table, Tail, Talk, Tan, Tand, Tea, Test, That, The, Then, Thin, Thirst, This, Time, To, Together, Too, Took, Tool, Tree, Twins, Two
Unsit, Up right, Us
Vegetable
Waiting, Walking, Want, Ward, Warm, Was, Way, We, Were, What, White, Who, Witness, Work
Yell, You
Zebras

STEM

Age, Alfalfa, Ant, Anything, Apples, At
Bad, Beam, Beetle, Behind, Big, Bitter, Black, Bloody, Blossom, Blow, Body, Boil, Boot, Born, Bowl, Boy, Bra Branches, Brand, Bread, Break, Breathes, Brook, Bulb, Bunch, Bush, But, Butter, Button, By by
Chlorophyll, Clip, Clothes, Clouds, Coffee, Coffee pot, Color, Cook, Cooking, Cool, Cord, Core, Cristy,
Damp, Dandelion, Den, Dig, Dog, Doing, Donkey, Don't, Door, Dope, Down, Drive, Dry
Easy, Eat, Ending, Evaporate, Evaporation
Fall, Farm, Fat, Father, Faucet, Filter, Fin, Fish, Fix,

Flour, Flow, Flows, Food, Foot, Fresh, Frost, Fuel, Fun, Funny
Gas, Girl, Go, Grape, Grass, Ground
Hand, Handle, Hard, Harsh, He, Head, Hell, Help, Hen, Hi, High, Hill, Hold, Hot water, House, Hurry
I, If, Ignorance, In
Kettle, King
Lake, Left, Lem, Lemon, Life, Light, Like, Lily, Lime, Look, Lot
Machine, Mad, Main, Make, Man, Me, Mean, Mellow, Monkey, Motor, Mountain, Move
Name, New, Nice, No, Nothing, Nut
Object, Of, One
Part, Part of flower, Part of plant, Peace, Peach, Peat, Petal, Petals, Petiole, Piano, Pistil, Pistol, Plan, Planet, Plans, Plants, Plants end, Pod, Point, Pole, Pop, Pot, Power, Puff, Pumpkin
Rain, Rat, Red, Rhubarb, Rise, River, Rivers, Rod, Room, Roots, Rope, Rough, Run
Science, Seat, See, Sew, Shoot, Short, Skiing, Skinny, Skip, Sky, Slender, Slim, Slow, Small, Smog, Smoky, So, Soft, Soup, Sow, Spray, Stamen, Stamp, Stand, Start, Steam iron, Steep, Step, Stigma of a plant, Still, Store, Straight, Straw, Strict, String, Stump, Suffix, Support, Sweat
Table, Tea, Teacher, Team, Tea pot, That, Thing, Think, Thought, Tip, Top, Trees, Trim, True, Tube
Vase, Vegetable, Vegetation
Walk, Want, Warm, Warm air, Water and gas, Weed, Wet, Wheat, Wind, Winter, Wire, Woman, Word, Work
Yarn, Yellow, Yes, You, Youth

STOMACH

Aches, Aching, Acids, Act, Agony, A grind, Am, Anacin commercial, Animal, A place where your food is, Appendix, Apple, Ate, Awful
Baby, Bag, Ball, Bath, Beer, Belch, Belly button, Belt, Billy, Birches, Black, Bladder, Bleach, Bleed, Blood, Bloody, Boats, Bodies, Body part, Bold, Bored, Born, Bowl, Boy, Bread, Breast, Brown, Bufferin, Burps, Butterfly, Button
Cage, Cancer, Candy, Car, Cardiac, Cat, Cave, Cavity, Chief, Child, Chin, Churn, Circle, Clothes, Coat, Cold, Colon, Color, Come, Complicated, Contentment, Cow, Cramp
Desk, Diagram, Did, Die, Digesting, Digestive, Doctor, Dog, Dogs, Dress, Dr. W. Mayo
Each, Earth, East, Endoderm, Eye
Feel, Finger, Fish, Fist, Five, Fluid, Food basket, Food container, Food is put, Fool, Foot, Frighten, Frog, Fun, Function, Funny
Gall bladder, Gastric, Gastric juices, Gee, Girdle, Girl, G.I. tract, Gizzard, Gland, Go, Green, Gullet, Gurgle
Had, Hand ache, Hands, Hat, Headache, Heart burn, Heat, Help, High, Him, Hit, Holder, Hold food, Holds, Hole, Hollow, Hot, House, Hurry, Hydrochloric acid
Icky, Indian, Ingestion, Inside of you, Inside your body, Internal, Iron, Ishy
Jelly
Kiss, Kissing
Lady, Leaves, Leg, Legs, Light, Like, Lion, Little, Lost, Lunch, Lung
Machine, Mad, Mark, Marvelous, Match, Me, Mean, Meanwhile, Meat, Medicine, Mess, Middle of body, Milk, Mind, Most, Moth, Mother, Movement, Much, Mush, My, Myself
Nail, Nausea, Neck, Nerves, Nice, Noises, Nose, Not, Nothing, Nourish
Oblong, Old, Organ of body, Organs, Ouch, Owl
Paints, Pancreas, Paper, Part, Part of human, Part of the body, Part of you, Part of your body, Peace, Physiology, Picture, Pig, Pill, Pills, Pink, Pit, Place for food, Plump, Poison, Pork, Pouch, Pretty, Pylorus
Rain, Ribs, Ride, Rod Egen, Rough, Rumble, Run
Same, School, Shoulders, Sickening, Sixteen, Slime, Slimy, Small intestine, Smart, Smell, Smoking, Smooth, Snack, So, Soap, Some, Something, Soreness, Speech, Spleen, Squishy, Steak, Stomach, Stomach hurting, Storage, Storm, Stove, Stumble, Suitcase, Swallow, System
Table, Tape worm, Teeth, Tender, That, Throw up, Tissue, To, Together, Tom, Tomato, Ton, Tongue, Tooth, Tough, Train, Trunk, Truth, Tubes, Tummy ache, Tums, Turning, Twist
Ugh, Ugly, Up, Upset stomach, Us
Veins, Viscera

Waist line, Waiting, Washing, Weight, Wetter, Where food goes, Wing, Wish, With
Yell, You, Yours, Yourselves, Yum, Yum yum
Zoology

STOVE

Ago, A place to cook, Apple, Ashes
Baking, Basement, Bath, Ben Franklin, Big, Blue, Boat, Bread, Brick, Bright, Bring, Burning, By
Cabin, Cake, Called, Candle, Cast iron, Cat, Charcoal, Clean, Cleaner, Clothes, Clove, Coals, Coke, Cold, Cooker, Cookies, Cook on, Cooks, Corn cob, Cover, Cut
Dials, Dirt, Dirty, Door, Doug, Drove
Ear, Eating, Electric, Electricity, Enamel, Even, Explosion
Fireplace, First, Five, Fix, Flame, Foot, Franklin, Freezer, Frig, Furniture
Glove, Good, Grill, Grills
Hamburgers, Handles, Hard, Hat, Hay, Head, Heating, Him, Hollow, Home, Hut
Ice, Iron Range
Keep warm, Kindle, King Arthur
Lake, Lamb, Lamp, Lantern, Lard, Large, Left, Leg, Legs, Lighted, Lighter, Love, Low
Machine, Make, Man, Match, Meals, Milk, Mon, Money, Mother, Move
Night, No, Nothing
Object, Oil, Old, Ouch, Out, Over
Pail, Part, Pat, Picture, Pig, Poker, Pop corn, Pot bellied, Pot belly, Pots, Pots and pans, Pounds, Problem
Red, Right, Roll, Room, Round, Rubbish
Shot, Shovel, Skating, Smell, Snow, Soft, Soot, Square, Steal, Steam, Stem, Steve, Steven, Stone, Stool, Stove, Stove pipe, Strong
Teach, Tea kettle, Them, Thief, Tim, Tree, Turkey, Two
Useful
Very
Warm food, Warn, Water, When, Wide, Winter, Woman, Work
Yellow, You

STREET

Accidents, Across, Ally, Altitude, And alleys, Any street, Anything, A place where cars go, Are, Asphalt, Automobile, Autos, Avenues, Away
Baby, Back, Balls, Baseball, Beard, Beat, Bed, Beet, Bicycle, Bike, Bikes, Birch, Bituminous, Black top, Black wide, Blair, Blaisdell, Bloomington ave., Boardman, Boulevard, Box, Boy, Brick, Bricks, Brown, Building, Bump, Bumpy, Bus
Calhoun, Call, Can, Candy, Cart, Cat, Cedar, Chambersburg, Chicago, Children, Chowen, Church, Cleaners, Clinton, Clothes, Club, Cobblestone, Cold, Colfax, Columbus, Come, Continuous, Corn, Corridor, Court, Crowded, Crystal
Dance, Dancer, Danger, Dead, Death, Della street, District, Down, Down town, Driving, Dry
Ear, Ears, East second, Eat, Eight, Eighteen, Eighth, Elm, Elms, Emerson, Empty, Ewing
Fall, Fast, Fella, Fern, Fifteen, Fifteenth ave., Fifth st., Fiftieth street, Fifty first, Fifty five, Fifty seventh, Fifty sixth, Fifty twenty, Fillmore, First, Football, Forty fifth, Forty first, Forty ninth, Forty sixth, Forty two, Fourth, Fremont, Friends, Fun
Girard, Gladstone, Go, Going home, Golf course, Good, Grand, Grass, Gravel, Gray, Green, Ground, Guard, Gutter, Gutters
Hair, Hall, Hayes, Heat, Heavy, Henn, Highland, Hill, Homes, Hoods, Hunt
Ice, Idaho, Irving
James, Jessie, Johnson, Juliet
Key, Kids, Kind
Laid, Lamp light, Lamp post, Lamps, Larue, Laurel ave., Lawn, Length, License, Life, Lighter, Light post, Like, Lincoln, Lines, Living, Loan, Lone, Lonely, Longfellow, Loud, Lovely
Man, Man hole, McKinley, Me, Meat, Meet, Men, Mile, Minnehaha, Montreal, Moon, Morgan, Mud, Music, My
Ne, Neighborhood, New Orleans, New York, N Huron, Nic, Nice, Nicollet, Nokomis, Now, Numbers
Oakland, Of, Oh, Oliver, Out, Outside
Pace, Paint, Paper, Parallel, Park, Park Ave., Parkway, Part, Pave, Paving, Pebble, Pedestrian, Penn, Pillsbury, Pipe, Pole, Police, Policeman, Polk, Portland, President, Prince, Princeton

Queen, Quiet
Race, Rag, Railroad, Railway, Rain, Read, River, Roads, Rock, Rocks, Rod, Rome Ave., Round, Rue, Rumble
Safe, Saint, Salt, Sand, Sargent, Scheffer, Seat, Second Ave., Second Avenue, See, Sewer, Seymour, Sheet, Sheridan, Sherwood, Sigh, Sign post, Sing, Singer, Sixth, Sleep, Sleet, Slippery, Smooth, Snelling, Speed, Spoon, Square, St., Standish, Stanford, State, Stevens, St. John's Ave., Stone, Stop, Store, Straight, Strait, Street, Street car, Street lamp, Street light, String, Suburban, Sugar, Sweep, Sweeper
Tarry, Tarrymore, Tarvia, That, The, There, Third Ave., Thirty five fifty Pierce, Thirty fourth Ave. So., Thirty one, Thirty sixth, Thomas, Tired, To, Tracks, Travel, Treat, Tree, Treet, Trouble, Truck, Trucks, Twenty eighth, Twenty eighth Ave., Twenty four, Two, Tyler
Up, Upton, Upton Ave.
Vacant, Village, Vincent
Wake, Walking, Wall, Washburn, Washington Ave., Way, WDGY radio station, Wet, Where I live, Winona
Xerxes
Year, Yellow line, Yosemite, You

SWEET

A apple is sweet, Air, Angel, Angry, Apples
Babies, Baby, Back, Bar, Bear, Bed, Beer, Berry, Big, Birds, Bites, Bitter sweet, Blue, Boys, Bread, Brittle, Broke, Brush, Brushing, Bubble gum, Butter
Calories, Candies, Candle, Car, Caramel, Cat, Cavities, Cheat, Cheerful, Cherries, Cherry, Clean, Clear, Coke, Cold, Come, Cooing, Cook, Cookie, Cookies, Corn, Cream, Cute
Dainty, Darling, Dave, Dear, Dessert, Dill, Dog, Dogs, Dull, Dumb
Easy, Eating, Enjoyable
Fast, Father, Faye, Feet, First, Fleet, Floor, Fragrant, Frosting, Fruits, Fudge
Gail, Go, Goat, Good smelling, Good tasting, Grapes, Gruff, Grumpy
Had, Hand, Happy, Hate, Hear, Heart, Heartful, Heat, Hill, Home, Horrible, Hunger, Hungry
Ick, Icy, Ishy
Jam, Jolly, Juice, Juicy
Karen, Kathy, Keen, Keep
Lady, Land, Lard, Light, Like, Likeable, Liked, Lime, Lips, Little, Long, Look, Lora, Lovable, Loving, Lovingly
Man, Marriage, Mary Lou, May, Maybe, Me, Meat, Meek, Meet, Mice, Mild, Milk, Miss Olson, Mom, Mommy, Mouth
Nancy, Neat, Nectar, No, No good, Nothing, Not nice, Not sour, Not sweet
One, Ouch
Pea, Pear, Pepper, Perfume, Person, Peter, Pickle, Pillow, Pineapple, Pink, Plan, Play, Pleasant, Pop, Potato, Prunes, Pudding
Quiet
Read, Refresh, Rice, Rich, Road, Roberta, Rolls, Rose, Rude
Saccharine, Sad, Salty, Sausage, Saw, Serene, Sharp, She, Short, Shower, Shrill, Sick, Silent, Sing, Six, Sleep, Small, Smart, Smelling, Smells, Smelly, Smile, Soil, Solid, Solemn, Something with sugar in it, Sore, Sorrow, Soul, Sound, Sounds, Sow, Spice, Spices, Spoon, Starchy, Stingy, Stop, Store, Strawberry, Street, Strong, Stuff, Sucor, Suite, Summer, Sundae, Sunshine, Sweat, Sweeten, Sweet lady, Sweet pea, Sweet pollen, Swore
Tardy, Tart, Tasteful, Tender, Tooth paste, Treat, Twenty
Unpleasant, Unsweet
Voice
Warm, Water, Wee, Wet, Wheat, Where, Whistle, Wife, Wine, Wonderful
You, Yum

SWIFT

Ache, Agile, Airplane, Airplanes, Alexander, And company, Animal, Antelope, Anxious, Armour, At, Atom, Author
Back, Bad, Bed, Beer, Better, Bike, Bite, Blow, Blue, Blur, Bow, Bread, Breeze, Brush, Bullet, Bunny, Butter, By
Calm, Candy, Canned, Canoe, Canon, Cars, Case, Change, Cheer, Cheetah, Chicken, Chief, Child, Chill, Class, Clean, Clever, Coast, Colorado River, Cool, Corvette, Cottage cheese, County, Cow, Cream, Crisco
Danger, Dangerous, Dart, Davis, Dear, Dove, Dragster, Drift
Ear, Eat, Efficient, Eggs, Even

Fair, Falcon, Family, Far, Faster, Fast moving, Fat, Feather, Female, First, Fish, Flash, Fleeting, Fleetness, Float, Flow, Flowing, Flyer, Flying, Ford, Forward, Fox, Fun, Funny

Gallant, Gazelle, Gentle, Girl, Give, Glide, Glory, Going, Graceful, Grease, Great, Greyhound

Hammer, Hand, Happy, Hare, Have, Hello, Hi, Hot, Hurry, Hurriedly, Hydroplane

Ice cream, If, In, It

Jet, Jupiter

Keep, Knife

Land, Lard, Last, Lazy, Leap, Level, Lift, Like, Lilliputian, Little, Living, Lizard, Log, Long, Loose, Lose, Low

Man, Me, Meals, Mean, Meet, Mellow, Men, Mercury, Messenger, Met, More, Mouse, Move, Moving, Mr. Payne, Murder, Mutt, My boat, Myself

Neat, Never, No, Nose, Not nice, Nun, Nut

Ocean, Off, Oh, One, Outside

Packing, Panther, Path, Patrol, People, Pig, Pigs, Play, Pleasant, Poet, Pony, Premium meat, Puck

Quiet, Quite

Race horse, Rake, Ran, Rapidly, Rapids, Red, Ride, Riding, River or plane, Rivers, Rocket, Roll, Rough, Run fast, Rushing

Sail, Sailing, Salt, Same, Sand, Sanford, Scarab, See, Serene, Sharp, Sheep, Shift, Show, Side, Silent, Simple, Singer, Sir, Skate, Skating, Slay, Sled, Sleek, Slick, Slim, Small, Smart, Smell, Smoothly, Snake, Snow, Softly, Song, Sooth, Sound, Sown, Sparrow, Speed boat, Stag, Steak, Steam, Stern, Store, Straight, Streak, Swan, Sweep, Sweet, Swift, Swiftly, Swim, Swing, Swiss

Talker, Test, Think, Thrift, Thrust, Tired, Tom Swift, Tone, Toni, Train, Turkey, Turn

Understandable

Was, Weaners, Weed, Weiner, Weiners, While, Whip, White, Wieners, With, Wood, Write

You

TABLE

Ashtray, At, Ate

Back, Ball, Bed, Beg, Bench, Black, Boards, Bottle, Box, Boy, Bread, Breakfast, Broad, Butter

Cable, Cake, Cap, Card, Chain, Chair lamp vase, Cheer, China, Chrome, Class, Clean, Coat, Coffee, Come, Cover

Deck, Dining, Dining room, Do, Dog, Door, Drawer, Drink

Eat on, Enamel

Fab, Fable, Fear, Finish, Flat surface, Flower center piece, Flowers, Fold, Food dishes people, Four, Four legs, Fun

Game, Glasses, Go, Good, Gray, Ground, Gum

Head, Height, House

Ink

Kettle, Knife

Lamps, Lay, Light, Little, Long, Low, Lunch

Mable, Mahogany, Man, Manners, Marble, Me, Meal, Meals, Mesa, Milk, Mink, Modern, Money, Mouse

Napkin, No

Oak, Object, Object for eating, Old

Paper, Part, Pencil, People, Person, Pies, Plateau, Plates, Pointers, Principal's desk, Put, Put things on

Queer

Rest

Sable, Said, Seat, Sheet, Shiny, Silver, Slat, Small, Something to eat on, Stable, Stand, Steal, Stool, Strong, Surface

Tab, Take, Talk, Tall, Task, Tax, Teacher, Thing, To, Towel, Tray, Trigonometry

Up, Useful

Varnish, Vase

Walnut, Warm, Water, White, Woman, Wooden, Wood grain, World, Write, Write on

TAKE

About, Accept, Ache, Acquire, Again, Age, Ake, All, Always, An, And, Anything, Apart, Apple, Arithmetic, As, At, Ate, Awake, Awhile

Bag, Baseball, Basket, Be, Being, Blue, Boats, Boots, Borrower, Bows, Boy, Brake, Break, Breath, Bright, Brought, Bug, Bus, By

Can have, Car, Careful, Care of, Caring, Cat, Catch, Charm, Children, Coat, Cold, Color, Comb, Cover, Crab, Cry

Dance, Date, Day off, Deposit, Do, Dog, Don't take, Down,

Draw, Drive, Drop

East, Easter, Egg, Eggs, Erase, Everything, Exam, Except, Extra

Fake, Fast, Father, Fetch, Fight, Find, Fine, Flowers, Fly, Food, For, Force, Forget, Forgot, Free, Fun

Gain, Garbage, Gather, Girl, Gives, Globe, Gone, Goods, Grab away, Grasp, Great, Groceries, Gun

Handle, Hat, Haul, Head, Heavy, Heed, His, House

If, Indoor, Is

Jobs

Kept

Lake, Late, Leaver, Leaves, Left, Lend, Let, Letter, Like, Little, Loan, Long, Loose, Loss, Lost, Love, Lunch

Man, Mine, Mom, Move, Movie, Much

Nail, Nap, Need, Never, New, Nice, No, None, Nothing, Not take

Offer, Okay, Old, Or, Our, Out steal, Own, Ownership

Package, Packages, Part, Peek, Pencil, People, Pet, Picture, Pills, Please, Pocket, Possession, Present, Pride, Purchase, Quick

Rake, Reach, Rent, Rest, Ride, Risk, Rob, Robber, Run

Sat, Save, See, Seize, Sell, Shake, Share, She, Shop lift, Show, Sister, Slow, Snack, Snatch, Snatching, Somewhere, Spelling, Stay, Stealing, Steal shop lift, Stolen, Stop, Store, Subtract, Suitcase, Sweater, Swiped

Table, Takeover, Taker, Takes, Tale, Tame, Taught, Teach, Tear, Tell, Test, Tests, Thank, Thanks, Thank you, Their, Then, These, Thief, Thing, Things, Those, Three, Throw, Tick, Together, Told, Tooth, To store, Tote, Town, Toy, Train, Try, Turn, Turns, Two

Up, Use, User

Verb

Wagon, Wait, Walks, Water, Way, Wear, Went, Who, Why, Width, Women, Wood, Wool, Word, Wrong

You're, Yours

TELL

About, Admit, Advise, Ah, Am, Ann, Another, Anyone, A part, Are, Arrow

Ball, Be, Bee, Be silent, Bible, Bicycle, Big, Bill, Blab, Boss, Boy, But, Buy, Buying

Call, Can, Car, City, Command, Communicate, Complain, Confess, Count

Daddy, Describe, Do, Dog, Donny, Don't, Don't tell, Drama

Eat, Eleven, Elf, Ell, End, Enemy, Everyone, Exclaim

Fall, Father, Feet, Film, Fingers, Flat, For, Fortune, Four, Friend

Gab, Gee, Gem, Girl, Go, Going to get them, Gone

Had, Hall, He, Heard, Hell, Help, Here, Hey, Hi, Hide, Hill, His, Hold, Home, House

I, Idea, If, Illustrate, Is

Jim, John

Keep secret, Know

Let, Lies, Live, Louder

Make, Man, May, Mell, Melt, Melvin, Men, Mention, Mess, Me why, Mill, Mom, Money, Mother, Music, My

Name, Narrate, Nell, News, No, Noise, No one, Not tell, Now, No where

Of, On, Order

Pen, Period, Person, Please, Pop, Put

Question, Quite

Radio, Rags, Read, Recite, Recount, Reply, Report, Request, Require, Reveal, Right, Run

Saw, Saying, School, Scream, Secrets, Sentence, Shatter, She, Shell, Shoot, Shut up, Silent, Sing, Sit up, Slow, Small, Smell, Snitch, Somebody, Someone, Soon, Sorry, Sound, Speaking, Speech, Spell, Spill, Spoke, Squeal snitch, Squeek, Stand, State, Stop, Store, Sun

Taddle, Tail, Talking, Talks, Talk squeal snicker, Tattle tale, Taught, Tea, Teach, Teacher, Teachers, Tell, Teller, Tells, Tell tale, Test, Than, Therefore, They, Think, Tick, Tile, Till, Tip, To, Toll, Took, Train, True

Uniform, Use, Utter

Verb, Voice

Wall, Want, Wax, Way, We, Went, Were, When, Where, Will, Wish, With, With hold, Women, Words, Would, Write

Yesterday, Your

THAT

Ace, Adjective, Adverb, All, Almost, Alright, An, Animal,

Another, Anything, Ape, Are, As, Ate
Baby, Bad, Bag, Ball, Balls, Be, Before, Beginning, Big,
  Bike, Bird, Bite, Brat, Bring, Brute, Bug, Building, Bus,
  Buzz
Calf, Came, Cane, Can't, Cap, Care, Cats, Chair, Child,
  Cite, Class, Clock, Clod, Coat, Comes, Come thing, Cone,
  Conjunction, Country, Cow, Crazy, Cried, Cry, Cry baby, Cut
Date, Demonstrative, Desk, Does, Doll, Don't, Dope
End, English, Evening, Every
Far, Fast, First, Fish, Food, Forever, French, Funny
Get, Go, Gone, Guess
Ha, Has, Has hundred calories in it, Have, Head, Hear, Hers,
  Hi, Hoe, Hog, Home, Hop, Horse, Hot, How
Ice, Idiot, If, Ish, Isn't, Item, It is, Its
Jerk, Just
Kid
Land, Lass, Let, Letter, Like, Little, Long, Look, Love
Make, Makes, Many, Map, Mate, May, Maybe, Mine, Monkey,
  Mother, Mouse, Mouth, Must
Neuter, Never, New, Nice, Night, Nor, Nose, Not, Note,
  Nothing, Noun, Nown, Nut
Oak, Of, Of course, Oh, OK, Old, On, Only, Open, Ore, Other,
  Out
Pacific, Page, Party, Pat, Pencil, People, Pertaining to,
  Picture, Pig, Plate, Pointing, Price, Pronoun, Puppy,
  Purse
Que, Question, Quite
Railroad, Right
Said, Sand, Scolding, Sentence, Shall, She, Ship, Shoe, Should,
  Side, Simile, Sister, Snow, Some, Somebodys, Song, Soon,
  Spat, Specific, Spelling, Spot, Starter, Store, Story, Street,
  Stuff, Stupid
Table, Take, Tap, Tat, Telling, Thank, Thanks, That, That is
  my car, Theirs, Therefore, There's, Thief, Thin, Things,
  Think, This one, Thou, Thought, Thumb, Thus, Thy, Tie,
  Top, Tough, Town, Toy, Trap, Tree, Try, Trying
Wall, Want, Well, What's, Wheel, Whew, White, With, Within,
  Woman, Women, Won't, Work, Would, Wow, Wrong
Yes, Yet, Your, Yours

THE

Adj, Adverb, Ah, Air, All, Also, Alter, Always, Amoeba,
  Animal, Animals, Answer, Ant, Anything, Apples, Are, Art,
  As, Ax
Bad, Bag, Band, Base, Bat, Bay, Bear, Bears, Beast, Became,
  Become, Bed, Bee, Bees, Before, Begin, Bell, Bible, Birds,
  Black, Blob, Boats, Bobby, Body, Books, Boot, Box, Bridge,
  Brother, Brown, Bus, But, Buy
Cad, Cake, Came, Camel, Can, Capitol, Cars, Cats, Certain,
  Chair, Chairs, Church, Circus, City, Class, Clock, Closer,
  Coat, Color, Come, Conj, Conjunction, Convent, Cows,
  Cry
Dam, Dark, Date, Days, Death, Definite, Der, Descriptive,
  Desk, Did, Die, Different, Dishes, Do, Dock, Does, Doesn't,
  Dogs, Donkey, Doors
Earth, Easy word, Egg, El, Everything
Fact, Fair, Fairy, Family, Farm, Farmer, Faster, Feet,
  Fellas, Fence, Field, Fiend, Fight, Finish, First, Fist,
  Foot, Form, Four, Fox, Friend, Front, Funny
Gang, Gender, Gifts, Girls, Goat, God, Good, Gov't, Grail,
  Grass, Great, Group, Gun, Guy
Ha, Hall, Happen, Have, Heading, Headless horseman, Heart,
  Heck, Help, Hen, Her, Hey, Hide, Hour, Houses, Hut
I, Ice, Impostor, Inauguration, Introduction, Item, Its
Judge, Jump
Kid, Kids, Kids outside, King, Kite, Kitten
Lab, Label, Lace, Lag, Land, Last, Late, Lawn, Le, Leg,
  Lemon, Let, Letter, Library, Life, Light, List, Living,
  Look, Lord, Lot
Mad, Make, Many, Mat, Matter, May, Means, Meet, Men, Mew,
  Might, Mike, Minute, Monkey, Monster, Moon, More, Mother,
  Mouse, Mouth, Movie, Music, My
Nail, Navy, News, Next, Night, No, Noise, Nothing, Noun,
  Now, No word blank, Number, Nut
Odds, Of, Offense, Oh, Oil, OK, Old, Once, Opening, Other,
  Over
Page, Paint, Palace, Paper, Part, Pass, Past, Peewee, Piano,
  Pie, Plane, Plate, Play, Poem, Priest, Prince, Problem,
  Pronoun, Purse, Put
Quarter back, Question, Quick

Rabbit, Race, Rain, Ran, Rat, Real, Reason, River, Road,
  Romance, Room
Sad, Saddle, Same, Saw, Say, Sheep, Ship, Shoes, Show, Sky,
  Sled, Slob, Small, Snob, Snowball, So, Some, Somebody,
  Song, Soon, Squirrel, Stand, Star, Start, Starting, Start
  sentence, Statement, Stop, Street, Stupid, Subject
Take, Talk, Talking, Tea, Teacher, Tee, Teen, Tell, Test,
  Than, That one, Theater, Themself, These, Thirteen, Tho,
  Thou, Though, Through, Throw, Tie, Together, Too, Town,
  Train, Tray, Treat, Trees, Truth, Two, Typing
U, Up, Us
Wagon, Walk, Wall, War, Was, Wedding, Week, Went, Were,
  Wharf, Where, Which, Why, Will, Wind, Winter, With,
  Women, Wonderful, Woods, Work, World, Would
Ye, Yes, Yet

THEN

About, Accident, Afterward, Alone, Alright, An, And forever,
  And now, Antithesis, As, As of, At that time, At the time,
  Away, A ways, Awhile
Bad, Become, Been, Began, Ben, Bent, Blank, Blue, Bob,
  Book, Bought, Boy, Boys, Bus
Cake, Capital, Car, Cause, Chair, Chalk, Choose, Class, Clock,
  Columbus, Comes, Corpse, Could, Crane, Crazy
Day, Days, Did, Die, Dog, Done, Donkey, Drive
Eat, End, English, Etc., Ever
Far, Fast, Fell, Finally, Find, First, Following, Forever,
  Four, Fun, Furthermore, Future
Gem, Get, Girl, Gone, Gray, Group, Groups, Gun
Happening, Happens, Happy, Has, Hat, Hay, Hear, Heard, Heat,
  Help, Hem, Hi, Hope, Hot, Hurry, Hymn
Ill, In
Jim
Knee
Late, Latter, Leave, Like, Line, Lion, Little, Live, Long, Long
  ago
Made, Mail, Many, Maybe, Mean, Minnesota, Moment, Money,
  Monkey, Movie, Must, My, Myself
Near, Nest, Nice, Night, Not, Note, Nothing, Now and then
Of course, Off, Offer, Office, Often, OK, Okay, Old, One time,
  On time, On to, Open, Or, Other, Out
Past time, Person, Pig, Play, Pop, Preposition, Presents,
  Promise, Pronoun, Purpose
Quit
Rather, Read, Reason, Result, Right away, Right now, Rope,
  Run
Salty, Sat, Saw, Say, School, Scream, Seen, Send, Sentence,
  She departed, Show, Since, Soft, Some, Someone, Someplace,
  Sometime, Somewhere, Spoon, Start, Still, Stop, Store,
  Story, Study, Summer, Sun, Swim
Table, Take, Taken, Tale, Talking, Teacher, Teeth, Tell, Ten,
  That minute, That time, The happened, Then, Thence, Then
  come, Then the people went away, These, They'll, Thin,
  Thing, Thirsty, Thou, Thought, Through, Thus, Thy, Tin,
  Today, Tree, Turn
Under, Until, Use
Wait, Watch, Way, Wear, Which, While, White, Who, Why then,
  With, Wren
Year, Yes, Yet, Yore

THERE

Abbreviation, Across, Afar, Air, All, All done, Also, Although,
  Always, Am, And, Animal, A place, Are girls, Aren't
Back, Ball, Be, Bear, Bed, Behind, Being, Belong, Beyond,
  Big, Boat, Book, Bout, But
Cabin, Can, Can't, City, Come, Comes, Console, Cool, Could
  be, Country, Cow, Crate, Curtain
Desk, Diamond, Dies, Dig, Direction, Dish, Distance, Do,
  Dog, Done, Down
Else where, Ever, Everywhere, Exists, Explaining
Fair, Fall, Fat, Feelings, Find, Finger, Finish, Flask, From,
  Full, Fun
Gail, Gate, Get going, Gets, Getting, Girl, Good, Got, Grass,
  Ground
Had, Hammer, Happy, Has, Hay, Heaven, Hide, High, Him,
  His, Hockey, Horse, Hot, How
I, I'm, In that place, Isn't, It goes, It is, Its
Kid, Kittens
Lake, Lamp post, Latter, Leaves, Lies, Life, Little, Live,
  Lives, Location

Mailbox, Man, Mane, Men, Mere, Middle, Might, Mine,
Missouri, Moms, Moo, Mountain, Moving things, Muscles
Near, New, Nice, No, Not, Not here, Not there, Nowhere
Of, Off, OK, Okay, Once, One, Or, Our, Out, Owner
Pacific, Park, Peace, Pear, Person, Phone, Pie, Pig, Pointer,
Pointing
Queen, Quite
Ranch, Reach, Right there, River, Road, Room
Saw, She goes, She is, Should, Show, Side, Sing, Sioux, Sit,
Snare, Some, Someone, Someplace else, Something, Some-
where else, Soon, Spain, Spanish, Spare, Sport, Stand,
Stare, State, Statement, Stood, Store, Story, Study, Summer,
Sun, Sure
Team, Tear, Thats, Theater, Therefore, There where the
people, These, They're, Thing, Things, Those, Though,
Time, To, Too, Towards, Town
Under, Upon, Us
Valley
Wait, Way, Went, Which, White, Who, Why, Within, Woods,
Work
Y, Yard, Yonder, You are, Young

THEREFORE

Acquaintance, Addition, After all, After that, Afterwards,
Against, Ago, Ah, Ahead, All, All right, Already, Alright,
Alternative, Altogether, Alway, Am, An, And furthermore,
And so on, Another thing, Answer, Answers, Any,
Anything, Anyways, Anywhere, Appropriate, As a result,
As much, As such, As though, Awards, Away, Awhile
Bad, Become, Been, Being, Between, Bewildered, Bible, Body,
Bomb, Book, Both, Boy, Bright, Buy, By
Cabin, Call, Cannon ball, Can't, Car, Care, Carrying, Catch,
Cause, Change, Child, Children, Church, Clean, Color,
Come now, Comet, Comprehension, Conclude, Cone, Con-
junction, Connect, Connection, Consideration, Constitution,
Continued, Contract, Contrary, Contrast, Corpse, Could,
Count, Course
Daddy, Day, Declaration of Independence, Deduction, Desk,
Did, Didn't, Done, Door, Doubt
Eat, End, Equals, Et cetera, Even, Ever, Ever after, Example,
Except, Exception, Exclaim, Excuse, Existence, Explain,
Express, Expression
Fact, Factories, Far, Farmer, Farther, Fast, Finally, Find,
First, Five dollars, Ford, Fore go, Fore head, Fore not,
Fore there, Forth, For that reason, Forward, Front, Funny
Geometry, Get, Gift, Girl, Give, God, Going, Gone, Goodby,
Got, Grown ups
Ha, Hair, Hand, Hat, Hate, Hear, Heard, Help, Here are,
Hereby, Here for, Here now, Here of, Here to, Here upon,
Hers, Hesitating, Hide, Hire, His, Hither, Hither to, Hither
to fore, Holiday, Home, Hospital
I am, I could, I'm, Important, Impossible, In, In addition, In
case of, In conclusion, Indirect, Information, In front, In
other words, Instance, Instead, Interfere, Introduction, Is
not, It is, It must, Its
Jail, Join, Judge, Just
Kids, King, Knees, Knowledge
Later, Laugh, Leave, Lesson, Let, Lets, Letter, Let us,
Lincoln, Literature, Long, Lose, Love
Mad, Man, Manual, Many, Marbles, March, Marry, Math,
Mathematics, May, Mean, Means, Mean while, Might, Milk,
Mind, Mine, Mistake, Modal, Moon, More, Mrs. Straka,
Much, Must, Myself
Nearer, Neatness, Next, Nice, Nine, None, Not fore, Not now,
Nov, Now as, Now as, Now then, Nuts
Objection, Obvious, Of course, Off, Office, Okay, Old, Once,
One, Only, On the other hand, Opinion, Or, Order, Ore,
Other, Otherwise, Other words, Our, Out, Over there
Paper, Past, Pause, Perhaps, Person, Peter, Pie, Pies, Please,
Point, Poor, Possible, Prepare, Pretentious, Probably,
Professor, Punished
Question, Questioning
Ready, Really, Remark, Remember, Represent, Resolve,
Resolved, Resulting, Results, Right, Romeo
Sad, Said, Sea, See, See it, See so, Semi colon, Sentence,
Shakespeare, Shop, Short hand, Should, Shouldn't, Singer, Sit,
Smart, So and so, So as, So far, So forth, Sold, Some, Some
how, Some more, Someone, Sometimes, Somewhere, So on,
Soon, So that, So what, Spanish, Speak, Speaking, Speed,
Spelling, Stand, Statement, Stop, Store, Story, String, Study,

Supper
Talk, Telling, That is, Theirs, Themes, Then fore, There
are, There art, Thereby, There come, There forth, There
from, There here, There how, There in, There know, There
not, There now, There on, There over, Theres, There to,
There upon, Therever, There was, There were, There will,
There with, Therout, These, Thesis, Thing, Think, Thorough,
Those, Thou, Though, Thought, Three, Through, Through
out, Thusly, Time, Today, To do, Together, Too, Tree,
Triangle, True, Truly, Twin meanings, Two, Twos
Ugly ward, Ultimatum, Understand, Unto, Up, Upon
Wait, Want, Was, Way, Wear, We are, Wedlock, Wee, Well,
Went, Whatever, What for, Whatsoever, Whenever, When
fore, Where after, Where of, Wherever, Whether, Who ever,
Who so ever, Why fore, Within, Wondering, Words, Work
Yes, Yet, You are, Young, Your, You're, Yours

THEY

A, Ail, Alot, Also, Always, And, Animals, As
Bath, Bay, Bet, Body, Both, Boy, Bring, But
Camels, Candy, Can't, Carry, Cat, Chased, Child, Church,
Class, Class mates, Climb, Company, Couldn't, Couple,
Cow, Crowded, Crowds, Crumbs, Cry
Dead, Didn't, Does, Dog, Don't, Down
Each, Eat
Face, Family, Fast, Fight, Find, Finger, Fun
Gang, Gave, Get, Give, Going, Great, Groups, Gun man, Guns,
Gut, Guy
Hard, Has, Heard, Heavy, Held, Helped, Herd, Hi, Hip, His,
How, Hurry
Indians
Jon K. H., Jump
Key, Knew, Know
Laugh, Left, Let, Lift, Like, Live, Look, Lot, Love, Lucky
Made, Martians, Mary and John, Masses, Men, Might, Miss,
Mob, Monster, More than one, Movie, My
Nay, Neighbor, Nice, Nine, No, Not, Note book
Oh, Other, Our, Ours, Out, Outer space, Own
Parents, Party, Pay, Peoples, Pick, Play, Played, Please,
Pool, Possession, Put
Right, Romans, Root
Same, Sat, Saw, Second, Several, Shall, She and he, Shot, Show,
Sick, Sie, Slid, Smile, So, Somebody, Something, Start,
Store, Story, Stupid
Take, Talk, Teachers, Tell, Telling, Than, Theirs, Themselves,
Theres, These, They, They'll, They're, They've, Thin,
Thou, Though, Thought, Three, Throw, Thy, To, Togetherness,
Too, Took, Try, Two people
Up
Valance
Walked, Want, Wear, Well, What, When, Whom, Whose, Why,
Win, Window, With, Won't, Word, Wore, Would, Wow, Write,
Wrong
Yes

THIEF

Action, Alarm, Al Capone, Alot, Anything, Article, Ass, Awes,
Awful
Bade, Bad guy, Bad man, Bag, Bang, Bar, Bastard, Be, Beast,
Bed, Beer, Beggar, Big, Bob Waade, Bomb, Book, Boys,
Brave, Bread, Break, Break in, Breaking in, Brief, Brooch,
Brother, Bruce, Bugle, Bum, Burglars, Butter, By
Cage, Can, Candle, Cap, Car, Cards, Care, Case, Chair,
Cheap, Cheater, Chef, Chicken, Citizen, Clever, Clod, Cold,
Collins, Con, Convict, Cook, Copper, Cops, Cowered, Crazy,
Creep, Criminals, Crock, Crooked, Cruel, Culprit
Dangerous, Death, Denny, Desk, Diamond, Dirty, Dirty rotten,
Disguise, Do, Dock, Doctor, Dog, Don, Don crook, Drink
Emil, Enemies, Enemy, England, Evil, Excitement
Face, Fair, Fall, Fat, Find, Food, Fourth, Fright, Fry, Fun,
Furtive
Gang, Gangster, Gas station, Gayle, Gems, Gentleman, German,
Get, Get away, Girl, Give, Giver, Going, Gone, Goodby,
Good guy, Goods, Grab, Guess, Guilt, Guilty, Guns, Gwen
Hair spray, Hand, Handy, Happy, Hard, Hat, Hate, He, Head,
Hear, Height, Help, Her, High, Him, Hire, Hit, Home,
Honesty, Hood, Hoodlum, Hope, Horizon, Horrid, Hose, Hot,
Hour, Hurt
I, Idiot, If, Indian, Indian giver, Ingrate, Insurance, Is, It
Jack, Jailer, Jam, Jeff, Jewel, Jim, Jim Anderson, Joe, Joker,

Judge, Jump

Kid, Kills, Kind, Kitchen, Knife, Know

Lady, Large, Larrie Labrie, Last, Law breaker, Lawless, Lawlessness, Lawyer, Leader, Leave, Left, Liar, Lie, Lieutenant, Life, Lift, Light, Lion, London, Loot, Lose, Lost

Mad, Many, Me, Mice, Mine, Miscreant, Monkey, Mr. Strand, My

Nail, Name, Neat, Nice, Night time, Nine, No, No good, Not, Not good, No thief, Now

OK, Open window, Outlaw

Pablo, Paddy wagon, Paint, People, Play, Poor, Priest, Prisoner, Prowler, Punishment

Quiet

Raid, Rat, Rat Dave Lindberg, Rave, Rebel, Red, Return, Rief, Right, Ring, Robbed, Robberies, Robbers, Robe, Roll, Ron, Ron Book, Roommate, Rubber

Sad, Safe, Sane, Savior, Scare, Scared, Scared man, Science, Scold, Scream, Scum, Sharp, Sheex, Sheriff, Shifty, Shoot, Shop lifter, Shot, Shout, Shut up, Sick, Silver ware, Sin, Six, Skimp, Skirt, Sleep, Smart, Smooth, Smuggler, Sneaker, Sneaking, Sneaky, Snicher, Sniff, Sold, Some, Sorry, Sped, Spend, Square, Steak, Steal things, Stealthily, Still, Strong, Stupid, Sumaratin, Sun, Suspect, Swift, Swipe, Swiped

Take away, Taken, Takes, Taking, Teeth, Television, Terrible, Their, Them, The Untouchables, Thief, Thieves, Thin, Thing, Things, Thirsty, Three, Thumb, Tie, Tom, Took, Took it, Tree, Trees, Trouble, Troubled, Truth, Turn, Two headed, Tyrant

Ugly, Unadjusted, Unthief, Us

Valuable, Villain

Wall, Want, Was, Water, Way, Wild one, Window, Windows, Write

Yes, You are

THINNER

A, Air, Apple, Are, Arm, Around, At, Atmosphere, Away

Back, Bad, Bar, Bean, Better, Big, Billy, Blade, Blood, Body, Bone, Box, Brake, Break, Broom, Brush

Came, Can, Candle, Car, Chicken, Christ, Clear, Cloth, Coat, Colder, College, Come, Consistency, Cooke, Cow, Cracker, Crackers

Dad, Daddy, Dark, Darker, Denser, Desk, Dime, Do, Dorothy, Dough, Dress

Easier, Eat, Eating, Every, Everyone, Exciting

Fade, Faint, Far, Fast, Faster, Fate, Father, Fattening, Female, Film, Fine, Finer, Fish, Flat, Fragile, Frail, Fun

Gas, Gasoline, Gets, Giraffe, Glaze, Goodby, Gooey, Gun

Hammer, Harder, Hat, Have, He, Health, Heart, Here, High, Him, Homer, Horse, Hot, How

If, In, Inn, Inner, Into, Iron, Is, It

Jack, Juice

Kerosene, Knew

Lacer, Lank, Large, Larger, Leather, Less thick, Lightning, Lil, Littler, Log, Lose, Loss

Ma, Mad, Make, Malnutrition, Meat, Meeker, Men, Mike, Milk, Miner, Mix, Mixer, Model, Molarity, Molasses, Mon, More, Mother, Much, Mule, My, Myrna

Nearer, Needle, Never, Next, Nicer, No, Noisy, Not, Not as thick, Not so fat, Now

Off, Oh, Oil, Old, Older, Old maid, One, Out, Over

Pain, Paint thinner, Pant, Pants, Part, Paul, Pencil, People, Pet, Piece, Pin, Ping, Pint, Plastic, Plate, Please, Plump, Point, Poison, Pole, Polish, Pretty, Pretzel

Rail, Rails, Rain, Ran, Read, Recipe, Red, Reduce, Reducer, Rod, Rope, Run, Runnier, Runny

Sally, Sauce, Saw, Scale, Scare crow, School, Scrawnier, Sealer, See, See through, Sewer, Shadow, Shaft, She, Shellac, Shiny, Short, Shorter, Silk, Sing, Sinner, Sister, Slenderer, Slice, Slices, Slobby, Slow, Smoother, Soap, Soft, Some girls, Soupy, Spinner, Splash, Spread, Stag, Starvation, Steal, Stiffer, Still, Storm, Stout, Stouter, Straight, Street, Strings, Stronger, Substance, Summer

Tan, Teacher, Terrible, Than me, That, Then you, Thermometer, They, Thicken, Thickest, Thickness, Thigh, Thing, Thinker, Thinner, Thins, This, Thread, Threw, Timer, Tinier, Tiny, To, Toast, Today, Tom Beck's hair, Tooth paste, Tooth pick, Transparent, Tree, Tress, Truck, Tub, Tubbier, Tummy, Turgid, Turn

Ugh, Unfat, Unthick

Varnish, Very, Vinegar, Viscosity, Vogue models

Waist, Walls, Warm, Waste, Waves, Were, Wet, Wetter, Whiter, Wiener, Wild, Will, Wine, Winter, Wire, Wish, With, Woman, Women, Wood, Word

Yes, Yet, You

THIRSTY

Aid, Around, At

Bad, Better, Beverage, Bird, Bitter, Blood, Book, Bottle, Brick, Bring

Cake, Came, Camel, Can, Car, Cat, Center, Chang, Class, Come, Cone, Cool, Cool aid, Creek, Cry, Cub, Cup

Dance, Dancing, Dart, Day, Dead, Dehydrated, Desire, Desire for water, Die, Dirty, Do, Doctor, Dog, Done, Drank, Draught, Drinking, Drink of water, Drowning, Drumming, Dryness, Dust, Dusty, Dying

Eraser, Europe

Famish, Faucet, Fed, Filled, First, Five, Folly, For, Fountain, Fresh, Friday, Friend

Gin, Glass of water, Glutton, Go, Gone, Gosh, Gulp

Hamm's, Handy, Health, Heat, Help, Hold, Home, H two O, Hurry

Ice, Ink, It

Juices, June

Kool aid

Lake, Large, Lash, Laugh, Let, Light, Like, Lips, Liq, Lunch, Lungs

Mean, Mice, Mine, Mommy, Moon, Mouth, Mrs.

Nail, Neat, Need, Needing, Nice, Nine, No, Not, Now, No water

Oasis, OK, Old, On, Orange, Orange juice, Oranges, Over

Parched throat, People, Person, Pig, Play, Porch

Quenched

Ran, RC, Real, Red, Right, Ring, River, Round, Rum, Run

Saliva, Salt, Sand, Satisfied, Saturated, See, Seven up, Sharp, She, Shoe, Sick, Six, Sky, Sleepy, Slow, Soda, Soft, Sometimes, Sore, Sound, Sour, Spend, Squirt, Starve, Starved, Starving, Store, Story, Strong, Susan, Swallow, Sweat, Sweaty, Sweet, Swelling, Swift

Taste, Tasty, Ten, The, They, Third, Thirst, Thirsty, Thirsty drink lot, Three, Throat dry, Throw, To drink, Tom, Tongue, Took, Tough, Toy, Tray, True, Trust, Try, Twenty

Uncomfortable

Want, Want a drink, Want water, Water way, Watery, Well Whistle, Wine, Worth

THIS

A, About, Again, Age, Alice, Alt, An, And that, Animal, Apple, Are, Arm, Article, At, Automobile, Awful

Base, Bat, Be, Because, Bell, Belong, Belongs, Bible, Bill, Blends, Blouse, Boat, Boot, Bother, Brother, Building, Buy

Cake, Call, Candy, Cane, Card, Cards, Certain, Chair, Character, Child, Clock, Close, Coat, Color, Comb, Come, Cook, Couch, Course, Cow, Crayon

Damn, Death, Definite, Dish, Do, Does, Dogs, Doll, Don't, Door, Down, Dress, Dusk

End, Ending, English, Este, Everything, Explaining

Face, Fast, Fell, Felt, Fence, Finger, Fire, Fish, Fly, Foam, Food, For, Fun, Funny

Game, Get, Go, Goes, Good, Grapefruit, Green, Gum, Gun, Guy

Had, Hand, Happen, Happened, Has, Hay, Head, Hear, Held, Her, Hers, Hill, Him, Hiss, Hit, Home, Hope, Horse, Hotel, Hour, How, Hurts

I, Idea, I.e. my hand, If, In, Instant, Is fun, Is it, Isn't, Is the end, Item, Its

Junk

Karen, Kid, Kind, Knife

Lady, Land, Language, Leg, Lesson, Letter, Life, Little, Look

Made, Make, Many, Matter, May, Means, Min, Minute, Mist, Mommy, Money, Month, Monument, Morning, Mother, Much, Myself

National, Nest, Never, Not, Number

Object or thing, On, One thing, Orange, Ours, Overland

Pace, Page, Pants, Particular, Pathetic, Pet, Picture, Piss, Please, Pocket, Point, Pointing, Pookie, Prayer, Present, Prize, Put

Question

Rag, Reading, Rich, Ring, Road, Room, Root beer, Rope

Same, Say, Sex, Shall, Shall last, Sheet, Shirt, Shoe, Shoes, Show, Showing, Side, Sidewalk, Ski, Skirt, Someone, Specific,

Stinks, Summer, Sweater

Tale, Telling, There's, Thieves, Things, Think, Though, Throw, Thus, Tiny, Toe, Toy, Trees, Two

Us

Valley, Vase, Verb, Very

We, Weapon, Weather, Week, When, Who, Why, Wills, Wise, Wish, World, Wow, Writes

Yard, Yes, You, Your

TO

Across, Address, Admire, After, Again, Ah, Aim, Alan, All, America, An, And me, Anne, Answer, Ant, Any, Are, Ask, Avoid it

Baby, Ball, Barn, Bed, Bees, Before, Began, Begin, Being, Besides, Billy, Bin, Birthday, Blew, Boo, Book, Boots, Both, Boy, Boys, Bring, Brother, Brought, Build a fire, But

Camping, Can, Car, Carry, Cat, Chair, Chippewa, Church, City, Class, Clean, Close, Cold, Company, Country, Cow

Desk, Destination, Deuce, Develop, Dick, Did, Die, Does, Down town, Dream, Drink, Duluth, Dumb

Each, English

Farm, Farther, Fat, Feet, Fight, Find, Fingers, Fit, Fly, Fore, Friend, Fun

Gather, Georgia, Gift, Girl, Gone, Grandma's, Grandmother, Group, Guns

Happy, Harm, Have, Heaven, Hell, Help, Hem, Hi, His, Ho, Hot

Ice cream, I'm, In addition, Infinite, Infinitive, In order, Into, Iron, Is

Jan, Jerry, Jim, Joining

Kathy

Lake, Lament, Lamp, Late, Laugh, Learn, Leave, Let, Like, Little, Love, Look, Lou, Low

Ma, Mail, Make, Man, Market, Marry, Mary, Match, Men, Mere, Minutes, Mit, Mom, Mommy, More, Morrow, Move, Movies, Mrs. Nielson

Name, Near, New York, Night, None, Not, Not one, No where

Often, Oh, Old, Open, Or, Out, Over, Ownership

Pair, Pairs, Pant, Part, Pat, Places, Play, Plus, Pot, Present, Proceed, Purpose, Purse, Put

Race, Rain, Real, Realize, Receive, Red, Reply, Right, Rise, Rocket, Room

Say, Science, Sea, Seem, Sending, Sent, She, Shoe, Shoot, Show, Slow, Small, So, Some, Somebody, Someplace, Something, Somewhere, Son, Soo, Soon, Speak, Stare, Stay, Stockings, Stop, Stove

Tan, Tea, Tell, Ten, Their, They, Thick, Thin, Thing, Through, Throw, Thus, Tie, Tight, Till, To, Today, Toes, Told, Tom, Tomorrow, Tone, Took, Toot, Tooth, Top, Tot, Touch, Tow, Toy, Train, Trouble, Tune, Two or two

Unconscious, Under, Undergo, Unto, Use

Valentine, Very, Visit

Walk, Want, Was, Wax, Wear, Went, Which, Whit, Why, Will, Win, Words, Work, Worm, Write

Years, Yes, Yet, Your

TOBACCO

Alabama, Alcohol, Angle, Animal, Ashes, Asthma, At, Athlete

Back, Bacon, Bad habit, Bag, Bar, Bed, Beer, Black, Bland odor, Boat, Boy, Boys, Bread, Brother, Brought, Burn, Butter, Buy

Cafe, Camel, Camels, Can, Candy, Can't stand, Car, Carmel, Cheap, Cheese, Cherry blend, Chesterfield, Chewed, Church, Cig, Cigar smoke, Cloth, Clue, Cocoa, Color, Company, Coneer, Consolation, Cotton, Cough, Country, Crap, Crazy, Crops, Cue

Date, Death, Die, Dirt, Dirty, Distasteful, Doctor, Down, Drink

Eating, Egg, Enjoyment, Evil

Farms, Fat, Fields, Fire, Fireless, Flavor, For smoking, Fresh, Fun

Garden, Garden or farm, Gas, Gin, Girl, Golden, Grain, Grandpa, Grandy, Grow, Growing, Grown, Gum, Gun

Ha, Habit, Happy, Harsh, He, Head, Heavy, History, Home, Hoods, Horrible, Hot, House

Ick, In, Indian, Indians, Insect, It

January, Junk

Kill, Know

Land, Land m, Leave, Life, Lighter, Like, Little, Long, Look, Loud, Lousy, LSMFT, Lucky, Lucky Strike, Lung, Lung cancer

Make, Man use, Many, Match, Mate, Me, Men, Mike Owen, Milk, Money, Mother

Name, Narcotics, New, New England, Newport, Nice, No good, Noise, Not good, Nothing

Odor, Oh, Old, Opium

Pall Mall, Paper, Paste, Pedro Ramos, People, Piece, Pig, Pinch, Place, Plane, Planet, Planets, Plantation, Plants, Pleasure, Poison, Poor, Powder, Product

Quiet

Relax, Rotten

Salems, Sam, Sand, Sauce, See, Sight, Sin, Smart, Smock, Smoke shop, Sneeze, Soft, Some, Something, Something to smoke, Soothing, South, Speak, Stars, Stimulant, Stink, Stinky smell, Stocking, Store, Story, Stove, String, Study, Substance, Sugar, Sweet

Tab Hunter, Tan, Tar, Tars, Telephone, Thanks, The, There, Thing, Thirty cents, Tick, Tobacco Road, Toboggan, Too, Top, Tough, Town, Tree, Through, Twenty cents

Ugh, Ugly, Unhealthy, Unnecessary, Use

Virginia

Wasteful, Weight, Wheat, Whiskey, Wood, Woods

You

TROUBLE

Able, Advice, A fight, Ahead, Aid, Air, All right, Alot, Alright, Ambulance, American, Angel, Angerous, Angriness, Anguish, Annoyance, Answer, Argent, Arm, Army, Arrest, Ashamed, Attack, Authority, Avoidable

Babies, Bad boy, Bad luck, Bad new, Bad or mischief, Bad sad, Bad things, Bank robbery, Barb, Basement, Bat, Battle, Beautiful, Bee, Behavior, Best, Better, Beware, Bill, Bills, Bird, Bit, Black, Black eye, Blue, Bob, Bobby, Bobo, Book, Bounce, Brake, Brat, Break a window, Brew, Broken, Broken glass, Broken window, Brown, Bumble, Busy, Butch, Butterflies, By

Calculus, Call, Camp, Cancer, Can't, Caps, Care, Carefree, Careful, Cares, Cars, Catastrophe, Caught, Cause, Chair, Chemistry, Child, Children, Chock, Chose, Church, Classes, Clean out, Cold, Comfortable, Concern, Conflict, Confused, Congo, Conscious, Contentment, Convict, Cookie jar, Cool, County, Course, Court, Cowboy, Cowboys, Crabby, Cracker balls, Crayons, Crime, Crises, Crook, Cross, Cruel, Crying, Customers

Dad, Damage, Dammit, Dark, Date, Dave Stri, Death, Deed, Deep, Definite, Dennis, Depend, Desk, Despair, Devil, Did something wrong, Dirt, Disadvantage, Disappointment, Discipline, Discord, Discouraged, Disgusted, Dislike, Disobey, Distress, Disturb, Do, Dog house, Dogs, Done, Done something wrong, Doris, Double play, Dream, Dr. Nelson, Dum da dum dum, Dutch

Early, Earth, Easily, Eileen, Embarrass, Embarrassment, Emotion, Enemy, Enjoy, Escape, Everywhere, Evil, Excellent

Face, Fact, Fail, Failure, Fall, Fan, Farm, Fast, Father, Fault, Feud, Few, Fighter, Fights, Find, Fired, Fish, Fit, Fitting, Five, Food, Foot, For, Forgot, Fortune, Free, Friendly, Fright, Frightening, Frown, Frustration

Gang, Gangster, Gangsters, Garage, Gary, Gas, Gay, German, Get, Get in, Getting it, Glass, Glen, Glen Lake, Go, God, Going, Goodby, Goodness, Grades, Great, Greatness, Grey, Grief, Ground, Gun

Hair, Happen, Happened, Happenings, Hard time, Harm, Hast, Hat, Have, Haven, Havoc, Hazard, Hazel, Head, Headache, Health, Heard, Heart, Heart ache, Hearted, Heck, Held, Helpful, Helping, Helpless, Here, High, Hit, Hoffa, Hold, Home, Homework, Honest, Hood, Hoodlum, Horrible, Horror, Horse, Hot, Hub caps, Hurricane, Hurry

Illness, In a fix, In danger, Innocence, Inside, Into, In trouble, Is, Ish

Jack, John, Jokes, Joy, Joys, Juvenile, Juvenile delinquent, Juveniles

Kathy, Kennedy, Khruschev, Kids, Killing, Kind, Know

Lad, Laos, Late work, Laugh, Lazy, Lecture, Lend, Lettuce, Licking, Light, Light hearted, Like, Lock, Locker, Look, Lose, Lots, Loud, Love, Luck, Lucky, Luke

Made, Madness, Manner, Many, Marriage, Math, Matter, Menace, Merry, Mice, Mickey, Middle East, Might, Mine, Mining, Mischievous, Miserable, Mistakes, Moon, More,

Motor, Mr. Bracket, Mr. Khrushchev, Muble, Mumble, Murder, My brother

Naught, Neat, Neck, Need, Neighbor, Nerves, Nicer, No good, Noise, Noisy, None, Nonsense, Not good, Not happy, Nothing, Not in trouble, Not nice, Not right, No trouble, Now, Nuisance, Nuts in the head

Ocean, Office, Oh, Oh no, Okay, Olson, One, Opposite, Order, Other, Outlaw, Out of trouble, Outsiders

Panic, Paper, Passed, Paul, Pay, Peaceful, Perfect, Pilet, Place, Play, Playing, Pleasant, Please, Pleasure, Plenty, Policeman, Policemen, Pool, Possie, Pranks, Pray, Predicament, Principle, Prison, Pump, Punish, Punished, Punt, Purpose, Purse, Puzzle, Puzzled

Quiet

Ran, Real, Record, Restless, Right, Ring, Riot, River, Rob, Robber, Robbers, Robbing, Rock, Rod Egen, Roused, Rows, Rubble, Rude, Rush, Russia, Russians

Sang, Satisfactory, Scare, Scream, Search, See, Seek, Seeker, Shakiness, Shoe, Shooters, Shooting, Shot, Should, Sicken, Side walk, Silent, Sin, Six, Sleep, Sleeping, Sleys, Slip, Snow, Soft, Soldier, Solution, Something, Sore, Sorrowful, Sort, Sound, Sour, Souring, Spanked, Speaking, Spelling, Spots, Stare, Start, Stealing, Stones, Stop, Stout, Stranger, Street, Stuck, Stumble, Suffering, Sun, Sunk, Sure, Sweet

Table, Talking too much, Tear, Tears, Tease, Teenager, Teenagers, Temper, Tension, Terror, Tests, That, The, Things, Think, Thought, Threat, Time, Tire, Tired, Tires, To, Toil, Tour, Traffic, Trap, Trial, Tribulation, Tried, Trouble, Troubles, Trouble shooter, Troublesome, Trout, True, Trusted, Turmoil, TV, Two, Two much

U.S., Unrest, Untroubled

Vandalism

Wagon, Want, Was, Watch, Watch out, Weak, Wealth, Weary, Well, Were, What, Wicked, Wish, Woe, Woman, Wonder, Wonderful, Word, Working, Worthless, Wrong doing, Wrongness, Wrongs

Yack, Yell, Yesterday, You, Young

US

A, Again, Alone, Always, Am, An, And me, Army, Ask, Asked, At

Bad, Bat, Be, Become, Bed, Before, Begin, Bill, Bit, Bob, Bob and Jim, Boo boo bear, Boy, Boy friend, Bruce, Bugs, Bunch, Bunny, Bust, But, Buy, Buying, By, By by

Came, Cars, Childrens, Chrisie, City, Class, Come, Cool, Cousin, Cute

Date, Dave, Dick and I, Did, Does, Donny, Down, Dust, Dusty

Ears, Eat, Eating, Everybody, Everyone, Everywhere

Face, Fast, Faster, Fellows, Fight, Find, Fine, Fingers, Finish, Fix, Folks, Fools, Forever, Forward, Four, Friend, From, Fus

Gang, Get, Girl, Gone, Good, Goodby, Guys

Had, Hair, Halitosis, Hand, Happen, Happy, Has, Have, Hear, Help, Herd, Here, His, Home, Horror, Horse, House, Humans

Ice, In, Into

Jack

Key

Leaving, Let, Lets, Like, Linger, Little, Live, Look, Lots, Lucy and me

Mad, Make, Makes, Man, Marriage, Marry, Me and John, Me and you, Men, Me you, Mike, Milk, Mine, Miss Banovetz, Money, More, More than one, Move, Mrs., Must, My, Myself

Nancy, Navy, Ne, Nice, Night, No, Nose, Not, Nous, Number

Object, Objective, Oh, One, Only, Others, Our gang, Over

Party, Pen, Persons, Play, Played, Please, Plural, Pop, Possessions, Pus

Rain, Right, Rocket, Ron, Rubber

Sea, Sell, Shall, Show, Sick, Slow, Smell, So, Some, Somebody, Something, Sometimes, Stand, State, States, Story, Stove, Students, Sure

Tacks, Take, Tea, Teach, Teacher, Tell, Than, The air, Their, Theirs, Theme, Therefore, Thin, Think, Thus, Today, Told, Tom, Took, Truth, Twins, Two or more, Two people

United States, Us, User, Uses, U.S. Grant, Using, Usually

Voice

Want, Well, Went, We uns, We we, What, When, Where, Whose, Will, Winter, With, Work, Write

Yellow, You me, You're, Yours

VERY

A, Abbreviate, Adj, Afraid, After, Again, Air, Airy, A little, Alligator, Almost, Alright, Although, Amount, Any, Are, At, Awful

Barrel, Barry, Beautiful, Beauty, Because, Becoming, Before, Berries, Best, Black, Book, Bow, Boy, Bright, Brilliant, Busy, Buy

Calm, Canary, Can't, Car, Celery, Certain, Certainly, Clean, Clearly, Color, Common, Complimentary closing, Considerate, Continue, Cry, Cute

Dare, Dead, Deep, Definite, Depends, Description, Desk, Diagram, Differ, Difference, Differs, Disappointing, Do, Dog, Done, Don't know, Dry, Dumb

Each, Early, Easy, Emphatic, English, Enjoy, Even, Everything, Exact, Excellent, Except, Exceptional, Exceptionally, Excessive, Expensive, Expert, Expression, Extra, Extraordinary, Extremes

Fair, Fairy, First, Five, Floor, Food, Forever, Friendly

Gary, Girl, Go, Gold, Gone, Grave

Happened, Hardly, Harry, Have, He, Heard, Her, Here, High, Him, Hoe, Hopeful, Horrible, How, Huge, Hungry, Hurry, Hurt

I, Idea, Ill, Import, Indeed, In particular, Insanitary, Interesting, Ish, It

Just

Kind, Kinds, Knew, Know

Lad, Larger, Last, Late, Left, Less, Letter, Letters, Liking, Look, Lost, Loud, Louse, Love, Lovely, Low, Luck

Maid, Make, Marry, Marvelous, Mary, May, Merely, Mild, Moment, Money, Mood, More, Mostly, Move, Mr., Much so, Music, Must

Neater, Nicely, No, Noisy, None, Not much, Not the same, Not very, Nut

Odd, Off, Oh, OK, On, Open, Over, Own

Particular, Peaceful, Pencil, People, Pepper, Persistent, Petty, Pig, Pistol, Plus, Poorly, Popular, Positive, Possible, Precise, Precisely, Pretty girls, Proud, Pure

Queer, Question

Rapid, Rational, Ready, Reason, Red, Reverend, Rich, Right

Sally, Salt, Scared, School, Sear, See, Sehr, Several, Shape, Shoe, Short, Show, Showy, Sick, Silly, Simple, Simply, Sincere, Sincerely, Six, Sky, Slight, Slightly, Sly, Softly, Solemn, Sometime, Sometimes, Somewhat, Sorry, Sort, Sound, Specific, Splendid, Sports, Star, Statement, Steady, Steel, Still, Strict, Strong, Strongly, Subtle, Such, Sudden, Surely, Surprise, Surprising, Sweet

Tall, Teacher, Tell, Terrible, Terry, Thankful, That, Their, Theme, Then, Thin, This, Thought, Thoughtful, Tight, Time, Tired, Touchy, Toy, Tree, Trees, Tremendously, Tres, Try, Trying, Two

Ugly, Unhappy, Unlikely, Unvariable, Urgent, Usual, Usually

Vale, Valuable, Variable, Varies, Varying, Varys, Vase, Vat, Veer, Very, Very good, Very much, Vicariously, Vitamins

Want, Wary, Way, Weak, Wearily, Weary, Weight, Weird, Welcome, Wet, What, Why, Wide, Wife, Will, Willingly, Wise, Wish, Woman, Wonderful, Words, Writing

Yards, Year, Yet, You are very nice, Young, Your

Zoo

WAS

Accident, Age, All, Also, Always, An, Ancient, And, Angry, Answer, Anything, Apple, Army, Ask, Asked, Ate

Bad, Band, Bandit, Bear, Become, Behind, Being, Big, Black, Brant, Bring, Broken, But

Can, Can't, Cat, Clean, Close, Course, Cover, Cow, Crazy, Crying

Dad, Death, Deceased, Did she, Died, Distinct, Dog, Doing, Dope, Dose, Dream

Easy, English, Enough, Every, Exist

Fact, Fair, Far, Father, Finally, Find, Fine, First, Fit, Flowers, Fore, Forget, Found, Friend, Friendly, From, Fun, Fuss

Gail, Game, Girl, Glad, Go, Got, Grave stone

Had been, Happening, Hard, Have, Have been, Hear, Heat, Height, Hello, Help, Hem, He was nice, History, Horrid, Hot, House, How, However

Idea, If, Inside, Interested, In the past, I was some place

Job, Jump, Just

Kidding, Know

Land, Last, Late, Latter, Like, Link, Little, Load, Longer,

Look, Lost, Lusts

Mad, Make, Man, Mat, May, Maybe, Mean, Meat, Minneapolis

Naughty, Near, New, No longer, No more, None, Not there, Nuts

Of course, Oh, OK, One, Ones, Own

Part time, Past tense, Pen, People, Person, Pig, Pin, Place, Places, Playing, Plus, Post, Previous, Purple

Questions, Quick

Ready, Really, Red, Remember, Right, Ring, Robber, Rocket, Ruined,

Same, Saying, School, Seen, Shall, Shiny, Should, Sick, Sickening, Single, Sit, Slow, So ever, Sold, Sometime, Sometimes, Somewhere, Soon, Sorrow, Sow, Still in, Still is, Story, Stupid, Sun, Sure, Surprised

Table, Take, Taken, Talking, Team, Ten, Tense, Than, Them, Think, Thinking, Time past, Tired, Tis, To be, Together, Told, Too, Try, Twas, Two, Typing

Used, Use to, Use to be, Usual

Verba

Walk, Wall, Wanted, War, Wash, Was not, Was she there, Was that, Was there, Way, Week, Well, Weren't, Whenever, Which, White, Will be, Winning, Wish, Won't, Work, Would, Would be, Write

Your, Yours

WE

A, Ain't, Al, Alone, Alot, Also, Always, Am, An, Aren't, Ate

Bags, Barb, Be, Became, Bee, Big, Bill, Buy, By

Car, Care, Cars, Children, Class, Coming, Companionship, Couple, Cow

Dating, Day, Dick and I, Did, Didn't, Dinner, Discomfort, Drove

Editorial, Enjoy, Everybody, Everyone

Face, Fair, Fast, Feel, Feet, Few, Five, Flee, For, French, Friend, Fun

Game, Gang, Get, Girl, Gone, Good

Happy, Hate, Having, He and I, Hear, Her, Here, He they, Hi, His, Humans, Hurry

If, Into, Is

Jumped

Karin, Key, Kids, Kiss

Learn, Lee, Left, Letters, Live, Looked, Lot, Lots

Made, Man, Married, Marry, May, Me and you, Meeting, Men, Milk, More than one, Moss

Nancy Larson, Ne, Need, Nostrum, Not, Number, Nuts

Obey, Observe, Often, Oh, Old, One, Order, Others, Out, Over, Own

Pair, Partners, Pea, Plane, Play, Played, Plus, Possession, Pronoun, Put

Race, Ready, Rest, Ride, Roast, Run

Said, Same, Sat, School, Sea, Shall, Silly, Sing, Sit, Sleep, Slowly, Smart, So, Soft, Some, Someone, Some people, Something, Somewhere, Stand, String, Study, Sue and I, Susan, Swim

Take, Take off, Talk, Tall, Tell, Test, Than, Thank, Thee, Their, There, They're, Though, Thought, Time, To, Togetherness, Too, Tow, Try

Understand

Very

Wake, Walk, We, We're, We are, Weather, Wed, Wee, Wee wee, We have, Well, Weren't, We've, Whom, Why, Wisconsin, Wise, Woe, Won't, Word, Would, Wow, Write, Wrote

Yes, You and I, You and me, Your, You've

WHAT

Activity, Adjective, Again, Alive, All, Altogether, Am, Amazed, And, Antidisestablishmentarianism, A nut, Anything, Arithmetic, As, Astonished, Ate

Baby, Ball, Bar, Be, Been, Before, Believe, Bird, Blanket, Blouse, Book, Books, Boys, But, By

Carry, Cars, Case, Chair, Citizen, Clock, Coat, Color, Come, Could, Cow, Crime, Cut

Dance, Day, Dead, Deaf, Depends, Describe, Desk, Didn't know, Different, Does, Doing, Door

Ear, Ears, Eh, Else, English, Even, Exclaim, Excuse, Expression

Fact, Felt, Fence, Find, Fire, Fool, Four letters, French, Fun

Get, Gives, Go, Goes, Good, Grammar, Green, Gut

Had, Hah, Happy, Has, Hath, Haven't, Heard, Hearing, Hearless, Heat, Heavens, Heh, Help, Hen, Her, Hi, Hill, Him,

His, Hit, Ho, Hog, Holler, Home, Hunt, Hut

Idiot, Importance, Insect, Interrogative, In the world, Isn't, Item, I've

Jig saw, Jon

Know

Lake, Leaf, Learned, Light, Light bulb, Like, Line, List, Listen, Lives, Long, Look, Looking, Lost

Mad, Make, Makes, Man, Many, Matter, May, Maybe, Mean, Means, Might, Mine, Monster, More, Mr. Anderson, My

New, News, Next, Nice, Nose, Not what, Noun

On, Or, Out, Outside, Over

Paper, Pardon me, Pencil, People, Person, Pig, Pigeon, Plant, Pot, Putt

Que, Quel, Questionable, Questions

Really, Reason, Red, Report, Ride, Right, Run, Runs

Saw, Say over, School, Secret, Shade, Shall, Should, Shut, Since, Six, Slow, So ever, Solid, Someone, Son, Soon, Sort of, So what, Spoon, Stop, Strut, Sure, Sweet

Talk, Tall, Than, That's, Their, There's, These, Think, Thinking, Thought, Through, Tot, Toy, Try

Understand, Understandles, Unknown, Up

Very

Wait, War, Was it, Wate, Wave, Way, Wear, Well, Wet, What are you doing, Whatever, Whats, Whatsoever, What what, Wheat, Wherefore, While, Whip, Whom, Wish, Wished, Woman, Women, World, Worry, Would, Wound, Wrong

Year, Yesterday

WHERE

About, Abouts, Accident, Adverb, Africa, Air, All, America, An, Ann, Any, Anyplace, A place

Back, Be, Bed, Been, Behind, Bewildered, Blank, Blow, Boat, Building

Calf, California, Can't, Care, Chair, Chapel, Church, City, Class, Classroom, Clean, Clothes, Cloths, Come

Dare, Dark, Day, Desk, Do, Dog, Dogs, Donde, Don't, Don't know, Drug store

Eat, Else, Ere, Every, Everywhere

Far, Fast, Father, Fence, Field, Fir, Florida, Food, Foot, Found

Garage, Girl, Goes, Golf, Good, Goodby, Good question, Greek, Grill, Grow

Happen, Hare, Has, Hat, Have, Hi, Hid, Hidden, Hiding, Him, His, Hit, Hook, How come, Huh, Hungry

If, I'm, In, Iowa, Is he, Is it, Is it question mark, Is she

Know

Lady, Land, Last night, Light, Listen, Live, Locate, Looking, Loves, Lunchroom

Man, Mar, Mare, Marry, Meow, Moon, More, Mouse, Movie, Moving, Mpls., Music, My

Never, Nice, Night, No, No place, Notes, Nut, Nuts

Of, Off, On, Once, One, Or, Orange, Or when, Our, Outside, Over someplace

Paper, Park, Party, Peak, People, Places, Preposition

Questioningly, Question mark, Questions

Read, Reason, Ring, Rise, River, Road, Ron, Room

See, Seen, Shall, She, Shirt, Shoes, Shot, Show, Sky, Snow, So, Some, Spot, State, Stick, Store, Strange place, Street, Sunset

Take, Talk, Tear, Than, That, Theater, Them, These, Those, Too, Toward, Town, Tree, Two

Under, Under there, Upon, Us

Want, Warm, Wash. D.C., Was it, Weird, Well, Weren't, What place, Whence, Where, Where abouts, Where at, Wherefore, Where meet, Where's, Wherever, While, Whom, Whose, With, Wonder, Wood, Wore, Work, World

Yonder

WHISKEY

Aa, Ach, A drink, Advertisement, Afraid, A hangover, Alcoholic, Alcoholism, Ale, And, Apartment

Bad tasting liquor, Barrel, Bars, Bartender, Bead, Beard, Bearded man, Beer joint, Beer or wine, Beverage drink, Bird, Biting, Black and white, Bond, Boot, Boot leg, Boot legging, Boss, Bottles, Bottom, Boy, Boys, Brand, Bread, Breath, Breathe, Brew, Bright, Brink, Bronze, Broom, Bum, Bunnys, Burning, Burp, Burping, Burr, Buzz

Cabin Still, Can, Canadian Club, Cerebral palsy, Cheer, Cheese, Children, Chug, Cigarettes, Clean, Coke, Cold, Collins, Cork, Cowboys, Crime, Cup

Danger, Dangerous, Daring, Dark, Day, Decadence, Despair,
Destructible, Ding, Disgust, Dislike, Distasteful, Dizzy,
Donkey, Door, Doug, Dress, Drinker, Drink good, Drink-
ness, Drinks, Drive, Drunkards, Drunker, Drunk person,
Dry, Dumb, During
Eat, Eliot Ness, Evil
Face, Faster, Fat, Father, Fine, Fire water, Fluffy, Fluid,
Food, Forbidden, Form, Friday, Friskey, Funny, Fuss
Girl, Glob, Gold, Good pick up, Grad, Grand dad, Grape,
Great
Hams, Hand, Hangover, Happiness, Happy, Hard, Harmful,
Harsh, Have, Haziness, Head, Health, Healthy, Heard, Hi,
Hic, Hiccoughs, High, Highball, Hill billy, Him, History,
Honey, Horrible, House, Hurry
Ice cubes, Ick, Icky, I don't think of it, If, Indians, Intoxicate,
Intoxicated, Intoxication, Is, Ishy, Ishy things
Jack, Joe, Joint, Juice, Jump, Junk
Kahn, Keg, Kennedy, Kitten
Lamp, Larry Labrie, Laugh, Law, Lay, Lazy, Licked,
Licorice, Life, Light, Liquor plastered, Loaded, Loud, Love
Make man drunk, March eleven, Me, Mean, Medicine, Men,
Mess, Milk, Mix, Money, Monkey, Moonshine, Morality,
Mouth, Music, Mustache, My dad
Naughty, Neat, Need, Never, Night club, Ninety proof, No,
Nose, Not good, Nothing
Oh boy, Oil, Old fashioned, Old Grand Dad, On, One,
One fifth, One hundred proof
Papa, Party, People, Person, Pin, Pint, Pirate, Plastered,
Pleasure, Poison, Poor, Potent, Prohibition
Radio, Raw, Reading, Red, Refreshment, River, Road,
Ron, Roses, Rot, Rot gut, Rough
Said, Saloon, Saturday, Seagram's, Seagram's Seven, See,
Seven Crown, Shame, Shave, She, Show, Sickness, Sin,
Sinful, Sing, Slow, Slurp, Smart, Smooth, Soda, Song,
Soothing, Sorrow, Sound, Sour dough, Sourness, Spread,
Sting, Stink, Straight, Street, Stupid, Swift
Taffy, Take, Tart, Taste, Tavern, These, Thing, Thirst,
Throw, Tickles, Tight, Time, To drink, Toy, Tricky,
Trouble
Ugh, Umm, Uncle, Us, Using
Vat sixty nine scotch, Vice, Vulgar
Wagon train, Want, Waste, Watching, Week, Whee, Wheeze,
Which, Whine, Whisk, Whiskers, Whiskey drunk,
Whispers, Whistle, White, Wild, Will, Win, Wind, Wish,
Wished, Wit, Work, Write, Wrong
Yes, Yum, Yummy

WHISTLE

Admire, Al Jolson, Aloud, Am, A noise, Apple, Are, Arm, At
a girl, Attract, A tune
Bag, Bait, Ball, Bark, Basketball games, Beat, Beautiful,
Bed, Beer, Betty, Big, Birds, Blast, Blind, Blonde, Blood,
Bloom, Blowing, Blows, Blue, Board, Bold, Bottle, Bow,
Box, Break, Breath, Breathe, Brisk, Brother, Brown, Brr,
Building, Bus, Buzz
Came, Canary, Can't, Car, Cat, Chair, Cheer, Child, Children,
Clean, Clear, Club, Coat, Cold, Comfortable, Command,
Cops, Corner, Crack, Crackers, Cry, Cute girl
Daughter, Dime store, Direction, Dock, Down, Duck
Ear, Eating
Fear, February, Female, Fingers, Fire, Flirt, Flu, Football,
Fox, Fresh male, Friend, Funny
Gaiety, Game, Gone, Good, Grapes, Grass, Grisel, Groan,
Gun, Guy
Hair, Hall, Hand, Hat, Have, Heard, Hello, Help, Hem, Hi,
High pitch, High sound, Him, Hit, Honk, Hope, House, How,
Humming, Hurt, Hymn
I can't, Inside, Instrument, Is
Jerk
Kid, Kiss
Lad, Lady, Lard, Laying, Less, Lightly, Like, Like it, Lip,
Listen, Little, Load, Lode, Loudly, Loud sound, Lousy,
Low, Lunch, Lunch time
Make noise, Male, Margie, Marry, Me, Melody, Men, Merry,
Metal, Mice, Missile, Mist, Moan, Mom, Money, Month,
Mon whistle, Motor, Mouse
Need, Nice, No, Noon, Nosey
Object, Ouch
Peep, Person, Pierce, Pitch, Plane, Plastic, Play, Plow,
Policewoman, Pucker, Pucker lips, Pulchritude, Pure, Purse

Quickly, Quiet, Quietly, Quit, Quite
Rabbit, Railroad, Rain, Red, Reed, Right, Ring, Run, Russ
Sail, Sailor, Sang, Santa Claus, School, Scout, Screech, See,
Sergeant, Sharpness, Sheer, Ship, Shirt, Short, Signal,
Singing, Sleep, Smile, Smoke, Smooth, Snack, Snob, Snore,
Softly, Somebody, Songs, Sore, Speak, Spit, Sports, Squirt,
Steam, Steel, Step, Store, Strips, Sweet, Symphony
Table, Take, Teacher, Thatch, The High and the Mighty, Thing,
Think, Thistle, Thrill, Through, Throw away, Time, Tin,
Tongue, Tree, TV
Vibration, Voice
Wait, Wale, Walk, Walking, Wear, Weave, Were, Whale, When,
While, Whine, Whiskey, Whist, Whistle, Whistled, Whistling,
White, Who, Whoo, Wild, Willow, Wise, Wish, Wood,
Wooden, Word, Wow, Wowee
Yankee Doodle, Yes, You, Your

WHITE

A color, Air, Angel, Angle
Bake, Beauty, Bernie, Bird, Bit, Bite, Blanket, Block, Boat,
Boy, Bread, Brick
Cap, Cashmere, Castle, Chair, Chalk, Church, Cleanliness,
Clothes, Coal, Collar, Colorful, Colors, Cool, Covers,
Cow, Crappy, Crayon, Creamy, Crystal
Darkness, Deer, Dirty, Doctor, Don't show good, Dot, Drink,
Duck
Egg
Fabric, Face, Fast, Feather, Feathers, Fell, Fence, Fight,
Fish, Floor, Flower, Flowers, Fluffy, Ford, Formal,
Fruit, Fun, Fur
Geese, Ghost, Girl, Gleaming, Gloves, Glow, Goat, God, Gold,
Good, Gray, Grey
Handsome, Hat, Heaven, Hi, High, Hot, Houses
Ice, It
Kitten
Lace, Lady, Lamb, Large, Light color, Linen, Love, Lovely
Marble, Marriage, Might, Mouse, Mt.
Nails, Neck, New, Night, Nile, No color, Nun
Object
Pale, Pant, Papers, Parrot, Perfect, Person, Place, Pond,
Pore, Print, Pureness
Rabbit, Rabbit cotton tail, Race, Rapids, Rat, Reflect, Ribbon,
Right, River, Rivers, Room, Rose
Salt, Same, Sand, Satin, Screen, Sharp, Sheep, Sheets,
Shimmering, Shiny, Shite, Show, Sick, Silk, Skiing, Skin,
Skirt, Sky, Slip, Slow, Small, Smear, Smooth, Snow flakes,
Sno white, Snow white, Something colorful, Space, Sparkle,
Spring, Startlingly, Stone, Stove, Summer, Sun, Sure,
Swan
Table cloth, Tea, Teeth, Thin, This, Tight, Tired, Towel,
Translucent, Transparent
Us
Vanilla, Veil, Virgin
Wait, Wall, Warm, Wash, Water, Waves, Wedding dress,
Wedding gown, Wedding, Were, Whistle, White, Wind, Window,
Winter, Woman, Women, Wonder, Wool, Wrong
Yes, You

WHO

A, And, Answer, Anyone, A person, Apple, Aren't, Are you,
Asked, Asking, At
Barbara, Be, Becomes, Bill, Bird, Bow, But
Called, Can't, Car, Carol, Cereal, Come, Could, Couldn't,
Cries
Dad, Dat, Day, Desk, Dick, Did it, Died, Dies, Doesn't, Dog,
Doll, Don, Done, Don't, Door, Dr. Dussers, Duane, Ducks,
Dunnit
Ears, Eat, Eisenhower, Exclamation
Faces, Father, Five, Fly, For, Forgot, For whom, Fought who,
Friend, Friends
Gets, Ghost, Girls, Gives, Go, Goes, Going, Good, Got, Gum,
Gun, Guns
Ha, Halloween, Hard, Has, Have, Heard, Here, Hers, Hey,
Hi, Hide, Hiding, Hit, House
Ike, I'm, Important, In, Isn't, Is who, Its
Jerry
Kids, Killed, Kittens, Know
Leaves, Left, Live, Long, Looks, Loot, Lots, Love
Many, Mary, Maverick, May, Maybe, Meet, Men, Mine, Mo,
Mon, Mother, My, Mystery

417

Needs, Never, New, None, No one, Nose, Not, Not who
Oats, Of, Owe, Owls, Owns
Pan, Patty, Pay, Persons, Phil, Picture, Pig, Plays, Pony,
  Pow, Prep, President, Puzzle, Puzzled
Question mark, Questions, Qui
Ran, Reason, Repeat, Room mate, Row, Roy
Saw, Seen, Shoe, Should, Show, Society, Something, Soon, Sort,
  Stars, Stopped, Stories, Stranger
Table, Tablet, Than, That's, Their, Theirs, Thing, Those,
  Though, To, Tree, Tries, Tuesday, TV
Unknown
Wants, Was that, Wear, Which one, Who, Who ever, Whole,
  Whoo, Who's who, Whowo, Witch, With, Wizard, Wolf, Woman,
  Women, Won, Wondering, Won't, Woo, World, Wound, Wow
Yes

WHY

Add, Also, Always, Am, And, Aren't, Asked
Baby, Bad, Because why, Bet, Betsy, Box, Boys, Brother, But,
  Buy, Bye
Cake, Cannot, Can't, Can you, Car, Child, Come, Confuse,
  Could, Could be, Cow, Curiosity, Curious
Day, Dead, Dear, Did he, Didn't, Die, Done, Donkey, Do not,
  Don't know, Dot, Do this, Doubtful, Dropped, Dye
English, Explain, Explanation, Expression
Fall, Far, Fast, Fault, Find, Fly, Folks, Fore, Forget,
  Forgot, For what, For what reason, Frown, Fry
Game, Gas, Gee, Genius, Girl, Got it, Green, Guess, Guy
Ha, Happy, Hard, Hats, Have, Have to, Hay, He, Hell, Help,
  Her, Here, Hey, Hide, Him, His, Ho
Idea, Intelligence, Interrogation, Isn't
Knew, Knot
Laughs, Lie, Like, Live, Look, Love
Mad, Mail, Man, Mat, May, Maybe, More, Most, Mother, MQ,
  Mystery
Neighbor, Night, Noise, Nothing, Numbers
Of course, Oh come, Oh why, OK, Okay, Only, Or, Out, Owl
Part, Patsy, Pest, Picture, Pie, Pig, Please, Porque, Problem,
  Puzzlement
Questionable, Questioned, Questions, Quiz
Ramsey, Reasons, Record, Reply, Rig, Right, Run, Rye
Sad, Said, Say, School, Science, See, Ship, Short, Should I,
  Shouldn't, Should they, Shut, Shut up, Sigh, Sing, Sister, Sky,
  Someone, Something, Sometimes, Soon, Start, Still, Stop,
  Store, Story, Stupid, Sure
Table, Tell, Thee, Them, Therefore, This, Thought, Thy, Tie,
  To, Today, Tongue, Too, Tree, Tube
Understand, Unknown
Very
Waist, Wander, Want to know, Warm, Warum, Water, Wear,
  When what where, Whither, Whom, Why, Why did you do it,
  Wind, Window, With, Wondering, Won't, Wouldn't, Writing
Y, Yellow, Your

WINDOW

Address, Apartment, Are
Bachelor, Ball, Bar, Bare, Baseball, Bat, Bath, Bay, Beaten,
  Beautiful, Bed, Belfry, Bird, Black, Blue, Book, Bough,
  Boy, Brake, Breakable, Bright, Brook, Building, Bunker
Cabin, Captiveness, Casement, Ceiling, Cell, Cellar, Cleaning,
  Clear glass, Clearness, Climb, Closed, Cloud, Crack
Day, Daylight, Dead, Dear, Die Fenster, Dirt, Divorce,
  Dog, Doll, Dome, Down, Drape, Drapes, Dress
Eagle
Face, Fall, Father, Fight, Fine, Flew, Floor, Flower pot,
  French, Fresh, From, Fun
Gas, Glass and pane, Glasses, Glow, Good, Got, Grass, Guess
Hall, Hard, Hear, Hello, Hose, Hot, House plan, Houses,
  Husband
Icy, In
Johnson
Lady, Lake, Land, Landscape, Lattice, Lean, Leave, Leaves,
  Little, Lock, Long, Low
Married, Meadow, Moon, Mountains, Mouse, Movie
Nature, Nice, None
Object, Old, Old woman, Openness, Open space, Orphan, Out
  of doors
Painting, Pair, Panel, Panes, Paper, Peeker, Peeper, People,
  Person, Pin, Pine, Place, Plain, Plan, Poor, Porch, Pretty,
  Proof, Purse

Reading, Reflection, River, Roof, Rough, Ruin, Rung
Sail, Scenes, School room, Sea, Seeing, Seen, See out, See
  thru, Selling, Sense, Shades, Shadow, Sheep, Shield, Shine,
  Shining, Shiny, Shop, Shopper, Shut, Shutter, Sight, Single,
  Sitting, Skill, Slide, Slip, Small, Smooth, Space, Spider,
  Spray, Spring, Stain, Still, Store, Storm, Street, Sunbeam,
  Sunlight, Sunny, Sunshine
Table, Thing, Three, Tickets, Tramp, Trees, TV
Ugly
Ventana, Vision
Washing, Watch, Water, Weather, White, Wide, Widow,
  Widower, Wife, Windes, Window pane, Windows, Window
  sill, Winter, Wiper, Women, Women not married, Wood, World
Yellow, You, You can see out of it

WISH

Airplane, Always, Angel, Answered, Apple, Apples, Asked,
  Asking, Attain, Attainment, A well, Awhile
Baby, Bad, Baseball bat, Bed, Beg, Beggar, Believe, Better-
  ment, Bicycle, Big, Bird, Blow, Bones, Book, Born, Boy,
  Boyfriend, Boys, Bright, Bring, Brown, Brush, Bum, By
Cake, Call, Came, Camping, Canada, Care, Castle, Cat,
  Catalog, Catalogue, Chair, Child, Church, Clear, Cloth,
  Clothes, Clouds, Club house, Cod, Coin, Coins, Cold, Come,
  Complain, Cry, Curse
Dancer, Danger, Dashs, Dave, Day, Day dreaming, Dead,
  Decide, Delightful, Demand, Design, Desired, Dick, Disher,
  Dive, Don't, Don't have, Don't wish, Doubt, Down, Dreamer,
  Dream of something, Dress, Drum
England, Ever, Everything, Expectation, Expert
Fable, Face, Fair, Fairies, Fairy tales, Faith, Fall, False,
  Fantasy, Fast, Fate, Fats, Find, Fine, Fingers, Flower,
  Foolish, Foot, Forever, Forget, For something, For
  something you want, Fortune, Fountain, Four, Friend,
  Fulfill, Fulfillment, Full, Futile, Future
Game, Get it, Get something, Ghost, Girls, Give, Given, Glad-
  ness, Glove, Go, Gone, Good things, Got, Gun, Gypsy
Had it, Hair, Hand, Hands, Happen, Happened, Hat, Hate,
  Having, Heaven, Help, Her, Here, Hinder, Ho, Holiday,
  Home, Hoped, Hope for something, Hopeless, Hopes, Horse
  shoe, Hot, House, How, However
Ick, Ideal, If, Imagine, Ish, It, I want
Jack, Joanne, Job, John, Joy
Kathy, Kids, Kiss, Knew, Knot, Know
Lady, Lake, Life, Lights, Liked, List, Longing, Long life,
  Look, Lots, Lucky
Mad, Make up, Man, Many, Marry, Maybe, Mean, Meet,
  Memory, Men, Mighty, Million, Millionaire, Mine, Miracle,
  Mirrow, Miss, Mist, Mother, Music, My, Myself
Name, Need, Never never, New, Nickel, Night, No, Non wish,
  Not, Nothing, Not wish, Now, Number
Obey, Obtain, Okay, Old, Order, Ox bone
Package, Pennies, People, Person, Piano, Pish, Plausible,
  Play, Please, Present, Presents, Pretend, Put away
Rabbit, Rain, Rainbow, Received, Remember, Request, Reveal,
  Right, Roberta, Room, Rum, Run
Sacred, Said, Say, School, Secret, Security, Shop, Shush,
  Shut up, Sigh, Sister, Sky, Slow, Small, Smart, Snow, Soap,
  Someone wishing, Something wonderful, Something you want,
  Son, Song, Sorrow, Sound, Star gaze, State, Stay, Story,
  Success, Suit, Summer, Superstitions
Table, Take, Tear, Terrible, Test, Thank, Thanks, There,
  Things, Thinks, Through, Time, Tooth, To want, Toy,
  Train, Treat, Tree, Trip, Truck, Try, Turkey bone, TV
Unnecessary, Upon, Urge
Vision
Wand, Wander, Wanted, Wanting, Want something, Was, Washy,
  Wealth, Wear, Were, Were not, What, When, When you
  want something, Which, Whisper, Whistle, White, Whiter,
  Why, Win, Window, Wine, Wipe, Wise, Wished, Wisher,
  Wishes, Wishful, Wishing bone, Wish well, Wishy, Witch,
  Wizard, Won, Wonderful, Won't, Word, Words, Work, Worker,
  World peace, Worry, Would, Would come true, Wrong
Yearn, Yep, You had something

WITH

Accompanying, Add, Addition, Against, Al, Along side, Alot,
  Altogether, Always, An, Anything, Apart, A person, Are,
  Arms, Around, As, Ask, Ax
Baby, Beach, Because, Behind, Being, Between, Bigger, Bill,

Black, Blank, Body, Book, Books, Both, Bowling, Brother, Brought, Bus, But, Butter

Cake, Can, Candy, Car, Carry, Cart, Chair, Chalk, Child, Children, Clothes, Color, Come, Company, Con, Conduct, Connect, Connected, Cousin, Cow, Crazy, Cream, Crowd

Date, Dave, Desk, Dick, Do, Donny, Down, Draw

Each, Ease, Easy, Elder, Else, Even, Every

Far, Fast, Faster, Fitch, Flat, For, Fork, From

Game, Gastropods, Get, Gloves, God, Good, Got, Go with, Grandmother, Gun, Gusto, Guy

Had, Hand, Hard, Has, Hasn't, Hat, Having, Heart, Held, Help, Hers, Hid, His, Hit, Home, How

If, I'm, Include, Irk, Is, Its

Jack, Jim, Joanne, Joe, Joining

Key, Kids, Kind, Knowledge

Lake, Late, Latin, Leave, Left, Length, Less, Life, Limit, Lit, Little, Live, Lonesome, Looking, Love

Math, Med, Mine, Miss, Mit, Mitt, Mom, Money, Mother, Myself

Name, Near, Never, Next, Next to, No, None, No one, Nope, Nothing, Not with

Off, Oh, Old, One, Onions, Others, Our, Outside, Over

Parents, Partner, Pills, Playground, Plus, Possession, Pride

Question

Radio, Ran, Reason, Rice

Said, Same time, Sane, Sang, Sat, School, See, Sentence, Set, Sharon, She, Shoe, Show, Side, Sister, Sit, Sitting, So, Soft, Some, Some else, Someone's, Soon, Spelling, Stand, Star, Stay, Still, Success

Tack, Taking, Teacher, Teeth, Tell, Their, They, Thing, Things, Those, Thou, Three, Through, Tick, Ticket, Time, Toy, Travel, Trust, Two people

Under, Until, Use

Walk, Warmth, Wasn't, Water, Way, Went, Were, Wheel, Which, While, White, Width, Will, Win, Wish, Witch, Wither, With hold, With it, With not, With someone, Won't, Words, Wrath, Writing

Yet, You are with someone, Yours

WOMAN

Adult, Ah, Aha, A lady, An, And, Angry, Animal, Apron, Arm, Arms, A sex, Attractive

Bardot, Bat, Being, Best, Betty, Big, Birth, Black, Blouse, Body, Bossy, Bow, Breasts, Butterfly, Buxom

Cape, Cat, Cautious, Chair, Chart, Chills, Clothing, Cloths, Coats, Cold, Comfort, Command, Cook, Cooking, Cooled, Cow, Creep, Cry

Dainty, Dance, Dark, Dish, Dog, Dogs, Dresses, Dressing, Dressy, Driver, Durable

Ethel, Exclamation mark, Eyes

Fair, Fashion, Fashionable, Feet, First, Flesh, Floor washer, Flowers, Friend, Friendly, Fur

Gal, Gentleness, Girdle, Gloves, Good looking, Graceful, Grandma, Grandmother, Great, Grown, Grown up

Hair do, Hand, Happy, Has, Hats, Head, Health, Hear, Heart, Heels, Her, Help, High, High heels, Holler, Home, House, House wife, Human being, Hunger, Husband

Inferior

Jacket, Janet, Jewels, Joan, Judy

Kathy, Kay, Kid, Kids, Kiss

Large, Laughter, Leg, Light, Little, Living things, Long, Long hair, Look, Looks, Loud

Ma, Mad, Main, Marilyn Monroe, Marriage, Married, Mate, Mature, Maturity, Mild, Mink, Miss, Miss America, Models, Mommy, Money, Monster, Mouth, Move, My mom

Nail, Nancy, Nice looking, Nose, Not man

Older girl

Picked, Place, Pleasant, Purse

Real, Ring, Romance, Round, Run

School, See, Sew, Shape, Shapely, She, Shirt, Shoe, Shoes, Sing, Sister, Sit, Skirt, Slave, Slender, Song, Spun, Stern, Store, Strength, Sweet

Tell, Terrific, Thin, Tress, Two

Ugly

Walk, Warm, Weak, Wear, What, Where, Whole, Wig, Wine, Wise, Wonder

Young

WORKING

Accomplish, Action, Acts, After school, Agh, Allowance, Always,

Ambition, Ambitious, Are, Asleep, At

Baby sitting, Back, Bad, Baloney, Bank, Beds, Bench, Best, Big, Blister, Blisters, Blow, Bore, Boring, Boss, Bowling, Box, Boy, Breathing, Brick laying, Bricks, Bridge, Broken, Broom, Brush, Bum, Business, Butcher

Callous, Can't, Car, Carpenter, Carpentry, Carrying, Carry out, Cars, Car wash, Cementing, Chemistry, Chores, Citizen, Clean, Clear, Clerking, Clothes, Clothing, Collapse, Comfort, Complain, Concentrating, Concentration, Condition, Construction, Construction zone, Crap

Daddy, Dayton's, Dentist, Desk, Difficult, Dig, Dirt, Dirty, Disable, Dish washing, Dislike, Ditch, Ditches, Doctor, Doing something, Don't like it, Do something, Dr., Drawing, Dread, Dreaming, Driving, Drudgery, Drunk, During, Duty

Earn, Eating, Employed, Energetic, English, Enjoy, Enjoying, Enjoyment, Exercise, Exert, Exhausted, Exhausting, Exhaustion

Factories, Farm, Farmer, Fast health, Fatigue, Fields, Finish, Fired, Fix, Fixed, Fixing, Fooling, Foolish, Forty hours, Forty hr. week, Free, Fried, Friend, Fun satisfaction

Garden, Gas station, Go, Goal, Going, Gone, Goofing, Grass, Grief, Grown, Grunt, Gymnastic

Habit, Habits, Hammering, Hands, Happening, Happy, Hard going, Hardship, Heat, Heavy, Helpful, Helping, High, Hire, Hit, Hole, Home, Homework, Hope, Horrid, Horse, House keeping, House work, How, Hurry, Husband

Ick, Illness, In, Industrious, Industry, Iron

Jobs, Jump

King

Lab, Ladder, Lading, Lawn mower, Laying bricks, Lay off, Lays, Laziness, Library, Life, Like, Little, Living, Lo, Lofting, Loitering, Looking, Lot, Lumber, Luch, Lying

Machine, Machinery, Machines, Machinist, Making, Male, Man hole, Manual, Masculine, Mean, Meat, Mechanical, Mining, Model, Mom, Mother, Movement, Muscles, Muscular work, My, My job, My place of employment

Nail, Navy, Necessary, Never, Nice, Night, Nine to five, Noise, None, Not fun, Not playing, Not resting, Now

Often, Oh, Old, Or

Pain, Painting, Paper, Papers, Parking, Past time, Payment, Pen, Perspiration, Perspire, Pizza, Plane, Planning, Plumbing, Pooped, Post office, Pound, Pounding, Print, Problem, Proletariat, Push, Pushing

Quickly, Quit

Racing, Railroads, Raking, Reading, Recreation, Relaxed, Rocking, Rough, Route, Run, Running

Salary, Satisfaction, Satisfactory, Saturday, Saving, Sawing wood, Scave, Scrub, See, Selling, Setting, Sew, Shape, Shoot, Shop, Sick, Sickening, Sign, Singer, Singing, Sit, Slavery, Slaves, Slum, So, Social Security, Soft, Sold, Song, Soon, Speed, Spelling, Standing, Station, Steel, Stiff, Still, Stocking, Straining, Street, Street cleaner, Street repairs, Strength, Strenuous, Strike, Strong, Struggle, Struggling, Student, Study labor, Subway, Sun, Supporting, Sweep, Sweeping, Sweet, Switch board

Task, Teacher, Tediousness, Terrible, Think, Thought, Tire, Tiredness, Tires, Tiresome, Tiring, Today, Together, Toiling, Took, Tool, Tough, Tractor, Train, Trouble, Truck, Typewriter

Ugh, Ugly, Unemployment, Uniform, Unpleasant, Unwork, Unworking, Up, Using

Vacation

Wages, Waiting, Wash, Water, Welding, Well, Wheat, When, Where, White collar, Windows, Wishing, Woman, Won't, Word, Worked, Worker, Working for money, Works, Work-shop, Write

Yard, Yelling

YELLOW

A color, Al Johnson, Amber, Angel, Anger, Ant, Apple, Art, Autumn, Average, Awake, Awful

Bad, Bag, Bananas, Bank, Barren, Bastard, Bead, Beauty, Bell, Bellow, Belly, Below, Big, Bill, Billow, Birds, Birth, Block, Blond, Bloom, Blouse, Bonanza, Born, Box, Boy, Braid, Braids, Breasted, Breed, Bridge, Bright color, Brightness, Bright sun, Brow, Buds, Bug

Cake, Calendar, Can, Canal, Caps, Careful, Caution, Cavalry, Chair, Chalk, Chick, Chicks, China, Church, Clear, Cloth, Clothes, Collar, Color of butter, Comfortable, Complimentary, Convertible, Cool, Core, Corn, Corn bread, Court, Cow,

Crayons, Curb, Curtain, Curtains
Dandelions, Danger, Day, Decadence, Desk, Dim, Dish, Doug, Dresses, Dress shoes, Duckling
Eat, Eggs, Exciting
Fairy, Fat, Favorite, Feather, Field, Find, Fire, Fires, Food, Forest, Fright
Gay, Gayness, Girl, Glass, Glossy, Goldfinch, Grapefruit, Grass, Gray, Greed, Gutless, Guts
Ham, Happy, Heart, Heat, Hen, Hollow, Homely, Honey, Hornet, Horse, Hot
Ick, Image, Indian, Intense, Ish, It
Jackson, Jap, Japanese, Jaundice, Jello
Kitchen
Lamp, Leave, Leaves, Light bulb, Lightness, Love, Low
Man, Marigolds, Me, Mellow, Melon, Mustard
Nelson, Nice, Nine, Not good, Nut
Paint, Painting, Paints, Pajamas, Pansy, Paper, Park, Parrot, Pastel, Pea, Peacefulness, Person, Petal, Petty, Phone book, Pig, Pillow, Plain, Poison, Primary, Pumpkin, Punk, Puppy, Pms
Rainbow, Raincoat, Ran, Read, Ring, Room, Rug
Sail, Sand, Scarf, Scarlet, Semaphore, Shoes, Shy, Sickness, Sign, Sissy, Sister, Skunk, Sky, Slow, Smoke, Son, Soothing, Spanish, Spring, Stomach, Stone, Stone park, Stop light, Stop sign, Stripe, Striped, Sucker, Sun flower, Sunny, Sunset, Swedes
Tall, Taxi, Think, Thursday, Tie, Tree
Ugh, Unclean, Uniform, Urine
Vase, Violet, Vivid, Volor
Warmth, Warning, Water, We, Wheat, Window
Yarn, Yell, Yeller, Yellow, Yolk, You

YOU

A, Advice, All, Alone, Also, Am, A man, Anyone, Appear, Aren't, Ate
Baa, Baby, Bad, Bat, Be, Belong, Big, Bill, Blonde, Blow, Blue, Body, Boo, Boredom, Bother, Boyfriend, Buddy
Can't, Cars, Cat, Children, Clod, Come, Command, Crazy, Creepy, Cry, Curse
Dan, Darrone, Dave, Dear, Did, Dog, Doing, Done, Door, Drink, Dumb
Ego, Everyone, Ewe, Eyes
Face, Faith, Families, Fear, Finger, Food, For, Friends
Gary, Generous, Good, Goofball
Had, Hair, Hand, Hands, Handsome, Haven't, Health, Himself, His, Hoe, Hoo, House, Housewife, How, Human
If, I'm, In, Instructer, Interesting, Is, Itself
Jack, Janet, Jeff, Jesus, Jimmy
Kay, King, Kool
Lady, Larry, Lips, Look, Looks, Lovely
Men, Mine, Miss Banovetz, Mother, Mr., Must, My
Name, Nancy, Neat, Need, Neighbor, Never, No good, Not, Nothing, Not me, Not you, Now, Nut, Nuts
Oh, Old, Only, Other, Ought, Our, Over, Ow

Paul, Pencil, Personally, Persons, Pig, Play, Point, Pointing, Pretty, Pronoun
Rat, Red
Sad, Saw, Sea, Second, Second person, Shall, Shoe, Shot, Show, Sister, Sit, Smart, So, Somebody, Son, Speak, Square, Stand, Start, Started, Stew, Stop, Susan, Susie, Swell
Table, Tell, Then, That, The, Thee, Their, Then, Thief, Thing, Think, Thou, Time, To, Toe, Two
Ugly, Use
Very, Vic, Vous
Was, Well, Were, What, When, Who, Whom, Why, Win, Woman, Word, Would
Yell, Yellow, Yes, You are nice, Young, You're, Yourselves, Youth

YOUNGER

A, At, Adolescent, Adult, Alan, All, Allen, Amoeba, Animals, Are, As
Babies, Bad, Bat, Beautiful, Better, Big, Bigger, Biggest, Birth, Body, Born, Bother, Boyhood, Boys, Boy than me, Brat, Brave, Bryce, But
Cars, Cheerful, Chest, Childish, City, Comparison, Complex, Cousins, Cry, Curt
Do, Daughter, Delinquent, Dim, Dog, Down, Dying
Early, Easy, Eat, Eldest, Enough, Everyone
Face, Farm, Faster, Fat, Father, Fay, Fifteen, Five, Folks, Fonder, For, Fresh, Fun
Game, Gemmules, Get, Girls, Go, Going, Good, Great, Grown
Handsome, Happier, Happy, Harder, He, Healthy, Help, Higher, Him, His, Ho, Hold, Hood, House, How, Hunger
Ill, Immature, Infant, Infantile, Infants, Innocent, Is, It
January, Junior, Juvenile
Karol, Kevin
Lady, Lamp, Less, Less old, Less wise, Life, Light, Like, Litter, Littlest, Lively, Long, Longer, Look, Looking, Love, Lovely
Mat, Mature, Me, Meet, Mike, Mind, More, Mother, Mouse
Nancy, Never, Nice, Nine, Not, Not as old, Not old, Now
On, Off, OK, Ones, Only, Other, Our, Out
Parents, Phil, Play pen, Pop, President, Prettier, Pretty, Punk
Ripe, Rosy
Said, Sandy, Sat, School, See, Seven, Shame, She, Short, Shorter, Shrimp, Sillier, Sissy, Sisters, Sit, Six, Six years, Smallest, Smarter, Smile, Song, Sophomore, Space, Spring time, Squirt, Still, Strong, Susie, Sweet
Table, Tall, Taller, Teen, Teenager, Test, Than I, Than me, That, The, Them, They, Thing, Think, Thirteen, This, Three, Time, Tinier, Tiny, To, Too, Tool, Too young, Tot, Twenty, Two
Under age, Up, Us
We, Weak, When, Wife, Wilder, With, Woman
Year, Yet, Young kid, Young un, Your, Youthful

RESPONSE INDEX

When entries run over to the top of the next column, the heading is repeated but underscored to indicate that it is a continued entry.

Alot, 81, 119, 121, 124, 127, 139, 174, 175, 181, 183, 185, 195
Aloud, 49, 72, 132, 156, 189
Alphabet, 1, 2, 7, 91, 119, 122
Alps, 37, 113
Already, 4, 5, 16, 17, 77, 82, 94, 118, 173, 184
Alright, 4, 5, 16, 37, 89, 94, 122, 169, 171, 173, 181, 183
Also, 1, 3, 4, 5, 6, 7, 8, 10, 11, 12, 16, 17, 27, 31, 45, 48, 65, 68, 76, 77, 84, 89, 92, 93, 94, 95, 110, 121, 122, 124, 125, 149, 152, 169, 170, 171, 172, 173, 174, 179, 183, 184, 185, 192, 195, 199
Altar, 129, 134
Alter, 4, 12, 170
Alternative, 4, 16, 27, 92, 125, 173
Although, 4, 8, 11, 16, 27, 45, 65, 76, 80, 89, 92, 125, 136, 172, 173, 183, 186
Altitude, 83, 163
Altogether, 4, 173, 186, 195
Aluminum, 54, 151
Alway, 4, 89, 124, 137, 173
Always, 1, 2, 4, 5, 6, 8, 10, 11, 12, 16, 17, 19, 27, 34, 39, 45, 46, 47, 58, 62, 65, 66, 76, 77, 88, 89, 90, 91, 92, 94, 95, 105, 110, 118, 122, 123, 124, 125, 126, 127, 130, 132, 139, 142, 148, 152, 167, 169, 170, 171, 172, 173, 174, 181, 182, 183, 184, 185, 192, 194, 195, 197, 199
Am, 1, 3, 5, 6, 7, 8, 10, 11, 12, 16, 17, 22, 31, 42, 43, 45, 55, 60, 61, 63, 73, 76, 78, 82, 85, 88, 89, 91, 92, 94, 101, 102, 108, 110, 116, 118, 119, 121, 122, 123, 125, 132, 144, 150, 152, 156, 158, 161, 168, 172, 173, 179, 182, 184, 185, 186, 187, 189, 191, 192, 199
Amazed, 3, 122, 186
Amber, 5, 6, 89, 198
Ambition, 6, 17, 52, 89, 197
Ambitious, 17, 197
Amble, 149, 150
Ambulance, 6, 109, 181
Amen, 1, 3, 6
America, 6, 9, 15, 40, 56, 57, 98, 121, 127, 154, 179, 187
American, 6, 7, 37, 40, 56, 57, 98, 134, 151, 154, 181
Amoeba, 170, 200
Among, 4, 12, 66, 147, 195
Amount, 119, 183
Amusement, 55, 127
Amy, 6, 79
An, 1, 2, 3, 4, 5, 6, 7, 8, 9, 11, 12, 16, 17, 27, 30, 31, 34, 42, 56, 60, 77, 91, 92, 93, 94, 95, 102, 104, 108, 109, 110, 116, 119, 120, 121, 122, 123, 125, 126, 128, 133, 150, 151, 152, 167, 168, 169, 170, 171, 173, 178, 179, 182, 184, 185, 187, 195, 196
Ancestor, 70, 134
Ancient, 19, 99, 106, 184
And, 1, 3, 4, 5, 6, 7, 8, 9, 10, 11, 12, 16, 17, 26, 27, 28, 31, 34, 35, 36, 40, 42, 43, 45, 47, 51, 54, 60, 61, 63, 65, 66, 70, 74, 76, 77, 79, 84, 88, 89, 91, 92, 93, 94, 95, 97, 102, 105, 108, 110, 111, 115, 116, 118, 120, 121, 122, 123, 124, 125, 126, 127, 130, 132, 134, 139, 140, 145, 148, 150, 156, 157, 159, 167, 169, 170, 171, 172, 173, 174, 178, 179, 182, 183, 184, 185, 186, 188, 191, 192, 195, 196, 199
Andre, 61, 95, 110

Andy, 8, 76, 78
Angel, 7, 9, 10, 23, 55, 111, 148, 164, 181, 190, 194, 198
Angels, 9, 10, 23, 55
Anger, 2, 4, 15, 17, 20, 23, 24, 36, 40, 47, 49, 55, 56, 68, 70, 90, 92, 96, 104, 107, 111, 115, 117, 129, 133, 148, 154, 155, 181, 198
Angle, 7, 9, 10, 23, 56, 57, 104, 123, 158, 180, 190
Angry, 2, 5, 6, 9, 10, 15, 17, ·20, 23, 38, 39, 47, 49, 86, 90, 96, 104, 107, 109, 120, 133, 136, 140, 145, 148, 152, 155, 164, 181, 184, 196
Anguish, 9, 181
Animal, 1, 2, 7, 9, 17, 22, 24, 28, 29, 33, 34, 38, 39, 40, 43, 53, 56, 69, 72, 73, 86, 87, 90, 95, 100, 101, 104, 105, 108, 109, 115, 127, 129, 133, 140, 143, 148, 149, 157, 158, 161, 165, 169, 170, 172, 178, 180, 196
Animals, 1, 13, 15, 17, 24, 29, 30, 35, 39, 53, 72, 86, 95, 100, 101, 104, 105, 111, 113, 127, 141, 143, 148, 157, 158, 170, 174, 200
Ankle, 64, 85, 97
Ann, 3, 6, 7, 8, 42, 69, 93, 109, 149, 168, 179, 187
Anne, 7, 179
Annie, 7, 72
Another, 1, 4, 6, 7, 8, 16, 17, 27, 31, 62, 77, 89, 92, 94, 121, 123, 125, 132, 168, 169, 173, 179, 195
Answer, 3, 4, 7, 8, 16, 27, 31, 34, 39, 40, 47, 58, 64, 65, 76, 88, 89, 92, 111, 119, 122, 125, 152, 156, 168, 170, 179, 181, 184, 186, 191, 192
Answered, 16, 194
Answers, 16, 119, 125, 173
Ant, 1, 3, 6, 7, 8, 9, 16, 29, 31, 34, 62, 92, 94, 95, 104, 125, 127, 134, 145, 149, 152, 156, 157, 160, 170, 179, 198
Antelope, 7, 137, 165
Ants, 2, 10, 127, 143, 157
Anvil, 7, 73, 81
Anxiety, 2, 9, 134, 181
Anxious, 17, 165
Any, 1, 4, 5, 6, 7, 8, 11, 27, 30, 40, 62, 68, 76, 77, 88, 89, 92, 95, 105, 111, 122, 124, 125, 126, 129, 142, 173, 179, 183, 187
Anyhow, 4, 8, 27, 82, 88, 89, 125, 142, 152, 173
Anyone, 11, 76, 89, 125, 154, 158, 168, 191, 199
Anything, 1, 3, 4, 7, 16, 22, 55, 65, 76, 77, 82, 89, 92, 94, 95, 111, 115, 121, 124, 125, 134, 136, 140, 151, 160, 163, 167, 169, 170, 171, 173, 175, 184, 186, 194, 195
Anytime, 5, 76
Anyway, 3, 4, 5, 16, 27, 76, 77, 88, 89, 92, 125, 152, 173
Anyways, 5, 27, 89, 173
Anywhere, 5, 12, 89, 173, 187
Apart, 4, 43, 60, 89, 108, 167, 168, 195
Apartment, 54, 62, 87, 131, 188, 193
Ape, 2, 7, 10, 17, 26, 100, 109, 146, 169
Apparent, 10, 17, 42
Appeal, 10, 16, 67, 155
Appear, 17, 26, 42, 43, 45, 62, 89, 132, 141, 199
Appearance, 10, 22, 42
Appears, 10, 95
Appendage, 63, 64, 74

Appendix, 52, 161
Appetite, 59, 67, 85, 90
Apple, 1, 3, 4, 6, 7, 8, 10, 11, 16, 20, 22, 25, 30, 32, 34, 35, 37, 52, 59, 62, 67, 68, 71, 75, 76, 77, 80, 83, 85, 89, 90, 93, 95, 98, 121, 124, 125, 127, 133, 138, 139, 142, 151, 153, 155, 159, 160, 161, 162, 164, 167, 168, 169, 170, 176, 178, 184, 189, 191, 194, 198
Apples, 7, 10, 20, 22, 30, 34, 37, 59, 67, 68, 71, 75, 80, 121, 138, 142, 155, 160, 164, 170, 194
Apply, 1, 7, 10, 67
Appreciate, 90, 156
Approach, 10, 17, 43, 45, 115
Apron, 7, 196
Arabia, 33, 99
Arch, 54, 64
Arctic, 20, 44
Are, 1, 3, 4, 5, 6, 7, 8, 11, 12, 16, 17, 25, 26, 27, 30, 33, 34, 35, 39, 42, 43, 45, 54, 57, 59, 60, 61, 62, 63, 65, 66, 69, 72, 75, 77, 82, 84, 85, 88, 89, 91, 92, 94, 95, 100, 105, 108, 110, 118, 119, 121, 122, 124, 125, 127, 132, 134, 141, 142, 143, 144, 148, 150, 152, 158, 159, 163, 168, 169, 170, 171, 172, 173, 174, 176, 178, 179, 182, 183, 184, 185, 186, 187, 189, 191, 192, 193, 195, 197, 199, 200
Area, 26, 41, 82, 158
Aren't, 4, 6, 7, 12, 17, 88, 90, 92, 94, 172, 174, 185, 191, 192, 199
Arf, 53, 156
Argue, 4, 9, 27, 47, 76, 89, 128, 152, 173
Arguing, 27, 128
Argument, 9, 27, 134
Arise, 10, 102, 159
Arithmetic, 8, 26, 34, 39, 58, 75, 77, 88, 119, 125, 131, 158, 167, 186, 197
Arizona, 66, 113
Ark, 50, 80
Arm, 6, 7, 22, 24, 27, 29, 34, 36, 38, 47, 63, 64, 73, 74, 79, 80, 81, 85, 102, 106, 109, 116, 127, 133, 144, 147, 151, 154, 155, 157, 161, 176, 178, 181, 189, 196
Armchair, 36, 46
Armed, 74, 154
Arms, 6, 10, 34, 36, 43, 45, 46, 63, 72, 79, 102, 106, 154, 195, 196
Army, 6, 7, 23, 40, 47, 56, 66, 72, 99, 128, 133, 136, 154, 181, 182, 184
Around, 1, 5, 8, 12, 16, 17, 19, 26, 31, 57, 66, 70, 93, 119, 121, 123, 126, 128, 137, 147, 158, 159, 176, 177, 195
Arrest, 40, 181
Arrive, 10, 17, 45, 108, 130
Arrived, 10, 17, 66, 77, 78
Arrow, 72, 106, 108, 119, 131, 165, 168
Arrows, 30, 72
Art, 1, 3, 6, 7, 12, 15, 23, 28, 29, 44, 50, 53, 57, 71, 108, 114, 117, 127, 134, 135, 170, 198
Article, 1, 7, 8, 62, 81, 95, 108, 121, 170, 175, 178, 186
Articles, 30, 142
Artist, 17, 52
As, 1, 3, 4, 6, 7, 8, 12, 16, 17, 27, 31, 35, 42, 43, 45, 58, 61, 65, 66, 72, 82, 85, 88, 89, 92, 93, 94, 95, 98, 100, 110, 118, 121, 125, 128, 130, 132, 141, 144, 148, 150, 152,

424

Boy, 135, 136, 137, 139, 140, 141, 142, 143, 144, 145, 146, 148, 149, 151, 152, 153, 154, 155, 156, 157, 158, 159, 160, 161, 163, 164, 165, 166, 167, 168, 169, 170, 171, 172, 173, 174, 175, 176, 177, 178, 179, 180, 181, 182, 183, 184, 186, 188, 189, 190, 191, 192, 193, 194, 195, 196, 197, 198, 199, 200
Boys, 2, 3, 5, 7, 8, 9, 13, 15, 20, 24, 27, 35, 38, 39, 43, 44, 48, 49, 53, 55, 60, 61, 65, 69, 72, 76, 78, 81, 84, 85, 90, 92, 97, 102, 107, 108, 109, 110, 111, 112, 114, 122, 124, 125, 127, 128, 130, 131, 136, 137, 141, 145, 149, 154, 158, 164, 170, 171, 174, 175, 179, 180, 181, 182, 185, 186, 187, 188, 189, 192, 194, 195, 200
Bra, 26, 102
Bracelet, 18, 38, 89, 125, 136
Braid, 2, 28, 133, 198
Braids, 69, 106, 198
Brain, 24, 38, 55, 70, 79, 89, 111, 160, 161
Brains, 77, 79, 111
Brake, 57, 108, 149, 167, 176, 181, 193
Branch, 22, 106, 160
Brand, 79, 111, 160, 188
Brandy, 20, 188
Brant, 76, 184
Brass, 101, 107
Brat, 13, 24, 26, 38, 39, 152, 158, 169, 181, 200
Brave, 2, 15, 17, 24, 40, 49, 56, 77, 80, 99, 104, 154, 175, 200
Bread, 2, 8, 18, 19, 20, 28, 29, 30, 31, 34, 37, 39, 44, 50, 51, 57, 59, 67, 68, 71, 75, 79, 80, 86, 90, 96, 98, 99, 106, 108, 115, 121, 131, 136, 138, 139, 142, 153, 160, 161, 162, 164, 165, 166, 175, 176, 180, 188, 190, 198
Break, 22, 25, 63, 75, 81, 87, 101, 108, 160, 167, 175, 176, 181, 189, 193
Breakfast, 25, 59, 67, 90, 115, 166
Breast, 13, 22, 26, 113, 144, 161
Breasts, 26, 196
Breath, 3, 14, 80, 81, 105, 122, 137, 155, 167, 188, 189
Breathe, 8, 105, 117, 137, 188, 189
Breathing, 137, 197
Bred, 28, 37, 56, 79, 133
Breed, 28, 37, 198
Breeze, 29, 37, 44, 58, 120, 132, 136, 165, 193
Brenda, 13, 110
Brew, 181, 188
Brick, 18, 37, 56, 75, 81, 87, 107, 117, 136, 147, 153, 158, 162, 163, 177, 190
Bricks, 34, 81, 87, 123, 133, 158, 163, 197
Bride, 10, 15, 17, 26, 29, 34, 56, 98, 190
Bridge, 1, 26, 36, 66, 68, 83, 89, 97, 102, 106, 121, 123, 126, 135, 141, 150, 170, 197, 198
Brief, 89, 105, 120, 145, 175
Bright, 3, 10, 15, 17, 22, 23, 24, 26, 27, 29, 42, 48, 50, 71, 79, 80, 87, 88, 96, 101, 103, 107, 111, 112, 114, 133, 141, 144, 151, 153, 160, 162, 167, 173, 183, 188, 190, 193, 194, 198
Brighter, 26, 42, 86, 108
Brightness, 71, 101, 103, 112, 114, 133, 198

Brilliant, 26, 103, 133, 183
Brine, 138, 139
Bring, 22, 26, 27, 30, 31, 34, 42, 43, 45, 49, 55, 62, 63, 65, 66, 68, 70, 77, 79, 82, 86, 102, 108, 139, 142, 150, 152, 162, 167, 169, 174, 177, 179, 184, 194, 195
Brink, 98, 188
Brisk, 44, 139, 189
Britain, 99, 104
Brittle, 75, 164
Broad, 21, 26, 42, 54, 69, 73, 81, 97, 106, 120, 127, 135, 154, 166, 176
Broader, 17, 42, 60, 176
Broke, 16, 30, 34, 35, 63, 72, 75, 80, 97, 108, 133, 136, 157, 164, 181, 193
Broken, 35, 36, 54, 63, 64, 101, 136, 181, 184, 193, 197
Brook, 31, 48, 75, 113, 126, 131, 135, 137, 160, 193
Broom, 34, 87, 115, 165, 176, 188, 197
Brother, 2, 8, 9, 13, 24, 26, 30, 35, 38, 39, 43, 49, 52, 72, 78, 81, 84, 85, 87, 90, 96, 97, 107, 110, 111, 116, 122, 127, 128, 129, 136, 140, 145, 147, 149, 154, 157, 158, 170, 175, 178, 179, 180, 181, 189, 192, 195, 200
Brothers, 5, 9, 24, 38, 39, 81, 87, 106, 140, 143, 145, 154, 200
Brought, 4, 24, 30, 31, 34, 62, 65, 66, 68, 77, 78, 89, 95, 108, 127, 142, 167, 179, 180, 195
Brow, 53, 198
Brown, 15, 16, 20, 21, 23, 24, 25, 29, 30, 33, 36, 37, 45, 48, 50, 51, 52, 53, 54, 55, 56, 57, 59, 62, 64, 69, 71, 72, 78, 79, 81, 87, 99, 100, 103, 104, 113, 115, 118, 130, 133, 135, 136, 141, 144, 153, 154, 160, 161, 163, 166, 170, 180, 181, 188, 189, 190, 194, 198
Brr, 44, 189
Bruce, 110, 111, 137, 175, 182
Bruise, 23, 75, 155
Brush, 14, 103, 123, 136, 142, 164, 165, 176, 194, 197
Brushes, 12, 142
Bryce, 39, 200
Bubble, 14, 19, 49, 55, 181
Bubbles, 14, 96
Bucket, 34, 68, 93
Bud, 8, 20, 22, 27, 29, 60, 69, 104, 111, 121, 129, 142, 157, 160
Buddha, 129, 134
Buddy, 24, 47, 154, 199
Buds, 22, 198
Bug, 1, 7, 15, 16, 18, 22, 29, 31, 32, 33, 46, 49, 57, 62, 67, 68, 75, 85, 86, 95, 104, 108, 117, 131, 136, 142, 149, 157, 158, 167, 169, 198
Bugged, 2, 23
Buggy, 1, 13, 18, 34, 35
Bugle, 23, 114, 175
Bugs, 2, 18, 29, 35, 67, 103, 149, 157, 182
Buick, 35, 87
Build, 26, 30, 34, 69, 73, 80, 87, 88, 108, 197
Building, 4, 15, 31, 40, 41, 43, 48, 54, 60, 73, 80, 82, 83, 87, 93, 95, 97, 106, 108, 111, 123, 126, 127, 158, 163, 169, 178, 187, 189, 193, 197
Buildings, 26, 41, 54, 83, 87, 158, 163
Built, 26, 72, 87, 108
Bulb, 22, 101, 103, 160
Bulbs, 12, 101
Bull, 2, 9, 27, 49, 52, 53, 59, 66, 72,

Bull, 102, 133, 140
Bulldog, 53, 70
Bullet, 72, 145, 165
Bully, 108, 136
Bum, 27, 40, 41, 66, 72, 115, 136, 175, 188, 194, 197
Bumble, 136, 181
Bumblebee, 29, 151
Bump, 16, 35, 43, 75, 79, 97, 113, 136, 150, 151, 155, 163
Bumps, 136, 151
Bumpy, 46, 57, 113, 136, 149, 151, 153, 163
Bun, 25, 27, 28, 59, 106, 112, 115, 140
Bunch, 1, 4, 10, 12, 67, 127, 136, 160, 182
Bundle, 13, 27, 34, 44
Bunny, 30, 32, 58, 61, 97, 130, 153, 165, 182
Bunnys, 153, 188
Bunting, 13, 136
Buoyancy, 80, 102
Burden, 34, 81, 102
Burger, 37, 139
Burglar, 3, 37, 40, 175
Burn, 3, 28, 63, 74, 86, 87, 101, 122, 138, 139, 145, 155, 162, 180
Burned, 63, 87
Burner, 123, 162
Burning, 44, 86, 101, 162, 188
Burp, 3, 188
Burr, 44, 188
Bury, 31, 34, 62
Bus, 1, 12, 16, 22, 30, 31, 35, 39, 41, 43, 47, 49, 70, 88, 89, 107, 123, 127, 137, 147, 149, 155, 157, 159, 163, 167, 169, 170, 171, 182, 184, 189, 195
Buses, 35, 41, 149
Bush, 22, 71, 136, 160
Business, 30, 85, 109, 197
Bust, 19, 79, 108, 182
Busy, 5, 35, 39, 41, 68, 94, 127, 128, 142, 163, 181, 183, 197
But, 1, 3, 4, 5, 6, 7, 8, 11, 12, 16, 17, 22, 26, 27, 28, 29, 30, 31, 33, 35, 43, 45, 58, 59, 60, 63, 65, 68, 72, 76, 79, 82, 84, 88, 89, 91, 92, 93, 94, 95, 100, 102, 116, 118, 121, 122, 124, 125, 126, 128, 141, 142, 144, 150, 152, 156, 158, 160, 168, 169, 170, 171, 172, 173, 174, 179, 182, 183, 184, 186, 191, 192, 195, 200
Butch, 13, 39, 53, 125, 133, 181
Butcher, 115, 197
Butt, 1, 11, 26, 27, 28, 29, 147
Butter, 3, 7, 15, 18, 20, 22, 25, 27, 28, 29, 30, 32, 37, 48, 52, 63, 72, 74, 77, 86, 95, 96, 109, 115, 121, 138, 139, 140, 151, 153, 155, 157, 158, 160, 164, 165, 166, 175, 180, 195, 198
Buttercup, 28, 198
Butterflies, 161, 181
Butterfly, 15, 27, 28, 151, 157, 158, 161, 196, 198
Buttermilk, 20, 28, 29, 155
Button, 1, 21, 27, 37, 47, 62, 66, 74, 92, 106, 115, 117, 121, 123, 129, 133, 152, 161
Buttons, 115, 119, 142, 152
Buy, 1, 5, 7, 12, 27, 30, 31, 32, 34, 35, 43, 49, 58, 62, 65, 68, 70, 77, 78, 82, 102, 105, 108, 116, 121, 123, 125, 126, 132, 141, 142, 144, 147, 150, 154, 159, 167, 168, 170, 173, 178, 180, 182, 183, 185, 192
Buyer, 5, 30, 142

428

Clothing, 10, 23, 30, 115, 133, 140, 142, 143, 144, 145, 196, 197
Cloths, 10, 30, 117, 123, 129, 140, 142, 144, 187, 196
Cloudy, 55, 111
Cloud, 10, 42, 44, 55, 56, 57, 60, 81, 83, 103, 107, 113, 153, 160, 190, 193
Clouds, 15, 23, 42, 47, 50, 55, 81, 83, 107, 113, 114, 141, 160, 190, 194
Cloudy, 42, 55
Clove, 115, 162
Clover, 71, 126
Clown, 96, 99, 108, 133
Club, 17, 40, 64, 72, 73, 79, 80, 93, 98, 104, 121, 131, 134, 150, 153, 163, 189
Clues, 27, 92, 125
Clumsy, 24, 144, 149, 150
Clutch, 30, 74
Coach, 36, 46, 101, 129, 147
Coal, 4, 21, 44, 46, 81, 86, 115, 162, 190
Coals, 86, 162
Coarse, 121, 136, 151, 153
Coast, 26, 120, 165
Coat, 7, 9, 15, 21, 23, 24, 26, 28, 30, 33, 34, 39, 40, 42, 43, 44, 46, 50, 51, 53, 69, 71, 74, 81, 84, 85, 86, 87, 95, 101, 106, 108, 109, 110, 113, 114, 115, 116, 121, 123, 124, 126, 127, 129, 133, 136, 137, 140, 143, 144, 145, 146, 148, 149, 151, 153, 161, 166, 167, 169, 170, 176, 178, 186, 189, 190, 196, 198
Coats, 30, 42, 44, 69, 144, 196
Cobbler, 115, 144
Cocoa, 20, 26, 86, 139, 180
Cocoon, 29, 157
Cod, 107, 194
Code, 119, 134
Coffee, 20, 21, 25, 28, 30, 37, 59, 86, 108, 123, 138, 145, 160, 162, 166, 177, 180
Coffin, 48, 146
Coin, 30, 56, 62, 79, 111, 194
Coins, 30, 194
Coke, 59, 77, 121, 159, 162, 164, 177, 188
Cold, 2, 3, 4, 6, 10, 14, 15, 17, 18, 20, 21, 23, 32, 34, 40, 44, 46, 48, 50, 51, 52, 54, 55, 57, 63, 64, 65, 67, 68, 71, 72, 74, 75, 76, 77, 79, 80, 81, 83, 86, 89, 90, 91, 94, 98, 101, 105, 106, 107, 108, 112, 113, 114, 115, 117, 119, 120, 123, 125, 126, 132, 133, 134, 135, 136, 138, 140, 142, 144, 146, 148, 149, 151, 152, 153, 154, 157, 158, 160, 161, 162, 163, 164, 167, 175, 177, 179, 181, 183, 188, 189, 190, 193, 194, 196
Colder, 20, 86, 176
Colds, 79, 86, 146
Collar, 21, 23, 53, 71, 115, 129, 133, 153, 190, 198
Collect, 30, 62, 142
College, 24, 26, 48, 176
Collie, 26, 53
Collins, 175, 188
Colonel, 47, 154
Color, 1, 4, 8, 15, 21, 22, 23, 29, 33, 35, 37, 39, 41, 42, 50, 51, 55, 57, 58, 62, 67, 71, 74, 86, 87, 89, 100, 101, 103, 107, 108, 115, 119, 133, 134, 135, 136, 141, 144, 153, 158, 160, 161, 167, 170, 173, 178, 180, 183, 186, 190, 195, 198
Colorado, 15, 113
Colored, 15, 29

Colorful, 15, 22, 23, 29, 55, 67, 71, 133, 190
Coloring, 71, 133
Colorless, 21, 190
Colors, 15, 21, 23, 29, 35, 50, 55, 67, 71, 87, 107, 119, 133, 141, 190, 198
Colt, 48, 72, 143, 144, 157
Columbus, 158, 163, 171
Coma, 8, 89, 148
Comb, 3, 45, 48, 79, 116, 136, 140, 167, 178
Come, 1, 2, 3, 4, 5, 7, 8, 10, 11, 12, 15, 16, 17, 26, 27, 28, 30, 31, 32, 34, 35, 39, 40, 42, 43, 46, 47, 49, 53, 54, 55, 58, 60, 61, 62, 63, 65, 66, 68, 70, 71, 76, 77, 78, 80, 82, 85, 87, 88, 89, 91, 92, 93, 94, 95, 97, 100, 101, 102, 103, 108, 110, 111, 114, 115, 117, 118, 119, 121, 122, 123, 124, 125, 126, 127, 128, 130, 131, 132, 134, 135, 136, 137, 143, 144, 149, 150, 152, 154, 157, 159, 161, 163, 164, 166, 167, 169, 170, 171, 172, 173, 174, 176, 177, 178, 179, 182, 183, 185, 186, 187, 189, 191, 192, 194, 195, 199
Comes, 5, 10, 17, 43, 45, 66, 78, 82, 92, 95, 100, 108, 150, 169, 171, 172, 191
Comfort, 2, 3, 14, 18, 19, 33, 36, 43, 46, 48, 55, 58, 59, 71, 80, 87, 90, 105, 115, 131, 135, 144, 146, 147, 148, 151, 153, 181, 196, 197
Comfortable, 3, 14, 17, 18, 33, 36, 46, 48, 59, 87, 115, 131, 143, 144, 147, 148, 151, 153, 157, 181, 189, 198
Comfortably, 46, 105
Comforting, 14, 46, 55, 134, 153
Comic, 3, 142
Coming, 4, 5, 6, 7, 10, 16, 17, 43, 45, 58, 66, 78, 84, 92, 94, 114, 126, 127, 128, 150, 185
Comma, 4, 8, 9, 16, 27, 89, 122, 173
Command, 5, 9, 27, 36, 40, 45, 68, 70, 74, 98, 99, 107, 108, 118, 136, 154, 156, 168, 189, 194, 196, 199
Commander, 47, 99, 154
Commandment, 19, 47
Commando, 47, 154
Commas, 89, 173
Comment, 3, 4, 27, 122, 152
Common, 27, 47, 76, 127, 147, 149, 158, 159, 183
Communicate, 156, 168
Communion, 25, 129
Communism, 90, 98, 127, 133, 134
Communist, 40, 90, 133
Community, 40, 41, 127
Compact, 27, 35, 145
Companion, 43, 195
Companionship, 43, 185
Company, 45, 77, 79, 88, 165, 174, 179, 180, 195
Compare, 11, 30, 125
Comparing, 11, 125
Comparison, 11, 125, 200
Complain, 92, 152, 168, 194, 197
Complete, 47, 98, 108, 126
Completely, 5, 76, 152
Complex, 41, 116, 200
Complexion, 15, 42, 71
Complicated, 58, 88, 119, 161
Composer, 31, 114
Compound, 8, 89
Con, 118, 142, 175, 195
Conceit, 91, 110
Concentration, 111, 197
Concern, 77, 108, 181
Concise, 42, 46

Conclude, 4, 8, 173
Conclusion, 4, 89, 92, 173
Concrete, 73, 136, 159, 163
Condition, 4, 11, 16, 27, 80, 89, 92, 152, 197
Cone, 45, 47, 169, 173, 177
Confederate, 126, 154
Confess, 129, 168
Confession, 127, 129, 134
Confidence, 2, 52, 58, 70
Confirmation, 19, 111, 134
Conflict, 9, 134, 181
Conform, 40, 143
Confuse, 119, 192
Confused, 42, 54, 55, 88, 181
Confusion, 9, 41, 88, 119, 127, 134, 181
Congo, 134, 135, 181
Conj, 8, 16, 27, 125, 170
Conjunction, 1, 7, 8, 11, 16, 27, 31, 89, 92, 125, 152, 169, 170, 173
Connect, 1, 4, 8, 27, 47, 89, 125, 173, 195
Connecting, 4, 8
Connection, 8, 16, 125, 173
Connie, 15, 46, 69, 91, 110
Conscious, 55, 111, 148, 181
Consequently, 16, 89, 152, 173
Considerate, 24, 183
Considering, 65, 89
Console, 46, 172
Constant, 5, 89
Constitution, 40, 61, 98, 173
Construct, 63, 108
Construction, 83, 149, 197
Consumer, 30, 142
Consuming, 30, 59
Contact, 43, 108
Contain, 93, 121
Contempt, 3, 9
Content, 3, 46, 90, 131
Contentment, 3, 59, 161, 181
Contest, 15, 156
Continents, 57, 120
Continue, 5, 7, 8, 17, 27, 89, 183
Continued, 8, 173
Continuous, 5, 163
Contract, 27, 173
Contraction, 6, 7, 11, 27
Contradiction, 27, 89
Contrary, 4, 89, 125, 173
Contrast, 27, 173
Control, 9, 47, 68, 108
Convent, 129, 170
Conversation, 34, 89, 156
Convertible, 35, 112, 198
Convey, 34, 102
Convict, 16, 40, 175, 181
Cook, 14, 25, 28, 32, 66, 69, 77, 86, 90, 92, 100, 102, 107, 108, 115, 136, 138, 151, 152, 160, 162, 164, 175, 178, 196
Cooked, 32, 136
Cookie, 25, 53, 67, 90, 98, 134, 139, 164, 167
Cookies, 25, 30, 68, 90, 94, 108, 139, 142, 162, 164
Cooking, 20, 28, 32, 59, 86, 108, 138, 160, 162, 196
Cool, 3, 7, 9, 10, 14, 23, 28, 36, 38, 42, 44, 46, 48, 51, 55, 57, 69, 71, 80, 83, 86, 92, 94, 95, 103, 112, 113, 120, 126, 127, 131, 135, 136, 138, 143, 145, 148, 149, 151, 153, 158, 160, 165, 172, 177, 181, 182, 183, 190, 193, 198
Cooled, 80, 86, 113, 196
Cooler, 42, 86
Cop, 40, 98, 131, 133, 140, 154, 175, 181, 189

Drove, 78, 150, 162, 185
Drown, 26, 49, 51, 71, 135
Drowning, 51, 135, 177
Drowsy, 10, 148
Drudgery, 34, 81, 197
Drug, 38, 81, 127, 188
Drugstore, 126, 187, 197
Druid, 129, 134
Drum, 55, 66, 73, 85, 107, 111, 114, 154, 160, 194
Drums, 107, 114
Drunk, 38, 59, 68, 73, 83, 84, 90, 148, 156, 177, 188, 197
Dry, 6, 14, 20, 25, 28, 42, 44, 49, 51, 57, 76, 86, 90, 94, 98, 106, 129, 130, 135, 136, 138, 139, 146, 149, 153, 160, 163, 177, 183, 188, 194
Dryer, 42, 86
Dryness, 25, 177
Duck, 21, 56, 90, 104, 111, 115, 122, 130, 143, 145, 146, 153, 189, 190, 198
Ducks, 72, 191
Due, 16, 17, 23, 26, 65
Dug, 42, 51, 53
Duke, 17, 53
Dull, 15, 20, 21, 23, 42, 44, 50, 71, 76, 81, 106, 111, 115, 131, 133, 134, 136, 139, 146, 149, 150, 151, 153, 155, 158, 164, 198
Duluth, 41, 66, 102, 179
Dumb, 1, 3, 4, 6, 8, 10, 17, 39, 47, 53, 69, 76, 79, 82, 93, 94, 95, 111, 114, 115, 124, 125, 128, 129, 136, 143, 149, 150, 151, 156, 158, 164, 179, 183, 188, 196, 199
Dummy, 1, 91
Dump, 1, 15, 32, 41, 101, 149, 158
Dungeon, 51, 104, 142
Durable, 75, 106, 196
During, 52, 188, 197
Dusk, 12, 178
Dust, 33, 41, 42, 57, 75, 112, 133, 157, 177, 182
Dusty, 41, 42, 154, 177, 182
Duties, 31, 40, 98
Duty, 33, 41, 42, 47, 81, 98, 197
Dwight, 15, 99
Dye, 23, 49, 80, 88, 105, 192
Dying, 59, 105, 128, 137, 146, 177, 200

Each, 3, 7, 32, 58, 65, 124, 125, 127, 154, 161, 174, 179, 183, 195
Eager, 9, 56, 76, 90
Eagle, 2, 7, 15, 23, 24, 26, 29, 57, 75, 136, 143, 156, 165, 193
Ear, 1, 10, 42, 51, 55, 57, 63, 64, 73, 74, 75, 79, 80, 81, 82, 85, 91, 95, 101, 107, 114, 116, 133, 139, 141, 153, 154, 156, 162, 163, 165, 168, 186, 189
Early, 18, 45, 58, 89, 103, 145, 155, 181, 183, 200
Ears, 14, 28, 53, 79, 82, 85, 107, 132, 163, 182, 186, 191
Earth, 5, 16, 17, 20, 23, 32, 33, 39, 43, 56, 66, 75, 81, 84, 96, 103, 105, 106, 108, 109, 112, 113, 123, 127, 134, 138, 139, 141, 153, 155, 161, 170, 181
Ease, 3, 12, 36, 46, 48, 58, 68, 75, 148, 151, 159, 181, 195
Eased, 46, 75
Easier, 42, 43, 45, 58, 61, 70, 76, 108, 128, 140, 167, 176
Easily, 3, 42, 46, 58, 75, 76, 102, 132, 140, 150, 151, 156, 181
East, 46, 57, 58, 61, 90, 105, 161, 167
Easter, 7, 58, 61, 96, 102, 167
Easy, 2, 3, 6, 10, 11, 15, 17, 20, 36,

Easy, 42, 43, 46, 47, 58, 61, 62, 70, 75, 76, 79, 81, 88, 95, 102, 103, 105, 108, 111, 119, 126, 128, 129, 130, 131, 132, 133, 136, 145, 147, 148, 149, 150, 151, 152, 153, 156, 160, 164, 165, 167, 181, 183, 184, 195, 197, 200
Eat, 1, 3, 5, 7, 9, 10, 12, 14, 17, 20, 21, 25, 26, 28, 29, 30, 32, 33, 36, 37, 39, 40, 47, 48, 53, 55, 56, 58, 59, 61, 63, 64, 66, 67, 68, 73, 74, 75, 76, 77, 79, 80, 81, 84, 87, 88, 90, 91, 93, 94, 96, 98, 100, 101, 104, 105, 107, 108, 110, 111, 114, 115, 116, 117, 118, 119, 123, 125, 127, 129, 130, 131, 132, 138, 139, 140, 141, 142, 143, 144, 145, 146, 147, 148, 150, 151, 154, 155, 156, 157, 160, 161, 162, 163, 164, 165, 166, 167, 168, 171, 173, 174, 176, 177, 180, 182, 187, 188, 189, 191, 198, 200
Eaten, 59, 76, 90
Eater, 25, 26, 32, 58, 104, 127, 138
Eating, 10, 20, 25, 28, 30, 32, 36, 37, 59, 60, 67, 90, 104, 105, 109, 115, 128, 139, 142, 148, 149, 151, 155, 158, 161, 162, 164, 166, 176, 180, 182, 189, 197
Eats, 21, 25, 32, 67
Edge, 26, 56, 75, 121, 136, 157, 158
Edges, 26, 136, 158
Education, 26, 48, 52, 80
Ee, 3, 122
Eek, 3, 50, 122, 140, 156, 157
Effect, 68, 146
Efficient, 58, 165
Effort, 76, 81, 107, 197
Egg, 1, 2, 7, 25, 26, 28, 29, 32, 37, 47, 56, 58, 59, 61, 66, 67, 75, 76, 79, 104, 105, 126, 138, 139, 142, 145, 151, 153, 155, 158, 167, 170, 180, 190, 198
Eggs, 20, 25, 28, 30, 34, 37, 39, 56, 58, 59, 61, 75, 80, 119, 126, 138, 142, 153, 165, 167, 198
Ego, 84, 91, 199
Eh, 3, 69, 122, 134, 186
Eight, 39, 63, 67, 73, 92, 104, 116, 119, 124, 125, 153, 157, 163
Eighteen, 69, 119, 163
Eileen, 9, 69, 181
Eisenhower, 154, 191
Either, 11, 27, 76, 89, 125
Elbow, 64, 74, 154
Elder, 38, 40, 109, 195, 200
Election, 40, 134
Electric, 30, 101, 103, 123, 162
Electricity, 56, 101, 103, 123, 138, 172
Elephant, 7, 8, 17, 81, 90, 99, 104, 111, 136, 149
Elephants, 100, 111
Elevation, 83, 113
Elevator, 51, 83, 102
Eleven, 24, 119, 120, 168
Elf, 116, 168
Elk, 135, 152
Else, 4, 7, 8, 16, 27, 63, 65, 82, 88, 89, 125, 152, 186, 187, 191, 195
Elvis, 99, 114
Embarrass, 131, 133, 181
Embarrassed, 71, 133
Emotion, 2, 9, 90, 96, 114, 181
Emotions, 9, 49
Emphatic, 122, 183
Empire, 99, 108
Empty, 21, 51, 79, 90, 131, 161, 163
Enamel, 162, 166
Enchanting, 55, 153
End, 5, 7, 8, 11, 16, 17, 20, 26, 27,

End, 31, 54, 56, 60, 61, 62, 64, 77, 79, 121, 126, 128, 133, 145, 160, 168, 169, 170, 171, 173, 178
Ending, 7, 55, 91, 98, 160, 178
Ends, 17, 152
Enemies, 9, 127, 175
Enemy, 9, 20, 40, 52, 69, 72, 98, 154, 157, 168, 175, 181
Energy, 80, 102, 137, 148, 197
Engine, 7, 35, 81, 86, 133, 136, 149, 152, 160
Engineer, 17, 47
England, 66, 99, 104, 115, 120, 158, 175, 194
English, 1, 4, 5, 6, 7, 8, 11, 12, 16, 31, 36, 37, 47, 65, 66, 77, 82, 85, 89, 94, 95, 111, 118, 121, 122, 125, 152, 155, 156, 158, 169, 170, 171, 173, 178, 179, 183, 184, 186, 192, 197
Enjoy, 15, 38, 46, 59, 80, 96, 105, 114, 128, 129, 181, 183, 185, 197
Enjoyable, 46, 58, 59, 114, 148, 164
Enjoying, 46, 128, 197
Enjoyment, 3, 46, 48, 55, 59, 63, 67, 69, 72, 112, 114, 128, 134, 180, 197
Enormous, 41, 57, 83, 113
Enough, 3, 4, 5, 27, 39, 59, 62, 76, 77, 86, 90, 94, 107, 124, 125, 136, 143, 145, 155, 158, 184, 200
Enter, 10, 17, 45, 54, 93
Envelope, 76, 89
Envy, 23, 71
Episcopal, 129, 134
Equal, 11, 98, 158
Equals, 94, 173
Equipment, 72, 73, 140
Er, 3, 122
Erase, 108, 167
Eraser, 26, 31, 39, 58, 158, 177
Errand, 65, 68
Escape, 26, 27, 134, 148, 181
Essential, 79, 134, 148
Etc., 7, 8, 16, 27, 119, 125, 152, 171, 173
Et cetera, 8, 118, 173
Eternally, 5, 105
Eternity, 5, 19, 66
Europe, 35, 56, 60, 66, 90, 99, 120, 177
European, 40, 127
Eve, 77, 105, 196
Even, 4, 5, 7, 8, 11, 12, 16, 20, 26, 27, 43, 60, 61, 68, 76, 89, 92, 98, 108, 117, 119, 125, 136, 150, 151, 152, 158, 162, 165, 173, 183, 186, 195
Evening, 7, 42, 50, 112, 131, 169
Ever, 4, 5, 6, 8, 11, 16, 43, 58, 61, 65, 66, 70, 76, 77, 88, 89, 91, 92, 94, 95, 105, 118, 122, 123, 124, 125, 126, 135, 151, 152, 156, 171, 172, 173, 183, 184, 186, 187, 191, 194
Evergreen, 15, 71, 113
Every, 4, 5, 8, 11, 27, 36, 43, 65, 76, 80, 88, 89, 94, 124, 126, 141, 156, 169, 176, 183, 184, 186, 187, 195
Everybody, 88, 92, 127, 182, 185
Everyday, 5, 105
Everyone, 12, 39, 40, 65, 89, 110, 124, 127, 141, 168, 176, 182, 185, 199, 200
Everything, 4, 5, 8, 15, 30, 57, 62, 77, 89, 111, 124, 167, 170, 178, 183, 194
Everywhere, 5, 63, 82, 89, 127, 134, 151, 172, 181, 182, 187
Evil, 21, 41, 90, 98, 104, 105, 134, 140, 141, 146, 157, 175, 180, 181, 188
Ewe, 143, 199

Handle, 102, 106, 124, 125, 160, 167
Handles, 54, 162
Hands, 24, 28, 34, 42, 43, 44, 63, 64, 69, 74, 79, 80, 85, 102, 108, 111, 115, 116, 136, 151, 153, 155, 159, 161, 194, 197, 199
Handsome, 10, 15, 16, 24, 26, 50, 74, 78, 99, 109, 151, 154, 190, 199, 200
Handy, 5, 39, 46, 58, 63, 73, 74, 76, 109, 117, 140, 175, 177
Hang, 63, 96, 98, 102, 126
Hanged, 68, 98
Hanging, 98, 157
Hang-over, 81, 148, 188
Hanky, 26, 44
Happen, 4, 5, 8, 10, 16, 17, 31, 55, 76, 88, 89, 92, 95, 96, 111, 122, 125, 170, 171, 178, 181, 182, 184, 186, 187, 194
Happened, 4, 10, 16, 17, 89, 92, 95, 122, 152, 171, 178, 181, 183, 184, 186, 194
Happening, 4, 5, 76, 94, 118, 171, 184, 197
Happenings, 55, 111, 181
Happens, 5, 17, 89, 95, 171, 186
Happier, 10, 58, 200
Happily, 9, 49, 105, 136
Happiness, 2, 9, 13, 20, 29, 38, 46, 48, 55, 69, 80, 87, 96, 103, 105, 111, 114, 116, 122, 134, 146, 181, 188, 194
Happy, 1, 2, 3, 4, 5, 6, 9, 10, 11, 13, 15, 17, 18, 20, 23, 24, 26, 34, 38, 39, 40, 42, 46, 48, 49, 55, 58, 59, 61, 62, 65, 68, 69, 71, 76, 80, 82, 87, 88, 89, 90, 95, 96, 97, 98, 103, 105, 108, 110, 111, 112, 114, 115, 116, 122, 125, 127, 128, 129, 130, 131, 132, 134, 139, 142, 146, 150, 154, 155, 164, 165, 171, 172, 175, 179, 180, 181, 182, 183, 184, 185, 186, 188, 189, 192, 194, 196, 197, 198, 200
Hard, 2, 3, 4, 6, 9, 11, 14, 15, 16, 17, 18, 20, 21, 22, 24, 25, 26, 27, 28, 31, 32, 33, 34, 35, 36, 37, 39, 40, 41, 42, 44, 46, 47, 49, 50, 51, 52, 54, 55, 56, 57, 58, 59, 60, 61, 62, 63, 64, 65, 69, 70, 73, 74, 75, 76, 79, 80, 81, 82, 83, 88, 89, 90, 94, 95, 97, 98, 99, 102, 103, 104, 105, 106, 107, 108, 109, 111, 112, 113, 114, 115, 116, 117, 119, 121, 124, 125, 126, 128, 129, 130, 131, 132, 133, 134, 136, 137, 138, 139, 140, 141, 142, 143, 144, 145, 146, 147, 148, 149, 150, 151, 152, 153, 154, 155, 156, 157, 158, 159, 160, 161, 162, 163, 164, 165, 166, 174, 175, 176, 177, 179, 181, 183, 184, 188, 189, 190, 191, 192, 193, 194, 195, 197
Harder, 17, 42, 43, 58, 60, 61, 75, 76, 97, 128, 150, 176, 200
Hardest, 58, 76
Hardly, 4, 27, 58, 61, 77, 125, 128, 129, 130, 132, 136, 150, 183
Hardness, 46, 75
Hardship, 46, 181, 197
Hardware, 73, 75
Hare, 76, 82, 105, 151, 165, 187
Hark, 56, 102
Harm, 2, 73, 74, 79, 85, 108, 127, 151, 179, 181
Harmful, 104, 157, 188
Harmony, 7, 20, 114, 181
Harp, 9, 25, 114, 117, 136
Harry, 34, 52, 84, 122, 181, 183
Harsh, 9, 20, 44, 47, 52, 71, 81, 107,

Harsh, 131, 132, 133, 136, 138, 139, 151, 153, 160, 164, 180, 188, 189
Has, 3, 4, 7, 8, 11, 16, 17, 59, 66, 68, 76, 77, 78, 79, 84, 85, 88, 94, 95, 116, 121, 126, 139, 144, 147, 152, 158, 169, 171, 172, 174, 178, 182, 184, 186, 187, 191, 195, 196
Hasn't, 77, 95, 195
Haste, 9, 108, 150
Hastily, 61, 130
Hat, 1, 3, 8, 9, 10, 12, 13, 14, 15, 21, 22, 23, 24, 29, 30, 34, 35, 36, 38, 40, 43, 44, 46, 47, 48, 50, 52, 53, 54, 58, 59, 60, 61, 62, 64, 65, 66, 68, 69, 71, 72, 73, 74, 75, 76, 77, 78, 79, 80, 82, 83, 84, 85, 86, 87, 88, 89, 93, 94, 95, 99, 100, 102, 108, 109, 110, 114, 115, 116, 117, 118, 119, 121, 123, 127, 129, 133, 142, 144, 145, 146, 152, 154, 159, 160, 161, 162, 166, 167, 169, 170, 171, 173, 175, 176, 178, 181, 186, 187, 189, 190, 194, 195, 196, 198
Hate, 2, 4, 9, 13, 14, 20, 24, 32, 33, 37, 39, 45, 46, 47, 52, 60, 69, 71, 75, 76, 80, 84, 85, 91, 96, 98, 100, 105, 108, 111, 114, 127, 128, 133, 143, 148, 149, 154, 157, 164, 173, 175, 181, 185, 188, 194, 197
Hateful, 9, 20
Hater, 31, 32
Hath, 9, 186
Hatred, 9, 20, 96
Hats, 30, 35, 39, 54, 127, 142, 144, 192, 196
Haul, 34, 126, 145, 151, 167
Have, 4, 5, 6, 7, 8, 10, 11, 12, 14, 16, 17, 18, 25, 27, 34, 35, 39, 42, 43, 49, 53, 55, 62, 63, 65, 68, 72, 73, 76, 77, 81, 82, 84, 88, 89, 91, 92, 95, 97, 100, 102, 103, 105, 107, 108, 110, 111, 115, 118, 119, 121, 122, 124, 125, 126, 127, 128, 132, 137, 138, 140, 141, 144, 152, 153, 156, 165, 167, 169, 170, 173, 174, 176, 179, 181, 182, 183, 184, 185, 186, 187, 188, 189, 191, 192, 194, 195, 199
Haven, 9, 56, 77, 181
Haven't, 76, 77, 132, 142, 186, 199
Having, 77, 89, 117, 158, 185, 194, 195
Havoc, 49, 181
Hay, 1, 3, 5, 18, 23, 31, 38, 40, 42, 43, 48, 51, 58, 59, 67, 77, 78, 84, 88, 96, 108, 115, 117, 122, 128, 139, 142, 144, 162, 171, 172, 174, 178, 192, 198
Haystack, 23, 117
Hazard, 17, 140, 149, 181
Haze, 42, 55
Hazy, 10, 17, 42, 55, 148
He, 1, 2, 3, 4, 5, 6, 7, 8, 10, 11, 12, 13, 14, 16, 17, 22, 24, 26, 27, 28, 30, 31, 34, 36, 38, 39, 43, 47, 49, 61, 63, 65, 66, 70, 72, 76, 77, 78, 82, 84, 85, 88, 89, 91, 92, 94, 95, 98, 101, 102, 105, 108, 109, 110, 112, 116, 117, 118, 119, 121, 122, 123, 124, 125, 126, 127, 128, 130, 131, 132, 134, 135, 137, 141, 142, 143, 144, 150, 152, 156, 157, 159, 160, 168, 169, 170, 171, 172, 173, 174, 175, 176, 178, 179, 180, 182, 183, 184, 185, 186, 187, 191, 192, 195, 199, 200
Head, 2, 9, 10, 11, 14, 18, 21, 25, 26, 27, 32, 34, 36, 37, 42, 44, 46, 47, 49, 52, 53, 54, 55, 56, 60, 63, 64, 70, 73, 74, 75, 76, 77, 78, 79, 80,

Head. 81, 83, 85, 87, 90, 91, 96, 99, 102, 103, 104, 107, 108, 109, 111, 114, 115, 116, 117, 120, 125, 126, 127, 129, 133, 134, 140, 142, 143, 144, 145, 146, 148, 151, 154, 155, 157, 158, 159, 160, 161, 162, 166, 167, 169, 175, 178, 180, 181, 188, 196
Headache, 46, 73, 79, 107, 146, 161, 181, 188
Headed, 75, 103
Heal, 7, 52, 64, 77, 80, 90, 144, 146
Healing, 52, 146
Health, 4, 14, 17, 20, 25, 28, 38, 40, 42, 46, 52, 59, 67, 73, 80, 90, 96, 98, 103, 105, 111, 113, 116, 134, 139, 146, 161, 176, 177, 181, 188, 196, 199
Healthful, 32, 59
Healthy, 10, 14, 17, 32, 46, 52, 76, 80, 109, 146, 188
Heap, 97, 143
Hear, 3, 5, 6, 7, 10, 12, 17, 21, 26, 27, 30, 31, 36, 42, 45, 47, 49, 53, 58, 62, 64, 66, 73, 75, 76, 77, 79, 81, 82, 84, 85, 94, 102, 104, 105, 107, 109, 111, 114, 115, 118, 123, 125, 126, 128, 129, 131, 132, 137, 141, 142, 143, 147, 149, 152, 153, 156, 159, 164, 168, 169, 170, 171, 172, 173, 175, 178, 182, 184, 185, 186, 187, 189, 193, 195, 196
Heard, 1, 10, 24, 43, 45, 49, 73, 75, 76, 77, 79, 80, 81, 82, 85, 91, 102, 107, 117, 126, 127, 128, 129, 132, 137, 141, 142, 143, 147, 151, 153, 156, 168, 171, 173, 174, 181, 183, 186, 188, 189, 191
Hearer, 42, 60
Hearing, 82, 186
Heart, 2, 7, 9, 29, 43, 49, 50, 52, 63, 64, 73, 74, 75, 79, 80, 81, 85, 89, 102, 103, 104, 105, 107, 109, 111, 116, 117, 124, 131, 133, 138, 140, 145, 146, 153, 154, 155, 156, 161, 164, 170, 176, 178, 181, 195, 196, 198
Heartburn, 32, 161
Hearted, 75, 103, 104, 153, 181
Hearth, 46, 57, 87, 101
Heat, 9, 13, 15, 43, 44, 46, 51, 56, 74, 79, 80, 81, 86, 87, 100, 101, 103, 115, 122, 123, 124, 133, 137, 146, 155, 156, 157, 160, 161, 162, 163, 164, 171, 177, 184, 186, 197, 198
Heater, 86, 162
Heating, 123, 162
Heave, 34, 81, 102, 107, 146, 153
Heaven, 5, 9, 15, 19, 23, 41, 48, 55, 57, 65, 66, 69, 81, 83, 96, 103, 105, 126, 134, 172, 179, 190, 194
Heavenly, 15, 55, 112
Heavens, 65, 112, 116, 122, 186
Heavier, 26, 42, 81, 86, 176
Heavily, 34, 76, 81, 102, 153
Heavy, 17, 18, 21, 25, 27, 34, 36, 46, 49, 51, 54, 58, 61, 72, 73, 75, 76, 77, 81, 86, 88, 89, 94, 102, 103, 104, 106, 107, 109, 112, 115, 123, 131, 132, 136, 140, 145, 149, 151, 153, 163, 167, 174, 176, 179, 180, 197
Heck, 3, 16, 65, 78, 86, 122, 170, 181
Heel, 34, 46, 52, 64, 79, 83, 144, 155
Heels, 83, 144, 196
Heidi, 110, 113
Height, 2, 9, 51, 79, 81, 83, 87, 97, 99, 102, 103, 106, 107, 112, 113, 115, 126, 129, 145, 152, 153, 159,

Height, 166, 175, 184

Held, 34, 52, 73, 74, 77, 79, 102, 174, 178, 181, 195

Hell, 2, 3, 19, 46, 64, 65, 66, 86, 93, 113, 122, 126, 129, 134, 142, 150, 160, 168, 179, 192

Hello, 3, 8, 16, 24, 30, 31, 66, 82, 83, 84, 88, 105, 110, 115, 122, 152, 165, 168, 184, 189, 193

Help, 1, 2, 3, 4, 5, 8, 10, 14, 16, 17, 18, 19, 27, 30, 34, 40, 42, 44, 46, 47, 49, 50, 51, 52, 54, 55, 58, 61, 62, 65, 71, 72, 74, 76, 80, 81, 82, 83, 86, 89, 90, 94, 96, 97, 98, 102, 104, 105, 107, 111, 113, 115, 117, 121, 122, 125, 127, 128, 129, 130, 134, 137, 138, 139, 140, 143, 146, 157, 159, 160, 161, 168, 170, 171, 173, 175, 177, 179, 181, 182, 184, 186, 189, 192, 194, 195, 196, 197, 200

Helper, 40, 52, 74, 76, 81, 129, 154

Helpful, 40, 46, 47, 48, 52, 58, 73, 74, 129, 134, 140, 154, 181, 197

Helping, 52, 66, 74, 111, 181, 197

Helpless, 13, 38, 74, 146, 181

Helps, 14, 52, 98, 122, 138, 154

Hem, 3, 8, 26, 108, 171, 179, 184, 189

Hen, 7, 18, 39, 58, 62, 87, 93, 115, 117, 125, 127, 128, 133, 160, 170, 171, 186, 198

Hence, 89, 173

Henry, 95, 99, 110, 122

Her, 1, 3, 4, 6, 7, 8, 9, 10, 11, 12, 15, 16, 17, 23, 26, 27, 30, 31, 33, 34, 35, 37, 42, 43, 45, 46, 47, 49, 53, 60, 61, 62, 65, 66, 68, 69, 74, 75, 76, 77, 78, 82, 84, 85, 86, 89, 91, 92, 93, 94, 95, 97, 102, 103, 105, 108, 110, 112, 115, 116, 118, 119, 121, 122, 123, 124, 125, 126, 127, 128, 132, 139, 141, 142, 146, 147, 152, 158, 159, 167, 168, 169, 170, 171, 172, 173, 174, 175, 178, 179, 182, 183, 184, 185, 186, 187, 191, 192, 194, 195, 196, 199

Herald, 9, 91, 140

Herb, 20, 32

Herd, 10, 75, 77, 82, 90, 115, 143, 153, 155, 174, 182

Herder, 143, 148

Here, 1, 3, 4, 5, 6, 7, 8, 10, 11, 12, 16, 17, 27, 30, 31, 34, 41, 42, 43, 45, 46, 47, 49, 51, 52, 57, 58, 60, 62, 63, 65, 66, 68, 70, 76, 77, 78, 82, 84, 85, 86, 88, 89, 91, 92, 93, 94, 95, 97, 102, 105, 107, 108, 110, 114, 115, 116, 118, 121, 122, 123, 124, 125, 126, 127, 128, 129, 131, 132, 133, 137, 139, 141, 142, 143, 147, 150, 152, 156, 159, 167, 168, 169, 170, 171, 172, 173, 174, 176, 178, 179, 181, 182, 183, 184, 185, 186, 187, 191, 192, 194, 195, 199

Hero, 7, 17, 82, 154

Hers, 5, 7, 17, 65, 77, 78, 82, 84, 85, 93, 94, 108, 116, 121, 124, 159, 169, 173, 178, 191, 195

Herself, 84, 108

He's, 65, 85

Hesitate, 27, 92, 152

Hesitating, 4, 89, 173

Hesitation, 16, 27, 92

Hey, 3, 31, 45, 62, 83, 122, 142, 168, 170, 174, 191, 192

Hi, 1, 3, 9, 10, 11, 12, 16, 19, 31, 42, 48, 49, 51, 52, 58, 75, 77, 79, 82, 83, 84, 85, 86, 87, 88, 91, 94, 97, 101, 102, 103, 106, 113, 116, 119,

Hi, 122, 124, 126, 129, 132, 134, 137, 139, 141, 149, 152, 156, 160, 165, 168, 169, 171, 174, 179, 185, 186, 187, 188, 189, 190, 191, 192

Hick, 122, 188

Hid, 10, 11, 50, 62, 97, 141, 157, 187, 195

Hidden, 48, 62, 132, 187

Hide, 2, 8, 10, 12, 34, 39, 47, 49, 60, 62, 63, 68, 71, 97, 102, 105, 141, 147, 168, 170, 172, 173, 181, 187, 191, 192

Hiding, 62, 128, 137, 187, 191

Hi-fi, 107, 114

High, 2, 4, 5, 9, 10, 17, 23, 26, 29, 31, 33, 34, 36, 38, 39, 47, 48, 49, 51, 54, 55, 56, 57, 61, 64, 66, 67, 69, 75, 79, 80, 81, 82, 83, 86, 87, 88, 90, 91, 97, 99, 101, 102, 103, 105, 106, 107, 112, 113, 115, 116, 119, 121, 122, 123, 124, 126, 127, 128, 129, 134, 136, 137, 140, 141, 144, 145, 147, 150, 152, 153, 155, 157, 159, 160, 161, 166, 172, 175, 176, 181, 183, 188, 189, 190, 192, 193, 196, 197

Higher, 26, 43, 61, 63, 83, 97, 102, 126, 200

Highest, 47, 83, 99

Highness, 37, 99

Highway, 35, 60, 66, 88, 99, 106, 134, 136, 151, 163

Highways, 35, 106

Hike, 97, 113

Hill, 23, 26, 28, 29, 41, 48, 51, 57, 60, 61, 64, 71, 72, 77, 79, 83, 87, 97, 98, 101, 104, 113, 115, 116, 123, 126, 134, 136, 137, 140, 143, 149, 150, 151, 156, 157, 159, 160, 163, 164, 168, 172, 178, 186

Hillbilly, 38, 114, 188

Hills, 15, 41, 57, 60, 71, 113, 126, 134, 136, 143

Hilly, 113, 136, 148, 151

Him, 1, 3, 4, 5, 6, 7, 8, 11, 12, 13, 15, 16, 17, 19, 24, 26, 27, 30, 31, 34, 35, 36, 43, 52, 55, 58, 60, 62, 65, 66, 68, 70, 76, 77, 78, 82, 84, 85, 88, 89, 91, 92, 94, 95, 97, 102, 104, 105, 108, 109, 110, 112, 116, 118, 119, 121, 122, 123, 124, 125, 126, 127, 132, 137, 139, 140, 141, 142, 144, 147, 148, 152, 154, 156, 159, 161, 162, 167, 168, 169, 170, 171, 172, 173, 174, 175, 176, 178, 179, 182, 183, 184, 185, 186, 187, 188, 189, 191, 192, 195, 199, 200

Himself, 17, 31, 78, 84, 85, 124, 199

Hind, 62, 81

Hip, 74, 97, 174

Hippopotamus, 81, 104

Hire, 45, 82, 172, 173, 175, 197

His, 3, 4, 6, 7, 8, 11, 12, 16, 17, 20, 27, 30, 31, 34, 45, 49, 52, 62, 65, 66, 67, 68, 74, 76, 77, 78, 82, 84, 85, 87, 88, 89, 91, 92, 93, 94, 95, 97, 108, 110, 116, 118, 120, 121, 122, 123, 124, 125, 127, 130, 132, 136, 142, 144, 152, 159, 167, 168, 169, 170, 172, 173, 174, 178, 179, 182, 184, 185, 186, 187, 189, 191, 192, 195, 199, 200

Hiss, 85, 178

History, 19, 26, 58, 72, 99, 108, 109, 111, 158, 180, 184, 188

Hit, 1, 2, 3, 9, 15, 20, 27, 34, 35, 47, 49, 53, 58, 60, 61, 66, 68, 70, 72, 73, 74, 75, 78, 80, 85, 88, 92, 93, 95, 97, 105, 112, 116, 122, 125, 128, 132, 145, 147, 149, 150, 155,

Hit, 156, 158, 161, 175, 178, 181, 186, 187, 189, 191, 195, 197

Hither, 45, 137, 173

Hitter, 20, 157

Hitting, 73, 137

Hive, 9, 105

Ho, 3, 6, 27, 70, 83, 88, 116, 122, 123, 152, 156, 179, 186, 191, 192, 194, 200

Hoarse, 6, 107, 133, 139, 159

Hobby, 29, 35, 72, 94, 108, 148

Hobo, 40, 49

Hockey, 75, 128, 172

Hoe, 68, 73, 88, 127, 132, 144, 152, 169, 183, 199

Hog, 1, 32, 53, 59, 94, 115, 169, 186

Hoist, 102, 116

Hold, 1, 11, 13, 17, 19, 26, 34, 43, 44, 46, 47, 51, 54, 58, 62, 63, 64, 65, 68, 74, 77, 81, 82, 86, 87, 94, 102, 108, 109, 115, 117, 121, 125, 142, 147, 156, 157, 160, 167, 168, 177, 181, 195, 200

Holder, 86, 154, 159, 161

Holding, 13, 34

Holds, 37, 161

Hole, 1, 4, 7, 11, 21, 26, 33, 37, 51, 57, 62, 63, 75, 77, 79, 83, 87, 93, 94, 106, 109, 112, 113, 115, 117, 118, 130, 136, 140, 144, 145, 154, 155, 158, 161, 193, 197

Holes, 25, 37, 54, 112, 144

Holiday, 58, 61, 96, 111, 122, 173, 194

Holiness, 19, 129, 134

Holland, 37, 144, 158

Holler, 3, 9, 37, 47, 49, 107, 122, 131, 156, 186, 189, 196

Hollow, 31, 49, 51, 75, 79, 161, 162, 198

Holly, 31, 53, 61, 69, 149

Holy, 4, 19, 29, 37, 44, 124, 129, 134, 150, 156

Home, 1, 3, 4, 5, 6, 8, 9, 10, 12, 13, 14, 15, 17, 18, 19, 25, 26, 27, 30, 31, 32, 33, 34, 36, 37, 38, 39, 41, 42, 43, 44, 45, 46, 47, 48, 53, 54, 57, 59, 60, 62, 66, 68, 70, 73, 77, 78, 79, 80, 82, 84, 85, 86, 87, 88, 89, 90, 91, 93, 94, 96, 97, 99, 100, 101, 102, 105, 108, 110, 111, 113, 114, 115, 116, 117, 118, 120, 121, 124, 126, 127, 128, 130, 131, 132, 134, 137, 142, 143, 144, 145, 146, 148, 154, 158, 159, 162, 163, 164, 167, 168, 169, 170, 171, 172, 173, 175, 177, 178, 179, 180, 181, 182, 184, 186, 187, 190, 193, 194, 195, 196, 197

Homely, 9, 13, 15, 46, 56, 89, 198

Homemade, 25, 108

Homer, 105, 176

Homes, 12, 30, 41, 54, 87, 132, 163

Homework, 5, 20, 58, 76, 111, 128, 136, 149, 181, 197

Homey, 48, 87

Honest, 38, 40, 52, 81, 89, 98, 111, 158, 175, 181

Honesty, 98, 111, 134, 175

Honey, 20, 25, 27, 29, 31, 37, 43, 53, 70, 88, 96, 164, 188, 198

Honk, 8, 35, 117, 189

Honor, 19, 20, 23, 56, 65, 85, 98, 99, 111, 154

Honorable, 40, 99, 129, 154

Hood, 35, 38, 39, 128, 129, 133, 136, 175, 181, 200

Hoodlum, 72, 129, 175, 181

Hoods, 35, 163, 180

Hook, 21, 72, 80, 187

Laughs, 88, 111, 192
Laughter, 3, 9, 38, 39, 69, 96, 107, 114, 127, 181, 196
Laundry, 81, 86
Laura, 110, 129, 145
Lava, 17, 77
Law, 19, 40, 47, 51, 52, 83, 98, 99, 107, 134, 147, 154, 175, 181, 188
Lawbreaker, 98, 175
Lawful, 5, 98
Lawlessness, 98, 175
Lawn, 26, 33, 41, 48, 53, 54, 71, 87, 88, 132, 134, 136, 163, 170
Laws, 19, 40, 98, 108
Lawyer, 17, 52, 89, 98, 175
Lay, 1, 13, 18, 31, 33, 34, 46, 58, 71, 89, 91, 97, 98, 102, 105, 109, 116, 121, 123, 128, 134, 136, 143, 147, 148, 159, 166, 188
Layer, 33, 52, 60, 120
Laying, 46, 123, 128, 137, 148, 153, 189, 197
Lazily, 46, 149, 150
Laziness, 46, 96, 149, 197
Lazy, 10, 17, 46, 55, 58, 75, 76, 81, 88, 102, 109, 128, 131, 135, 145, 146, 148, 149, 150, 153, 154, 165, 181, 197, 198
Lead, 18, 34, 47, 72, 74, 79, 81, 102, 105
Leader, 6, 26, 40, 47, 79, 98, 99, 104, 114, 129, 154, 175
Leadership, 40, 47
Leaf, 11, 22, 32, 71, 117, 154, 160, 180, 186
League, 40, 75, 98
Leak, 81, 156
Lean, 48, 55, 71, 106, 159, 176, 193
Leap, 51, 84, 96, 97, 137, 143, 148, 150, 165
Learn, 13, 17, 19, 42, 48, 58, 88, 104, 105, 108, 111, 114, 119, 121, 129, 131, 132, 134, 150, 179, 185
Learned, 52, 132, 186
Learning, 19, 111, 128, 134, 149
Least, 12, 76, 155
Leather, 21, 36, 42, 75, 136, 144, 151, 153, 154, 176
Leave, 5, 7, 8, 17, 22, 27, 30, 31, 34, 45, 66, 68, 70, 71, 77, 89, 102, 105, 106, 108, 118, 126, 132, 136, 141, 144, 150, 159, 160, 167, 171, 173, 175, 179, 180, 193, 195, 198
Leaves, 15, 26, 32, 71, 97, 133, 160, 161, 163, 167, 172, 180, 191, 193, 198
Leaving, 23, 30, 31, 66, 81, 182
Lecture, 156, 181
Led, 47, 64, 132, 133
Ledge, 31, 83, 143, 193
Lee, 78, 141, 156, 158, 185
Left, 8, 27, 32, 34, 39, 43, 54, 64, 66, 74, 77, 78, 81, 91, 95, 102, 106, 115, 121, 122, 124, 130, 132, 136, 150, 159, 160, 162, 167, 174, 175, 183, 185, 191, 195
Leg, 7, 9, 15, 18, 24, 32, 36, 40, 53, 56, 57, 63, 64, 69, 74, 79, 83, 85, 97, 106, 109, 115, 116, 129, 130, 137, 143, 144, 145, 147, 151, 154, 157, 159, 160, 161, 162, 166, 170, 178, 196
Legend, 17, 19
Legs, 6, 18, 24, 26, 36, 53, 61, 63, 64, 66, 69, 74, 79, 83, 85, 97, 106, 109, 116, 127, 133, 137, 143, 144, 147, 149, 157, 159, 161, 162, 166, 196
Leisure, 46, 58, 148, 197
Lemon, 20, 32, 66, 67, 155, 159, 160,

Lemon, 164, 170, 198
Lemonade, 142, 177
Lemons, 20, 59, 67, 138, 155
Lend, 26, 31, 77, 103, 117, 142, 167, 181
Length, 26, 35, 51, 60, 64, 83, 106, 111, 145, 163, 195
Lengthy, 106, 145
Leo, 99, 104, 106
Leopard, 104, 130
Less, 4, 8, 10, 27, 42, 46, 58, 60, 66, 76, 77, 102, 124, 150, 176, 183, 189, 195, 200
Lesser, 26, 58, 60
Lesson, 19, 47, 58, 111, 114, 129, 132, 144, 173, 178
Lessons, 111, 114
Lest, 10, 45, 58
Let, 3, 4, 7, 16, 17, 26, 27, 42, 43, 45, 55, 58, 63, 64, 65, 66, 68, 70, 72, 75, 77, 80, 93, 94, 97, 102, 105, 108, 110, 118, 119, 125, 127, 144, 147, 150, 152, 156, 167, 168, 169, 170, 173, 174, 177, 179, 182, 186
Lets, 2, 3, 8, 17, 45, 51, 62, 94, 118, 121, 141, 152, 173, 182
Letter, 1, 4, 5, 6, 7, 8, 12, 31, 32, 42, 54, 62, 66, 68, 91, 94, 111, 116, 119, 122, 124, 128, 140, 141, 144, 145, 155, 167, 169, 170, 173, 178, 179, 183
Letters, 1, 11, 16, 19, 32, 34, 79, 95, 119, 125, 169, 183, 185
Lettuce, 25, 30, 32, 37, 48, 54, 71, 75, 79, 139, 181
Level, 9, 39, 62, 83, 117, 120, 151, 165
Lever, 102, 140
Liar, 92, 129, 175
Liberty, 40, 56, 98, 103, 121, 154
Librarian, 131, 132
Library, 19, 42, 83, 131, 132, 170, 197
License, 35, 68, 119, 142, 163
Lick, 28, 45, 63, 105, 138, 139, 146
Licorice, 106, 188
Lid, 102, 139, 162
Lie, 3, 16, 17, 18, 27, 31, 46, 47, 49, 58, 59, 76, 89, 92, 97, 102, 104, 105, 113, 115, 116, 122, 123, 146, 147, 148, 150, 159, 168, 175, 192
Lies, 33, 82, 111, 168, 172
Lieutenant, 47, 154, 175
Life, 2, 5, 7, 13, 15, 17, 18, 19, 22, 25, 26, 27, 34, 38, 39, 41, 46, 48, 52, 55, 57, 58, 65, 71, 80, 84, 85, 87, 96, 98, 100, 102, 103, 105, 106, 109, 111, 112, 116, 121, 127, 129, 133, 134, 137, 138, 141, 145, 146, 157, 160, 163, 170, 172, 175, 178, 180, 181, 186, 188, 194, 195, 197, 200
Lift, 17, 27, 34, 49, 60, 62, 63, 74, 81, 84, 92, 97, 102, 105, 141, 165, 167, 174, 175
Lifted, 34, 81, 102
Lifting, 30, 34, 74, 102
Lifts, 34, 102
Light, 1, 3, 5, 10, 14, 15, 18, 19, 21, 23, 25, 26, 27, 29, 31, 33, 34, 35, 41, 42, 43, 44, 46, 50, 51, 55, 56, 58, 59, 60, 61, 66, 67, 69, 70, 71, 74, 75, 76, 77, 79, 81, 83, 87, 88, 90, 92, 93, 96, 97, 101, 102, 103, 105, 106, 111, 112, 114, 115, 119, 121, 123, 125, 130, 131, 133, 134, 136, 138, 140, 141, 143, 145, 147, 148, 149, 150, 151, 153, 156, 157, 158, 160, 161, 162, 163, 164, 165,

Light, 166, 170, 175, 176, 177, 180, 181, 183, 186, 187, 188, 190, 193, 196, 198, 200
Lighter, 26, 42, 50, 58, 61, 86, 101, 103, 125, 153, 162, 163, 176, 180
Lighthouse, 103, 120
Lightly, 76, 189
Lightness, 103, 198
Lightning, 2, 9, 61, 103, 165, 176
Lights, 35, 41, 50, 54, 101, 114, 119, 121, 123, 153, 163, 194
Like, 1, 2, 3, 4, 5, 6, 9, 10, 11, 13, 15, 16, 17, 19, 20, 21, 24, 26, 27, 30, 32, 33, 35, 37, 38, 39, 40, 41, 42, 43, 46, 47, 48, 50, 52, 53, 55, 57, 58, 59, 60, 62, 65, 66, 67, 68, 69, 71, 76, 77, 79, 80, 83, 84, 85, 87, 88, 89, 90, 91, 92, 93, 94, 95, 96, 97, 98, 100, 102, 105, 107, 108, 109, 110, 111, 114, 118, 119, 121, 122, 125, 127, 128, 129, 131, 133, 134, 137, 140, 141, 142, 144, 148, 151, 152, 155, 157, 158, 159, 160, 161, 163, 164, 165, 167, 169, 171, 174, 177, 179, 180, 181, 182, 183, 184, 185, 186, 189, 192, 194, 195, 197, 199, 200
Likeable, 13, 154, 164
Liked, 132, 164, 194
Likely, 11, 76, 94, 183
Liking, 59, 183
Lily, 22, 36, 160,
Limb, 64, 74, 79, 101, 160
Lime, 20, 59, 71, 155, 160, 164
Limit, 26, 41, 106, 195
Limited, 76, 124
Limp, 74, 88, 97, 101, 150
Lincoln, 35, 40, 98, 111, 159, 163, 173
Linda, 13, 53, 69, 110, 124, 145
Line, 9, 25, 26, 27, 31, 56, 79, 92, 105, 106, 111, 119, 120, 136, 141, 145, 151, 152, 158, 159, 160, 163, 171, 186
Linen, 18, 151, 190
Liner, 26, 105, 120
Lines, 18, 26, 35, 114, 119, 151, 158, 163
Lining, 26, 151, 161
Link, 36, 184
Lion, 2, 7, 9, 13, 29, 46, 90, 96, 99, 100, 104, 107, 113, 134, 137, 143, 150, 161, 171, 175
Lions, 31, 100
Lip, 79, 116, 189
Lips, 3, 63, 66, 79, 84, 86, 95, 116, 133, 156, 164, 177, 189, 199
Lipstick, 69, 133, 142, 151
Liquid, 28, 42, 96, 98, 138, 153, 176, 177, 188
Liquor, 20, 46, 75, 83, 177, 188
List, 14, 30, 68, 85, 106, 111, 114, 123, 124, 170, 178, 186, 194
Listen, 7, 9, 47, 52, 58, 82, 107, 108, 111, 114, 118, 119, 131, 132, 140, 141, 156, 168, 186, 187, 189
Lit, 34, 50, 84, 95, 101, 102, 103, 105, 118, 147, 195
Literature, 19, 173
Litter, 13, 20, 28, 100, 200
Little, 1, 2, 3, 4, 6, 7, 10, 11, 13, 15, 16, 17, 18, 20, 22, 23, 24, 27, 29, 32, 35, 37, 38, 39, 41, 42, 43, 45, 48, 49, 51, 53, 55, 57, 58, 60, 63, 64, 65, 69, 71, 72, 74, 76, 77, 79, 83, 86, 87, 88, 89, 92, 93, 94, 95, 100, 101, 102, 103, 106, 107, 108, 109, 110, 111, 113, 116, 117, 121, 124, 125, 127, 131, 132, 134, 135, 138, 139, 140, 143, 144, 145, 147, 149, 150, 152, 153, 155, 157, 158,

Little, 159, 161, 164, 165, 166, 167, 169, 170, 171, 172, 176, 178, 179, 180, 182, 183, 184, 189, 193, 195, 196, 197, 200

Littler, 176, 200

Live, 4, 5, 6, 17, 26, 27, 31, 40, 41, 45, 46, 48, 49, 52, 55, 57, 63, 65, 66, 70, 72, 76, 77, 78, 80, 82, 87, 88, 94, 100, 102, 105, 106, 112, 121, 124, 125, 127, 128, 134, 138, 143, 158, 163, 167, 168, 171, 172, 174, 179, 182, 185, 186, 187, 191, 192, 195

Lively, 39, 61, 105, 114, 130, 200

Liver, 105, 115, 135, 161

Lives, 78, 94, 105, 172, 186

Living, 6, 40, 41, 46, 48, 57, 58, 59, 80, 87, 100, 102, 105, 109, 127, 128, 157, 163, 165, 170, 197

Lizard, 29, 71, 95, 105, 165

Llama, 34, 143

Lo, 3, 83, 107, 152, 153, 197

Load, 1, 26, 34, 35, 49, 51, 76, 81, 102, 104, 106, 107, 124, 126, 131, 132, 156, 158, 184, 189

Loaded, 72, 81, 154, 188

Loading, 34, 132

Loaf, 25, 46, 55, 58, 153, 197

Loafing, 48, 128, 197

Loan, 142, 163, 167

Locate, 62, 141, 187

Location, 12, 62, 66, 82, 172, 187

Lock, 21, 54, 72, 153, 181, 193

Locked, 54, 73, 93

Locker, 28, 54, 115, 181

Lode, 145, 153, 189

Lodge, 51, 102, 153

Lofty, 29, 56, 83

Log, 34, 48, 75, 81, 87, 97, 106, 126, 136, 145, 165, 176

Logs, 48, 53, 81

Lollipop, 24, 146

London, 41, 60, 158, 175

Lone, 3, 5, 9, 47, 48, 51, 106, 108, 124, 131, 145, 163

Lonely, 2, 10, 15, 17, 21, 23, 27, 41, 50, 83, 84, 89, 92, 105, 106, 107, 112, 124, 131, 132, 146, 163

Lonesome, 2, 6, 17, 23, 50, 60, 83, 94, 106, 124, 154, 195

Long, 1, 2, 4, 5, 6, 8, 11, 12, 14, 15, 16, 17, 18, 19, 20, 22, 23, 24, 25, 26, 31, 33, 34, 35, 38, 41, 42, 44, 45, 46, 47, 48, 49, 51, 54, 55, 57, 60, 61, 62, 63, 64, 65, 68, 69, 72, 73, 74, 75, 77, 79, 81, 83, 84, 87, 88, 89, 94, 97, 102, 103, 105, 106, 107, 108, 110, 111, 117, 119, 120, 121, 124, 129, 130, 131, 134, 135, 137, 141, 142, 143, 144, 145, 147, 148, 149, 150, 151, 152, 155, 156, 157, 158, 159, 160, 162, 163, 164, 165, 166, 167, 169, 171, 173, 175, 176, 179, 180, 183, 184, 186, 188, 189, 191, 193, 194, 196, 197, 200

Longer, 17, 26, 43, 58, 60, 61, 105, 106, 118, 136, 141, 147, 150, 176, 184, 200

Longfellow, 106, 163

Longing, 106, 111, 194

Longways, 51, 106

Look, 3, 4, 5, 6, 7, 10, 11, 12, 15, 16, 17, 19, 20, 27, 30, 31, 35, 38, 39, 42, 43, 45, 47, 52, 54, 55, 56, 58, 59, 60, 61, 62, 64, 65, 66, 68, 69, 72, 76, 79, 80, 81, 82, 83, 85, 87, 88, 89, 93, 95, 96, 100, 101, 102, 103, 105, 106, 107, 108, 110, 111, 112, 114, 115, 117, 118, 119, 121, 122, 125, 126, 127, 128, 132,

Look, 134, 140, 141, 143, 144, 146, 147, 149, 150, 152, 156, 159, 160, 164, 167, 169, 170, 171, 172, 174, 178, 179, 180, 181, 182, 183, 184, 185, 186, 187, 189, 192, 193, 194, 196, 199, 200

Looked, 10, 62, 77, 78, 84, 132, 159, 185

Looking, 6, 10, 15, 17, 30, 62, 80, 83, 141, 146, 150, 157, 159, 186, 187, 193, 195, 197, 200

Lookout, 2, 104, 122, 181, 193

Looks, 2, 10, 15, 17, 24, 77, 79, 80, 95, 140, 191, 196, 199

Loose, 10, 17, 30, 34, 43, 62, 64, 65, 68, 77, 102, 108, 121, 144, 146, 165, 167

Loot, 144, 175, 191

Lora, 15, 69, 164

Lord, 19, 26, 78, 84, 99, 107, 116, 129, 134, 170

Lose, 10, 17, 22, 30, 43, 47, 62, 68, 77, 84, 105, 108, 111, 144, 165, 167, 173, 175, 176, 181

Loser, 43, 61

Loss, 34, 62, 99, 111, 167, 176

Lost, 2, 3, 4, 10, 17, 21, 22, 34, 39, 43, 58, 60, 61, 62, 63, 68, 77, 78, 102, 105, 107, 108, 111, 121, 124, 125, 127, 142, 143, 149, 150, 161, 167, 175, 183, 184, 186, 187

Lot, 1, 5, 30, 31, 34, 35, 39, 53, 54, 58, 59, 66, 76, 77, 81, 87, 105, 107, 110, 113, 121, 124, 127, 134, 152, 158, 160, 170, 174, 183, 185, 197

Lotion, 13, 74, 120, 151

Lots, 1, 5, 11, 16, 30, 35, 39, 53, 54, 63, 76, 77, 81, 87, 100, 119, 121, 124, 126, 127, 174, 181, 182, 183, 185, 191, 194

Loud, 2, 9, 10, 17, 18, 22, 27, 31, 33, 34, 35, 36, 38, 39, 41, 42, 47, 49, 51, 53, 55, 71, 72, 73, 74, 76, 81, 84, 86, 96, 97, 99, 104, 105, 113, 114, 115, 118, 122, 129, 130, 131, 132, 133, 135, 136, 140, 145, 146, 148, 150, 152, 153, 156, 163, 164, 175, 180, 181, 183, 188, 189, 196

Louder, 3, 6, 17, 42, 49, 107, 131, 132, 156, 168

Loudly, 49, 76, 128, 130, 131, 132, 156, 189

Loudness, 107, 114, 131

Lounge, 18, 36, 46, 147

Louse, 87, 99, 183

Lousy, 10, 32, 46, 111, 180, 189

Lovable, 10, 13, 38, 112, 153, 164

Love, 2, 3, 5, 6, 7, 9, 11, 13, 15, 16, 18, 19, 22, 23, 24, 28, 31, 32, 35, 38, 39, 43, 45, 46, 47, 48, 50, 51, 53, 55, 57, 58, 59, 60, 62, 63, 65, 66, 68, 69, 71, 74, 75, 76, 77, 78, 80, 82, 84, 85, 87, 88, 91, 92, 93, 96, 100, 102, 103, 105, 106, 108, 109, 110, 111, 112, 114, 116, 118, 120, 121, 124, 127, 128, 129, 131, 133, 134, 141, 144, 146, 148, 150, 151, 152, 153, 162, 164, 167, 169, 173, 174, 179, 181, 182, 183, 185, 188, 190, 191, 192, 194, 195, 196, 198, 199, 200

Loved, 2, 96, 111

Lovely, 3, 6, 10, 13, 15, 17, 19, 20, 22, 23, 29, 38, 43, 55, 57, 69, 71, 74, 79, 89, 96, 111, 112, 114, 120, 124, 153, 163, 164, 183, 190, 196, 199, 200

Lover, 55, 84, 114

Loves, 95, 105, 187

Loving, 5, 6, 9, 38, 46, 111, 164

Low, 17, 31, 34, 35, 36, 42, 44, 51, 61, 64, 70, 75, 81, 83, 86, 87, 88, 89, 96, 97, 98, 101, 102, 104, 105, 106, 107, 113, 118, 122, 124, 125, 126, 129, 130, 131, 132, 139, 144, 145, 149, 150, 151, 152, 153, 155, 156, 158, 162, 164, 165, 166, 179, 183, 189, 193, 198

Lower, 34, 43, 52, 60, 61, 83, 97, 102, 147, 149, 156

Lowly, 10, 124, 132, 150

Loyal, 40, 53, 98, 99, 129

Loyalty, 40, 98

Luck, 27, 54, 58, 62, 65, 66, 80, 96, 111, 116, 121, 140, 157, 181, 183, 194

Lucky, 6, 17, 53, 58, 62, 65, 81, 87, 117, 119, 174, 180, 181, 194

Lug, 34, 81, 102

Lullaby, 13, 31

Lumber, 37, 48, 81, 87, 119, 121, 136, 142, 197

Lump, 75, 96, 97, 103, 138, 151

Lumps, 37, 75

Lumpy, 36, 136, 151, 155

Lunar, 57, 112

Lunch, 12, 25, 30, 37, 46, 59, 67, 90, 111, 161, 166, 167, 177, 189, 197

Lunchroom, 59, 82, 118, 187

Lung, 3, 161, 180

Lungs, 161, 177

Lutheran, 129, 134

Luxurious, 46, 153

Luxury, 33, 46, 87, 148

Lying, 18, 30, 46, 65, 128, 148, 197

Lynne, 55, 66, 69

Ma, 3, 6, 11, 28, 30, 48, 60, 108, 110, 176, 179, 196

Mable, 117, 166

Machine, 2, 9, 26, 35, 41, 52, 72, 73, 81, 117, 127, 152, 154, 160, 161, 162, 197

Machinery, 72, 197

Machines, 58, 72, 197

Mad, 2, 3, 4, 5, 6, 8, 9, 10, 16, 17, 20, 21, 25, 32, 33, 39, 40, 41, 46, 47, 48, 52, 54, 56, 58, 68, 74, 75, 76, 77, 79, 81, 90, 96, 98, 99, 104, 107, 108, 109, 115, 118, 122, 124, 127, 128, 131, 133, 136, 137, 140, 149, 150, 152, 154, 155, 157, 160, 161, 164, 170, 173, 175, 176, 177, 181, 182, 183, 184, 186, 192, 194, 196, 197

Madame, 6, 29

Made, 2, 9, 17, 18, 20, 25, 31, 42, 66, 74, 76, 77, 78, 79, 88, 90, 91, 108, 115, 119, 121, 126, 149, 155, 157, 171, 174, 178, 181, 185

Madison, 41, 158

Madness, 9, 20, 41, 96, 181

Magazine, 46, 69, 80, 142

Magic, 10, 17, 21, 31, 33, 51, 64, 65, 88, 194

Magician, 10, 130

Magnificent, 15, 52, 56, 113, 120

Mahogany, 36, 166

Maid, 78, 87, 108, 116, 183

Mail, 12, 24, 31, 34, 66, 109, 156, 171, 179, 192

Mailbox, 93, 172

Main, 47, 86, 113, 120, 160, 163, 196

Maine, 11, 15

Majestic, 15, 56, 99, 104, 113

Majesty, 56, 85, 99, 104

Major, 47, 154

Make, 6, 7, 8, 10, 17, 18, 20, 21, 30, 31, 35, 43, 45, 47, 48, 52, 55, 56,

Mount, 113, 115, 159
Mountain, 15, 21, 27, 45, 46, 48, 51,
56, 57, 64, 71, 75, 81, 83, 87, 89,
97, 110, 112, 113, 115, 123, 126,
127, 131, 134, 135, 136, 143, 151,
160, 172, 190
Mountainous, 113, 136
Mountains, 15, 48, 57, 60, 71, 83,
113, 126, 135, 136, 193
Mountie, 98, 154
Mouse, 1, 2, 7, 10, 16, 21, 22, 29, 36,
37, 50, 56, 58, 62, 86, 87, 94, 96,
99, 100, 103, 104, 105, 107, 109,
110, 112, 113, 114, 115, 116, 117,
122, 124, 131, 132, 140, 145, 146,
157, 165, 166, 169, 170, 187, 190,
193, 200
Mouth, 3, 8, 9, 13, 20, 25, 29, 49, 59,
63, 64, 74, 79, 85, 88, 89, 90, 104,
107, 114, 122, 131, 135, 145, 151,
156, 157, 158, 161, 164, 168, 169,
170, 177, 180, 188, 189, 196
Move, 1, 5, 6, 10, 27, 31, 33, 34, 35,
41, 43, 45, 47, 54, 57, 60, 61, 63,
64, 66, 68, 70, 74, 77, 79, 81, 93,
94, 97, 100, 102, 105, 108, 126,
127, 129, 130, 132, 135, 137, 142,
147, 149, 150, 159, 160, 162, 165,
167, 179, 182, 183, 196
Moved, 34, 37, 95
Movement, 34, 63, 68, 74, 114, 148,
149, 150, 161, 197
Moves, 57, 95, 131
Movie, 2, 4, 5, 8, 10, 15, 18, 29, 42,
47, 48, 50, 55, 66, 70, 72, 86, 93,
95, 104, 144, 154, 157, 167, 170,
171, 174, 187, 193
Movies, 36, 50, 72, 104, 123, 141, 142,
179
Moving, 35, 43, 57, 61, 63, 66, 69, 70,
74, 105, 110, 135, 137, 149, 150,
165, 187, 197
Mow, 70, 82, 84, 88, 89, 112, 118
Mpls., 40, 41, 66, 187
Mr., 35, 40, 84, 85, 98, 109, 121,
183, 199
Mr. Engle, 158, 186
Mr. Payne, 158, 165
Mrs., 89, 105, 118, 139, 152, 156,
177, 182
Mrs. Straka, 89, 173
Mrs. Trand, 159, 175
Mt., 15, 83, 190
Mt. Rushmore, 83, 111, 113
Much, 4, 5, 6, 11, 40, 42, 58, 59, 60,
61, 63, 67, 76, 77, 81, 86, 88, 89,
92, 108, 118, 125, 127, 139, 142,
146, 150, 152, 161, 167, 173, 176,
178, 179, 181, 183
Mucky, 25, 42
Mud, 3, 21, 24, 27, 42, 51, 53, 57, 62,
63, 75, 106, 108, 111, 115, 135,
153, 154, 157, 163
Muddy, 42, 57, 135, 154
Muffin, 115, 157
Mug, 7, 36
Mule, 11, 104, 114, 115, 149, 176
Multiply, 119, 121
Mum, 72, 131, 132
Mumble, 49, 115, 181
Mummy, 2, 115
Mumps, 77, 80, 116, 146, 155
Murder, 2, 9, 16, 50, 72, 96, 98, 165,
175, 181
Muscle, 6, 34, 74, 75, 80, 81, 102,
109, 151, 161
Muscles, 68, 73, 80, 81, 102, 109, 136,
161, 172, 197
Muscular, 26, 80, 84, 109
Mush, 7, 25, 115, 152, 161

Mushy, 28, 37, 115, 153
Music, 2, 3, 4, 5, 10, 15, 16, 18, 22,
29, 32, 44, 50, 55, 57, 59, 63, 75,
83, 96, 97, 98, 106, 107, 109, 111,
113, 115, 116, 128, 131, 132, 149,
151, 152, 153, 155, 159, 163, 164,
168, 170, 183, 187, 188, 189, 194
Must, 5, 6, 11, 16, 17, 47, 77, 85, 88,
89, 91, 95, 108, 114, 115, 119, 124,
125, 127, 134, 152, 169, 171, 173,
174, 182, 183, 185, 192, 199
Mustache, 52, 109, 188
Mustard, 20, 198
Musty, 42, 144, 157
Mut, 27, 86, 115
Mute, 115, 156
Mutt, 27, 53, 115, 165
Mutter, 28, 115
Mutton, 25, 27, 37, 44, 74, 101, 115,
143, 148
My, 1, 3, 4, 5, 6, 7, 8, 10, 11, 12, 15,
16, 17, 18, 19, 20, 24, 25, 26, 27,
30, 31, 34, 35, 37, 42, 43, 45, 49,
54, 55, 58, 60, 61, 62, 63, 65, 66,
68, 76, 77, 84, 85, 87, 88, 89, 91,
92, 93, 94, 95, 97, 98, 102, 105,
108, 110, 111, 114, 116, 119, 121,
122, 123, 124, 125, 126, 127, 128,
130, 131, 134, 137, 139, 141, 142,
144, 147, 150, 152, 155, 156, 159,
160, 161, 163, 167, 168, 169, 170,
171, 173, 174, 175, 176, 178, 179,
182, 184, 185, 186, 187, 191, 192,
194, 195, 197, 199
Myself, 4, 6, 11, 17, 24, 31, 38, 39,
40, 46, 49, 64, 65, 68, 69, 74, 79,
80, 84, 89, 91, 109, 110, 111, 116,
124, 145, 149, 161, 165, 171, 173,
178, 182, 194, 195, 199
Mysterious, 21, 50, 51, 135
Mystery, 2, 9, 55, 62, 112, 191, 192
Myth, 19, 55, 92, 116, 134, 143

NaCl, 138, 139
Nail, 11, 54, 63, 64, 73, 74, 75, 79,
91, 106, 117, 136, 140, 145, 157,
161, 167, 170, 175, 177, 196, 197
Nails, 33, 54, 58, 63, 73, 74, 136,
144, 190
Naked, 14, 41, 44
Name, 2, 5, 6, 7, 8, 9, 13, 17, 19, 24,
26, 37, 38, 40, 41, 46, 48, 56, 58,
60, 63, 65, 69, 73, 77, 78, 84, 85,
86, 89, 91, 94, 96, 98, 99, 104,
106, 107, 110, 111, 115, 116, 119,
121, 125, 132, 133, 134, 136, 139,
147, 155, 157, 159, 160, 163, 168,
170, 175, 178, 179, 180, 188, 191,
194, 195, 199
Names, 110, 119, 158
Nancy, 13, 15, 55, 69, 91, 110, 164,
182, 196, 199, 200
Nap, 18, 33, 46, 85, 115, 128, 131,
148, 167
Narcotics, 142, 180
Narrow, 18, 26, 43, 51, 63, 83, 106,
135, 140, 145, 163, 176
Narrower, 26, 43, 176
Nasty, 9, 20, 38, 52, 139, 157
Nation, 40, 41, 90, 99, 127, 158
Nations, 121, 127
Native, 24, 40, 61, 127
Natural, 40, 42, 47
Naturally, 16, 76
Nature, 15, 22, 29, 57, 71, 113, 121,
131, 193
Naught, 65, 181
Naughty, 9, 38, 72, 108, 119, 128,
129, 175, 181, 184, 188
Nausea, 146, 161

Navy, 23, 47, 72, 118, 120, 154, 170,
182, 197
Nay, 34, 174
Ne, 163, 182, 185
Near, 5, 6, 7, 10, 11, 12, 17, 26, 31,
36, 41, 42, 43, 45, 52, 60, 66, 68,
70, 76, 82, 88, 89, 93, 104, 105,
108, 112, 118, 121, 123, 124, 125,
126, 132, 147, 152, 153, 159, 171,
172, 179, 183, 184, 187, 195
Nearby, 31, 43, 60, 82
Nearer, 26, 42, 43, 45, 60, 89, 173,
176
Nearest, 43, 60
Nearly, 4, 5, 6, 43, 76, 183
Nears, 43, 60
Neat, 3, 5, 9, 10, 15, 19, 24, 29, 35,
42, 43, 48, 55, 65, 69, 76, 80, 87,
89, 94, 101, 107, 110, 112, 115,
117, 119, 123, 124, 129, 131, 133,
134, 136, 151, 154, 157, 158, 164,
165, 175, 177, 181, 183, 188, 196,
199
Neater, 17, 42, 58, 89, 183
Neatness, 10, 54, 173
Necessary, 19, 92, 134, 138, 197
Necessity, 64, 74, 90
Neck, 43, 56, 74, 79, 85, 106, 108,
112, 116, 154, 159, 160, 161, 181,
190
Necklace, 62, 69
Need, 5, 10, 14, 18, 29, 38, 46, 65,
68, 76, 77, 79, 80, 88, 90, 96, 100,
117, 124, 134, 148, 152, 157, 167,
177, 181, 185, 188, 189, 194, 199
Needed, 22, 80, 98, 111, 117, 148
Needing, 90, 177
Needle, 52, 62, 73, 80, 97, 106, 140,
152, 157, 176
Needles, 52, 152
Needs, 90, 191
Negative, 76, 125
Neglect, 46, 124
Negro, 21, 40, 50, 94, 109, 127, 136
Neighbor, 17, 40, 43, 84, 87, 105,
174, 181, 192, 199
Neighbors, 127, 141
Neither, 27, 60, 76, 88, 89, 118, 124,
125
Nell, 7, 168
Nelson, 52, 198
Nephew, 13, 24, 38
Nerves, 2, 29, 97, 131, 132, 161, 181
Nervous, 2, 9, 10, 17, 29, 46, 147,
156, 181
Ness, 30, 50
Nest, 29, 52, 56, 62, 104, 119, 157,
171, 178
Net, 27, 29, 33, 42, 68, 80, 94, 108,
140, 157
Neuter, 95, 155, 169
Never, 1, 2, 3, 4, 5, 6, 8, 10, 11, 16,
17, 27, 31, 34, 42, 43, 45, 46, 49,
54, 58, 60, 62, 66, 68, 76, 77, 78,
88, 89, 90, 91, 92, 94, 95, 102, 105,
106, 110, 118, 121, 122, 124, 125,
126, 127, 130, 132, 137, 142, 145,
148, 149, 150, 152, 154, 156, 165,
167, 169, 171, 173, 176, 178, 181,
183, 184, 185, 186, 187, 188, 191,
192, 194, 195, 197, 199, 200
Nevertheless, 4, 27, 89, 173
New, 3, 4, 6, 8, 10, 11, 13, 17, 19, 22,
23, 25, 30, 32, 33, 35, 36, 42, 43,
63, 65, 66, 68, 72, 76, 82, 87, 90,
96, 101, 108, 112, 114, 115, 118,
121, 122, 124, 127, 130, 140, 144,
152, 153, 160, 162, 167, 169, 172,
179, 180, 183, 184, 186, 190, 191,
194, 200

452

457

459

460

461

Threw, 4, 7, 27, 39, 60, 150, 176
Thrift, 30, 165
Thrill, 69, 96, 189
Throat, 3, 42, 44, 79, 146, 161, 177
Throng, 99, 127
Through, 3, 4, 8, 11, 12, 21, 26, 31,
34, 42, 43, 45, 54, 59, 60, 70, 75,
76, 77, 88, 93, 97, 102, 105, 111,
124, 126, 127, 132, 136, 137, 141,
147, 170, 171, 173, 179, 186, 189,
193, 194, 195
Throughout, 4, 173
Throw, 4, 8, 9, 12, 16, 34, 60, 62,
68, 70, 73, 102, 117, 126, 127, 136,
167, 170, 174, 177, 178, 179, 188
Thrown, 99, 132
Thru, 4, 42, 45, 137
Thud, 81, 107
Thumb, 63, 66, 71, 73, 74, 117, 119,
169, 175
Thump, 53, 63, 97
Thunder, 2, 107, 148
Thunderbird, 35, 46
Thursday, 21, 198
Thus, 4, 7, 8, 11, 16, 27, 58, 65, 88,
89, 93, 124, 130, 152, 169, 171, 173,
178, 179, 182
Thusly, 99, 173
Thy, 1, 8, 31, 77, 116, 145, 169, 170,
171, 174, 192
Tick, 12, 95, 117, 167, 168, 180, 195
Ticket, 30, 98, 195
Tickets, 30, 142, 193
Tickle, 64, 139, 157
Tide, 96, 111, 112, 120, 135, 150
Tie, 8, 11, 23, 24, 26, 49, 71, 78, 84,
85, 91, 107, 109, 116, 124, 133,
144, 149, 169, 170, 175, 179, 192,
198
Ties, 49, 144
Tiger, 2, 100, 104
Tight, 10, 20, 43, 50, 63, 74, 75, 81,
101, 106, 136, 143, 144, 145, 147,
148, 179, 183, 188, 190
Tile, 14, 33, 158, 168
Till, 4, 5, 57, 102, 168, 169, 179
Tilt, 26, 78, 102
Tim, 84, 137, 154, 162
Timber, 20, 72
Time, 1, 4, 5, 7, 10, 11, 12, 13, 16
17, 18, 19, 22, 24, 26, 27, 30, 31,
34, 40, 42, 45, 50, 57, 58, 60, 61,
62, 65, 66, 70, 72, 76, 77, 82, 83,
85, 89, 91, 92, 93, 94, 96, 100,
101, 102, 105, 106, 108, 111, 114,
116, 118, 119, 121, 123, 124, 127,
128, 129, 130, 131, 132, 134, 135,
136, 137, 145, 148, 149, 150, 151,
152, 154, 156, 158, 159, 167, 168,
169, 170, 171, 172, 173, 176, 178,
181, 183, 184, 185, 186, 188, 189,
194, 195, 197, 199, 200
Times, 5, 31, 111, 119, 121, 126, 158
Timid, 2, 132
Tin, 20, 35, 48, 84, 91, 93, 95, 116,
154, 171, 176, 189
Tine, 26, 117
Tinier, 176, 200
Tiny, 3, 13, 29, 38, 69, 100, 117, 145,
153, 176, 178, 200
Tip, 36, 53, 63, 79, 131, 160, 168
Tiptoe, 131, 132
Tire, 35, 49, 143, 144, 148, 149, 181,
197
Tired, 2, 3, 4, 5, 6, 9, 17, 18, 23, 34,
36, 44, 46, 49, 55, 59, 60, 61, 63,
64, 68, 80, 81, 90, 91, 97, 106, 110,
121, 122, 128, 131, 132, 134, 137,
143, 144, 146, 147, 148, 149, 150,
154, 155, 156, 159, 163, 165, 177,

Tired, 181, 183, 184, 190, 197
Tiredness, 148, 197
Tires, 35, 181, 189
Tiresome, 81, 106, 197
Tiring, 106, 147, 149, 197
Tis, 85, 94, 184
Tissue, 108, 153, 161
Tissues, 80, 153
Title, 116, 121, 170
To, 1, 3, 4, 5, 6, 7, 8, 9, 10, 11, 12,
16, 17, 20, 23, 26, 27, 30, 31, 34,
35, 41, 42, 43, 45, 46, 48, 49, 51,
54, 58, 60, 63, 64, 65, 66, 67, 68,
70, 72, 77, 78, 82, 84, 85, 88, 89,
91, 92, 93, 94, 95, 96, 97, 108,
110, 115, 118, 119, 121, 122, 123,
124, 125, 126, 128, 130, 131, 132,
134, 135, 137, 139, 141, 142, 144,
147, 150, 151, 152, 156, 159, 161,
163, 166, 167, 168, 169, 170, 171,
172, 173, 174, 176, 178, 179, 180,
181, 182, 184, 185, 186, 187, 191,
192, 195, 199, 200
Toast, 25, 28, 37, 75, 90, 139, 176
Toaster, 25, 28, 86
Tobacco, 37, 81
Today, 4, 5, 10, 11, 17, 42, 43, 44,
45, 49, 58, 80, 82, 86, 88, 89, 90,
105, 118, 121, 124, 126, 127, 128,
149, 150, 156, 171, 173, 176, 179,
182, 192, 197
Todd, 35, 76, 127
Toe, 41, 63, 64, 72, 74, 79, 117, 122,
144, 152, 158, 178, 179, 199
Toenail, 64, 67
Toes, 13, 43, 63, 64, 73, 74, 77, 79,
132, 144, 179
Together, 4, 5, 7, 8, 10, 11, 31, 36,
43, 45, 46, 66, 68, 76, 82, 88, 94,
96, 102, 103, 105, 108, 123, 124,
127, 128, 132, 134, 147, 148, 156,
159, 161, 167, 170, 173, 174, 179,
182, 184, 185, 195, 197
Togetherness, 4, 8, 43, 127, 174, 185,
195
Toil, 73, 81, 181, 197
Toilet, 14, 27, 79, 147
Told, 16, 19, 40, 47, 64, 77, 125, 152,
156, 167, 168, 179, 182, 184
Tom, 6, 7, 8, 9, 22, 24, 34, 38, 50,
66, 69, 78, 79, 82, 84, 91, 106,
107, 110, 112, 132, 134, 161, 165,
175, 177, 179, 182
Tomato, 20, 32, 37, 98, 133, 138, 139,
151, 161
Tomatoes, 32, 138, 139, 155
Tommy, 24, 39, 72, 99
Tomorrow, 2, 4, 5, 17, 31, 41,. 45, 49,
55, 66, 118, 121, 124, 171, 179
Ton, 27, 81, 102, 106, 107, 115, 138,
161
Tone, 41, 42, 107, 114, 153, 165, 179,
189
Tong, 73, 106
Tongue, 3, 20, 52, 64, 79, 133, 136,
138, 139, 144, 156, 161, 177, 189,
192
Tonic, 142, 155
Tonight, 4, 18, 45, 105, 112, 132, 148
Tony, 48, 102, 110, 154
Too, 3, 4, 6, 8, 9, 10, 11, 12, 16, 17,
26, 27, 42, 43, 54, 58, 63, 64, 65,
66, 70, 72, 75, 77, 78, 81, 82, 84,
85, 88, 89, 93, 94, 96, 97, 102,
108, 110, 113, 121, 124, 125, 130,
136, 139, 143, 144, 150, 151, 152,
155, 156, 159, 169, 170, 171, 172,
173, 174, 179, 180, 182, 183, 184,
185, 187, 192, 195, 199, 200
Took, 10, 34, 63, 66, 72, 73, 95, 108,

Took, 112, 122, 127, 140, 141, 159,
167, 168, 174, 175, 177, 179, 182,
195, 197
Tool, 27, 31, 72, 73, 74, 76, 80, 81,
108, 116, 140, 158, 159, 197, 200
Tools, 63, 73, 108, 140, 197
Toot, 64, 67, 104, 179, 189
Tooth, 4, 13, 33, 52, 56, 64, 80, 104,
151, 155, 161, 164, 167, 179, 194
Top, 1, 5, 12, 14, 21, 35, 36, 42, 43,
47, 48, 51, 54, 57, 73, 79, 81, 83,
87, 93, 99, 102, 113, 115, 118, 123,
126, 128, 136, 147, 151, 153, 155,
157, 160, 162, 166, 169, 179, 180
Topography, 113, 136
Tops, 61, 99
Tore, 65, 108, 125, 158
Torn, 10, 17, 20, 76, 86, 144
Torrent, 120, 135
Tot, 13, 38, 39, 69, 179, 186, 200
Tote, 34, 102, 167
Tots, 39, 108
Touch, 3, 43, 63, 74, 75, 76, 77, 81,
86, 93, 102, 123, 131, 136, 141,
147, 151, 153, 179
Touched, 63, 76
Touching, 43, 153
Tough, 2, 4, 5, 9, 20, 24, 46, 49,
56, 58, 66, 73, 74, 75, 76, 78, 81,
88, 104, 107, 115, 121, 136, 139,
145, 151, 153, 154, 161, 169, 177,
180, 181, 197
Tour, 136, 181
Tow, 22, 27, 35, 70, 81, 125, 145,
152, 179, 185
Toward, 4, 12, 43, 45, 60, 65, 66, 70,
150, 179, 187
Towards, 11, 12, 31, 45, 66, 172, 179
Towel, 14, 49, 73, 74, 85, 136, 153,
166, 190
Tower, 1, 41, 63, 83, 103, 113, 134
Town, 4, 12, 26, 31, 35, 40, 41, 48,
49, 52, 57, 60, 63, 66, 70, 72, 87,
93, 99, 105, 106, 118, 121, 126,
127, 136, 158, 163, 167, 169, 170,
172, 179, 180, 187
Towns, 35, 40
Toy, 1, 7, 13, 24, 29, 30, 31, 35, 38,
39, 53, 62, 63, 68, 72, 73, 77, 82,
85, 94, 95, 96, 104, 108, 116, 121,
124, 128, 133, 140, 142, 154, 158,
167, 169, 177, 178, 179, 183, 186,
188, 189, 194, 195
Toys, 1, 13, 24, 30, 31, 33, 35, 38,
39, 63, 72, 77, 108, 128, 142, 154
Track, 32, 35, 61, 64, 73, 83, 97,
106, 111, 137, 139
Tracks, 35, 163
Tractor, 26, 52, 81, 102, 197
Trade, 30, 35, 142
Traffic, 35, 41, 70, 149, 150, 163, 181
Trail, 98, 106, 113, 136
Trailer, 35, 87, 106, 142
Trailers, 35, 87
Train, 1, 4, 23, 26, 31, 32, 35, 43,
53, 60, 61, 77, 81, 103, 106, 107,
111, 113, 116, 121, 123, 127, 130,
137, 139, 149, 150, 152, 160, 161,
165, 167, 168, 170, 179, 189, 194,
197
Tramp, 40, 101, 137, 193
Tranquil, 131, 148
Tranquility, 13, 48
Transparent, 10, 42, 103, 176, 190,
193
Transportation, 34, 35, 120
Trap, 1, 31, 169, 181
Trash, 11, 32, 40
Travel, 26, 31, 34, 35, 41, 45, 60, 61,
66, 70, 72, 90, 93, 103, 113, 120,

466